REAL ESTATE LAW

Concepts and Applications

REAL ESTATE LAW

Concepts and Applications

THERON R. NELSON
University of North Dakota

THOMAS A. POTTER
University of North Dakota

WEST PUBLISHING COMPANY
Minneapolis/St. Paul New York Los Angeles San Francisco

Production Management: Michael Bass & Associates
Copyediting: Ellen Thomas
Text and Cover Design: Lois Stanfield, LightSource Images
Cover Image: Photograph by Arthur Furst © 1993
Composition: BookMasters, Inc.

West's Commitment to the Environment

In 1906, West Publishing Company began recycling materials left over from the production of books. This began a tradition of efficient and responsible use of resources. Today, up to 95 percent of our legal books and 70 percent of our college and school texts are printed on recycled, acid-free stock. West also recycles nearly 22 million pounds of scrap paper annually—the equivalent of 181,717 trees. Since the 1960s, West has devised ways to capture and recycle waste inks, solvents, oils, and vapors created in the printing process. We also recycle plastics of all kinds, wood, glass, corrugated cardboard, and batteries, and have eliminated the use of Styrofoam book packaging. We at West are proud of the longevity and the scope of our commitment to the environment.

Printing and Binding by West Publishing Company.

Photo Credits
Chapter 1: Stock·Boston/Mike Mazzaschi; chapter 2: Stock·Boston/Fredrik Bodin; chapter 3: Stock·Boston/Peter Menzel; chapter 4: Stock·Boston/Hazel Hankin; chapter 5: Stock·Boston/Michael Dwyer; chapter 6: Stock·Boston/Lionel Delevigne; chapter 7: Gregory Martin/SuperStock; chapter 8: Stock·Boston/Tom Cheek; chapter 9: Stock·Boston/Michael Dwyer; chapter 10: Charles Orrico/SuperStock; chapter 11: Courtesy of West Educational Publishing; chapter 12: FPG International/Ron Chapple; chapter 13: Courtesy of National Real Estate Service; chapter 14: Stock·Boston/James Holland; chapter 15: Courtesy of National Real Estate Service; chapter 16: Stock·Boston/Spencer Grant; chapter 17: FPG International/Mike Valeri; chapter 18: P.I. Productions/SuperStock; chapter 19: Stock·Boston/Eric Neurath.

01 00 99 98 97 96 95 94

8 7 6 5 4 3 2 1 0

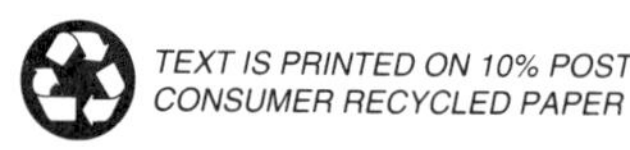

Library of Congress Cataloging-in-Publication Data
Nelson, Theron R. (Theron Ray), 1946-
Real estate law : concepts and applications / Theron R. Nelson, Thomas A. Potter.
p. cm.
Includes index.
ISBN 0-314-02824-2
1. Real property—United States. 2. Vendors and purchasers—United States. 3. Real estate business—Law and legislation—United States. 4. Real estate development—Law and legislation—United States.
I. Potter, Thomas A. II. Title.
KF570.N35 1994
346.7304'3—dc20 93-36562
[347.30643] CIP

CONTENTS

PREFACE

The study of legal issues as they apply to the acquisition, financing, and sale of real estate can be a fascinating endeavor. The creation of a text that can be used for investigating the law as it applies to real estate transactions presents the authors with a number of important and difficult decisions.

The first decision is whether the text should be written as an aid to students who intend to study about the law or for students whose intention is to study the law itself. The majority of the established texts in this area employ the first approach. Most real estate law texts contain an exhaustive catalogue of black letter law, containing a mind-numbing array of rules, organized by chapter and major topic headings, which students are expected to memorize. We have chosen the second approach in this book. It is designed to assist students in studying *concepts* of law, as they are *applied* to transactions involving real property.

We believe that studying the law itself is easier and certainly more satisfying than memorizing lists of rules. Moreover, the rules of the real estate industry have begun to change quite rapidly in the last twenty years. Legal rules that students memorize today defining the environmental liability of landowners and mortgage lenders, for example, are changing so rapidly that by the time students need to put that knowledge to use a new set of rules will apply. The same observation can be made with respect to rules defining the liability of real estate brokers and salespersons, regulations affecting various securities that represent ownership in real property, and a host of other areas that constitute the daily work environment of real estate professionals. For these and many other reasons, it seems appropriate to create a text designed to assist students in learning how and why the law is created. This knowledge can be more easily used to form a set of expectations about how various social, economic, and political forces can be expected to change the law in the future, when the knowledge students acquire today will actually be put to use.

Each chapter in the book begins with material describing the broad outlines of a particular body of law that can be expected to apply to typical transactions in real property. Interwoven in this material are *Key Points* that illustrate particular points and summaries of relevant cases. This material is followed by a set of more comprehensive cases in which students can observe judges interpreting and applying the concepts described in the text material to particular facts of relevance to real estate professionals. Although the concepts of law outlined in the text are important, the applications of legal principles to be found in the cases, Key Points, and case summaries provide the vehicles that students may use to form their own expectations about how the law will treat various issues in the future.

The next set of difficult decisions relates to the coverage that the text should offer. The range of legal issues that affect the ownership, financing, and transfer of real property is extremely broad. We have attempted to include as much of this range as possible in the coverage of issues contained in this book. The breadth of coverage required for a real estate law text necessarily limits the depth of the investigation into the specific areas of law that real estate professionals must be familiar with.

The text begins with coverage of basic legal concepts that provide the foundation for understanding the more complex issues the modern real estate professional must face that are introduced gradually in the book. The material in this book also provides information on the history of many of our modern legal concepts. Although this history is interesting in itself, its inclusion is based on the need for students to understand the progression in legal concepts over many hundreds of years. The accepted legal concept of today is often in reality a much refined and revised version of an ancient rule. It is much easier to understand a modern concept if you have at least some knowledge of how and why society adopted the idea and which other approaches have been tried.

We have consistently attempted to provide students with the material needed to answer two important questions. The first question is "When do I need to consult an attorney?" Many of the legal issues that confront real estate professionals are routine and repetitive in nature. Navigating these "safe harbors" does not usually require the skills of a licensed attorney. However, the law of averages dictates that real estate professionals will occasionally become involved in more difficult legal issues that do require the specialized skill and knowledge of an attorney. Learning to recognize the exceptions is one of the key skills required of real estate professionals.

The second question that this text seeks to answer is, "What should I ask the attorney to do for me?" The skills and knowledge of legal practitioners are expensive. Knowing how to use this resource effectively is an important skill for real estate practitioners. Armed with knowledge of basic legal concepts and information about current applications of these concepts to real estate transactions and an ability to know when and how to use legal help, the reader is able to approach even the most difficult legal question with confidence.

Chapter Features

Each chapter in the book follows the same basic format and includes the same set of features:

Key Terms—Each chapter begins with a set of important terms that are defined and discussed in the chapter. This set of terms helps students to focus on the central concepts of the chapter.

Learning Objectives—In addition to the key terms, a set of learning objectives is included to help students know when they have mastered the key concepts discussed in the chapter.

Key Points—At various places throughout each chapter, the reader will find boxed inserts containing illustrative examples of key points discussed in the chapter.

Case Summaries—In addition to the more complete cases contained at the end of each chapter, brief summaries of additional cases are included to illustrate specific key points.

Discussion Questions—A set of questions designed to test the reader's knowledge of the material covered is included at the end of each chapter. These questions can be used as the basis for classroom discussions or as assignments for outside work.

Cases—Each chapter contains several cases selected to illustrate the major points discussed in the chapter. Although older, "classic" cases are used in some instances, most of these cases are examples of current judicial logic.

Case Reflections—Each case concludes with a series of questions designed to foster discussion on the major points raised in the case.

Glossary—The first time a *Key Term* is introduced in a chapter, a definition is included in the margin—a style called a "running glossary." This allows readers to have ready access to definitions of all key terms. In addition, a complete glossary, which includes all key terms and many additional terms, is contained at the end of the text.

Text Organization

The text is organized in four sections beginning with information on basic legal concepts and building toward an in-depth look at the rapidly evolving role of the real-estate professional.

I. Concepts in Property Ownership—This section provides an introduction to real estate law. Distinctions between real and personal property, the various estates in real property, methods of co-ownership, and limitations on fee simple ownership are discussed.

II. Transferring Ownership of Real Property—Real estate professionals are most frequently involved in legal matters surrounding the process of transferring ownership rights. This section of the text covers the methods by which ownership may be transferred, the process of preparing and recording deeds, and mortgages and other documents that may affect title. Because each parcel of property has a history of ownership, before actually transferring ownership at the closing process, titles must be researched. Thus this section of the text includes information on title searches, abstracts, and title insurance as well as details on conducting a formal title closing procedure.

III. The Role of the Real Estate Professional—The first two sections of the text provide information on the legal framework for ownership and transfer of ownership rights in real property. Part III provides a look at how these legal concepts are applied by real estate professionals. Agency relationships are discussed in some detail. Because the legal environment for real estate professionals is fraught with perils, two chapters are devoted to areas of potential liability. Fair housing, agency, antitrust, and environmental issues are discussed in detail. The legal pressures these liability issues are producing are leading to some structural changes within the real estate industry. These are discussed in the final chapter of this section.

IV. Legal Aspects of Real Estate Development—The text continues with material on three additional areas of interest to real estate professionals: land use regulation, product liability and homeowner's warranties, and real estate as a security. Each of these areas has already produced changes that affect real estate professionals, often in profound ways. The text concludes with a look at the trends in real estate law and where the industry appears to be heading.

Additional Features

A complete *Instructor's Manual* is available for adopters of this text. The manual includes chapter outlines, answers to all chapter and case questions, case briefs for all included cases, a test bank, and additional information on real estate law in California, Texas, Ohio, Illinois, New York, and Florida provided by a team of legal professionals in these states.

ABOUT THE AUTHORS

Theron R. Nelson is Associate Professor and Chair of the Department of Finance at the University of North Dakota. A 1983 graduate of Georgia State University with a Ph.D. in Real Estate, Dr. Nelson is a past president of the American Real Estate Society, currently serves on the Board of Directors for the organization, and serves as coordinator of real estate pre-licensing education for the state of North Dakota. Dr. Nelson is the author of three additional books, serves on the editorial boards of several academic and professional journals, and has written numerous articles that have appeared in publications including the *Journal of Real Estate Research*, the *American Real Estate and Urban Economics Association Journal, The Real Estate Educators Association Journal*, and *The Appraisal Journal*.

Dr. Thomas A. Potter began his academic career at Southern Methodist University in Dallas Texas. Before graduation there, he transferred to the University of Colorado at Boulder, where he received a Bachelors degree in Finance. He graduated from the University of Colorado College of Law in 1974 and entered the active practice of law immediately after passing the Colorado Bar examination.

In 1979, Dr. Potter returned to the University of Colorado and was awarded a Ph.D. degree in Finance. He has been a member of the finance faculty at the University of North Dakota since 1981. In addition to his legal practice and teaching experience, Dr. Potter has been an active investor in commercial and residential real estate properties for over twenty years. He currently teaches finance, real estate law, and strategic management at the University of North Dakota. In his spare time, Dr. Potter is the owner and CEO of a restaurant capable of seating more than 200 patrons for fine dining and dinner theater entertainment.

REAL ESTATE LAW

Concepts and Applications

PART

1

CONCEPTS IN PROPERTY OWNERSHIP

EQUAL JUSTICE UNDER LAW

CHAPTER

1

INTRODUCTION

LEARNING OBJECTIVES

After reading this chapter, you should be able to:

1. Describe the differences between common law and civil code legal systems
2. Describe the federal system of government employed in the United States
3. Describe the trial process used by the American legal system to resolve disputes
4. Read a judicial opinion and understand the legal significance of the ruling contained in the opinion

KEY TERMS

Civil Code Legal Systems

Common Law Legal Systems

Judicial Opinions

Legislative Enactments

Judgment

Constitutions

Supreme Law of the Land

Diversity Jurisdiction

Legal and Equitable Remedies

Stare Decisis

Complaint and Answer

Summary Judgment

WHAT IS A LEGAL SYSTEM?

There is no body of law that can correctly be described as "real estate law." Instead, practitioners in the real estate industry must be conversant with many different areas of law. Obviously, the law of real property will affect the outcome of every real estate transaction. In addition, the law of contracts will be invoked whenever real estate practitioners agree to buy, sell, or lease real property. The law of agency determines the rights and duties of real estate brokers, salespeople, and their clients. The law of secured transactions, debtor's rights, and creditor's remedies will be applied to any transaction that includes mortgage financing. Constitutional law is regularly applied to zoning and land use issues, which are of primary importance to real estate practitioners. The developing area of environmental law is beginning to have a significant impact on the way real estate practitioners conduct their business. Finally, securities law is now being applied to many aspects of the real estate industry.

The intent of this book is to weave these disparate strands of law together into a comprehensible body of knowledge that real estate practitioners can use to protect themselves against unexpected calamities. The strategy employed in the book is to begin with a broad conceptual overview of the basic legal principles that affect real estate practitioners, followed by examples of the ways specific areas of the law are applied to particular categories of real estate transactions.

Much of the text material in Part I is devoted to the historical development of the legal principles that form the modern law of real property. In addition, the chapters in Part I introduce many of the jurisprudential concepts that provide the intellectual foundation of legal rights in real and personal property that the law of property attempts to define.

The guiding principle of this book is that people generally cannot fully understand what the law is without first discovering how the law was created. The legal system currently employed in the United States is the product of an evolutionary process that began many thousands of years ago and is continuing in the present. In accordance with this guiding principle, our investigation of the various areas of law that affect the real estate industry will begin with an overview of the social and empirical forces that led to the creation of the abstract body of thought referred to as "the law."

History of Legal Systems

The archeological record of human culture indicates that legal systems came into being whenever a group of people learned to domesticate crops and livestock. The earliest recorded legal system is the Code of Hammurabi, named for a Sumerian king who lived in a region contained in the modern nation of Iraq. The Sumerian kingdom reached its peak of power and population some six thousand years ago. The foundation of this early superpower was the abundant food supply produced in fields irrigated by the two great rivers of the area, the Tigris and the Euphrates.

It is surely not an accident that the earliest recorded legal code was developed in the earliest agricultural society. Laws are only necessary for people who must stay in one place to tend a crop and thus depend upon the harvest of the crop to insure their survival. Farmers must protect the growing crop from the ravages of livestock, wild animals, and other people. Moreover, since farmers must devote almost all of their time to planting, cultivating, and harvesting, they must be able to trade the part of the crop they do not eat for other goods produced by those who do not farm. This complex web of human relationships seems to require a complex set of rules and obligations to regulate the conduct of the people involved.

Wherever people learned to harness the land and make it produce food, legal systems were created. New laws regulated the conduct of those who produced the food and those who ate the food produced by others. Many of these legal systems were little more than oral traditions, which after a time simply became customs that everyone in the village was supposed to know about and comply with. Other systems were more formal; and in societies that possessed a written language, the formal systems were almost always written down.

Different Forms of Legal Systems

Beginning about twenty-five hundred years ago, the Roman Civil Code, the written legal system of the Roman Empire, replaced the legal systems of all the cultures within a week's travel of the Mediterranean Sea. Today, the majority of people on earth live in a nation whose legal system is modeled after the Roman Civil Code. These legal systems rely on carefully drawn, complex statutes drafted by national legislatures, which define the rules of conduct every citizen is expected to live by. The statutes adopted by legislatures in **civil code systems** are closely akin to what Americans think of as contracts; that is, civil code statutes are essentially written agreements, designed to cover all contingencies and specify exactly what each party to the contract must do in the case of each contingency. The implied agreement is that all citizens will behave in the ways specified in the statute and that the government will punish those citizens who refuse to behave in the manner prescribed by the statute.

Civil Code Legal Systems A type of legal system which relies mainly on laws drafted by national and regional legislatures to regulate the behavior of citizens.

KEY POINTS

Most Latin American nations, including Mexico, use a civil code legal system. In 1985, an experienced real estate developer from Colorado purchased a home in Puerto Vallarta, Mexico. The developer planned to use the home for vacation trips by himself and his family.

In 1989, the developer rented the vacation home to a local Puerto Vallarta family for a six-month period, during the summer and fall, when the owner planned to be in the United States. The lease expired on a Mexican national holiday, so as a courtesy to the family the owner waited until the following day to reclaim possession of the home. The developer reports that to his horror he was informed that the legal status of the family occupying the home changed from "tenant" to "occupant" when the owner failed to reclaim possession on the last day of the lease. Further, there are no provisions of the Mexican civil code that permit the removal of an "occupant" from a residential building. At last report, the owner was still attempting to recover possession of his vacation home.

Moral: Differences in legal systems across international boundaries are at least as important as differences in the language spoken.

Common Law Legal System A type of legal system which relies mainly on the legal opinions produced by judges to regulate the behavior of citizens.

The primary alternative in the modern world to the civil code legal system is the **common law system** employed by England, the U.S., and many other nations that were at one time a part of the worldwide British Empire. In the common law system, laws enacted by parliaments or legislatures (statutes) are intentionally broad, general statements of what is right and what is wrong. For example, the Sherman Antitrust Act, a major piece of legislation that had directly affected the actions of thousands of businesses in this country, says simply, "Every contract, combination in the form of trust or otherwise, or conspiracy, in restraint of trade or commerce among the several states, or with foreign nations, is declared to be illegal . . ." Such broad, sweeping language seems to ask more questions than it answers. What does it mean to restrain trade? What constitutes a conspiracy? Which transactions fall under the heading of commerce among the several states and which do not? These questions are extremely important, since the penalty for violating the Sherman Antitrust Act can run into millions of dollars. How can anyone decide if a proposed course of action is legal or illegal, when the statute is so broad and general?

The answer is that specific statements of what behavior is punishable and what behavior is not punishable will not appear in most of the statutes adopted by legislatures in common law countries. Rather, the answers to such specific questions are to be found in the actions and decisions of judges, who over the years apply the statutes on a case-by-case basis to particular facts as they arise in the life of the nation. The reliance on **judicial opinions** rather than legislative enactments to define what is acceptable and what is punishable in a society is the major difference between common law systems like our own and civil law systems that exist elsewhere. It also explains why American law students spend most of their time studying judicial opinions, while Swedish law students spend their time studying the **legislative enactments** of the Swedish Parliament.

Judicial Opinions A legal document which explains how the law should be applied to the actions of the parties to a law suit, and describing the reasoning process employed by the judges who issued the opinion.

With this background, we are now prepared to ask and answer two important questions. First, what is the purpose of a legal system? Second, how might a nation design procedures to accomplish that purpose.

PURPOSE AND PROCEDURES OF A LEGAL SYSTEM

Legislative Enactments Laws established by Congress, or various state legislatures; Judges are required to interpret and apply the common law in the manner prescribed by legislative enactments.

The fundamental purpose of any legal system is to protect us from each other. In the process, a good legal system offers an additional advantage: knowledge of the laws allows us to plan ahead, relying on the assumption that other people will, in general, behave the way the legal system says they should behave. When the driver of a car approaches a green light at an intersection, he can feel some confidence that driving through the intersection will not be a fatal act, since a red light will be stopping traffic moving the other way through the intersection. When someone signs a contract to buy a house, the legal system allows the buyer to believe that she will actually own the house in the near future. Even if the seller changes her mind, the buyer can expect a court to force the seller to hand over the keys and vacate the premises. Without this knowledge, a buyer would be reluctant to contract for a mortgage, sell the home she currently occupies, hire a moving company, or do anything at all in preparation for moving into the new home.

A relatively modern development is the notion that the purpose of a legal system extends to protecting the citizens of a nation from exploitation or abuse by the governmental power of the nation. The U.S. Constitution was written for the purpose of creating a legal system in which the power of government was expressly limited to a few purposes that were deemed legitimate by the members of the Constitutional Convention.

Settling Disputes

In the process of extending protection to each member of society from all other members and from society itself, a legal system must provide a sound and available mechanism for resolving disputes. And it is here that we must begin to look for procedures that will enable a legal system to accomplish its purpose of protecting citizens and allowing them to plan for the future. Imagine, if you will, the following events (which actually occurred in a college dormitory many years ago). Student B borrowed $20 from student L, who lived down the hall, and promised to repay the loan at the end of the month when student B received his paycheck. The end of the month came and went, and predictably no payments on the loan were offered. Student L, in high dudgeon, crept into Student B's room one dark night and confiscated the borrower's typewriter to hold as collateral until he decided to repay the loan. As luck would have it, Student B did not discover the typewriter was missing until the night before a term paper was due. In a panic, Student B asked up and down the hall if anyone had seen his typewriter and found to his horror that it was being held hostage against the payment of the $20 debt owed to Student L.

A resident adviser was attracted by the noise of the argument that ensued in Student L's room and found the two students about to come to blows over possession of the typewriter. In order to avoid the threatened violence, the resident adviser ruled on the spot that the typewriter must be returned immediately and admonished Student B to pay his obligation with the first twenty dollars that came into his possession. Both deeds were apparently performed on schedule, since the resident adviser heard nothing more about the dispute.

In later years, the same resident adviser began to study the law and heard his professors repeating over and over the mantra of legal scholarship: "the law does not permit self-help remedies." Each time this phrase was uttered, the resident adviser–law student remembered the violence that was threatened when Student L attempted to help himself by obtaining a mechanical hostage to trade for repayment of legal debt. After many years of reflection, that resident adviser–law student remains convinced that meaningful mechanisms for resolving disputes between people are an essential requirement for a functioning legal system.

The form of the dispute resolution mechanism is much less important than its availability. Indeed, every nation has developed a mechanism that reflects its own unique cultural heritage and political history. However, the existence of a consistent and reliable method for resolving disputes remains the hallmark of an advanced legal system.

Procedures in Court Trials

In the United States, the dispute resolution procedures provided by our common law system are found almost entirely in the courts. Every American who believes he or she has been wronged by another person, or by an agency of government, is required to either shrug off the injury or bring the dispute before a court of competent jurisdiction (a technical legal term that identifies the particular courthouse where the disagreement must be aired).

Once brought before a court, the dispute resolution procedure occurs in two separate stages. Figure 1.1 outlines the litigation process. First, a jury (or occasionally the trial judge acting, with the consent of both parties, as a jury) will listen to evidence presented by both sides and determine what actually happened to cause the dispute. When all of the evidence has been presented by both parties to the dispute, the second phase of the dispute resolution mechanism begins. The trial judge will decide, based upon his or her legal training, how the law should treat the behavior of the parties in the lawsuit. The trial judge may decide that, based on the evidence, the defendant has not done anything unlawful and that the lawsuit should be dismissed. If the trial judge decides that the evidence does give the plaintiff a right to complain about the defendant's behavior, then further proceedings will be necessary.

The trial judge will instruct the jury to examine the evidence and decide on two things. First, the jury will be asked to determine exactly who did what to whom, by examining the evidence produced at the trial. The jury will also be told that when they have completed this first task, they must decide what, if anything, the defendant should be required to do to repair the damage. After the jury has considered both of these questions, following the instructions given to them by the trial judge, they will report their verdict.

After the jury delivers the verdict, the trial judge has two remaining choices. The judge can accept the verdict of the jury and enter a legal order requiring the defendant to pay the damages awarded by the jury. Or, if the trial judge believes that the jury did not follow their instructions and so reached the wrong conclusion, the judge can overturn the verdict of the jury. If the trial judge decides that the jury was clearly wrong in reaching their verdict, a Judgment NOV (*non obstante verdictum*) will be entered by the court. When the trial judge enters a **judgment** on the jury's verdict, or a judgment notwithstanding the verdict of the jury, the trial comes to an end.

Judgment
An order issued by a trial judge providing a legal conclusion to the controversy which resulted in a law suit. The conclusion prescribed by the judgment is binding on all the parties to the law suit.

After the trial is completed, the losing side has a right to appeal to another set of judges. The appellate judges will examine the case and decide whether or not the trial judge made any mistakes in his or her conclusions about the law as it applies to the parties to the action. If the appeals court concludes that no mistakes were made, it will affirm the judgment of the trial court. If the appeals court finds errors of law in the case, it will overrule the trial court and may order the parties to try the lawsuit over again. The party who loses at the first appeal can ask yet another appeals court to take a look at the case. This time, however, the still-higher appeals court can refuse to look at the case, and the judgment of the first appeals court will stand.

These procedures offer everything an injured party could want, along with a whole lot more. The primary benefit of our legal system is that disputes are resolved in an atmosphere of courtesy and propriety. The entire operation is designed to prevent violence or bloodshed of any kind, and it usually functions as intended. The physical strength and courage of the parties to the lawsuit are not important; the entire proceeding is handled by their attorneys, who are skilled in the courtroom dance of mind-to-mind combat, in order to avoid the messier hand-to-hand kind of combat. The drawback, of course, is that it will probably take years to get the final answer to the question, and it will undoubtedly cost a lot of money.

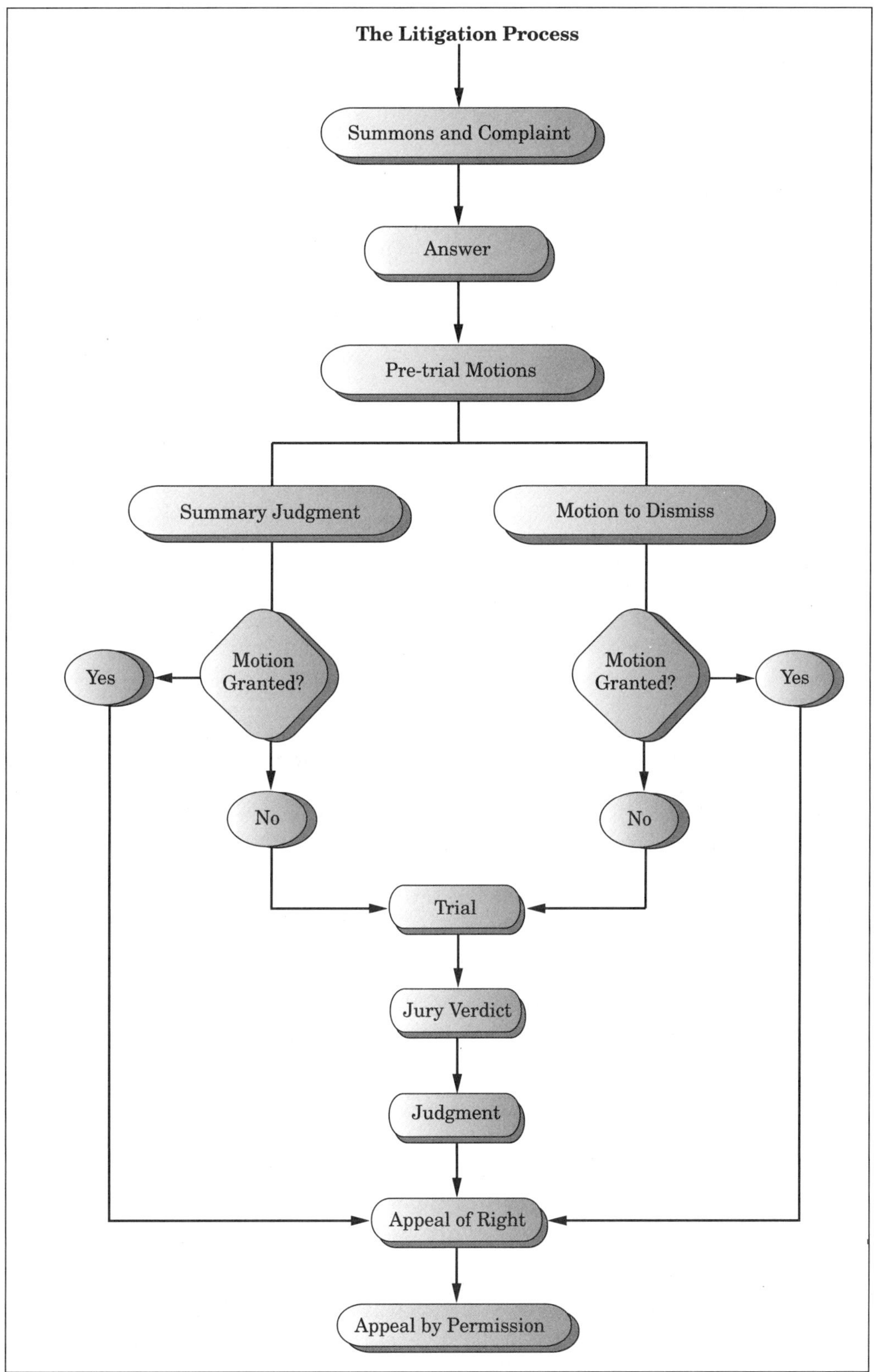

FIGURE 1.1 THE LITIGATION PROCESS

KEY POINTS

In general, the length of time required to settle a dispute with a law suit is three to five years. Both sides of the dispute should expect to spend more than $10,000 in legal fees. If the losing side appeals the jury's decision, add another three years and another $10,000 in legal fees. A primary reason for studying real estate law is to learn to recognize and avoid transactions that will probably result in long and expensive legal proceedings.

SOURCES OF REAL ESTATE LAWS

Constitutions The basic document of government which describes the powers, procedures and limitations of governmental actions.

Supreme Law of the Land The legal doctrine established in the United States Constitution that the laws of the Federal Government take precedence over the laws adopted by the government of any state.

Diversity Jurisdiction The authority granted to Federal Courts by the U.S. Constitution to hear and resolve controversies between citizens of two or more different states.

The basic governing document of our country is the United States Constitution. America did not become a nation in 1776, when the original colonies declared their independence from the government of England. Instead, the nation we inhabit today came into being in 1789, when the **Constitution** was ratified (accepted) by the thirteen original states. The combination of a single federal government, whose influence and sovereignty extend over the territory of each state, aided and extended by the authority of each of the individual states in the Union, was a unique experiment in the 1700s and remains virtually unique today.

Article VI of the Constitution states that it, along with all laws made under its provisions, "shall be the **supreme Law of the Land**." The federal government, which is to make and execute the supreme law of the land, is composed of three distinct branches: the legislative branch, the executive branch, and the judicial branch as illustrated in Figure 1.2.

Article I establishes Congress as the legislative body of the federal government. Section 8 of the legislative article lists several law-making powers that the Congress will have under the Constitution. Most important for our purposes are the power to regulate interstate commerce and the power to establish uniform bankruptcy laws to be applied in every state. Article II establishes the president as the head of the executive branch of the federal government. Presidential powers include command of all military forces together with the power to appoint supreme court justices and other federal judges as well as officers and managers for the various federal agencies established by Congress. Finally, Article II requires the president to "take care that the Laws be faithfully executed . . ."

Article III vests the judicial power of the United States in one "supreme Court, and in such inferior Courts as the Congress may . . . ordain." The inferior courts ordained by Congress include the ten circuit courts of appeals, the federal district courts, and several specialized courts like the tax court. Under Article III, the kinds of cases that can be submitted to the federal courts are limited. The most usual route for gaining entry to the federal court system is the **diversity jurisdiction:** "controversies between two or more States—between a State and Citizens of another State—[or] between citizens of different states." Another major route for entering the federal court system is cases involving the Constitution or the laws of the United States.

Finally, the Tenth Amendment to the Constitution reserves all powers not expressly given to Congress or the executive branch to the states. It is this amendment

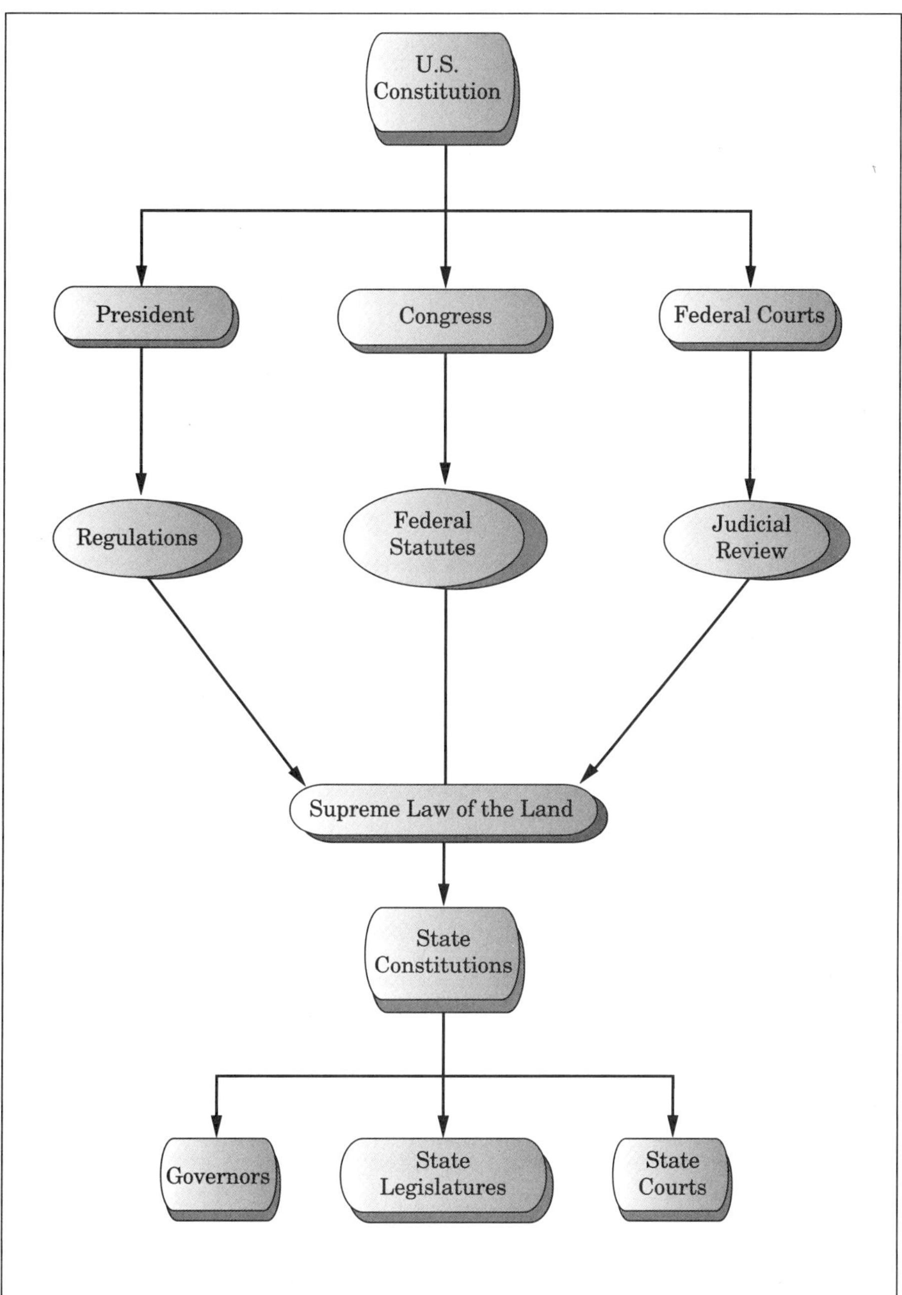

FIGURE 1.2 ORGANIZATION OF THE BRANCHES OF THE US GOVERNMENT

that rounds out the picture of the federal form of government that we see today. Congress may pass laws that do not violate any provision of the Constitution and are necessary or appropriate to any of the powers granted to Congress by the Constitution. Since these laws are the supreme law of the land, state legislatures may not pass, and state officials cannot enforce, any laws that contradict the federal statutes or violate the U.S. Constitution. However, in all areas not specifically mentioned by the Constitution, states are permitted to make and enforce their own rules within the borders of the state.

Our independent judicial system exists to monitor all of the laws and regulations adopted by the federal government and by each of the fifty state governments. The Supreme Court, as well as the lower federal courts, are empowered to declare any federal law that violates the Constitution as void. The federal court system may also strike down any state law or regulation that violates either the Constitution or a valid federal law.

Judicial systems have been created in all fifty states and for the most part are modeled on the federal system. Like the federal courts, state courts may declare any law passed by the state legislature invalid if it violates the federal constitution, the state constitution, or any valid federal statute. Both federal and state courts are required to interpret and enforce statutes that do not violate the supreme law of the land. It is this judicial process of interpreting and applying the laws of the land that will be the focus of study in this book.

The federal system of government that we enjoy today was not created in a vacuum. Legal systems have been part of human life for thousands of years; a tremendous wealth of legal history and philosophies of human behavior was available to the framers of the Constitution. At their convention in Philadelphia, the framers thought through this wealth of knowledge, applied it to their own experience, and fashioned a document that they hoped would regulate the public life of a great nation for many years.

Since all of the framers entered the world as citizens of England (albeit second-class colonial citizens), the legal system they were most familiar with was the common law system of England. Like so many other aspects of American life, the common law system traces its origin to the problems encountered by William of Normandy, who in 1066 conquered the island of Britain and declared himself its king.

Development of English Common Law

A thousand years ago, life was much slower and probably less complex than the life we live in the twentieth century. With some notable exceptions, the population of Europe and the British Isles lived in small groups or tribes, each relatively isolated from the others. Each group (numbering from a few hundred to a few thousand people) was presided over by a chief or elder, whose two primary responsibilities were to rally and organize the tribe against invasions from neighboring tribes and to settle disputes within the tribe before they could lead to violence and bloodshed among its members.

William of Normandy was one of those rare chieftains who dared to expand his leadership over a larger group distributed over a wider area. Since most of Europe was already taken, William decided to cross the English Channel and make his move on the island of Britain. The rest, as they say, is history.

As soon as William had established himself as king of all England, he set about the task of making that kingship a reality. As the chief of a tribe that numbered in the hundreds of thousands and was scattered around an island that took days to cross, William had to find new ways of discharging his twin responsibilities. The methods he employed to rally and organize his subjects in order to ward off invasions led to the development of real property ownership, which we will investigate in Chapter

3. The methods he and his successors employed to settle disputes among their many subjects eventually formed a system that came to be known as "English common law."

With their subjects scattered across the width and breadth of England, it was clearly impossible for the early English monarchs to attend personally to each and every dispute that arose in England. Hence, they soon began appointing groups of able assistants to appear in their behalf and judge disputes throughout the kingdom. Each of these assistants (who, for obvious reasons, were called judges) held court in the cities and towns of England on a regular basis. Eventually, the judges were armed with a set of writs from the king that could be used to settle the arguments that came before them. For example, if a judge determined that farmer Brown had stolen a pig from farmer Smythe, he would give Brown a writ, which everyone understood to be the written command of the king, instructing Brown to return the pig to Smythe.

In theory, the king's judges could pack in their briefcases a set of blank writs that would exactly fit every problem that came before them. Once the judge learned what had happened, he would find a writ that directed the guilty party to return the property, or pay money to the victim, or both. Each writ would, of course, serve as the king's direct command to his guilty subject and result in precisely the proper punishment to fit the crime.

In practice, not every problem that came before the judges could be neatly resolved by one of the available writs. There always seemed to be exceptions and special circumstances making it unfair to resolve a dispute with any of the king's writs that the judge had in his briefcase. Eventually, these exceptions were channeled into a different path that led to a hearing before the chancellor.

The chancellor was an official selected by King William (and his successors) whose job it was to assist the king directly in the management of the affairs of the kingdom. Because the chancellor worked with the king on a daily basis, the monarch trusted him more thoroughly than he trusted the judges. As a result, the chancellor was empowered to decide what would be a fair or equitable way to resolve those disputes that could not be handled by the issuance of a writ. Over the centuries, this parallel system of resolving disputes based on wide-ranging notions of fairness became known as the courts of equity, to distinguish them from the courts of law, where disputes were settled by filling in the blanks of an existing writ.

Today, the distinction between courts of law and courts of equity has all but disappeared; the language of the law nonetheless retains the distinctive words that were employed in the twelfth century to mark the differences between the two systems of justice. In most American courtrooms, you can apply to the same judge for **legal remedies** (for example, an order from the judge requiring the defendant to pay money to compensate for the damage he or she has caused) or for **equitable remedies** (usually an order for specific performance, which requires the defendant to do what he or she promised to do.) But even today, most judges will state that equitable remedies are not available unless the plaintiff has no adequate legal remedies. Whenever we read that sentence in a judge's opinion, we can almost hear the early English kings saying, "Don't bother me with your problems if one of my law judges can take care of it."

Legal Remedies
The right of the plaintiff in a law suit to obtain an order requiring the defendant to pay a sum of money for damages when the defendant has committed a legal wrong against the plaintiff.

Now, what does all of this have to do with English common law? The connection is both simple and subtle. Whenever the chancellor agreed to hear a dispute because it could not be settled with the legal writs available at the time, he was of course

Equitable Remedies
The right of a plaintiff in a law suit to obtain a judicial order requiring the defendant to perform, or refrain from performing, a specific act. Equitable remedies are only available to plaintiffs whose injury cannot be repaired by the payment of money damages.

Stare Decisis
The legal principle which requires judges in each controversy to apply the law to the facts of the controversy in the same way the law was applied to similar facts in the past.

required to explain why the decision he gave was an equitable one. Over the years, the chancellor and his assistants piled up a fairly large body of written opinions explaining how and why particular disputes were resolved. At the same time, the law judges were busy writing up their reasons for issuing or refusing to issue particular writs as a result of the disputes that came before them. Each of these written opinions became an individual brick to be used in building the huge palace of ideas called English common law. Since each judgment issued by one of the king's employees carried the force of the king's command to his obedient subjects, the notion of stare decisis rapidly attached itself to the decisions. This Latin phrase, translated as "the decision stands," was a shorthand way of saying to the people, "By this decision, the king has spoken and the king expects to be obeyed." The notion of stare decisis was a handy one from the king's point of view, for it enhanced his power and reputation as the person who, through his judicial employees, provided a way for his subjects to settle their arguments without having to fight each other.

Stare decisis was also a handy notion from the point of view of the king's subjects. First of all, every plaintiff who won a judgment could say, quite correctly, "The king is now on my side, and you are required to obey the king's command." More important, stare decisis allowed the parties to a dispute to insist that the judge at their trial must reach the same conclusion as the judge in a previous trial when the events that led to the previous trial were the same as those that led to the current proceedings. In this way, stare decisis allowed the creation of a consistent and understandable body of law. Anyone who took the trouble to study and understand this body of law that all the king's subjects held in common could predict, with reasonable certainty, what would happen to him under almost any circumstances.

The framers of the U.S. Constitution had the benefit of over five hundred years of experience with this system of common law, and they applied the knowledge gained from that experience to the construction of the governing document for the new nation they intended to create. The framers certainly expected Congress and the state legislatures to pass laws that would become the skeleton of the American common law, and Congress has willingly obliged. But the framers clearly assumed that the federal judges called for in the Constitution, assisted by the judges in all of the state court systems, would provide the flesh of common law to cover the bare bones of legislation. To their credit, the system that the constitutional framers expected to create has worked just about the way they expected it to work. When Americans study the law, they study the written opinions of judges, which provide the living fabric of our common legal system.

Since the meaning and impact of American real estate law are found almost entirely in the written opinions of judges, we turn our attention next to a discussion of the format of these written opinions.

STUDYING JUDICIAL OPINIONS

Every judicial opinion was, once upon a time, an argument between two or more people. To learn more about the way arguments can develop into the case law of judicial decisions, let's examine the case of *Memphis Development v. Factors, Inc.* (616 F.2d 956, 6th Cir. 1980). The argument that led to this opinion started shortly after Elvis Presley died. A group of people in Elvis's hometown of Memphis, Tennessee, decided to erect a statue in honor of the singer. In order to raise money to have the statue built, the Memphis Development Foundation decided to give an eight-inch pewter replica of the statue to everyone who donated $25 or more toward the cost of erecting the statue. This arrangement sounded pretty innocent, but a problem developed almost immediately. Factors, Inc., a corporation organized under the laws of New York State, had paid $150,000 for the right to exploit the name and likeness of Elvis Presley after he died. Apparently, when Factors heard about the plans for the Memphis statue, they sent a letter to Memphis Development informing them that the sale of the pewter replicas of Elvis's statue would be in violation of Factors's property rights.

At this point, one of several things might have happened. Memphis Development Foundation could have decided to leave well enough alone and agreed with Factors that the sale of the pewter replicas was wrong. In this case, there would have been no argument, no lawsuit, and no opinion. Or, Memphis Development could have decided to ignore the warning and sell the pewter replicas anyhow. This would probably have resulted in a lawsuit in which Factors sued Memphis Development to protect the investment of $150,000 Factors had made for the right to profit from the name and likeness of Elvis Presley. In the actual event, Memphis Development decided that the best defense is a good offense and sued Factors. They filed the lawsuit in federal district court, since it was a lawsuit involving citizens of two different states.

In general, a lawsuit must be filed in the state where the defendant lives. To avoid giving the defendant a "home court" advantage, out-of-state plaintiffs will often try to have their lawsuits heard in federal court rather than the courts of the defendant's home state. So it was in this case.

Memphis Development asked the federal district judge to declare in advance that Memphis Development had the legal right to distribute pewter replicas of the proposed Elvis statue in exchange for $25 or more. This lawsuit, like every lawsuit, was started when the plaintiff filed two documents with the court. The first document is the **Complaint**. Just as the name implies, the plaintiff states in the Complaint exactly what it is that the defendant has done wrong and requests (or demands) that the court enter a judgment that undoes or repairs the wrong that the plaintiff claims to have suffered.

Complaint and Answer The major pleadings which describe the nature of the controversy between the parties to a law suit.

The second document required for a lawsuit is the Answer from the defendant. The **Answer** can be short and sweet, as in "The Defendant in this action appears and denies each and every allegation of the plaintiff's complaint." Or, the answer may admit some things that are obviously true (for example, Factors might be willing to admit that the plaintiff is a nonprofit organization formed under the laws of Tennessee) but deny any allegations of wrongdoing. The answer may also contain a counterclaim, in which the defendant alleges that the plaintiff has done wrong and asks the court to enter a judgment that undoes or repairs the damage the defendant claims to have suffered.

Once the Answer is filed, the lawsuit is under way. A trial date will be set, and the parties will get themselves ready to appear in the courthouse and attempt to prove the claims they made in their respective pleadings. A burden of proof is always placed on the plaintiff to show: (a) that the facts alleged in the Complaint are true, and (b) that these facts establish a claim against the defendant for a legal wrong that can be undone or repaired by an order from the judge granting the relief the plaintiff has requested.

Sometimes the argument can be resolved without a trial. For example, the judge may decide that even if all the facts alleged in the Complaint are true, the defendant still has not done anything that would entitle the plaintiff to a judgment. In this case the judge will dismiss the Complaint for failure to state a claim on which relief can be granted, and the lawsuit comes to an end. Or, the parties may agree as to exactly what happened but still argue about the legal meaning of these facts. In that case, the trial judge will decide what the legal meaning of the facts is and enter a **summary judgment**. This is apparently what happened in the Memphis Development case. After agreeing that the facts were exactly as described above, the parties asked the judge to decide what the legal meaning of those facts was. And the trial judge decided that all of the facts, taken together, meant that Memphis Development Foundation could erect the statue if they wanted to but that they could not distribute the pewter replicas in exchange for money.

Summary Judgment An order of a trial judge which disposes of the controversy that resulted in a law suit prior to the trial of the law suit. A Summary Judgment can only be granted when the judge finds, as a matter of law, that there is no dispute about the facts of the controversy.

Once the trial judge enters his or her findings, the trial phase of the lawsuit ends. The losing party at this stage has the right to appeal the judge's decision to a higher court. In the federal court system, appeals from decisions at the district (trial) court level automatically go to the circuit court of appeals. Virtually all of the cases that you will study in this book will be opinions of appeals courts. That is because at the appeal stage, the only issue the court will think about is the legal meaning of the facts that were found to be true at the trial. It is these decisions about the legal significance of the established facts in a controversy that create the body of law we will be examining.

In order to make it easier for you to understand what the cases you will be studying mean, we recommend that you write a brief for each case. The case brief should have five sections. Each brief should identify clearly and succinctly the names of the parties to the action, the cause of action brought by the plaintiff, the nature of the proceedings in the lower courts, the decision of the appeals court, and the reasoning used by the appeals court in reaching its decision. The authors' brief for the Memphis Development Corporation case is included at the end of this chapter to provide an example of the recommended form.

The material in this book consists of text followed by cases. The purpose of the text portions is to introduce you to the legal theories that judges use to decide what the legal significance of the facts in a controversy ought to be. These discussions provide a framework that should help you understand the nature and operation of the legal principles that affect real estate transactions. Then, having mastered the basic principles, you will learn about real estate law by studying the cases included at the end of each chapter. By watching judges actually interpreting (and in some cases making) the legal principles that form American common law, you will thereby gain a much deeper insight into the fabric and meaning of real estate law.

CONCLUSION

This chapter has examined the origin and nature of legal systems used by various cultures around the world. We focused on some of the differences between the common law legal system, employed in the U.S., Canada, and Great Britain, and the civil law legal system, employed in much of Latin America and Europe.

Chapter 1 also examined the development of dispute-settlement procedures employed in the Anglo-American system of common law. The historical differences between the English courts of equity and courts of law were described, and the modern practice of unifying equity and law in the same court was explained.

Chapter 1 then described the federal system of constitutional governance employed in the United States. The relationship between the Supreme Law of the Land embodied in the U.S. Constitution and the acts of the United States Congress was depicted in relationship to the power and authority of state governments operating under the constitutional framework adopted in 1789.

Finally, Chapter 1 examined the procedures employed by the parties to a lawsuit together with the appeals of the decision that often follow a lawsuit. The chapter ended by recommending a form for studying decisions of appellate courts, in order to quickly discover the law embodied in those opinions.

MEMPHIS DEVELOPMENT FOUNDATION V. FACTORS ETC., INC.

616 F.2d 956 (Sixth Circuit, 1980)

MERRITT, Circuit Judge.

This appeal raises the interesting question: Who is the heir of fame? The famous have an exclusive legal right during life to control and profit from the commercial use of their name and personality. We are called upon in this diversity case to determine whether, under Tennessee law, the exclusive right to publicity survives a celebrity's death. We hold that the right is not inheritable. After death the opportunity for gain shifts to the public domain, where it is equally open to all.

I.

Elvis Presley died in Memphis on August 16, 1977. To honor him, the Memphis Development Foundation, a Tennessee non-profit corporation, laid plans to erect a large bronze statue of Presley in downtown Memphis. The Foundation solicited public contributions to pay for the sculpture. Donors of $25 or more received an eight-inch pewter replica of the proposed statue from the Foundation. The District Court held that the heirs and assigns of Presley retained his exclusive right of publicity after his death. It held that the exclusive right to exploit Elvis Presley's name and likeness currently belongs to Factors Etc., Inc., the assignee of Elvis Presley's "right of publicity." The District Court thus enjoined further distribution of the replicas by the Foundation. Prior to his death, Presley had conveyed the exclusive right to exploit the commercial value of his name and likeness to Boxcar Enterprises in exchange for royalties. . . . Two days after Presley's death, Boxcar sold a license to use its rights to Factors for $150,000. Presley's father agreed to the sale on behalf of Elvis' estate.

The Foundation instituted this action seeking a declaratory judgment that Factors' license does not preclude distribution by the Foundation of the pewter replicas and that the Foundation has the right to erect the Presley statue. Factors in turn by counterclaim seeks damages and an injunction against further distribution of the replicas by the Foundation. Factors claims that the Foundation is selling the statuettes for $25 apiece, and thus appropriating Factors' exclusive right to reap commercial value from the name and likeness of Elvis Presley.

The District Court issued an injunction against the Foundation. The injunction allows the Foundation to build the Presley memorial but prohibits it from manufacturing, selling or distributing any statuette bearing the image or likeness of Elvis Presley, or utilizing commercially in any manner or form the name, image, photograph or likeness of Elvis Presley.

II.

At common law, there is a right of action for the appropriation or unauthorized commercial use of the name or likeness of another. An individual is entitled to control the commercial use of these personal attributes during life. But the common law has not heretofore widely recognized this right to control commercial publicity as a property right which may be inherited.

* * *

Tennessee courts have not addressed this issue directly or indirectly, and we have no way to assess their predisposition. Since the case is one of first impression, we are left to review the question in the light of practical and policy considerations, the treatment of other similar rights in our legal system, the relative weight of the conflicting interests of the parties, and certain moral presuppositions concerning death, privacy, inheritability and economic opportunity. These considerations lead us to conclude that the right of publicity should not be given the status of a devisable right, even where as here a person exploits the right by contract during life.

III.

Recognition of a post-mortem right of publicity would vindicate two possible interests: the encouragement of effort and creativity, and the hopes and expectations of the decedent and those with whom he contracts that they are creating a valuable capital asset. Although fame and stardom may be ends in themselves, they are normally by-products of one's activities and personal attributes, as well as luck and promotion. The basic motivations are the desire to achieve success or excellence in a chosen field, the desire to contribute to the happiness or improvement of one's fellows and the desire to receive the psychic and financial rewards of achievement. As John Rawls has written, such needs come from the deep psychological fact that the individuals want the respect and good will of other persons and "enjoy the exercise of their realized capacities (their innate or trained abilities), and this enjoyment increases the more the capacity is realized, or the greater its complexity." (Footnote omitted.) According to Rawls: (Such) activities are more enjoyable because they satisfy the desire for variety and novelty of experience, and leave room for feats of ingenuity and invention. They also evoke the pleasures of anticipation and surprise, and often the overall form of the activity, its structural development, is fascinating and beautiful. *A Theory of Justice* 426–27 (1971). Fame is an incident of the strong motivations that Rawls describes. The desire to exploit fame for the commercial advantage of one's heirs is by contrast a weak principle of motivation. It seems apparent that making the right of publicity inheritable would not significantly inspire the creative endeavors of individuals in our society.

IV.

On the other hand, there are strong reasons for declining to recognize the inheritability of the right. A whole set of practical problems of judicial line-drawing would arise should the courts recognize such an inheritable right. How long would the "property" interest last? In perpetuity? For a term of years? Is the right of publicity taxable? At what point does the right collide with the right of free expression guaranteed by the first amendment? Does the right apply to elected officials and military heroes whose fame was gained on the public payroll, as well as to movie stars, singers and athletes? Does the right cover posters or engraved likenesses of, for example, Farah Fawcett Majors or Mahatma Gandhi, kitchen utensils ("Revere Ware"), insurance ("John Hancock"), electric utilities ("Edison"), a footbal stadium ("RFK"), a pastry ("Napoleon"), or the innumerable urban subdivisions and apartment complexes named after famous people? Our legal system normally does not pass on to heirs other similar personal attributes even though the attributes may be shared during life by others or have some commercial value. Titles, offices and reputation are not inheritable. Neither are trust or distrust and friendship or enmity descendible. An employment contract during life does not create the right for heirs to take over the job. Fame falls in the same category as reputation; it is an attribute from which others may benefit but may not own.

* * *

The question is whether the specific identification and use of the opportunity during life is sufficient to convert it into an inheritable property right after death. We do not think that whatever minimal benefit to society may result from the added motivation and extra creativity supposedly encouraged by allowing a person to pass on his fame for the commercial use of his heirs or assigns outweighs the considerations discussed above.

Accordingly, the judgment of the District Court is reversed and the case is remanded for further proceedings consistent with the principles announced above.

SAMPLE BRIEF

MEMPHIS DEVELOPMENT V. FACTORS INC.

Cause of Action

Plaintiff Memphis Development sued Factor's Inc., demanding a declaratory judgement that defendant's licensing rights do not preclude the plaintiff from erecting a statue of Elvis Presley and selling pewter replicas of the statue. Defendant counterclaimed for damages and injunction prohibiting the sale of the statue replicas.

Proceedings

Federal District court, in a diversity action, ruled that plaintiff was not entitled to declaratory relief. The District court also granted an injunction against Memphis Development on the defendant's counterclaim.

Facts

Prior to his death, Elvis Presley conveyed the exclusive right to exploit the commercial value of his name and likeness to Boxcar Enterprises. After his death, Boxcar conveyed a license to use these rights to Factors, Inc. Plaintiff, a Tennessee non profit corporation, planned to solicit money to erect a large bronze statue of Presley in Memphis. To encourage donors, the plaintiff agreed to provide a small pewter replica of the statue to everyone who contributed $25 or more for the construction of the monument.

Issue

Is the exclusive legal right to profit from commercial exploitation of a deceased person's name or accomplishments a property interest which can be sold or passed by inheritance?

REASONING AND HOLDING

Recognizing a property right of publicity which survives the death of a famous person advances two different interests of society; the encouragement of creativity and effort, and the creation of a valuable capital asset which the heirs of a famous person can hope to profit from after his or her death.

On the other hand, such a property right would raise a large set of practical problems for courts to solve which do not exist in the absence of an inheritable right to profit from the fame of a decedent. In balancing the benefits and problems of recognizing such a property right, the Sixth Circuit concluded that the problems far outweighed the benefits, and therefor refused to recognize a proprietary interest in the name or fame of Elvis Presley.

Reversed and remanded.

Gateway Center
MOTOR LODGE
Red Coach

CHAPTER

2

REAL AND PERSONAL PROPERTY OWNERSHIP

LEARNING OBJECTIVES

When you finish reading this chapter, you should be able to:

1. Describe what is meant by the statement "This is my car"
2. Describe the differences between real property and personal property
3. Understand the scope of ownership rights attached to a parcel of real property

KEY TERMS

Natural Law
Civil Law
Real Property
Personal Property
Annexation
Severance
Fixtures
Trade Fixtures
Air Rights
Mineral Rights

As late-twentieth-century Americans, we swim in a rich and complex sea of ownership relations. Because the ownership of property is such a fundamental part of our lives, we are often unaware of the full meaning of apparently simple statements such as "This is my car." In fact, the claim of ownership expressed by this statement is a large and complicated notion that has been hammered out by trial and error over many hundreds of years.

The purpose of this chapter is to step back and carefully examine the meaning of various ownership claims. In the process, we will discover that the Anglo-American system of property law used in this country has played and continues to play an important role in the tremendous growth of material wealth that has marked the continuing social experiment as we call America. We will begin our investigation by considering the work of some of the great legal philosophers who have contributed significantly to our understanding of the nature of property.

CONCEPTS OF PROPERTY

Natural Law A philosophy of law which seeks to examine the natural order of things and relationships in the world, in order to define the meaning of legal principles. In practice, Natural Law philosophies are most concerned with the duties and obligations of citizens in a society.

Jeremy Bentham was a philosopher who wondered about the difference between **"natural law"** and "civil law." Natural law, according to Bentham, is the set of rules governing the activities of people in the natural order of things; for example, it is part of natural law that people who do not eat will die. Civil law refers to the set of rules people make up for themselves to determine how they will relate to one another. An example of a rule of **civil law** is the popular English dictum, "He who killeth a man while he is drunk, shall be hanged while he is sober."

During the late 1600s and early 1700s, a tremendous debate occurred in Europe and England over the relative merits and meaning of natural and civil law. The framers of the U.S. Constitution studied this debate carefully for ideas to help them structure a new nation on a new continent. In the following passage, Bentham summarized some of these ideas that frame our basic system of government:

> The better to understand the advantages of law, let us endeavour to form a clear idea of *property*. We shall see that there is no such thing as natural property, and that it is entirely the work of law.
>
> Property is nothing but a basis of expectation; the expectation of deriving certain advantages from a thing which we are said to possess, in consequence of the relation in which we stand towards it.
>
> There is no image, no painting, no visible trait, which can express the relation that constitutes property. It is not material, it is metaphysical; it is a mere conception of the mind.
>
> To have a thing in our hands, to keep it, to make it, to sell it, to work it up into something else, to use it—none of these physical circumstances, nor all united, convey the idea of property. A piece of stuff which is actually in the Indies may belong to me while the dress I wear may not. The aliment which is incorporated into my very body may belong to another, to whom I am bound to account for it.
>
> The idea of property consists in an established expectation; in the persuasion of being able to draw such or such an advantage from the thing possessed, according to the nature of the case. Now this expectation, this persuasion, can only be the work of law. I cannot count upon the enjoyment of that which guarantees it to me. It is law alone which

> permits me to forget my natural weakness. It is only through the protection of law that I am able to inclose a field, and to give myself up to its cultivation with the sure though distant hope of harvest. . . .
>
> Property and law are born together, and die together. Before laws were made there was no property; take away laws and property ceases.
>
> (*Quoted in Cribbet, Fritz, and Johnson,* Cases and Materials on Property, *6th ed.* [*Foundation Press, 1984*])

Civil Law
A philosophy of law which seeks to determine the ways things should be in order to construct a set of legal principles which results in a "just" society. In practice, Civil Law philosophies are most concerned with protecting the rights and privileges of citizens in a society.

The debate between the proponents of natural law and civil law did not end in the eighteenth century. During the early years of this century, several scholars developed a philosophy in which law is thought of as a system of "juro-correllatives." According to this framework, the generic "rights" that people have in a functioning legal system actually have four different aspects, called "rights (in the strict sense)," "powers," "liberties," and "immunities." Each of these aspects of generic legal rights has a corresponding (or correlative) feature that exists in the legal system. For example, the correlative of a right (in the strict sense) is the duty of all other persons not to interfere with the exercise of that right. The correlative of a power is the nonright of all other persons to interfere with the use of that power, and so on.

Roscoe Pound, the late dean of the Harvard Law School, used this philosophy to argue against the position of a man named Duguit, who was a proponent of a natural law theory of property. The following passage is taken from an article published by Dean Pound in the *American Bar Association Journal* in 1939. The tone of the article clearly reflects the tumult and turmoil experienced by the world in the opening days of the Second World War.

> Rights, liberty, property, law, four ideas which grew up in contests with arbitrary personal rulers, are losing ground and as we are told by many, will disappear in the society of the future. It is significant that they are losing [ground] with the rise of the new [theories which suggests that governments have the absolute right to control the activities of their citizens]. . . .
>
> Duguit tells us that there are no such things as rights. There are only social functions. . . . "Liberty," says Duguit, "is a function." He adds: "Today each person is considered as having a social function to fulfil and therefore is under a social duty to develop to the greatest possible extent his physical, intellectual and moral personality in order to perform his function most effectively."
>
> . . . [However, according to the civil philosophy of law] property involves six rights: a *jus possidendi* or right of possessing, a right in the strict sense; a *jus prohibendi* or right of excluding others, also a right in the strict sense; a *jus disponendi* or right of disposition, what we should now call a legal power; a *jus utendi* or right of using, what we should now call a liberty; a *jus fruendi* or right of enjoying the fruits and profits; and a *jus abutendi* or right of destroying or injuring if one likes—the two last also what today we should call liberties. Thus at least half of the content of a right of property is liberty—freedom of applying as one likes, free of legal restraint. But, says Duguit, "property is not a right, it is a social function. The owner, that is to say the possessor of wealth, by the fact of his possession, has a social function to perform." If he does not perform it, the state is to intervene and compel him to employ [his wealth] "according to its nature."
>
> (*Pound, "The Law of Property and Recent Juristic Thought,"* ABA Journal *25 (1939): 993–98*)

The contests with arbitrary personal rulers that Pound alluded to are real contests that have continued throughout most of the history of human civilization. The American Revolution was a significant, but by no means final, chapter in the history of such contests. Tension between the natural law philosophy of property as a thing that imposes social duties upon its owner and the civil law philosophy of property as the cornerstone of individual liberty still exists today, in virtually the same form in which that tension has existed for the past three hundred years.

KEY POINTS

Environmental law, a rapidly expanding field that will be examined in Part III, rests largely upon a natural law understanding of property rights. One example is the comprehensive body of wetland regulations. Swamps and marshes play an important environmental role as habitat for many plant, animal, and fish species, as well as providing a natural filter capable of trapping and removing pollutants from groundwater. Current wetland regulations are founded upon the belief that real property owners have a duty to maintain these important ecological systems intact for the benefit of everyone in society. The existence of social duties to be borne by property owners is one of the hallmarks of natural law philosophy.

In the cases you will study in this and the following chapters, you will see (if you look closely) a process that can adjust and relieve these tensions without violence or bloodshed. Along the way, you may also develop your own views on the meaning of ownership and your own perceptions of the role of property in the life of a nation.

CATEGORIES OF PROPERTY

Real Property The set of ownership rights and duties which are associated with land and buildings.

Personal Property The set of ownership rights and duties which are associated with everything which is not real property.

The law of property makes a distinction between two broad categories of property: **real property** and **personal property**. The category of personal property includes anything capable of being moved from one place to another. Automobiles, stereos, kitchen utensils, and the like are all items of personal property. The category of real property includes land, buildings, and other permanent items that cannot be moved from one place to another. This division sounds simple, but in practice it can become quite confusing.

For example, if you were to drive by a vacant lot on a spring day and notice piles of lumber, drywall, and wiring on the ground, you would be correct in assuming that all of the items in the piles are personal property. They can easily be loaded into a truck and removed to some other location. In fact the law will treat these piles of building materials as personal property, belonging to the contractor who placed them on the lot. This is just another way of saying that the piles of material do not belong to the owner of the land. Now, if you were to drive by the same lot five months later, you might find that the piles of building materials were gone, while a house now stands on the previously vacant lot. The house is clearly real property, and it belongs to the same person as the lot beneath the house. This common occurrence might lead you to ask, "When did the piles of personal property belonging to the contractor become real property (a house) belonging to the landowner?"

Another example will add to the mystery. Suppose you drive through the country one day in August and chance to see a field of wheat ripening in the summer sun. Since the wheat plants are attached to the ground as firmly as the farmhouse you see in the distance, it seems reasonable to conclude that the wheat crop, like the house, is part of the real property belonging to the owner of the land. Three weeks later, you drive by the same field and see a person who is not the owner of the land loading the harvested wheat into a truck and driving away with it. This occurrence might lead you to ask, "When does something that is part of the land become personal property that belongs to someone other than the land owner?"

The mystery is solved by defining two terms that the law uses in order to determine when property changes from real to personal or vice versa. Personal property becomes real property when it is **"annexed"** to the real estate. Real property becomes personal property when it is **"severed"** from the real estate. Determining whether a particular item has been annexed to or severed from a parcel of land is usually the same as deciding which person in the world has the right to claim, "This is my carpeting" or "Those are my grapes."

Annexation
The legal principle which defines the mechanical processes required to convert an item of personal property into a fixture.

Fixtures

A **fixture** is an item of personal property that has become part of the real estate where it is located. The owner of the land is always the owner of the fixture. In general, courts will use a two-prong test to determine if an item of personal property has become a fixture:

a. The item has been securely attached to the land or to a building located on the land.
b. From the circumstances, it is clear that the intention to make the item part of the real estate existed at the time it was attached to the realty.

Severance
The legal principle which defines the mechanical processes required to convert an item of real property into personal property.

When both conditions are met, courts will usually conclude that the item has been annexed to the property and has therefore become a fixture that belongs to the owner of the real estate. Some courts have begun to require a third condition for annexation: that the property be adapted for or applied to the particular use or function of the real estate. As an example, a gas pump securely attached to the driveway of a filling station would pass the "applied-to-use test," while the same gas pump attached to the back lot of a car dealership would not pass the test.

Merritt-Chapman v. Mauro

Fixtures
Items which become real property through the process of attachment to land or buildings.

Trade Fixtures

The doctrine of **trade fixtures** is an unfortunate misnomer that applies only to commercial real estate leases. When a tenant rents a building for the purpose of conducting a trade or business on the leased premises, the tenant will often spend substantial amounts of money adding the specialized equipment needed to conduct the business. At the end of the lease, the question arises as to who owns the equipment installed by the tenant. If the items of personal property are fixtures, then they belong to the landlord, even though the tenant paid for the purchase and installation of the equipment. Courts have been reluctant to provide such a windfall to landlords

Consiglio v. Carey

Trade Fixtures The legal doctrine applied to items of personal property installed in or upon real property which is leased for the purpose of conducting a trade or business. Items of personal property which meet the trade fixture definition retain their character as personalty, even though they are securely attached to a parcel of land or to a building.

and have developed the doctrine of trade fixtures to prevent such a result. Courts have developed a four-part test for circumstances such as these:

a. The tenant leased the premises for the purpose of conducting a trade or business.
b. The equipment was purchased and installed by the tenant on or after the day the tenant was allowed to enter the premises.
c. The equipment was actually used in the tenant's trade or business conducted on the leased premises.
d. The equipment can be removed without substantial damage to the premises.

When items of property meet these conditions, courts will generally decide that the items are trade fixtures, which means that the property is really not a fixture at all. Since it is clear from the circumstances that the tenant did not intend for the equipment to become part of the landlord's property, then the installation fails part (b) of the two-part annexation test above. "Trade fixture" is simply a short-hand term for personal property that has been installed in, but not annexed to, a commercial building. And, since annexation did not occur, the commercial tenant can legally remove the equipment at the end of the lease.

Modern Trends

During and after the Great Depression of the 1930s, many courts began gradually to extend the doctrine of trade fixtures. The most usual extension was to apply the notions underlying the doctrine to personal property attached to premises by tenants who occupy a building for residential purposes rather than for strictly commercial purposes.

In some jurisdiction, judges seized upon the adapted-to-use test for trade fixtures. These courts tended to find that items of personal property added by tenants to an apartment were adapted to the residential use of the apartment and should thus be treated in the same way as trade fixtures in a commercial property. (Remember that trade fixtures remain the personal property of the commercial tenant. By extension, items attached to the premises of an apartment will remain the personal property of the residential tenant.)

Courts in other jurisdictions approached the problem by analyzing the annexation test. Recall that the second part of the test was that the owner of the personal property intended for it to become part of the real property at the time the personal property was attached to the realty. These courts would often decide that a tenant in an apartment lacked the required intention when he or she installed cabinets, appliances, or other goods in an apartment to make it more livable. Since the intention was lacking, the property was not annexed. Since the property was not annexed, it did not become a fixture and so remained the personal property of the tenant.

While these developments have probably created a more equal justice between landlords and tenants, they have also managed to muddy the waters surrounding the issue of when personal property will become real property. As a general rule, personal property affixed to real estate by the owner will usually be treated as a fixture, thus belonging to the owner of the realty. Personal property affixed to real estate by a tenant after taking possession of the property under a lease will be treated as personal property that the tenant can remove at the expiration of the lease. But there are exceptions to both of these general rules.

The amount of effort required to remove the disputed property from the real estate, as well as the damage that will result from the removal, remain important factors. As the amount of effort and damage involved in removing an item increases, courts become more willing to treat the item as part of the real estate, belonging to the owner of the real property. Furthermore, not all states recognize the rights of tenants to remove property they have installed to the same degree. Some states lean more in the direction of protecting tenants' rights, while others lean more toward the rights of landlords. As a result, when someone asks whether "a particular item in a building is an item of personal property belonging to the tenant," the answer is a definite "maybe."

CONTRACT DEFINITIONS

"Maybe" is not the kind of term we would associate with the idea that property is a clear set of rights and expectations, as Dean Pound described it earlier. This is the first of many examples we will encounter where the law of property needs to be clarified by resorting to the law of contracts. Whenever the parties to a real estate transaction agree with each other on the items to be included in the transaction, courts can be expected to honor the agreement. Confusion and uncertainty arise most frequently when parties to a transaction have been careless in making an agreement that both parties are expected to honor.

Leases are contracts for the possession of a parcel of real property during a definite time period. We will examine leases more thoroughly in Chapter 4. For now, it is enough to mention that every lease should contain a clause spelling out the ownership of property attached to the rented premises by the tenant. The following three examples illustrate the range of expectations that can be created by a carefully drawn contract.

1. All items of personal property installed by the tenant within the demised premises are, and shall remain the property of the tenant. The tenant shall have the right to remove any such items of property installed during the period of this lease within a reasonable time after the expiration of the lease.
2. All items of personal property which are or become attached to any wall, ceiling or floor within the demised premises become, by virtue of their attachment, the property of the landlord. The tenant shall not remove any items from the premises at the expiration of the lease except the furniture, clothing and household goods which belong to the tenant.
3. All items of personal property installed by the tenant within the demised premises are, and shall remain the property of the tenant. The tenant agrees to remove all such items before the expiration of the lease. The tenant further agrees to reimburse the landlord for the actual cost of repairing any damage resulting from the installation or removal of an item of personal property installed by the tenant.

Obviously, the first example would be the favorite choice of tenants; the second example would be preferred by landlords; while the third example represents a compromise between the two extremes. A lease that contains language similar to one of these examples leaves no room for doubt about the ownership of any item within the rented premises. When the lease is silent on this issue, then any disputes about ownership will have to be resolved by a court. In that case, the final resolution of the dispute is likely to remain unclear for a substantial period of time.

The issue of what is a fixture and what is personal property can also arise in the sale of a parcel of real estate. Is the dining room chandelier a fixture that will remain with the house when the new owner takes possession, or is it an item of personal property that the present owners are allowed to remove and take to their new home? To avoid disputes of this kind, a good real estate sales contract will include a paragraph similar to the following:

> Property includes garden bulbs, plants, shrubs and trees, all storm doors and windows, detachable vestibules, screens, awnings, window shades, blinds (including venetian blinds), curtain rods, traverse and drapery rods, lighting fixtures and bulbs, plumbing fixtures, hot water tanks and heating plant (with any burners, tanks, stokers, and other equipment used in connection therewith) and liquid gas tank and controls (if property of seller); permanently installed sump pump, television antenna, incinerator, built-in dishwasher, garbage disposal, ovens, cook-top stoves, and central air conditioning equipment, basketball hoop, mailbox, wall-to-wall carpeting, attached linoleum, attached garage door opener and controls, if any used on said premises, and also the following personal property:

A blank line usually follows the preceding paragraph, where the buyer may add any additional items of property that are to be included with the sale of the real estate. In addition, the present owner is free to line out any of the printed items (e.g., the basketball hoop) to exclude them from the sale. But once the buyer and the seller have agreed to a list of items that are included and a list of items that are excluded, then each party knows exactly what to expect from the transaction.

Severance

There are times when an item of real property becomes personal property through removing the item from the land where it is found. Growing crops, timber, valuable minerals, and (in some states) oil and gas are examples of property that may be transformed from real property into personal property by severance.

Courts generally rely on the Uniform Commercial Code (UCC) provisions for guidance in working with property that is severed from real estate. The UCC states that minerals, structures on land, and the materials in the structures are all real property until the seller of the property severs it from the land. (Severance occurs when the property is removed from the surrounding land so that it can be put on a truck and moved away.) Crops and other growing things are treated as personal property from the moment the owner of the item agrees to sell the produce of the land. Crops and other growing things are treated as goods by the UCC regardless of whether the buyer or the seller will sever them from the land.

THE SCOPE OF REAL PROPERTY

As we have already discovered, the statement "This is my car" is a great deal more complex than it appears to be. As Dean Pound pointed out in the excerpt at the beginning of this chapter, a statement of ownership involves six different legal principles. Stating that this car is mine is a convenient way of saying that I have the right to use the car, possess the car, exclude others from the car, sell the car, rent the car, and drive it over a cliff when I get tired of the car.

KEY POINTS

In California (and probably in many other states) if you drive your car over a clif you may be held legally responsible for violating numerous antipollution regulations. The spill of oil, gasoline, and hydraulic fluids that would most certainly accompany such an activity would probably result in personal liability for fines and cleanup costs that would run into several thousands of dollars. It is never safe for real estate practitioners to ignore the conflict between natural law philosophies, which are mainly concerned with the social duties of property owners, and civil law philosophies, which are mainly concerned with the rights of property owners.

The statement "This is my land" is even more complex. To begin with, this statement includes the six generic legal rights that are included with the ownership of a car. In addition, the nature of the thing that is owned is more complex when the property is land rather than a car. With real property, the claim of ownership extends not only to the soil enclosed by the boundaries of the property (the land itself) but also includes all of the buildings and other structures annexed to the soil, the trees, bushes, and other growing things found on the land, the minerals beneath the surface of the land, and more. For example, we should ask who owns the water in the creek that flows across a piece of property. We might also ask how far the right to exclude others from the surface of the land extends above and below the surface. Is someone who digs a tunnel underneath my land trespassing? How about someone who flies an airplane over the roof of my house? Is the pilot a trespasser? The answers to these questions will go a long way toward defining the meaning of the statement "This is my land."

Air Rights

Air Rights
The exclusive right to occupy, use and enjoy the air above a parcel of real property.

Cujus est solum ejus est usque ad coelum et ad infernos (Whoever owns the soil also owns to the heavens and to the depths). This ancient doctrine of real property ownership is still part of the American law of property. An Iowa judge observed, "The title of the owner of the soil extends not only downward to the center of the earth, but upward *usque ad coelum,* although it is, perhaps, doubtful whether owners as quarrelsome as the parties in this case will ever enjoy . . . their property in the latter direction" (*Hannabalson v. Sessions,* 90 N.W. 93 (Iowa, 1902)).

The plaintiffs owned 2.8 acres of land near an airport outside of Greesboro, North Carolina. They lived on the property, and raised chickens there. During WW II, the U.S. government leased the airport for use by military aircraft. The glide path to the runway used by bombers and fighters passed directly over the plaintiffs property, at a height of 67 feet above the roof of the house. The noise from aircraft taking off and landing at the airport rendered the plaintiff's property uninhabitable.

The Supreme Court relied upon the Air Commerce Act of 1926 in holding that the U.S. government has complete and exclusive national sovereignty in the navigable air space above the continental U.S. However where, as in this case, the use of the navigable airspace renders the surface of the ground unusable, the Supreme Court held that a taking has occurred which requires the government to compensate the land owner for the loss of surface use. U.S. v. Causby, 328 U.S. 256 (1946)

The ownership right of excluding others from the air above the soil and of using the air above one's property did not become particularly valuable until after the Civil War. However, as cities grew ever larger and the population density within cities increased, development patterns began to change. Buildings grew taller in order to accommodate and house ever larger numbers of people within a reasonable distance from the city center. New construction methods and improved building materials led to the development of "skyscraper" buildings, which are now the hallmark of a large urban area.

As the sky filled with buildings, experiments in vertical subdivisions were undertaken in the nation's largest cities. For example, 896 apartments were built by a developer over railway lines located near the center of Chicago. Later, the Pan Am building was constructed in the air space above the Grand Central railway station in New York City. A motel and office complex has been built above the Massachusetts Turnpike right-of-way in Boston. In each case, the owner of the soil increased the value of the real property held by selling or leasing the right to build something in the air above the property.

From these experiments, two concepts have been added to the law of property. "Airspace" is now defined as the space above a given plane that contains a point that is a measured distance above the ground. For example, "all the space that is above a horizontal plane thirty-five feet above the northwest corner of Blackacre" will define an airspace. "Air rights" are an ownership right that includes the exclusive right to occupy an airspace.

When thinking about air rights, two things must be kept in mind. First, the owner of Blackacre can convey rights only to the air that is above Blackacre. Even though the airspace description might appear to include airspace above a neighboring parcel, the right to occupy airspace can only be acquired from the owner of the land beneath the airspace.

Second, an air right is valuable only when the owner of the air right obtains an easement from the surface owner for support of the structures to be built in the air space. Even though the building will only occupy the space more than thirty-five feet above the northwest corner of Blackacre, the building will have to touch the ground somewhere. Provisions for support of the structures in the air space must be made at the time the air space is created.

Mineral Rights The legal principles which define the ownership rights and duties of the person who removes (or will be permitted to remove) minerals beneath the surface of a parcel of real property.

Mineral Interests

The owner of the soil also owns "to the depths of the earth." Often, valuable mineral deposits are found beneath the surface; thus the owner of the soil can obtain greater value from that ownership by selling the right to exploit and remove the mineral deposits found within the ground.

Mineral interests can be created in either of two forms: a **mineral right** or a mineral lease. The sale of a mineral right conveys absolute title to the minerals in the ground. The mineral right can convey ownership in all of the minerals found in the ground or only in specific minerals such as sand and gravel or coal. Finally, mineral rights can be created either by grant (the owner of the surface sells the underground minerals to another) or by reservation (the owner sells the surface to another but retains the ownership of the underground minerals after the sale).

Brent v. Corbin

A mineral lease conveys the right to remove minerals for a specified time period only. In this case, the lessee becomes the owner of only those minerals that are actually removed during the period of the lease. All the minerals that remain at the end of the lease still belong to the owner of the soil. Mineral leases usually require a royalty payment to the surface owner, based upon the quantity of minerals removed by the lessee.

Mineral interests have the capacity to interfere significantly with the use and enjoyment of the surface of the land. Minerals can be removed by surface operations (open-pit mines, for example) or by subsurface mining and tunneling. Surface operations involve moving all of the soil above the valuable mineral deposits and transporting it to another location. After the valuable minerals have been exposed, they are dug out of the ground and loaded on trucks or train cars for transport to the mills and refineries where the minerals are processed. Even for minerals that lie close to the surface (e.g., sand and gravel), the extraction process will involve a great deal of noise, dust, and heavy truck traffic over the surface.

Plaintiffs owned the coal beneath a tract of land. The plaintiffs sued for an injunction requiring the owner of the surface to sign a written consent form permitting the plaintiff to enter the surface of the land and commence mining operations. The plaintiff argued that the consent of the surface owner was necessary to obtain a permit to mine the coal which it owned.

The Supreme Court of Pennsylvania held that the consent of the surface owner was not required, because the deed which conveyed the coal to the plaintiff included "the free and uninterrupted right and right of way into, upon, over, under and through the said land at such points and in such manner as may be necessary or convenient for the purpose of all operations in connection with [the development, processing and marketing of the plaintiff's coal.] Since the owner of the coal already possessed rights to use the surface in mining operations, the permission of the surface owner was not required by the Pennsylvania mining law. Sedat, Inc. v. Fisher, 617 A.2d 1 (Pa., 1992).

When minerals are removed by subsurface mining, the noise and dust problems are of little concern. However, the removal of large quantities of minerals can leave huge, open caverns underground that may eventually cave in and cause the surface of the land to drop by several feet. This settling action is usually sufficient to destroy any houses or other buildings that were constructed above the location of the cave-in.

Because the exploitation of mineral interests can affect the use and enjoyment of the surface, great care must be exercised when dealing with properties in which the mineral rights have been severed from the surface ownership. The nature and circumstances of the mineral rights conveyance must be examined thoroughly. Prospective owners of land with mineral interests severed from the surface ownership will want to know what kind of protection they might have against the hazards of mineral extraction. In particular, prospective owners will want to find out what rights they will have to limit the activity of the mineral rights holders on the surface. If valuable minerals are present under the surface, the prospective owner will have to develop a strategy to minimize the damage and discomfort that inevitably accompany mining operations.

KEY POINTS

A subdivision in the mountains of western Colorado was developed in the early 1970s on land that had previously been used as a cattle ranch. In 1968 the owner of the ranch sold all of the minerals beneath the soil to a mining company. The deed conveying the minerals to the mining company allowed the mineral owner to remove soil, to build and maintain roadways, and to pile rocks and other mine tailings anywhere on the surface of the property. In addition, the conveyance allowed the mining company to avoid responsibility for any subsidence or movement of the surface soil caused by underground cave-ins.

A geologist has informed you that commercial quantities of coal can be found approximately one thousand feet below the surface of the land. Would you be willing to buy one of the houses in that subdivision? If not, where does that leave the developer of the subdivision?

Oil Leases

Oil is a special case of underground mineral because it is a liquid. As a result, oil located beneath the surface of Whiteacre will often migrate across property lines when oil is being removed from Blackacre, the property next door. Because of the nature of oil, some states have recognized that oil cannot be owned until it is removed from the ground. Other states hold that oil, like any mineral, can be subject to absolute ownership.

The difference between the two views is not an important one, since all states recognize the rule of capture. This rule holds that the owner of the surface has the right to appropriate oil and gas from any wells drilled on the surface, whether or not the oil has migrated from an adjacent property. The rule of capture is the only reasonable way to identify the ownership of oil and gas. Once the oil is brought to the surface by a well, it is impossible to determine if the oil has migrated to the well from another person's land or not.

The rule of capture insures that the owner who pumps oil out of the ground the fastest will get the most oil. Owners who would prefer to leave the oil in the ground and recover it later run the risk of losing their oil to neighbors who are pumping out the underground reserve as rapidly as possible. The federal government has recognized that the capture rule has the potential to distort the economic incentives for finding and removing oil. As a result, the production of oil is intensively regulated in this country. One purpose of the regulatory scheme is to limit the rate at which wells are allowed to remove oil from the ground. These limitations are designed to insure that oil that is not needed in the market today will remain in the ground until it is needed in the future.

Water Rights

The final topic of real property ownership is the right to use water found on or beneath the surface of the land. Water rights can be determined under either the riparian theory or the prior appropriation doctrine.

Riparian Theory

The riparian theory of water usage is part of the ancient common law of England. This approach to water prevails in most of the states east of the Mississippi River, where the abundant rainfall resembles the climatic conditions of England. Riparian lands are those lands that touch a flowing stream of water. The owner of riparian lands has a right to use the water from the stream in any way that does not unreasonably harm the owner of riparian lands downstream. (Some states use a slightly more restrictive test: the owner of riparian lands may use the water in any way that does not interfere with the natural flow of the stream.) Where water is plentiful, the riparian approach to water rights works reasonably well. In the arid western regions of the nation, however, another approach was required.

Boylan v. Van Dyke

> The owners of the lots bordering Lake Beulah all took their property via a 1939 deed which contained an easement in favor of the non-riparian owners in a subdivision near the lake. The deed reserved an easement to the non-riparian owners granting the "the right . . . to use the lake shore for boating, bathing and kindred purposes."
>
> In 1989, the riparian owners removed a dock which had been erected by the non-riparian owners, and informed the residents of the lots which did not abut the lake that they would no longer be permitted to use the lake shore. The non-riparian owners sued for an injunction prohibiting the riparian owners from interfering with the rights they enjoyed under the easement. The Wisconsin Court of Appeals affirmed a judgment for the defendants, holding that "the case law has made it clear that non-riparian owners have no riparian rights." The Supreme Court of Wisconsin reversed, holding that "one who acquires land abutting a body of water may acquire no more [rights] than are conveyed by the deed." The easement to use the lake shore for boating and swimming reserved those rights to the non-riparian owners. Stoesser v. Shore Drive Partnership. 494 N.W. 2d 204 (Wis, 1993)

Prior Appropriation Doctrine

Under this approach, the first person to apply water to a beneficial use acquires the right to use the water. By applying water to a beneficial use (e.g., irrigation) one becomes the owner of the quantity of water so applied. In many western states, this ownership is recognized in the form of a "water right" that permits the holder to withdraw a stated quantity of water from a named source each year.

Colorado was among the first states to completely reject the riparian theory and adopt a strict prior appropriation law for water usage. As a result, virtually every drop of water in the state is now the subject of an ownership right, in the form of an "adjudicated water right." A brief description of the Colorado system will serve to illustrate the workings of the prior appropriation doctrine.

Water rights are measured by the acre-foot, a volume of water sufficient to cover an acre of land to a depth of one foot. A water right permits the owner to withdraw a fixed number of acre-feet of water from a named river or ditch. Water rights are adjudicated by the water court, an administrative tribunal that meets regularly for the purpose of administering all the water rights held in the state and resolving disputes between the owners of the rights.

The water court performs its function by using maps prepared in the office of the state water engineer. The water maps identify all of the natural water courses in the state. The maps also identify all of the ditches constructed for carrying water from a natural stream, lake, or reservoir to other locations. The water maps also provide information on the average rate of flow in each water course, measured in acre-feet per year.

A water right is obtained by removing unappropriated water from a river or ditch and applying it to a beneficial use, usually irrigation or municipal water supply purposes. After a statutory period, the person appropriating the water can apply to the water court for an adjudicated water right. The water court will examine the records to insure that the water appropriated does not belong to a prior water right. (In other words, the court will determine that all of the prior adjudicated water rights add up to an amount that is less than the water normally flowing through the stream or ditch from which the applicant has been appropriating the water requested for adjudication.)

Once a water right has been adjudicated, it becomes a valuable property that can be bought, sold, and enforced by the owner. If the owner of an adjudicated water right fails to apply the water to beneficial uses for a statutory period, the water right will be considered abandoned. The water covered by abandoned rights is returned to the unappropriated water supply in the state, so that a new user will be able to apply for an adjudicated right to use the water.

While the prior appropriation system seems to be cumbersome and unwieldy, it has served the west very well. For example, the Colorado River rises in the high mountains of western Colorado and flows through four states before reaching the Pacific Ocean near Mexicali, on the border between California and Mexico. Along the way, virtually all of the water in the river is removed by the owners of various water rights. Such intensive use of a resource that is scarce and precious in the west is the result anticipated by those who created the prior appropriation system of water law.

CONCLUSION

Property is a creature of law. The claim of ownership embodied by the statement "This is mine" is really just a set of expectations as to how I will be able to use the thing and benefit from it in the future. The existence of a legal system that recognizes my claim of ownership makes these expectations realistic and important.

The system of American property law recognizes the claim of ownership when applied to the soil of a particular real estate parcel. The claim of ownership is also extended to the air above the soil and the minerals beneath the soil. Finally, the American system of property law makes a distinction between the ownership rights in real property and the ownership rights in personal property. We have also reviewed circumstances where the claims of ownership in personal property and real property collide with each other.

DISCUSSION QUESTIONS:

1. Distinguish between real property and personal property. Cite some examples of each.
2. When does personal property become real property? When does real property become personal property?
3. What is a fixture? Who holds legal ownership of a fixture? How do the courts determine whether an item is personal property or a fixture?
4. Define trade fixture. What is the doctrine of trade fixtures? What is it intended to prevent?
5. Briefly explain a situation in which real property becomes personal property. What is this called? Describe the two UCC provisions designed to assist parties working with severed property.
6. Distinguish between airspace and air rights.
7. Name the two forms in which a mineral interest can be created. What does each convey?
8. Briefly explain the two methods by which mineral rights are created.
9. Why is it so difficult to identify ownership of oil? Define the rule of capture. What is the problem with this rule?
10. Describe the two ways in which water rights can be determined.

PETER A. CONSIGLIO ET AL. V. GEORGE CAREY

421 N.E.2d 1257 (Mass., 1981)

Ownership of trade fixtures

ARMSTRONG, Justice.

During the summer seasons from 1975 through 1978, the defendant operated a restaurant called Dorsie's Steak House in a woodframe building at 183 Main Street in West Yarmouth. He paid the plaintiffs rents which escalated from $4,500 the first year to $8,500 in 1978. In the spring of 1979 the parties discussed the possibility of purchase and sale and apparently arrived at an understanding that the defendant would purchase the building and roughly an acre of land (the plaintiffs owned twenty-six acres) for $195,000. But the defendant then dragged his feet, and on June 8, 1979, the plaintiffs' counsel wrote a letter notifying the defendant, who had no written lease, that the rent would be increased to $35,000 per month as of July 8, 1979. The plaintiff Consiglio testified that the purpose of the letter was to induce the defendant to go through with the purchase, but by early July the plaintiffs learned that the defendant was preparing to move the restaurant to another building roughly a mile away.

The plaintiffs then brought the present action to enjoin the defendant from removing the restaurant equipment from the premises. . . . A trial was held in September, and the judge ruled that the defendant owned and had been entitled to take all of the equipment that he had removed from the premises between July 3 and July 11; that six major items of equipment which were claimed by the defendant but which remained on the premises were "trade fixtures affixed to the realty" and could not be removed by the defendant; and that the defendant should pay the plaintiffs $8,250 in addition to what they had already been paid as rent for 1979.

The defendant appealed from the judgment and contends that that portion of the judgment is erroneous which enjoined him from removing the six items of equipment. He does not contend that the determination of additional rental was erroneous. The plaintiffs did not appeal.

The six items of equipment are a walk-in freezer, a compressor which supplies the cold air to the freezer, two air conditioners, a dishwasher, and a bar. . . . Only one of the six contested items was on the premises when the defendant began his tenancy: namely, the dishwasher, which the defendant purchased from the prior occupant, Carl's Restaurant, Inc., along with many of the other items which the judge ruled the defendant had properly removed from the premises in July. The defendant purchased the two air conditioners and installed them in two of the three window casings on the street side of the building. The units were large; their installation necessitated removal of the sash from each casing. The walk-in freezer and the compressor were purchased by the defendant from a restaurant supply company. The freezer was twelve feet high, too high to be brought into the building. It was installed at the back wall of the building on an insulated concrete slab. A hole was cut in the rear wall of the building to provide access to the freezer door. A plywood shell was erected around the freezer to protect it from the sun and weather. The freezer itself is "portable", in the sense that a person using only an "Allen set wrench" can break it down into panels for easy transportation and reassembly. The compressor, bought at the same time, is also located outside the building and is attached only to the freezer. The defendant built the bar in 1979, shortly before the dispute which led to his departure. The nature of its attachment to the building does not appear in the recorded evidence, but the judge, who took a view, made a general finding that each of the items in question is attached to the realty.

* * *

A determination that the items are affixed to the realty does not, however, dispose of the case, as it might, for example if the items had been installed by the owner of the realty, and the dispute was with a purchaser of the realty, or between the owner as mortgagor and a mortgagee. Greene v. Lampert, 274 Mass. 386, 174 N.E. 669 (1931). "Many articles annexed by a tenant can be removed by him which, if annexed by the owner, become part of the realty and pass under a deed or mortgage." Smith v. Bay State Sav. Bank, 202 Mass. at 485, 88 N.E. 1086, and cases cited. At an early date it was "established by the cases, that things which the tenant has at his own expense affixed to the freehold for purposes of ornament or domestic convenience, or for purposes of trade, business or manufactures, may be removed by him before the expiration of his term. The right of removal depends upon the mode in which the thing to be removed is annexed to the freehold, and the effect which its removal would have upon the premises. It may be exercised in such a case, wherever it is not contrary to any prevailing usage, and causes no material injury to the estate, and where the thing can be removed without losing its essential character or value as a personal chattel." Hanrahan v. O'Reilly, Mass. 201, 203 (1869). . .

The distinction was of importance in early practice chiefly in the selection of the appropriate common law form of action. In Guthrie v. Jones, it was held that a tenant dispossessed by the landlord during the term of tenancy could not recover the value of his trade fixtures in an action of tort for conversion (trover), because the fixtures, although removable by the tenant, were not personalty.

That the cited cases are not notably recent is not an indication of their obsolescence but merely shows that settled law breeds little litigation. For more modern statements, see Restatement (Second) of Property, Landlord & Tenant, sec. 12.2(4), Comments r and s, and Illustrations 28 and 29 (1977); 5 Am. Law of Property s 19.11 (1952).

Applying these principles to the present case, we think it is clear that the items in dispute, except the dishwasher, are tenant's fixtures, having been installed by the defendant during his tenancy for the purpose to which he was putting the rented premises, and that they can be removed without damage to the items themselves and with only such damage to the premises as falls within the principles of [the cases cited previously]. As to that damage, the defendant has an obligation to restore the premises to the condition they were in before the tenancy, reasonable wear and tear excepted, and that obligation requires him to restore the sash which was removed to permit installation of the air conditioners, to remove the plywood shell and the foundation for the walk-in freezer (assuming that the plaintiffs desire this removal), and to restore the wall to its former condition. These obligations can be enforced by a requirement in the judgment that defendant post security for their proper performance, see Restatement (Second) of Property, sec. 12.2(4), Comment s, or they may be enforced in a separate action for damages.

The record does not enable us to determine whether the dishwasher is a tenant's fixture. It was purchased by the defendant from the prior tenant, Carl's Restaurant, Inc., but an officer of that corporation was not permitted to testify concerning its acquisition. It is unnecessarily speculative to attempt to infer that the dishwasher was installed by Carl's Restaurant, Inc., solely from the fact that it treated the dishwasher as its personal property by selling it to the defendant, when the matter may be made certain by direct evidence. If, on a rehearing, which need not extend beyond this question except in the discretion of the rehearing judge, it should be shown that the dishwasher was installed by Carl's Restaurant, Inc., and was thus removable by it during its tenancy, . . . we think that it would retain its character as a tenant's fixture if sold during that time to the next tenant. Otherwise it would, after expiration of the time allowed, become the property of the landlord. Natural Autoforce Ventilator Co. v. Winslow, 215 Mass. 462, 463, 102 N.E. 705 (1913). The judgment is reversed, and the case is remanded for further proceedings in accordance with this opinion.

So ordered.

Case Reflections

1. The walk in freezer was a large item securely attached to the real estate. Why was the tenant allowed to remove this item?
2. What was the question of fact which remained unresolved concerning the ownership of the dishwasher in the building?
3. What difference did it make to the appeals court that the property in dispute was used in the tenant's business?

OBERJUERGE RUBBER COMPANY V. STATE TAX COMMISSION OF MISSOURI

674 S.W.2d 186, (Mo., 1984)

Taxation of trade fixtures

SNYDER, Judge.

This is an appeal from a judgment which reversed a decision of the appellant State Tax Commission. The Commission included the value of two overhead cranes in the assessment of the value of respondent Oberjuerge Rubber Company's real property. The trial court found that the cranes were "trade fixtures" and as such should be assessed as personal property. The Commission appeals. The judgment is reversed and remanded.

* * *

Oberjuerge owns an office and warehouse building in St. Louis County. When the structure, which is a pre-engineered steel building referred to as a Butler building, was built, it was designed for the installation of two overhead cranes. Crane beams were included, the building columns were designed to bear the cranes, the footings were made heavy enough to support the cranes, and the building was built to a height designed to accommodate the cranes.

The cranes themselves were installed after the Butler building was completed. The overhead cranes move back and forth on tramrails which are located on opposite sides of the building and run the length of the building. The tramrails are supported by the crane beams in the ceiling and the crane beams in turn are supported by building columns. The cranes are electrically wired into the beams, but are removable.

The useful life of the two cranes, one a ten ton and the other a fifteen ton crane, is approximately fifteen years. The fair market value of the cranes as of the date of the assessment was $93,046.90. The fair market value of the Oberjuerge real property, including the cranes, was $1,237,842.00.

The St. Louis County tax assessor included the value of the cranes as part of the value of the realty. Oberjuerge appealed this assessment to the Commission, which upheld the assessment on the ground that the cranes were fixtures. A fixture is taxable as realty. Sec 137.010(3) RSMo.1978 (1983 Cum.Supp.). The St. Louis County Circuit Court reversed the Commission and from this judgment the Commission appeals.

* * *

In cases of common ownership, in which the annexor owns both the land and the attached chattel, the elements of a fixture are annexation to the realty, adaptation to the location, and the intent of the annexor at the time of the annexation. (Citations omitted.) The last element is generally regarded as the most important. Whether the annexor intended at the time of the annexation to make the article a permanent accession to the land is an objective test, to be determined from the annexor's acts and conduct and the surrounding facts and circumstances. *See* Bastas v. McCurdy, 266 S.W.2d 49, 51–52 (Mo.App.1954).

* * *

It has previously been shown that the proper test of a fixture in the common ownership cases . . . is the intention test, objectively applied. What would the reasonable person consider part of the land so as to pass with a deed or mortgage? It seems only proper that the same test should apply here. If the fixture is apparently part of the realty, the assessor is justified in relying on its appearance regardless of the existence of secret agreements for retention of title or a right of removal under the doctrine of trade fixtures. If the parties wish to avoid the more drastic consequences of the rule they need only give the assessor proper notice of separate ownership of such fixtures.

* * *

The issue is thus whether Oberjuerge annexed the overhead cranes to the realty, adapted them to the location and intended at the time of the annexation to make the cranes permanent accessions to the land.

The cranes were only slightly attached to the building because they were electrically wired into the beams and moved about along the tramrails. That the annexation may be slight or easily displaced will not, however, prevent an article from being a fixture if the article is adapted to the proper use of the building and was placed in the building by the owner with the intent of forming a part of the special object and design for which the building was constructed. (Citations omitted.) Thus, the undisputed facts point to annexation of the cranes to the building.

The element of adaptation is also proved by essentially undisputed facts. The building was designed and constructed so that the cranes could be used in it. The cranes perform an important function in moving about Oberjuerge's stock in trade, rubber conveyor belts. The overhead cranes are thus adapted to the proper use of the building and fulfill part of the special object and design for which the building was constructed.

The last element, intent, is of paramount importance. (Citations omitted.) Here, intent may be inferred from the fact that the cranes were suited for use in the building, which was specifically designed to use and accommodate them. *See* Banner Iron Works v. Aetna Iron Works, *supra.* Moreover, Oberjuerge's operations manager testified that the cranes were installed for use in the business and are actively used in the business.

Some evidence was adduced which might lead one to infer a lack of intent: Oberjuerge apparently treated the cranes separately from the building for federal income tax purposes and the building was constructed before the cranes were purchased. There was, however, substantial and competent evidence to support the Commission's finding of intent.

The overhead cranes are thus fixtures. Oberjuerge argues, however, and the circuit court found, that the cranes are trade fixtures, *cf.* Blackwell Printing Co. v. Blackwell-Wielandy Co., 440 S.W.2d 433, 438[6] (Mo.1969), and therefore taxable only as tangible personal property. This court declines to exempt Oberjuerge's cranes form the real property tax as trade fixtures. The overhead cranes are not trade fixtures. The distinction between ordinary fixtures and trade fixtures applies only in the context of the landlord-tenant relationship. Cusack v. Prudential Insurance Co., 192 Okl. 218, 134 P.2d 984, 989[7] (1943). "The doctrine of trade fixtures . . . is not applicable in the case of annexations made by the owner of the land." 35 Am.Jur.2d, Fixtures sec. 3 (1967).

The judgment of the circuit court is reversed and remanded and the Circuit Court directed to enter judgment affirming the decision of the Commission.

Case Reflections

1. Did the court rule that the cranes in Oberjuerge's building were personal property or real property?
2. Suppose Oberjuerge sells the building. Would the company be allowed to remove the cranes before delivering possession to the new owner? Why or why not?
3. Which was more securely attached to the building: the overhead crane in the Oberjuerge case or the walk in freezer in the Consigliari case? Why was the overhead crane held to be real property, while the walk in freezer was held to be personal property?

MERRITT-CHAPMAN AND SCOTT CORPORATION V. NICHOLAS MAURO ET AL.

368 A.2d 44, (Conn., 1976)

Annexation tests of fixtures

LOISELLE, Associate Justice

The plaintiff, Merritt-Chapman & Scott Corporation, brought this action to determine its rights in and to bowling equipment located in a building formerly owned by the defendant Nicholas Mauro, who had mortgaged it to the plaintiff's predecessor in interest in 1964. The plaintiff claims that it acquired title to this bowling equipment by virtue of the strict foreclosure of the mortgage in 1968. Mauro claims that this equipment had been excluded from the mortgage, that it was personalty and that title remained in him after foreclosure. After a trial to the court, judgment was rendered in favor of Mauro on all issues. On appeal, the plaintiff challenges the court's conclusion that the bowling equipment was not a fixture and the court's ruling in admitting certain parol evidence offered to prove Mauro's intention to exempt the bowling equipment from the mortgage.

The findings of the trial court, as corrected, may be summarized as follows: In 1960 or 1961, the defendant Nicholas Mauro purchased property known as the Enfield Plaza shopping center from its financially troubled owner, who had been unable to complete construction and who has rented only 60 percent of the center although the whole complex had been substantially completed. At the time the center included an unrented and unimproved area which Mauro unsuccessfully attempted to rent before he decided to turn it into a bowling alley. The unrented portion of the complex later occupied by the bowling alleys had been completed to the extent that a concrete floor had been laid but no ceiling or air conditioning had been installed. This unfinished condition would enable the owner to install the kind of flooring, ceiling and lighting that would be desired by a prospective tenant.

Thereafter, on September 28, 1962 Mauro contracted by conditional bill of sale with the defendant Brunswick Corporation to purchase the bowling equipment, the title to which is in issue here. The conditional bill of sale stated that the bowling equipment and accessories were to be located at the shopping center and would not be altered, modified or removed without the written consent of Brunswick. The total purchase price of the equipment was $267,711.06, of which $245,760 was to be paid in sixty-four monthly installments of $3840 each, with 6 percent interest thereon. Despite these terms, the purchase price was not paid in full until February, 1971. At the time of the purchase Brunswick required the defendant Mauro to obtain a consent agreement from Society for Savings, the holder of a first mortgage on the Plaza property, which stipulated that the bowling equipment "shall at all times be considered personal property and not attached to the real estate on which they are installed." The conditional bill of sale was filed in the Enfield land records, along with a financing statement which listed the bowling equipment and stated that this equipment was "affixed or to be affixed to real property," i.e., the Enfield Plaza shopping center.

* * *

[The court described the significant and expensive work required to prepare the space for the installation of the bowling lanes, and concluded with the following observation.] The bowling lanes may be removed by cutting them in two places, carrying them out in three sections on edge through a door and placing them on a flatbed trailer. Similarly, pinsetters may be disassembled, taken out through a regular doorway and loaded onto trucks. Removal of all of the lanes would take a ten-man crew ten days, and reinstallation would require eighty-five man-hours per lane.

The bowling equipment and restaurant area were completed and opened for business by the end of 1962; they were operated by or under Mauro until 1966, when they were rented to a tenant.

In July or August of 1964, Mauro applied for a loan of one million dollars from the Industrial Finance Corporation, the plaintiff's predecessor in interest. That loan was consummated in August, 1964, within two weeks of receipt of Mauro's application, and was secured by a mortgage on ten commercial properties, including the Enfield Plaza shopping center. . . .

The plaintiff's mortgage included a 'fixture clause' following the description of the ten mortgaged properties which stated that the mortgage was to include "insofar as the same are, or can by agreement of the parties be made, a part of the realty, all structures, fixtures and appliances now or hereafter on the described premises, or used therewith. . . . "

* * *

The plaintiff claims that the trial court erred as a matter of law in concluding that the bowling equipment was not covered under the fixture clause of the 1964 mortgage but was instead personalty, title to which remained in Mauro.

* * *

In Lesser v. Bridgeport-City Trust Co., 124 Conn. 59, 198 A. 252, an action against a mortgagee who had foreclosed a mortgage secured by land and a building specially adapted for bowling alleys, the court stated the general rule: "There is a strong tendency as between mortgagor and mortgagee to hold that such articles are a part of the realty; whereas, in the case of landlord and tenant or other holder of a limited term, the tendency is the other way. The reason for this rule is that the owner of the equity is presumed to make improvements for the permanent benefit of the property, while a mere tenant is more likely to make them for his personal convenience." The court also said that especial stress should be given to whether a building was specially adapted to certain uses. "If so adapted, then the instrumentalities to carry out those purposes are ordinarily considered a part of the realty." *Ibid.* Further, in that case, the court considered whether the postannexation acts of the owners and operators confirmed an intention, at the time of annexation, to make the alleys a part of the realty. All facts found, with one exception, fulfilled every condition from which an intention would be presumed to make the personal property—the bowling alleys—a part of the realty. The exception was a conditional sale contract under which the original owners bought the alleys and equipment. Under the contract the alleys, as between vendor and vendee, were to be considered as personal property. In that case the vendor's security interest arising under the contract had been extinguished by the payment of the debt prior to the foreclosure and the "situation (was) the same as if no conditional bill of sale had been given." The court concluded that, under all the facts, the alleys, as a matter of law, were fixtures.

* * *

In the present action, the alleys were installed by the owner, thereby creating a presumption that he intended the alleys to be for the permanent benefit of the property. The bowling equipment was also bulky and considerable effort would be required to remove it from the building. Any other building would have to be specially prepared to use the equipment. *See* Capen v. Peckham, *supra.*

* * *

It is true, as stated in Lesser v. Bridgeport-City Trust Co., *supra,* that an article may retain it chattel character between a vendor and vendee but remain real property as between a mortgagor and mortgagee. Such evidence, however, although not conclusive, may be considered with other evidence presented, especially when at the time of foreclosure by the mortgagee, the vendor's security interest had not been extinguished by the payment of the debt. The alleys could not have been deemed to be realty as to all concerned. (Citation omitted.)

Contrary to the situation in Lesser in which the court placed "especial stress" on the fact that the building was specially adapted to bowling alleys, the building in this case, as constructed, was not adapted to bowling alleys, but the alleys were installed in a vacant area in a shopping center already built and adapted to produce rental income from any source.

In Webb v. New Haven Theatre Co., 87 Conn. 129, 133, 87 A. 274, the court found that one of the important factors tending to show an intent to annex permanently was that the removal of the installed articles would render the building practically useless for the purpose for which it was constructed and used.

Furthermore, acts subsequent to the installation of the alleys tend to confirm an intent that the alleys were to remain personalty. When the alleys were rented to a tenant, the rental was split, that is, rent was specifically charged for the space in the premises and rent was specifically charged for the use of the alleys. This arrangement continued after the foreclosure of the plaintiff's mortgage on August 12, 1968. After that date, the tenant only paid the plaintiff as owner of the premises for the use of the space. As the vendor of the alleys was not fully paid at the time of the foreclosure of the plaintiff's mortgage in August, 1968, Mauro continued to pay the vendor for the alleys after the foreclosure until they were paid in full in February, 1971. Mauro, or his tenants, paid the taxes, assessments and insurance premiums for the alleys as personalty before the foreclosure and, after the foreclosure, for the years 1969, 1970 and 1971. Furthermore, Mauro, after the foreclosure, spent from $25,000 to $28,000 for additional equipment on the alleys. All of these acts could be considered as confirming an intention that the bowling alley equipment placed in the vacant area of the shopping center was to remain personalty. (Citations omitted.)

"A question of intent is a question of fact, the determination of which is not reviewable unless the conclusion drawn by the trier of fact is one which cannot reasonably be reached." International Brotherhood v. Commission on Civil Rights, 140 Conn. 537, 543, 102 A.2d 366, 369; McDermott v. McDermott, 97 Conn. 31, 35, 115 A. 638. It cannot be held that the court was in error in concluding upon all the evidence that the intention of Mauro, objectively manifested as of the date when the bowling equipment was installed in the shopping center, and confirmed by later actions, was that such equipment remain personalty.

There is no error.

Case Reflections

1. The bowling equipment in this case cannot be removed from the building without substantial work and considerable damage to the both the premises and the equipment. Why did the court rule that the bowling equipment was not included by the lien of the mortgage on the building where the equipment was located?
2. The court states: "It is true, that an article may retain its chattel character between a vendor and vendee but remain real property as between a mortgagor and mortgagee." What does the judge mean by this statement?

GORDON R. BRENT ET AL. V. BILL R. CORBIN

173 So.2d 430 (Miss., 1965)

Mineral Interests

ETHRIDGE, Justice.

This is a suit by vendors of real property, Gordon R. Brent and Allen C. Thompson, Jr., against the vendee, Bill R. Corbin, for the recovery of earnest money under a contract of sale. The contract provided for a warranty deed with a merchantable title. The vendee stopped payment on the earnest money check because vendors did not own the minerals. The Chancery Court of Yazoo County agreed with that position, held vendors were unable to comply with the contract of sale, and dismissed their bill of complaint. We affirm that decree. . . . On or about December 14, 1962, [the parties] executed in Memphis, Tennessee, a sale and purchase contract, on a form printed for a title insurance company. Corbin gave his check for $5,000 as earnest money and in part payment. The parties did not insert a legal description of the property, but referred to "1670 acres, more or less, owned by seller" in Yazoo County, Mississippi. This was all of the land owned by Brent in Yazoo County. The printed contract provided that seller agreed to convey the real estate "by good and sufficient warranty deed."

* * *

The contract stated: "It is understood and agreed that if the title is not good and cannot be made good within a reasonable time after written notice has been given that the title is defective, specifically pointing out the defects, then this earnest money which has been deposited with the undersigned agent (Thompson) shall be returned to the purchaser and the usual commission shall be paid the agent by the seller." If the title was good, and purchaser failed to pay for the property, seller had the right to cancel the contract and retain the earnest money. Also: "The purchaser accepts the said real estate in its existing condition, no warranties or representations having been made by the seller or the agent which are not herein expressly provided." And further, "Title to be conveyed subject to all restrictions, easements and covenants of record, and subject to zoning ordinances or laws of any governmental authority."

Corbin employed an attorney to represent him and to examine the title. He found that most of the minerals were owned by persons other than the vendors. . . . Closing the sale was delayed, pending negotiations about co-ordinating payment dates and examination of title. After the attorney examined the title and determined that vendors did not own the minerals, he orally advised Brent that Corbin would not purchase the property for that reason. No written notice of defect to the title was given. Brent had not deposited the earnest money check, so Corbin withdrew the funds from his account, thus effectively stopping payment on it.

* * *

First. A contract to convey a merchantable title to land by a general warranty deed implies an obligation to convey a perfect, fee-simple title, unless restricted by other clauses. (Citations omitted.) In the instant case Brent agreed to convey the property "by good and sufficient warranty deed," which would be "a good and merchantable title." Since he did not own most of the minerals, he could not convey them. Hence he could not comply with the terms of his contract. A defect of title sufficient to constitute unmarketability can consist of outstanding mineral rights. (Citations omitted.) Appellants argue that the contract excepted minerals not owned by the vendors. It provided that the purchaser accepted the land "in its existing condition." This pertains not to the status of the title to the minerals in place, but to the existing condition of the land and improvements on it. The agreement also stated that title was to be conveyed "subject to all restrictions, easements and covenants of record." This was not an exception of the minerals, but a reference to restrictions upon use of the surface.

* * *

Appellants do not contend that they would have been able to cure the title by purchasing the considerable amount of outstanding minerals within a reasonable time. Although this land appears to be some distance from any producing oil wells, Yazoo County for many years has had oil production. *Cf.* Van Landingham v. Jenkins, 207 Miss. 882, 43 So.2d 578 (1949).

Affirmed.

KYLE, P.J., and JONES, PATTERSON and INZER, JJ., concur.

Case Reflections

1. Why was the seller's title defective in this case?
2. The seller argued that the buyer had agreed to accept the property "subject to all restrictions, easements and covenants of record." Why did the court not require the buyer to accept the property subject to the outstanding mineral interests?

BOYLAN V. VAN DYKE

806 P.2d 1024 (Mont., 1991)

Riparian rights

WEBER, Justice.

This cause of action arose when the defendants constructed a pond. Plaintiff, W. Boyd Boylan (Mr. Boylan) filed suit alleging that the pond interfered with his use of a ditch which traverses that area. The District Court for the Eighteenth Judicial District, Gallatin County, found that the pond had no effect on the flow of water in the ditch and that Mr. Boylan did not suffer any damages as a result. From that decision, Mr. Boylan appeals. We affirm in part and reverse in part.

The issues before us are: 1. Did the District Court err in concluding that defendants did not unlawfully interfere with Mr. Boylan's ditch easement?

* * *

Mr. Boylan is a retired rancher and the owner of approximately 252 acres located north of the defendants' property. Defendants, Arnold and Ann Van Dyke are husband and wife and the parents of Larry Van Dyke. Defendants, Larry and Berna Sue Van Dyke, husband and wife own what will be referred to hereinafter as "Tract A." Larry and Berna Sue are the sole shareholders and directors of the Van Dyke Irrigation Service, Inc. Larry manages the corporation which engages in irrigation related construction and installation of irrigation related equipment, such as pipes, headgates, flumes, and the like.

In the spring of 1988, defendants Larry and Berna Sue Van Dyke constructed a one-acre pond on their land where Spring Creek intersects an irrigation ditch known as Tudor Lane Ditch. The construction of the controversial pond occurred on Tract A on or about May 17, 1988, until approximately May 22, 1988, prior to the irrigation season for 1988. Pond construction involved placement of a dam across the Tudor Lane Ditch and excavation of approximately 600 feet of ditch to form the pond.

* * *

In August of 1989, the Court viewed the premises and saw a full flow from the diversion point in Dry Creek into the pond of defendant and out of the pond of the defendant through the rather sophisticated but very satisfactory headgate that was fully opened when the Court viewed it during the irrigation season. . . . The Court walked over to where the flumes were installed, and the waters of the Spring Creek were fully flowing into the pond and would naturally flow out of the pond into the Tutor Lane Ditch together with the waters of Dry Creek. Therefore, the Complaint of the plaintiff that they were deprived of the waters of Spring Creek is dispelled. . . .

If in the future the dam would break, and the plaintiff would suffer damages as a result thereof, clearly the plaintiff at that time would have a cause of action, but there is certainly no damages proved now at this point about the construction of the dam.

* * *

I.

Did the District Court err in concluding that defendants did not unlawfully interfere with Mr. Boylan's ditch easement?

Mr. Boylan maintains that the construction of the pond was an unlawful interference with his ditch easement. He maintains the pond deprived him of irrigation water for his land and reduced the value of his land to half of what it was worth prior to construction of the pond and the destruction of his ditch. He argued that his son, Doug Boylan, who was a tenant on his ranch was no longer able to make a living on the ranch because of a significant reduction in available water since the pond's construction.

Defendants maintain that the ditch caused no interference with Mr. Boylan's ditch right or easement. They further maintain that the ditch has the same carrying capacity after construction of the pond as it did before. Defendants urge that after the construction of the pond Mr. Boylan receives the same amount of water, if not more, than he did before. Defendants contend Mr. Boylan has essentially the same maintenance chores required of him before the pond's construction. They urge that maintenance is actually easier now due to installation of improved headgates. Finally, defendants urge that Mr. Boylan sustained no damages during the course of construction, nor is he likely to sustain any in the future.

The standard of review for a judge sitting without a jury, pursuant to Rule 52(a), M.R.Civ.P., is that the court's findings shall not be set aside unless clearly erroneous. Thus, when the District Court's findings are based on substantial credible evidence, they are not clearly erroneous. Downing v. Grover (1989), 237 Mont. 172, 772 P.2d 850.

The District Court correctly noted that Mr. Boylan's son, Doug, is not a party to this lawsuit. The District Court further noted that the Van Dyke pond had nothing to do with Mr. Boylan's shortage of water in his ditch during the month of July, but rather that the shortage was caused by an upstream user, exercising his full right to Dry Creek water for the first time that Doug Boylan testified he could remember. After reviewing the record in this case, it is clear that there is no evidence to support Mr. Boylan's claims. We conclude that the District Court's findings of fact are not clearly erroneous. We hold that the District Court was correct in concluding that defendants did not unlawfully interfere with Mr. Boylan's ditch easement.

II.

Did the District Court err in denying Mr. Boylan's motion to refer determination of his water rights to the Water Court?

As pointed out in the above stated facts, Mr. Boylan requested that the District Court request that the water court adjudicate his rights, defendants' rights and the rights of people not parties to the lawsuit. As defendants correctly point out, Mr. Boylan did not raise the water rights question in his complaint; the District Court specifically excepted such issues from trial; the issue was not raised in the Pretrial Order; and it was expressly waived by Mr. Boylan at the start of the trial. A reviewing court will not hold a trial court in error for a procedure in which the appellant acquiesced at trial. In re Marriage of West (1988), 233 Mont. 47, 758 P.2d 282. We conclude that the District Court correctly narrowed the focus of its review to whether the pond interfered with Mr. Boylan's use of the Tudor Land Ditch and any damages so caused. We hold that the District Court did not err in denying Mr. Boylan's motion to refer determination of his water rights to the Water Court.

* * *

Affirmed in part. Reversed in part.
TURNAGE, C.J., and BARZ, HARRISON and McDONOUGH, JJ., concur.

Case Reflections

1. Why did the court determine that the defendant's pond did not interfere with the flow of water to the plaintiff's property?
2. Why did the court refuse to adopt the plaintiff's request that the matter be adjudicated by the water court?

CHAPTER

3

ESTATES IN FEE SIMPLE

LEARNING OBJECTIVES:

After reading this chapter, you should be able to:

1. Describe the development of the modern concept of real property ownership
2. Distinguish between rights of ownership and rights of possession in real property
3. Identify the important components of the bundle of rights that is real property ownership

KEY TERMS

Allodial Ownership

Feudal Rent

Fee Simple Absolute Estate

Ownership Rights

Possessory Rights

Fee Tail Estate

Future Interest

Life Estate

HISTORICAL DEVELOPMENT OF ESTATES IN LAND

Allodial ownership A set of absolute ownership rights in land which was created by the Roman Civil Code.

At the beginning of the present millennium, two different systems of land "ownership" were employed side by side on the continent of Europe. The older of these two systems was the **allodial** structure of ownership, which was descended from the civil code employed by the Roman Empire. Under Roman law, real property was owned absolutely, so that the person in possession of the land had no obligation to pay any rent or provide any services as the price for possession. This absolute right to the possession of land was meaningful only as long as the legal system of the Roman Empire and the military might of the Roman legions stationed throughout the Empire were available to protect the allodial ownership rights enjoyed by Roman citizens.

By the sixth century, the city of Rome had been sacked repeatedly by marauding tribes of warriors, and the Empire had all but disintegrated. The rule of law, which for centuries had been maintained by the governmental genius of Rome, was replaced by the rule of combat. In this new order, the strongest and ablest military commanders captured and exploited whatever areas of land they were able to hold by force of arms. During these turbulent centuries a new form of landholding known as feudalism was created, which neatly matched the needs and interests of two classes of people.

Farmers and herders needed the protection of military chieftains to make sure that a crop planted in the spring would not be stolen when harvested in the fall. The military chieftains required the food produced by the farmers in order to feed their troops and required the services of armed knights, soldiers, and archers for the armies that provided the protection.

By the year 1000, a complex web of relationships between soldiers, military leaders, farmers, tradesmen, and herders had developed in order to accommodate the needs and abilities of each group. The right to possess and enjoy land was at the heart of these relationships. In general, the land belonged to a military chieftain, who agreed to defend it against any hostile force. In return, the occupant of the land agreed to provide military services or food to the owner as a **feudal rent**. It is not clear whether people originally understood the feudal rents as payments made in return for the right to occupy the land, or in return for the protection provided by the feudal overlord. The distinction was probably meaningless anyway, since the right to possess the land had no value without the protection offered by the overlord. As a result, everyone began to think of the feudal rents as payments made only in return for the right to possess the land.

Feudal tenure The right to possess and enjoy land which belongs to a military overlord. The feudal tenure was created in Europe after the collapse of the Roman Empire.

In 1066 one of the more successful military chieftains, William, duke of Normandy, invaded the island of Britain. At the time of the invasion, Britain was already populated by several hundred thousand people, who had given their allegiance to one or more of the kings who ruled and protected various parts of the island. William defeated the forces of Harold, one of the most powerful kings on the island, and sent word that from that day forward all Britons would recognize William as their king. Most of the inhabitants of Britain, who lived beyond the reach of William's forces, refused to comply with his request. This refusal angered William and led him to declare all the lands of the island forfeit to him. Thus William established himself as the high king of all Britain. The only remaining detail was to take possession of all his new lands and begin collecting the feudal rents due to him as overlord of the island.

In order to accomplish this, William established a system of feudal relationships of the kind he had been familiar with in Normandy. As new lands were subdued and the inhabitants acknowledged William as their king, the Conqueror established one of his top commanders as a "tenant in capite" (chief tenant). This new overlord held a vast section of newly conquered land from the king in exchange for the annual service of a large number of knights and soldiers owed to the king. The tenant in capite would then proceed to carve his holding up into smaller parcels, each given to a trusted lieutenant known as the "mesne tenant" (intermediate tenant). Each mesne tenant was sworn to provide the tenant in capite with a portion of the knights and soldiers owed to the king. The mesne tenants would in turn give portions of their lands to others in exchange for feudal rents, until the bottom rung of the ladder was reached, the "tenant paravail." In general, the tenants at the bottom occupied only enough land to support a single family after payment of the feudal rents.

The two most important kinds of tenure in the English feudal system that William created were military tenure and socage tenure. Those who held land in military tenure were required to serve a certain number of days in the armed forces of the tenant's feudal lord. When the tenant in military service died, his tenure in the land also came to an end. Since the services of the tenant were no longer available to his lord after the tenant's death, the lord was required to find a new tenant for the land to take the place of his departed soldier. Often, the son or other heir of the deceased tenant would apply to the feudal lord for appointment as the replacement tenant. Frequently, the new claimant would offer a sum of money to the overlord, to help the lord see more clearly why the claimant would be a good choice for the new tenancy. This customary payment made on the death of a feudal tenant is still with us in twentieth-century America, in the form of inheritance taxes paid whenever real property is transferred to the heirs of the owner at his or her death.

KEY POINTS

The numerous areas of American law that affect the outcome of real estate transactions require practitioners to remember thousands of individual facts and legal principles. The thesis of this book is that recalling the social forces that created this bewildering array of facts and legal principles is a powerful aid to remembering how the law will be applied to a given transaction.

Socage tenure, another form of the feudal relationship, anticipated by some six hundred years the famous remark of Napoleon that "an army travels on its stomach." When soldiers are in the field they must eat three times each day, but they have no means for producing the food they must consume. Socage tenants held their land in return for a definite quantity of some agricultural commodity produced on the land. This food then became available to feed not only the army but also the family of the feudal lord who received the socage payment.

Within a century after William's invasion, the island of Britain had been fairly thoroughly pacified, and the need for both military service and supplies for the army had been dramatically reduced. As a result, it became customary for tenants to pay a monetary rent to their overlords, in lieu of the military service or crops that had previously been required by the feudal relationship. Increasingly over the years the money was used to hire professional soldiers for the few military tasks remaining and to purchase supplies for the army in the organized markets that began to grow in Britain under William's reign.

At the same time pressures began to build within the feudal system that would change it dramatically and ultimately replace the system altogether. After William and his sons firmly established themselves as monarchs of an island nation, the people turned their attention away from military affairs and toward the business of creating vast wealth. Since land was the ultimate source of wealth, it was important for land to remain in a family for generations, so that each generation in turn could add to the land and enjoy the fruits of what had already been accomplished. This desire led to increasing levels of strife and conflict between tenants and overlords in the feudal system.

Slowly but surely the ancient model of absolute ownership, the *allodium* of Roman civil law, began to return to the memories of Britons. The feudal interests of tenants had replaced the allodial estates of absolute ownership in Europe and England only because the dangers of military conquest by others had required the protection of feudal overloads. When the danger passed, as it had in Britain after two centuries of Norman rule, the appeal of absolute ownership in allodial estates quickly began to reassert itself.

As early as 1225 a feudal tenant had agreed to give possession of his lands to another person. At the death of the transferring tenant, his son and heir obtained appointment as the successor tenant from the overlord and sued to regain possession of the land transferred by his father. The court that heard the case ruled that since the father had conveyed the land along with a covenant of quiet enjoyment, the son was barred from ever possessing the land. This decision created a means for landowners to sell their property during their lives and preclude its inheritance by children. It happened that the interest possessed by the tenant who made the conveyance was called a fee simple interest. The term "fee" was derived from the Norman term "enfeoffment," which described the creation of a feudal tenancy. When the right to possess the feudal tenancy descended to the present owner's heirs without conditions, the fee was said to descend "simply," giving rise to the term "fee simple" to describe an inheritable right of possession that endures forever.

By creating a method for a tenant in fee simple to transfer an absolute right to possess land, the judges in *D'Arundel's Case* established a new feudal tenancy that became the fee simple absolute estate we are investigating in this chapter. The final historical observation to be made here is that 160 years after William the Conqueror established the English feudal system, English judges were deciding on methods for creating absolute rights of possession in the king's land. The ancient notion of allodial ownership had already supplanted the feudal notion of tenants occupying the king's land only for as long as the tenant was able to pay the feudal dues. No one would have suggested in 1225 that the tenants who were arguing over the possession of the land actually owned the land, since the ownership remained with the king. But the notion of the king's "ownership" had already become a somewhat pale and symbolic artifact. The important issues in 1225 were not who owned the land but rather who had the right to possess and enjoy the land and for how long a tenant could preserve those rights of possession and enjoyment.

Another two hundred years would be required before English law generally recognized the concept of estates in land (rights of possession and enjoyment that belong to an owner different from the king) rather than tenancies in lands of the king. During the four hundred-odd years that English concepts of real property law evolved from the feudal interests imposed by William I into the allodial patterns of individual ownership, most of the concepts of real property law we are studying today were developed. A clear understanding of these topics is difficult without an appreciation of the social and political forces that forged them in the first place.

THE BUNDLE OF RIGHTS

For example, the conventional definition of the estate in **fee simple absolute** is "the largest bundle of rights that an owner of land can possess." While this definition is accurate in all respects, it seems to ask more questions than it answers. What exactly is a bundle of rights, and what does it have to do with owning a house? Do rights actually come in bundles of different sizes? How does one possess such an invisible bundle of undefined rights?

Fee Simple Estate The largest bundle of ownership rights available in the American law of real property.

> Tedesco owned a farm in Deerfield Township, New Jersey. Shack was an attorney employed by Camden Regional Legal Services, Inc., a non-profit corporation chartered in New Jersey under an act of Congress to provide legal services to migrant farm workers. Tejeras was employed by another non-profit corporation created to provide health services to migrant farm workers.
>
> Shack and Tejeras went to Tedesco's farm to meet with two migrant workers housed there in a migrant worker's camp. They drove past numerous "No Trespassing" signs on the road which crossed the farm. Tedesco met them at the entry to the dirt lane leading to the migrant worker's camp, and demanded to know their business.
>
> After some heated conversation, Tedesco stated that Shack and Tejaras would be permitted to meet with the migrant workers they had come to see in Tedesco's office. The owner refused to allow Shack or Tejaras to go into the migrant worker's camp where the workers were housed. When Shack and Tejaras refused to accept these conditions, Tedesco summoned a state trooper. After Tedesco signed a written complaint against them, Shack and Tejeras were arrested for trespass. They were subsequently convicted of the offense by the Municipal Court of Deerfield Township.
>
> On appeal, the Supreme Court of New Jersey reversed the conviction, stating " . . . we are satisfied that under our State law the ownership of real property does not include the right to bar access to governmental services available to migrant workers and hence there was no trespass with the meaning of the penal statute." The court continued, holding "[p]roperty rights serve human values. They are recognized to that end, and are limited by it. Title to real property cannot include dominion over the destiny of persons the owner permits to come upon the premises." State of New Jersey v. Shack and Tejaras 277 A. 2d 369 (N.J., 1971)

Ownership Rights The generic term applied to each of the individual rights included in the fee simple bundle of rights.

Possessory Rights The portion of the fee simple bundle of rights which allows the holder to possess, use and enjoy land in the present.

The ownership of land was separated from the rights to occupy and enjoy the use of the land as long as feudalism flourished in England. This separation of **ownership rights** and **possessory rights** forms the basis of our modern idea of ownership as the power to exercise a particular set of rights with respect to a piece of property. And yes, rights do come in bundles of different sizes.

According to one leading authority[1], there are at least four dimensions that can be used to distinguish the size of one bundle of rights from that of another bundle of rights in a parcel of real property. These dimensions are possession, duration, the degree of beneficial enjoyment to which the owner of an interest in land is entitled, and the number of persons who are entitled to the benefits.

Possession and Duration

Some estates give the owner the right to possess and occupy the land in the present. Other kinds of estates provide the owner only with a right to enter and possess the land at some time in the future. The duration of a present possessory interest is infinite for some estates in land. For other estates, the right to possession ends with the death of a person, the occurrence of a stated event, or the passage of a particular number of years. There is even one estate in land, the tenancy at sufferance, in which the present possessory interest exists on a moment-to-moment basis.

Rights of Beneficial Enjoyment

In some of the ownership estates, the owner of the present possessory interest receives all of the use and beneficial enjoyment of the property. Owners of these estates may exclude all others from entering the land, may build, tear down, or abandon structures, harvest crops, remove sand, gravel, or minerals and sell them—in short, may do all of the things that we associated with "ownership." The owner of an estate that is less than a fee simple absolute will typically have less than all of the rights of beneficial enjoyment that belong to the fee simple estate.

Persons Entitled to Benefits of Ownership

Finally, estates in land can be held by a single individual, a legal entity (e.g., a corporation or a partnership), or by a group of individuals. The effect of multiple ownership on the rights included in various estates in land will be examined more closely in Chapter 5. The remainder of this chapter will examine the various bundles of rights included in the fee simple absolute, fee simple conditional, and life estates.

KEY POINTS

The material that follows in Part I will be much easier to comprehend if the reader seeks to discover which ownership rights are included in the bundle of rights described by a particular estate in land. The sale of a fee simple absolute estate always involves the transfer of the entire bundle of rights from the present owner to a new owner. All other transactions can be traced to a date in the past when the owner of the fee simple absolute estate transferred only a portion of the fee simple ownership rights to another person.

[1] See *Powell on Real Property*, vol. 2 P1 (Matthew Bender, New York, NY, 1991).

ESTATES OF PERPETUAL OWNERSHIP RIGHTS

By the year 1600, the legal fiction that all of the land in England belonged to the king had finally expired. That fiction was replaced by a set of property laws that recognized the perpetual ownership rights of individuals other than the king. But the experience gained during the period when the ownership of land remained separate from the possession of land carried over to the new understanding of property law. In the feudal system, the royal owner of land gave the right to possess the land to others in exchange for feudal rents. In the modern system, the individual landowner may also bargain away the right to possession of the land in exchange for a rental payment.

As a result, the person who currently has the right to possess real property may not be the owner of the property. For now, it is enough to say that the right to possess property that is owned by someone else will always have two characteristics: (1) the right of possession continues only for as long as the required rents are paid; and (2) the right of possession, even when the rents are paid, will end at some definite date in the future.

On the other hand, true ownership estates continue for an indefinite or infinitely long period of time. We will examine leasehold estates (those that will terminate at some definite date in the future) and life estates (those that will terminate at an indefinite time in the future) in Chapter 4. The remainder of this chapter will examine various kinds of fee simple estates (ownership estates of potentially infinite length).

Fee Simple Absolute Estates

The fee simple absolute estate is an interest in land with a potentially infinite duration. The estate includes a right of present possession, and the owner of the possessory interest enjoys the full use and benefit of the land. The duration of the estate is potentially infinite because the rights enjoyed by the owner of the estate can be conveyed without reducing any of the rights. In other words, the particular individual identified as the owner of the fee simple absolute estate in a particular piece of property may, and often will, change frequently. But the existence of the estate continues forever into the future, serenely disregarding the changing names of its owners. (Remember how the ownership of a piece of property and the right to possess and enjoy the property became separated after peace was restored to England in the 1200s; vestiges of that separation still remain in American property law of the late twentieth century.)

Cole v. Steinlauf

The owner of a fee simple absolute interest in a piece of real property can convey the interest to another person by writing a deed containing the words "To A and his heirs." The words "and his heirs" (or "and her heirs") are called words of inheritance, which at one time performed a quasimagical function in the transfer of possessory interests in land. Recall that after *D'Arundel's Case* in 1225, a method existed for conveying an absolute and perpetual right to possess a parcel of land to another person. This kind of absolute conveyance was, in the feudal world of the 1200s, an aberration, the kind of thing that people would not ordinarily attempt to accomplish. Therefore, a formula was needed to allow judges to determine if a particular grantor had intended to convey the rights to possession absolutely, or only for a time. The formula that ultimately gained acceptance was a conveyance made not only to a living person but also to all the future heirs of that person.

W. J. Wooten conveyed a parcel of real property to his daughter Allie Walker. One part of the deed, called the "granting clause" contained the following information: "Know All Men by These Presents, that I, W. J. Wooten of Blythewood S.C. desire to convey to Allie Walker this tract of land (100) acres to have and to hold her natural life, at her death it is to revert to heirs of her body."

A second clause of the deed, called the "habendum clause" read as follows: "To Have and To Hold all and singular the premises before mentioned unto the said Allie Walker her Heirs and Assigns forever."

When Allie Walker attempted to sell the property conveyed to her by W. J. Wooten's deed, several relatives objected to the sale, arguing that she possessed only a life estate. On appeal, the court held "The granting clause in the subject deed gave the property to 'to Allie Walker,' and contained no words of inheritance. Thus a life estate by implication was granted to Allie Walker. Since the granting clause did not make a complete disposition of the title to the property, resort must be had to the habendum clause for the purpose of ascertaining the quantity of the estate intended to be conveyed. The habendum contained the traditional words of inheritance, and therefore had the effect of enlarging the life estate conveyed by the granting clause into a fee simple." Wayburn v. Smith 239 S.E. 2d 890 (S.C., 1977)

Such a conveyance was clearly intended to be effective for a period well beyond the lifetime of the parties to the agreement. If the grantor intended that the right to possess Blackacre would extend not only to the living grantee, but to his posterity as well, then the only reasonable conclusion was that the grantee intended to convey the rights to possession absolutely. The words of inheritance soon became a required incantation; without them, a conveyance was not powerful enough to transfer the right to possess Blackacre absolutely to another person. The requirement for words of inheritance has been eliminated from the real property law of most states, but the practice of including appropriate words of inheritance in deeds continues to be almost universally followed.

Fee Tail Estates An arachaic ownership estate which allows the owner to possess, use and enjoy land during his or her life; at the death of the fee tail tenant, the ownership estate automatically passes to the children of the decedent.

Fee Tail Estates

The fee simple absolute estate we know today was born in 1225 and reached maturity in the late 1400s. Along the way, another development took root that represents almost a mirror image of *D'Arundel's Case.* That case created a mechanism for transferring possessory interests in real property which had the effect of cutting off the inheritance of the grantor's children. The generation gap was no smaller in 1310 than it is today, and many a landowner in England discovered a new problem to worry about: "Suppose my dissolute, no-good son sells all of the family's property after I am gone, and leaves my poor grandchildren penniless and starving." The landed gentry became convinced that a way must be found to prevent this terrible occurrence, and in due course it was. Before his death, the Duke of Clarendon could entail the family property by conveying the right to possess Whitehall to "Clive, my good for nothing son, and the heirs of his body."

By limiting the inheritance of the right to possess Whitehall to the heirs of Clive's body (i.e., his children, grandchildren, and so on), the grantor expressed his intention that the property remain in the family. As a result, Clive had the exclusive right to possess Whitehall during his lifetime, but at his death the right of possession was automatically transferred to his oldest living child. This child, grandchild of the original Duke of Clarendon, would then have the right to possession until he or she died; the possessory interest would go to the next generation, and so on. (Note: There were a number of limitations to and variations on this basic scheme, resulting from several legal principles that were part of English property law in 1450 but are no longer in force today. We can safely ignore these issues.)

The scheme worked reasonably well as long as each generation of the original grantor produced offspring. The problem arose when an owner of the present possessory interest died without living children or grandchildren to inherit the interest. Upon the death of the last living lineal descendant of the original grantor who created the entail, there appeared to be no one who owned the right to possess Whitehall.

During the height of the feudal period, an unowned right to possession was always troubling and potentially dangerous. The feudal rents, especially military service, were only due from the tenants who owned the right to possess particular lands. An unoccupied estate produced no knights or soldiers, leaving a gap in the king's army. For that reason, English property law abhorred an unowned right of possession in the same way that nature abhors a vacuum. And sooner or later, the fee tail estate was almost guaranteed to produce an unowned present possessory interest.

This problem was addressed by deciding that when the lineal descendants of a grantor who created an entailed estate finally died out, the possessory interest would revert to the original grantor, the old Duke of Clarendon in our example. The difficulty, of course, was that the old duke was always dead when his line failed and often had been dead for quite a while. As a result, the collateral heirs (nieces, nephews, cousins, and their descendants) of the old duke became the new owners of the possessory interest in Whitehall. This arrangement was fine as an abstract theory of where present possessory interests go when their owners die, but in practice it became a nightmare. An entire literary genre, the Victorian novel, flourished by describing the trials and tribulations of great-grandnephews of old dukes who spent their lives attempting to wrest possession of an entailed estate from a vicious family of interlopers who had purchased the estate from the last lineal descendant of the old duke. Every one of these stories included hidden deeds, purloined wills, and court cases that went on for generations.

Because of the nightmarish consequences resulting from attempts to entail a parcel of real property, most American jurisdictions refused to recognize the entail. By 1850, the general rule in the U.S. was that a conveyance "To A and the heirs of his body" creates a fee simple absolute estate. The actual mechanics of creating a fee simple absolute estate from an attempted fee tail conveyance will vary among the states. But regardless of the forms used, the fee tail estate is now of historical importance only.

Fee Simple Defeasible Estates

Fee simple conditional estates are first cousins of the fee tail and share many of the undesirable characteristics of the family. Nevertheless, conditional estates are still recognized in the U.S. and England, which makes them an important component of the study of real estate law.

The purpose of the fee tail estate was to permit a grantor to control the disposition of his or her property by limiting its ownership to direct lineal descendants. The purpose of the fee simple conditional estate is to control the use of a piece of property after the grantor has relinquished ownership of the property. For example, Mrs. Howell might be contemplating the development of a piece of land she owns near the edge of town. If a school is located near the parcel, then it will be easier to sell the houses that she expects to build on the parcel. To accomplish this end, she can convey an acre of her land "to the independent school district and its successors and assigns, so long as the land is used for the operation of a school."

Mahrenholz v. School Board

Like the fee simple absolute, the estate conveyed here is potentially of infinite duration. As long as a school is operated on the property, the estate continues. However, the moment the school on the property ceases operation, the estate ceases to exist, and the ownership of the parcel reverts to Mrs. Howell. This form of conveyance creates an estate known as a fee simple determinable, with the possibility of reverter. The language of the conveyance keeps the estate alive only so long as the condition is continuously met. Should the condition ever fail to be met, then the ownership of the property instantaneously "springs back" or reverts to Mrs. Howell, by operation of law. Just as with the fee tail, Mrs. Howell will probably have died before the condition fails and the ownership of the property reverts to her. In that case, the ownership of the parcel will be passed along to her heirs who are alive at the instant of reversion, using the rules of inheritance we will explore in Chapter 7.

In 1934, the Kinney Land and Cattle Company conveyed 790 acres to the State of Kansas. The warranty deed contained the following reversion clause: "It is further agreed and understood by and between the parties hereto that the premises herein described are to be used by the party of the second part as a public forestry, fish and game preserve and recreational state park, and in so using the said premises a lake of at least 150 acres is to be constructed thereon, and said premises are to be used and maintained for purposes aforesaid, and if the party of the second part fails to so use and maintain said premises, then and in that event the title to the said property hereinbefore described shall revert to the party of the first part, its successors or assigns."

The property was used continuously by the State of Kansas for the required forestry and recreation purposes. A lake was constructed on the property. However the size of lake never reached the required minimum of 150 acres. In 1970, the heirs of the Kinney Land and Cattle Company shareholders sued to recover title to the property. The heirs argued that the State had failed to use the property for the purposes set forth in the deed, causing the property to revert to the heirs of the original grantors.

The trial court granted the State's motion for summary judgement, and the plaintiffs appealed. The appeals court affirmed the summary judgement. "Under the circumstances, we hold that the trial court correctly held that the State of Kansas had not forfeited its title to the land simply because the quantity of water contained in the lake has not been sufficient to completely fill an area of 150 acres." Kinney v. State of Kansas 710 P.2d 1290 (Kansas, 1985)

Johnson v. Wheat Ridge

The attorney for the school district may be uncomfortable with this conveyance and will probably make a counterproposal. Mrs. Howell could also convey the property "to the independent school district and its successors and assigns. Provided however, that if the property is used for purposes other than maintaining a school, the grantor and her heirs shall have a right of entry and repossession." This conveyance will create a fee simple with condition subsequent (see Table 3.1). In this case, if the property is used for purposes other than maintaining a school, the estate continues in existence and the school district remains as the owner. In order to

TABLE 3.1 DEFEASIBLE FEE ESTATES

Fee Simple Determinable

Grantor retains a reverter interest

If limitations in the grant are violated, fee simple absolute title reverts to Grantor (or the heirs of the Grantor) by operation of law

Created by the words "To B, so long as the property is used for ________________ purposes; otherwise, title to the property shall revert to the Grantor."

Fee Simple Condition Subsequent

Grantor retains a right of reentry

If the limitations in the grant are violated, the Grantor (or the heirs of the Grantor) must petition a court to transfer title back to them.

Created by the words "To B, on the condition that the property is used for ________________ purposes; otherwise, the Grantor may reenter and retake possession."

recover ownership of the parcel from the school district, Mrs. Howell (or her heirs) will have to apply to a court for permission to reenter the land and recover its possession. Even though this application will certainly be granted by the court, the school district remains the owner of the parcel if Mrs. Howell or her heirs fail to make the application.

Future Interests

Some ownership estates in real property do not give a right to possess the property in the present. Instead, the **future interest** estates provide a right to enter and possess the property at some time in the future. Two of the future estates are created by the conditional fee estates just discussed: the reverter interest of the fee simple defeasible and the right of entry associated with the fee simple with condition subsequent. These interests are thought of as "inchoate" interests, because a right of possession in the future may not exist in the present. As long as a school is maintained on the property in the preceding example, a right to future possession does not presently exist.

Future Interests
An estate in land which conveys no ownership rights to the holder until a stated event in the future has occurred.

Those interests that include a present right to possess real property at some future date are referred to as vested interests. The most common example of a vested future interest is the remainder interest created when a **life estate** is created. (Life estates will be discussed in more detail in Chapter 4.) If a husband conveys a parcel of property "to my wife Helen during her life, and then to my son William and his heirs," William will have a vested remainder interest in the parcel. At Helen's death, William will be the owner of a fee simple absolute estate in the property. If William should die before Helen, then William's heirs will be the fee simple owners of the property. The interest is called a remainder because the fee simple absolute estate of the husband has been carved up into two bundles of rights. The life tenant Helen has the present possessory interest in the property as long as she remains alive, and she

Life Estate
A bundle of ownership rights which last only until the death of the owner.

TABLE 3.2 FUTURE INTERESTS

Vested Interests

Remainder Interest

"To A for life, and then to B and his heirs"

Contingent Remainder

"To A for life, and then to B if B is living, and if B is not living then to C and her heirs."

Contingent Remainder Subject to Open

"To A for life, and then to my children who survive A." (As long as the Grantor remains alive, the possibility that the Grantor will have more children leaves the contingent remainder subject to open.)

Inchoate Interests

Right of reverter created by the grant of a fee simple determinable estate

Right of reentry created by the grant of a fee simple conditional estate

Dower

Curtesy

also has the right to the beneficial enjoyment of the property during her lifetime, subject to a few limitations which will preserve the value of the property for William. The remainder of the fee simple absolute rights that do not belong to the life tenant Helen are conveyed to the remainderman William.

The remainder interest in this example is vested, because either William or his heirs will have the full fee simple estate in the parcel on the death of the life tenant Helen. Suppose the conveyance was "to my wife Helen during her life, and then to my children who are living at the time of Helen's death." William is one of those children and he now possesses a remainder interest, but the interest is not vested. Before William can claim his possessory interest, he must first outlive Helen. But no one can know for sure which person will outlive the other until one of them dies. If Helen dies first, then William, along with his surviving brothers and sisters, will obtain a vested remainder interest at the same instant that they all come into the present possessory interest of the remainder. If William dies first, then his interest in the property is extinguished, and William's heirs will not be entitled to a possessory interest in the parcel after Helen dies. (See Table 3.2.)

Dower and Curtesy

Fee simple absolute estates that are owned by married people may be subject to additional inchoate future interests. At common law, a widow had the right to inherit one-third of the real property owned by her husband at the date of his death. This common law future interest was referred to as a dower interest. The interest was inchoate because the wife had to both outlive her husband and remain legally married to him at the time of his death in order to acquire her present possessory interest.

Husbands had a similar interest in any real property belonging to their wives, known as the curtesy interest.

The inchoate dower interest retained its attachment to the fee simple absolute estate of the husband as long as the wife remained alive and married. If the husband attempted to convey his ownership estate without the permission of his wife, her dower interest was included as a limitation on the conveyance. At the death of her husband, his widow would be entitled to claim her dower interest in the property, even though the husband had conveyed the property to another before his death. The only way to defeat the dower interest was to obtain the wife's permission for the conveyance of the property during the life of the husband. This permission was usually obtained by requiring the wife to sign the deed conveying her husband's property.

One can well imagine that many husbands, being unable to obtain their wives' approval for the sale of property, would begin to think of various ways the dower interest might be defeated. The courts generally approved of such efforts, because the consequences of the dower interest were potentially very difficult to deal with. Every time a married man conveyed real property without his wife's consent, a new opportunity for a lawsuit was created. Widows began popping up all over the countryside, demanding their one-third interest in property conveyed away years before the death of their husbands.

In general, the courts were willing to agree that the dower interest attached only to real property actually owned by the husband at the date of his death. But this general conclusion was hedged about carefully with limitations and exceptions. If, for example, a husband retained the ownership and control of substantial real property throughout his life but attempted to convey the property away on his deathbed, equity courts were usually willing to set the conveyance aside as a fraud against the surviving widow.

England abolished the dower interest early in this century, apparently deciding that the restraint on alienation posed by the inchoate dower interest was more trouble than it was worth. Many American states retain the interest in one form or another. In these states, whenever a purchaser hopes to acquire a fee simple absolute title through a conveyance from a married person, the signatures of both spouses should be included on the deed.

CONCLUSION

The bundle of ownership rights incorporated in the concept of estates in land includes the rights of present and future possession, together with the rights of use and beneficial enjoyment by the owner of the present possessory interest. In the fee simple absolute estate, all of these rights are present for a period that is potentially infinite.

Portions of the fee simple absolute bundle of rights can be repackaged and sold, providing a wide range of possibilities for the use and development of real property. By selling or exchanging portions of the infinite duration of the fee simple absolute estate, or portions of the rights to possession and enjoyment, real estate developers can realize substantial profits and manage the risks of development. The succeeding chapters of the text will discuss these possibilities in more detail.

DISCUSSION QUESTIONS

1. Around the year 1000 A.D., two different systems of land ownership were prevalent in Europe. What were they? How did they differ?
2. What is a tenure? Define socage tenure and military tenure.
3. According to Powell, what are the four dimensions that can be used to distinguish the size of one bundle of rights from another? Give examples of each.
4. Define the fee simple absolute estate. What rights does this estate include? How is a fee simple absolute interest conveyed?
5. What are the mechanics of the fee tail estate? What were some problems with this type of transfer? How do courts view a fee tail estate in the U.S.?
6. Distinguish between the purpose of the fee tail estate and that of the fee simple conditional estate.
7. Identify the primary difference between a fee simple defeasible with the possibility of reverter and a fee simple with condition subsequent.
8. What is a future interest? Differentiate between "inchoate" and "vested" interests.
9. Define both dower and curtesy interests. What are the implications of purchasers to real estate in states that retain these interests?

COLE V. STEINLAUF

136 A.2d 744 (Conn., 1957)

Fee Simple Absolute words of limitation

WYNNE, Chief Justice.

There is no dispute as to the facts. The case presented a single question of law. The only evidence was the deed which was part of the defendant's chain of title. The plaintiffs and the defendant entered into a contract for the sale of real estate situated in Norwalk. The plaintiffs were named as purchasers and the defendant as seller. The contract provided that if the seller was unable to convey title to the premises free and clear of any defect of title, the purchasers had the option of rejecting the seller's deed. In the event of such a rejection, all sums paid on account, together with reasonable fees for the examination of the title, were to be repaid to the purchasers. The plaintiffs paid the defendants $420 as a deposit when the contract was executed. They engaged an attorney to examine the title before the closing date of July 1, 1955. The attorney discovered that the deed had been executed in New York on October 22, 1945, to a predecessor in title of the defendant. It appears from the deed that it ran to the grantee "and assigns forever." No mention was made of "heirs" as would be customary and necessary in a fee simple conveyance made in Connecticut. The plaintiffs refused to accept the defendant's deed on the ground that the 1945 deed did not mention the heirs of the grantee. They made demand upon the defendant for a return of the $420 deposit plus expenses for the search of the title, which it was stipulated amounted to $50. The demand was refused, and the instant suit was thereafter brought.

The trial court found the issues for the defendant, holding that General Statutes § 7087 validated the 1945 deed and that the claimed defect in it did not render the defendant's title unmarketable.

The issue for determination is whether the 1945 deed operated to convey the totality of the fee to the grantee without a flaw or defect which would render the title offered to the plaintiffs unmarketable. To create an estate of inheritance in land by deed, it is necessary to use the word "heirs." Chapper v. New York, N. H. & H. R. Co., 62 Conn. 195, 202, 24 A. 997, 17 L.R.A. 420. Where the common-law rule is in effect, as it is in Connecticut, a grant to a grantee "and his assigns forever" vests only a life estate in the grantee. 19 Am. Jur. 474. A deed can be reformed to vest a fee in a grantee where the word "heirs" is omitted if it can be determined from the clearly expressed intent of the parties that a fee was intended. Chamberlain v. Thompson, 10 Conn. 243, 253. It is impossible to determine the intent of the parties to the 1945 conveyance in this proceeding, for the reason that the necessary parties are not all before the court. It was not the function of the trial court to try the title. Rather, it was to determine whether the title offered was from reasonable doubt, in law or in fact. Frank Towers Corporation v. Laviana, 140 Conn. 45, 53, 97 A.2d 567.

Another relevant factor is the fact that a title searcher must make his analysis of a title from the information appearing of record. The inquiry in the present case, therefore, should be whether the alleged defect in title is one which leaves the record title free from reasonable doubt, or on the contrary, is one which puts a purchaser to the test of proving intent from sources outside the record.

A deed purporting on its face to have been attested in another state, in the absence of anything in it to the contrary, will be deemed, prima facie, to have been executed, acknowledged and delivered in that state, thus making General Statutes, § 7087 prima facie applicable. New Haven Trust Co. v. Camp, 81 Conn. 539, 542, 71 A. 788. The effect of § 7087 is to provide that a deed purporting to convey land in Connecticut, if executed and acknowledged in, and according to the laws of, a foreign state, will be treated as validly executed and acknowledged even though the execution and acknowledgment may not be in conformity with the law of Connecticut. *See* Farrell Foundry v. Dart, 26 Conn. 376, 380. But this has nothing to do with the estate, if any, created by the deed. The effect of the statute is limited to curing defects in the form or manner of execution or acknowledgment.

* * *

Here, the deed objected to on its face conveyed only a life estate under law, although it would convey a fee simple under the law of New York. Whether in a court action the deed could be constructed as conveying a fee simple would depend, not upon § 7087, but upon the law of Chamberlain v. Thompson, *supra*, and New Haven Trust Co. v. Camp, *supra*. Whether the proof which would be essential in order to apply the law of those cases would be available is uncertain. In any event, we are not concerned with the actual estate conveyed but with the marketability of the title.

However far the cases cited by the defendant may go in proving that the title conveyed was a fee simple, that is not the issue. It is not whether the property was in fact the defendant's to convey absolutely but whether there is enough doubt in the chain of title to bring the plaintiffs up short and make them think twice before buying a lawsuit at a future time to determine title. Perhaps the court at a future time would find good title, but the plaintiffs do not have to gamble on that. The trial court erred in treating this as a title problem rather than as one to determine whether the plaintiffs were justified in refusing to take a chance on the title as revealed on the face of the Norwalk town records. It cannot be said that this title was marketable under our rule.

There is error, the judgment is set aside and the case is remanded with direction to render judgment for the plaintiffs for $470 and costs.

Case Reflections

1. What is the effect of the Connecticut statute analyzed by the court (General Statutes § 7087)?
2. Why did the court rule that the Connecticut statute failed to render the plaintiff's title merchantable?

MAHRENHOLZ
V.
COUNTY BOARD OF SCHOOL TRUSTEES OF LAWRENCE COUNTY

417 N.E.2d 138 (Ill., 1981)

Fee Simple Defeasible estate

JONES, Justice

This case involves an action to quiet title to real property located in Lawrence County, Illinois. Its resolution depends on the judicial construction of language in a conveyance of that property.

* * *

On March 18, 1941, W. E. and Jennie Hutton executed a warranty deed in which they conveyed certain land, to be known here as the Hutton School grounds, to the Trustees of School District No. 1, the predecessors of the defendants in this action. The deed provided that "this land to be used for school purposes only; otherwise to revert to Grantors herein." W. E. Hutton died intestate on July 18, 1951, and Jennie Hutton died intestate on February 18, 1969. The Huttons left as their only legal heir their son Harry E. Hutton.

The property conveyed by the Huttons became the site of the Hutton School. Community Unit School District No. 20 succeeded to the grantee of the deed and held classes in the building constructed upon the land until May 30, 1973. After that date, children were transported to classes held at other facilities operated by the District. The District has used the property since then for storage purposes only.

* * *

On May 7, 1977, Harry E. Hutton, son and sole heir of W. E. and Jennie Hutton, conveyed to the plaintiffs all of his interest in the Hutton School land. This document was filed in the recorder's office of Lawrence County on September 7, 1977. On September 6, 1977, Harry Hutton disclaimed his interest in the property in favor of the defendants. This disclaimer was in the form of a written document entitled "Disclaimer and Release." It contained the legal description of the Hutton School grounds and recited that Harry E. Hutton disclaimed and released any possibility of reverter or right of entry for condition broken, or other similar interest, in favor of the County Board of School Trustees for Lawrence County, Illinois, successor to the Trustees of School District No. 1 of Lawrence County, Illinois. The document further recited that it was made for the purpose of releasing and extinguishing any right Harry E. Hutton may have had in the "interest retained by W. E. Hutton and Jennie Hutton* * * in that deed to the Trustees of the School District No. 1, Lawrence County, Illinois dated March 18, 1941, and filed on the same date * * *." The disclaimer was filed in the recorder's office of Lawrence County on October 4, 1977.

* * *

The plaintiffs filed a third amended complaint on September 13, 1978. This complaint recited the interests acquired from [other owners of parcels adjoining the school district land] and from Harry Hutton. On March 21, 1979, the trial court entered an order dismissing this complaint. In the order the court found that the

> [W]arranty deed dated March 18, 1941, from W. E. Hutton and Jennie Hutton to the Trustees of School District No. 1, conveying land here concerned, created a fee simple subject to a condition subsequent followed by the right of entry for condition broken, rather than a determinable fee followed by a possibility of reverter.

Plaintiffs have perfected an appeal to this court.

The basic issue presented by this appeal is whether the trial court correctly concluded that the plaintiffs could not have acquired any interest in the school property from . . . Harry Hutton. Resolution of this issue must turn upon the legal interpretation of the language contained in the March 18, 1941, deed from W. E. and Jennie Hutton to the Trustees of School District No. 1:

> this land to be used for school purpose only; otherwise to revert to Grantors herein.

In addition to the legal effect of this language we must consider the alienability of the interest created and the effect of subsequent deeds.

* * *

Consequently this court must determine whether the plaintiffs could have acquired an interest in the Hutton School grounds from Harry Hutton. The resolution of this issue depends on the construction of the language of the 1941 deed of the Huttons to the school district. As urged by the defendants and as the trial court found, that deed conveyed a fee simple subject to a condition subsequent followed by a right of re-entry for condition broken. As argued by the plaintiffs, on the other hand, the deed conveyed a fee simple determinable followed by a possibility of reverter. In either case, the grantor and his heirs retain an interest in the property which may become possessory if the condition is broken. . . . The type of interest held governs the mode of reinvestment with title if reinvestment is to occur. If the grantor had a possibility of reverter, he or his heirs become the owner of the property by operation of law as soon as the condition is broken. If he has a right of re-entry for condition broken, he or his heirs become the owner of the property only after they act to re-take the property.

It is alleged, and we must accept, that classes were last held in the Hutton School in 1973. Harry Hutton, sole heir of the grantors, did not act to legally retake the premises but instead conveyed his interest in that land to the plaintiffs in 1977. If Harry Hutton had only a naked right of re-entry for condition broken, then he could not be the owner of that property until he had legally re-entered the land. Since he took no steps for a legal re-entry, he had only a right of re-entry in 1977, and that right cannot be conveyed [*by a deed*]. On the other hand, if Harry Hutton had a possibility of reverter in the property, then he owned the school property as soon as it ceased to be used for school purposes. Therefore, assuming (1) that cessation of classes constitutes "abandonment of school purposes" on the land, (2) that the conveyance from Harry Hutton to the plaintiffs was legally correct, and (3) that the conveyance was not pre-empted by Hutton's disclaimer in favor of the school district, the plaintiffs could have acquired an interest in the Hutton School grounds if Harry Hutton had inherited a possibility of reverter from his parents.

The difference between a fee simple determinable (or determinable fee) and a fee simple subject to a condition subsequent, is solely a matter of judicial interpretation of the words of a grant. . . . A fee simple determinable may be thought of as a limited grant, while a fee simple subject to a condition subsequent is an absolute grant to which a condition is appended. In other words, a grantor should give a fee simple determinable if he intends to give property for so long as it is needed for the purposes for which it is given and no longer, but he should employ a fee simple subject to a condition subsequent if he intends to compel compliance with a condition by penalty of a forfeiture. School District No. 6 v. Russell (1964), 156 Colo. 75, 396 P.2d 929.

. . . In the 1941 deed, though the Huttons gave the land "to be used for school purpose only, otherwise to revert to Grantors herein," no words of temporal limitation, or terms of express condition, were used in the grant.

The plaintiffs argue that the word "only" should be construed as a limitation rather than a condition. The defendants respond that where ambiguous language is used in a deed, the courts of Illinois have expressed a constructional preference for a fee simple subject to a condition subsequent. (Citation omitted.) Both sides refer us to cases involving deeds which contain language analogous to the 1941 grant in this case.

We believe that a close analysis of the wording of the original grant shows that the grantors intended to create a fee simple determinable followed by a possibility of reverter. Here, the use of the word "only" immediately following the grant "for school purpose" demonstrates that the Huttons wanted to give the land to the school district only as long as it was needed and no longer. The language "this land to be used for school purpose only" is an example of a grant which contains a limitation within the granting clause. It suggests a limited grant, rather than a full grant subject to a condition, and thus, both theoretically and linguistically, gives rise to a fee simple determinable.

The second relevant clause furnishes plaintiffs' position with additional support. It cannot be argued that the phrase "otherwise to revert to grantors herein" is inconsistent with a fee simple subject to a condition subsequent. Nor does the word "revert" automatically create a possibility of reverter. But, in combination with the preceding phrase, the provisions by which possession is returned to the grantors seem to trigger a mandatory return rather than a permissive return because it is not stated that the grantor "may" re-enter the land. *See* City of Urbana v. Solo Cup Co. (4th Dist. 1979), 66 Ill.App.3d.45,22Ill.Dec.786, 383 N.E.2d 262.

The terms used in the 1941 deed, although imprecise, were designed to allow the property to be used for a single purpose, namely, for "school purpose." The Huttons intended to have the land back if it were ever used otherwise. Upon a grant of exclusive use followed by an express provision for reverter when that use ceases, courts and commentators have agreed that a fee simple determinable, rather than a fee simple subject to a condition subsequent, is created.

* * *

We hold, therefore, that the 1941 deed from W. E. and Jennie Hutton to the Trustees of School District No. 1 created a fee simple determinable in the Trustees followed by possibility of reverter in the Huttons and their heirs. Accordingly, the trial court erred in dismissing plaintiffs' third amended complaint which followed its holding that the plaintiffs could not have acquired any interest in the Hutton School property from Harry Hutton. We must therefore reverse and remand this cause to the trial court for further proceedings.

We refrain from deciding the following issues: (1) whether the 1977 conveyance from Harry Hutton was legally sufficient to pass his interest in the school property to plaintiffs, (2) whether Harry Hutton effectively disclaimed his interest in the property in favor of the defendants by virtue of his 1977 disclaimer, and (3) whether the defendants have ceased to use the Hutton School grounds for "school purposes."

REVERSED and REMANDED

KARNS and HARRISON, JJ., concur

Case Reflections

1. Why did Harry E. Hutton sell his interest in the property to both the plaintiffs (on May 7, 1977) and to the defendants (on September 6, 1977)?
2. If the original grant created a fee simple determinable title, what interest did Harry Hutton convey to the plaintiffs? What interest was conveyed if the original grant created a fee simple condition subsequent?
3. How did the court decide what ownership estate was created by the original grant from Harry E. Hutton's parents?

JOHNSON V. CITY OF WHEAT RIDGE

532 P.2d 985 (Colo., 1975)

Fee Simple Conditional estate

ENOCH, Judge.

Plaintiff, Paul Johnson, Appeals from a judgment of the district court dismissing his quiet title action. We affirm.

The property at issue consists of land formerly owned by the late Judge Samuel W. Johnson which was conveyed by him in two parcels as a gift for use as a public park. These parcels were subsequently conveyed by the original donees to the City of Wheat Ridge (City).

Plaintiff, as executor and heir of the estate of Judge Johnson, alleges that the interest conveyed to the City had terminated by reason of the failure of the original donees and the City to satisfy certain conditions set forth in the deeds. At the conclusion of the evidence the court determined that all the conditions save one had been met, that the action was barred by the applicable statute of limitations, and that plaintiff was barred by laches.

The property was conveyed by Judge Johnson in two transactions. A parcel of approximately five acres was conveyed to the Wheat Ridge Lions Foundation in 1955. A second parcel of approximately 14 acres was conveyed in 1957 to Jefferson County, for the custody and management of the Wheat Ridge Recreation District. In 1958 Judge Johnson consented in writing to the conveyance of the five acre parcel to Jefferson County on behalf of the Wheat Ridge Recreation District, subject to the conditions contained in the original deed. An interest in both parcels was transferred to the City when the City was incorporated in 1969.

Each of the original deeds contains conditions that the property must be used for a public park to be named "Johnson Park." The 1957 deed contains additional conditions, i.e., that, within certain time limits, the grantee shall provide a road into the land, clear away fire hazards, and make available a public water supply and lavatories on the premises. Each deed also contains the following language:

> In the event that any of the conditions set out above are not compiled with the failure to comply shall constitute a condition subsequent terminating the estate of the grantee and its assigns in and to all of the real property, land, above described, and the Grantor, his heirs and assigns may re-enter and take possession of said premises.

The court's determination that all of the conditions had been met except one is supported by the evidence and will not be disturbed on review.

The one condition which had not been met was the installation of a public water supply and lavatory facilities on the larger of the two parcels within the required two years from the date of the conveyance. The breach of this condition, however, does not entitle plaintiff to relief. The breach of a condition subsequent does not cause title to revert automatically to the grantor or his heirs, and the use of judicial proceedings to enforce a resulting power to terminate is governed by the statute of limitations in C.R.S.1963, 118-8-4, Wolf v. Hallenbeck, 109 Colo. 70, 123 P.2d 412. C.R.S.1963, 118-8-4, provided that no action may be maintained,

> to enforce the terms of any restriction concerning real property . . . unless said action be commenced within one year from the date of the violation for which the action is sought to be brought or maintained.

The applicable one year statute of limitations started to run from December 13, 1959, which was two years after the date of the deed and was the end of the period within which the conditions were to have been met. Therefore, though this one condition had not been met, the plaintiff's right of action is effectively barred by the statute of limitations.

Judgement affirmed.

BERMAN and VanCISE, J.J. concur.

Case Reflections

1. What interest in land belonged to the plaintiff in this case? Why?
2. The plaintiff was not permitted to retake possession of the land conveyed by his father. Why not?

NOW OPEN
OFFICE SPACE
ALL SIZES
CALL
B.SMITH
W.WEINBAUM
867•5900
COLDWELL BANKER
Pavilion

CHAPTER

4

ESTATES FOR YEARS

LEARNING OBJECTIVES

After reading this chapter, you should be able to:

1. Describe the differences between life estates and leasehold estates in real property
2. Identify the key terms that should be included in a residential lease
3. Identify the key terms that should be included in a commercial lease

KEY TERMS

Life Tenant

Lease Tenant

Waste

Holdover Tenancy

Sublease

Assignment

Escalator Clause

Net Leases

The potential duration of an estate in land is the most important criterion for distinguishing freehold estates from estates for years. The ownership interests examined in Chapter 3 could potentially endure forever. The interests examined here terminate at some point in the future. If an ownership interest will be extinguished at the end of some person's life, the interest is known as a life estate. Leasehold estates are interests in land that terminate after a defined number of years or months.

As we consider these ownership interests, it is important to keep one central fact in mind. Life estates and leasehold estates are both "subdivisions" of the fee simple absolute estate. To put it another way, these estates are created when some of the sticks in the fee simple "bundle of rights" are separated from the bundle and given to another person to hold for a period of time. Eventually, however, the sticks will be returned to the fee simple bundle, and the undivided ownership of the property will once again reside in the holder of the fee simple estate.

Life tenant The owner of a present possessory interest in real property which continues until the death of the life tenant.

The major difference between the life estate and the leasehold estate is the number of sticks transferred from the fee simple bundle to the life tenant or lease tenant. **Life tenants** enjoy virtually all of the rights that belong to the holder of the fee simple estate. Life tenants may occupy and enjoy the property, exclude others from the property, collect the rents, plant and harvest crops, and sell their life tenancy. The only limitation on the rights of a life tenant is the duty to leave the property in good condition at the death of the life tenant. As a result, the fee simple estate all but disappears during the term of a tenancy for life. The fee simple ownership rights vanish into the remainder interest. As we saw in the previous chapter, the remainderman has no present rights in the property. The only ownership interest left over from the creation of a life estate is the right to enter and possess the property at the unknown date in the future when the life tenant dies.

Lease tenant The owner of a present possessory interest which ends at a definite date in the future.

On the other hand, owners of a leasehold interest receive virtually none of the property rights of the fee simple owner. The **lease tenant** often possesses nothing more than the bare right to occupy the premises and exclude others therefrom. In all but the most unusual circumstances, lease tenants will not have the right to collect rents from the property. In our discussion of fixtures in Chapter 2, we saw that lease tenants must be very careful about spending money to make changes in the property. It is also possible for the landlord (fee simple owner) to forbid the tenant to sell his or her possessory interest in the property. As a result, the fee simple owner retains many (sometimes most) of the important ownership rights during the period of a leasehold tenancy.

KEY POINTS

Even though the leasehold estate includes little more than the right to possess the property, it is by far the most common method of "ownership" for business purposes. The right of possession is the most important of the ownership rights for the conduct of a trade or business. Leasehold estates remain the most cost-effective method of acquiring this property right.

LIFE ESTATES

Life estates are created by conveying land "To A, for life and then to B." This is the normal formula for creating a life estate in A, with the remainder in B. Another form of the life estate, called a life estate "per autre vie," is created by a conveyance "To A, to have and to hold so long as B remains alive, and at B's death to C."

The primary purpose of a life estate is to control the descent of property after the death of the owner. For example, a husband and wife may agree to execute mutual wills. Both parties agree to leave their home "To my spouse for life, and then to our children." (The exact wording of the clauses in each document will probably be more florid than this example, but the effect of the prose will be the same.) As long as neither party changes his or her will before death, then the following events are guaranteed: the surviving spouse will enjoy the ownership of the home, and the children will become the owners when both parents have died.

Viva Lilliston left her farm to her daughter under the terms of a will which included the following terms and conditions:

> Item Twelve: I give and devise my farm situated on the Seaside from Locustville, in the County of Accomack, State of Virginia . . . to my daughter Margaret Lilliston Edwards, upon the conditions, set out in Item Fourteen. . . . .
>
> Item Fourteen: all gifts made to my daughter Margaret L. Edwards, individual and personally, under Items Eleven and Twelve of this Will, whether personal estate or real estate, are conditioned upon the said Margaret L. Edwards keeping the gift or devise herein free from encumbrances of every description, and in the event the said Margaret L. Edwards shall attempt to encumber same or sell her interest, or in the event any creditor or creditors of said Margaret L. Edwards shall attempt to subject her interest in the gift or devise herein made to the payment of the debts of the said Margaret L. Edwards, then and in that event the interest of said Margaret L. Edwards therein shall immediately cease and determine, and the gift or devise shall at once become vested in her children, viz: Betty Belle Branch, Beverly Bradley, John R. Edwards, Bruce C. Edwards, Jill A. Edwards and Jackie L. Edwards, in equal shares in fee simple.

After her mother's death, Margaret L. Edwards asked her children for permission to sell the farm she received from Viva Lilliston. All of the children except Barbara Bradley agreed to the sale. The objection of Barbara Bradley apparently terminated the negotiations for the sale. When Margaret L. Edwards died approximately one year later, her will devised the sum of $1.00 to her daughter Barbara Bradley, and divided the farm equally among her remaining children.

Barbara Bradley argued that the will of Viva Lilliston created a life estate in Margaret Edwards, with the remainder of her children in equal shares. Barbara's brother John Edwards argued that the will of Viva Lilliston conveyed a fee simple with condition subsequent to Margaret Edwards. Since the conditions were not violated during Margaret Edward's lifetime, she possessed a fee simple interest in the property at her death.

The court ruled that the conditions imposed by the will of Viva Lilliston would be void as an unreasonable restraint on Margaret Edwards power to sell or mortgage the property. By examining other provisions of the will, the court determined that Viva Lilliston clearly intended to preserve her property for the benefit of her grandchildren, while allowing her daughter Margaret Edwards to have the use and benefit of the property until her death. The court concluded that the will was intended to convey a life estate to Margaret Edwards, with a remainder to her children. Edwards v. Bradley 315 S.E.2d 196 (VA, 1984)

Why is a life estate required to guarantee these results? Why couldn't the husband and wife in our example simply leave their ownership interest in the home to the surviving spouse and agree that the surviving spouse would bequeath the home to the children? The answer is that a surviving spouse who is the fee simple owner of the home can sell it before the children have a chance to inherit it. The use of a life estate eliminates this possibility. It is a fundamental principle of the law that a person can convey only the ownership interest he or she actually possesses. If the surviving spouse is a fee simple owner, the sale of that interest will cut off the children. However, a life tenant can only sell the right to possess and enjoy the property while the tenant is alive. At the death of the surviving spouse, the children become fee simple owners, even if the surviving spouse sold the home prior to his or her death. Any purchaser would acquire only the right to possess and enjoy the home until the death of the surviving spouse.

Carlton v. Wilson

A life estate per autre vie is sometimes used to provide for the care of a severely disabled child, after the death of the parent. Suppose that a husband and wife have four children. The oldest child, Dianne, is severely retarded. As a result she is unable to adequately manage her affairs, and her parents want to provide support for her after their death. The youngest child, Sammy, has agreed to look after his sister when their parents are no longer able to. Suppose further that the parents own an office building that produces rents large enough to provide for Dianne's needs, if properly managed. The parents might be tempted to convey the office building "To our son Sammy, so long as Dianne is alive, and then to our children who survive Dianne."

While this arrangement has the potential to provide support for Dianne during her life, it has some drawbacks. Once Sammy becomes the life tenant of the building, he has the right to collect the rents from the building. If Sammy later decides to spend the rent money for his own needs, he may do so. Even if Sammy is under a moral obligation to use the rent money to provide for Dianne's support, he is under no legal obligation to do so. Even worse, Sammy may fail to outlive his older sister Dianne. If Sammy dies while Dianne is still living, the life tenancy will pass to Sammy's heirs. These heirs may prove to be either unwilling or unable to manage the building for the care and support of Dianne.

In 1984 Leola Hale and Lynda Gay Campos sold a home and a lot located in Bemis, Tennessee, to Ruth R. Davis and her children, Barnie Gene Davis and Nancy Davis Winsett. The deed names the mother as a life tenant in the property with Barnie Gene Davis and Nancy Davis Winsett named as remainderman. In September of 1988, Barnie Gene Davis died naming his wife Peggy Anita Davis as the executrix of his estate. In his will Barnie Gene Davis bequeathed all of his property to his wife Peggy.

Shortly after the death of her son, Ruth Davis moved into a nursing home. She decided that she had no further use for the property in question, and quitclaimed her interest to Nancy in exchange for $50. Thereafter, Peggy filed a lawsuit asking the court to declare the state of the ownership interests in the house after these transactions.

The trial court applied the doctrine of merger in holding that Nancy and Peggy became tenants in common in the fee simple ownership of the property after the deed from Ruth to Nancy. The merger doctrine states that when the same person becomes the owner of both a life estate and a remainder interest in the same property, the two estates will be merged into a fee simple interest. The trial court also held that Nancy could take no actions which would adversely affect the title of her co-tenant Peggy. As a result, when Nancy became vested with the fee simple title, the same title vested in her co-tenant Peggy.

The Court of Appeals approved the reasoning of the trial court, but reversed the decision on other grounds. Evidence at the trial showed that Nancy and Barney had entered into an agreement to use all of their jointly held property for the support of their mother Ruth Davis. After Ruth moved into a nursing home, Nancy had leased the property and applied the rents to the support of Ruth. As a co-tenant in fee simple, Peggy had the right to demand one half of the rental payments received on the property.

As a result, the Court of Appeals held that applying the doctrine of merger to these facts would be inequitable and would defeat the intention of the grantor Ruth Davis. The Court of Appeals decided that the quitclaim deed from Ruth Davis to her daughter Nancy conveyed a life estate pur autre vie, measured by the life of the grantor Ruth Davis. Davis v. Winsett 1991 WL 236848 (Tenn.App., 1991)

Because the life estate per autre vie is subject to these limitations, it is seldom used in modern practice. If the parents were to convey the building to a bank as trustee for the benefit of Dianne, then they would be able to rest easier after the transaction. The bank trustee in this case would have a legally enforceable obligation to manage the building competently and use the rents from the property for Dianne's support. Further, if the trust document is carefully drawn, there is no danger of the trustee failing to outlive Dianne. Even if the original trustee should fail or close before Dianne's death, a successor trustee would be found to take over the management of the property. Because trust arrangements eliminate many of the very real dangers posed by the life estate transaction in our example, they are the most usual method of providing support for a child who is severely disabled.

KEY POINTS

Trust agreements generally provide more flexibility in the use of property than life estates or other limited conveyances can provide. Suppose that five year after the death of Dianne's parents, market conditions change and the rents from the office building begin to decline. As the fee simple owner of the property, a trustee could sell the building and replace it with a more suitable investment. It is doubtful that Sammy, as a tenant for the life of Diane, would be able to find a buyer for such a limited ownership interest.

Rights and Duties of a Life Tenant

A life tenant can exercise virtually all of the ownership rights available to the fee simple owner until the expiration of the life tenancy. When the estate is measured by the life of the tenant, then the life tenant can be regarded as the fee simple owner of the property during his or her lifetime. A life tenant enjoys the exclusive right to possess and use the property. All rents from the property belong to the life tenant. Finally, the life tenant may sell the ownership rights to another party, who will then enjoy them as long as the life tenant remains alive.

The ownership rights of a life tenant are subject to two important limitations. The first, obviously, is that a life tenancy usually cannot be passed by inheritance, as a fee simple estate can. An ordinary life tenancy expires at the death of the life tenant. As a result, there are no ownership rights remaining for the heirs of the life tenant to inherit. The fee simple ownership estate simply passes by operation of law to the one who holds the remainder interest. A question of inheritability arises when the tenant of a life estate per autre vie dies before the person whose life measures the duration of the life estate. "Since the life estate by definition is not an inheritable estate, does it follow that no one is entitled to the land during this interval and that, accordingly, the first person who takes possession cannot be [removed]? With undeniable logic, the English courts so held, though they permitted this unsatisfactory situation to be avoided by the designation of a 'special occupant' in the instrument creating or transferring a life estate. E.g., if land was conveyed to 'B and his heirs for the life of C,' B's heir was entitled to the land as special occupant. One of the numerous clauses of the Statute of Frauds (adopted by Parliament in 1677) provided that a life estate not ending with the death of its owner could be devised, and, if not devised, should pass as [an item of personal property through the life tenants estate] in the absence of a special occupant. According to the Restatement of Property sec. 151 (1936) the common law rule in the United States is identical with the Statue of Frauds provision."[1]

Melms v. Pabst Brewing

Waste
The legal doctrine which requires a life tenant to maintain the real property possessed by the life tenant in a state of good repair, for the benefit of holder of the remainder interest.

The rights of ownership enjoyed by a life tenant are subject only to the duty not to commit **waste**. Since the ownership of the property will eventually be transferred to the holder of the remainder interest, the life tenant must take care to guard the value of the property until it is surrendered to the remainderman. At common law, a life tenant who caused or permitted any changes to the property was guilty of waste. The rule arose at a time when the use of land did not change appreciably during the normal lifetime of an individual. As a result, the strict prohibition of changes to the property did not interfere substantially with a life tenant's rights to use and enjoy the property.

In our modern industrialized world, however, the pace of change has increased dramatically. Today it is not uncommon for a parcel of land to move from agricultural to residential, commercial, and industrial uses within the lifetime of a single life tenant. The old common law rule that strictly prohibited changes in the property during the tenure of a life tenant thus began to interfere with the ownership rights of such tenants. Modern courts have responded to this development by amending the common law rule of waste. Today, the rule is more accurately stated by saying that a life tenant who causes or permits any deterioration of the property or its improvements has committed waste.

Moore v. Phillips

LEASEHOLD ESTATES

Leasehold estates are the final and the smallest ownership estates recognized in American property law. While the fee simple absolute estate represents the largest bundle of rights that a landowner can possess, the leasehold estate comprises the

[1] Cribbet, Johnson, Findley, and Smith, *Property—Cases and Materials,* 6th ed. (Foundation Press, 1990), 237.

smallest bundle of ownership rights. At common law, the fee simple and life estates were known as freehold interests. The possessor of these estates held the land free from the present ownership interests of any other person. The leasehold was a temporary expedient, designed to last for only a few years or even a single growing season. The ownership rights of the lease tenant were always held subject to the contemporaneous interest of the owner of the fee simple or life estate from which the leasehold was created.

Modern leases represent an interesting marriage of two branches of the law. The leasehold interest was originally created in the agricultural economy of the late Middle Ages. At that time the leasehold estate was treated as an ownership interest in land, governed by the rules of property law. During the industrial revolution a new branch of law, the law of contracts, emerged. Gradually, the principles of contract law (which define the creation and enforcement of obligations between the parties to an agreement) were grafted onto the ownership rights of the leasehold estate. As a result, the rights and duties of modern lease tenants are determined as much by principles of contract law as they are by the law of property.[2]

Creation of a Leasehold Interest

In modern practice, a leasehold interest is most often created by a written agreement between the owner of the fee simple estate in the leased premises (the landlord) and the holder of the leasehold estate (the tenant). This written agreement will be enforced as a contract between the parties. If the tenancy is to last for more than a year, the Statute of Frauds in most states will require a written agreement signed by the party to be charged with performing the agreement. Many of the difficulties in the landlord-tenant relationship can be traced to defects in the written agreement that forms the basis for the relationship. When disagreements between the landlord and the tenant arise over topics that are not covered by the lease, judges often look to the ancient law of property to find principles that will help them resolve the dispute. We will examine leaseholds according to this pattern. We begin our investigation by describing the terms that should be included in a good lease. Next, we will ask what happens when a poorly written lease fails to include one or more of these important terms.

The lease contracts we will examine can be divided into two general groups: residential leases and commercial leases. Residential leases define the landlord-tenant relationship for property used as housing for individuals and families. Commercial leases are the more important category in terms of dollar values. These agreements provide the basis for most of the economic activity in our economy. A substantial portion of the retail stores, warehouses, offices, and factories that constitute the business core of the U.S. economy occupy spaces rented under the terms of a commercial lease.

A good lease permits both parties (landlord and tenant) to understand in advance what they can expect during the lease tenancy, as well as what will be expected of them during the period of the tenancy. At a minimum, the lease should state the

---

[2] For a detailed analysis of this process, see Alex M. Johnson, Jr., "Correctly Interpreting Long Term Leases Pursuant to Modern Contract Law: Toward a Theory of Relational Leases," *Virginia Law Review* (May 1988): 751.

precise times at which the tenancy will begin and end. The lease must also describe the space that the tenant will have the right to occupy during the period of the lease. Finally, the lease should state the total rent owed by the tenant for the entire period of the lease, and describe the installments (usually monthly) by which the tenant will be expected to pay the rent.

KEY POINTS

Many first-time apartment dwellers are surprised to learn that a one-year lease on an apartment, at a monthly rental of $500, obligates the tenant to pay $6,000 to the landlord. The tenant is always free to move out of the apartment, but moving out during the term of the lease does not always end the obligation to pay the full amount of the rent reserved by the lease. As long as the landlord meets his or her obligations under the lease, the tenant will be required to pay the full year's rental.

Residential Leases

Most apartment houses and rental houses use a standard form lease drafted by the attorney for the owner. As a result, these leases tend to be written in ways that protect the landlord's interests carefully and may therefore ignore the needs of the residential tenant. Prospective tenants should review these documents carefully to avoid frustration and difficulty after moving into a house or apartment. Landlords can use a well-written lease as a marketing tool to attract tenants to the property and keep the dwellings full. The following areas are the most frequent sources of difficulty in landlord-tenant relationships.

Gokey v. Bessette

MAINTENANCE. In general, it is the duty of the apartment landlord to keep the property maintained and functioning. Broken appliances, heating, air conditioning, and plumbing are a primary source of dissatisfaction to tenants. A residential lease should contain a provision that requires the landlord to repair these items within a stated time after notice by the tenant that something in the apartment is not working. On the other hand, damage to the premise caused by the tenant (e.g., broken mirrors, holes in the wall, burned carpeting) are the responsibility of the tenant.

KEY POINTS

When the landlord fails or refuses to make repairs in an apartment, the tenant is often faced with a difficult dilemma. If the bathroom toilet overflows every time it is flushed, the tenants will find life in the apartment to be very unpleasant. An unscrupulous landlord might be inclined to wait until the tenants run out of patience and pay the repair bill themselves. Can the tenant deduct the cost of the repairs from the next month's rent payment?

DAMAGE DEPOSITS. Landlords will often require tenants to provide a damage deposit before moving in, to protect the landlord from incurring costs to repair damage caused by the tenant. The lease should state the amount of deposit required and should also state that the deposit will be returned to the tenant after the expiration of the lease. Most states have adopted statutes that require landlords to return all of a tenant's damage deposit within thirty days after the lease expires. These statutes authorize landlords to deduct only the actual cost of repairing damage and require the landlord to provide the tenant with a written statement of the costs. Many states provide penalties that the tenant may recover from a landlord who fails to return the damage deposit in accordance with the statute.

KEY POINTS

Shortly after the State of Colorado adopted the nation's first security deposit law an inexperienced landlord rented a basement apartment in her home to a husband and wife, who were both practicing attorneys. The tenants did substantial damage to the apartment, and on moving out said to the landlord, "We are sorry about the shape we left your apartment in. Feel free to keep our damage deposit to help pay for the repairs." The landlord was required to replace the carpeting, repair several holes in the walls, and repaint the entire apartment, at a cost of $500. The landlord retained the $300 damage deposit, as the tenants had suggested, but she failed to send a written notice within thirty days explaining the reasons for keeping the deposit, as required by the new statute.

Thirty-two days after they moved out, the tenants sued the landlord for return of their damage deposit, citing her failure to provide the required written notice. The security deposit statute permitted tenants who did not receive the required written notice to recover the amount of the security deposit, plus three times the amount of the deposit as a penalty, and attorney's fees. The tenants recovered a judgment against the landlord for approximately $2,000.

HOLDING OVER. If the tenant remains in the apartment at the expiration of the lease, a **hold over tenancy** will be created. This is an area in which the newer law of contracts may conflict with ancient property law. The best way to avoid conflict is for the lease contract to prohibit holding over. The lease should require the tenant to remove all personal belongings and vacate the apartment on or before the day the lease expires. A tenant who wishes to remain in the apartment can always do so by signing a new lease several weeks before the current lease expires.

Hold Over Tenancies
The real property interest which is created when a lease tenant remains in possession of the premises after the expiration of the lease period.

COMMON AREAS. Many apartment projects provide swimming pools, clubhouses, laundries, garages, and other amenities for their residents. These common areas should be identified in the lease. In addition, the hours or operation and rules for using the common areas should be included in the written contract. If the apartment lease also includes a garage or storage area for the private use of an apartment tenant, the location of the facility should be specified (e.g., "garage unit F").

LATE PAYMENT PENALTIES. It is not unusual for landlords to charge interest on rent payments that are not received on time. If interest is to be charged, the lease must state the annual or monthly interest rate that will be owed on rent installments that are late. The rent installment is typically due on the first day of the month and becomes late after the expiration of a grace period. The grace period should be at least ten days and in many cases will extend until the end of the month.

Nylen v. Park Doral Apts.

SUBLEASING. At common law, the ownership interest of a leasehold tenant could be assigned or sold to another person before the expiration of the tenancy. However, the owner of the freehold interest could prohibit such a sale if he or she chose to do so, and the common law of property rights would enforce the prohibition. Under the law of contracts, any party to a contract may assign his or her rights under the agreement to another person but cannot assign any of the duties owed under the agreement without the consent of the party to whom the duty is owed. The marriage of these similar doctrines from different legal theories can cause mischief in modern leasing practice.

Sublease
An agreement by which a lease tenant agrees to permit another person to use all or a portion of the right of present possession which belongs to the lease tenant.

The best way to eliminate potential conflicts is to prohibit any **sublease** or assignment of the leased premises in the contract that creates the leasehold tenancy. If the contract fails to prohibit subleasing or assignment, then there will arise the possibility of confusion and frustrated expectations. Let us examine two scenarios that illustrate how such a possibility might be realized under a residential lease that fails to prohibit subleasing. In each scenario, we will assume that an apartment tenant occupies the apartment under a one-year lease that begins at 9:00 A.M., January 1, and ends at 12:00 midnight on December 31 at a monthly rent of $400.

First, suppose that the lease tenant decides to rent a spare bedroom in the apartment to a friend. The tenant and the friend agree that they will share the rent equally. On February 1, both the tenant and the friend give the landlord their checks for $200 each, and the landlord cashes them. This occurs each month until June, when the friend stops paying his portion of the rent. When the landlord demands the unpaid portion of the rent from the tenant, the tenant may reply: "I subleased half of the apartment to my friend, so I only owe half of the rent, and my half is paid. You will have to talk to my friend if you want the other half."

Second, suppose that the tenant takes a new job in another city and moves out of the apartment at the beginning of May, after the May rent has been paid. Since the tenant still owes $2,400 in rent for the remaining six months of the lease, he will try to find another person to take over the lease on the apartment. Assume that the tenant finds a new person willing to move into the apartment, and the new person pays the rent in June, which the landlord accepts. Again, the new party stops making rent payments in July, and the landlord (after some searching) locates the original tenant and demands the unpaid rent from him. In this case the tenant may claim, "I assigned my interest in the property to your new tenant. Since you accepted the **assignment**, I don't owe you any more rent."

Assignment
An agreement by which a lease tenant sells to another person the right of present possession enjoyed by the lease tenant, for the remaining period of the leasehold estate.

Because the lease was silent on the issue of subletting the premises, a judge may be required to sort out the relative merits of the positions maintained by all of the parties involved. The judge has a number of avenues available for the sorting process. He or she may decide to apply the common law of real property to the case. Under this approach, the tenant has the right to sell or assign all or any portion of the leasehold rights to another person, unless the transfer was prohibited at the beginning of the lease term. Since the lease was silent on the issue of subletting, there was no prohibition. Therefore, both the sublease in the first scenario and the assignment in the second scenario are valid. And, since the tenant has parted with all or a portion of the ownership interest, the tenant has also escaped the obligation to pay rent, since no one has a duty to pay rent or property he or she does not "own" as a leasehold tenant.

Or, the judge may decide to apply the law of contracts to the transactions. Under this approach, the tenant may assign the right to occupy the apartment (or one bedroom in the apartment) to someone else without the landlord's consent. However, the tenant may not assign the duty to pay rent on the apartment unless the landlord consents to the assignment. But in both scenarios, the landlord (or the landlord's bookkeeper) accepted a rent check from a stranger to the lease. A judge would not be wrong to conclude that this acceptance of the rent constitutes a consent to the assignment of the tenant's duty to pay rent under the contract. This line of thinking would also lead to a judgment for the tenant.

The theories of both property and contract law also provide grounds for holding the tenant responsible for the unpaid portion of the rent in both scenarios. Under a real property theory, a judge might decide that the tenant's actions were not sufficient to convey a portion of the leasehold estate to the other person. If there was no conveyance, then the tenant remains the "owner" of the leased premises and is still under the duty to pay rent. Under a contract theory, the judge would examine the intent of the parties. From all the circumstances, the judge might conclude that the landlord and tenant did not intend to create a method by which the tenant could escape the obligation to pay all of the rent. The absence of such an intent will prevent the tenant from escaping the contractual obligation to pay all of the rent called for in the lease contract.

When the lease is silent with respect to subleasing, the scenarios present four possible outcomes. Either party may prevail under either of two legal theories. If, on the other hand, the lease had prohibited subleasing or assignment by the tenant, the number of outcomes would be reduced to one. Under both the property law approach and the contract law approach, the attempt to assign any portion of the leasehold interest of the tenant is void from the beginning. The third party in each scenario remains a trespasser from the landlord's point of view. The landlord may evict the third party at any time or allow the party to remain as long as it suits the landlord to do so. The tenant will remain obligated to pay the rent until the term of the lease expires.

The prohibition of subleasing fully protects the landlord. Is it of any benefit to the tenant? At the very least, such a provision does no harm. The preceding discussion makes it clear that attempting to sublease or assign a residential unit will produce a fairly large set of highly uncertain outcomes. The best way to avoid this uncertainty is to avoid subleasing entirely.

Commercial Leases

Leasehold interests in property intended for retail, office, and other commercial uses present some complexities that are usually not present in residential leases. These additional issues arise from several considerations that are important to commercial firms but have no significance to a residential tenant.

Retailers have long been aware that the volume of business they can expect depends in large measure on the location of the store. The second most important variable is the length of time the store has been in a particular location. Other commercial users of property have similar reasons for staying in the same location for many years. For example, manufacturers have to halt production in order to move to a new location. As a result, commercial leases usually have a much longer term than residential leases. A five-year lease with an option to renew for an additional five years is a fairly standard minimum term for a commercial lease. Lease terms of up to twenty five years are not unheard of in commercial settings. Because the future is always uncertain, the extended lease terms desired by commercial tenants require more sophisticated methods of dealing with unknown future events at the time the lease contract is signed.

The specialized needs of commercial tenants raise a second issue of complexity in commercial leasing practice. Residential tenants require a fairly standard space with a kitchen, a bathroom, and some storage space. The only variations in residential spaces are in the level of amenities. The equipment and facilities required by a grocery store, however, are very different from the requirements of an accounting firm. Tailoring the rented space to the exact needs of a commercial tenant must be accounted for in the written lease that governs the use of the space. Each of these issues will require terms in a commercial lease that are not ordinarily necessary in a residential lease.

ESCALATOR CLAUSES. Because commercial leases have long terms, conditions are likely to change during the term of the lease. Often these changes would make it appropriate for the landlord to charge a higher rental. The tenant, on the other hand, would like to have the rent remain constant for the entire term of the lease. A convenient way to resolve this conflict is to include a clause in the lease that allows the monthly rent to increase at regular intervals during the term of the lease.

Escalator Clause The provision of a commercial lease which permits increases in the rent paid by the tenant during the period of the lease.

The simplest form of the **escalator clause** is a constant percentage increase to be applied every year. For example, the lease may include a provision making the monthly rent increase by 3% in January of each year during the term of the lease. While the constant escalator possesses the virtue of simplicity, it fails to incorporate changes in the rental market that would make an adjustment in the rent appropriate. To accommodate these unforeseeable events, many commercial leases use a formula in the escalator clause.

The simplest formula is to tie the monthly rent to changes in the consumer price index. An increase in this index means that the real cost of the tenant's rent has declined along with the real income of the landlord. In theory, if the rent is adjusted periodically to reflect changes in the price level, the real cost and real income of the parties will remain roughly constant. In practice, constructing a verbal formula in the lease that will accomplish this objective is very difficult. An example of one such formula is included in the commercial lease form in the appendix to this chapter.

Another variant of the escalator clause in a commercial lease is a percent-of-sales provision. All other things being equal, business managers tend to prefer variable costs over fixed costs. Because the level of future sales is always uncertain, managers need to be able to adjust their costs in order to earn a profit on any level of sales. Variable costs are, by definition, costs that automatically adjust to changes in sales.

As long as the landlord receives a fixed base rent that covers the cost of owning the leased premises, the landlord will also be attracted by the possibility of earning a higher rent when the tenant does well. As a result, many commercial landlords are willing to negotiate a percent-of-sales lease, which allows the tenant to keep a substantial part of the total rent expense in the variable cost column.

Creating a percent-of-sales formula in a commercial lease may be difficult to accomplish in practice. Before the tenant occupies the property, the parties must agree on a formula that will be used to compute gross sales. For example, if vending machines are installed on the premises, will the proceeds from the sales of those machines be included in gross sales? In addition, the landlord will require some assurance that the tenant is reporting the sales accurately and paying all the rent due from the percent-of-sales computations. Finally, the lease should specify when the percent of sales is to be paid. Many businesses do not know what their sales for January are until March, when sales for the quarter are added up. The normal accounting practices of the tenant must be reflected in the percent-of-sales procedures written into the lease. Examples of percent-of-sales clauses are provided in the Appendix.

Borchert v. Webb

NET LEASE TERMS. Maintenance, utility costs, and property taxes are the three largest expense items in the budget of the typical commercial landlord. Further, the size of these expense items will often depend on the activities of the tenant. For example, the tenant may use the air conditioner to keep the temperature at a chilly 70° in the summer and run the heating plant to maintain a toasty 78° in the winter. These activities will result in a dramatic increase in utility costs to the landlord, while the benefits of the additional costs accrue only to the tenant. As a result, most commercial leases require the tenant to pay the utility costs associated with the property. A lease that requires the tenant to pay for utilities is often referred to as a **net lease**.

Net Leases Commercial leases in which the lease tenant is required to pay for some or all of the expenses of owning the property.

Maintenance costs can also become a significant item in a commercial lease. Many commercial tenants install a number of specialized fixtures for the conduct of their business on the leased premises. Each of these fixtures can be expected to increase the costs of maintaining the property. Landlords are usually eager to impose the cost of maintenance on the tenant who receives the benefit of the maintenance. A lease that requires the tenant to pay for both maintenance and utilities is referred to as a net, net or double net lease. An additional complication can arise when equipment in the building reaches the end of its useful life and needs to be replaced rather than repaired. A well-written double net lease will require the tenant to "repair or replace all plumbing fixtures, trade fixtures, furnishings, interior walls, carpeting, and other contents of the building during the term of the lease."

Property taxes constitute a source of great uncertainty in the commercial lease setting. It is probably safe to conclude that property taxes will increase during the typical commercial lease; but when and by how much is unknown. Landlords have only three options in the face of the expected increase in property taxes. The first option is to charge a higher rent to offset the reduction in net income that can be expected during the term of the lease. The second is simply to accept the reduced return. The third is to include property tax increases as part of an escalator clause that will trigger an increase in the rent paid by the tenant whenever property taxes rise.

Market conditions will often prevent landlords from adopting the first alternative. Landlords are understandably reluctant to accept the second alternative. As a result, the inclusion of property tax increases in the escalator clause of the lease is the most popular solution.

It is a short step from this alternative to simply requiring the tenant to pay the property taxes. Most tenants would be reluctant to pay for a property tax increase under the terms of an escalator clause, unless they also receive a rent decrease in the (perhaps unlikely) event that property taxes decline. If the rent is to be adjusted every time the taxes on the property are changed, it makes more sense for the parties to agree that the tenant will simply pay the taxes, thus obviating the need for frequent rental adjustments. In exchange, a sophisticated landlord would be willing to agree to a lower constant rent, since the risk of changes in the property tax has been passed to the tenant. Commercial leases that require the tenant to pay for maintenance, utilities, and property taxes are referred to as net, net, net or triple net leases.

SUBLEASING. The issue of subleasing has already been discussed in the context of residential leases. The problem arises with more force in the context of commercial leasing. When a commercial tenant builds a successful business in a rented location, the tenant may often decide to sell the business and move on to other pursuits. The common law rights of a leasehold tenant permit the assignment of the lease to a third party, unless assignment is prohibited by the terms of the lease.

Commercial landlords are well advised to include a term in the lease that prevents the assignment of the tenant's leasehold interest. The rents that provide the return to the landlord will only be paid if the business conducted on the leasehold premises is successful. In addition, the landlord will usually be faced with a large monthly mortgage payment on the leased building, which he or she may not be able to pay if the rent flows are interrupted. Commercial landlords have nothing to gain and much to lose when their tenants assign a leasehold interest to a new and untried manager, who may or may not be successful in operating the business. Landlords are understandably eager to prohibit the assignment or subleasing of their property by an established tenant.

On the other hand, commercial tenants will be unable to realize the value they have created in their business activities if they are prevented from transferring the business to another party in exchange for cash. Commercial tenants will therefore usually insist on a lease provision giving them the right to assign the lease. The subleasing clause in the Appendix represents a frequent compromise between the conflicting interests of the parties.

Carma executed a 10 year lease on commercial property in San Francisco. Several years into the lease, the tenant notified the landlord that it intended to sublet 80% of demised premises. The lease permitted the tenant to sublease the property only with the permission of the landlord, which permission would not be unreasonably withheld.

The lease also contained a termination clause which allowed the landlord to ". . . terminate the lease and enter into a new lease covering the Premises with the intended assignee or sublessee or with any other person. . . . in such event, tenant shall not be entitled to any portion of the profit, if any, which the landlord may realize on account of any such termination or reletting."

When the landlord elected to terminate the lease after the tenant's notice of intent to sublease, the tenant sued alleging the landlord had breached its contract and failed to act reasonably. The trial court held that the termination provision of the lease was void as an unreasonable restraint on alienation and entered a judgment for the tenant of approximately $450,000.

The California Supreme Court reversed the decision. The Supreme Court noted that the tenant had leased the property at a rental of $22 per square foot, and had agreed to sublease virtually all of the space at a rental of $33.32 per square foot. As a result of this transaction, the tenant expected to realize an annual profit on the sublease of $10,323 per year. The Supreme Court ruled that a lease provision which prohibits long term commercial tenants from reaping the profits created by an increase in market rents was not an unreasonable restraint. Carma Developers, Inc. v. Marathon Development California, Inc. 826 P.2d 710 (CA, 1992)

HOLDOVER TENANCIES. At common law, the leasehold tenant became a trespasser on the landlord's property at the end of the lease term. As long as the landlord did not object to the tenant's presence, the tenant was free to remain. The tenant holding over, however, like any trespasser, was obliged to leave whenever the landlord decided that the tenant's presence was no longer desirable.

In modern practice, this somewhat harsh rule has been softened. Most states have now adopted statutes that define that privileges of a lease tenant who remains in the property after the expiration of the lease term. Although there are slight variations among the states, the general rule is that a tenant holding over will be treated as being a periodic tenant on the property. If the original lease term was for a period of one year or less, the tenant will become a month-to-month tenant after the expiration of the lease. That is, when the tenant pays the monthly rental, the tenant will have the right to remain on the property for the rest of the month. If the original term of the lease was for more than a year, the tenant will become a year-to-year tenant. In this case, the payment of one month's rent gives the tenant the right to remain on the property for a full year, so long as the remaining monthly rents are paid on time. The monthly rent due for a holdover tenant is equal to the rent paid for the last month of the lease under which the tenant originally occupied the property.

In addition, most states have adopted statutes requiring landlords to give tenants advance notice that they will be evicted from the property. If the tenancy is for less than a year, the tenant cannot be evicted until thirty days after the landlord gives notice that the tenant must vacate the premises. If the tenancy is for a year or more, six months' notice will usually be required. Again, these time limits are established by statute in each state, so there is some variation in the notice required among the states.

RIGHTS AND DUTIES OF LANDLORDS AND TENANTS

We conclude this chapter with a brief look at the rights and duties of the parties to a lease agreement. In general, all tenants have a duty to pay the required rent, to use the property in the manner described in the lease, and to perform any additional obligations included in a written lease agreement. All landlords have a duty to protect the tenant's quiet enjoyment of the property. In other words, landlords may not interfere with the tenant's use of the property in any way, unless the actions of the tenant violate the terms of the lease agreement. It is customary to include a provision in written leases allowing the landlord or the landlord's agent to enter the premises at reasonable times and inspect them for damage. In the absence of such a provision, a residential tenant may usually refuse to allow the landlord to enter and inspect before the term of the lease expires. Commercial tenants, especially those who invite members of the general public into their locations, are usually required to allow the landlord to enter and inspect the premises during normal business hours.

Implied Warranties of Habitability

Residential landlords have incurred an additional duty during the last fifty years. Because residential landlords provide housing for their tenants, courts have been willing to impose additional burdens on these landlords that benefit the people who live in their properties. Most states now require landlords to maintain residential properties in a safe and functional manner. All the appliances and plumbing fixtures in a dwelling must be in working order. The landlord bears the duty to repair them, unless the tenant has agreed to do so in writing.

In addition, the landlord may not permit accumulations of trash, garbage, or other filth on the property. Infestations of rats, insects, or other vermin must be corrected by the landlord. In general, the implied warranty of habitability requires a residential landlord to maintain a clean and safe environment for the tenants. If a landlord fails to discharge any of these duties, most courts have allowed tenants to stop paying rent until the problem is corrected.

Eviction

When a tenant fails to perform any of the duties required by the lease agreement, the landlord may institute proceedings to remove the tenant. The most frequent cause for eviction is the nonpayment of rent. Like any other lawsuit, an eviction proceeding begins when the tenant is served with notice that he or she will be required to vacate the premises within the notice period provided by the state statute.

The notice served on the tenant must state the reasons why the landlord is seeking to evict the tenant. In addition, the notice must inform the tenant of the time and place where a judge will hear evidence to determine whether the tenant should be removed or not. Due process requires that the tenant be given an opportunity to appear and explain why an order for eviction should not be entered. For example, the tenant may come to the court at the time indicated in the notice and give evidence that the landlord has breached the implied warranty of habitability. If the warranty has been breached, then the nonpayment of rent is excused, and the judge will refuse to issue an order of eviction.

In addition, the tenant usually will be given the opportunity to cure the breach of the lease agreement that the landlord has stated as grounds for eviction. If the landlord has begun the eviction proceedings because the tenant is behind in the rent, for example, the tenant will be allowed to pay the past due amounts and remain in the property.

The moral of the story is that eviction is difficult, expensive, and time-consuming activity. And the outcome of an eviction effort is not always what the landlord had in mind when the proceeding was initiated. That is why the landlord's best defense is to screen tenants carefully and accept only those who appear able and willing to meet their obligations under the lease. In addition, it is important to use a written lease agreement that spells out the rights and duties of both parties clearly and completely.

CONCLUSION

In this chapter, we have reviewed the major differences between a life tenancy and a leasehold tenancy. We noted that the leasehold tenancy, for all its importance to modern commerce, comprises the smallest bundle of ownership rights. We have also examined the marriage of real property and contract law that defines the modern leasehold estate. The rights and duties of landlords and tenants will be determined by the terms of the written lease agreement that the parties sign. We have seen that when the lease is silent as to important elements of the landlord-tenant relationship, ancient doctrines of real property law may be used to resolve disputes between the parties. Finally, we have examined some of the state statutes that may modify the rights and duties of the parties to a leasehold interest, especially when the party involved is residential in nature.

DISCUSSION QUESTIONS

1. Distinguish between a life estate and a leasehold estate.
2. What is the major difference between the estates described in Question 1?
3. State the purpose of the life estate. What are two ways in which a life estate can be created? When might a life estate per autre vie estate be used?
4. Name two limitations that ownership rights of a life tenant are subject to. What is the modern legal definition of "waste"?
5. As a potential tenant, what information should one look for when going over a residential lease agreement?
6. With reference to commercial leases, what is an escalator clause? What are some variations on this type of clause?
7. Distinguish between a net lease and a net, net (or double net) lease.
8. When is a holdover tenancy created? What determines how long the holdover tenancy will last?
9. State the duties of the residential landlord under the implied warranty of habitability

MELMS ET AL.
V.
PABST BREWING CO.

79 N.W.2d 738 (Wis., 1899)

The doctrine of waste

This is an action for waste, brought by reversioner against the defendant, which is the owner of an estate for the life of another in a quarter of an acre of land in the city of Milwaukee. The waste claimed is the destruction of a dwelling house upon the land, and the grading of the same down to the level of the street. The quarter of an acre of land in question is situated upon Virginia street, in the city of Milwaukee, and was the homestead of one Charles T. Melms, deceased. The house thereon was a large brick building built by Melms in the year 1864, and cost more than $20,000.

At the time of the building of the house, Melms owned the adjoining real estate, and also owned a brewery upon a part of the premises. Charles T. Melms died in the year 1869, leaving his estate involved in financial difficulties. After his decease, both the brewery and the homestead were sold and conveyed to the Pabst Brewing Company, but it was held in the action of Melms v. Brewing Co. 93 Wis. 140, 66 N.W.,244. that the brewing company only acquired Mrs. Melms' life estate in the homestead, and that the plaintiffs in this action were the owners of the fee, subject to such life estate.

The homestead consists of piece of land 90 feet square, in the center of which the aforesaid dwelling house stood. It clearly appears by the evidence that after the purchase of this land by the brewing company the general character of real estate upon Virginia street about the homestead rapidly changed, so that soon after the year 1890 it became wholly undesirable and unprofitable as residence property. Factories and railway tracks increased in the vicinity, and the balance of the property was built up with brewing buildings, until the quarter of an acre homestead in question became an isolated lot and building, standing from 20 to 30 feet above the level of the street, the balance of the property having been graded down in order to fit it for business purposes.

The evidence shows without material dispute that, owing to these circumstances, the residence, which was at one time a handsome and desirable one became of no practical value, and would not rent for enough to pay taxes and insurance thereon; where as, if the property were cut down to the level of the street, so that it was capable of being used as business property, it would again be useful, and its value would be largely enhanced. Under these circumstances, and prior to the judgment in the former action, the defendant removed the building, and graded down the property to about the level of the street, and these are the acts which it is claimed constitute waste.

The action was tried before the court without a jury, and the court found, in addition to the facts above stated, that the removal of the building and grading down of the earth was done by the defendant in 1891 and 1892, believing itself to be the owner in fee simple of the property, and that by said acts the estate of the plaintiffs in the property was substantially increased, and that the plaintiffs have been in no way injured thereby. Upon these findings the complaint was dismissed, and the plaintiffs appeal.

WINSLOW, J. (after stating the facts). Our statutes recognize waste, and provide a remedy by action, and the recovery of double damages therefor (Rev.St. 1898, 3170 *et seq.*); but they do not define it. It may be either voluntary or permissive, and may be of houses, gardens, orchards, lands, or woods (*Id.* 3171); but, in order to ascertain whether a given act constitutes waste or not, recourse must be had to the common law as expounded by the text-books and decisions.

In the present case a large dwelling house, expensive when constructed, has been destroyed, and the ground has been graded down, by the owner of the life estate, in order to make the property serve business purposes. That these acts would constitute waste under ordinary circumstances cannot be doubted. The following definition of "waste" was approved by this court in Bandlow v. Thieme, 53 Wis. 57 9 N.W. 920: "It may be defined to be any act or omission of duty by a tenant of land which does a lasting injury to the freehold, tends to the permanent loss of the owner of the fee, or to destroy or lessen the value of the inheritance, or to destroy the identity of the property, or impair the evidence of title." And in Brock v. Dole, 66 Wis. 142, 28 N.W. 334, it was also said that "any material change in the nature and character of the buildings made by the tenant is waste, although the value of the property should be enhanced by the alteration."

These recent judicial utterances in this court settle the general rules which govern waste without difficulty, and it may be said, also, that these rules are in accord with the general current of the authorities elsewhere. But, while they are correct as general expressions of the law upon the subject, and were properly applicable to the cases under consideration, it must be remembered that they are general rules only, and, like most general propositions, are not to be accepted without limitation or reserve under any and all circumstances.

Thus the ancient English rule which prevented the tenant from converting a meadow into arable land was early softened down, and the doctrine of meliorating waste was adopted, which without changing the legal definition of waste, still allowed the tenant to change the course of husbandry upon the estate if such change be for the betterment of the estate. . . . It is now well settled that, while such change may constitute technical waste, still it will not be enjoined in equity when it clearly appears that the change will be, in effect, a meliorating change, which rather improves the inheritance than injures it.

* * *

This element will be found in all the definitions of waste, namely, that it must be an act resulting in permanent injury to the inheritance or future estate. It has been frequently said that this injury may consist either in diminishing the value of the inheritance, or increasing its burdens, or in destroying the identity of the property, or impairing the evidence of title. The last element of injury so enumerated, while cogent and persuasive one in former times, has lost most, if not all, of its force, at the present time. It was important when titles were not registered, and descriptions of land were frequently dependent upon natural monuments, or the uses to which the land was put; but since the universal adoption of accurate surveys, and the establishment of the system of recording conveyances, there can be few acts which will impair any evidence of title.

But the principle that the reversioner or remainder-man is ordinarily entitled to receive the identical estate, or, in other words, that the identity of the property is not to be destroyed, still remains, and it has been said that changes in the nature of the buildings, though enhancing the value of the property, will constitute waste if they change the identity of the estate. Brock v. Dole, *supra*.

* * *

The case now before us, however, bears little likeness to such a case, and contains elements so radically different from those present in Brock v. Dole that we cannot regard that case as controlling this one.

There are no contract relations in the present case. The defendants are the grantees of a life estate, and their rights may continue for a number of years. The evidence shows that the property became valueless for the purpose of residence property as the result of the growth and development of a great city. Business and manufacturing interests advanced and surrounded the once elegant mansion, until it stood isolated and alone, standing upon just enough ground to support it, and surrounded by factories and railway tracks, absolutely undesirable as a residence, and incapable of any use as business property. Here was a complete change of conditions, not produced by the tenant, but resulting from causes which none could control.

In the absence of any contract, express or implied, to use the property for a specified purpose, or to return it in the same condition in which it was received, a radical and permanent change of surrounding conditions, such as is presented in the case before us, must always be an important, and sometimes a controlling, consideration upon the question whether a physical change in the use of the buildings constitutes waste. In the present case this consideration was regarded by the trial court as controlling, and we are satisfied that this is the right view.

Judgment affirmed.

Case Reflections

1. What are the duties which a life tenant owes to the holders of the remainder interest?
2. Why did the court find that destruction of the house of the plaintiff's property did not violate those duties?

MOORE
V.
PHILLIPS

627 P.2d 831 (Kan., 1981)

Duties of a life tenant

PRAGER, Justice Presiding:

This is a claim for waste asserted against the estate of a life tenant by remaindermen, seeking to recover damages for the deterioration of a farmhouse resulting from neglect by the life tenant. The life tenant was Ada C. Brannan. The defendant-appellant is her executrix, Ruby F. Phillips. The claimants-appellees are Dorothy Moore and Kent Reinhardt, the daughter and grandson of Ada C. Brannan.

The facts in the case are essentially as follows: Leslie Brannan died in 1962. By his will he left his wife, Ada C. Brannan, a life estate in certain farmland containing a farmhouse, with remainder interests to Dorothy Moore and Kent Reinhardt. Ada C. Brannan resided in the farmhouse until 1964. She then rented the farmhouse until August 1, 1965, when it became unoccupied. From that point on, Ada C. Brannan rented all of the farmland but nobody lived in the house. It appears that from 1969 to 1971 it was leased to the remaindermen, but they did not live there. It is undisputed that the remaindermen inspected the premises from time to time down through the years. In 1973, Ada C. Brannan petitioned for a voluntary conservatorship because of physical infirmities. In 1976, Ada C. Brannan died testate, leaving her property to others. Dorothy Moore and Kent Reinhardt were not included in Ada's bounty. From the record, it is clear that Ada C. Brannan and her daughter, Dorothy Moore, were estranged from about 1964 on. This estrangement continued until Ada Brannan's death, although there was minimal contact between them from time to time.

After Ada Brannan's death, Dorothy Moore and Kent Reinhardt filed a demand against the estate of Ada Brannan on the theory of waste to recover damages for the deterioration of the farmhouse. The total damages alleged were in the amount of $16,159. Both the district magistrate and the district judge inspected the premises and found deterioration due to neglect by the life tenant. The district court found the actual damages to the house to be $10,433. The executrix of Ada's estate denied any neglect or breach of duty by Ada Brannan as life tenant. She asserted the defenses of laches or estoppel, the statute of limitation and abandonment. These affirmative defenses were rejected by the district magistrate and the district judge, except the defense of laches or estoppel which the district magistrate sustained. On appeal, the district judge found that the defense of laches or estoppel was not applicable against the remaindermen in this case. Following entry of judgment in favor of the remaindermen, the executrix appealed.

It is important to note that the executrix does not contend, as points of error, that the life tenant was not responsible for deterioration of the farmhouse or that the action is barred by a statute of limitations. The amount of damages awarded is not contested. In her brief, the executrix-appellant asserts four points which essentially present a single issue: Whether the remaindermen, by waiting eleven years until the death of the life tenant before filing any claim or demand against the life tenant for neglect of the farmhouse, are barred by laches or estoppel?

The executrix contends, in substance, that laches and estoppel, although considered to be equitable defenses, are available in an action at law to recover damages. She points out that, under K.S.A.58-2523, a remainderman may sue to prevent waste during the life of the tenant while the life tendency is still in existence. She then notes that the remaindermen inspected the premises on numerous occasions during the eleven years the property was vacant; yet they made no demand that the farmhouse be kept in repair. They waited until the death of the life tenant to bring the action, because they would not be faced with Ada's testimony which might defeat their claim.

The remaindermen, in their brief, dispute certain factual statements made by the executrix. They agree that the remaindermen had very limited contact with the life tenant after the estrangement. They contend that there is evidence to show the vast majority of the damage to the house occurred during the last two to three years of the life tenancy and that Dorothy Moore did, in fact, express concern to her mother about the deterioration of the house 15 or 20 times during the eleven-year period. They contend that mere passage of time does not constitute laches and that, in order to have laches or estoppel, the person claiming the same must show a detrimental change of position or prejudice of some kind. They argue that the executrix has failed to show any prejudice, since the fact of waste and deterioration is clear and undisputed and there is nothing the testimony of the life tenant could have added on that issue had she been at the trial. As to the failure of the remaindermen to file an action in the lifetime of the life tenant, the remaindermen argue that claimants had been advised to avoid contact with Ada Brannan unless it was absolutely necessary and that they did not want to make a claim during her lifetime since it would have only made a bad situation worse. They maintain that they had good reasons to wait until Ada's death to assert the claim.

In order to place this case in proper perspective, it would be helpful to summarize some of the basic principles of law applicable where a remaindermen asserts a claim of waste against a life tenant. They are as follows:

1. A life tenant is considered in law to be a trustee or quasi-trustee and occupies a fiduciary relation to the remaindermen. The life tenant is a trustee in the sense that he cannot injure or dispose of the property to the injury of the rights of the remaindermen, but he differs from a pure trustee in that he may use the property for his exclusive benefit and take all the income and profits.
2. It is the duty of a life tenant to keep the property subject to the life estate in repair so as to preserve the property and to prevent decay or waste. 51 Am.Jur.2d, Life Tenants and Remaindermen § 259, pp. 546–548. Stated in another way, the law imposes upon a tenant the obligation to return the premises to the landlord or remaindermen at the end of the term unimpaired by the negligence of the tenant. (Citations omitted.)
3. The term "waste" implies neglect or misconduct resulting in material damages to or loss of property, but does not include ordinary depreciation of property due to age and normal use over a comparatively short period of time.
4. Waste may be either voluntary or permissive. Voluntary waste, sometimes spoken of as commissive waste, consists of the commission of some deliberate or voluntary destructive act. Permissive waste is the failure of the tenant to exercise the ordinary care of a prudent man for the preservation and protection of the estate. 78 Am.Jur.2d, Waste § 3, p. 397.
5. The owner of a reversion or remainder in fee has a number of remedies available to him against a life tenant who commits waste. He may recover compensatory damages for the injuries sustained. He may have injunctive relief in equity, or, in a proper case, may obtain a receivership. The same basic remedies are available against either a tenant for years of a life tenant.
6. By statute in Kansas, K.S.A.58-2523, "[a] person seized of an estate in remainder or reversion may maintain an action for waste or trespass for injury to the inheritance, notwithstanding an intervening estate for life or years." Thus a remainderman does not have to wait until the life tenant dies in order to bring an appropriate action for waste.
7. Where the right of action of the remainderman or landlord is based upon permissive waste, it is generally held that the injury is continuing in nature and that the statute of limitations does not commence to run in favor of the tenant until the expiration of the tenancy. Under certain state statutes, it has been held that the period of limitation commences at the time the waste is committed. (citations omitted)
8. There is authority which holds that an action for waste may be lost by laches. Harcourt v. White, 28 Beavan's 303, 54 Eng.Reprint 382 (1860); 78 Am. Jur.2d, Waste § 38, p. 424. Likewise, estoppel may be asserted as a defense in an action for waste. The doctrines of laches and estoppel are closely related, especially where there is complaint of delay which has placed another at a disadvantage. Laches is sometimes spoken of as a species of estoppel. Laches is a wholly negative thing, the result of a failure to act; estoppel on the other hand may involve an affirmative act on the part of some party of the lawsuit. The mere passage of time is not enough to invoke the doctrine of laches. Each case must be governed by its own facts, and what might be considered a lapse of sufficient time to defeat an action in one case might be insufficient in another. Laches, in legal significance, is not mere delay, but delay that works a disadvantage to another. The defense of laches may be applied in actions at law as well as in equitable proceedings. Laches is an equitable defense and will not bar a recovery from mere lapse of time nor where there is a reasonable excuse for non-action of a party in making inquiry as to his rights or in *asserting* them.

* * *

The basic question for our determination is whether the district court erred in holding that the defense of laches or estoppel should not be applied in this case. We have concluded that the district court did not commit error in its rejection of the defense of laches or estoppel under the circumstances of this case. In reaching this conclusion, we have noted the following factors: The evidence is clear that the life tenant, Ada Brannan, failed to carry out her duty as life tenant and quasi-trustee to keep the property in reasonable repair. The claim of waste does not arise out of any act on the part of the remaindermen. Preservation of the property was the responsibility of the life tenant. There was evidence to show that the vast majority of the damage to the farmhouse occurred during the last two or three years of the life tenancy. The fact that the permissive waste occurred was proved beyond question. If the life tenant had been alive, she could not very well have disputed the fact that the property has been allowed to deteriorate. Hence, any delay in filing the action until after Ada's death could not have resulted in prejudice to her executrix. There is no evidence in the record to support the defense of estoppel.

The judgment of the district court is affirmed.

Case Reflections

1. In what way did the life tenant breach her duties to the holders of the remainder interest?
2. Why was the breach of duty not excused in this case?

CARLTON
V.
WILSON

665 S.W.2d 356 (Mo., 1984)

Life Estate per autre vie

PREWITT, Judge.

Plaintiff sought the proceeds of a fire insurance policy, now deposited in the circuit court, and to quiet title to the real estate on which the insured dwelling had been situated. Following non jury trial, the trial court determined that defendant was entitled to all of the proceeds and that plaintiff and defendant owned equally a life estate in the real estate for the life of defendant, with the remainder in plaintiff.

Defendant was previously married to plaintiff's mother, Levon E. Wilson. Levon E. Wilson had been the sole owner of the real estate. On December 15, 1973, during their marriage, she and defendant signed a warranty deed purporting to convey to plaintiff an interest in the real estate. Following the legal description of the property the following words were typed: "It is understood by all parties that the first parties (grantors) reserve a life estate in the above described real estate." Absent the language quoted the deed would have conveyed to plaintiff title in fee simple without any reservations.

Levon E. Wilson died on March 2, 1978. Previous to her death the house was insured against fire and other perils by an insurance policy showing as the named insureds defendant and Levon Wilson. When the policy came up for its annual renewal in November of 1978 defendant refused to pay the premium until the policy was changed to his name alone. The insurance company made the change. Two months later the policy was again changed to reflect the insureds as defendant and his new wife. All premiums on the policy following Levon Wilson's death were paid solely by defendant. On June 9, 1979, a house on the property was totally destroyed by fire. Following the fire and the filing of this action the insurance company paid the proceeds of the policy into the Cedar County Circuit Court for it to determine the proper recipient.

Plaintiff's first point contends that the trial court erred in finding that defendant had an interest in the real property. She asserts that the effect of the reservation in the deed was to reserve to Levon E. Wilson a life estate in her measured by her life. Defendant contends that the deed reserved an additional life estate for Levon E. Wilson measured by the life of defendant as an estate per autre vie; that is, for the life of another. He asserts that when Levon E. Wilson died that life estate passed to plaintiff and defendant as Levon E. Wilson's only heirs.

* * *

Plaintiff claims that the clear intent to be drawn from the deed is that Levon E. Wilson wanted to make a fee simple conveyance to her daughter and to reserve a life estate for herself only. She contends that the "use of the word 'grantors' in connection with the reservation of the life estate is clearly an inadvertent use of the plural and a typist error" and that the only reason defendant joined in the deed was to relinquish his prospective marital rights to plaintiff. Plaintiff asserts that Levon E. Wilson would not have intended to reserve a life estate in defendant because of the possibility that their marriage might have been dissolved and she would not have "intended to reserve a right for such an ex-husband to occupy the premises after the marriage no longer existed."

* * *

There was no evidence that any language in the deed was there because of inadvertence or error. The dissolution argument fails because defendant's interest is acquired not by the deed, but as an heir, and had the marriage been dissolved prior to Levon E. Wilson's death, he would not have acquired any interest in the property. On the basis of the record before us, we have to conclude that Levon Wilson died intestate and that defendant, her surviving spouse, and plaintiff, her only child, acquired an equal interest in the life estate for defendant's life as tenants in common. See sec. 474.010, RSMo 1978. The remainder is in plaintiff.

We next discuss whether plaintiff, as the owner of the remainder is entitled to any portion of the insurance proceeds. Certain applicable principles are set forth in Farmers' Mut. Fire & Lightning Ins. Co. v. Crowley, 354 Mo. 649, 190 S.W.2d 250 (1945). "If a building has been insured prior to the creation of a life tenancy and is afterwards destroyed, the property is in effect converted into personalty and the life tenant is entitled only to a life estate in the proceeds of the insurance contract." 190 S.W.2d at 251. However, if a life tenant insures the property in his own name and for his own benefit and pays the premiums from his own funds, he is entitled to proceeds of the insurance upon a loss absent a stipulation in the instrument creating the life estate or an agreement binding him to keep the premises insured for the remainderman's benefit. *Id.* 190 S.W.2d at 251–252. *See also* Michigan Fire & Marine Ins. Co. v. Magee, 240 Mo.App. 767, 218 S.W.2d 151 (1949); Underwood v. Fortune, 9 S.W.2d 359 (Mo.App.1928). There was no requirement in the deed and no other agreement that defendant would procure insurance on the house for plaintiff's benefit.

In Farmer's Mut. Fire & Lightning Ins. Co. v. Crowley, *supra,* Mary Crowley had insured a dwelling on her land. She died during the term of the policy, having devised a life estate to her husband, remainder to her nieces and nephews. After her death, at the husband's request, the insurance company attached a "rider" to the policy, recognizing that the interest of Mary Crowley had ceased and the title was now in the name of the husband. After her death the husband paid the cost of the insurance. The court stated that it was "clear" that by the procurement of the insurance company's "rider," after the life estate became vested, a new contract of insurance was effectuated and as the husband procured the contract of insurance in his own name as insured and paid for it, he was entitled to the proceeds. Such a new contract was entered into here and plaintiff as owner of the remainder had no interest in the proceeds. The facts in Crowley and Michigan Fire & Marine Ins. Co. v. Magee, *supra,* are similar to these and based on the principles they state we must determine this question against plaintiff.

Plaintiff is not entitled to share in the proceeds because she is a tenant in common of the life estate. Insurance procured separately against loss by a cotenant does not inure to the benefit of another cotenant. Crabtree v. Maupin Seed Co., 294 S.W. 433, 435 (Mo.App.1927).

* * *

The judgment is affirmed.

Case Reflections

1. Describe the exact nature of the real property interests created by the wording of the deed to the plaintiff.
2. What does the court mean by the statement "If a building has been insured prior to the creation of a life tenancy and is afterwards destroyed, the property is in effect converted into personalty and the life tenant is entitled only to a life estate in the proceeds of the insurance contract." Does this seem like a good rule?

3. Suppose the defendant spends the proceeds of the insurance settlement on a new home located in different city. Would the plaintiff have any grounds for complaint? Should the plaintiff seek an order requiring the defendent to use the insurance settlement for the purpose of rebuilding the home which was destroyed?

GOKEY V. BESSETTE

580 A.2d 488 (Vt., 1990)

Landlord's duty to maintain premises

GIBSON, Justice

I.

Plaintiff landlord, who brought an action for unpaid rent, appeals from a district court decision denying relief and awarding defendant tenants damages and attorney's fees for breach of an implied warranty of habitability and retaliatory eviction. We affirm in part and reverse in part.

The parties entered into an oral agreement for the rental of a mobile home starting in September of 1985 at a monthly rent of $400. The tenants paid for electric service to the mobile home, but the landlord paid for the electricity for a nearby barn, in which the tenants were allowed to store their freezer. The trial court found that during the tenancy a variety of problems developed, including water leakage into the home through the roof, which was fixed by the tenants, power failures due to a faulty transformer, and a furnace breakdown. More serious was a break in the sewer line serving the premises, which remained unresolved from February to June of 1986 and resulted in water surfacing from the system. The trial court found that the "landlord's response [fell] short of an adequate response. Foul odor filled the trailer and unhealthy fluids lay underneath the trailer for long periods of time." Defendant stopped paying rent as of June 1, 1986. The court found that final repair to the septic system came later in June, 1986, only after a visit from the town health officer, prompted by defendants. On June 6, 1986, prior to the repair, plaintiff gave notice to quit, effective August 1, 1986. The court found that after defendants stopped paying rent, plaintiff locked the barn where the freezer was located and shut off the power, causing the loss of $300 worth of food. Defendants vacated the premises on October 31, 1986, approximately one month after the plaintiff had sold the mobile home.

Plaintiff thereafter sued for unpaid rent, and defendants counterclaimed for damages, alleging violations of plaintiff's duty to provide habitable premises. The court concluded that because of the failure to correct the sewage problem and other continuing defects, plaintiff had violated his warranty of habitability, validating defendants' claim to return of the rent paid for the period from February to June, 1986, some $1600. In addition, the court awarded defendants $300 for the loss of the freezer food, $800 for the "discomfort and distress for the lockout of the barn for the months June to October, 1986," $1600 for the retaliatory eviction under 9 V.S.A. § 4465[1], and $700 in attorney's fees, for a total of $5,000. Plaintiff contends that the total award was actually $6,600, since the $5,000 total does not include the forgiveness of rent due for June through September, 1986, resulting from dismissal of plaintiff's complaint. The present appeal followed.

II.

Plaintiff argues first that the trial court erred in concluding that the eviction was retaliatory simply

[1] 9 V.S.A. § 4465 states in relevant part:

(a) A landlord of a residential dwelling unit may not retaliate by establishing or changing terms of a rental agreement or by bringing or threatening to bring an action against a tenant who:

(1) has complained to a governmental agency charged with responsibility for enforcement of a building, housing or health regulation of a violation applicable to the premises materially affecting health and safety.

because it followed defendants' complaints to the town health officer about the sewage problems. He maintains that he affected the repairs promptly and that they were approved by the town health officer. The eviction, he argues, was the result of nonpayment of rent.

Defendants do not deny that the timing of the complaint to the health officer and of the eviction notice were central to the court's decision on retaliatory eviction, but they respond that the events, taken as a whole, amply support the court's conclusion that the eviction was in retaliation for notification of the health officer. We agree. The trial court found that plaintiff had failed to comply with his duty to provide a habitable dwelling. Consequently, the withholding of the rent, which occurred after four months of inaction by plaintiff and prior to the repair, was allowable under our holding in Hilder v. St. Peter, 144 Vt. 150, 162, 478 A.2d 202, 209–10 (1984), and under 9 V.S.A. § 4458 (a) (1). Plaintiff's argument that eviction was for the nonpayment of rent would appertain only if the trier of fact had concluded that there had been no breach of the landlord's duties. (Citations omitted.) The trial court made detailed findings to the contrary, however; absent a showing that these findings were not supported by credible evidence or that the trial court abused its discretion in concluding that the landlord had violated his statutory and contractual obligations to defendants, these findings must stand. . . .

Given the findings that plaintiff had failed to perform his obligations to defendants and that defendants were justified in withholding their rent payments, the trial court could reasonably conclude that the eviction was retaliatory. See 9 V.S.A. § 4465(a) (2). In urging that he believed he had legal basis for the eviction—the nonpayment of rent—and, consequently, intended no retaliation plaintiff argues for a subjective test for a retaliatory eviction. While animus or bad motive may properly be considered in evaluating what is "retaliatory," the statute does not contemplate use of a subjective test. A subjective test would effectively establish such a high burden of proof for tenants that the benefit the Legislature intended to confer would be an illusion. In determining what is and is not retaliatory, the events must speak for themselves. (Citations omitted.)

In the present case, the eviction action against defendants followed a long course of disagreements over the condition of the rental premises, generated by plaintiff's failure to provide habitable premises. See Hilder v. St. Peter, 144 Vt. at 159, 478 A.2d at 208. There was ample evidence to support the trial court's conclusion that the eviction action and the closure of access to the barn—which constituted "changing terms of a rental agreement" within the meaning of 9 V.S.A. § 4465(a)—were retaliatory. If plaintiff simply wished to recover the rent he believed due him, and which defendants had withheld after June 1, 1986, he could have limited his action to that claim. It is not the purpose of sec. 4465 to bar a landlord from bringing a good-faith action to recover unpaid rent. Plaintiff, however, having failed to provide habitable premises and having conceded that significant corrective action was eventually required, should not be surprised that the court would construe as retaliatory his attempt to oust his tenants after four months of contention over the condition of the premises.

III.

Plaintiff next argues that since he repaired the sewer system within a reasonable time, the court erred in awarding damages for breach of the implied warranty of habitability. In essence, plaintiff argues that he fixed the premises within a reasonable time after notice. The trial court found otherwise based on ample evidence to support its finding that, due to the septic system failure, the want of proper heating, and a leaky roof, plaintiff had failed to maintain habitable premises.

IV.

Plaintiff also asserts that the damages awarded by the trial court were not supported by the evidence or the law. His principal argument is that the trial court awarded $1600 twice, once for the "discomfort of living in an unsanitary dwelling from February to June, 1986," and a second time "for the stress and discomfort of having to endure the frustration of a retaliatory eviction." The heart of plaintiff's claim is that the emotional injury attributable to the failure to repair the sewer system and the emotional injury from the retaliatory eviction were, in effect, the same injury, and that "the tenants are not entitled to this double recovery." Even though the amount of each recovery was the same ($1600), the recovery was not double. The events giving rise to the emotional damage were not contemporaneous with, nor did they concern, the same occurrence. Defendants experienced the strain and suffering resulting from the unsanitary conditions from February to June, 1986. With or without a subsequent retaliatory eviction, that emotional injury was complete when the septic system was finally repaired on June 17, 1986. The retaliatory eviction followed the withholding of the June 1st rental payment and caused an entirely different injury—not the risk of illness from flowing sewage and an assault on the olfactory senses, but rather the injury of eviction from a dwelling which has finally been made habitable. The two injuries differed in time and nature.

V.

Plaintiff is correct, however, that there was no basis on the record to deny his claim for rent from June 17 to September 30, 1986. Defendants remained on the premises during this period, after the sewer line repair had been completed. None of the defendants' theories apply to this period of occupancy. The violation of the implied warranty of habitability was addressed by the forgiveness of rent for February, March, April, and May 1986, and the court awarded damages for the retaliatory eviction, the loss of food, and the discomfort and distress associated with the lockout from the barn.

The court provided no rationale for denial of plaintiff's claim for rent from June 17 through September 30, and defendants do not suggest any rationale in their brief. Consequently, plaintiff is entitled as a matter of law to rent in the amount of $1,370.95 for this period.

VI.

Plaintiff next argues that the attorney's fee allowance of $700 was unsupported by any evidence on the record. The trial court concluded "from the file, the complexity of the factual and legal issues presented and the competence of counsel that his services equal at least $700." Plaintiff, however, offered no evidence as to the value of those services.

We have always required counsel to present evidence in support of any request for attorney's fees. (Citations omitted.) Without abrogating our longstanding practice in the usual case, we hold that when the fee requested is not large, it is within the discretion of the trial court to award a reasonable fee without requiring the submission of evidence. We make no attempt, however, to establish a dollar amount below which a trial court may dispense with the taking of evidence; that decision is one that must depend on the facts of the individual case.

We believe this is one of those cases. The amount involved is not substantial for the complexity of the case, and we do not believe it would serve any useful purpose to remand this matter solely for the taking of evidence as to the reasonableness of the attorney's fee. Trial courts have wide discretion in fixing the reasonable value of legal services, and the fee allowed by the court will ordinarily not be disturbed unless there is "strong evidence of excessiveness or inadequacy." (Citations omitted.) There is no claim that the fee awarded herein was excessive or unreasonable, and we find no abuse of discretion on the part of the trial court.

The total amount of defendants' award, including attorney's fees, comes to $5,000, and is thus within the $5,000 jurisdictional limit of the district court. *See* 4 V.S.A. sec 437.

The dismissal of that portion of plaintiff's complaint seeking recovery of rent from June 17 through September 30, 1986 is reversed, and plaintiff is awarded judgment in the amount of $1,370.95 on his complaint. The judgment of $5,000 in favor of defendants on their counterclaim is affirmed. Accordingly, defendants are awarded judgment in the net amount of $3,629.05.

Case Reflections

1. What are the elements of the implied warranty of habitability?

2. The court decided that the landlord was entitled to rent for the period in which the defendants occupied the premises after the repair to the sewer line and septic system. What risks do tenants face when they refuse to pay monthly rent, arguing that the premises are not habitable?

NYLEN V. PARK DORAL APARTMENTS

535 N.E.2d 178 (Ind., 1989)

Tenant's Duty to pay rent

HOFFMAN, Judge.

Susan Nylen, Elizabeth Lewis, Julie Reed, Lucy Reed, Ronald Nylen, and Boyd Lewis, the defendants-appellants, appeal from a trial court decision for Park Doral Apartments, the plaintiff-appellee, in a suit for ejectment and damages. After hearings on the issues of eviction and damages, the trial court ordered ejectment and the payment of delinquent rent, future rent, late fees, attorney fees and consequential damages. The appellants contend that the trial court's judgment is contrary to law.

The facts relevant to this appeal may be summarized as follows. Susan Nylen, Elizabeth Lewis and Julie Reed, students at Indiana University, executed a Rental Agreement with Park Doral Apartments for a term from August 26, 1986 until August 19, 1987. Performance of the lease was secured by a deposit in the amount of $420.00, constituting pre-payment of rent for the last month of the lease term, and by the signatures of Ronald Nylen, Boyd Lewis and Lucy Reed as co-signers.

At the end of the fall semester, Julie Reed moved out of the apartment and in February of 1987, she refused to pay any further rent. Susan Nylen and Elizabeth Lewis remained in possession of the apartment, paying only two-thirds of the total rent due for the month of February. Park Doral Apartments filed suit for ejectment of the tenants for failure to pay rent in full for the month of February.

While the ejectment proceedings were pending, Susan Nylen and Elizabeth Lewis made a payment of $280.00 for the rent due in March. Subsequently, on March 10, 1987, the trial court ordered Nylen and Lewis to pay full rent or vacate the premises. They vacated the apartment, pursuant to court order, on March 13, 1987.

A final hearing on the issue of damages was held on September 14, 1987. The trial court awarded delinquent rent owed plus the balance of rent due under the lease from the time of Nylen and Lewis' eviction. The delinquent portion of the rent was $140.00 per month for February and March, and the balance of the remainder of the lease was $420.00 per month for April through July. The court also awarded $362.00 in late fees, $600.00 in attorney fees and $75.24 in consequential damages. Total relief awarded by the court, set off by the $420.00 security deposit, was $2,577.24 plus the costs of the action.

The issues raised on appeal challenge that portion of the trial court's judgment awarding damages to Park Doral Apartments:

1. whether the trial court's award of future rents is contrary to law because eviction terminated the lease and abrogated all contractual obligations under the lease;
2. whether the trial court's judgment is contrary to law, because the court permitted Park Doral Apartments to pursue inconsistent remedies of eviction and recovery of post-ejectment rents;
3. whether the trial court's award of future rents is contrary to law, because it violates the doctrine of mitigation of damages;
4. whether the trial court's award of late fees is contrary to law, because such fees are punitive in nature and therefore unenforceable; and
5. whether the trial court's judgment is contrary to law, because the lease is unconscionable and therefore unenforceable.

* * *

Mindful of the appropriate standard of review, this Court will consider first the appellants' argument that an award of future rents is contrary to law. According to the appellants, eviction served to abrogate all covenants in the Rental Agreement, including the savings clause set out in Paragraph 3 of the lease:

> 3 . . . Eviction of tenant for a breach of lease agreement shall not release tenant from liability for rent payment for the balance of the term of the lease.

The appellants maintain that termination of the lease by an order of ejectment terminated their liability for rents accruing in the future. It is a general rule that a tenant will be relieved of any obligation to pay further rent if the landlord deprives the tenant of possession and beneficial use and enjoyment of any part of the demised premises by an actual eviction. (Citations omitted.) However, an exception to the general rule exists when the lease includes a savings clause expressly providing that termination shall not affect the accrual of liability for rent. (Citations omitted.)

[The court provided an extended discussion as to whether this exception to the general rule is recognized in Indiana. The court concluded that the exception is recognized in state law.]

Therefore, this Court concludes that the award of future rents based on Paragraph 3 of the Rental Agreement was not contrary to law.

The second issue raised on appeal concerns whether the lower court erroneously permitted Park Doral Apartments to pursue inconsistent remedies. "The test of such inconsistency of remedies has its basis in the factual background which constitutes the cause of action. If the assertion of one cause of action involves the repudiation of another, then the modes of redress are inconsistent. If the one cause of action admits a state of facts, and the other denies the same facts, the remedies sought by such actions are inconsistent." Kimmel v. Captain (1940), 107 Ind.App. 621, 626, 24 N.E.2d 435, 437.

According to the appellants, Park Doral Apartments could not seek both an order of ejectment and recovery of rent for the balance of the lease term. The appellants maintain that the suit for ejectment brought by Park Doral Apartments operated as a denial of the Rental Agreement, thereby barring recovery under the savings clause of the lease. That argument reflects a basic misunderstanding as to the nature of a suit for ejectment.

Ejectment is the appropriate means of recovering possession of leased premises from a tenant for non-payment of rent or forfeiture of the lease by a breach of its conditions, where the lease stipulates or the law provides that the landlord may re-enter for such non-payment or breach. Adams v. Holcomb (1948), 226 Ind. 67, 73, 77 N.E.2d 891, 893. A suit for ejectment does not constitute a denial that a lease agreement exists, but it is a means of enforcing the lease. Thus the ejectment action brought by Park Doral Apartments did not preclude recovery of future rents under the savings clause. Because the remedies of ejectment and recovery of post-ejectment rents are consistent, the trial court properly allowed concurrent pursuit of those remedies. See 28 C.J.S. Election of Remedies § 3b (1941) (where remedies are concurrent and consistent, a party may pursue one or all of such remedies until satisfaction is had).

For their third allegation of error, the appellants suggest that the lower court's judgment violates the doctrine of mitigation of damages. The appellants first argue that they were discharged from liability for post-ejectment losses, because the evidence disclosed an exacerbation rather than mitigation of damages. The appellants reason that there was a failure to mitigate damages when Park Doral Apartments sought to evict Susan Nylen and Elizabeth Lewis, instead of permitting them to continue in possession while paying only two-thirds of the rent due per month. There is no authority for the proposition that a landlord must tolerate a breach of lease terms in order to mitigate its damages, and this Court declines to endorse such a premise. In the alternative, the appellants aver that enforcement of a savings clause in a lease subverts the doctrine of mitigation of damages. This Court cannot reach such a conclusion.

The doctrine of mitigation of damages creates an obligation on the part of the landlord to use such diligence as would be exercised by a reasonably prudent man under similar circumstances to re-let the premises, if possible, in order to mitigate damages resulting from the tenant's breach of lease. State v. Boyle (1976), 168 Ind.App. 643, 646, 344 N.E.2d 302, 304. The obligation exists even if there is no mandatory re-letting clause in the lease. See Hirsch et al. v. Merchants Nat'l Bk. (1975), 166 Ind.App. 497, 336 N.E.2d 833. Further, courts have recognized and enforced the doctrine of mitigation of damages while at the same time sustaining savings clauses.

Id.; *see also* Grueninger, *supra,* 413 N.E.2d 1034.

In the instant case, there was evidence before the trial court that Park Doral Apartments used due diligence to re-let the premises. The manager of the apartments had placed a series of advertisements in the Indiana Daily Student newspaper. In response to the advertisements, three persons came to view the apartment. Subsequently, the manager reduced the monthly rental rate in an effort to find a tenant. Considering the evidence most favorable to the judgment, this Court holds that the award of future rents based on a savings clause was not contrary to law as a violation of the doctrine of mitigation of damages.

* * *

The appellants next challenge the trial court's award of late fees to Park Doral Apartments. That award was based on a provision of the Rental Agreement which stated:

> The tenant(s) understand and agrees that the rent will be due and payable on the 1st day of each month at the designated address and should said rent not have been paid by the 1st day of the month, the landlord reserves the right to require a $2.00 per day, per person late fee. . . .

The appellants characterize Paragraph 2 of the lease as a penalty, while Park Doral Apartments maintains that the paragraph is a liquidated damages provision. In determining whether a stipulated sum payable on breach of a contract constitutes liquidated damages or a penalty, the facts, the intention of the parties and the reasonableness of the stipulation under the circumstances of the case are all to be considered. Melfi v. Griscer Ind., Inc. (1967), 141 Ind.App. 607, 611, 231 N.E.2d 54, 57. Where the nature of the agreement is such that a breach would result in damages which are uncertain and difficult to prove, that a breach would result in damages which are uncertain and difficult to prove, and where the stipulated sum payable on breach is not greatly disproportionate to the loss likely to occur, then that fixed sum will be accepted as liquidated damages and not as a penalty. Harris v. Primus (1983), Ind.App., 450 N.E.2d 80, 83.

The evidence before the lower court showed that the damages incurred by Park Doral Apartments for late rent were dependent upon several variables: the number of tenants in an apartment, each tenant's share of the rent, the ability to locate the breaching tenant and the lateness of the particular share of rent. According to the manager of the apartments, a tenant's failure to pay rent on time created extra work for the management in sending notices, preparing weekly rent delinquency report, calling the tenant and using and preparing additional cash journals. There was also testimony concerning loss of interest income when rental payments are delinquent.

The question whether a contractual provision stipulating damages in the event of a breach is a valid liquidated damages clause or a penalty is purely a question of law for the court. Mandle v. Owens (1975), 164 Ind.App. 607, 610–611, 330 N.E.2d 362, 364. The trial court's determination that Paragraph 2 of the Rental Agreement is an enforceable liquidated damages provision cannot be deemed to be contrary to law.

The appellants argue in the alternative that the fees for late payments could not extend beyond the time of the appellants' ejectment. By operation of the savings clause in the Rental Agreement, the appellants' liability for rent was preserved for the balance of the lease term. Because the appellants continued to be liable for rental payments, the trial court properly awarded late fees for the balance of the lease term.

* * *

Park Doral Apartments contends that it is entitled to appellate attorney fees, based upon Paragraph 3 of the Rental Agreement. That paragraph states in pertinent part:

> 3. If the tenant(s) defaults in the performance of any of the covenants of this lease agreement and by reason thereof the Landlord employs the

> services of an attorney to enforce performance of the covenants by the tenant, to evict the tenant, to collect monies due from the tenant, or to perform any service based upon default, then, in any of said events the tenant does agree to pay a reasonable attorney's fee and all expenses and costs incurred by the landlord pertaining thereto. . . .

Traditionally, courts in Indiana declined to award appellate attorney fees based upon contractual provisions requiring the payment of such fees. The reason for denial was that the provision authorizing the award of attorney fees was deemed to have been merged into the judgment. Thus the contractual authorization no longer existed. *See,* e.g., McCormick v. Falls City Bank (7th Cir.1892), 57 F. 107. Recently, Indiana courts have excepted appellate attorney fees from the general rule of merger. (Citations omitted.) The doctrine of merger no longer precludes an award of appellate attorney fees.

The appellants seek to limit the recent trend of awarding appellate attorney fees to cases involving parties with equal bargaining power. When there is disparity in bargaining power, the appellants reason that an award of appellate attorney fees would have a chilling effect on future appeals taken by individual tenants. This Court is not persuaded that disparity in bargaining power necessitates a departure from precedent allowing the recovery of reasonable attorney fees incurred in defending an appeal.

Therefore, Park Doral Apartments may recover appellate attorney fees. The preferred procedure, however, is for the trial court to hear the evidence and determine a reasonable fee when the appeal has been concluded. At that time, Park Doral Apartments may properly present its position concerning what constitutes a reasonable fee.

Accordingly, the judgment of the trial court is affirmed, but the case is remanded for a hearing on appellate attorney fees.

Case Reflections

1. How did the two room mates who remained in the apartment after Julie Reed moved out become liable for a larger monthly rent?
2. Why did the court allow the landlord to recover rent payments which did not become due until after the tenants were evicted?
3. Define the landlord's duty to mitigate damages after evicting a tenant. Why did the court reject the defendant's argument that the landlord breached this duty by refusing to allow the two remaining tenants to remain in the apartment at a reduced rent?

BORCHERT ENTERPRISES, INC.
V.
WEBB

584 S.W.2d 208 (Tenn., 1978)

Computation of Gross Sales

SUMMERS, Judge.

The defendants-appellees, E. H. Webb, Jr., and Ann Thomas Webb, are the owners of certain real property in Davidson County, Tennessee, which is occupied by the plaintiff-appellant, Borchert Enterprises, Inc. The property in question was leased by the defendants to Scooter Stores, Inc., on May 8, 1971. On August 21, 1975, Scooter Stores, Inc. assigned the lease to the plaintiff, and the defendants approved the assignment.

Thereafter, some controversies arose between the plaintiff and the defendants, and a lawsuit was filed by the plaintiff against the defendants. The defendants counterclaimed against the plaintiff. The case was heard below by the chancellor without a jury. The plaintiff appealed only one of the rulings of the chancellor and assigned the following error: The chancellor erred in holding that the term "gross sales" includes income received from pinball machines.

The clause in the lease which is in dispute is as follows: Lessee, in addition, agrees to pay to Lessor as additional rental a sum equal to two (2%) percent of the gross sales in excess of Two Hundred Thousand ($200,000.00) Dollars per annum, excluding sales tax and money order sales, said payments to be made annually, within forty-five (45) days from each annual anniversary of this lease. Lessee agrees to provide to Lessor annually a Certified Public Accountant's report of sales to substantiate the payments made hereunder.

When the sublease was assigned by the defendants to the plaintiff, the plaintiff was engaged in the operation of a convenience market. Later, in October of 1975, the plaintiff placed in the convenience market several pinball machines. The defendants contend that the income generated by these pinball machines is included within the term "gross sales"; the plaintiff contends that the revenue from the pinball machines is not properly included within the term "gross sales." On this point the chancellor ruled as follows:

7. That receipts from pinball machines located on the leased premises are included in the term "gross sales" as said term is used in the lease and must be included in determining the amount of gross sales in excess of Two Hundred Thousand Dollars ($200,000.00) per annum upon which the plaintiff is required by the lease to pay an additional rental of two percent (2%) provided, however, that the pinball receipts which are to be included in the term "gross sales" are those actually received by Borchert Enterprises, Inc.; stated another way, the term "gross sales" includes the fifty percent (50%) of the net profits from the pinball machines and does not include the portion of pinball machines taken out by the owners of the pinball machines". The 1975 Supreme Court case of Bob Pearsall Motors, Inc. v. Regal Chrysler-Plymouth, Inc., 521 S.W.2d 578, also involves the interpretation of a sublease. Justice Henry in that case said:

The cardinal rule for interpretation of contracts is to ascertain the intention of the parties and to give effect to that intention, consistent with legal principles. It is the Court's duty to enforce contracts according to their plain terms. Further, the language used must be taken and understood in its plain, ordinary and popular sense. (Citations omitted.)

The courts, of course, are precluded from creating a new contract for the parties. Dubois v. Gentry, 182 Tenn. 103, 184 S.W.2d 369 (1945). The definition of a sale under T.C.A. 47-2-105(1) is: " . . . A 'sale' consists in the passing of title from the seller to the buyer for a price. . . . " In playing pinball machines there is nothing that passes from a seller to a buyer. This activity is considered an amusement and not a sale. The sales that are reported to the state and on which sales tax is paid do not include receipts from pinball machines. At the time that the lease was drawn up between the defendant and the original lessee, pinball machines were not in the lessee's place of business. We cannot say the parties contemplated the inclusion of revenue from pinball machines in gross sales. It was only after the sublessee, the plaintiff herein, had been in possession of the property for several months that pinball machines were placed therein.

The term "gross sales" would appear to this court to be limited to transactions which are actually considered sales. Had the language in the lease been gross revenue, income, receipts, earnings, receivables or payments, this court would have no doubt that the income from the pinball machines would be included in computing the additional rent due. However, the use of the word "sales" tends to limit the kind and quality of income to be used in calculating the additional rental.

From the testimony in the bill of exceptions we find that the plaintiff took no part in drafting the instrument in question. The defendants and Scooter Stores, Inc. negotiated the terms of this lease. It is also settled law in Tennessee that any ambiguity in a contract is settled against the drafter of that contract. (Citations omitted.)

Therefore, this court sustains the assignment of error of the plaintiff and reverses that portion of the chancellor's ruling from which the plaintiff appealed. We find that the income received from the pinball machines should not be included as part of the "gross sales" referred to in the lease agreement.

* * *

Therefore, it is the ruling of this court that the judgment of the chancellor holding that the pinball machine receipts should be computed in the "gross sales" of the lessee is overruled. The assignments of error of the defendant are without merit. The judgment of the lower court shall be reversed in its ruling from which the plaintiff appealed. The costs of this cause shall be assessed against the defendants.

Case Reflections

1. What is the difference between "gross sales" and "gross revenues"?
2. Suppose that the defendant was required to pay sales tax on the proceeds received from the pinball machines. Would this have made a difference in the court's conclusion? Why or why not?

WATER MUSIK
BOSTON, MA.

CHAPTER

5

CO-OWNERSHIP OF REAL PROPERTY

LEARNING OBJECTIVES

After reading this chapter, you should be able to:

1. Identify the characteristics of seven different forms of common ownership of real property
2. Recognize the advantages and disadvantages of each of the different forms of common ownership

KEY TERMS

- Tenancy in Common
- Partition
- Joint Tenancy
- Right of Survivorship
- Limited Liability
- Partnership
- Limited Partnership
- Cooperative
- Condominium

In the preceding chapters, we examined the rights of ownership that are included in the fee simple absolute estate. We also looked at various subdivisions of the bundle of rights, which form other recognized estates in real property. In this chapter, we will ask what happens when the ownership rights of an estate in real property belong to more than one person at the same time. Co-ownership of real property has a long history in Anglo-American law, and the forms for this kind of ownership have been well established for many years.

When more than one person claims an ownership right in the same property at the same time, each owner is referred to as a cotenant. Each cotenant will possess what is termed an undivided fractional interest in the property. A common example is a husband and wife who jointly own the house they reside in. Each member of the couple will typically own an undivided one-half interest in the home.

It is not necessary for each cotenant to own an equal undivided interest in the property. For example, the owner of an apartment house could convey an undivided one-fourth interest to each of two children. After these transactions, the original owner will retain an undivided one-half interest, while the children each own a one-fourth interest. The only requirement is that the fractional interests of all cotenants must add up to one.

RIGHTS AND DUTIES OF COTENANTS

The owner of an undivided interest in real property may use and enjoy the entire property in any manner that is consistent with the estate possessed by the cotenant. For example, if three people each own undivided interests in a fee simple estate, all three cotenants may occupy all or any portion of the premises. None of the cotenants may exclude any of the other cotenants from using or enjoying any part of the property. However, any of the cotenants may exclude the rest of the world from the property.

Maas v. Lucus

The cotenants are jointly and severally liable for real estate taxes on the property. That is, each cotenant can be required to pay all of the property taxes owed to a taxing authority. In the event any cotenant pays more than his or her aliquot share of the taxes, then that cotenant may bring a collection action to require the remaining owners to reimburse their shares of the taxes to the cotenant who paid the original amount.

Any cotenant may undertake a mortgage against the jointly owned property without obtaining the consent of the other coowners. (However, lenders almost always require the signatures of all co-owners before they will advance funds against a mortgage. This practice of the trade places an effective practical limitation on the legal rights of a cotenant to use the property as security for a debt.) If the proceeds of the mortgage are used to construct improvements on the property, then we must ask whether the remaining cotenants will be required to repay the mortgage. If all of the joint owners signed the note that created the debt secured by the mortgage, then the answer is yes. (That is why lenders commonly require all signatures.) If one or more of the cotenants are left off the note and mortgage, there is some diversity among the states as to the liability of cotenants who are not parties to the loan.

The general rule is that cotenants are not liable for mortgage payments unless the cotenant is a party to the loan agreement. Most states will allow the cotenant who contracted the mortgage to apply all of the rents from the improvement to the mortgage loan payment. Some states require a cotenant who has built an improvement on the property to share the profits from the improvement with the other cotenants, after the mortgage payment and operating expenses have been deducted from the rent on the improvement. Other states will allow a cotenant who improves the land at his or her own expense to keep all of the revenues generated by the improvement.

KEY POINTS

The variation in law from state to state illustrates the conflict over money than often occurs among co-owners of real property. It is reasonable to expect that people who own an interest in the same parcel of real property will eventually develop different ideas as to how the property should be developed or utilized. It is not uncommon for one of the common owners to become frustrated by such a difference of opinion and decide to take matters into his or her own hands. When one common owner expends effort or money to improve the property, a true dilemma is created for the legal system.

On the one hand, it does not seem just to require a common owner to share the fruits of his or her efforts with other owners who made no contribution to the improvement. On the other hand, it does not appear just to deprive the remaining common owners of their share of the income produced by their property, since the right to receive the income produced by real property is perhaps the core ownership right. The variation in the law among states simply reflects the different values and priorities used by judges in resolving this dilemma.

Any cotenant may sell his or her undivided interest in the property at any time. The purchaser of an undivided interest simply becomes a new cotenant with the remaining joint owners. This is the feature of common ownership that often makes cotenancy a difficult form of ownership for property held as an investment. Most people prefer to avoid doing business with strangers. However, the right of any cotenant to sell his or her undivided interest in an investment property can result in the introduction of a total stranger to the remaining cotenants of the original investment group when one cotenant sells his or her interest.

To avoid this undesirable outcome, groups of cotenants may agree between themselves that none of them will sell his or her interest in the property without the permission of the other cotenants. Agreements of this type must be carefully drawn, however. The American law of property, following the English pattern, does not permit unreasonable restraints to be placed upon the alienation (sale) of land. Any agreement that unreasonably restrains the alienation of land will be held void as against public policy. Some of the cases at the end of this chapter will explore the issue of restraints on alienation in more detail.

INHERITABILITY OF JOINT OWNERSHIP RIGHTS

So far, we have concluded that common ownership of a fee simple estate in real property is not very different from ownership by a single person. One area where com-

Tenancy in common A form of multiple ownership of real property in which each tenant in common owns an undivided interest in the property. At the death of any tenant in common, the undivided interest will pass to the heirs of the deceased owner.

Bailey v. Parker

Partition A legal proceeding which ends the common ownership of real property by dividing the real property into as many portions as there are undivided interests, and distributing the portions to each of the tenants in common or joint tenants. At the conclusion of a partition proceeding, each of the former joint or common tenants receives the sole ownership of property distributed through partition.

mon ownership may differ from individual ownership is the inheritability of the ownership interest. When a fee simple estate is possessed by a single owner, the ownership rights in the property will pass to the heirs of the owner at his or her death. The ownership rights of a cotenant in a fee simple estate may or may not pass to the heirs of the cotenant at death. The right to designate an heir to the property at the death of the cotenant marks the difference between a tenancy in common and a joint tenancy with right of survivorship.

Tenancy in Common

The most common form of joint ownership is the **tenancy in common**. In fact, the description of ownership rights in the previous section was written with this form of ownership in mind. The undivided interest of a tenant in common is an inheritable estate. At the death of a tenant in common, the undivided interest he or she owns will pass to the heirs designated by the will of the deceased tenant. If the tenant in common died intestate (without a valid will), then the undivided interest in the property will pass to the heirs of the tenant under the rules of intestate succession described in Chapter 7.

The inheritability of the undivided interest of a tenant in common provides a second method for introducing a new owner to the common ownership arrangement. Recall that in the previous section, we mentioned that tenants in common can sell their undivided interest in the property. We also mentioned that tenants in common who wish to avoid taking a stranger into their midst can agree among themselves that no tenant will sell his or her interest without the permission of the other tenants. If carefully and correctly drawn, such agreements provide some protection against this unwanted eventuality. However, there is no agreement that can prevent the inheritance of an undivided property interest on the death of a tenant in common. As a result, tenancy in common is not a suitable ownership arrangement for people who wish to hold investment property in common with a group of people they have selected and with no one else. Fortunately, other more suitable ownership forms are available; they will be discussed later in this chapter.

Partition

Because the tenancy in common is so likely to produce a stranger in the midst of the common ownership of the tenants, it is not unusual for cotenants to wish they could escape from their fellow owners. The equitable remedy of **partition** was created to permit such an escape.

At any time, any cotenant can apply to a court for an order of partition. It is generally held that each cotenant has an absolute right to have the property partitioned by a court. Cotenants may agree among themselves not to exercise this right, and courts will generally hold the cotenants to their agreement if it is reasonable to do so. For example, cotenants who purchase raw land for the purpose of building an apartment house may agree not to partition the land for three years after it is acquired. Since it is reasonable to believe that building and renting the apartments may require a period of three years, a court would probably enforce the agreement not to partition the land until development is complete.

In the absence of an agreement not to partition (or, if the court finds that the agreement is unreasonable), an order for partition will be entered at the request of any cotenant. The only remaining issue is whether the property is to be partitioned in kind or by sale.

If the property can be divided equitably among the cotenants, the court will usually order a partition in kind. For example, if a 160-acre wheat field is owned by two tenants in common, each with an undivided one-half interest in the property, partition in kind may be appropriate. The court could divide the wheat field into two 80-acre parcels and give one parcel to each cotenant. If the property is not readily divisible, the court will order partition by sale. Again, using the apartment house example, the court would order the cotenants to list the property for sale and accept the highest offer received within a reasonable time. The proceeds from the sale will be divided among the cotenants on the basis of their fractional interests in the property.

Schneider v. Schneider

Flippo v. Wilson

Joint Tenancy A form of multiple ownership of real property in which each joint tenant owns an undivided interest in the property. At the death of any joint tenant, the undivided interest will pass to the surviving joint tenants.

Joint Tenancy with Right of Survivorship

Joint tenancy is a special case of tenancy in common. The undivided interest of a joint tenant is not inheritable. Instead, the undivided interest of a joint tenant passes automatically to the surviving joint tenants at the death of any joint tenant. If there is more than one surviving joint tenant, then they will share equally in the undivided interest of the decedent. This automatic transfer of the property interest at death is called the **right of survivorship**.

KEY POINTS

The use of joint tenancy with right of survivorship as a means to avoid probate is a popular seminar topic. In Chapter 7, we will examine the probate procedures required to dispose of one's property after death. It is true that these procedures are both expensive and time consuming. It is also true that property owned in joint tenancy will not be subject to probate proceedings, since title to the property automatically passes to the surviving joint tenant. As a result, the supervision of a court in probate proceedings is not necessary for this property.

However, there is more to this topic than meets the eye. For example, many items of personal property (refrigerators, furniture, and the like) are not sold with documents that provide evidence of the title to the articles. At the death of the owner, it is not clear whether such property was owned exclusively by the decedent, owned in common by the decedent and someone else, or owned by the decedent as a joint tenant with right of survivorship. As we will see in the next section, it is extraordinarily difficult to insure that all property owned by a decedent will pass to another person under the right of survivorship. Prudence requires that anyone wishing to obtain this result must consult a competent attorney.

Joint tenancy imposes an automatic restraint on alienation. As a result, the common law took a dim view of the arrangement and imposed a number of restrictions on its creation. Blackstone's *Commentary* was a comprehensive review of the English common law of property, published in the late 1600s. Blackstone wrote that the creation of a joint tenancy required a fourfold unity of time, title, interest, and possession. That is, the joint tenants must have acquired their ownership at the same

TABLE 5.1

	Joint Tenancy	Tenancy in Common
Right of survivorship	Yes	No
Severed by sale of one tenant's interest	Yes	No
All tenants liable for taxes	Yes*	Yes*
All tenants entitled to share in the rents	Yes*	Yes*
All tenants liable for mortgage payments	Yes*	Yes*

*Subject to special circumstances described in the text

Right of Survivorship The rule of real property law which causes the ownership interest of a joint tenant to pass to surviving joint tenants at the death of any joint tenant.

instant in time; they must have the same degree of title to the property (e.g., fee simple absolute); they must have the same undivided interest in the property (two joint tenants must each own an undivided one-half interest); and the tenants must have identical rights of possession in the property.

The fourfold unities were applied by English and American courts for several centuries after Blackstone described them. The result of this doctrine was to make life more complicated for many people. Suppose that a young man who owns a house decides to marry. In addition, he would like to own the house as a joint tenant with his new wife. If the young man simply conveys an undivided one-half interest in the house to his wife, as a joint tenant with right of survivorship, he will not achieve the result he had hoped for. The unity of time will be violated by the deed, since the husband acquired his interest in the property before the wife did. As a result, the couple will be treated as tenants in common in the land, not as joint tenants.

In 1947, Joyce King conveyed the King Farm to her two sons and their wives with the following language:

"... [to] Harry L. Michael and Bertha Michael, his wife, tenants by the entireties and Ford W. Michael and Helen M. Michael, his wife, as tenants by the entireties, with right of survivorship ..."

Harry Michael died prior to 1962, survived by his wife Bertha and by two sons, Ford and Robert. Bertha Michael died testate on November 26, 1963. Her will appointed her two sons as co-executors of her estate, and devised her interest in the King Farm to Robert. During the administration of the estate, a dispute arose as to the what, if any, interest Bertha Michael owned in the King Farm.

Ford Michael argued that the original deed from Joyce King created a joint tenancy with right of survivorship between all of the four grantees named in the deed. Under this construction, Ford's aunt and uncle became the sole owners of the King Farm at Bertha's death. Robert argued that the deed created a tenancy in common between the two married couples, each couple holding its one half undivided interest as tenants by the entireties. Under this construction, Bertha would own an undivided one half interest in the farm at her death.

In choosing between these constructions, the court observed: "At common law, joint tenancies were favored, and the doctrine of survivorship was a recognized inci dent to a joint estate. The courts of the United States have generally been opposed to the creation of such estates, the presumption being that all tenants hold jointly as ten ants in common, unless a clear intention to the contrary is shown."

The usual method for creating a joint tenancy is the use of the phrase "joint tenants, with a right of survivorship, and not as tenants in common." Although the deed in question did use the phrase "right of survivorship," the court determined that this phrase applied only to the ownership interests of each pair of spouses, and did not apply to the tenancy between the spousal pairs. As a result, the court concluded that Bertha Michael owned an undivided one half interest in the King Farm at her death. In Re Estate of Michael, 218 A.2d 338 (Penn., 1966)

The only way for our young man to accomplish his object is through the use of a "straw deed." The creation of a joint tenancy under these circumstances requires a two-step process when the fourfold unities are enforced. First, the owner must convey the house to a straw man (his attorney, the president of the local bank, or some other trustworthy individual). The straw man then immediately conveys the house back to the husband and wife, as joint tenants with right of survivorship. In this way, the fourfold unities can be preserved, and the new couple can get on with their lives.

In this century, American legislators have grown impatient with many of the ancient forms and practices of property law. Most states have passed laws abolishing the fourfold unities as a requirement for the creation of a joint tenancy with right of survivorship. But even in those states that do not require unity of time, title, interest, and possession for the creation of a joint tenancy, the tenancy in common is still the preferred construction of deeds and wills. If two or more people want to own real property as joint tenants, they should make sure that the deed conveying the property to them makes that clear. The granting clause of the deed should convey the property "To A and B and their heirs, as joint tenants with the right of survivorship, and not as tenants in common."

Finally, we need to ask whether a joint tenant can sell his or her undivided interest in the property. The answer is yes, but contains a qualification. When a joint tenant sells his or her undivided interest in the property, the joint tenancy is severed. The new owner will be a tenant in common with the former joint tenants.

Lawrence and Matilda Fox were married on May 6, 1949. In 1950, they purchased a home as joint tenants with right of survivorship. In 1954, Lawrence Fox murdered his wife. Three days later he conveyed the home, valued at $20,000, to his attorney. Matilda Fox's daughter by a prior marriage sued to invalidate the transfer of the home to Lawrence Fox's attorney. She argued that the murder of her mother prevented Lawrence Fox from acquiring Matilda Fox's title to the real estate through the right of survivorship.

The law is well established that a murderer has no right to receive the proceeds of an insurance policy on the life of his victim, and has no right to receive property devised by the will of a victim. Some courts have held that this general rule does not apply to the right of survivorship, because a joint tenant is deemed to own the entire property at the date of the original conveyance, and does not acquire any additional property interest at the death of a joint tenant.

The Illinois Supreme Court termed this argument a legal fiction."Before the murder [Lawrence Fox], as a joint tenant, had to share the profits of the property, and his right to complete ownership . . . was contingent upon surviving his wife; whereas, after [the murder] he became the sole owner of the property . . . " As a result of this analysis, the court concluded that Lawrence Fox had destroyed the right of survivorship and retained only the title to his undivided one half interest in the home. Bradley v. Fox, 129 N.E. 2d 699 (Ill., 1955)

Tenancy by the Entirety

The tenancy by the entirety is an archaic form of joint tenancy that can be owned only by two people who are husband and wife. The ownership rights of tenants by the entirety are identical to the ownership rights of joint tenants. The entirety includes the right of survivorship that is the hallmark of the joint tenancy. Most states have abolished this form of ownership by statutes that make the tenancy by the entirety equivalent to a joint tenancy with right of survivorship.

OTHER FORMS OF CO-OWNERSHIP

The limitations of tenancies in common and joint tenancies for investment purposes were mentioned in previous sections. We return to this issue now, in order to examine some forms of common ownership that are more satisfactory for investment purposes. The primary motivation for common ownership of investment property is the large expense involved in creating real property investments.

The cost of constructing an apartment house, office building, or factory can range from several hundred thousand to hundreds of millions of dollars. Few people (if any) have personal financial resources large enough to pay for these costs by themselves. Most real estate developments larger than a duplex unit will require several people to pool their resources in order to have enough money to complete the project.

Limited Liability The legal doctrine which holds that the liabilty of shareholders in a corporation, or limited partners in a limited partnership, is limited to the amount each shareholder or limited partner has invested in the entity.

Corporate Ownership

Corporations are artificial "persons" created by law for the purpose of carrying out business or charitable activities. In general, anything that a real person can legally do is something that a corporate "person" can also do. This includes the ownership and development of real property.

There are a number of advantages to the corporate form of ownership. First among them is the **limited liability** of the shareholders. A new corporation is formed when a group of people contribute money to the organization in exchange for shares of stock issued by the firm. Since the corporation is a "person" in the eyes of the law, it is solely responsible for paying any debts it may incur. A shareholder is not obligated to pay any debt owed by the corporation unless the shareholder agreed to guarantee the debt at the time the corporation incurred it.

KEY POINTS

The limited liability feature of corporate ownership is largely theoretical for the typical real estate venture. Virtually all real estate developments require the use of mortgage funds. And the bankers who provide the mortgage funds will generally require the shareholders of a corporation to guarantee personally the repayment of the loans. In practice, limited liability is available only to shareholders of large, established corporations with a history of many years of profitable operations.

In addition, corporations are a very flexible form of ownership. The corporate form allows the owners to designate one or a few people to manage the affairs of the business. This corporate management team is authorized to make all decisions regarding the development and management of the property without consulting the owners. Clearly, as the number of people who must be consulted on a decision increases, the number of opportunities for disagreement also increases. By limiting the number of decision makers managing the affairs of the corporation, this form of ownership can avoid the problem of too many cooks spoiling the broth.

A third advantage of corporate ownership is the ease with which investors may enter and leave the project. The ownership of a real property investment held in the corporate form is represented by the capital stock issued by the corporation. If an investor becomes dissatisfied with the project or simply wants to recover the investment and move on, he or she may do so simply by selling his or her shares. While U.S. securities laws do place limitations on the ability to sell shares, investors in a corporation can usually find ways to avoid such limitations without breaking the law.

The addition or deletion of investors has no effect on the ownership of the project. Ownership remains at all times in the corporation, independent of the current list of shareholders. Changes in shareholders will usually have no impact on the management of the project, since the management is employed by the corporation and not by the shareholders. The ease with which investors may enter and leave a project held in corporate form overcomes the major drawback to the tenancy-in-common form of ownership.

The primary disadvantage of corporate ownership lies in the adverse income tax treatment of revenues and earnings from the project. Since a corporation is a "person," it must pay tax on all of the earnings it generates. The shareholders are also taxed on the earnings when they are distributed from the corporation in the form of dividends. This double taxation reduces the returns realized by investors in a real estate development. In addition, real estate investments offer a number of tax benefits to the owners of the property. If the corporate form is used, these benefits accrue to the corporation and are thus unavailable to the investors. Because of the income tax implications of the corporate form of ownership, it is not widely used for investment purposes.

Partnerships

The **partnership** form of ownership overcomes the tax disadvantages of corporate ownership. This form of organization, however, is only slightly better than the tenancy in common from the perspective of managing the development of a real estate investment.

Unlike the corporation, a partnership is not a legal "person." Rather, a partnership is simply a legal relationship between two or more natural persons. As such, the partnership does not pay any taxes. All of the income or losses of the partnership belong to the partners. The partnership agreement will determine how the partners divide the income and losses among themselves.

In almost all states, the partnership relation is governed by the Uniform Partnership Act (UPA). The UPA assumes that the partners will all sign a written agreement at the time the partnership is formed. As a result, it is both foolish and economically dangerous to enter into a partnership relation without a well-drafted partnership agreement.

Partnership
A legal relationship between two or more people which is formed for the purpose of owning real property or conducting a trade or business. Each of the partners is individually liable for payment of all of the partnership debts.

The major drawback to the partnership form is the unlimited liability of the partners. Under the UPA, any partner can obligate all of the partnership members to repay any debts contracted in the name of the partnership. In a very real sense, joining a partnership amounts to handing a stack of blank checks to each of the other partners. The UPA contains provisions that may allow partners to escape liability for debts that did not involve the partnership business. But the burden of proof is usually on the partner who has been asked to pay for a debt he or she did not incur. And, if the debt was properly incurred and used for partnership business, there is no escape allowed.

The partnership form can be used to prevent strangers from joining in the ownership of a real property investment, which makes it an improvement over the tenancy in common. However, the cost of this privilege may be a large one. When any partner dies, retires, or withdraws from the partnership, the partnership is then dissolved. The UPA states that the partnership agreement will determine what happens after a partnership is dissolved. In the absence of a partnership agreement, the UPA requires that dissolution be followed by a winding up of the partnership affairs. Winding up means that all partnership property must be sold, all debts repaid, and any surplus funds distributed to the partners.

The partnership form of ownership is used for the majority of real estate investments. The hazards described above can be controlled by a carefully written partnership agreement. As long as all of the partners remain honest and ethical in their dealings with each other, a carefully constructed partnership is a viable form for real property development.

Limited Partnerships

Limited Partnership A partnership arrangement in which there are two types of partners — general and limited — which offers the limited partners liability protection.

Limited partnerships are the most recent development in the law. This form offers the tax benefits of a true partnership along with the limited liability features of the corporate form of ownership. The Uniform Limited Partnership Act (ULPA) has been adopted by virtually all of the states. The provisions of the ULPA govern the relations of the parties in a limited partnership.

While a general partnership can be created on the basis of oral agreements among the parties, a limited partnership cannot exist without a written partnership agreement. The ULPA requires each limited partnership to have at least one general partner, who is liable for all debts and obligations of the partnership. The general partner can be a corporation if the parties choose to make it so. There is no limit on the number of limited partners who can belong to the partnership. Further, the addition or deletion of a limited partner does not dissolve the limited partnership.

The affairs of the limited partnership must be managed by the general partners, or by the duly elected officers of the corporate general partner if that form has been selected. Any limited partner who takes an active role in the management of the affairs of the partnership becomes a general partner. Limited partners, like shareholders in a corporation, are not personally liable for any of the debts or obligations of the limited partnership.

The income and losses of the limited partnership are divided between the general partners and the limited partners in the manner specified in the partnership agreement. The share belonging to the limited partners will be divided equally among the limited partnership shares outstanding. Each limited partner must own at least one limited partnership share and may own more than one share if he or she chooses.

The limited partnership provides a flexible vehicle for real property investment, combining the advantages of the corporate and partnership forms while avoiding many of their disadvantages. As a result, this form of ownership is perhaps the best choice for real estate developments that require large sums of cash to be raised from a group of twenty or more investors who do not know each other well enough to become general partners. The primary drawback to this form of ownership is that the limited partnership shares will almost certainly be classified as securities. In Chapter 17, we will examine the host of complex issues raised by the sale of securities.

Washburn v. 166 E. 96th St. Owner Assoc.

Co-ownership of Residential Property

Co-operative apartment houses and **condominium** developments represent two relatively recent developments in the common ownership of residential property. Co-ops are a variation on the theme of corporate ownership of real property. Condominiums are a specialized form of tenancy in common.

Co-operative
A corporation which is formed for the purpose of owning and maintaining an apartment building. The shareholders of the corporation are limited to the occupants of the residential unts in the development owned by the cooperative.

Co-operative Apartment Houses

We have already discussed the reasons why developers might choose a corporate form of ownership for the development and management of a large apartment project. Corporations were designed to facilitate the management of large financial commitments using funds raised from a diverse group of individuals. The shareholders of the corporation will expect the management of the firm to collect enough rents from the project to provide a fair return to the shareholders, after payment of both corporate and personal taxes.

Now, suppose that the tenants of the apartment house become the shareholders of the corporation that owns the apartment project. In this case, the shareholders who expect a fair return on their investment are the same group who pay the rent to provide the return. Suppose further that the corporation is granted an exemption from the obligation to pay taxes on the income it earns. The gross rent of such a co-operative venture could be as much as twenty percent less than the rent required by a taxable corporation owned by investors who are not tenants in the building.

Rent reduction is the primary motivation for the creation of a co-operative association to own residential real property. If a co-op were required to pay taxes on any income it realizes, then the tenant owners would establish a rent that just covers all expenses, leaving no income to be taxed. However, this theoretical ideal is very difficult to achieve in practice. The expenses of maintaining and operating an apartment building vary from year to year, while tenants prefer to pay a constant rent each year. In addition, many expenditures required for the maintenance of an apartment building (e.g., periodically replacing the roof or making principal payments on the mortgage) are not recognized as expenses for income tax purposes.

It would be much easier if co-ops could collect some extra rent and put these amounts aside as a reserve for maintenance and mortgage amortization, without being required to pay taxes on these amounts. The internal revenue code permits this procedure for a co-operative association organized in compliance with the requirements of the code. Co-ops are formed as not-for-profit organizations and are allowed to maintain reasonable reserves for maintenance and mortgage amortization without

Condominium
A form of multiple ownership in which each condominium owner receives a fee simple absolute estate in an individual air space unit (either a dwelling or an office space) and an undivided interest as tenant in common in the lands and structures which are within the boundaries of the condominium development and outside of the individual air space units.

paying taxes on the reserves as they are accumulated. As a result, tenants in a co-operative building can expect to pay significantly lower rents than tenants in buildings that are operated for profit by investors other than the residents.

Condominium Developments

Suppose a developer builds a twelve-unit apartment house on a one-acre parcel of land. Suppose further that the market conditions at the time the project is completed will produce rents that will justify a value of the project equal to $360,000, or $30,000 per apartment. However, the developer believes that the units in the project can be sold to various individuals and families at an average price of $40,000 per unit, or a total of $480,000 for the entire project.

Clearly, the developer would prefer to sell these units, rather than renting them, because the sale of the individual units produces a much higher profit. By filing a condominium declaration, the developer can realize the profit enhancement available from selling the units instead of renting them. A condominium declaration is a lengthy legal document that must be filed for record in order to create a condominium development.

The declaration includes a description of the land on which the development is located. In addition, the declaration will contain architectural drawings identifying the size and location of each of the units in the condominium development. Finally, the condominium declaration establishes an owners' association to manage and maintain the common areas of the development. Initial bylaws for the operation of the owners' association, including the initial charges and dues for membership, must be included in the condominium declaration.

Gazdo Properties v. Lang

The plaintiff was a resident of a large condominium development located near a golf course. During 1980, numerous residents of the development became victims of car thefts, burglaries and robberies. The plaintiff's unit was burglarized in April of 1980. As a result, she requested the condominium board to install additional security lighting to guard against the increasing number of crimes committed against residents of the development. The following month, plaintiff requested permission from the condominium board to install additional security lighting at her own expense. The board did not formally respond to either request.

In August of 1980, plaintiff installed, at her own expense, additional security lighting which she believed would protect her from further crime. The board immediately wrote her a letter demanding the removal of the security lighting because it violated the condominium association's architectural covenants. Plaintiff responded by asking the board's permission to leave the lighting in place until the condominium board could arrange for adequate security lighting. This request was denied by the board. On October 1, 1980, the condominium board sent the plaintiff a letter instructing her to remove the exterior lighting she had installed, and to the restore the association property (the exterior walls of the unit) to its original condition on or before October 6. On the afternoon of October 8, following extended discussions with the site manager concerning security lighting, the plaintiff disconnected the electric circuit to which the exterior lighting was wired, leaving her unit in total darkness. That night, she was raped and robbed.

The California Court of Appeals ruled that these allegations were sufficient to state a cause of action for negligence against the condominium board and the individual directors. The court ruled that condominium boards are held to the same standard of care as any landlord of residential property. Whether the board in this case had breached that duty of care was a question of fact which would require a trial.

The court also ruled that the facts stated a cause of action against the individual directors. The complaint alleged that the directors had actual knowledge of the dangers posed by the increasing level of crime in the development, and took actions which actually increased the risk of injury faced by the plaintiff. The court cited the well settled principle of law that a director who actually votes for the commission of a tort [in this case, negligence] is personally liable, even though the wrongful act is performed in the name of the corporation. Frances T. v. Village Green 723 P.2d 573 (Cal., 1986)

Purchasers of a unit in the condominium acquire fee simple title to one of the "airspace units" in the building. An airspace unit is defined as all of the air between the center lines of the exterior walls of a unit. The exact dimensions of each airspace unit are given in the architectural drawings that are part of the condominium declaration. The common areas of the development are everything that is not included within the airspace of one of the condominium units. This will normally include the roof and outside walls of the structure, as well as the grounds, parking areas, lobby areas, and hallways between the airspace units. In addition to the fee simple title to the airspace unit, purchasers also receive an undivided fractional interest as tenants in common in the common areas.

CONCLUSION

In this chapter, we have examined seven different forms for common ownership of real property. These forms include tenancy in common, joint tenancy, partnerships, limited partnerships, corporations, co-operative associations, and condominiums.

Tenancy in common and joint tenancy are most frequently used for the common ownership of property held for personal rather than business purposes. The major difference between these forms is the inheritability of the real property interest. When a tenant in common dies, his or her ownership interest will pass to the heirs of the tenant in common. When a joint tenant dies, his or her ownership interest will pass to the surviving joint tenants.

Partnerships are the primary method for owning business or commercial real estate when the property will be developed by a small group of people who know each other well and have done business together in the past. The partnership form allows the tax benefits of real property ownership to be enjoyed by the partners personally. However, great care must be exercised in selecting partners, because each partner will be personally liable for all the debts and obligations of the partnership.

Limited partnerships and corporations are the primary vehicles for very large real estate development efforts. Both of these forms allow the owners to limit their liability to the amount they have invested in the corporation or limited partnership. The primary difference between corporations and limited partnerships is the income tax consequences of each. Corporations, as separate legal "persons," must pay tax on the income earned by the real property development before the income is distributed to the share holders. Limited partnerships, on the other hand, permit the limited partners to recognize income or losses on their personal tax returns without any additional tax burden at the limited partnership level.

Co-operative associations and condominium developments represent methods of common ownership for owner-occupied residential property that can significantly reduce the costs of such ownership.

DISCUSSION QUESTIONS

1. Define cotenant. What does a cotenant possess? Do the interests of cotenants have to be equal?
2. Describe the rights and duties of a cotenant.
3. What is a tenancy in common? What is the potential problem with this type of joint ownership?
4. Why was the right of partition created? Distinguish between partition in kind and partition by sale.
5. Briefly describe a joint tenancy with the right of survivorship. Blackstone, in the early 1600s, put some restrictions on the creation of a joint tenancy that are still used in some states today. What are they?
6. What are some advantages of corporate ownership? What is the primary disadvantage?
7. State the major differences between the partnership and the corporate form of ownership.
8. How does a limited partnership work?
9. Distinguish between a co-operative apartment house and a condominium development.

BAILEY V. PARKER

492 So.2d 1175 (Fla., 1986)

Partition of tenancy in common

SHIVERS, Judge.

This case involves an appeal of a final judgment ordering the partition of real property held by appellant and appellee as tenants in common. We affirm the order of partition, but reverse and remand the order of accounting between the parties.

The facts of this case are as follows. Appellant, Mrs. Bailey, and appellee, Mr. Parker, began living together in 1978, in a home which Mrs. Bailey owned prior to buying the subject property. During that time, Mrs. Bailey was housing several children and adults for both HRS and the Veterans Administration and was in need of a larger house. In January of 1981 the parties moved into the Smyrna Street house which is the subject of this appeal. Bailey continued to house several adults and children and also sporadically rented out a small cottage located on the new property.

The Smyrna Street house was purchased for \$49,470. A \$7,000 loan was taken out by Mrs. Bailey in her name alone, \$5,000 of which was used as the down payment of the house. A \$19,000 existing mortgage on the property was assumed and the sellers took back a purchase money mortgage in the amount of \$25,500. The monthly payment on the existing and purchase money mortgages is \$495.81. The warranty deed grants the property to "Christine Bailey, single, and Lee O. Parker, single." According to Bailey, the only reason Parker's name was placed on the warranty deed was because the two planned to be married, and it would save Bailey the trouble of changing the deed later. According to Mr. Parker, the two never discussed marriage but had a "business relationship" with regard to purchasing the home.

At the trial, Mrs. Bailey testified that Parker paid her approximately $125 every two weeks until September of 1981, after which he began paying $200 every two weeks. However, Bailey contended that the money was applied by her toward the purchase of groceries, not toward the purchase of the property. She stated that Parker paid $225 toward insurance on the home, but did not contribute to taxes. She admitted that she did not contribute any VA, HRS, or rent income to Parker.

According to Mr. Parker's testimony, Mrs. Bailey was given $250–$300 of Parker's salary every two weeks. Parker testified that he considered himself responsible for repaying the loans incurred on the home, and that it was his belief that the money given to Mrs. Bailey was being applied toward all household expenses, including taxes and loan payments. Parker stated that Bailey handled the payment of all household bills and the collection of all VA, HRS, and rent checks. Parker lived in the house until April of 1983, at which time (according to Parker) Mrs. Bailey "kicked him out" and changed the locks. Parker contributed no more money to Bailey after that time.

On June 30, 1983, Parker filed an action against Bailey seeking partition of the property and an accounting for the rental of the property since the date of Bailey's sole occupancy. . . . Without a discussion of the calculations used to make its decision, the court found the contributions of the parties to be "equal and offsetting" except with respect to the down payment made by Bailey in the amount of $7,000, and the mortgage, taxes, and insurance payments made by Bailey subsequent to the parties' separation in April 1983. Bailey was thus granted a special interest in Parker's one half interest, equal to (1) one half the ratio of $7,000 to the purchase price of the property, and (2) one half the mortgage, taxes, and insurance payments made by Bailey after May 1, 1983.

Although we affirm the court's order of partition, we find the final judgment to be in error in several respects with regard to the accounting between the parties. First, the law is clear that it is the obligation of each tenant in common to pay one half of all property expenses, including mortgage payments, taxes, insurance, and necessary repairs, except when a cotenant has sole possession of the property and is receiving all the profits therefrom. (Citation omitted.) Assuming the trial court relied on Mrs. Bailey's testimony regarding the amount of Parker's monetary contributions, and found Parker to have contributed as little as $250 per month (approximately one half the monthly payment on the two mortgages) there is competent, substantial evidence to hold that Parker is still accountable to Bailey for one half of the down payment. However, the record indicates that the amount of the down payment was $5,000, not $7,000. Further, Parker should be held accountable for one half of the amount of $5,000, not one half the ratio of the down payment to the purchase price.

Second, the court failed to make a finding as to Parker's accountability for one half of the taxes and insurance paid by Bailey during the time Parker was in possession of the property.

Third, since the record indicates that Mrs. Bailey was in sole possession of the property after April 1983 and that she received all rents and profits derived from the property after that time, the court erred in ordering Mr. Parker to account to Bailey for one half the mortgage, taxes, and insurance paid by Bailey after May 1, 1983.

Last, the law is clear that where a cotenant has exclusive possession of property owned as tenants in common, and uses the property for this own behalf and does not receive rents or profits therefrom, the tenant in possession is not accountable to the tenant out of possession unless the tenant in possession holds the property adversely or as the result of ouster or its equivalent. In order to prove ouster, a tenant in common must show acts by the tenant in possession inconsistent with, and exclusive of, the rights of the cotenant and knowledge by the cotenant of the tenant in possession's acts. The record in this case shows that an ouster of Parker by Bailey occurred in April of 1983. Therefore, Bailey must be held accountable to Parker for one half the rental value of the property after the ouster.

Accordingly, the final judgment is affirmed in part, reversed in part, and remanded for further proceedings consistent with this opinion.

BARFIELD, J., concurs.
ZEHMER, J., dissents with written opinion.
ZEHMER, Judge, dissenting.

I would reverse and remand for redetermination of the respective interests of the parties in the property. Although the trial court properly found that the parties held the property as tenants in common, the evidence before the court established anything but an intention that each hold a one-half interest therein. The record reflects that appellant supplied far more than one-half of the consideration for the acquisition and maintenance of the property, and there is a complete lack of evidence to establish that she made a gift of a one-half interest to appellee. In my view, the trial court erroneously applied a legal presumption to arrive at the equal division of interests when the record before it completely negated such presumption and warranted a factual determination of the respective interests based on relative contribution of consideration.

Case Reflections

1. The majority opinion held that the co-tenants owned undivided one half interests in the property. The dissent argued that the facts indicate some other fractional interest. Which opinion seems right to you? Why?
2. Suppose Mr. Parker had decided to move to a new home, and Mrs. Bailey had simply said, "well, its up to you." Would those facts change the outcome of the case? Why or why not?
3. What could the parties have done at the time they purchased the house to avoid this lawsuit?

MAAS V. LUCAS

349 A.2d 655 (Md., 1975)

Duties of tenants in common

LOWE, Judge.

A proverb, much used in a part of England where estates do not long stay in one family, declares: "The father buys, the son builds, the grandchild sells and his son begs." . . . The father, appellant here, bought and also built upon property, one-half interest in which he (and his former wife) had conveyed to his two children as tenants in common pursuant to a marriage dissolution in 1943. Sometime after the conveyance he improved a garage on the back lot of the property by building two apartments over it.

The father instituted a suit in the Circuit Court for Baltimore County for sale in lieu of partition. In addition to the value of his one-half interest he sought reimbursement for the improvements and contribution from the children for the mortgage he had paid off after they had become half owners. All issues on appeal relate to the distribution of the funds received from a sale of the property. When the sale was first held under court order, the children's bid of $80,000 was accepted as the highest. However, even though time extensions were obtained to permit compliance with the contract of sale, they were forced to default. The trustees again offered the parcels for sale at public auction under order of the court " . . . to resell the property described in this proceeding at the risk and expense of the Defendants (the children)." The resale brought a purchase price of $95,500, which was $15,500 higher than the original purchase price bid at the first sale by the children. The questions having to do with the distribution of proceeds from that sale, here raised by appeal and cross-appeal, are:

1. Should the father be compensated for the improvements he had constructed (two apartments)?
2. Should the children be awarded one-half of the apartment rentals during their co-tenancy (and between the first and second sale)?
3. Who is entitled to the $15,500 increase in the purchase price after the children defaulted?
4. Is the father entitled to contribution for discharging the prior mortgage?

The chancellor did not compensate the father for the value of the apartments, finding that the father had not met his burden of proof. However, he sought to balance the equities somewhat by denying the children an allowance for rentals therefrom during the co-tenancy. The children were awarded the amount of money by which the final purchase price exceeded the price at the initial sale upon which they had defaulted, and were also allowed the rental payments for the apartments between the dates of the two sales. The chancellor also compelled contribution from the children for one-half of the cost of discharging a mortgage which was paid off by the father soon after the creation of the co-tenancy.

THE LAW

"A circuit court may decree a partition of any property . . . on the . . . petition of any . . . tenant in common. . . . If it appears that the property cannot be divided without loss or injury to the parties interested, the court may decree its sale and divide the money resulting from the sale among the parties according to their respective rights. . . . " Real Property Art. 21, § 14-107. . . .

"In matters of partition," says Judge Story, "a Court founds itself upon its general jurisdiction as a Court of equity, and administers its relief, ex oequo (sic) et bono according to its own notions of general justice and equity between the parties." 1 Story's Equity Juris., §656 b.

Recently, the Court of Appeals has again described the latitude allowed an equity court in distributing the proceeds of a partition sale. Judge Horney wrote for the Court in Bowers v. Balto. G. & E. Co., 228 Md. 624, 629, 180 A.2d 878, 881:

> With respect to a sale (in lieu of partition) . . . , we repeat what was probably first said in Story v. Johnson, 1 Y. & C.Ex. 538 (1835), 2 Y. & C.Ex. 586 (1837), that the "Court, in decreeing a partition, does not act ministerially and in obedience to the call of those parties who have right to partition, but founds itself upon its general equitable jurisdiction," and will "adjust the equitable rights of all the parties interested in the estate."

Notwithstanding the broad discretion allowed the chancellor, there are certain general principles and guidelines to which he must adhere.

1. Improvements

One such principle relates to the compensation to which a co-owner may be entitled for the value of any improvement he has put upon the property. The chancellor below observed that:

Although there is no Maryland case directly in point the general rule of law seems to be that a co-tenant who makes a substantial improvement to the property, such as the apartments constructed by George Maas, is entitled to be compensated, but only to the extent to which the improvements are shown to have enhanced the value of the property at the time of sale. . . . The burden is on the tenant who makes the improvements to show that they enhanced the value of the property, and it is in this respect that the plaintiff has failed to support his claim. . . . The plaintiff here relies on the testimony of Mr. Harry Riepe, an experienced and well known appraiser, but this court has read his testimony carefully and at no time did the witness ever state that at the time of sale the property was more valuable because of the construction of the apartments over the garage on the rear portion of the tract.

Appellant agrees in this brief that:

> If this assertion by the Trial Court is factually correct, Appellant may not prevail on this point of his appeal.

We find the court's assertion to be correct both legally and factually. While it may be true that there is "no Maryland case directly in point . . . " there is certainly Maryland authority espousing the principle as being the law of Maryland. In Williams v. Harlan, 88 Md. 1, 5, 41 A. 51, 52 the Court said: "There can be no question that as between Wm. H. Greenway, and his co-tenants he would be entitled to a lien for the amount expended by him on improvements and repairs made upon the joint property with their knowledge or at their request or in good faith for the benefit of all. This doctrine is fully settled by all the authorities. Mr. Pomeroy in his Equity Jurisprudence, section 1239 says: 'When two or more persons are joint-owners of real or other property, and one of them in good faith, for the joint benefit, makes repairs and improvements upon the property which are permanent, and add a permanent value to the entire estate, equity may not only give him a claim for contribution against the other joint-owners with respect to their proportional shares of the amount thus expended, but may also create a lien as security for such demand upon the undivided shares of the other proprietors.'"

A review of the testimony of appellant's expert witness affirms Judge Raine's observation. The testimony elicited was based upon replacement cost rather than on the amount by which the property was enhanced by virtue of the improvements at the time of sale. We certainly find no abuse of discretion in rejecting the testimony as failing to establish a foundation for compensation. (Citations omitted.)

2. Rent

Although a co-tenant is normally entitled to an accounting for rent for three years prior to suit, Colburn v. Colburn, 265 Md. 468, 474, 290 A.2d 480, the chancellor refused to award to the children any rent which accrued prior to the first sale. In doing so, he expressly exercised his broad equity discretion in distributing the proceeds of a partition sale, as heretofore noted. The chancellor's opinion said:

> Ordinarily, one co-tenant must account to the other for rents received from third parties. On the other hand the court has the power to adjust the equities between the parties. Even though the facts in McLaughlin v. Barnum, 31 Md. 425, are different this court reaches the same result, for to do otherwise would be inequitable. Where the costs of the improvements were borne by George Maas and contribution to him has been denied herein, it would be a gross inequity to deprive him of the net rental income. As pointed out by the defendants it would be inequitable, if not outrageous, to deny the children an offset for the rents against an allowance to the father of the credit for improvements. It would be equally inequitable to deny the father's claim for improvements, but to allow the children to share in the rental income that flowed solely from the improvements.

We find no error.

* * *

3. Overage

Upon default following their successful bid at the first sale, the children, by decree, bore the risk that the resale might bring less than the bid they had defaulted upon. Mealey v. Page, 41 Md. 172, 183. Fortune smiled on them, however, and the resale brought more, not less, than their original bid. The chancellor awarded the children the $15,500 excess, and we think properly so.

Miller, Equity Procedure, sec. 526 explains the resale procedure under Chapter XXVI entitled "SALES UNDER DECREES," citing Mealey, *supra*, as authority: "sec. 526. Disposition of proceeds of sale.—When a re-sale is made the proceeds are to be disposed of as follows: the costs, fees and expenses of the resale, including the proper commissions, are to be deducted; and also the amount of the original purchase money due, with interest from the date of the first sale to the date of the receipt of the purchase money of the second sale. The proceedings for a re-sale, after final ratification, treat the first contract as binding on the original purchaser. The property is re-sold as the property of the defaulting purchaser, and at his risk. He is therefore entitled to any excess in the proceeds of sale at the re-sale, just as he would be responsible for any deficiency. The purchaser is to be charged with the whole purchase money and costs of the re-sale, and credited with the payments he has made, and with the proceeds of the second sale. If the latter amounts are not sufficient to pay the sum for which the property was first sold, the purchaser is to be charged with the deficiency. The application of the cash paid as a credit on his purchase is in no sense a forfeiture inasmuch as he is entitled to any surplus which may remain." (Footnotes omitted.)

The chancellor followed this directive to the letter.

* * *

The same ratio decidendi was applied by the chancellor to the rents for the period between the two sales. That ruling is supported by rulings of the Court of Appeals from at least as early as 1868, until at least as late as 1968. In Farmers' Bank of Md. v. Clarke, 28 Md. 145, 156 it was stated:

> As the purchaser is made to bear all loss by depreciation subsequent to the time of sale, he

should be entitled to all profit that he may be able to make of the property after that time.

* * *

4. The Mortgage Pay Off

At the time of the dissolution of the marriage in 1943, appellant and his wife conveyed the property by straw deeds to a straw party who reconveyed it to appellant and his children as tenants in common. Both straw conveyances warranted the property specially and contained covenants that the grantors (parents) had done: "no act, matter or thing whatsoever to encumber the property hereby conveyed."

There was in existence at that time, however, a mortgage on the property executed by the real grantors, appellant and his wife (as opposed to the straw party to whom they had represented that warranty). Less than one year later, appellant discharged the mortgage by full payment of the $4,770 balance due. The children did not assume any obligation under the mortgage, nor was the mortgage assigned to appellant upon discharge for subrogation or otherwise. The payment was made and full release recorded.

Citing Hogan v. McMahon, 115 Md. 195, 203, 80 A. 695, 698, appellees, as cross-appellants, recognize that:

> Where a tenant in common discharges a mortgage upon the joint property, equity treats him as an assignee of the mortgage as against his co-tenant's interest in the property, and, this though no actual assignment is made.
>
> They further concede (this time, citing Aiello v. Aiello, 268 Md. 513, 302 A.2d 189) that the right of contribution can be enforced by obtaining an assignment, or by asserting a right of subrogation as a surety, or by enforcing an equitable lien against the co-tenant's interest. See also annotation, 48 A.L.R.2d 1305.

However, they contend that the father no longer has such relief available because of the lapse of over 25 years after he had a right to seek such relief. They base this conclusion on one or all of three equitable and legal reasons: laches, limitations and/or estoppel. They argue that the court below erred in awarding the father contribution for the discharge of the mortgage, although the chancellor's motivations were unquestionably equitable:

> it would be inequitable, even outrageous, to allow the children to force their father to assume the whole burden of the mortgage when they received the benefit of his payment discharging the mortgage.

Notwithstanding that "courts of equity do not hesitate to adapt their methods to the exigencies of justice or to protect the equitable rights of those concerned . . . ," Myers, *supra*, 139 Md. at 613, 116 A. at 455, there is a barrier which even the "exigencies of justice" may not penetrate.

Here a presumption of a gift to appellant's infant children, . . . by his having paid off the mortgage, is bolstered by deeds declaring the property was conveyed unencumbered. The children were the objects of the father's natural bounty which "is of itself a circumstance sufficient to raise an inference that a gift was intended. . . . " (Citations omitted.) In light of the total absence of evidence to overcome the inference of a gift, the express conveyance "without encumbrances" from the parents through a straw party, and the release of the mortgage by the father with no attempt to secure a right to contribution by subrogation, assignment or lien, no equitable right in the father has been shown entitling the chancellor to balance the equities by forcing the children to contribute to the pay off of the mortgage which occurred more than 20 years prior to the distribution.

* * *

Judgment affirmed in part and reversed in part.

Case Reflections

1. Partition is an equitable remedy. Does this mean that a judge can refuse to order a partition after a co-tenant has requested this remedy? Why or why not?
2. Do you agree with the law stated in this case that tenants in common are only entitled to compensation for improvements to the property when the improvement increases the value of the property? Why or why not?
3. Why were the children not permitted to share in the rental income from the improvements which was earned prior to the first sale, but were given credit for the rental income which was earned between the first and second sales?

SCHNEIDER
V.
SCHNEIDER

389 N.W.2d 835, 132 (Wis. 1986)

Agreements prohibiting partition

EICH, Judge.

John J. Schneider appeals from a summary judgment dismissing his action to partition real estate. The dispositive issue is whether the action is barred by an agreement executed by Schneider, his brother Allen and their wives, each of whom had an ownership interest in the property. We conclude that the agreement precludes the action, and we therefore affirm.

* * *

In 1978, Schneider and his brother Allen acquired title to an undivided one-half interest in the family farm as tenants in common. Their wives were named with them in the deed. All four then signed an agreement restricting sale of the property. The agreement allows one brother to sell his half interest in the farm only with the other's consent and, failing that, only after first giving the other the right to purchase it. The "buy-out" price is established by the terms of the agreement. It sets $130,000 as the value of the farm for the year 1978 and directs the brothers to "stipulate the agreed value" annually thereafter. The stipulated figure forms the basis for calculating the value of the brothers' interests, should either wish to sell. In the event no such stipulation is reached in a given year, the agreement provides that the preceding year's valuation shall control. Upon the death of one brother, his interest is automatically transferred to the survivor. Each agreed to maintain life insurance in a designated amount for the purpose of compensating a deceased brother's estate for the survivor's acquisition of his interest. The agreement does not contain a termination date.

The deed to the farm listed as grantees "John J. Schneider and Janet B. Schneider, as owners of an undivided one-half (1/2) interest as tenants in common, as well as tenants in common with Allen E.Schneider and Carol J. Schneider as owners of an undivided one-half interest as tenants in common."

The introductory paragraph of the agreement describes the wives, along with their husbands, as "owners of an undivided one-half interest" in the property "as tenants in common." The substantive terms of the document, however, state that only Schneider and his brother are "parties" to its terms. Throughout the agreement, the terms "party" or "parties" are referred to in the masculine gender. The confusion is compounded by the fact that the concluding paragraph of the agreement, which refers to the "parties . . . hav[ing] hereunto set their hands," is followed by the signatures of not only Schneider and his brother but the wives as well. As if this weren't enough, the complaint alleges (and the answer admits) that when Schneider and his wife were divorced in 1983 their interests in the property were "changed from that as [*sic*] joint tenants to that of tenants in common."

While it would seem that the confusing language concerning the wives' interest in the land and their status under the agreement would figure in the arguments, the parties have ignored these questions, as do we.

In 1983, John Schneider decided to sell his interest in the farm. In the five years the agreement had been in existence, however, the brothers had never finalized any annual stipulation as to the value of the property. When John could not agree with Allen on the 1983 value, he commenced this partition action. Allen and his wife and John's former wife (they are now divorced) were named as defendants. They raised the agreement as a defense, relying on § 842.02(1), Stats., which provides that anyone who owns an interest in land in common with others may sue to partition that interest "unless an action for partition is prohibited . . . by agreement between the parties for a period not to exceed 30 years."

Allen and the wives argued, and the trial court agreed, that even though the agreement was silent as to its duration, it did not violate the thirty-year restriction because it had been in existence for only six years. While we disagree with the court's reasoning, we reach the same conclusion: the agreement is a defense to the partition action, and the complaint was properly dismissed.

John argues that because the agreement contains no termination date, it is, on its face, one that "exceeds 30 years" within the meaning of sec. 842.02(1), Stats., and thus does not defeat his action.

As a general rule, when a contract is of indefinite duration, we will imply a reasonable time for performance. Courts are reluctant to interpret contracts as providing for some perpetual or unlimited right unless the document itself clearly states that that is the intention of the parties. Interpretations which avoid construing a contract to have an indefinite duration are preferable. (Citations omitted.)

The introductory paragraphs of the agreement state that its purpose is to retain ownership of the Schneider family farm in John and Allen "or the survivor of them." To this end, the brothers agreed to restrict "the right of either party to sell or otherwise dispose of his interest in the . . . real estate during his lifetime, and to further provide for the purchase by the other of his interest . . . in the even of the death of one of the parties."

The contract is not indefinite. By its terms, it cannot be effective beyond the death of one brother. Admittedly, it is not known whether this "automatic" termination will occur within thirty years of the document's signing. But, the agreement is terminable by either party at any time. Either may liquidate his interest: (1) with the other's consent, or, failing that; (2) by selling to the other brother under the "buy-out" provisions. If the nonselling brother's consent is withheld, he is given a sixty-day option to purchase the seller's interest at a price to be calculated under the terms of the agreement. If he exercises the option, the sale is to him; if he fails to exercise the option, the selling brother is free to dispose of his interest as he wishes. A brother wishing to dispose of his undivided interest may thus do so at will under the agreement; the sale will be either to his brother under the buy-out clause, or to a third party upon the brother's consent or failure to exercise the contractual sixty-day option.

The right of a cotenant to partition and convey his or her interest in real property is favored in the law; it is often said to be a matter of right. It is also recognized, however, that one may validly agree not to partition. Because the law frowns on restrictions on the alienability of property, such agreements, to be valid, cannot extend for an unreasonable length of time. Section 842.02(1), Stats., effects a similar compromise between these competing policies by establishing the "reasonable time" beyond which such agreements may not extend. Thus, an agreement which prohibits partition for a period of thirty years or more is invalid, while one with a lesser prohibition is enforceable and may bar the action.

In this case, the agreement does not prohibit either party from partitioning and selling his interest. It merely conditions that right on compliance with the consent and sixty-day option-to-purchase procedures. We conclude, therefore, that the agreement is valid under sec. 842.02(1), Stats., and the respondents' motion to dismiss was properly denied.

Judgment affirmed.

Case Reflections

1. Under the Wisconsin statute cited by the court, and agreement not to partition land which extends for thirty years or more is invalid. Why did the Wisconsin legislature adopt such a statute?
2. The court ruled that the agreement in this case did not violate the statute. Do you agree? Why or why not?

FLIPPO
V.
NELSON

792 P.2d 99 (Okla., 1990)

Partition in kind

BRIGHTMIRE, Chief Judge.

The issue presented for review in this partition action is whether the trial court's in kind allocation of subject land in accordance with the commissioners' final report was clearly unfair and inequitable as to the objecting plaintiff under the evidence.

We hold that it was and modify the final decree.

I.

The orientational background facts are that the plaintiff Dorothy Flippo, formerly Shannon, is the daughter of the late L.D. Shannon who died testate leaving an estate consisting of, among other things, several pieces of real estate located in various counties in the state. The decedent's will was probated and his land was distributed August 4, 1976, to the defendant trustees of two trusts created by the terms of the will, one of which was called "My Wife's Trust Estate" and the other "My Residuary Trust Estate." The trustees are Barlow Nelson and Yandell Shannon, the plaintiff's mother. The trusts were each devised a one-half interest in the decedent's real estate. The plaintiff and her sister, Darlene Kay Gelino, a defendant, were made equal beneficiaries of the assets of "My Residuary Trust" with distribution of one-third of the corpus at ages 35, 40 and 45.

The plaintiff's late father, L.D. Shannon, executed his last will in 1963. It was probated and the estate distributed in 1976. Not long thereafter the trustees of the estate trusts conveyed a 40-acre tract located in Section 7, T17N, R10E, Creek County, Oklahoma, to the plaintiff and a 40-acre tract in the same section to her sister, defendant Gelino. The two tracts were separated by an 80-acre tract owned by the trusts.

After acquiring her 40 acres the plaintiff started up a dairy farm business which she and her son operated. Early on the plaintiff received permission from her mother to run her cattle on the adjoining 80 acres for both grazing and watering and has so used the acreage through the years.

On June 13, 1985, the plaintiff filed this action asking that the real property held by the Shannon trusts be partitioned in kind if practical and if not then sold and the proceeds distributed. The trustees answered asking the court to refuse to grant partition relief, or else order the property sold. Commissioners were appointed January 15, 1986. They issued a partial report March 19, 1986, appraising certain improved real estate situated outside Creek County, and certified it could not be divided in kind without great injury to the parties. The report was not objected to and the property was eventually sold pursuant to a court order and the funds distributed by the court. On May 24, 1988, the commissioners filed their final report saying they "found that partition of [the remaining real] property can be made among the said parties according to their respective interests as determined and ordered by [the court] without manifest injury to said parties, and we have accordingly partitioned the said property as follows, to wit:"

"To [the] Trustees of 'my wife's trust'" a 10-acre tract and a 30-acre tract in Cherokee County, a 120-acre tract and a 30-acre tract in Creek County (near Depew, Oklahoma) ad an 80-acre tract in Creek County (the Kellyville tract that adjoins the plaintiff's farm);

"To Darlene Kay Gelino" an 80-acre tract and a 40-acre tract in Creek County;

"To [plaintiff] Dorothy Ann Flippo" a 130-acre tract (near Depew, Oklahoma) some 25 or so road miles away from her dairy farm.

The plaintiff filed an objection to the report based on the fact that as a matter of equity she should be allotted the 80 acres which adjoin her dairy farm to the west and on which she has been running her cattle with the permission of her mother for many years; and that it will work an economic hardship on her if the tract is not allotted to her. Both the trustees and Gelino objected to the plaintiff's objection.

The matter was heard June 1, 1988.

* * *

At the conclusion of the testimony the trial court seemed to brush aside the evidence of injury to the plaintiff by the commissioners' recommended allocation and entered an order affirming the report of the commissioners. Regarding the plaintiff's request that she be allotted subject 80-acre tract for the operation of her dairy, the trial court stated:

> I can certainly understand that she would like to have her dairy operation right where it is, but I am not convinced that arrangements could not be worked out elsewhere for this same operation. I think she has got other property to go to, or she would have the option to purchase the very eighty or the very forty that has been discussed here if she sells some of her other property. I don't know of any reason that hasn't been shown

> to this Court why the trustees would not sell this eighty to her. Anyway, not being convinced that the Commissioners' Report is anything other than fair and equitable, I'm going to deny the objection, enter an Order confirming the Report of the Commissioners and deed or deeds are ordered issued in accordance with the recommendations of the Commissioners.

Thus it is apparent that the trial court reached the conclusion it did partly on the basis of speculation and evidence not in the record. In its "Final Decree" the trial court "decreed that the said report of the commissioners is hereby in all things ratified, confirmed, and approved by the Court," overruled the plaintiff's objection thus denying her the equitable relief she sought and ordered the property divided in kind in accordance with the commissioners' final report.

The plaintiff appeals contending she has been substantially prejudiced by the ruling.

II.

The dispositive issue is whether the plaintiff made a showing of being substantially prejudiced by the allocation. We hold she did.

First we should review the fundamental law applicable to partition proceedings. They are governed by 12 0.S. 1981 and Supp.1989 ss 1501 through 1517. The right to partition is absolute and the proceeding is of equitable cognizance. Keel v. Keel, 475 P.2d 393 (Okl.1970). Partition in kind is favored, and the court for "good and sufficient reasons" may direct the commissioners "to allot particular portions to any one of the parties." 12 O.S.1981 s 1507.

In his bench statement quoted earlier the trial judge said he had "not heard any testimony that would indicate that [the commissioners' allocation] is not a just or equitable partition between the parties." In making this statement his focus must have been on land values because he then emphasized the fact that the "respective values are the same," suggesting that the plaintiff's obvious special need for the 80-acre tract was of little or no equitable significance. Finally, the judge spoke in terms of "substituting" his opinion for that of the commissioners and states "that's all I would be doing . . . substituting my opinion, and there wouldn't be any reason for the appointment of the Commissioners."

We believe the trial court misperceives its judicial responsibility in partition proceedings. The court has the statutory authority, and, indeed, the duty, to direct what the commissioners do. Here the court gave the commissioners no directions. They took it upon themselves to determine how the property was to be divided—whether in kind or by sale—and for that which was to be divided in kind, the commissioners decided to whom it was to be allotted. Thus when the plaintiff made her objection she invoked the judicial power of the court to make an equitable determination of how the tracts should be allotted. 12 O.S.1981 s 1516. It was error for the trial court to abdicate this duty by taking the position that performance of its judicial function would somehow destroy the need for commissioners. The commissioners were appointed to perform certain administrative functions under the direction of the court. Their report was, in substance and effect, findings of fact as to values and a recommendation to the court as to whether the property could be fairly divided in kind or not. Absent an objection by one or more of the parties, the court would ordinarily be expected to accept the commissioners' report and adjudicate the issues in accordance with it. But if there is an objection the court must resolve the issue and render a judgment.

In this case we are of the opinion the court did hear testimony that indicated the commissioners' report was not just, equitable, fair or necessary with respect to the allotment to the plaintiff. Indeed, it appears to us that for some undisclosed reason the commissioners went out of their way to avoid allocating subject 80-acre tract to the plaintiff. Under the undisputed evidence the commissioners' allocation of subject property appears to have been rather arbitrary, or at least inequitable.

Contrary to what the trial judge stated, there is no evidence the plaintiff has other suitable property to go to or that it would be cost efficient to move an established dairy operation. She is established on her 40-acre tract and has been for more than ten years. Her mother has let her use the 80-acre tract during that period. There is no evidence that the trustees have offered to sell the 80 acres to the plaintiff as the trial court implied they should, but the comment suggests a recognition that the plaintiff should have the property—a recognition that invokes the principle that equity will do that which should have been done.

The ultimate fact is, therefore, that the plaintiff presented "good and sufficient reasons" for allocating subject 80 acres to her as contemplated by statute. She has shown she has been injured by the commissioners' allocation. And this has not been disputed by anyone.

III.

It is therefore our opinion that the trial court's failure to sustain the plaintiff's objection to the commissioners' recommended allocation and to award the plaintiff the 80 acres adjoining her dairy farm plus the north 30 acres of the Depew tract in lieu of the 130 acres the commissioners allotted to her, was an abuse of discretion which substantially prejudiced the plaintiff. . . .

As to the remaining allotments, the decree is affirmed.

REIF and STUBBLEFIELD, JJ., concur.

Case Reflections

1. The court states that "certain improved real estate" owned in common by the parties could not be partitioned in kind, and therefore ordered that the property be sold. However, the unimproved farm property was partitioned in kind. How might improvements to real property make partition in kind inequitable?
2. When ordering a partition in kind, is the court required to consider any issues beyond the market value of the parcels each party will receive after partition?

GAZDO PROPERTIES CORP.
V.
LAVA, et. al.

565 N.Y.S.2d 964 (1991)

Duties of condominium associations

MARGARET TAYLOR, Judge:

The issue to be determined in this case is whether, pursuant to the Multiple Dwelling Law ("MDL") and the Housing Maintenance Code ("HMC"), the owners of individual condominium units or the Board of Managers (and Managing Agent) of a condominium building are responsible for correcting violations inside individual condominium units. For the reasons set forth below, the court finds that an owner of a condominium unit is an owner as defined by the relevant statutes and is, therefore, responsible for the maintenance, repair and correction of code violations within the unit.

Petitioner Gazdo Properties Corp. owns apartment units 1E and 3F at 2900 Ocean Avenue, Brooklyn, a building owned in condominium. Respondents Mark Lava, Irwin Rothkein, Carl Brill, Marilyn Rosenblatt, Corrine Heslin, Eli Marinofsky, Francis Cole, and Sy Weiss make up the Board of Managers of the building. Respondent Edward L. Waldman is the building's Managing Agent.

Petitioner, by Order to Show Cause dated May 2, 1990, commenced a tenant action seeking an order directing respondents to correct six violations of State and City housing codes, which were documented in an inspection report dated August 29, 1989. Two violations existed in common areas of the building, while four were alleged to be inside individual units not owned by petitioner or respondents. Petitioner also asked for civil penalties and for a finding of personal liability against each respondent.

On June 14, 1990 respondents moved to dismiss the petition on the grounds that it failed to state a cause of action, that the petitioner lacked standing to bring the proceeding and that the real parties in interest were not joined. At the court's request, additional moving papers were submitted specifically addressing the question of whether the Board of Managers and the Managing Agent of a condominium or the unit owners are responsible for the correction of violations of the MDL and/or the HMC where the violations exist within individual units.

Condominiums are governed by the Condominium Act, Article 9-B of the Real Property Law

("RPL") ss 339-d through 339-ii. Pursuant to RPL sec. 339-u, "[t]he operation of the property shall be governed by by-laws. . . . " The by-laws of the subject premises at 2900 Ocean Avenue provide, in Article 5, Section 5.1(A), that maintenance and repairs of the interiors of the individual units are the responsibility of the individual unit owner: ". . . all . . . maintenance, repairs and replacements, whether structural or nonstructural, ordinary or extraordinary[,] . . . in or to any Unit and all portions thereof . . . shall be performed by the owner of such Unit at such Unit Owner's cost and expense. . . . " By-laws of 2900 Ocean Condominium, sec. 5.1(A). Similarly, the by-laws provide that "all . . . maintenance, repairs and replacements . . . in or to the Common Elements shall be performed by the Condominium Board as a Common Expense." *Id.*, sec. 5.1(A) (ii).

The Condominium Act provides that a " '[u]nit owner' means the person or persons owning a unit in fee simple absolute. . . . " RPL sec. 339-e(16); that "[e]ach unit, together with its common interest, shall for all purposes constitute real property[,]" RPL sec. 339-g; and that "[e]ach unit owner shall be entitled to the exclusive ownership and possession of his unit." RPL sec. 339-h. Such provisions also reflect case law holdings that "[a] condominium is a single real property parcel with all the unit owners having a right in common to use the 'common elements' with separate ownership confined to the individual units which are serially designated." Kaufman and Broad Homes of Long Island, Inc. v. Leter M. Albertson, 73 Misc.2d 84, 341 N.Y.S.2d 321 (Sup.Ct.Suff.Co.1972). The unit owner enjoys "fee simple ownership of [the] unit or apartment . . . " Gerber v. Town of Clarkstown, 78 Misc.2d 221, 222, 356 N.Y.S.2d 926 (Sup.Ct.Rockl.Co.1974).

This is, thus, a different type of real property ownership than a cooperative holding, where proprietary tenants or shareholders own shares in the cooperative corporation, which ownership entitles them to occupy particular defined apartments.

As an owner in fee simple, the condominium unit owner fits the definition of "owner" provided in both the Multiple Dwelling Law and the Housing Maintenance Code (ss 4(44) and 27-2004(a) (45), respectively):

> The term "owner" shall mean and include the owner or owners of the freehold of the premises or lesser estate therein, a mortgagee or vendee in possession, assignee of rents, receiver, executor, trustee, lessee, agent, or any other person, firm or corporation, directly or indirectly in control of a dwelling. Under the MDL, the owner of a premises is responsible for keeping it in good repair and for complying with the law's provisions. MDL sec. (1). And under the HMC, the owner is to "keep the premises in good repair . . [and] be responsible for compliance with the requirements of this code . . . " HMC sec. 27-2005.

The Condominium Act provides as follows in the section entitled "Effect of other laws" (RPL sec. 339-ee):

> Any provision of the multiple dwelling law, the multiple residence law, or any state building construction code as to multiple residences pursuant to the provisions of article eighteen of the executive law, requiring registration of the owner or other person having control of a multiple dwelling shall be deemed satisfied in the case of a property submitted to the provisions of this article by registration of the board of managers, such registration to include the name of each unit owner and the designation of his [*sic*] unit; each unit owner shall be deemed the person in control of the unit owned by him [*sic*], and the board of managers shall be deemed the person in control of the common elements, for purposes of enforcement of any such law or code, provided, however, that all other provisions of the multiple dwelling law or multiple residence law, otherwise applicable, shall be in full force and effect. (Emphasis added.)

Thus, although RPL sec. 339-ee of the Condominium Act does not specifically address the effect of the Housing Maintenance Code on the unit owners and the Board of Managers of a condominium and only refers to the Multiple Dwelling Law, the Multiple Residence Law and state building construction codes, it is evident that when the various provisions of the Condominium Act, the by-laws of the condominium (provided for by the Condominium Act) and the MDL are construed together, the legislature intended that the correction of all code violations within an individual condominium unit be the responsibility of the unit owner and not the Board of Mangers and the Managing Agent. The Board and the Managing Agent are not by definition owners of each unit in a condominium building.

It would defeat the entire purpose of the legislature in enacting the Condominium Act carefully delineating the different responsibilities of unit owners and the Board, including the correction of code violations in RPL sec. 339-ee, if courts were required to hold unit owners, and not the Board, responsible for MDL violations inside the units but deem the same or similar violations of the HMC inside the units the responsibility of the Board. That could not have been the intention of the legislature when it enacted the Condominium Act is particularly clear when one considers the virtually identical purposes of the MDL and the HMC, their definitions of "owner" and the obligations the MDL and the HMC impose on "owners." MDL sec. 4(44); HMC sec. 27-2004(a)(45).

The court, therefore, finds that code violations inside individual condominium units must be corrected by the unit owner, including violations of the Housing Maintenance Code. The Board of Managers and the Managing Agent are not responsible for maintenance or repairs inside the individual units nor are they liable for correcting MDL or HMC violations inside the units. They are responsible only for the common areas.

The petition, as it relates to violations inside the individual units, is dismissed with prejudice for failure to state a cause of action. Since the two violations relating to the common areas were repaired during the pendency of this proceeding, the petition relating to those violations is likewise dismissed with prejudice. Thus, the entire petition is dismissed with prejudice. In view of this decision, there is no need to reach the other grounds raised in the motion to dismiss.

Case Reflection

1. What kinds of regulatory problems are created by the condominium form of ownership?

WASHBURN V. 166 EAST 96TH STREET OWNERS CORP.

564 N.Y.S.2d 115 (1990)

Co-operative ownership arrangements

MEMORANDUM DECISION.

Judgment, Supreme Court, New York County (Norman A. Mordue, J.), entered July 7, 1989, which declared, inter alia, that plaintiff was entitled to exclusive use of the roof area surrounding and adjacent to his cooperative apartment and which awarded plaintiff damages and attorneys' fees, unanimously affirmed, with costs.

In 1978, plaintiff rented apartment 16-D, a duplex penthouse type apartment which occupied the sixteenth floor rear portion of the subject building. Thereafter, and subsequent to the conversion of the premises to cooperative ownership in 1981, plaintiff enjoyed the exclusive use of the 830 square foot terrace which surrounded the lower portion of the apartment. Plaintiff had purchased 1,225 shares of cooperative stock and obtained the proprietary lease for his apartment which recited, in pertinent part, that the apartment should include ". . . a portion of the roof adjoining a penthouse, the Lessee shall have and enjoy the exclusive use of . . . that portion of the roof appurtenant to the penthouse. . . . " In 1982, the cooperative board undertook repairs which included portions of the roof area occupied by plaintiff. Objection was voiced by persons who were of the opinion that the roof area adjacent to plaintiff's apartment was common property. Upon the completion of the roof repairs in May of 1982, pursuant to newly promulgated House Rules and over plaintiff's objections, the cooperation board seized almost two thirds of plaintiff's roof terrace. The area was declared common property and plaintiff was denied his exclusive possession by the placement of tables and chairs thereon.

The credible evidence adduced at trial established that 302 of the 1,225 shares purchased by plaintiff represented the entire roof terrace area. This expert opinion was amply supported by the fact that all other one bedroom "D" line apartments were allocated an average of only 600 shares in the prospectus. Furthermore, the conduct of both plaintiff and defendant's predecessor clearly indicates that the original leasehold included the exclusive use of the roof terrace area (see generally Shepherd v. Seril, 118 A.D.2d 422, 499 N.Y.S.2d 85), which consequently we hold to be appurtenant to plaintiff's apartment within the meaning of the proprietary lease.

We conclude that the conduct of the defendant constituted an actual partial eviction of plaintiff and further, subjected his remaining tenancy to a substantial loss of the quiet enjoyment of his leasehold and to the troublesome necessity of the underlying law suit and the instant appeal.

Accordingly, we affirm the judgment appealed from and remand the matter to Supreme Court only for the purpose of establishing the proper amount of attorney's fees and disbursements to be awarded plaintiff as a result of having to respond to this appeal.

Case Reflection

1. If the roof appurtenant to the plaintiff's apartment was his own seperate property, why did the cooperative board make repairs to that portion of the roof?

CHAPTER

6

LIMITATIONS OF FEE SIMPLE OWNERSHIP

LEARNING OBJECTIVES

After reading this chapter, you should be able to:

1. Identify and discuss the duties owed by real property owners to the owners of adjacent parcels of land
2. Identify and discuss the duties owed by real property owners to people who come onto the land
3. Identify and discuss the various kinds of easements that can be created by voluntary agreement between property owners or by operation of law.

KEY TERMS

Nuisance

Easement

Covenant

Abatement

Physical Injury

Legal Injury

Affirmative Defense

License

Dominant Tenement

Servient Tenement

Promissory Estoppel

The title of this chapter serves as a reminder that no one possesses absolute rights in the American legal system. The fee simple ownership estate represents the largest bundle of rights available under the law. But even this largest of all bundles is subject to some limitations.

The general limitation on the rights of fee simple owners is summarized by the Latin maxim *sic utere tuo, et alieunum non laedas.* Loosely translated, this maxim advises owners to "use your own property as you will, and avoid injuring the property of other owners." A famous English case of the last century, *Rylands v. Fletcher,* was one of the earliest cases to apply this theory. In that case, Fletcher operated a coal mine on his property. After some years, the mine became flooded. Eventually, water from the mine formed an underground stream running beneath the land of Rylands. The flow of the water undermined the soil on Rylands' property and caused the surface of the land to sink noticeably. Fletcher was required to compensate Rylands for the injury to his land, since landowners have a duty not to injure the property of their neighbors.

This general duty not to injure the physical property of others surrounds a number of more specific duties owed by landowners. The doctrine of **nuisance** was developed to prevent activities by property owners that interfere with the use or quiet enjoyment of neighboring lands. In addition, the common law has always imposed various duties on landowners to avoid injuring people who happen to be on the property. We will examine both of these issues in detail here.

Nuisance Activities of a landowner which interfere with the use or quiet enjoyment of neighboring parcels of real property

Finally, there are a number of nonpossessory property rights recognized by the law that may limit the ownership rights in a parcel of land. **Easements** and **covenants** can be created that impose duties on one landowner while conferring rights in the property to adjacent owners. These property rights can be distinguished from the nuisance obligations and the duty of care owed to others on the land by virtue of the fact that the property rights were created by a voluntary agreement at some time in the history of the property. For example, Blackacre may be subject to an easement allowing the owner of the adjacent parcel to cross Blackacre in order to reach the highway. This arrangement was originally created with the consent of the owner of Blackacre. Each subsequent purchaser of Blackacre will also be deemed to have consented to this arrangement that allows the neighbor to cross the land in order to reach the highway.

Easement A real property interest which gives the owner of the easement the right to subject the real property of another to a defined use or restriction on use

On the other hand, landowners are not required to consent to the common law duties of avoiding injuries to other people or their property. Every landowner has these duties, whether he or she agrees to accept them or not. In this chapter, we will first examine the duties imposed by law. Then we will take up the limitations on ownership that fee simple holders may create by voluntary arrangements.

Covenant An agreement between two or more landowners which limits or restricts the ownership rights of the parties to the agreement

NUISANCE DOCTRINES

Every property owner has a general legal duty not to injure the property of another. The doctrine of nuisance is one of the specific forms of this general legal duty. A nuisance can be either a public or a private nuisance. In most states, public nuisances are defined by statutes (at the state level) or ordinances (at the city or county government level). As a result, the public nuisance remedies vary widely among the states, reflecting the unique geographic, economic, and population circumstances of the states.

Public Nuisance

When a landowner uses a parcel of land in a manner that violates a public nuisance statute or ordinance, two questions present themselves: What can be done about the offensive use, and who has the power to begin proceedings to eliminate the offensive use? The answer to the first question is the easier of the two. All states provide for the **abatement** of a public nuisance. Most public nuisance statutes permit a court to issue an order prohibiting the offensive use, subsequent to a lawsuit establishing that the landowner has violated public nuisance statute.

Towne v. Porter Township Board

Abatement A judicial act or order which is intended to terminate the activities of a land owner which have been declared to create a nuisance

> Rosebud's English Pub was created in 1976 and 1977 by an extensive remodelling of a leased building in downtown San Francisco. The city building department issued a construction permit, and conducted numerous on site inspections of the work during the remodelling. When completed, the remodelled building violated handicap access requirements. The city building department mistakenly believed that these requirements were imposed only on new construction, and did not apply to remodelling projects. The architects and contractors responsible for the work did not mention the requirements of handicap access, and the owners of the restaurant were not independently aware of these requirements.
>
> In 1978, a person in a wheel chair was unable to use the public telephone in Rosebud's, because the phone was located on the second floor with no means of wheel chair access from the first floor. A complaint was lodged with the state Department of Rehabilitation, and an investigation was commenced. When Rosebud's refused to comply with the demands from the city to provide handicap access in its premises, the restaurant was declared a public nuisance. When Rosebud's continued to refuse to provide handicap access, the city filed suit to abate the nuisance. The State of California joined the suit also demanding that Rosebud's comply with the state handicap access laws.
>
> Rosebud's argued that the city was estopped from demanding compliance, because city inspectors remained silent when they had a duty to inform Rosebud's that its work was in violation of state law. The court ruled that estoppel against the city was moot, because the state was a party to the action, and the elements required for the defense of estoppel were lacking as against the state. City and County of San Francisco v. Grant Company 227 Cal. Rptr. 154 (CA, 1986)

The injunction order that a court issues has its roots in the equity courts of England. Since injunction is an equitable remedy and not a legal remedy, courts may use more discretion in deciding whether or not to issue an injunction. Equity courts exist to reach the "best" or "fairest" result, considering all of the circumstances. Historically, judges were free to consider both the benefits of the use that violates a nuisance statute and the harm caused by the use. Under this "balancing of interests" test, a judge may decide that the good outweighs the harm and refuse to issue the injunction. For example, if the nuisance complained of is smoke and noise from a factory that is the town's largest employer, a court of equity may decide that the benefit of the livelihoods obtained from the factory outweigh the harm from its operation. The court may order some reasonable actions to reduce the impact of the harm but still allow the factory to continue in operation. In recent years, many statutes have been amended to reduce the freedom courts have used in balancing the interests of the community while dealing with a public nuisance.

KEY POINTS

The definition of a public nuisance is one of the few elements of the law of rea property that has undergone noticeable change in the last one hundred years. At common law, a public nuisance was generally not defined by statute or ordinance. Rather, a public nuisance was defined as the activities of a landowner that injured everyone in the neighborhood in the same way. In the course of the current century, the common law doctrine of public nuisance has been substantially replaced by the zoning ordinances and land use regulations adopted by local government units. In current practice, these local ordinances define the activities of landowners that will be deemed harmful to everyone else in the neighborhood.

The second question, who has the power to begin proceedings to abate a public nuisance, has even more answers than the first question. In some states, only a public official designated by the nuisance statute or ordinance has the necessary "standing" to bring a public nuisance action. In other states, private citizens may sue to abate a public nuisance only if they can show some special or unique injuries not shared by the public at large. These states may limit private citizens to the legal remedy of damages. That is, private citizens who sue a landowner for using his or her land will be entitled only to receive money as compensation for the damage caused by the offending land use. In these states, private citizens may not obtain an injunction to prohibit the offensive use in the future. Then again, a few states allow private citizens to "stand in the shoes" of a public official and sue for an injunction to abate a public nuisance.

Private Nuisance

When the activities of a landowner damage only one or a few neighboring parcels, the actions will constitute a private nuisance. Foul odors, noise, dust, and dirt are just a few examples of the varieties of private nuisance to be found in the cases. The judicial treatment of the thousands of nuisance cases presented to the courts presents a bewildering array of different approaches and shifting outcomes. In order to make sense of the private nuisance doctrine, we must focus on two issues. The first issue is the nature of the injury complained of in a nuisance action. The second is the presence of an effective defense to the action.

Physical Injury Injury to land or personal property of another person

The injury created by a private nuisance can be either physical or legal. **Physical injuries** include actual damage to buildings or other property located on the land belonging to the private nuisance plaintiff. For example, suppose the plaintiff builds a swimming pool in the backyard. Some years later, the roots from a willow tree planted on the parcel next door grow through the wall of the pool in search of water. As another example, suppose paint droplets from an auto body shop drift into the wind across the property line, damaging the finish of cars parked on the used car lot next door. In each of these cases, the plaintiff will go to court complaining of a physical injury to property resulting from the existence of a private nuisance on the defendant's land.

Legal injuries diminish the value of property by interfering with the plaintiff's right to use and enjoy his or her property, free from any interference caused by the activities of neighbors. Feedlots and slaughterhouses are known to create unbearable odors and to attract large quantities of flies and other insects. The presence of such conditions can make property unsuitable for residential purposes, even though they result in no physical damage to any property on adjoining parcels. Plaintiffs who find their homes virtually uninhabitable as the result of a new feedlot operation will go to court complaining of the legal injury caused by the defendant's use of land.

Legal Injury Interference with the use or quiet enjoyment of another person's real property

Carrs Beach Amusement Company, Inc. v. Annapolis Roads Owners Association, Inc. et al.

Understanding the nature of the injury complained of in a private nuisance suit will help to predict the judicial response to the complaint. When the injury complained of is physical in nature, we can expect a judge to order the defendant to pay money damages to compensate for the injury. However, when the injury is legal in nature, money damages may not provide adequate compensation to the plaintiff. The legal remedy of money damages is designed to restore the plaintiff to the status quo ante, the position the plaintiff was in before the injury occurred. In the swimming pool example, a contractor could be found who would dig up the ground around the pool, remove the offending willow roots, and install a barrier to prevent a recurrence of the problem. When the holes in the pool are repaired, the plaintiff will be back in business, as if the physical injury had never occurred. A damage award, sufficient to pay for these activities, will provide an adequate remedy.

When the injury complained of is legal in nature, however, money damages may not be enough to return the plaintiff to the status quo ante. Even if the defendant in the feed lot example pays the full market value of the house to the plaintiffs, the house will remain uninhabitable. Simply requiring the plaintiffs to sell their house to a feedlot operator and move somewhere else does not provide an adequate legal remedy. When no adequate legal remedy exists, courts are willing to grant equitable relief. (Recall from Chapter 1 that law courts and equity courts were originally separate systems. Further, plaintiffs were not allowed to bring their suits before the equity courts unless they could show that no adequate remedy was available from the law courts.)

When the injury complained of in a nuisance action is legal in nature and money damages are not enough to restore the plaintiff to the status quo ante, then courts will issue an injunction prohibiting the defendant from continuing the activity that caused the injury. There are some cases, moreover, where both legal and equitable relief will be granted. In the auto body shop example above, a damage payment will be sufficient to restore the plaintiff used car dealer's property to the status quo ante. However, it is reasonable to believe that every time the wind blows, the plaintiff will have to come back to court to ask for additional money damages. To prevent this unhappy eventuality, the judge may be inclined to issue an order requiring the defendant to build a larger paint booth and refrain from painting cars outdoors in the future.

Whenever a judge decides that money damages for nuisance are not an adequate remedy, the judge becomes empowered to enter the realm of equitable relief. Equitable remedies are fashioned from broad notions of justice and fairness. These very general notions must be applied to the specific circumstances of the parties to the nuisance action. Here is one explanation for the apparent diversity of decisions in private nuisance actions. Each decision reflects the unique circumstances of the parties to the action, following the general notion that people who cause injuries to the property rights of others must be held accountable. The equitable nature of many private nuisance suits also explains the **affirmative defenses** that are often raised by the defendant.

Affirmative Defense A defense which must be raised by the defendant in a law suit in order to excuse the action complained of the plaintiff. The burden of proof in establishing an affirmative defense rests on the party who asserts it

"Coming to the nuisance" is a doctrine that a defendant may assert in order to escape liability for the injury complained of. One who buys a lot and builds a home near an existing feedlot can expect to find the living conditions there somewhat undesirable. In such a case, it would appear that the injury complained of results more from the plaintiff's decision to build than it does from the defendant's operation of the feedlot. In this case, fairness may require that the defendant be permitted to continue the activities complained of in the nuisance suit.

Courts will also use a balancing-of-interests test in considering what, if any, equitable relief should be granted in a nuisance action. If a nuisance activity has value to the community as a whole, either because of the jobs provided by the nuisance activity or the benefit of the outputs from the activity, a court can weigh these benefits against the burden on the plaintiff caused by the activity. If justice or fairness to the community requires that the activity be continued, the equity court will look for ways to permit continuation that are least injurious to the plaintiff.

DUTIES TO PERSONS ON THE LAND

In the previous section, we examined the duty of landowners not to injure the property of others. In this section, we examine the duties of care owed to people who come onto the property for various reasons. As we will see, the degree of the duty owed to other people depends largely upon their connection with the owner or the occupant of the property.

Duty to Trespassers

Anyone who walks onto the property of another without the consent of the owner is a trespasser on the property. Since the connection between an owner and a trespasser is almost nonexistent, the duty owed to trespassers is also small. Owners have the duty merely to avoid intentional harm to trespassers. An owner violates this duty by constructing any kind of trap or other dangerous instrumentality that is designed to deter trespassers by injuring them.

> Defendant's were the owners of a farm house in Monroe County Nebraska. The house was unoccupied. For a period of ten years, trespassers regularly broke into the house, breaking windows, stealing household items and "messing up the property in general." The defendants posted no trespassing signs, boarded up the windows, and made the property as secure as possible, but none of these efforts succeeded in deterring trespassers.
>
> In June of 1967, the defendant placed a loaded 20 gauge shotgun in the bedroom of the farm house, and rigged the gun with wire so that it would discharge when the bed-

room door was opened. One month later the plaintiff and an accomplice broke into the house once again. The plaintiff opened the bedroom door, and the gun discharged. Much of the plaintiffs lower leg, including the tibia, was blown away by the shotgun blast.

The plaintiff sued for damages resulting from the injury, and recovered a large judgment against the defendant. On appeal, the Supreme Court of Nebraska sustained the damage award. In the words of a leading expert on the law of personal injury, " . . . the law has always placed a higher value upon human safety than upon mere rights in property. [I]t is the accepted rule that there is no privilege to use any force calculated to cause death or serious bodily injury to repel the threat to land or chattels . . . " Katko v. Briney 183 N.W. 2d 657 (NE, 1971)

Duty to Licensees

At common law, judges made their living by drawing fine distinctions between various classes of people and then assigning a particular duty to everyone in a particular class. Historically, the category of licensee was placed between the category of trespasser (one who was on the land without the consent of the owner) and invitee (one who entered the land at the request or invitation of the owner). **Licensees** would include the UPS driver, the kid who delivers your pizza, and the letter carrier who brings the mail.

License
A personal property interest which permits the owner of the license to enter the land of another for specific purpose

Licensees have a stronger connection with the owner than trespassers, since the owner typically receives some benefit or service from the presence of the licensee. Accordingly, the duty of the owner toward a licensee is slightly greater. At common law, owners had the duty to keep the portion of the premises where licensees normally enter free from artificial conditions which pose an unreasonable risk of injury. For example, suppose a homeowner hired a contractor to repair the foundation of the house. The contractor digs a large hole directly under the mailbox and then covers the hole with a tarp to keep the rain out. When the letter carrier arrives for the regular mail delivery, there is an unreasonable risk of injury caused by the disguised hazard directly below the mailbox.

The modern trend has been to eliminate the distinctions between licensees and other persons on the property and to substitute a standard of reasonableness. When a licensee appears on the property unexpectedly, many courts will consider it reasonable for an owner merely to refrain from intentional injury to the licensee. When the licensee appears on the property at regular and predictable times, these courts will hold owners to the same standard of care owed to invitees.

Duty to Invitees

Invitees are by definition guests on the property who appear at the request of the owner. The connection between the owner and an invitee is again stronger than the connection with trespassers and licensees; thus the law imposes a still higher duty toward members of this class.

The owner of the property has a duty toward invitees to use reasonable care to keep the property free from dangerous defects that pose a risk of injury. In determining whether an owner has acted reasonably or not, courts will examine the magnitude of the risk—How likely it is that someone would be injured by a broken faucet handle or a defective shower door?—as well as the utility of the risk—How expensive would it be for the owner to repair the defect?

In addition, an owner has a duty to warn invitees of dangerous conditions on the property which the owner is aware of. For example, if the property has an open well in the backyard, the owner has a duty to warn all invitees of its location, so that they can avoid falling into the well. At common law, simply giving the warning was sufficient to protect the owner from liability for injuries suffered by a guest on the property. The modern trend is to inquire whether the warning given by the owner was reasonable and adequate in the circumstances.

Business Invitees

Modern courts have developed a new classification that was not part of the common law scheme: the business invitee. Customers in a store, tenants in an apartment house, and probably students at a university are all business invitees. Members of this class are on the premises at the express or implied invitation of the owner. Furthermore, the invitation was extended by the owner in the hope of achieving an economic benefit from the presence of the business invitees.

Owners of property have a duty to use reasonable care to insure that business invitees remain free of injuries while on the premises. This duty includes the obligation to remove any hazards from the premises within a reasonable time or as soon as the owner, or an employee of the owner, becomes aware of them. To put it another way, if the owner does not become aware of a hazard in a reasonable time, then the duty of due care owed to the customers has been breached, and the owner will be held liable for any injuries that result.

The law in this area is beginning to change. The old common law classifications are giving way to a general standard of reasonableness. However, the courts continue to use the older classifications to a greater or lesser degree in deciding what expectations of owners are reasonable in the circumstances. Clearly, a standard of care that is reasonable toward a trespasser would not be a reasonable for a customer in a grocery store. While this new standard evolves, a clear understanding of the common law scheme of duties is a useful guide to identifying the behaviors of various owners that will be deemed reasonable in the circumstances of the case.

Trespassing Children

Because young children are often unable to evaluate the risks of injury to themselves, special rules are applied to them. In 1873, the U.S. Supreme Court introduced the doctrine of attractive nuisance to American law. This doctrine held that when children were attracted to a dangerous condition by their natural curiosity, the owner of the property would be held liable for any injuries the children suffered.

Beaston v. James Julian

Currently, few states recognize the attractive nuisance doctrine. In most jurisdictions, it has been replaced by a four-part test contained in the Second Restatement of Torts. The test is set forth in one of the cases at the end of this chapter. We can summarize it here by saying that property owners have a duty to keep children out of harm's way on their land whenever there is reason to believe that children might, while playing, come onto the land.

VOLUNTARY LIMITATIONS ON OWNERSHIP

There are a number of nonpossessory interests in land that can be created to increase the value or utility of real property. Each of these interests, while created with the consent of the owners, will provide rights for people who are not the owners to make limited use of the land without first obtaining the owner's permission.

Easements

Virtually all easements are created to adjust the needs of people who own neighboring parcels of land. As a result, easements can be either positive or negative rights. A positive (or affirmative) easement permits the owner of the easement to use a specified portion of another owner's land for a specific purpose. A negative easement permits the owner to prohibit a specific use on the property burdened by the negative easement.

The most common example of an affirmative easement is an easement of way. Suppose that A owns a parcel of land that is two miles from the nearest road. B owns the land between A's parcel and the highway. In order to make any use of the parcel, A must have a way of getting to the land from the highway. The simplest way for A to meet this need is to purchase an easement from B permitting A to travel across B's land whenever the need arises.

An easement for light and air provides an example of a negative easement. Suppose the Chadwicks want to install a set of solar panels on their home in a residential subdivision. The Cadwalladers own the parcel immediately to the south of the Chadwicks' home. At the moment, the Cadwalladers' parcel is vacant, but they have expressed the intention to build a house on the lot. The Chadwicks are concerned that a house might block the sun during a portion of the day, reducing the efficiency of the solar heating device the Chadwicks' plan to install. The Chadwicks would be wise to purchase an easement from the Cadwalladers prohibiting the erection of any structure that prevents the sun from reaching the solar panels to be installed on the Chadwicks' residence. This prohibition creates a negative easement.

In both of these examples, it is clear that the easement benefits one parcel of land and burdens another parcel. In the easement-of-way example, the benefit flows to A (because access to that parcel is assured by the easement) while the burden falls on B, who is required to allow anyone who has business on A's land to cross over the easement. In the negative-easement example, the Chadwicks receive the benefit, while the Cadwalladers bear the burden.

KEY POINTS

The majority of easements are voluntary arrangements between owners of adjacent parcels of land. The purchase of an easement is, in many ways, identi cal to the purchase of a parcel of land. In general, landowners are not required to sell an easement in their property. The most usual method for acquiring an easement is to offer a cash inducement large enough to gain the agreement of the owner whose property will be burdened by the easement.

The land that benefits from an easement is called the **dominant tenement,** while the land that bears the burden of the easement is called the **servient tenement.** The easements themselves are referred to as appurtenant easements. An easement appurtenant is a real property interest that belongs to the owner of the dominant tenement. As the ownership of the dominant tenement changes, the ownership of the easement will also change.

Shingleton v. N.C.W.R.C

However, some easements involve only a servient tenement and do not have a dominant parcel. Virtually all of the residential and commercial lots in American cities are subject to a utility easement. The easement permits utility firms to place gas, electric, telephone, and other lines within the utility easement. Employees of the various utilities are also permitted to enter the land for repairs, maintenance, or new construction on the easement. Clearly, the parcels that are served by the utilities are all servient tenements, since they all bear the burden of the easement. However, there is no parcel of land that qualifies as a dominant tenement, receiving the benefit of the easement. Utility easements are one example of easements in gross. Easements in gross are personal property interests. Usually, these easements are extinguished at the death of the owner.

Dominant Tenement The parcel of land which receives the benefit of an easement

Servient Tenement The parcel of land which is required to bear the burden of an easement

Creation of Easements

Easements can be created in one of three ways: by deed, by implication, or by prescription.

EASEMENTS CREATED BY DEED. The most common mode of creation of easements is by deed. Many courts refer to these as easements created by express grant. In the case of the negative easement to insure sunlight for solar heating panels discussed previously, the easement will be created by a deed from the Cadwalladers to the Chadwicks. The deed will recite that the owners of the dominant tenement have a right to sunlight and that the owners of the servient tenement will remove any structures, trees, or other obstruction that interferes with that right. Of course, the Cadwalladers will expect to be paid in exchange for conferring this benefit on the Chadwicks. Since the easement is appurtenant, each new owner of the dominant tenement will be entitled to the benefit, and each new owner of the servient tenement will be required to accept the burden of the easement.

Easements are more commonly created in the deed that transfers title to either the dominant or servient tenement. Suppose O is the owner of a forty-acre parcel of land. The eastern boundary of the land is a county road. The other three borders of the parcel adjoin the lands of other owners. If O decides to sell the eastern half of the parcel, the twenty-acre piece he retains will be landlocked, with no means of reaching it. In the habendum clause of the deed conveying the eastern half of the property, O will reserve an easement to cross the land in order to reach the county road. On the other hand, if O decides to sell the western, landlocked, portion of the property, then the buyer will insist that the conveyance include the express grant of an easement of way across the property retained by O.

EASEMENTS CREATED BY IMPLICATION. Easements can be created by the implication of prior use or by the implication of necessity. Easements by implication are not voluntary arrangements. However, under certain conditions the owner of the servient tenement will be presumed by law to have agreed to the easement.

Assume that O, the owner of the forty-acre parcel, has lived in a house on the western edge of the parcel for twenty-five years. Assume further that a gravel road, which runs from the front of the house to the county road on the eastern boundary of the parcel, has always been the means of ingress and egress to the house. O now sells a ten-acre parcel, which includes the land the house is on, to B. B's new home is landlocked. There is no way for B's family to reach the home without trespassing on O's land or the land of someone else. B should have insisted on the grant of an easement to use the road that O had always used to reach the house. However, B never had the chance to study real estate law and didn't realize that an easement would be required.

B discovers the magnitude of the error one day when the family comes home to find a new gate across the road, bearing a conspicuous NO TRESPASSING sign. Since the land originally belonged to one owner, O, and since the road was obvious and in use when O sold a portion of the land to B, then O's consent to an easement for the use of the road will be implied, on the basis of the prior use of the road.

Even if no road and no house existed, an easement by implication would still be created. If B simply purchased a ten-acre plot in the northwest corner of O's cornfield, there would be no prior use to imply an easement of way. However, even in this case, O's consent to an easement will be implied by the necessity of the easement. Whether an easement by implication is created by prior use or simply by necessity, the law always implies that the parties intended to create the easement but simply forgot to attend to the details required to do so.

EASEMENTS CREATED BY PRESCRIPTION. An easement by prescription can arise whenever a person makes open, notorious, and hostile use of the land of another, under a claim of right, for a statutory period of years. Suppose that the Addams family buys a house that was built in 1945. The house next door was built in 1942. The driveway to the Addams' house was installed in 1950. In 1990, a new purchaser of the house next door discovers that a part of the Addams' driveway actually lies on the neighboring parcel. The fact that the Addams and their predecessors in title had used the driveway openly and notoriously for over forty years will be enough to establish a prescriptive easement for the benefit of the current owners of the old Addams family home.

Wagner v. Fairlamb

Boulder Medical Arts v. Waldron

Use of Easements

As we have seen, the owner of a servient tenement that is burdened by an easement has given up a portion of the right to quiet enjoyment of the property. The owner of the servient tenement must permit others to come onto his or her property in accordance with the terms of the easement. As circumstances and land use patterns change over the years, servient tenement owners may discover that the burden of the easement across their land is more than they bargained for.

A shopping center developer built a shopping mall on two parcels of land. One parcel fronted on Oracle Road. The other parcel, known as the Foster parcel, was east of the Oracle Road parcel, and was accessible only by an easement over the Tucson Mall Ring Road. The easement had been granted to the defendant developer by the plaintiff. When Neffson learned that plans for the new shopping mall permitted access from the Foster parcel to the Oracle Road parcel, the plaintiff sued to enjoin such use. The trial court granted summary judgment to the plaintiff and entered an injunction prohibiting use of the easement until such time as the mall was altered to prevent use of the easement by shoppers utilizing that portion of the mall not situated on the dominant estate.

The summary judgment was affirmed on appeal. The court observed that "[i]t is elementary law that an easement cannot be extended by the owner of the dominant tenement to other land owned by him adjacent to or beyond the land to which it is appurtenant, for such an extension would constitute an unreasonable increase of the burden of the servient tenement." DND Neffson Company v. Galleria Partners 745 P.2d 206 (AZ, 1987)

Suppose that S sells a landlocked parcel of 120 acres, currently being used for agricultural purposes. S, being an honorable person, also conveys an easement of way across his property allowing the purchaser of the farmland to cross the land adjacent to the county road with the farm equipment necessary to plant and harvest crops on the 120-acre parcel. Both parties expect that the traffic across the easement will consist of an occasional tractor during planting and harvest season and perhaps a few trucks during the fall months.

Now suppose that the farmer resells the land a few years later to a real estate developer. The developer proceeds to build streets, curbs, and gutters on the landlocked 120-acre parcel and then builds and sells five hundred new homes. In the process, the developer also lays down asphalt paving on the easement of way S granted to the developer's predecessor in title and names the new street Orchard Lane. Since Orchard Lane is still the only way for people to gain access to the new subdivision, the burden imposed on S will increase significantly.

S originally agreed to allow an occasional tractor and a few grain trucks to pass over his land within the boundaries of the easement of way. After the subdivision is built and the houses are all sold, S will discover that perhaps a thousand cars a day are passing over the easement. Does S have any right to complain about this dramatic change in circumstances? Fortunately, the answer to that question is yes.

The law is very clear that the owner of an easement may not increase the burden imposed on the servient tenement beyond the amount and kind of use that the original parties to the easement agreed upon. Courts are quick to hold that an increase in the amount of traffic over an easement or a change in the kind of traffic over an easement is unlawful. The usual remedy provided by courts is an injunction, prohibiting the owner of the easement from using the easement in ways that are not consistent with the original terms of the easement.

Termination of Easement Rights

State v. McNutt

As the preceding section suggests, the existence of easement rights to use a portion of another's property without permission may pose real hazards to subsequent purchasers of a servient tenement. It seems reasonable to ask whether the owner of a servient tenement can ever escape the burden imposed by easement rights in the property.

The law of real property recognizes two methods for extinguishing the burden of easement rights against the owner of a servient tenement. One method is the operation of Marketable Title Acts. Marketable title statutes have been adopted in virtually all of the states. These statutes will be examined in more detail in Chapter 10. The other circumstance that will terminate the rights of an easement owner is the abandonment of the easement.

We have already seen that changing land use patterns will change the needs and desires of landowners. As cities expand, new roads are built, new streets are created, new water and sewer lines are extended, and so on. Property that was a landlocked agricultural field in 1932 might very well become the center of a large commercial district sixty years later.

Even within the confines of an existing city, the continuous sale and purchase of real property can be expected to result in changes to the boundaries of property belonging to a single owner. For example, A might purchase a landlocked parcel in an industrial park, reserving an easement of way across the land of the seller. Three years later, A purchases an adjoining parcel that fronts on another street in the industrial park. Since the expanded parcel owned by A is no longer landlocked, it would not be surprising to discover that A no longer uses the easement of way over the neighboring property. It would be tempting to say that A has abandoned the easement under these circumstances and conclude that the easement rights against the owner of the servient tenement should be extinguished. However, courts have been extremely cautious in reaching that conclusion.

All state courts require more than simple non-use of an easement in order to conclude that the property rights of the easement owner have been abandoned. Most state courts will insist that the owner of an easement has not abandoned his or her rights to use of the servient tenement unless the owner has behaved in a way that clearly indicates an intent to abandon those rights. For example, if the easement owner builds a structure on the dominant tenement that would make it impossible to use the easement rights in the servient tenement, the majority of states would agree that the easement has been abandoned.

Lague, Inc. v. Royea

A minority of states apply the doctrine of **promissory estoppel** in determining whether or not an easement has been abandoned. Under this doctrine, the owner of the servient tenement is required to change his or her position in reliance upon the statements or actions of the easement owner. For example, assume that E owns an easement of way across the land of the nextdoor neighbor H. Years ago, E built a new driveway on the other side of the property and has not used the easement since then. One fine spring day, H says to E, "I am thinking about building a new garage for our house that will block your easement across our property. Is that all right with you?"

Promissory Estoppel An obligation which arises when a promise is made which the promisor should reasonably expect to induce action or forbearance of a definite and substantial character on the part of a promisee, and which does induce such action or forbearance. The obligation is binding if injustice can be avoided only by its enforcement

If E replies by saying, "Sure, I never use the easement anymore," then the easement will become abandoned as soon as H begins construction on the garage. Note that under the estoppel doctrine, two events are required for abandonment of an easement. The first event is justifiable reliance by the servient tenement owner on the words or actions of the easement holder. The second event is a change in the position of the servient tenement owner as a result of the reliance. In our example this second event does not occur until H spends time or money on the construction of the garage.

OTHER NONPOSSESSORY INTERESTS

Covenants running with the land, profits, and licenses are the remaining nonpossessory interests that can be created in land. Any agreement that "touches or concerns" the land of two or more owners who are not cotenants will usually be deemed a covenant running with the land. Subdivision covenants are the most frequent example. Almost all residential subdivisions are subject to a set of covenants that were created when the land in the development was first laid out into building lots. The covenants usually place restrictions on the kind of buildings that can be erected on the lots and often prohibit commercial activities of any kind within the subdivision.

Mustang Fuel corporation obtained easements to install and operate a natural gas pipeline from numerous property owners. At the time the easements were created, an Oklahoma statue provided that "whenever any gas pipeline crosses the land or premises of any one outside of a municipality, said corporation shall, by request of the owner of said premises, connect said premises with a pipeline and furnish gas to said consumer at the same rate as charged in the nearest city or town." Most of the landowners who conveyed an easement for the pipeline to Mustang fuels relied upon this statute to request connection with the pipeline on their property. Nine of the land owners demanded that the easement grant include an express provision requiring Mustang to sell them natural gas at the same rate as charged in the nearest city or town.

The statute was declared unconstitutional in 1978. Shortly after that decision, Mustang notified most of its customers that their contract to purchase natural gas would be terminated. The land owners sued to enjoin the threatened termination. The trial court determined that the plaintiffs fell into two groups: the larger group who had not expressly reserved the right to purchase gas in the original right of way easement grant, and the small group who made such an express reservation. Only the nine land owners with express reservations in their easements were awarded permanent injunctive relief.

On appeal, the Supreme Court of Oklahoma affirmed the trial courts judgment. The express reservations of the right to purchase gas were held to be covenants running with the land. "A covenant running with the land is one relating to the land, or as more commonly said one which touches and concerns the land itself, so that its benefit or obligation passes with the ownership [of the land]." Since the covenants to supply natural gas created benefits and obligations to both parties arising out of the use of the land for a natural gas pipeline, the covenants were held to run with the land. Richardson v. Mustang Fuel Corporation 772 P.2d 1324 (OK, 1989)

Runyon v. Paley

Like any real property interest, subdivision covenants (in fact, any covenant that touches or concerns the land) are binding and enforceable against the parties who originally agreed to the covenants and against all of their successors in title. As the years roll by, covenants can become increasingly onerous burdens on the ownership of real property. When owners who are many years removed from the parties who originally agreed to restrictive covenants in a deed seek relief from those covenants, courts are generally sympathetic.

When one or more of the covenants in an old deed have been violated and no one has objected to the violation, courts are likely to find that the covenants are no longer enforceable. For example, assume that all of the houses in a particular subdivision were acquired by deeds that restrict the use of the property of single-family residential homes. Furthermore, the restrictions prohibit the construction of any fences more than four feet tall, prohibit the conduct of any business on any lot within the subdivision, and require that all houses be set back at least twenty-five feet from the boundaries of the lot.

Fifteen years after the subdivision was established, one of the residents built a six-foot fence around the backyard in order to contain a very agile German shepherd with the habit of jumping over fences less than six feet tall. No one in the subdivision objected to the fence, because all of the neighbors were glad to have the dog at last contained within its own yard.

Twenty years after the subdivision was built, another neighbor opened a beauty parlor in the garage of his home. The neighbors did object to this violation of the subdivision covenant and went to court asking for an injunction against the beauty parlor owner that would prevent him from operating the business in his home. Much to the surprise of the plaintiffs, the beauty parlor operator pointed to the six-foot fence down the street and claimed that since the covenant prohibiting fences more than four feet tall had been violated, all of the subdivision covenants were now unenforceable. Much to the chagrin of the plaintiffs, the trial judge agreed with the owner of the beauty parlor and held that by not enforcing the covenant prohibiting tall fences, the neighbors had waived their rights to enforce any of the subdivision covenants.

KEY POINTS

Subdivision covenants are used in many areas as a substitute for zoning ordinances. Covenants restricting the use of land within the boundaries of a subdivision to single family residential homes can be just as effective as a zoning ordinance that accomplishes the same purpose. The major drawback to such "private zoning" schemes is their lack of flexibility. As cities grow and evolve, land use patterns constantly change. Public zoning statutes can be amended to reflect those changes as they occur. However, subdivision covenants may become null and void whenever changes to the covenants are attempted.

A profit is the right to come on the land of another and remove sand, gravel, timber, or crops. In the modern view, profits are treated as equivalent to an easement. Like any easement, a profit may be either appurtenant or in gross.

Finally, a license is simply the permission granted by the owner of a parcel allowing another to come upon the land for a particular purpose. Generally, such permission is revocable at the will of the owner. Further, the permission is valid only for the person who receives the license from the owner. As such, a license cannot be sold to any other person. A ticket to a concert provides the holder with a license to enter the premises where the concert is being held. If the ticket holder attempts to sell the ticket to another person, the purchaser is technically not entitled to enter. However, since all tickets look alike, in practice the license is extended to all people who present the correct piece of cardboard at the door.

CONCLUSION

In this chapter, we have examined the limitations imposed on the rights of fee simple owners. These limitations include duties imposed on land owners by operation of law, and duties which land owners may choose to voluntarily assume.

A nuisance is any use of one's own property which injuries the property of another. Public nuisances include violation of applicable zoning and health regulations. Private nuisances include all actions which damage property of another (physical injuries) or diminish the right to the use and quiet enjoyment of someone else's property (legal injuries).

Easements, covenants, profits and licenses are all examples of voluntary arrangements in which the owner of real property agrees to permit others to make limited use of a portion of the property. The right to use the property of another is itself a real property interest.

DISCUSSION QUESTIONS:

1. Describe the doctrine of nuisance and list the two types of nuisance. What items define public nuisance?
2. Two questions arise when a landowner uses a parcel in a manner that violates the nuisance laws. What are they? Define abatement.
3. Give some examples of parties who may have the power to begin abatement proceedings.
4. What is a private nuisance? There are two issues inherent in the discussion of private nuisances; name them.
5. The injuries created by a private nuisance can be either physical or legal. What does each of these entail? Describe the remedies courts may apply to each of these situations.
6. State two ways in which a party violating the nuisance doctrine may escape liability.
7. Define trespasser, licensee, invitee, and business invitee. Give examples of each.
8. What duty of care does a landowner owe each of the parties named in Question 7?
9. Children are a special category of "persons on the land." What doctrine applies to them and what does it hold?
10. Define the terms positive and negative easement, giving an example of each. Also define dominant tenant, servient tenant, and easement in gross.
11. Name and describe the three ways in which an easement can be created.
12. Other than easements, what are the remaining nonpossessory interests in land? Define each of them.

SHINGLETON
V.
NORTH CAROLINA WILDLIFE RESOURCES COMMISSION

133 S.E.2d 183 (NC, 1963)

Easements appurtenant and in gross

MOORE, Justice.

The State of North Carolina owns a large body of land in Pender County, known as the Holly Shelter Wildlife Area. It is managed by the North Carolina Wildlife Resources Commission. No public roads or highways adjoin or cross any portion of the Wildlife Area involved in this action. The roads within the area are owned by defendants and used in connection with wildlife management.

There was a dispute between defendants and plaintiff Shingleton with respect to the ownership and location of certain lands within the boundaries of the Area. A suit was instituted, but before trial a compromise settlement was reached. Pursuant to the compromise agreement, plaintiff herein conveyed to the State a portion of the land in dispute and the State deeded to Shingleton a portion. After these deeds were executed and delivered, a consent judgment was entered reciting generally the execution and delivery of the deeds, the payment of a sum of money by the State, and the satisfactory settlement of the matters in controversy, and the action was dismissed.

The said conveyance by the State to plaintiff herein was by quitclaim deed. It conveyed to J. A. Shingleton and 'his heirs and assigns' 110 acres situate in Topsail Township, Pender County. This land is described by metes and bounds, and lies entirely within, and a considerable distance from, the boundaries of the Wildlife Area. Immediately below the description are the following easement provisions:

"The party of the first part reserves from this conveyance the right to maintain and use the roads existing on the above described lands; and the said J. A. Shingleton is hereby granted the right to use the roads existing on other lands of the Wildlife Resources Commission for the purpose of ingress and egress to and from the above described lands by the most direct route." The present controversy "arose when the plaintiff's (J. A. Shingleton's) brother and other kinsmen were attempting to go over (the) road in question which leads from the public road through the Wildlife Refuge of the defendants by the most direct route to the plaintiff's land and * * * defendants placed a locked gate at the entrance to the road in question and mounted armed guards to keep out all persons except plaintiff."

Plaintiff contends the right-of-way granted him by the State is an easement appurtenant. Defendants contend it is an easement in gross and may be used and enjoyed only by J. A. Shingleton personally. J. A. Shingleton instituted the present action to have determined his rights under the grant of easement, and makes allegations which, he contends, entitles him to injunctive relief.

Trial by jury was waived and the judge made findings of fact and conclusions of law and entered judgment. It was adjudged that the easement granted by the State of the plaintiff "is an unlimited easement appurtenant to plaintiff's land, given to plaintiff for his use and the use of his agents, servants, employees, licensees, and the public generally who have not been refused permission to use the easement by the plaintiff," and "that the defendants, their agents, servants and employees * * * are enjoined from interfering by gate or otherwise with the use of said easement or road as herein provided."

An appurtenant easement is one which is attached to and passes with the dominant tenement as an appurtenance thereof; it is owned in connection with other real estate and as an incident to such ownership. An easement in gross is not appurtenant to any estate in land or not belonging to any person by virtue of his ownership of an estate in other land, but is a mere personal interest in or right to use the land of another; it is purely personal and usually ends with the death of the grantee. . . . If an easement is in gross there is no dominant tenement; an easement is in gross and personal to the grantee because it is not appurtenant to other premises. *ibid.*, pp. 626–7. An easement in gross attaches to the person and not to land. 89 A.L.R. 1189.

. . . Whether an easement is appurtenant or in gross is controlled mainly by the nature of the right and the intention of the parties creating it, and must be determined by the fair interpretation of the grant * * * creating the easement, aided if necessary by the situation of the property and the surrounding circumstances. * * * In case of doubt, an easement is presumed to be appurtenant and not in gross. 17A Am.Jur., Easements, § 12, p. 628.

Defendants contend that the easement of ingress and egress granted by them is in gross and personal to J. A. Shingleton. The grant does not use the term "appurtenant" nor the term "in gross." It does not qualify plaintiff's right by use of such terms as "personally" or "in personal." The language of the grant is that 'the said J. A. Shingleton is hereby granted the right * * * "The fact that the words "heirs and assigns" are not inserted after the name of the grantee does not control interpretation. G.S.§ 39-1; 28 C.J.S. Easements § 4c, p. 637.

* * *

It seems clear that the reservation of easement is appurtenant to the lands retained by the State. In the absence of express provision in the grant restricting the easement to the personal use of plaintiff, the presumption is that it is an easement appurtenant to plaintiff's 110-acre tract. Moreover, the situation of the property and the surrounding circumstances indicates beyond question that an easement appurtenant was intended. The original controversy, in the settlement of which the deed was given, arose from conflicting claims of rights and title to lands. The record does not disclose that plaintiff has ever claimed any personal rights, apart from land ownership, in the Wildlife Area. The deed conveys to plaintiff a tract of land which, without some adequate access over defendants' lands, would be completely cut off from any public or private road. The grant of easement was so clearly connected with the conveyance of the 110-acre tract that in the deed it follows immediately the description of the land. The words "ingress" and "egress" as used in the grant of easement show clearly it was intended that the easement is connected with and is to be used for the benefit of the land.

The road in question is appurtenant to the land in fact, and leads from the land across the Wildlife Area to the public road beyond. Apart from the ownership of the 110-acre tract, the easement is worthless. If plaintiff did not own this land he would have no business or interest of any kind within the Wildlife Area. The land was conveyed to plaintiff in fee. It is not reasonable to conclude that the State would undertake to grant and plaintiff to accept a right of access to the land which would end at the death of plaintiff and render the land thereafter inaccessible and worthless. Furthermore, it is not reasonable to suppose that plaintiff could, acting alone, cut and remove timber from his land or cultivate, harvest and remove crops, or make other beneficial use of the land. Certainly the parties did not intend that plaintiff's heirs, devisees or assigns should have no access to the property. We hold that the easement granted by the State to plaintiff is appurtenant to plaintiff's land described in the deed.

* * *

The judgment below will be modified in accordance with this opinion.

Modified and affirmed.

Case Reflections

1. Why did the State of North Carolina decide to interpret the easement as a personal property interest of J. A. Shingleton?

WAGNER V. FAIRLAMB

379 P.2d 165 (CO, 1963).

Easement by necessity

SUTTON, Justice.

Defendants in error, who were plaintiffs in the trial court will be referred to as plaintiffs in this opinion. They alleged that they have a right-of-way for a recently constructed road to the south half of the Bradley claim across mining property owned by defendant. The issues were made by an amended complaint and the answer thereto. Trial was had to the court with an advisory jury, with the result that plaintiffs obtained judgment for the right-of-way claimed plus damages of $150.00. The judgment entered was based upon the existence of an implied easement, stemming from a common grantor, one A. E. Reynolds, who in 1919 had conveyed the north half of the Bradley claim to defendant's predecessor in title.

Plaintiffs' pleadings alleged several reasons why they were entitled to the claimed easement of right-of-way. The trial court narrowed the issues to those of whether a right-of-way had arisen by (1) implication or (2) by prescriptive use. The advisory jury found in the affirmative on both issues, but in its findings of fact the court concluded there was insufficient evidence to support the special verdict on adverse possession. It adopted, however, the jury's verdict as to a right-of-way by "implication" (meaning thereby one by preexisting use).

* * *

The several assigned grounds for reversal lead us to conclude that the entire dispute can be resolved by answering the following two questions:

1. Does the evidence prove all the elements necessary to establish either an implied easement by way of pre-existing use or a way of necessity?
2. The trial court having decreed that the defense of laches for failure to assert an alleged way of necessity for many years was not applicable because of generally poor economic conditions in the mining industry in the area in question, of which the court took judicial notice, did it thereby commit error?

The law has long recognized the interest in land known as an "easement" and that it can take several forms. One is the actual or express easement that appears in a deed or contract for the sale of land. This form is easy to recognize and usually not difficult to apply if fully described. A second type is the implied easement, which creates problems for both litigants and the courts. It is one not expressed by the parties in writing, but which arises out of the existence of certain facts implied from the transaction. Generally implied easements have not been looked upon with favor by the courts. Under some circumstances and facts, however, they are recognized. See 1 Thompson, Real Property, §§ 390 and 394 (prem. ed. 1939).

Implied easements have been subdivided into those which are implied due to a grant and those implied from a reservation. The former moves in favor of the grantee and the latter in favor of the grantor. Some courts have treated such easements differently. *See* 3 Tiffany, Real Property, § 791 (3rd ed.).

In 1 Thompson *supra,* § 396, at page 647, the necessary elements to prove an implied easement are set forth as:

> "(1) Unity and subsequent separation of title; (2) obvious benefit to the dominant and burden to the servient tenement existing at the time of the conveyance; (3) use of the premises by the common owner in their altered condition long enough before the conveyance to show that the change was intended to be permanent; and (4) necessity for the easement."

It seems well to point out here that Thompson's four detailed requirements apply essentially to an implied easement by pre-existing use, for his third ground is not necessary for the existence of an implied easement by way of necessity as will more fully hereinafter appear. In any event an examination of this record reveals that the evidence does not support the trial court's finding of an implied easement by way of pre-existing use since at best a terminated intermittent rather than a permanent use was shown. However, if the record discloses that that court arrived at the correct result for the wrong reason we will not set aside its judgment. Scott v. Bohe, 81 Colo. 454, 256 P. 315 (1927). Thus, we need to consider further the facts and the law applicable to this case.

* * *

We must next consider whether this record discloses the applicability of the doctrine of implied easement by way of necessity. This rule has recently been recognized in Colorado in Martino v. Fleenor, 148 Colo. 136, 365 P.2d 247 (1961), and is controlling in this case if the facts warrant its application as we conclude they do.

An implied way of necessity arises when the owner of a parcel of land conveys and grants part thereof to another, which leaves the remainder of the land without ingress or egress, except over the part conveyed. In such case reservation of a way of necessity is implied. The most common application of the doctrine occurs, however, when it is implied with the grant, i.e., where the lands conveyed are without ingress or egress except over lands retained. In such a case the lands retained are held to be subject to an easement in favor of the grantee. *See* 17A Am.Jur. Easements, § 58.

It appears from the foregoing authorities that generally there are three requirements to be met before a way of necessity can be said to exist: The first requires that the original ownership of the entire tract be held by a single grantor prior to a division thereof. As previously noted, all of the Bradley claim originally was owned by A. E. Reynolds who conveyed away the north one-half thereof. The second requires that the necessity existed at the time of the severance. The evidence here indicates that in 1919, as at the present time, the south half of the Bradley was virtually inaccessible except by the route now in dispute. The third requirement is that the necessity for the particular right-of-way be great. Here the testimony of several residents of the Telluride area, as well as that of an expert witness (all borne out by the photographs in evidence), was to the effect that this is a very mountainous, rocky area with steep canyon walls, where roads at best are hazardous, expensive and dangerous to build. Documents in evidence support plaintiffs' contention that plaintiffs' road as now constructed is under all the circumstances the only practical method of affording ingress and egress for the purpose of mining or otherwise using the south half of the Bradley. And, based upon conflicting evidence and its view of the area during the course of the trial, the trial court found that this road was necessary and that the necessity existed in 1919 as well as today. In this connection we take cognizance of the fact that some authorities have held that a way of necessity cannot exist merely because the land is too steep or too narrow for a reasonable route. *See* 2 Thompson, *supra,* § 534. We hold that the rule as applied to property like this means a practical inability to have access any other way than by a way of necessity. Accord: Crotty v. New River & Pocahontas Consol. Coal Co., 72 W.Va. 68, 78 S.E. 23, 46 L.R.A.,N.S., 156. For this purpose the law assumes that no person intends to render property conveyed inaccessible for the purpose for which it was granted. And, of course the reverse is also true, i.e., that he does not intend to render lands retained inaccessible. The scope and type of the use, present and future, varies with the necessity. *See* 2 Thompson, *supra,* § 550 (perm. ed. 1939).

* * *

We turn now to the alleged error urged by defendant based on the trial court's taking judicial notice of the depressed condition of the mining industry during at least part of the period involved.

In this regard it should be pointed out that laches does not apply to a way of necessity for the law is clear that a way of necessity can remain dormant without affecting the right. 2 Thompson, *supra,* § 533. Thus, we need not determine whether the judicial notice of mining conditions was error for it was immaterial.

The judgment is affirmed.

Case Reflections

1. What are the legal requirements for creation of an easement by necessity?
2. How do these requirements mesh with the court's observation that "the law assumes that no person intends to render property conveyed inaccessible for the purpose for which it was granted"?

BOULDER MEDICAL ARTS, INC.
V.
WALDRON
500 P.2d 170 (CO, 1972)

Easement by prescription

SILVERSTEIN, Chief Judge.

This is an appeal from a decree and judgment in favor of plaintiff, Boulder Medical Arts, Inc., (Medical Arts) in which a public highway—or alley—was declared to exist over the north ten feet of land owned by defendants, Mr. and Mrs. Waldron (Waldrons), in Boulder, Colorado. The decree also permanently enjoined interference with the use of the alley by the public.

The easement was asserted to exist under the following provisions of C.R.S.1963, 120—1—1: "The following are hereby declared to be public highways: (3) All roads over private lands that have been used adversely without interruption or objection on the part of the owners of such lands for twenty consecutive years."

In this appeal the Waldrons assert that the judgment should be reversed because the use was not shown to be adverse, but was, in fact, permissive. We do not agree, and affirm the judgment.

The evidence disclosed that the alley runs in an east-west course along the north edge of the Waldrons' land, extending west to 10th Street, which street is approximately 200 feet west of the west boundary of Waldrons' land. The Waldrons acquired title in 1946. Medical Arts owns the property to the north of that owned by the Waldrons. According to the evidence, their lands are separated by a strip of land ten feet wide which, apparently because of a surveying error, was not included in the land owned by either of the parties.

It is undisputed that, for several years prior to 1946 and at all times subsequent thereto, the area which included this ten foot strip and the north ten feet of the Waldrons' land, and that of their neighbors, was used by members of the public for foot and vehicular traffic without interruption or objection. Further, it is undisputed that the line of the alleyway has been certain and definite from before 1946 to the present. In 1954 the Waldrons built a fence along the south line of the ten foot strip. Mr. Waldron testified that this was done in order to conform with the fences of his neighbors between 10th Street and his land.

The only issue here is whether the use was adverse or permissive. In Shively v. Board of County Commissioners, 159 Colo. 353, 411 P.2d 782, the Supreme Court stated, "When testing the sufficiency of the evidence to support a finding of title by prescription the party asserting the same is aided by a presumption that the character of the use of adverse where such use is shown to have been made for a prescribed period of time. (Citing cases.) The rule is no different with the respect to presumptive rights gained by the public under the statute herein cited. (C.R.S.1963, 120—1—1(3))."

The presumption is, of course, rebuttable, and when the presumption arose from the facts established in the instant case, it became incumbent on the Waldrons to overcome the presumption. Martino v. Fleenor, 148 Colo. 136, 365 P.2d 247.

This the Waldrons failed to do. They rely primarily on the fact that no one affirmatively asserted to them a claim of right to use the alleyway. However, there is no testimony that anyone who used the roadway sought, obtained, or was given consent to use it.

The failure to interrupt or object to the public use of the alleyway for over twenty years cannot, without more, be equated to permissive use. Were this the case, the statute would be rendered meaningless since it requires that the use be both adverse and without objection.

The Waldrons rely on Starr v. People, 17 Colo. 458, 30 P. 64, which set forth certain criteria to establish a public highway by prescription. Among these were acts by the owner which evidenced an intent to set apart the land for public use as a road, or such conduct on his part as would estop him from denying such intention. Here the Waldrons built a fence along the south boundary of the asserted right of way thus setting apart the alleyway from the rest of their land in conformance with the existing line of fences set up by their neighbors.

The finding of the trial court was supported by the evidence. Under such circumstances, all presumptions are in favor of the trial court's findings, and the record should be reviewed in the light most favorable to the successful party. Allen v. First National Bank, 120 Colo. 275, 208 P.2d 935.

DWYER and PIERCE, JJ. concur.

Case Reflections

1. What are the legal requirements for creation of an easement by prescription?
2. How do these requirements differ from the circumstances leading to an easement by necessity?

LAGUE, INC.
V.
ROYEA

568 A.2d 357 (Vt., 1989)

Abandonment of easements

MAHADY, Justice.

Defendants constructed a truck stop on their parcel of land in the Town of Berlin. Plaintiff owned two deeded and recorded rights of way through the parcel. One right of way, sixty feet wide, passed through the center of defendants' property from the street to the back boundary line. The second, thirty feet wide, passed through the front of the property. Both rights of way were depicted in maps on file in the land records. Defendants' construction encroached upon plaintiff's rights of way.

The trial court concluded that plaintiff had abandoned the rights of way and entered judgment in favor of defendants. We reverse and remand for a new trial.

I.

The trial court made no finding that defendants relied upon the claimed abandonment of the rights of way. During construction defendants placed fuel pumps within the thirty-foot right of way. Their restaurant extends twenty feet into the sixty-foot right of way, and a garage extends ten to fifteen feet into the same right of way. The testimony of defendants at trial strongly indicated that they took such action in reliance upon their surveyor's erroneous opinion that the rights of way had been extinguished, not in reliance upon a belief that the easements had been abandoned by plaintiff. The first issue is therefore squarely presented: May an easement be extinguished by abandonment absent reliance by the owner of the servient tenement upon acts of abandonment on the part of the owner of the easement?

The clear weight of authority does not require such reliance although a minority of jurisdictions hold "that an indication of intention to abandon the easement is not effective to extinguish the easement unless the owner of the servient tenement is induced thereby to make expenditures or otherwise to alter his position, thus in effect making the question of abandonment a question of estoppel." 3 H. Tiffany, The Law of Real Property s 825, at 388 (3d ed. 1939). The Restatement adopts the majority view. Restatement of Property § 505 (1944).

Vermont has long recognized the principle of abandonment. Rogers v. Stewart, 5 Vt. 215, 216–17 (1833). We have been clear that an easement acquired by deed cannot be extinguished by nonuse alone, no matter how long it continues. However, our precedents as to the requirement of reliance are confusing and inconsistent. Initially, we clearly adopted the minority view and held that an abandonment must "originate in, or be accompanied by, some unequivocal acts of the owner, inconsistent with the continued existence of the easement, and showing an intention on his part to abandon it; and the owner of the servient estate must have relied or acted upon such manifest intention to abandon the right so that it would work harm to him if the easement was thereafter asserted." [Citations omitted.]

The seeds of future confusion were sown in Nelson v. Bacon, 113 Vt. 161, 32 A.2d 140 (1943).

In that case we set forth the rule that "to establish an abandonment there must be, in addition to nonuser, acts by the owner of the dominant tenement conclusively and unequivocally manifesting either a present intent to relinquish the easement or a purpose inconsistent with its future existence," but [the opinion in that case] did not refer to reliance. *Id.* at 172, 32 A.2d at 146.

* * *

Therefore, from 1956 to 1966, it appeared that we had embraced the majority rule. In 1968, however, there was an explicit return to the minority position. Quoting Mason, we emphasized the requirement of reliance and reaffirmed the holding of Sabins. Massucco v. Vermont College Corp., 127 Vt. 254, 258, 247 A.2d 63, 65–66 (1968). Scott and Sargent were distinguished. *Id.*

Since that time, relying on Massucco, we have continued to apply the minority rule with its requirement of reliance. Timney v. Worden, 138 Vt. 444, 446, 417 A.2d 923, 925 (1980); Russell v. Pare, 132 Vt. 397, 406, 321 A.2d 77, 83 (1974).

This rule clearly merges the doctrine of abandonment with that of estoppel. Tiffany at s 825. Even without a requirement of reliance, the difficulty of proving intent to abandon an easement is such that its application is often impractical. *Id.* Indeed, the very impracticality of the doctrine has stirred some criticism. *See,* e.g., Note, 11 Columm.L.Rev. 777, 778 (1911). It therefore appears that the majority rule, adopted by the Restatement, is the wiser one.

Accordingly, we hold that reliance by the owner of the servient estate is not required to establish an abandonment of an easement. In doing so, we reaffirm our previous statements of the rule in Nelson, Scott, Sargent and Welch. Insofar as they are inconsistent with our holding today, Mason, Sabins, Massucco, Russell and Timney are expressly overruled.

It follows that the trial court's application of the rule as set forth in Sargent was correct. The absence of reliance was not fatal to the finding of an abandonment of the easement.

II.

Although "[w]e realize that the question whether there has been an abandonment . . . is one of fact," Sabins v. McAllister, 116 Vt. at 308, 76 A.2d at 110, a trial court is nonetheless required to make findings and conclusions, helpful for appellate review, which indicate to the parties and to this Court not only what was decided but how the decision was reached as well. Harman v. Rogers, 147 Vt. 11, 19, 510 A.2d 161, 166 (1986). The record below fails to do this.

The burden on the party claiming an abandonment of an easement is a heavy one: Such an abandonment may be established only by "acts by the owner of the dominant tenement conclusively and unequivocally manifesting either a present intent to relinquish the easement or a purpose inconsistent with its future existence." Nelson v. Bacon, 113 Vt. at 172, 32 A.2d at 146. On this record it is not clear whether the trial court applied this " conclusive and unequivocal" standard. Therefore, a new trial is required.

Reversed and remanded.

Case Reflections

1. What kinds of kinds of evidence should the defendants offer at the new trial which might show some " unequivocal acts of the owner" of the easement that constitute abandonment of the easement?
2. Why is non-use alone insufficient to constitute the abandonment of an easement?
3. Explain the difference between the minority rule that the owner of the servient tenement must rely on the acts of the easement owner, and the majority rule which does not require such reliance.

STATE EX REL. FISHER V. McNUTT

597 N.E.2d 539 (OH, 1992)

Increasing the burden of an easement

GWIN, Judge.

Defendants-appellants, Donald and Patty McNutt ("appellants"), appeal from the judgment entered in the Muskingum County Court of Common Pleas permanently enjoining appellants from interfering with the use of an easement located on their property and owned by plaintiff-appellee, state of Ohio, Department of Natural Resources ("state").

Facts

In 1958, the state acquired a right-of-way easement by deed from the United States of America. The original grant of this easement was made in 1887 by Stuart (Stewart) Fauber, appellant's predecessor in title, to his neighbor Ella (Ellie) Harmer, the state's predecessor in title. The original grant provided:

"Stuart °ΔFauber
To
Ella Harmer

Know all men by these presents, that we Steward Fauber and Chestina Fauber husband and wife of the County of Muskingum and State of Ohio in consideration of the sum of one dollar and other considerations to us paid by Ellie Harmer of said County and State the receipt whereof is hereby acknowledged do hereby grant to said Ella Harmer her heirs and assigns a right of way across the west half of the North East quarter of section thirty three township thirteen range twelve in Salt Creek Township, Muskingum, Ohio. Said right of way is described as follows. Being fifteen feet wide and beginning on the east line of the land of said Fauber, where the private road crosses said land, thence along said South line to the point where the lands of Harmer, Evans, Clapper, and Fauber join. Said right of way is for road purposes only.

At the time of the original grant of the easement, Fauber owned the fee simple title to approximately eighty acres of property located northeast of Harmer's 77.7 acres of fee simple property. The easement was duly recorded and followed an unbroken chain of title.

In 1958, the state acquired Harmer's original 77.7 acres and an additional 4,764.60 acres of adjacent property from the United States government. In 1967, appellants acquired Fauber's original property, including that portion of the property servient to the right-of-way easement. Subsequent disputes concerning the location and extent of the state's easement on appellants' property caused the state to file an action seeking injunctive relief against appellants. The dispute concerning the location of the easement was resolved between the parties and is not at issue here. However, the dispute concerning the scope and extent of the easement remains. The state, through the Ohio Department of Natural Resources, Division of Forestry, intends to use its easement, for road purposes, in managing the forest located not only on Harmer's original 77.7 acres, but the entire 4,842.30 acres of land known as Blue Rock State Forest. The forest management includes, but is not limited to: boundary maintenance; inspection, measurement and inventory of trees; timber stand improvement; timber harvest; enforcement of forest laws by forest officers; protection of forest from fires; prevention, detection and suppression of forest insects and disease; scouting and correcting forest tree seeds; recreation management, inspection, development, maintenance of forest facilities and trails; mineral management by authorized agencies; examination for scientific research into endangered or threatened plant or wild life, hydrology concerns, unique geographical features; and any other activity necessary for prudent forest management.

The state claims its use of the easement is not limited to Harmer's original 77.7 acres because the original grant of the easement was silent as to whether the easement was for the sole benefit of Harmer's property, and did not specifically reference Harmer's fee simple title of 77.7 acres of property. This ambiguity, the state asserts, allows the court to consider the surrounding circumstances at the time of the grant so to give effect to the parties' intentions regarding the extent of the easement. Upon construing the surrounding circumstances and the ambiguous language contained in the grant most strongly in favor of the state (the grantee of the easement), as the law requires, the state claims it may use its easement to conduct its forest management on the entire 4,842.30 acres and such does not constitute an unreasonable increase in burden to appellant's servient property. It is appellants' position that the state can use its easement of right of way for ingress and egress across appellants' property, but such use should be limited to the 77.7 acres. Appellants claim the original grant of the easement unambiguously limited the grantee's use of the easement to the 77.7 acres owned by Harmer at the time the easement was granted.

The trial court, after "having reviewed the pleadings, memoranda of law, arguments of counsel, the evidence and exhibits filed by the parties," entered judgment, findings of fact and conclusions of law consistent with the state's position. Appellants timely appealed.

* * *

[A]ppellants claim the trial court's judgment permitting the state to use the easement to gain access to thousands of acres of land adjacent to the original 77.7 acres was contrary to law, an abuse of discretion, and against the manifest weight of the evidence. The parties agree that the original grant between Fauber and Harmer created an easement appurtenant. As such, appellants' property, whereon the easement exists, is the servient tenement, the land upon which the obligation rests, and the state's 77.7 acres is the dominant tenement, the estate in land to which the right of the easement belongs. The dispute in this case centers upon whether the state may use its easement located on appellants' property to provide forest management not only for the 77.7 acres owned by the original grantor of the easement, but also for the additional 4,764.60 acres of adjacent property.

The general rule of law regarding the use of easements appurtenant was set forth in Berardi v. Ohio Turnpike Comm. (1965), 1 Ohio App.2d 365, 372–373, 30 O.O.2d 385, 389–390, 205 N.E.2d 23, 28–29:

> 'An easement can be used only in connection with the estate to which it is appurtenant and cannot be extended by the owner to any other property which he may then own or afterward acquire, unless so provided in the instrument by which the easement is created, and the fact that such property is within the same enclosure as the lot to which the easement is appurtenant makes no difference in the application of the rule. Accordingly, a right of way cannot be used by the owner of the dominant tenement to pass to other land or premises adjacent to or beyond that to which the easement is appurtenant * * *.' In Methodist Protestant Church v. Laws (1893), 4 Ohio C.D. 562, 566, 7 Ohio C.C. 211, 220, affirmed (1896), 55 Ohio St. 662, 48 N.E. 1114, the Hamilton County Court of Common Pleas noted the following law concerning easements appurtenant:
>
> * * *
>
> "No man can impose a new restriction or burden on his neighbor by his own act, and for this reason. 'An owner of an easement cannot, by altering his dominant tenement, increase his right.' Goddard [on Easements], 280."
>
> * * *
>
> "A right of way appurtenant to the dominant tenement can be used only for the purpose of passing to or from their tenement. It cannot be used for any purpose unconnected with the enjoyment of the dominant tenement, neither can it be assigned by him to a stranger, and so be made a right in gross. Nor can he license a stranger to use the way when he is not going to and from the dominant tenement." Goddard, 321.
>
> * * *

In this case, the grant in which the easement was created did not provide that the owner of the dominant tenement could use the right of way across appellants' servient tenement to pass to the state's other land adjacent to or beyond that to which the easement is appurtenant. Accordingly, the law specifically proscribes the state's extended use of the easement in question. However, apparently cognizant of this rule, the trial court found the grant of the easement to be ambiguous because of its silence as to whether the easement was for the sole benefit of the property belonging to the original grantee, i.e., Harmer. We find as a matter of law the original grant of the easement to be unambiguous, and the trial court erred in finding otherwise. Here, the original grant of the easement in 1887 specifically was entitled "Stuart Fauber to Ella Harmer." The first sentence of that grant provided that the Faubers "in consideration of the sum of one dollar and other considerations * * * do hereby grant to said Ella Harmer, her heirs and assigns a right of way across" their property. Contrary to the trial court's finding of silence, we find the grant speaks loudly as to which property was to benefit from the easement.

Assuming arguendo that the original grant of the easement was ambiguous, the evidence before the trial court was overwhelmingly contrary to the court's finding that the state's plan to use the easement to conduct forest management on the entire 4,842.30 acres of land "does not constitute an unreasonable increase in burden." In reaching this finding, the trial court looked to the surrounding circumstances at the time the grant was created for the purpose of giving effect to the intentions of the parties with regard to the extent of the easement. *See* Methodist Protestant Church, *supra.* Under the undisputed facts of this case, the surrounding circumstances at the time the easement was created were as follows: (1) Fauber granted to Harmer a right-of-way easement across Fauber's property to a specific location; and (2) Harmer owned fee simple title to 77.7 acres of property. Reasonable minds looking at this evidence could only conclude that intentions of the original grantee and grantor of the easement were that the right of way would only be used for ingress and egress to Harmer's 77.7 acres. Furthermore, the state's plan to use the right-of-way easement to conduct forest management on the entire 4,842.30 acres of land would enhance the burden on appellants' servient estate by sixty times. This certainly is an unreasonable increase in the burden to the servient estate and could not have been intended by the original grantor and grantee.

For these reasons, we reversed the judgment entered in the Muskingum County Court of Common Pleas, and pursuant to App.R. 12(B), hereby enter judgment for appellants and order the state to restrict its use of the right-of-way easement to only the 77.7 acres of property originally owned by Harmer. We sustain appellant's first, second, third, fourth, sixth, seventh and eighth assignments of error.

For the foregoing reasons, the judgment entered in the Muskingum County Court of Common Pleas is reversed and we hereby enter judgment for appellants and order the state to restrict the use of the aforementioned easement to the 77.7 acres of property originally owned by Harmer.

Judgment reversed.

PUTMAN, P. J., and MILLIGAN, J., concur.

Case Reflections

1. The court observed that "No man can impose a new restriction or burden on his neighbor by his own act, and for this reason an owner of an easement cannot, by altering his dominant tenement, increase his right." Explain why this restriction is an important element of the law of easements.
2. Do you believe the addition of 4,000 acres of wilderness area will really change the burden imposed upon the easement across McNutt's land?

TOWNE V. PORTER TOWNSHIP BOARD

460 N.W.2d 596 (MI, 1990)

Public nuisance doctrines

MCDONALD, Judge.

Defendants Dennis and Sherrie Harr appeal as of right from an October 24, and December 8, 1988, circuit court opinion and order finding plaintiffs, as private property owners, proper parties to institute an action to abate a public nuisance stemming from the Harrs' erection of a pole building in violation of local zoning ordinances and ordering abatement of the same. We reverse.

Although the Harrs raise several issues on appeal, we find one issue dispositive. The Harrs claim private citizens, such as the instant plaintiffs, have no standing to secure an abatement of a nuisance per se under the Township Rural Zoning Act where the citizens cannot prove special damages. We agree. The use of land in violation of local ordinances constitutes a nuisance per se, M.C.L. § 125.294; M.S.A. § 5.2963(24).[1] This statute further provides that the township board enacting the ordinances shall administer and enforce the same and that the court shall order such nuisance abated. Thus, pursuant to the statute, any violation of a local township zoning ordinance constitutes a nuisance per se and is to be ordered abated by the court upon an action being brought by the officials designated to administer and enforce the ordinance.[1]

Given the purpose for which zoning ordinances are enacted and enforced, we believe a nuisance arising from the violation of the same must by its very nature constitute a "public" nuisance. Generally, a public nuisance gives no right of action to an individual and must be abated by the appropriate public officer. However, our Supreme Court has long recognized the propriety of private citizens bringing actions to abate public nuisances, arising from the violation of zoning ordinances or otherwise, when the individuals can show damages of a special character distinct and different from the injury suffered by the public generally. Morse v. Liquor Control Comm., 319 Mich. 52, 29 N.W.2d 316 (1947); Plassey v. S. Loewenstein & Son, 330 Mich. 525, 48 N.W.2d 126 (1951). Enactment of M.C.L. § 125.294; M.S.A. § 5.2963[24], rendering buildings erected in violation of local zoning ordinances nuisances per se, does not vitiate a private individual's long standing right to bring an action to abate a public nuisance. Indian Village Ass'n v. Shreve, 52 Mich.App. 35, 216 N.W.2d 447 (1974). Instead, the statute's designation of all buildings erected in violation of local ordinances as nuisances per se reduces the quantity of proofs required of an individual to prove a public nuisance, as the existence of the nuisance may be established merely by showing a violation of the ordinance. Thus, individuals need not prove a nuisance in fact, as the zoning violation renders the building a nuisance per se. Bruggeman v. Minster, 42 Mich.App. 177, 201 N.W.2d 344 (1972); Indian Village, *supra*. However, contrary to plaintiffs' assertions on appeal, neither Bruggeman nor Indian Village relieves an individual bringing suit to abate a public nuisance from the burden of proving special damages. Any such attempt by this Court to do so would necessarily fail, as an individual's proof of special damages has been a long standing requirement under Michigan's common law, dating back at least as far as 1872. *See* Clark v. Lake St. Clair & New Up-River Ice Co., 24 Mich. 508 (1872), *see also* Morse, *supra*, and Plassey, *supra*.

In the instant case the trial court's findings indicate plaintiffs failed to prove special damages resulting from the Harrs' violation of the zoning ordinance. Plaintiffs therefore had no standing to bring the instant suit to abate the nuisance, and

---

[1] Uses of land, . . . in violation of local ordinances or regulations adopted under the authority of this act are a nuisance per se. The court shall order the nuisance abated and the owner or agent in charge of the dwelling, building, structure, tent, trailer coach, or land is guilty of maintaining a nuisance per se. The township board shall in the ordinance enacted under this act designate the proper official or officials who shall administer and enforce that ordinance and provide penalties for the violation of the ordinance.

the trial court's order granting plaintiffs said relief must be vacated.

Although it is seemingly unjust to deny the plaintiffs standing to seek abatement of the instant nuisance, we note that plaintiffs are not without recourse. However, plaintiffs' recourse must be achieved through their township officials who under the statute are given no discretion but to enforce the local zoning ordinances.

Reversed.

Case Reflections

1. Does it appear that Michigan law allows private citizens to "stand in the shoes" of public officials in enforcing zoning laws under the public nuisance doctrine?
2. Who is required to bring the action which results in enforcement of zoning ordinances in the state of Michigan? Why do you suppose Michigan has adopted this rule?

CARR'S BEACH AMUSEMENT COMPANY, INC. V. ANNAPOLIS ROADS PROPERTY OWNERS ASSOCIATION, INC. ET AL.

160 A.2d 598 (MD, 1960)

Private nuisance

PRESCOTT, Judge.

Carr's Beach Amusement Company, Inc. (Carr's), the defendant-appellant, leases some fifteen acres of water-front property in Anne Arundel County, upon which it operates a public bathing beach and amusement park. As a result of suit being instituted against it by complaining owners of nearby residential properties, it was enjoined from "operating and maintaining their loud-speakers or public address systems at such excessive levels of sound volume as to penetrate the private homes of the individual plaintiffs herein so as to disturb the comfortable enjoyment of their said homes by the said plaintiffs or any of them, and subject to the further order of this Court."

The position taken by the appellant is rather unusual and extraordinary. It concedes that if the plaintiffs are entitled to an injunction, the form and scope of the chancellor's decree are correct. It almost concedes that its conduct of the amusement park has, in a legal sense, constituted a nuisance, stating that it will, "not simply concede but strongly suggests that a public beach and amusement park such as Carr's beach . . . would be, under any circumstances, a matter of some inconvenience and annoyance from the point of view of nearby residents." It admits it is familiar with the rule stated in the case of Meadowbrook Swimming Club, Inc. v. Albert, 173 Md. 641, 197 A. 146 (which will be mentioned later), but goes on to argue that the "plaintiffs came to the alleged nuisance," and, if this be considered with all of the other circumstances of the case, and the principle of balancing conveniences and inconveniences (some law books now refer to this principle in terms of the gravity of the harm weighed against the utility of the activity causing the harm. 1 Harper and James, Law of Torts, § 1.24; Restatement, Torts, Sections 826–828.), had been properly applied, then the court should not have issued its injunctive decree. In other words, its contention is, that even if it has been conducting its business so as to maintain a legal nuisance, this Court should sanction a continuation of that nuisance under the particular circumstances of this case.

That part of appellant's argument which deals with the plaintiff's "coming to the nuisance" may be disposed of summarily. The only complaint against the operation of the defendant's business is the excessive sound volume emanating from the loud-speakers and public address systems. At least two of the plaintiffs (and perhaps more of the predecessors in interest of the plaintiffs) had built and occupied substantial and costly homes before Carr's was established. The predecessor in interest of the plaintiff, Beall, built his home in 1928, and, at that time, though Carr's was in existence, there was testimony that it was conducted in an orderly and quiet manner. Thus, it is seen that, at least, some of the plaintiffs had constructed and occupied their dwellings long before there were any disturbing noises from Carr's, and, therefore, did not "come to the nuisance," so, whatever may have been the legal effect, if any, had they in fact done so, need not be discussed nor considered further.

The only other reasons advanced by the appellant as to why the principle of balancing conveniences and inconveniences should be applied are that it has some $135,000 invested in its enterprise, and the operation of the amusement park is a public benefit, which it insists will be lost if the injunction stands, as it will be forced out of business. We do not deem it necessary to make a lengthy or comprehensive exposition of the above principle; for, obviously, the instant case does not present a proper factual background for its application. Generally where the question is affected by a public interest, if the inconvenience or loss resulting to a complainant from the continuance of a nuisance will be slight as compared with the inconvenience to the public or the loss to the defendant resulting from its abatement, equity will, ordinarily, refuse relief. Huebschmann v. Grand Company, 166 Md. 615, 621, 172 A. 227; 1 Harper and James, *op. cit.*, § 1.24, p. 74; Restatment, Torts, §§ 826–828. *Cf.* Lichtenberg v. Sachs, 213 Md. 147, 131 A.2d 264 and Dundalk Holding Co. v. Easter, 215 Md. 549, 137 A.2d 667, cases that involved encroachments upon properties, not nuisances.

In the case at bar, the nearby property owners, presumably, had an equal, if not greater, investment in their properties than the investment of the defendant: one of the plaintiffs testified that his property had cost him more than $37,000. And the chancellor found that the inconvenience to the plaintiffs was not "slight," but that the loud noises caused "actual physical discomfort to the plaintiffs" and "seriously" interfered with the ordinary comfort and enjoyment of their properties as dwellings (findings that we will later affirm). No element of estoppel is present here. And it is very difficult to conceive how the chancellor's decree is going to "force the appellant out of business." It simply prevents the operation of the loud-speakers and public address systems at excessively high sound levels. With the nearest residence some 1200 feet from where the bands play in the amusement park, there would seem to be little need for the amplification system to be set so high as to annoy seriously persons of ordinary tastes and sensibilities, in order for the public to continue to patronize the place.

The case was, we think, properly decided by the chancellor. It would serve no useful purpose to set forth in detail the evidence presented by the parties. It will suffice to say that the testimony was taken in open court, and the chancellor found "that the sound system on the defendant's premises is operated in such a manner to cause actual physical discomfort to the plaintiffs and to seriously interfere with the ordinary comfort and enjoyment of their properties as dwellings." Upon the record as it is presented to us, we certainly cannot hold that he was clearly in error, which we would be required to do in order to reverse his findings of fact. Rule 886.

This brings the case squarely within the ambit of the leading case of Meadowbrook Swimming Club, Inc. v. Albert, *supra,* 173 Md. 641, A. 146. That case, as the instant one, involved a nuisance to nearby residents caused by loud noises emanating from skilled musicians conducting an orchestra. The Court, 173 Md. at page 645, 197 A. at page 148, stated:

> The rule which must control is whether the nuisance complained of will or does produce such a condition of things as in the judgment of reasonable men is naturally productive of actual physical discomfort to persons of ordinary sensibilities, tastes, and habits, such as in view of the circumstances of the case is unreasonable and in derogation of the rights of the party (citations) subject to the qualification that it is not every inconvenience that will call forth the restraining power of a court. The injury must be of such a character as to diminish materially the value of the property as a dwelling and seriously interfere with the ordinary comfort and enjoyment of it.

* * *

Decree affirmed, with costs.

Case Reflections

1. Was the injury complained of here a physical or a legal injury?
2. The homes of the plaintiffs were apparently built after the amusement park was created, but before the loud speaker system was installed. Will homeowners who purchased their property after the loudspeakers began operating be barred by the "coming to the nuisance" defense? Why or why not?

BEASTON
V.
JAMES JULIAN, INC.

120 A.2d 317 (DE, 1956)

Landowner's duties to children

HERRMANN, Judge.

The question is whether the complaint reflects the breach of a duty by the defendants from which liability for the death of the plaintiffs' decedent may arise.

It is alleged in the complaint that the defendant James Julian, Inc. was engaged in the construction of a sewer which ended in a pit in an open field, the land of the defendant Wilmington Manor, Inc. It is averred that the pit was twelve feet long, five feet wide and five feet deep, that it had no outlet and that it was located about 300 feet from the end of the street on which the child, age four years, resided. It is alleged that while the child was playing around the pit she fell into it and drowned in rain water which had accumulated therein to the depth of five feet.

As a "First Cause of Action," it is alleged that the defendant James Julian, Inc. "knew or should have know that this area was used by the children of the neighborhood as a play area" and that the defendant Wilmington Manor, Inc. "knew or should have known of the use of this area as a play area for the children residing in the neighborhood, and acquiesced in this use." It is further averred that the defendants "knew or should have known that this pit was alluring to children" and that they knew or should have known that "unless adequate safeguards or reasonable caution were taken children coming on the premises, in and about the pit, would be endangered." It is further alleged that the defendants maintained "an attractive nuisance in that they knew or should have known that the open pit was alluring to children and endangered them, but in spite of this, failed to exercise reasonable care" in that they failed to maintain fences or a watchman.

In the "Second Cause of Action" the complaint contains repetition of the allegations that the defendants knew or should have known that the area in which the pit was located was used by children of the neighborhood as a play area and that the owner acquiesced in this use. It is further asserted that the defendants "knew or should have known that neighborhood children were in the habit of playing in the open field, and in spite of this, failed to take any precaution" in that they failed to maintain fences or a watchman.

The defendant [1] contends that this action is founded upon the " attractive nuisance" doctrine and that, since that doctrine has not been adopted in this jurisdiction, the complaint fails to state a claim upon which relief can be granted. *See* Civil Rules 8(a), 9(b), and 12(b) (6), Del.C.Ann.

Although the term "attractive nuisance" appears in the complaint, the classical doctrine of attractive nuisance is not involved in this case because the plaintiffs do not contend that the child was enticed or lured upon the premises by the attraction of the pit. It appears from the complaint that the child entered upon the premises because she was accustomed to play there. It is not contended that the pit presented a condition that would be likely to attract children to come upon

[1] The pending motion is presented by the defendant James Julian, Inc. only. Therefore, reference is to the one defendant.

the premises. Ordinarily, liability is not imposed under the doctrine of attractive nuisance where the attraction is discoverable only after a trespass. It has been said that to come within the doctrine of attractive nuisance, a condition must invite the trespass, not merely invite after the trespass. Under the classical doctrine, in those jurisdictions where it has been adopted, the possessor of land is held bound to anticipate the presence of children upon his premises, and to exercise care for their safety, because the instrumentality or condition is one that would be likely to attract them to come upon the premises. *See* 38 Am.Jur. "Negligence" § 153; *compare* Weinberg v. Hartman, 6 Terry 9, 65 A.2d 805, 809. This is not the situation reflected by the complaint in the instant case.

I am not required, therefore, to pass upon the important question of whether the attractive nuisance doctrine, as introduced in this country by Sioux City & P. R. Co. v. Stout, 17 Wall., U.S., 657, 21 L.Ed. 745, has or should become part of our jurisprudence. The existence of the doctrine has been acknowledged by this Court in four reported cases. (Citations omitted.) In none of these cases, however, was the doctrine found applicable and nowhere does it clearly appear that the doctrine has been either adopted or rejected in this jurisdiction. Although not required to decide the question because I find the doctrine inapplicable here, I take the occasion to interpose a caveat and to note that the attractive nuisance doctrine has been rejected by most of our neighboring jurisdictions. (Citations omitted.)

The attractive nuisance doctrine aside, this case is governed by the rules which have been formulated and generally accepted to determine the duty and degree of care owed to a trespassing child. It is a general rule that ordinary care must be exercised to prevent injury to a trespasser whose presence upon the premises is reasonably to be anticipated. *See* 38 Am.Jur. "Negligence" §§ 109, 112. It is also generally accepted that the age of a child may require a possessor of land to take precautions not required for the protection of an adult. *See* 38 Am.Jur. "Negligence" § 118. When one knows or should know that children are likely to trespass upon premises where there is a condition likely to be dangerous to them, a duty of reasonable care arises toward such children even though they are trespassers. If the person maintaining such condition knows or should know that the presence of trespassing children is to be expected, he is bound to anticipate them and to exercise reasonable care to avoid injury to them. The care to be exercised is such care as is reasonable and prudent under all of the circumstances, having in mind the probability that children, because of their youth, may not discover the condition or may not realize the risk involved in intermeddling with it or in entering the area endangered by it. *See* Wolfe v. Rehbein, 123 Conn. 110, 193 A. 608.

The applicable rule is set forth in the Restatement of Torts, § 339, as follows:

> A possessor of land is subject to liability for bodily harm to young children trespassing thereon caused by a structure or other artificial condition which he maintains upon the land, if
>
> a. the place where the condition is maintained is one upon which the possessor knows or should know that such children are likely to trespass, and
> b. the condition is one of which the possessor knows or should know and which he realizes or should realize as involving an unreasonable risk of death or serious bodily harm to such children, and
> c. the children because of their youth do not discover the condition or realize the risk involved in intermeddling in it or in coming within the area made dangerous by it, and
> d. the utility to the possessor of maintaining the condition is slight as compared to the risk of young children involved therein. (Citations omitted.)

Since the attractive nuisance doctrine is not applicable in this case, further consideration need not be given to the defendant's argument that ponds, pools, streams and other bodies of water are not within the scope of that doctrine. *See* 56 Am.Jur. "Waters" § 436; 65 C.J.S., Negligence, s 29(12)j. It is for the trier of fact to decide whether the pit of water in this case constituted a condition "involving an unreasonable risk of death or serious bodily harm" within the various facets of the rule expressed in Restatement § 339.

There is no merit to the contention that the defendant James Julian, Inc. had no duty of reasonable care for the child's safety because it was neither the owner nor the possessor of the land.

In view of the foregoing, it does not appear to a certainty that the plaintiffs may not recover under any reasonably conceivable set of circumstances susceptible of proof. Accordingly, the complaint may not be dismissed for failure to state a claim upon which relief can be granted.

Case Reflections

1. What is the duty owed by land owners to trespassing children? Why is this duty larger than the duty not to intentionally injure an adult trespasser?
2. The defendant in this case was not the owner of the land where the child was injured. Did that make a difference?
3. Can the owner of the land be held liable for the injuries caused by the work performed by James Julian? What should a land owner do to protect themselves against liability for injury caused by contractors on the land?

RUNYON
V.
PALEY

416 S.E.2d 177 (NC, 1992)

Subdivision covenants

MEYER, Justice.

This case involves a suit to enjoin defendants from constructing condominium units on their property adjacent to the Pamlico Sound on Ocracoke Island. Plaintiffs maintain that defendants' property is subject to restrictive covenants that prohibit the construction of condominiums. The sole question presented for our review is whether plaintiffs are entitled to enforce the restrictive covenants.

On 17 May 1937, Ruth Bragg Gaskins acquired a four-acre tract of land located in the Village of Ocracoke bounded on the West by the Pamlico Sound and on the east by Silver Lake. By various deeds, Mrs. Gaskins conveyed out several lots, which were later developed for residential use. One and one-half acres of the sound-front property, part of which is at issue here, were conveyed by Mrs. Gaskins and her husband to plaintiffs Runyon on 1 May 1954. On 6 January 1960, the Runyons reconveyed the one and one-half acre tract, together with a second tract consisting of one-eighth of an acre, to Mrs. Gaskins. By separate deeds dated 8 January 1960, Mrs. Gaskins, then widowed, conveyed to the Runyons a lake-front lot and a fifteen-foot-wide strip of land that runs to the shore of Pamlico Sound from the roadway separating the lake-front and sound-front lots. This fifteen-foot strip was part of the one and one-half acre parcel that the Runyons had reconveyed to Mrs. Gaskins.

The next day, 9 January 1960, Mrs. Gaskins conveyed the remainder of the one and one-half acre parcel to Doward H. Brugh and his wife, Jacquelyn D. Brugh. Included in the deed of conveyance from Mrs. Gaskins to the Brughs was the following:

> BUT this land is being conveyed subject to certain restrictions as to the use thereof, running with said land by whomsoever owned, until removed as herein set out; said restrictions, which are expressly assented to by [the Brughs], in accepting this deed, are as follows:
>
> (1) Said lot shall be used for residential purposes and not for business, manufacturing, commercial or apartment house purposes; provided, however, this restriction shall not apply to churches or to the office of a professional man which is located in his residence, and
>
> (2) Not more than two residences and such outbuildings as are appurtenant thereto, shall be erected or allowed to remain on said lot. This restriction shall be in full force and effect until such time as adjacent or nearby properties are turned to commercial use, in which case the restrictions herein set out will no longer apply. The word "nearby" shall, for all intents and purposes, be construed to mean within 450 feet thereof.
>
> TO HAVE AND TO HOLD the aforesaid tract or parcel of land and all privileges and appurte-

> nances thereunto belonging or in anywise thereunto appertaining, unto them, the [Brughs], as tenants by the entirety, their heirs and assigns, to their only use and behoof in fee simple absolute forever, [b]ut subject always to the restrictions as to use as hereinabove set out.

Prior to the conveyance of this land to the Brughs, Mrs. Gaskins had constructed a residential dwelling in which she lived on lake-front property across the road from the property conveyed to the Brughs. Mrs. Gaskins retained this land and continued to live on this property until her death in August 1961. Plaintiff Williams, Mrs. Gaskins' daughter, has since acquired the property retained by Mrs. Gaskins.

By mesne conveyances, defendant Warren D. Paley acquired the property conveyed by Mrs. Gaskins to the Brughs. Thereafter, defendant Warren Paley and his wife, defendant Claire Paley, entered into a partnership with defendant Midgett Realty and began constructing condominium units on the property. Plaintiffs brought this suit, seeking to enjoin defendants from using the property in a manner that is inconsistent with the restrictive covenants included in the deed from Mrs. Gaskins to the Brughs. In their complaint, plaintiffs alleged that the restrictive covenants were placed on the property "for the benefit of [Mrs. Gaskins'] property and neighboring property owners, specifically including and intending to benefit the Runyons." Plaintiffs further alleged that the "restrictive covenants have not been removed and are enforceable by plaintiffs."

Defendants moved to dismiss the lawsuit, and plaintiffs thereafter moved for summary judgment. Following a hearing on both motions, the trial court granted defendants' motion to dismiss for failure to state a claim upon which relief could be granted and, pursuant to Rule 54(b), rendered a final judgment after having determined that there was no just reason for delay in any appeal of the matter. The Court of Appeals affirmed the trial court, concluding that the restrictive covenants were personal to Mrs. Gaskins and became unenforceable at her death. Judge Greene dissented in part, concluding that the dismissal of plaintiff Williams' claim was erroneous.

At the outset, we note that at the hearing on plaintiffs' and defendants' motions, the trial court allowed plaintiffs to present evidence of matters outside the pleadings. Because it is not clear whether the trial court excluded this evidence in ruling on defendants' motion to dismiss, the trial court's order must be treated on appeal as a partial summary judgment for defendants. [1] N. C. R. Civ. P. 12(b) (6).

Having considered the evidence presented to the trial court, we conclude that plaintiff Williams presented sufficient evidence to show that the covenants at issue here are real covenants enforceable by her as an owner of property retained by Mrs. Gaskins, the covenantee. Accordingly, we reverse that part of the Court of Appeals' decision that affirmed the trial court's dismissal of plaintiff Williams' claim. However, we agree with the Court of Appeals that the covenants are not enforceable by the Runyons, and we therefore affirm that part of the Court of Appeals' decision that concerns the dismissal of the Runyons' claim.

It is well established that an owner of land in fee has a right to sell this land subject to any restrictions he may see fit to impose, provided that the restrictions are not contrary to public policy. Sheets v. Dillon, 221 N. C. 426, 431, 20 S. E. 2d 344, 347 (1942). Such restrictions are often included as covenants in the deed conveying the property and may be classified as either personal covenants or real covenants that are said to run with the land. See 5 Richard R. Powell, Powell on Real Property P 673 (1991) [hereinafter Powell on Real Property]. The significant distinction between these types of covenants is that a personal covenant creates a personal obligation or right enforceable at law only between the original covenanting parties, 5 Powell on Real Property P 673[1], at 60-41, whereas a real covenant creates a servitude upon the land subject to the covenant ("the servient estate") for the benefit of another parcel of land ("the dominant estate"), Cummings v. Dosam, Inc., 273 N. C. 28, 32,

---

[1] Plaintiffs Runyon also alleged claims against defendants for breach of a settlement agreement and for willful and intentional trespass to real property. These claims were not subjects of the trial court's order and are therefore not before this Court.

159 S. E. 2d 513, 517 (1968). As such, a real covenant may be enforced at law or in equity by the owner of the dominant estate against the owner of the servient estate, whether the owners are the original covenanting parties or successors in interest.

I. REAL COVENANTS AT LAW

A restrictive covenant is a real covenant that runs with the land of the dominant and servient estates only if (1) the subject of the covenant touches and concerns the land, (2) there is privity of estate between the party enforcing the covenant and the party against whom the covenant is being enforced, and (3) the original covenanting parties intended the benefits and the burdens of the covenant to run with the land. [Citations omitted.]

A. Touch and Concern

As noted by several courts and commentators, the touch and concern requirement is not capable of being reduced to an absolute test or precise definition. *See* Neponsit Property Owners Ass'n v. Emigrant Indus. Sav. Bank, 278 N. Y. 248, 256–58, 15 N. E. 2d 793, 795–96, reh'g denied, 278 N. Y. 704, 16 N. E. 2d 852 (1938); Charles E. Clark, Real Covenants and Other Interests Which "Run With Land" 96 (2d ed. 1947) [hereinafter Clark, Real Covenants]. Focusing on the nature of the burdens and benefits created by a covenant, the court must exercise its best judgment to determine whether the covenant is related to the covenanting parties' ownership interests in their land. Clark, Real Covenants 97.

For a covenant to touch and concern the land, it is not necessary that the covenant have a physical effect on the land. It is sufficient that the covenant have some economic impact on the parties' ownership rights by, for example, enhancing the value of the dominant estate and decreasing the value of the servient estate. It is essential, however, that the covenant in some way affect the legal rights of the covenanting parties as landowners. Where the burdens and benefits created by the covenant are of such a nature that they may exist independently from the parties' ownership interests in land, the covenant does not touch and concern the land and will not run with the land. [Citations omitted.]

Although not alone determinative of the issue, the nature of the restrictive covenants at issue in this case (building or use restrictions) is strong evidence that the covenants touch and concern the dominant and servient estates. As recognized by some courts, a restriction limiting the use of land clearly touches and concerns the estate burdened with the covenant because it restricts the owner's use and enjoyment of the property and thus affects the value of the property. A use restriction does not, however, always touch and concern the dominant estate. To meet the requirement that the covenant touch and concern the dominant estate, it must be shown that the covenant somehow affects the dominant estate by, for example, increasing the value of the dominant estate.

In the case at bar, plaintiffs have shown that the covenants sought to be enforced touch and concern not only the servient estate owned by defendants, but also the properties owned by plaintiffs. The properties owned by defendants, plaintiff Williams, and plaintiffs Runyon comprise only a portion of what was at one time a four-acre tract bounded on one side by the Pamlico Sound and on the other by Silver Lake. If able to enforce the covenants against defendants, plaintiffs would be able to restrict the use of defendants' property to uses that accord with the restrictive covenants. Considering the close proximity of the lands involved here and the relatively secluded nature of the area where the properties are located, we conclude that the right to restrict the use of defendants' property would affect plaintiffs' ownership interests in the property owned by them, and therefore the covenants touch and concern their lands.

B. Privity of Estate

In order to enforce a restrictive covenant as one running with the land at law, the party seeking to enforce the covenant must also show that he is in privity of estate with the party against whom he seeks to enforce the covenant. 5 Powell on Real Property P 673[2]; 7 Thompson on Real Property § 3155, at 84. Although the origin of privity of estate is not certain, the privity requirement has been described as a substitute for privity of contract, which exists between the original covenanting parties and which is ordinarily required to enforce a contractual promise. 3 Tiffany Real Property § 851, at 451 n. 32. Thus, where the covenant is sought to be enforced by someone not a party to the covenant or against someone not a party to the covenant, the party seeking to enforce the covenant must show that he has a sufficient legal relationship with the party against whom enforcement is sought to be entitled to enforce the covenant.

For the enforcement at law of a covenant running with the land, most states require two types of privity: (1) privity of estate between the covenantor and covenantee at the time the covenant was created ("horizontal privity"), and (2) privity of estate between the covenanting parties and their successors in interest ("vertical privity"). William B. Stoebuck, Running Covenants: An Analytical Primer, 52 Wash. L. Rev. 861, 867 (1977) [hereinafter Stoebuck, 52 Wash. L. Rev. 861]. The majority of jurisdictions have held that horizontal privity exists when the original covenanting parties make their covenant in connection with the conveyance of an estate in land from one of the parties to the other. 7 Thompson on Real Property § 3155, at 85, and cases cited therein. A few courts, on the other hand, have dispensed with the showing of horizontal privity altogether, requiring only a showing of vertical privity. [Citations omitted.]

Vertical privity, which is ordinarily required to enforce a real covenant at law, requires a showing of succession in interest between the original covenanting parties and the current owners of the dominant and servient estates. As one scholar has noted:

> The most obvious implication of this principle [of vertical privity] is that the burden of a real covenant may be enforced against remote parties only when they have succeeded to the covenantor's estate in land. Such parties stand in privity of estate with the covenantor. Likewise, the benefit may be enforced by remote parties only when they have succeeded to the covenantee's estate. They are in privity of estate with the covenantee. Stoebuck, 52 Wash. L. Rev. 861, 876.

We adhere to the rule that a party seeking to enforce a covenant as one running with the land at law must show the presence of both horizontal and vertical privity. In order to show horizontal privity, it is only necessary that a party seeking to enforce the covenant show that there was some "connection of interest" between the original covenanting parties, such as, here, the conveyance of an estate in land.

In the case sub judice, plaintiffs have shown the existence of horizontal privity. The record shows that the covenants at issue in this case were created in connection with the transfer of an estate in fee of property then owned by Mrs. Gaskins. By accepting the deed of conveyance, defendants' predecessors in title, the Brughs, covenanted to use the property for the purposes specified in the deed and thereby granted to Mrs. Gaskins a servitude in their property.

To review the sufficiency of vertical privity in this case, it is necessary to examine three distinct relationships: (1) the relationship between defendants and the Brughs as the covenantors; (2) the relationship between plaintiff Williams and the covenantee, Mrs. Gaskins; and (3) the relationship between plaintiffs Runyon and Mrs. Gaskins. The evidence before us shows that the Brughs conveyed all of their interest in the restricted property and that by mesne conveyances defendant Warren Paley succeeded to a fee simple estate in the property. Thus, he is in privity of estate with the covenantors. Any legal interests held by the other defendants were acquired by them from defendant Warren Paley. As successors to the interest held by defendant Warren Paley, they too are in privity of estate with the covenantors. Plaintiff Williams has also established a privity of estate between herself and the covenantee. Following the death of Mrs. Gaskins, the property retained by Mrs. Gaskins was conveyed by her heirs to her daughter, Eleanor Gaskins. Thereafter, Eleanor Gaskins conveyed to plaintiff Williams a fee simple absolute in that property. The mere fact that defendants and plaintiff Williams did not acquire the property directly from the original covenanting parties is of no moment.

Regardless of the number of conveyances that transpired, defendants and plaintiff Williams have succeeded to the estates then held by the covenantor and covenantee, and thus they are in vertical privity with their successors in interest. Such would be true even if the parties had succeeded to only a part of the land burdened and benefitted by the covenants. 5 Powell on Real Property P 673[3], at 60-85 to -86; 5 Restatement of Property §§ 536, 551 (1944). Plaintiffs Runyon have not, however, made a sufficient showing of vertical privity. The Runyons have not succeeded in any interest in land held by Mrs. Gaskins at the time the covenant was created. The only interest in land held by the Runyons was acquired by them prior to the creation of the covenant. Therefore, they have not shown vertical privity of estate between themselves and the covenantee with respect to the property at issue in this case. Because the Runyons were not parties to the covenant and are not in privity with the original parties, they may not enforce the covenant as a real covenant running with the land at law.

C. Intent of the Parties

Defendants argue that plaintiff Williams is precluded from enforcing the restrictive covenants because the covenanting parties who created the restrictions intended that the restrictions be enforceable only by Mrs. Gaskins, the original covenantee. According to defendants, such a conclusion is necessitated where, as here, the instrument creating the covenants does not expressly state that persons other than the covenantee may enforce the covenants. We disagree.

* * *

We conclude that the language of the deed creating the restrictions at issue here is ambiguous with regard to the intended enforcement of the restrictions. The deed from Mrs. Gaskins to the Brughs provided that the property conveyed was being made "subject to certain restrictions as to the use thereof, running with said land by whomsoever owned, until removed [due to a change of conditions in the surrounding properties] as herein set out. "As noted by the dissent in the Court of Appeals, this provision unequivocally expresses the parties' intention that the burden of the restrictions runs with the land conveyed by the deed. In the habendum clause of the deed, the parties also included language providing that the estate granted shall be "subject always to the restrictions as to use as hereinabove set out." We conclude that the language of the deed creating the restrictions is such that it can reasonably be interpreted to establish an intent on the part of the covenanting parties not only to bind successors to the covenantor's interest, but also to benefit the property retained by the covenantee.

* * *

Applying these principles as well as the rules of construction used to determine the parties' intent that a covenant run with the land, which likewise apply here, we conclude that plaintiffs Runyon have failed to show that the original covenanting parties intended that they be permitted to enforce the covenants either in a personal capacity or as owners of any land they now own. The Runyons were not parties to the covenants, and neither they nor their property are mentioned, either explicitly or implicitly, as intended beneficiaries in the deed creating the covenants or in any other instrument in the public records pertaining to defendants' property. Although they own property closely situated to defendants', in an area which was primarily residential at the time the restrictive covenants were created, they did not acquire their property as part of a plan or scheme to develop the area as residential property. In fact, they acquired their property free of any restrictions as to the use of their property. Finally, the Runyons purchased their property prior to the creation of the restrictive covenants at issue here, and thus they cannot be said to be successors in interest to any property retained by the covenantee that was intended to be benefitted by the covenants.

* * *

For the reasons stated herein, we conclude that the restrictive covenants contained in the deed from Mrs. Gaskins to defendants' predecessors are not personal covenants that became unenforceable at Mrs. Gaskins' death but are real covenants appurtenant to the property retained by Mrs. Gaskins at the time of the coveyance to defendants' predecessors in interest. As a successor in interest to the property retained by Mrs. Gaskins, plaintiff Williams is therefore entitled to seek enforcement of the restrictive covenants against defendants. We therefore reverse that part of the Court of Appeals' decision that affirmed the trial court's dismissal of plaintiff Williams' claim and remand this case to that court for further remand to the Superior Court, Hyde County, for further proceedings not inconsistent with this opinion. We further conclude that the Runyons have not proffered sufficient evidence to show that they have standing to enforce the restrictive covenants, either personally or as owners of any land intended to be benefitted by the restrictions. We therefore affirm that part of the Court of Appeals' decision that affirmed the trial court's dismissal of the Runyon's claim.

Affirmed in part, reversed in part, and remanded.

MITCHELL and WEBB, JJ., concur in the result.

Case Reflections

1. In what way did the condominium construction proposed by the defendants violate the covenants contained in the deed from Mrs. Gaskins?
2. Why do you suppose Mrs. Gaskins inserted these covenants in her deed? Why do you suppose her grantees agreed to the covenants?
3. What tests did the court use in deciding that the covenants at issue here "touch and concern" the land?

PART

2

TRANSFERRING OWNERSHIP OF REAL PROPERTY

CHAPTER

7

METHODS OF TRANSFERRING INTERESTS IN LAND

LEARNING OBJECTIVES

After reading this chapter, you should be able to:

1. Define and discuss the requirements for a valid contract to sell or purchase real property
2. Identify the legal documents required to establish the transfer of real property ownership after the death of the owner
3. Identify the elements required to gain title to real property under the doctrine of adverse possession

KEY TERMS

Adverse Possession

Eminent Domain

Contract

Offer

Acceptance

Counteroffer

Consideration

Revocation

Rescission

Estoppel

Intestate Succession

Testate Succession

Inter Vivos Gift

The first part of this book looked closely at the nature of the claim "This land belongs to me." Part I found that the claim of ownership in real property incorporates and summarizes a broad array of legal rights and duties. Part I also talked at some length about various ways that the fee simple absolute bundle of rights can be broken up and repackaged into smaller bundles of rights. Each of these smaller bundles can be sold in the marketplace in order to increase the total value of the property.

Adverse Possession A legal doctrine which permits a natural person to acquire title to real property by the continuous, open and hostile possession of the property.

This part of the book will focus on the process of selling all, or any portion, of the fee simple absolute bundle of rights. This chapter will define the legal principles that determine whether the current owner has successfully transferred an ownership interest to another person. This first chapter of Part II will deal primarily with the theory of transferring ownership claims. The remaining chapters in this part will look more closely at the art and practice of transferring ownership interests in real property.

An interest in real property can be transferred voluntarily by the current owner or may be transferred without the owner's consent. Voluntary transfers include sales, gifts, and bequests (a gift that occurs at the death of the giver). Involuntary transfers include changes in ownership resulting from the doctrine of **adverse possession** or from the exercise of the power of **eminent domain.**

Eminent Domain The right of governmental entities to take private property for public use or benefit.

In the normal course of events, the sale of an interest in real property has two phases. The first phase is the creation of a binding **contract** between the seller and the buyer, which spells out the rights and the duties of each party. The most important duty of the seller is to prepare and deliver a deed capable of transferring a marketable title in the property to the buyer. The most important duty of the buyer is to pay the price agreed to in the contract. The second phase of a real estate transaction occurs in a process known as the closing. Normally, both parties will perform the obligations incurred under their contract at the closing. Deeds will be examined more closely in Chapter 8. Chapter 9 will examine the impact of mortgages and other liens. The closing process will be described in Chapters 10 and 11. This chapter will focus on the first phase of a voluntary real estate transaction: the creation of the contract.

Contract A legally enforceable agreement between two or more persons.

ELEMENTS OF CONTRACT LAW

Offer Any written or oral communication which is sufficiently definite in its terms as to indicate that the person making the offer intends to become bound by its terms.

A contract is simply a legally enforceable agreement between two or more people. The important words in that definition are "legally enforceable." Most people make casual agreements every day that they do not expect to result in a lawsuit. One roommate might say to another, "I'll do the dishes tomorrow night if you will do them tonight." Or, you might tell a friend, "Call me next week, and I will buy you lunch." Neither speaker would expect to be sued if he or she fails to do the dishes or buy the lunch. But, in the right context, each of these statements could ripen into a binding contract that would form the basis for a successful (if somewhat frivolous) lawsuit. Clearly, then, we should stop to consider the circumstances which cause a written or spoken promise to become a legally enforceable obligation.

Formal Requisites for a Contract

A contract requires an offer, an acceptance, and a consideration. Whenever all three of these elements are present in the communications between two people, a contract will spring into existence.

An **offer** is any verbal or written communication that is sufficiently definite in its terms to manifest an intent on the part of the offeror to be bound by the terms of the offer. The terms of an offer generally include:

a. The specific performance or payment that the offeror intends to make
b. The price or other payment the offeror expects to receive in exchange for performing the agreement
c. The amount of time the offer will remain open

In determining whether a legally enforceable contract exists, courts will examine the words of the offeror to see if they measure up to the requirements of a valid offer. If reasonable people who read or hear the words of the offeror can agree on what the offeror intended, courts will usually conclude that the words constitute a valid offer. If the last term (the amount of time the offer will remain open) is missing, courts will usually infer that acceptance within a "reasonable time" will be sufficient to create a legally enforceable agreement.

An **acceptance** is any act or communication that manifests agreement to all the material terms of the offer. When a valid acceptance is made, the contract springs into being. Both the offeror (the person who made the initial offer) and the offeree (the person who accepted the offer) will be legally obligated to perform the duties defined by the terms of the offer.

Very often in real estate contracts, an offeree will accept all of the terms of the offer except one. The buyer may, for example, agree to purchase the house on the date requested in the offer and accept all of the requirements demanded by the seller, but change the price that the offer requires. Since the offeree has changed one of the material terms of the offer (the price for the house), the offer has not been accepted. Instead, the buyer will have made a **counteroffer** to the seller. No contract will be created unless the seller now accepts the counteroffer of the buyer. The seller may in turn propose a new price between the original offer price and the counteroffer price. This process can continue until both parties agree on a price (which then becomes an acceptance of the final counteroffer) or until one party decides to terminate the

Beall v. Beall

Acceptance
Any act or communication which responds to the terms of an offer and creates a binding contract incorporating all of the material terms of the offer.

Counter-Offer
Any communication, either writtten or oral, which responds to the terms of an offer by changing or amending one or more of the material terms of the offer. A counter-offer does not create a contract until it is accepted by the party receiving the counter-offer.

KEY POINTS

Near the end of the last century, a gentlemen attending a wedding encountere his sixteen-year-old nephew. The gentleman said, "Nephew, if you do not smoke any tobacco before your twenty-first birthday, I will pay you $100." Five years later the nephew, who had indeed refrained from smoking, demanded the promised payment. When the surprised uncle refused to pay, the nephew filed a lawsuit. The court decided that the communication from the uncle constituted a valid offer, which the nephew had accepted. The court ordered a judgment for the nephew in the amount of $100, the payment promised in the contract.

negotiation. Whenever an acceptance of a counteroffer occurs, a binding contract will be created. But if the parties never agree on the price, no contract will spring into existence.

KEY POINTS

The standard procedure for negotiating the price of a house begins when the buyer signs a real estate contract form describing (among other things) the house the buyer desires to purchase and the purchase price the buyer is willing to pay. When this document is delivered to the seller (or to the real estate broker acting as the seller's agent), the document itself constitutes an offer to make a binding contract.

The seller can make a counteroffer by simply drawing a line through the price typed in the form, writing a new, higher price, and placing his or her initials near the change entered on the contract form.

The buyer can accept this counteroffer merely by placing another set of initials near the new price written in the contract by the seller. The initials placed on the contract form by the parties are not legally necessary for a contract to be created. But they are used by careful practitioners to serve as evidence of the fact that both parties are aware of, and have assented to, the new price.

Consideration Any promise or performance which is made in exchange for a promise or performance by the another party to a contract.

Consideration is the last of the formal requisites for the existence of a legally enforceable contract. Consideration is any promise or performance that is made in exchange for a promise or performance by the other party to a contract. Consideration is almost always present in a contract for the sale of real estate. The essence of such a contract is a promise by the owner to convey title to the buyer and a promise by the buyer to pay the purchase price for the property. Each of these promises is valid consideration that will support the contract created when the offer was accepted. The buyer's promise to pay the purchase price is valid consideration, even if the value of the property is much smaller (or larger) than the price agreed to by the parties. The fact that one of the parties has made a bad bargain does not change the legally enforceable nature of a contract.

KEY POINTS

Courts are generally willing to accept any "bargained for exchange" as valid consideration to support a contract. A mutual exchange of promises (I promise to give you a valid deed if you promise to pay me $50,000) clearly meets this test. Other forms of consideration include rendering personal services, actually paying a sum of money, or the forbearance of a legal right. The nephew in the case discussed above had a legal right to smoke tobacco before his twenty-first birthday. By forbearing to exercise that right in exchange for the promise to pay money made by the uncle, the nephew provided the consideration required to support the contract.

Unilateral Contracts

Under some circumstances, the acceptance of an offer is made by providing the consideration requested by the offer. Such circumstances give rise to legally enforceable agreements called **unilateral contracts.**

Unilateral Contracts Legally enforceable agreements in which one party to the contract is not required to perform under the agreement until the other party has completed the performance required by the agreement.

The typical real estate contract is composed of two promises. The seller promises to deliver a deed to the property at some definite date in the future, and the buyer promises to pay the agreed-upon price at that future date. Both the buyer and the seller incur an obligation to perform their promises when the offer is accepted.

But suppose an owner makes the following offer: "You can live in my house as long as you pay me $1,000 on the first day of each month. And, if you stay there for five years, paying the rent on time each month, I will give you the deed to the house." Here, the owner has made an offer that can ripen into no fewer than sixty-one unilateral contracts. The first part of the offer allows the tenant to live in the house for a month whenever the rent is paid on the first day of the month. The tenant is never obligated to pay the rent, because the offer from the owner does not, by its terms, require the tenant to stay for any length of time. But every month, when the tenant pays the rent, the owner's offer to allow the tenant to live in the house is accepted, creating a valid contract.

In addition, after sixty months of rental payments, the tenant can demand a deed to the house from the owner, because the tenant will then have accepted the second part of the offer. It is easy to see why the law calls this form of contract unilateral. Each month for sixty months the owner becomes liable to perform a promise, when the tenant accepts the owner's offer by paying the requested rent. The obligation is only on one side, since the tenant can withdraw from the arrangement at any time.

Contractual arrangements like this offer a standing invitation to trouble. Suppose the owner decides not to give the tenant a deed at the end of the fifth year. The owner is now in breach of the contract to deliver a deed, and the tenant can go to court to force the owner to make good on the promise. Even worse, suppose the owner and the tenant have a fight at the end of the fourth year, and the owner decides to throw the tenant out. Does the tenant have a leg to stand on?

The answer is a definite "maybe." Unilateral contract offer number 61 made by the owner of the house was the offer to deliver a deed if the tenant remains in the house for five years and pays rent of $1,000 on the first day of each month. As soon as the tenant accepts this offer, a binding contract has been created. With a bilateral contract, the instant of acceptance is usually easy to find. When the offeree says "I accept," the contract is formed, and both parties are legally bound to perform their obligations.

But a unilateral contract is accepted by actually performing the duties requested by the offer. Clearly, when the tenant has made sixty monthly payments on the rent, the offer to give a deed to the tenant has been accepted. But how about when the tenant has made fifty-nine rental payments? Isn't that close enough to sixty that the offer should be deemed accepted? What about fifty-eight rental payments? Forty-two rental payments?

An offer to create a unilateral contract generally does not provide a clear instant in time when the offer can be considered to be accepted. Acceptance begins when the offeree starts to perform and is complete when the offeree concludes the performance. In between those dates, it is not clear whether the offer has been accepted or not. In determining whether an offer for a unilateral contract has been accepted, courts will look at all of the surrounding circumstances, weigh the equities, examine the reasonableness of the parties' actions, take a deep breath, and decide yes or no.

Clearly, an offer for a unilateral contract creates a great deal of uncertainty for both the offeror and the offeree. In the field of real estate transactions, the uncertainty is multiplied because the time required for the performance that creates acceptance of the offer is usually long. Once the offeree embarks upon the performance requested by the offer, courts become reluctant to release the offeror from the duties that will be owed when the offer is accepted. For this reason, the careful real estate practitioner will always set a definite time limit for the acceptance of any offer to make a contract.

Revocation and Rescission

Anyone who makes an offer for a contract will become legally bound to perform the promises contained in the offer at the instant the offer is accepted. That fact should cause some anxiety on the part of anyone who makes an offer for a contract. Before an offer is communicated, the offeror should consider and answer two important questions. The first is "When will it be safe for me to assume that my offer has not been accepted, so that I will be free to make other arrangements with my property?" The second is "What will happen to me if I change my mind after I communicate the offer?"

The answer to the first question is fairly straightforward. The offeror is protected by simply including a date by which the offer must be accepted as one of the terms of the offer. If no acceptance has occurred by the time the date specified in the offer goes by, then the offer becomes void. The answer to the second question, however, is more problematic.

Revocation

Revocation The withdrawal of an offer by the person making an offer. Revocation can occur at any time prior to the instant that the offer is accepted

An offer can be revoked by the offeror at any time prior to its acceptance by an offeree. If the **revocation** is effective, then the offeror is off the hook, since the offer becomes void when it is revoked. Clearly, then, an offeror needs to know how to make an effective revocation of the offer to have any hope of changing his or her mind after an offer has been communicated.

Revocation is effective whenever it is communicated to an offeree using the same medium that was used to communicate the offer. If the offer was made in writing, then the revocation should also be in writing. (Notice the word "should" in the previous sentence. There are circumstances in which an oral revocation is sufficient to void a written offer. But it is never wise to depend on circumstances for protection.) In addition, the revocation must be communicated to the offeree before the offeree accepts the offer. (Remember that at the instant of acceptance, the offer becomes a contract, and contracts are never revocable.)

The twin requirements that revocation be communicated to the offeree before acceptance and that it be communicated by the same medium used to communicate the offer have led to some interesting lawsuits. Suppose S sends a written offer to sell an apartment house to B in a letter mailed on June 1. The offer states that acceptance must be made by June 30, or the offer will become null and void. B reads the offer, thinks it over, and mails an acceptance to S on June 15. On June 16, B receives a letter from S revoking the offer. The revocation letter is postmarked June 14. S receives the letter accepting the offer from B on June 17, and breaks into a cold sweat. Has a contract been created?

The law of contracts holds that the acceptance of an offer is effective when it is communicated to the offeror, while the revocation of an offer is effective when it is received by the offeree. When the mails are used, several days may elapse between the sending and receiving of an acceptance or a revocation. Courts have adopted the "mailbox" rule to deal with this problem.

An acceptance will be considered as communicated when the offeree places the letter in a mailbox with sufficient postage to reach the offeror. At that point, the offeree has done everything required to communicate acceptance. On the other hand, the revocation is not effective until it appears in the offeree's mailbox, since revocation must be received by the offeree before acceptance has occurred. Under this rule, a contract will be created, because B put the acceptance letter in a mailbox one day before the revocation letter appeared in B's mailbox.

KEY POINTS

Whenever an offer to buy or sell real estate is communicated through the mails, the mailbox problem will arise. The offeror can be protected from this rule by stating in the offer that the offer becomes void unless notice of acceptance is *received by the seller* at or before midnight of a given date. Since the date of acceptance is a material term of the offer, this agreement must be met in order for a contract to be created.

Rescission

There are two special circumstances that may allow one party to a contract to escape the legally enforceable obligations required by the agreement. These circumstances are fraud and mutual mistake of fact.

Recission The legal doctrine which excuses both parties to a contract from performing the agreement, when the agreement was procured by fraud, or when both parties are mistaken as to the existence or lack of existence of a material fact.

Fraud occurs when one party to the agreement makes an intentional misrepresentation of a material fact that is intended to mislead the other party and induce that party to enter into the contract. For example, a prospective home buyer might ask the owner if the house has ever had water in the basement. In fact, the present owner has been required to clean up water damage in the basement of the home on three separate occasions. But the owner replies, "No, we have never had any problems with water in this house. You can rest assured that this basement never floods." Relying on the owner's statement, the buyer makes an offer to purchase the house, which the owner accepts with alacrity.

The following spring, when the buyer discovers that she has been misled, she will bring an action to rescind the contract. If the buyer can satisfy the jury that the former owner knew about the water problem, that he intentionally lied to the buyer about the problem, and that the buyer was reasonable in believing the seller's lie, then the court will order a **rescission.** The buyer will be entitled to receive her money back from the seller, and the seller will get the house back from the buyer.

A mutual mistake of fact occurs when both parties believe that a material fact in the transaction is true, when in reality the material fact is not true (or vice versa).

Mosher v. Mayacamas

Consider a rural home that draws water from a well on the property. The well was drilled at the request of the current owner to a depth of seventy-five feet. At the time the well was drilled, the owner was told that a large underground aquifer lay beneath the surface of the land at a depth of seventy feet. As a result, the owner believes that the well is taking water from the underground aquifer and can therefore be expected to produce all of the water required for the home.

When the owner sells the home, the purchaser is informed that the well is dependable, since the owner believes it takes water from a large underground lake containing millions of gallons of water. One year later, the well runs dry, and a geologist is summoned by the purchaser. After detailed analysis, the geologist reports to the purchaser that the boundary of the large aquifer both parties believed was supplying the well is actually one-half mile east of the property. In fact, the well on the property was taking water from a small underground pool that is now empty.

If a jury were to decide that the purchaser acted reasonably in failing to summon the geologist before the transaction was completed, then the trial judge would be required to order a rescission of the contract. On the other hand, if the jury decided that a reasonable purchaser would have called a geologist prior to closing, then the judge would not order a rescission. One of the cases at the end of chapter presents the full three-part test for the availability of rescission due to mutual mistake of fact. For now, it is enough to say that the careful practitioner should not rely on rescission as a method of escaping from a bad bargain except in the most unusual circumstances. It is always better for a purchaser to gather all the information required to determine the quality of the bargain before accepting the offer.

Void
An agreement which is unenforceable against any party, because the agreement violates public policy.

The Statute of Frauds

In 1677, the English Parliament adopted the Statute of Frauds, which required certain agreements to be in writing and to be signed by the person charged with performing the agreement. (Fraudulent claims against landowners and others were apparently becoming a problem in England.) The approach of the Statute of Frauds seems simple enough. No one will be compelled to honor an agreement to sell his or her home unless written evidence of the agreement can be produced by the putative buyer.

KEY POINTS

Occasionally, an unscrupulous seller will attempt to increase the selling price of a home by building what appears to be an additional bathroom. The extra bathroom will be framed in, painted, and fixtures will be installed, but the fixtures will not be connected to the water and sewer lines in the house. While the fake may be attractive to look at, it is completely useless.

An unwary buyer who is fooled by the appearance of the bathroom will have a hard time rescinding the contract. There is no mutual mistake of fact, since the seller was well aware of the lack of function in the bathroom. Fraud will be hard to prove, because the seller will take care to be out of the house when prospective purchasers are looking at it. The best protection for the buyer is to turn on each water faucet in the house during the inspection, to verify that water does flow into the fixture and the drain does carry the water away.

Each of the fifty American states has also adopted its own unique version of the original Statute of Frauds. While real estate contracts are covered by a statute of frauds in every state, the particular terms of the statutes vary somewhat. In some states, the statute requires that the price to be paid, the description of the property, and the date for closing be specified in writing. Other states allow enforcement of a written memorandum even though one or more of the terms of the agreement were given orally. Some state statutes make oral agreements for real estate transactions **void,** whereas other state statutes make oral agreements merely **voidable.**

Voidable An agreement which cannot be enforced against one of the parties, because that party lacked the capacity to make a valid contract, or because the agreement is so unreasonable that it shocks the conscience of the court where enforcement is sought.

A statute of frauds requires the wise practitioner to insist on a formal written consent in every real estate transaction. It is never safe to rely on the fact that the other party to an agreement will perform as expected unless the agreement is in writing and signed by the other party. In addition, the wise practitioner should avoid the temptation to use the statute of frauds as a means for escaping liability under a real estate contract. Suppose O orally agrees to sell his house to B for $60,000. Three weeks later, B delivers $60,000 in cash to O and requests the deed. Each year, a surprisingly large number of people in such a position decide to keep the money and refuse to deliver the deed. Their argument is that since the contract was not in writing, the promise to deliver the deed cannot be enforced.

Courts have had no trouble in deciding that an oral contract for the sale of real property is specifically enforceable under these conditions. Judges generally hold that since O accepted the payment for the house, he is **estopped** from denying the validity of his agreement to convey title to the house.

KEY POINTS

The equitable doctrine of estoppel has been given wide application in the law of property. There is a strong temptation during negotiations with another party to offer grudging assent to various requests from the other side in order to keep the negotiating process alive. This temptation should always be resisted. If the other side changes its position, justifiably relying upon an offer that was intended solely to keep the negotiation alive, the person making the offer may be required to perform as was indicated.

Real Estate Options

Recall from our earlier discussion that an offer to sell real estate can be revoked at any time prior to acceptance. At first glance, a real estate option appears to be an exception to this general rule. An option allows the buyer to purchase a particular parcel of real estate for an agreed-upon price at any time during the option period. The owner of the parcel is not allowed to withdraw from the option prior to the expiration date specified by the option agreement.

Such an arrangement sounds like an irrevocable offer to sell, but in fact, a real estate option is a bilateral contract that requires an offer, an acceptance, and must be supported by consideration.

Estoppel An equitable doctrine which requires a party to render a promised performance when another party has changed his or her position as a result of justifiable reliance upon the promise made by the party to whom the doctrine of estoppel is applied.

In general, the holder of the option offers to pay a sum of money in the present in exchange for the right to purchase the property at the option price at any time during the period of the option. If the owner of the land accepts this offer, the holder of option pays the option price in exchange for the promise to sell in the future. The consideration given by the holder of the option is the payment of the option premium. The consideration given by the owner of the land is the promise to convey the land at the option price if requested.

GIFTS AND INHERITANCE OF REAL PROPERTY

The remaining categories of voluntary real estate transfers include gifts and inheritance. At common law, people entitled to inherit property from a decedent fell into one of three classes. *Heirs* were the natural descendants of the decedent, who would receive property if the decedent did not have a will. *Legatees* were those who received money or other personal property under the terms of a valid will that was in force on the date of the decedent's death. *Devisees* included those who received title to real property under the terms of a valid will.

In modern practice, these distinctions are not particularly important. Real estate practitioners are more interested in the processes used to transfer title from a decedent to the heirs or devisees of the decedent. We will see in Chapter 8 that the strength of a real estate title purchased by a real estate practitioner will always be equal to the strength of the title owned by the seller. Therefore, when any seller in the chain of title acquired his or her title by devise or inheritance, the purchaser must be able to ascertain the strength of the title acquired. When all of the procedures required for transferring title to real property at the death of the owner have been followed, the heirs of the decedent receive a valid title to the property. If one or more of the required procedures is not followed, the title to the property will be defective. Therefore, it is necessary to understand the legal proceedings required to transfer a valid title to real property from a decedent to the heirs or devisees of the decedent.

Intestate Succession The transfer of property to the heirs of a decedent who died without a valid will.

Testate Succession The transfer of property to the devisees and legatees of a decedent who died leaving a valid will.

Succession Procedures

When a person who owns real property dies without a valid will, title to the property will be transferred under the laws of **intestate succession.** When a valid will is in effect at the date of the decedent's death, his or her property will be distributed under the laws of **testate succession.** The Uniform Probate Code (UPC) has been adopted by virtually all of the states. This uniform code establishes the procedures for determining the descent of property under both intestate and testate succession.

The UPC requires that a personal representative be appointed as soon as possible after the death of a person who owns property. The personal representative must perform four tasks in the proper order. The first task is to make a thorough inventory of the decedent's property and prepare a list of all debts owed by the decedent at the date of death. The second task is to determine the names and addresses of all parties who may be entitled to receive property from the estate of the decedent. The third task is to pay all of the just debts and taxes owed by the estate. The personal representative may sell various assets of the estate to raise the cash required for these payments, if that becomes necessary. The fourth task is to make a final distribution

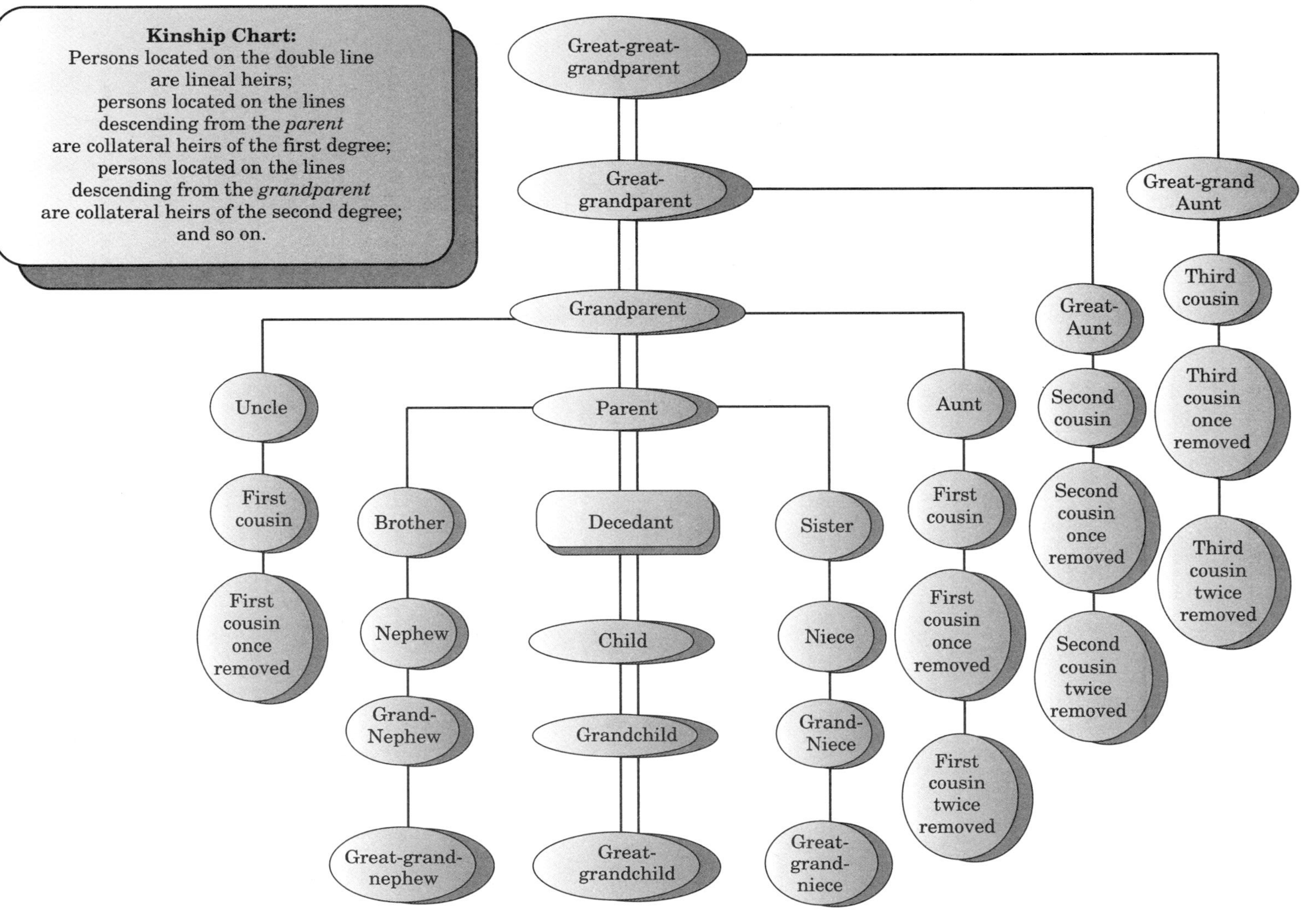

FIGURE 7.1 KINSHIP CHART

of the remaining assets of the estate to the persons who are entitled to receive the assets, after all debts and taxes owed by the estate have been paid by the personal representative.

Estate of Beason v. North

As the personal representative goes about these tasks, he or she will generate a fairly sizable paper trail. The efforts of a personal representative are always closely supervised by a judge who specializes in the administration of decedents' estates. All but the most routine actions of the personal administrator will require permission of the supervising judge. The personal representative must submit written motions or petitions asking the judge to approve the payment of debts, the sale of any assets, or the distribution of assets. The judge will respond to each request with a written order granting or denying permission to the administrator to take the requested action.

When the petitions of the personal representative and the orders of the judge are filed for public record, these documents will form the basis for transferring a valid title from the decedent to the new owner. Four documents are particularly important for establishing a valid record of title in real property. These documents are:

1. *Death Certificate.* This document establishes the date of the decedent's death. All real property owned by the decedent on the date of death will be part of the decedent's estate.
2. *Appointment of a Personal Representative.* This document is usually titled "Letters of Administration" for intestate estates, or "Letters Testamentary" for testate estates. The letters will always contain the name and address of the person who is legally empowered to sell or distribute the property of the estate.
3. *Final Order of Distribution.* This document will name the people who are entitled to receive the decedent's property and identify the parcels each heir or devisee receives with an adequate legal description. In some cases, the property will be described in a similar document, an Order for Sale. When the personal representative is required to sell property in order to pay debts, the court will order the property to be sold rather than distributed to the heirs or devisees.
4. *Personal Representative's Deed.* The deed from the personal representative to the purchaser, heir, or devisee is the document that actually conveys title to the grantee. However, the deed may be void if one of the first three documents is missing. For that reason, it is always good practice to insist on seeing the first three documents in the public record before accepting the deed as valid.

Verifying the strength of an ownership claim to real estate is always more difficult when the claim of ownership is based upon a transfer of title from a decedent. Because of this difficulty, many states have adopted statutes that protect good faith purchasers from irregularities in the administration of an estate. These statutes generally prohibit the heirs of a decedent from contesting a conveyance to a good faith purchaser when the conveyance results from a judicial order that appears to be valid. Such a statute protects a good faith purchaser for value whenever an order for sale and a deed from the personal representative appear in the public record. However, even in these jurisdictions, the presence of a death certificate and letters of administration will reduce the chance of a lawsuit against the purchaser.

Bessie Burkes died intestate in 1977. Her niece was appointed as personal representative for the estate. On December 5, 1977, the probate court ordered that a subdivision lot owned by Mrs. Burkes at the time of her death be sold by Grace Lyday. The next day, a personal representatives deed was delivered to Mrs. Lyday, pursuant to the order of the probate court.

Billie Gene Burkes was the son and only heir of Bessie Burkes. At the time of her death, he was incarcerated in the Georgia state penitentiary. Upon his release in 1984, he sued Grace Lyday seeking a decree vesting title to the property in him, and seeking the fair rental value of the property from and after December 6, 1977. The trial court awarded Burkes title to the property, and ruled that Grace Lyday had no interest in the property.

On appeal, the Georgia Supreme Court reversed the ruling. The court held that an order of a court for the sale of property, which is valid on its face, cannot be overturned after the time for appeal of the order has expired. Burkes v. Lyday 405 S.E. 2d 472 (GA, 1991)

Transfers by Gift

An **inter vivos gift** is a conveyance of real property made during the life of the owner. At common law, it was difficult to make an inter vivos gift of real property because of the ancient requirement that a deed must be supported by consideration. Recall that when our system of real property law was being formed, all of the land in England belonged to the king. As a result, the earliest deeds did not convey what we now consider to be the ownership of the parcel. After the conveyance, the king retained the ownership of the land. The deed merely conveyed the right to occupy the land.

***Inter Vivos* Gift**
The transfer of property by a living donor who receives no compensation in exchange for making the transfer.

The feudal right of occupancy was more in the nature of a contractual right than an ownership right. Therefore, a deed during the feudal period (to the extent deeds were used in that era) represented an assignment of the contractual right to occupy the land in return for payment of the feudal levies. Since the entire transaction involved contract rights, it seemed appropriate that the transaction require some consideration to support the mutual promises embodied in the deed.

In modern practice, the deed that conveys title to real property is separate from the contract between the parties for the conveyance. As a result, many states have abolished the requirement that deeds be supported by consideration. Even so, it is very common for a deed conveying property by inter vivos gift to recite that the conveyance is made "in consideration of one dollar plus other good and valuable consideration."

The most important question today concerns the time at which a gift becomes effective. The answer is that a gift becomes effective when a valid deed is delivered to the recipient of the gift. The next chapter will consider the requirements of a valid deed more closely. The present issue is when delivery of the deed occurs.

In matters of law, it is frequently the case that apparently simple answers involve a host of very difficult factual issues. The delivery of a deed to complete the process of making an inter vivos gift is one of those cases. Suppose that Cosima wants to give a house she owns to her daughter Carmen. She prepares a valid deed to the house, naming Carmen as the grantee. Now consider each of the following alternative factual circumstances.

1. Cosima gives the deed to Carmen at lunch one day and tells her, "The house belongs to you now."
2. Cosima tells Carmen over lunch one day, "I have prepared a deed giving my house on Elm Drive to you. The deed is in the top righthand drawer of my desk. You may pick it up whenever you like."
3. Cosima tells Carmen over lunch one day, "I have prepared a deed giving my house on Elm Drive to you. The deed is in my safe-deposit box. One day soon we will have to go to the bank together and retrieve it."
4. Cosima puts the deed in the top right hand drawer of her desk. However, she does not tell Carmen that the deed has been prepared. One day, while having lunch with Carmen, Cosima chokes on a piece of walnut torte and dies.

Under the first set of facts, Cosima has made an actual physical delivery of the deed. The gift becomes effective at the instant Carmen receives the piece of paper. Under the second set, Cosima has made a constructive delivery of the deed. Since Carmen knows where the deed is and can retrieve it without trespassing, delivery will be considered complete. Once again, Carmen becomes the owner of the house.

The third set of facts might or might not constitute a constructive delivery of the deed. If Carmen has her own key to the safe-deposit box and is authorized to enter the box without Cosima's presence, then constructive delivery has occurred. If Cosima has the only key to the box, then there will be no delivery of the deed, and hence the gift will not become effective. Finally, according to the fourth set of facts, the gift fails for lack of delivery. When Cosima dies, the house on Elm Drive will become part of her estate, along with all of the other property Cosima owned at the date of her death.

A parcel of real property, jointly owned by the plaintiff and her mother, had been erroneously included in a trust created by attorney Catherine Carter, the sister of the plaintiff and mother of the defendant. Plaintiff and her mother (who was also the grandmother of the defendant) successfully sued to have the trust dissolved, and the conveyance of the property declared a nullity.

While this lawsuit was in progress, the grandmother executed a quit claim deed to the property in favor of the defendant, and gave the deed to her attorney to hold until the litigation over the trust was completed. The grandmother died prior to the completion of that lawsuit.

On appeal, the Supreme Court of Florida ruled that no delivery of the deed had occurred. The court observed that the test of a valid delivery is whether or not the grantor of the deed reserved the right to change his or her mind. In this case, the court concluded that the grandmother gave the deed to her attorney to hold conditionally. By so doing, the grandmother reserved her right to change her mind, and a delivery of the deed did not occur. Howarth v. Moreau 430 S.2d 576 (FL, 1983)

INVOLUNTARY TRANSFERS OF REAL PROPERTY

We have already seen that property rights in the United States are never absolute rights. Individual property rights are and have always been subordinate to the needs of society at large. The governmental power of eminent domain allows society, through its duly elected representatives, to make use of any property required for public safety or convenience.

In addition, it is possible for the owner of a parcel of real estate to lose the rights of ownership in the parcel through negligence or inattention. The doctrine of adverse possession allows a trespasser to gain ownership of property under certain conditions. This involuntary transfer to ownership is extremely important. Owners are expected and required to remove trespassers from their property within a reasonable time. Whenever an owner fails to discharge this duty, the owner may be required to surrender the property to the trespasser.

Eminent Domain

Real property can be taken for public use from private owners under the governmental power of eminent domain. The U.S. Constitution requires that governments pay "just compensation" for all property and further requires that the owners of property condemned for public use be afforded due process of law. The due process requirement is met when three conditions are fulfilled:

1. The owner receives actual notice that his or her property is to be condemned for public use
2. The owner of the property is given an opportunity to appear before a court of competent jurisdiction to protest the proposed condemnation
3. If the condemnation occurs, the owner is given an opportunity for a full hearing to present evidence establishing the amount of just compensation that the condemning agency will be required to pay

The State of Alaska condemned a portion of the property adjoining the plaintiffs property in order to widen Dimond Road from two lanes to six lanes. In the process, the plaintiff's shopping center was hidden from the view of motorists on the newly widened highway. The plaintiff's claimed damages in the amount of $461,817 resulting from the loss of visibility. The trial court denied the claim, holding that loss of visibility as a result of state condemnation actions is not compensable as a matter of law.

The Alaska Supreme court reversed the summary judgment and ordered a trial on the matter. The Supreme Court reviewed the evidence, and found that the Diamond D shopping center was partially hidden by an increase in the elevation of railroad tracks adjacent to Dimond Road. The earth berms required to raise the elevation of the tracks were all built on the property of the Alaska Railroad. The court held that loss of visibility to the plaintiff as a result of constructions on the property of the Alaska Railroad were not compensable.

However, the State of Alaska also condemned a portion of the plaintiffs property for use in the road widening. The grade of this land was reduced in order to allow the new road to pass under the railroad tracks. The Supreme court held that reduction in the visibility of the plaintiff's shopping center resulting from construction on land which it previously owned, and lost through condemnation, is compensable. Diamond D Properties v. State of Alaska 806 P.2d 843 (Al, 1991)

Most states have adopted statutes that authorize various governmental agencies to condemn private land for use by the public. When a governmental agency condemns private land for public use, using the procedures for condemnation set forth in the statute, the second due process requirement will be satisfied. In these "quick take" procedures, the enabling statute renders the owner's protest void as a matter of law. The only issue remaining is the amount of compensation to be paid. Due process requires that the owner of the condemned property be afforded a full hearing on this issue.

Nollan v. Cal. Coastal

Governmental agencies must pay just compensation only when property is "taken" for public use. In this century, courts have spent a great deal of time deciding precisely when the actions of a governmental agency rise to the level of a taking that requires the payment of compensation. Early in the century, the U.S. Supreme Court decided that zoning regulations do not constitute a taking, even if they prohibit a potentially valuable use of the property. (This issue will be examined in more detail in Chapter 15.) As a result, many government agencies find themselves faced with intriguing possibilities.

Whenever a unit of government can dedicate the use of private land to public purposes through creative zoning regulations, the governmental unit can escape the payment of compensation to the private landowner. Whenever this occurs, benefits to the public are created at no expense to the public. However, the individual owner of the land that is now dedicated to public use may not be as happy about the situation. The best remedy for such an aggrieved property owner is to appeal to the courts, demanding that the governmental unit either pay for the property dedicated to public use or remove the restriction that results in public use of the property.

When confronted with such a request, the courts will carefully examine the circumstances to determine whether or not the actions of the governmental unit rise to the level of a taking. Courts generally examine the reasonableness of the regulations. In the process, the court can be expected to weigh the benefit to the public against the harm to the private landowner. A taking will be deemed to occur only when the regulation prohibits any reasonable use of the land by the owner.

Adverse Possession

The doctrine of adverse possession has its roots in the experiences of ancient landowners. Before the invention of modern surveying techniques, property boundaries were often ill defined and difficult to recognize. If Blackacre included "all of the land on the western bank of the Wavy River, from the cart ford to the crest of Piny Hill," a neighbor would be hard pressed to determine the exact location of the western boundary of Blackacre. Presumably, the line lay somewhere west of the crest of Piny Hill, but exactly where might remain a mystery. Under these conditions, it seemed quite reasonable to allow the neighbors to work out the exact boundary locations among themselves.

Even worse, written records of property ownership were somewhere between incomplete and nonexistent during the initial five hundred years of the growth of English property law. It was not at all uncommon in the 1400s to find a family occupying a plot of ground under an oral grant from the previous occupant or as a result of a written grant that had been destroyed in a fire. To prevent endless disputes between parties over the ownership of land, English courts decided that a person who occupied land for a sustained period while claiming ownership would be deemed the owner of the land. English judges saw no reason to put aside the ownership rights of persons in possession of the land simply because the original grant of ownership had been lost.

This "lost grant" theory of ownership has been more or less incorporated into modern adverse possession statutes adopted in each of the states. The statutes generally state that any person who possesses land will become the owner of the land after the passage of a certain number of years. The possession must be "hostile, open, notorious, continuous and under a claim of right," and must last for the number of years required by the particular state statute.

A landowner who is confronted with continuous trespass by a neighbor (or by anyone else) faces a series of very delicate decisions. In order to gain ownership of the land, the trespasser must occupy the land under conditions of hostility. If the owner agrees to permit the trespasser to remain on the property, then the adverse possession clock may not begin to run. The owner's permission to the trespasser removes the element of hostility required to gain title by adverse possession.

Sutton v. Miller

On the other hand, many courts have decided that when a trespasser remains in open and notorious possession for the required number of years, the possession will be presumed to be hostile. The owner will then be required to overcome this presumption by offering evidence sufficient to persuade a jury that the trespasser was aware of and accepted the owner's permission to remain on the land.

If the owner does nothing, the adverse possession clock will begin to tick. At the end of the statutory period, the trespasser can bring an action to claim title to the land and to evict the former owner from the premises. The best way for owners to protect themselves from loss by adverse possession is to bring the matter to court immediately after the trespass begins. By asking the court for an order ejecting the trespasser from the disputed land, the owner will be able to prevent the transfer of title by adverse possession.

Adverse possession issues are present whenever a practitioner purchases or sells a parcel of land bounded by a fence or roadway on any side. If the fence or road has been in existence for more than the statutory period, then it has probably become the actual property line. If the fence is placed inside the original property line, the lot has almost certainly become smaller by virtue of the adverse possession doctrine.

CONCLUSION

In this chapter, we have examined many of the procedures required to transfer some or all of the ownership rights in real property to another person. Most voluntary conveyances of real property interests begin with the execution of a contract between the buyer and the seller. We saw that the contract must be supported by valid consideration and must comply with the statute of frauds adopted by the state where the real property is located.

The chapter also examined conveyances made as gifts from the owner to the recipient of the ownership interests. These gifts can be made during the lifetime of the donor (an inter-vivos gift) or at the donor's death. When property is transferred after the death of the owner, required documents must be placed in the public record to insure that the heir or devisee of the ownership interest receives a valid title to the property. The two most important of these documents are a death certificate and letters of administration.

Finally, the chapter reviewed two circumstances in which the owner of real property will be required to convey away the ownership interest involuntarily. These involuntary conveyances occur as a result of the public right of eminent domain, or as a result of the doctrine of adverse possession.

DISCUSSION QUESTIONS

1. Name two ways in which an interest in real property can be transferred. Give examples of each.
2. Define a contract. What are the formal requisites for a binding contract? Define each.
3. Differentiate between a unilateral and a bilateral contract. When is each considered accepted?
4. What are the two requirements for legal revocation of an offer? When does a revocation become effective as opposed to an acceptance? Answer the latter question assuming the mails are used.
5. Name the two circumstances that may allow one party to escape from, or "rescind," the legal obligations required by an agreement.
6. What did the original Statute of Frauds require? What are some of the versions of this statute used in the United States today?
7. The UPC requires that a personal representative be appointed as soon as possible after the death of a person who owns property. The personal representative then must perform four tasks. What are they?
8. When transferring ownership title from a decedent to a new owner, four documents are particularly important for establishing a valid record of title in real property. Name and describe each of them.
9. Define inter vivos gift. When does a gift become effective?
10. What is eminent domain? The U.S. Constitution requires that governments afford victims of eminent domain due process of law. What are the conditions of due process?
11. What is the "lost grant" theory of ownership as applied to adverse possession?

MOSHER V. MAYACAMAS CORPORATION

263 Cal.Rptr. 373 (1989)

Recission for mutual mistake of fact

FACTS

In 1976, plaintiff and his brother, Roger L. Mosher, invested in a townhouse at Lake Tahoe. Each held an undivided one-half interest. Roger Mosher thereafter managed the investment, organizing several trades which resulted in the brothers' ownership of three Lake Tahoe properties by the time of the transaction at issue in this case.

In 1982, Roger Mosher proposed that appellant Mayacamas Corporation (an entity formed to engage in investments for Roger Mosher and his family) buy out plaintiff's interest in the properties. After a period of negotiation, plaintiff accepted appellant's proposed price of $502,750 (less assumed debt of $312,750, leaving a net due to plaintiff of $190,000 with $50,000 down and the remainder to be paid with interest over five years). The contract of sale was prepared by Roger Mosher in his capacity as Chief Executive officer of appellant.[1] Following execution of the contract on October 12, 1982, appellant made the down payment and paid $40,000 principal and $10,500 interest over the next two years.

Beginning in early 1985, property values at Lake Tahoe declined drastically. For purposes of plaintiff's motion for summary judgment, it was undisputed that a principal cause of the decline was impending federal tax legislation (later enacted as the Tax Reform Act of 1986) which substantially eliminated tax benefits for secondary residences. Appellant subsequently liquidated the properties acquired under the contract for approximately $115,000 and ceased making payments to plaintiff.

On April 30, 1986, plaintiff filed his complaint for breach of contract, seeking the balance of the purchase price plus accrued interest and costs. Appellant filed a cross-complaint seeking rescission on the basis of mistake of fact as to the valuation of the property and failure of consideration. In its opposition to plaintiff's motion for summary judgment, appellant also suggested that the trial court could reform the contract to express what it alleged to be the parties' mutual intent that the parties share the risk of any post-sale diminution in the value of the properties. The trial court found as a matter of law that plaintiff was entitled to full performance of the contract.

* * *

Appellant contends that summary judgment should not have been granted because three triable issues of material fact were presented: whether there was a mistake of fact with respect to the valuation of the properties, whether there was a "basic assumption" by the parties at the time of entering into the contract that the tax benefits generated by the properties would continue indefinitely, and whether the parties intended to share the risk of any subsequent decline in value. The trial court found as a matter of law that appellant failed to establish the existence of any of these issues. We agree.

Mistake of fact justifying relief from the obligations of a contract is defined in Civil Code section 1577 as follows: "Mistake of fact is a mistake, not caused by the neglect of a legal duty on the part of the person making the mistake, and consisting in: 1. An unconscious ignorance or forgetfulness of a fact *past or present,* material to the contract; or, 2. Belief in the *present* existence of a thing material to the contract, which does not exist, or in the *past* existence of such a thing, which has not existed." (Emphasis added.)

Appellant asserts that the valuation of the Lake Tahoe properties which formed the basis of the 1982 contract was grossly overstated, an assertion which might raise a triable issue of fact were it supported by evidence that the valuation was overstated at the time of the sale. However, the entire thrust of appellant's claim appears to be that the valuation was rendered mistaken by subsequent events, i.e., the adverse tax legislation which began affecting Lake Tahoe real estate in 1985 and

[1] Roger Mosher is also an attorney.

was ultimately enacted in 1986, nearly four years after the parties' transaction.

As the underscored language in Civil Code section 1577 makes clear, there is no legal authority for appellant's position. Absent evidence that the existence of a future contingency (e.g., continuation of tax benefits) is an assumption of the contract (about which more in a moment), the defense of mistake of fact must be premised on past or present facts about which the parties are ignorant or mistaken. There was no evidence presented to the trial court that the valuation of the properties proposed by appellant itself in 1982 was erroneous in light of facts then or previously in existence.

Smith v. Zimbalist (1934) 2 Cal.App.2d 324, 38 P.2d 170, cited by appellant, is distinguishable and actually demonstrates the illogic of appellant's argument. In Smith, an internationally famous violinist contracted to purchase two violins, believed by both buyer and seller to be a "Guarnerius" and a "Stradivarius," at a price commensurate with their supposed value. He later discovered that the violins were not genuine and ceased making payments. The trial court excused further performance on the ground of mutual mistake of fact as to the identity of the violins.

The distinction between the present case and Smith is self-evident. The violins never were what they were believed to be; they never had the value which the parties imputed to them. By contrast, the only evidence before the trial court here was that the value of the Lake Tahoe properties was diminished by events occurring years after the sale. Adoption of appellant's argument would expose virtually any unprofitable contract to legal attack upon the later occurrence of unforeseen adverse events.

Perhaps aware of the havoc a literal acceptance of its mistake of fact contention would wreak, appellant also argues that there are triable issues of fact as to whether the parties assumed a continuation of favorable tax treatment of the properties and resultant high valuation in entering into the contract and as to whether they intend to share the risk of any post-sale economic adversity. In its brief opposing summary judgment, appellant alleged that "[t]he basic assumption under which the parties were operating was that the second home marketplace would not be destroyed as a result of government intervention." Appellant also argued that since the parties' original business relationship was a "50/50 deal" it must have been their intention that the risks attendant to the 1982 transaction would be shared equally.

Unfortunately, appellant produced no competent evidence as to either of these issues. The parties' written agreement, prepared by Roger Mosher, contained no language to that effect, nor was there evidence of any oral agreement or understanding. At most, as the trial court noted, there "may have been the unrevealed subjective view of Mayacamas."

As the trial court correctly observed, appellant's predicament has resulted, as a matter of law, from an "error in judgment" rather than a mistake of fact or failure of consideration. (*See,* M. F. Kemper Const. Co. v. City of L.A. (1951) 37 Cal.2d 696, 703, 235 P.2d 7.) Appellant chose to enter into the subject contract knowing that tax benefits were a major aspect of the value of the properties and presumably knowing that the availability of such benefits could be affected by future legislation, yet it made no provision with respect to tax matters in the contract which its own chief executive officer prepared. The risk of a mistake in such circumstances clearly was borne by appellant. (*See,* Rest.2d Contracts, § 154.) Because there was insufficient evidence to entitle appellant to avoid, rescind or reform the contract, the trial court properly granted summary judgment.

The judgment is affirmed.

Case Reflections

1. What is the difference between an "error in judgment" and a "mistake of fact"?
2. What reason does the court give for refusing to allow Mayacamas to escape its contractual obligations because of the error in judgment committed by its officers?

SUTTON
V.
MILLER

592 A.2d 83 (Pa., 1991)

Adverse Possession

Appeal is taken from a final decree in Equity awarding appellees, through adverse possession, fee simple title to a parcel of land adjoining appellants' lot. In addition, appellees received mandatory injunctive relief compelling appellants to replace appellees' fence (previously removed by appellants) at a location where it had remained from 1957–1985. With modification, we affirm.

The relevant facts as found below by the Honorable George Kiester, S.J., specially presiding, are as follows: Appellees, Edward Delos, et ux., are the current owners of a parcel of land located in Clay Township, Butler County (co-appellees Sutton are the former owners of the Delos lot and are responsible for commencing litigation). Appellants, Paul and Betty Miller, own an adjoining parcel. Without the aid of a survey, sometime between 1953–1957 the Suttons constructed a fence dividing the lots. Comprised of electrified barbed wire and locust and steel posts, the fence was built for the purpose of pasturing cattle on the Sutton property—the fence being within eyesight of the Miller residence. Thereafter, between 1957–1985 the Millers repeatedly verbalized disagreement concerning the propriety of the Sutton fence, as located, as demarcating the true boundary line between the lots. Nevertheless, apart from a letter sent in 1957 by appellants' attorney expressing the Millers' dissatisfaction with the location of the fence, and apart from numerous verbal protestations by the Millers, the Millers never initiated legal proceedings to resolve the boundary dispute. In 1985 they did, however, remove the Sutton fence (without the Suttons' consent) and replace it with another fence located pursuant to a survey conducted by W. J. McGarvey, R.P.E., the differential representing the disputed property herein.

* * *

(The court next provided an extensive discussion on the correct legal procedures to be used in adverse possession cases. They concluded that when the plaintiff is in possession of the disputed property, the correct legal proceeding is an action to quiet title in the name of the plaintiff. However, when the defendant is in possession of the disputed property, then the plaintiff must bring an action in ejectment to remove the defendant from the land. In this case, the court found that the defendant came into possession of the disputed property when the second fence was built. As a result, the correct procedural posture is an action in ejectment. Finally, the court decided to accept the pleadings in the case as stating a cause of action for ejectment.)

II.

It has long been the settled rule of this Commonwealth that one who claims title by adverse possession must prove that he had actual, continuous, exclusive, visible, notorious, distinct, and hostile possession of the land for twenty-one years. Each of these elements must exist, otherwise the possession will not confer title. (Citations omitted.)

Appellants' argument [against the existence of an] adverse possession distills to the following: The Miller position is that permissive use no matter how long it may continue cannot be considered adverse. [Citation omitted.] If the original possession, as in this case, the original placement of the fence, is permissive, with the understanding that a survey would need to be conducted at some point, the mere passage of time, however long, would not convert this permissive possession into an adverse or hostile one.

* * *

"The ongoing complaints of Miller, the discussion with all parties concerned, the nature of the land and all of the facts would indicate that the property was not obtained by adverse possession since it was not a hostile taking but rather the fence existed in Miller's mind until a survey could be obtained to establish the right property line."

Appellants' Brief at 11–12.

Recently, the elements of adverse possession have been refined (not redefined) so as to create a presumption that where "all other elements of adverse possession have been established, hostility will be implied, regardless of the subjective state of mind of the trespasser." Tioga Coal v. Supermarkets Gen. Corp., 519 Pa. 66, 546 A.2d 1, 5 (1988) ("it is inconceivable that if an adverse possessor actually takes possession of land in a manner that is open, notorious, exclusive and continuous, his action will not be hostile to the true owner of the land . . ."); *see also* Schlagel v. Lombardi, 337 Pa.Super. 83, 486 A.2d 491, 494 (1984) (Pennsylvania follows the majority rule in that "a sufficiently notorious possession will always be enough to alert an owner[;] . . .hostility is implied if all other elements have been established") (citing Lyons v. Andrews, 226 Pa.Super. 351, 313 A.2d 313, 316–17 (1973)). Where, however, possession is held under rather than against the record title holder it cannot ripen into title. Upon this belief we have held that where a sufficiently notorious possession exists to alert the "true" owner of an adverse claim, it will then be incumbent upon said owner to establish "permissive" use. Satisfaction of the requisite elements of adverse possession, and the issue of "permissive" use, are questions of fact for, in this instance, the Chancellor and will not be reversed on appeal unless marked by a clear abuse of discretion or an erroneous application of the law.

Where, as here, appellants concede that plaintiff-appellees' possession was open, notorious, exclusive and continuous, hostility will be implied. *See* Tioga, *supra.* At this point, the burden shifts to appellants to prove use was not hostile, but permissive.

Fundamentally, appellants misconceive the test of "permissiveness" (and "hostility"), even though their suggestion that possession cannot be hostile where it is "permissive" is unquestionably sound. To begin, appellants make the bald assertion that placement of the fence was "with the understanding that a survey would need to be conducted at some point." No such oral understanding or agreement was found by the Chancellor, and correctly so, as this claim is thoroughly belied by the record. Not only was there lacking an acknowledgment by appellees of superior title in appellants, (citation omitted) but rather appellees at all times believed ownership to the disputed parcel was in them. Appellees' claim as to the fence demarcating the proper boundary, despite appellants' repeated complaints, belies any claimed recognition that they were holding at sufferance to appellants' rights. Moreover, we are at pains to understand how appellants can in one breath argue both permissive possession by appellees and, at the same time, argue that appellants have continuously registered complaints concerning appellees' possession, but to no avail. Turning to appellants' argument against a finding of "hostility" because "the fence existed in Miller's mind until a survey could be obtained to establish the right property line," we simply note that to the extent the test of hostility focuses of intention, it is with appellees' intention not appellants'. *See* Schlagel v. Lombardi, 337 Pa.Super. 83, 486 A.2d 491, 494 (quoting Vlachos v. Witherow, 383 Pa. 174, 118 A.2d 174, 177 (1955)) ("While the word 'hostile' has been held not to mean ill will or hostility, it does imply the intent to hold title against the record title holder."); *see also* Robin v. Brown, 308 Pa. 123, 162 A. 161 (1932). In sum, today we reaffirm that property rights are defined by law; appellants' failure to seek legal recourse within the statutory period, see 42 Pa.C.S.A. § 4430, amounts to legal acquiescence in the superiority of appellees' rights in the parcel. The chancellor appropriately found "hostility" present as well as a failure by appellants to prove "permissive" use.

Accordingly, the final decree is affirmed with modification to reflect that appellees, in Ejectment (as amended), have proved superior title to the disputed parcel through adverse possession and are entitled to immediate possession. That portion of the decree awarding mandatory injunctive relief remains unchanged.

Decree affirmed with modification.

Case Reflections

1. The court states the majority rule that open, notorious and continuous possession of land is presumed to be hostile to the owner of the land. How does this presumption affect the outcome of the case?
2. Does the adverse possession doctrine strike you as good law? When the Delos family purchased the Sutton's land, where do you suppose they believed the boundary of their property was located?

3. Now that the court was determined that the original (Sutton) fence was located on property belonging to the Delos family, will the Miller's become liable for the damage caused by removal of the Sutton fence?

BEALL V. BEALL

434 A.2d 1015 (MD, 1981)

Offers, acceptance and consideration

In this case we are called upon to decide, after a brief discussion of the reasons a purported option to purchase land does not satisfy the requirements of the statute of frauds, a question of first impression: [1] whether a bare offer by husband and wife to sell land held as tenants by the entirety survives the death of one of the tenants.

We summarize the facts. Calvin and Cecelia Beall were husband and wife, who in 1956 purchased as tenants by the entirety a 1/2 acre parcel of land, from John and Pearl Beall, Calvin's father and mother. The rectangular parcel is the subject of this dispute and is bound on three sides by a much larger plot of land (130 to 145 acres in size), at that time also owned by Calvin's parents and known as the Beall farm. Calvin had worked the Beall farm since leaving high school and had shared the fruits of his labor with his parents.

In February of 1968, Carlton Beall, a second cousin to Calvin, contracted to purchase the Beall farm from Pearl Beall, then widowed. At about the same time, Carlton obtained a written, three-year option to purchase Calvin and Cecelia's parcel for $28,000. This option recited consideration of $100.00 which was paid by check to Calvin. In February of 1971 the parties executed a new option for five years, on the same terms as the first, which again recited consideration of $100.00. Carlton never exercised either option, but in 1975 four lines were added to the bottom of the 1971 agreement which purported to extend it for three additional years. Calvin and Cecelia signed this addendum, which reads as follows:

As of October 6, 1975, we, Calvin F. Beall and Cecelia M. Beall, agree to continue this option agreement three more years February 1, 1976 to February 1, 1979.

/s / Calvin Beall

/s / Cecelia Beall

Calvin died in 1977.

In May of 1978, Carlton advised Cecelia by letter that he was accepting the offer to sell and would be in a position to settle within thirty (30) days. Cecelia responded that she was unwilling to sell for $28,000. In September of 1978, Carlton again notified her of his intent to purchase and advised her of the settlement date. Again Cecelia refused and declined to attend the settlement. Thereafter, Carlton filed suit in the Circuit Court for Prince George's County seeking specific performance. That court granted Cecelia's motion to dismiss on the ground that the 1975 agreement was unsupported by consideration and was therefore unenforceable. Carlton appealed to the Court of Special Appeals, which reversed and remanded the case for a new trial directing the circuit court to determine whether there was a valid, unrevoked offer to sell the property in dispute and, if so, whether there was a proper acceptance of that offer sufficient to create a contract specifically enforceable in equity. 413 A.2d 1365. We granted Cecelia's petition for certiorari to decide the important issues presented.

The first question we must address is whether there arose a binding agreement between Carlton on the one hand and Calvin and Cecelia on the other. An option is a continuing offer to sell by the optionor which cannot be withdrawn by him during the stated period. (citation omitted) An option is not a mere offer to sell, however, but a binding agreement if supported by consideration. The optionee has what is termed a power of acceptance, and when he accepts the offer in the prescribed manner, the option is thereby exercised

[1] Our research has revealed no reported case in the United States or Great Britain which has addressed this issue.

and a binding bilateral contract of sale is created. Moreover, when the optionee indicates his intention to exercise the option and tenders the amount of the purchase price, he has performed under the option and is entitled to specific performance [of the bilateral sales contract].

It is conceded in the instant case that the only offer Calvin attempted to accept was the offer made in the extension agreement of 1975. The key, then, to deciding whether Carlton may require Cecelia to convey to him depends upon whether a binding option contract was formed in 1975 or whether, if not, there was nevertheless a valid offer to sell outstanding at the time he attempted to effect his acceptance in 1978.

Cecelia maintains that enforcement of the alleged contract of 1975 is barred by the statute of frauds. The statute is codified in Maryland Real Property Code (1974, 1980 Cum.Supp.), § 5-104, which provides that

> (No) action may be brought on any contract for the sale or disposition of land or of any interest in or concerning land unless the contract on which the action is brought, or some memorandum or note of it, is in writing, and signed by the party to be charged or some other person lawfully authorized by him.

An option to purchase land concerns the sale of land and is, therefore, governed by the statute of frauds. See Farley v. Null, 244 Md. 567, 224 A.2d 448 (1966); Bank v. Hurst Estate, 187 Md. 333, 50 A.2d 133 (1946). To render a contract enforceable under the statute of frauds, the required memorandum must be:

1. a writing (formal or informal);
2. signed by the party to be charged or by his agent;
3. naming each party to the contract with sufficient definiteness to identify him or his agent;
4. describing the land or other property to which the contract relates; and
5. setting forth the terms and conditions of all the promises constituting the contract made between the parties. (Citations omitted.)

In sum, we have stated that the statute of frauds requires a memorandum for the sale of real estate to contain all the elements of a valid contract.

The chancellor below observed, and we agree, that reference to the various agreements between the parties readily provides most of the elements not contained in the 1975 addendum. The property to be sold was ascertainable; the parties involved were identifiable; the duration of the option was specified; and the purchase price was certain. Thus, the memorandum of agreement, by itself or by reference to earlier agreements, contained all the elements of a valid option contract except one: consideration for Calvin and Cecelia's extension of the offer to sell.

It is fundamental that in order for a contract to be binding it must be supported by consideration. Totally absent from the 1975 memorandum is any recitation of consideration for Calvin and Cecelia's extension of their offer to sell for three additional years. It would appear, therefore, that the memorandum does not fulfill the requirements of the statute and that the underlying agreement is unenforceable. Carlton argues, however, that the extension contract is nevertheless enforceable in his action for specific performance under the equitable doctrine of part performance. He asserts that the consideration for the extension was his forbearance upon exercising his 1971 option, which, in October 1975, was good until February 1976.

It has generally been accepted in Maryland that forbearance to exercise a legal right is sufficient consideration to support a promise. (Citations omitted.) However, when forbearance is offered as evidence of part performance sufficient to escape the operation of the statute of frauds it must be such as would not ordinarily have taken place in the absence of the alleged contract and therefore is not reasonably explicable on some other ground. If the part performance asserted consists wholly of forbearance to act, the fact is less likely to be evidential in character than when it consists of affirmative action. 2 Corbin, Contracts § 430, at 473–74. (10, 11) This Court has stated that part performance is adequate to remove the bar of the statute of frauds when there is "full and satisfactory evidence" of the terms of the agreement and the acts constituting part performance. (Citations omitted.) Furthermore, we have held that the part performance itself "must furnish evidence of the identity of the contract; and it is not enough that it is evidence of some agreement, but it must relate to and be unequivocal evidence of the particular agreement. . . ." Semmes v. Worthington, 38 Md. 298, 326–27 (1873)

Here Carlton offered the following testimony as evidence of his forbearance: BY MR. GARNER:

Q: Now, Mr. Beall, would you tell the Court, what were the circumstances under which the October 6th, 1975, the four lines on the bottom left-hand corner of Exhibit 9 were signed?

A: It was my mutual agreement that the contract be continued, and a mutual agreement of Cecelia as well as Calvin anmyself. And this was added and executed by them to continue this agreement. And for that reason in 1975 *this* four lines were written by my wife, she typed it in.

Q: Prior to the execution of the October 6th, 1975 those four lines on October 6th, 1975, had you expressed your intention to exercise your option?

A: Prior to that, in 1970, I expressed my desire to exercise the option.

Q: Then did you at any time subsequent to 1970 express

A: In 1975 I expressed my interest in exercising my option.

Q: And to whom did you express that?

A: I expressed it to Calvin and Cecelia.

Q: What was their reaction to that?

A: In 1971, Cecelia's reaction was that, let's take I'm ready to go, let's relocate. And, of course, in their discussion between them and I said, "You people decide what you want to do."

The question and the request was that we continue that I continue the option. And at that point I informed them that I did not have a copy of it, and in order to continue it, if they loaned me their copy I would have it typed so it could be properly executed and we could continue it. And we talked about a period of five years at the time.

And for that reason this was typed by my wife, and was executed, too, that time.

In 1975 Calvin had been sick, and was sick and the question was could he continue. It was never raised, he was sick.

And I also expressed my interest in this time, should exercise my option that if I still wanted the farm worked and wanted to continue it, and it was by mutual agree ment by he and Cecelia that this would be continued. And this was extension was placed on this agreement, signed by them. And I did not sign it because I didn't see the need for it.

Q: But you agreed to it, did you not?

A: I agreed to it. And they continued to work the farm.

Q: When was that agreement signed, the four lines?

A: October the 6th.

Also adduced at trial was the fact that Calvin had worked this farm from 1956 until 1968, sharing the profits of his labor with his parents. From 1968 until his death, he continued to work the farm for Carlton, relieving him from paying the taxes and all expenses incident to farming. It is not certain, therefore, that Carlton's election to postpone acceptance of the offer was an act which he would not have done in the absence of Calvin and Cecelia's extension of the offer to sell their land. As a matter of fact it is clearly explainable on the ground that he wished Calvin to continue working the farm without regard to his interest in purchasing the subject property.

Since it is uncertain what Carlton's forbearance in fact related to, part performance has not been sufficiently established in order to take the 1975 agreement out of the operation of the statute of frauds. Thus, the purported extension of the option in 1975 was not a binding contract but merely an offer, which could be revoked at any time prior to acceptance. James L. Kernan Co. v. Cook, 162 Md. 137, 142, 159 A. 256 (1932).

Carlton argues that, even if the extension agreement was unenforceable as a contract but was merely a bare offer, he accepted this offer before it was withdrawn, thereby creating a binding contract between the parties which the court may enforce. Apparently what Carlton does not reckon with is the effect of Calvin's death in 1977 upon this offer, based upon the fact that Calvin and Cecelia owned the property in question as tenants by the entirety.

The general rule is that the death of an offeror revokes his offer or causes his offer to lapse. (Citations omitted.) Therefore, after death, the formation of that "apparent state of mind of the parties which is embodied in an expression of mutual consent" is rendered impossible.

Cecelia asserts that the offer at issue was made by a single unit, tenants by the entirety, and, that when Calvin died the marriage of Calvin and Cecelia was terminated and operated as the legal death of the offeror, which, according to the long established rule, caused the offer to lapse. Carlton's rejoinder is that the offer to sell was signed by two individuals, each of whom had an interest in the whole, and that while the death of Calvin operated as a revocation of his offer to sell and terminated his interest, his death neither (1) terminated the offer made by Cecelia, an offer over which she retained, as an individual and as from the outset, the unrestricted power to revoke; (2) increased her interest, see Columbian Carbon Co. v. Knight, 207 Md. 203, 114 A.2d 28, 51 A.L.R.2d 1232 (1955); nor (3) destroyed her capacity to convey. In other words, Carlton suggests the effect of the death of Calvin was merely to free the estate from his participation. See Lang v. Commissioner, 289 U.S. 109, 53 S.Ct. 534, 77 L.Ed. 1066 (1933), affirming 61 F.2d 280 (4th Cir. 1932). Such a view, however, flies in the face of common law principles regarding the nature of an offer and the attributes of an estate held by the entirety.

Maryland retains the estate of tenancy by the entirety in its traditional form. Columbian Carbon Co. v. Knight, *supra*. By common law, a conveyance to husband and wife does not make them joint tenants, nor are they tenants in common; they are in the contemplation of the law but one person, and hence they take, not by moieties, but by the entirety. Neither can alienate without the consent of the other, and the survivor takes the whole. (Citations omitted.) Tenancy by the entirety may not be severed by the consent of one of the parties or by their individual judgment creditors during their joint lives; except in the case of absolute divorce, during the lifetime of both tenants their estate may be terminated only by the joint action of both and a conveyance by both to a third person. Eastern Shore Bldg. & Loan Corp. v. Bank of Somerset, 253 Md. 525, 253 A.2d 367 (1969).

While the individual interests of each will be protected by a court of equity under appropriate circumstances, *see,* e.g., Colburn v. Colburn, 262 Md. 333, 278 A.2d 1 (1971), on appeal after remand, 265 Md. 468, 290 A.2d 480 (1972) (wife entitled to one-half the income from property held by the entireties), when a husband and wife act together with respect to property held as tenants by the entirety, they are required, under traditional legal principles, to be of one mind. Calvin and Cecelia signed a 1976 addendum not in their purely individual capacities but as a team. They acted together in making but a single offer to convey. The correct focus, then, is not upon the individual powers and capacities of Calvin and Cecelia with respect to their survivor interests, but upon the powers and capacities of each in their respective roles as tenants by the entirety.[2]

Thus, our adoption of the "team" approach is as much occasioned by practical considerations as it is upon theory. Nevertheless, the fact that each had an interest in the whole, as opposed to only part, is one of the features which distinguishes this case from Ritchie v. Rawlings, 106 Kan. 118, 186 P. 1033, 1035 (1920), which involves an offer to distribute the proceeds of an estate in a manner different from that provided in the will, and holds that acceptance of an offer must be communicated during the life of all the parties.

With respect to the nature of the offer, it has been held that:

The continuation of an offer is in the nature of its constant repetition, which necessarily requires someone capable of making a repetition. Obviously this can no more be done by a dead man than a contract can, in the first instance, be made by a

[2] This approach is conceptually dissimilar to that proffered by Mrs. Beall, although both approaches lead to the same conclusion. Her approach focuses on the fiction of "oneness" and enables the analysis to proceed as though the offer had been made by the tenancy itself. Were divorce instead of death the triggering event, however, we fear Mrs. Beall's approach might lead to anomalous results.

dead man. (Pratt v. Trustees of Baptist Soc., *supra*, 93 Ill. at 478–79.)

Viewing the offer of tenants by the entirety as being made by a team rather than the two individuals who make up this team provides a solution in the instant case. The continuation of an offer made in this fashion depends upon the continuous assent of both tenants, for neither can continue an offer to sell without the continued assent of the other. Here, in the absence of consideration to support an option, the vitality of the offer made by Calvin and Cecelia depended upon the continued assent of each; upon Calvin's death, his assent was no longer viable. Hence, the offer lapsed upon the death of Calvin Beall. After his death, one of two events was necessary to the formation of a contract in the instant case: (1) a renewal by Cecelia of the lapsed offer to sell, which offer was accepted by Carlton Beall, or (2) an offer to buy made by Carlton, which offer was accepted by Cecelia. Neither of the above sequences of events took place. We conclude that when Carlton sent his letter of acceptance in May of 1978 there was no viable offer for him to accept. Calvin's death had effectively caused the offer to lapse. We hold, therefore, that no enforceable contract was formed between the parties.

* * *

Judgment of the court of special appeals reversed; the case remanded to that court with instructions to affirm the judgment circuit court Prince George's County. Appellee to pay the costs.

Case Reflections

1. Is an option to purchase real estate a binding contract?
2. To serve as consideration which supports a binding contract, a forbearance to act must be a bargained for exchange. What evidence from the trial did the court rely on in holding that Calvin's decision not to exercise his legal right to purchase the property was not adequate consideration to support the option contract?
3. The written memorandum was sufficient under the Statute of Frauds to constitute an offer to sell the property. Was the offer revoked prior to acceptance? Why or why not?

ESTATE OF BEASON V. NORTH

811 P.2d 848 (KA, 1991)

Testate succession

This appeal arises from proceedings involving the estates of Macy Virgil Beason and Caroline Hearting Beason which were consolidated with a quiet title action. The trial court quieted title to the disputed land in favor of Albert and Eunice North, set aside a deed, and determined that a codicil to Caroline Hearting Beason's will would not be admitted to probate.

In order to understand the issues, it is necessary to give background information and the procedural history of what has occurred in the case. Readers are informed that this dispute is over four sections of land in Trego County owned by Macy and Caroline Beason, which will be referred to in this opinion as Hearting-Beason II (HB II). The dispute is between the North family (who managed the Beasons' farming operation) and nieces and nephews of the Beasons. The original farm and ranch, Hearting-Beason I (HB I), and other assets devised to the Kansas State University Foundation are not in dispute. Macy Beason and Caroline Hearting Beason were husband and wife. They had no children. They lived in Trego County and, starting with a section inherited from Caroline's parents, they developed a large farm and ranch operation along with other assets. During the last 25 to 30 years of their lives, they had no close family relationships. Since 1981, the ranching on HB I had been done by the North family. The Beasons were pleased with the way that the Norths farmed the land. In July 1987, the Beasons purchased four additional sections of land (HB II) for the purpose of eventually giving it to Albert and Eunice North.

After several revisions, Macy and Caroline executed a will on August 15, 1987, entitled "Joint and Mutual Will," giving HB II to the Norths and giving HB I and all other property to The Kansas State University Foundation, with a life estate reserved for the survivor.

Within half an hour of executing the will, Macy executed a deed to HB II, giving it to himself and Caroline as joint tenants with right of survivorship and not as tenants in common. This deed was not introduced into evidence at any of the proceedings, although it was testified to by one of the drafters of the will and deed. Macy had purchased HB II at public auction and Caroline's name had not been placed on the deed at that time.

A codicil to the will was executed on February 25, 1988, which provided that in the event the Norths predeceased the Beasons, HB II would go to the Norths' sons, Arliyn and Daryl.

Macy Virgil Beason died on August 28, 1988, and shortly thereafter his estate proceedings were opened. At this point, Caroline was 91 and in a hospital in Random. Steve Beason and C. Wade Beason (nephews of Macy) removed Caroline from the hospital in Ransom and took her to a hospital in Hays, and then to a series of other hospitals, ending in Kansas City, Missouri. While in Hays, Caroline filed for a voluntary conservatorship, attempting to have Muriel Faith Cook (one of Macy's nieces) appointed as conservator.

Three of Macy's nephews and nieces (Steve Beason, Nixie Koelling, and Muriel Faith Cook) filed an objection to the appointment of the Norths as executors of Macy's estate. At the hearing on the admission of the will to probate on October 7, 1988, these three appeared personally and through an attorney. (Another nephew appeared personally.) The court admitted the will and codicil to probate and made a minor correction to a land description.

The next day, October 8, 1988, Caroline executed a deed for all four sections of HB II to "all nieces and nephews of Macy V. Beason who survive him & all nieces and nephews who survive grantor at the time of her death in equal, undivided shares (per capita)," and granted herself a life estate. Several days later, Caroline executed a power of attorney in favor of C. Wade Beason and Steve Beason. The deed was not recorded until January 10, 1989.

Shortly after this, in an order with the same case number of Macy's probate case, the court executed a restraining order against Macy's nieces and nephews prohibiting them from exercising custody or control over Caroline and directing that she be returned to the hospital in Ransom. After several days of legal maneuvers, a guardian ad litem was appointed for Caroline and an order was issued directing the return of Caroline to the Ransom Hospital.

Also at this point, Caroline executed a codicil to her will naming various nieces and nephews as executors and changing paragraph 3, which originally gave four sections of HB II to the Norths, to leave it to all her nieces and nephews who survived her and to the nieces and nephews of Macy who survived him. Macy's will was admitted to probate on November 1, 1988. No appeal was taken. . . .On September 20, 1989, Caroline died, and her estate was soon opened.

* * *

A quiet title suit was filed by the Norths personally and as executors of the estate. The petition was filed under the caption of both Beasons' estates and given the same case numbers. (The trial court granted a motion to consolidate the estate cases for the purposes of the quiet title action.) The petition lists all 34 of Macy's nephews and nieces as parties to be served. The Norths alleged that by virtue of a certain deed (the deed executed by Caroline giving HB II to Macy's and her nieces and nephews), the defendants claimed an interest in the property. The Norths alleged that the trial court's decision in Macy's estate was res judicata and that when Caroline executed the deed she was incompetent and under undue influence of the defendants.

Six nieces and nephews answered the quiet title suit. We believe five of them were parties to the July 20, 1989, hearing where the trial court determined they were not heirs, devisees, or legatees of Macy and struck their pleadings and barred them from further participation in the lawsuit.

* * *

There are 42 defendants named in the quiet title action, 34 of whom are allegedly nieces and nephews of Macy Beason. In the Journal Entry of

Judgment Quieting Title, cancelling the deed from Caroline Hearting Beason to all the nieces and nephews and holding the codicil to her will "ineffectual," the judgment was against all of the nieces and nephews. The trial court held that the issue of whether the wills of the Beasons are joint, mutual, and contractual "has been decided, that no appeal has been taken, and that the issue is res judicata. The parties here contesting the will were present at the hearings, were represented by counsel, and no appeal was taken from the Orders entered." In quieting title in favor of the North family (Albert, Eunice, Daryl and Arliyn—although the latter two do not appear to be devisees under the Beasons' will unless their parents predeceased the Beasons), the trial court also held that the deed and codicil to Caroline Hearting Beason's will was obtained by undue influence and persuasion and that Caroline Hearting Beason was incapable of making a valid warranty deed or will when the instruments were executed.

The trial court previously based its decision to quiet title, cancel the deed, and hold the codicil ineffectual on the fact that the nieces and nephews had appeared in Macy's probate proceeding and did not appeal the trial court's decision not to allow them to participate. The trial court reasoned they were, therefore, bound by the trial court's later decision that the wills were joint, mutual, and contractual, and anything Caroline Hearting Beason did inconsistent with Macy's will was ineffectual.

* * *

When Macy Beason died, and his estate was opened, the nieces and nephews of Macy and his wife were not legatees or devisees under the will; nor were any of them heirs of Macy because as long as his wife was alive and they had no children, she was his sole heir. Consequently, the nephews and nieces were not entitled to notice and had no standing to challenge the probate proceedings. In re Estates of Estes, 239 Kan. 192, 196, 718 P.2d 298 (1986).

By allowing a quiet title action to the inserted in the middle of two probate proceedings, the trial court effectively defeated the intent and purpose of the probate code for the orderly administration of estates. The place to determine whether the wills are joint, mutual, and contractual is in the pending probate proceedings, not in a quiet title action. It is not the result that requires reversal. It is the procedure used in this case that requires reversal.

When estates are still pending and the court has not assigned interests in real estate, a quiet title action is not a proper method of eliminating persons who may be entitled to share in estate property and who have not had an opportunity to have their day in court.

Here, the trial court has quieted title in the Norths while proceedings relating to a codicil to Caroline Hearting Beason's will are still pending. The court has, by using the wrong procedure (quiet title), denied at least one of the appellants his day in court.

We do not hold that a quiet title action cannot be brought by an estate. It can, under proper circumstances. We simply hold that title to real estate that is subject to an ongoing or pending probate proceeding should first have the claims of heirs, devisees, and legatees decided in the probate proceedings and title assigned to the proper party pursuant to the probate code. Then, if a quiet title suit is necessary, it may later be brought as part of the probate proceedings.

* * *

Reversed and remanded with directions to set aside the judgment in the quiet title action and to proceed with the orderly administration of the decedents' estates.

Case Reflections

1. If you were the probate judge supervising the administration of the Beason estate, how would you proceed?

NOLLAN V. CALIFORNIA COASTAL COMMISSION

483 U.S. 825, 107 S. Ct. 3141 (1987)

Land use regulation and eminent domain

I.

SCALIA, *Justice.*

The Nollans own a beachfront lot in Ventura County, California. A quarter-mile north of their property is Faria County Park, an oceanside public park with a public beach and recreation area. Another public beach area, known locally as "the Cove," lies 1,800 feet south of their lot. A concrete seawall approximately eight feet high separates the beach portion of the Nollans' property from the rest of the lot. The historic mean high tide line determines the lot's oceanside boundary.

The Nollans originally leased their property with an option to buy. The building on the lot was a small bungalow, totaling 504 square feet, which for a time they rented to summer vacationers. After years of rental use, however, the building had fallen into disrepair, and could no longer be rented out. The Nollans' option to purchase was conditioned on their promise to demolish the bungalow and replace it. In order to do so, under California Public Resources Code secs. 30106, 30212, and 30600 (West 1986), they were required to obtain a coastal development permit from the California Coastal Commission. On February 25, 1982, they submitted a permit application to the Commission in which they proposed to demolish the existing structure and replace it with a three-bedroom house in keeping with the rest of the neighborhood.

(The Nollans were informed that the permit would be issued subject to the requirement that they allow the public an easement to cross their lot on the ocean side of the concrete sea wall. They appealed the decision of the Coastal Commission to the California courts, and eventually to the U.S. Supreme Court)

II.

Had California simply required the Nollans to make an easement across their beachfront available to the public on a permanent basis in order to increase public access to the beach, rather than conditioning their permit to rebuild their house on their agreeing to do so, we have no doubt there would have been a taking. To say that the appropriation of a public easement across a landowner's premises does not constitute the taking of a property interest but rather, (as Justice Brennan contends) "a mere restriction on its use," is to use words in a manner that deprives them of all their ordinary meaning. Indeed, one of the principal uses of the eminent domain power is to assure that the government be able to require conveyance of just such interests, so long as it pays for them. (Citations omitted.) Perhaps because the point is so obvious, we have never been confronted with a controversy that required us to rule upon it, but our cases' analysis of the effect of other governmental action leads to the same conclusion. We have repeatedly held that, as to property reserved by its owner for private use, 'the right to exclude [others is] 'one of the most essential sticks in the bundle of rights that are commonly characterized as property.' " Loretto v. Teleprompter Manhattan CATV Corp., 458 U. S. 419, 433, 102 S. Ct. 3164, 3175, 73 L. Ed. 2d 868 (1982), quoting Kaiser Aetna v. United States, 444 U. S. 164, 176, 100 S. Ct. 383, 391, 62 L. Ed. 2d 332 (1979). In Loretto we observed that where governmental action results in "[a] permanent physical occupation" of the property, by the government itself or by others, "our cases uniformly have found a taking to the extent of the occupation, without regard to whether the action achieves an important public benefit or has only minimal economic impact on the owner." (Citations omitted.) We think a "permanent physical occupation" has occurred, for purposes of that rule, where individuals are given a permanent and continuous right to pass to and fro, so that the real property may continuously be traversed, even though no particular individual is permitted to station himself permanently upon the premises.

* * *

Given, then, that requiring uncompensated conveyance of the easement outright would violate the Fourteenth Amendment, the question becomes whether requiring it to be conveyed as a condition for issuing a land use permit alters the outcome. We have long recognized that land use regulation does not effect a taking if it 'substantially advance[s] legitimate state interests" and does not "den[y] an owner economically viable use of his land," Agins v. Tiburon, 447 U. S. 255, 260, 100 S. Ct. 2138, 2141, 65 L. Ed. 2d 106 (1980). *See also* Penn Central Transportation Co. v. New York City, 438 U. S. 104, 127, 98 S. Ct. 2646, 2660, 57 L. Ed. 2d 631 (1978) ("a use restriction may constitute a 'taking' if not reasonably necessary to the effectuation of a substantial government purpose").

Our cases have not elaborated on the standards for determining what constitutes a "legitimate state interest" or what type of connection between the regulation and the state interest satisfies the requirement that the former "substantially advance" the latter. They have made clear, however, that a broad range of governmental purposes and regulations satisfies these requirements. (Citations omitted.) The Commission argues that among these permissible purposes are protecting the public's ability to see the beach, assisting the public in overcoming the "psychological barrier" to using the beach created by a developed shorefront, and preventing congestion on the public beaches. We assume, without deciding, that this is so—in which case the Commission unquestionably would be able to deny the Nollans their permit outright if their new house (alone, or by reason of the cumulative impact produced in conjunction with other construction) would substantially impede these purposes, unless the denial would interfere so drastically with the Nollans' use of their property as to constitute a taking.

* * *

The Commission argues that a permit condition that serves the same legitimate police-power purpose as a refusal to issue the permit should not be found to be a taking if the refusal to issue the permit would not constitute a taking. We agree. Thus, if the Commission attached to the permit some condition that would have protected the public's ability to see the beach notwithstanding construction of the new house—for example, a height limitation, a width restriction, or a ban on fences—so long as the Commission could have exercised its police power (as we have assumed it could) to forbid construction of the house altogether, imposition of the condition would also be constitutional. Moreover (and here we come closer to the facts of the present case), the condition would be constitutional even if it consisted of the requirement that the Nollans provide a viewing spot on their property for passersby with whose sighting of the ocean their new house would interfere. Although such a requirement, constituting a permanent grant of continuous access to the property, would have to be considered a taking if it were not attached to a development permit, the Commission's assumed power to forbid construction of the house in order to protect the public's view of the beach must surely include the power to condition construction upon some concession by the owner, even a concession of property rights, that serves the same end. If a prohibition designed to accomplish that purpose would be a legitimate exercise of the police power rather than a taking, it would be strange to conclude that providing the owner an alternative to that prohibition which accomplishes the same purpose is not.

The evident constitutional propriety disappears, however, if the condition substituted for the prohibition utterly fails to further the end advanced as the justification for the prohibition. When that essential nexus is eliminated, the situation becomes the same as if California law forbade shouting fire in a crowded theatre, but granted dispensations to those willing to contribute \$100 to the state treasury. While a ban on shouting fire can be a core exercise of the State's police power to protect the public safety, and can thus meet even our stringent standards for regulation of speech, adding the unrelated condition alters the purpose to one which, while it may be legitimate, is inadequate to sustain the ban. Therefore, even though, in a sense, requiring a \$100 tax contribution in order to shout fire is a lesser restriction on speech than an outright ban, it would not pass constitutional muster. Similarly here, the lack of nexus between the condition and the original purpose of the building restriction converts that purpose to something other than what it was. The purpose then becomes, quite simply, the obtaining of an easement to serve some valid governmental purpose, but without payment of compensation. Whatever may be the outer limits of "legitimate state interests" in the takings and land use context, this is not one of them. In short, unless the permit condition serves the same governmental purpose as the development ban, the building restriction is not a valid regulation of land use but "an out-and-out plan of extortion."

Reversed.

BRENNAN, Justice (Dissenting)

Appellants in this case sought to construct a new dwelling on their beach lot that would both diminish visual access to the beach and move private development closer to the public tidelands. The Commission reasonably concluded that such "buildout," both individually and cumulatively, threatens public access to the shore. It sought to offset this encroachment by obtaining assurance that the public may walk along the shoreline in order to gain access to the ocean. The Court finds this an illegitimate exercise of the police power, because it maintains that there is no reasonable relationship between the effect of the development and the condition imposed. The first problem with this conclusion is that the Court imposes a standard of precision for the exercise of a State's police power that has been discredited for the better part of this century. Furthermore, even under the Court's cramped standard, the permit condition imposed in this case directly responds to the specific type of burden on access created by appellants' development. Finally, a review of those factors deemed most significant in takings analysis makes clear that the Commission's action implicates none of the concerns underlying the Takings Clause. The Court has thus struck down the Commission's reasonable effort to respond to intensified development along the California coast, on behalf of landowners who can make no claim that their reasonable expectations have been disrupted. The Court has, in short, given appellants a windfall at the expense of the public.

I.

There can be no dispute that the police power of the States encompasses the authority to impose conditions on private development. It is also by now commonplace that this Court's review of the rationality of a State's exercise of its police power demands only that the State "could rationally have decided "that the measure adopted might achieve the State's objective. (Citations omitted.) In this case, California has employed its police power in order to condition development upon preservation of public access to the ocean and tidelands. The Coastal Commission, if it had so chosen, could have denied the Nollans's request for a development permit, since the property would have remained economically viable without the requested new development. Instead, the State sought to accommodate the Nollans' desire for new development, on the condition that the development not diminish the overall amount of public access to the coastline.

* * *

"The term 'police power' connotes the time-tested conceptional limit of public encroachment upon private interests. Except for the substitution of the familiar standard of 'reasonableness,' this Court has generally refrained from announcing any specific criteria. The classic statement of the rule in Lawton v. Steele, 152 U. S. 133, 137 [14 S. Ct. 499, 501, 38 L. Ed. 385] (1984), is still valid today: '. . . [I]t must appear, first, that the interests of the public . . .require [government] interference; and, second, that the means are reasonably necessary for the accomplishment of the purpose, and not unduly oppressive upon individuals.' Even this rule is not applied with strict precision, for this Court has often said that 'debatable questions as to reasonableness are not for the courts but for the legislature . . .'"

* * *

II.

The fact that the Commission's action is a legitimate exercise of the police power does not, of course, insulate it from a takings challenge, for when "regulation goes too far it will be recognized as a taking." Pennsylvania Coal Co. v. Mahon, 260 U. S. 393, 415, 43 S. Ct. 158, 160, 67 L. Ed. 322 (1922). Conventional takings analysis underscores the implausibility of the Court's holding, for it demonstrates that this exercise of California's police power implicates none of the concerns that underline our takings jurisprudence. In reviewing a Takings Clause claim, we have regarded as particularly significant the nature of the governmental action and the economic impact of regulation, especially the extent to which regulation interferes with investment-backed expectations. Penn Central, 438 U. S., at 124, 98 S. Ct., at 2659. The character of the government action in this case is the imposition of a condition on permit approval, which allows the public to continue to have access to the coast. The physical intrusion permitted by the deed restriction is minimal. The public is permitted the right to pass and re-pass along the coast in an area from the seawall to the mean high tide mark. This area is at its widest 10 feet, which means that even without the permit condition, the public's right of access permits it to pass on average within a few feet of the seawall. Passage closer to the 8-foot high rocky seawall will make the appellants even less visible to the public than passage along the high tide area farther out on the beach. The intrusiveness of such passage is even less than the intrusion resulting from the required dedication of a sidewalk in front of private residences, exactions which are commonplace conditions on approval of development.

* * *

Finally, the character of the regulation in this case is not unilateral government action, but a condition on approval of a development request submitted by appellants. The State has not sought to interfere with any pre-existing property interest, but has responded to appellants' proposal to intensify development on the coast. Appellants themselves choose to submit a new development application, and could claim no property interest in its approval. They were aware that approval of such development would be conditioned on preservation of adequate public access to the ocean. The State has initiated no action against appellants' property; had the Nollans not proposed more intensive development in the coastal zone, they would never have been subject to the provision that they challenge.

Examination of the economic impact of the Commission's action reinforces the conclusion that no taking has occurred. Allowing appellants to intensify development along the coast in exchange for ensuring public access to the ocean is a classic instance of government action that produces a "reciprocity of advantage." Appellants have been allowed to replace a one-story 521-square-foot beach home with a two-story 1,674-square-foot residence and an attached two-car garage, resulting in development covering 2,464 square feet of the lot. Such development obviously significantly increases the value of appellants' property; appellants make no contention that this increase is offset by any diminution in value resulting from the deed restriction, much less that the restriction made the property less valuable than it would have been without the new construction. Furthermore, appellants gain an additional benefit from the Commission's permit condition program. They are able to walk along the beach beyond the confines of their own property only because the Commission has required deed restrictions as a condition of approving other new beach developments. Thus, appellants benefit both as private landowners and as members of the public from the fact that new development permit requests are conditioned on preservation of public access.

I respectfully dissent.

Case Reflections

1. Justice Scalia's majority opinion likens the grant of a public easement across the Nollans property as a condition for obtaining a building permit to charging a fee for permission to shout fire in a crowded theater. How would you explain this simile to someone who has never studied law?
2. How does the majority opinion define the connection required by the Constitution between regulations imposed by state governments and the legitimate state interests which those regulations advance?
3. Do you agree with Justice Brennan's argument that the development restriction is minimal, since the public already has the right to walk along the beach below the high tide line, which is "only a few feet" from the Nollan's seawall?

957 RECORD OF DEEDS 957 GENESEE COUNTY 957
RECORD OF DEEDS 958 GENESEE COUNTY 958
RECORD OF DEEDS 959 GENESEE COUNTY 959
RECORD OF DEEDS 960 GENESEE COUNTY 960
RECORD OF DEEDS 961 GENESEE COUNTY 961
RECORD OF DEEDS 962 GENESEE COUNTY 962
963 RECORD OF DEEDS 963 GENESEE COUNTY 963
964 RECORD OF DEEDS 964 GENESEE COUNTY
975
976
977
978
979
980
981
982

CHAPTER 8

PREPARATION AND RECORDING OF DEEDS

LEARNING OBJECTIVES

After reading this chapter, you should be able to:

1. Identify and discuss the requirements for a valid deed
2. Recognize defects in a deed that could make the instrument invalid
3. Describe the process required for a buyer to obtain full record title to a parcel of real property

KEY TERMS

- Livery of Seisin
- Warranty Deed
- Quitclaim Deed
- Granting Clause
- Habendum Clause
- Metes and Bounds
- Subdivision Plat
- Record Title
- Race Statutes
- Notice Statutes
- Good Faith Purchaser for Value

A deed is the actual physical record of property ownership in modern real estate practice. When a deed has been properly executed and delivered to the grantor, conveyance of the title to the property described in the deed has occurred. Once the deed is deposited for record with the appropriate officer, it becomes evidence to all the world that title to the property described in the deed is now vested in the person named as the grantee of the deed.

The distinction between the conveyance of title and the public record of title is an important one. The grantee in a deed may enforce ownership rights in the property only against those persons who know about the existence of the deed. The grantor of the deed will always know about the existence of the deed, since the grantor prepared, executed, and delivered it to the grantee. As a result, the grantee may always enforce the ownership rights conveyed by the deed against the grantor.

KEY POINTS

The central thesis of this book is that legal rights are of no value unless the pe son who possesses a right can enforce it against anyone who might be inclined to interfere with the exercise of the right. That is why real estate practitioners must constantly ask two questions:

1. How can valuable ownership rights in real property be acquired?
2. What must be done to make those valuable rights enforceable after they are purchased?

Suppose an unscrupulous grantor delivers a deed conveying one piece of property to two different buyers on the same day. Both grantees have legally enforceable ownership rights against the scoundrel who sold the property twice. But can either grantee enforce ownership rights against the other? The answer to that question can only be determined by a lawsuit.

Each of the fifty states has adopted some form of recording statute to aid judges and juries in the process of sorting out the ownership claims asserted by people who each hold a different deed to the same property. The fact that every state has recognized the need for such a statute means that real estate practitioners must be constantly on guard in a purchase transaction. In this chapter, you will learn how make sure that you actually get the ownership interest you paid for when you purchase real property.

DEEDS

Livery of seisin The ancient method of transferring the right to possess and enjoy land, used in England during the feudal period.

The modern deed is the result of an evolutionary process that is nearly one thousand years in length. The beginnings of this process can be found in the practices and purchases of the feudal period in England. During the years following the Norman conquest of England in 1066, the right to possess land was transferred in a ceremony known as **livery of seisin.** The ceremony required the "seller" and the "buyer" of the possessory rights to go on the land together, in the company of witnesses. There, the seller would hand the buyer a twig from a tree, or a clod of earth, or some other artifact symbolizing the possession of the land. As the seller handed the artifact to the buyer, he was also required to say certain well-recognized words of conveyance.

The words of the seller, in the presence of witnesses, were all that was required to effect the conveyance of the rights of possession in the land. However, it is not unreasonable to infer that the solemn nature of the proceedings, together with the formal nature of the required words, lent an air of mystery and magic to the ceremony. Certainly the law judges in early English courts treated the words as if they had the potential for magic. If the seller stated "and I do hereby covenant and agree with B and his heirs that they shall have the use and enjoyment of these lands forever," then judges were prone to decide that an estate in fee simple absolute had been conveyed. Different incantations would lead judges to find that different kinds of possessory interests had been created by the livery of seisin ceremony.

The obvious result of this procedure was to place tremendous importance on the words of conveyance used by the grantor. In the 1500s the livery of seisin ceremony was largely displaced by written documents, which are the direct ancestors of contemporary deeds. Even though the early ceremony of conveyance was replaced by the writings of later centuries, the quasi-magical importance of the words used in the writings was retained until very recently. Today, most states have adopted statutes requiring only simple, direct phrases to effect the legal transfer of property interest. But most deed forms still present an abundance of flowery language, echoing the rich history of property law.

Warranty Deed
A deed conveying title to real property in which the grantor warrants that he or she actually possesses the title being conveyed. Warranty deeds are most commonly used to transfer title in exchange for payment of a purchase price.

Warranty and Quitclaim Deeds

The vast majority of deeds used in current real estate practice are either warranty deeds or quitclaim deeds. A **warranty deed** contains covenants made by the grantor to the grantee that guarantee (warrant) that the grantee will have a valid legal title upon receiving the deed. A quitclaim deed does not contain these warranties.

Grantees will obviously prefer to receive a warranty deed, since the title guarantees offered by the deed are clearly an advantage to the grantee. A grantor who delivers a **quitclaim deed** does not promise that the grantor has any ownership interest in the property. The only effect of a quitclaim deed is to insure that the grantor has no ownership interest after the quitclaim deed is recorded.

Quitclaim Deed
A deed which releases any title to the real property described in the deed which the grantor may own. Quit claim deeds are used primarily to correct defects in the record title to real property.

Deed clauses

A warranty deed will usually have seven different clauses. The wording required for each clause varies from place to place, being determined by the statutes in effect in the state where the property is located. This chapter will discuss a deed form that should be valid in every state. The form we will be using contains more words than would be required by any one state, in order to include all of the words that might be required by any state. The words inserted in brackets at various places are not part of the deed form but are there only to simplify our discussion of the various clauses.

KEY POINTS

Quitclaim deeds are preferred in three different situations. The first is the nee to remove a cloud from the record title to real property. Clerical mistakes in the documents that compose the record title to a parcel of land often result in the incomplete or incorrect transfer of ownership interests. As a result, the present owner's title may be subject to claims from a relative of a former owner or some other stranger. The quitclaim deed is the only deed form that can be used to correct such defects.

The second most common use of quitclaim deeds is in mortgage foreclosures and the administration of a decedent's estate. The representative of the lenders in a foreclosure action and the personal representative of a decedent often do not have title to the property they are conveying. As a result, they must convey title with a quitclaim deed, backed by a court order requiring the conveyance.

Finally, government agencies transferring title to real property frequently use the quitclaim deed to accomplish the transfer. Enabling statutes that govern transactions by various units of government may prohibit the issuance of a warranty deed, or the governmental agent in charge of the conveyance may simply be unwilling to obligate the public purse to the payment of title warranties.

Granting Clause The words in a deed which actually convey an ownership estate in real property from the grantor to the grantee of the deed.

Habendum Clause The words in a deed which describe the nature of the ownership estate conveyed from the grantor to the grantee. Any limitations on the ownership estate should be included in the habendum clause.

GENERAL WARRANTY DEED

[Premises Clause]

THIS INDENTURE MADE, this ______day of ________,19___, between (name of grantor), of (grantor's address), party of the first part, and (name of grantee), of (grantee's address), party of the second part:

WITNESSETH, that the party of the first part, in consideration of the sum of_____ Dollars, to him in hand paid by the party of the second part, the receipt whereof is hereby acknowledged,

[Granting Clause]

does hereby grant, bargain, sell, and convey unto the party of the second part, his heirs and assigns, forever, all that tract or parcel of land lying and being in (city, county and state) and described as follows, to wit: (legal description)

[Habendum Clause]

To have and to hold the same, together with all the lands, tenements, hereditaments and appurtenances thereunto belonging or in any wise appertaining, to the party of the second part, his heirs and assigns, forever.

[Warranty Clause]

And the party of the first part, for himself, his heirs, executors and administrators, does hereby covenant with the party of the second part, his heirs and assigns, that the party of the first part is well seised in fee of the lands and premises aforesaid; that he has good right to sell and convey the same in manner and form aforesaid; that the same are free from any and all liens and encumbrances, except [most deed forms have a space to insert title defects the grantee is required to accept]; and that he and his heirs, executors and administrators will warrant and forever defend the same to the party of the second part, his heirs and assigns, against the lawful claims and demands of all persons.

[Testimonium Clause]

In witness whereof, the party of the first part has hereunto set his hand and seal the day and year first written above.

_______________________________(Seal)

In the presence of

____

____

[Acknowledgment Clause]

Know all men by these presents, that on the—— day of——, 19—, the persons whose names are subscribed above appeared before me and in my presence subscribed their names to the within General Warranty Deed, and acknowledged to me personally that they have signed the same as their own free and voluntary acts.

____

Notary Public

(my commission expires________)

A quitclaim deed is similar in form to a warranty deed, except that warranty clause of the warranty deed is not included in the quitclaim form. (This is the primary distinction between a quitclaim and a warranty deed.) In addition, the granting clause of a quitclaim deed is usually worded differently from the granting clause of a warranty deed. The following is typical for the granting clause of a quitclaim deed:

> does by these presents remise, release and quitclaim unto the party of the second part any and all right, title and interest which the party of the first part may own or possess in or to that certain parcel of land described as follows . . .

Most beginning students of real estate law express a fond wish that the language used in deeds could be simpler. After studying some of the cases that wrestle with the difficult problems created by minor variations in the language of a deed, however, many students give up this wish. As we mentioned earlier, many of the words in these deed forms could be safely removed from the document and the deed could still satisfy the deed statute of the state where the property is located. The difficulty is that the practitioner would have to study the statutes (and perhaps the cases) of that state to discover *which* words could be safely removed. Furthermore if the grantee in the deed were from a different state, he or she might be accustomed to seeing the words that were removed to conform with the statute of the state where the property is located. The grantor would then be required to convince the grantee that the deed was in fact valid under the laws of the state where the property was located. As a result, it is often easier to simply accept the musical cadences of the standard deed forms presented above.

Victor and Irene Queathem were married for over 50 years, and had no children. In 1977, they executed mutual wills leaving all of their property to the surviving spouse, and at the death of the surviving spouse to their nieces and nephews. Irene died in 1978.

After Irene's death, Victor became increasingly withdrawn, and his health began to deteriorate. He added the name of Cordell Queathem, one of his nephews, to his bank accounts. From 1979 until Victor's death in 1981, Cordell managed all of Victor's financial affairs. On September 2, 1980, Victor quitclaimed his interest in his farm, valued at $278,000, to Cordell Queathem and his wife Betty. At the time the deed was executed, Victor was hospitalized with diabetes and prostate cancer. He died one year later.

After Victor's death, the remaining nieces and nephews sued to have the deed to Cordell cancelled, and have the farm returned to Victor's estate. The plaintiffs argued that Victor lacked the mental capacity required to execute a valid deed, and that he was subject to the undue influence of Cordell Queathem, the grantee of the deed.

The appeals court observed "[t]the cancellation of a deed is an extraordinary proceeding in equity and in order to justify such cancellation, the evidence in support thereof must be clear, cogent and convincing." Although the evidence at trial indicated that Victor was at times disoriented, depressed and forgetful, there was also evidence in the record that Victor was not confused on the day the deed was executed. In particular, Victor's doctor testified that he was mentally competent. On the basis of the record, the appeals court agreed that the plaintiff's failed to meet the burden of proof with respect to mental incapacity.

The court also agreed the confidential relationship between Victor and Cordell, by itself, did not constitute proof that Cordell had unduly influenced Victor's decision to convey the property to him. Absent any other evidence that Cordell had acted improperly, the court affirmed the judgement of the trail court refusing to cancel the deed. Queathem v. Queathem 712 S.W. 2d 703 (Mo., 1986)

Deed Problems

Knell v. Price

Errors or omissions in any of the seven clauses in a warranty deed can lead to difficulties in establishing the current ownership of the property. Therefore, practitioners should always examine a deed carefully before accepting the document in exchange for the purchase price to be paid in the transaction. This examination is usually performed by an attorney; however, even attorneys can make mistakes. Because the use of correct and sufficient language in the deed conveying the property interest is of crucial importance to the purchaser, it is a good idea for the purchaser to review the document along with the attorney.

Defects in title created by the inappropriate use of language in a deed usually come from one of three sources. The most usual problem comes from an incorrect property description in the granting clause. The second source is the use of language in the granting and habendum clauses that is not sufficient to convey the estate desired by the purchaser. Often this problem occurs when the language of the granting clause conveys the desired estate, while the language of the habendum clause is only sufficient to convey a lesser estate. Any conflict between the words of the granting clause and the words of the habendum clause is an open invitation to a lawsuit against the purchaser.

Consider a deed prepared in 1927 that conveyed property known as Bunker Hill Farm to the owners' daughter, Emma M. Hinton, during her lifetime, and then to the natural heirs of her body forever—to her as long as she might live, then at her death to the natural heirs of her body, if any of the children of her body might then be living; and if no natural heir or heirs of her body might survive her, then at her death to the nearest heirs of her body or blood relatives.

The habendum clause provided "to have and to hold and defend unto her, the aforesaid Mrs. Emma M. Hinton, party of the Second Part, her natural lifetime, then to the children of her body, if any survive her, if no child of her body survives her, then and in that case at her death to her nearest blood relatives, as above, forever." The life tenant Emma

M. Hinton died on August 6, 1966, survived by one child, George O. Hinton, and by a deceased son's children, Harvey A. Hinton and J. Warner Hinton, III.

George O. Hinton brought this suit seeking a construction of the deed. By a final decree, the trial court held that the deed conveyed a one-half remainder interest to the child George O. Hinton and a one-quarter remainder interest each to the grandchildren Harvey A. Hinton and J. Warner Hinton, III. *Hinton v. Hinton* 165 S.E.2d 386. (Va., 1984)

Property Descriptions

In order for a deed to accomplish a valid conveyance of title, the document must fully describe the property. Judges are fond of saying that the identity of the property conveyed "must be ascertainable within the four corners of the instrument." That is, by reading the property description in the deed, the judge must be able to determine the exact location of all of the property boundaries. Over the years, three different forms of property description have been developed to meet this legal requirement.

Metes and Bounds Descriptions

The oldest form of property description is the **metes and bounds** formula. The description begins with a well-defined landmark that is easy to locate on the ground. From there, the metes and bounds description continues with a series of "calls," directing the reader of the description to move a given distance in a given direction from the last point of reference. By beginning at the landmark identified in the description and following the directions carefully, it is possible to actually trace the property lines on the ground. The following is a very simple metes and bounds description of a corner lot in a city subdivision:

> Beginning at the southeast corner of the intersection of Oak and Chestnut streets in the City of Chance, County of Last and State of Confusion; thence easterly along the southern border of Oak Street, a distance of 105' 3"; thence south, 3 deg. east a distance of 78' 4 1/2"; thence west, 2 deg. south a distance of 108 feet more or less to the eastern boundary of Chestnut Street; thence northerly along the eastern boundary of Chestnut Street a distance of 82 feet more or less to THE TRUE POINT OF BEGINNING.

By actually going to the intersection of Oak and Chestnut streets and following the directions given above, anyone can trace the physical boundaries of this lot on the surface of the earth. As a result, the property will be adequately described within the four corners of the deed that contains this description.

Lawyers Title Insurance Company v. Nash

By a deed dated February 27, 1951 Berchenko conveyed to Fulton County, Georgia "a 28 foot strip to make said road a 50 foot road: to be known as Climax Place." The deed further recited that the road ran from Stewart Avenue "in an easterly direction a distance of approximately 1,075 feet to Cheshire Avenue". At the time of the conveyance, Berchenko owned property on both sides of a 22 foot dedicated public road identified in the plat map as Climax Place. At the time the deed was executed, the grantor was the owner of two tracts, one fronting the south side of Climax Place 195 feet, and the other fronting the north side of Climax Place 1035 feet. Although the deed recited that the conveyance was made by "We, the undersigned property owners" only Berchenko's signature appeared on the deed. All of Berchenko's property was annexed by the City of Atlanta in 1952.

Metes and Bounds
A method of describing the physical boundaries of real property by starting at an identifiable location on the ground (The True Point of Beginning), and instructing the reader to travel a given distance in a prescribed direction.

In 1955, Berchenko conveyed his land on the north side of Climax place to the plaintiff. Two years later, the City of Atlanta ordered the plaintiff to remove two structures which were built within a 28 foot strip of land lying on the north side of Climax Place. The Supreme court of Georgia observed that "from the allegations of the petition as set out in the foregoing statement of facts, it would seem to appear that the grantor intended to convey a strip of land on the south side of Climax Place 28 feet by 195 feet, whereas the City of Atlanta and the grantee contend that the deed in question conveyed a strip of land on the north side of Climax Place 28 feet by 1035 feet." The court ruled that the deed from Berchenko to Fulton County (and by implication its successor the City of Atlanta) failed to convey any property because "no surveyor, however expert, could take the description contained in the instrument just mentioned, and, by the aid of any extrinsic evidence, locate the precise body of land." City of Atlanta v. Atlanta Trailer City Trailer Park 102 S.E. 2d 23 (Ga., 1958)

Federal Land Survey

Most of the lands west of the Ohio River were surveyed by the U.S. government during the last century. The records created in this monumental task are still used as the basis for property descriptions in many western states. The survey was conducted by dividing all of the land in the survey area into townships, which are square grids six miles long on each side. As a result, each township contains 36 square miles of land.

The townships are numbered by the distance from a principal meridian of longitude and a principal baseline of latitude. (The principal meridians and baselines were established in 1795, shortly after the U.S. Constitution was ratified by the original thirteen states.) Under this scheme, Township 1 North, Range 1 West would be found at the northwest corner of the intersection of one of the principal meridians and a principal baseline. As the survey moves north from the baseline, the township numbers increase. As the survey moves west from the principal meridian, the range numbers increase. Township 41 north, Range 50 west is a 36-square-mile tract of land. The southeast corner of the tract is supposed to be exactly 120 miles north of the principal baseline and 294 miles west of the principal meridian.

Townships are divided into thirty-six numbered sections. Each section contains one square mile of land, which is equal to 640 acres. The section number scheme is depicted in Figure 8.1.

Since a section of land is equal to 640 acres, a quarter section (e.g., the SW 1/4 of section 22) is equal to 160 acres. Dividing the quarter section into quarters once again (e.g., NE 1/4 of the NW 1/4 of section 22) results in a 40 acre parcel. The smallest parcel that can conveniently be described by referring to the federal land survey is about 2.5 acres (e.g., the SE 1/4 of the NE 1/4 of the SW 1/4 of the SE 1/4 of section 22) (see Figure 8.2).

Shopping centers, factories, farms, and subdivision developments ordinarily involve parcels that are substantially larger than 2.5 acres. As a result, the federal land survey is a useful and convenient method for describing land in most development settings. However, the typical residential building lot is approximately 1/5 of an acre. Individual lots for commercial use are often even smaller. The federal land survey does not provide a convenient means of describing parcels as small as these. A widely used alternative is the lot and block description for individual parcels located in a developed area of a town or city.

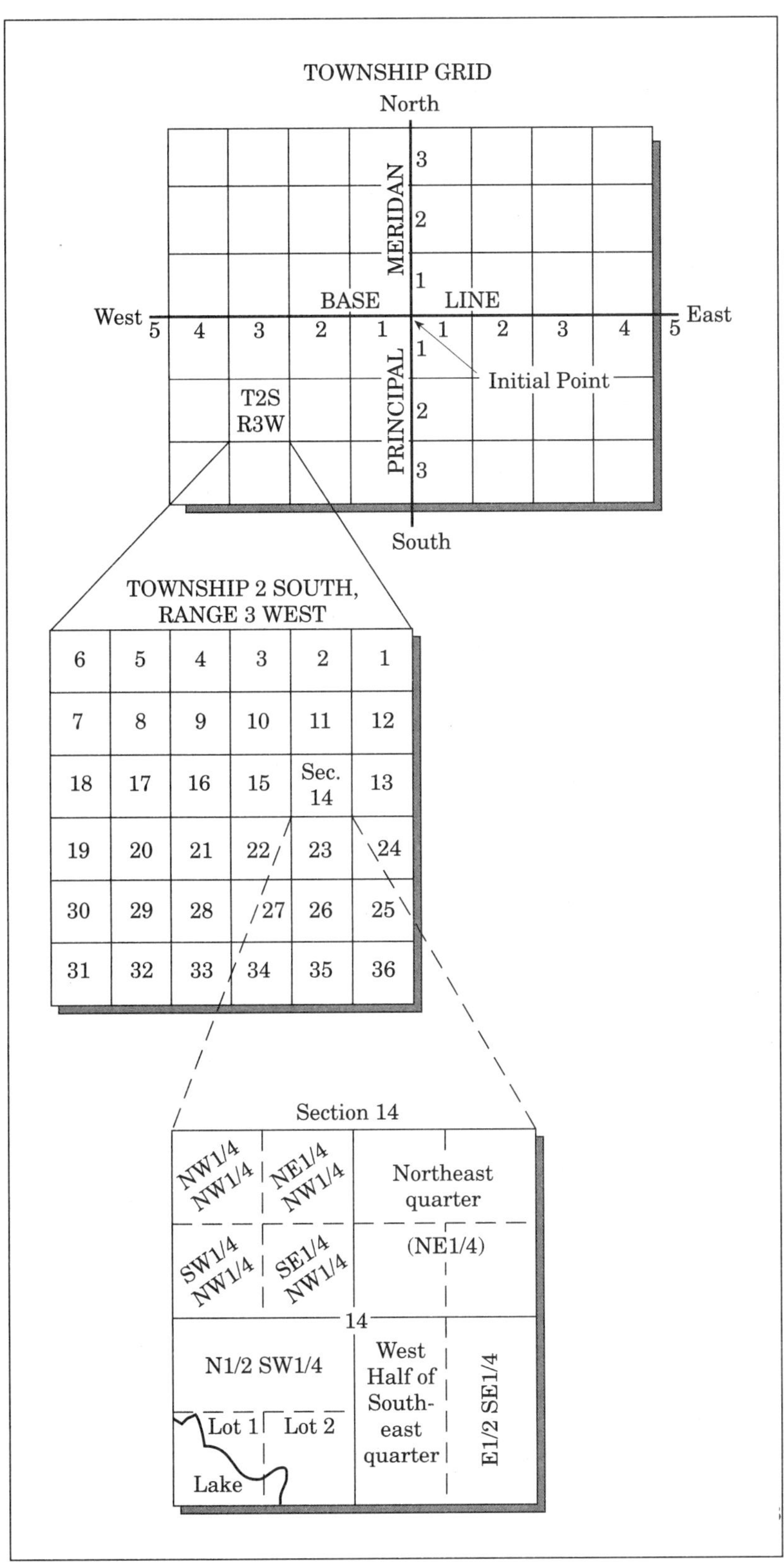

FIGURE 8.1 SECTION NUMBERS

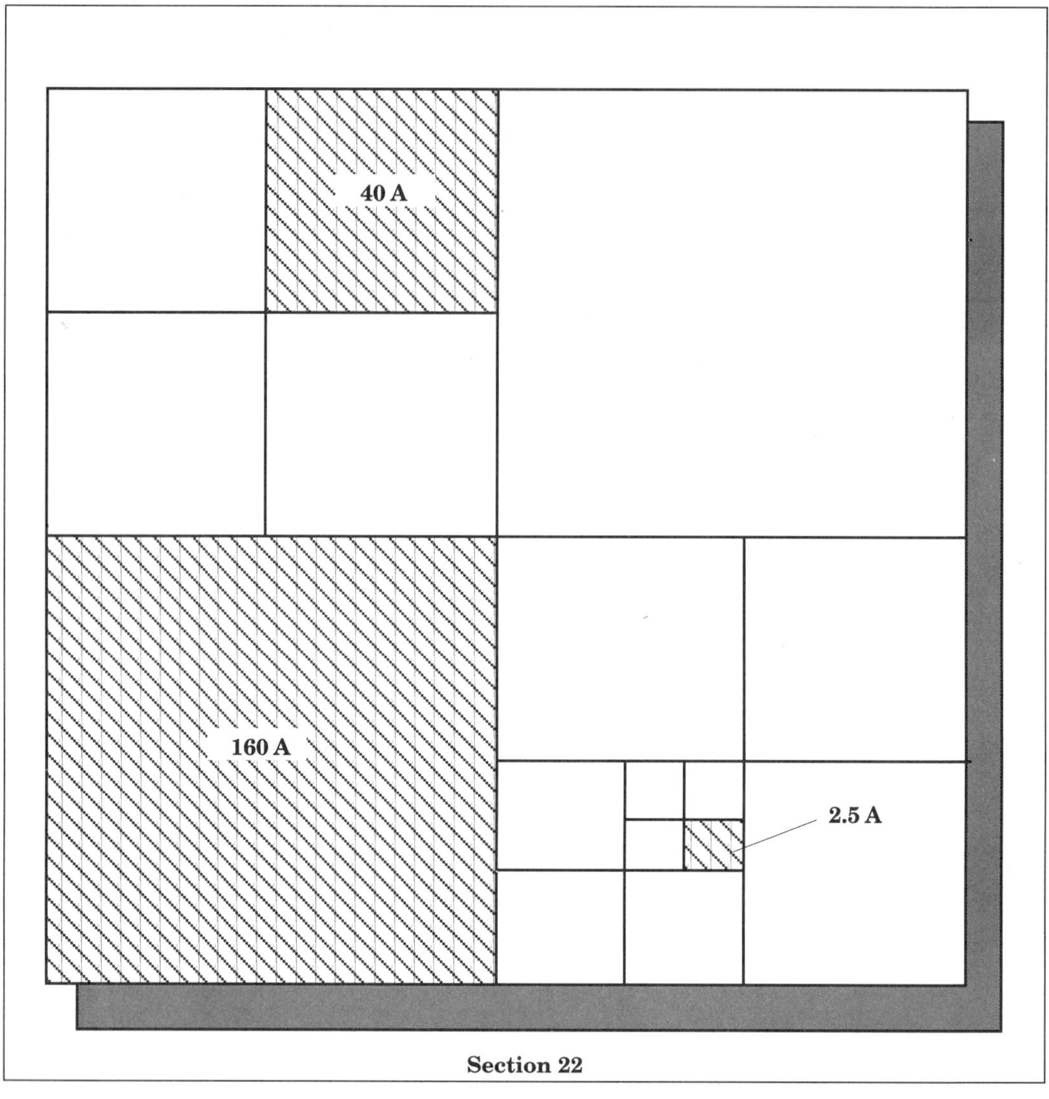

FIGURE 8.2 SECTION 22

KEY POINTS

Much of the federal land survey was conducted with fairly crude methods designed to produce a large number of section corners per day. A favored method was to tie a white cloth to the wheel of a wagon containing the section and township corner stakes. Assuming the wagon wheel was four feet in diameter, the wheel would turn just over 416 times per mile. The driver of the wagon would start out heading east, while the second member of the survey team rode in the wagon, counting the turns of the wheel. Every 416th turn, more or less, the second team member would toss out a corner stake. The third member of the team would drive the stake into ground, to mark the section or township corner. At the end of the day, the survey team would drive six miles south, and repeat the process while heading west on the following day. Errors in this process occurred most frequently during the middle of the day, when the warmth of the sun could cause the second team member to drowse and lose count of the wheel turns.

Lot and Block Numbers

A **subdivision plat** is a large set of documents that is filed for record whenever the owner of a parcel of raw land hopes to develop the property into individual lots for either residential or commercial buildings. One of the documents included in the subdivision plat is a complete legal description of the boundaries of the subdivision. The description is typically a metes and bounds description. However, the surveyor who prepares the legal description usually refers to the section and township numbers from the federal land survey that includes the parcel.

Subdivision Plat
A document filed for record with an official of a local government unit which contains a map of all the building lots in the subdivision, and lists any restrictive covenants which apply to real property contained in the subdivision.

A second document included in the plat is a detailed map showing all of the streets, alleys, and building lots that the owner proposes to develop over time. Each block in the subdivision will be given a number on the plat map, and each of the lots in every block will be given a lot number. A complete legal description for any of the lots in the platted subdivision can be given by the lot and block numbers, along with the name of the subdivision (e.g., "Lot 5, Block 12 of the Sunnyside Terrace Addition to the City of Found, County of Lost and State of Confusion, according to the plat thereof ").

Note that the name of the subdivision must be included in the legal description. That is because most cities have numerous subdivisions, each with blocks numbered from 1 to N and lots in each block numbered from 1 to M. As a result, there are probably dozens of homes in every town that are located on Lot 5, Block 12, of somebody's subdivision. The platting process ensures that each subdivision is given a unique name, so that inclusion of the name will provide the unique description for each parcel in any platted subdivision.

The name of the city must be included in the description. While every subdivision in a particular town or city is given a unique name, there may be several cities with a Sunnyside Terrace addition platted within the municipal boundary.

Parker v. Pittman

The name of the state is required as well. It is possible (perhaps probable) that a Sunnyside Terrace addition is platted in both Las Vegas, Nevada, and in Las Vegas, New Mexico. The name of the county is always included to guard against the possibility that two cities in the same state have the same name and that each city has a subdivision of the same name.

Addresses in a Legal Description

Every lot in a platted subdivision will be assigned an address by the U.S. Postal Service or by the city that contains the subdivision. This address is never sufficient to describe the property in a deed but should always be included with the property description if it is known at the time the conveyance is made.

The address of the property serves as a unique identifier of the location of the property. If nothing else, the postman needs to know where to deposit mail addressed to the occupant of 3625 Chestnut Street. However, the address says nothing about the dimensions of the parcel or the locations of its boundaries. Because the address alone does not give enough information to locate the actual boundaries of the property on the ground, the address of the property is never a sufficient legal description.

Why, then, should the address always be included with the description if the address is known? Suppose you decide to buy the house at 3625 Chestnut Street, and you agree to pay the current owners more money than you have ever seen in your life. In return, you receive a deed conveying a fee simple absolute title to "Lot 12, Block 5 of the Sunnyside Terrace Addition to the City of . . . , commonly known as

3625 Chestnut Street." Three years after you move in, you discover that your house is actually located on Lot 12 of Block 6 in the Sunnyside Terrace addition. For three years, you have been making mortgage payments on somebody else's home!

Fortunately, since the street address was included in the deed, you can apply to the local court to issue an order reforming the deed. The judge will do so gladly, since the deed clearly contained a clerical error. The inclusion of the street address makes it clear from the deed that the grantors intended to convey the lot in Block 6.

However, if the legal description did not include the street address, the judge will be less eager to issue an order reforming your deed. You will probably be asked to locate the grantors and produce their sworn testimony that they intended to convey your house to you. If the grantors cannot be found, the judge will require you to produce evidence from some other source indicating that your property actually belongs to you. Whatever happens, you will devoutly wish that your deed had included the street address.

A Final Word of Warning

Our discussion of the available legal description processes, accompanied by the crisp, clean figures on the pages of this book, suggests that the process is a precise science. The reality of legal descriptions is far from precise. We have already alluded to the possibility of clerical errors in transcribing a long and complex legal description onto a deed. But even when the description is correctly entered on the deed, the actual property boundaries may be different from the boundaries described.

If a fence, driveway, or alley abuts the property, it may be that this visible boundary is not located exactly on the property line described in the deed. If the visible boundary had been in place for a sufficiently long time, the doctrine of adverse possession will cause the location of the property boundary to shift from the described property line to the visible boundary.

In addition, mistakes are bound to occur in the process of transferring the boundary descriptions from a map to the ground. For example, a section of land in the federal land survey is supposed to contain exactly 640 acres. But due to measurement errors, most sections actually contain somewhat more or somewhat less than the prescribed 640 acres of land. As a result, a parcel of land described as "the E 1/2 of the NE 1/4 of Section 22, containing 80 acres more or less" is a very apt description. If a buyer purchases this parcel of $80,000, the actual price per acre will depend upon whether the parcel contains more or less than 80 acres.

Recall also that lot and block descriptions are based upon the dimensions contained in a subdivision map that was probably drawn before any of the streets or blocks actually existed. In the development process, the developer attempts to create an actual subdivision that looks exactly like the planned subdivision described in the plat. But, once again, errors in measurement and perhaps changes in the development plan will occur during the development process. These errors and amendments will result in actual property lines that are slightly (or perhaps significantly) different from the property lines described in the plat map.

As a result, there is no substitute for a thorough physical inspection of the property. Every purchaser should carefully examine the legal description of the parcel involved and verify that the actual boundaries of the property correspond to the description of the boundaries. If the inspection reveals significant differences between the actual dimensions of the parcel and the dimensions described in the deed, the purchaser will have grounds to rescind the contract.

Names of Parties

The premises clause of the deed identifies the grantor and grantee in the conveyance. Suppose one of the names is misspelled. Or suppose that the grantor in the deed is identified as "Samuel A. Parsons," while the record owner of the property is "A. Samuel Parsons." Will such discrepancies cause the conveyance to fail?

Fortunately, courts are less fussy about the names of parties than they are about the description of the property. As long as the parties to the deed can be ascertained with reasonable certainty, judges are usually content to find that the deed conveys title from the person identified as the grantor to the person identified as the grantee. Here, as always, an ounce of prevention is worth several pounds of cure. The wise practitioner will always make sure that the name of the grantor in a deed corresponds exactly to the name of the record owner of the property.

> In 1921, George Rigby deeded a parcel of land to the "Colored Library and Civic Imp. Ass'n." The purpose of the deed was to provide a library for the Black community of Ormond Beach because the segregated white-only library was unavailable to the Blacks. After a few years, probably after the white-only rules were lifted from the other library, the "Colored Library" ceased operation. The building became unoccupied and its disuse and disrepair led the appellees to seek a better use for the property.
>
> However, no legal entity by the name of the Colored Library and Civic Imp. Ass'n. ever existed. In 1986, one of the plaintiffs decided to build a car wash on the premises. He, along with other community members, filed a law suit requesting the court to quiet title in the plaintiffs as officers of the Colored Library and Civic Improvement Association of Ormond, Volusia County, Florida. A second group of citizens filed an answer to the complaint, alleging that they had been selected by the black community of Ormond Beach, Florida, to establish an organization to take title to the property. The trial court struck the answer filed in the case, and ordered title quieted in the plaintiffs.
>
> On appeal, the Florida Supreme Court ruled that the 1921 conveyance by George Rigby was void, because the grantee of that deed did not exist. As a result, the Florida Supreme Court decided that title to the property belonged to the heirs of George Rigby. Daniels v. Berry 513 So.2d 250 (Fl., 1987)

Granting Clause

The words "grant, bargain, sell and convey" in the granting clause of a deed are all terms of art. Collectively, they are referred to by courts as "words of purchase." The precise meanings of these terms are rooted in the experience of the feudal and common law periods of English property laws. The distinctions among these terms is rapidly disappearing, but it is probably still too soon to be safe in deleting one or more of these terms of art from the granting clause of a deed. In the not-so-distant past, a deed that used only the term "sell" in a granting clause might have to be supported by consideration to be valid. Or, a deed that used only the term "grant" in the clause might be sufficient to pass a life estate to the grantee, but not a fee simple estate. There is only one safe generalization that can be made about words of purchase: extra words of purchase will be ignored by courts and thus will do no harm. But if a required word of purchase is missing, a court may seize upon that fact to determine the nature of the estate conveyed by the deed. Thus, the use of all four terms of art will never do harm and may be a benefit.

Words of limitation in the granting clause define the nature of the estate conveyed by the deed. As we have seen, the words "and his heirs" indicate the conveyance of a fee simple absolute estate, while the words "for life" indicate the conveyance of a life estate.

When the grantor intends to convey a complex set of ownership rights (e.g., a life estate to my wife, with a contingent remainder to my children and a vested remainder subject to divestiture to my grandchildren), the words of limitation in the granting clause become very difficult to describe. In such circumstances, a deed begins to look more like a will. As a result, we strongly recommend that complex future interests be created by drafting a will or trust instrument rather than a conveyance by deed.

Habendum Clause

The only requirement of the habendum clause is that the words of limitation used in the habendum exactly match the words of limitation employed in the granting clause. Failing to meet this simple requirement can be expected to result in a very expensive lawsuit with a highly uncertain result. Again, the words of limitation in the habendum clause are more likely to cause difficulty when the ownership rights conveyed by the deed are complex and difficult to interpret. The most appropriate method for creating complex future estates in land is a will or an inter vivos trust agreement.

RECORDING STATUTES

As is so often the case, the development of written documents to provide evidence of the ownership of real property created new problems in the process of solving old problems. The Statute of Frauds was adopted by the English Parliament in 1677 in order to reduce the confusion that had resulted from ownership claims based upon oral statements. Oral statements made by people who want to obtain (or hang onto) valuable ownership rights are notoriously unreliable. At best, human beings tend to remember the facts that strengthen their claims of ownership, while forgetting those facts that weaken the claim. If the stakes are high enough and the risks of detection low enough, many people are willing to lie in order to get what they want.

By requiring written evidence for a claim of property ownership, the Statute of Frauds eliminated the difficulties caused by the faulty or selective memories of people contending for the ownership of a parcel of land. But the Statute, like any statute, was not able to eliminate dishonesty on the part of people who execute and deliver written documents. It was still possible for a dishonest owner to sell a parcel of land to two different people and deliver an apparently valid deed to each of them. Further refinements in the law were needed to address this very real difficulty.

Each state has adopted a recording statute that judges can use to sort out the claims of ownership in real property when two or more people hold apparently valid deeds to the same parcel. The practical effect of these statutes is to change the date at which full legal title to property is actually conveyed to a new owner. At common law, title was conveyed to a new owner when the deed was delivered. Under the recording statutes, only a "bare" legal title is conveyed by the delivery of the deed. The ownership claims from this bare legal title can only be asserted against those people who have notice that the deed was delivered. (Generally, a person has notice of a fact when the person either knows or reasonably should know of the fact.)

Fees-Krey, Inc. v. Page

When a deed is recorded, following the directions for recording provided by the state statute, the bare legal title blossoms into a "full" or **"record" title.** Once a deed is recorded, everyone in the world will have notice of the deed, because anyone in the world can (and should) discover the existence of the deed by inspecting the public records.

"Record" Title The ownership of real property which can be found by searching the public records of real property conveyances.

The formulas used by various states in determining which of two competing deed holders will become the record owner of a property can be divided into three groups. Two states (North Carolina and Louisiana) have adopted "pure race statutes." Of the remaining forty-eight states, half use a "pure notice" formula and the other half use a hybrid known as the "race/notice" formula. In order to understand how these statutory formulas differ, we will examine the outcome of the following fact setting under each of the three statutes.

> *Monday:* O, the record owner of an office building, sells the property to B, an unsophisticated buyer, for $120,000 in cash. O delivers the deed for the property to B and says, "Here is your deed. If you would like to leave it with me, I will record it for you." B agrees, thanking O for his courtesy.
>
> *Tuesday:* O gives a deed for the same property to S, his son. The deed states that the grantor has received $10 and other good and valuable consideration.
>
> *Wednesday:* S deposits his deed with the County Clerk and Recorder, as required by the recording statute in effect.
>
> *Thursday:* O deposits the deed to B with the same official.

Race Statutes Recording statutes which award the record title in real property to the first person who records an instrument conveying the title.

Under a pure **race statute,** S will become the record owner of the office building. S won the race to the courthouse and as a result has obtained the record ownership of the property. To make matters worse, poor B cannot even sue for a refund of the purchase price. O has performed all of his obligations, according to the letter of the contract between O and B. O delivered the deed, as required by the contract for the sale. And O did record the deed, just as he promised he would. Under a pure race formula, the guilty party is B, who failed to record his interest soon enough to cut off the ownership interests of other parties. (Perhaps this result is the reason that the pure race statute is such a rarity.)

Notice Statutes Recording statutes which award the record title in real property to the last good faith purchaser for value who records an instrument conveying the title.

Under a pure **notice statute,** B's chances will improve. If B can prove that S had notice of the transaction between B and the father of S, then B will receive the record title to the office building. If S knew or should have known that his father had already sold the office building, then the conveyance to S is void.

Under a race/notice statute, the same result would occur. By being the first to record, S wins the race to the courthouse and is presumed to be the record owner. However, if O can demonstrate that S had notice of the earlier sale, the presumption will be overcome, and O will be entitled to the record ownership of the property.

Under both the notice and the race/notice statutes, B will have an additional string for his bow. Most states apply their recording statutes only in favor of a **good**

Good Faith Purchaser for Value
A person who gives money or some other thing of value in exchange for the conveyance of a real property interest, and has no notice or knowledge of any competing claims in the real property purchased.

faith purchaser for value. If S knew of the previous transaction, then he is not a good faith purchaser. In addition, since S apparently did not pay for the property, he did not purchase for value. Most states have decided that a donee (one who receives the property as a gift) is not entitled to the protection of the recording statute.

We can summarize this discussion with the following set of rules.

1. Under a pure race statute, the first grantee to record a deed becomes the record owner of the property.
2. Under a race/notice statute, the first good faith purchaser for value (who may or may not be the first grantee) to record a deed becomes the record owner.
3. Under a pure notice statute, the last good faith purchaser for value becomes the record owner. (Note: any grantee who purchases in good faith and for value can become the last good faith purchaser for value by recording a deed. Why?)

Regardless of the statute adopted by the state where the property is located, it is imperative to record the deed immediately after the closing. In addition, it is necessary to check the public records immediately before the closing, in order to make sure that no other deeds to the property have been recorded. Only by following these two practices can a purchaser be certain that not one else will be able to assert an ownership claim that will be given priority over the ownership claim of the purchaser.

CONCLUSION

In this chapter we have examined the requirements for a valid deed, capable of conveying a marketable title to real property. We have analyzed both quitclaim and general warranty deeds and discussed the clauses generally found in each type of deed. We also discussed events that might cause a conveyance to fail because of insufficiencies in the deed. It was noted that the description of the property conveyed must be adequate to allow the actual boundaries of the property to be determined by referring only to the description in the deed. The effect of conflicts between the granting and the habendum clause of a deed were also examined. We also noted that misspellings in the names of the parties to a deed will generally not defeat the conveyance the deed is intended to make, as long as the actual parties can be determined with reasonable certainty. Finally, we discussed the impact of state recording statutes on the conveyance of title to real property.

DISCUSSION QUESTIONS:

1. Describe the "livery of seisin" ceremony used to transfer ownership of land during the feudal era.
2. Explain the difference between a warranty deed and a quitclaim deed.
3. Where in a general warranty deed is inappropriate use of language most likely to create a defect in the title?
4. Name the oldest form of property description. How is a parcel identified using this method?

5. Give an overview of the federal land survey process. In what area of the United States was the federal land survey widely used? Are there any disadvantages to using this method?
6. What property identification method is best suited for residential developments? How does this method work? Identify items that must be included in this type of description.
7. Why is the street address not a sufficient legal description of the property transferred in a deed?
8. What does the premises clause of a general warranty deed do? What does the court use as a general rule when discrepancies pertaining to the names of the parties in the contract arise?
9. Give one generalization that can be made about words of purchase. What are "words of limitation" intended to do?
10. There are three types of recording statutes used in the United States today. Name each and specify who becomes the record owner of property under each statute. Define "good faith purchaser for value."

KNELL V. PRICE

569 A.2d 636 (Md., 1990)

Conflict between granting and habendum clauses

CHARLES E. ORTH, Judge, Specially Assigned.

The drama which was revealed by the institution of this case in the Circuit Court for Kent County had a cast of three: William A. Knell—the husband, Violet E. Knell—his wife, and Jesse Annabelle Price—the "other woman." After some 22 years of marriage, Mr. and Mrs. Knell separated. The terms of the separation were never spelled out in a written agreement, nor did the separation ever culminate in a divorce. When Mr. and Mrs. Knell went their separate ways, Mr. Knell's way was to live with Miss Price. For 27 years, thereafter, until Mr. Knell's death on 12 July 1987, he and Miss Price enjoyed a relationship akin to that of a marital status, but it was not imprinted with the legality which would have been bestowed by a marriage. . . .

At the time of Mr. Knell's death, the couple were living in a dwelling in Rock Hall, Kent County, Maryland, purchased by Mr. Knell about 10 years before for $34,000. The property was conveyed to him alone, in fee simple absolute, by a deed from the sellers dated 16 October 1978. On 19 December 1978 two deeds, prepared at the instance of Mr. Knell by Anthony Libersky, Mr. Knell's attorney, were executed and duly recorded, transferring the property. Each deed recited that the conveyance was "for good and valuable consideration" but noted that there was "no monetary consideration." The first deed conveyed the property in fee simple to Libersky, designated therein as "Trustee." The second deed, by its granting clause, conveyed the property to Mr. Knell in fee simple. The habendum, however, read:

> TO HAVE AND TO HOLD the said lot or parcel of land and premises, unto and to the use of the said William A. Knell for and during the term of his natural life, with the full power unto him to sell, mortgage, lease, convey and dispose (except by Last Will and Testament) of the whole and entire estate in the same property at any time he may deem expedient, without the purchaser or purchasers, mortgagee or mortgagees, lessee or lessees, or other persons taking title from him, being required to see to the application of the purchase or mortgage money, or the consideration paid for the disposal of said property; it

> being also the intention of these presents that the exercise by said William A. Knell of the powers hereinbefore enumerated and granted unto him, when and as exercised shall operate upon and there shall pass hereunder unto the grantee or grantees, mortgagee or mortgagees, lessee or lessees, or other persons taking title, not only the life estate hereby created but also the interest and estate in remainder hereinafter mentioned and hereby created; and immediately upon the death of the said William A. Knell, without having disposed of said property in the exercise of the powers aforesaid, or as to so much of the same as may remain, unto and to the use of Annabelle Price, her heirs and assigns, in fee simple.

Inasmuch as Mr. Knell died without having disposed of the property in exercise of the powers given him in the habendum clause, Miss Price considered that the property passed to her in fee simple at Mr. Knell's death. Mrs. Knell thought otherwise. She filed a complaint in the Circuit Court for Kent County seeking a judgment declaring that the habendum clause of the deed "in so far as it purports to give [Miss Price] the fee simple ownership of the . . . property at the death of [Mr.] Knell [was] void," so that the property became a part of Mr. Knell's estate. The court "adjudged, ordered, declared and decreed that":

1. The habendum clause in the deed from Libersky to Knell accurately reflected the true intent of William Knell. Accordingly, the straw deeds together had the effect of creating a life estate in William Knell and a remainder interest in Jessie Annabelle Price.
2. The transfer was not a fraudulent conveyance and therefore a valid transfer of title.
3. William Knell therefore died owning a life estate with a remainder interest in Jessie Annabelle Price.
4. Upon the death of William Knell, the property passed by operation of law to Jessie Annabelle Price in fee simple absolute. The property therefore is not includable in the estate of William Knell.

Having so declared, the court stated that it was "unnecessary for the Personal Representative of the estate of William Knell to take any further action to effectuate a transfer of title of the property."

Mrs. Knell was not content. She appealed to the Court of Special Appeals. It affirmed the judgment. Knell v. Price, 77 Md.App. 331, 550 A.2d 413 (1988). Still not satisfied, Mrs. Knell sought our review. We granted her petition for the issuance of a writ of certiorari and ordered that the case be certified to us. The petition presented two questions:

1. Whether a conflict between the granting and habendum clauses of a deed should have been resolved in favor of the granting clause?
2. Were the deeds executed by the deceased husband and trustee in December 1978 for purposes of defrauding [Mrs. Knell] of her statutory share in her deceased spouse's estate?

In the circumstances of this case, the answer to the first question is "no" and the answer to the second question is "yes."

The Granting Clause v. The Habendum Clause

It is not disputed that the granting clause and the habendum are not harmonious and cannot be reconciled. Ordinarily, we have abided by the general rule that where the granting clause and the habendum clause are in conflict, the granting clause will prevail. (citations omitted) The traditional reasoning behind this result is that such an habendum clause is considered repugnant to the granting clause. More broadly, the repugnancy doctrine states that as between any two clauses, if the second is repugnant to the first, the former controls. No consideration is given to the overall intention of the parties to the deed. This doctrine operates as a matter of law and not as a principle of construction. . . . The general rule may be tempered, however, in certain circumstances. Tiffany continues:

> But inharmonious provisions should be reconciled and effect given to all of them so far as that is possible by reasonable interpretation. Otherwise, provisions repugnant to what is determined to be the intention of the parties should be rejected.

* * *

Ordinarily, the rule which prefers the granting clause to an inconsistent habendum is applied when a deed must be construed with exclusive reference to its own terms. It is the purpose of the rule to determine which of the two conflicting provisions in the deed shall prevail when the deed itself does not solve the problem. But when the real and specific intention is evident from the process of conveyance of which the particular deed forms a part, there is no occasion to utilize the conventional rule of construction just mentioned. The deed containing the habendum under inquiry must be construed in connection with the preceding grant, in immediate pursuance of which it was executed and delivered. The only actual consideration for either deed was the patent purpose of the first grantor to invest himself with a different title from that which he already held. That purpose is as plainly demonstrated by the coincident execution of the two deeds, as if it had been definitely stated in both instruments. The application of the rule invoked in this case is not required by any uncertainty arising from conflicting expressions of intention in a deed which must be separately considered, but it would frustrate the palpable design of dual and interdependent conveyances and render them entirely meaningless and useless.

* * *

Under the special conveyancing conditions presented in this case it is permissible and proper to apply the cardinal rule that a deed should be so construed as to effectuate the intention of the parties, if that result is possible without violation of any principle of law. (Citation omitted.)

* * *

The Rights of a Surviving Spouse

Maryland Code (1974, 1989 Cum.Supp.), § 3-203 of the Estates and Trusts Article (ET) provides in pertinent part:

> (a) General.—Instead of property left to him by will, the surviving spouse may elect to take a one-third share of the net estate if there is also a surviving issue, or a one-half share of the net estate if there is no surviving issue.
>
> (b) Limitation.—The surviving spouse who makes this election may not take more than a one-half share of the net estate.

It is "settled law that a widow is entitled to no part of her husband's estate except that of which he died seized or possessed." Grove v. Frame, 285 Md. 691, 695, 402 A.2d 892 (1979), and cases therein cited at 695–696, 402 A.2d 892. As we have seen, the conveyancing here had the effect of reducing the size of Mr. Knell's estate at his death by excluding the real property. See ET § 1-301. Prior to 1970, our decisions dealing with the right of a husband to transfer his personal property recognized that he had this right "provided that he relinquishes all dominion and control over the property during his lifetime." . . . Rabbitt v. Gaither, 67 Md. 94, 104–]105, 8 A. 744 (1887), stated: "[A] husband may alienate his personal property and his equitable interest in land, either by sale or gift, without the concurrence or assent of his wife, and if the transfer be absolute and unconditional, and without any reservation of interest in, or control over, the property to himself, and if the possession be parted with or delivered in pursuance of the conveyance, it is valid even though his intent and purpose in making it, may have been to deprive his wife of her dower or thirds therein, provided there be no fraudulent participation on the part of the grantee or donee in such intent or purpose. In fact, this power of the husband over such property, has been so long recognized by the courts, and so often exercised, as to have become not only a well-established principle of law, but a settled rule of property upon which a large number of titles depend. But on the other hand, if the transfer be colorable merely, that is to say, if it be a mere device or contrivance by which the husband does not part with the absolute dominion over the property during his life, but seeks thereby to defeat the claims of his widow at his death, the law pronounces it a fraud upon her rights, and this fraud may be proved and established by his retention of possession, during his life, by a reservation of an interest to himself on the face of the conveyance, or by an outside agreement or arrangement between him and his grantee or donee, to the effect that he shall receive the benefit of, or have control over, the property, during his life, or by any other fraudulent participation on the part of the grantee or donee to aid him in his purpose of defeating the rights which the law gives to his widow upon his death."

* * *

It has always been recognized that a husband, in the absence of statutory regulation like that in the case of dower, has an unqualified right to give away his personal property [and now, his real property] during his life time, even though the effect is to deprive the wife of her statutory share. But if the gift is not absolute and unconditional and the donor retains dominion and control over the property during his lifetime, the courts have held that the gift is colorable and may be set aside.

See Shimp v. Huff, 315 Md. 624, 556 A.2d 252 (1989).

It may be that "[n]o general and completely satisfactory rule to determine the validity or invalidity of transfers alleged to be in fraud of marital rights has yet been evolved in this State." Whittington, 205 Md. at 14, 106 A.2d 72. *See* Klosiewski v. Slovan, 247 Md. 82, 88, 230 A.2d 285 (1967). But here, it is perfectly clear that Mr. Knell retained control of the property during his lifetime by establishing a life estate in himself with unfettered power in him, while living (except by will), to dispose of all interests in the property in fee simple. He did not part with the absolute dominion of the property during his life. His conveyance, through a straw man, of the remainder of the property was not complete, absolute, and unconditional. The law pronounces this to be a fraud on the marital rights of Mrs. Knell. His reluctance to relinquish control over the disposition of the property during his lifetime defeated his intention.

JUDGMENT OF THE COURT OF SPECIAL APPEALS REVERSED;

Case Reflections

1. Suppose Mr. Knell had sold the house prior to his death. Would Mrs. Knell have any rights in the property after his death?
2. Suppose Mr. Knell had sold the house prior to his death. Would Miss Price have any rights in the house?
2. What could Mr. Knell have done differently to insure that the house will belong to Miss Price if she outlives him?

LAWYERS TITLE INSURANCE CORPORATION V NASH.

396 S.E.2d 284 (Ga., 1990)

Errors in the legal description

Appellant appeals the order of the trial court granting appellee's motion for summary judgment and denying appellant's summary judgment motion in this case involving the breach of warranty of title to property.

Appellant issued a title insurance policy to Corner Cupboard Craft Shops, Inc. ("Craft Shops") insuring the property in question. Craft Shops had acquired the property from James F. Smith and Shirley M. Smith ("Smiths") who had acquired the property from appellee. Appellant argues that appellee conveyed more property than he in fact held title to in his deed to Smith and Smith in turn conveyed this additional property to Craft Shops. Craft Shops ultimately forfeited this additional property to another party, and appellant paid the resulting claim to Craft Shops. Appellant, as subrogee of the rights of Craft Shops under the policy, seeks to recover the value of this forfeited property from appellee, alleging a breach of warranty of title to Craft Shops, a successor in title to appellee.

Specifically, appellant argues that the legal description of the property in the deed to appellee describes the southern boundary of the property as fronting 50 feet along an alley, whereas the deeds to Smith and Craft Shops describe the same southern boundary as fronting 100 feet along the alley. Appellant includes in the record numerous surveys, copies of the deeds and an affidavit of a title examiner to support its contention that the disputed property to which appellee did not have title was included within the description of the property that appellee conveyed and warranted in his deed to Smith and in the deed from Smith to Craft Shops. Appellee presented his own affidavit in support of his position that none of the land in the disputed area was included in the deed from appellee to Smith.

1. Although the trial court gave no explanation for its decision, it appears that one question to be determined is the sufficiency of the legal description in the deed from appellee to Smith. The sufficiency of a property description is a question of law for the court; the identity of the property is a question of fact. McCann v. Miller, 177 Ga.App. 53, 54(2), 388 S.E.2d 509 (1985). We cannot say that the legal description at issue was insufficient as a matter of law. " 'Perfection in legal descriptions of tracts of land is not required. "If the premises are so referred to as to indicate . . . [the grantor's] intention to convey a particular tract of land, extrinsic evidence is admissible to show the precise location and boundaries of such tract. The test as to the sufficiency of the description of property contained in a deed is whether or not it discloses with sufficient certainty what the intention of the grantor was with respect to the quantity and location of land therein referred to, so that its identification is practicable." [Cits.]' " *Id.* at 54, 338 S.E.2d 509. Further, it must be determined if the deed contains sufficient "keys" to clarify any indefiniteness in the description. Wisener v. Gulledge, 251 Ga. 419, 421, 306 S.E.2d 642 (1983).

The legal description of the property contains several distance calls which are rendered indefinite by the phrase "more or less" and by running to undefined points; further, the general directional calls, such as "northwesterly" and "southeasterly," are unspecific. However, the description references a plat which contains two keys to clarify the intention of the grantor. A scale of 1 inch to 200 feet and a designation for north appear on the plat. Applying these two keys to the configurations on the plat, the exact distances and directions, as well as the property conveyed, can be identified. *See* Grant v. Fourth Nat. Bank of Columbus, 229 Ga. 855(2), 194 S.E.2d 913 (1972).

2. Appellee apparently bases his motion for summary judgment on the argument that no genuine issue of material fact exists because the documents disclose that the disputed property was not included in his deed to Smith. Appellee supported his motion with a copy of the deed and his own affidavit which contains no explanation but simply restates his contention. Appellant submitted copies of all relevant documents and plats as well as an affidavit of an expert title examiner who analyzed in detail the legal descriptions to support the assertion that the disputed property was in fact conveyed by appellee. After a review of the record, we conclude that appellee did not pierce the appellant"s pleadings and did not carry his burden to show that there exists no genuine issue of material fact. Waits v. Makowski, 191 Ga.App. 794(1), 383 S.E.2d 175 (1989). Accordingly, we reverse the grant of appellee"s motion for summary judgment and affirm the denial of appellant"s motion for summary judgment.

Judgment affirmed in part and reversed in part.

Case Reflections

1. Do sellers of real property need to exercise any degree of caution to insure that the legal description in the deed they deliver is accurate, or is that responsibility imposed only on the buyer of real property?
2. Can you think of any reason to save a title insurance policy after the property covered by the policy is sold?

PARKER V. PITTMAN

197 S.E.2d 570 (NC, 1952)

Reformation of a deed

This is a civil action in which plaintiff seeks judgment declaring her to be the owner of record of a one-half undivided interest in a certain tract of real property or, in the alternative and if the court should declare plaintiff owner of record of less than a one-half interest, to correct and reform a deed dated 5 April 1962 recorded in Book 995, page 25, of the Cumberland County Registry so as to vest in plaintiff a one-half interest. Jury trial was waived and the court found the facts.

Certain of these, as to which there is no dispute, may be summarized as follows: By recorded deed dated 5 September 1945 the property in question, being a lot and building located in the City of Fayetteville, was conveyed to Dr. R. L. Pittman and wife, Grace S. Pittman, and to Raymond L. Pittman, Jr., subject to the outstanding right of one Maggie Williford Williamson to receive the rents therefrom during her natural life. It is admitted that this deed conveyed an undivided one-half interest in the property to Dr. and Mrs. Pittman as tenants by the entirety and an undivided one-half interest to Raymond L. Pittman, Jr., both interests being subject to the outstanding life estate.

By recorded deed dated 6 November 1947 Maggie Williford Williamson conveyed her life estate to Pittman Realty Company. As part of the consideration for this deed the grantee corporation covenanted to pay to Maggie Williford Williamson from the rents from the property the sum of $250.00 monthly throughout her life, during which time she shall have a lien on the property as security for such monthly payments. By deed dated 10 January 1948 and recorded in Book 512, page 91, of the Cumberland County Registry, Pittman Realty Company conveyed all of its right, title and interest in the land, being the identical interest which had been conveyed to it by Maggie Williford Williamson by her deed dated 6 November 1947, to Dr. R. L. Pittman and wife, Grace Sykes Pittman, the grantees in this deed covenanting to make the $250.00 monthly payments from the rents to Maggie Williford Williamson throughout her lifetime as set forth in her deed to Pittman Realty Company. Grace S. Pittman died testate on 8 September 1961, her will dated 18 June 1958 containing a provision devising her interest in the subject property to her daughter, Margaret Blue Parker, the plaintiff herein.

By deed dated 5 April 1962 recorded in Book 95, page 25, Cumberland County Registry, Dr. R. L. Pittman executed and recorded a deed to Raymond L. Pittman, Jr., (defendant herein) and Margaret Blue Parker (plaintiff herein), conveying the subject property, in which the words of conveyance are as follows: "WITNESSETH, That said party of the first part in consideration of other good and valuable considerations and the sum of Ten Dollars, to him paid by parties of the second part the receipt of which is hereby acknowledged, have bargained and sold, and by these presents do grant, bargain, sell and convey to said parties of the second part, their heirs and assigns, to each a 1/2 undivided interest as tenants in common in and to a certain tract or parcel of land in Cross Creek Township, Cumberland County, State of North Carolina, adjoining the lands of ______ and others and bounded as follows, viz:"

There then appears a metes and bounds description of the property, after which the following reference is made:

"And being the same property conveyed to R. L. Pittman and Grace Sykes Pittman (Grace Sykes Pittman is now deceased) by deed from Pittman Realty Company, duly recorded in the Cumberland County Registry in Book 512, page 91." The habendum and warranty clauses in this deed are as follows:

"TO HAVE AND TO HOLD to each a one-half undivided interest as tenants in common the aforesaid tract or parcel of land, and all privileges and appurtenances thereto belonging to the said parties of the second part, their heirs and assigns, to their only use and behoof forever.

"And said party of the first part for himself and his heirs, executors and administrators, covenants with said parties of the second part, their heirs and assigns, that he is seized of said premises in fee and has right to convey in fee simple; that the same are free and clear from all encumbrances and that he does hereby forever warrant and will forever defend the said title to the same against the claims of all persons whomsoever."

This deed also contains a recital to the effect that the grantees covenanted to pay Maggie Williford Williamson $250.00 monthly from the rents on the property throughout her life. Dr. R. L. Pittman died testate on 1 August 1963, his will and a codicil thereto, both dated in 1958, making no specific mention of the subject property, but making provision for a testamentary trust of the residue of the testator's estate.

In addition to the foregoing findings of fact, as to which there is no dispute, the trial court made the following finding of fact to which defendants excepted:

> 8. That in the execution of the said deed, at the time Dr. R. L. Pittman made the aforesaid deed to the plaintiff and defendant dated April 5, 1962, he intended to make such conveyance as would vest an equal interest in fee simple in plaintiff and defendant in and to the subject property as tenants in common.

Based upon the foregoing findings of fact the trial court made conclusions of law in substance as follows: Prior to the death of Grace S. Pittman, she and her husband, Dr. R. L. Pittman, were owners as tenants by the entirety of (1) a life estate in the property for the life of Maggie Williford Williamson, subject to the latter's right to receive $250.00 monthly from the rents, and (2) an undivided one-half interest in the remainder; that Raymond L. Pittman, Jr., at that time owned the other one-half undivided interest in the remainder; that on the death of Grace S. Pittman, her husband, Dr. R. L. Pittman, as surviving tenant by the entirety, became owner of the same interest as had previously been owned by the two of them as tenants by the entirety, and no interest in the property passed by the will of Grace S. Pittman; that by his deed dated 5 April 1962 recorded in Book 995, page 25, Dr. R. L. Pittman "clearly intended for the plaintiff and defendant each to be vested with an equal undivided one-half interest in fee simple in said property as tenants in common, with the provision that the payment of the monthly rental to Maggie Williford Williamson be continued"; and that said deed, "as intended by the grantor, Dr. R. L. Pittman, conveyed to Margaret Blue Parker, a one-half undivided interest in fee and conveyed to Raymond L. Pittman, Jr. and Margaret Blue Parker, each a one-half undivided interest in the life interest and estate, and thereupon said life interest and estate of Maggie Williford Williamson was merged with the remainder in fee and both grantees became the owners of equal undivided interests in fee in and to the said lot subject only to the covenant to pay monthly rental."

Upon these findings of fact and conclusions of law, the court entered judgment decreeing that plaintiff, Margaret Blue Parker, and defendant, Raymond L. Pittman, Jr., "are each the owners of an equal one-half undivided interest in fee simple in and to the Hay Street lot described in deed recorded in Book 995, page 25, Cumberland County Registry, subject to the right to monthly rental of Maggie Williford Williamson."

From this judgment, defendants appealed.

PARKER, Judge.

In her amended complaint plaintiff alleged that there was a "mutually agreed upon" testamentary plan between Grace S. Pittman (who was the mother of plaintiff and of the defendant, Raymond L. Pittman, Jr.) and Dr. R. L. Pittman (who was stepfather of the plaintiff and father of said defendant) "to give the plaintiff and defendant Raymond L. Pittman, Jr., a one-half undivided interest each in the property in question"; that following the death of Grace S. Pittman, Dr. Pittman "employed attorneys for the express purpose of making a deed which would convey a one-half undivided interest in this property to the plaintiff, and vest in the plaintiff and the defendant, Raymond L. Pittman, Jr., a one-half undivided interest each in the property"; that "through error and oversight" Dr. Pittman failed to mention to the attorneys the fact that Raymond L. Pittman, Jr., was already vested with a one-half undivided interest in the remainder; and that because the attorneys were "inadvertent" to this fact, they prepared the deed "without limiting the conveyance to the defendant, Raymond L. Pittman, Jr., to a one-half interest in the life estate only by express terms and language, so as to vest in the plaintiff and the defendant, Raymond L. Pittman, Jr., a one-half life undivided interest each in and to the life estate and remainder interest in said property as was intended by all of said parties."

If a deed fails to express the true intention of the parties it may be reformed to express such intent only when the failure is due to the mutual mistake of the parties, to the mistake of one party induced by fraud of the other, or to mistake of the draftsman. "The mistake of one party to the deed or instrument alone, not induced by the fraud of the other, affords no ground for relief by reformation." Crawford v. Willoughby, 192 N.C. 269, 134 S.E. 494. Even where appropriate grounds for reformation are asserted, "(w)hen a solemn document like a deed is revised by court of equity, the proof of mistake must be strong, cogent and convincing." Hege v. Sellers, 241 N.C. 240, 84 S.E.2d 892. In the present case plaintiff alleged mistake of the draftsman as grounds for the equitable relief or reformation, but her proof failed to support her allegations.

Plaintiff's evidence consisted solely of copies of recorded deeds in the chain of title, copies of the wills of her mother and stepfather, and her own testimony. The provisions in the two wills, neither of which is in the chain of title or otherwise directly affects title to the property involved, do not support plaintiff's allegations that there was a "mutually agreed upon" testamentary plan. Had the property passed under either will, the result would not have been to vest title in the manner for which plaintiff now contends. Her own testimony was confined principally to descriptions of the recorded documents and throws no light on the circumstances surrounding the preparation, execution, or delivery of the deed dated 5 April 1962 which she seeks to interpret or to reform. Plaintiff's proof being totally deficient to establish any grounds for reformation of that instrument, the trial court quite correctly did not grant that equitable relief, but limited its judgment to a legal interpretation of the instrument as drawn. In interpreting the legal effect of the instrument, however, in our opinion the trial court committed error.

In construing a deed and determining the intention of the parties, ordinarily the intention must be gathered from the language of the deed itself when its terms are unambiguous. Smith v. Smith, 249 N.C. 669, 107 S.E.2d 530. Only when the meaning of the language is in doubt may resort be had to evidence outside of the deed in order to determine the true intent of the grantor. 3 Strong, N.C. Index 2d, Deeds, § 11, p. 257. Here, not only was the language in the deed unambiguous, but there was simply no other evidence from which the grantor's intent might be found. Necessarily, therefore, we are limited in this case to the language contained in the deed itself in order to determine its legal effect.

At the time Dr. Pittman executed the deed dated 5 April 1962 he owned (1) a life estate in the property for the life of Maggie Williford Williamson (subject to the latter's right to receive $250.00 monthly from the rents of the property during her lifetime) and (2) a one-half undivided interest in the remainder. His son, Raymond L. Pittman, Jr., owned the other one-half undivided interest in the remainder. The trial court interpreted the deed dated 5 April 1962 as conveying (1) the life estate in equal shares to each of the two grantees and (2) the grantor's one-half interest in the remainder to only one of the two grantees, to the exclusion of the other. The deed itself, however, makes no such provision but throughout treats each of the two grantees equally. The language of the deed being clear and unequivocal, it must be given effect according to its terms, and we may not speculate that the grantor intended otherwise. "The grantor's intent must be understood as that expressed in the language of the deed and not necessarily such as may have existed in his mind if inconsistent with the legal import of the words he has used." Pittman v. Stanley, 231 N.C. 327, 56 S.E.2d 657. Any other rule makes for too great instability of titles.

The judgment appealed from is reversed and this cause is remanded to the Superior Court in Cumberland County for entry of judgment in conformity with this opinion.

Reversed and remanded.

Case Reflections

1. Why did the appeals court find that the granting clause in the deed was free of any ambiguties?
2. Why did the court in Parker v. Pittman refuse to consider the circumstances surrounding the execution of the deed, when the court in Knell v. Price held that the circumstances surrounding the execution of the deed were controlling?

FEES-KREY, INC.
V.
PAGE
591 P.2d 1339 (CO, 1979)

Race and Race-Notice Recording Statutes

This is a quiet title action. Plaintiffs, Fees-Krey, Inc., appeal from a judgment quieting title in defendant, Page, Jr., on his counterclaim to a 2% overriding royalty on an oil and gas lease. Defendant never recorded his interest pursuant to the Colorado Recording Act, sec. 38-35-109, C.R.S.1973, and plaintiffs subsequently acquired the lease without notice of defendant's overriding royalty. Neither plaintiffs nor any grantees prior to plaintiffs recorded their interests in the lease. [All of the parties to the lease recorded their interests with the Bureau of Land Management, and not with the County Clerk and Recorder, as required by the recording statute.] Plaintiffs contend that sec. 38-35-109, C.R.S.1973, is a pure notice statute, and that therefore plaintiffs have priority over defendant, because plaintiffs acquired their interest without notice. Defendant argues that the statute is a race-notice statute, or, in the alternative, that plaintiffs had constructive notice of defendant's interest by virtue of defendant's having recorded his interest in the records of the Bureau of Land Management.

We hold that the statute is a pure notice statute and that recording with the Bureau of Land Management does not constitute constructive notice of a prior interest. Because defendant's interest is cut off by his failure to record, we need not decide whether it was extinguished by merger of leasehold interests in the hands of a subsequent grantee.

* * *

The issue whether sec. 38-35-109, C.R.S.1973 is a pure notice or a race-notice type of statute is critical in this case because the characterization will determine the priority between the competing interests. An overriding royalty carved out of the working interest in an oil and gas lease is an interest in real property, Hagood v. Heckers, 182 Colo. 337, 513 P.2d 208 (1973); Globe Drilling Co. v. Cramer, 39 Colo.App. 153, 562 P.2d 762 (1977), and is therefore subject to the rules of priority of the Recording Act. If the statute is a race-notice type, a subsequent purchaser will prevail over a prior unrecorded interest only if he purchases without notice and records his interest before the prior interest is recorded. Even if the prior interest is never recorded, the subsequent purchaser must record his own interest before he can assert priority. Thus defendant would have priority here because plaintiffs, though subsequent purchasers without notice, failed to record. If, on the other hand, the statute is a pure notice statute, a subsequent purchaser who purchases without notice of a prior interest prevails over a prior unrecorded interest even though the subsequent purchaser does not record. Thus, plaintiffs, having purchased without notice of defendant's overriding royalty, would prevail under a notice type statute.

To support his argument that the statute is a race-notice type, and that plaintiffs cannot prevail without having first recorded their interest, defendant cites Eastwood v. Shedd, 166 Colo. 136, 442 P.2d 423 (1968), and Plew v. Colorado Lumber Products, 28 Colo.App. 557, 481 P.2d 127 (1970) wherein the courts either characterized or implicitly treated the statute as a race-notice statute. In neither case, however, was the characterization of the statute directly in issue. In Eastwood the issue was whether a donee was protected by the statute; in Plew the question was whether the statute protected a subsequent purchaser who had not yet paid full value, but who had recorded his contract of purchase. In neither case had the prior purchaser recorded before the subsequent purchaser recorded his interest. In both cases the subsequent party in interest would have had priority under either a notice or a race-notice type statute.

Because the characterization of the statute was dictum in Eastwood and was not directly addressed in Plew, we do not feel constrained to adopt the race-notice label without close analysis of the statute. After careful consideration of the language and purpose of the statute, we are convinced that the better construction is as a pure notice statute.

Section 38-35-109, C.R.S.1973, reads as follows:

> All deeds, powers of attorney, agreements, or other instruments in writing conveying, encumbering, or affecting the title to real property . . . may be recorded in the office of the county clerk and recorder of the county where such real property is situated and no such instrument or document shall be valid as against any class of persons with any kind of rights, except between the parties thereto and such as have notice thereof, until the same is deposited with such county clerk and recorder. In all cases where by law an instrument may be filed, the filing thereof with such county clerk and recorder shall be equivalent to the recording thereof.

The purpose of the statute is to "render titles to real property and every interest therein more secure and marketable." Section 38-34-101, C.R.S.1973. Thus we must liberally construe the statute:

> with the end in view of rendering such titles absolute and free from technical defects so that *subsequent purchasers and encumbrancers by way of mortgage, judgment, or otherwise,* may rely on the record title and so that the record title of the party in possession is sustained and not defeated by technical or strict constructions. Section 38-34-101, C.R.S.1973. (Emphasis added.)

The statute reads like a pure notice statute, and the language is similar to pure notice statutes in other jurisdictions. (Citations omitted.) For example, the Illinois recording act, which is generally considered as a notice statute, provides that:

> All deeds, mortgages and other instruments of writing which are authorized to be recorded, shall take effect and be in force from and after the time of filing the same for record, and not before, as to all creditors and subsequent purchasers, without notice; and all such deeds and title papers shall be adjudged void as to all such creditors and subsequent purchasers, without notice, until the same shall be filed for record. Ill.Rev.Stat. ch. 30, § 29 (Smith-Hurd, 1969).

By contrast, language in race-notice statutes, such as Michigan's, specifies that the subsequent purchaser must first record before he can have priority: "Every conveyance of real estate within this state hereafter made, which shall not be recorded as provided in this chapter, shall be void as against any subsequent purchaser in good faith, and for a valuable consideration, of the same real estate, or any portion thereof, *whose conveyance shall be first duly recorded.*" Mich.Stat.Ann. § 26.547 (1970) (M.C.L.A. § 565.29). (Emphasis added.)

Because sec. 38-35-109, C.R.S.1973, does not specifically state that to assert priority a subsequent purchaser must record his interest, as well as acquire it without notice, we construe the statute liberally to protect those who take without notice of a prior unrecorded interest.

Our decision is buttressed by the fact that a pure notice statute serves to protect subsequent purchasers, allowing them to rely on the record title as it exists at the time of their purchase. The danger of a race-notice statute is that a prior interest holder who has failed to record may cut off the claim of a subsequent purchaser who relied on the record at the time of his closing but has not yet had time to record his own instrument. *See* Note, The Colorado Recording Act: Race-Notice or Pure Notice? 51 Den.L.J. 115 (1974). Characterizing the statute as a pure notice rather than race-notice statute will encourage purchasers to record their interests as soon as acquired. Although a subsequent purchaser need not record to protect his interest against prior unrecorded interests, unless he does record, his interest may be cut off by a purchaser subsequent to him.

Defendant contends that even if the statute is a pure notice statute, plaintiffs had constructive notice of the overriding royalty because it was recorded in the office of the Bureau of Land Management. We disagree. Recording in the office of the Bureau of Land Management is constructive notice only if so recognized by state law. Bolack v. Underwood, 340 F.2d 816 (10th Cir. 1965). There is nothing in the Colorado statutes which indicates any intent of the General Assembly that such federal records constitute constructive notice to a person acquiring an interest in property in Colorado. Because the purpose of sec. 38-35-109, C.R.S.1973, is to strengthen record title by the recording in the County Clerk and Recorder's office, and because recording of a royalty interest with the Bureau of Land Management is only for the purpose of verifying the holdings of the assignee, 43 C.F.R. § 3106.4 (1977), we hold that recording with the Bureau of Land Management is not sufficient to constitute constructive notice of an interest in real property. Bolack v. Underwood, *supra;* Dame v. Mileski, 80 Wyo. 156, 340 P.2d 205 (1959). Having determined that § 38-35-109, C.R.S.1973, is a pure notice statute and that recording with the Bureau of Land Management is not constructive notice of an interest in real property, we find that plaintiffs acquired their interest in the oil and gas lease free of the unrecorded overriding royalty reserved by defendant.

The judgment is reversed and the cause is remanded with directions to enter judgment quieting title in plaintiffs to the 2% overriding royalty, and to order that all funds held in escrow pending this appeal be paid to plaintiffs.

Case Reflections

1. Why was the Colorado Supreme Court required to decide whether the Colorado Recording Act was a pure notice or a race notice statute?
2. Why did the plaintiffs (who were the last purchasers) argue for a pure notice statute, while the defendant argued that the statute was a race notice statute?

FORECLOSURE
AUCTION
JEROME J. MANNING
& CO., INC.

CHAPTER

9

MORTGAGES, LIENS, AND OTHER DOCUMENTS AFFECTING TITLE

LEARNING OBJECTIVES:

After reading this chapter, you should be able to:

1. Recognize and discuss the differences between a mortgage, a lien, and a security interest in personal property
2. Recognize the circumstances that can lead to the loss of ownership of real property through the actions of a lien holder against the owner of the property
3. Identify the steps in a mortgage foreclosure proceeding

KEY TERMS

- Lien
- Uniform Commercial Code
- Security Interest
- Lis Pendens
- Foreclosure
- Mortgagor
- Mortgagee
- Equity of Redemption
- Strict Foreclosure
- Deed of Trust
- Default
- Junior Lien Holders
- Foreclosure by Public Sale

Since the dawn of history, people have been borrowing from and lending to each other. In the very earliest human civilizations, these loan transactions involved crops, animals, and other necessities for life and productive labor. In later societies, money was developed as a medium of exchange to replace the more cumbersome barter arrangements. Today the typical loan transaction involves a payment of money from a lender to a borrower, in exchange for the written promise of the borrower to repay the loan, usually with interest.

It has always been true, and it is true today, that the moment the lender gives the money over to the borrower, the lender runs the risk of losing all of the money delivered, plus the interest on the money. If the borrower turns out to be unable (or simply unwilling) to repay the loan, the lender will lose money. In order to reduce the risk of loss, lenders have always looked for some form of security to protect themselves against the dangers of a borrower's becoming unable or unwilling to repay the loan.

Real property owned by the borrower provides an excellent source of security. So long as the value of the real property is greater than the amount of the debt, even the most unwilling borrower would prefer to pay the loan when the alternative is the loss of the valuable real property. And, if the borrower turns out to be willing but unable to pay, then the secured lender can take over the ownership of the property. Again, if the value of the property exceeds the amount of money owed to the lender, then the lender will be protected against the risk of loss.

While this arrangement is easy to understand in the abstract, the implementation of actual real property security arrangements presents a host of difficult and complex problems. For example, agreements that secure the promise to repay money in the future are most valuable when the borrower becomes unable to keep the promise. However, the borrower who is unable to repay one creditor usually has several creditors demanding repayment. And all of these creditors may have secured their loans with the same piece of property. When all of the creditors come to court demanding that the borrower surrender the property to them, judges will need a set of rules for deciding which creditor's claim will have priority over the claims of other creditors.

In addition, the value of the property securing the promise to repay will usually be more than or less than the amount of the unpaid debt. If the value of the property is more than the amount of the unpaid debt, it would not be fair to the borrower to allow the creditor sell the property and keep the added profit. If the value of the property is less than the amount of unpaid debt, will the borrower be required to make up the difference? Once again, judges need a set of rules to answer all these questions in a manner that provides substantial justice to all parties in light of the circumstances of the case.

Finally, there are some transactions in which the creditor gives the borrower something of value that is not money. A skilled carpenter may work to build a house, expecting to be paid for the work when it is finished. A lumberyard might deliver materials to a construction site that are then incorporated into a building. Again, the lumberyard expects to be paid after the materials are delivered and used. The carpenter and the lumberyard have both made "loans" to the owner of the real property, even though the thing loaned was goods or services instead of money. All states have adopted statutes that allow these creditors to obtain a security interest in the real property benefited by their efforts if the owner fails to pay for the goods or services.

In this chapter, we will examine many of these issues closely. When you have finished reading the chapter, you should have a clearer understanding of the rules judges use to assign priorities among various creditors who claim to have a secured interest in real property. You should also have a clearer understanding of the procedures used by creditors to realize the value of their secured interests.

Lien
The legally enforceable right to compel a debtor to sell property encumbered by the lien and apply the proceeds of the sale against the principle and interest owed on a debt.

LIENS

In current practice, a **lien** is a nonpossessory interest in real property that secures the obligation of the property owner to make a money payment to the lien holder. Until very recently, liens against personal property also existed. In the last few decades, all states have adopted the **Uniform Commercial Code** as the statute governing transactions in most personal property. The UCC defines a lien against personal property as a **"security interest."** In almost all cases a lien against personal property is, strictly speaking, a security interest as defined in Article 9 of the UCC. Today, liens against personal property that are not legally defined as security interests governed by the terms of the UCC are so rare that we can safely ignore them. True liens (real property interests *not* governed by the UCC) can arise through any of three mechanisms.

Uniform Commercial Code
Uniform statute adopted in most states which governs commercial transactions.

Judgment Liens

When the plaintiff in a lawsuit prevails, he or she will obtain a judgment against the defendant. If the judgment requires the defendant to pay a sum of money, the plaintiff can record the written document and obtain a lien against all of the property owned by the defendant. The lien of a judgment is often required to compel the defendant to make the payments ordered by the court. If the defendant were willing to make the payments, a lawsuit would not have occurred.

The judgment lien allows the plaintiff (now called the judgment creditor) to obtain an order to sell the defendant's (or judgment debtor's) real property to raise the cash required to satisfy the judgment. The only way for the judgment debtor to avoid this unpleasant outcome is to make the cash payments required by the judgment.

The judgment lien attaches to all property owned by the judgment debtor, but it attaches only to the property owned by the debtor. This leads to an intriguing possibility. Suppose that when a lawsuit is filed, the defendant transfers all of his or her property to another person (a spouse, close relative, or friend). The transfer makes

Security Interest
The legally enforceable right to repossess and sell personal property which was previously purchased or financed in a transaction governed by the Uniform Commercial Code.

KEY POINTS

In most states, a judgment creditor can levy on the personal property of a judgment debtor very quickly. The usual procedure is to summon the judgment debtor to court, and in the presence of a judge ask the debtor to identify the location of all bank accounts, securities, automobiles, and other property owned by the debtor. The procedure usually ends with the attorney for the judgment creditor asking the judgment debtor to hand over the keys to the car that the debtor drove to the court appearance. The creditor is then free to use that car until the title is transferred from the debtor to the creditor.

the defendant "judgment proof" since there will be no property left for the plaintiff to sell in order to satisfy a judgment.

Lis Pendens A notice filed for record which informs the public that the owner of real property is, or might become, the defendant in a law suit which may affect the title to the real property.

The **lis pendens** notice is one method for preventing a defendant from becoming judgment proof. The lis pendens is a document stating that a lawsuit is (or soon will be) pending against the owner of real property. When filed for record, the lis pendens produces a cloud on the record title of the real property belonging to the person named as the actual or potential defendant in the notice. A grantee of real property from an owner named in a lis pendens notice may take the property subject to a future judgment lien of the person filing the notice.

All states have also adopted statutes that prohibit "fraudulent conveyances." The statutory formulas vary somewhat from state to state, but the basic theme of the statutes is the same everywhere. When a conveyance of real property is made by a person who hopes to become judgment proof in order to escape paying a debt, the conveyance will usually be voided by a court. Upon application by a creditor, the court may set aside the fraudulent conveyance and determine that the fraudulent grantor is still the owner of the property. In order to escape the operation of a fraudulent conveyance statute, the grantee may be required to prove that he or she was a good faith purchaser for value, without notice of the creditor's claim against the grantor.

Whenever a grantee actually pays a cash price for the property that is reasonably close to the fair market value of the asset purchased, most courts are reluctant to void the transaction. If the price paid is significantly less than fair market value, or if the purchase substitutes creative financing for a cash payment of the price, courts will look more closely at the conveyance. In these cases, the grantee may be asked to prove that he or she had no notice of the creditor's claims against the grantor at the time of the purchase.

This requirement often poses formidable problems of proof. A grantee has actual notice of another creditor's claim when he or she has received, or should have looked for, notification. Documents filed by creditors, including mortgages, lis pendens, UCC financing statements, and other similar papers provide actual notice to all the world of the creditor's claim against a grantor of property. Further, grantees may be charged with having constructive notice of an adverse claim to the property if, from all of the facts known to the grantee at the time of the transfer, the grantee had reason to know that an adverse claim to the property existed. Proving that any of these conditions exist is somewhat difficult. Proving that none of these conditions existed is much more difficult.

Statutory Liens

When people in the construction trade provide goods or services to the owner of real property, they run the risk of not being paid for whatever they have delivered. For example, the carpenter who spends five days remodeling a kitchen has clearly conveyed a benefit on the owner of the home and expects to be paid an agreed-upon wage after the remodeling is completed. Likewise, the lumberyard that sold the materials used by the carpenter has provided a benefit to the owner of the house and will expect to be paid at the end of the month.

Because property owners have often failed or refused to pay for the goods and services purchased and added to their property, all states have adopted statutes that create a lien against the real property in these circumstances. Mechanic's liens and materialman's liens can be enforced by filing an appropriate document for record within the time limits established by the statute. (The time limit is usually six months after the mechanic has completed the work or six months after the materialman has completed delivery of all the goods giving rise to the lien.) Once the document, in the form prescribed by the statute, has been filed, the lien attaches to the real property. Even if the owner who contracted with the carpenter or the lumberyard sells the property before the lien document is filed, the lien will attach to the property and may be valid against the new owner.

KEY POINTS

The risks of nonperformance exist on both sides of any transaction involving improvements to real property. Every attorney has heard a story similar to the following tale.

A young working-class couple owned a home with a full but unfinished basement. One day they decided to hire a friend who worked as a carpenter to remodel the basement. The homeowners agreed with their friend that a new bedroom, bathroom, and family room would be built in the basement, at a total cost of $15,000. The homeowners went to a local bank and obtained a home equity loan to pay for the improvements. When the loan closed, the homeowners delivered the check to the carpenter, who promised to start work immediately.

Six weeks later, the homeowners consulted an attorney. The "friend" never did begin work on the basement remodeling project as promised. Worse, the carpenter had declared personal bankruptcy and moved to a new city. The only advice the attorney could offer was to continue making payments on the home equity loan. The homeowners had already lost the money they paid to their carpenter in advance. But they were still at risk of losing their home as well if the bank was required to foreclose on the home equity loan.

Once the lien attaches to the property, it can be enforced by **foreclosure** proceedings. We will examine foreclosure in more detail later in this chapter. For now it is enough to say that the lien holder may be able to obtain a court order that directs the sheriff of the county where the property is located to sell the property to the highest bidder. The proceeds of the sale will first be used to satisfy the claims of the lien holder. Any remaining proceeds will be delivered to the person who was removed from ownership by the foreclosure sale.

Foreclosure The process a lender must use to compel a borrower to sell real property and apply the proceeds of the sale towards the payments due to the lender.

The idea that a purchaser can be removed from ownership of property through the foreclosure of a statutory lien is a disquieting notion. To prevent this unhappy result, prospective purchasers must take positive steps to protect their interests. First, the buyer much check the public records and verify that no mechanic's lien statements have been filed on or before the date on which the buyer pays the purchase price and takes possession of the property. However, since a mechanic's lien statement can be filed as much as six months after the work that gave rise to the lien was performed, simply checking the public records will not be sufficient in all cases.

In addition, the purchaser should insist on a statement from the seller that no construction work has been performed on the property being sold within the time limit allowed for the filing of a statutory lien. The purchaser should also make a thorough inspection of the premises, looking for evidence of recent work performed by tradespeople who might be entitled to file a statutory lien. The performance of these actions will be required for a buyer to qualify as a good faith purchaser for value. By attaining this status, a buyer can expect to be immunized from the effect of a statutory lien filed after the buyer takes possession of the property.

Tax Liens

Most real property in the United States is subject to ad valorem property tax (a tax computed by referring to the value of the property). These taxes always become payable on the same day each year. The particular day ad valorem taxes for the year are payable is defined by statute in each state. If the taxes remain unpaid after the due date, the property will become subject to a tax lien.

The procedures for enforcing tax liens vary from state to state. In general, the tax lien attaches to the property on the date tax payments become due. If the taxes remain unpaid for a period of one month to one year after the due date, then the taxes will be sold at a public auction. The buyer at the auction receives a tax certificate, with a face amount equal to the unpaid taxes and bearing interest at a stated rate. In most states, the taxing authority can refuse to sell a tax certificate for an amount less than the unpaid taxes.

During the "redemption period," which lasts from one to five years depending upon the state statute, the owner of the property may redeem the taxes by paying the holder of the tax certificate the amount of unpaid taxes plus accrued interest. If the taxes are not redeemed within the time period allowed, then the holder of the tax certificate will generally become the owner of the property.

Mortgagor The owner of real property who gives a mortgage against the property in exchange for cash or something else of value.

Mortgagee A lender who receives a mortgage against real property to secure the future repayment of a debt to the lender contracted by the owner of the real property.

MORTGAGES

While statutory liens are an important source of defects in the title to real property, mortgages are far more common and a good bit more difficult to understand. Even the terminology of mortgage financing is hard to grasp at first. Court opinions defining the rights of borrowers and lenders in a mortgage transaction usually refer to **mortgagors** and **mortgagees.** These archaic terms refer to the borrower and lender, respectively, in a mortgage transaction. As you read the cases at the end of this chapter (and perhaps even as you read the remainder of this chapter) you will probably want to keep a piece of paper handy with the following formulas on it:

mortgagor = borrower
mortgagee = lender

These terms arose during the fourteenth century. At that time, a mortgage deed transferred the title to land from the mortgagor (the grantor in the mortgage deed) to the mortgagee (the grantee in the mortgage deed). The title conveyed in a mortgage deed of that time was essentially a fee simple defeasible title. The mortgagee received the present possessory interest to the property and could evict the grantor and take possession of the land at any time. However, since the mortgagee was required to apply any rents or profits from the land against the money owned by the mortgagor, this option was almost never exercised.

The title to the land was defeasible because the mortgagor retained the right to pay a stated sum of money on the *law day* and, by making the payment, extinguish the ownership interest of the mortgagee. The sum of money the mortgagor was required to pay would usually be the amount the mortgagee paid for the deed plus interest. These early mortgages were crude but effective. When lenders advanced money in exchange for a mortgage deed, they could rest assured that they would either receive their money back on the law day or become the fee simple owner of the property transferred by the mortgage deed. As long as the mortgagee was careful about the amount of funds advanced to the mortgagor, the lender would be indifferent between these outcomes.

As always, the law judges enforced the early mortgages exactly as they were written. If the mortgagor came to court on the law day and paid the sum of money described in the mortgage deed, then the ownership of the mortgagee was defeated. If not, the mortgagor became a common trespasser on the property of the mortgagee.

But suppose that the mortgagor was robbed on his way to make the law day payment required to extinguish the ownership interest of the mortgagee and as a result lost the family homestead? There was no remedy in the law courts, since the law judges could not ask why the payment was not made. The law judges were only empowered to ask if the payment had been made. Many borrowers in this situation would take their cause to the king's equity courts, where questions of fairness and justice could be dealt with more broadly. There, the dispossessed borrower would plead for permission to repay the debt at a date after the law day and thereby *redeem* the property from the mortgagee's possession.

Equity of Redemption In modern practice, this term refers to the difference between the fair market value of real property and the amounts currently due and owing to any mortgagees who have rights to the real property. At common law, the equity of redemption was the right of a borrower to redeem the property from the mortgagee after a foreclosure of the mortgage.

Within a generation or so, equity courts routinely ordered mortgagees to accept late payments on mortgage debts and convey the ownership of the property to the mortgagor. This procedure became so common, it was given the name **equity of redemption.** In modern practice, equity refers to the difference between the value of a mortgaged property and the balance of the debt due under the mortgage. This shorthand term merely describes the circumstances under which a borrower would find it profitable and desirable to exercise the equity of redemption.

While this development represented a great victory for borrowers, it raised a host of vexing questions for lenders. Once the law day passed with the mortgage debt unpaid, the mortgagee would not know if the mortgagor intended to redeem the property or not. This uncertainty caused lenders to launch a counterattack in the equity courts. After a default occurred, it became common practice for mortgagees to request the equity judge to enter an order requiring the mortgagor to redeem the property on or before a given date, usually six months to a year after the default occurred. The lender would also ask the equity judge to warn the mortgagor that the equity of redemption would be *foreclosed* on that date if the mortgagor failed to redeem. As a result of this proceeding, the mortgagee could once again determine the precise date on which the title to the property would ripen into a fee simple absolute title, free of the defeasibility feature of the mortgage deed and its attendant equity of redemption.

Strict Foreclosure The process by which the mortgagee in a title theory jurisdiction acquires the fee simple title to the real property encumbered by a mortgage. After a strict foreclosure, the mortgagee acquires a title which is subject only to the mortgagor's right of redemption.

This procedure, known as **strict foreclosure,** is still in use in a few states today. By far the most common procedure for terminating the equity of redemption is **foreclosure by public sale.** Foreclosure by sale offers some advantages to borrowers who lack the cash to repay their debts, even though the property they own is

Foreclosure by Public Sale
The process by which the mortgagee in a lien theory jurisdiction is empowered to sell the real property encumbered by a mortgage, and apply the proceeds of the sale to the unpaid balance of the mortgage.

worth more than the amount of the unpaid mortgage debt. Under strict foreclosure, the mortgagee becomes the owner of the property, at a "price" equal to the unpaid balance of the debt. Under foreclosure by sale, there is reason to hope that bidders will offer to pay the full market value of the property. Any proceeds from the sale over and above the unpaid debt can then be salvaged for the borrower.

As the pendulum swung between borrowers and lenders over the centuries required for these developments, it became more and more evident that a mortgage was something other than the conveyance of title to real property. After the equity of redemption and the process of foreclosure by public sale had emerged, it began to be clear that a mortgage was really just another form of a lien securing the performance of a borrower's obligation to pay. As a result, judges began to treat mortgages less like an ownership interest in land and more like a lien against the property to secure the repayment of a debt.

When a judge thinks about the effect of a mortgage in terms of its impact on the ownership of land, he or she is using a title theory approach to the instrument. On the other hand, judges who analyze a mortgage in terms of its effect upon the record title to the property are using a lien theory approach. While some states retain the ancient title theory of mortgage deeds, the majority of states today use a lien theory approach to mortgages.

Maglione v. Banc Boston Mortgage Corporation

Public Trustee Deeds

Deed of Trust
A document conveying a power to sell real property to a public official (the Public Trustee) whenever the owner of the property fails or refuses to pay the sums due to a lender whose note is secured by the deed of trust.

The public trustee deed represents a modern blending of the two mortgage theories developed over the previous five hundred years. Most states have now made statutory provisions for a financing instrument commonly known as a "note and **deed of trust.**" The promissory note referred to by this term contains the agreement between the borrower and the lender. The agreement spelled out by the note will indicate the amount of money borrowed, the interest rate to be paid by the borrower, the repayment terms, and other pertinent items. In order to secure the borrower's performance under the note agreement, the borrower will execute a deed conveying real property to an appointed official known as the public trustee.

By virtue of the public trustee deed, the legal title to the property is vested in a government official, who holds the property in trust for the parties to the note that must accompany the deed. The ownership of the public trustee reflects the ancient title theory approach to mortgage transactions. However, the ownership rights of the public trustee are severely restricted by the trust agreement that created the trustee's ownership. The sole ownership right the trustee is empowered to exercise in the property is the power to sell the property upon the request of the lender.

It is fair to ask why states have gone to such lengths to create what appears to be a very cumbersome procedure. Why in the world should there be a need for an appointed official of government to hold a bare legal title to all mortgaged property in a particular county? The answer is that the public trustee deed is a good compromise between the ancient title theory of mortgages, which allows lenders to collect their money through strict foreclosure, and the more modern lien theory of mortgages, where lenders must collect their money through foreclosure by public sale.

In the next section we will examine foreclosure proceedings in more detail. There, you will see that strict foreclosure is an easier and speedier remedy for lenders than foreclosure by public sale. However, you will also discover that foreclosure by sale offers some protection to borrowers that is missing in the strict foreclosure proceedings. Public trustee deeds were created as an attempt to provide the best of both worlds in a single legal structure. The public trustee's power of sale provides a remedy that is almost as easy and speedy as strict foreclosure, which is a good thing from the lender's perspective. However, since the public trustee is always required by statute to exercise the power of sale in a regulated public manner, the borrower can potentially receive all of the protection afforded by sale foreclosure proceedings. The value of the protections afforded to the borrower depends upon the degree of judicial oversight required by the state statute.

George Tobin and others published notice that property subject to a deed of trust would be offered for public sale to satisfy an unpaid secured debt. The sale was originally scheduled for December 7, 1972, but was repeatedly postponed. The sale actually occurred on January 12, 1973. The property, with a fair market value estimated at $36,000 was sold for $26,700

The plaintiffs had intended to bid at the public sale, but apparently were unable to do so because the sale was not held at the time and place named in the notice of sale. They sued the public trustee and others, demanding damages for expenses incurred in preparing a bid, lost profits and punitive damages.

The plaintiffs alleged fraudulent misrepresentation of the date and time of the advertised public sale, in order to conduct the actual sale of the property in secret. The California court of appeals held that the complaint stated a cause of action against the defendants. The court also ruled that the plaintiffs were entitled to recover the expenses of preparing a bid in reliance on the notice of public sale, and would be entitled to receive punitive damages if they were able to prove that the defendants had intentionally misrepresented the time and place of the sale. The court cited the rule in California that "a [public] trustee or [secured lender] may be held liable in damages to the [borrower] or his successor in interest for conducting an illegal, fraudulent or oppressive sale." That rule does not preclude recovery by a prospective bidder for damages sustained as a consequence of a public trustee's deceit. Block v. Tobin 119 Cal. Rptr. 288 (1975)

Mortgage Liens

A mortgage creates an encumbrance on the fee simple title to real property on the date that the mortgagor and mortgagee contract for the mortgage. As with any other ownership interest, the rights of a mortgagee can only be enforced against persons with notice of those rights. (Recall that the rights of a mortgagee can properly be called "ownership rights" only in those states that use a title theory approach to mortgages.) When a mortgage deed or trust deed is filed for record, all the world will have notice of the mortgagee's rights in the property encumbered by the mortgage.

If property encumbered by a recorded mortgage is sold, the new owner will take the property subject to the encumbrance. In the event payments on the mortgage are not made, the lender will have the right to foreclose the mortgage and evict the new owner. One of the primary purposes of the closing process, described in Chapter 11, is to insure that all mortgages that encumber the property transferred at the closing are paid in full before the new owner takes possession. Obviously, the payment of all mortgages against the property will require that the price paid by the purchaser be at least equal to the balance due on all mortgages encumbering the property. For this reason, the use of mortgage financing imposes some risks on borrowers as well as on lenders.

When the highest price a willing buyer would pay for a parcel of real property is less than the outstanding balance of the mortgages encumbering the property, the current owner will have a negative equity. If title to the property is transferred to a new owner, the current owner will be required to add personal funds to the price paid by the purchaser in order to satisfy the claims to the mortgages.

In cases where the equity in a property is small or negative, the parties may want to use the outstanding mortgage balances as a portion of the consideration to be paid by a purchaser. If the lender gives consent, a purchaser can take title to mortgaged property by agreeing to assume the mortgage. That is, the purchaser takes over all of the obligations that the prior owner had under the mortgage. In return for assuming the obligation to make all future payments, the purchaser will receive credit against the purchase price in an amount equal to unpaid principal balance of any mortgages assumed.

As an alternative, the purchaser may take the property subject to the mortgage. In this case, the purchaser acknowledges that if future payments on the mortgage are not made, the property will become subject to foreclosure. In order to prevent foreclosure, the parties usually agree that the purchaser will make all future payments on the mortgage. However, the purchaser who takes the property subject to the mortgage has no personal obligation to make future payments. Each month, the purchaser can decide to continue making payments or allow the mortgagee to proceed with foreclosure. Purchasers of property subject to a mortgage will also expect to receive credit on the purchase in an amount equal to the unpaid balance of the mortgages.

Mortgage Terms

Over the years mortgage forms have developed that provide a great deal of flexibility in the security arrangements needed by borrowers and lenders in a variety of circumstances. Like snowflakes, no two mortgage loans are exactly alike. The size of the loan secured by a mortgage, the use of the loan proceeds by the borrower, the value and nature of the collateral mortgaged, and the circumstances of the parties will be different in each loan transaction.

As a result, most mortgage forms include a set of standard provisions common to all transactions and are then augmented by the inclusion of particular mortgage terms that reflect the needs and circumstances of the parties to the agreement. The standard mortgage clauses describe the property securing the debt and recite the amount, interest rate, and repayment terms of the debt. Additional clauses can be mixed and matched with the standard mortgage provisions to create a security arrangement exactly matching the needs and positions of the parties to the loan. The Appendix to this chapter includes samples of four of the more common special provisions that appear in mortgages.

After Acquired Property Clauses

When the borrower has taken out a mortgage to finance the purchase of a new home, the home will typically contain kitchen cabinets, appliances, a central heating system, and other amenities of modern life. If any or all of these items are removed by the borrower after a default on the mortgage debt, the value of the lender's security may be substantially reduced. While all such items that were in the house on the date the mortgage was recorded are probably subject to the lien of the mortgage, new appliances, cabinets, and central heating plants purchased after the mortgage is recorded may not be subject to the lien of the mortgage. In order to prevent the removal of standard household items from the premises during a foreclosure proceeding, lenders often include an after acquired property clause in the text of the mortgage document.

First National Bank v. Fink

Such a clause is even more important when the collateral is a commercial building. It is reasonable to expect that a commercial occupant will purchase significant new or replacement items of equipment for the conduct of the business located in the mortgaged premises. Lenders are understandably eager to insure that the lien of their mortgage also includes equipment necessary to the commercial activity in the mortgaged premises that was purchased after the date the mortgage was recorded.

Future Advance Clauses

Another common mortgage form is the construction loan. A developer who owns a parcel of vacant ground will usually need to obtain mortgage financing in order to pay for the cost of erecting a house or commercial building on the property. It is the practice of the construction industry to pay for work after it is completed. As a result, the construction lender will typically file the mortgage for record prior to the date construction begins and advance funds to pay for various phases of the construction after each phase is completed. The first advance made by the construction lender may occur after the foundation of the new building is complete. The next advance might be made after the exterior walls and the roof are in place, and so on.

Adamson Construction v. First Federal Savings and Loan

A future advance clause is an essential term of a construction mortgage. Generally, the lien of a mortgage will only secure debts owed by the mortgagor on the date the mortgage is executed. On the date a construction mortgage is executed, the mortgagor may owe nothing to the lender, because no advances on the construction loan have been made on that date. The future advances clause in a recorded mortgage alerts the world that the property owned by the mortgagor will be encumbered as security for a debt that will be created after a date of the mortgage. For a construction mortgage, this notice is sufficient to change the general rule and bring the property under the lien of the construction lender's mortgage.

A future advances clause may also be included in mortgages that are not related to the construction of improvements to real property. However, as the case at the end of this chapter points out, the results of such clauses in mortgages not involving construction loans may be less than the lender had hoped for.

Acceleration Clauses

Virtually all of the promissory notes that are secured by real estate mortgages require monthly payments of principal and interest to be made over a long period of time. Thirty-year mortgages are not uncommon for residential properties. If a borrower stops making monthly payments three years after the note is executed, a question arises as to how much money the lender would be entitled to receive in a foreclosure proceeding. By the terms of the note, the borrower is not required to repay the remaining principal for another twenty-seven years.

The acceleration clause removes this ambiguity by stating that in the event of default, the borrower can be required to repay the full principal balance, with interest, immediately. The lender is then entitled to recover this amount in a foreclosure proceeding.

Due on Sale Clauses

Because real estate mortgages typically have terms of fifteen to thirty years, it is reasonable to expect that interest rates will change significantly during the term of the mortgage. When interest rates rise, borrowers who have contracted for a long-term debt with a fixed interest rate will make money. The principal and interest payments on a thirty-year fixed-rate mortgage at 7 percent are $332.65 per month for a $50,000 mortgage. At 10 percent, the monthly payment on the same mortgage would be $438.78. Under these conditions a prospective buyer could, in theory, take over the payment of the low-interest first mortgage, contract for a second mortgage at 12 percent for fifteen years in the amount of $8,000, and still have a smaller total monthly mortgage payment than the buyer would have with a new first mortgage at 10 percent. As a result, the price a willing buyer would pay could be as much as $8,000 larger when the buyer can assume the existing mortgage.

> Fidelity Savings and Loans made numerous mortgages on real property located in California. Each of the mortgages contained a due on sale clause. The plaintiffs had each purchased a property on which Fidelity held a mortgage. Fidelity was not notified of any of these transactions. When Fidelity became aware of the plaintiff's purchases, Fidelity informed them that the due on sale clause in the mortgage would be enforced. Each purchaser was notified that Fidelity would accept an agreement to increase the interest rate on the mortgages to the prevailing market rate. The purchasers refused to agree, and Fidelity commenced foreclosure proceedings.
>
> The purchasers filed suit to prevent the foreclosures, arguing the California courts had previously ruled that due on sale clauses constitute an unreasonable restraint on alienation, and are therefore void as against public policy. The district court found for Fidelity, but the court of appeals reversed. The U.S. Supreme Court then granted certiorari.
>
> The U.S. Supreme court held that the Federal Home Loan Bank Board had preempted regulation of federally chartered thrift institutions like Fidelity. Further, the FHLBB had adopted a regulation which empowered federal savings and loan associations to include a due on sale clause in their mortgages. Because federal regulations preempt state laws and court rulings, the California ruling invalidating due on sale clauses was invalid under the supremacy clause of the U.S. constitution. Fidelity Federal Savings and Loan v. De La Cuesta 458 U.S. 141 (1982)

When borrowers make money on changes in interest rates, lenders lose money. As a result, lenders routinely include a due on sale clause in mortgages, in order to prohibit transactions of the kind described above. The due on sale clause forces the buyer to negotiate with the lender on the assumption of the mortgage. In general, real estate lenders will allow creditworthy buyers to assume an existing mortgage whenever the interest rate on the mortgage is adjusted to reflect current market conditions.

Default
The failure or refusal to comply with any material term or condition of a mortgage, or the promissory note which the mortgage secures.

Mortgage Foreclosure

Whenever a mortgagor fails to make any of the payments required by the terms of a promissory note executed by the borrower in favor of the lender, a **default** has occurred. The occurrence of a default arms the lender (mortgagee) with several options.

KEY POINTS

The "wraparound" mortgage is a financing device used occasionally as an attempt to escape the effects of a due on sale clause. In the circumstances described above, the buyer might be tempted to arrange for second mortgage financing and proceed with the purchase of the house without advising the existing mortgage lender about the transaction. The buyer would then take possession of the house, make payments directly to the second mortgage lender, and make payments to the seller in an amount equal to the monthly installments on the existing first mortgage. The seller in turn pays the first mortgage lender.

Such an arrangement is both unethical and inherently dangerous. The most likely outcome is that the seller fails to make payments on the first mortgage, requiring the buyer to either refinance the home at current market rates or lose the house to foreclosure proceedings. The next most likely outcome is that the lender will discover the transaction and demand payment of the first mortgage under the due on sale clause. Again, the buyer will be required to either refinance or lose the home.

The mortgagee's first option is to do nothing, in hopes that the default will be cured in the near future and no further problems with the loan will occur. It is customary for lenders to send a defaulting borrower a rather stern letter, warning the mortgagor that the default must be cured immediately or the property will become subject to a foreclosure proceeding.

If the warning letter does not obtain results and the default remains uncured, the mortgagee will have to begin to consider foreclosure proceedings. In general, a foreclosure proceeding begins when a mortgagee files a foreclosure lawsuit with a court of competent jurisdiction. The mortgagee is typically required to notify the mortgagor and all other persons who claim an interest in the mortgaged property that the foreclosure of the mortgage lien is imminent. The required notice is given by delivering a copy of the mortgagee's complaint together with a copy of a summons notifying the defendants in the foreclosure action that they must appear in person at the courthouse to present their objections to the proceedings. As always, if a defendant receives the summons and complaint and subsequently fails to appear as ordered, the court will conclude that the defendant has no objection to the foreclosure proceedings requested by the mortgagee.

A foreclosure action extinguishes the mortgage lien of the mortgagee who initiates the action. In addition, the foreclosure proceeding will extinguish the lien of any mortgages and judgments that are "junior" to the lien of the mortgagee who initiates a foreclosure. In the next section, we will examine in more detail the rules for determining priorities among various liens in a single parcel of real property. For now, it is sufficient to remember that owners of real property may contract for several different mortgages on the same parcel of property. In general, each new mortgage lien will be junior (or subordinate) to the lien of any mortgages created at an earlier date.

Once a foreclosure action is begun, the lien of the mortgagee who initiates the action, together with the liens of all junior mortgagees who are notified of the foreclosure action, will be terminated. During the proceedings, the trial judge will examine the promissory note executed by the borrower in favor of the foreclosing mortgagee. The borrower will also be given an opportunity to present evidence that he or she has complied with all of the terms of the note and is not in default as the lender alleged in the complaint. Once the trial judge becomes satisfied that a default has in fact occurred, an order of foreclosure will be entered.

Strict Foreclosure Proceedings

In states that apply the title theory of mortgages, the mortgagee becomes the owner of the property on the date of the foreclosure order, subject to the mortgagor's equitable right of redemption. If the mortgagor does not redeem the property within the period allowed by statute, then the mortgagee acquires a fee simple absolute title to the property. This relatively simple procedure becomes quite complicated, however, when either of two circumstances surrounds the strict foreclosure proceeding.

If the market value of the mortgaged property is greater than the total amount due to the mortgagee (including principal, accrued interest, and other costs), then the mortgagee can expect to receive more than the unpaid debt when the property is sold. This potential for a windfall gain to the mortgagee, acquired at the expense of the mortgagor, has always caused problems in strict foreclosure states. In theory, the mortgagor can protect his or her interests by redeeming the property. In practice, this is often impossible. As a result, many strict foreclosure states have created an equitable doctrine of appropriation. This doctrine requires the mortgagee to pay the mortgagor a sum of money equal to the fair market value of the property less the amount due to the mortgagor from the foreclosure proceedings. The payment is usually not due until the property is actually sold by the mortgagee who has acquired title through strict foreclosure.

A&M Realty v. Dahms, Jr.

Rockwood Realty mortgaged property to the plaintiff Ganbaum. Rockwood then sold the property to Edith Levine, who acquired the title subject to the lien of Ganbaum's mortgage. The mortgage included an assignment of rents clause which included the following language: "the mortgagor hereby assigns to the mortgagee the rents, issues and profits of the premises as further security for the payment of said indebtedness . . . "

Levine failed to make payments on the mortgage, and Ganbaum foreclosed. Ganbaum also demanded damages in the amount of $31,180.64 from Levine. Ganbaum argued that Levine had received rent from the property for two years, while failing to pay the property taxes, sewer and water charges on the property. As a result, Ganbaum was required to pay these amounts after recovering the property in the foreclosure.

The trial court granted summary judgment against Ganbaum. The court argued that a mortgage in the state of New York represents only a lien against real property. "The common law doctrine that the mortgagee held title [to the mortgaged premises] or any incidents thereof has long ago been abolished." Since the assignment of rents clause in the mortgage represented an attempt to acquire an incident of title by the mortgagee, the court ruled that the assignment clause was void because it contradicted the stated public policy of New York. Ganbaum v. Rockwood Realty 308 N.Y.S. 2d 436 (1970)

Junior Lien Holders Persons who hold liens in property which is encumbered by other liens which will be given priority in foreclosure or bankruptcy proceedings.

The second circumstance that complicates stricture foreclosure proceedings is the presence of **junior lien holders** in the property. Recall that a foreclosure proceeding will extinguish the lien of the foreclosing mortgagee, as well as all liens that are junior to the lien foreclosed. Since the ownership of the property is transferred to the foreclosing lien holder in a strict foreclosure proceeding, the junior lien holders are left with neither the property nor their liens. To prevent the complete dissolution of the rights of other secured creditors in the foreclosed property, strict foreclosure states usually provide a statutory method whereby junior lien creditors can redeem the property from senior lien creditors after a foreclosure.

The order of foreclosure will state the amounts due and owing to each of the creditors whose liens are extinguished in the foreclosure proceeding. The same order will convey title in the property to the holder of the senior lien foreclosed in the action, subject to various rights of redemption. Any junior creditor may redeem the property from a senior creditor by depositing a cash payment equal to the amount due the senior creditor with the court where the foreclosure action was heard. When such a cash payment is received, the court will issue a redemption certificate to the redeeming junior lien creditor and pay the cash to the senior creditor in order to satisfy the unpaid debt.

The holder of the redemption certificate will then be entitled to receive an amount equal to the cash paid for the certificate, plus the amount due on his or her own secured debt from any other lien creditor (or the mortgagor) who wishes to redeem the property. When several liens against the property have been foreclosed, lien creditors can be expected to continue redeeming the property until the payment required for the next redemption exceeds the market value of the property.

When the redemption period finally comes to an end, six to twelve months after the foreclosure order, the holder of the last redemption certificate will become the fee simple owner of the property. In most cases, the holder of the redemption certificate will apply to the court for an order directing that a deed to the property be properly prepared and executed, naming the last redemptioner as grantee in fee simple absolute. In most states, the grantor of the deed will be the sheriff of the county where the property is located. Some states use other public officials to take possession of the foreclosed property and deliver title to the holder of the redemption certificate. In any case, the foreclosure proceeding comes to a final end with the delivery of the appropriate deed.

Foreclosure by Public Sale

The redemption and appropriation procedures required by strict foreclosure proceedings are the result of many hundreds of years of battle between borrowers and lenders. Many states in this country have decided that these procedures are more cumbersome than they need to be. Courts and legislatures in these states have seized upon the lien theory approach to mortgages in order to simplify the procedures used to protect all parties to a secured loan. In these states, foreclosure proceeds by public sale.

United Oklahoma Bank v. Moss

The appropriation doctrine was required under title theory mortgage procedures in order to protect borrowers from losing the value of their equity of redemption. The redemption procedures just described are necessary to protect the interests of various secured lenders who have interests in the same parcel of land when one of the liens on the parcel is foreclosed.

Both of these interests are nicely balanced when a mortgage lien is foreclosed by offering the property to the highest bidder in an advertised public sale. In theory, the successful bidder at the sale will agree to pay all that the property is worth, without regard to the unpaid loan balances secured by the mortgage in foreclosure. If the property is worth more than the secured debt, then the sale price will pay the secured lender in full and the excess will be delivered to the borrower shortly after the sale. This result is exactly what the appropriation doctrine was designed to achieve.

When more than one mortgage lien is foreclosed, the holder of each lien has an opportunity to bid on the property. Usually the holder of the first (most senior) mortgage lien will appear at the sale and bid the full amount owed, hoping that someone else at the sale will make a higher offer. If this hope is realized, then the senior lien holder will receive cash from the sale in an amount equal to the unpaid debt. If no one outbids the senior lien holder, then the lien on the property will be replaced by the senior lien holder's ownership of the property.

The senior lien holder will also have taken care to foreclose the liens of all junior secured creditors. (Recall that the liens of all mortgagees who receive notice of a foreclosure action will be extinguished in the foreclosure.) Senior lien holders should take this action to guard against the possibility of becoming the owner of the property at the foreclosure sale if no one appears at the sale to make a higher bid. The person who acquires the property as a result of a foreclosure sale will receive an ownership interest that is subject to any mortgage liens that were not extinguished in the foreclosure. Therefore, the prudent senior mortgagee will take care to extinguish all the liens that might interfere with his or her ownership interest after the foreclosure sale.

In order to protect their interests, junior lien holders must also appear at the sale and make their own bids on the property. In order to examine the bidding strategies available to junior lien holders more closely, let us analyze the following hypothetical example. B is the owner of a home. Since purchasing the home, B has borrowed money from three different people and secured each loan with a mortgage on the home. The dates and original and unpaid amounts of the mortgages are provided in Table 9.1.

TABLE 9.1

Date	Original Loan	Unpaid Balance
10/31/87	$75,000	$73,450
4/1/88	$35,000	$36,200
6/5/90	$25,000	28,570
	$135,000	$138,220

The unpaid balance amounts include, as always, accrued interest, attorney's fees, and other costs. For the second and third mortgages, these additional costs are larger than the amount paid against the principal of the note. That is why the unpaid balances for both junior liens exceed the original amount of the loan.

Assume that the fair market value of the house is $135,000. Assume further that the foreclosure petition was filed by the first mortgagee, the holder of the note dated 10/31/87. Since the value of the property is well in excess of the amount owed on the first mortgage, that lien holder will confidently open the bidding at the foreclosure auction with a bid of $73,450. If no one else bids a higher price, the first mortgagee will become the owner of a house worth substantially more than the amount owed on the note.

Under these circumstances, the second mortgagee can also be expected to enter a bid on the property. The second mortgagee here should bid $109,650 for the house. This bid just covers the amount owed on the two senior mortgages. The second mortgagee will be required to pay $73,450 in cash to the first mortgagee. The holder of the second mortgage can receive credit for the rest of the purchase price by surrendering the claim against the owner for the unpaid balance of the mortgage.

It would be a serious mistake for the second mortgagee to bid less than $109,650 for the house. Suppose the second mortgagee decides to bid only $73,451. That will be enough to outbid the first mortgagee but not enough to be sure that the second mortgagee will be paid what is owed. Another bidder could offer $80,000 for the house and become the owner the property. The first $73,450 of this amount will be paid to the first mortgagee, and the remaining $6,550 will be paid to the second mortgagee, leaving an unpaid balance on that claim of $29,650. This amount will be an unsecured debt of the borrower, since the second mortgage was extinguished during the foreclosure proceedings. Whether or not this amount can be collected from the borrower is unclear.

Only by bidding the full amount of the first and second mortgage claims can the junior mortgagee be sure that he or she either will become the owner of the property (if no one else submits a higher bid) or will be paid in full from the proceeds of the foreclosure sale (if some one else does submit a higher bid).

This requirement poses a genuine dilemma for the third mortgagee. Since the fair market value of the property is less than the amount owed on the three mortgages, the third mortgagee will probably lose money on this transaction.

Further, because the fair market value of the property is very close to the amount owed on all three mortgages, the third mortgagee's decision is even more complicated. The third mortgagee has at least three options. The first is to bid nothing at the sale. This is the lowest-risk option and probably provides the smallest expected payment to the third mortgagee. The second mortgagee can be expected to bid $109,650 on the property, for the reasons outlined above. The third mortgagee will then be required to invest this additional amount in cash in the property in order to have any opportunity of becoming the owner. By refusing to bid, the third mortgagee can avoid this additional financial commitment. However, by electing not to bid, the third mortgagee also surrenders the security interest in the property.

A second option is to bid $138,220, the full amount owed on all three loans. It is virtually certain that this bid will be successful, and the third mortgagee will become the owner of the property. It is absolutely certain that the third mortgagee will be required to pay nearly $110,000 in cash for the property. Unfortunately, the amount of cash the third mortgagee might realize by reselling the property is highly uncertain. It is possible that the third mortgagee would not be able to resell the property for a price large enough to recover the required initial investment of $110,000.

A third option is to submit a bid of $130,000, which is just below the market value of the property. By following this alternative, the third mortgagee is hoping that someone else at the sale will enter a slightly higher bid, resulting in an immediate cash payment to the third mortgagee. The amount of payment the third mortgagee can expect to receive is the difference between the $109,650 owed to the two senior lien holders and the final amount bid for the property at the foreclosure sale. While this amount is less than what is owed, it may be greater than the payment the third mortgagee could expect under the other two options.

We can readily see from this discussion that the amount of risk borne by junior lien holders is substantially larger than the risk facing the holder of a first mortgage. First, junior lien holders may be required to pay out substantial sums of money to protect their interest if a senior mortgagee forecloses the liens on the property. In addition, the benefit to be received by these additional payments may be small or nonexistent when the market value of the property is very close to the total amount owed on all the outstanding mortgage liens. The additional risk borne by junior lien holders explains the significantly higher interest rates customarily charged for second and third mortgages.

CONCLUSION

In this chapter, we reviewed the historical development of mortgages. The original title theory of mortgages is still a part of American property law in many states. We have also examined the distinctions between the title theory of mortgages and the more modern lien theory which many courts apply.

The most difficult area of mortgage law relates to the foreclosure process. Under a title theory of mortgages, the foreclosure proceeding itself is simple and straightforward. However, difficulties often arise in applying the proceeds of any subsequent sale of foreclosed property among the various holders of mortgages on the property, and with the original borrower under the mortgages. In lien theory states, the foreclosure process is more difficult and time consuming. However, the application of the proceeds from a foreclosure sale is easy to grasp.

Mortgages always create a cloud upon the title to real property. A title encumbered by a mortgage is not marketable, unless the mortgage is released during the closing process we will examine in Chapter 11.

DISCUSSION QUESTIONS

1. What is the definition of a lien? Name the three primary types of liens.
2. How does a judgment lien arise? What does a judgment lien allow a plaintiff to do?
3. Why is a lis pendens notice important? What is a fraudulent conveyance, and how do courts usually deal with them?
4. When do statutory liens arise? What are the two types of statutory lien? What happens if the owner who contracted with the mechanic or materialman sells the property before the lien is filed?
5. Describe the general procedure most states use when enforcing property tax liens.
6. Distinguish between the terms mortgagor and mortgagee.
7. What is the equity of redemption, and how does it relate to the law day?

8. How does a strict foreclosure procedure work? What is the purpose of strict foreclosure?
9. Explain the public trustee deed system. What ownership right does the public trustee hold?
10. When does a foreclosure procedure officially begin? What obligation is the mortgagee required to satisfy? How are junior liens treated in a foreclosure proceeding?
11. In states that apply the title theory of mortgages, the mortgagee becomes the owner of the property on the date of the foreclosure order, subject to the mortgagor's equitable right of redemption. However, two circumstances can severely complicate this procedure. What are they? How is each situation handled?
12. There is only one bid a lienholder can submit to insure that he or she will either become the owner of the property or be paid in full from the proceeds of a foreclosure sale. What is it?

MAGLIONE V. BANCBOSTON MORTGAGE CORPORATION

29 Mass.App.Ct. 88, 557 N.E.2d 756 (1990)

Lien theory v. title theory of mortgages

Insofar as the plaintiffs have "a claim of a right to title to [the] real property" in question, it is as second mortgagees. The question presented is whether a judge may order the dissolution of a lis pendens recorded by a mortgagee upon condition that the mortgagor or a competing mortgagee place in escrow, or bond, the amount due on the note. We hold that a judge may do so.

Ordinarily, the presence of an undischarged mortgage (at least a recent one) in a record chain of title will serve as well as a lis pendens in discouraging transactions in the encumbered property. What provokes the lis pendens issue in this case is that the plaintiffs, the Magliones, are disputing whether they or the defendant BancBoston Mortgage Corporation ("BancBoston") have a priority of lien in land in Sudbury, which we shall refer to as the "locus." The mortgagor, a real estate developer, has defaulted on its mortgage debt. BancBoston, which became the first mortgagee at the time the developer acquired the property from the Magliones, has foreclosed on the equity of redemption and desires to sell the locus. For reasons which need not detain us, the Magliones contest whether BancBoston continued to enjoy first mortgage status. They commenced an action in Superior Court asking for a declaration of their status, i.e., whether junior or senior, as a mortgagee and for other relief.

In connection with their action the Magliones filed a motion that the judge before whom the action was pending endorse on their memorandum of lis pendens a finding that "the subject matter of the action constitutes a claim of a right to title to real property or the use and occupation thereof . . . ." G.L. c. 184, § 15, second par., as appearing in St.1985, c. 809. A judge of the Superior Court allowed the motion, and the plaintiffs saw to it that the memorandum of lis pendens was recorded.

* * *

Literally, in Massachusetts, the granting of a mortgage vests title in the mortgagee to the land placed as security for the underlying debt. The mortgage splits the title in two parts: the legal title, which becomes the mortgagee's, and the equitable title, which the mortgagor retains.

* * *

In practical terms, the difference between a "lien theory" and a "title theory" as to the nature of a mortgage is that under the latter the mortgagee may enter into possession of the mortgaged premises upon default and before foreclosure, whereas under the "lien theory" there is no right of possession; the mortgagee must await sale of the mortgaged property and obtains satisfaction of the mortgagor's debt from the proceeds of sale. Osborne, Mortgages ss 13–16 (2d ed. 1970).

The right of possession gives the mortgagee under a "title theory" regime slightly better control of foreclosure proceedings. *See* Mendler, Massachusetts Conveyancers' Handbook § 5:7.01, at 114 (3d ed. 1984). If other means are available to satisfy the debt, the vesting of legal title in the mortgagee is without practical significance. [By virtue of the proceedings below], the debt owed the Magliones has been secured. The mortgagee's title, only a means to assure payment of an underlying debt, is without further relevance or force. To ascribe a right to title to the locus on the part of the Magliones becomes an exercise in the elevation of form over substance. The pending litigation between the Magliones and BancBoston will determine whether the Magliones are entitled to the $70,000 and will determine some other issues not here relevant; it will not adjudicate who has a right to title to the locus or the use and occupation of it. Third parties who are transferees of the locus do not need notice of the litigation. *See* G.L. c. 184, § 15; Debral Realty, Inc. v. DiChiara, 383 Mass. 559, 560–561, 420 N.E.2d 343 (1981).

Affirmed.

Case Reflections

1. Describe the differences between a title theory mortgage and a lien theory mortgage.
2. Was the argument between the parties in this case about the right to possess the property which secured the mortgage in question, or about the right to possess the proceeds from the sale of the property?

A & M REALTY
V.
DAHMS

217 Conn. 95, 584 A.2d 466 (1991)

The doctrine of appropriation in a strict foreclosure

This is a suit on a promissory note. The disposi-tive issues are: (1) whether the trial court correctly applied the equitable doctrine of appropriation in determining the sums due on the note; and (2) whether the trial court abused its discretion in the value it assigned to certain real property that had been the subject of a prior foreclosure action. We conclude that: (1) there is mathematical error in the application of the appropriation doctrine; and (2) the value assigned to the real property is within the broad discretion reposing in the trial court in such instances. We therefore order that the judgment be modified accordingly.

On April 22, 1985, the plaintiff, A & M Realty, sold to the defendants, Albert J. Dahms, Jr., and Lee Tyrol, real property located at 611 Palisado Avenue, Windsor, for $375,000. To pay the purchase price, the defendants borrowed $260,000 from The Windsor Bank and Trust Company (bank) secured by a first mortgage on the Palisado Avenue premises. The defendants paid the balance of the purchase price by executing their $215,000 promissory note payable to the plaintiff. As security for this second note, the defendants gave a purchase money second mortgage on the Palisado Avenue premises. The plaintiff disbursed the balance of the proceeds of the $215,000 note, approximately $100,000 after adjustments, to the defendants in cash.

On April 6, 1987, the defendants having failed to make the payments due on the first mortgage, the bank obtained a judgment of strict foreclosure. The defendants failed to redeem on the law day assigned to them. On May 19, 1987, the law day assigned to the partnership, the plaintiff redeemed the property by paying the bank $297,000 in full satisfaction of the defendants' debt due the bank. As of that date, title to the premises became absolute in the plaintiff. On July 10, 1987, the defendants having failed to make the payments due on the second mortgage note, the plaintiff began the present action seeking the balance due on this instrument. The defendants filed a counterclaim alleging an unjust enrichment in that the value of the Palisado Avenue premises exceeded not only the amount paid to the bank to redeem the property, but also the amount due the plaintiff on the second mortgage note. On October 25, 1989, the trial court rejected the defendants' counterclaim as to the value of the property, and rendered judgment for the plaintiff to recover $253,013.35, the balance that it found due on the note after applying the equitable doctrine of appropriation that allowed a credit $38,000 to the defendants.

The defendants appealed to the Appellate Court and the plaintiff cross appealed. We thereafter transferred the matter to ourselves pursuant to Practice Book § 4023.

The defendants first claim that the trial court erred in its application of the doctrine of appropriation. Specifically, the defendants claim that the trial court miscalculated the amount due the plaintiff in applying the doctrine. The doctrine of appropriation applies where the value of the property at the time of redemption equals or exceeds the amount of the debt or debts involved. Bugg v. Guilford-Chester Water Co., 141 Conn. 179, 182, 104 A.2d 543 (1954). If the value of the land is greater, application of the doctrine may extinguish the debt or debts and prevent further action on the underlying notes.

Once a mortgagor loses the right to redeem, the "judgment of strict foreclosure . . . constitutes an appropriation of the mortgaged property to satisfy the mortgage debt." *Id.* "The appropriation of the real estate, however, [does] not pay the debt in full unless the value of the real estate equaled or exceeded the amount of the debt; otherwise, it was only a payment pro tanto." *Id.*; 55 Am.Jur.2d, Mortgages § 904.

In the present case, the trial court determined that the property's value at the time of redemption exceeded the amount paid by the plaintiff to redeem and, therefore, the defendants were entitled, under the appropriation doctrine, to an equitable credit on the sums owing on the note. In the calculation of the credit due the defendants, however, based on the predicate facts found, there was mathematical error that had the effect of debiting the defendants twice for the approximately $100,000 cash that they received at the closing thereby erroneously reducing the equitable credit by $100,000.[1] A modification of the judgment is therefore necessary.[2]

The defendants next claim that the trial court erred in finding the value of the Palisado Avenue premises to be $435,000 as of May 19, 1987, the date of redemption. Specifically, the defendants argue that the trial court was required to accept their appraiser's $515,000 estimate of the property's value as this figure was within $10,000 of the $525,000 sum that the plaintiff actually realized upon the subsequent sale of the premises on July 13, 1988.

---

[1] The trial court found that: "[t]he defendants at the closing got a cash benefit of $100,000.00. By virtue of plaintiffs paying the Bank the defendants also received a benefit of $297,000.00. The sum of those two benefits of $397,000.00. When the fair market value of the property ($435,000.00) is compared with that sum the court finds that the difference is $38,000.00. . . .

"The court finds the present debt calculated as follows:

Principal amount of @215,000.00 reduced by 24 payments	$211,356.50
Equitable credit	(38,000.00)
	$173,356.50
Interest on unpaid principal balance	44,511.70
Late Charge	2,145.15
Attorney fees	33,000.00
TOTAL:	253,013.35

[2] The correct calculations are:

Credit	Due Plaintiff	Due Defendant
Redemption	$297,000.00	
Market Value		$435,000.00
Note Balance	211,356.50	
Interest	44,511.70	
Late Charges	2,145.15	
Attorneys Fees	33,000.00	
Total	$588,013.35	
Less FMV	435,000.00	
Due Plaintiff	$153,013.35	

The trial court heard conflicting evidence on the issue of valuation. John Kenny, the plaintiff's appraiser, testified that the fair market value of the property was $435,000. Kenny, who had actually viewed the property, testified that it was in poor condition and in need of repair. He derived his estimate of the value based upon his observations, an examination of the sales prices of comparable properties and also upon a capitalization of this property's income. William Betts, the defendant's appraiser, testified that the fair market value of the property was $515,000. Betts, who had never viewed the property, based his estimate of the fair market value upon the assumption that the property's condition and quality of construction were average. Further, there was evidence that required repairs would significantly decrease the appraised value. There was no evidence as to what, if anything, was done to the property after its redemption and prior to the subsequent sale for $525,000 on July 13, 1988. Further, there was no evidence as to the financial terms of this subsequent sale.

"While it is true that a recent sale of the subject realty resulting from 'fair negotiations between a desirous buyer and a willing seller . . .' will ordinarily be the most reliable indicator of fair market value, the particular facts of this case [or the absence of them,] remove it from this general rule." New Haven Savings Bank v. West Haven Sound Development, 190 Conn. 60, 71, 459 A.2d 999 (1983). Since there was no evidence presented as to the condition of the property at resale or the terms of the agreement that led to its subsequent resale, the trial court was well within its inherent discretion in adopting the estimate of value furnished by Kenny, the only expert who had actually viewed the property.

"Ultimately, the determination of the value of the land depended on the considered judgment of the [trial court], taking into account the divergent opinions expressed by the witnesses and the claims advanced by the parties. . . . There is nothing to show that in determining the value of the plaintiffs' land the [trial court] misapplied or overlooked, or gave a wrong or improper effect to, any test or consideration which it was his duty to regard." Bennett v. New Haven Redevelopment Agency, 148 Conn. 513, 516, 172 A.2d 612 (1961). In its cross appeal, the plaintiff argues that it has the option of pursuing a deficiency judgment in equity in the bank's foreclosure action or pursuing an independent legal action on its underlying promissory note. *See* First Bank v. Simpson, 199 Conn. 368, 375, 507 A.2d 997 (1986); Hartford National Bank & Trust Co. v. Kotkin, 185 Conn. 579, 581, 441 A.2d 593 (1981). Because it elected to pursue its remedy at law in a separate suit upon the note, the plaintiff claims that this barred the trial court from applying any equitable principles, especially the doctrine of appropriation, in determining the sums due on the note.

This argument implies that there is a separability between actions in law and equity that is in some fashion inviolate and that the selection of an action at law precluded the trial court from applying equitable principles in determining the amount due on the note. While there may be an historical basis for the administration of legal and equitable claims by separate tribunals in separate actions in other states, this is not the case in Connecticut. *See* 22. Swift, Digest (1823) pp. 14–15. "Whatever may have been the rule when actions in equity were separately heard and determined, it does not conform to our present practice where both legal and equitable issues may be joined, heard and determined in one action, and where both legal and equitable relief may be had in the Superior Court." Gaul v. Baker, 105 Conn. 80, 84, 134 A. 250 (1926).

The judgment is affirmed, and the matter is remanded, however, with direction to modify the amount awarded the plaintiff in accordance with this opinion.

Case Reflections

1. Why is the appropriation doctrine needed in states which use the title theory approach to mortgages?
2. How did the trial judge err in applying the appropriation doctrine to the facts of this case?
3. Why did the court sustain the trial judge's use of $435,000 as the market value of the property for purposes of applying the appropriation doctrine?

UNITED OKLAHOMA BANK V. MOSS

793 P.2d 1359 (Okla. 1990)

Foreclosure by public sale proceedings

The husband-debtor's ex-wife tenders two issues for our decision in this appeal: (1) Does the husband's mortgage of non-homestead property they owned together, given without the wife's knowledge or consent, have priority over the lien impressed in her favor by the divorce decree? and (2) Did the foreclosure sale comply with Oklahoma law? We answer the first question in the affirmative insofar as it applies to the husband's prior (pre-mortgage) interest in the property and in the negative insofar as it affects the wife's prior (pre-divorce) interest in the premises. Our response to the second question is in the negative.

ANATOMY OF LITIGATION

In 1975 Ted (husband) and Peggy (wife) Moss mortgaged certain Cleveland County real estate which they owned together.[1] This mortgage was subsequently assigned to City National Bank of Ft. Smith, Arkansas (CNB). In 1982 and 1983 the husband and a woman posing as his wife executed additional mortgages on that property to First Continental Bank of Del City (FCB). Unchallenged here are the trial court's findings that the wife did not sign these mortgages, received no benefit from the loans, and thus bears no obligation to FCB. The FDIC is successor to the interest of FCB.

A.

The couple divorced in 1984. The husband was awarded the property in contest as part of the decree-effected division of spousal assets. It was set apart to him "subject to mortgages and encumbrances of record and further subject to a lien in favor of Peggy L. Moss in the amount of $395,000.00."

Husband subsequently defaulted on the CNB and FCB loans. The trial court concluded that by force of the "after-acquired title doctrine," CNB's mortgage and "all other mortgages pertaining to this land" were impressed upon all of the husband's interest in the property, including the half interest he acquired through the divorce decree. The court gave CNB a judgment against the husband and the wife. The first-lien status of CNB's mortgage is not disputed. The court also gave judgments to the FDIC and to the wife against the husband. Because it was later in time, the wife's decree-conferred lien received third priority—one that is to follow CNB's lien and those of FDIC. The first appeal (No. 70,129) tenders the wife's challenge to the decreed priority of the FDIC's mortgage liens over her equitable lien. The priority contest between the FDIC's mortgage liens and the wife's equitable lien presents a question of first impression.

B.

The trial court ordered the liens to be foreclosed and the property sold. Three component appraisers appointed by the Cleveland County sheriff valued the land at $300,000 for its existing agricultural use. Prior appraisals secured at FDIC's request—one of which was made within weeks before the sale—estimated a significantly higher market value for the property.[2] Another, ordered by the wife, suggested the market value would be appreciably enhanced by the premises' sale as two parcels[3] and by taking into account their potential use for sand, gravel, and topsoil excavation.[4]

[1] The wife referred to her ownership quantum as a "one-half undivided interest." Her testimony is neither disputed by the record nor contested by the parties, but its exact meaning is unclear.

[2] The values ranged from $651,750 to $1,189,000.

[3] The property consisted of two distinct parcels contiguous only at one corner.

[4] This appraisal suggested a value of $986,500.

The FDIC bought the property for $200,000; the trial court confirmed its purchase. The second appeal (No. 71,364) challenges the court's approval of the foreclosure sale to FDIC. At the confirmation hearing, the trial court found that (a) the $300,000 appraisal was less than fair market value; (b) it was disproportionate to fair market value; and (c) the appraisal was influenced by the scheduled sale of the property at a sheriff's sale. The court ruled that it would not hold itself bound by any of its findings and conclusions when establishing the credit to be given the husband on a motion for deficiency judgment.

The trial court held further that the sale could not be set aside unless the price was so low as to shock its conscience and (sic) the buyer's conduct could be characterized as tainted by an element of unfairness. Although the trial court found that FDIC knew the property was worth significantly more than the bid price, it could ascribe no unfairness to FDIC's actions. During the pendency of this appeal, FDIC filed a "stipulation and confession of error" admitting that (a) the sale price was grossly inadequate, (b) the appraisal and sale were irregular, and (c) the trial court misstated the law when confirming the sale.

* * *

[The actual priorities of the various liens were complicated by the transfer of the wife's one-half interest to the husband in the divorce proceedings. After an extended discussion of this problem, the court concluded:]

In short, each of these contesting parties has a second lien on a one-half interest in the tract and a third lien in the other half.

II.

Alleged Error in the Order Confirming Foreclosure Sale

The wife seeks to reverse the trial court's order which confirmed the sale to the FDIC for two-thirds of the value assessed by the sheriff's appraisers. FDIC filed herein a stipulation confessing error by conceding that the sale price was grossly inadequate, the appraisal and sale were irregular, and the trial court misstated the law when confirming the sale. CNB (uncontested senior lienholder) opposes this confession, urging that the sale be confirmed.

Confirmation of a foreclosure sale is largely within the discretion of the trial court. Its order will not be disturbed unless abusive of lawful discretion. The FDIC's confession calls for an examination of the record. It is not binding on this court and cannot alone support the order's reversal. Solemn judicial acts are not vulnerable to appellate nullification at a party appellee's will. Nevertheless, the confession may be used to assist in determining error in the challenged confirmation order.

A confirmation's reversal is proper when (1) the sale price is so grossly inadequate that it shocks the conscience of the court; (2) the sale price is grossly inadequate and the sale is tainted by additional circumstances; or (3) the result is inequitable to one or more of the parties before the court, whether owner, purchaser, or creditor. (citations omitted)

The trial court incorrectly assumed that gross inadequacy of sale price could not be the sole ground for refusing to confirm a foreclosure sale, even if that inadequacy "shocked the conscience" of the court. On this record, we cannot be certain that the trial judge's wrong assumption of the applicable norm of law did not affect his ruling.

Nonetheless, the FDIC—the party who stands to lose the most from a vacation of the sale—concedes that the price paid was "grossly inadequate" and admits an irregularity in the sheriff's failure to appraise the two parcels both separately and together and to sell them in the manner which would result in obtaining the best price. The record clearly supports the FDIC's confession. We therefore give it our approval and remand the cause for re-appraisal and re-sale.

Even if no confession had been filed, there is good reason here to reverse the confirmation order. When the trial court confirmed the sale, the wife's lien was in "last place"; now as to one-half of the tract her lien stands second in the rank of priority. This change alone counsels that the critical issues tendered at the confirmation hearing call for a different assessment. A result that might have then appeared equitable would not be so now in light of the changed priorities. The wife's advanced rank in the order of priority gives her a greater stake in the proceeds at re-sale.

The trial court's order determining priority is affirmed in part and reversed in part, and the order confirming sale is reversed; the cause is remanded for further proceedings not inconsistent with today's pronouncement.

All the Justices concur.

Case Reflections

1. Why should a trial judge be required to approve a foreclosure by sale? What are the standards judges should use in approving or vacating foreclosure sales?
2. Compare the results of a judicially supervised foreclosure sale to the application of the appropriation doctrine in the Maglione case. Which procedure would you prefer if you were a lender? Which procedure would you prefer if you were a borrower?

PINEDA V. PMI MORTGAGE INSURANCE COMPANY

843 S.W.2d 660 (TX, 1992)

Private Mortgage Insurance

Jesse and Zenaida Pineda (the "Pinedas") appeal from a summary judgment granted in favor of PMI Mortgage Company ("PMI") on its deficiency claim and on the counterclaim of the Pinedas, and from the denial of the Pinedas' cross-motion for partial summary judgment on their claims.

The Pinedas executed a note in the original principal sum of $64,300, dated October 7, 1981, payable to the order of Houston First American Savings Association in monthly installments of $655.22, commencing December 1, 1981, together with interest thereon at the rate of 11.875% per annum. The note was secured by a Deed of Trust, of even date therewith, covering certain real property in Harris County, Texas. The Pinedas defaulted in their payments pursuant to the note and foreclosure resulted. The substitute trustee conveyed the subject real property to United Savings Association of Texas, "successor to Houston First American Savings Association" by deed dated June 23, 1986. United Savings Association assigned the original note to PMI on May 29, 1990, pursuant to a subrogation and assignment agreement. The note was endorsed to PMI by United Savings Association on August 22, 1990.

PMI, by "Commitment for Insurance," dated August 28, 1981, advised Houston First American Savings Association that it would insure the Pinedas' loan in the amount of $64,300. The Commitment provided in relevant part: In consideration of the premium set forth below, your application has been examined and with reliance on representations therein, the Company hereby issues to you a Commitment for Insurance of the loan herein described, subject to the terms and conditions on the reverse side hereof, and subject to any special or general conditions that may be set forth below. In consideration of the payment of premium set forth below, the Company hereby insures the lender against loss of the mortgage loan hereinafter described, subject to the terms and conditions contained on the reverse side hereof.

The real property securing the sale brought $58,646.42 at the foreclosure sale, leaving a deficiency of $14,170.04. PMI received a claim on the policy of insurance from United Savings Association for payment on the policy that had been theretofore issued by PMI to Houston First American Savings Association as set out in the "Commitment for Insurance." The claim ($19,789.24) was paid by PMI to United Savings Association on September 11, 1986. The deed of trust required the Pinedas to pay to the original noteholder in monthly installments, in addition to payment on the note and payments for taxes and assessments, "one-twelfth of yearly premium installments for mortgage insurance." The Pinedas, the mortgagors, paid the monthly (one-twelfth of the yearly) mortgage insurance premiums to the original noteholder and mortgagee, or its successor, until date of default. The mortgagee paid the mortgage premiums to PMI.

PMI'S SUMMARY JUDGMENT

The Pinedas contend in their first point of error that the trial court erred in granting summary judgment in favor of PMI on its claim as a noteholder. They advance numerous arguments in support of their contentions.

First, the Pinedas argue that their note was completely paid off by proceeds of the trustee's sale plus the claim paid by PMI to its insured lender, leaving no deficiency on which PMI could sue. What PMI paid to the old United Savings Association of Texas, was the claim for payment on a policy of insurance that had been issued by PMI to Houston First American Savings Association, the original lender. The uncontroverted summary judgment evidence was that PMI paid a percentage of the original lender's total submitted claim. The uncontroverted affidavit of David Peterson, part of PMI's summary judgment proof, reflected that "[t]he payment made to the lender by PMI was based upon a claim presented by the lender to PMI pursuant to its policy of insurance and was not made on behalf of the borrowers to extinguish the deficiency." PMI's claim payment was pursuant to its contractual obligation to the lender under the lender's policy of insurance. The Pinedas' characterization of PMI's claim payment as payment on the Pinedas' behalf or of the Pinedas' deficiency obligations to the lender ignores the summary judgment proof, commercial reality of the relationship between PMI and its insured lender, and the nature of private mortgage insurance as held in Texas cases on the subject. The Pinedas' first point of error is internally inconsistent. On the one hand, they contend that the note was completely paid off so no deficiency remained on which PMI could sue; on the other hand, they state: the issue is not whether the deficiency was paid but whether this payment by PMI to the note holder should be applied against the Pinedas' indebtedness. In other words, may the note holder or its assignee, recover the same deficiency twice?

The uncontroverted summary judgment evidence showed that after PMI paid the lender's claim pursuant to PMI's mortgage insurance policy, the lender then assigned to PMI all rights the lender had against the borrowers under the loan documents and negotiated and transferred the Pinedas' note to PMI. The lender was paid its claim and never recovered "the deficiency," even though the amount of money paid in the claim exceeded the amount of the deficiency. In consideration of PMI's payment of the lender's claim, the lender assigned its rights under the loan documents to pursue claims for deficiency, and otherwise, against the Pinedas. Thus, PMI, the present note holder, has not sought to "recover the same deficiency twice." Nor has PMI, prior to the filing of this lawsuit, sought to recover any deficiency against the Pinedas and therefore could not have sought to "recover the same deficiency twice."

The Pinedas further argue that they were "insureds," in privity with PMI or otherwise beneficiaries of the mortgage insurance policy PMI issued to the lender. Indeed, each of the cases the Pinedas cite in their first point of error necessarily relies on some sort of privity or beneficiary status. Two Texas cases, which we follow in deciding the issue presented in the first points are Hunt v. Jefferson Sav. & Loan Ass'n, 756 S.W.2d 762 (Tex.App.—Dallas 1988, writ denied), cert. denied, 489 U.S. 1079, 109 S.Ct. 1532, 103 L.Ed.2d 837 (1989), and Shields v. Atlantic Fin. Mortgage Corp., 799 S.W.2d 441 (Tex.App.—El Paso 1990, no writ) both of which recognize and hold that the mortgage insurance in these cases was for the benefit of the lender and not the borrower. . . . In Shields, the Court said:

> The mortgage insurance was for the benefit of the Appellee [Jefferson Savings] and not for the Appellants [Borrowers]. As stated in Hunt v. Jefferson Savings and Loan Association, 756 S.W.2d 762 (Tex.App—Dallas 1988, writ denied): "No contract existed giving Hunt a right to an offset for private mortgage insurance, nor is there a requirement at law for an offset. Hunt's position is outside the contractual agreements between the parties and wholly unsupported by the law.
>
> Shields, 799 S.W.2d at 444.

Furthermore, private mortgage insurance carriers are regulated in Texas by Tex.Ins.Code.Ann. art. 21.50 (Vernon Supp.1992) which only authorizes mortgage insurance companies to insure lenders, not borrowers. After a careful review of the record, we conclude that the Pinedas were neither insureds under the policy, nor in contractual privity with PMI. Nor were they beneficiaries under the PMI policy of insurance to Houston First Savings Association, the lender. The summary judgment evidence was uncontroverted that the private mortgage insurance was for the benefit of the lender and not for the Pinedas.

* * *

We have carefully reviewed and considered all points of error which have been brought forward by the Pinedas. They are overruled. The judgment of the trial court is affirmed.

Case Reflections

1. Since the Pinedas paid the premiums for the mortgage insurance policy, does it seem right that they should also be required to pay the balance of the mortgage?
2. Why would a borrower be willing to pay premiums on an insurance contract where the lender is the beneficiary of the policy?

L. M. ADAMSON CONSTRUCTION COMPANY V. FIRST FEDERAL SAVINGS AND LOAN ASSOCIATION OF ANDALUSIA

519 SO.2d 1036 (Fl., 1988)

Conflicts between mortgage and other liens

This is an appeal from a final judgment of foreclosure finding the liens of appellee's construction mortgage and appellee's purchase money mortgage to have priority over appellant's mechanic's lien. We affirm in part, reverse in part and remand.

Fusco-Waldrop Associates, Inc. (FW), owner of lots 35 and 36 of Seabreeze subdivision, contracted with appellant/L. M. Adamson Construction Company for the latter to build a restaurant on the property. Needing more property for the restaurant, FW entered into a lease with option to purchase lots 33 and 34 of Seabreeze and an additional parcel of land from the owner, Gulf Mortgage Systems, Inc. (Gulf). (The land subject to the lease will hereinafter be referred to as lots 33 and 34.) The lease contained a provision prohibiting FW from placing improvements on the land. The lease was recorded on July 6, 1982.

On July 2, 1982, FW and First Federal Savings and Loan Association of Andalusia (First Federal) entered into a construction loan agreement wherein FW executed and delivered a promissory note in the sum of $1,200,000 secured by a mortgage (hereinafter "construction mortgage") on lots 35 and 36 and on FW's leasehold interest in lots 33 and 34. This construction mortgage was recorded on July 6, 1982. In order to induce First Federal to make the construction loan, Adamson executed a lien subordination agreement whereby Adamson agreed to subordinate to the construction mortgage any and all liens with respect to lots 35 and 36. Lots 33 ad 34 are not covered by the subordination agreement. A notice of commencement describing all four lots was recorded on July 6, 1982, but subsequent to the recording of the construction mortgage.

Thereafter, FW decided to exercise its option to purchase lots 33 and 34 from Gulf and FW's purchase of such lots was closed in November, 1982. In connection therewith, FW gave Gulf a $305,000 promissory note secured by a purchase money mortgage on lots 33 and 34 which was recorded on November 18, 1982.

In February, 1983, appellant completed performance of the contract. Its final draw request was not honored by FW and appellant filed a claim of lien for $303,000.

FW defaulted on the construction mortgage in July, 1983 and on the purchase money mortgage the following month. In October, 1983, First Federal acquired by assignment the Gulf purchase money mortgage.

Subsequently, First Federal sued to foreclose both the construction and purchase money mortgages. The trial court entered a final judgment of foreclosure finding both mortgages to have priority over Adamson's mechanic's lien.

Appellant first contends that the trial court erred in determining that its mechanic's lien is junior and inferior to the Gulf purchase money mortgage in regard to lots 33 and 34.

Appellant's claim of lien was, of course, filed subsequent to the purchase money mortgage. However, Section 713.07(3), Florida Statutes (1981), provides that a mechanic's lien "shall have priority over any conveyance, encumbrance or demand not recorded against the real property prior to the time such lien attached." Section 713.07(2) provides that mechanic's liens "attach and take priority as of the time of recordation of the notice of commencement." The notice of commencement in the instant case was filed several months prior to the purchase money mortgage. The statute does not provide any exception for purchase money mortgages.

Contrary to the suggestion of First Federal (assignee of the subject purchase money mortgage), appellant's mechanic's lien was not limited to FW's leasehold interest. Although it is true that such interest was all that FW had in lots 33 and 34 at the time appellant's lien attached (i.e. when the notice of commencement was filed), Section 713.10 provides in pertinent part, that the mechanic's lien extends to the right, title and interest of the person who contracts for the improvement (in this case FW) "as such right, title, and interest exists at the commencement of the improvement or is thereafter acquired in the real property." (e.s.)

However, First Federal asserts that purchase money security interests have traditionally been accorded highest priority regardless of the time of filing and that the statutory provisions of Chapter 713 should not be read to abrogate that rule. First Federal asserts that Van Eepoel Real Estate Co. v. Sarasota Milk Co., 100 Fla. 438, 129 So. 892 (1930) supports such proposition. In that case, the purchase money mortgage was not recorded until after the mechanic completed his work. The mortgagor finally recorded and, shortly thereafter, the mechanic recorded his lien. Under the statutes then in effect, the mechanic's lien was perfected when a claim of lien was filed. Notices of commencement did not exist. However, because the mortgagor caused the mechanic to work on the property under the assumption that it was unencumbered, the Supreme Court held that the mechanic's lien had priority. It is not the holding in Van Eepoel upon which First Federal relies but rather the following principles stated therein:

> The views herein expressed, affording the mechanic's lien priority, do not conflict with the general rule that a purchase-money mortgage, made simultaneously with the conveyance to the mortgagor, takes precedence over any lien arising through the mortgagor, though the latter be prior in point of time. [Citations omitted.]
>
> * * *
>
> [This] rule . . . holding the purchase-money-mortgage superior to the mechanic's lien, is applied in cases where the mechanic's lien is acquired for work done at the instance of the purchaser, and without the acquiescence of the vendor, prior to the execution of the mortgage.

The statutes with which we deal are different in that the lien attaches and takes priority as of the time of the recordation of the notice of commencement. Sections 713.07(2) and (3), Florida Statutes (1981). In addition, in the instant case, there is no recording problem. Rather, the purchase money mortgage did not exist at the time the notice of commencement was filed. The contractor's work was underway before the mortgage was executed. Van Eepoel does not conflict with our application of the current mechanic's lien law. The contractor who performed work without notice of the purchase money mortgage was given priority. Under the present law, mechanics rely on the notice of commencement to establish their priority. To rule against the mechanic's lien in this case would place a more onerous burden on mechanics than is contemplated by Chapter 713.

Neither do we find that the lease provision purporting to prohibit construction on the leased property prevented the appellant from asserting his priority in this case. Section 713.10, quoted in part above, further provides: When an improvement is made by a lessee in accordance with an agreement between such lessee and his lessor, liens shall extend also to the interest of such lessor. In the absence of fraud on the part of the lessor, the interest of the lessor shall not be subject to liens for improvements made by the lessee when the lease is recorded and the terms of the lease expressly prohibit such liability.

This statute merely informs us that had the option not been exercised, i.e., had Gulf maintained its ownership interest in lots 33 and 34, the mechanic's lien would not have extended to that interest as there was a recorded instrument prohibiting construction on the property. However, since the property was transferred to FW, it became an interest in property "thereafter acquired in the real property" by Fusco and thus subject to the mechanic's lien.

In the remaining issue, appellant asserts that the trial court erred in holding that the First Federal construction mortgage had priority over appellant's mechanic's lien as to lots 33 and 34. Although the construction mortgage was recorded prior to the notice of commencement, appellant seeks reversal on the basis that the lien of First Federal's construction mortgage did not attach to lots 33 and 34 until mortgagor/FW became owner of such lots when it exercised its option to purchase. And, appellant says, First Federal's lien being based upon an after-acquired property theory, its lien is junior to appellant's mechanic's lien since the notice of commencement was recorded prior to First Federal's exercise of its option to purchase. Appellant relies upon ITT Industrial Credit Co. v. Regan, 487 So.2d 1047 (Fla.1986), a Uniform Commercial Code case.

First Federal vigorously asserts that appellant has failed to preserve the above point for appellate review. We agree that appellant has waived such point. At the conclusion of the evidence, appellant clearly stated its position:

> MR. FLEMING [Appellant's counsel]: [W]e agree that if you can't—if you don't find for us on equitable subordination or equitable lien theory, then we did not prevail in any sense as to the [construction] mortgage. Our only argument on relation back and purchase money mortgage related to the purchase money mortgage itself. So they would be first as to the [construction mortgage]; we would be second as (*sic*) the mechanic's lien; and they would be third as to the purchase money mortgage that they acquired under our alternative theories.

Notably absent is any assertion of the kind which appellant now seeks to make regarding an after-acquired property theory. As to the "equitable subordination" or "equitable lien theory" referred to above by counsel, the trial court found against appellant on such theories and appellant does not assert error on appeal therefor.

Insofar as the judgment erroneously held the purchase money mortgage to have priority over appellant's mechanic's lien, we reverse and remand for the entry of an amended judgment consistent with this opinion. We affirm the judgment insofar as it found the construction mortgage to have priority over appellant's mechanic's lien.

Reversed in part, affirmed in part, and remanded.

Case Reflections

1. What steps should the construction lender have taken to avoid conflict with the mechanics lien?
2. Suppose the construction mortgage had been filed before the construction contract was signed and the contractor was able to file the notice of commencement. What steps would the contractor need to take to insure full payment for the work done?

FIRST NATIONAL BANK IN WICHITA
V.
FINK

736 P.2d 909 (Ka., 1987)

"After Acquired Property" clauses in a mortgage

This appeal involves the priority of liens in a mortgage foreclosure action. The facts in the case are not in dispute and essentially are as follows: The defendants, Marion J. Fink and Deloris M. Fink, are the mortgagors on two mortgages covering the same real estate located in Sedgwick County. This dispute is between the First National Bank in Wichita (Bank), the plaintiff/appellant, and Robert H. Souders, the defendant/appellee, who are the holders of mortgages on the property.

The mortgage liens were created as a result of loans made to the Finks in the following chronological order:

On November 22,1977, the Finks borrowed money from the First National Bank in order to purchase certain real estate. The defendants signed a promissory note in the principal amount of $24,506 plus interest, and executed a mortgage on the real estate described as follows:

> Lot 4, North Half of Lot 5, Block 10 Beverly Manor, Sedgwick County, Kansas.

The mortgage, which was recorded on January 26, 1978, contains a future advance clause or "dragnet clause," which provided as follows:

> (7) That this mortgage secures the payment of any and all existing and future notes, loans, advances and any renewal or renewals of note/s and each and all of the payments and obligations thereunder, even though the indebtedness of Mortgagors to Mortgagee from time to time be reduced below the maximum amount above stated or be paid in full and if Mortgagee shall thereafter make loans or advances to Mortgagors, such loans or advances thereafter made shall nevertheless be secured by this mortgage until this mortgage is released of record.

On July 30, 1979, the Finks executed a second mortgage on the same real estate in favor of defendant Souders in the principal amount of $30,000 plus interest. This second mortgage was recorded on August 23, 1979.

On or about October 28, 1983, and January 23, 1984, the Bank made two additional loans to the Finks in the principal amounts of $6,472 and $13,144, respectively. The Finks executed a promissory note and a mortgage to the bank for each loan. On the face of both the 1983 and the 1984 notes, the parties agreed as follows:

> SECURITY AGREEMENT
>
> FOR VALUABLE CONSIDERATION, Borrower hereby grants unto Bank a security interest in the property (Collateral) described below together with any and all additions thereto, substitutions therefor, and proceeds therefrom:
>
> DESCRIPTION OF COLLATERAL
>
> Real estate mortgage dated November 22, 1977, on the following described property:
>
> Lot 4, North Half of Lot 5, Block 10, Beverly Manor, Sedgwick County, Kansas.

The Finks defaulted on their loans, and the Bank brought an action on the notes and for foreclosure of its mortgage. Defendant Souders was made a party along with other creditors not involved in this appeal. A dispute arose between the First National Bank and Souders as to the priorities of their respective mortgage liens.

The district court found that the Bank's mortgage lien had priority over the mortgage lien of Souders only as to the amount of any unpaid balances due on the original 1977 loan. The court ruled that the Bank made the later loans to the Finks with notice of defendant Souders' intervening mortgage and that reference to the 1977 mortgage on the face of the 1983 and 1984 notes would not defeat the priority of Souders' lien. The trial court established the order of priority between the mortgage liens of the Bank and Souders as follows: (1) The unpaid balance of the Bank's 1977 purchase money mortgage in the amount of $9,152 plus interest; (2) defendant Souders' mortgage in the amount of $39,182 plus interest; (3) the Bank's 1983 note in the amount of $8,617 plus interest; and (4) the Bank's 1984 note in the amount of $14,886 plus interest.

The Bank perfected a timely appeal, and the case was transferred to the Supreme Court for determination.

* * *

It is the position of defendant Souders that the subsequent loans made by the Bank to the Finks in 1983 and 1984 were not secured by the 1977 mortgage, because the subsequent advances were made for unrelated business purposes, were optional, non-obligatory loans, and were made by the Bank with notice of the Souders' 1979 mortgage lien. The trial court adopted, in substance, the position of defendant Souders.

We should first consider the Kansas statutes and previous cases on the subject. K.S.A. 58-2336 . . . provides for the securing of future advances in the following language:

> 58-2336. Liens of mortgages securing loans upon real estate; providing for the securing of future advances; priority of lien. Every mortgage or other instrument securing a loan upon real estate and constituting a lien or the full equivalent thereof upon the real estate securing such loan, according to any lawful or well recognized practice, which is best suited to the transaction, may secure future advances and the lien of such mortgage shall attach upon its execution and have priority from time of recording as to all advances made thereunder until such mortgage is released of record: Provided, That the lien of such mortgage shall not exceed at any one time the maximum amount stated in the mortgage." (Emphasis supplied.)

The trial court in this case relied on K.S.A. 58-2222, which provides, in substance, that a mortgage shall from the time of filing the same with the register of deeds for record impart notice to all persons of the contents thereof; and all subsequent purchasers and mortgagees shall be deemed to purchase with notice.

The appellate courts of Kansas have discussed the effect of future advance clauses in mortgages on several occasions. In Potwin State Bank v. Ward, 183 Kan. 475, 327 P.2d 1091 (1958), the question on appeal was the priority between a mortgage given to secure future advances and a mechanic's lien covering labor and materials for the construction of a house on the mortgaged premises after the recording of the mortgage but before the making of advances by the mortgagee. The mortgage was given in connection with a loan for the construction of the house. This court held that a mortgage to secure future advances is valid and will be judicially enforced. Advances made under such a mortgage, at least if made pursuant to an agreement to make them, have priority over mechanic's liens which attach after the recording of the mortgage but before the making of the advances.

* * *

In Emporia State Bank & Trust Co. v. Mounkes, 214 Kan. 178, 519 P.2d 618 (1974), this court again recognized the validity of a future advance provision or dragnet clause. It was held that future advances made pursuant to a dragnet clause fall within the contemplation of the parties and are secured under the mortgage containing such clause. Dragnet clauses are not, however, highly regarded in equity and shall be carefully scrutinized and strictly construed.

* * *

Based upon the Kansas statutes and the cases cited above, we have no hesitancy in holding that the trial court erred in finding that mortgage lien of defendant Souders was prior to the liens created by the Bank's 1983 and 1984 notes, each of which specifically stated on the face of the instrument that it was secured by the prior 1977 mortgage. The priority of the Bank's lien is limited, however, to the principal of the 1977 mortgage, $24,506.39 plus interest thereon, as required by K.S.A. 58-2336. The lien of the Souders mortgage is held to be prior to any sums owing the Bank in excess of that amount.

The judgment of the district court is reversed and remanded for further proceedings.

Case Reflections

1. The second mortgage holder argued that later advances were not secured by the first mortgage because "the subsequent advances were made for unrelated business purposes, were optional, non-obligatory loans, and were made by the Bank with notice of the Souders' 1979 mortgage lien." What do you think about the merits of Souders position?
2. The court compromised by limiting the priority of the first mortgage lien to the original principal amount of the 1977 mortgage, plus interest. Does this compromise seem reasonable in light of Souders' argument?

CHAPTER

10

ABSTRACTS, TITLE SEARCHES, AND TITLE INSURANCE

LEARNING OBJECTIVES

After reading this chapter, you should be able to:

1. Explain the role of title abstracts, attorney opinions, and title insurance policies in guaranteeing the title purchased in a real estate transaction.
2. Identify the title defects that are not covered by title insurance or other methods of inspection.
3. Understand the mechanics of marketable title acts

KEY TERMS

Patent

Grantee Index

Grantor

Title Abstract

Attorney Opinions

Title Insurance

Marketable Title

After a thorough study of the nature (and pitfalls) of real property ownership, many students take a solemn vow never to become entangled in the web of ownership arrangements we have described so far. After considering the myriad ways of real estate purchaser can pay sizable amounts of money in exchange for less than the purchaser bargained for, it is not unusual for students to decide to remain totally outside the realm of real estate transactions.

Fortunately, there are methods and procedures that real estate purchasers can follow to prevent the calamities we have examined thus far. In this chapter, we will examine the methods used to investigate the state of the title to a parcel of real property.

CHAIN OF TITLE

The fee simple absolute estate is an ownership interest in real property that endures forever. A chain of title is forged by identifying the individual owners of this perpetual estate from the date of its creation to the present. The chain of title begins with a grant of fee simple ownership in a parcel made by a sovereign to a particular individual. In most states, this initial sovereign grant will be a federal **patent**. Along the Atlantic coastline, the initial sovereign grants were made by the king of England during the colonial period of our history. Our investigation of the concept of a chain of title must begin, therefore, with a brief review of the processes that resulted in the modern United States.

Patent
A grant of fee simple absolute title in land which belongs to a sovereign nation at the time the patent is issued.

At the time of the Revolutionary War, virtually all of the land in the original thirteen colonies was owned by people who claimed their land under a royal charter issued by the English monarch in order to develop and exploit the resources to be found in the new world. Little more than a century later, the sovereignty of the United States of America spread out from the narrow strip of land along the eastern seaboard to encompass virtually all of the temperate latitudes of the North American continent. In the process, millions of square miles were added to the "public domain" lands, unsettled territory that became the property of the United States government. Congress adopted several different strategies for encouraging the settlement and development of these vast, unexplored new lands. The earliest of these strategies were various Homestead Acts adopted by Congress during the 1800s. Although the specific provisions of the Homestead Acts changed from time to time, the basic outline remained constant. Anyone who built a house on the public domain lands, remained on the property for a stated period of time (three to five years), and cultivated a crop became entitled to a federal homestead patent. The patent conveyed a fee simple absolute title to the individual who met the requirements of the Homestead Act. The size of the parcel conveyed varied from time to time, with amendments to the Act, but the majority of the homestead patents conveyed title to a quarter section (160 acres) of land.

As settlers poured into the public domain lands, Congress recognized the need for dependable rail transportation in the new territories. Beginning in the 1860s Congress passed a series of Railway Acts to encourage the construction of rail lines, which would ultimately link the Atlantic and Pacific coasts of the nation. By virtue of these measures, railway companies received patents conveying a section of land for each mile of rail laid over the public domain lands.

Knight agreed to purchase a home for $450,000. Under the terms of the contract, he deposited $40,000 with Devonshire Co., the realtor representing the seller, as earnest money for the transaction. Devonshire procured a title insurance commitment which listed the reservation of a mineral right to the United States government as an exception to the title policy. Knight refused to accept the title, and sued Devonshire for a refund of the earnest money deposited.

The Colorado court observed that a marketable title is one which is "reasonably free from such doubts as will affect the market value of the estate; one which a reasonably prudent person with knowledge of all the facts and their legal bearing would be willing to accept." The mineral right retained by the United States on the property in question was created when the U.S. government granted the property to the Union Pacific railroad in 1883. All railroad patents issued between 1866 and 1904 contained substantially the same mineral reservation. The U.S. Supreme Court ruled in 1914 that the issuance of such a patent constituted a conclusive determination by the Land Department that the lands granted were non-mineral in character.

By virtue of the U.S. Supreme Court decision, the Colorado Supreme Court ruled that the mineral reservation did not render the title to the property unmarketable. Knight v. Devonshire Co. 736 P. 2d 1223

KEY POINTS

The various mining acts adopted by Congress provide the most interesting variations on the theme of patent grants. The mining acts permitted any person to stake a mining claim on public domain lands. The person who staked out a mining claim, by literally driving stakes into the ground at the corners of the parcel, became entitled to the exclusive use and possession of the land within the claim boundaries. This right of exclusive possession continued as long as a required amount of "development" work was performed within the boundaries of the claim. The development work included drilling exploration holes, building structures on the claim, and other activities defined by various amendments to the federal mining acts.

If valuable mineral deposits were discovered within the boundaries of the claim, then a federal mining patent could be obtained, granting fee simple ownership of the parcel to the person who applied for and received the patent. But even if valuable minerals were never discovered, the right to exclusive occupancy of the claim remained in effect until the claim was abandoned.

As a result, the location of a mining claim creates a perpetual right to the exclusive use and occupancy of a parcel of land belonging to the United States government. There are thousands of cabins and vacation homes built in the mountains of the western states on unpatented mining claims. While the "owners" of these improvements may be evicted at any time by the U.S. government, the title to the property is good against all other persons.

Finally, Congress adopted several mining acts, which provided federal patents for smaller parcels of land (usually less than one acre) wherever valuable minerals were discovered on public domain lands. These federal patents, issued under one of the many acts of Congress, provide the starting point for uncovering the links in the chain of title for real property in regions of the country that were originally part of the public domain lands of the United States.

Each patent names a specific grantee as the owner in fee simple absolute of the property described in the patent. The complete chain of title is uncovered by tracing the conveyances made by the original patent grantee and by all of the subsequent grantees up to and including the current owner. Title researchers use a set of specialized index volumes to perform this task.

Grantor/Grantee Indices

Whenever a deed (or other document affecting the title to real property) is filed for record, the recording official enters a notation about the document in two specialized indexes. The information includes the reception number of the document (which a title researcher needs in order to locate the document in the public record), a brief description of the property conveyed, and the name of both the grantor and grantee identified in the document. The grantor index contains this information for each recorded document, arranged in alphabetical order under the last name of the grantor. The grantee index arranges the information alphabetically by the last name of the grantee.

In order to trace the chain of title to a particular parcel, a researcher begins by looking up the name of the current owner in the **grantee index.** When the deed to the present owner is located, the researcher will begin a search for the grantor of the present owner's deed in the grantee index. Once that name is located, a new grantor in the chain of title will be revealed. Eventually, the researcher will reach the end of the trail when the grantee index reveals the name of the person who first acquired title to the property by virtue of a federal patent or royal charter.

Grantor/ Grantee Index A record of deeds, mortgages and other documents affecting title to real property which records the documents alphabetically by the names of the parties to each document.

After reaching this bedrock level in the chain of title, the researcher must begin a new search, working forward through the **grantor index.** To be sure that the present owner's title is valid, the researcher must verify that each grantor in the chain of title conveyed the property only to the succeeding grantee in the chain. If the researcher discovers any conveyances to someone outside the present owner's chain of title, the conveyance must be noted as a potential cloud on the title.

Along the way, the researcher will almost certainly discover that various owners have conveyed mortgages during the history of the property. Each of these mortgages must be examined, and a document releasing the lien of each mortgage must be found. Any mortgages not released in the public records will also be noted as potential clouds on the present owner's title.

Each of the deeds in the chain of title will also be examined carefully. The title researcher must insure that a valid fee simple absolute estate has been conveyed to the present owner. Therefore, each deed must be examined for the grant of easements that might burden the property, reservations of life estates, dower interests or other future interests, or other irregularities in the deed that might result in an impairment of the title. Any irregularities uncovered by the search are also carefully noted as potential clouds on the current owner's title.

ABSTRACTS, TITLE OPINIONS, AND TITLE INSURANCE

The bedrock of land titles in the United States is federal patents or royal charters. These original conveyances occurred more than one hundred years ago in most parts of the country and up to three hundred years ago in some areas along the Atlantic coast. As the original grant recedes into the distant past, the number of documents in the chain of title to a parcel of property continues to grow.

It is not unusual to discover that the chain of title to a parcel of real property is composed of several hundred separate documents. It is also not uncommon to discover that many of the chain of title documents have been destroyed by earthquake, fire, or flood and are thus unavailable for inspection by a title researcher. Because the mere passage of time will inevitably increase the cost and difficulty of establishing the chain of title to real property, several specialized procedures have been developed to facilitate chain of title research.

Title Abstracts

Once a document has been filed for record, the impact of the document on the chain of title is both permanent and unchanging. While each document in the chain of title must be examined once, no document needs to be examined more than once. A **title abstract** is a record of title examinations that have been performed at various times during the history of a parcel of real property. An abstract is used to identify the documents in the chain of title that have previously been examined. As a result, the title researcher only needs to locate and examine the documents filed for record since the last title examination contained in the abstract.

Title Abstract
A written history of all documents filed for record which affect the ownership rights to a particular parcel of real property.

An abstract certified to the date of the closing provides acceptable evidence that the current owner of a parcel has a good title, free and clear of any liens or encumbrances not listed in the abstract. The certification process involves tracing the chain of title backwards through the grantee index to the owner of the property on the previous certificate date provided in the abstract. (Typically, that owner will be the immediate predecessor in title to the current owner, so that only one deed will be required from the grantee index.) Then the abstracter traces the chain of title forward through the grantor index, looking only for documents filed for record on or after the previous certification date. The abstracter will identify each of these documents and provide a brief description of the documents on pages added to the back of the abstract.

When this work is completed, the abstracter will insert a statement certifying that all documents affecting the title to the property that were filed for record on or before the certification date are identified in the abstract. Anyone who examines the abstract can determine whether or not the person claiming to be the owner of the parcel on the certification date possesses a valid title, free and clear of liens or encumbrances.

Johnson was the successful bidder on a parcel of real property offered for sale by auction. Under the terms of the auction announcement, Johnson deposited 20% of the bid price as earnest money for the sale. The balance was due 10 days after the sale. The terms of the auction required the seller to deliver a deed, and to furnish evidence of marketable title to the property on or before the date the final payment was due.

The auction occurred on November 26. The seller delivered an abstract of the title on December 5, one day prior to the date the buyer was required to pay the balance of the purchase price. The abstract revealed that the property was encumbered by a mortgage in the amount of $19,100, and was also encumbered by several tax liens. Johnson declared the title to be unmarketable, and refused to pay the balance of the bid price.

When the sellers refused to return the earnest money paid at the time of the sale, Johnson sued. The court determined that the liens disclosed by the abstract rendered the title to the property unmarketable, and ordered the return of the earnest money deposit. Johnson v. Malone. 42 So.2d 505 (AL, 1949)

Attorney Opinions

This examination is usually performed by an attorney. Anyone is free to examine an abstract and form an opinion about the state of the title revealed by the abstract. However, communicating an opinion about the state of a title revealed by an abstract to another person constitutes the active practice of law. Only attorneys licensed to practice law may perform that role.

In examining an abstract, the attorney will perform several checks. Every mortgage identified in the abstract should be accompanied by a lien release, also identified in the abstract. The attorney will also examine each of the deed descriptions in the abstract to make sure that no easements, mineral interests, or other encumbrances were conveyed to persons outside the chain of title.

When all of these checks have been completed, a formal written **attorney opinion** is issued stating that the record title to the parcel is free and clear of any and all liens and encumbrances. The title opinion usually contains a number of exceptions (e.g., utility easements, subdivision covenants, and tax liens), which describe limitations on ownership rights that people normally expect to bear in twentieth-century America.

Attorney Opinion An opinion formed by reviewing the documents included in a title abstract of the property, and concluding that record title to the parcel belongs to the individual named in the opinion. The opinion will also mention any liens or encumbrances which may be asserted against the title of the record owner of the property.

Title Insurance

The certified abstract and attorney's opinion are a reasonable means of assuring a clear title to prospective purchasers of real property. By limiting the search and examination process to only those documents filed for record in the relatively recent past, abstracts eliminate a tremendous amount of effort from the title search process. The opinion of a qualified legal practitioner is usually enough to guarantee that the purchaser will not be faced with an unpleasant surprise after paying for the property.

However, even these procedures leave room for improvement. Abstracts can easily be lost or destroyed. While the cost of updating an abstract from the last certification date is usually modest, the cost of preparing a new abstract can run into several thousands of dollars.

And, since attorneys are human, they can make mistakes during the examination process and render an opinion that title to the property is clear, when in fact the title is subject to an outstanding lien or encumbrance of record. While it is true that an attorney who mistakenly certifies a title as clear is liable for malpractice, it may not always be possible to locate the attorney to obtain a damage award compensating for any loss suffered by the purchaser.

To overcome these defects, several companies began offering **title insurance** around the turn of the century. Today, virtually all real estate transactions are covered by a title insurance policy that protects the purchaser against defects in the record title to real property.

Title Insurance An insurance policy which will pay the record owner of real property for any damage suffered as a result of liens or encumbrances of record against the property, unless the damage flows from a defect in record title which was excluded from the policy coverage.

As the name implies, a title insurance policy pays for damage or loss suffered by the owner of real property that was caused by a defect in the record title to the property. However, a title policy is not a pure insurance agreement. A title policy does not protect a property owner against random or unexpected events the way a fire insurance policy does. Instead, it merely guarantees that the issuing company has inspected the chain of record title and believes it to be free from any defects or encumbrances of record.

Firstland purchased a tract of vacant land in an existing subdivision. The subdivision lots were each encumbered by a set of restrictive covenants. Prior to Firstland's purchase, the restrictive covenants were amended to permit construction of a planned unit development. Firstland purchased a title insurance policy from Lawyer's Title which excepted the original subdivision covenants, and the amendments to the covenants, from coverage under the policy.

After Firstland completed the purchase, the subdivision covenants were amended a second time. The second amendment restricted the use of Firstland's lots, causing economic damage to the developer. Firstland sued to recover the damage from its title insurance policy.

The court observed that "The risks [covered by] title insurance end where the risks of other kinds begin." Since the amendment to the restrictive covenants which resulted in damage to the plaintiff occurred after the title policy was purchased, the issuer was not liable for those damages. Firstland argued that the second amendment was not a "subsequent event", because that amendment related back to the subdivision covenants which were in existence at the time the policy was purchased. The court rejected this argument, noting that damage resulting from the restrictive covenants in effect at the time the policy was issued were excepted from the coverage of the policy. Firstland Village Assoc. v. Lawyer's Title Insurance Co. 284 S.E. 2d 582 (S.C. 1981)

Crawford v. Safeco Insurance

Title insurance companies normally issue a title commitment one to two weeks before the date the purchaser has agreed to pay for the property and take possession. The commitment binds the title company to issue a title policy after the required premium is paid. In addition, the title commitment will require the purchaser to record a deed (and perhaps other documents) before the title company is required to issue the policy. These documents will complete the conveyance of the title insured from the current owner to the policy beneficiary.

The title commitment also contains a schedule of exceptions, defects in the record title that the policy will not cover. If these exceptions are limited to utility easements, subdivision covenants, and the lien of the seller's mortgage, they do not constitute a cloud that would render the title unmarketable. As we will see in the next chapter, the seller's mortgage will be paid and released at the closing, so that lien will not exist when the title policy is actually issued. Utility easements and subdivision covenants normally benefit the owner of the property; thus a prospective purchaser cannot refuse to accept property solely because of these items.

Barter v. Palmerton School Disrict

Occasionally, the schedule of exceptions will reveal unexpected defects in the record title that the buyer was not aware of. The buyer will take the property subject to these outstanding interests, and any damage suffered by the buyer as a result of these defects will not be covered by the title policy. Such unexpected exceptions in the title commitment serve as a warning that the seller's title may be unmarketable. Under these conditions, the buyer may have the right to refuse to purchase unless the seller cures the defects noted by the title company.

Title policies are a decided improvement over abstracts and title opinions. In general, title insurance policies are less expensive than the older forms of title assurance. This is true because title companies have developed extremely efficient procedures for searching and evaluating title chains. In addition, since the policies are issued by large, well-established insurance companies, buyers can rely on the policy for protection in the event that a mistake was made in evaluating the chain of record title. This is an important feature, since defects in the record title often do not come to light until many years after a purchaser has paid for and entered into possession of a parcel of real property.

KEY POINTS

Any owner of real property who makes a conveyance of the ownership rights in the property by a warranty deed will be well advised to retain the title insurance policy issued on the real property when it was purchased. Recall that a warranty deed makes the grantor responsible to all subsequent owners of the property for any damage caused by a title defect.

If a title defect comes to light years after a conveyance by warranty deed, when a subsequent grantor attempts to reconvey the property, then a chain of lawsuits can be expected. The owner who suffers loss from a defect in title will sue his or her grantor under the title warranties given in the deed. That defendant will probably sue the previous grantor, and so on until the grantor whose period of ownership produced the title defect is found. Each of these defendants will devoutly wish they still had the title insurance policy issued on the date they entered the chain of title.

As years go by, the risk of loss arising from a breach in the warranty of title contained in a deed decreases. But the risk never disappears completely until the time period for action under the state marketable title act has passed.

Marketable Title Acts

To understand how defects in the record title can remain hidden for years, consider Figure 10.1. When Mr. Johnson sold his farm in 1926, he excluded the one-acre parcel of land surrounding the farmhouse near the northeastern corner of the property. In addition, being the prudent person that he was, Mr. Johnson expressly reserved an easement of way across his former property, allowing access to the farmhouse from the county road north of the farm. A clearly defined, two-lane gravel road marked the boundaries of the easement.

By 1965, several things had happened in the area. Both the Johnson farm and the original Johnson farmhouse had changed hands several times. The house itself had been extensively remodeled and had increased dramatically in value. In addition, the population of a nearby town had grown, and the city limits were approaching the Johnson farm from the east.

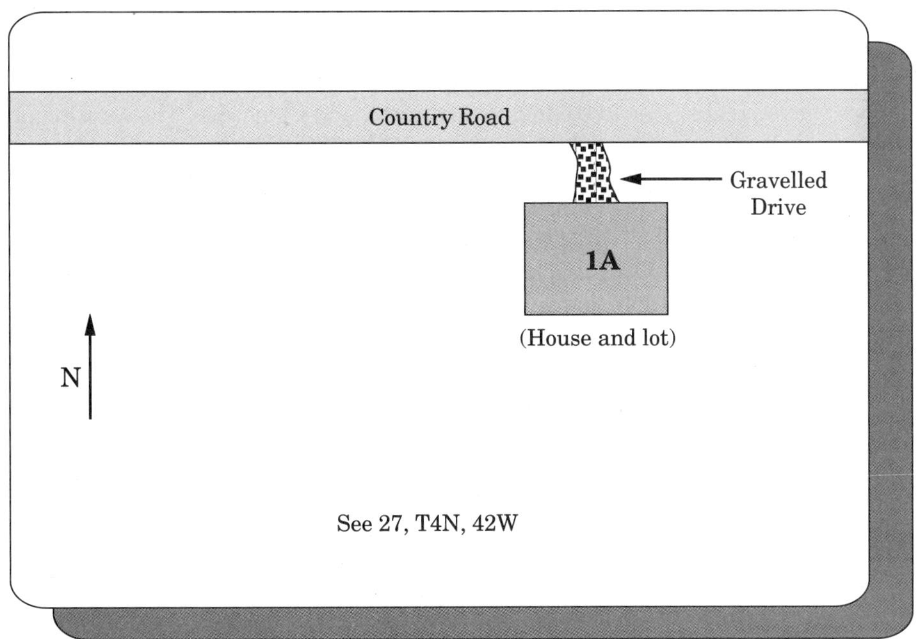

FIGURE 10.1 JOHNSON FARM, 1926

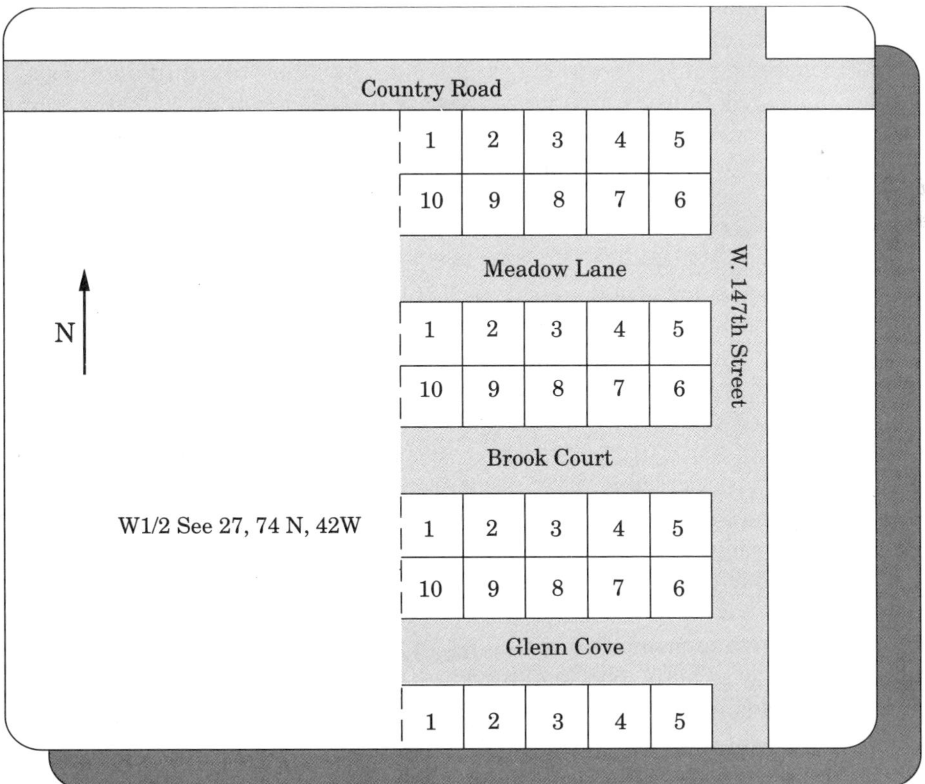

FIGURE 10.2 SHADY ACRE SUBDIVISION PLAT (EAST 1/2 OF OLD JOHNSON FARM, 1975)

In 1970, a real estate developer purchased the east half of the old Johnson farm, intending to build a subdivision that would eventually contain thirty-five luxury homes on large lots. The developer recorded a subdivision plat with the county and built three paved roads, Meadow Lane, Brook Court, and Glen Cove. The location of these dedicated public roads is shown in Figure 10.2. (The Johnson farmhouse and its surrounding land became lot 7 in Block 1 of the subdivision plat.) One of the lots in the subdivision plat, located along the county road forming the northern boundary of the property, was burdened by the easement of way leading to the old Johnson farmhouse. The location of this lot (Lot 4 Block 1) also appears in Figure 10.2.

The owners of the old Johnson farmhouse were not particularly concerned about these developments. Since Meadow Lane was a paved road, providing convenient ingress and egress to their property, the owners began to use that route whenever they went to town. The graveled road of the original easement was used only occasionally, when the owners intended to travel west from their property.

In 1983, a new house was built on lot 4. The kitchen and garage of the new structure occupied a portion of the land reserved for the easement of way in the 1926 deed from Mr. Johnson. The owners of the original Johnson farmhouse said nothing about the obstruction, since they had become accustomed to entering and leaving their property over the paved roads of the subdivision.

However, in 1986 the Johnson farmhouse was sold once again. The new owners discovered that the easement attached to their property had been blocked by the house on lot 4 and decided to take action, perhaps hoping to reap a windfall gain from the situation. The owners of the Johnson farmhouse notified the owners of lot 4 that the kitchen and garage of the home on that lot were obstructing a valid easement and would have to be removed.

With mounting panic, the owners of lot 4 consulted their title insurance policy. With enormous relief, they verified that the easement claim advanced by the Johnson farmhouse owners was not listed in the exceptions to the record title that the policy would not cover. Gratefully, the lot 4 owners notified their title insurance company to expect a call from their neighbors to the south, concerning a small problem with a recorded easement across their land. After some stormy negotiations, the title insurance company agreed to pay the owners of the Johnson farmhouse $25,000 in return for a document abandoning the easement across lot 4.

An internal investigation by the title insurance company revealed that the easement had been inadvertently left off the subdivision plat when it was created back in 1970. This error probably occurred because none of the deeds to the original Johnson farm executed after 1944 mentioned the easement across the farm from the old farmhouse.

As was the usual practice, title policies written on lots within the subdivision were not checked for defects in the record title prior to the date of the subdivision plat. It was normally safe to assume that the subdivision developer had a clear title to all of the land in the plat at the time the plat was filed. By limiting the search of the record title to the years since the subdivision plat, title companies were able to charge competitive premiums for the coverage provided and still remain safe from claims on virtually all of the policies issued.

However, circumstances like those described occur with enough regularity to disturb the sleep of title insurance executives. As a result, the title insurance industry has developed and advocated a model **Marketable Title** Act, which has been adopted by most states. This model act limits the lifespan of nonpossessory interests in land to a period of forty years after the interest is recorded. In adopting the model act, states have changed the time limit for recorded interests to be valid from periods as short as twenty years and as long as fifty years. However, most states have retained the other major features of the model act without significant modification.

Kirkman v. Wilson

The central concept of the marketable title acts, as adopted by the states, is the "root of title." The root of title is the first conveyance to the current owner, or to a predecessor of the current owner, in the chain of title, which occurred more than forty years ago (in the model act). In states that have adopted the Marketable Title Act, only those interests recorded after the date the root of title is established will be valid.

Since none of the deeds to the old Johnson farm recorded after 1946 mentioned the reservation of the easement, the easement rights mentioned in the previous example will expire in 1986. In order to protect their easement, the owners of the Johnson farmhouse are required to file a new record of the easement every forty years, so that evidence of the interest will always be available during the period after the root of title is established.

Marketable Title A title that is free from liens and encumbrances and which a reasonable purchaser, well informed as to the facts and their legal significance would, in the exercise of ordinary prudence, be willing to accept and ought to accept.

Marketable title acts do not extinguish property interests that are possessory in nature. For example, one who acquires title to real property by open, continuous, and hostile use will retain this title as long as the use continues. Marketable title acts cut off only those interests which rely upon documents in the chain of title. These documents must appear of record after the root of title date in order for the interest to continue.

Marketable title acts perform the function for which they were designed; of relieving title researchers from the burden of examining ancient documents each time a conveyance of real property is made. However, since these statutes do not cut off property interests acquired by use or possession, they do not relieve purchasers of the duty to make a thorough inspection of the premises prior to closing. This inspection must include a search for any evidence of hostile or adverse use of the property by strangers. Even in states that have adopted a marketable title act, prescriptive easements and adverse possession interests will remain as clouds on the title as long as the open and notorious use of the property continues.

Torrens Title Systems

McClaskey v. Bumb & Muellert Farms, Inc

Even though the title insurance industry has managed to create a set of useful procedures for working with the problems created by long chains of record title, others outside the industry have long called for further improvements. One candidate frequently advanced as a potential improvement is the Torrens title system. According to one authority,[1] these procedures were first developed by Sir Robert Torrens, an Australian barrister, more than one hundred years ago. In many ways, the Torrens system resembles the procedures used in most states to identify the record owner of an automobile.

A certificate of title to a motor vehicle is issued by an official of local government, usually the clerk and recorder of the county where the owner chooses to register the vehicle. Whenever a car is sold, the owner is required to endorse the title over to the purchaser. The purchase takes the endorsed title to the proper official, and a new

[1]Baxter Dunaway, **The Law of Distressed Real Estate,** part F, chapter 27, section 12.

certificate of title is issued to the new owner. In the event that the automobile is pledged as security for a loan, the lender will inform the registering official in the county and request that the title certificate be issued with the amount of the lien printed on the back. Generally, the lender will hold the certificate of title until the loan is repaid, to prevent any unauthorized sale of the vehicle while the loan remains outstanding.

In a Torrens title systems, each parcel of real property is given a certificate of title closely resembling a motor vehicle certificate of title. The certificate can be expected to identify the current owner of the parcel and to contain mention of all mortgages outstanding against the parcel. Because the local government officials who issue Torrens certificates guarantee that the information on the certificate is accurate, the need for exhaustive searches of the chain of record title to the property is eliminated. In theory, then, Torrens title registration should provide a means of verifying the present state of title to real property that is both quicker and less expensive than traditional means.

While the system has worked well for automobiles, title certificates of the kind recommended by Sir Robert have not enjoyed wide usage in this country. Although the convenience and ease of use in a Torrens system is a clear advantage, the system appears to have very large startup costs. Before the initial title certificate can be issued, in order to bring a parcel into the Torrens system, a complete search of the record title must be conducted. Before a government official becomes willing to guarantee the state of title to a parcel, he or she must be absolutely convinced that the actual title conforms to the guarantee of the Torrens certificate. Apparently the initial cost of registering a parcel in the Torrens system has been too large to justify widespread use of this method.

CONCLUSION

In this chapter we have reviewed the procedures and documents required to insure that the purchaser of real property receives a marketable title to the property purchased. The preparation of an abstract and attorney's opinion of title is one method for ascertaining the state of a title to be transferred. A title insurance policy is a desirable alternative to the abstract and opinion method.

The use of a grantor/grantee index in the title search process was described. Then we discussed the impact of marketable title acts. Because defects in the title to real property can lie dormant for many years, owners of property who have made conveyances by warranty deed were advised to retain their title insurance policies after making a conveyance.

DISCUSSION QUESTIONS

1. Define chain of title. Where does a chain of title usually begin? Who or what were the initial sovereign grants made by the United States?
2. Name and describe three types of legislation that assisted in the settlement and development of the U.S. in its early stages.

3. What is contained in the grantor and grantee indexes?
4. How does one perform a complete chain of title search?
5. What is a title abstract? What does a title abstract identify, and what does it provide? How does it facilitate the chain of title research process?
6. When an attorney examines an abstract, he or she will perform several routine checks. What do these checks consist of? What is an attorney opinion?
7. What does a title insurance policy pay for? What does title insurance implicitly guarantee?
8. Define title commitment and schedule of exceptions. Name some items that are normally included in the schedule of exceptions.
9. The Marketable Title Act, adopted by most states, makes the job of title researchers considerably less difficult. Briefly discuss the act and state how it saves title researchers time.
10. How would a Torrens title system for real property operate? Why has the Torrens system not yet been applied to real property in the U.S.?

BARTER
V.
PALMERTON AREA SCHOOL DIST.

581 A.2d 652 (PA, 1990)

Definition of marketable title

In this action to recover a deposit made pursuant to the terms of a contract for the sale of real estate, the trial court determined that the seller's title was unmarketable as a matter of law and entered summary judgment in favor of the buyer for the deposit which he had made. After careful review, we reverse and remand for further proceedings.

Peter Barter is the assignee of Frank J. Horwith, who purchased at public sale, on October 1, 1988, the Delaware School Property on Delaware Avenue in Palmerton, Carbon County. The written agreement contained a provision that if the Palmerton Area School District could not deliver marketable title to the school property, the deposit of $23,500.00 (ten percent of the purchase price of $235,000.00) would be returned to the purchaser. Alleging that the School District did not have marketable title to the school property, Barter refused to accept a deed and demanded a refund of his deposit. When the refund was not forthcoming, he commenced an action at law to recover the same. The School District filed an answer in which it denied that its title was unmarketable and alleged that Barter had breached the contract by refusing to close. After Barter had filed a reply to the new matter contained in the School District's answer, he filed a motion for summary judgment.

* * *

The pleadings disclose that the Delaware School consisted of lots 6, 8, 10, 12, 14, 16, 18, 20, 22 and 24 Delaware Avenue (400 x 190) on Plan of Palmer Land Company, a subsidiary of the New Jersey Zinc Company. It was the Palmer Land Company which had developed the Borough of Palmerton, and all titles to land in the Borough chain back to the Palmer Land Company. The school district's predecessor, the School District of the Township of Lower Towamensing, purchased lots 18, 20, 22 and 24 from Palmer Land Company in June, 1908. The deed, however, was not recorded and is now lost. The remaining lots were purchased from the Palmer Land Company by deeds dated March 26, 1921 and August 2, 1927. These deeds were duly recorded.

Unsigned copies of the deeds for lots 18, 20, 22 and 24 were found in the records of Horsehead Industries, Inc., the successor to Palmer Land Company, and were made available to Barter prior to the closing date. Quitclaim deeds were requested and were being prepared when the date of closing arrived. Between 1908 and the date of sale on October 1, 1988, a school building was situated on the lots in question, and subsequently acquired property was enclosed by fencing. The property was used continuously for school purposes without any claims being asserted against the title. Finally, the School District asserted, Barter had refused to accept title for economic reasons and not because of any alleged defect in the title.

A marketable title is one that is free from liens and encumbrances and "which a reasonable purchaser, well informed as to the facts and their legal bearings, willing and ready to perform his contract, would, in the exercise of that prudence which businessmen ordinarily bring to bear upon such transactions, be willing to accept and ought to accept." 77 Am.Jur.2d Vendor and Purchaser, § 131 (1975). A title is not marketable if it is such that the grantee may be exposed to the hazard of a lawsuit. LaCourse v. Kiesel, 366 Pa. 385, 77 A.2d 877 (1951); Bonebrake v. Koons, 333 Pa. 443, 5 A.2d 184 (1939). However, where there is no color of outstanding title which might prove substantial, and there is no reasonable doubt either at law or in fact concerning the title, the mere possibility of some future litigation concerning it does not prevent the title from being good and marketable. Rice v. Shank, 382 Pa. 396, 115 A.2d 210 (1955).

A break in the chain of the vendor's title caused by an unrecorded deed which has been lost is calculated to raise the doubts of a reasonably prudent person and, in the absence of explanation, is enough to render his title unmarketable. 77 Am.Jur.2d Vendor and Purchaser, § 151 (1975). *See*: Ewing v. Plummer, 308 Ill. 585, 140 N.E. 42 (1923); Irving v. Campbell, 121 N.Y. 353, 24 N.E. 821 (1890). However, it has also been held that where the land, for which an unrecorded deed which has been lost or destroyed, has continued in the possession of the vendor for a long period of time, the purchaser may be compelled to accept the title. Wade's Heirs v. Greenwood, 41 Va. 497 (1843).

Moreover, a title depending on adverse possession may constitute a title that is not only good but also marketable. Medusa Portland Cement Co. v. Lamatina, 353 Pa. 53, 44 A.2d 244 (1945); Smith v. Windsor Manor Co., 352 Pa. 449, 43 A.2d 6 (1945).

* * *

It is apparent, therefore, that upon a trial the school district may be able to prove a title which is not only good but marketable as well. In view of the facts now appearing of record, the appellant school district must at least be given an opportunity to prove that its title was good and marketable. It must be given an opportunity to explain the unrecorded deed and establish its title. We hold, therefore, that when the record is viewed in the light most favorable to the non-moving party, as we are required to do, there remain issues of undetermined fact and that the trial court's summary holding that appellant's title was unmarketable as a matter of law was erroneous.

Reversed and remanded.

Case Reflections

1. Would you be willing to pay $235,000 for property when the seller of the property cannot produce a deed proving the seller's ownership?
2. Why did the court decide the marketability of the school district's title was a question of fact, since the school district could not produce a valid deed to demonstrate ownership of a significant portion of the property to be purchased by the plaintiff?

PARKER V. MACHEN

567 So.2d 739 (LA, 1990)

Action to quiet title in a purchaser

Before NORRIS, LINDSAY and HIGHTOWER, JJ.

The plaintiffs sued for judgment recognizing themselves as the sole owners of a tract of land they bought from the defendants. In the alternative, they sought restitution of the purchase price and attorney fees. From a judgment declaring plaintiffs the sole owners of the property and assessing attorney fees and costs, the defendants appeal. We affirm the parts of the judgment recognizing the plaintiffs' ownership, clearing the title and assessing costs but reverse the part that awards attorney fees.

FACTS AND PROCEDURAL POSTURE

Mr. and Mrs. Parker bought from Curtis Machen and his wife a tract of land in Madison Parish in October 1983. The sale was by warranty deed and the price was $39,100. At the closing, Curtis Machen was represented by his brother, Richard Machen, who is an attorney in Slidell; the Parkers paid him for title insurance in favor of the lender, Tallulah State Bank. Richard Machen indicated without exception that there were no title problems. According to Mrs. Parker, Curtis Machen mentioned at the closing that something might once have been wrong with the title but his brother Richard had cleared it up.

The Parkers got their loan from Tallulah State Bank but fell behind in payments. As a matter of convenience, they deeded the property to their CPA, Mr. May, in April 1987 for $41,301. The Parkers continued to pay the Tallulah State Bank note, apparently through Mr. May as an intermediary. Both Mr. May and the Parkers were actively seeking a genuine purchaser. They eventually found a prospective buyer, a Mr. Johnson, who hired attorney Michael Lancaster to research the title and render an opinion.

Mr. Lancaster felt the title was not merchantable for the following reasons. The property was originally owned by W.J. Machen, who died in 1978; his heirs opened his succession and listed this property as an asset. Curtis Machen, the Parkers' vendor, was one of six legitimate children of W. J. Machen; Richard Machen was another. W. J. Machen was married only once, but after a divorce he lived in open concubinage for 25 years with a woman named Adela King. By this common-law union there were four illegitimate children. After W. J. Machen's death, Curtis Machen filed in the succession proceedings an affidavit of death and heirship that listed all the children, six legitimates and four duly acknowledged illegitimates; however, the judgment of possession itself placed only the legitimate children in possession of the succession assets. (The other legitimate heirs later sold their portions to Curtis, who was the Parkers' actual vendor.)

The judgment of possession, dated December 14, 1982, came over two years after the decision of Succession of Brown, 388 So.2d 1151 (La.1980), which recognized the constitutional right of illegitimates to share in their parent's succession. Also filed in the succession proceeding was W. J. Machen's holographic will that gave a [life estate in] the property to Adela King, but the judgment of possession omitted this too. Because the judgment of possession omitted the illegitimate heirs and ignored the [life estate], Mr. Lancaster found the title strongly suggestive of litigation and unmerchantable. Because of this opinion the prospective purchaser did not buy.

Mr. May reconveyed the land to the Parkers. Mrs. Parker testified that they attempted to get quit claim deeds from the illegitimate children but these refused. The Parkers brought this suit in January 1988 against Curtis Machen and his wife, the actual vendors; his four surviving legitimate siblings (including the attorney, Richard Machen); the six children of a predeceased legitimate brother; the four illegitimate siblings; and Adela King. The Parkers requested judgment declaring them the sole owners of the property and dissolving the [life estate] in favor of Adela King. Alternatively, and only if their title could not be cleared, they prayed for a money judgment of $46,000, representing in effect restitution of the purchase price plus $7,000 spent on improvements, plus costs and attorney fees. The prayer for attorney fees was affixed only to the request for a money judgment.

Richard Machen represented most of the defendants. He filed an exception of no right of action based on LSA-R.S. 9:5630 (see below). He also attached a copy of an affidavit dated August 7, 1979, in which Adela King renounced her [life estate]; this affidavit had never been filed in the succession record or the conveyance records. After a hearing in August 1988, the trial court overruled the exception.

The matter went to trial in March 1989. The Parkers and Curtis Machen testified to the facts outlined above. Richard Machen added that he never intended to divest his illegitimate brothers and sisters of their share of the property; he simply overlooked Succession of Brown, even though 99% of his practice is real estate work. He also thought his brother Curtis paid for the title insurance he provided to Tallulah State Bank, even though the settlement statement plainly showed otherwise.

The trial court found that when defendant Curtis Machen signed the affidavit of death and heirship, he knew about his illegitimate siblings; in fact, he had full knowledge of the title problems because he had attempted to get a loan from Southern National Bank but the bank refused, citing the illegitimates' claims. The court also found that defendant Richard Machen had received a fee from the Parkers for the latters' title insurance policy, and should have known of the title defects. The court agreed that the illegitimate heirs' claims against the Parkers had been prescribed under R.S. 9:5630; it found, however, that the plaintiffs could not have known about Adela King's affidavit, which was not disclosed until two months after suit was filed. Thus there was a cloud on the title when the plaintiffs filed suit and they were entitled to judgment against all defendants declaring the plaintiffs to be the rightful owners of the property.

* * *

By their second assignment [of error] the Machens urge the trial court erred in finding that the Parkers' title was unmerchantable; they argue the suit to quiet title was unnecessary and the judgment improper.

Louisiana jurisprudence still recognizes the action to quiet title. Walmsley v. Pan American Petr. Corp., 244 La. 513, 153 So.2d 375 (1963);

Harrison v. Alombro, 341 So.2d 1165 (La.App. 1st Cir.1976), writ denied, 343 So.2d 1063 (La.1977). Under this jurisprudence, a person who claims to be the owner of an immovable may bring an action to confirm his title. Standard Homes, Inc. v. Prestridge, 193 So.2d 100 (La.App. 2d Cir. 1966). The requirements of the action to quiet title are:

1. Claim of ownership;
2. Existence of clouds;
3. Description of property; and
4. Prayer for cancellation of the clouds.

The plaintiffs easily satisfied three of these elements of the action; the only issue now is whether they proved the existence of "clouds." The trial court, in holding that the title was "unmerchantable," specifically found that the omitted [life estate] was a cloud on the title. Property has a merchantable title when it can be readily sold or mortgaged in the ordinary course of business by reasonable persons familiar with the facts and questions involved. A title is unmerchantable when it is suggestive of litigation. (Citations omitted.) True, the claims of these unrecognized heirs would be barred by R.S. 9:5630. However, this title chain reveals what appears to be a blatant omission of certain heirs' rights. On this basis, a reputable lawyer had termed the title "questionable" and refused to give a clear title opinion; he felt that other title lawyers in the area would reach the same conclusion. One loan and at least one prospective sale had fallen through because of these problems. The omitted heirs, when approached about an amicable solution, had proven intractable, and their attitude was suggestive of litigation. The trial court concluded that in this state of affairs the property could not be readily sold or mortgaged in the ordinary course of business by reasonable persons familiar with the facts. We certainly will not disturb the trial court's finding of a cloud on the title. The relief granted was appropriate.

* * *

Affirmed in part and reversed in part.

Case Reflections

1. Suppose the trial judge had found that the title of the illegitimate heirs and the life estate held by Adela King were valid encumbrances, so that the Parkers did not have a fee simple title to the property. Would the Parkers be able to recover the money they had spent to buy and improve the property? Why or why not?

ONO
V.
COOS COUNTY

792 P.2d 476 (OR, 1990)

Seller's obligations to provide marketable title

Plaintiffs purchased several parcels of real property from defendant Coos County (county) under a land sale contract. After discovering that a mortgage lien previously had been recorded against the property, they brought this action for declaratory judgment, seeking recovery for the amount of the mortgage lien. The trial court entered judgment in their favor, and county appeals. We reverse and remand.

On September 21, 1984, pursuant to ORS chapter 312, county instituted tax foreclosure proceedings against several parcels of land that are the subject of this dispute. As permitted by former ORS 312.040(1), it served notice on persons interested in the property by publication only. On October 29, 1985, after county complied with all applicable procedures, the tax collector deeded it the land. In January, 1986, this court held that notice of a tax foreclosure proceeding by mere publication, pursuant to former ORS 312.040(1), did not satisfy the due process rights of an assignee of a recorded beneficial interest in the property being foreclosed. Seattle-First National Bank v. Umatilla Co., 77 Or.App. 283, 713 P.2d 33, rev. den. 300 Or. 704, 716 P.2d 758.

On April 30, 1986, plaintiffs purchased the parcels from county at a public auction under a land sale contract, which provided, in pertinent part: "Upon payment of the total purchase price of the property provided herein, and the performance of the Purchaser of all the terms, conditions and provisions hereto, the County shall deliver to the Purchaser a *good and sufficient quitclaim deed* conveying the property to the Purchaser." (Emphasis supplied.)

Plaintiffs later discovered that, in 1981, a mortgage lien had been recorded on a portion of the property. After negotiating with the mortgage holders for its payment and release, they brought this action to recover the amount paid. On stipulated facts, the trial court entered judgment for plaintiffs. County argues that the trial court erred in construing the contract language a "good and sufficient quitclaim deed" to require county to convey an unencumbered fee simple title. According to county, use of the term "quitclaim" effectively disclaims any obligation to guarantee marketable title. The phrase "good and sufficient," it argues, simply means that the deed must be in form adequate to convey whatever title that county holds.

We agree. There are no Oregon cases construing the requirement in a land sale contract that the vendor provide "a good and sufficient quitclaim deed." However, in Thompson v. Hawley, 14 Or. 199, 207, 12 P. 276 (1886), the Supreme Court set forth the following rule:

> [W]here the terms of the contract are such as to bind the grantor to convey by good and sufficient deed, or to make a good and sufficient conveyance, he can only perform his agreement by making a deed that will pass a good title. But if it clearly appears from the contract itself, or from the circumstances accompanying it, that the parties had in view *merely such conveyance as will pass the title which the vendor had, whether defective or not,* that is all the vendee can claim or insist upon. (Emphasis supplied.)

In this case, the parties did not agree that county would convey by "good and sufficient deed." Instead, they agreed that county would deliver "a good and sufficient quitclaim deed." By definition, a quitclaim deed is one that passes whatever title, interest or claim that the grantor may have in the described property, without warranting the validity of the title or containing any other covenants of title. *See* Black's Law Dictionary 1417 (4th ed. rev. 1968); ORS 93.865. Because "it clearly appears from the contract itself" that the parties agreed that defendant would execute a conveyance that would "pass the title which the vendor had, whether defective or not," plaintiffs cannot require a deed that warrants them marketable title.

As county points out, however, the "exceptions" relied upon by the trial court either were described in statutes or were part of the property description. The reference to municipal liens,[3] for example, gave plaintiffs notice of a municipal corporation's statutory right to redeem property foreclosed by the county. *See* ORS 312.280. Similarly, the language regarding land use laws[4] was required by ORS 93.040(1) (amended by Or. Laws 1983, ch. 718, § 2, Or.Laws 1985, ch. 719, § 1, and Or.Laws 1989, ch. 366, § 1). Finally, the reference to the rights of the public in property below the mean high water line[5] was part of the property description. Given their origin, we do not view inclusion of those provisions to be inconsistent with a disclaimer of warranties.

Reversed and remanded.

Case Reflections

1. Why did the county agree to convey the property by quit claim deed?
2. Did the purchasers at the auction, who received a quit claim deed, get what they paid for?

[3]The contract provided that "[p]urchaser assumes responsibility for any and all municipal liens."

[4]The contract contained the following language: This instrument does not guarantee that any particular use may be made of the property described in this instrument. The Purchaser should check with the appropriate City or County Planning Department to verify approved uses.

[5]The property descriptions incorporated into the contract for each parcel ended with the notation, "Subject to the rights of the public in and to any part thereof lying below the mean high water line."

KIRKMAN
V.
WILSON
390 S.E.2d 698 (NC, 1990)

The effect of marketable title acts

This is a declaratory judgment action in which plaintiffs seek a judgment declaring them fee simple owners of a tract of land in Craven County, ejecting defendants and giving plaintiffs possession of the property.

The parties agree that fee simple title to all of the land in question was vested in A. E. Kirkman some time before 22 August 1936. A. E. Kirkman died testate on 11 May 1941. In his will dated 22 August 1936, he devised all of his property to his son, G. C. Kirkman "to have and to use during his life time [*sic*], with out [*sic*] the right or privilege [*sic*] to sell or convey the said relstate [*sic*] in any form or manner," with the remainder left to the children of his son, G. C. Kirkman. Plaintiffs are the sons of G. C. Kirkman who were living at the time of their grandfather's death.

A. E. Kirkman's original will was filed in Folio Number 27 in the Office of the Clerk of Superior Court in Craven County but was also recorded by transcription in Will Book K, page 27 in the Craven County Clerk's Office. The transcription in Will Book K erroneously included that the property was devised to G. C. Kirkman "with the right or privilege to sell or convey" the property. Between January 1947 and October 1949, G. C. Kirkman and wife, Sabrah L. Kirkman (also known as

Sabrah E. Kirkman, Sabrah Elizabeth Kirkman and Sabra Elizabeth Kirkman), conveyed in fee simple all the lands inherited by general warranty deeds. Each defendant here claims title as a direct result of mesne conveyances from G. C. Kirkman and Sabrah L. Kirkman.

G. C. Kirkman died on 13 November 1982. Plaintiffs brought this action in 1985 claiming superior title in the tracts of land by virtue of the vested remainder interest allegedly granted by A. E. Kirkman's will. Defendants argue that plaintiffs' interests was extinguished by the Marketable Title Act. In 1984 the error in the transcription of A. E. Kirkman's will was corrected in Will Book K, page 27 at the foot of the original transcription. At trial, the trial judge found that several defendants were listed on the tax records as owners of the real property in issue and had been listed as owners for more than 30 years next preceding the institution of this action. The trial judge also found that none of plaintiffs were listed on the tax records as owners or had paid the taxes. The trial judge further found that defendants were bona fide purchasers for value when they acquired the property and had no notice of plaintiffs' claim until the institution of this suit. The trial judge concluded that "[a]ny rights of the plaintiffs in the lands owned by A. E. Kirkman at the time of his death, as vested remainderman under the Will of A. E. Kirkman, have been extinguished by Chapter 47B of the General Statutes of North Carolina (Real Property Marketable Title Act)." Plaintiffs appeal.

* * *

Plaintiffs' sole assignment of error is the trial court's conclusion that the North Carolina Real Property Marketable Title Act extinguished that vested remainder interest. Plaintiffs argue that the "application of the Act so as to extinguish Appellant's vested remainder in fee would be unconstitutional under both the United States and North Carolina Constitutions." Plaintiffs also argue that even if the application of the North Carolina Real Property Marketable Title Act can extinguish appellants' vested remainder in fee, appellants' inter-est is excepted from extinguishment pursuant to North Carolina General Statutes section 47B-3(1).

I. NORTH CAROLINA REAL PROPERTY MARKETABLE TITLE ACT

Initially, we note that "[t]he Real Property Marketable Title Act was enacted by the General Assembly of North Carolina in an effort to expedite the alienation and marketability of real property." Heath v. Turner, 309 N.C. 483, 488, 308 S.E.2d 244, 247 (1983) citing Note, North Carolina Marketable Title Act Section 47B-2(D)—Proof of Title—Relief at Last for the Plaintiff Instituting Land Actions, 10 W.F.L.Rev. 312 (1974).

G.S. 47B-2 provides:

> Marketable record title to estate in real property; 30-year unbroken chain of title of record; effect of marketable title.
>
> (a) Any person having the legal capacity to own real property in this State, who, alone or together with his predecessors in title, shall have been vested with any estate in real property of record for 30 years or more, shall have a marketable record title to such estate in real property.
>
> (b) A person has an estate in real property of record for 30 years or more when the public records disclose a title transaction affecting the title to the real property which has been of record for not less than 30 years purporting to create such estate either in:
>
> (1) The person claiming such estate; or
>
> (2) Some other person from whom, by one or more title transactions, such estate has passed to the person claiming such estate;
>
> with nothing appearing of record, in either case, purporting to divest such claimant of the estate claimed.
>
> (c) Subject to the matters stated in G.S. 47B-3, such marketable record title shall be free and clear of all rights, estates, interests, claims or charges whatsoever, the existence of which depends upon any act, title transaction, event or omission that occurred prior to such 30-year period. All such rights, estates, interests, claims or charges, however denominated, whether such rights, estates, interests, claims or charges are or appear to be held or asserted by a person sui juris or under a disability, whether such person is natural or corporate, or is private or governmental, are hereby declared to be null and void.

(d) In every action for the recovery of real property, to quiet title, or to recover damages for trespass, the establishment of a marketable record title in any person pursuant to this statute shall be prima facie evidence that such person owns title to the real property described in his record chain of title. (1973, c. 255, s. 1; c. 881; 1981, c. 682, s. 11.)

"A person seeking to establish marketable record title under the Act must directly or through predecessors in title establish a root of title that is at least 30 years old. This is done by tracing back to a 'title transaction' located at or beyond the 30 year period." P. Hetrick, Webster's Real Estate Law in North Carolina, section 508.3 (rev.ed.1988). "The term 'title transaction' means any transaction affecting title to any interest in real property, including but not limited to title by will or descent, title by tax deed, or by trustee's, referee's, commissioner's, guardian's, executors', administrator's, or sheriff's deed, contract, lease or reservation, or judgment or order of any court, as well as warranty deed, quitclaim deed, or mortgage."

Whether the North Carolina Real Property Marketable Title Act [hereinafter Act] can extinguish vested remainders has not been determined in this State. In order to facilitate the transferability and marketability of real property, the Act requires that a person claiming a right, estate, interest or charge which is non-possessory and would be extinguished by the Act to register that interest in the county's Register of Deeds' Office. G.S. 47B-4. In order to protect the rights of those with non-possessory interests in property in the years immediately following the Act's enactment, the 1973 Act did not become effective against those interests created prior to the Act's enactment until three years after the enactment of the Act. G.S. 47B-5. Nothing in the Act indicates that the General Assembly intended to except vested remainders from its application. The only exceptions are stated in G.S. 47B-3 which enumerates the rights left unaffected by the Act. While G.S. 47B-3 does not explicitly list vested remainders, we infer that vested remainders are exempted if they are "disclosed by . . . the muniments of title of which such 30 year chain of record title is formed" provided they are referred to specifically by reference to book and page of recorded title transaction which imposed, transferred, or continued those rights, estates, interests, claims, or charges. G.S. 47B-3(1); *see also* Town of Winton v. Scott, 80 N.C.App. 409, 342 S.E.2d 560 (1986), aff'd, 318 N.C. 690, 351 S.E.2d 298 (1987).

Here the record does not indicate that plaintiffs registered their interest pursuant to G.S. 47B-4. Accordingly, in order for plaintiffs' interest to be preserved, the interest must be revealed in the muniments of title during the 30 year period. Because plaintiffs' vested remainder here resulted from devise of the life estate to G. C. Kirkman in the Kirkman will, if any of the deeds in each respective defendant's 30 year record chain of title refers to A. E. Kirkman's will specifically by book and page number, plaintiffs' interest would then be revealed in the muniments of title and plaintiffs' vested remainder would survive as to that defendant's competing claim.

II.

We now examine the record chain of title of each defendant to ascertain if plaintiffs' interest appears in the muniments of title thereby excepting their interest from extinguishment by operation of the Act.

First, we note that this action for declaratory judgment was instituted on 22 January 1985. Pursuant to G.S. 47B-1 et seq. this is the operative date for determining the record chain of title. The 30 year period would have commenced on 22 January 1955. If a title transaction has not occurred on this date, we then proceed to the next earliest title transaction before commencement of the 30 year period. If plaintiffs' interest does not appear in any instrument in the record chain of title executed from the last title transaction to the date of purchase of that property, plaintiffs' vested remainder is extinguished and defendants are entitled to remain in possession of the property. *See also* P. Hetrick, Webster's Real Estate Law in North Carolina, Section 508.3 (rev. ed. 1988).

A. Defendant Elvira Johnson

Defendant Elvira Johnson acquired her property on 4 November 1949. This was the first title transaction beyond the 30 year period. The deed conveying the property to Johnson specifically refers to the A. E. Kirkman will probated on 17 May 1941 and appearing in Will Book K, at page 27, in the Office of the Clerk of Superior Court of Craven County. Since the will containing plaintiffs' interest is found in defendant's record chain of title, plaintiffs' interest with respect to this particular defendant is excepted from the Act and is not extinguished.

* * *

[The court then made similar examinations of the title held by three other defendants, and reached the same conclusion.]

E. Defendants Ernest F. Boyd and wife, Sybil E. Boyd

Defendants Ernest and Sybil Boyd received their property on 5 March 1962 from Jimmy and Janice Morris. The next title transaction following the expiration of the 30 year period was the conveyance from G. L. and Addie Wilson to Dennis and Cora Bailey on 10 September 1952. None of the deeds in defendants' record chain of title specifically refers to the Kirkman will. Accordingly, plaintiffs' interest was extinguished by operation of the Act.

* * *

[The court concluded its analysis by examining the titles of each of the other defendants and finding that the vested remainder interest either was or was not extinguished by the Act based upon the presence or absence of mention of the Kirkman will in the defendant's chain of title.]

III. Constitutionality of the Act

* * *

After careful review of the record before us, we find that it does not affirmatively reveal that the constitutionality of the Act was raised, discussed, considered or passed upon by the court below . . . . [Since the] constitutionality of the Act was not properly raised before the trial tribunal . . . we decline to discuss it for the first time on appeal.

Case Reflections

1. It appears that the defendants whose "root of title" included mention of the A. E. Kirkman will lost their property to Mr. Kirkman's grandchildren. How could these defendants have prevented this outcome?
2. It appears that A. E. Kirkman's grandchildren forfeited their ownership rights to defendants whose root of title did not include mention of the Kirkman will. What should the grandchildren have done to prevent this outcome?

MCCLASKEY V. BUMB & MUELLER FARMS, INC.

547 N.E.2d 302 (Ind., 1989)

Conflicts between the seller's warranty of title and the Marketable Title Act

STATEMENT OF THE CASE

Cross-complainant-appellant, Marvin Randall McClaskey (McClaskey), appeals the trial court's granting of summary judgment in favor of the defendants, M. R. Hudson, A. B. Hudson, and Mary Hudson Vandergrift (the Hudsons).

We reverse.

STATEMENT OF THE FACTS

On December 21, 1983, the Hudsons conveyed a parcel of real estate to McClaskey by a warranty deed. Prior to this conveyance, the State of Indiana (the State) had acquired a 125-foot highway easement over this real estate. The warranty deed McClaskey received, however, did not reveal the existence of the State's highway easement.

As part of the project to make U.S. 41 a limited access highway, the State initiated condemnation proceedings against McClaskey seeking to appropriate and condemn that portion of McClaskey's real estate which abutted U.S. 41. Noting the exclusion of the 125-foot easement, McClaskey cross-claimed against the Hudsons alleging they breached their warranty of title. Both parties moved for summary judgment. The trial court granted Hudsons' motion, denied McClaskey's motion, and McClaskey subsequently perfected this appeal.

ISSUE

McClaskey presents the following issue for our review:

Whether the trial court erred in concluding that the Hudsons did not breach their warranty of title.

DISCUSSION AND DECISION

* * *

McClaskey argues that the Hudsons breached their warranty of title because their deed failed to disclose a highway easement held by the State. The Hudsons counter that they transferred a marketable title which is sufficient under the Marketable Title Act and thus have complied with the requirements of Indiana law. *See* IND.CODE 32-1-5-1 thru -10.

It is undisputed that the Hudsons conveyed the real estate to McClaskey by warranty deed. Under a warranty deed, the transferor guarantees that the real estate is "free from all encumbrances and that he will warrant and defend the title to the same against all lawful claims." IND.CODE 32-1-2-12. The existence of a highway easement constitutes as breach of a covenant against encumbrances. Burk v. Hill (1874), 48 Ind. 52.

In the present case, the real estate was encumbered by a highway easement in favor of the State. The Hudsons' deed failed to reveal the existence of this easement. Thus, as a matter of law, the Hudsons breached their warranty of title. *Id.*

Although the Hudsons conveyed the real estate by warranty deed, they contend that McClaskey was only entitled to a marketable title. The Hudsons rely upon Indiana's Marketable Title Act to support their contention. This reliance is misplaced.

* * *

The Hudsons contend that since U.S. 41 was in existence at the time of the conveyance to McClaskey, McClaskey was under a requirement to make a reasonable inquiry concerning the extent of the easement before he purchased the real estate covered by the warranty deed.

If we were to accept the Hudsons' position, IND.CODE 32-1-2-12, which provides for warranties of title, would be completely abrogated by the Marketable Title Act. Where two statutes speak to the same general subject, they should be harmonized, and if possible, each given effect. Bell v. Bingham (1985), Ind.App., 484 N.E. 2d 624, 627. To harmonize the statutes, we hold that the Marketable Title Act relieves the covenants imposed by a warranty deed only to the extent that a claim or interest is extinguished by the Marketable Title Act. If a claim or interest is not extinguished by the Act, the Act has no effect on the guarantee contained in the deed. This construction furthers the purpose of both the Act and IND.CODE 32-1-2-12. Furthermore, the trial court specifically found that McClaskey did not have actual knowledge of the easement and the existence of the easement was not disclosed in his abstract of title. Record at 25. As noted by our supreme court over a century ago.

> [T]he reason the person insists on covenants for title, or a warranty of quality or quantity, is because he either knows or fears that the title is not good or that the article lacks in quantity or quality. If he were perfectly assured on those questions, he would seldom be tenacious in obtaining a covenant or a warranty. (Citation omitted.)

The judgment of the trial court is reversed and the cause remanded with instructions for the trial court to enter summary judgment for McClaskey and against Hudson.

Case Reflections

1. The court observed "the Marketable Title Act relieves the covenants imposed by a warranty deed only to the extent that a claim or interest is extinguished by the Marketable Title Act." Do you agree with this position? Why or why not?

CRAWFORD V. SAFECO TITLE INSURANCE COMPANY

585 So.2d 952 (FL, 1991)

Title Insurance policy terms

This cause is before us on appeal from a final order dismissing appellants' first complaint with prejudice. The issues are: (1) whether the complaint states a cause of action for breach of title insurance policy; and (2) whether the complaint states a cause of action for negligent misrepresentation.

The complaint states that in March 1984, appellants secured from appellees a title insurance binder incident to their purchase of real property located in Walton County, Florida. The binder, incorporated into the complaint, contained exceptions for rights or claims of parties in possession not shown by the public records and boundary line disputes which would be disclosed by an accurate survey. To secure the elimination of the boundary dispute exception from the policy, appellants paid an extra premium for research of the records and secured an up-to-date survey (hereinafter Richardson Survey), which they furnished to appellees.

In July 1984, appellees issued the title insurance policy, and the closing took place. The policy, incorporated into the complaint, provided that: The Company, at its own cost and without undue delay, shall provide for the defense of an insured in all litigation consisting of actions or proceedings commenced against the insured to the extent that such litigation is founded upon an alleged defect, lien, encumbrance, or other matter insured against by this policy.

The policy contained an exception for rights or claims of parties in possession not shown by the public records, boundary-line disputes which would be disclosed by an accurate survey, and encroachments shown in the Richardson Survey.

Shortly after the closing, a neighboring landowner notified appellants of her claim, under a deed of record, to a portion of the property described in the policy. The neighboring landowner then fenced approximately one-half acre of the property described in the policy. Appellants notified appellees of the claim but received no response. Subsequently, appellants retained their own counsel and filed suit to quiet title to the disputed property. The neighboring landowner counterclaimed to quiet title to this property. Appellants prevailed in their action to quiet title.

Appellants brought suit against appellees based upon appellees' failure to participate in the quiet-title action. Under Count I, appellants seek to recover their attorney fees and costs expended in the quiet-title action, plus consequential damages. Under Count II, appellants seek damages for misrepresentation of the quality of their title. On appellees' motion, the trial court dismissed the complaint with prejudice.

Appellees argue, and the trial court found, that under the above-quoted policy language, appellants cannot recover under Count I since they, rather than the adjoining landowner, commenced the quiet-title action.

We need not decide whether appellees' obligations under the policy are strictly limited, as appellees contend, to defense of suits brought against the insured, because the complaint here alleges that the adjoining landowner has asserted a counterclaim seeking to quiet title. The assertion of this counterclaim brought the quiet title action within the policy language requiring appellees to provide for the defense of appellants "in all litigation consisting of actions or proceedings commenced against [appellants]."

In dismissing the complaint with prejudice, however, the trial court expressly found that the adjoining landowner's claim was not a title defect within the meaning of the policy for three reasons, viz.: (1) the claim was that of a party in possession not shown by the public records; (2) the claim was in the nature of a boundary dispute which should or would have been disclosed by an accurate survey of the premises; and (3) the Richardson Survey would have disclosed the claim.[1] The first

[1]The Richardson survey is not part of the record and, in any event, should not have been considered on motion to dismiss, which is limited to the four corners of the complaint.

finding overlooks the allegation in the complaint that the adjoining landowner's claim was based on a deed of record. All three reasons, however, are findings of fact. In considering a motion to dismiss the trial court must take all material allegations of the complaint as true and must confine itself strictly to the allegations within the complaint's four corners. Shahid v. Campbell, 552 So.2d 321, 322 (Fla.1st DCA 1989); Bryant v. Coordinated Programs, Inc., 534 So.2d 932 (Fla. 1st DCA 1988); Platte' v. Whitfield Realty Company, Inc., 511 So.2d 720, 721 (Fla. 1st DCA 1987). We therefore reverse as to Count I.

In Count II, appellants allege, in pertinent part, that they purchased title insurance in lieu of obtaining an abstract and relied upon the commitment to determine the quality of title prior to closing the transaction. Appellants further allege that appellees failed to undertake a reasonable search and examination of title in accordance with Section 627.7845(1), Florida Statutes, and that appellees' failure to undertake the search or to disclose the defects shown in the public records and Richardson Survey caused them damages.

In dismissing Count II with prejudice, the trial court determined that because the claims were not defects within the meaning of the policy, appellants could not recover based upon appellees' failure to disclose them. This was error.

In Shada v. Title and Trust Company of Florida, 457 So.2d 553, 557 (Fla. 4th DCA 1984), petition for review denied, 464 So.2d 556 (Fla.1984), the court stated:

> We see no reason why the principle applicable to an abstractor [imposing a duty of reasonable care to the purchaser in disclosing record title defects] should not be applied to a title insurance company where it undertakes the duty to schedule record title defects. The use of a title insurance binder or commitment instead of an abstract and an attorney's opinion of title has become commonplace. A title insurance company has a duty to exercise reasonable care when it issues a title binder or commitment and its failure to do so may subject it to liability in either contract or tort.

The title insurer must disclose even those defects exempted by the commitment language where those defects were known to the insurer at the time of closing. Daniel v. Coastal Bonded Title Company, 539 So.2d 567, 568 (Fla. 5th DCA 1989). Accordingly, we reverse the order dismissing the instant complaint with prejudice and remand for further proceedings consistent herewith.

Case Reflection

1. What material facts must the plaintiff prove at trial in order to recover a judgment from the defendant?

CHAPTER 11

CLOSING AND SETTLEMENT PROCEDURES

LEARNING OBJECTIVES

After reading this chapter, you should be able to:

1. Identify the source and significance of all of the items entered on a real estate settlement sheet
2. Discuss the duties of a real estate closing agent
3. Perform the real estate tax proration calculations required for a real estate closing

KEY TERMS

Settlement Statement

Certified Check

Cashier's Check

Closing Agent

Tax Proration

Lender's Escrow Account

The successful conclusion of a real estate transaction is often the most difficult and certainly the most complex portion of the process. Before the purchaser pays the purchase price and takes possession of the property, several things must happen.

First, all clouds and encumbrances against the title to the property must be removed. This will usually require the closing agent to identify the documents required to "clean up" the record title and then to correctly prepare these documents in advance of the closing. Second, the clear record title must be properly conveyed from the seller to the purchaser by preparing and recording the deed called for in the purchase agreement. Finally, the seller will need to collect the funds due to his or her account after payment of the expenses of sale; these funds must be collected from the buyer in a form that is not subject to dishonor or revocation after the title documents are recorded.

The problem the real estate closing designed was to solve is a chicken and egg kind of difficulty. At the instant a seller submits his or her deed for recording, the seller gives up ownership of the property. If for any reason a seller is unable to recover the purchase price expected from the sale, he or she will wind up with no money, no house, and very dismal prospects for finding a new place to live. For this reason, sellers are usually advised not to present their deed for recording until they have received the purchase price expected in the form of cash or some cash equivalent.

Buyers, however, face a similar problem. Once a buyer delivers the amount of cash (or cash equivalent) required for the purchase, the cash will be gone forever. If the buyer fails to receive a clear title to the property, then it is the buyer who winds up with little or no money, no house, and dismal prospects for a place to live. Buyers therefore are also well advised not to pay the money for the purchase of a new home until the title has been cleared up and the seller has recorded the deed.

Neither the seller nor the buyer will want to be the first one to perform the obligations incurred when the contact for sale of the property is signed. For this reason, a closing procedure must be used that solves the problem of who goes first, the buyer or the seller. The closing procedure permits both parties to go at the same time. The closing agent holds the money from the buyer and checks the documents from the seller in order to be sure that everything is in order. When everything checks out, the closing agent then pays the buyer's funds over to the seller at the same time as the seller's documents are recorded.

KEY POINTS

When the Empire State Building in New York City was sold during the late 1960s, the closing process is said to have required signatures on nearly three thousand documents. The actual closing was attended by over two hundred people, all of whose signatures were required on one or more of the closing documents.

The attorneys for the parties to the transaction rehearsed the closing procedure for a week prior to the actual closing date. The purpose of the rehearsals was to verify that the individual assignments made to each member of the army of clerks assisting in the closing would in fact obtain all required signatures on each of the closing documents.

While this process sounds pretty simple, it can be enormously complex, especially when commercial properties are involved. The additional ownership interests and creative financing methods used with commercial property often cause exponential growth in the number of documents required to deliver a clear title and secure the buyer's financing. Because commercial real estate closings can be expected to create great difficulties requiring weeks or months of an attorney's time to resolve, we will begin the discussion in this chapter by considering only the residential real estate closing. When the basic requirements of residential closing procedures have been reviewed, we can examine some of the more common additional complications that arise in a commercial closing.

THE REALTOR'S OBLIGATIONS AT CLOSING

Part III of this book will analyze in detail the rights and obligations of licensed real estate professionals. In this chapter, we will become acquainted with some of these concepts by examining the functions realtors are expected to perform in a residential closing.

KEY POINTS

The obligations of real estate professionals actually begin at the time the purchase contract is signed and end when the closing is successfully completed. Several years ago, a Georgia real estate broker obtained the signature of a reluctant home purchaser by inserting an additional provision in the contract requiring the lawn on the property to be mowed on the closing date.

At the time appointed for the closing, the seller, the broker, the mortgage lender, and two attorneys arrived at the designated place for the closing, but the purchaser failed to appear. Finally, the broker called the purchaser to ask why he had not arrived for the closing. The buyer responded, "I thought the closing was canceled, because I drove by the house on my way to meet with you and the lawn had not been mowed."

The frantic broker raced home, loaded his lawnmower in the trunk of his car, and in the heat of a Georgia afternoon fulfilled the final remaining obligation of the seller under the terms of the contract.

We begin by noting that in current practice, Realtors® are legally obligated to represent the interests of sellers of property. Realtors® who attempt to represent the interests of a buyer run the risk of being found in breach of their obligations to the seller. This fact can take buyers by surprise. It is not uncommon for buyers to believe that when they seek out a Realtor[r] and request assistance in finding a new home, the realtor they are working with will represent their interests. This mistaken belief on the part of the buyer is most likely to cause mischief at the closing. Buyers, especially first-time homeowners, are often intimidated and confused by the pile of documents presented to them for signature at closing. It is only natural for buyers to ask "their"

Realtor® to explain the meaning of all those pieces of paper. It is equally natural for Realtors® to want to help the buyer understand the nature of the documents presented to them, and assist the buyer in feeling comfortable about signing the documents and paying the purchase price.

As agent of the seller, the Realtor® is under the obligation to prepare a set of docu-ments that, when presented at the closing, will obligate the buyer to pay for the property. The seller, and therefore the Realtor®, have a personal and pecuniary interest in conveying a marketable title to the buyer. In the course of performing these duties on behalf of the seller, the Realtor® will of course be required to work with the buyer and to offer assistance to the buyer in obtaining mortgage funds in order to pay for the property.

However, when responding to a buyer's questions at the closing, the Realtorr must be very careful. As agent of the seller, the Realtor® is always free to explain how a particular document serves the seller's interest in conveying a marketable title to the buyer. The Realtor® is also free to suggest that when a marketable title is delivered, the buyer is obligated to pay for the property and accept the title. Finally, the Realtor® is free to describe, in general terms, what the requirements for a marketable title are and to describe the steps that have been taken to provide a marketable title in the transaction at hand.

However, if the buyer should ask whether or not the documents at this closing are enough to convey a marketable title, a careful Realtor® must refuse to answer that question, for two reasons. First, the question calls for a legal opinion that a Realtor® is not licensed to provide. Second, any answer the Realtor® may give has the potential to create a conflict of interest. Since the Realtor® represents only the seller in a real estate transaction, the Realtor® is prohibited from offering the buyer any assistance beyond what is necessary to obtain the buyer's payment for the property. As a result, sophisticated purchasers know that they must decide for themselves whether or not the title received in a real estate closing is marketable. If there is any doubt, the careful practitioner will seek the advice of a competent attorney.

SETTLEMENT STATEMENTS

Even the simplest residential real estate closing is a fairly complex transaction. Cash will be received at the closing both from the buyer and from the lender who is financing the purchase. Cash will be paid from the closing to the seller, to the real estate brokers who are entitled to commissions, to the registrar of deeds for recording the documents of title, and probably to another lender, who had financed the previous purchase of the home by the current seller. In addition, there will be a number of prorations applied to the cash payments for real estate taxes, utilities, and other items. The **settlement statement** (often referred to as the settlement sheet) is the real estate document that makes it possible to quickly and accurately determine how much cash the buyer must bring to the closing and how much cash the seller can take home from the closing after all the expenses of transferring the title have been paid.

Settlement Statement
A statement of charges and payments made by the buyer and seller at a real estate closing.

The easiest way to visualize the function of a settlement sheet is to imagine a large cast-iron pot on the table at the closing. The buyer brings enough cash to the closing to pay for the house as well as all additional expenses of the sale that are the buyer's responsibility. The closing process begins when the buyer places the required amount of cash in the pot. The closing agent will then take cash out of the pot in order to pay the expenses of the transaction. For example, the closing agent may take $3,000 out of the pot and give it to the real estate broker for his or her commission on the sale. The agent will also take money out of the pot to pay for recording the deed, the mortgage, and other documents of title that are required to complete the transaction. When all of the expenses of sale have been paid, the seller is entitled to whatever money is left in the pot, and the buyer has become the new owner of the house.

Obviously, the amount of cash required for the purchase of a home is so large that most people would feel uncomfortable bringing enough currency to the closing to fill up the pot. Some other means of accomplishing the same result without carrying $80,000 in currency into the closing room will be required.

A **certified check** is an excellent substitute for the currency required. A certified check is created when the buyers go to their bank and present a check drawn on their account in the amount needed to pay for the new home and other closing expenses. The bank then withdraws enough money to cover the check from the buyers' account and places the money in a separate account the bank uses for that purpose. At the same time, a bank officer stamps the face of the check "Accepted for Payment." Thereafter, anyone can take the accepted check to the bank that certified it and collect the amount of money written on the check directly from the accepting bank. (Most banks today are unwilling to certify checks, because banking regulations require them to hold funds payable against certified checks in separate accounts that cannot be invested to earn interest for the bank. As a result, virtually all real estate closing payments are made with **cashier's checks.** A cashier's check is simply a check drawn on the funds belonging to the issuing bank. Courts have generally held that a cashier's check is equivalent to a certified check.)

The escrow account of the **closing agent** makes a good substitute for the cast-iron pot on the table in our example. The settlement sheet is nothing more than a record of deposits made by the buyer into the escrow account of the closing agent (the money put into the pot) and checks written against the escrow account to pay the expenses of the transaction and provide the seller with the net proceeds of the sale (the money taken out of the pot).

To construct a proper settlement sheet, all that is required is a list of expenses to be paid by the purchaser, together with a list of expenses to be paid by the seller. We will examine these items in more detail in Part III. For now it is enough to say that all items payable by the purchaser are entered on the settlement sheet as deposits to the escrow account, and all items payable by the seller are entered as checks written on the escrow account. The final item, the amount paid to the seller, is the amount that makes the total checks written on the escrow account exactly balance with the total deposits made to the escrow account for the closing. Another way to say this is to make sure that the escrow agent does not make any money or lose any money on the closing. The total amount of the checks paid against the escrow account should be exactly equal to the total amount of deposits made to the escrow account, so that the pot will be empty when the closing is completed.

The settlement sheets now required by federal regulations include a number of shortcuts and column totals that may obscure the "one check per expense amount" scheme of the settlement sheet. But the basic logic of settlement sheets, as we have explained it here, remains unchanged. Let us now examine the expense amounts that are included in the settlement sheet.

Certified Check
A check which has been certified for payment by the bank the check is drawn on. The bank certifies the check by removing the funds needed for payment from the maker's account, and holding the funds in separate account for payment to the person who presents the check.

Cashier's Check
A check which is drawn by a depositary institution against funds held on deposit with the Federal Reserve or with another commercial bank.

Closing Agent
The person who collects, holds and disburses all the funds required for a real estate closing. The closing agent may also file all documents required to complete the transfer of record title which occurs at the closing.

Allocating Expenses between the Parties

The general rule is that the expenses of transferring title to the buyer will be paid by the seller, while the expenses of ownership after the transfer of title will be paid by the purchaser. However, the parties to the sale may agree to divide the expenses in any way they choose. That is why the preparation of a settlement sheet begins with an examination of the contract for the sale of the real property involved. Unless the contract specifies another arrangement, the parties to the sale will each be responsible for the following expenses.

Expenses to Be Paid by the Seller

The expenses usually allocated to the seller in a real estate closing include the following:

1. The cost of a certified abstract or title insurance policy showing marketable title to the property in the seller
2. The cost of recording the seller's deed to the buyer
3. The cost of recording any other document (e.g., a lien release or a satisfaction of mortgage) that are required to deliver a clear title to the buyer
4. Real estate brokerage commissions
5. Principal and interest to the date of closing on the seller's mortgage(s)

Expenses to Be Paid by the Buyer

The following expenses are generally charged to the purchaser, unless the contract provides for a different allocation:

1. A legal opinion of the title demonstrated by the certified abstract (if a title policy is not purchased by the seller)
2. Mortgagee's title insurance to protect the interest of the lender (if required)
3. Hazard insurance on the property
4. Expenses related to obtaining new mortgage financing on the property, such as appraisal fees, credit report charges, and loan origination fees

Analyzing the Contents of a Settlement Statement

The most widely used form for settlement sheets is the HUD-1 Settlement Statement. Figure 11.1 shows a completed HUD-1 statement for a hypothetical real estate sale. The scheduled date for the closing is August 25. We will walk through the settlement sheet one line at a time, explaining the entries on each line.

Cash Due from Buyer

Line 303 identifies the total amount of cash the buyer must bring to the closing. When the buyer contributes this sum of cash to the pot and the lenders add the additional amount of the new mortgage loans, there will be just enough money to purchase the house and pay all of the bills that become due at the closing.

A. SETTLEMENT STATEMENT

U.S. Department of Housing and Urban Development

OMB No. 2502-0265 (Exp. 12-31-86)

B. Type of Loan

1. ☐ FHA 2. ☐ FmHA 3. ☐ Conv. Unins. 4. ☐ VA 5. ☐ Conv. Ins.	6. File Number	7. Loan Number	8. Mortgage Insurance Case Number

C. Note: This form is furnished to give you a statement of actual settlement costs. Amounts paid to and by the settlement agent are shown. Items marked "(p.o.c.)" were paid outside the closing; they are shown here for information purposes and are not included in the totals.

D. Name and Address of Borrower	E. Name and Address of Seller	F. Name and Address of Lender

G. Property Location	H. Settlement Agent	
	Place of Settlement	I. Settlement Date

J. Summary of Borrower's Transaction		K. Summary of Seller's Transaction	
100. Gross Amount Due From Borrower		**400. Gross Amount Due To Seller**	
101. Contract sales price	105,000.00	401. Contract sales price	105,000.00
102. Personal property	2,200.00	402. Personal property	2,200.00
103. Settlement charges to borrower (line 1400)	6,177.68	403.	
104.		404.	
105		405.	
Adjustments for items paid by seller in advance		**Adjustments for items paid by seller in advance**	
106. City/town taxes to		406. City/town taxes to	
107. County taxes to		407. County taxes to	
108. Assessments to		408. Assessments to	
109.		409.	
110.		410.	
111.		411.	
112.		412.	
120. Gross Amount Due From Borrower	113,377.68	**420. Gross Amount Due To Seller**	107,200.00
200. Amounts Paid By Or In Behalf Of Borrower		**500. Reductions In Amount Due To Seller**	
201. Deposit or earnest money	5,000.00	501. Excess deposit (see instructions)	
202. Principal amount of new loan(s)	70,000.00	502. Settlement charges to seller (line 1400)	6,835.00
203. Existing loan(s) taken subject to		503. Existing loan(s) taken subject to	
204.		504. Payoff of first mortgage loan	73,486.28
205. Second lien mortgage	3,000.00	505. Payoff of second mortgage loan	
206.		506.	
207.		507.	
208.		508.	
209.		509.	
Adjustments for items unpaid by seller		**Adjustments for items unpaid by seller**	
210. City/town taxes 216.20 to 8/25/91	140.38	510. City/town taxes 216.20 to 8/25/91	140.38
211. County taxes 1,085.08 to 8/25/91	704.56	511. County taxes 1,085.08 to 8/25/91	704.56
212. Assessments 740.26 to 8/25/91	480.66	512. Assessments 740.26 to 8/25/91	480.66
213.		513.	
214.		514.	
215.		515.	
216.		516.	
217.		517.	
218.		518.	
219.		519.	
220. Total Paid By/For Borrower	79,325.60	**520. Total Reduction Amount Due Seller**	81,646.88
300. Cash At Settlement From/To Borrower		**600. Cash At Settlement To/From Seller**	
301. Gross Amount due from borrower (line 120)	113,377.68	601. Gross amount due to seller (line 420)	107,200.00
302. Less amounts paid by/for borrower (line 220)	(79,325.60)	602. Less reductions in amt. due seller (line 520)	(81,646.88)
303. Cash ☒ **From** ☐ **To Borrower**	$34,052.08	**603. Cash** ☒ **To** ☐ **From Seller**	$25,553.12

Previous Edition is Obsolete HUD-1 (3-86)

ISC/CHSSXX//0786/HUD-1 (3-86)/LASER Page 1 of 2 RESPA, HB 4305 2

FIGURE 11.1 SETTLEMENT STATEMENT

The cash required from the buyer includes the contract price for the house, entered on line 101. In addition, the parties in this transaction agreed that the buyer would pay an additional $2,200 to the seller in exchange for the kitchen appliances. These appliances were originally excluded from the sale in the contract. Later on, the buyer and seller agreed that the appliances could remain with the house if the buyer paid for them. This payment for additional personal property is entered on line 102.

Line 103 contains the amount of additional settlement charges computed on page 2 of the HUD-1 forms. We will see how that figure is derived when we examine page 2 of the settlement sheet, which appears in Figure 11.2.

On lines 201–9, the buyer receives credit for payments that have already been made or payments that will be made at the closing by the buyer's banks. In this case, the buyer deposited $5,000 as earnest money when the contract was signed, and that amount appears on line 201. The buyer has arranged for a first mortgage of $70,000 and gets credit for that amount on line 202. The buyer has also arranged for a second mortgage of $3,000, which appears on line 205. If the buyer had agreed to assume an existing mortgage on the house, the unpaid balance of that loan at the closing date would appear on line 203. In this case, there is no mortgage assumption, so line 203 is blank.

Tax Prorations

Proration of Taxes The division of property tax payments between the buyer and seller of real property subject to the tax. The division is based on the number of days during the year that each party occupied the property.

Lines 106–8 *and* lines 210–12 are provided for the **proration of taxes** between the buyer and the seller. Since tax prorations are the most difficult and complicated part of the settlement sheet preparation, we will take a minute to discuss the theory of tax proration before investigating the practice of the art.

In order to determine the correct amounts to be entered in each tax proration line on the settlement sheet, the settlement agent must answer four questions:

1. Have the property taxes and special assessments from the previous calendar year been paid on the date of the closing?
2. Will the amounts of special assessments for the current calendar year be available before the date of the closing?
3. Will the amount of the property taxes for the current year be available on the date of the closing?
4. Will the property taxes and special assessments for the current year be paid on the date of closing?

The answer to each of these questions will depend on the date the closing is held. Every state has adopted statutory procedures for determining and announcing the assessed valuation, mill levy, and special assessments for every parcel of real property. The statutes always contain a date on which the taxing authority is required to make this information available to the public. If the closing occurs before the new tax information is required to be released, then the answers to questions 2 and 3 above will be negative. When the closing occurs after the deadline for announcements of tax information, the answers to these questions will be in the affirmative. The closing statements we are examining assume that taxes are paid in arrears, that is, the taxes owed on real property for the current year are determined on December 15, near the end of the year. The current year's taxes and special assessments become due and payable in February, after the year for which the taxes apply has ended.

L. Settlement Charges		
700. Total Sales/Broker's Commission based on price $ 105,000 @ 6 % = 6,300	Paid From Borrowers' Funds at Settlement	Paid From Sellers' Funds at Settlement
Division of Commission (line 700) as follows:		
701. $3,150 to Listing Broker		
702. $3,150 to Selling Broker		
703. Commission paid at Settlement		6,300.00
704.		
800. Items Payable In Connection With Loan		
801. Loan Origination Fee 1.5 %	1,050.00	
802. Loan Discount 1.0 %	700.00	
803. Appraisal Fee 350 to Appraisal Associates	350.00	
804. Credit Report 75 to Credit Bureau	75.00	
805. Lender's Inspection Fee		
806. Mortgage Insurance Application Fee to		
807. Assumption Fee		
808. Processing Fee 125	125.00	
809.		
810.		
811.		
812.		
813.		
814.		
815.		
816.		
817.		
900. Items Required By Lender To Be Paid In Advance		
901. Interest from 8/25/91 to 10/5/91 @$ 22.05 /day	904.05	
902. Mortgage Insurance Premium for 12 months to 9/1/92	150.00	
903. Hazard Insurance Premium for 1 years to 9/1/92	415.00	
904. years to		
905.		
1000. Reserves Deposited With Lender		
1001. Hazard insurance 2 months@$ 34.60 per month	69.17	
1002. Mortgage insurance 2 months@$ 8.33 per month	16.66	
1003. City property taxes 10 months@$ 18.02 per month	180.20	
1004. County property taxes 10 months@$ 90.42 per month	904.20	
1005. Annual assessments 10 months@$ 61.69 per month	616.90	
1006. months@$ per month		
1007. months@$ per month		
1008. months@$ per month		
1100. Title Charges		
1101. Settlement or closing fee 150.00 to Settlement Agent	75.00	75.00
1102. Abstract or title search 225.00 to Abstract Titles		225.00
1103. Title examination 300.00 to		
1104. Title insurance binder 150.00 to		150.00
1105. Document preparation 75.00 to		
1106. Notary fees 7.50 to		7.50
1107. Attorney's fees 375.00 to Ernie the Attorney	300.00	75.00
(includes above items numbers: 1103, 1105)		
1108. Title insurance 125.00 to ALTA Company	125.00	
(includes above items numbers:)		
1109. Lender's coverage $ 70,000		
1110. Owner's coverage $105,000		
1111.		
1112.		
1113.		
1200. Government Recording and Transfer Charges		
1201. Recording fees: Deed $ 3.00 ; Mortgage $ 3.00 ; Releases $ 3.00	6.00	3.00
1202. City/county tax/stamps: Deed $ 10.50 ; Mortgage $	10.50	
1203. State tax/stamps: Deed $ 105.10 ; Mortgage $	105.00	
1204.		
1205.		
1300. Additional Settlement Charges		
1301. Survey to		
1302. Pest inspection to		
1303.		
1304.		
1305.		
1400. Total Settlement Charges (enter on lines 103, Section J and 502, Section K)	$6,177.68	$6,835.00

Buyer	Date	Seller	Date
Buyer SS#		Seller SS#	
Buyer	Date	Seller	Date
Buyer SS#		Seller SS#	

ISC/CHSSXX//0786/HUD-1 (3-86)/LASER Page 2 of 2

FIGURE 11.2 SETTLEMENT STATEMENT, PAGE 2.

KEY POINTS

The actual ad valorem property taxes that the buyer will be required to pay after taking possession are computed by multiplying the certified mill levy fo the property by the taxable value of the property. The taxable value is a fraction of the fair or market value of the property as determined by the local assessor, whose job it is to assess the value of each parcel of property within the boundaries of a taxing district.

It is fairly common for property assessments to lag behind changes in actual market values by several years. As a result, the price agreed to by the buyer of a parcel may be substantially greater than the value of the parcel established by the assessor's office. In those states where property taxes are paid in arrears, a large difference between the assessed value of a property and the purchase price of that property can cause a nasty surprise for the buyer.

A large difference between the assessed value of a property and the actual purchase price of the property will often trigger an increase in the valuation used to compute the property taxes. The increase in taxable value will of course result in the buyer being required to pay substantially more taxes than expected.

When property is to be purchased at a price significantly greater than the assessed value, the prudent buyer should take steps to avoid this outcome. If the closing cannot be delayed until a date when the assessed value of the property for the year of purchase will be certified, the buyer should insist on the use of a method for computing the taxes to be prorated to the seller that recognizes the actual tax amount the buyer should expect to pay.

The answer to our first question (Have the taxes and special assessments for the previous year already been paid?) is important, because these taxes are not prorated between the buyer and the seller. The prior year's taxes and assessments are the responsibility of the seller alone. If the taxes and assessments have been paid, they are disregarded. If they have not been paid, the amount due will be deducted from the seller's proceeds and paid to the county treasurer during the closing.

Taxes and special assessments for the current year must be prorated between the parties, since the buyer and seller will both occupy the property for a portion of the current year. Each party is responsible for the payment of the taxes and assessments that accrue during the portion of the year they occupied the property. The only problem is determining the exact amount of the total taxes and assessments to be allocated between the parties.

We will assume that Figure 11.1 was prepared for a closing that will occur before the date when special assessments, assessed valuation, and mill levies are announced but after the date that tax payments for the previous year are due. The settlement agent called the county treasurer's office and obtained the following information regarding the property taxes on the property being purchased:

1. Yes, the taxes for the prior year have been paid. (The answer to this question was obtained by asking the county treasurer if any delinquent taxes are outstanding against the property. The county treasurer reported that there were none.)

2. No, the special assessments for the current year have not yet been announced. Therefore, the settlement agent will calculate the proration based upon the special assessments from the previous year.
3. No, the amount of the property taxes for the current year are unknown. Again, these taxes will be prorated on the basis of last year's property tax amount.
4. No. The county treasurer reports that the taxes for the current year remain unpaid. The current year's taxes are not delinquent, because they are not required to be paid until next year.

The total property taxes and special assessments paid on the property for last year were $2,041.54. This amount breaks down as $216.20 for city property taxes, $1,085,08 for county and school district taxes, and $740.26 for special assessments. All of these amounts must be allocated between the buyer and the seller based on the number of days in the current year that each party occupied the premises. August 25 is the 238th day of the year, leaving 127 more days in the year.

Since the buyer takes possession of the property on August 25, the seller occupied the premises for 237 days. Dividing each of the tax amounts by 365 (to obtain the tax per day for each category) and multiplying by the 237 days the seller occupied the property results in the total credit the buyer should receive for property taxes and special assessments that accrued during the portion of the year that the seller was in possession. These amounts are entered on lines 210–12 of the HUD-1 Settlement Sheet as a reduction in the amount of cash due from the buyer. We can now breathe a huge sigh of relief, because the buyer's portion of page 1 of the settlement sheet is completed, with one minor exception.

Line 103 contains the entry for the total settlement charges, computed on page 2 of the HUD-1 form. Earlier in this analysis, we skipped over that line; now is the time to return to it. And, since we have been discussing the tax proration process, the best place to enter page 2 is at lines 1003–5. These lines also include settlement charges to the buyer that are related to the property taxes and special assessments on the property.

Remember that the estimated taxes and special assessments for the current year, in the amount of $2041.54, must be paid by the buyer when the current year's taxes become due. The taxes will be paid out of an escrow account maintained by the lender. In order to make sure that the **lender's escrow account** contains enough money to pay the taxes next February, it is necessary to put some money aside for the payment now. Eight months of the year have already passed as of the date of the closing, so the lender has the right to require that the escrow account begin with a deposit reflecting that amount. In addition, since the amount of taxes and special assessments that will be due next February is not known at the date of the closing, the lender is permitted to demand up to two additional months of "cushion" in the escrow account. As a result, page 2 of the HUD-1 form indicates a deposit to the escrow account of $1701.28, which is ten months of the estimated taxes and special assessments. These amounts are entered by category in lines 1002–4. If the property were a condominium or townhouse, with an annual membership fee, ten months of that annual assessment would be entered on line 1006.

Lender's Escrow Account Funds held by mortgage lenders which will be used to pay property tax bills and insurance premiums when those items become due in the future.

At first glance, it appears that the buyer is now being required to pay the taxes on the property that accrued during the first eight months of the year, while the seller was in possession. In reality, that is not the case. The taxes due while the seller was in possession were subtracted from the amount the buyer owes on page 1 of the form and added to the amount the buyer owes on page 2 of the form. The net effect of these offsetting entries is a wash to the buyer. However, the $1,325.60 of taxes prorated to the seller are subtracted from the money due the seller and paid to the lender for inclusion in the escrow account. As a result, the amount deposited in the escrow for taxes and special assessments is composed of roughly eight months of taxes taken from the seller's money, along with the two-month cushion charged to the buyer. When the tax payments are actually made, the monthly escrow charge to the buyer will be adjusted to reflect the actual demand made upon the escrow account.

Proration of Taxes Paid in Advance

In many states, property taxes are paid in advance at the beginning of the year. The proration process for taxes paid in advance is identical to the process described above for taxes paid in arrears. The only difference is the placement of the adjustment items on the settlement sheet. When the closing occurs after the tax payment date, the taxes for the remaining portion of the year are items paid by the seller in advance. The prorated amounts are calculated using the number of days remaining from the date of closing until December 31 and are entered on lines 106–08 on page 1 of the settlement sheet. The net effect of this adjustment is to cause the buyer to reimburse the seller for the taxes already paid during the portion of the year the buyer is in possession of the property.

Other Closing Costs

The remaining closing costs are computed on page 2 of the HUD-1 form. The real estate commission is computed in line 700 and allocated between the listing and the selling broker on lines 701 and 702. The total commission is charged to the seller on line 703.

Lines 801–4 contain normal expense items that are charged by all lenders in connection with a mortgage loan. The specific amount for each of these items is determined by the lender and furnished to the settlement agent prior to the closing. Unless the parties have agreed otherwise, the costs of obtaining mortgage financing are paid by the buyer and are included in the buyer's settlement charges on page 2. The only exception to this rule is the VA (Veterans Administration) funding fee on line 806. When the property is purchased with a VA mortgage, the seller is required to pay the points on the mortgage. This requirement should be included in the contract for the sale of the home and should come as no surprise to the seller.

Line 901 contains the "odd days interest" computation. It is a fairly standard practice in the mortgage industry to give the buyer a month or two of grace before the first payment on the mortgage becomes due. However, this practice does not involve any charity on the part of the lender, because the buyer is required to pay interest on the money in advance for the period of time between the date the loan is advanced (the date of the closing) and the date the first payment on the mortgage is due. The daily interest amount is computed by first multiplying the amount of the loan by the annual interest rate on the loan. (This calculation results in the annual interest payment due on the initial principal balance.) Next, the annual interest is divided by 365 days to compute the daily interest. (Some lenders may use the "financial year" of 360 days to compute the annual interest. Dividing by 360 instead of 365 increases the daily interest figure by a few pennies for most loans.) The amount of "odd days interest" is included on line 901 as an additional settlement cost to the buyer.

If the buyer has financed the property with either an FHA (Federal Housing Administration) loan or a conventional loan covered by a Private Mortgage Insurance policy, the amount of the premium will appear on line 902. For conventional insured mortgages, the premium for the first year of insurance will be paid in advance. In addition, two months of insurance premium will be added to the escrow account on line 1002.

The last portion of the settlement charge statement relates to the cost of furnishing evidence of marketable title and conveying title to the buyer. The costs of abstracting, title examination, and the title insurance binder are usually paid by the seller to fulfill the obligation of offering a marketable title at the closing. It is also the seller's obligation to prepare the deed and to pay the title insurance premium for the owner's coverage. The buyer usually pays the title insurance premium for the lender's policy.

The usual practice is for the seller to pay the recording fees for all documents that must be recorded to provide a marketable title at the time of closing (e.g., the release of the seller's mortgage on the property), while the buyer pays the recording fees for all other documents. Generally, the buyer is also responsible for payment of the tax stamps attached to the deed at the time of recording.

Summary of Seller's Transaction

The adjustments for the seller's proceeds from the closing are the same as the adjustments for the buyer's charges we have just reviewed, with a few exceptions. On page 1 of the HUD-1 form (Figure 11.1), the amount due to the seller begins with the contract price for the real property and any personal property included in the bargain. Lines 503–5 reflect the payments the seller must make on existing encumbrances in order to deliver a clear title at the closing. These amounts will be withheld from the seller and paid to the holders of the encumbrances in exchange for a release of the mortgages. All other settlement charges to the seller from page 2 are inserted in line 502.

We have now reached the "bottom line" of the settlement sheet. In the buyer's column, line 303 indicates the total amount of cash the buyer must bring to the closing and line 603 the total amount of cash the seller will receive at the closing.

COMMERCIAL REAL ESTATE CLOSING

A commercial real estate closing includes everything we have discussed so far, plus a whole lot more. It is usually the case that commercial properties are held in the name of a corporation, partnership, or other form of common ownership. Proper written authorization for the sale of property held in a common ownership arrangement must be obtained form the seller in order to prove the validity of the deed conveying title to the buyer.

Commercial property is usually encumbered by a lease (often by numerous leases to a variety of tenants.) Each of these leases must be carefully examined, because the new owner, as landlord, will almost certainly be bound by the terms and conditions of the existing leases.

Finally, many commercial properties are encumbered by a series of mortgages, some of which the buyer will assume during the purchase and some of which will be paid off at the closing. Each of these documents must be carefully examined and the payoff amounts listed in the settlement sheets thoroughly scrutinized. It is not unusual to find that commercial property is also encumbered by liens against individual shareholders of the corporation (or members of the partnership) that holds record title to the property. Each of these liens must be discharged during the closing and the amount of the lien deducted from the sale proceeds delivered to the individual against whom the lien existed.

Identifying the items that must be resolved in a commercial closing and preparing the documents required for the resolutions is a time-consuming and difficult task. Only the most seasoned practitioners have the skills and knowledge required to perform these activities. In general, both the buyer and the seller in a commercial real estate closing are well advised to retain the services of an attorney who is knowledgeable in this rather specialized field.

ESCROW CLOSING

An escrow closing is a specialized case of the general closing procedures we have discussed in this chapter. In a "normal" closing, the buyer and seller simply gather in one place at the time appointed for the closing and exchange the documents and payments required to complete the transaction. Both parties examine the settlement sheet, review and sign the required documents, and approve the payment of the purchase price and the delivery of the deed. The settlement agent delivers the documents and checks to the appropriate recipients during this process, and the conveyance is accomplished when the parties leave the closing room.

In an escrow closing, the parties perform exactly the same activities. However, the settlement agent does not deliver any documents or checks to the parties at the conclusion of this initial meeting. Instead, the money from the buyer, along with all the required documents, are held in an escrow account. The escrow agent then follows a set of specific instructions over a period of from three to six months. During the period of the escrow agreement, the escrow agent will pay off the mortgages, obtain the mortgage lien release documents, and perform any other duties required by the escrow agreement. The escrow usually closes after the period for filing a mechanic's lien has elapsed. The final duty required of the escrow agent is to check that no such liens have been filed. If that is the case, the escrow agent will send the remaining funds to the seller and record the deed to the buyer, and the escrow account will be closed.

The escrow agent is bound by the duty to use due care in following all of the instructions contained in the escrow agreement. If these instructions are followed to the letter, the conveyance of the property will be completed without any surprises to either party.

CONCLUSION

This chapter has discussed the procedures required to close a real estate transaction. We noted that a closing is necessary because neither the buyer nor the seller would be willing to perform his or her obligations until the other party has performed. The closing process allows both sides of the transaction to perform their obligations at the same time.

The chapter also discussed the use and construction of the settlement statement. The settlement statement is required to insure that the buyer brings sufficient money to the closing to pay all of the costs of the transaction for which he or she is responsible. In addition, the settlement statement indicates the net proceeds that will be due to the seller after payment of all costs for which the seller is responsible.

DISCUSSION QUESTIONS:

1. Several things must happen before a purchaser takes possession of a property. Name them.
2. What difficulty is the real estate closing process designed to overcome? How does the closing process accomplish this?
3. What is the obligation of the realtor—as an agent of the seller—at closing?
4. Name some items a broker is free to discuss with a buyer at closing. What is one question a broker must refuse to answer? Why?
5. Explain the purpose of the settlement statement, as well as what is required to construct it.
6. Distinguish between the expenses paid by the seller and the expenses paid by the buyer in a real estate closing.
7. The settlement agent must answer four questions in order to determine the correct amount of taxes owed by each party to the closing. What are these questions?
8. How are the previous year's taxes and assessments handled during the closing procedure? How is this different from the allocation of taxes and special assessments for the current year?
9. What additional issues does a commercial real estate closing involve that a residential closing does not?
10. How does an escrow closing differ from a "normal" closing?

GRAY V. BOYLE INVESTMENT COMPANY

803 S.W.2d 678 (TN, 1990)

Closing agent's duty of care

This is a suit by purchasers of real estate to recover the purchase price paid. Plaintiffs, Willie E. Gray and wife, Carrie M. Gray, filed their complaint . . . against defendants, Dorothy L. Lester, Boyle Investment Company, Grover McCormick, as Executor of the Estate of Porter Thomas, and Grover McCormick, individually, and Dunlap Cannon, III, attorney, individually.

The complaint alleges that plaintiff contracted on August 3, 1983, to purchase the property known as 3182 Winslow Street in Memphis, Tennessee, and that the title to the property was recorded in the name of Porter Thomas, who was then deceased.

. . . The Grays allege that the closing of the transaction occurred on August 10, 1983, and that, at the time, they delivered a check for the closing in the amount of $11,063.02 and were given keys to the property together with copies of the closing papers.

The complaint further avers that after the closing the Grays began repairs on the property and upon the completion of the repairs discovered that the locks on the house had been changed and a note had been placed on the door notifying them that the holder of the first mortgage had foreclosed on the property and that the property had been sold to an individual named Jimmy Carter. They aver that they had no knowledge of any pending foreclosure and that they had no knowledge that the mortgage on the property (which they were to assume) was in arrears.

* * *

Plaintiff's proof established that defendant Dorothy Lester is a real estate agent affiliated with Boyle Investment Company and had a listing contract to sell the residence at 3182 Winslow which was signed by Lovie Hicks, who was the sole beneficiary of the Porter Thomas' Estate. . . . Prior to the signing of the contract, defendant Lester had spoken to Jerry Whitehurst at the Veterans Administration and was informed that the mortgage loan on the property was in arrears and that a payment of $404.00 would bring the matter up to date. She was advised that foreclosure proceedings had been instituted and she informed defendant Grover McCormick, the Executor of the Porter Thomas Estate, and Dunlap Cannon, III, the closing attorney, of the arrearage in the mortgage loan payments and the imminent foreclosure. After the contract of sale was signed on August 3, defendant Lester turned the matter over to Dunlap Cannon as the closing attorney.

* * *

Boyle Investment Company contends that there was no breach of duty on its part and that its agreement was limited to that stated in the contract which was to hold the earnest money in trust subject to the terms of the contract. It is undisputed that defendant Lester was at all pertinent times acting as the agent, servant and employee of Boyle and thus Boyle is bound by the actions of Lester. The proof is undisputed that Lester knew foreclosure proceedings were in progress at the time she procured the execution of the contract by and between the plaintiffs and the seller. The proof is also undisputed that defendant Lester failed to inform plaintiffs of this fact, thus the plaintiffs were deprived of an opportunity to make an election as to whether to enter into the contract, and even more so, deprived of their opportunity to protect their interest by seeing that the foreclosure was halted. It was only after the foreclosure had occurred that plaintiffs received any notice whatsoever. * * * The trial court erred in dismissing the case as to defendant Lester and correctly held against [Lester's employer] defendant Boyle.

As to defendant Cannon, the closing attorney, the proof is undisputed that he charged plaintiffs an attorney's fee and purported to close the transaction whereby plaintiffs would acquire title to the property in question. Where attorneys charge all parties for services in connection with a real estate transaction, there is nothing unusual or harsh in requiring the exercise of reasonable care toward all concerned. Stinson v. Brand, 738 S.W.2d 186

(Tenn.1987). It is clearly shown that Cannon knew the property was in the midst of foreclosure proceedings, that he never informed the plaintiffs of this fact and that he accepted from the plaintiff more than $11,000 in order to close the transaction and then disbursed the funds to the other defendant Grover McCormick pursuant to the settlement sheet presented at closing.

* * *

It appears to this court that when an attorney handling a real estate transaction takes money from a purchaser to remit to a seller and, at the time of closing, knows that the property is in foreclosure, but fails to advise purchasers of the foreclosure and takes no corrective measures to protect the purchasers' investment, the attorney is guilty of clear and palpable negligence. Cannon did not testify in his own behalf nor did he introduce any proof in this cause to rebut plaintiffs' proof. The trial court erred in dismissing plaintiffs' case as to Cannon.

* * *

The events leading to the dispute occurred in August, 1983. Suit was filed in December, 1983, and the trial was not held until June, 1986, almost three years after suit was filed. The case was then held under advisement for approximately two years, which brought the wheels of justice to at least a slow grind, if not a full stop. Approximately five years from the time suit was filed a final judgment was entered. Plaintiffs' plight has been compounded by the long delay, for which we can find no satisfactory explanation in the record.

We also note that the trial court's intent to return the parties to status quo is not accomplished by the amount of the judgment awarded. Plaintiffs were awarded $11,063.02 for the amount paid for the purchase of the property, but the record reflects that this is the amount paid by the plaintiffs at closing. Plaintiffs had previously paid $500 earnest money which, together with the cash payment made at closing, constitutes a total cash payment of $11,563.02 made by plaintiffs. They are entitled to a recovery of this amount. In summary, the judgment of the trial court in favor of the defendants, Lester, McCormick and Cannon is vacated and the judgment awarding attorney's fees is vacated. The judgment of the trial court is modified to award judgment to the plaintiffs against defendants, Dorothy L. Lester, Boyle Investment Company, Grover McCormick, individually and as the Executor of the Estate of Porter Thomas, and Dunlap Cannon, III, for $11,563.02 plus prejudgment interest of $4,464.17, plus additional costs of $1,139.04 for a total of $17,166.23. Costs of the appeal are assessed against appellees, Boyle, Lester, McCormick and Cannon. The case is remanded to the trial court for such further proceedings as may be necessary.

Case Reflections

1. What should the closing agent have done to prevent this lawsuit?

LAND TITLE COMPANY OF ALASKA, INC. V. ANCHORAGE PRINTING INCORPORATED

783 P.2d 767 (Alaska, 1989)

Apparent authority to sell commercial real estate

Land Title Company of Alaska, Inc. ("Land Title") appeals from a judgment of the superior court holding it liable to Anchorage Printing, Inc. ("Anchorage Printing") as a result of Land Title's negligence in the closing of a land sale transaction. For the reasons set forth below, we remand the case with instructions to vacate the judgment against Land Title.

I.

Anchorage Printing initiated this action to set aside an unauthorized purchase of real estate made by the corporation's secretary-treasurer, Michael Rhodes. Anchorage Printing is a closely-held corporation owned by the three sons of Charles Herbert (Herb) Rhodes, who served as president of the corporation. Charles Gregory (Greg) Rhodes served as vice-president and general manager. Michael Rhodes served as secretary-treasurer and acted as shop foreman. Christopher Rhodes acted as pressman. All three sons were also directors, and each held one-third of the corporation's voting stock.

In late 1985, Herb and Greg Rhodes noted that Michael Rhodes was exhibiting bizarre behavior resulting from his impending divorce. On February 2, 1986, Michael was admitted to Alaska Psychiatric Institute after an episode in which he appeared close to suicide. He was released on February 4, 1986, with the recommendation that he receive inpatient psychiatric treatment, but the Rhodes declined this option.

In March 1986, Thomas O'Connor, a real estate agent with Commercial Investment Brokers, Inc. ("Commercial Investment"), learned that Michael Rhodes was interested in property surrounding Anchorage Printing's shop. O'Connor, acting on behalf of Howard and Fusako Wright, approached Michael concerning the Wright's property. Michael met several times with O'Connor and another agent for Commercial Investment. On March 19, 1986, they entered into an earnest money agreement for the purchase of the Wrights' property. Michael gave the Wrights an Anchorage Printing corporate check for $2,000 as earnest money.

According to the terms of the agreement, the transaction was to close no later than April 1, 1986. Anchorage Printing was to be the purchaser, and Land Title was to act as the closing/escrow agent. Prior to the signing of the closing documents, Land Title's escrow supervisor Phyllis Newcombe contacted O'Connor and asked him who would be signing for Anchorage Printing and if there was a corporate resolution available. O'Connor testified that Newcombe told him that a corporate resolution was necessary and that Newcombe would obtain the resolution. Newcombe testified that she discussed with O'Connor the need for a corporate resolution, but that O'Connor, rather than herself, had agreed to obtain it. The signing of documents took place at the office of Land Title on March 28, 1986. O'Connor attended the signing with the Wrights. The Wrights signed first. Michael Rhodes signed after the Wrights had left. Newcombe testified that when Michael appeared she asked him whether he had a corporate resolution, and he stated that he had none but would obtain one. On April 1, 1986, Newcombe recorded the documents according to the escrow instructions without having received a resolution from Michael Rhodes.

On April 23, 1986, Newcombe spoke with Greg Rhodes, general manager of Anchorage Printing, and asked him for the corporate resolution. Greg responded that he knew nothing of the transaction and that there was no corporate resolution. On May 16, 1986, counsel for Anchorage Printing wrote to Land Title, advising it that Michael had no authority to act for Anchorage Printing in the transaction. The Wrights declined to rescind the sale, and Anchorage Printing brought suit against the Wrights, Commercial Investment, and Land Title.

II.

A trial was held before Superior Court Judge Milton M. Souter sitting without a jury. The court found that Anchorage Printing was not negligent and that Michael Rhodes was not incompetent. The court concluded that Michael Rhodes did not have express, inherent, implied, or apparent authority to buy the property. The court held that real estate agent O'Connor and broker Vern Padgett had a duty to determine if Michael had authority to purchase the property. . . . The superior court set aside the sale and pursuant to Civil Rule 82, held Commercial Investment, Land Title, and the Wrights jointly and severally liable for Anchorage Printing's attorney's fees and costs.

. . . Land Title appeals.

III.

A. The trial court found that Land Title, through Phyllis Newcombe, gratuitously undertook to obtain the corporate resolution authorizing the sale. The court concluded that by negligently failing to obtain the resolution and then allowing the transaction to be closed and the documents recorded Land Title was liable to Anchorage Printing in tort. The trial court specifically found that had Land Title sought to obtain the resolution before the closing the unauthorized acts of Michael Rhodes likely would have been discovered and the transaction cancelled.

* * *

[The] evidence fails to establish that Newcombe undertook any duty to obtain the resolution before she closed the transaction by recording the executed documents. Nor do the facts present any reliance by Commercial Investment on Newcombe's obtaining the documents. O'Connor did not object to the signing of the documents by Michael Rhodes when O'Connor knew that Rhodes had not brought the resolution with him. O'Connor testified that he believed at the time of the closing that a resolution was necessary, but he failed to take any action demonstrating this belief. Nor does the evidence show that O'Connor expected Newcombe to obtain the resolution before the recording of the transaction. The fact that Newcombe inquired about the resolution after the recording of the documents is immaterial.

While O'Connor had a duty as agent of the sellers to verify the authority of Michael Rhodes to purchase the property, we conclude that the evidence presented in the record before us fails to demonstrate that Newcombe promised to assume or actually undertook this duty. We therefore conclude that the superior court's finding of a voluntary undertaking by Land Title is clearly erroneous.

We reverse the judgment of the superior court holding Land Title jointly and severally liable for Anchorage Printing's costs in setting aside the transaction and remand the case for entry of judgment in according with this opinion.

Reversed and remanded for further proceeding in accordance with this opinion.

Case Reflections

1. Suppose Michael Rhodes had agreed to sell the property where Anchorage Printing is located. Would Anchorage Printing be allowed to rescind the transaction?
2. Suppose Michael Rhodes had produced a corporate resolution signed by himself as Secretary/Treasurer of the corporation. Would Anchorage Printing be allowed to rescind the purchase in that case?

PART

3

THE ROLE OF THE REAL ESTATE PROFESSIONAL

CHAPTER

12

AGENCY RELATIONSHIPS

LEARNING OBJECTIVES

After reading this chapter, you should be able to:

1. Understand the relationships between agents, subagents, and principals and how these relationships are formed.
2. Recognize when and why an individual must be licensed by the state to perform certain duties relating to real estate transactions and what constitutes ethical behavior for these individuals.
3. Describe the four basic types of listing contracts commonly used in real estate.
4. Appreciate the negotiation process that occurs between buyers and sellers and the role of the agent in this process.
5. List the major aspects of a properly drawn purchase contract.

KEY TERMS

Fiduciary Relationship
Licensing Laws
Independent Contractor
Reciprocity Agreement
Code of Ethics
Standards of Practice
Procuring Cause
Agency Disclosure
Subagency Optional
Buyer Brokerage
Offer and Acceptance
Equitable Conversion
Marketable Title
Misrepresentation

The previous section of this book described the process of transferring ownership in real property. The complex legal environment in which these transfers take place is made much more complex by the characteristics of the marketplace and the need to negotiate. The essence of a real estate transaction is, of course, the transfer of ownership rights, or some other rights, from one party to another. Because real estate ownership is often facilitated by the use of borrowed money, additional parties may become involved in the transaction. Generally both the seller of a parcel and the prospective buyer will have lenders to deal with. For the buyer, this usually means that yet another party, an appraiser, will need to become involved. This involvement is necessitated by the lender's need to have assurance from a third party that the property will provide adequate collateral for the loan about to be made. These relationships are illustrated in Figure 12.1.

This market environment, when combined with the legal process of title transfer described in Part II of this book, makes even a "normal" real estate transaction too complex for the average participant to attempt without assistance. Thus the use of representatives has become commonplace. There are other, and possibly better, forms for the legal relationships in real estate brokerage found elsewhere in the world. In the United Kingdom, estate agents are generally paid 1–2 percent commissions by sellers to "inventory" property, which is done primarily by displaying listings in the window. In Germany, the *Bundesverband Ring Deutscher Makler,* which is the largest real estate professional association, uses a model in which the purchaser

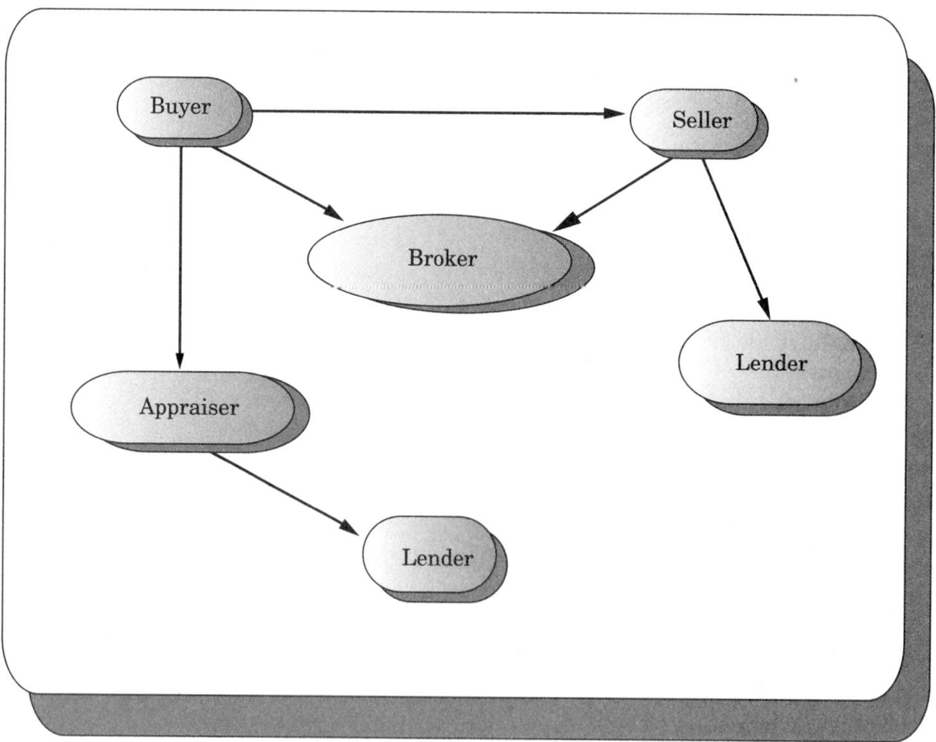

FIGURE 12.1 MARKET RELATIONSHIPS

generally pays the commission. Similarly, Norwegian purchasers often pay commissions. In Greece, agents tend to be dual agents paid by both parties or single agents paid by either the seller or buyer.

KEY POINTS

Our notions of the process of selling or purchasing a house do not always trans late well in other parts of the world. In the Far East, for example, the notion of placing "for sale" signs on property is abhorrent. Prospective buyers must contact a real estate agent, who then makes appointments with sellers for "suitable" buyers. Century 21 Real Estate has opened several offices in Japan and has found that adapting methods that are successful in the U.S. to the Japanese culture can be a difficult process at best.

In many instances, the notion of representing one or both parties is rejected in favor of the role of an intermediary not bound to either party. Such is the case in Italy, where the *agenti immobiliari* is not bound to either party, and, absent an agreement by the seller to pay the entire commission, the seller pays 2 percent and the buyer pays 1 percent under Italian law. The same model is used in Turkey except that each party pays 2 percent.[1]

Velten v. Robertson

In the U.S., the single agency model dominates. This form of relationship has many pros and cons. In the next chapter, we examine many of the emerging problems with the agency model. In this chapter, our goal is to describe the nature of the agency relationship—what an agent is, how relationships are created, the need to license agents, the effect of multiple listing service (MLS) agreements, and dual agency and buyer brokerage issues.

Fiduciary Relationship A relationship based upon trust and confidence between an agent and principal.

AGENTS DEFINED

Pilling v. Eastern and Pacific Enterprises Trust

Anyone who represents the interests of one person in dealings with others is an agent. As we will see, this sweeping definition can sometimes present problems. For example, a written contract is not always necessary to create an agency relationship. Sometimes things that we say or do can *imply* the existence of such a relationship. This is especially important in real estate because the issue of "Whom does the agent represent?" has become a critical one in recent years.

There are usually two essential ingredients in an agency relationship: First there is the creation of a ***fiduciary relationship.*** This relationship is one of trust—the party being represented, called a principal, must trust that the agent will do as instructed and will not cause him any harm. The second ingredient is that of competence. The principal generally hires an agent to represent him because that agent has

[1]This material is based on a summary by Jay Ball of Northeastern University of a book by E. P. Conser, *Real Estate—European Style* (New York: Exposition Press, 1976).

some special skills or knowledge that will help the principal. These two ingredients are obviously related in that the principal must *trust* that the agent actually has the competence to assist in the transaction. The central notion of trust in fiduciary relationships leads to a number of duties owed by an agent to the principal. These duties are described in Table 12.1.

When the agent has the right to act on behalf of the principal, the relationship is sometimes called a *general agency.* When the agent must operate within specific guidelines, and may not obligate the principal, the relationship may be called a *special agent.* Real estate brokers and salespeople, because they must act within the limits of the listing contract, are usually special agents. This distinction, however, does little to protect the agent from any breech of fiduciary duties to the principal.

TABLE 12.1 FIDUCIARY DUTIES OWED A PRINCIPAL

Duty	Definition
Loyalty	The agent must act at all times in the best interest of the principal. The agent may do nothing that may cause harm to the position of the principal.
Obedience	An agent must obey all lawful instructions of the principal.
Disclosure	An agent must reveal all relevant information to the principal that may have a material effect on the purpose of the contract. In the case of purchase contracts, this specifically means any information the agent may have regarding the willingness of the purchaser to accept a counteroffer.
Confidentiality	An agent must keep confidential any information that might weaken the principal's bargaining position. For example, the agent may not reveal or imply to a purchaser that the principal may be willing to accept an offer at less than the asking price.
Accounting	An agent must provide an accurate accounting of all monies that are a part of the transaction. In most instances, the agent is required by state statute to maintain a separate account, which contains only monies belonging to the parties in the transaction, and to avoid commingling the agent's money with that of the parties.
Reasonable Skill and Care	An agent must exercise reasonable skill and care in executing the terms of the contract. The principal and all parties to the contract have the right to expect a reasonable level of skill and a diligent application of that skill.
Diligence	An agent must diligently pursue the interests of the principal and not be negligent in any dealings on behalf of the principal.

REGULATORY ENVIRONMENT

Most participants in real estate transactions, especially those involving single-family homes, are vulnerable to abusive practices. An unscrupulous agent would be in a position to do great harm to a principal. Remember that the principal *trusts* the agent and believes that the agent possesses skills and knowledge that will be used to the advantage of the principal. In an effort to protect the public, all states have enacted some form of ***licensing laws***, which impose a set standards on those acting as real estate brokers. The right to require the attainment of a license flows from the *police power* of a state. Police powers authorize the state to protect the health, safety, and welfare of its citizens. Thus the licensing laws are present to protect all members of the public, not just the principal in an agency relationship. This often creates a problem for agents. As we have seen, agents may do nothing to harm the position of their principals. It is not difficult to imagine how this duty may conflict with their duties, under licensing laws, to protect the public. Take, for example, a situation in which an agent has accepted a listing contract for a single-family residence. After the listing contract has been signed, but before any offers to purchase have been made, it comes to the attention of the agent that a fast food chain has acquired the lot directly across the street with the intention of building an outlet on it. The agent is now in a position of possible conflict of obligations. Her fiduciary duties to the principal prohibit actions that would potentially harm the position of the principal. Certainly it could be argued that making a statement to each purchaser regarding the future fast food restaurant could be construed as harming the principal's bargaining position. To withhold this information, however, may violate the agent's obligations under licensing laws to protect the public. The potential for conflicts of this type seems to be increasing and is described in detail in Chapter 13.

Licensing Laws
State Statutes which define the requirements for licensure, acceptable conduct of licensees, and establish a means of control.

Each state has also established some type of regulatory entity, often called a real estate commission, to oversee and implement the licensing laws. They do this by promulgating a set of rules and regulations that interpret the laws, carry the force of law, and provide specific information on how agents must conduct their affairs.

KEY POINTS

Most states now require some level of education before obtaining a real estate sales license. The level of required prelicensure education is usually measured in terms of classroom hours and varies from zero to a high of 180 in two states. The average is fifty-four hours, or sixty-four if the states that do not require prelicensing education are excluded. A few states require that compulsory education be obtained during the first year of licensure, but this practice seems to be waning.

Licensure Requirements

Although each state has adopted some form of licensing statute for real estate brokers and salespersons, the requirements for obtaining a license differ from state to state. Table 12.2 provides a brief overview of these requirements for each state. There is always a distinction made between *salespersons* and brokers. In a few states, there may be an additional category, such as an *associate broker.* Persons holding a sales license are authorized to work only under the direction of a broker. In this chapter, we simply use the term *agent* when the distinction between broker and salesperson is not important to the discussion. Most states have adopted some form of the model license law developed by the National Association of License Law Officials (NARELLO). The NARELLO model specifies twelve common requirements for licensure:

1. Completion of an application form.
2. Attainment of a minimum age level.
3. Attainment of minimum education, usually specific to real estate sales and brokerage operations.
4. Passing some form of written examination.
5. Having a sponsoring broker (for sales licenses) who agrees to hold the salesperson's license.
6. Payment of certain fees.
7. A photograph of the applicant.
8. The applicant's fingerprints (sometimes required).
9. Payment into a recovery fund or, in some instances, the procurement of a bond in a specified amount.
10. A credit report from an approved credit reporting agency.
11. Satisfaction of minimum residency requirements.
12. Completing minimum experience requirements (for broker's licenses).

TABLE 12.2 EDUCATION AND EXPERIENCE REQUIREMENTS FOR LICENSEES

	Salesperson's		**Broker's**		
	Prelicensing Education	*Continuing Education*	*Experience Required for Broker's License*	*Additional Prelicensing Education*	*Continuing Education*
Alabama	45 hours	12 hours per 2 years	2 years full time	60 hours	12 hours each 2 years
Alaska	20 hours	20 hours/2 years	2 years	15 hours	20 hours/2 years
Arizona	90 hours	24 hours every 2 years	3 years	90 hours	24 hours every 2 years
Arkansas	60 hours	6 hours/year	2 years—may be waived for education	None	6 hours/year
California	45 plus 90 within 18 mos.	45 hours every 4 years	2 years within last 5 years	RE courses	45 hours every 4 years

TABLE 12.2 EDUCATION AND EXPERIENCE REQUIREMENTS FOR LICENSEES *(continued)*

	Salesperson's		**Broker's**		
	Prelicensing Education	*Continuing Education*	*Experience Required for Broker's License*	*Additional Prelicensing Education*	*Continuing Education*
Colorado	72 hours	24 hours	2 years	48 hours	24 hours
Connecticut	30 hours	12 hours within 2 years	2 years	60 hours	12 hours within 2 years
Delaware	93 hours	15 hours per 2 years	5 years and 30 sales	90 hours	15 hours per 2 years
D.C.	45 hours	12 hours/ 2 years	2 years	135 hours	12 hours/ 2 years
Florida	63 hours	14 hours per 2 years	1 year	72 hours	14 hours per 2 years
Georgia	75 hours	6 hours/ year	3 years	60 hours	6 hours every year
Hawaii	40 hours	10 hours./ 2 years	2 years	46 hours	10 hours./ 2 years
Idaho	90 hours	12 hours./ 2 years	2 years	90 hours	12 hours./ 2 years
Illinois	30 hours	12 hours	1 year	60 hours	12 hours
Indiana	54 hours	16 hours	1 year	54 hours	16 hours
Iowa	30 hours	36 hours in 3 years	2 years	60 hours	36 hours in 3 years
Kansas	30 hours	12 hours per 2 years	2 years	24 hours	12 hours per 2 years
Kentucky	96 hours or 6 college credits	6 hours	2 years	96 in RE plus 144 in electives	6 hours
Louisiana	90 hours	8 hours	2 years	150 hours	8 hours
Maine	39 hours	12 hours	2 years	45 hours	12 hours
Maryland	45 hours	12 hours per 2 years	3 years	135 hours	12 hours per 2 years
Massachusetts	24 hours	None	1 year	30 hours	None
Michigan	40 hours	6 hours per year	3 years	90 hours	6 hours per year
Minnesota	90 hours	15 hours every year	2 years	None	15 hours every year
Mississippi	90 hours or 2 GRI credits	8 hours every 2 years	1 year	120 hours	8 hours every 2 years

TABLE 12.2 EDUCATION AND EXPERIENCE REQUIREMENTS FOR LICENSEES *(continued)*

	Salesperson's		**Broker's**		
	Prelicensing Education	*Continuing Education*	*Experience Required for Broker's License*	*Additional Prelicensing Education*	*Continuing Education*
Missouri	60 hours	12 hours	1 year	48 hours	12 hours
Montana	60 hours	15 hours	2 years	60 hours	15 hours
Nebraska	60 hours	12 hours/2 years	None	6 courses	12 hours/2 years
Nevada	90 hours or 6 college credits	30 hours first 2-year period, 15 hours per subsequent 2-year period	8 years	58 semester hours	30 hours first 2-year period, 15 hours subsequent 2-year period
New Hampshire	None	3 hours	1 year	None	3 hours
New Jersey	75 hours	None	2 years	90 hours	None
New Mexico	60 hours	30 hours every 3 years	2 years	150 hours	30 hours every 3 years
New York	45 hours	45 hours	Yes	90 hours	45 hours/4 years
North Carolina	30 hours	None	2 years	90 hours	None
North Dakota	30 hours	24 hours every 3 years	2 years	60 hours	24 hours per 3 years
Ohio	120 hours	30 hours every 3 years	2 years	120 hours	30 hours every 3 years
Oklahoma	45 hours	21 hours	2 years	75 hours	21 hours
Oregon	90 hours	24 hours every 2 years for first renewal, 12 hours every 2 years thereafter	3 years	60 hours	24 hours every 2 years
Pennsylvania	60 hours	14 hours	3 years	240 hours	14 hours
Rhode Island	None	None	None	90 hours or 1 year experience	None
South Carolina	30 hours	30 hours within first year of licensure	See education	90 hours and 3 years experience or 5 years experience	None

TABLE 12.2 EDUCATION AND EXPERIENCE REQUIREMENTS FOR LICENSEES (*continued*)

	Salesperson's		Broker's		
	Prelicensing Education	*Continuing Education*	*Experience Required for Broker's License*	*Additional Prelicensing Education*	*Continuing Education*
South Dakota	40 hours	24 hours per 2 years	2 years	60 hours	24 hours per 2 years
Tennessee	60 hours	16 hours per 2 years	3 years	60 hours	None
Texas	180 hours	15 hours./ 2 years	2 years	630 hours	15 hours/ 2 years
Utah	90 hours	12 hours	3 years	120 hours	12 hours
Vermont	None	4 hours	1 year and 6 closed transactions	8 hours	4 hours
Virginia	60 hours	8 hours/ 2 years	3 years	180 hours	8 hours/ 2 years
Washington	30 hours	30 hours/ 2 years	2 years	90 hours	30 hours/ 2 years
West Virginia	90 hours	7 hours	2 years	90 hours	7 hours
Wisconsin	72 hours	12 hours	None	36 hours or 20 semester hours	12 hours
Wyoming	30 hours	45 hours every 3 years	2 years	30 hours	45 hours per 3 years

Source: National Association of Real Estate License Law Officials, *Digest of Real Estate License Laws 1993*. Subject to change.

Independent Contractor Status

As mentioned earlier, persons holding a real estate salesperson's license are authorized to work only under the direct supervision of a sponsoring broker. It is common practice for state licensing commissions to issue sales licenses only directly to the sponsoring broker. The broker retains liability for actions, certainly any fraudulent actions, taken by a salesperson under his direction.[2] Although this arrangement may sound much like an employer–employee situation, this is often not the case.

In many instances, brokers prefer to have all salespersons operate as ***independent contractors*** rather than employees. Although this arrangement limits the degree of control that the broker may exercise over the activities of salespersons, it provides a number of benefits for the broker. The broker avoids the necessity of withholding federal and state income taxes, making payments into state unemployment systems, providing a retirement pension system, providing medical insurance as well

Independent Contractor An individual working under the direction of another who exercises a limited degree of control.

[2] In other words, the broker serves as the agent, and salespersons act in the role of subagents.

as other expenses. This allows a broker to maintain working relationships with a larger number of salespersons.

The distinction between employees and independent contractors is not always clear-cut. In *Black v. Department of Labor and Industries of the State of Washington* (854 P.2d 46, 1993), the Court of Appeals upheld a finding that real estate brokerage firms must pay industrial insurance premiums for real estate agents even though they are independent contractors. Under Washington law, an independent contractor is a "worker" if "the essence of [the contract] is his or her personal labor for an employer." The court applied three factors to determine if the essence of the contract is personal labor: the necessity of the independent contractor to provide machinery or equipment, an inability to perform the contract without assistance, and the employment by the independent contractor of others to do part or all of the contracted work. Finding that real estate agents fail to meet any of these standards, the brokerage firm was found liable for past due insurance premiums.

Reciprocity Agreements

Reciprocity Agreement Agreements between regulatory agencies of states to recognize the licenses issued by other states.

A common problem for real estate agents who live near a state border is the need to obtain a license in more than one state. Generally the agent must be licensed in the state in which her place of business is located. The ability to work in neighboring states is eased by the existence of ***reciprocity agreements*** between the regulatory agencies of the states. In essence, these agreements recognize the license of neighboring state(s) either in full or in part. Figure 12.2 contains an example reciprocity agreement between neighboring states.

A nonresident broker regularly engaged in the real estate business as a vocation and who maintains a definite place of business and is licensed in some other state, which offers the same privileges to the licensed brokers of this state, may not be required to maintain a place of business within this state. The commission shall recognize the license issued to a real estate broker by another state as satisfactorily qualifying him/her for license as a broker; provided, that the nonresident broker has qualified for license in his/her own state and also that the other state permits licenses to be issued to licensed brokers in this state. Every nonresident applicant shall file an irrevocable consent that suits and actions may be commenced against such applicant in the proper court of any county of the state in which a claim for relief may arise, in which the plaintiff may reside, by the service of any process or pleading authorized by the laws of this state, on any member of the commission, said consent stipulating and agreeing that such service of such process or pleading shall be taken and held in all courts to be as valid and binding as if due service had been made upon said applicant in this state. The consent shall be duly acknowledged. Any service of process or pleading shall be by duplicate copies, one of which shall be filed in the office of the commission and the other immediately forwarded by registered mail to the last known main office of the applicant to whom said process or pleading is directed, and no default in any such proceedings or action shall be taken except upon affidavit or certificate of the commission, that a copy of said process or pleading was mailed to the defendant as herein required, and no judgment by default shall be taken in any such action or proceeding until after thirty days from the date of mailing of such process or pleading to the nonresident defendant.

FIGURE 12.2 EXAMPLE RECIPROCITY AGREEMENT

Exceptions to Licensing Requirements

Any person who attempts to sell, list for sale, negotiate, or in any fashion hold himself out to be a broker or salesperson is covered by licensing laws. A person, partnership, association, or corporation, or any regular employees thereof, may perform acts that would normally require a license so long as the acts pertain only to property owned (or leased) by them. This usually includes bank employees and public officials performing their regular duties.

Attorneys at law are also generally exempt from license requirements when the actions relate directly to a proceeding in which the attorney is participating; for example, trust administration, bankruptcy proceedings, or receiverships. Thus any person serving as a receiver, trustee, executor, or guardian is often exempt from the need to carry a license.

Revocation of Licenses

Each state has established a set of actions that can lead to the suspension or revocation of real estate licenses. Although the specific acts vary, they generally include many of the following items:

Alley v. Nevada Real Estate Division

1. Making a material false statement in the application for licensure.
2. Making a substantial and willful misrepresentation in a transaction that injures any party.
3. Making a false promise in attempting to influence, persuade, or induce a party to commit an action that injures the party.
4. Acting as a dual agent without the knowledge and consent of both parties.
5. Mishandling funds belonging to others (including failure to account for or remit, commingling with the agent's own funds, failing to use an account in an appropriate institution).
6. Conviction for any felony or a misdemeanor involving theft, forgery, embezzlement, obtaining money under false pretenses, bribery, larceny, extortion, conspiracy to defraud, or similar offense.
7. Claiming or taking a secret or undisclosed commission or other compensation.
8. Failing to produce any material requested by the real estate commission during an investigation by the commission.
9. Offering property for sale or lease without authorization from the owner or an agent of the owner.
10. Discriminating based on race, color, religion, or national origin.
11. Failure to provide a copy of any document pertaining to a transaction to any person whose signature appears on the document.
12. Paying a fee or commission to any person who is not licensed or authorized to receive such compensation.
13. Failing to disclose an interest, direct or indirect (including options), in any property listed through the office of the licensee.
14. Failure to provide a fixed expiration date on a written listing contract and to provide the principal with a copy of the contract.

15. Failure to deliver in a timely fashion to the seller a complete, detailed closing statement.
16. Accepting a commission split as a real estate salesperson from any person not licensed as a real estate broker (or a person who falls into one of the licensing exceptions).
17. Allowing, as a real estate broker, any person to act as a salesperson who is not properly licensed as such.
18. Failure to reduce an offer to purchase to writing and to deliver all such offers to the seller in a timely fashion.
19. Any other conduct that constitutes dishonesty or fraudulent conduct, whether relating to licensed activities or not.

Code of Ethics

Code of Ethics A statement of professional behavior to which all members of the National Association of REALTORS adhere.

Real estate agents who belong to the National Association of Realtors(r) (NAR) subscribe to a ***Code of Ethics*** that sets standards for professional practice. Many courts and licensing commissions have viewed the Code of Ethics as having the force of law for those persons who hold themselves out to be Realtors®. Thus, although the code is not a law per se, members should treat it as such in dealing with their clients or customers. In addition to the Code of Ethics, the NAR also publishes ***Standards of Practice,*** which are not a part of the Code itself,but are "interpretations" of the Code describing the professional conduct required in specific situations. The Code of Ethics, including the "numbered cases" found in interpretations of the Code, and the Standards of Practice provide a reasonably comprehensive set of guidelines for conduct.

KEY POINTS

During their November 1992 national meeting, the National Association of Realtors® took a close look at their Code of Ethics. A total of fifty-four changes were made to the existing Code of Ethics and its accompanying Standards of Practicc. Although some of the changes were done to improve the wording, many were substantive and reflect the current state of change prevalent in the industry. Many of the changes address issues such as buyer's brokerage, arbitration of disputes, and other evolving topics that may change the role of real estate agents in many fundamental ways during the rest of this decade. Appendix 12.2 contains the current Code of Ethics and Standards of Practice, which took effect in January 1993.

Standards of Practice Specific examples of acceptable conduct under the REALTOR's Code of Ethics.

CREATING AGENCY RELATIONSHIPS

The relationships between parties to a real estate transaction can sometimes become confusing. It is not always clear where legal obligations exist. A widely quoted 1983 Federal Trade Commission study found that 72 percent of buyers surveyed thought that they were represented by the selling agent. Even when only one agent (the listing agent) was involved in a sale, 31 percent of the buyers thought that they were represented by that agent. In co-operative sales, 82 percent of the sellers thought that the selling agent (who is their subagent) represented the buyer.[3] Many agents also become confused as to who their principal is. Obviously it is difficult to protect the interests of your principal if you do not know who it is. Figure 12.3 provides a description of the nature of these relationships in a "typical" real estate transaction.

The most common way for an agency relationship to be formed is for a written *listing agreement* to be created between a seller (often called a *vendor*) and an agent. Most state license statutes, or the rules and regulations implementing them, require that all listing agreements be in writing. The agreement should identify the property as well as terms and conditions under which the property may be sold (including the price, commission to be paid, signatures of all parties involved, and a definite expiration date). The reason for requiring such written agreements is to avoid questions concerning when an agency relationship was formed and what parties are involved.

Rohauer v. Little

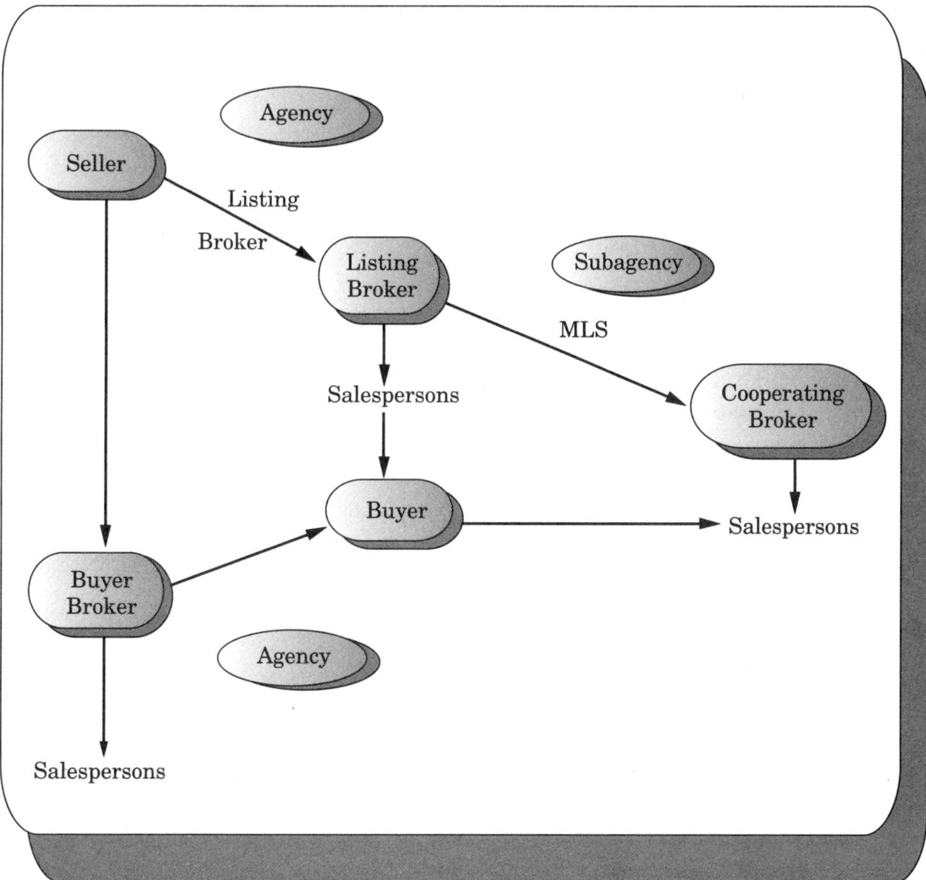

FIGURE 12.3 RELATIONSHIPS IN A REAL ESTATE TRANSACTION

[3] Federal Trade Commission, *The Residential Real Estate Brokerage Industry* (Washington, D.C.:

Procuring Cause

The object of the listing contract is to obtain a buyer who is *ready, willing, and able* to purchase the property at a price, and on terms, acceptable to the seller. When this has been accomplished, the agreed-upon commission or fee has been earned.[4] In order for an agent to make a valid claim for compensation, however, he must be able to demonstrate that he was the primary and ***procuring cause*** of the sale. There are numerous situations in which this can be in dispute. For example:

Procuring Cause The actions necessary to cause a transaction to take place.

When a property has been shown by more than one agent to the same buyer.

When a property is first shown as an "open house" and later by a different agent.

When the agent provides the owner with the name of a potential buyer.

When a buyer learns of a listing through the efforts of an agent (e.g., sees the agent's signs or advertisements) but contacts the seller directly.

The rules that apply in instances involving disputes between the seller and agent revolve around the ability of the agent to demonstrate that the buyer learned of the listing through his efforts. When several agents are involved, the successful agent must demonstrate that the buyer was unwilling to continue to work with the original agent, negotiations were broken off, or some sort of disagreement developed. In general, however, the agent must demonstrate that his efforts predominated the negotiation process. In other words, it is not sufficient simply to present an offer that was primarily developed by another agent or to make only a few minor changes.

> The concept of procuring cause can extend even beyond the initial transaction. In *Coldwell Banker First Realty, Inc. v. Kane* (491 N.W.2d 716, 1992), a broker was awarded a sales commission for a sale of property even though an intervening sale had taken place. Coldwell Banker had found a tenant for a building under a contract which called for a commission to be paid not only for finding a tenant, but for any eventual sale to the tenant. The building was eventually sold to a third party who then sold the building to the tenants. Although there was never a contract between the third party and Coldwell Banker, the court held that Coldwell Banker was still the procuring cause of the sale and was thus owed a sales commission by the original owner.

Types of Listing Contracts

Swallows v. Laney

Although there are numerous variations, there are just four basic types of listing contracts in common use today. Each form offers certain benefits and problems for the parties. Often the choice is a matter of market conditions (i.e., does a "seller's market" or "buyer's market" exist?). The most appropriate choice may also depend on the role the seller wishes to play in the process, the existence of any current offers to purchase, or other similar factors. Three of these listing forms, the open, ex-

---

[4]Although the commission or fee is earned when a meeting of the minds between seller and buyer has taken place, the listing agreement generally stipulates that the commission or fee will be paid at closing. This is a convenience for the seller because the seller will not realize any proceeds until closing takes place and also insures that nothing will go wrong with the arrangement. This is often called a "no deal, no commission" clause.

clusive agency, and exclusive right to sell, are described here. The fourth common listing agreement, the *multiple listing service* agreement, is described later in the chapter.

Open Listing

There is no reason, absent an agreement between the seller and agent, that a seller may not sign listing agreements with more than one agent. Thus in the absence of a written listing agreement, most courts will find that an open listing situation exists. Under this form of listing arrangement, the first agent to procure a buyer, unless the seller produces a buyer first, will earn the commission. Although open listings are common in commercial property transactions, they are not generally used in the sale of single-family homes.

Exclusive Agency Listing

Most agents are not willing to extend the time, money, and effort necessary to sell a property without some reasonable assurance that their efforts will be rewarded. Thus most agents prefer to use some form of an exclusive listing, giving them sole authority to produce a buyer. Although this does not necessarily avoid all procuring cause arguments, owing to the use of subagency arrangements, it does provide the agent with an assurance that a commission will be earned if she is able to locate a buyer. This form of listing contract reserves the right to sell by the owner. In other words, no other agent may claim a commission,[5] but the owner may sell the property and not owe a commission, provided that the agent was not the procuring cause of the transaction.

Exclusive Right to Sell Listing

Given the opportunity, virtually any agent will prefer to obtain this type of listing. This is simply because any sale, even by the owner of the property, will cause a commission to be earned. Thus disputes over the issue of procuring cause between owner and agent are avoided. Of course, the seller may wish not to use this form of listing if a potential buyer is known before creating the listing agreement. Figure 12.4 is an example of an exclusive right to sell contract.

Verbal Contracts

It is not always necessary for a written agreement to exist for an agency relationship to be created. Section 26 of the *Second Restatement of Agency Law* prepared by the American Law Institute states that

> . . . the authority to do an act can be created by written or spoken words or other conduct of the principal which, reasonably interpreted, causes the agent to believe that the principal desires him to so act on the principal's account.

---

[5]Should the owner sign another listing contract while an exclusive listing is in effect and the second agent procures a buyer, a commission will be owed to both agents.

EXCLUSIVE LISTING CONTRACT

This contract involves the property at (address) ______

______ City ______ State ______

(legal) ______

"I" means seller: ______

"YOU" means real estate broker: ______

LISTING

1. As seller, I give you the exclusive right to sell the property for the price of $ ______ on these terms: (Cash unless otherwide noted) ______
2. Personal property included ______
3. REAL property excluded ______
4. This contract starts ______, 19______ and ends 11:59 p.m. on ______, 19______. In exchange, the broker agrees to list the property for sale.
5. Sign permitted on property - Yes______ No______ Lock Box - Yes______ No______
6. The seller has a contract with NSP, REA, fuel tank rental or water softener contract - Yes______ No______ Terms: ______

SELLER'S DUTIES

As seller I will:

(a) cooperate with broker in selling the property;
(b) promptly tell broker about all inquiries received about the property;
(c) Provide and pay for any inspections and reports if required by city or state;
(e) provide the buyer an updated abstract of title, owner's duplicate certificate of title and registered property abstract or title insurance to the property as required by the earnest money agreement;
(f) warrant all appliances, heating, air conditioning, wiring, and plumbing located on said premises will be in proper working order at date of closing.

I have the full and legal right to sell the property and will sign all closing documents (including a warranty deed or contract for warranty deed) necessary to transfer to the buyer full and unquestioned ownership of the property, or as required by the earnest money agreement.

NOTICE

THE COMMISSION RATE FOR THE SALE, LEASE, RENTAL OR MANAGEMENT OF REAL PROPERTY SHALL BE DETERMINED BETWEEN EACH INDIVIDUAL REAL ESTATE BROKER AND ITS CLIENT.

BROKER'S COMMISSION

As seller, I will pay the broker a commission of ______ % of the selling price or a minimum of ______ upon the happening of any of the following events:

(a) at the closing of the sale, if I sell or agree to sell the property before this contract ends, even if another broker or I sell the property without your assistance;
(b) if you present a buyer who is willing and able to buy the property at the price and terms required in the contract, but I refuse to sell;
(c) if within______ days after the end of this contract I sell or agree to sell the property to anyone who:
    (1) during this contract made inquiry of me about the property and I did not tell you about the inquiry;
    (2) during this contract made an affirmative showing of interest in the property or was physically shown the property by you;
    (3) if the real estate agent has provided me with a prospect list within 72 hours after the end of this contract, and I sold to some person on that list.

I understand that I do not have to pay your commission if I sign another valid listing contract after the expiration of this contract, under which I am obligated to pay a commission to another licensed real estate broker.

NOTICES ABOUT MY REAL ESTATE

As of this date, I have not received notice from any municipality, government agency, or homeowners association about the property that I have not told you about, and I agree to promptly tell you of any notices of the type that I receive:

General real estate taxes and any installments of special assessments shall be paid as follows: ______

FORFEITURE OF EARNEST MONEY

If a buyer of the property defaults and as a result forfeits the earnest money, you will get______% and I will get______% of the earnest money.

I do______ do not______ authorize you to allow subagents. I do______ do not______ authorize you to allow agents representing a buyer to market my property and to share your commission with an agent's broker unless otherwise noted as an addendum to this agreement. The above information will be submitted to the Multiple Listing Service.

Acceptance Date: ______, 19______
Broker Firm ______
By (Agent) ______
Agent Phone # ______ Home
______ Office

Owner ______
Owner ______
Owner's Address ______
City ______
Phone # ______ Home ______ Office

FIGURE 12.4 EXCLUSIVE LISTING CONTRACT

Thus the act of walking into a real estate agency and requesting help in locating a suitable house may be sufficient to create an agency relationship. When the property that the buyer decides to purchase is covered by a listing agreement with the same or co-operating broker, the agent finds himself trying to represent both the buyer and the seller. Some courts have adopted what might be called a "first contact" rule, by which the broker becomes the agent of the party who first employs him [*Wise v. Dawson,* 353 A.2d 207 (Del. Super. Ct. 1975) and *Menzel v. Morse,* 362 N.W. 2d465 (Iowa 1985)].

Agency Disclosure Rules

Because of the potential conflict between "first contact" rules and listing agreements, participants in real estate transactions are often confused by the lack of ***agency disclosure***. Buyers often believe that the salesperson who is showing them properties, assisting in the negotiation process, holding earnest money deposits, helping to find a suitable lender, arranging for the transfer of title, and so forth is, in fact, working for them. This is certainly a reasonable conclusion to draw and is one that many agents reach as well. This is especially true when the property the buyers select is one listed by a different firm. The subagency relationships shown in Figure 12.3 are generally created either through a series of agreements between agents or, more likely, through the use of a *multiple listing service.*

Agency Disclosure A statement made to interested parties which indicates the existence of an agency relationship.

Many states have now adopted some form of mandatory disclosure of agency that must be presented, in writing, to all parties in a transaction. Although the specific rules vary from state to state, as seen in Table 12.3, generally the disclosure must be made with or before the first written document is prepared. In most instances, this document is an offer to purchase made by the potential buyers. Figure 12.5 contains an example disclosure statement.

Unfortunately, because the buyers may have relied on the agent in selecting the property and deciding on the offer amount, this may amount to closing the barn door after the horse has left. Thus it is still incumbent upon agents to avoid possible conflict-of-interest situations by disclosing as soon as reasonably possible the existence of an agency relationship with the seller.

Given the high degree of confusion that has existed in the marketplace concerning whom agents represent, it is not surprising that one study indicates that 50 percent of all lawsuits filed against real estate agents involve some aspect of agency disclosure.[6] A series of lawsuits filed in Minnesota (discussed in Chapter 19) are based in part on claims of inadequate agency disclosure. The court has been asked to certify one of these cases as a class action suit, and, because some of the claims are being brought under the RICO (Racketeer, Influence and Corrupt Organization) Act, which permits treble damages, one estimate of potential damages has been set at more than $240 million.

[6]Wolf, Guy P., and Marianne M. Jennings, "Seller/Broker Liability in Multiple Listing Service Real Estate Sales: A Case for Uniform Disclosure." *Real Estate Law Journal,* Summer 1991, pp. 22–53.

TABLE 12.3 STATE AGENCY DISCLOSURE RULES

State	Rule
AL	Special language required in sales contract.
AK	Initial disclosure; confirmation in sales contract.
AZ	Selling agent makes disclosure to buyer.
CA	Mandatory disclosure form at initial stage plus confirmation in contract.
CO	Initial disclosure plus confirmation in sales contract.
CT	Initial disclosure plus confirmation in sales contract.
DE	Initial disclosure plus confirmation.
DC	Buyer to sign notice of agency status.
FL	Written disclosure prior to sales contract.
GA	Specific language before or at time of sales contract.
HI	Initial disclosure plus confirmation in sales contract.
ID	Required agency disclosure brochure; special confirmation in contract.
IL	Written disclosure to unrepresented party; timing at broker's discretion.
IN	Written disclosure that selling agent represents seller if not buyer's agent.
IA	Initial disclosure plus confirmation in sales contract.
KS	Initial disclosure plus confirmation in sales contract.
LA	Make clear for which party licensee acts.
ME	Written disclosure to party not represented.
MD	Written disclosure that represent seller (unless written buyer agency agreement).
MA	Written notice to buyer using approved language.
MI	Initial disclosure plus written contract; buyer's agency must be written.
MN	Written disclosure in contract.
MS	Written disclosure in contract.
MO	Written disclosure; presumed to be seller's agent unless written agreement.
MT	Written disclosure no later than offer.
NE	Written disclosure that represent seller unless buyer agency agreement.
NV	Initial disclosure plus confirmation in sales contract.
NY	Make clear for which party broker acts.
ND	Written disclosure; presumed to be agent of seller.
OH	Mandatory disclosure form; presumed to be agent of seller.
OK	Initial disclosure plus confirmation in sales contract.
PA	Initial disclosure that broker is agent of seller or agent of buyer.
RI	Mandatory disclosure form to be signed by buyer and seller, with agents initialing their agency status.
SC	Mandatory disclosure form.
SD	Written disclosure prior to signing sales contract.
TN	Initial disclosure as soon as practicable; written disclosure prior to preparation of offer.
TX	Written disclosure on initial contract using agency disclosure form.
UT	Initial disclosure with written disclosure in sales contract.
VT	Disclose to buyer that agent represents seller, unless a buyer agency agreement.
VA	Written disclosure at earliest practical time.
WA	Initial disclosure plus confirmation in sales contract.
WV	Written agency disclosure.
WI	Disclosure at time buyer's or seller's needs and objectives are discussed; need seller authorization to permit subagency.
WY	Initial disclosure as soon as practicable with written confirmation in sales contract.

Source: Based on a similar table by John Reilly, which appeared in the Summer 1992 (Vol II, No. 2, p. 3) issue of *Advise & Counsel,* the official publication of the National Association of Counselors.

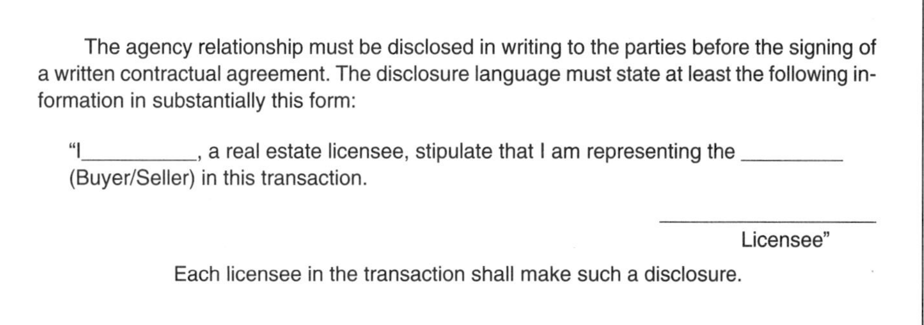

The agency relationship must be disclosed in writing to the parties before the signing of a written contractual agreement. The disclosure language must state at least the following information in substantially this form:

"I__________, a real estate licensee, stipulate that I am representing the _________ (Buyer/Seller) in this transaction.

Licensee"

Each licensee in the transaction shall make such a disclosure.

FIGURE 12.5 EXAMPLE AGENCY DISCLOSURE STATEMENT

Multiple Listing Service Agreements

Most areas of the U.S. now use some form of a multiple listing service (MLS). These services have vastly improved the provision of services to all parties in real estate transactions. They provide a central registry of information on properties listed for sale when seeking a suitable property for a potential buyer. They also allow agents to assure the widest possible exposure for properties listed for sale. Buyers know that agents have access to far more properties than the specific firm might have listed, and sellers know that they are employing not just a single agent or firm but all members of the MLS. In short, it is a service too good to give up.

KEY POINTS

A Federal Trade Commission study conducted in 1983 found that 92 percent o all sellers who used a real estate broker had their properties listed on a multiple listing service. Since real estate brokers are employed by about 81 percent of all sellers of single-family homes, it is clear that the use of a MLS is extremely important for effective sales of homes. Would the inability to join a local MLS result in a real estate agent being placed at an unfair competitive disadvantage in the marketplace? This issue is discussed in Chapter 13.

Virtually all MLS systems except in California[7] use some form of subagency agreement as a part of the listing process. Basically an agent listing a property for sale in the MLS retains the exclusive agency, or exclusive right to sell, characteristics but agrees to a predetermined commission split with any agent who sells the property. In other words, all agents in the system *automatically* become subagents of the seller.[8] An agent may believe, based on his desire to help a buyer find a suitable property, that

[7]The situation in California changed when antitrust issues, based on the refusal to allow a part-time broker to participate in a MLS, were introduced. This issue is described in more detail in Chapter 13.

[8]This is now in the process of changing, however. The *Report of the Presidential Advisory Group on Agency* recommended abolishing the use of mandatory subagency MLS contracts. More information on this report and its recommendations may be found in Chapter 19.

Subagency Optional An offer made by one broker to another to accept or reject a subagency relationship

Buyer Brokerage An agency relationship which is created between a potential property buyer and a broker

the buyer is, or should be, his principal. Thus the agent may offer advice on such things as offering price and terms of sale. The seller, who has in effect hired the agent as a result of the MLS agreement, may not look favorably on an agent who suggests that a buyer offer less than the seller desires.

In some areas, primarily in California, sponsoring MLS organizations have developed "**subagency optional**" forms of the basic MLS agreement. In effect, these agreements allow an agent to choose whether or not he wishes to function as a subagent of the seller or as an agent for the buyer. This latter form of agency is now becoming popular as "**buyer brokerage**" services.

BUYER BROKERAGE

It should be apparent at this point that the typical buyer in a real estate transaction is generally the only unrepresented party. The seller often has an entire set of agents and subagents representing her interests as a result of MLS agreements. Lenders use appraisers and other professionals to safeguard their interests. Only the buyer comes to the table without representation. As was noted previously, licensing statutes are designed to protect the public and, combined with the trends now seen in the courts to insure consumer protection, provide a reasonable set of safeguards for buyers.

For some real estate agents and buyers, this is not enough. They feel the need to represent or be represented directly in the negotiation process. The concept of *buyer brokerage* was created to fill this gap in the provision of brokerage services. In essence, the agent creates a contractual obligation with the buyer (who becomes the principal for this agent) to provide services in locating, negotiating, and assisting with the financing of a suitable property.[9]

All of the fiduciary responsibilities owed by an agent to her principal apply to this relationship. Because the concept of buyer brokerage is relatively new, at least in the area of residential sales, it is important for the agent to disclose her agency relationship to all parties as soon as practical. These disclosures should be made to other agents, who are likely to make statements, thinking that the agent is a subagent of the seller, that could violate their own fiduciary obligations.

DUAL AGENCY

An agent who represents both parties in a transaction is known as a *dual agent* and owes fiduciary obligations to both. Because the seller and buyer are generally in an adversarial position, it is difficult for an agent to serve as a true dual agent. Although dual agency situations are not prohibited, they must be disclosed to both parties. An undisclosed dual agency, even if unintentional, will result in, at a minimum, a lost commission for the agent and could easily result in a damage suit.

[9]The buyer brokerage concept is explored in depth in Chapter 15.

Often an agent creates a dual agency situation inadvertently by attempting to represent the best interests of both parties. This seemingly laudable goal may in fact be a violation of the agent's fiduciary duties to his principal. The agent may be attempting to serve as a *middleman,* or a person who simply brings two parties with mutual interests together. Unfortunately, in most instances, the "middleman exception" does not apply to real estate agents. This is because these agents have been retained to provide not only factual information (which could fall within the middleman role), but also assistance, advice, and counsel. As discussed in Chapter 13, the dual agency issue is a difficult one for real estate agents to deal with.

NEGOTIATION PROCESS

At the heart of most real estate transactions is a negotiation process between the purchaser (or, in general terms, the *client*) and the seller. It could be said that the primary role of the real estate agent is to assist in this negotiation process in a fashion that provides the best results for the principal without harming the rights of the purchaser. Given the regulatory environment described earlier in this chapter and the increasing liability exposure of real estate agents (as described in Chapter 13), this is often a difficult proposition.

From the agent's point of view, the negotiation process can be considered successful when a purchaser has made an offer that the seller accepts. If this ***offer and acceptance*** is done in a fashion that is not inherently unfair to either party,[10] then a binding agreement between the parties has been formulated.

Offer and Acceptance Initial communication by the offeror in contract formation process that, if accepted by the offeree, results in the creation of a binding contract

Conditions for Acceptance

When an offer has been made by one party to another, the accepting party may not make any changes to the offer. If the seller makes any changes at all, even minor changes, to the purchase offer, then the offer has not been accepted. Rather the seller has in effect rejected the offer and made a *counteroffer* to the purchaser. This counteroffer must then be accepted by the purchaser. This process of offer and counteroffer often proceeds through several rounds before a final agreement on all points.[11]

As a general rule, it is not necessary to redraft the entire contract each time a minor change has been made. The initials of all parties to the contract near the change signify an offer and acceptance of the change. Most licensing regulations, however, require that when the changes are "material or extensive," a clean copy of the document should be prepared.

Merely signing the offer does not complete the acceptance process. The acceptance must be communicated to the purchaser. Although this is not usually a

[10]The consent of the parties must be real, and the terms of the contract must reflect the true intention of the parties. These conditions are often referred to as "reality of assent."

[11]Some commentators refer to this as the "mirror-image" rule of contract law. In other words, the acceptance must mirror the offer in all respects.

problem, in a situation in which time is of the essence, as it is with an offer to purchase, delivery of the acceptance can become critical. To be safe, the agent should personally deliver the accepted offer to the purchaser as quickly as possible. If the purchaser has a representative, such as a buyer's broker, then delivery to the agent will generally constitute acceptance by the purchaser. Remember, however, that most agents are actually subagents of the seller, not agents of the buyer, and delivery to the agent with whom the purchaser has been working may not constitute acceptance.

PURCHASE CONTRACTS

The most important item in a real estate transaction is a properly drawn and executed purchase contract. All of the efforts to create agency relationships, to define the rights and obligations of the principal and agent, and so forth are predicated on completing the transaction. The object of the relationship is to find a suitable buyer and consummate a transaction. No commission will be earned until this object is achieved. Thus it is important to take a detailed look at the parts of a purchase contract and the issues involved.

Statute of Frauds

Although it would be nice to be able to do business based on just a handshake, the absence of a written agreement leaves too much room for unscrupulous activity. Thus the *Statute of Frauds* became law in England in 1677. As its name implies, the Statute was intended to prevent frauds in many types of dealings. Specific among these are the " . . . sale of lands, tenements, or hereditament, or any interest concerning them. . . . " Thus all contracts dealing with real estate must be in writing if they are to be enforceable.[12]

Contract Provisions

A contract to purchase real property must contain numerous provisions. These are listed with a brief note about the significance and importance of each. Figure 12.6 is a sample purchase contract.

Date

Purchase contracts contain an offer to purchase a specific property at a stated price. The offer, however, should not be allowed to stand open for an extended period of time. To do so would allow the seller to use the offer as a negotiating tool to produce better offers from other prospective buyers. Thus this contract, similar to many others in real estate, is usually a *time is of the essence* contract. The offer will

[12]To avoid problems with a strict interpretation of the statute, courts have developed the concept of "part performance" of an oral contract. Although the specifics vary, if the purchaser makes improvements on the property, takes possession of the property, and pays a portion of the purchase price, the contract may be enforceable.

REALTOR®

From the Office of:

STANDARD FORM PURCHASE AND SALE AGREEMENT

Member Greater Boston Real Estate Board

This ______________ day of ______________ 19 ____

1. PARTIES *(fill in)*

hereinafter called the SELLER, agrees to SELL and

hereinafter called the BUYER or PURCHASER, agrees to BUY, upon the terms hereinafter set forth, the following described premises:

2. DESCRIPTION *(fill in and include title reference)*

3. BUILDINGS, STRUCTURES, IMPROVEMENTS, FIXTURES *(fill in or delete)*

Included in the sale as a part of said premises are the buildings, structures, and improvements now thereon, and the fixtures belonging to the SELLER and used in connection therewith including, if any, all venetian blinds, window shades, screens, screen doors, storm windows and doors, awnings, shutters, furnaces, heaters, heating equipment, stoves, ranges, oil and gas burners and fixtures appurtenant thereto, hot water heaters, plumbing and bathroom fixtures, electric and other lighting fixtures, mantels, outside television antennas, fences, gates, trees, shrubs, plants, and, if built in, air conditioning equipment, ventilators, garbage disposers, dishwashers, washing machines and driers; and
but excluding

4. TITLE DEED *(fill in)*
**Include here by specific reference any restrictions, easements, rights and obligations in party walls not included in (b), leases, municipal and other liens, other encumbrances, and make provision to protect SELLER against BUYER'S breach of SELLER'S covenants in leases, where necessary.*

Said premises are to be conveyed by a good and sufficient deed running to the BUYER, or to the nominee designated by the BUYER by written notice to the SELLER at least seven days before the deed is to be delivered as herein provided, and said deed shall convey a good and clear record and marketable title thereto, free from encumbrances, except
(a) Provisions of existing building and zoning laws;
(b) Existing rights and obligations in party walls which are not the subject of written agreement;
(c) Such taxes for the then current year as are not due and payable on the date of the delivery of such deed;
(d) Any liens for municipal betterments assessed after the date of this agreement;
*(e)

5. PLANS

If said deed refers to a plan necessary to be recorded therewith the SELLER shall deliver such plan with the deed in form adequate for recording or registration.

6. REGISTERED TITLE

In addition to the foregoing, if the title to said premises is registered, said deed shall be in form sufficient to entitle the BUYER to a Certificate of Title of said premises, and the SELLER shall deliver with said deed all instruments, if any, necessary to enable the BUYER to obtain such Certificate of Title.

7. PURCHASE PRICE *(fill in); space is allowed to write out the amounts if desired (provide for payment by certified or Bank's Check acceptable to the SELLER, if required)*

The agreed purchase price for said premises is
dollars, of which
$ have been paid as a deposit this day and
$ are to be paid at the time of delivery of the deed in cash, or by certified, cashier's, treasurer's or bank check.
$
$ TOTAL

FIGURE 12.6 A SAMPLE PURCHASE CONTRACT

8.	TIME FOR PERFORMANCE; DELIVERY OF DEED *(fill in)*	Such deed is to be delivered at o'clock M. on the day of 19 , at the Registry of Deeds, unless otherwise agreed upon in writing. It is agreed that time is of the essence of this agreement.
9.	POSSESSION and CONDITION of PREMISES. *(attach a list of exceptions, if any)*	Full possession of said premises free of all tenants and occupants, except as herein provided, is to be delivered at the time of the delivery of the deed, said premises to be then (a) in the same condition as they now are, reasonable use and wear thereof excepted, and (b) not in violation of said building and zoning laws, and (c) in compliance with the provisions of any instrument referred to in clause 4 hereof. The BUYER shall be entitled to an inspection of said premises prior to the delivery of the deed in order to determine whether the condition thereof complies with the terms of this clause.
10.	EXTENSION TO PERFECT TITLE OR MAKE PREMISES CONFORM *(Change period of time if desired).*	If the SELLER shall be unable to give title or to make conveyance, or to deliver possession of the premises, all as herein stipulated, or if at the time of the delivery of the deed the premises do not conform with the provisions hereof, then any payments made under this agreement shall be refunded and all other obligations of the parties hereto shall cease and this agreement shall be void and without recourse to the parties hereto, unless the SELLER elects to use reasonable efforts to remove any defects in title, or to deliver possession as provided herein, or to make the said premises conform to the provisions hereof, as the case may be, in which event the SELLER shall give written notice thereof to the BUYER at or before the time for performance hereunder, and thereupon the time for performance hereof shall be extended for a period of thirty days.
11.	FAILURE TO PERFECT TITLE OR MAKE PREMISES CONFORM, etc.	If at the expiration of the extended time the SELLER shall have failed so to remove any defects in title, deliver possession, or make the premises conform, as the case may be, all as herein agreed, or if at any time during the period of this agreement or any extension thereof, the holder of a mortgage on said premises shall refuse to permit the insurance proceeds, if any, to be used for such purposes, then, at the BUYER'S option, any payments made under this agreement shall be forthwith refunded and all other obligations of all parties hereto shall cease and this agreement shall be void without recourse to the parties hereto.
12.	BUYER'S ELECTION TO ACCEPT TITLE	The BUYER shall have the election, at either the original or any extended time for performance, to accept such title as the SELLER can deliver to the said premises in their then condition and to pay therefor the purchase price without deduction, in which case the SELLER shall convey such title, except that in the event of such conveyance in accord with the provisions of this clause, if the said premises shall have been damaged by fire or casualty insured against, then the SELLER shall, unless the SELLER has previously restored the premises to their former condition, either (a) pay over or assign to the BUYER, on delivery of the deed, all amounts recovered or recoverable on account of such insurance, less any amounts reasonably expended by the SELLER for any partial restoration, or (b) if a holder of a mortgage on said premises shall not permit the insurance proceeds or a part thereof to be used to restore the said premises to their former condition or to be so paid over or assigned, give to the BUYER a credit against the purchase price, on delivery of the deed, equal to said amounts so recovered or recoverable and retained by the holder of the said mortgage less any amounts reasonably expended by the SELLER for any partial restoration.
13.	ACCEPTANCE OF DEED	The acceptance of a deed by the BUYER or his nominee as the case may be, shall be deemed to be a full performance and discharge of every agreement and obligation herein contained or expressed, except such as are, by the terms hereof, to be performed after the delivery of said deed.
14.	USE OF PURCHASE MONEY TO CLEAR TITLE	To enable the SELLER to make conveyance as herein provided, the SELLER may, at the time of delivery of the deed, use the purchase money or any portion thereof to clear the title of any or all encumbrances or interests, provided that all instruments so procured are recorded simultaneously with the delivery of said deed.
15.	INSURANCE **Insert amount (list additional types of insurance and amounts as agreed)*	Until the delivery of the deed, the SELLER shall maintain insurance on said premises as follows: *Type of Insurance* — *Amount of Coverage* (a) Fire * $ (b) Extended coverage * (c)
16.	ASSIGNMENT OF INSURANCE *(delete entire clause if insurance is <u>not</u> to be assigned)*	Unless otherwise notified in writing by the BUYER at least seven days before the time for delivery of the deed, and unless prevented from doing so by the refusal of the insurance company(s) involved to issue the same, the SELLER shall assign such insurance and deliver binders therefor in proper form to the BUYER at the time for performance of this agreement. In the event of refusal by the insurance company(s) to issue the same, the SELLER shall give notice thereof to the BUYER at least two business days before the time for performance of this agreement.

FIGURE 12.6 A SAMPLE PURCHASE CONTRACT (*continued*)

17.	ADJUSTMENTS *(list operating expenses, if any, or attach schedule)*	Collected rents, mortgage interest, prepaid premiums on insurance if assigned as herein provided, water and sewer use charges, operating expenses (if any) according to the schedule attached hereto or set forth below, and taxes for the then current year, shall be apportioned and fuel value shall be adjusted, as of the day of performance of this agreement and the net amount thereof shall be added to or deducted from, as the case may be, the purchase price payable by the BUYER at the time of delivery of the deed. Uncollected rents for the current rental period shall be apportioned if and when collected by either party.
18.	ADJUSTMENT OF UNASSESSED AND ABATED TAXES	If the amount of said taxes is not known at the time of the delivery of the deed, they shall be apportioned on the basis of the taxes assessed for the preceding year, with a reapportionment as soon as the new tax rate and valuation can be ascertained; and, if the taxes which are to be apportioned shall thereafter be reduced by abatement, the amount of such abatement, less the reasonable cost of obtaining the same, shall be apportioned between the parties, provided that neither party shall be obligated to institute or prosecute proceedings for an abatement unless herein otherwise agreed.
19.	BROKER'S FEE *(fill in fee with dollar amount or percentage; also name of Broker(s))*	A broker's fee for professional services of is due from the SELLER to the Broker(s) herein, but if the SELLER pursuant to the terms of clause 22 hereof retains the deposits made hereunder by the BUYER, said Broker(s) shall be entitled to receive from the SELLER an amount equal to one-half the amount so retained or an amount equal to the broker's fee for professional services according to this contract, whichever is the lesser.
20.	BROKER(S) WARRANTY *(fill in name)*	The Broker(s) named herein warrant(s) that he (they) is (are) duly licensed as such by the Commonwealth of Massachusetts.
21.	DEPOSIT *(fill in, or delete reference to broker(s) if SELLER holds deposit)*	All deposits made hereunder shall be held by the broker(s) subject to the terms of this agreement and shall be duly accounted for at the time for performance of this agreement, provided however that in the event of any disagreement the broker(s) may retain said deposits pending instructions mutually given by the SELLER and the BUYER.
22.	BUYER'S DEFAULT; DAMAGES	If the BUYER shall fail to fulfill the BUYER'S agreements herein, all deposits made hereunder by the BUYER shall be retained by the SELLER as liquidated damages unless within thirty days after the time for performance of this agreement or any extension hereof, the SELLER otherwise notifies the BUYER in writing.
23.	SALE OF PERSONAL PROPERTY *(fill in and attach list or delete entire clause)*	The BUYER agrees to buy from the SELLER the articles of personal property enumerated on the attached list for the price of $ and the SELLER agrees to deliver to the BUYER upon delivery of the deed hereunder, a warranty bill of sale therefor on payment of said price. The provisions of this clause shall constitute an agreement separate and apart from the provisions herein contained with respect to the real estate, and any breach of the terms and conditions of this clause shall have no effect on the provisions of this agreement with respect to the real estate.
24.	RELEASE BY HUSBAND OR WIFE	The SELLER'S spouse hereby agrees to join in said deed and to release and convey all statutory and other rights and interests in said premises.
25.	BROKER AS PARTY	The broker(s) named herein, join(s) in this agreement and become(s) a party hereto, in so far as any provisions of this agreement expressly apply to him (them), and to any amendments or modifications of such provisions to which he (they) agree(s) in writing.
26.	LIABILITY OF TRUSTEE, SHAREHOLDER, BENEFICIARY, etc.	If the SELLER or BUYER executes this agreement in a representative or fiduciary capacity, only the principal or the estate represented shall be bound, and neither the SELLER or BUYER so executing, nor any shareholder or beneficiary of any trust, shall be personally liable for any obligation, express or implied, hereunder.
27.	WARRANTIES AND REPRESENTATIONS *(fill in); if none, state "none"; if any listed, indicate by whom each warranty or representation was made*	The BUYER acknowledges that the BUYER has not been influenced to enter into this transaction nor has he relied upon any warranties or representations not set forth or incorporated in this agreement or previously made in writing, except for the following additional warranties and representations, if any, made by either the SELLER or the Broker(s):

FIGURE 12.6 A SAMPLE PURCHASE CONTRACT (*continued*)

28.	CONSTRUCTION OF AGREEMENT **delete "triplicate" and substitute "quadruplicate" if required.*	This instrument, executed in triplicate*_______________ is to be construed as a Massachusetts contract, is to take effect as a sealed instrument, sets forth the entire contract between the parties, is binding upon and enures to the benefit of the parties hereto and their respective heirs, devisees, executors, administrators, successors and assigns, and may be cancelled, modified or amended only by a written instrument executed by both the SELLER and the BUYER. If two or more persons are named herein as BUYER their obligations hereunder shall be joint and several. The captions and marginal notes are used only as a matter of convenience and are not to be considered a part of this agreement or to be used in determining the intent of the parties to it.
29.	LEAD PAINT LAW	The parties acknowledge that, under Massachusetts law, whenever a child or children under six years of age resides in any residential premises in which any paint, plaster or other accessible material contains dangerous levels of lead, the owner of said premises must remove or cover said paint, plaster or other material so as to make it inaccessible to children under six years of age.
30.	ADDITIONAL PROVISIONS	The initialed riders, if any, attached hereto, are incorporated herein by reference.

________________________________ ________________________________

SELLER (or spouse) *SELLER*

________________________________ ________________________________

BUYER *BUYER*

____

Broker(s)

EXTENSION

Date_______________

The time for the performance of the foregoing agreement is extended until___________________ o'clock________________M. on the__________________________ day of ___________________19____, time still being of the essence of this agreement as extended. In all other respects, this agreement is hereby ratified and confirmed.

This extension, executed in triplicate, _______________________________ is intended to take effect as a sealed instrument.

________________________________ ________________________________

SELLER (or spouse) *SELLER*

________________________________ ________________________________

BUYER *BUYER*

____

Broker(s)

[D4880]

FIGURE 12.6 A SAMPLE PURCHASE CONTRACT (*continued*)

automatically terminate if not accepted within a specified time period. Many commentators also suggest that, once the offer has been accepted, a series of time limits be set for the completion of such things as the delivery of title by the seller, purchaser's evaluation of the sufficiency of title evidence (i.e., a determination as to the marketability of the title), correction by the seller of any title defects, closing, and possession. Many of these items are discussed subsequently in more detail.

Parties

Because the essence of a contract is to bind two or more parties to perform certain acts in the future, the parties to the contract must be unambiguously defined. This includes the full names of all parties as well as any aliases; the marital status, so that all spouses may join the contract to avoid problems with dower or courtesy rights; and if a legal entity, such as a corporation or partnership, executor, or agent acting for another, is involved, full information about the entity and the authority to sign.

Property Description

The object of the contract is to purchase a specific property or properties; thus an accurate, unambiguous description of the property must be included in the contract. It would be best to include a complete, accurate legal description, but courts have been quite lenient in interpreting incomplete property descriptions.[13] Remember to include all items that are to be transferred as a part of the transaction. Include any personal property that is to be included and fixtures (to avoid problems later).

Price

Because both parties to a contract must obligate themselves, the purchase price must be clearly stated in the contract. The total purchase amount does not necessarily need to be stated, but it must be easily computed based on additional information (such as the number of acres to be included in the transaction and a price per acre).

Method of Payment

In addition to price, it is best to describe what method of payment is to be used. A certified check, bank draft, or similar instrument offers the most protection to the seller. This avoids nonsufficient funds (NSF) problems as well as the possibility of the buyer deciding for some reason to stop payment of a check.

Schackai v. Lagreco

Contingency Clauses

Perhaps the only rule in real estate transactions is that everything is negotiable. Thus when drafting an offer to purchase, it is perfectly permissible to insert contingency

[13]There is a provision in law known as the *Parol Evidence Rule* that if a written document is meant by the parties to be a final agreement, any additional agreements between the parties that are not put in writing may not be used in court to change the written agreement. Thus the parol evidence rule would prohibit any changes to a description in a contract but would allow additional information to be used to clarify a description.

clauses to benefit either party. For example, it is common to make the transaction contingent on the ability of the purchaser to obtain suitable financing. Of course, the term *suitable* leaves the door open for the buyer to back out and would force a court to decide when financing was reasonably suitable. Courts generally interpret contingency clauses so as to require a good faith effort of the party that stands to benefit from the clause. Any reasonable clause, however, may be included; for example, an appraised value at least equal to the offer price; making the offer contingent on the sale of the purchaser's current house; or requiring certain acts, such as painting or landscaping, to be done by the seller.

Risk of Loss

It is reasonable to assume that when an offer to purchase a property is made, the property will be delivered in the same condition it was in when the offer was made. In fact, a purchaser may wish to insert a provision requiring the seller to make certain improvements to the property. Once a binding agreement, such as a properly executed and accepted offer to purchase, is in place, the doctrine of ***equitable conversion*** holds that "what ought to be done is regarded as done." Thus the seller should receive the agreed-upon purchase price, and the purchaser should receive the property.[14]

Equitable Conversion Doctrine which holds that "what ought to be done is regarded as done" when a binding agreement is in place.

Under this concept, the terms and conditions of the contract are binding on the heirs of both parties. Thus even the death of either party does not end the contract. As a general rule, this concept works well. It would be unfair to allow an agreement to dissolve as a result of a change in circumstances. It would also be unfair to place the burden on the purchaser for an action before closing; for example, if the property should be damaged by fire, flood, or storm. Under the equitable conversion doctrine, the purchaser would have to bear the loss. Because most purchasers do not place insurance on the property until the closing date, such a loss could be catastrophic.

To avoid this situation, some states have adopted the *Uniform Vendor and Purchaser Risk Act,* which places the risk of loss on the seller until title or possession has been transferred (or the purchaser causes the damage). Even in these states, however, a clause should bc inserted into the purchase contract stating that all risks will remain with the seller until closing.

Possession

In keeping with the theme already expressed, the date on which the purchaser may take possession of the property is generally negotiable. If the property is vacant, possession could be immediate. In some instances, the seller may need a considerable amount of time before moving. Often possession is tied to the date of closing. It is not usually a good idea to allow a seller to stay in residence after the property has been sold. This creates potential problems in getting the former owner out on schedule and with potential damage to the property. By the same token, the owner runs a risk by allowing the purchaser to take possession before closing. This risk is mitigated

[14]Before closing, the seller's interests are regarded as personal property even though title has not yet been transferred. The purchaser's interests are transformed into real property rights at the time of acceptance.

to some extent, however, by the earnest money being held by the agent. Should the need arise to have either party take or remain in possession until a date not in concert with the closing date, the use of a short-term lease may avoid potential problems with eviction.

Marketable Title

A title that a reasonably prudent buyer would accept is considered to be a good, clear, perfect, or **marketable title.** The seller is not obligated to prove that the title being offered is marketable. Thus to protect his interests (even when a title search has been done or title insurance is in place[15]), the purchaser should specify the need for the seller to provide proof of clear title. By the same token, the presence of easements or restrictive covenants may make the title unmarketable for the seller. Thus a clause stating that the property is "subject to all easements and restrictions of record" will avoid many potential problems. This clause may be especially important when zoning or building code issues becomes involved. Such might be the case when the purchaser plans to use the property in a fashion other than the current use.

Marketable Title
A title that is free from liens and encumbrances and which a reasonable purchaser, well informed as to the facts and their legal significance would, in the exercise of ordinary prudence, be willing to accept and ought to accept.

Can a seller use an inability to deliver marketable title as a way to avoid completing a transaction? That is the issue in *Kelly v. Leucadia Financial Corporation* (846 P.2d 1238, 1992) in which a purchaser asked a court to force a seller to honor a purchase agreement in which the buyer agreed to accept the property "as is," and elected to waive any defects in title. The seller, a lender who had taken title as a result of a default on loans secured by the property, had entered into litigation with neighboring property owners regarding a boundary line dispute. The buyer agreed to take over the litigation and wished to proceed with the purchase.

Why would a seller under these conditions not wish to proceed with a sale? It turns out that the seller wanted to convey to property to another buyer, presumably at a higher sales price, and used the title problem as a way to avoid the earlier transaction. Holding that specific performance (i.e., forcing one party to complete a contract) is an appropriate remedy for purchasers against sellers, the court ordered the lender to complete the transaction and that the purchaser was entitled to a price abatement for the failure of the seller to deliver marketable title.

Type of Deed

The issues surrounding the type of deed to be provided (see Chapter 8 for information on types of deeds) should be addressed in the purchase contract. When the contract is silent on this issue, the appropriate state statute will determine the minimum deed requirements. Although some states require that a general warranty deed be furnished, a few require only a quitclaim deed. Remember that the quitclaim form of deed provides no warranties for the purchaser. To avoid this unhappy situation, the type of deed required of the seller should be specified in the purchase contract.

Earnest Money Deposit

It has become customary and expected that when a purchaser makes a formal offer to purchase a property, the offer will be accompanied by a sum of money as evidence

[15]The entire area of title evidence, including title insurance issues, is discussed in Chapter 10.

of the purchaser's "good faith." Although this deposit it not necessary to a binding contractual arrangement, many sellers are reluctant to accept an offer, particularly one for less than the asking price, without some evidence that the purchaser is serious. Although the seller has other remedies for nonperformance of a purchase contract (as described in Chapter 13), often a seller simply keeps the earnest money deposit in the event that the purchaser fails to complete the transaction. Thus it is important to the seller that the purchaser be at some risk should he have a change of heart.

Closing Date and Place

The closing ceremony marks the exact time and place at which title is to be officially transferred from the seller to the purchaser by the act of conveying the required type of deed. Although all parties are generally anxious to have this take place, it is necessary to allow sufficient time for all of the preliminary activities to be completed without any undue haste. As has been noted many times in this text, the legal environment for real estate ownership is often treacherous. It is always a good idea to allow time for problems to be identified, evaluated, and corrected. The majority of problems by owners can be avoided by a careful, deliberate process of review before closing. As mentioned earlier, most purchase contracts specify certain dates or time limits for the completion of acts before and including closing. In some instances, time may not be of the essence in closing a transaction. A reasonable delay in performance may not breech the contract so long as the noncomplying party has acted in good faith. Thus it may in some instances be appropriate to err on the side of caution in preparing for closing.

Prorating Expenses

Owning real property involves many ongoing expenses. Items such as property taxes, insurance, and utilities take one of two forms. Most expense items are *prepaid.* The benefits are not received until payment has been received. Some items, however, are paid in arrears (i.e., after the benefits have been received). These items are usually referred to as *accrued expense* items. In the absence of an agreement, the purchaser will benefit from any unused prepaid items, and the seller would benefit from accrued expenses. In the interest of fairness, these items are almost always apportioned into the *pro rata* shares of the seller and purchaser. In other words, each should pay in proportion to the benefits enjoyed. More information on prorating is found in Chapter 11.

Signatures

A contract not signed by all parties (or agents authorized to act on behalf of the parties) is at least arguably not binding on any party not signing. Thus all parties to the contract need to indicate their desire to execute the contract by signing it. In most instances, it is not necessary to have witnesses or to use a notary public. Nor do most states require the use of a seal.[16] If an agent claims authority to sign for one of the

---

[16]A few form contracts may contain the letters *L.S.* This stands for the Latin *locus siligis,* meaning "place of the seal."

parties, it is a good idea to have her produce documentary evidence of this authority at the time of signing.

ADDITIONAL ISSUES CONCERNING PURCHASE CONTRACTS

Although a carefully drawn offer to purchase will resolve most problems before they ever occur, there are a few issues that cannot be covered by the written document itself. These issues concern the rights and obligations of the parties at various times in the negotiation process. The regulatory environment described earlier in this chapter exists primarily to insure a fair, equitable treatment of all parties. It is the responsibility of the agent to insure that all contracts, especially any offers to purchase, correctly reflect the wishes of the parties involved. The agent must insure that the documents are complete, correct, and meet all requirements concerning form. Although the agent is charged with these responsibilities, the system of law must make provisions to protect parties who may be injured in any way during the process.

Mistakes

A basic tenant of contract law holds that a mutual mistake voids any contract. This is not to say, however, that either party may simply claim that a mistake has been made and thereby void the agreement. As a general rule, each party will be held to the terms of the agreement regardless of the intention. Thus typographical errors can be disastrous. An additional zero can change an offer of $1,000 per acre into $10,000 per acre. Thus it is imperative that all parties as well as the agent(s) involved check all contracts carefully before signing them.

Misrepresentation

When a property has been misrepresented in some material fashion by one party or, in many instances, by the agent of that party, there is likely to be an objection by the other party. If, for example, the seller represented a property as containing "50 acres more or less" when in fact a survey reveals a total of only 30 acres, the property has been misrepresented. If the **misrepresentation** was intentional, the act was one of fraud. Unintentional misrepresentation can be caused either by negligence or by mistake. Generally when a material misrepresentation has been made by either party, the offended party may void the agreement and, if damages can be shown, may seek restitution.

Misrepresentation
Statements or actions, whether intentional or not, which create a false impression in the mind of another and which may affect the purchase or sale decision.

Duress

Any action taken against the "free will" of a person may be canceled. This includes making or accepting an offer to purchase. If either party can demonstrate that the offer or acceptance was made under a threat of harm, whether physical or emotional, then the contract will not stand. In similar fashion, if one party is in a dominant position and uses *undue influence* to coerce another party to take an action against his free will, the action may be rescinded.

CONCLUSION

The relationship created between agent and principal, because of the degree of trust and confidence required by both parties, is very special in the law. Agents have an obligation to act in the best interests of their principals at all times. Real estate brokers, because they act as agents for members of the public, must meet licensure requirements established by the state and follow a set of very specific rules which govern their actions. These rules require the use of contractual agreements that are designed to protect the interests of all parties in real estate transactions.

Real estate transactions begin with a written listing agreement between a seller and a broker that specifies the obligations and limitations of each party. To avoid problems caused by the fiduciary obligations of agents to principals, agents must disclose their legal relationship to other parties in transactions. For example, agents representing the seller in a transaction must disclose that fact to potential purchasers. Because one of the primary roles of real estate agents is to assist in the negotiation process between buyer and seller, agency disclosure is critical.

Purchasers communicate their position through the use of purchase contracts. Although buyers may be represented by agents, the most common current practice is to have only the seller represented. Thus, seller agents are often involved in assisting buyers complete purchase agreements. Obviously, this practice can, and often does, lead to problems—mostly caused by misunderstandings about the proper role of the real estate broker in an agency relationship.

DISCUSSION QUESTIONS

1. Define the term agent. Name and describe the two essential ingredients in an agency relationship.
2. Distinguish between general agency and special agency. Under which category do real estate brokers usually fall?
3. What are the licensing requirements for a broker and a salesperson in your state? (Refer to Appendix 12.1.)
4. What parties are generally exempt from state licensing requirements?
5. List the items generally included in a listing agreement.
6. When is the commission agreed upon by the agent and principal said to be earned? If a dispute over who earned the commission should arise, what must an agent do to render his claim for compensation valid?
7. List and describe the four common forms of listing agreements.
8. What are the conditions that must be met before an offer is legally accepted?
9. What impact does the Statute of Frauds have on real estate transactions?
10. List and briefly describe the significance of the numerous provisions that may be included in a purchase contract.
11. Name the circumstances under which a contract for real estate may be voided.

VELTEN V. ROBERTSON V. ZIMMERMAN

671 P.2d 1011 (Colorado Court of Appeals, 1983)

Breach of fiduciary duties

In January of 1979, Derrick Zimmerman, a real estate salesman, contacted seller to inquire about her willingness to sell a 10-unit apartment building. The seller would not agree to give the salesman an exclusive listing on the property, but, because seller indicated that she might consider selling the building, the salesman then contacted the buyers to inquire about their interest in the property.

Together with the salesman, the buyers prepared a receipt and option agreement. The salesman obtained the buyers' signatures on this contract. The salesman then presented this contract to the seller at her home and obtained her signature. The seller proposed a number of changes to the contract and an addendum was prepared. Two days later, the salesman also obtained the buyers' and seller's signatures on the addendum.

Neither the contract nor the addendum contained a provision which would require the seller to pay the salesman a commission because the salesman had indicated to the seller that he would be compensated by the buyers. In lieu of a cash commission, the buyers offered "to execute a note and deed of trust [secured by the property] in favor of [the salesman] in the sum of $5,000." The buyers also agreed that in the event the property were to be sold within the next year, the salesman would be entitled to 50% of the profits. Neither the salesman nor the buyers disclosed the details of this arrangement to the seller.

The seller refused to close because she believed that her request for a financial statement from the buyers constituted a counteroffer which was not accepted. . . .

[1] The seller contended before the trial court . . . that the trial court erred in granting specific performance to the buyers because the salesman failed to disclose his personal financial interest in the property and that, because the salesman was her agent as well as the buyers', this was a breach of his fiduciary duty of disclosure. We agree.

In M.S.R., Inc. v. Lish . . . we examined the elements of an agency relationship with a salesman. In Lish, the broker "contacted the defendant [seller] and told her he had procured a buyer, he prepared the contract, he obtained the signatures of the parties, and his employer . . . was to receive a broker's commission under the terms of the contract." After consideration of the above factors, we held that the broker was, as a matter of law, the agent of the seller.

[2] Here, the salesman is also, as a matter of law, the seller's agent. The evidence is uncontradicted that the salesman contacted the seller, and obtained the signatures of both the buyers and the seller. The only difference between Lish and the present case is that in Lish the "commission" was to be received from the seller, rather than from the buyers, as here. However, the establishment of an agency relationship does not stand or fall on a determination of whether a commission was to be paid.

[3] As an agent of the seller and the buyers, the salesman "has a fiduciary duty to act with the utmost faith and loyalty on behalf of his principal[s]." This duty requires the agent to make a "full and fair disclosure. . . . " If, as here, the agent by the conveyance will acquire an equitable or beneficial interest in the property, then the agent must specifically disclose the nature of that interest to his principals. If he does not do so, specific performance cannot be ordered. . . . Here, the salesman did not disclose the nature of his financial interest to the seller. The buyers were both parties to the contract which gave the beneficial interest to the salesman, and they may not now seek to disavow their responsibility for the salesman's failure to disclose this interest to the seller.

The judgment granting specific performance in favor of the buyers is reversed.

Case Reflections

1. For what reasons did the Appellate Court rule that the broker was also an agent of the seller?
2. What fiduciary duty owed the seller did the agent breach?

SWALLOWS V. LANEY

102 N.M. 81, 691 P.2d 874 (Supreme Court, 1984)

Action for specific performance of sales contract

. . . This case involves an important question . . . in New Mexico: whether a fiduciary relationship between a real estate broker or salesperson and his principal may continue to exist under certain circumstances after the expiration of a written listing agreement.

The Laneys entered into two exclusive right to sell listing agreements with Western Farm Management Company for the sale of three tracts of land . . . Swallows was the real estate salesman who arranged the listings. He was unable to sell any of the tracts prior to the termination date of the written listing agreements on October 15, 1980.

In early February 1981, Swallows and the Laneys entered into negotiations concerning the possible purchase by Swallows of [a] . . . parcel. . . .

[1][2][3] An owner-broker relationship is clearly established during the term of a listing agreement. . . . It is well-established in New Mexico law that a real estate agent stands in a fiduciary relationship with his principal and must reveal all facts within his knowledge which might affect his principal's decisions, rights, and interests. . . . As a fiduciary, a broker or salesperson holds a position of great trust and confidence and must act in utmost good faith. . . .

The National Association of Realtors in the Preamble to its Code of Ethics recognizes the trust placed on members of its profession. . . . This code is applicable to all members of New Mexico's regional Boards of Realtors.

[4] Strict adherence to these fiduciary duties and obligations by a real estate broker or salesperson is especially important when the broker or salesperson buys the listed property for himself. The opportunity for overreaching by the broker or salesperson, or for taking advantage of facts and information within his specialized knowledge, is great. For this reason, this Court has previously recognized, when a real estate broker or salesperson buys listed property from his principal *before* the listing has expired, that: In addition to the duty to disclose his interest as a purchaser, a real estate broker is under a legal obligation to make a full, fair, and prompt disclosure to his employer of all facts within his knowledge which are or may be material, or which might affect his principal's rights and interest or influence his action relative to the disposition of the property. . . .

[5][6]We conclude that the fiduciary relationship between a real estate broker or salesperson and his principal may, under certain circumstances, exist in the absence or after the expiration of a written listing agreement. To determine whether particular circumstances give rise to such a relationship, a court should consider the following factors, among others, to be relevant:

1. The course of conduct between the real estate broker or salesperson and the principal.
2. The extent to which the broker or salesperson holds himself out to the principal as a real estate advisor and confidant.
3. The degree of the principal's dependence on the broker or salesperson for advice.
4. The sophistication of the principal in real estate matters.
5. The familiarity of the principal with the value of the subject property. . . .

[8] We are not suggesting that once a real estate broker or salesperson has acted as agent for the sale of a property, he may not purchase it himself. What we do hold is that having once acted as agent, the broker or salesperson has the additional obligation of full and complete disclosure of all pertinent facts within his knowledge concerning the property if the fiduciary relationship between the agent and principal has continued to exist. If this is not done, the negotiations concerning the purchase of the property might be unequal, and the realtors' ideals of fairness, high integrity, and strict moral conduct could be jeopardized. . . .

[11] If a breach in fiduciary duty is found, the transaction is void as against public policy whether the broker has profited thereby or not. . . . For this

reason alone, Swallows is prevented from specifically enforcing the contract. . . .

The district court is affirmed on all issues.

Case Reflections

1. Why did defendant Laney back out of the sale before plaintiff Swallows?
2. State the issue before the Appellate Court in this case. What judgment did it render?

SCHACKAI V. LAGRECO

350 So.2d 1244 (Court of Appeal, Fourth Circuit, 1977)

Claim for commission earned

Appellant, Morris Vaccarello, a real estate agent, appeals from the trial court's denial of his claim for a commission allegedly due. The sale on which the commission depended was never consummated because the proposed vendors, Nuncio Lagreco and Lucy Lagreco, were not able to deliver title consistent with the property description in the purchase agreement. . . .

The basic facts are not seriously contested: Appellees had a previous listing agreement with Vaccarello covering the same property which is here involved. Sometime after expiration of that agreement, appellant secured a subsequent listing of the property. At that time, there was some discussion and apparent disagreement between Nuncio and Lucy concerning the dimensions of the property. Lucy believed it measured 192 feet in width; Nuncio thought it was 144 feet. Vaccarello accepted Lucy's version and put the 192 foot measurement down in the listing agreement. This measurement was inconsistent with the first listing, which showed the lesser dimensions. According to Nuncio Lagreco, who could not read and who could only write his name, the document was not read to him and he did not know the measurement specified therein when he signed it. . . . It is uncontested that a subsequent title examination showed that the true width of the property was 147 feet, and, thus, the sale was never consummated because of vendors' inability to deliver merchantable title to a 192 foot wide lot as per the listing agreement.

It is appellant's contention that this case is governed by the following:

> Where, as was the case here, the broker's contract was to find a purchaser, his right to his commission is dependent upon whether he has found and produced one, who is able, ready, and willing to buy on the terms prescribed by his principal. When the broker produces such a purchaser, he is entitled to his commission, although the sale is not consummated, because of the inability of the vendor to comply with his offer. . . . *The broker, in such a case, in the absence of notice to the contrary, has the right to act upon the assumption that his principal has a marketable title. . . .* (emphasis added)

Appellant further contends that actual knowledge of a defect in vendors' title is required, and that inferential notice such as to put him on inquiry is an insufficient basis for denying his commission.

Here, the real estate agent had accepted a prior listing of the identical property with obviously conflicting dimensions. The fact that, without the aid of the prior listing, he remembered that it excluded the Picarrello tract and changed the original draft of the second listing to so provide, suggests that he had actual knowledge of the dimensions from the prior listing. Even were this not so, the argument between the Lagrecos as to the dimensions of the property, which occurred in appellant's presence, and the existence of conflicting dimensions in the prior listing in his own files should certainly have alerted him to the probability of error in the second listing.

Under the circumstances of this case, failure to ascertain the correct measurements of the property constituted a breach of the duty of a real estate agent "to act strictly in conformity with his authority and in good faith and with reasonable care, skill, and diligence." . . . Professor

Yiannopoulos, in an examination of the civil law authorities on brokerage, concludes:

> Even where the broker undertakes no obligation to act, he is bound by certain obligations resulting from the principle of good faith and he is held to a certain standard of conduct. He is obliged to conduct the entrusted business in good faith, to promote the interests of his principal, and to protect him from possible losses. He must at once notify the principal with regard to all doubts or reservations he may have concerning the person of the prospect, *the quality of the object of the transaction,* and any other aspects capable of producing loss. In all cases he should act according to the directions of his principal. The principal, on the other hand, is under an obligation to inform the broker that the transaction is concluded, whether or not as a result of the broker's activity, so that unnecessary efforts may be avoided.

. . . The real estate agent need not be a seer nor a title examiner, but, nevertheless, he is required to act with due diligence where, as here, such circumstances exist as to alert a reasonable broker to reconcile an apparent discrepancy in the description of the property to be listed before allowing his principals to bind themselves to sell property of doubtful dimensions.

The judgment of the trial court is affirmed, at appellant's cost.

Case Reflections

1. Briefly describe the events leading up to the initial lawsuit filed by the agent Vaccarello.
2. How did the Appellate Court decide the commission issue?

Yiannopoulos, "Brokerage, Mandate, and Agency," 19 L.L.R. 777, 788–789 (1959) (emphasis added) (footnotes omitted).

ALLEY
V.
NEVADA REAL ESTATE DIVISION

94 Nev. 123, 575 P.2d 133 (Supreme Court, 1978)

Use of a "double escrow scheme"

This is an appeal from a district court order affirming the decision of the Nevada Real Estate Division and its Advisory Commission to permanently revoke the real estate broker's license held by Jerry L. Alley. . . .

Here, the record of the administrative proceedings establishes . . . that Alley had received a secret profit of $2,000 for himself, and others, by utilizing a "double escrow" scheme.[1]

In a "double escrow," the broker or salesman purchases a principal's property in the first escrow, and sells it to a third party at a profit in a second escrow without a full disclosure to both the principal and the third party. The escrows close at the same time and the broker or salesman thereby uses the proceeds from the sale in the second escrow to purchase his principal's property. The broker or salesman receives a commission on the sale in the first escrow and a secret profit on the closing in the second escrow. . . .

> A broker when pursuing his own interest cannot ignore those of his principal and will not "be permitted to enjoy the fruits of an advantage taken of a fiduciary relationship, whose dominant characteristic is the confidence reposed by one in another." (Citation omitted.)

The law does not allow the agent who also has a right to purchase to wait until someone makes an offer of an amount in excess of the agreed purchase price and then elect to purchase the property at the lesser price without informing the owner of the higher offer, and, after the agent has obtained the consent from the owner to buy the property, then immediately sell it for the higher price as his own property.

---

[1]Specifically, the Commission found Alley's conduct to be in violation of . . . certain Rules and Regulations of the Commission; and, portions of the Real Estate Code of Ethics.

The administrative determination to permanently revoke Alley's license finds ample support in the record . . . Accordingly we affirm the order of the district court.

Case Reflections

1. Explain the "double escrow scheme" employed by Alley.
2. Of the six fiduciary duties owed a principal (see Table 12.1), which did the agent Alley breach?

PILLING V. EASTERN AND PACIFIC ENTERPRISES TRUST and V. RENTON MORTGAGE & ESCROW, INC.

702 P.2d 1232 (Court of Appeals, Division 1, 1985).

Does an agency relationship continue beyond the time when a commission is earned?

On January 13, 1977, Dorothy Pilling listed her home for sale with Benton Realty, through its salesperson, Pauline Courey. The listing agreement provided for a multiple listing of the property through Real Estate Multiple, Inc. (REMI), of which respondent Renton Realty was a member. Arnold Hernandez, a real estate salesman employed by Renton Realty, noticed Pilling's listing in REMI and brought it to the attention of one Myron J. Stewart. Stewart owned Renton Mortgage and Escrow, Inc., and Eastern and Pacific Enterprises Trust, among other enterprises. . . . Hernandez and Stewart viewed Pilling's property, and Hernandez informed Pilling that Stewart, on behalf of Eastern and Pacific Enterprises Trust, wanted to make an offer to purchase. Pilling directed Hernandez to discuss the offer with her son-in-law, Ronald Goodmansen, who was the branch manager of a mutual savings bank and an experienced mortgage loan officer. . . .

The sale closing on April 11 was held in the offices of Renton Mortgage and Escrow. Pilling was accompanied at the closing by her listing real estate agent, Pauline Courey, of Benton Realty. Goodmansen, Stewart, Thompson, and Hernandez were not present. Instead of executing a real estate contract, Pilling signed two warranty deeds, and took back deeds of trust. She later testified that she did not understand what a deed of trust was. . . .

DUTY TO DISCLOSE

The Washington Supreme Court has held that the real estate brokerage firm with whom property is listed for sale becomes the agent of the seller for the purpose of finding a purchaser; from this agency relationship arises the duty and the obligation on the part of the listing broker, as well as on the part of any subagents, to exercise the utmost good faith and fidelity toward the seller in all matters falling within the scope of employment. . . .

[2][3] Hernandez concedes that this duty exists, but contends that the duty applies only to a listing broker. This contention is without merit. In a multiple listing situation, the selling broker is an authorized subagent of the listing broker. . . . Thus, a selling agent in a multiple listing system also owes the seller the same duties owed by the listing broker. . . .

[4] . . . Pilling's lack of reliance on Renton Realty did not relieve the company, Thompson, or Hernandez from their obligation to act in her best interest:

> It is of no consequence, in this regard, that the broker may be able to show that the breach of his duty of full disclosure and undivided loyalty did not involve intentional or deliberate fraud, or did not result in injury to the principal, or did not materially affect the principal's ultimate decision in the transaction. . . .

[5][6] . . . Knowledge of the agent is imputed by law to the principal. . . . Therefore, Goodmansen's knowledge of Stewart's connection to the company is imputed to Pilling.

[7][8] Thompson and Hernandez had a duty of full disclosure and were not relieved of that duty in

respect to Stewart's ownership of Renton Mortgage and Escrow simply because Pilling learned of it through another source. An agent is subject to liability for loss caused to the principal by any breach of duty. . . . The trial court found on substantial evidence that Goodmansen's knowledge was imputed to Pilling and that any failure to communicate by Hernandez or Thompson was not the cause of her loss. . . .

SCOPE OF AGENCY

[10] Pilling next argues Thompson and Hernandez breached their fiduciary duty by failing to monitor the closing of the transaction in order to assure it was done in accordance with the contract. Implicit in such an argument is the contention that the agency relationship between the seller and the listing broker or his subagents extends to the date of closing. . . . [T]his case, where the commission is earned when the broker produces a ready, able and willing buyer who signs a contract acceptable to the seller. . . .

[11] The scope of the agency between the seller and the broker is defined by the agent's purpose, which is to find a purchaser. . . .

[12][13] . . . [W]e conclude that there is no legal basis for asserting that the seller-broker agency relationship between the seller and the listing broker or his subagents extends to the date of closing. . . .

Judgment affirmed.

Case Reflections

1. On what grounds did plaintiff Pilling sue defendants Eastern and Renton? How did the Trial Court rule?
2. How does the scope of agency, as defined by the Appellate Court, affirm the judgment of the Trial Court?

ROHAUER V. LITTLE

736 P.2d 403 (Supreme Court, 1987)

Receipt by agent is not receipt by buyer

I.

. . . Floyd D. and Joyce G. Little entered into an exclusive listing agreement with the real estate brokerage firm of Coldwell Banker whereby Coldwell Banker, through its salesperson Dorothy Porter, undertook to sell the Littles' property in Arapahoe County, Colorado. In June 1981, Rhonda Gorenz, another salesperson in the same Coldwell Banker office in which Porter was employed, received a telephone call from the employer of Frank G. Rohauer, informing her that Rohauer was moving from Houston, Texas, to Denver and would need assistance in finding a home. . . . After several visits to the Littles' home, the Rohauers decided to make an offer to purchase it. . . .

On June 18, 1981, Gorenz prepared a receipt and option contract incorporating the Rohauers' offer to purchase the Littles' property for $400,000 in cash or certified funds, of which $20,000 was to be tendered as earnest money. . . . The Littles rejected the offer, but informed Gorenz that they would be willing to sell their home for $425,000. This price, which was agreeable to the Rohauers, was written into the receipt and option contract, after which the Littles and Frank Rohauer initialed the changes and signed the contract.

The receipt and option contract acknowledged receipt of the $20,000 earnest money, to be held in escrow by Coldwell Banker as part payment for the property, and included the following provisions:

> 3. An abstract of title to said property, certified to date, or a current commitment for title insurance policy in an amount equal to the purchase price, at seller's option and expense, shall be furnished the purchaser on or before July 10, 1981. . . .

Porter received the commitment from Transamerica Title Insurance Company at the Coldwell Banker office on July 7, 1981, and notified Gorenz of the receipt on the same date. The Rohauers, however, were not notified of the receipt of the title insurance commitment at this time and did not receive the commitment until a copy arrived by mail at their Houston home on July 15, 1981. By that time, the Rohauers had already stopped payment on their earnest money check and had advised Gorenz on July 14 that they were meeting with legal counsel and would probably not proceed with the purchase. The Rohauers failed to appear at the closing on July 20, 1981, and the Littles sold their home in November 1981 to other purchasers for $430,000.

The Littles brought suit against the Rohauers, claiming that the Rohauers had breached their contract by not proceeding with the closing and that they (the Littles) were entitled to the $20,000 earnest money as liquidated damages. The Rohauers defended on the basis that their duty of performance never arose, since the Littles had failed to furnish them with the title insurance commitment by July 10, 1981, as required by the contract. . . .

II.

The significance of the agency issue to the proper resolution of the case is obvious. If . . . Coldwell Banker, through its salesperson Rhonda Gorenz, was the Rohauers' agent when the title commitment was delivered to Coldwell Banker on July 7, 1981, then the Littles complied with their contractual obligation and the Rohauers breached the contract by failing to proceed with the closing, since receipt of the title commitment by the agent would necessarily be imputed to the principal. . . .

. . . [T]here can be no question that an agency relationship exists between Rhonda Gorenz, the salesperson of the listing broker, and the Littles, the sellers. . . .

A proper resolution of this case turns on whether, notwithstanding the agency relationship existing between the salesperson of the listing broker and the sellers, an agency relationship may also exist simultaneously between the salesperson of the listing broker and the purchasers. . . . The rules of the Colorado Real Estate Commission contemplate the possibility of a dual agency only where there is an agency contract between the purchaser and the real estate licensee, full written disclosure is given to all parties to the transaction, and the parties consent in writing to the dual arrangement. . . .

[1] The potential conflicts of interest on dual representation lead us to conclude that in the absence of written disclosure of the dual agency and the express written consent of all parties to the transaction, a salesperson of the listing broker may not simultaneously represent both the seller and the purchaser in the same real estate transaction. In the absence of such disclosure and consent, the salesperson of the listing broker is an agent of the seller only and not an agent of the purchaser. We hasten to add that the absence of an agency relationship between the purchaser and the salesperson of the listing broker will not necessarily leave the purchaser unprotected in his dealings with the salesperson. . . .

B.

[2] . . . Since the Rohauers never gave written consent to Gorenz to act as their agent in connection with their contemplated purchase of the Little home, Gorenz was not acting as their agent when she received the title insurance commitment at Coldwell Banker's office on July 7, 1981.

The judgment is thus affirmed in part . . .

Case Reflections

1. Briefly outline the events which occurred up to Rohauer backing out of the sale. Clarify all relationships between the parties involved.
2. What is the issue in this case? From what point of view do the Littles see this issue?
3. Does a dual agency exist in this case? Why or why not?

CHAPTER

13

LIABILITY OF REAL ESTATE PROFESSIONALS: AGENCY AND ANTITRUST ISSUES

LEARNING OBJECTIVES

After reading this chapter, you should be able to:

1. Describe the "due care" standard of behavior for real estate agents.
2. Understand how the concept of *caveat emptor* has gradually evolved into what might now be called *caveat vendor*.
3. Recognize the distinctions between fraud, misrepresentation, and allowable "puffing."
4. Explain why "price fixing" in the context of a restraint of competition has been a major issue in real estate brokerage.
5. Understand how a "closed" multiple listing service can be a restraint to normal market operations.

KEY TERMS

Due Care Standard

Caveat Emptor

Strict Liability

Caveat Vendor

Fraud

Breach of Contract

Puffing

Dual Agency

Commingling of Funds

Securities

Price Fixing

Anticompetitive Practices

Multiple Listing Service

Boycotts

For real estate professionals, no other aspect of doing business is as difficult, and frightening, as the potential liability exposure they face. Almost every facet of the real estate industry—brokerage, appraisal, property management, development, construction, and mortgage lending, to name only the largest segments—has seen a rising tide of litigation. For many real estate professionals, the concept of *risk reduction* has taken on far greater importance than at any time in history.

The areas of potential liability exposure in the real estate industry are almost too numerous to mention. In this chapter, we take a close look at two areas that, in combination with those discussed in Chapter 14, make the legal environment difficult and confusing for most professionals: agency and antitrust issues. In Chapter 14, we continue the discussion of liability with a look at fair housing and environmental issues. As important as these four major areas are, however, they do not even come close to encompassing all aspects of legal liability. Issues that evolve from land use regulation, for example, are discussed in Chapter 16 and the emerging areas of product liability and securities laws in Chapters 17 and 18. The complex legal environment relating to landlord-tenant rights and obligations has already been discussed in Chapter 4.

These areas, similar to most aspects of law, cannot really be broken down into clearly defined areas. Fair housing laws have an obvious impact on landlord-tenant issues. In addition, many of the most difficult issues in land use regulation, brokerage, and mortgage lending are tied in some way to fair housing concepts. Even within this chapter, the agency issues that are discussed lead directly to many of the problems in antitrust liability. Thus the categories listed here are useful only as a method for organizing the concepts. Case law recognizes no such categories.

AGENCY ISSUES

Easton v. Strassburger

A strong argument could be made that nearly all liability exposure for real estate brokers has its basis in some aspect of agency law. Primarily at issue are the *fiduciary obligations* owed by an agent to his principal, which were described in Chapter 12: loyalty, obedience, disclosure, confidentiality, accounting, reasonable skill and care, and diligence. Recall that the central issue in any fiduciary relationship is one of *trust.* An individual must be able to rely on a person in a fiduciary relationship, whether we are talking about a banker, accountant, attorney, or real estate agent. Thus any action, or inaction, by the fiduciary that causes harm to the individual creates a potential liability exposure for the fiduciary.

Due care standard Standard of conduct which applies to the actions of an agent when dealing with his principal and the public.

Recall also that for real estate brokers, the obligations are reinforced (some might even say expanded) by licensure requirements of the states and the Code of Ethics promulgated by the National Association of Realtors. Both are based on the concept of consumer protection brought about by the supposition that most participants in real estate transactions are ill informed and, quite possibly, naive.[1] This notion provides a basis for understanding the expansion of the definition of the ***due care standard*** in real estate brokerage.

[1] Although this argument is valid for residential transactions, most courts have been reluctant to make the same assumptions about parties to commercial, particularly large, real estate transactions. Thus brokers have often been able to rely on a "sophisticated buyer" (or seller) defense.

Caveat Emptor

The ancient rule of ***caveat emptor,*** or simply "buyer beware," was the standard of care in real estate brokerage for most of recorded history. Over the last twenty years, this standard has evolved into one approaching **strict liability**. During the 1970s and 1980s, additional requirements were gradually added to the role of the broker. The duty to speak accurately grew into the doctrine of negligent misrepresentation and, at least in some jurisdictions, to an affirmative obligation to inspect and reveal any and all material facts. The affirmative disclosure rule is often said to be based on the rules laid down in *Easton v. Strasburger*[2] [512 Cal. App. 3d 90, 199 Cal. Rptr, 3d 383 (1984)] and *Gouvera v. Citicorp Person to Person Financial Center* [101 N.M. 572, 686 p2d 262 (N.M. App. 1984)]. These cases reinforced the duty of real estate agents to conduct a "reasonably diligent and competent" inspection of residential property on behalf of potential buyers.[3] Keep in mind that this obligation exists even when the agency relationship is between the broker and the seller. Thus it may now be more appropriate to refer to the legal environment as one of ***caveat vendor***, or "seller beware."

Caveat Emptor Literally, "Let the buyer beware." Often the standard of conduct in real property transactions.

Strict Liability Liability created based upon an injury to a party regardless of intent or fault. Negligence is not an element in determining strict liability.

KEY POINTS

Customer satisfaction is essential in avoiding legal problems in any service industry. Satisfied customers are far less likely to file complaints than are dissatisfied customers. *Consumer Reports,* the popular magazine, frequently conducts surveys in which consumers are asked to indicate their level of satisfaction with a product or service. In their 1989 survey of nearly 72,000 readers, they found that real estate brokerage had one of the lowest overall satisfaction rates they had ever seen. Typical service companies leave only about 10 percent of their customers dissatisfied, whereas real estate firms left nearly 20 percent of their clients less than satisfied with their service. In addition, nearly one-third of the more than 56,000 people who had recently used a real estate brokerage firm reported trouble of one kind or another. The most common complaints were that the agent did not earn the commission, pressured for a lower sale price too soon, did not show or advertise the house as promised, or was not an effective negotiator (*Consumer Reports,* July 1990, pp. 460–464).

Fraud and Deceit

Reed v. King

When a property has been misrepresented in some material fashion by one party or, in many instances, by the agent of that party, there is likely to be an objection by the other party. If, for example, the seller represented a property as containing "50 acres more or less" when in fact a survey reveals a total of only 30 acres, the property has

Caveat Vendor Literally, "Let the seller beware." May represent an emerging standard of conduct in real property transactions.

[2] This case is included at the end of this chapter.

[3] The California Legislature enacted California Civil Code 2079 *et seq.,* recognizing the duty of a real estate agent to "inspect and disclose" to the buyer of residential real property of one to four units based on the *Easton* ruling.

Fraud
Deceitful practice with intent to deprive another of his right, or in some fashion do him injury.

Breach of contract
The failure by one party to live up to the terms of a binding contract.

been misrepresented. If the misrepresentation was intentional and involves a material fact, the act was one of ***fraud***.[4] When no intent to misrepresent can be shown, the act must have been the result of negligence or a mistake.

Fraud can occur only when a factual misrepresentation of a material nature has been made. The notion of what is material is more easily defined in terms of what is *not* material. A fact that has little or no impact on the value of the property or did not play a major role in a decision-making process will not form the basis for damages. In similar fashion, the distinction between fact and opinion is often unclear. Opinions generally include such things as predictions and promises. A promise is often the basis for a contractual agreement and, if broken, may form the basis for a **breach of contract** claim, as discussed later in this chapter, but is seldom the basis for a claim of fraud.

KEY POINTS

One of the most unusual misrepresentation cases involves a house that was de clared to be haunted "as a matter of law" by the Appellate Division of the State Supreme Court of New York. The purchasers, claiming to be "the victims of ectoplasmic fraud" and that the agent "hadn't said boo about the house being haunted," asked to have the $650,000 purchase contract rescinded and their $32,500 binder returned. Because the house had been the subject of articles in *Reader's Digest* and the local newspaper, and Kreskin had asked permission to perform a seance in the house, the court was "moved by the spirit of equity" to allow the purchasers to break the contract. Although the purchasers had agreed to take the property "as is," the court noted that the sellers had failed to deliver a "vacant" house as the contract required. The court also noted that, although buyers can call termite inspectors and structural engineers to check the condition of the house, it is more difficult in the field of paranormal phenomena. After all, asked the court, "Who you gonna call?"

Puffing
Statements of opinion made by salespersons or brokers regarding features or characteristics of a property being offered for sale.

Many people believe that salespersons have a natural tendency to inflate the quality and desirability of their products. This process, often called **"puffing,"** results in statements meant to place the property in its best light. In most instances, puffing will not form the basis for fraud, even if what is said is not literally the truth. This is due to the nature of such statements as opinions rather than facts and the belief that most adults have the ability to discount or ignore obviously inflated opinions. Real estate agents, however, are given much less tolerance by courts for puffing based on the position of trust they enjoy, the presumption of expertise based primarily on the licensing laws, and the naive nature of the parties to the transaction. Like so many things in law, the definitions of materiality and fact are decisions to be determined by the court based on the particulars of the situation.

[4] Some people make a distinction between *actual* fraud or deceit, when it is based on an intentional deception, and *constructive* fraud, when the deception was unintentional.

Liability for damages for real estate agents can occur even when the injured party is simply viewing a property. In *Smith v. Inman Realty Company* (846 S.W.2d 819, 1992), an agent holding an open house agreed to allow an individual to also view a partially completed home next door to the open house. The agent accompanied the visitor who, while viewing a bathroom that had no windows, stepped into a hole cut in the floor for a heating and air conditioning vent and injured her left foot causing her to miss over forty days of work. The trial court awarded Smith $7,500 from the sub-contractor but dismissed the suit against the real estate agent. An appeal of the dismissal resulted in a judgment that "[p]ossessors of property and those acting on their behalf owe a duty of reasonable care to patrons and invitees. . . . This duty includes (1) the duty to maintain the premises in a reasonably safe condition, . . . (2) the duty to inspect the premises to discover dangerous conditions reasonably recognizable by common experience and ordinary prudence, . . . ; and (3) the duty to either remove or to warn of the dangerous condition the possessor knows or should reasonably know about."

The duty to inspect, described previously, serves to help define the liability exposure of the agent in situations involving fraud. The court will ask if a "reasonably competent" professional should have been aware of the discrepancy that forms the basis for the claim. In other words, an agent may not simply rely on the fact that the information was provided by the seller as the basis for liability protection. The court will impose a duty to conform to a standard of professional and ethical conduct when dealing with the public. Thus the problem for the agent is one of definition. There are no strict rules that define the boundaries of acceptable behavior by an agent. What, for instance, constitutes a "reasonably diligent and competent" inspection? At what point is an agent obligated to seek out confirmation of seller-provided information?

KEY POINTS

Most claims against real estate agents come from buyers of properties. One re port suggests that buyers make 75 percent of all claims against agents, sellers make 12 percent of claims, and other third parties make the remaining 13 percent. It is also interesting to note that 81 percent of all liability insurance claims are based on residential property transactions.

Misrepresentation

An agent who presents information, even information that she honestly believes to be true, which turns out to be false has misrepresented the property. Any misrepresentation of a material fact will provide grounds for rescinding the agreement. If damages can be demonstrated, most misrepresentations will also form the basis for a damage award. Although some courts still accept the so-called innocent misrepresentation defense when awarding damages, many do not. The notion of consumer protection is one in which the goal is to provide protection for the damaged party. If the agent played a role in causing damage to a party, even though she may have acted honestly, the injured party must still be compensated.

The general rule relating to when conditions must be disclosed to purchasers allows sellers and their agents to remain silent about conditions that are reasonably observable by all parties so long as they do not actively attempt to conceal such conditions. In *Fullington v. Meadows* (1993 WL 166287) purchasers of two lots in a new subdivision, one of whom had already constructed a new home on his lot, sued the developer, real estate agent, and builder when they discovered that a sink hole was located on the property line between the two lots. The buyers discovered the existence of the sink hole only after heavy rainfall caused water to erupt from the sink hole and flood the basement of the new house.

The court agreed that the developer did not actively try to conceal the existence of the sink hole. Because the hole had been filled in, however, the court decided that the purchasers could not have known about its existence and, since the developer admitted knowledge of the sink hole and had specifically located the property line on it to avoid constructing houses near it, found for the buyers. Both buyers recovered the original price of their lots and the buyer who had constructed a home was awarded an amount equal to the cost of the home, a total of over $81,500.

Many courts rely on a determination of *negligence* by an agent in deciding when damages will be awarded. Negligence is often the result of a violation of one or more of the fiduciary duties owed to a principal. The disclosure rules described earlier, however, have tended to expand the notion of negligence to include parties other than the principal. Thus the legal environment is quickly approaching a strict liability standard in which any action that results in harm to any party will lead to liability exposure for the agent.

KEY POINTS

Although all claims of misrepresentation, even those involving ghosts, must be taken seriously, a Vermont case pushed the liability concept to a new level. After the first substantial snowfall of the year, the new owners of a home turned on the gas-powered deicer under the steep driveway of their new home and went to bed. The couple and their 23-month-old daughter died in their sleep from carbon monoxide fumes seeping from the faulty gas heater in the adjoining garage. The seller of the house was charged with three counts of involuntary manslaughter for failing to tell the buyers the heater was malfunctioning. Although rare, homicide charges can be filed in connection with the sale of a home.

Dual Agency

Dual Agency Created when an agent represents two parties who are in an adversarial relationship.

When an agent sets out to represent both parties in a transaction, the relationship is called a **dual agency.** Dual agencies can, of course, be intentionally created, and there are situations in which they are a legal, normal means of conducting business. The primary requirement in creating such relationships is one of disclosure. Both parties must know that the agent is acting in a dual capacity. In real estate brokerage, dual agency situations, at least ones that were intentionally created, are rare. A look at the fiduciary obligations owed by an agent to a principal provides a fairly good explanation as to why this is the case. Many of the obligations are difficult, if not impossible, to fulfill when the agent represents two parties who are in adversarial positions.

Unfortunately, many dual agency situations are created by accident. The material in Chapter 12 on forming agency relationships illustrates how this might happen. Some real estate brokers see their role not as that of a traditionally defined agent with the attendant fiduciary obligations but as a "go-between" or facilitator. Although a compelling argument can be made for assuming this role, the fact is that virtually all court rulings have defined the relationship as one involving agency concepts. The notion of the broker as a middleman is one that is not accepted. The reasons for this are numerous but primarily involve the same issues already described—protection of a naive, trusting public.

Property House v. Kelley

Mishandling of Funds

In Chapter 12, a list of common grounds for license revocation found in state licensing statutes was presented. In addition to the types of actions that would constitute fraud, several involve violations of fiduciary obligations. The most common violation is probably one involving some mishandling of client funds. Although some violations are technical in nature (e.g., not using an approved banking institution, not maintaining records in the proper format), some may constitute the basis for a claim against the agent.

Generally an agent must act in a fashion similar to a bank when dealing with money that belongs to someone else. After all, agents and bankers are both serving as fiduciaries. What this means in practice is that the agent must keep all such money in accounts separate from those of the agent or agency. No funds may be placed, even temporarily, in a private account of an agent or an operating account of the agency. To do so constitutes a **commingling of funds.**

Commingling of Funds Allowing monies held by a broker as trustee to be mixed with other funds of the broker or firm.

Even minor errors involving escrow accounts can lead to penalties. Although a hearing officer found an unauthorized $50 withdrawal from an escrow account to have been inadvertent, the broker was given one year of probation and fined $500 for the action. The broker appealed and in *Schumacher v. Department of Professional Regulation, Division of Real Estate* (611 So.2d 75, 1992), the court found that the Division acted in excess of its discretion and dismissed the charge. What is interesting about this case is not the fact that the broker ultimately prevailed, but that the real reason for the rather severe penalty was due to the failure of the broker to "promptly produce her records" for review. Even though its penalty was set aside, the Division seems to have sent a pretty clear message to brokers that requests for records must be responded to promptly.

Breach of Contract

A contract is, in essence, a promise made by two or more parties to do some act at some point in the future in exchange for some form of compensation. The many aspects of contract law are obviously well beyond the scope of this discussion, but the basic premise is not. When a seller signs a listing contract or a buyer signs a purchase contract, all of the parties to the agreement, including agents when used, are bound by its terms and conditions.

A purchase contract, for example, obligates a buyer to complete the purchase of a property. Failure to do so would constitute a breach of the contract. When the refusal to complete the contract was caused by an action of the seller or seller's agent, however, the buyer may be in a position to rescind, rather than breach. Often the complaint against a buyer will be based on a breach of contract issue that the buyer will defend with a misrepresentation or fraud counterclaim. If the misrepresentation was made by an agent, not only will the agent find himself drawn into the dispute, but also he could easily end up as the only loser. In many instances, courts will find that two parties (e.g., the seller and the agent) contributed to the problem and will assess damages claims against each.

Securities Issues

Securities Investment contracts which meet the criteria for being considered a security.

One of the more troublesome issues in real estate brokerage is inadvertently slipping over into the area of **securities** dealing. A security, for example, shares of stock or bonds, is basically an investment medium. Although the purchase of real estate, even an owner-occupied, single-family residence, has many investment attributes, it is not technically a security instrument. To sell securities, a dealer, or broker, must carry a license, just as a real estate broker must. The problem is that these are not the same licenses. Thus a real estate broker who sells a house based, at least in part, on claims about its investment characteristics may have ventured into the securities law area. This is an area with rapidly growing applications in real estate, as is discussed in Chapter 18.

The primary issue for real estate agents, in the context of liability exposure, is one of defining the difference between a statement of opinion concerning the property ("I think this is a good neighborhood where housing will rise in value") and one primarily concerning an investment ("This house will be a great investment for you"). The first is not actionable as fraud because no factual statement was made, although even here some courts use a "higher standard" of conduct for real estate transactions. The latter statement may well result in an actionable complaint based on the position of trust the agent occupies—particularly if the claim turns out not to be true.

During the 1970s, many real estate agents made the mistake of establishing transactions using "creative financing" techniques. These creative techniques often used a short-term loan from the seller, which was to be replaced with a new first mortgage when interest rates dropped. Unfortunately, in many instances, the rates did not drop as predicted by the agents who put the deals together. When this happened, sellers were forced to extend the financing to buyers for a longer time period, often causing chain reactions in other transactions, or buyers faced losing the property. Obviously many agents found themselves in court, often on the losing end.

ANTITRUST ISSUES

The second major area of liability exposure for real estate professions, primarily brokers and salespersons, involves antitrust issues. Antitrust legislation has one of the longest records of any business law area. Beginning with the Sherman Antitrust Act in 1890, Congress has been concerned about the effects of acts which tend to limit free enterprise. Table 13.1 summarizes much of this legislative history.

Brokerage Commission Structures

The Federal Trade Commission (FTC) has long been concerned with the commission structure in real estate brokerage firms. In particular, the issue of **price fixing**, in

TABLE 13.1 FEDERAL ANTITRUST LEGISLATION

1890	**Sherman Antitrust Act** Outlawed monopolies as well as contracts, combinations, and conspiracies that restrain trade.
1914	**Clayton Act** Regulated price discrimination, tying contracts, exclusive dealing arrangements, requirements contracts, reciprocal deals, and acquisition of stock of another company.
	Amendments to the Clayton Act
1936	***Robinson-Patman Act*** Regulated seller-induced price discrimination, buyer-induced price discrimination, and price discounts (i.e., advertising allowances, brokers discounts).
1950	***Celler-Kefauver Amendment*** Regulated acquisition of assets as well as stock of another company.
1976	***Hart-Scott-Rodino Antitrust Improvement Act*** Required large firms to prenotify Federal Trade Commission (FTC) of intentions to merge.
1914	**Federal Trade Commission Act** Declared unfair methods of competition to be illegal; established the FTC.
	Amendments to the FTC Act
1938	***Wheeler-Lea Act*** Prohibited deceptive acts and practices as well as unfair methods of competition.
1973	***Alaska Pipeline Act*** Increased penalty for violating a cease and desist order; allowed injunctive relief.
1975	***FTC Improvement Act*** Expanded idea of trade regulation rules; expanded remedial powers of FTC.

State of Washington v. Black

he context of a restraint of competition, has been a major issue. When a commission structure is fixed by some agreement among individuals or firms who are, or should be, competitors, free and open competition ceases to exist in a meaningful fashion. This situation is obviously detrimental to consumers and is thus a concern of Congress. Real estate brokers have often found themselves in situations that, at least on the surface, resemble a fixed price structure.

Price Fixing Actions by competing firms to mutually agree upon a fee or commission structure which will be charged by all firms in the market.

There can be no doubt that the Sherman Antitrust Act applies to real estate brokerage, that issue was effectively settled by the Supreme Court in 1950 in *United States v. National Association of Real Estate Boards,* 339 U.S. 485, 70 S.Ct. 711 (1950). The only issue that remains is to what extent, if any, price fixing occurs in real estate brokerage. The National Association of Realtors® (NAR) is concerned enough about this issue to provide training materials to local Boards cautioning against any discussion of commission structures with competitors. Their advice is simply to leave any conversation when the subject of commissions rates, fees, or prices is raised. The advice is sound for two reasons: first, to avoid creating a price fixing situation in the first place and, second, to avoid being pulled into a suit. The latter situation happens when the FTC uses its most common form of information gathering—the offering of immunity from prosecution for help in developing a case against others. Thus anyone who brings up the subject of commission rates is, or certainly should be, suspect.

KEY POINTS

In a case that *Business Week* (January 20, 1992, p. 78) said "could cut home prices," a predominately black brokers' organization, called the Empire Real Estate Board, charged the local Board of Realtors with illegally "tying" products by requiring membership in NAR as a condition for use of the board-owned multiple listing service (MLS), engaging in a group boycott, and conspiring to monopolize the MLS market in south Atlanta. The Court of Appeals upheld the tying and group boycott claims and denied a request for a rehearing. The U.S. Supreme Court refused to hear the case; thus it currently applies only in a few southern states. Several similar suits, however, are now being filed in other parts of the U.S. Some estimates of the total effect on the current $25 billion paid each year in commissions suggest that, were all multiple listing services to be opened, as much as $10 billion a year in reduced commissions would result.

Agency and Subagency Issues

Marin County Board of Realtors v. Palsson

Anticompetitive Practices Actions by competitors whereby they agree to cooperate in the marketplace to form effective monopolies.

The second major area of antitrust concern is that of **anticompetitive practices,** or the creation of effective monopolies. This occurs when, in a particular market area, especially a small market, a single organization controls the market to a large extent. This does not mean that a single brokerage firm dominates the market. Although this would also be a problem, it rarely if ever occurs. Rather an organization to which the majority, often an overwhelming majority, of real estate brokers belong effectively controls access to the market by controlling access to membership in the organization. For example, if a local Board of Realtors operates the only **multiple listing service** (MLS) in the area and allows access to the MLS only to members, nonmembers are placed at a severe competitive disadvantage.

This is a complex issue that involves aspects of antitrust and, in most areas, notions of agency law as well. Many people point to a California case, *Marin County Board of Realtors v. Palsson* (549 P.2d 833) in 1976 as a turning point in the issue of monopolies. In this case, included at the end of this chapter, the issue was whether or not the local Board of Realtors could deny membership to an individual and thus deny him access to the only effective MLS in the area. The court held that:

> The board's rules denying access of nonmembers to the multiple listing service must be eliminated, although nonmembers may be charged a reasonable fee for use of the service consistent with the per-capita costs of operation. In addition, as long as membership in the board is necessary for employment by an active member, the board should be enjoined from enforcing or promulgating any bylaw or other rule which conditions associate membership . . . (*id.* at 845)

This ruling effectively ended the control by Boards of Realtors over MLS systems in California and, to the extent that MLS access is a major benefit of membership in the Board, took away a major enticement to membership. To avoid a repeat of this situation in other states, NAR responded by making a change in the nature of standard MLS agreements. Conceptually a MLS is an information gathering and sharing device that allows participants to know about all property available for sale in the area served by the system. This is a major competitive advantage and has become an essential aspect of the real estate brokerage business. Although an agreement concerning the split of commissions or fees is an integral part of MLS arrangements, a legal relationship between participants is not essential.

Multiple Listing Service A cooperative agreement between brokers to share listings and split commissions.

The standard MLS agreement[5] (except in California), however, now uses a system of agency and subagency agreements as described in Chapter 12. In effect, any participant who uses the MLS becomes an automatic subagent of the listing agent. Although not essential to the operation of a MLS, NAR justifies this arrangement by pointing out the fiduciary nature of the agency relationship. The listing agent, as a fiduciary, has significant obligations to the principal. The only way to ensure that these obligations will be upheld when a MLS is employed is to make all participants parties to the original agency agreement. In addition, NAR points out that because only members of NAR are bound by the Code of Ethics, membership must of necessity be limited to NAR members to ensure ethical behavior by all MLS participants.

Although this line of reasoning has some appeal, the agency liability issues described earlier in this chapter combined with the antitrust issues inherent in a monopolistic situation (compounded by the use of standard contracts—although the commission rate is not, or certainly should not be, printed on the form) are causing many brokers to reevaluate the current use of agency and subagency relationships.

KEY POINTS

Some commentators have taken the position that the real estate brokerage industry, primarily because of the use of multiple listing services owned by local Boards of Realtors, suffers from a high degree of anticompetitive practices. These practices, it is claimed, have resulted in the "artificially high" brokerage commission rates prevalent in the industry. One author even claims that the "real" commission rate would be closer to 2 percent if all restrictions to fair trade were removed from the industry (E. Lesly, "How Your Realtor Rips You Off," *The Wall Street Journal,* November 30, 1990). Although estimates vary a great deal, one estimate puts the total "excess commissions" figure at $26 billion a year.

Boycotts and Conspiracies

The final antitrust issue is one of unfair methods of competition. Many states have enacted legislation modeled after the Federal Trade Commission (FTC) Act. These statutes, often called Consumer Protection Acts, are designed to protect the public

[5] This type of contract is being eliminated based on recommendations made by the *Presidential Advisory Group On Agency,* whose report is described in Chapter 19.

from firms using unfair methods of competition. Although most applications of these Acts involve products rather than services, there is no question about the relevance of these Acts to real estate brokerage services.

Boycott An agreement not to use a firm's services. Permissable if done by customers, but generally illegal if done by competitors.

Any action that results in an elimination or reduction of competition is unlawful under these Acts. For example, the legality of an agreement to **boycott** the products or services of a firm depends on who is doing the boycotting. If the boycott is by customers, then under most circumstances the action would not violate antitrust Acts. If, however, the group boycotting is composed of competitors, then the actions are generally unlawful. Boycotts by competitors are often designed to force a competitor to change his business practices or, in the extreme, drive him out of the market. Such boycotts may be characterized by courts as *conspiracies,* and when such actions violate antitrust laws, they also constitute an unfair method of competition under FTC Acts.

In real estate brokerage, many such boycotts have taken place or been attempted. Usually the target is a competing firm that begins to offer discount fees or services. In an effort to maintain the current commission structure, competing firms may refuse to show any property listed by the offending broker and refuse to allow brokers using such fee structures to participate in the MLS. There is an obvious overlap between the notion of an unfair methods of competition claim and an antitrust violation. Yet each is a potential violation of a different set of laws, and each constitutes a separate claim of wrongdoing.

CONCLUSION

In this chapter, we have examined the major sources of liability exposure for real estate professionals. In the Chapter 14, we continue this discussion with an examination of two related topics—fair housing issues and environmental contamination problems. Real estate professionals must be prepared to cope with the liability exposure created by the complex regulatory environment surrounding fair housing and environmental concerns. As pointed out earlier, nearly all potential liability exposure for real estate professionals flows at least indirectly from the agency issues discussed here and in Chapter 12. Until and unless the agency structure used in real estate is significantly altered, real estate professionals will continue to find themselves exposed to significant liability potential.

DISCUSSION QUESTIONS

1. Describe the elements included in a fraudulent real estate transaction. When is a fact material?
2. Distinguish between misrepresentation and negligence.
3. How must an agent act when dealing with money belonging to another party?
4. Why must real estate agents be concerned with securities laws?
5. One major area of liability exposure for real estate professionals involves antitrust issues. Give a brief overview of the three areas concerning antitrust and the real estate professional.

6. Explain why linking membership in an organization such as the National Association of Realtors to gaining access to a multiple listing service may have a significant impact on the cost of housing.
7. What is meant by a "boycott"? How is a boycott different from a "conspiracy," and why is this distinction important?

REED
V.
KING

193 Cal. Rptr. 130 (Court of Appeal, Third District, 1983)

Psychologically impacted property

In the sale of a house, must the seller disclose it was the site of a multiple murder? Dorris Reed purchased a house from Robert King. Neither King nor his real estate agents (the other named defendants) told Reed that a woman and her four children were murdered there ten years earlier. However, it seems "truth will come to light; murder cannot be hid long." (Shakespeare, Merchant of Venice, *Act II, Scene II.) Reed learned of the gruesome episode from a neighbor after the sale. She sues seeking rescission and damages. . . .*

FACTS

. . . King and his real estate agent knew about the murders and knew the event materially affected the market value of the house when they listed it for sale. They represented to Reed the premises were in good condition and fit for an "elderly lady" living alone. They did not disclose the fact of the murders. At some point King asked a neighbor not to inform Reed of that event. Nonetheless, after Reed moved in neighbors informed her no one was interested in purchasing the house because of the stigma. Reed paid $76,000, but the house is only worth $65,000 because of its past. . . .

DISCUSSION

Does Reed's pleading state a cause of action? Concealed within this question is the nettlesome problem of the duty of disclosure of blemishes on real property which are not physical defects or legal impairments to use. . . .

The trial court perceived the defect in Reed's complaint to be a failure to allege concealment of a material fact. . . . As appears, the analytic pathways to these conclusions are intertwined. [1] Concealment is a term of art which includes mere nondisclosure when a party has a duty to disclose. . . . Accordingly, the critical question is: does the seller have duty to disclose here? Resolution of this question depends on the materiality of the fact of the murders.

[2] In general, a seller of real property has a duty to disclose: "where the seller knows of facts *materially* affecting the value or desirability of the property which are known or accessible only to him and also knows that such facts are not known to, or within the reach of the diligent attention and observation of the buyer, the seller is under a duty to disclose them to the buyer."[1] . . . This broad statement of duty has led one commentator to conclude: "The ancient maxim caveat emptor ('let the buyer beware.') has little or no application to California real estate transactions." . . .

[3] [4] Whether information "is of sufficient materiality to affect the value or desirability of the property . . . depends on the facts of the particular case." . . . Materiality "is a question of law" . . . Three considerations bear on this legal conclusion: the gravity of the harm inflicted by non-disclosure; the fairness of imposing a duty of discovery on the buyer as an alternative to compelling disclosure, and its impact on the stability of contracts if rescission is permitted.

Numerous cases have found non-disclosure of physical defects and legal impediments to use of real property are material. . . . Should this variety

[1] The real estate agent or broker representing the seller is under the same duty of disclosure. . . .

of ill-repute be required to be disclosed? Is this a circumstance where "non-disclosure of the fact amounts to a failure to act in good faith and in accordance with reasonable standards of fair dealing [?]" . . .

If such an "irrational" consideration is permitted as a basis of rescission, the stability of all conveyances will be seriously undermined. Any fact that might disquiet the enjoyment of some segment of the buying public may be seized upon by a disgruntled purchaser to void a bargain . . .

The murder of innocents is highly unusual in its potential for so disturbing buyers they may be unable to reside in a home where it has occurred. This fact may foreseeably deprive a buyer of the intended use of the purchase. Murder is not such a common occurrence that buyers should be charged with anticipating and discovering this disquieting possibility. Accordingly, the fact is not one for which a duty of inquiry and discovery can sensibly be imposed upon the buyer.

. . . If information known or accessible only to the seller has a significant and measurable effect on market value and, as is alleged here, the seller is aware of this effect, we see no principled basis for making the duty to disclose turn upon the character of the information. . . .

[5] [6] Reputation and history can have a significant effect on the value of realty. "George Washington slept here" is worth something, however physically inconsequential that consideration may be. Ill-repute or "bad will" conversely may depress the value of property. . . .

The judgment is reversed.

Case Reflections

1. Which fiduciary obligation(s) did plaintiff Reed claim the defendent breached? What was the Trial Court's initial ruling?
2. What issue was the Appellate Court asked to decide in this case?
3. What line of reasoning did the Appellate Court use to overturn the Trial Court's decision?

EASTON V. STRASSBURGER

199 Cal. Rptr. 383 (Court of Appeal, 1984)

Misrepresentation and the affirmative duty to disclose

The Superior Court . . . entered judgment in favor of purchaser on negligence cause of action brought against real estate broker and broker appealed. The court of Appeal . . . , held that: (1) duty of a real estate broker, representing the vendor, to disclose facts includes the affirmative duty to conduct a reasonably competent and diligent inspection of the residential property listed for sale and to disclose to prospective purchasers all facts materially affecting the value or desirability of the property that such an investigation would reveal; (2) verdict finding real estate broker negligent in connection with damage sustained by purchaser of residential property which was damaged by massive earth movements was supported by substantial evidence; . . .
Affirmed in part and reversed and remanded with instruction in part.

FACTS

. . . [T]he record discloses the following facts: The property which is the subject of this appeal is a one-acre parcel of land located in the City of Diablo. The property is improved with a 3,000 square foot home, a swimming pool, and a large guest house. Respondent purchased the property for $170,000 from the Strassburgers in May of 1976 . . . Appellant was the listing broker in the transaction.

Shortly after respondent purchased the property, there was massive earth movement on the parcel. Subsequent slides destroyed a portion of the driveway in 1977 or 1978. Expert testimony indicated that the slides occurred because a portion of the property was fill that had not been properly engineered and compacted. The slides caused the foundation of the house to settle which in turn caused cracks in the walls and warped doorways. After the 1976 slide, damage to the property was so severe that although experts appraised the value of the property at $170,000 in an undamaged condition, the value of the damaged property was estimated to be as low as $20,000. Estimates of the cost to repair the damage caused by the slides and avoid recurrence ranged as high as $213,000.

. . . It is uncontested that . . . agents conducted several inspections of the property prior to sale. There is also evidence they were aware of certain "red flags" which should have indicated to them that there were soil problems. Despite this, the agents did not request that the soil stability of the property be tested and did not inform respondent that there were potential soil problems.

During the time that the property was owned by the Strassburgers there was a minor slide in 1973 involving about ten to twelve feet of the filled slope and a major slide in 1975 in which the fill dropped about eight to ten feet in a circular shape fifty to sixty feet across. However, the Strassburgers did not tell [the agents] anything about the slides or the corrective action they had taken.

Respondent purchased the property without being aware of the soil problems or the past history of slides.

In December of 1976 respondent filed suit against appellant, the Strassburgers, and three other named defendants.[1] As against appellant, respondent alleged causes of action for fraudulent concealment, intentional misrepresentation, and negligent misrepresentation. . . .

The action was tried before a jury. . . . The jury returned a special verdict finding that all named defendants had been negligent, and assessed damages of $197,000. . . .

DISCUSSION

. . . We are concerned here only with the elements of a simple negligence action; that is, whether appellant owed a legal duty to respondent to use due care, whether this legal duty was breached, and finally whether the breach was a proximate cause of appellant's injury . . .

[1] [2] . . . Appellant does not contend that it was under no duty to exercise due care to prevent injury to respondent[2] . . .

[3] [4] [5] It is not disputed that current law requires a broker to disclose to a buyer material defects known to the broker but unknown to and unobservable by the buyer . . . The issue, then, is whether a broker is negligent if he fails to disclose defects which he should have discovered through reasonable diligence. Stated another way, we must determine whether the broker's duty of due care in a residential real estate transaction includes a duty to conduct a reasonably competent and diligent inspection of property he has listed for sale in order to discover defects for the benefit of the buyer. . . .

. . . If a broker were required to disclose only known defects, but not also those that are reasonably discoverable, he would be shielded by his ignorance of that which he holds himself out to know. . . . Such a construction would not only reward the unskilled broker for his own incompetence, but might provide the unscrupulous broker the unilateral ability to protect himself at the expense of the inexperienced and unwary who rely upon him. In any case, if given legal force, the theory that a seller's broker cannot be held accountable for what he does not know but could discover without great difficulty would inevitably produce a disincentive for a seller's broker to make a diligent inspection. Such a disincentive would be most unfortunate, since in residential sales transactions the seller's broker is most frequently the best situated to obtain and provide the most reliable information on the property and is ordinarily counted on to do so.

. . . Definition of the broker's duty to disclose as necessarily including the responsibility to conduct a reasonable investigation thus seems to us warranted by the pertinent realities. . . . It seems relevant to us, in this regard, that the duty to disclose that should be known is a formally acknowl-

[1] These three defendants—San Ramon Builders, George Sauer, and H.M. Bull—were sued for negligent construction only.

[2] Despite the absence of privity of contract, a real estate agent is clearly under a duty to exercise reasonable care to protect those persons whom the agent is attempting to induce into entering a real estate transaction for the purpose of earning a commission . . .

edged professional obligation that it appears many brokers customarily impose upon themselves as an ethical matter. Thus, The Code of Ethics of the National Association of Realtors . . . includes . . . the provision that a broker must not only "avoid . . . concealment of pertinent facts," but "has an affirmative obligation to discover adverse factors that a reasonably competent and diligent investigation would disclose." . . .

In sum, we hold that the duty of a real estate broker, representing the seller, to disclose facts, . . . includes the affirmative duty to conduct a reasonably competent and diligent inspection of the residential[3] property listed for sale and to disclose to prospective purchasers all facts materially affecting the value or desirability of the property that such an investigation would reveal.

. . . Real estate agents hold themselves out to the public as professionals, and, as such, are required to make reasonable use of their superior knowledge, skills, and experience within the area of their expertise . . . Because such agents are expected to make use of their superior knowledge and skills, which is the reason they are engaged, and because the agents in this case were or should have been alert to the signs of soil problems earlier described, the jury was well within the bounds of reason when it concluded that a reasonably diligent and competent inspection of the property would have included something more than a casual visual inspection and a general inquiry of the owners. . . .

[3] We express no opinion here whether a broker's obligation to conduct an inspection for defects for the benefit of the buyer applies to the sale of commercial real estate. Unlike the residential home buyer, who is often unrepresented by a broker, or is effectively unrepresented because of the problems of dual agency . . . , a purchaser of commercial real estate is likely to be more experienced and sophisticated in his dealings in real estate and is usually represented by an agent who represents only the buyer's interests . . .

Case Reflections

1. State the issue presented to the Appellate Court.
2. Describe the duty of disclosure as defined in Chapter 12. What duties did the Appellate Court add to this definition?

PROPERTY HOUSE, INC.
V.
KELLEY

68 Haw. 371, 715 P.2d 805 (Supreme Court, 1986)

Failure to disclose a dual agency situation

Action was instituted by broker to recover real estate commissions from vendors in connection with two separate transactions. . . . (2) breach of the duty of full disclosure by real estate broker when the agency was dual and broker did not obtain the consent of both principals after full disclosure operated to deprive broker of its right to a commission.
As to . . . count II, reversed.

SYLLABUS BY THE COURT

. . . 3. A real estate agent bears a duty to make a full, fair, and timely disclosure to the principal of all facts within the agent's knowledge which are, or may be, material to the transaction and which might affect the principal's rights and interests or influence his actions.

4. A dual agency is permissible only where the real estate agent obtains the consent of both principals after full disclosure.

5. The breach by a real estate broker of the duty of full disclosure deprives him of his right to a commission.

6. Under Hawaii law, there is no exception to the real estate broker's duty of full disclosure for "finders" or "middlemen" who merely bring parties together so that they may negotiate their own contract, and who have no power to and do not negotiate the terms on which the principals deal. . . .

A.

On July 31, 1979, Property House and Roy Kelley entered into an exclusive listing agreement for the sale of the Coral Seas and Reef Lanai hotels . . .

Some time after receiving the exclusive listing, Property House entered into an agreement with Jay H. Shidler (hereinafter "Shidler") to represent him as a potential buyer of the hotels. . . .

B.

. . . [4] [5] The rules of agency apply to the relationship between a real estate broker and principal. . . . The law imposes upon a real estate broker a fiduciary obligation comprised of utmost good faith, integrity, honesty, and loyalty, as well as a duty of due care and diligence. . . . In particular, a real estate agent bears a duty to make a full, fair, and timely disclosure to the principal of all facts within the agent's knowledge which are, or may be, material to the transaction and which might affect the principal's rights and interests or influence his actions. . . .

[6] In Jenkins v. Wise . . . we recognized the requirement that a principal must have knowledge of and consent to the purchase by a real estate agent of property which he has been authorized to sell, or else the transaction would be voidable by the principal.

Similarly, in Silva v. Bisbee . . . the court recognized that, absent full disclosure to the client, it was a breach of fiduciary duty for a real estate broker to sell the client's property to a party in which the broker had a pecuniary interest.

[7] A dual agency is therefore permissible only where the agent obtains the consent of both principals after full disclosure. . . .

[8] The breach of the duty of full disclosure by Property House deprives it of its right to a commission. . . . These consequences follow even though the principal ignorant of the duplicitous agency cannot prove actual injury to himself or that the agent committed an intentional fraud. . . .

C.

. . . [9] A "finder" or "middleman" is one whose employment is limited to bringing parties together so that they may negotiate their own contract. . . . On the other hand, "a broker, in addition to the duties of a 'middleman,' is employed to use discretionary authority for the benefit of his employer and to act for his best interests."

[10] Even if Property House acted merely as a "middleman" in this transaction, we choose not to recognize a "middleman" exception to the real estate broker's duty of full disclosure. The disclosure and consent requirements, while certainly not burdensome, serve to reduce the risk of misconduct by an intermediary. By keeping all parties fully informed, they reduce the potential for misunderstanding and dispute. . . .

Case Reflections

1. What is a "middleman"? How does the role of a middleman differ from that of an agent?
2. Why did the Court refuse to recognize a "middleman" exception to the agency duty of full disclosure?
3. How was a dual agency created in this instance? Why did a failure to disclose the nature of the situation result in a loss of commissions for the agent even without proof of damages?

MARIN COUNTY BOARD OF REALTORS, INC. V. PALSSON

130 Cal. Rptr. 1, 549 P.2d 833 (Supreme Court, 1976)

Denial of access to MLS as an antitrust violation

We decide here for the first time the extent to which the state antitrust law circumscribes the practices of a multiple listing service operated by a county board of realtors. We conclude that the Marin County Board of Realtors has violated the Cartwright Act . . . by limiting its membership to persons primarily engaged in the real estate business and by denying nonmembers access to its multiple listing service.

The board is an incorporated real estate association affiliated with the California Real Estate Association and the National Association of Real Estate Boards. . . . Three-fourths of the brokers actively engaged in selling residential real property in Marin County were members of the board. The board provides a number of benefits to its members, the most important of which is the only multiple listing service for residential property operating exclusively in Marin county . . .

The listings are available only to active and associate board members, who are prohibited by the board's bylaws from disseminating published listings to nonmembers. Although each active member may cooperate with nonmember brokers in selling his own listing, the actual extent of such cooperation is negligible . . .

Eugene Palsson, a licensed real estate salesman, applied to the board for membership after obtaining employment with an active member. His application was denied because the board found that Palsson, an airline flight engineer, did not meet the requirements of one of the board's bylaws which provided that an associate member must be "primarily engaged in the real estate business." This provision was enforced through sanctions against an active member sharing offices with or employing a person denied membership in the board. Thus, a salesman denied membership was also denied employment with 75 percent of the residential brokers in Marin County.[1] . . .

I

While neither of the parties raise the issue, the California Association of Realtors (CAR), in an amicus brief, maintains that the Cartwright Act does not apply to the sale of services. This theory, raised here for the first time, appears to be contrary to federal and state authority. Indeed, the United States Supreme Court has expressly held that the Sherman Act applies to the activity of real estate brokers. . . .

III

. . . The threshold question is whether the practices of the board should be judged per se violations of the Cartwright Act or reviewed under the "rule of reason" standard. In general, only unreasonable restraints of trade are prohibited. . . . However, "there are certain agreements or practices which because of their pernicious effect on competition and lack of any redeeming virtue are conclusively presumed to be unreasonable and therefore illegal without elaborate inquiry as to the precise harm they have caused or the business excuse for their use." . . . Among these per se violations is the concerted refusal to deal with other traders, or, as it is often called, the group boycott. . . .

IV

Under the rule of reason standard, pursuant to the salutary purposes of the antitrust law, we must analyze the economic effects of the board's practices and then consider possible justifications for the practices. . . . Antitrust laws are designed primarily to aid the consumer. . . .

[1] Since a salesman must be employed by a broker in order to sell real estate . . . ,denial of membership and employment substantially hinders a salesman from pursuing a career in the real estate field.

Another beneficiary of antitrust law is the competitor himself. The preservation of competition, while indirectly aiding society by producing lower prices and higher quality goods and services, directly aids the scrupulous trader by insuring him a fair opportunity to compete on the market. . . .

Viewed in the light of these purposes, the practices of the board pose serious anticompetitive dangers both to licensed real estate salesmen and brokers and to consumers. . . .

Moreover, the "primarily engaged" rule inflicts particularly severe economic detriment on a part-time salesman. Denied membership in the board, he may not be employed by three-fourths of the residential real estate brokers in Marin County. And, unless employed by a licensed broker, he may not legally sell real estate. . . . Thus both rules seriously hamper a nonmember's ability to compete effectively in the real estate industry.

The buyer or seller of a home also suffers by the board's practices, although this injury is somewhat less evident. It may be argued that consumers are not being denied any housing information; all they must do is engage the services of a board member with access to the multiple listing service. . . . Consumer choice is thereby narrowed. A person wishing to sell or buy a home may believe that a particular nonmember is more competent than available members. But if the consumer wishes to have ready access to a large market in a short period of time, he may be forced to deal with a less desirable member broker or salesman.

This narrowing of choice may have an effect on the commissions a consumer must pay for brokerage service. . . .

We must weigh these anticompetitive effects against the possible justifications for the board's practices. The primary rationale for denying nonmembers access to the multiple listing service appears to be that the board has a right to make membership desirable by providing attractive benefits. . . . An association may, for example, require membership eligibility for participation in an educational seminar, even when the seminar may provide an economic benefit.

An association's freedom to exclude nonmembers from its activities is not absolute. It must yield to antitrust laws when (1) its activities begin to correspond directly with and touch upon the business activities of its members; and (2) the association has the power to shape and influence the economic environment of its particular market. . . . While the Marin County Board of Realtors may permissibly provide some exclusive benefits to its members, access to the multiple listing service is so essential to nonmembers if they are to compete effectively that such access must be granted to all licensed salesmen and brokers who choose to use the service. . . .

In this case, the board claims that its "primarily engaged" rule operates to further the professional and ethical competence of the real estate profession, surely a legitimate goal. A full-time salesman, maintains the board, will be more likely to educate himself on developments in the field and will have more time to devote to his clients.

This rationale can be challenged on two grounds. First, the purported necessity for the "primarily engaged" rule is minimal in light of the extensive state regulation of the real estate industry. . . . While the existence of regulatory statutes does not per se preempt the field and prevent the Marin County board from setting its own internal standards, the legislatively enacted scheme does call into question the professional need for the board to act as an extragovernmental agency. . . .

Second, the board has failed to establish that the "primarily engaged" rule facilitates an increase in professional or ethical competence in all or most cases. . . .

Even if the board's assumptions about part-time salesmen were empirically valid in many cases, the "primarily engaged" rule is too broadly drawn in light of its anticompetitive effects. If the board seeks to encourage further professional education and devotion to clients, the board could consider regulations aimed directly at those goals. . . .

V

. . . The board's rules denying access of nonmembers to the multiple listing service must be eliminated, although nonmembers may be charged a reasonable fee for use of the service consistent with the per-capita costs of operation. In addition, as long as membership in the board is necessary for employment by an active member, the board should be enjoined from enforcing or promulgating any bylaw or other rule which conditions associate membership on primary engagement in the real estate industry.

Case Reflections

1. On what grounds did the Board of Realtors refuse membership to the defendant?
2. Why did the refusal of membership put the defendant at a distinct disadvantage to salesmen who were members of the board?
3. How does the "primarily engaged" rule violate antitrust laws?

STATE OF WASHINGTON V. BLACK

676 P.2d 963 (Supreme Court, 1984).

Conspiracy to eliminate price competition

. . . On June 14, 1978, the State Attorney General filed this civil antitrust action against 14 Spokane area real estate brokers and the Spokane Board of Realtors. The complaint alleged that the defendants combined and conspired to eliminate price competition . . . and engaged in unfair methods of competition . . .

Respondents are all members of the Spokane Multiple Listing Service (MLS). Under the MLS rules, member brokers submit their listing contracts to the MLS which in turn publishes the pertinent information for use by other members. Any member broker is authorized to sell an MLS listing to a prospective buyer. A sale of property which is listed by one broker but sold by another is known in the industry as a "cross-sale." When a cross-sale is made, the listing broker splits part of its commission with the selling broker. The MLS policy during and prior to 1977 was to publish the total commission rate and the commission split which was offered to a selling broker in the event of a cross-sale. Testimony at trial indicated that prior to the time in question, most, but not all, brokers charged a 6 percent commission on new construction and a 7 percent commission on resale homes. The standard commission split between the listing and selling brokers was 50/50. . . .

The present controversy arose in May 1977 as a response to the adoption of a new marketing program instituted by Victor Lewis Realty (Lewis), known as the "Seller's Choice" program. Under this program, a property seller was given two options. The seller could agree to pay a 5 percent commission and receive the usual brokerage services. If the seller was willing to do some of the work, the seller could opt to pay a flat fee of $750. . . . The program was designed to attract the "for sale by owner" seller. If a seller who opted to pay the flat fee was unhappy with the do-it-yourself arrangement, the seller could convert the contract to a full-service commission arrangement.

The initiation of the Seller's Choice program triggered an immediate reaction throughout the Spokane real estate market. The trial court found that it also generated a great deal of confusion. . . . Lewis made it clear . . . that all Lewis listings, including flat fees, would continue to be listed through the MLS and that the commission split on a cross-sale was 50/50. Lewis continued to offer 6 and 7 percent commissions in addition to his seller's choice options. Testimony at trial indicated that other brokers could not determine from the MLS information submitted by Lewis whether a particular listing was flat fee or commission without first contacting Lewis. Testimony further indicated that even though Lewis' salespeople were not obligated to show flat fee listings, sales people from other brokerages felt it was their duty to show any home which was of interest to a prospective buyer. Thus, other brokers faced the possibility of providing full services on flat fee listings in return for half of the $750 fee. The trial court found that $375 was not enough to meet expenses in such a transaction. Even with a 5 percent commission, the trial court found that only companies with low overhead, such as Lewis, could economically survive.

Prior to the adoption of the Seller's Choice program, each of the respondent brokers maintained a 50/50 commission split policy with Lewis. Beginning in June and continuing for the next 3 months,

Lewis received letters from nine Spokane brokers . . . reducing their commission splits with Lewis Realty. On June 22, 1977, respondent Black indicated it would pay a flat rate of $250 on any Black-Lewis cross-sales—regardless of the actual commission. Respondent Tupper announced it would pay only 10 percent of the commission. Respondent Sullivan reduced its split to 90/10 while respondent Hege reduced its split to 85/15. At trial, respondents explained that the new splits were necessary to equalize the commission shares paid to Lewis with what they could expect to receive from Lewis. Testimony at trial showed that flat fee listings comprised a significant percentage of all Lewis listings following adoption of the Seller's Choice program and further that almost half of the Lewis flat fee listings were sold by other brokers. Testimony at trial also indicated that during the same period, respondents Black and Tupper changed their commission split policies with other real estate brokers. . . .

I. UNFAIR METHODS OF COMPETITION . . .

. . . The State urges that even where there is no conspiracy, anticompetitive unilateral conduct is sufficient to find a . . . violation. The State further argues that there is "overwhelming" evidence from which to conclude that respondents' reduced commission splits were in fact unfair and anticompetitive.

[1] Our State Consumer Protection Act . . . is patterned to a large extent after federal trade regulation statutes. . . .

[W]e conclude that the only conduct which could possibly constitute an unfair method of competition was the respondent brokers' individual action in sending letters to Victor Lewis announcing a reduced commission split. It is clear from the record that these letters were written in response to the Lewis Seller's Choice program. The trial court concluded, however, that the letters were written for legitimate business reasons and thus did not constitute an unfair method of competition. . . .

A reduction in commission splits may not be the fairest way to do business; however, we find that the trial court's finding of fact and conclusions of law are supported by the evidence. We therefore affirm the trial court's disposition of this issue.

II. THE 1974 CONSENT DECREE

[9] In 1974, the State Attorney General brought a civil antitrust action against Black and other Spokane realtors for what was alleged to be an attempt to fix a standard commission rate of 7 percent for resale contracts. The case was settled before trial and as part of the settlement, James S. Black Co. entered a consent decree which enjoined him from certain conduct related to price fixing. . . .

The 1974 consent decree is phrased in broad terms prohibiting even the indirect recommendation or suggestion of uniform commissions. The evidence at trial shows that by adopting a reciprocity basis for commission splits, Black made it clear to other brokers that if they wanted 3.5 percent of the selling price as a commission split, they would have to maintain a 7 percent commission with a 50/50 split. This conduct violates the literal terms of the 1974 consent decree regardless of whether it also constitutes an unfair method of competition . . .

Case Reflections

1. Why did the State believe that reduced commission splits were "anticompetitive"?
2. If listings in the MLS were labeled as to which were under the "Seller's Choice" program, would this solve the problem in this case? Why or why not?
3. What is the significance of the earlier consent decree for Black? If all firms had been subject to this decree, would this case have had a different outcome?

DIOXIN
HERE
DANGER
WORLD'S LARGEST
DIOXIN DUMP
150 FT.
FOR SALE
TO
THE HEARTLES
EPA

CHAPTER

14

LIABILITY OF REAL ESTATE PROFESSIONALS: FAIR HOUSING AND ENVIRONMENTAL ISSUES

LEARNING OBJECTIVES

After reading this chapter, you should be able to:

1. Describe the major areas of liability exposure for real estate professionals.
2. Appreciate the critical role that real estate plays in the area of race relations and all forms of discrimination.
3. Define the concepts of "blockbusting" and "racial steering" and explain why these practices have been banned.
4. List the major legal sources of environmental liability.
5. Describe the potential techniques for managing environmental risk.

KEY TERMS

Familial Status

Blockbusting

Racial Steering

Sign Ordinances

Handicapped Access Rules

Credit Discrimination

Redlining

Hazardous Substances

CERCLA

Potentially Responsible Party

SARA

Innocent Landowner Defense

Due Diligence Reviews

Indemnification Clause

The agency structure used in the real estate industry and the liability exposure that accompanies it require that persons working with real estate become intimately familiar with the major types of legislation that relate to real property transactions. Two of the most important areas of legislation are those regarding housing discrimination and environmental protection. These issues are important not only to real estate professionals, but also to everyone. These are issues that affect the way we live now and how we will live in the future. They affect not only us, but also our children and grandchildren. The issues discussed in this chapter transcend concerns about potential liability exposure and get to the heart of our society. The liability issues discussed here merely represent the degree of importance we as a society have placed on these topics.

Both of the topics discussed in this chapter are evolving at a somewhat rapid pace. Those working with real property must pay close attention to the shifting legislative and judicial standards in these areas. Risk reduction strategies for real estate professionals contain four basic components:

Education—avoid mistakes by knowing the regulatory landscape.

Risk anticipation—identify problem properties or clients, make necessary disclosures in a systematic fashion, and keep client expectations at reasonable levels so as to avoid dissatisfaction later.

Risk control—monitor all transactions and follow up all complaints or concerns using predefined resolution techniques.

Risk shifting—use insurance and warranty programs when possible, keep accurate records that detail the sources of all information, and use or advise the use of third-party professionals whenever possible.

The first step in devising an effective risk reduction strategy is to gain an understanding of the legal environment. This chapter concentrates on some of the most important sources of liability exposure for real estate professionals.

FAIR HOUSING ISSUES

The U.S. has had a long, troubled history with respect to civil rights. Even before its inception, the country struggled with moral issues involving individual rights and freedoms. That struggle, far from being settled, continues today in many aspects of our society. Real estate, particularly housing, represents much of what Americans hold dear. Although outdated in syntax, the notion that "a man's home is his castle" has taken tangible form in many of our laws, customs, and traditions.

The application of civil rights concepts to the area of real estate is perhaps one of the most important long-term issues facing the U.S. The prospect of an integrated society rests, to a large extent, on our ability to live together as neighbors. Thus housing has always played a prominent role in helping this nation move forward in terms of race relations.

Discrimination, however, does not involve only racial issues: Issues involving women (particularly in the granting of credit), physically and mentally handicapped individuals, and even children play major roles in this area. This section begins with a brief review of major civil rights legislation as it applies to real estate and then looks at the some of the specific areas of concern.

Civil Rights Acts

Although the Thirteenth Amendment to the Constitution abolished slavery in 1865, the history of civil rights laws really begins with the first civil rights act signed in 1866. This act, which still has major importance today, was the first of several acts passed during this time period and generally referred to as the Civil War laws. It was not until the 1960s, however, that the civil rights movement began, based, at least in the early years, on a belated enforcement of these Civil War laws. Perhaps the most famous of these cases, at least in terms of its impact on real estate, is that of *Jones v. Alfred H. Mayer, Co.* [392 U.S. 409, 20 L.Ed. 2d 1189, 88 S.Ct. 2186 (1968)], in which the Supreme Court held that the 1866 statute "... was intended to bar all racial discrimination, private as well as public, in the sale or rental of property, ..." The timing of this decision is interesting in light of the next piece of federal legislation to be passed that had a major impact on real estate transactions—the Civil Rights Act of 1968 [1]. Title VIII of this act, commonly called the Fair Housing Act (42 U.S.C. Sec. 3604 *et seq.*), is specifically aimed at eliminating discriminatory actions involving housing patterns.

The 1968 act made it illegal to discriminate against persons based on race, color, religion, sex, or national origin in the sale, rental, of financing of dwellings. At the time this act was passed, the U.S. was in a state of social unrest and faced patterns of racial discrimination in many areas. Thus the primary emphasis in passing the 1968 act was in announcing a national policy of nondiscrimination, primarily with respect to race. Figure 14.1 is a form developed by the Department of Housing and Urban Development (HUD) for reporting claims of discrimination.

During the late 1960s and into the 1970s, many real estate agents attempted to take advantage of the pattern of "panic selling" that often existed when all-white neighborhoods became integrated for the first time. This practice, clearly prohibited by the Fair Housing Act, evolved into more subtle attempts to maintain or create certain racial patterns.

By the mid-1980s, other forms of discrimination, long present but of lesser importance than race relations, needed to be addressed by Congress. Thus the 1968 act was amended in 1989 to include a ban on discrimination based on **familial status** or handicaps, either physical or mental.

Familial Status Provisions in the Fair Housing Amendments Act (1989) which prohibit discrimination against families and individuals with children in most housing situations.

Blockbusting and Steering

When white homeowners faced the prospect of living in integrated neighborhoods for the first time, many feared that a disintegration of the economic and social fabric of their lives would take place. These fears, at least the economic aspects, proved to be unfounded over time. During the early years of neighborhood integration, however, many real estate agents fed upon and encouraged these fears in hopes of generating large numbers of sales—all of which would, of course, generate commissions.

[1]The only dissenting opinions in the case were based on a belief that the new act so diminished the importance of the case that is should not be heard.

Housing Discrimination Complaint

Please type or print this form - Don't write in the shaded area

U.S. Department of Housing and Urban Development
Office of Fair Housing and Equal Opportunity

OMB Approval No. 2529-0011 (exp. 1/31/92)

Public reporting burden for this collection of information is estimated to average one hour per response, including the time for reviewing instructions, searching existing data sources, gathering and maintaining the data needed, and completing and reviewing the collection of information. Send comments regarding this burden estimate or any other aspect of this collection of information, including suggestions for reducing this burden, to the Reports Management Officer, Office of Information Policies and Systems, U.S. Department of Housing and Urban Development, Washington, D.C. 20410-3600 and to the Office of Management and Budget, Paperwork Reduction Project (2529-0011), Washington, D.C. 20503.

Instructions: Read this form and the instructions on reverse carefully before completing. All questions should be answered. However, if you do not know the answer or if a question is not applicable, leave the question unanswered and fill out as much of the form as you can. Your complaint should be signed and dated. Where more than one individual or organization is filing the same complaint, and all information is the same, each additional individual or organization should complete boxes 1 and 7 of a separate complaint form and attach it to the original form. Complaints may be presented in person or mailed to the Regional Office covering the State where the complaint arose (see list on back of form),any local HUD Field Office, or to the Office of Fair Housing and Equal Opportunity, U.S. Department of HUD, Washington, D.C. 20410.

This section is for HUD use only.

Number :

Filing Date :

(check √ applicable box) : ☐ Referral and Agency (specify) ☐ Systemic ☐ Military Referral

Jurisdiction : ☐ Yes ☐ No ☐ Additional Info

Signature of HUD personnel who established jurisdiction:

1. Name of Aggrieved Person or Organization (last name, first name, middle initial) (Mr.Mrs.Miss,Ms.)

Home Phone : ( )

Business Phone : ( )

Street Address (city, county, State & zip code)

2. Against whom is this complaint being filed? Name (last name, first name, middle initial)

Phone No.: ( )

Street Address (city, county, State & zip code)

Check (√) the applicable box or boxes which describe(s) the party named above.

☐ Builder ☐ Owner ☐ Broker ☐ Salesperson ☐ Supt. or Manager ☐ Bank or other Lender ☐ Other

If you named an individual above who appeared to be acting for a company in this case, check (√) this box ☐ and write the name and address of the company in this space:

Name:

Address:

Name and Identify others (if any) you believe violated the law in this case

3. What did the person you are complaining against do? Check (√) all that apply and give the most recent date these act(s) occurred in block No. 6a below.

☐ Refuse to rent, sell, or deal with you
☐ Falsely deny housing was available
☐ Engage in blockbusting
☐ Discriminate in broker's services
☐ Other (explain)
☐ Discriminate in the conditions or terms of sale, rental occupancy, or in services or facilities
☐ Advertise in a discriminatory way
☐ Discriminate in financing
☐ Intimidated, interfered, or coerced you to keep you from the full benefit of the Federal Fair Housing Law

4. Do you believe that you were discriminated against because of your race, color, religion, sex, handicap, the presence of children under 18, or a pregnant female in the family or your national origin? Check (√) all that apply:

☐ Race or Color: ☐ Black ☐ White ☐ Other
☐ Religion (specify)
☐ Sex: ☐ Male ☐ Female
☐ Handicap: ☐ Physical ☐ Mental
☐ Familial Status: ☐ Presence of children under 18 in the family ☐ Pregnant female
☐ National Origin: ☐ Hispanic ☐ Asian or Pacific Islander ☐ American Indian or Alaskan Native ☐ Other (specify)

5. What kind of house or property was involved?
☐ Single-family house
☐ A house or building for 2, 3, or 4 families
☐ A building for 5 families or more
☐ Other, including vacant land held for residential use (explain)

Did the owner live there? ☐ Yes ☐ No ☐ Unknown

Is the house or property: ☐ Being sold? ☐ Boing rented?

What is the address of the house or property? (street, city, county, State & zip code)

6. Summarize in your own words what happened. Use this space for a brief and concise statement of the facts. Additional details may be submitted on an attachment.
Note: HUD will furnish a copy of the complaint to the person or organization against whom the complaint is made.

6a. When did the act(s) checked in Item 3 occur? (include the most recent date if several dates are involved)

7. I declare under penalty of perjury that I have read this complaint (including any attachments) and that it is true and correct.

Signature & Date :

X

Previous editions are obsolete.

form **HUD-903** (6/90)
ref. Handbook 8020.1

FIGURE 14.1 HOUSING DISCRIMINATION COMPLAINT FORM

What Does the Fair Housing Amendments Act of 1988 Provide?

The Fair Housing Act declares that it is national policy to provide fair housing throughout the United Sates and prohibits eight specific kinds of discriminatory acts regarding housing if the discrimination is based on race, color, religion, sex, handicap, familial status or national origin.

1. Refusal to sell or rent or otherwise deal with a person.
2. Discriminating in the conditions or terms of sale, rental, or occupancy.
3. Falsely denying housing is available.
4. Discriminatory advertising.
5. "Blockbusting" -causing person(s) to sell or rent by telling them that members of a minority group are moving into the area.
6. Discrimination in financing housing by a bank, savings and loan association, or other business.
7. Denial of membership or participation in brokerage, multiple listing, or other real estate services.
8. Interference, coercion, threats or intimidation to keep a person from obtaining the full benefits of the Federal Fair Housing Law and/or filing a complaint.

What does the Law Exempt?
The first three acts listed above do not apply **(1)** to any single family house where the owner in certain circumstances does not seek to rent or sell it through the use of a broker or through discriminatory advertising, nor **(2)** to units in houses for two-to-four families if the owner lives in one of the units.

What Can You Do About Violations of the Law?
Remember, the Fair Housing Act applies to discrimination based on race, color, religion, sex, handicap, familial status, or national origin. If you believe you have been or are about to be, discriminated against or otherwise harmed by the kinds of discriminatory acts which are prohibited by law, you have a right, within 1 year after the discrimination occurred to:

1. **Complain to the Secretary of HUD** by filing this form by mail or in person. HUD will investigate. If it finds the complaint is covered by the law and is justified, it will try to end the discrimination by conciliation. If conciliation fails, other steps will be taken to enforce the law. In cases where State or local laws give the same rights as the Federal Fair Housing Law, HUD must first ask the State or local agency to try to resolve the problem.

2. **Go directly to Court** even if you have not filed a complaint with the Secretary, The Court may sometimes be able to give quicker, more effective, relief than conciliation can provide and may also, in certain cases, appoint an attorney for you (without cost).

You Should Also Report All Information about violations of the Fair Housing Act to HUD even though you don't intend to complain or go to court yourself.

Additional Details. If you wish to explain in detail in an attachment what happened, you should consider the following:

1. If you feel that others were treated differently from you, please explain the facts and circumstances.

2. If there were witnesses or others who know what happened, give their names, addresses, and telephone numbers.

3. If you have made this complaint to other government agencies or to the courts, state when and where and explain what happened.

Racial/Ethnic Categories

1. **White (Non Hispanic)** - A person having origins in any of the original peoples of Europe, North Africa, or the Middle East.

2. **Black (Non Hispanic)** - A person having origins in any of the black racial groups of Africa.

3. **Hispanic** - A person of Mexican, Puerto Rican, Cuban, Central or South American or other Spanish Culture or origin, regardless of race.

4. **American Indian or Alaskan Native** - A person having origins in any of the original peoples of North America, and who maintains, cultural identification through tribal affiliation or community recognition.

5. **Asian or Pacific Islander** - A person having origins in any of the original peoples of the Far East, Southeast Asia, the Indian Subconti nent, or the Pacific Islands. This area includes, for example, China, Japan, Korea, the Philippine Islands, and Samoa.

You can obtain assistance (a) in learning about the Fair Housing Act, or (b) in filing a complaint at the HUD Regional Offices listed below:

Region I - BOSTON (Connecticut, Maine, Massachusetts, New Hampshire, Rhode Island, Vermont)
HUD - Fair Housing and Equal Opportunity (FHEO)
Boston Federal Office Building, 10 Causeway Street
Boston, Massachusetts 02222-1092

Region II - NEW YORK (New Jersey, New York, Puerto Rico, Virgin Islands)
HUD-Fair Housing and Equal Opportunity (FHEO)
26 Federal Plaza
New York, New York 10278-0068

Region III - PHILADELPHIA (Delaware, District of Columbia, Maryland, Pennsylvania, Virginia, West Virginia)
HUD - Fair Housing and Equal Opportunity (FHEO)
Liberty Square Building, 105 S. 7th Street
Philadelphia, Pennsylvania 19106-3392

Region IV - ATLANTA (Alabama, Florida, Georgia, Kentucky, Mississippi, North Carolina, South Carolina, Tennessee)
HUD- Fair Housing and Equal Opportunity (FHEO)
Richard B. Russell Federal Building, 75 Spring Street, S.W.
Atlanta, Georgia 30303-3388

Region V - CHICAGO (Illinois, Indiana, Michigan, Minnesota, Ohio, Wisconsin)
HUD - Fair Housing and Equal Opportunity (FHEO)
626 West Jackson Boulevard
Chicago, Illinois 60606-6765

Region VI - FORT WORTH (Arkansas, Louisiana, New Mexico, Oklahoma, Texas)
HUD - Fair Housing and Equal Opportunity (FHEO)
1600 Throckmorton, P.O. Box 2905
Fort Worth, Texas 76113-2905

Region VII - KANSAS CITY (Iowa, Kansas, Missouri, Nebraska)
HUD - Fair Housing and Equal Opportunity (FHEO)
Professional Building, 1103 Grand Avenue
Kansas City, Missouri 64106-2496

Region VIII - DENVER (Colorado, Montana, North Dakota, South Dakota, Utah, Wyoming)
HUD - Fair Housing and Equal Opportunity (FHEO)
Executive Tower Building, 1405 Curtis Street
Denver, Colorado 80202-2349

Region IX - SAN FRANCISCO (Arizona, California, Hawaii, Nevada, Guam, American Samoa)
HUD - Fair Housing and Equal Opportunity (FHEO)
450 Golden Gate Avenue
San Francisco, California 94102-3448

Region X - SEATTLE (Alaska, Idaho, Oregon, Washington)
HUD - Fair Housing and Equal Opportunity (FHEO)
Arcade Plaza Building, 1321 Second Avenue
Seattle, Washington 98101-2058

Privacy Act of 1974 (P.L. 93-579)
Authority: Title VIII of the Civil Rights Act of 1968, as amended by the Fair Housing Amendments Act of 1988, (P.L. 100-430).

Purpose: The information requested on this form is to be used to investigate and to process housing discrimination complaints.
Use: The information may be disclosed to the United States Department of Justice for its use in the filing of pattern or practice suits of housing discrimination or the prosecution of the person who committed the discrimination where violence is involved; and to state or local fair housing agencies which administer substantially equivalent fair housing laws for complaint processing.

Penalty: Failure to provide some or all of the requested information will result in delay or denial of HUD assistance.

Disclosure of this information is voluntary.

For further information call the Toll-free Fair Housing Complaint Hotline 1-800-424-8590.
Hearing Impaired persons may call (TDD) 1-800-543-8294.

form **HUD-903**

FIGURE 14.1 HOUSING DISCRIMINATION COMPLAINT FORM (*continued*)

Village of Bellwood v. Dwivedi

Blockbusting The practice of enticing minorities to move into segregated neighborhoods in hopes of creating panic selling.

Some agents, not satisfied with simply profiting from these racially motivated fears, set out to create situations in which panic selling by white homeowners would take place. They did this by enticing a black family, usually with a bargain price that they subsidized, to move into an all-white area. The agents then informed the neighbors of the impending arrival of the black family and encouraged them to sell while they could. This practice, called **"blockbusting"** was specifically targeted by a section of the Fair Housing Act (42 U.S.C. sec. 3604(e)), referred to as the "antiblockbusting" provision.

In time, the racially motivated fears began to diminish—in part as a result of the prohibition of blockbusting techniques—as housing values did not collapse, and the social fabric of neighborhoods was not destroyed by the process of integration. It would be nice to think that the end of blockbusting signaled the end of housing discrimination, but, sadly, this is far from the case.

Sometimes it becomes hard to tell the "good guys" from the "bad guys." A recent case highlights the often confusing tangle of motives involved with attempts to end the effects of housing discrimination. A Chicago organization, the South Suburban Housing Center (SSHC) enacted an affirmative marketing plan to prevent a feared return to segregation in a south Chicago neighborhood. The plan required real estate agents to make special efforts to generate interest from white buyers for homes in an area that was increasingly becoming all black. The local and National Association of Realtors (NAR) challenged the plan as an exercise in racial steering in *South-Suburban Housing v. Greater South Suburban Board of Realtors* (935 F.2d 868, 1991).

In a complex ruling that also included complaints about "anti-solicitation" ordinances which prohibit real estate agents from approaching persons who have placed their names on a list maintained by city clerks, and the reenactment of a sign ordinance (which was then withdrawn again), the court ruled that the affirmative marketing plan did not violate the Fair Housing Act because it was an effort to add potential buyers, not restrict access in any way. Most of the NAR's problem with the plan, it should be noted, was caused by fears that it would violate their own "voluntary marketing agreement" entered into with HUD. Thus we have several groups, all presumably working toward the same goal of nondiscrimination in housing, waging a lengthy court battle over who's plan is better.

The antiblockbusting provisions of the Fair Housing Act effectively put an end to such overt practices. The process of discrimination, however, simply took on a more subtle character. In many instances, real estate agents make assumptions about where people "want" to live. When these assumptions are based on expressed de-

KEY POINTS

A recent study[2] indicates that racial discrimination is far from a thing of the past. Using 3800 paired tests, or audits, twenty-five metropolitan areas were tested. Each pair consisted of a white couple and either a black or hispanic couple posing as buyers or renters with the same educational and income levels. In 8 percent of the cases, black or Hispanic buyers were not even allowed to see an agent (these rose to 15% for blacks and 12% for Hispanics when renting). In addition, black and Hispanic renters and buyers were often shown fewer units or given less favorable terms. Finally, steering was reported in 21 percent of the test cases.

sires, this process is not only legal and proper, but also an important part of the brokerage function. When those assumptions are based on racial characteristics, even subtle ones such as income (which is often directly correlated with race), the process becomes discriminatory. Actions by real estate agents that lead to housing patterns based on, or influenced by, race maintain the vestiges of a segregated society. Thus the practice of **racial steering,** which consists of any actions by agents that tend to promote or maintain racial housing patterns, is prohibited by the Fair Housing Act.

Racial Steering The practice of showing certain properties for sale or rent to specific racial groups only.

In defense of real estate agents, however, it should be pointed out that the line between steering based on race and trying to serve the client is often difficult to define. Clearly a refusal to show housing in "white" areas to black buyers (or vice versa) is a violation. When a client does not express a desire for certain areas, the agent must not assume that certain areas are "more suitable" than others. Nor can an agent directly ask if the buyers have a preference based on the racial composition of the area. Agents can, and should, ask questions regarding the physical characteristics of the property desired, the location characteristics that apply to access concerns (e.g., nearness to schools and shopping), and the price range desired.The problems of blockbusting and racial steering have led some communities to attempt an intervention in the market operations. These efforts have been aimed at preventing the effects of racial discrimination.

The traditional, and still actively used, method of documenting a racial steering case is the use of "testers." A recent case illustrates the dangers of steering for real estate agents. In *City of Chicago v. Matchmaker Real Estate Sales Center* (982 F.2d 1086, 1992), several agents in a real estate firm were found guilty of racial steering based on housing shown to five sets of testers. The agents were ordered to pay each tester $1,000, the organization which sponsored the testers $16,500 for frustration of its purpose and another $25,000 in punitive damages, and over $160,000 in costs and fees. The ruling found all defendants to be joint and severally liable for these penalties thus providing a very substantial penalty for the real estate agents.

Sign Ordinances

One way to limit panic selling is to prohibit the placement of "For Sale" and "Sold" signs in the yards of houses. The idea behind the ordinances that prohibit such signs is that many times homeowners will create a panic situation by reacting to the presence of such signs.

This approach, however, has received little, if any, support from courts. Although noting that the concerns addressed by **sign ordinances** are legitimate and important, First Amendment (i.e., free speech) issues generally preclude such an approach. In addition, the courts have noted that the sign ordinance approach is not a particularly effective method of achieving racial integration because it closes ". . . only one method of communication while leaving ample alternative channels open" (*Linmark Associates, Inc. v. Township of Willingboro* [*97 S.Ct. 1614* (*1977*)]).

Sign Ordinances City ordinances that prohibited the placement of "for sale" signs in the yards of houses in an attempt to limit racially motivated panic selling.

[2]Conducted by The Urban Institute and Syracuse University for the Department of Housing and Urban Development during the spring and summer of 1989.

Discrimination Against Families with Children

Shellhammer v. Lewallen

In a national survey of discrimination based on familial status, HUD found that 25 percent of all rental units did not allow children, 50 percent were subject to restrictive policies that limited the ability of families to live in those units, and almost 20 percent of families were living in homes they considered less desirable owing to restrictive practices. Until the Fair Housing Amendments took effect in March, 1989, no federal law provided comprehensive protection to families with children who suffered discrimination in housing.

KEY POINTS

An issue that is becoming increasingly important is that of sexual harassment in housing. A survey done in 1986[3] of 150 public and private housing centers agencies, and organizations across the U.S. found 300 reports of sexual harassment. The true total, based on evidence that only between 2 and 4.4 percent of all similar incidents are ever reported, was estimated to be between 6,818 and 15,000. A case that received little notice when it was heard has now become a focus of attention in this area. In this case (*Shellhammer v. Lewallen,*, included at the end of this chapter), the Appellate Court allowed a claim under the Fair Housing Act for the first time and, although a class action request was denied, opened the door for suits claiming sexual harassment in housing.

Betsey v. Turtle Creek Associates

Several challenges to "all-adult" policies had been raised based, before the amendments, on racial grounds. Housing units in predominately white neighborhoods restricted children at a rate of 28.9 percent compared with 17.5 percent in predominately black neighborhoods, and newer units were more likely to have restrictions[4]. Because ethnic and racial groups are more likely to have children, courts maintained that actions could be brought on racial grounds, even by nonminority tenants. Thus Congress was faced with *de facto* court-imposed limitations on familial discrimination.

The new amendments broadly define the categories of persons included in the protection given families with children. A "family" may consist of a single individual, where as "familial status" means one or more individuals under 18 years of age who are living with a parent or guardian with legal custody or a person designated in writing as having custody. Familial status also extends to any person who is pregnant or in the process of securing legal custody of a minor.

Although reasonable government regulations, such as building codes or zoning ordinances, that place limits on the maximum number of occupants permitted to live in a dwelling are lawful, private restrictions are presumed to be prohibited. HUD has announced that owners and managers could devise reasonable occupancy standards

---

[3]Regina Cahan, "Home Is No Haven: An Analysis of Sexual Harassment in Housing." *Wisconsin Law Review,* 1987, pp. 1061-1093.

[4]Comments of Senator Dominici, *Congressional Record,* S10553 (daily ed. August 2, 1988).

based on factors such as the size and the number of bedrooms and the overall size of the dwelling. The burden will be on the owner or manager, however, to show that the standard does not unreasonably restrict housing for families with children and any doubt should be resolved against the landlord.

The only exemption in the Amendments is for "housing for older persons," which includes three categories:

1. Housing provided under any state of federal program specifically designed and operated to assist the elderly.
2. Housing intended for, and solely occupied by, persons 62 years or older.
3. Housing intended and occupied by at least one person 55 years of age or older that meets regulations developed by HUD.

The amendments also have a grandfather clause, which exempts buildings under the second and third categories that have some residents who do not meet the new age requirements, so long as the new occupants are required to meet the age requirements.

Two existing occupancy restriction methods previously upheld by court decisions must now be reevaluated based on the amendments. The first, based on the *Village of Belle Terre v. Boraas* [416 U.S. 1 (1974)] decision, bases a definition of family on issues of "blood, adoption, or marriage" and is likely to be invalidated. The provision effectively restricts unrelated persons from sharing living quarters (except when limited to two persons who live and cook together). The second approach, based on the Mount Laurel[5] decisions, restricts the ability of cities to limit the building of low-income housing. These methods involve zoning ordinances, as opposed to private limitations, and are discussed in more detail in Chapter 16.

Discrimination Against the Handicapped

In the early 1970s, handicapped persons joined the push for civil rights. The movement resulted in the passage of numerous state and federal laws, notably the Rehabilitation Act of 1973, designed to protect the handicapped. As with families with children, Congress found that widespread stereotyping of persons with handicaps resulted in their frequent exclusion from housing. Thus the 1989 amendments to the 1968 Fair Housing Act also included prohibitions against discrimination based on physical or mental handicaps.

The term "handicap" is defined as:

1. A physical or mental impairment that substantially limits one or more major life activities.
2. Having a record of such an impairment.
3. Being regarded as having such an impairment.

Current, illegal use of or addiction to a controlled substance is specifically excluded from the definition, although alcoholism is not. The coverage is also extended to persons who have a mentally retarded relative who will not live with the tenant but who might visit the tenant from time to time.

---

[5]*South Burlington County NAACP v. Township of Mount Laurel* [92 N.J. 158, 456 A.2d 390 (1983)].

KEY POINTS

Although the Fair Housing Act expressly excludes current users of illegal drug from coverage, a recent case (*United States v. Southern Management Corp.* [955 F.2d 914, 1992]) held that the Fair Housing Act prohibits discrimination by landlords against recovering drug addicts participating in structured rehabilitation programs. A Federal Appeals Court upheld an order requiring an apartment management firm to lease units to drug and alcohol abuse program participants. According to the court, the "negative reactions of others" to the former drug problem leads to discrimination. Recovering addicts are thus considered to be handicapped individuals protected on account of their former addiction even if that addiction has no current effect on their ability to function.

The third category, persons who are perceived to have a handicap, greatly expands the coverage of amendments. For example, a landlord may not refuse to lease to a person who appears to be retarded or to a gay person because he might have acquired immunodeficiency syndrome (AIDS). The amendments cover not only people who might have AIDS, but also those who are actually infected with the AIDS virus (or any disease that although contagious, is not easily transmitted). So long as a "reasonable accommodation" by the landlord eliminates the risk of harm to others, the person must be accepted.

Finally, the amendments require that covered multifamily dwellings designed or constructed after March 13, 1991, must meet design and construction requirements so as to make them **accessible to handicapped persons**. The requirements apply to multifamily buildings of four or more units if the building has an elevator as well as to "ground floor" units in other buildings consisting of four or more units. Not only must the dwelling units be accessible, but also all public use and common areas.

Handicapped Access Rules Provisions in the Fair Housing Amendments which require all multifamily dwellings constructed after March 1991 to be accessible to handicapped persons.

Americans with Disabilities Act

The Fair Housing Act applies only to residential real estate. The Americans with Disabilities Act, signed into law on July 26, 1990, prohibits discrimination based on disability in employment, provision of government services, transportation provided by public or private entities, places of public accommodation and commercial facilities, and telephone services available to the public. Title III, which went into effect on January 26, 1992 (and extended to even the smallest companies on January 26, 1993), requires places of public accommodation and commercial facilities to remove architectural barriers where it is "readily achieveable."

Alterations begun after January, 1992, must be made accessible to the "maximum extent feasible." Exceptions will be granted only when it is "virtually impossible" to comply with the standards. New construction is held to a higher standard, and exceptions are allowed only when they would be "structurally impracticable" in those rare instances when unique features of terrain prevent the incorporation of accessibility features.

The Justice Department regulations established priorities for removing architectural barriers: (1) providing access from sidewalks or parking areas, (2) providing access to those areas where goods or services are offered to the public, (3) providing access to restroom facilities, and (4) other measures necessary to provide full access. The guidelines that implement the act are specific and require, for example, doorways to be of adequate width (generally 36 inches or more); ways provided to circumvent stairs and heavy doors; adequate parking for disabled within short distances of buildings; furniture arrangements that allow clear paths to all service points and restrooms; adequate restroom facilities; and avoiding the use of separate entrances and elevators, which may tend to segregate the disabled. The act also provides for monetary damages for individual victims of discrimination, including out-of-pocket expenses and pain and suffering.

Credit Discrimination

The Fair Housing Act includes in its coverage acts involving the financing of dwellings. It seems clear that Congress recognized that **credit discrimination** can take place not only in the ability to purchase or rent property, but also in the ability to obtain the financing necessary to complete the transaction. Few, if any, challenges, however, have been made under the Fair Housing Act. Rather, specialized legislation aimed at lending institutions has provided the basis for most legal actions.

Credit Discrimination The refusal to grant or extend credit based upon race, sex, religion, or other characteristics.

There are really two basic, although interrelated, issues with regard to lending practices. The first is a denial of credit by an institution based on a protected characteristic (e.g., race, color, religion, sex, national origin, and, after the 1989 Amendments, familial status or having a handicap). Such a denial, unless the lending institution can demonstrate risk factors not related to one of these characteristics, is clearly unlawful. The second is one based, not on the characteristics of the would-be borrower, but on the location of the property for which a loan is sought.

The latter practice of denial of loans, or making loans with higher costs, based on the location of property was at one time a common practice for lenders. Simply put, lenders made their job a bit easier by ruling out areas where property or neighborhood conditions did not seem favorable. Once again the distinction between a valid fiduciary obligation to make only prudent, safe loans came into conflict with discriminatory effects. Without making any assumptions about possible racial or ethnic discriminatory intents, it became clear that the effect of such **"redlining"** practices was to deny credit on race-related grounds.

Redlining The practice of refusing to make loans in certain areas due to economic and/or racial composition. Often noted on maps by drawing a red line around the area.

Several legislative efforts have been aimed at this area—most notably the Home Mortgage Disclosure Act (1975), the Equal Credit Opportunity Act (1976), the Community Reinvestment Act (1977), and the National Neighborhood Policy Act (1978). The Magnuson-Moss Warranty–Federal Trade Commission Improvement Act in 1979 also relates to these issues. All of this legislation was aimed at preventing the decline and facilitating the revitalization of neighborhoods.

In addition to lenders, both real estate agents and appraisers have been drawn into this arena. Appraisers base their judgments of market value at least in part on neighborhood factors. To the extent that racial composition, especially racial transitions from segregated to integrated (and often back to segregated, although with a different racial group), has an impact on value, appraisers incorporated these factors in their opinions. Unfortunately, this can become a circular argument. If appraisers indicate that racial characteristics have an impact on property values, then lenders, buyers, and sellers are affected by this pronouncement. It truly becomes a "chicken and egg" question: Are appraisers simply reporting on the situation, as they have maintained, or does their reporting in fact influence the situation, as the Justice Department maintains?

After a long, painful argument, the appraisal industry agreed to eliminate all references to racial composition from its textbooks and other course materials and to take a position officially that racial characteristics of neighborhoods should not enter into value judgments. In similar fashion, real estate agents, by the process of racial steering described earlier, also have a major impact on market conditions for housing. Thus each group is constantly exposed to liability for statements or actions that have a discriminatory effect on the housing market.

ENVIRONMENTAL ISSUES

The final liability issue to be discussed in this chapter, although by no means the least important, is that of environmental liability. The field of environmental law promises to be one of the fastest growing areas in law and, because it has obvious relationships to land, poses a major threat for real estate professionals in all fields. We are really just now beginning, as a nation, to understand the magnitude and implications of actions that have been taken for granted in the past. The industrial revolution marked not only the beginning of a new era in productivity for many nations, but also it marked the beginning of a steady deterioration of the environment. Issues relating to business organizations, labor relations, marketing and advertising, production methods, and inventory control have been well documented. The byproducts of all this economic activity, however, often include unwanted, potentially harmful material.

Hazardous Substance Substances listed in 40 CFR Table 302.4 which can trigger CERCLA liability. There are currently well over 1,000 substances listed.

The process of disposing of such unwanted materials has been largely ignored for the last century. Only now are we beginning to understand, based on new technology and a heightened awareness, the impact that careless disposal of potentially **hazardous material** can have on our environment and, in turn, on our ability to live safe, healthy lives.

Legal Sources of Environmental Liability

Until the 1980s, the sale and transfer of real property contaminated with hazardous wastes was not considered a problem, unless the contamination was severe enough to limit the intended use of the property. With the environmental legislation passed in the last decade, virtually every real estate transaction can be affected to some degree by the assessment and allocation of liabilities associated with potential environmental contamination. Table 14.1 contains a summary of the major federal legislation that creates the legal sources of environmental liability.

CERCLA Comprehensive Environmental Response, Compensation, and Liability Act (1980). Created the "superfund" to respond to releases of hazardous materials.

Although all of the legislation summarized in Table 14.1 potentially has an impact on real estate transactions, the **Comprehensive Environmental Response, Compensation, and Liability Act (CERCLA)** significantly changed the rules of the game for real estate. CERCLA defines **"potentially responsible parties,"** or PRPs, who may be liable for cleanup costs, to include:

1. The owner and operator of a vessel or facility.
2. Any person who at the time of disposal of any hazardous substance owned or operated any facilities at which such hazardous wastes were disposed of.
3. Any person who arranged for disposal or treatment of hazardous waste.
4. Any person who accepted hazardous waste for transport to treatment, storage, or disposal (TSD) facilities.

Potentially Responsible Party
Individuals defined by CERCLA who may potentially be liable for all costs associated with the removal of hazardous materials from a site.

TABLE 14.1 FEDERAL ENVIRONMENTAL LEGISLATION

	Water Pollution
1899	**Rivers and Harbors Act** First federal legislation aimed at protecting the navigability of waterways. Prohibits the discharge of "refuse" into navigable waters of the U.S.
1948	**Water Pollution Control Act**
1956	**Amendments**
1965	**Water Quality Act**
1972	**Federal Water Pollution Control Act** First act to set specific goals for clean water.
1977	**Amendments (Clean Water Act)** The first major amendment; it established three specific goals: (1) eliminating pollutant discharges into navigable waters by 1985; (2) achieving by 1983, wherever attainable, water quality that is swimmable and fishable and allows for recreational uses; and (3) prohibiting the discharge of pollutants in toxic amounts. Additional amendments were added in 1981 and 1987.
1974	**Safe Water Drinking Act** Passed as an amendment to the Public Health Service Act, the act is intended to protect aquifers and other drinking water sources from contamination.
	Air Pollution
1955	**Air Pollution Control Act**
1963	**Clean Air Act** Established partial restraint of motor vehicle emissions. Allowed only limited federal enforcement.
1967	**Air Quality Act** Added stationary source emission standards, but did not establish complete restraint and also allowed only limited federal enforcement.
1970	**Amendments to Clean Air Act** Adopted a radical, completely restructured approach by instituting a permitting program, establishing specific standards, giving the states responsibility for achieving those standards.
1977	**Amendments to Clean Air Act** Included a national policy to prevent significant deterioration of the air quality.
1990	**Amendments to Clean Air Act** Major revision that added muscle to the setting of state standards (including substituting federal standards and punitive actions against states), tougher tailpipe emission standards, air toxics standards, and some controversial acid rain regulations.
	Solid Wastes
1965	**Solid Waste Disposal Act**
1970	**Resource Recovery Act**
1976	**Toxic Substances Control Act** Empowers the Environmental Protection Agency to require testing of chemical substances entering the environment and to regulate them when necessary. Tests measure a chemical's carcinogenic (cancer causing), teratogenic (birth defect causing), and mutagenic (genetic damaging) properties.

TABLE 14.1 FEDERAL ENVIRONMENTAL LEGISLATION *(continued)*

1976	**CERCLA** Legislation passed in response to the Love Canal (New York), Valley of the Drums (Kentucky), Times Beach (Missouri), and similar problem areas. Created a fund of money, the "superfund," to respond to releases of hazardous substances.
1986	**SARA** Added an "innocent landowner defense" to liability for cleanup expenses. A "due diligence review" must be performed to demonstrate lack of knowledge concerning contamination.
1986	**Asbestos Hazard Emergency Response Act** Amended the Toxic Subtance Control Act issuing regulations defining what response must be taken in school buildings.

PRPs are potentially liable for:

1. All costs of removal or remedial action incurred by the U.S.government or a state or an Indian tribe,
2. Any other necessary costs of response incurred by any other person.
3. Damages for injury to, destruction of, or loss of natural resources, including the reasonable costs of assessing injury, destruction, or loss resulting from a release of toxic material.
4. The costs of any health assessment or health effects study carried out.

Liability exposure incurred under CERCLA has the following characteristics:

1. It is retroactive because PRPs are liable for acts or omissions occurring well before CERCLA was enacted in 1980.
2. It is strict because it is irrelevant that all legal requirements were fully met or that due care was exercised.
3. It may be joint and several because one party may be liable for more than his share under any fair allocation and may in fact be held liable for the entire site cleanup.
4. It is eternal because even after site cleanup, a responsible party may be liable for some previously undiscovered problems.
5. It may be personal and can be applied to both corporate entities and to individuals.

CERCLA liability is subjected to a limited number of defenses. These defenses include establishing that the release and subsequent damage was caused by:

1. An act of God.
2. An act of war.
3. An act or omission of a third party, such as acquiring the land by inheritance or a government entity acquiring the land by escheat, involuntary acquisition, or eminent domain.

Innocent Landowner Defense

The **Superfund Amendments and Reauthorization Act (SARA)** added an additional line of defense, the **"innocent landowner defense."** Under this defense, a current owner may not be liable for cleanup costs, provided that he can establish that he did not know of any existing contamination when he purchased the property and had no reason to know of the contamination. The second condition, that he had no reason to know, is met by conducting what has come to be called a **"due diligence environmental review"** of the property before purchase.

SARA Superfund Amendments and Reauthorization Act (1986) which added the "innocent landowner" and "third party" defenses to CERCLA.

To meet the due diligence standard, a purchaser must ask the current owner five questions:

1. What is the current owner's specialized knowledge or experience?
2. What is the relationship of the purchase price to the value of the property if uncontaminated?
3. What is commonly known or reasonably ascertainable information about the property?
4. What is the obviousness of the presence or likely presence of contamination at the property?
5. What is the ability to detect such contamination by appropriate inspection?

Innocent Landowner Defense A current landowner may not be liable for clean-up costs due to hazardous materials if he can establish that he did not know, and had no reason to know, of the contamination.

Note that there is no defense available to any party that disposes of any hazardous substance while an owner. Also, and of major importance to real estate professionals, the innocent landowner defense is not available if a broker has knowledge of a release of hazardous materials on a site, even though she fails to share that knowledge with the purchaser.

One area of potential liability exposure that has caused a great deal of controversy and that continues to be examined is that of lenders. An additional defense to liability, called the "third-party defense," is based on the definition of an "owner or operator" contained in the act. A person " . . . who, without participating in the management of a vessel or facility, holds indicia of ownership primarily to protect his security interest in the vessel or facility . . . " is specifically excluded from the definition. The exemption is obviously aimed at third-party lenders who do not operate the facility.

Due Diligence Reviews The environmental inspection of a property necessary to rely upon the "innocent landowner" defense against liability claims for hazar-dous materials found on a site.

The issue becomes a great deal more complicated, however, when the owner/operator of a facility containing hazardous wastes defaults on the loan. If the lender takes title by purchase at a foreclosure sale, which it normally would to protect its investment, does the exemption cease to exist? If it does, then lenders have little protection under the third-party defense. The definition of ownership in this context is examined in the *U.S. v. Maryland Bank & Trust Company* case, included at the end of this chapter.

To use the innocent purchaser defense, lenders may need to establish a set of rules and monitor the borrower's use of the property. These rules may include restrictions on use, compliance and reporting requirements, and inspection rights. Thus, if the lender must foreclose, the lender will be in a better position to have the knowledge of buyer's use that the court likely will impute. Figure 14.2 is a sample certificate for use in monitoring buyer's use.

United States v. Maryland Bank & Trust

Because of the confusion in this area, the Environmental Protection Agency issued its "final rule" on lender liability under CERCLA on April 29, 1992. Basically under this rule, lenders may engage in permitted activities in five areas: (1) loan inception activities, (2) monitoring the security interest, (3) workout activities with problem loans, (4) foreclosure activities, and (5) post-foreclosure activities. Unless the lender exercises direct decision-making control with regard to the handling or

Borrower:____
(name as it appears on the loan documents)

Address:____
____
(if this is a new address please check here:____)

Date:________________

Legal description and address of property subject to mortgage (property):
COMPLETED BY LENDER
____
____
____
____

This certificate is to be filed every six(6) months by the Borrower and is solely for the purpose of determining, in the event [LENDER] must sometime in the future foreclose on the Property, if Borrower's use of the Property could subject [LENDER] to liability for environmental law violations. [LENDER] does not by requiring the filing of this Certificate participate in the financial management of the Property or Project to a capacity to influence the Borrower's treatment of hazardous substances or other similar decisions.

The Borrower hereby certifies that, to the best of its knowledge, information and belief, each of the following statements is accurate and does not omit any material fact necessary to prevent it, or this Certificate generally, from being misleading:

1. The planned and existing stuctures on and uses of the Property consist of:
____
____
(collectively, the "Project")
2. The Borrower knows of no (a) defect in any of the permits, licenses or approvals which have heretofore been issued in connection with the Project, (b) unfulfilled representation or agreement made in connection with the issuance of said permits, licenses or approvals, but not disclosed on the face thereof, or (c) condition to the granting of such permits, licenses or approvals, but not disclosed on the face thereof.
3. The Borrower has no actual knowledge of any facts constituting either (a) a violatio of law with respect to the constuction or operation of the Project, or (b) a violation of any of the permits, licenses or approvals heretofore issued with respect to the Property or the Project. The Borrower has not received any notice of violation with respect to the Property or Project. No governmental official has notified the undersigned that said official intends to issue or seek any such notice of violation or order that a violation be corrected.
4. To the best of Borrower's knowledge after due investigation, there are no actions, suits, proceedings, or investigations pending or threatened against or affecting the

FIGURE 14.2 SAMPLE CERTIFICATE

This certificate is provided as a sample only. It is not intended to constitute legal advice or counsel. Legal advice should be sought when financing any property or project.

Property, the Project or the undersigned (nor to the best of the Borrower's knowledge after due investigation, is there any basis therefor) in any court or before any arbitrator of any kind or before any federal, state, municipal, or other governmental department, commission, board, bureau or instrumentality.

5. To the best of Borrower's knowledge after due investigation, there are no unsatisfied judgments, decrees or settlements against or affecting the Property, the Project or the Borrower (nor to the best of the Borrower's knowledge after due investigation, is there any basis therefor) in any court or before any arbitrator of any kind or before any federal, state, municipal, or other governmental department, commission, board, bureau or instrumentality.

6. To the best of Borrower's knowledge after due investigation, no hazardous substances have been, or are being, stored, disposed, transported, used or released onto the Property or any adjoining property.

7. Exhibit No. 1 hereto is an accurate and complete list of all of the persons and entities who or which are currently occupying space upon the Property and their respective current uses. No uses are being made of the Property except as set forth in Exhibit No.1 hereto.

The Borrower hereby re-affirms that:

1. Borrower will use the Property in compliance with all applicable laws, rules, and regulations.
2. Borrower will not store, dispose, transport, use or release any hazardous substance onto the Property.
3. [LENDER] shall receive copies of all notices of violations, correspondence, and pleadings on environmental conditions relating to the Borrower or the Property.
4. [LENDER] may enter the Property and Project in order to inspect for any violation of law with respect to hazardous substances.

IN WITNESS WHEREOF, the undersigned has executed this Certificate as the date and year first written above.

[BORROWER]

By :____________________________

Title:____________________________

FIGURE 14.2 SAMPLE CERTIFICATE (*continued*)

disposal of hazardous substances or exercises control of day-to-day decision making on a level comparable to a manager of the firm, the third-party defense will be available. The post-foreclosure permitted activities definitions also provide clear guidelines for lenders to avoid the problem seen in the *Maryland Bank & Trust Company* case.

Sources of Contamination[6]

As of July, 1990, there were 1,056 specific substances plus many more generic process waste streams that can triger CERCLA liability. These items are contained in a list published as 40 CFR Table 302.4 and are constantly being updated. Thus recent

[6]The authors would like to acknowledge the assistance of Mike Swanson of the Energy and Environmental Research Center for his contributions to this section.

TABLE 14.2 MAJOR SOURCES OF CONTAMINANTS

Underground Storage Tanks (USTs)

It is estimated that there are more than 8 million underground storage tanks in the U.S. and that 2 million are covered by the new regulations. Up to 25% of these tanks may be leaking. Before the recent enactment of the Environmental Protection Agency regulations on USTs, the common practice was to install bare steel tanks and piping in the ground. Without corrosion protection, these UST systems tend to act as a weak battery by creating a small electric potential, which causes a flow of electricity that will slowly corrode away portions of the tank and piping. New UST regulations require certification of proper installation of piping for tanks installed after December 22, 1988. Errors in backfilling and compacting, especially when the piping was not installed by the manufacturer of the tank but was assembled at the time of installation by a local contractor, leads to failure of the piping systems. Because leaking fuel has a tendency to follow utility lines, there is a significant fire and explosion hazard when it enters basements or other open areas. In addition, leaking tanks can contaminate the local groundwater, and, if undetected, leaks can travel substantial distances and contaminate nearby properties. The cost of cleaning up this kind of damage can easily be hundreds of thousands of dollars. Spills and overflow are secondary potentially significant problems associated with UST systems. Careless operation of UST systems have caused contamination problems in the vicinity of USTs. Even if a nonleaking tank system has been removed from the ground, its prior existence and location is a matter of interest to a potential purchaser for this reason.

Septic Tanks and Cesspools

Approximately 800 billion gallons of wastewater each year are discharged from septic tanks and cesspools into the environment, making septic tanks and cesspools the largest discharger of wastewater to soils. As a result, these water treatment systems are the most frequently reported source of groundwater contamination. As a result of poor location, design, construction, or maintenance, it is expected that only 40% of all existing septic tanks are functioning properly. Adding to this problem is the fact that the design life of these septic tank systems is approximately 10-15 years, and many systems have exceeded their usable life, leading to significant groundwater contamination.

Radon Gas

Evidence is accumulating that indicates that radon may be second only to smoking as a leading cause of lung cancer. It has been estimated that some 20,000 Americans die each year from radon-induced lung cancer. The detection and abatement of radon contamination in a building are relatively easy and inexpensive (radon mitigation for a high-radon house averages approximately $1000) in most cases.

Radon is an invisible, colorless, radioactive gas that results from the breakdown of minute quantities of naturally occurring uranium in soils. Radon gas can enter a building through any direct airway between the soil and the building, such as cracks in the concrete slab, gaps between the concrete slab and block foundation, through drain tiles connected to sump holes, through hollow block walls via mortar joints or cracks, and simply through the pores in block wall itself. Also, any gaps around pipes that penetrate through a cement floor can also allow radon gas an entry point into a building. With so many entry points into a house, it is difficult to block all of them and will not likely drop the radon gas levels to an acceptable range without use of more effective techniques.

Urea-Formaldehyde

Urea-formaldehyde foam insulation (UFFI) is thermal insulation material that has been extensively used since 1970. This material would be pumped into the spaces between the walls of a building, where it would harden to form a solid layer of insulation. Formaldehyde has been shown to cause cancer in animals and is assumed to also cause cancer in humans. It can also cause asthma attacks; skin rashes; and watery burning eyes, noses,

TABLE 14.2 MAJOR SOURCES OF CONTAMINANTS *(continued)*

and throats. Thus the Consumer Product Safety Commission banned the use of UFFI in 1982. This ban on UFFI was overturned by the U.S. Fifth Circuit Court of Appeals in 1983 owing to insufficient evidence to prove its risk to human health, and sufficient evidence has not been gathered to reinstate the ban. Scientific reports have shown that after UFFI is installed, formaldehyde emissions become minimal and pose little human health risk. Because of all the bad publicity, however, UFFI has greatly diminished in popularity, and many people do not want to expose themselves to it.

Lead

Too much lead in the human body can cause serious damage to vital organs, such as the brain, kidneys, nervous system, and red blood cells. The detrimental health effects are related to the level of exposure and the age at which a person is exposed. Those at highest risk, even from small amounts of lead, are infants and small children. The known effectson humans range from subtle biological effects caused by low levels of exposure to acute neurological and toxic effects—even death—at very high levels.

Lead can be introduced primarily through two sources: (1) lead paint and (2) lead in drinking water. Lead was a primary ingredient of many paints used in the U.S. from approximately 1940 until their banning in 1980. Therefore any building that was constructed or remodeled in this time frame has a much higher probability of having lead paint. Lead can also get in the air from any renovation in which lead paint is removed by scraping, sanding, or heating with an open flame. Unfortunately, lead dust is so fine it quite often passes right through a vacuum cleaner filter, only to be reintroduced to air each time the carpet is vacuumed.

Levels of lead in drinking water are generally very low leaving the water treatment plant or wells (depending on the well), but the water tends to leach lead from pipes as it travels to its final destination. This lead comes from lead pipes, lead solder used to connect copper pipes, and lead used in the manufacture of plumbing fixtures, leading to the passage of the 1986 Safe Drinking Water Act amendment, which eliminated the use of lead pipe and required the use of lead-free solder and flux beginning in June 1988. Fortunately, as pipes and fixtures get older, they become coated with other minerals that inhibit the release of lead into the water. Studies have shown that the most dangerous levels of lead are experienced in the first two years, and after five years the levels are reduced substantially. Therefore given enough time, the problem of lead in drinking water will disappear without any abatement action.

Wetlands

The acquisition of property containing regulated wetlands can appreciably affect the value of a property by preventing development. There is no clear definition of wetlands but the U.S. Army Corps of Engineers has defined wetlands as: "those areas that are inundated or saturated by surface or ground water (either fresh or salt) at a frequency and duration sufficient to support vegetation adapted for life in saturated soil conditions. Wetlands include such areas as swamps, marshes, bogs, estuaries, certain unique pond systems, and inland and coastal shallows."

Care should be taken as part of the "due diligence" process to determine whether property is now or has ever been in the past included in regulated wetlands. A purchaser may incur liability for restoration or mitigation of unpermitted fill activities by the previous owners, even when the purchaser was unaware of the unpermitted activities.

Drinking Water

Drinking water obtained from private wells is susceptible to a variety of problems because well water is rarely treated before use. There is a relatively high probability that the well water could be contaminated with pollutants from waste disposal systems located near a well whenever the system is not completely treating the waste stream. Well water is also susceptible to contamination from hazardous wastes discharges on or near the site and from pollutants that can travel substantial distances via underground aquifers. Water-born

TABLE 14.2 MAJOR SOURCES OF CONTAMINANTS *(continued)*

diseases are another potential problem that can be found in well water. Water-borne diseases have also broken out among customers of public works systems (generally small, less than 3,330 persons).

Polychlorinated Biphenyls (PCBs)

PCBs were widely used in transformers and other electrical equipment and were also used in printing inks. Although the production of PCBs was outlawed in 1976, transformers that contained PCBs were allowed to remain in operation throughout their useful life. PCBs have been shown to be toxic, especially when ingested. An additional danger from PCBs is the extremely toxic byproducts that are formed in low-temperature fires involving PCB-containing electrical equipment. Because of their high stability and low water solubility, PCB contamination of soils increases the cost of cleanup. Areas where electrical equipment was used, worked on, or disposed of are areas of particular concern.

Asbestos

Asbestos was once considered a modern wonder material because of its insulation, soundproofing, strength, and fire-retardant qualities. It is now considered a major environmental problem owing to the release of asbestos fibers when any asbestos-containing material (ACM) is disturbed. If these air-borne fibers are inhaled into the lungs, they remain there throughout a person's lifetime, and premature death or disablement may result. Scientific evidence suggests that children are at greater risk of developing asbestos-related cancer owing to their faster metabolic rate, increased activity, and the long latency period after exposure to asbestos for physical problems to develop. This greater risk led to the passage of the Asbestos School Hazard Abatement Act.

Environmental Protection Agency surveys estimate that ACM can be found in approximately 31,000 schools and in 733,000 other public and commercial buildings in the U.S. The presence of asbestos in a building does not necessarily endanger the health of the building's occupants. As long as the ACM is not disturbed and remains in good condition, exposure is unlikely. When building maintenance, repair, renovation, or other activities disturb ACM, however, asbestos fibers are released, creating a potential hazard to occupants.

Miscellaneous Environmental Hazards

Miscellaneous environmental hazards that can have a detrimental effect on human health, thereby affecting property evaluations include:

1. Carbon monoxide, nitrogen dioxide, and respirable particulates from unvented kerosene and gas heaters and improperly installed chimneys and flues for wood stoves and fireplaces.
2. Agricultural pollution from animal wastes, fertilizers, pesticides, and herbicides.
3. Organic vapors from household application of pesticides to control insects, rodents, termites, and fungi.
4. Odors from nearby industrial facilities.
5. Noise from nearby airports, railroads, highways, and commercial and industrial sites.

issues of the *Federal Register* need to be monitered for recent additions to the list. Information on the most prevalent sources is contained in Table 14.2.

Environmental Due Diligence

As noted earlier, SARA added an "innocent landowner" defense available to purchasers who can demonstrate a lack of knowledge concerning the presence of hazardous materials. To use this defense, a purchaser must show that she (1) did not

KEY POINTS

Sometimes environmental contamination can "sneak up" on building owners. One group of high-rise office buildings and hotels in the Washington, D.C., are is built on a site that was at one time an oil storage facility. Although the storage facility had been gone for many years and the site showed no signs of contamination, problems began to occur a few years after construction in the area was completed. Liquids spilled on the earth soak into the soil. Over time, these substances will "percolate" back to the surface. Most of the new buildings have underground parking facilities, the lower floors of which have problems with petroleum fumes and, in a few instances, actual accumulations of petroleum products. Thus these floors must be constantly monitored and cleaned and fans used to insure against a buildup of fumes that might explode. Obviously these floors are now closed to any public use.

know that the property was contaminated at the time of purchase, (2) reacted responsibly to the contamination when found, and (3) had made reasonable inquiries into the past uses of the property before acquisition in a effort to determine if the property was contaminated. There is no standard format or guideline on what constitutes a "reasonable inquiry" using an environmental assessment. Most environmental assessments, however, are conducted in a phased manner. These phases are designed so information obtained in earlier phases is used in determining the scope of the subsequent phases. Generally the purchaser should take the lead in conducting the environmental assessment because the purchaser is the one exposing himself to the largest change in environmental risk. The lender, however, will often require the environmental assessment as a part of loan documentation. Due diligence environmental evaluations usually contain from one to three phases, depending on what is found during each phase. Figure 14.3 summarizes the sources of information that may be used during each phase.

KEY POINTS

Horror stories concerning environmental contamination of properties abound. One executive tells the story of having complied with new state regulations that require the placement of "monitoring wells" near underground storage tanks when the tanks reach a certain age. In this instance, the required wells had been placed on a convenience store property that sold gasoline products. Shortly after the new wells had been drilled and the monitoring equipment installed, a gasoline delivery was made to the site. After the truck driver had been inside eating a donut for awhile, one of the employees asked him why it was taking so long to fill the underground storage tanks. The driver then went to check his pumping equipment and returned to say that it appeared to be working fine and had pumped several thousand gallons already. The clerk was puzzled by the amount pumped because he did not think the tank capacity was that large. The driver replied that he assumed new storage tanks had been installed since the fill pipes were new. As you might have already guessed, the driver was, in fact, pumping gasoline directly into one of the new monitoring wells. Several days, and many thousands of dollars, later, most of the gasoline had been recovered. More than 1,000 gallons of gasoline, however, was lost in the underground aquifers of the area.

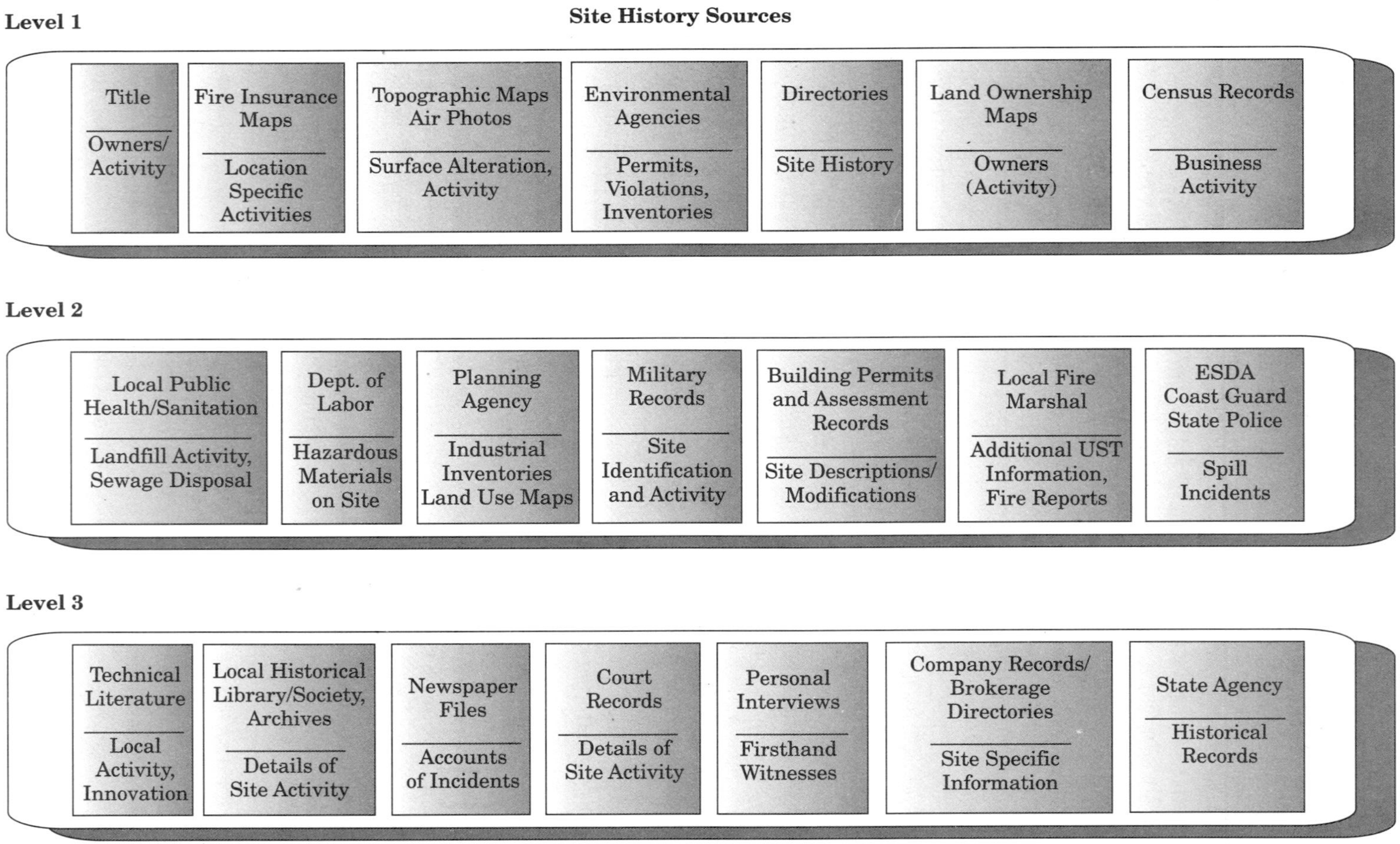

Site History Sources

Level 1

Title — Owners/Activity
Fire Insurance Maps — Location Specific Activities
Topographic Maps Air Photos — Surface Alteration, Activity
Environmental Agencies — Permits, Violations, Inventories
Directories — Site History
Land Ownership Maps — Owners (Activity)
Census Records — Business Activity

Level 2

Local Public Health/Sanitation — Landfill Activity, Sewage Disposal
Dept. of Labor — Hazardous Materials on Site
Planning Agency — Industrial Inventories Land Use Maps
Military Records — Site Identification and Activity
Building Permits and Assessment Records — Site Descriptions/Modifications
Local Fire Marshal — Additional UST Information, Fire Reports
ESDA Coast Guard State Police — Spill Incidents

Level 3

Technical Literature — Local Activity, Innovation
Local Historical Library/Society, Archives — Details of Site Activity
Newspaper Files — Accounts of Incidents
Court Records — Details of Site Activity
Personal Interviews — Firsthand Witnesses
Company Records/Brokerage Directories — Site Specific Information
State Agency — Historical Records

FIGURE 14.3 SITE HISTORY SOURCES

Role of Phase I Evaluation

Phase I is frequently referred to as a preliminary evaluation, or initial screening assessment. This phase involves a review of reasonably available information to determine the need and range of analytical review and testing of a site. Typically a Phase I assessment will consist of a review of public records, a site visit, a review of environmental records maintained by the company operating the site, interviews and questionnaires with personnel familiar with the site on its prior uses and operations, and comparison of past aerial site photographs with current site photographs. The Phase I assessment will also address the potential for contamination occurring from adjacent properties. A typical Phase I investigation will require approximately four weeks and range in cost from $3,000 to $10,000.

Some would advocate a less expensive and quicker Phase I investigation using only a form. Such an inspection, currently available in some areas for about $125 to $250, might use a form such as that shown in Figure 14.4.

Role of Phase II Evaluation

If the Phase I review turns up evidence of possible site contamination or violations of environmental laws, then a Phase II investigation is justified. The Phase II investigation would be tailored to the results reported from the Phase I investigation. Although there is no standard definition of what constitutes a Phase II assessment, the courts have ruled the unless the thoroughness of the investigation is appropriate with the level of suspicion caused by the Phase I assessment, an innocent landowner defense is not allowable. The elements of a Phase II investigation include soil sampling, water sampling (including ground and surface water if there is a pond, creek, stream, or lagoon on the property), laboratory analysis of any soil and water samples, and testing of any underground storage tanks. It is not feasible to test for every possible contaminant in every location of a site; thus this phase should sample at the locations suggested for the possible contaminants listed in the Phase I review.

The time this assessment can take ranges from 5 to 15 weeks and can cost from $10,000 to more than $50,000 depending on the amount of sampling and analyses required. Deep groundwater monitoring can substantially increase the costs of this investigation.

Role of Phase III Evaluation

If after completing a Phase II investigation and learning a site is contaminated, the purchaser still wants to continue with the acquisition process, provided that the proper terms can be reached, a Phase III evaluation is warranted. A Phase III evaluation involves performing a detailed evaluation of a known contaminated site for purposes of executing a remedial cleanup action. The purchaser and seller can decide to clean up the property before closing the transaction, the seller can pay for the cost of cleanup after the purchaser has taken possession, or the seller can discount the property enough to entice the purchaser to assume the risk of cleanup. The assessment generally takes an extremely long time because the remediation of the contamination usually takes place in accordance with a remedial action plan approved by the lead governmental agency.

UNIFORM ENVIRONMENTAL RISK SCREENING REPORT

File No.

Client			
Client Address			
Property Address			
City	County	State	Zip
Lender			
Firm Name			
Address			

The undersigned Underwriter/Appraiser/Inspector, acting as Environmental Risk Screener for the client, has made an inspection of the property and the area surrounding the property for the purpose of screening for apparent hazardous substances and detrimental environmental conditions. This report enumerates what inspections and/or test(s) were made and what apparent hazardous substances and detrimental environmental conditions were discovered. This report also contains recommendations for additional inspections and tests.

(The reported results of the inspection and these recommendations are not intended to preclude the client from obtaining a complete hazardous substance and detrimental environmental conditions audit together with the appropriate tests made by a professional hazardous substance and detrimental environmental conditions inspector and/or engineer.)

The following checked items indicate sources used by the undersigned Environmental Risk Screener to perform a screening of the property to discover the existence of apparent hazardous substances and detrimental environmental conditions:

_____ Building Specifications
_____ Historical Aerial Photos
_____ Current Aerial Photos
_____ Title History
_____ Site Survey
_____ Interviews with Local Fire, Health, Land Use or Environmental Enforcement Officials
_____ Neighborhood Zoning Maps
_____ Neighborhood Land Use Maps
_____ List of Commercial Tenants On-site
_____ Verification of Public Water and Sewer
_____ Interviews with Builder, and/or Property Manager
_____ Other ____________________

ASBESTOS

The following checked items indicate additional specific investigations made by the Environmental Risk Screener.

_____ Dated Building Construction or Rehabilitation Specifications
_____ Engineer's or Consultant's Asbestos Report _____ Other ____________________

Below is a summary of my History and Record Check, Field Observation, Available Test Results and my Comments & Recommendations.

Summary of my Field Observations: ____________________

Known Tests and Results: ____________________

Comments & Recommendations: ____________________

PCBs (Polychlorinated Biphenyls)

The following checked items indicate additional specific investigations made by the Environmental Risk Screener.

_____ Utility Transformer Records _____ Site Survey Transformers
_____ Site Soil and Groundwater PCB Test Results _____ Other ____________________

Below is a summary of my History and Record Check, Field Observation, Available Test Results and my Comments & Recommendations.

Summary of my Field Observations: ____________________

Known Tests and Results: ____________________

Comments & Recommendations: ____________________

Page 1

FW 70ES Test Version 4A-3/90 1989 Forms and Worms, Inc., 315 Whitney Ave., New Haven, CT 06511 1(800)243-4545 National Association of Environmental Risk Auditors Item #115100

FIGURE 14.4 UNIFORM ENVIRONMENTAL RISK SCREENING REPORT

UREA (Formaldehyde)

The following checked items indicate additional specific investigations made by the Environmental Risk Screener.

_____ Urea-Formaldehyde Foam Insulation Survey _____ Other _____

Below is a summary of my History and Record Check, Field Observation, Available Test Results and my Comments & Recommendations.

Summary of my Field Observations: _____

Known Tests and Results: _____

Comments & Recommendations: _____

LEAD PAINT

The following checked items indicate additional specific investigations made by the Environmental Risk Screener.

_____ Lead Paint Survey _____ Other _____

Below is a summary of my History and Record Check, Field Observation, Available Test Results and my Comments & Recommendations.

Summary of my Field Observations: _____

Known Tests and Results: _____

Comments & Recommendations: _____

DRINKING WATER

The following checked items indicate additional specific investigations made by the Environmental Risk Screener.

_____ Lead in Drinking Water Test _____ Other _____

Below is a summary of my History and Record Check, Field Observation, Available Test Results and my Comments & Recommendations.

Summary of my Field Observations: _____

Known Tests and Results: _____

Comments & Recommendations: _____

AIR POLLUTANTS

The following checked items indicate additional specific investigations made by the Environmental Risk Screener.

_____ Interior Air Test Results _____ Other _____

Below is a summary of my History and Record Check, Field Observation, Available Test Results and my Comments & Recommendations.

Summary of my Field Observations: _____

Known Tests and Results: _____

Comments & Recommendations: _____

Page 2

'W 70ES Test Version 4A-3/90 1989 Forms and Worms, Inc., 315 Whitney Ave., New Haven, CT 06511 1(800)243-4545 National Association of Environmental Risk Auditors Item #115100

FIGURE 14.4 UNIFORM ENVIRONMENTAL RISK SCREENING REPORT (*continued*)

RADON

The following checked items indicate additional specific investigations made by the Environmental Risk Screener.

_____ Water Utility Records
_____ On-site Radon Test Results
_____ Gas Utility Records
_____ Other_____

Below is a summary of my History and Record Check, Field Observation, Available Test Results and my Comments & Recommendations.

Summary of my Field Observations: _____

Known Tests and Results: _____

Comments & Recommendations: _____

UST's (Undergound Storage Tanks)

The following checked items indicate additional specific investigations made by the Environmental Risk Screener.

_____ Oil, Motor Fuel and Waste Oil Systems Reports
_____ Site Soil and Groundwater Test Results
_____ Site Tank Survey
_____ Other_____

Below is a summary of my History and Record Check, Field Observation, Available Test Results and my Comments & Recommendations.

Summary of my Field Observations: _____

Known Tests and Results: _____

Comments & Recommendations: _____

WASTE DISPOSAL

The following checked items indicate additional specific investigations made by the Environmental Risk Screener.

_____ Site Soil and Groundwater Test Results
_____ Other _____

Below is a summary of my History and Record Check, Field Observation, Available Test Results and my Comments & Recommendations.

Summary of my Field Observations: _____

Known Tests and Results: _____

Comments & Recommendations: _____

WASTE SITES

The following checked items indicate additional specific investigations made by the Environmental Risk Screener.

_____ NPL sites which might effect the subject property
_____ CERCLIS/HWDMS sites within_____ miles of the subject property
_____ Site soil and/or groundwater test results: _____
_____ State EPA site lists for neighborhoods (within _____ mile radius)
_____ Other_____

Below is a summary of my History and Record Check, Field Observation, Available Test Results and my Comments & Recommendations.

Summary of my Field Observations: _____

Known Tests and Results: _____

Comments & Recommendations: _____

Page 3

FW 70ES Test Version 4A-3/90

1989 Forms and Worms, Inc., 315 Whitney Ave., New Haven, CT 06511 1(800)243-4545
National Association of Environmental Risk Auditors

Item #115100

FIGURE 14.4 UNIFORM ENVIRONMENTAL RISK SCREENING REPORT *(continued)*

ADDITIONAL ENVIRONMENTAL HAZARDS

The following checked items indicate additional sources, tests, investigations and inspections made by the Environmental Risk Screener and not reported in the previous separate sections of this report.

_____ Other ________________________ _____ Other ________________________

_____ Other ________________________ _____ Other ________________________

Below is a summary of my History and Record Check, Field Observation, Available Test Results and my Comments & Recommendations.

Summary of my Field Observations: ________________________

Known Tests and Results: ________________________

Comments & Recommendations: ________________________

SUMMARY

The following is a summary of the investigations, inspections and tests made by and/or considered by the Environmental Risk Screener together with a summary of the Environmental Risk Screener's recommendation: ________________________

SPECIAL DISCLOSURE WHEN ENVIRONMENTAL SCREENING IS MADE AS PART OF A REAL ESTATE APPRAISAL

WHEN NO APPARENT HAZARDOUS SUBSTANCES OR DETRIMENTAL CONDITIONS ARE FOUND

_____ 1. As a result of this inspection, which did not reveal any apparent significant hazardous substances or apparent significant detrimental environmental conditions and based on the undersigned's overall knowledge of the area in which the property is located, the undersigned has elected to make this a "Full Scope" appraisal as defined in the Uniform Standards of Professional Appraisal Practice. The value estimated in this report is based on the assumption that the property is not negatively affected by the existence of hazardous substances or detrimental environmental conditions. Should an inspection or tests made by a professional hazardous substances and detrimental environmental condition inspector and/or engineer reveal the existence of hazardous substances and/or detrimental environmental conditions the value estimates would not be valid.

WHEN ONE OR MORE HAZARDOUS SUBSTANCES OR DETRIMENTAL CONDITIONS ARE FOUND

_____ 2. Hazardous substance(s) and/or detrimental environmental conditions were found by the undersigned and described in this report. It is assumed that it is possible to remove the hazardous substance(s) and/or eliminate the detrimental environmental conditions. The value estimated in this report is based on the assumption that all hazardous substances and detrimental environmental conditions have been eliminated or rendered harmless.

_____ 3. The hazardous substance(s) and/or detrimental environmental conditions found by the undersigned and described in this report make it impossible for the appraiser to estimate the value of the property without the collaboration of a professional environmental risk auditor. At the present time, without the needed significant additional information, it is impossible to estimate the value of the property in keeping with the USPAP.

Additional Comments: ________________________

Environmental Risk Screener

Signature ________________________

Name ________________ Date ________

Reviewed by

Signature ________________________

Name ________________ Date ________

_____ Did _____ Did not inspect property

FW-70ES Test Version 4A 3/90

1990 Forms and Worms Inc., 315 Whitney Ave., New Haven, CT 06511 1(800)243-4545
Approved by National Association of Environmental Risk Auditors

Item #115100

FIGURE 14.4 UNIFORM ENVIRONMENTAL RISK SCREENING REPORT *(continued)*

Environmental Risk Management

Each party to a transaction, including third parties, such as lenders and real estate agents, needs to be aware of potential environmental liability exposure. Although many times the following suggestions are in direct conflict with each other, they are provided as suggestions for each of these parties.

Purchaser Risk Management

For a purchaser of real estate, the due diligence review described earlier generally provides the basis for a sound risk management program. Purchase contracts involving potentially contaminated property should, however, contain a few additional clauses:

Indemnification Clause A contract provision designed to protect one party from potential liability due to conditions not due to their actions.

1. In addition to the standard broad indemnification provisions, the purchaser should have a separate, specific **environmental indemnification**, which should extend to any and all liabilities imposed on the purchaser for environmental conditions of the property not due to the actions of the purchaser. This indemnification should not be limited in time period or monetary amount, although the seller will try to negotiate some limits. The indemnification should also contain a provision that it is the seller's duty to defend the purchaser in any subsequent litigation and to pay for all legal costs, but the purchaser may want to retain some control over such litigation and contacts made with the government agencies.
2. The purchaser should try to have the seller represent and warrant as much as possible about the property. Items the contract could represent and warrant are that (a) no release of CERCLA-defined hazardous substances has occurred; (b) no potential environmental liabilities exist on the property; (c) no litigation or administrative hearing regarding environmental problems on the property has occurred; (d) no past environmental liens have been placed or currently exist on the property; (e) no correspondence from government agencies with respect to the property was received; (f) all necessary environmental permits have been acquired; and where possible (g) no hazardous substances have been used, generated, manufactured, stored, transported to or from, or disposed on, under, or about the property or will be before closing. The buyer should heed which warranties the seller will not make, as possible indications of possible kinds of environmental contamination. Warranties should be "to the best of the seller's knowledge after a thorough and diligent review and investigation by the seller."
3. The contract should retain the right of access to the property to perform a proper environmental assessment.
4. The purchaser should retain the right of rescission in which the purchaser may at any time after execution of the contract but before closing decide not to close owing to environmental problems and still receive a refund of the earnest money deposit.

When faced with the often huge costs associated with cleaning up environmental con-taminants, some property owners find themselves wishing they had never purchased the property. This raises the issue of rescinding the purchase as a way out of the problem. In *Donahey v. Bogle* (987 F.2d 1250, 1993) the buyers of a contaminated site were faced with several hundred thousand dollars of clean up costs. Unwilling to incur these costs, even with the prospect of eventual recovery from the former owners, the buyer attempted to rescind the purchase on the basis that the environmental contaminants on the property constituted an encumbrance to clear title. The court held that, although environmental contaminants may diminish the value of property, they do not constitute an encumbrance because they do not affect title. Since they had knowledge of the contamination, and thus could not claim the innocent landowner defense, the buyers found themselves liable for clean up costs along with former owners.

KEY POINTS

Even the old adage to "never look a gift horse in the mouth" may not hold whe dealing with real estate. One nature conservancy organization accepted as a gift some land that had previously been used as a farm. The existing structures were to be removed and the area set aside as a permanent animal refuge. As the team of volunteers worked to clean up the former farm buildings, one volunteer came across a barrel in a storeroom in the barn. The barrel was rolled out into the barn, but before dumping its contents, the volunteer decided to ask one of the conservancy staff what to do. As it turned out, the barrel contained a pesticide that is now on the Environmental Protection Agency hazardous substances list, and, to make matters worse, the state the farm was located in had no acceptable site for disposing of the material. The conservancy organization was faced with either leaving the barrel in a structure for some indefinite time period or having it transported several thousand miles to one of the few disposal sites available in the U.S. Because the transportation and disposal costs would have been extremely high, the barrel still remains in a secure structure (built just for the barrel) on the site. After another barrel of the same substance turned up on another donated site, the organization prepared a set of strict environmental inspection guidelines that must now be followed before accepting any more gifts.

Seller Risk Management

Although a seller is liable under CERCLA with essentially no avenue for escape, there are several procedures a seller can implement to reduce his CERCLA liability and allocate these risks to other PRPs. The seller should obtain from the purchaser written certification that the purchaser has examined the property and is accepting it "as is." This will probably not completely eliminate the seller's liabilities under CERCLA but may help reduce the seller's contributions for future cleanup costs. The seller needs to make sure that adequate disclosure is made of all items not discovered by the buyer that will materially and adversely affect the buyer. Any items not disclosed that can affect the buyer's ability to operate the facility, pose an adverse health risk, or impose substantial economic costs on the buyer can result in costly future litigation under various fraud or negligent representation torts. With this in mind, the seller should try to observe the following guidelines in drafting representations and warranties in the sales contract:

1. The seller should represent and warrant as little as possible about the compliance of the facilities with existing laws and regulations and should expressly except all known noncompliances.
2. The seller should represent and warrant as little as possible about the validity and renewability of environmental permits.
3. The seller should represent or disclose existing environmental conditions that may require the buyer to invest additional funds or may impose additional liabilities on the buyer.
4. The seller should try to have his monetary obligation under the indemnity defined in terms of some maximum exposure in dollars.
5. The seller should try to limit the indemnity and representation obligations to a set period of time.
6. The seller should try to obtain change of law provisions that clearly transfer all risk of change of law to the buyer.
7. The seller should avoid providing indemnities for claims or causes of action that can be resolved or avoided by having the buyer modify current operations or equipment.
8. The seller should obtain from the buyer broad indemnification for post-closing incidents caused in whole or in part by the buyer.

Real Estate Broker, Agent, and Appraiser Environmental Risk Management

In general, environmental liabilities are attached to past and present owners and operators of real estate or facilities. Those involved in the transfer of real estate, however, should minimize their potential liabilities. Real estate developers and other professionals may arguably be liable under CERCLA or common law theories of negligence. *Tanglewood East Homeowners v. Charles-Thomas, Inc.* [849 F.2d 1568 (1988)] raises issues about the potential liabilities for developers, construction companies, real estate agents, and brokers. In this case, soils contaminated with creosote and other wood preservative chemicals from a former wood preservative facility at the site were moved about the property as part of the normal construction activities. The court held that those responsible for the movement of the soil acted as parties who arranged for disposal. Under this theory, many developers, construction companies, real estate companies, and other institutions may face liability for having arranged to move contaminated material (i.e., disposed of hazardous materials at the site). Another source of CERCLA liability for a broker is when a deal is structured such that a broker acts as an intermediary who takes possession of the property for a short period. Once a broker becomes an "owner" of the property, even for just a day, the broker has become exposed to liability for any future costs of cleanup.

If a broker has knowledge of environmental problems or restrictions on the property that are material, the broker's failure to disclose them will constitute fraud, provided that the problems are such that a purchaser would not have discovered these problems during a reasonable investigation of the property.

Hiring a contractor to dispose of hazardous wastes would normally absolve the producer of those wastes from liability for a contaminated site. In *Shockley v. Hoechst Celanese Corporation et. al.* (1993 WL 241179 (4th Cir. (S.C.))) the court found the producer of wastes to be liable for the eventual clean-up of the site of a company employed to dispose of the wastes. In this case, the court held that the company producing the wastes intentionally employed the disposal company knowing that it was likely to involve contamination of the disposal company's site and, ultimately, the surrounding property. In effect, the court refused to allow the producer of wastes to avoid liability by simply moving the wastes to an independent contractor (owned by a former employee) unlikely to properly handle the hazardous material.

The broker may reduce his risk of liability in several ways. First, the real estate broker should make no representations concerning the condition of the property or the appropriateness of the property for a particular use. Second, a broker should recommend that an environmental assessment be performed using consultants selected by the buyer or seller or both. The broker should not select the environmental consultant to avoid liability if the consultant should prove negligent. If the parties decide not to conduct an environmental assessment, a duty to investigate may still remain with the broker. He should at least question the seller to determine prior uses of the property and any problems that may exist as a result of these prior uses. The broker should independently investigate the property, confirm the prior uses of the property, and investigate the prior uses of the adjacent properties. The broker should also check to see if there are any restrictions associated with the property and if there are any environmental liens against the property. If any environmental problems are revealed in these investigations, the broker should disclose this information to the prospective purchasers in writing. If the broker represents the seller, the seller's approval is needed before this information can be released. Disclosure of this information without the seller's approval can be considered a breach of the broker's fiduciary obligation. If the seller refuses to give this permission, a broker should seriously consider withdrawing from the transaction.

If a serious environmental problem is discovered, there is a legal obligation to report the problem to the appropriate federal and state authorities. A broker should give the seller the opportunity to report the problem to these agencies. If the seller refuses, a broker's safest, most responsible policy is to report the problem. Third, indemnity provisions, which eliminate the obligation on the part of the broker to investigate the property independently for environmental problems or restrictions and acknowledge that the purchaser will not rely on the broker to perform such an investigation, should be added to the transaction documents. Fourth, brokers should obtain liability insurance as a protection against liabilities arising out of the sale of property with environmental problems.

There is no significant case law that addresses the extent to which real estate appraisers may be held liable for failure to recognize environmental hazards. Appraiser liability, however, is generally the same as that for brokers. One theory of liability is based on an opinion rendered without an adequate inspection of the property. An appraisal without considering information in the public records regarding the environmental condition of the property might be considered negligent. The integration of as much "due diligence" as possible into the appraisal process and limitations on the potential liability and indemnification of an appraiser should be included in standard appraisal contracts.

CONCLUSION

The material in this chapter, although it is written in terms of the liability risks facing real estate professionals, serves to illustrate the central role that real property law plays in our society. Issues of fair housing really strike at the heart of race relations—if we cannot live together, then we are unlikely to ever abolish race discrimination. In similar fashion, our willingness to live side-by-side with people of all physical and mental abilities is crucial to our growth as a society.

Just as we must pay increasing attention to how we live with each other, we must also pay increasing attention to how we treat the property we live on. Perhaps more than any other issue, environmental protection will shape our way of life in the coming decades. Once again, land is central to our approach to dealing with contamination. It has often been said that "under all lies the land." It follows, then, that how we treat the land is an all important issue for our society.

The legal system is simply a reflection of the goals and values of our society. Commitment to resolving issues can be measured by the strength of our laws, and the vigor with which we enforce them. The areas of fair housing and environmental protection are, using these criteria, of vital importance to us and are likely to remain so.

DISCUSSION QUESTIONS

1. What was the significance of *Jones v. Alfred H. Mayer*? How did Title VIII of the Civil Rights Act of 1968 affect real estate transactions?

2. Describe the blockbusting process. How does this differ from racial steering?

3. In 1989, Amendments were made to the Fair Housing Act prohibiting discrimination based on physical or mental handicaps. What is the definition of "handicap" as used in the amendments? What parties is the definition extended to in order to cover?

4. With regard to lending and credit discrimination, the Fair Housing Act prohibits two practices. What are they?

5. The Comprehensive Environmental Response, Compensation, and Liability Act (CERCLA) has a tremendous impact on real estate transactions involving environmental issues. What parties does this act define as "potentially responsible" for cleanup costs? What are these parties potentially liable for?

6. Under CERCLA, a limited number of defenses are available that allow parties to escape liability. Name them.

7. The Superfund Amendments and Reauthorization Act (SARA) added an additional line of defense to the ones outlined in CERCLA, called the "innocent landowner defense." Describe this defense, and explain what is meant by a "due diligence environmental review."

8. Explain the third-party defense. Who is this defense designed to protect?

9. Due diligence environmental evaluations can contain up to three steps, depending on what is found during each phase. Describe the three phases, outlining what evaluation techniques are used during each.

10. Real estate brokers run the risk of being charged with fraud if environmental problems should arise after sale of a property. Discuss some ways in which a broker may reduce his or her liability.

VILLAGE OF BELLWOOD V. DWIVEDI

895 F.2d. 1521 (Seventh Circuit, 1989-1990)

Blockbusting and racial steering

The defendants in this civil rights suit—a real estate brokerage firm (Raj Realty), its owner (Chandra Dwivedi), and two of its employees—appeal from a judgment . . . and an injunction. The defendants had been charged with violating two statutes. The first . . . , part of the Civil Rights Act of 1866, grants all citizens of the United States the same rights as white people with respect to property. The second, . . . part of Title VIII of the Civil Rights Act of 1968, forbids (so far as potentially relevant to this case) making a dwelling unavailable to any person because of his race, . . . ; discriminating on racial grounds against any person in the provision of services in connection with the sale of a dwelling, . . . ; or falsely representing to any person because of his race that any dwelling is not available for inspection or sale. . . . The parties agree that . . . each . . . forbid[s] racial steering by real estate brokers, but they do not agree on what "racial steering" is.

A suburban community of some 20,000, located thirteen miles west of downtown Chicago, Bellwood was once all white but by the time of trial in 1987 was 45 percent black. The adjoining suburbs continue to have very few black residents. Many people in Bellwood are concerned that if the percentage of blacks in the community continues to increase, a point will soon be reached where the remaining whites become so uncomfortable that they exit en masse, making the community all black. The Village has energetically employed the legal tools available to it to prevent this "tipping" from taking place. . . .

Raj Realty opened in Bellwood in 1982. More than 90 percent of its customers are black, and this has been true from the agency's inception. In 1985, officials of the Village, learning that 80 percent of the Village's new residents were black, decided to investigate a number of real estate agencies, including Raj Realty, to determine whether any of them were steering black home seekers to Bellwood and white ones to the adjoining suburbs. . . . The Council hired both black and white couples to serve as "testers." Twenty-eight of these couples went to Raj Realty, posing as customers. Their reports convinced the Council that Raj Realty was encouraging blacks to buy in Bellwood and whites to buy in the other suburbs—more precisely that Raj Realty was encouraging blacks to buy in east Bellwood and whites in west Bellwood (which is still mainly white) as well as in the white suburbs that surround Bellwood . . .

[16][17] 3. . . . Only one tester couple dealt with Chaudhary and their testimony was the entire evidence against him. The couple was black, and testified that several times while they were looking in the listings book at homes in other suburbs, Chaudhary took the book out of their hands and turned it back to the Bellwood section. This evidence was insufficient to justify a rational jury in concluding that Chaudhary had engaged in racial steering. Steering implies different treatment of testers of different races. A broker determined to "steer" all customers, of whatever race, to a particular neighborhood is not guilty of racial steering, because he is not treating the races differently. If a white tester couple had also testified about their treatment by Chaudhary, and their testimony had shown that he was not eager to sell them a house in Bellwood, then the verdict against him could stand. But as far as the evidence shows, he was

treating this couple the way he treated every other couple—trying to sell them houses in the area with which he was most familiar, the area in which the real estate agency was located: Bellwood. He did not refuse the show the couple houses in white suburbs, and did actually show them a house in one of those suburbs.

4. . . . Suppose a real estate broker falsely states to a black customer that no homes are for sale in Village X, which is primarily white, and he does so because the customer is black, so that the statement is a deliberate, racially motivated falsity. . . . This is deliberate conduct, and unquestionably it is racial steering.

[18]Misrepresentation is not the only species of racial steering. If a broker simply refuses a customer's point-blank request to show him a house in a neighborhood that the broker wants to reserve for persons of a different race, this is steering even though there is no misrepresentation. . . . A point-blank refusal is not necessary; any effort to discourage will do. . . .

[19][20][21] . . . To test what unintentional racial steering might mean, we put the following hypothetical case to the plaintiffs' counsel. A black person comes to Raj Realty and tells the agent that he wants to know the racial composition of the various communities in the listings books because he wants to live in an integrated community. The agent answers that Bellwood is integrated but that the other suburbs are white, and he proceeds to show the customer only houses that are for sale in Bellwood. In such a case the real estate agent would not be trying to "steer" (in some invidious sense that might ground legal liability) a black person to a community that already had a large black population, unless the agent would have refused to cooperate equally if that person wanted to live in a white community. The agent would simply be trying to give the black person what that person wanted. Yet if many black people would prefer to live in an integrated community, the effect of the agent's conduct, in combination with similar conduct by other real estate agents, could be to "tip" the community, transforming it from integrated to resegregated; or, more realistically, to fail to prevent tipping. . . .

[24] . . . [T]he broker who refuses to show the customer a property in which the customer is interested and does so not because he dislikes persons of the customer's race but because he fears being boycotted by persons of a different race if he refuses to abide by the community's racial mores. Such a broker is discriminating against his customer on grounds of race and therefore violates the statute. But our first broker, the broker who responds to the customer's desires, is not discriminating against the customer, or denying the customer a dwelling, or misrepresenting to the customer the unavailability of a dwelling. The statue does not require a broker to endeavor to make his customers better people by withholding information that they request about the racial composition of the communities in which the broker sells houses. It does not impose liability for failing to promote integration, or for failing to coordinate individual integrative acts that have an aggregate resegregative effect. If the broker treats all his customers the same, regardless of race, he is not liable. . . .

[28] . . . [W]e note that the defendants were catering to blacks, not to whites. Was it not therefore in the defendants' pecuniary interest to sell homes anywhere to blacks? If that drove whites out, all the better for the defendants' pocketbooks, since there would be more homes to sell to blacks. Although the defendants may have hoped that if enough blacks moved into Bellwood the remaining whites would leave in a panic and there would be even more homes to sell to blacks, there is no evidence that they harbored this intent and none that they engaged in "blockbusting"—that is, tried to induce whites to sell their homes by telling them that other whites were leaving and the community would soon be virtually all black. . . .

CASE REFLECTIONS

1. Define "blockbusting" and "racial steering."
2. What, from a business standpoint, did the defendant have to gain by engaging in the aforementioned illegal practices?

SHELLHAMMER and SHELLHAMMER V. LEWALLEN and LEWALLEN

770 F.2d 167 (Sixth Circuit, 1985)

Sexual Harassment in Housing

Thomas and Tammy Shellhammer appeal the decision of the district court denying them part of the relief they sought under the Fair Housing Act, . . . and denying their motion for class certification. We affirm.

In March 1982, Thomas and Tammy Shellhammer entered into a month-to-month tenancy for the rental of an apartment owned by the appellees, Norman and Jacqueline Lewallen. Shortly after they moved into the apartment, Norman Lewallen approached Tammy Shellhammer, while she was cleaning an apartment for him, and asked her to pose for nude pictures for him. Shellhammer refused and informed her husband of the incident. Approximately one month later, when Norman Lewallen had again taken Tammy Shellhammer to clean one of his vacant apartments, Lewallen asked her to have sexual relations with him and offered to pay her money for that purpose. She again refused and reported the occurrence to her husband.

In July of that same year, the Shellhammers and the Lewallens had a dispute over payment of rent. The Shellhammers claimed that the Lewallens were responsible for providing a working refrigerator, and they wanted to use that month's rent to procure a new refrigerator. The Lewallens apparently maintained that they were not responsible for the refrigerator. In any case, rent was not paid in a timely manner, and the Lewallens instituted eviction proceedings. The Shellhammers were forced to move to a new apartment and to incur larger rent payments.

On October 26, 1982, the Shellhammers filed suit against the Lewallens claiming that they had been deprived of rights secured by the Fair Housing Act. . . . The Shellhammers styled their claim as a class action on behalf of themselves and others similarly situated who had inquired about, applied for, and/or rented presently or in the future dwelling units owned or managed by the Lewallens. On February 7, 1983, the Shellhammers filed a motion to certify the class.

On November 7 and 8, 1983, the magistrate, who had been assigned the case at the parties' consent, held a trial on the Shellhammers' individual claims without first ruling on the Shellhammers' class certification motion. . . .

On November 22, the magistrate entered his decision in the case. He found that the Shellhammers were asserting two distinct legal theories for liability. First, they were arguing that Lewallens' sexual harassment created an offensive environment for their tenancy. Second, the Shellhammers were claiming that the Lewallens had made their tenancy subject to sexual consideration. By analogizing their claim to a Title VII action . . . , the magistrate found that both theories of relief stated viable legal claims under the Fair Housing Act. Having recognized the viability of the plaintiffs' claim, the magistrate then considered whether the Shellhammers had factually proven their claims. With respect to the Shellhammers' "hostile environment" claim, the magistrate found that the plaintiffs had failed to carry their burden of proof.

The magistrate stated:

> With reference to plaintiff's first claim—that the landlord's conduct subjected her to a hostile environment as a result of her sex, it is clear that she has failed to satisfy the elements of this claim as defined above. She points to two requests during the three or four months of her tenancy. This does not amount to the pervasive and persistent conduct which is apredicate to finding that the sexual harassment created a burdensome situation which caused the tenancy to be significantly less desirable than it would have been had the harassment not occurred. The plaintiffs, therefore, are not entitled to relief on the first aspect of her claim.

With respect to the Shellhammers' second claim—that they had been evicted because Mrs. Shellhammer had rebuffed Mr. Lewallen's sexual advances, the magistrate found the Shellhammer's had factually proven their claim. The Shellhammers were eventually awarded $7,410 for this claim.

On March 22, 1984, the magistrate issued another opinion in the case dealing with the plaintiff's motion for class certification. The magistrate found that the Shellhammers would not be the proper representatives of a class that included all females, and where applicable, their spouses, who had inquired about, applied for, and/or rented dwelling units owned or managed by the Lewallens because such a class was too broadly defined. The magistrate found that the Shellhammers could only represent those persons who had been denied occupancy or evicted because they refused to assent to Mr. Lewallens' demands for sexual favors. . . .

Having limited the class to those persons who had been denied occupancy or were evicted because of their refusal to assent to Mr. Lewallen's sexual demands, the magistrate found that such a class did not meet the numerosity requirement. . . . In support of this finding, the magistrate noted that the evidence available in the case indicated that only twelve members belonged to this class. The magistrate therefore refused to certify a class on this ground.

In this appeal, the Shellhammers argue the magistrate erred in two ways. First, they claim he erred in not finding the Lewallens liable under their "hostile environment theory." Second, they challenge the magistrate's refusal to certify a class.

. . .

In this case, we do not believe an error had clearly been committed. The magistrate simply concluded that the appellees' conduct in this case, when considered in light of the length of the appellants' tenancy, did not created such a hostile environment as to require liability. This was a rational decision that we shall not disturb.

With regard to appellant's second claim of error, we understand the appellant's claim to encompass two distinct arguments. First, the appellants are arguing that their district court erred in making a liability determination on the plaintiffs' individual claims before ruling on their motion for class certification. Second, they are asserting that the magistrate erred in finding that they did not meet the numerosity requirement.

We do not believe that the magistrate's ruling on the plaintiffs' individual claims before deciding the class certification requires reversal. . . .

We also find no reversible error in the magistrate's refusal to certify the class because the plaintiffs failed to meet the numerosity requirement. . . . [W]e shall only reverse a trial court's class action determination if it abuses . . . discretion. We shall only find an abuse of discretion if we have a "definite and firm conviction that the court below committed a clear error of judgment in the conclusion it reached upon a weighing of the relevant factors." . . .

The magistrate did not abuse his discretion in this case. After determining the scope of defendant's liability on plaintiffs' individual claims, the magistrate quite logically limited the class to those who had been evicted or denied occupancy for refusing to assent to Mr. Lewallen's sexual demands, as had the Shellhammers. Having so limited the class, the magistrate formulated what appears to be a reasonably accurate number of twelve persons who fit within this class. Twelve persons is not such a great number that joinder would be infeasible, as most courts have concluded . . .

The decision of the magistrate is thus affirmed.

Case Reflections

1. The Fair Housing Act prohibits discrimination based on race, color, religion, sex, familial status or national origin in "the sale or rental of . . . a dwelling." How do the claims of the Shellhammers fit within this prohibition?
2. Why do you think the Magistrate in the Trial Court refused to certify the claims of the plaintiffs as a class action? Do you think it is possible that a future court might allow a class action suit in a similar situation?

UNITED STATES V. MARYLAND BANK & TRUST COMPANY

632 F.Supp. 573 (District Court, 1986)

Does the third party defense apply after foreclosure?

This case presents the novel question of whether a bank, which formerly held a mortgage on a parcel of land, later purchased the land at a foreclosure sale and continues to own it, must reimburse the United States for the cost of cleaning up hazardous wastes on this land, when those wastes were dumped prior to the bank's purchase of the property. The United States instituted this action pursuant to . . . the Comprehensive Environmental Response, Compensation, and Liability Act of 1980 (CERCLA) . . . to recover the expenses incurred by the United States Environmental Protection Agency (EPA) for removal of hazardous wastes from the toxic dump site known as the McLeod property or the California Maryland Drum site . . . Named as defendant in this suit is the Maryland Bank & Trust Company (MB & T), the owner of the property since May, 1982, and before that, the mortgagee of the tract beginning in December, 1980.

FACTS

From July 7, 1944 to December 16, 1980, Herschel McLeod, Sr. and Nellie McLeod owned the piece of property now the subject of this litigation . . . The parties have dubbed this property the California Maryland Drum site or "CMD site." During the period of the McLeod's ownership, the McLeods engaged in a business relationship with the Maryland Bank & Trust Co., the contours of which are disputed by the parties. It is undisputed, however, that during the 1970s, MB & T loaned money to Herschel McLeod, Sr. for two of his businesses—Greater St. Mary's Disposal, Inc. and Waldorf Sanitation of St. Mary's, Inc. The bank knew that McLeod operated a trash and garbage business on the site, but the record does not state at what point the bank became aware of this. During 1972 or 1973, McLeod permitted the dumping of hazardous wastes on the CMD site. . . . In 1980, Mark Wayne McLeod applied for a $335,000 loan from MB & T to purchase the CMD site from his parents. On or about September 2nd of that year, MB & T sent Farmers Home Administration a request for loan guarantees relating to the McLeod loan . . . FmHA issued Loan Note Guarantees for 90 percent of the loan on January 2, 1981.

Mark Wayne McLeod purchased the CMD site on December 16, 1980 through the MB & T loan, but soon failed to make payments on the loan. Consequently, MB & T instituted a foreclosure action against the CMD site in 1981 and purchased the property at the foreclosure sale on May 15, 1982 with a bid of $381,500. MB &T then took title to the property. From that date to the present, MB & T has been the record owner of the CMD site. FmHA continues to be a 90 percent guarantor of that loan. On June 20, 1983, Mark Wayne McLeod informed Walter E. Raum, Director of Environmental Hygiene for St. Mary's County Department of Health, of the existence of dumped wastes on the CMD site. After inspecting the site the following day, the State of Maryland contacted the EPA. Tests were conducted to identify the substances. On the basis of test results, the EPA requested and received funding to conduct a removal action under CERCLA. The agency notified MB & T president John T. Daugherty that MB & T would be given until October 24, 1983 to initiate corrective action at the site or EPA would use its funds to cleanup the wastes. The bank declined the EPA's offer, so the agency proceeded to clean the site itself, removing 287 drums of chemical material and 1180 tons of contaminated soil at a cost of approximately $551,513.50. After completing the cleanup, the EPA sent a letter to MB & T President Daugherty summarizing the costs incurred in the response action and demanding payment. To date, MB & T has not tendered payment. This action ensued. . . .

DISCUSSION

The question central to both the defendant's and the plaintiff's motion for summary judgment concerns . . . whether Maryland Bank & Trust is an "owner and operator" . . . Additionally, Maryland Bank & Trust has raised in its answer an affirmative defense . . . the so-called "third-party defense."

Essentially, MB & T contends that as a former mortgagee of the property which it has purchased at a foreclosure sale, it is exempted from liability under CERCLA, even though it might be a "person who has owned, operated, or otherwise controlled activities" at the site.

[1] A. . . . It is undisputed that MB & T has been the owner of the facility since May, 1982. The parties dispute whether the bank has been the operator of the facility since that time. The dispute over the term "operator" is not determinative, however, for the Court holds that current ownership of a facility alone brings a party within the ambit of subsection (1). . . . An examination of the legislative history, sparse as it is, and the lone relevant case convinces the Court to interpret the language of subsection (1) broadly to include both owners and operators. . . .

B. The definition of "owner or operator" . . . excludes from liability "a person, who, without participating in the management of a vessel or facility, holds indicia of ownership primarily to protect his security interest in the . . . facility." MB & T disclaims liability on the basis of this exemption. . . .

[2] . . . MB & T contends that it is entitled to the benefit of this exclusion because it acquired ownership of the CMD site through foreclosure on its security interest in the property and purchase of the land at the foreclosure sale. The government asserts that the bank is not entitled to the exemption as a matter of law. The Court finds the government's position more persuasive and holds that MB & T is not exempted from liability . . . The exemption . . . covers only those persons who, at the time of the cleanup, holds indicia of ownership to protect a then-held security interest in the land. . . .

Under the scenario put forward by the bank, the federal government alone would shoulder the cost of cleaning up the site, while the former mortgagee-turned-owner would benefit from the cleanup by the increased value of the now unpolluted land. At the foreclosure sale, the mortgagee could acquire the property cheaply. All other prospective purchasers would be faced with potential CERCLA liability, and would shy away from the sale. Yet once the property has been cleared at the taxpayers' expense and becomes marketable, the mortgagee-turned-owner would be in a position to sell the site at a profit.

In essence, the defendant's position would convert CERCLA into an insurance scheme for financial institutions, protecting them against possible losses due to the security of loans with polluted properties. Mortgagees, however, already have the means to protect themselves, by making prudent loans.[1] Financial institutions are in a position to investigate and discover potential problems in their secured properties. For many lending institutions, such research is routine. CERCLA will not absolve them from responsibility for their mistakes of judgment. . . .

II. The Third Party Defense . . .

Section 107(b)(3) establishes an affirmative defense for a person otherwise liable . . . , the so-called third party defense. Section 107(b) (3) provides:

> There shall be no liability under subsection (a) of this section for a person otherwise liable who can establish by a preponderance of the evidence that the release or threat of release of a hazardous substance and the damages resulting therefrom were caused solely by—(3) an act or omission of a third party other than an employee or agent of the defendant, or than one whose act or omission occurs in connection with a contractual relationship, existing directly or indirectly with the defendant, . . . if the defendant establishes by a preponderance of the evidence that (a) he exercised due care with respect to the hazardous substance concerned, taking into consideration the characteristics of such hazardous substance, in light of all relevant facts and circumstances, and (b) he took precautions against foreseeable acts or omissions of any such third party and the consequences that could foreseeably result from such acts or omissions. . . .

[1]The mortgagees also have the options of not foreclosing and not bidding at the foreclosure sale. Both steps would apparently insulate the mortgagee from liability.

Defendant MB & T raised this defense in its answer . . . The United States has asserted . . . that MB & T cannot meet its burden of proof for this defense. . . .

Case Reflections

1. Why did the United States of America bring suit against Maryland Bank and Trust Co.?
2. How did the defendant come to acquire the parcel of land in question?
3. Why did Maryland Bank and Trust claim it was exempt from liability? Why did the Court side with the plaintiff?

BETSEY V. TURTLE CREEK ASSOCIATES

736 F.2d 983 (Fourth Circuit, 1983-1984)

Discrimination Against Families with Children

Turtle Creek Associates, et al., the partnerships and partners who own and manage a three-building, high-rise apartment complex in Silver Spring, Maryland, known as The Point, issued eviction notices to many of the tenants of Building Three, allegedly to institute an all-adult rental policy. Plaintiffs, tenants of Building Three, most of whom are black and most of whom have children residing with them . . . sued the owners and managers for alleged violations of the Fair Housing Act of 1968 . . . Plaintiffs' theory was that defendants acted with a racially discriminatory intent in seeking to evict them and that the evictions would have a disparate racial impact, both in violation of the Act. . . .

I.

The Point consists of three high-rise buildings constructed in the 1960s. Prior to September of 1979, the buildings, though they shared common facilities, had different owners. In late 1979, Turtle Creek acquired all three buildings and began a systematic effort to upgrade the properties. At the time Turtle Creek acquired The Point, Building Three was generally considered to be more desirable than its counterparts . . .

Shortly after their acquisition of the complex, Turtle Creek instituted a series of new policies including: substantial rent increases, eviction notices based on alleged incidents of vandalism, and a change in the security staff. In May of 1980, eviction notices were sent to all families with children residing in Building Three. Tenants were required to move by August 1, 1980 or earlier if their leases had an earlier expiration date. Tenants who agreed to move in sixty days were given the right to move into comparable apartments in one of the other buildings, subject, however, to availability. Turtle Creek attempts to justify these evictions by contending that an "all-adult" conversion was necessary to reduce the vacancy rates in the complex.

In July of 1980, this action was instituted. Plaintiffs alleged a pattern of harassment against the black tenants at The Point, and they asserted a "deliberate and systematic effort to alter the racial character" of the property. The "all-adult" conversion policy resulting in eviction notices to families with children in Building Three was described as one part of a broad systematic effort to alter the racial composition of the complex. . . .

II

. . . [2][3] In order to prevail in a discriminatory impact case under Title VIII, plaintiffs, members of a discrete minority, are required to prove only that a given policy had a discriminatory impact on them as *individuals*. . . . Accordingly, we conclude that plaintiffs are not required to show a discriminatory impact on anyone but the existing minority residents of Building Three. . . .

[4] The correct inquiry is whether the policy in question had a disproportionate impact on the minorities in the total group to which the policy was applied . . .

The conversion policy affects only the occupants of Building Three. Thus, we see no merit in the argument that the effects of the conversion should be judged with reference to The Point as a whole.

III.

From this record we think that there is little question that the all-adult conversion policy for Building Three had a substantially greater adverse impact on minority tenants. At the time when Turtle Creek began issuing eviction notices under the conversion policy, 62.9 percent of the tenants with children in the building were black and an additional 5.4 percent were other non-whites or Hispanic. In total, 54.3 percent of the non-white tenants in the building received termination notices as opposed to only 14.1 percent of the white tenants.

When the statistics are converted to reflect the total number of individuals affected, the results are even more striking. Of the total number of men, woman and children living in Building Three, 74.9 percent of the non-whites were given eviction notices while only 26.4 percent of the whites received such notices. Under these circumstances, we believe a disparate impact is self-evident.

Case Reflections

1. This case was brought as a claim of racial discrimination. Would this be necessary under current law?
2. On what basis was racial discrimination claimed?

Catalog of Homes
A COMPLETE GUIDE TO HOMES, LAND & FARMS
Catalog of Homes
A COMPLETE GUIDE TO HOMES, LAND & FARMS
NEW • NEW • NEW

CHAPTER 15

EMERGING FORMS OF REAL ESTATE PRACTICE

LEARNING OBJECTIVES

After reading this chapter, you should be able to:

1. Evaluate the critical elements in an exclusive buyer agency contract.
2. Understand the concept of "breaking up" the traditional full-service brokerage practice into subsets of specific services.
3. Recognize the various forms of franchise and network agreements and the major issues in selecting an appropriate type of franchise.
4. Define the various roles a broker may play in a transaction.
5. Appreciate the distinctions between traditional real estate brokerage models and those in common use in the securities brokerage industry.
6. Evaluate the role that can be played by mandatory seller disclosure statements and the potential impact such statements may have on the liability exposure of real estate agents.

KEY TERMS

Discount Brokerage
Flat Fee Brokerage
Assignment by Buyer
Relocation Networks
Buyer Warranty Programs
Seller Assurance Programs
Franchise Disclosure Statement
Uniform Franchise Offering Circular
Referral Networks
Negotiator
Middleman
Arbitrator
Agency Theory
Mandatory Seller Disclosure

In Chapters 12, 13, and 14, the traditional agency relationship and the potential problems with that legal form were described. In this chapter, we conclude Part III with a look at some emerging forms and concepts in real estate practice. The concept of *buyer brokerage* was described briefly previously. Here we look more closely at the contractual relationships involved in operating as an agent for the buyer. We also look closely at the creation and operation of *franchise agreements.* At one time, the creation of franchises was believed to be the new wave in real estate brokerage and, similar to many retailing operations, would soon dominate the market. This has not come to pass for many reasons. Here we examine the benefits and costs, from a legal perspective, of franchise agreements.

Discount Brokerage Term applied to brokers who offer a limited set of services for a generally lower fee or commission.

Another emerging concept is that of **discount** or *unbundled services* brokerage. Another version of this approach is ***flat fee*** brokerage. These concepts and others like them challenge the basic structure of the real estate brokerage industry and have not always met with acceptance by either brokers or consumers. Finally, we compare the agency model prevalent in real estate brokerage with that seen in the securities brokerage area. The differences are examined in terms of what the securities brokerage model may have to offer real estate brokers.

Flat Fee Brokerage A brokerage firm which charges, rather than a commission, a predetermined fee for service.

BUYER BROKERAGE

The traditional agency relationship in real estate brokerage, as described in some detail in Chapter 12, involves a contractual agreement with the seller. The fiduciary relationship thus created between the broker (agent) and seller (principal) often leaves the buyer in a vulnerable position. Although as we have seen the buyer is protected by the actions of licensing laws and the Realtor's *Code of Ethics,* many believe that this is insufficient. Thus the use of agents to represent the buyer is beginning to become common.

Buyer brokerage has been fairly common in commercial and industrial real estate transactions for some time. A 1989 survey by the National Association of Realtors found that at least 30 percent of all real estate companies have had agents

KEY POINTS

Many people have begun to point out the potential ethical, and possible legal, problems associated with having agents within the same firm representing buyers and sellers. Can, for example, one agent in a firm fully represent a buyer in negotiations with a seller when the seller is represented by another agent in the same firm? Do the parties in such a transaction have adequate representation, or does the primary focus of the negotiation process become creating a deal that benefits the real estate firm? These questions and many others like them are beginning to appear, especially in smaller markets where no exclusive buyer agency exists. Although there are, at the very least, some significant ethical problems involved in this type of situation, it has already begun to happen in real estate brokerage firms.

involved in residential buyer brokerage. Barry M. Miller, founder of "The Buyer's Market," which specializes in buyer representation, describes buyer brokerage as "... the revolution of the 1980s,"[1] which will become institutionalized in the 1990s. A buyer's agent may assist in reviewing proposed contracts, negotiating to obtain the best price and terms, and insuring that the physical property has been inspected.

Unfortunately, the use of an additional agent may create almost as many problems as it solves. For example, issues of compensation, conflicts of interest, disclosure, and completion of contract must all be addressed. Some claim that the use of buyer brokers only increases the costs of a transaction and does little, if anything, to improve it. Other hail buyer brokerage as the single most important development in real estate brokerage this century. Who is correct? Is buyer brokerage just a means to insure work for more agents, or is it the salvation of buyers?

It is too early in the development of this form of brokerage to answer these questions with any degree of certainty. As we have seen, however, the current seller agency model leaves much to be desired. Thus the advent of buyer brokerage will, if nothing else, at least focus more attention on the issues involved.

Exclusive Buyer Agency Contracts

The discussion of buyer brokerage in this chapter assumes that the agent is to serve as the exclusive agent for the buyer. In other words, the agent does not also represent sellers in transactions. To do so, or even to have a firm with some agents representing sellers while others represent buyers, is to invite problems. The fiduciary duties of an agent, as described in Chapter 12, make such a mixed role difficult, if not impossible.

No single, standard buyer agency contract form has yet emerged. The basic issues that must be addressed, however, are fairly clear. Each of these issues is described here. Figure 15.1 provides one version of an exclusive buyer agency contract.[2] Not all buyer agency contracts, assuming one is even available in your location, will contain these clauses. But the basic approach will likely be similar to that shown here.

Effect of Exclusive Buyer Agency Contract

The first issue to be addressed is that of defining the role of the buyer broker. This is especially important at this stage because such contracts are still uncommon. The basic obligations of the agent and buyer need to be spelled out. Buyers may be unfamiliar with the nature of a buyer agency, as might other brokers and sellers. As is the case with agents representing sellers, the agent wants to insure a commission if a transaction takes place. Thus any efforts to circumvent the agent must be prohibited.

---

[1]As quoted in a NAR *News Release,* "Buyer Brokerage Practice Gains Popularity with Realtors," November 27, 1989.

[2]Figure 15.1 is based on a draft contract form considered by the Colorado Real Estate Commission.

EXCLUSIVE BUYER AGENCY CONTRACT

THIS IS A LEGAL INSTRUMENT. IF NOT UNDERSTOOD, LEGAL, TAX OR OTHER COUNSEL SHOULD BE CONSULTED BEFORE SIGNING.

____
(Place)

____
(Date)

____
[Name(s) of Buyer(s)]

("Buyer") hereby appoint(s)____________________________________

____
(Broker's Name and Address)

("Broker") as Buyer's exclusive agent for the purpose OF ASSISTING BUYER TO ACQUIRE INTERESTS IN REAL PROPERTY AS INDICATED in Section 2 and under the terms specified herein.

1. Effect of Exclusive Buyer Agency Contract. By appointing Broker as Buyer's exclusive agent, Buyer agrees to conduct all negotiations for SUCH property through Broker, and to refer to Broker all inquires received from real estate brokers, salespersons, prospective sellers, or any other source during the time this contract is in effect. Buyer agrees that any Broker compensation which is conditioned upon the acquisition by Buyer of interests in real property, whether by lease or purchase, will be earned by Broker whenever such interests are acquired by Buyer DIRECTLY OR INDIRECTLY, without any discount or allowance for any efforts made by Buyer or by any other agent of Buyer in connection with the acquisition of such interests by Buyer.

2. PROPERTY. THE PROPERTY SHALL SUBSTANTIALLY MEET THE FOLLOWING REQUIREMENTS OR BE OTHERWISE ACCEPTABLE TO BUYER:

("PROPERTY")

3. Time of Commencement and Duration of Agency. Broker's authority as Buyer's exclusive agent shall begin______________ , 19____ , and shall continue until THE EARLIER OF______________, 19____, or completion of the purpose(s) of agency as set forth in Section 2.

4. Broker's Representations and Services. Broker will use REASONABLE efforts to locate Property, to procure acceptance of any offer to purchase or lease Property AND TO ASSIST IN THE COMPLETION OF THE TRANSACTION. Broker shall make submissions to Buyer describing and identifying properties appearing to substantially meet the criteria set forth in Section 2, for the consideration of Buyer.

5. Costs of Services or Products Obtained from Outside Sources. Broker will not obtain or order products or services from outside sources unless Buyer HAS agreed to pay for them when payment is due. (Examples: surveys, soil tests, RADON TESTS, title reports, PROPERTY INSPECTIONS)

FIGURE 15.1 EXAMPLE OF AN EXCLUSIVE BUYER AGENCY CONTRACT

6. Compensation of Broker. In consideration of the services to be performed by Broker, Buyer SHALL pay Broker as follows:

[Instruction: If any of the forms of compensation set forth in subsections (b), (c), or (d) will not be used, write "N/A" in the blank(s) of such subsection(s).]

(a) Maximum fee. The total fees PAYABLE UNDER subsections (b), (c) and (d) BELOW shall not exceed the greater of $________________ or__________ % of the purchase price of the real property acquired pursuant to this contract.

(b) Success fee. Buyer SHALL pay Broker a fee equal to the greater of $____________ or__________ % of the purchase price.

The SUCCESS FEE IS conditioned upon completion of the PURCHASE OF THE PROPERTY DESCRIBED in Section 2 hereof, or the acceptance by Buyer of a transaction not in compliance with the CRITERIA specified in Section 2 hereof BUT WITHIN THE PURVIEW OF THIS CONTRACT. This fee is payable upon closing of the transaction(s), subject to the provisions of Section 7. This fee shall apply to transactions made during the original term of this contract or made during any extension(s) of such and shall also apply to transactions made within_________ days after this contract expires or is terminated if the property acquired by Buyer was SHOWN OR SPECIFICALLY PRESENTED in writing to Buyer by Broker during the original term or any extension(s) of the term of this contract.

BUYER IS OBLIGATED TO PAY BROKER'S FEE IN ADDITION TO THE PURCHASE PRICE. HOWEVER, BROKER IS AUTHORIZED AND INSTRUCTED TO REQUEST PAYMENT OF BROKER'S FEE IN ANY OF THE FOLLOWING INDICATED METHODS:

( ) BY SELLER FROM THE PURCHASE PRICE.
( ) BY LISTING BROKER.
( ) OTHER: ______________________________

(c) Hourly fee. Buyer SHALL pay Broker at the rate of $__________ per hour for time spent by Broker pursuant to this contract, to be paid to Broker when billed to Buyer:

(d) RETAINER fee. Buyer SHALL pay Broker a nonrefundable RETAINER fee of $________ due and payable upon signing of this contract. THIS AMOUNT ( ) SHALL ( ) SHALL NOT BE CREDITED AGAINST THE MAXIMUM FEE.

(e) Other:

7. Failure to Close. If a seller fails to close with no fault on the part of Buyer, the success fee provided in Section 6(b) shall be waived. If BUYER IS AT FAULT, such success fee will not be waived, but will be due and payable immediately. Broker SHALL NOT be obligated to advance funds for the Buyer in order to complete a closing.

8. Disclosure of Broker's Role. At the time of initial contact Broker shall inform all prospective sellers and their agents with whom Broker negotiates pursuant to this contract that Broker is acting on behalf of a buyer-principal.

9. Disclosure of Buyer's Identity. Broker ( ) does ( ) DOES NOT have Buyer's permission to disclose Buyer's identity to third parties without prior written consent of Buyer.

10. Conflicting Interests. BUYER AGREES THAT BROKER SHALL NOT BE REQUIRED TO DISCLOSE TO BUYER INFORMATION KNOWN TO BROKER CONCERNING PROPERTIES OR PERSONS REPRESENTED BY BROKER AS AGENT FOR OTHER BUYERS OR FOR OWNERS OF PROPERTIES.

FIGURE 15.1 EXAMPLE OF AN EXCLUSIVE BUYER AGENCY CONTRACT *(continued)*

11. Assignment by Buyer. No assignment of Buyer's right under this agency contract and no assignment of rights in real property obtained for Buyer pursuant to this agency contract shall operate to defeat any of Broker's rights under this contract.

12. Nondiscrimination. The parties agree not to discriminate against any prospective seller or lessor because of the race, creed, color, sex, marital status, national origin, FAMILIAL STATUS, HANDICAP, RELIGION OR ANCESTRY of such person.

13. Attorneys' Fees. In case of litigation OR ARBITRATION concerning the rights of Buyer or Broker pursuant to this contract, the parties agree that reasonable attorneys' fees SHALL BE AWARDED to the prevailing party.

14. Modification of this Contract. No modification of any of the terms of this contract shall be valid, binding upon the parties, or entitled to enforcement unless such modification has first been reduced to writing and signed by the parties.

15. Entire Agreement. This contract constitutes the entire agreement between the parties relating to the subject thereof, and any prior agreements pertaining thereto, whether oral or written, have been merged and integrated into this contract.

16. A DISCLOSURE OF BUYER'S FINANCIAL QUALIFICATIONS. **BUYER AGREES THAT ANY FACTS ACTUALLY KNOWN BY BROKER RELATIVE TO BUYER'S QUALIFICATION FOR A LOAN REQUIRED FOR THE PURCHASE OF THE PROPERTY MUST BE DISCLOSED BY BROKER TO ANY PROSPECTIVE SELLER.**

OR

BUYER ACKNOWLEDGES THAT BROKER, IF ASKED, MUST DISCLOSE TO ANY PROSPECTIVE SELLER OR HIS AGENT FACTS ACTUALLY KNOWN BY BROKER RELATIVE TO BUYER'S QUALIFICATION FOR ANY LOAN REQUIRED FOR THE PURCHASE OF THE PROPERTY.

17. Multiple Buyers. BUYER ACKNOWLEDGES THAT BROKER MAY PRESENT THE SAME PROPERTIES TO OTHER BUYERS AS BROKER PRESENTS TO BUYER AND, IN SUCH EVENT, THIS ACTION SHALL NOT BE DEEMED A CONFLICT OF INTEREST.

18. Additional Provisions.

19. Copies of Agreement. This Contract is executed in multiple copies and Buyer acknowledges receipt of a copy of this Contract signed by the Broker.

20. Counterparts. If more than one person is named as a Buyer herein, this Contract may be executed by each Buyer, individually, and when each Buyer has executed a copy of this Listing Contract, such copies taken together shall be deemed to be a full and complete contract between the parties.

Accepted____________________	____________________
(Broker)	(Buyer)
By ____________________	____________________
	(Buyer)
Address: ____________________	Address____________________
____________________	____________________
Phone: ____________________	Phone: ____________________

FIGURE 15.1 EXAMPLE OF AN EXCLUSIVE BUYER AGENCY CONTRACT (*continued*)

Property

This section spells out the type of property the buyer is interested in. Although this sounds quite simple, there are numerous issues involved. If the description is too specific, the agent will have difficulty locating an appropriate property and will leave the issue of contract completion in doubt. A loosely written description, however, may leave the buyer in the position of paying a fee (see the section on compensation later) even though no suitable property was located.

Date and Duration of Agency

Like any contract, buyer brokerage contracts must begin on a specified date and end on the completion of the task or a specified date. Again, issues of compensation come into play here. In a traditional seller relationship, the contract is completed when a ready, willing, and able buyer is found at a specified price. The completion requirement for a buyer broker, however, is much less clear. Thus it is more tempting for the buyer to allow the contract to expire in hopes of avoiding the payment of a fee. One major problem in buyer brokerage is that of the "reluctant buyer", who refuses to accept property. This has long been a problem for seller agents who often spend many hours and days showing properties to buyers who are not really serious about making a purchase. For seller agents, such buyers are a nuisance. For buyer brokers, such buyers can lead to serious problems.

Broker's Representations and Services

At some point in the contract, the obligations of the broker in fulfilling the contract need to be spelled out.

Schaechter v. Regency Properties, Inc.

Costs of Services or Products Obtained from Outside Sources

In most transactions, additional products or services (e.g., environmental inspections, surveys, title searches) are needed. This clause simply informs the buyer that the broker is not agreeing to pay for them.

Compensation of Broker

This is probably the single most important clause in this type of contract. It spells out the conditions under which compensation will be due the broker. The form shown here has five types of possible compensation. Not all of these will be used in each contract. Quite the opposite, the contract form was designed to allow the broker and buyer to clarify the particular type of relationship desired. The basic compensation package is often based on a maximum fee (stated either in dollar amount or percentage of purchase price). This maximum fee could be composed of a *success fee* payable upon a successful completion of the contract; an *hourly fee* based on time spent by the broker; a *retainer fee,* which is in effect an advance payment; or some other basis for payment.

Note the clause that places the obligation to pay on the buyer and indicates that the compensation due is in addition to the purchase price. The broker is generally authorized, however, to seek an agreement from the seller or seller's broker to pay the buyer brokerage fee. Because the selling broker would ordinarily split the commission with another broker anyway, such an agreement is not as unlikely as it might seem.

Agreements between a seller, or seller's broker, and a buyer's broker in which the seller agrees to pay the commission of the buyer broker can lead to problems in the event the buyer defaults. In *Chan v. Tsang* (1 Cal.App.4th 1578, 3 Cal.Rptr.2d 14, 1992) the buyer refused to complete a transaction in which he was represented by a broker. The seller, under the terms of the purchase agreement, was entitled to retain the deposit of $20,000 as liquidated damages. An addendum to the purchase agreement stipulated that the broker representing the buyer would receive 2 1/2% of the $4 million purchase price or $100,000. Because the sale never took place, the seller refused to pay the broker as did the buyer. A trial court awarded the broker one-half of the liquidated damages, or $10,000, and everyone appealed. On appeal, the seller was awarded the entire $20,000 and the broker was awarded his agreed upon commission of $100,000 to be paid by the buyer based on the concept of an implied promise by the buyer to complete the transaction so that the broker can collect his commission.

KEY POINTS

Some early, highly unscientific information indicates that the use of a buyer's agent may provide some definite benefits. This evidence suggests that, on average, buyers working with traditional seller's agents pay about 96 or 97 percent of the asking price for home purchases. Purchasers working with a buyer's agent, however, pay only an average of about 91 percent of asking price. Thus, if the average sales price is about $100,000 in many markets, using a buyer's agent could save the purchaser about $5000 to $6000. It is not clear from these reports, however, if a buyer's brokerage fee has been included in the 91 percent figure. If not, the potential savings is reduced to about $2000.

Failure to Close

This clause spells out the conditions on which the success fee will be payable. In essence, it provides an escape for buyers when sellers default and helps to solve the "reluctant buyer" problem described earlier.

Disclosure of Broker's Role

This clause makes a disclosure of the agency relationship to all affected parties mandatory. As discussed earlier, many people may be confused by the concept of buyer brokerage and may disclose inappropriate information in the mistaken belief that the broker is a subagent of the seller.

Disclosure of Buyer's Identity

In most instances, the identity of the buyer is not an issue. There are situations, however, when the buyer uses a broker primarily because he wishes to remain anonymous. In fact, many of the early uses of what we now call buyer brokerage took place when a buyer did not wish to be revealed. Usually this was for business reasons, but concealment to avoid racial discrimination has also been known to take place.

Conflicting Interests

This clause attempts to minimize the potential conflict of interest problems that can arise when a broker is representing more than one client. For example, two clients have expressed essentially the same property preferences. Can the broker effectively represent both buyers in negotiating for properties? The potential conflict when the broker is also serving as seller broker is obvious and should be avoided. In smaller markets, however, this may not always be practical. Remember that most brokers have many agents working with them. Thus it is likely that some could represent sellers while others represent buyers. In a situation in which **MLS** contracts are used, the potential for conflicts of interest is quite high.

This type of clause is essentially untested. It is clear that a broker cannot establish an agency relationship with a buyer and then take steps that would hurt that buyer's position. The guidelines in this area have not yet been established, however. Thus the 1990s will likely see a great deal of litigation to define more clearly the rights and obligations of buyers and their agents.

Assignment by Buyer

This clause operates to help insure payment of all fees earned by the broker. One simple way to defeat a success fee, for example, is to have a third party purchase the property. Perhaps your brother is looking for a property. You could sign a buyer brokerage contract, have the broker locate an acceptable property, negotiate a good price, and then inform your brother of all details of the property. Your brother could then approach the seller, make an offer, which, by the way, would not include payment of fees to the buyer broker, and "steal" the property from you. Thus your brother gets a good deal on a purchase, you allow the buyer brokerage contract to expire, and the buyer broker is left with little if anything to show for his efforts. Keep in mind that the bulk of a buyer brokerage fee is represented by the success fee. This clause allows the broker to collect a fee from your brother to whom you assigned your rights.

Assignment by Buyer Process of transferring contract rights to another person.

Additional Issues in Buyer Brokerage

The remainder of Figure 15.1 contains clauses relating to nondiscrimination, attorney's fees, and other fairly standard items. The only other major issue is that of disclosure. The agency relationship, as discussed earlier, must always be disclosed to avoid confusion. But what about characteristics of the buyer? Must the agent disclose financial information about the buyer? It is clear that a seller's agent is responsible for insuring that a buyer is financially capable when submitting an offer to a seller. Failure to do so could injure the seller. Thus it would appear that information about the financial capacity of the buyer must be provided. If the buyer does not provide it, then the buyer's broker must if requested. Note that two forms of this clause are shown in Figure 15.1. The second form makes disclosure contingent on a request for information.

Murray v. Hayden

Another area of disclosure is also of some importance. As we have seen in previous chapters, the seller or the seller's agent is responsible for disclosing information about the property. Although many questions remain concerning the exact nature of what must be disclosed, it is clear that any known problems with the property must be made known to the buyer. If the seller's agent has disclosure responsibilities, does the buyer's agent share these? Because the buyer's agent is present to safeguard the buyer's interests, the logical answer would appear to be yes. On further reflection, however, it may occur to you that the buyer's agent does not have the same information, nor access to such information, as the seller's agent. Thus courts, even in California, where mandatory disclosure is in effect, have held that the disclosure obligation does not extend to brokers representing the buyer.

BREAKING UP THE BROKERAGE SERVICE PACKAGE

In one sense, buyer brokerage departs from traditional brokerage practice by changing the set of services offered. A "full-service" seller's agent provides assistance in setting an appropriate listing price, advertising the property, finding interested buyers, qualifying potential buyers, showing the property, arranging financing, and assisting with the closing of the transaction. A buyer's broker, along with shifting representation from the seller to the buyer, eliminates some of these services.

A few brokers during the last decade or so have begun looking at the standard set of services offered. Are there any additional services that could or should be offered? By the same token, are there some services that sellers may not value? The basic question then is "Does every seller want the same set of services?" Any marketer would be quick to answer no to such a question. Virtually every area of retailing and selling recognizes the presence of market segments. Why then have real estate brokers continued to offer a single product to all customers?

Many sellers, for example, want some sort of "do-it-yourself" information rather than paying for full services. Probably the biggest problem for sellers who do not use an agent is finding suitable buyers. Thus some brokerage firms offer a referral service. Rather than having agents show the property, the buyer is simply given information about the property and the seller is informed of the buyer's interest. In this fashion, a brokerage firm can reduce costs by letting sellers do at least some of the work.

Discount Brokerage Term applied to brokers who offer a limited set of services for a generally lower fee or commission.

As we have seen in Chapter 13, however, problems can arise in this area. When a **"discount" broker** has allowed buyers direct access to MLS information, conflicts with full-service brokers often result. The antitrust implications of this have already been discussed. In this chapter, we look at this area in terms of the limits to marketing techniques and pricing decisions. This is an area in which, like law, medicine, and banking, changes in services and products, advertising, and pricing are inevitable.

A broker who wishes to change the set of services offered has two basic choices: add new services (either with or without raising costs) or eliminate some current services. The latter approach was the first one experimented with by brokers. Similar to securities brokers, some real estate brokers have attempted to provide minimum services packages and discount prices. This approach has met with limited success. For the most part, buyers are uninterested in such brokerage firms. Most buyers perceive the provision of brokerage services, similar to those of travel agents, to be "free." Discount brokers save only the seller money. To the extent that these savings are passed along to buyers, discount brokers offer a useful service to buyers. In many instances, however, buyers do not believe that they are going to save any money when a discount broker is used by the seller. Thus discount brokers have faced market resistance from buyers as well as animosity from competing full-service brokers.

Brokers then began to turn to the notion of adding benefits for seller or buyers to the existing package. In many instances, these efforts have resulted in real benefits for market participants. Such innovations as mortgage locator services and **relocation networks** have resulted from these efforts. Owing to the nature of the legal environment, however, there are strict limits on the types of benefits that brokers can offer (see *Coldwell Banker Residential Real Estate Services, Inc. v. New Jersey Real Estate Commission* [242 N.J.Super. 354, 576 A.2d 938] in this chapter for an example of a failed marketing scheme). Brokers also face limits on the types of services they can offer and be paid for (see *Mortgage Bankers Association of New Jersey v. New Jersey Real Estate Commission* [506 A.2d 733] in this chapter for an example of the problems dual commissions can create).

Relocation Networks A system which provides member brokers with referrals of sellers and/or buyers by brokers in other parts of the country.

Perhaps the most important concepts to emerge thus far from these experiments in brokerage services are those of seller guarantees and **buyer warranties.** For sellers, the biggest fear is an inability to sell the property. Thus some brokerage firms have begun to provide programs of guaranteed purchase of the property. These **"seller assurance"** programs are, of course, most popular in weak markets. For sellers, these programs allow them, even in fairly strong markets, to complete plans for moving and purchasing a new home with the assurance that a specified minimum purchase price will be available at a specified date. For brokers, such plans involve the risk of having to hold a property during a weak market (or sell it at a loss) versus the additional business that may result from offering such a program.

Coldwell Banker Residential Real Estate Services, Inc v. New Jersey Real Estate Commission

For buyers, the biggest fear is having problems with their new home. The provision of some sort of insurance or warranty program is a major benefit. Chapter 17 takes a closer look at these Home Owner Warranty (HOW) Programs.

Mortgage Bankers Association of New Jersey v. New Jersey Real Estate Commission

BROKERAGE FRANCHISES AND NETWORKS

Franchising has become so commonplace that we scarcely notice the profound change that the process has had on our way of life. By acquiring a franchise, a local businessperson can affiliate with a large national, or even international, firm, thus obtaining the benefits of the large firm while retaining a high degree of control over the enterprise. It is essentially impossible for a customer or client to know if a business, whether it is a fast food restaurant, a retail clothing store, or stock brokerage firm, is independently owned and carries a franchise or is part of a large national firm (i.e., a company-owned outlet). Most "chains" are composed of both locally owned franchises and company-owned outlets.

Buyer Warranty Programs Various programs designed to provide some degree of protection for property purchasers.

Franchising first became popular in real estate brokerage in the 1970s. Many people predicted that franchising would sweep the industry and small, local, independent real estate brokerage firms, like retail grocery stores before them, would become things of the past. Although franchising has continued to be a major force in the industry, the revolution has yet to occur. The reasons for this are many and, for the most part, outside the scope of this text. Our concern here is with the legal issues involved in creating, maintaining, and ending franchise agreements. Some of the

Seller Assurance Programs Programs adopted by some brokers to provide a guaranteed minimum purchase price if a buyer is not located within a specified time period.

issues discussed elsewhere in this text also apply here. Franchising law includes the areas of advertising, antitrust, intellectual property, licensing, the Uniform Commercial Code, contracts, covenants not to compete, and product liability.[3]

Franchises Defined

Most of us think of a franchise as a store or other outlet. In fact, the franchise, in a legal sense, " . . . is the agreement between the parties, and not the business operated by the franchisee." (*Coast to Coast v. Gruschus* [667 P.2d 619 (Wash. 1983)]) In marketing terms, a franchise is a form of "vertical distribution." In many ways. franchising is analogous to landlord–tenant relationships in which the rental stream paid by the tenant builds equity for the landlord. In franchising, the income stream generated by the franchisee generates equity for the franchisor. In both instances, however, both parties stand to benefit.

For the franchisor, the creation of a network of franchise outlets offers the opportunity to build a strong, recognizable image for his product or service. It is this very image that is of value to the franchisee. Much of the appeal of a franchise for the customer is the knowledge about the product or service that can be obtained. What the franchisor offers is a set of standards that apply to every phase of operation of the business. From product development to personnel policies, the franchisee must meet certain standards and follow a set of guidelines or risk losing the use of the product name. In similar fashion, the franchisor must be careful not to damage the image of the product or service by a proliferation of franchise outlets, which can easily become poorly controlled.

As we shall see, one of the critical issues in franchise law is that of control. The franchisor must insure quality standards are met, and this often includes providing managerial advice to franchisees, while not exercising day-to-day control over the

KEY POINTS

Most of us claim to be unaffected by the presense of a franchise when we select which brokerage firm we will use. Several surveys in this area have indicated that consumers, at least when it comes to selecting a real estate brokerage firm, claim not to care if the firm is franchised or not. The results of the selection process, however, show quite the opposite. In nearly every case, franchised firms have larger market shares than nonfranchised firms and are seen as either "more professional" or as having a "better reputation" in the area. It could simply be that more successful firms tend to become franchised. Or perhaps people like to think that firm image and other marketing "ploys" have no effect on them, when in fact they do.

[3]For an excellent, comprehensive treatment of franchise law, see Chapter 10 "Primer in Franchising Legal Compliance" in *The Complete Guide to Marketing and the Law* by Robert J. Posch, Jr. (Englewood Cliffs, NJ, Prentice Hall, 1988 with 1990 Cumulative Supplement).

operation. The issue of control is critical because of its relationship to liability exposure. One of the cases in this chapter (*Salisbury v. Chapman Realty*) deals with the limits of control in a franchise agreement.

Salisbury v. Chapman Realty

Because the concept of a franchise is so broadly defined, the Federal Trade Commission (FTC) has promulgated, after almost eight years of study, a rule regulating the practice of franchising (16 C.F.R. 436). Most states have adopted similar legislation.[4] Two basic types of franchises are included in the rule's coverage—package and product franchising. A *product franchise* allows the franchisee to distribute a product manufactured under the control of the franchisor. A *package franchise* provides a prepackaged business format, including rules of operation and quality control. In the real estate brokerage industry, a third form of franchise agreement has been created. The hybrid *"conversion franchising"* concept was first popularized by Century 21 Real Estate Corporation. This is an agreement with an existing independent business to become a franchisee. Thus it is not a package franchise, since the business already has a set of operating rules, nor is it a product franchise.

Franchise Disclosure Statement

One of the major issues in franchise regulation is that of unequal bargaining positions. The franchisor has the benefit of a large organization with considerable expertise, whereas the potential franchisee is generally inexperienced and at an obvious disadvantage. To assist the potential franchisee, the FTC rule requires that franchisors provide a variety of detailed up-front disclosures. One of two forms may be used for the disclosure: the older format, known as the ***Uniform Franchise Offering Circular*** (UFOC), which contains twenty-three items, or the twenty-item form developed by the FTC.

Franchise Disclosure Statement A statement required by the FTC which discloses information about the franchisor, obligations the franchisee will incur, and important terms of the franchise agreement.

Both forms contain three types of information:

Information relating to the franchisor.

Obligations the contract will impose on the franchisee.

Important terms contained in the franchise agreement.

Franchising Issues

Payment of Fees

Uniform Franchise Offering Circular An older format still used for providing the required disclosure of information by franchisors to potential franchisees.

Although there are numerous issues addressed by the disclosure requirement, perhaps the most important is that of funds required of the franchisee.

1. *Initial fees*—a nonrefundable fee usually paid on signing the agreement.
2. *Continuing royalties*—usually a percentage of gross revenues, often on a sliding scale. There are a number of potential problem areas in defining applicable gross revenues because they must result from, through, by, or on account of the franchise operation. For example, a real estate broker may also do some appraisal or property management work. Should this be included in gross revenue for purposes of computing royalty payments?

[4]Twenty-two states have laws requiring presale disclosure in connection with the sale of franchises, and twenty-three have adopted business opportunity laws.

3. *Advertising fee*—also usually based on a percentage of gross revenue. The contract should define the minimum level of support to be provided and the types of advertising to be used. Issues of control may also be important. For example, the type, level, and timing of advertising should be customized to the local market.
4. *Training fee.* Certain initial courses should be included in the initial franchise fee (although travel costs are generally not included). To insure quality control, the franchisor may offer training courses, some of which may be required as a condition of maintaining the franchise.

Real Estate Commissions in many state have rules relating to permissable types of advertising by brokers, salespersons and firms. In general, these rules cause few problems and are simply designed to insure that the public is made aware of the identity of the responsible broker. In some instances, however, these rules can come into conflict with requirements of franchisors. In *Century 21 Real Estate of Northern Texas v. Arkansas Real Estate Commission* (611 S.W.2d 515, 1981) a Commission rule which required the broker's name to appear equally prominant with the franchisor lead to a Supreme Court of Arkansas ruling striping the Commission of the authority to regulate advertising. Partly in response to this finding, other states reviewed their rules concerning advertising to develop better ways to deal with franchise advertising.

Grant of Franchise and Licenses

The issue here is one of exclusivity. Will other franchises be granted in your territory? How many sites are included in your agreement? Are there any legal challenges to other current franchise agreements?

Territory

Most franchise agreements provide rights to an exclusive territory. The franchisor will reserve the right to grant franchises outside the territory, and the franchisee is usually prohibited from operating, without written permission, outside the defined territory. Not all franchise agreements, however, provide exclusive territorial rights. Many franchisees have been "burned" by nonexclusive franchise agreements. The use of nonexclusive territories is common in real estate brokerage, at least for certain franchisors.

Confidential Information

Certain information provided by the franchisor (e.g., forms, management procedures, training manuals) may not be disclosed by the franchisee.

Termination of the Franchise Agreement

The final major issue is that of conditions for terminating the franchise agreement. Depending on the circumstances, either the franchisor or franchisee may be looking for a way to end the relationship. If the franchisor believes that a better franchise agreement is possible (e.g., one with a smaller territory, thus allowing the placement of more franchisees), he may look for ways to void the contract. In similar fashion, if the franchisee finds that the agreement has not done what was hoped for, he may look for ways to get out of the payment of the ongoing royalties and other fees. The *Ciampi v. Red Carpet Corporation of America* case in this chapter illustrates certain aspects of the termination process.

Ciampi v. Red Carpet Corporation of America

Additional Issues in Franchising

Several related issues deserve mention in this section. Keep in mind the motivating forces relating to the formation of franchise agreements. For real estate brokerage franchisees, the primary motivations are name recognition, economies of scale, and referrals. Included in the economies of scale area are those of training, management, and other forms of expertise. In some instances, access to mortgage money is also an issue. This has led some to look for ways of achieving the same types of benefits without the costs and risks of franchising.

Referral Networks

By franchising, the local broker gains access to automatic referrals by member brokers in other parts of the U.S. When a person is moving, a franchised firm can handle not only the sale of the current property, but also the purchase of a new property in a different location. This is a powerful marketing tool and has led to the development of alternate methods of creating sources of referrals. In effect, a partial franchise is established by joining a **referral network.** Members of these networks agree to provide other members with information on persons moving to their territory. Thus, one of the benefits of franchising is gained without actually becoming franchised. For some real estate brokers, referrals are the primary benefit of franchise agreements. For them, joining a referral network is a low-cost, effective alternative to franchising.

Referral Networks A system which provides member brokers with referrals of sellers and/or buyers by brokers in other parts of the country.

"Local Franchises" and Mergers

In response to the increasing franchising trend, many local firms sought alternative relationships that might offer some of the same benefits at lower cost. For some small firms, the answer was to merge into a single larger firm. The large firm would then offer some of the same name recognition features as a franchise, at least on a local basis. In some instances, the individual firms remained in their original locations, and in others, the mergers resulted in new, common facilities.

The agreements between firms took many different forms. In some cases, the firms formally merged into a single new firm. In other cases, the firms in essence created a local franchise arrangement that allowed member firms to leave the group under certain circumstances. In any event, the desire was to gain some of the benefits enjoyed by franchised firms: economies of scale in training, purchasing, and advertising; enhanced name recognition; greater specialization, without taking on all of the additional costs of maintaining a national franchise agreement. There are a number of potential antitrust issues involved in these types of agreements, and care must be exercised to avoid restraint of trade charges.

Many brokers believed, and still believe, that a real estate brokerage firm need not have the same degree of national name recognition as, say, a fast food outlet. All, or at least most, of the essential benefits of franchising may be gained through some combination of using a referral network, a national mortgage locator service, and, if appropriate, merging with other local firms.

NEW THEORIES ON BROKERAGE FUNCTIONS AND RESPONSIBILITIES

The brokerage model used in real estate has evolved from one in which the buyer was at some risk (i.e., the *caveat emptor* approach) to one in which the broker has come to be at some risk. The changing nature of the environment for real estate brokerage has prompted a number of people to question the appropriateness of the traditional agency model. Alternative concepts, such as the negotiator model, the arbitrator model, and the middleman model, have been examined in the context of real estate brokerage.

In this section, we look briefly at each of these models and look at the approach used in the securities brokerage area for clues that may help the real estate industry extricate itself from its current predicament.

Agents and Brokers Defined

Before we view alternative models for real estate brokers, it may be useful to review the definitions of an agent and a broker. The term *agent* has many definitions, most of them referring to particular situations. *Black's Law Dictionary* (6th Edition) defines an agent as:

> A person authorized by another (principal) to act for or in place of him; one intrusted with another's business. *Humphries v. Going,* D.C.N.C., 59 F.R.D. 583, 587. One who represents and acts for another under the contract or relation of agency (q.v.). . . . One who undertakes to transact some business, or to manage some affair, for another, by the authority and on account of the latter, and to render an account of it. One who acts for or in place of another by authority from him; a substitute, a deputy, appointed by principal with power to do the things which principal may do. . . . One authorized to transact all business of principal, or all of principal's business of some particular kind, or all business at some particular place. *Farm Bureau Mut. Ins. Co. v. Coffin,* 136 Ind.App. 12, 186 N.E.2d 180, 182.

Notice the sweeping language of this definition. Interestingly, *Black's* defines a real estate agent specifically as:

> Person whose business it is to sell, or offer for sale, real estate for others, or to rent houses, stores, or other buildings, or real estate, or to collect rent for others.

Thus the concept of a buyer's agent has not yet made it into the world of legal definitions. It is also interesting to note that we commonly refer to people who transact real estate sales not as agents but as brokers. *Black's* defines a broker as:

> An agent employed to make bargains and contracts for a compensation. A dealer in securities issued by others. *White v. Financial Guarantee Corporation,* 13 Cal.App.2d 93, 56 P.2d 550, 553. A middleman or negotiator between parties. A person dealing with another for sale of property. A person whose business it is to bring buyer and seller together. One who is engaged for others, on a commission, to negotiate contracts relative to prop-

> erty. *North Carolina Real Estate Licensing Board v. Aikens,* 31 N.C.App. 8, 228 S.E.2d 493, 496. An agent of a buyer or a seller who buys or sells stocks, bonds, commodities, or services, usually on a commission basis. The term extends to almost every branch of business, to realty as well as personalty.
>
> Ordinarily, the term is applied to one acting for others but it also applicable to one in business of negotiating purchases or sales for himself.
>
> . . .
>
> Real estate broker. Persons who procure the purchase or sale of land, acting as intermediary between vendor and purchaser, and who negotiate loans on real-estate security, manage and lease estates, etc. *Latta v. Kilbourn,* 150 U.S. 524, 14 S.Ct. 201, 37 L.Ed. 1169. A broker employed in negotiating the sale, purchase, lease, or exchange of lands on a commission contingent on success. A person engaged in business to such an extent that it is his vocation or partial vocation.

Thus a "broker" is merely a specific type of agent. It is interesting, however, that the definition includes the terms "middleman" and "negotiator" as well. As we shall see in the following discussion, many courts have gone to great lengths to differentiate between these terms, which have been lumped together here.

Broker as Negotiator

The essential outcome of any real estate transaction is the transfer of ownership, or some right of ownership, from one party to another. The process is one in which many factors must be agreed upon, not the least of which is the price (or rent) to be paid. Obviously this is a process that often involves some negotiation between parties. Thus the real estate agent (or broker) generally finds that her role at some point becomes that of a **negotiator.**

Negotiator
One who represents another in deliberations, discussions or conferences upon the terms of a proposed agreement.

Black's defines a negotiation as a:

> . . . process of submission and consideration of offers until acceptable offer is made and accepted. *Gainey v. Brotherhood of Ry. and S.S. Clerks, Freight Handlers, Exp. & Station Emp.,* D.C.Pa., 275 F.Supp. 292, 300. The deliberation, discussion, or conference upon the terms of a proposed agreement; the act of settling or arranging the terms and conditions of a bargain, sale, or other business transaction.

The image of a real estate agent as a negotiator seems an appropriate one at various stages of the sales process. Unfortunately, however, this label does little to alter the essential obligations of an agent. Thus shifting to the notion of a real estate negotiator would be little more than a semantic difference.

Real Estate Brokers as Middlemen

Middleman
An individual whose function it is to bring together a seller and a buyer but who does not enter into the negotiating process.

An exception exists in agency theory from the normal fiduciary obligations for those who serve as middlemen during a transaction. Despite numerous attempts to use this exception (some of which are documented in Chapter 12), the so-called **middleman** exception does not generally apply to real estate brokers.

To understand why, we need to understand the role of a true middleman. *Black's* defines a middleman as:

KEY POINTS

Some commentators have suggested that a mediation process be established to settle disputes in a less formal fashion. A clause would be inserted in the purchase agreement requiring mediation efforts to settle disputes before any legal action. This approach would use an "alternative dispute resolution center" to select a mediator and conduct the mediation process. The mediator would not become an advocate for either party, would maintain strict confidentiality, and would maintain order during the process. The arbitration process described later in this chapter is one version of a mediation process.

> One who merely brings parties together in order to enable them to make their own contracts.
>
> An agent between two parties; an intermediary who performs the office of a broker or factor between seller and buyer, producer and consumer, land-owner and tenant, etc. One who has been employed as an agent by a principal, either express or implied. . . .

Once again notice the use of the term *agent* prominently in this definition. A middleman is, once again, only a special form of an agent. Thus the exception beckons to those who, while serving as agents, find a violation of fiduciary obligations charge leveled at them. The first sentence in this definition, however, effectively closes the door on real estate brokers by specifying that the parties are to " . . . make their own contracts." Obviously a broker cannot serve as any type of negotiator, or even as a salesperson, and preserve any hope of using a middleman defense against liability claims.

The only way in which a broker could function as a middleman would be to leave both parties unrepresented in the transaction. This model has little appeal in the marketplace because it reduces the broker to one who acts simply as a finder and leaves the most difficult portions of the transaction in the hands of the parties. The collection of substantial brokerage commissions for this level of service would be difficult at best.

Real Estate Brokers as Arbitrators

Arbitrator A neutral person whose function it is to hear the claims of parties and render a decision.

The final approach that has been suggested is that of an arbitrator. An **arbitrator** serves as an umpire, or referee, in disputes and is defined as:

> A neutral person either chosen by the parties to a dispute or appointed by a court, to hear the parties' claims and render a decision. . . .

If the negotiation process is viewed as a dispute over the terms and conditions of sale or lease, then the arbitrator model may have some validity. Similar to the middleman role, however, it can leave both parties unrepresented. The notion of *neutrality* is, once again, not a compelling one in the context of real estate negotiations. The arbitrage model reduces the role of the broker in much the same fashion as the middleman model.

Recently, however, a dispute resolution process using the services of the American Arbitration Association has been adopted in several locations around the U.S. A voluntary arbitration procedure is established in the purchase agreement, which provides a specific process for dealing with buyer or seller disputes. Many agents favor this type of model because it helps to shift the focus of the dispute away from the agent and thus reduces the potential for liability exposure. Although this approach is new, and thus not much information is available concerning its effectiveness, it holds a great deal of promise for the industry. Figure 15.2 is a sample copy of the "Arbitration Rules" typically used in this process.

Arbitration proceedings may only be reviewed by courts for errors of fact or law. Upholding an arbitrator's findings in *Hall v. Trompas* (20 Cal.Rptr.2d 404, 1993), the court admonished lower courts not to review arbitral proceedings because they are not designed for full judicial review. In other words, unless a clear error of fact or law has occured, the court system may not second guess the findings of an arbitrator. The case described here involved a ruling favoring the seller of a property against a broker for failing to adequately disclose information about a purchaser's financial condition after the buyer defaulted while purchasing a property.

Securities Brokerage Model

Those who function as brokers in the securities area serve much the same function as those in the real estate field yet generally manage to escape the liability burdens of the latter. How, one might ask, does this occur? The answer to this question lies in the structure of the securities industry and does offer some possible lessons for the real estate industry.

In the securities field, much is made of the distinction between those who act as *brokers* and those who act as *dealers.* In many instances, participants act as both. Once again it may be useful to view the definitions of these terms:

> Broker-dealer. A securities brokerage firm, usually registered with the S.E.C. and with the state in which it does business, engaging in the business of buying and selling securities to or for customers.
>
> Securities broker. Brokers employed to buy and sell for their principals stocks, bonds, government securities, etc. Any person engaged in the business of making transactions in securities for the account of others, but does not include a bank. *Securities Exchange Act of 1934,* § 3. A person engaged for all or part of his time in the business of buying and selling securities, who in the transaction concerned, acts for, or buys a security from or sells a security to a customer. *U.C.C.* § 8–303.
>
> A person who acts as an agent for a buyer or seller, or an intermediary between a buyer and seller, usually charging a commission. A broker who specializes in shares, bonds, commodities or options must be registered with the exchange where the specific securities are traded. A broker should be distinguished from a securities dealer who, unlike the broker, is in the business of buying or selling for his own account.

Home Buyer Home Seller Arbitration Rules

Adopted by the American Arbitration Association and the North Dakota Association of REALTORS®

As amended and in Effect April 1, 1991

American Arbitration Association

Introduction

Each year in, thousands of real estate transactions take place. Occasionally disputes develop over these business transactions. The Home Buyer/Home Seller Arbitration Rules have been prepared in response to an express need for an efficient voluntary arbitration procedure to resolve these disputes privately, promptly, and economically.

The American Arbitration Association and the Association of REALTORS® have developed these arbitration procedures to meet the consumer and real estate agents needs in resolving disputes. The rules contain specific procedures for the selection of arbitrators with appropriate expertise, including both those affiliated with the real estate industry and those who are not. Another feature is that the system is less formal than litigation. In addition each arbitration is held at the property in question.

These features, as well as others contained in the rules, will assist parties in resolving disputes fairly and efficiently.

To Initiate The Arbitration of Disputes:

All parties must sign the arbitration clause as provided in the purchase agreement:

HOME BUYER/HOME SELLER ARBITRATION SYSTEM: ANY CLAIM OR DEMAND OF SELLER(S), BUYER(S), BROKERS(S) OR AGENT(S), OR ANY OF THEM, ARISING OUT OF OR RELATING TO THE PHYSICAL CONDITION OF THE PROPERTY COVERED BY THIS PURCHASE AGREEMENT (INCLUDING WITHOUT LIMITATION CLAIMS OF FRAUD, MISREPRESENTATION, WARRANTY AND NEGLIGENCE), SHALL BE SETTLED BY BINDING ARBITRATION IN ACCORDANCE WITH THE RULES, THEN IN EFFECT, ADOPTED BY THE AMERICAN ARBITRATION ASSOCIATION AND THE ASSOCIATION OF REALTORS.® A REQUEST FOR ARBITRATION MUST BE FILED WITHIN 6 MONTHS OF THE DATE IN WHICH THE RELEVANT FACTS REGARDING THE CLAIM WERE DISCOVERED OR COULD REASONABLY HAVE BEEN DISCOVERED. THIS IS A SEPARATE VOLUNTARY AGREEMENT BETWEEN THE PARTIES AND BROKERS/AGENTS WHICH SHALL SURVIVE THE DELIVERY DEED OR CONTRACT FOR DEED PROVIDED FOR IN THIS PURCHASE AGREEMENT. FAILURE TO AGREE TO ARBITRATE DOES NOT AFFECT THE VALIDITY OF THIS PURCHASE AGREEMENT. THIS DISPUTE RESOLUTION SYSTEM IS ONLY ENFORCEABLE IF ALL PARTIES TO THE PURCHASE AGREEMENT AND BROKERS/AGENTS HAVE AGREED TO ARBITRATE AS ACKNOWLEDGED BY INITIALS BELOW. UNDERSTAND THAT, IF YOU SIGN THIS AGREEMENT TO ARBITRATE, THE RULES OF ARBITRATION WILL REPLACE OTHER LEGAL REMEDIES, INCLUDING ACCESS TO THE COURT SYSTEM, WHICH YOU MAY HAVE. IF YOU HAVE ANY QUESTIONS ABOUT YOUR RIGHTS, CONSULT AN ATTORNEY.

Buyer/Seller Arbitration Rules

1. Agreement of Parties

These rules have been adopted by the American Arbitration Association (AAA) and the Association of REALTORS® to govern arbitration of disputes between seller(s), buyer(s) and agent(s) arising out of or relating to the physical condition of property covered by a purchase agreement executed by the parties. These rules shall also apply whenever the parties have agreed to arbitrate under them. They apply to the extent that they are not inconsistent with applicable statutes or with the agreement of the parties. The parties shall be deemed to have agreed to these rules in the form obtaining at the time the arbitration is initiated.

2. Initiation of Arbitration Proceedings

The party seeking arbitration must first obtain a Request for Arbitration form from the AAA by calling OR by contacting the Local Board of REALTORS in your area.

Arbitration under an arbitration provision in a contract may be initiated in the following manner.

(a) The initiating party shall prepare a written notice to the other party of its intention to arbitrate (Demand), which notice shall contain a statement setting forth the nature of the dispute, the amount involved, if any, the remedy sought, and

(b) Shall file at one of the following AAA locations: , four (4) copies of said notice, together with three (3) full copies of the purchase agreement, together with the appropriate administrative fee as provided in the Administrative Fee Schedule.

The AAA shall give notice of such filing to the other party. If so desired, the party upon whom the Demand for Arbitration is made may file an answering statement in duplicate with the AAA within ten (10) days after notice from the AAA, in which event said party shall simultaneously send a copy of the answer to the other party. If no answer is filed within the stated time, it will be assumed that the claim is denied. Failure to file and answer shall not operate to delay the arbitration.

3. Appointment of Arbitrator

The AAA shall appoint a single Arbitrator from its panel of persons knowledgeable in the sale of residential real estate, subject to the provisions of Rule 6.

4. Number of Arbitrators

The dispute shall be heard and determined by one Arbitrator unless the AAA, in its discretion, directs that a greater number of Arbitrators be appointed.

FIGURE 15.2 SAMPLE COPY OF ARBITRATION RULES

5. Qualifications of an Arbitrator

No person shall serve as an Arbitrator in any arbitration in which that person has any financial or personal interest in the result of the arbitration.

Prior to accepting an appointment, the prospective Arbitrator shall disclose to the AAA any circumstances likely to prevent a prompt hearing or to create a presumption of bias. Any party to the arbitration that has a factual objection to the service of an Arbitrator shall notify the AAA in writing, at the earliest opportunity. Upon receipt of such information, the AAA shall immediately replace the Arbitrator or communicate the information to the parties for their comments.

6. Appointment from Panel

(a) Claims in excess of $2,500. In arbitrations where the claim exceeds $2,500, the Arbitrator shall be appointed in the following manner: Immediately after the filing of the demand submission, the AAA shall submit simultaneously to each party to the dispute and identical list of three (3) names of persons chosen from the panel. Each party to the dispute shall have 10 days from the mailing date in which to strike one name, number the remaining names to indicate the order of preference, and return the list to the AAA. If a party does not return the list within the time specified, all persons named therein shall be deemed acceptable. From among the persons who have been approved on both lists, and in accordance with the designated order of mutual preference, the AAA shall appoint an Arbitrator to serve. If the parties fail to agree on any of the persons named, or if acceptable Arbitrators are unable or unwilling to act, for any reason, the AAA shall have the power to make the appointment from among other members of the panel without the submission of additional list. (In the event of multiparty arbitration, the AAA may increase the number of potential Arbitrators and divide the strikes so as to afford an equal number of strikes to each adverse interest.)

(b) Claims of $2,500 or less. In arbitrations where the claim is $2,500 or less, the Arbitrator shall be appointed in the following manner: Immediately after the filing of the demand or submission, the AAA shall appoint an Arbitrator, chosen from the panel. AAA shall notify the parties of the Arbitrator and shall enclose a biographical statement of the Arbitrator. The parties to the arbitration shall retain the right, provided in Rule 5, to submit a factual objection to the service of an Arbitrator.

7. Notice to Arbitrator of Appointment

Notice of the appointment of the Arbitrator shall be mailed to the Arbitrator by the AAA, together with a copy of these rules, and the signed acceptance of the Arbitrator shall be filed prior to the opening of the first hearing.

8. Administrator

When parties agree to arbitrate under these rules, they thereby constitute the AAA the administrator of the arbitration. The authority and the obligations of the administrator are prescribed in the agreement of the parties and in these rules.

9. Delegation of Duties

The duties of the AAA under these rules may be carried out through Case Administrators or such other officers or committees as the AAA may direct.

10. Office of Tribunal

The general office of this Tribunal is the Office of the AAA.

11. Change of Claim

After filing of the claim, if either party desires to make any new or different claim, such claim shall be made in writing and filed with the AAA and a copy thereof shall be mailed to the other party, who shall have a period of seven (7) days from the date of such mailing within which to file an answer with the AAA. After the Arbitrator is appointed, however, no new or different claim may be submitted except with the Arbitrator's consent.

12. Initiation Under Submission

Parties to any existing dispute may commence an arbitration under these rules by filing at the Office of the AAA two (2) copies of a written agreement to arbitrate under these rules (Submission), signed by the parties. It shall contain a statement of the matter in dispute, the amount of money involved, if any, and the remedy sought, together with the appropriate administrative fee.

13. Time and Place of Hearing

The hearing will be held at the home site whenever possible or at such other suitable place as the Arbitrator may designate. (a.) Claims in excess of $2,500. In arbitrations where the claim exceeds $2,500, the Arbitrator shall fix the time of the hearing, notice of which must be given to the parties at least 14 days in advance. Appearance at the hearing waives any defect in this notice requirement.

(b.) Claims of $2,500 or less. In arbitrations where the claim is $2,500 or less, the AAA shall fix the time of hearing, notice of which must be given to the parties at least 14 days in advance. Appearance at the hearing waives any defect in this notice requirement.

14. Vacancies

The AAA is authorized to appoint another Arbitrator if a vacancy occurs or if an appointed Arbitrator is unable to serve promptly.

15. Representation by Counsel

Any party may be represented by counsel. A party intending to be so represented shall notify the other party and the AAA of the name and address of counsel at least five (5) days prior to the date set for the hearing at which counsel is first to appear. If a party fails to give five (5) days notice, as required by this rule, the Arbitrator upon request of another party or upon the initiative of the Arbitrator, may adjourn the hearing to a later date.

16. Audio/Stenographic Record

Any party wishing an audio or stenographic record shall make such arrangements and shall notify the other parties of such arrangements in advance of the hearing. The requesting party or parties shall pay the cost of such record.

17. Discovery

The voluntary exchange of information between the parties is encouraged. Formal discovery is discouraged except that a party is entitled, upon receipt, to:

(a.) exchange of supporting documentation; and,
(b.) other exhibits to be offered at the hearing.

18. Attendance at Hearings

The Arbitrator shall maintain the privacy of the hearings unless the law provides to the contrary.

FIGURE 15.2 SAMPLE COPY OF ARBITRATION RULES (*continued*)

All persons having a direct interest in the arbitration as well as representatives are entitled to attend hearings. The arbitrator shall have the power to require the exclusion of any witness, other than a party or other essential person, during the testimony of any other witness.

19. Adjournments

The Arbitrator may take adjournments upon the request of a party or upon the Arbitrator's own initiative and shall take such adjournment when all of the parties agree thereto.

20. Oaths

Before proceedings with the first hearing or with the examination of the file, each Arbitrator may take an oath of office, and if required by law, shall do so. The Arbitrator has discretion to require witnesses to testify under oath administered by any duly qualified person or, if required by law or demanded by either party, shall do so.

21. Order of proceedings

A hearing shall be opened by the filing of the oath of the Arbitrator, where required, and by the recording of the place, time, and date of the hearing, the presence of the Arbitrator and parties, and counsel, if any, and by the receipt by the Arbitrator of the statement of the claim and answer, if any.

The Arbitrator may, at the beginning of the hearing, ask for statements clarifying the issues involved.

The complaining party shall then present its claim and proofs and its witnesses, who shall submit to questions or other examination. The Arbitrator has discretion to vary this procedure but shall afford full and equal opportunity to all parties for the presentation of any material or relevant proofs.

Exhibits, when offered by either party, may be received in evidence by the Arbitrator.

The names and addresses of all witnesses and exhibits in order received shall be made a part of the record.

22. Arbitration in the Absence of a Party

The arbitration may proceed in the absence of any party which, after due notice, fails to be present or fails to obtain an adjournment. An award shall not be made solely on the default of a party. The Arbitrator shall require the party who is present to submit such supporting evidence as the Arbitrator may require for the making of an award.

23. Evidence

The parties may offer such evidence as is relevant and material to the dispute and shall produce such additional evidence as the Arbitrator may deem necessary to an understanding and determination of the dispute. An Arbitrator may subpoena witnesses, documents or other evidence upon the request of any party, or independently.

The Arbitrator shall be the judge of the relevance and the materiality of the evidence offered. All evidence shall be taken in the presence of the Arbitrator and all of the parties, except where any of the parties is absent, in default or has waived the right to be present.

24. Evidence of Affidavit and Filing of Documents

The Arbitrator may receive and consider the evidence of witnesses by affidavit, but shall give it only such weight as the Arbitrator deems it entitled to after consideration of any objections made to its admission.

All documents not filed with the Arbitrator at the hearing, but arranged for at the hearing or subsequently by agreement of the parties, shall be filed with the AAA for transmission to the Arbitrator. All parties shall be afforded opportunity to examine such documents.

25. Applicable Law

These rules shall be subject to the Uniform Arbitration Act,

26. Inspection or Investigation

Whenever the Arbitrator deems it necessary to make an inspection in connection with the arbitration, the Arbitrator shall direct the AAA to advise the parties of such intention. The Arbitrator shall set the time and AAA shall notify the parties thereof. Any party who so desires may be present at such inspection. In the event that one or both parties are not present at the inspection, the Arbitrator shall make an oral or written statement identifying the sites inspected to the parties and afford them an opportunity to comment.

27. Conservation of Property

The Arbitrator may issue such orders as may be deemed necessary to safeguard the property which is the subject matter of the arbitration without predjudice to the rights of the parties, or the final determination of the dispute.

28. Close of Hearings

The Arbitrator shall ask whether parties have any further proofs to offer or witnesses to be heard. Upon receiving negative replies, the Arbitrator shall declare the hearing closed.

29. Waiver of Rules

Any party who proceeds with the arbitration after knowledge that any provision or requirement of these rules has not been complied with and who fails to state objections thereto in writing shall be deemed to have waived the right to object.

30. Serving of Notices

Any papers or process necessary or proper for the initiation or continuation of an arbitration under these rules may be served upon any party (a) by mail addressed to such party or its attorney at its last known address, or (b) by personal service, or (c) by telephone followed by written confirmation.

31. Time of Award

The award shall be rendered promptly by the Arbitrator and, unless otherwise agreed by the parties, not later than twenty-one (21) working days from the date the hearing is closed.

32. Form of Award

The award shall be in writing and shall be signed by the Arbitrator. Findings of the Arbitrator shall be in summary form.

FIGURE 15.2 SAMPLE COPY OF ARBITRATION RULES *(continued)*

33. Scope of Award

The Arbitrator may grant any remedy or relief which the Arbitrator deems just and equitable and within the scope of the agreement of the parties, including, but not limited to, specific performance of a contract.

34. Award Upon Settlement

If the parties settle their dispute during the course of the arbitration, the Arbitrator, upon their request, may set forth the terms of the agreed settlement in an award.

35. Delivery of Award to Parties

Parties shall accept as legal delivery of the award the placing of the award or a true copy thereof in the mail by the AAA, addressed to such party at its last known address or to its attorney, or personal service of the award, or the filing of the award in any manner which may be prescribed by law. Application for modification or correction of an award shall be governed by

36. Release of Documents for Judicial Proceedings

The AAA shall, upon the written request of a party, furnish to such party, at the party's expense, certified facsimiles of any papers in the AAA's possession that may be required in judicial proceedings relating to the arbitration.

37. Expenses

The expenses of witnesses, expert witnesses, or reports for either side shall be paid by the party producing such witnesses or reports.

38. Interpretations and Application of Rules

The Arbitrator shall interpret and apply these rules insofar as they relate to the Arbitrator's powers and duties. All other rules shall be interpreted and applied by the AAA, as administrator.

39. Limitation of Actions

Any request for arbitration must be filed within six (6) months of the date in which the relevant facts regarding the physical condition of the property were discovered or could reasonably have been known to the party requesting arbitration.

40. Administrative Fee Schedule

An administrative fee shall be filed by the requesting party based on the following fee schedule:

Amount of Claim Fees

$1 to $2500 $250

$2501 to $50,000 $400

$50,001 and up $600

The administrative fee shall be reimbursed if the requesting party prevails at the conclusion of the arbitration. (The non-prevailing party shall be required to pay the administrative fee.)
The arbitrator will be compensated $100.00 for each case completed.

A refund of $100 will be made by the AAA if the matter is withdrawn or settled by the parties prior to the scheduling of a hearing.

No refund will be made in cases where filing fee is $250.

If there are more than two parties represented in the arbitration, an additional 10% of the administrative fee will be due for each additional party.

$100 is payable by a party requesting/causing its first postponement of a hearing.

$200 is payable by a party requesting/causing its second or subsequent postponement of a hearing.

41. Applications to Court and Exclusion of Liability

(a) No judicial proceeding commenced by a party relating to the subject matter of the arbitration shall be deemed a waiver of the party's obligation to arbitrate.

(b) Neither the AAA nor any Arbitrator in a proceeding under these rules is a necessary party in judicial proceedings relating to the arbitration.

(c) Parties to these rules shall be deemed to have consented that judgment on the arbitration award may be entered in any federal or state court having jurisdiction thereof.

(d) Neither the AAA, nor any Arbitrator shall be liable to any party for any act or omission in connection with any arbitration conducted under these rules.

(e) These rules are not intended to apply to commission disputes. Any commission disputes between Real Estate brokers or agents, who are members of the Association of REALTORS® shall be resolved in the manner provided in Article 14 of the REALTORS® Code of Ethics.

FIGURE 15.2 SAMPLE COPY OF ARBITRATION RULES (*continued*)

In the regulation of the securities industry, those who serve as dealers only, making "arm's length" transactions, are held to a somewhat different standard than those who serve as brokers (who are subjected to a set of fiduciary duties). To understand these relationships, it is necessary to take a look at the history of the regulation of brokers, dealers, and broker-dealers in the securities market.

"Shingle" Theory

In 1939, the Securities and Exchange Commission (SEC) established that securities dealers, previously believed to have no obligations to customers, would be held to a standard of fairness. Specifically the SEC was concerned over the practice of charging customers, most of whom were not knowledgeable about the operation of the securities market, prices considerably higher than market prices. This, said the SEC, was fraudulent dealing. This standard, which came to be known simply as the "Shingle Theory," was upheld by the courts and rapidly became accepted as the standard of practice for dealers.

"Trust and Confidence"

In later cases, the SEC began to establish a standard relating to the conflict between investment advice as a broker and the sale of securities as a dealer. This standard came to be known as the "trust and confidence," or implied agency, theory. In essence, individuals licensed as broker-dealers have an inherent conflict of interest when advising clients to purchase securities. In such instances, the broker-dealer must, under the implied agency theory, disclose the cost to the dealer of the securities offered for sale and the "best price" at which they could be obtained. In effect, the SEC established a fiduciary obligation (and thus the term "implied agency") for broker-dealers who gain the "trust and confidence" of their customers. Failure to make such disclosures was ruled to be fraud.

Although this standard has been in existence since the 1940s, the prior shingle theory is relied on more heavily because of the necessity of establishing the nature of the relationship between the broker-dealer and the customer under the trust and confidence theory.

Agency Theory in Securities Markets

In the mid-1940s, the SEC seemed to make an attempt to apply basic agency principles to securities dealers. This was done primarily by ruling that dealers who accepted orders for specifically recommended securities and filled these orders by going into the market, rather than selling from the firm's inventory, were brokers subject to an obligation to make disclosures regarding commissions and actual prices paid for securities. Although this series of rulings caused great consternation in the securities markets, the SEC went more then forty years before relying on "good old-fashioned **agency theory**" again in a 1988 case,[5] in which a broker-dealer was cited for failing to make adequate disclosures of industry practices even though its actions were permissible and the customer was a highly sophisticated portfolio manager.

Agency Theory Concepts of fiduciary responsibility based upon agency law.

[5]This case, known as the Manning case (Exchange Act Release No. 25887, [1988–89 Transfer Binder] Fed. Sec. L. Rep. (CCH) P 84,303 [July 6, 1988]) involved a branch office of E. F. Hutton failing to execute a "limit order" while making transactions of its own stock. This practice, called "trading ahead," is allowed in the over-the-counter market.

Applications to Real Estate Brokerage Practices

This brief overview of the standards of practice that apply in the securities market was intended only to provide a basis for comparison to agency theory as it is currently applied to real estate brokers. You may have noticed that in the previous discussion, no mention was made of the need to disclose specifics about the securities themselves. The commonly accepted standard in this regard is that securities brokers must make reasonable efforts to recommend securities that are suitable for a particular customer. These standards, known simply as the "know your customer" and "suitability" standards, imply a certain level of fiduciary obligation to customers. This obligation, however, in no way implies that the securities themselves will live up to expectations. Investing in securities of any sort is, after all, a risky business.

Why, you might ask, are securities brokers allowed to operate on a set of agency doctrines that involve making reasonable recommendations to customers but that do not involve them directly in making disclosures about the products themselves? The answer is the disclosure requirements the SEC imposes on the issuers of the securities. Each security offered for sale has disclosure information in the accompanying registration statement and "prospectus" prepared by a third party. This information is thus available for inspection by any investor and shifts the burden of disclosure from the broker to the prospectus preparer. If such a shift could be accomplished in the real estate brokerage area, a similar improvement in the ability to function as a true market maker might take place.

The most promising approach to making such a shift appears at this point to be that of a revised inspection approach. Such inspections are not uncommon in the residential real estate market. They are conducted by third parties for a fee and are sometimes a part of a "Home Owner's Warranty" (HOW) program. If the inspection process were to be expanded to encompass all necessary items and be made a mandatory part of the sales process, brokers might find themselves relieved of disclosure obligations.

Mandatory Seller Disclosure Statements

As a result of the increased disclosure requirements that have followed the *Easton*-type rulings discussed in the preceding chapters, the pressure to have sellers provide complete information has increased. In mid-1991, the National Association of Realtors (NAR) began a national campaign to lobby state legislatures to enact **mandatory seller disclosure** acts. These acts, patterned after similar acts in California and Maine, would require the disclosure of all pertinent facts by sellers of residential property, including information concerning the physical condition of the property, environmental hazards (e.g., lead-based paint, asbestos, and radon), and zoning and building code violations. In addition, some have pushed for the inclusion of "nuisances" (e.g., noisy neighbors, traffic patterns) such as those disclosed on the California form. A more controversial area of disclosure requirements concerns the history of the property. As we have seen, even events such as murders that were committed in a property or a belief that the property might be "haunted" can affect market value. Thus such information, if the form is to be effective, must be disclosed. Figure 15.3 contains an example transfer disclosure form.

Mandatory Seller Disclosure A statement containing information about the physical condition of the property, environmental hazards, building and zoning code violations provided by the seller.

REAL ESTATE TRANSFER DISCLOSURE

This disclosure statement concerns the real property located at is to the best of the sellers knowledge and is not a warranty of any kind by the seller or any Agent representing any Party in this transaction, and is not a substitute for any inspections or warranties the buyer may wish to obtain.

A. GENERAL INFORMATION:

(1) When did you purchase the home?

(2) Have you lived in this home for the past 12 months? Yes______ No______

(3) Has there been any flood or other disaster(s), ie. hail, fire, at the property? Yes______ No______

If yes, give details of what happened and when. ____________________

(4) During your ownership has the structure been altered? (For example, additions, altered roof lines, changes to load bearing walls.) Yes______ No______ If yes, please specify what was done, when and by whom (owner or contractor)

(5) Was a building permit issued? Yes______ No______

(6) Is the property suitable for year round use? Yes______ No______

B. STRUCTURAL SYSTEMS: Do any of the following conditions currently exist or have they previously existed?

(1) THE BASEMENT

(a) Foundation problem	Yes______	No______	(e) Drainage system problem	Yes______	No______
(b) Flooding	Yes______	No______	(f) Cracked floors/walls	Yes______	No______
(c) Wet Walls	Yes______	No______	(g) Sewer backup	Yes______	No______
(d) Leakage/seepage	Yes______	No______	(h) Other	Yes______	No______

Give details to any question answered "yes". ____________________

(2) THE ROOF

(a) What is the age of the roofing material? __________ Comments: __________

(b) Has there ever been interior damage from ice buildup? Yes______ No______

(c) Has there ever been any leakage, condensation, or other problem? Yes______ No______

(d) Have there ever been any repairs or replacement made to the roof? Yes______ No______

Give details to any question answered yes. ____________________

C. HEATING, PLUMBING, ELECTRICAL AND MECHANICAL SYSTEMS:

The following are in working order **and shall be at time of closing** unless marked "no". Cross out items not included.

	YES	NO		YES	No		YES	NO
Range			Intercom			Central Heating System		
Oven			Garage Door Openers			Central Air Conditioning		
Hood			Garage Door Controls			Wall Air Conditioner(s)		
Refrigerator			Vent Fans/Fixtures			Furnace Humidifier		
Microwave			Security Systems			Electronic Air Purifier		
Dishwasher			Smoke Detectors			Supplemental Heaters		
Freezer			Central Vacuums			Solar Collectors		
Washer			Door Bell			Fireplace & Equipment		
Dryer			Window Treatments			Pool & Equipment		
Trash Compactor			Water Heater			Woodburning Stove		
Garbage Disposal			Sump Pump			Incinerator		
Plumbing System			Drainage System			Water Softener		
Toilet Mechanisms			Satellite Dish			Lawn Sprinkler System		
Private Well			TV Antenna/Cables			Septic Tank		
Cistern			Electrical Systems			Drain Field		
Comments:								

D. LAND USE AND PROPERTY CONDITION:

Does the building contain any asbestos material? (ie. pipe insulations, ceiling tile) Yes______ No______ If yes what is its

FIGURE 15.3 EXAMPLE OF A REAL ESTATE TRANSFER DISCLOSURE FORM

condition? ______________________________

If applicable, when was the last time the Septic Tank was pumped out? ______________________________

Are there keys for all the locks? Yes ______ If not which ones are missing? ______________________________

Are you aware of any of the following existing?

Encroachments? Yes ______ No ______ Soil problems? Yes ______ No ______ Diseased trees? Yes ______ No ______

Rodent infestation? Yes ____ No ____ Insect infestation? Yes ____ No ____ Restrictions on the use of the land? Yes ____ No ____

Easements other than utility or drainage easements which do not interfere with present improvements? Yes ______ No ______

Is the property located in a designated flood plain? yes ______ No ______

What is the condition of the driveway & sidewalk? ______________________________

Comments. ______________________________

E. ENVIRONMENTAL DISCLOSURE:

Has the home been tested for Radon? No ______ Yes ______ If yes, when ______________ Type of test: Charcoal Canister ______________

Other: ______________________________ Results: ______________________________

Does the insulation in the building contain urea formaldehyde foam? Yes ______ No ______ Unknown ______

Date insulation installed: ______________ type: ______________ Company: ______________

Is there an unused buried fuel tank, septic tank, or cistern on the property? Yes ______ No ______

Has it been sealed in accordance with EPA directives? Yes ______ No ______

Is there a well on the property? Yes ______ No ______

If yes, is it currently being used? Yes ______ No ______ and is it certified? Yes ______ No ______

If no, has it been sealed according to State regulations? Yes ______ No ______

When was the well water last tested? ______________

Is there an addendum showing a map of the well locations? Yes ______ No ______

Comments: ______________________________

F. OTHER KNOWN DEFECTS:

Are there any other known defects in or on the property? Yes ______ No ______ If yes, explain. ______________________________

G. SELLERS STATEMENT: (To be signed at time of listing)

We/I, owner(s) of the property at ______________________________
certify the above statements to be true to the best of our knowledge and give permission to Listing Broker to disclose
this information to the prospective buyers. We also give the prospective buyer permission to have the house
professionally inspected at buyers expense.

Date: ______________________ **Seller:** ______________________

Date: ______________________ **Seller:** ______________________

IT IS UNDERSTOOD THAT THE PROPERTY IS NOT NEW AND THE PRICE REFLECTS ITS WORN CONDITION.

K. BUYERS ACKNOWLEDGEMENT: (To be signed at time of purchase agreement.

We/I, the Buyer(s) do acknowledge receipt of the Sellers Property Disclosure Statement and agree that no representation
regarding the condition of the property has been made, other than those made above. **LISTING BROKER AND AGENTS MAKE NO
REPRESENTATIONS AND ARE NOT RESPONSIBLE FOR ANY CONDITIONS EXISTING IN THE PROPERTY.**

Date: ______________________ **Buyer:** ______________________

Date: ______________________ **Buyer:** ______________________

L. SELLER'S ACKNOWLEDGEMENT (To be signed at time of purchase agreement.)

We/I hereby certify that the present condition of all items is the same as so noted above.

Date: ______________________ **Seller:** ______________________

Date: ______________________ **Seller:** ______________________

M. BUYER'S CLOSING INSPECTION

We have inspected the property prior to closing and find all items to be in the same condition as disclosed by the
seller and the property is in a "broom clean" condition.

Date: ______________________ **Buyer:** ______________________

Date: ______________________ **Buyer:** ______________________

We waive our right to have a final inspection.

Date: ______________________ **Buyer:** ______________________

Date: ______________________ **Buyer:** ______________________

FIGURE 15.3 EXAMPLE OF A REAL ESTATE TRANSFER DISCLOSURE FORM (*continued*)

Will such mandatory disclosure relieve real estate brokers of liability? The answer, based on cases such as *Tennant v. Lawton* [26 Wash. App. 701, 615 P.2d 1305 (1980)], *Prichard v. Reitz* [178 Cal. App. 3d 465, 223 Cal. Rptr. 734 (1986)], *Bevins v. Ballard* [655 P.2d 757 (Alaska 1982)], and *Johnson v. Geer Real Estate Co.* [239 Kan. 324, 720 P.2d 660 (1986)], all of which found that a broker cannot rely on seller-provided information without verification, would clearly indicate that brokers will continue to have disclosure liability. Why then is NAR pushing for such legislation? Although we can only speculate as to their motives, it would appear that NAR believes that mandatory seller disclosure, even though it does not provide complete protection, is a large step in the right direction. This belief, based on all that you have seen here, would appear to be correct.

Will mandatory seller disclosure acts, assuming that NAR is at least partially successful, lead eventually to third-party inspection or warranty acts? Only time will tell, of course, but the trend appears to be in this direction. The result may be a market where buyers are better protected, brokers face fewer liability concerns, and the real estate market is allowed to operate more effectively.

CONCLUSION

The real estate brokerage industry in the United States has changed little in the last 100 years. The rapid pace of change now taking place is a reflection not only of current pressures facing the industry, but the need for change which has been building for many years. Change is taking place in every aspect of the industry—from the nature of the legal relationships between parties, to the organizational structure of individual firms. Some would say that the very nature of the real estate brokerage industry is changing to such an extent that the concept of brokerage as we have come to know it will cease to exist. Such a view may be a bit extreme, but the pace and degree of change should not be underestimated.

Just as the banking industry is undergoing dramatic changes, the real estate brokerage industry must adapt to changes in our society. Buyers are increasingly less willing to be unrepresented in real estate transactions. As sellers find themselves facing buyers armed with representatives, the nature of the traditional real estate firm has come under pressure. Simply continuing to provide listing and negotiating services may not be sufficient to retain market shares.

Thus real estate brokers find themselves facing the prospect of a diminishing market position and an increasing level of liability exposure. In response, new ideas about the most appropriate legal relationship have begun to emerge. The traditional concept of agency representation may give way to some version of the real estate broker as middleman or negotiator. In similar fashion, real estate firms have looked for new ways to position themselves in the marketplace. Just as the "mom-and-pop" grocery stores of the 1950's were pushed out of the market by the concept of a "supermarket," real estate firms may be split into two groups—small, customized service firms, and large, full-service firms offering appraisal, financing and other services in addition to traditional representation.

DISCUSSION QUESTIONS

1. List several services a buyer broker may provide.
2. What does the exclusive buyer agency contract ensure?
3. Briefly explain the importance of the first eleven clauses contained in the exclusive buyer agency contract shown in Figure 15.1.
4. Aside from those outlined in question number 3, disclosure is the only other major issue pertaining to an exclusive buyer agency contract. Why is the area of disclosure so important?
5. A broker who wishes to change the set of services offered has two basic choices. Discuss the success of each of these options.
6. Explain the concepts of seller guarantee and buyer warranty.
7. What are some advantages to a local businessperson of entering into a franchise agreement?
8. Distinguish between *product franchise* and *package franchise.* What type of franchising is used in the real estate brokerage industry?
9. Name and describe the types of fees the franchisee may be required to pay under a franchise agreement.
10. Define the concept of a "middleman" in a transaction. Why does this concept generally not apply to real estate transactions?
11. Although the role of an arbitrator has little appeal for real estate brokers, would the use of an outside arbitrator to settle disputes offer any advantages?
12. Explain the role of the registration statement and prospectus in the sale of securities. Would mandatory seller disclosure forms play a similar role in real property transactions?

MURRAY V. HAYDEN

259 Cal.Rptr. 257 (Court of Appeal, First District, 1989)

Duty to inspect by buyer broker

Purchasers of a house which contained concealed defects sued the sellers of the residence, a brokerage firm that acted for both them and the sellers, and the brokerage firm employee who acted as their broker. The Contra Costa Superior Court, . . . , granted broker's motion for summary judgment, and purchasers appealed. The Court of Appeal . . . held that purchaser's broker owed no duty to inspect premises.

Affirmed.

Appellants suffered damages as a result of concealed defects in a single-family residence they purchased. Among the defendants named in a complaint to recover appellants' damages, was respondent, who acted as appellants' "agent and broker" for the purchase of the residence. Appellants alleged respondent was negligent in that she failed diligently to inspect the residence. The trial court sustained respondent's demurrer.

STATEMENT OF FACTS AND PROCEDURAL HISTORY

. . . Appellants Mark and Roberta Murray purchased and thereafter occupied a single family residence in Walnut Creek, on or about September 18, 1979. Sometime after moving into the residence, the Murrays began to notice "cracks, distress and deterioration." In October or November, 1985, they submitted a claim to their homeowner's insurance carrier. A consultant retained by the insurance carrier reported: (1) The residence had been built over expansive clay without making adequate provision for surface drainage; (2) a severely distressed original foundation was incorporated into the newly built residence; and, (3) two different foundation systems had been used, which acted differently, resulting in "undue distress and deterioration."

The Murrays sued the group of individuals who built and then sold the residence. The Murrays also sued "Stephen R. Payne, Realtors," a "real estate brokerage" firm that acted for both them and the sellers. The Murrays' complaint, in the Sixth Cause of Action for "Real Estate Agent/Broker Negligence," named as defendants, several agents who worked for Stephen R. Payne, Realtors, including respondent Hayden. Hayden acted as the Murrays' "agent and broker." . . . The other agents acted for the sellers. The Sixth Cause of Action alleged the real estate agent defendants were negligent in that they failed to conduct a reasonably competent and diligent inspection of the residence before its sale.

The trial court sustained Hayden's demurrer to the complaint and dismissed the action as to Hayden. The court found no duty on the part of Hayden, acting as the buyer's broker, to conduct an inspection.

The Murrays appeal. . . .

DUTY TO INSPECT

[1] "[T]he duty of a real estate broker, representing the seller, to disclose facts, . . . includes the affirmative duty to conduct a reasonably competent and diligent inspection of the residential property listed for sale and to disclose to prospective purchasers all facts materially affecting the value or desirability of the property that such an investigation would reveal." (Easton v. Strassburger [1984] . . .)

The Murrays seek to extend the holding in Easton to include a duty on the part of the real estate broker representing the buyer to conduct a reasonably competent and diligent inspection. Whether Hayden owed a duty to the Murrays to conduct an inspection is a question of law.

The facts in Easton are similar to those in the present case. Earth movement caused damage to a single-family residence. The homeowners sued the sellers, the builders, and the listing broker (a corporation). All defendants were found negligent. The broker's negligence was premised on its agents' failure to conduct further investigation after their inspections revealed certain "red flags" which indicated there might be soil problems. . . ."

In affirming the finding of broker negligence, the Easton court reasoned "the seller's broker is most frequently the best situated to obtain and provide the most reliable information on the property and is ordinarily counted on to do so." . . . Imposing a duty to inspect on the seller's broker would protect buyers from unethical brokers and provide accurate information to make an informed decision. . . . Many buyers "justifiably believe the seller's broker is also protecting their interest . . . " A significant benefit is conferred on buyers, with relatively little burden placed on the broker. . . .

[2] The Murrays point out that Hayden, as their agent, had certain fiduciary obligations to them, including the duty to use reasonable care, diligence and skill in carrying out her duties. . . . The buyer's agent has a duty to investigate before making any representations. . . .

[3] . . . Hayden notes the buyer's broker usually does not have easy access to the property, or to information about the property. Since the seller's broker already has a duty to inspect pursuant to Easton, it would be a duplication of effort to impose the same duty on the buyer's broker, according to Hayden. The Legislature reacted to Easton by adding Civil Code sections 2079–2079.5. . . . [1] Civil Code section 2079 provides, in relevant part: "It is the duty of a real estate broker . . . to a

[1]"It is the intent of the Legislature that this act codify and make precise the holding in Easton v. Strassburger . . . The Legislature finds that the imprecision of terms in the

prospective purchaser of residential real property . . . to conduct a reasonably competent and diligent visual inspection of the property offered for sale and to disclose to that prospective purchaser all facts materially affecting the value or desirability of the property that such an investigation would reveal, if that broker has a written contract with the seller to find or obtain a buyer or is a broker who acts in cooperation with such a broker to find and obtain a buyer." . . .

Civil Code section 2079 does not expressly impose any obligations on brokers representing the buyer. It does impose the duty to inspect on "co-operating" brokers, also known as "selling" brokers. "A 'selling agent' is an agent participant in a multiple listing service who acts in cooperation with a listing agent and who sells, or finds and obtains a buyer for, the property." . . . Cooperating brokers are considered subagents of the seller though it is possible for a cooperating broker to be also an agent for the buyer. . . .

In the final analysis, we can find no compelling reason for extending the duty to conduct an inspection to a broker representing the buyer. Hayden's points have merit. The seller's broker is in a better position to conduct an inspection, and there would be a duplication of effort were such a duty imposed on the buyer's broker. The trial court's conclusion that Hayden had no duty to conduct an inspection of the Walnut Creek residence will be affirmed.

The Order is Affirmed.

Easton case and the absence of a comprehensive declaration of duties, standards, and exceptions has caused insurers to modify professional liability coverage of real estate licensees and has caused confusion among real estate licensees as to the manner of performing the duty ascribed to them by the court, and that it is necessary to resolve and make precise these issues in an expeditious manner. The Legislature finds that it is desirable to facilitate the issuance of professional liability insurance as a resource for aggrieved members of the public, and declares that the provisions of this act are, and shall be interpreted as, a definition of the duty of care found to exist by Easton v. Strassburger, and the manner of its discharge." . . .

Case Reflections

1. On what grounds did plaintiff Murray sue defendant Hayden? How did the trial court rule?
2. What was the issue to be decided by the Appellate Court in this case?
3. Why did the Appellate Court rule that the buyer broker has no duty to inspect the premises before the purchase?

SCHAECHTER V. REGENCY PROPERTIES, INC.

497 N.Y.S.2d 793 (Supreme Court, Appellate Division, Fourth Department, 1985)

Commission due to buyer's broker

Purchaser who breached contract to purchase real property brought action against broker, who brought third-party action against vendors. The supreme Court . . . ordered escrow deposit returned to purchaser, dismissed broker's counterclaim, and held that vendors were liable for broker 's commissions. On appeal, the Supreme Court, Appellate Division, held that: (1) purchaser's refusal to perform contract to purchase rendered him liable to broker for commissions, and (2) release executed by vendors extinguished vendor's rights against purchaser but did not cut off right of purchaser's broker to proceed against purchaser. Reversed and remitted.

MEMORANDUM

In this action by plaintiff, who breached a contract to purchase real property procured for him by defendant, his broker, and owned by third-party defendants, it was error to order the escrow deposit returned to plaintiff, to dismiss defendant's counterclaim, and to hold that the sellers, third-party defendants, were liable for defendant's broker's commissions. Absent express exclusion of the broker's right, where a buyer employs a broker who procures an agreement which the buyer fails or refuses to perform, the buyer is liable for the commissions the broker would have earned if the agreement had been executed . . . That is true even where the contract or the usual practice contemplates that the seller will pay the commissions . . . and where there is only an implied contract of employment between the buyer and the broker and the buyer has not expressly undertaken to pay commissions . . .

[1] Plaintiff enlisted the services of defendant to find a house. Through defendant's efforts, plaintiff contracted to purchase the home of third-party defendants but subsequently breached the contract. His refusal to perform the contract renders him liable to Regency for the commissions it would have earned had the contract been executed even in the absence of an express agreement by plaintiff to pay commissions and even though Regency expected that the commissions would be paid by the sellers . . .

[2] The trial court correctly found that third-party defendant sellers' rights against the buyer were extinguished by the release which they executed and that they therefore had no claim to the amount held in escrow. The release extinguished any other remedies the sellers might have had but did not cut off the right of the buyer's broker to proceed against the buyer. Regency's counterclaim against the buyer should thus be reinstated and the matter remitted for trial to determine the amount of commission to which Regency would have been entitled under the contract of sale.

Judgment unanimously reversed on the law and facts with costs, defendant's counterclaim reinstated and matter remitted to Supreme Court for further proceedings, . . .

Case Reflection

1. From this case, there is an important lesson to be learned pertaining to the payment of brokerage commissions. What is this lesson?

COLDWELL BANKER RESIDENTIAL REAL ESTATE SERVICES, INC. V. NEW JERSEY REAL ESTATE COMMISSION

In the Matter of COLDWELL BANKER BEST BUYER AND BEST SELLER PROGRAM.

242 N.J. Super. 354, 576 A.2d 938 (Appellate Division, 1990)

Use of inducements and promotions in real estate brokerage services

Real estate broker appealed from ruling of the Real Estate Commission, determining that broker's discount coupon promotion program was impermissible. The Superior Court . . . held that merchandise coupons offered by real estate broker to residential buyers and sellers were "prizes" within meaning of statute prohibiting real estate promotions involving a prize.

Affirmed.

This matter is here for the second time. It involves the question whether plaintiffs' proposed discount coupon promotion program is legally permissible. The New Jersey Real Estate Commission ruled that it was not. We affirm. Plaintiff (CB) is a real estate broker, wholly owned by Sears Roebuck. In 1983 it inquired of the Commission whether a described promotional program would be lawful. The Commission Director replied that there would be legal objection to the program, because regulations prohibited brokers from making free promotional offerings. In 1985 and 1986, the Commission considered whether to rewrite the regulation, decided not to, and instructed staff to enforce it after adequate notification to brokers.

CB started a Chancery Division suit to bar enforcement, and to declare the underlying statutory provisions unconstitutional. . . . [T]he Commission held four days of hearings. It issued its thirty-page decision on February 28, 1989, including factual findings which we briefly summarize. CB is a licensed real estate broker. It seeks to institute a program of providing to home sellers who list with CB and to home buyers who purchase through CB discount coupons for Sears merchandise.

CB has 58 owned and 26 franchised offices in New Jersey. . . . CB has developed what it calls the

Best Seller and Best Buyer Plans . . . The current version of the Best Seller Plan includes a booklet of Sears merchandise coupons conferring discounts of specific dollar amounts (as contrasted with percentages) on regular and sale items. . . . The coupons are given to sellers upon listing with CB. Sears absorbs all the "costs" other than printing.

The Best Buyer Plan also includes discount and specific merchandise coupons. They are earned by signing a contract to buy a home through a CB broker, and do not depend on the consummation of the purchase. Sears absorbs all "costs" other than printing. . . .

The coupons are nontransferable, but the restriction is not enforced by CB or Sears. There is no requirement that the Sears merchandise relate to the home bought or sold or to real estate at all.

The coupon books are offered as a marketing strategy designed to maximize profits and market share of Sears and CB. As the Commission said;

> Unsophisticated sellers or buyers or relocating buyers unfamiliar with real estate brokers in a particular area might choose a Coldwell Banker office based on the offer of the Coupon Book.

A State-employed expert on consumer protection testified to program details which prompted the Commission to find that "the proposed Best Seller and Best Buyer Coupon programs have elements which may tend to mislead consumers." Finally, the Commission found that the programs operate "as an extraneous inducement to consumers" to buy or sell through CB for reasons other than the quality of the professional services of the broker. The Public Advocate is particularly concerned that the Coupons also serve as extraneous inducements to buyers to purchase homes based upon the opportunity to receive coupons instead of the quality and suitability of the home itself.

On the basis of the evidence before it, the Commission concluded that the coupon programs would not . . . make any false promises, substantial misrepresentations, . . . or false promises. That conclusion is not challenged by any party before us.

The Commission made two additional determinations, however, which were adverse to CB. The first was that the coupon program would violate [statute], which prohibits [u]sing any plan, scheme or method for the sale or promotion of the sale of real estate which involves a lottery, a contest, a game, a prize, a drawing, or the offering of a lot or parcel of lots or parcels for advertising purposes; . . .

The Commission concluded that the coupons constituted a prohibited "prize." The other determination was that the coupon program would violate [statute] which prohibits, [p]aying any rebate, profit, compensation or commission to anyone not possessed of a real estate license; . . .

[1] . . . CB argues that a "prize" in that provision must be taken to mean the subject of a gamble. CB points out that all of the other prohibited items involve lotteries, drawings, and other like promotions containing an offensive element of chance. The Sears coupons have no such element. There is no helpful legislative history.

[2] We agree with the Commission that statutory words should be read according to their ordinary meanings, consistent with context and legislative history. . . . One of the meanings of the word "prize" in ordinary use is "a novelty or other premium given with merchandise as an inducement to buy." . . . The most familiar example is the "prize" in the box of Crackerjacks. . . .

The evil addressed . . . is the capacity of extraneous inducements to distract the residential buyer and seller from the material elements of their decisions to list, sell and buy their homes. To many buyers and sellers, these are among the most significant financial decisions they face. Distracting gimmickry creates dangers which are the legitimate concern of the Legislature and the Commission. The occupation of a real estate broker is permeated by considerations of public policy, and is subject to regulation "to protect the public from fraud, incompetence, misinterpretation, sharp or unconscionable practice." A broker is a fiduciary, and is required to exercise good faith and primary devotion to the interests of the principal. . . .

Promoting listings and sales by sweetening the real estate deal itself does no violence to the relationship. Extraneous inducements, however, can take the buyers' or sellers' eyes off the ball.

[3]We are not persuaded by CB's complaint that barring its coupon program is an improper regulation of competition. It may have the effect of restricting competitive advantages by narrowing the range of inducements that may be offered to buyers and sellers. But, the side effect does not inval-

idate laws reasonably designed to bar practices which encourage inappropriate consumer behavior. Similarly, permitting brokers to provide home warranty programs and other free offerings ancillary to the real estate transaction itself is not inconsistent with the goal of barring extraneous and distracting inducements to deal. . . . We confess some difficulty seeing a major distinction between CB's coupon program and aspects of Century 21's Preferred Client Club. However, lines have to be drawn somewhere, and this is not a regulatorily unreasonable place to draw it. . . .

Case Reflections

1. Describe the "Best Seller" and "Best Buyer" promotions developed by Coldwell Banker.
2. What two statues did the Commission conclude the coupons violated? Did the Appellate Court agree or disagree? What other issue did the Appellate Court address?

THE MORTGAGE BANKERS ASSOCIATION OF NEW JERSEY V. NEW JERSEY REAL ESTATE COMMISSION

506 A.2d 733 (Supreme Court of New Jersey, 1985–86)

Charging multiple fees in a real estate transaction

Association of mortgage bankers and brokers appealed from declaratory ruling of Real Estate Commission concluding that real estate broker's double compensation for services rendered in respect to both sale and financing was not statutorily barred. The Superior Court, . . . reversed and real estate broker appealed. The Supreme Court . . . held that: . . . (2) department of banking has authority to regulate real estate brokers in connection with their business activities as licensed mortgage bankers and mortgage brokers. Reversed and remanded.

In this case we are asked to consider the validity of a declaratory ruling by the New Jersey Real Estate Commission (Commission) that N.J.S.A. 45:15–17(i)[1] does not preclude a real estate brokerage firm that earns a commission from the seller in a real estate transaction from also receiving compensation for its role in placing or originating the mortgage financing necessary to consummate the real estate transaction. . . .

I.

In 1983 both the First Boston Capital Group, Inc. (First Boston) and the Mortgage Bankers Association of New Jersey (MBA), a trade association comprised primarily of mortgage bankers and mortgage brokers, asked the Commission for a ruling as to the proper interpretation of N.J.S.A. 45:15–17(i). First Boston had formulated a mortgage-financing program known as "Shelternet" to assist New Jersey real estate brokers in organizing mortgage-origination companies, either directly or through affiliates. First Boston anticipated that it would employ its capital resources to participate in the New Jersey mortgage market by purchasing at a discount mortgage loans originated by the participating real estate brokers and their mortgage-company affiliates. First Boston requested the Commission to rule that its Shelternet program did not violate the Real Estate Brokers Licensing Act . . . (Act), when the participating brokers placed mortgage loans with their affiliated mortgage company and simultaneously received commissions for effecting the related sales transaction. MBA sought a ruling from the Commission that the Shelternet program was prohibited by the Act. . . .

[1]N.J.S.A. 45:15–17(i) prohibits a licensed real estate broker from [c]ollecting a commission as a real estate broker in a transaction, when at the same time representing either party in a transaction in a different capacity for a consideration.

[T]he Commission rendered its advisory opinion on April 24, 1984, in which it concluded that:

> The Commission shall not consider it a violation . . . when a duly licensed real estate broker receives fees for services rendered in more than one capacity in a single transaction.

. . . In reversing the Commission's declaratory ruling, the Appellate Division majority observed:

> [T]he only question remaining is whether the broker's double compensation in receiving a commission from the seller and a consideration for placing or granting the buyer's purchase money mortgage loan comes within the statutory prohibition. It does if the sale and mortgage transaction are, effectively, components of the same transaction and if the broker represents more than one party to the transaction. The intervenors contend that the broker, in placing the mortgage, does not represent any party to the transaction other than the seller for two reasons: first, because the mortgage transaction is separate from the sales transaction, and second, because the broker in placing the mortgage loan is paid by the lender or receives profit as the lender and does not therefore "represent" the buyer as borrower.

[W]e are convinced that the two transactions are so closely entwined, so interdependent and have so great a potential for conflict of interest and self-dealing on the part of the broker as to require the conclusion that at least for purposes of this statute they are each a part of the single, overall transaction which takes place when a purchaser buys real estate financed by a purchase money mortgage loan.

We are also persuaded that in that overall transaction a broker receiving a commission from the seller would also be "representing either party in a different capacity for a consideration" if he is also paid by the borrower or lender for his services in the mortgage transaction. . . .

A. The Regulatory Context

[2] [3] It is undisputed that real estate brokers may also function, subject to licensure, as mortgage bankers or mortgage brokers. . . .

B. The Real Estate Broker's Function

. . . [T]he Commission's jurisdiction was apparently invoked to consider only whether a real estate broker who has earned a commission from a seller can function and be compensated in the same transaction as the issuer of the buyer's mortgage, either directly or through an affiliated company.[2] . . .

The Commission broadly approved the right of real estate brokers to receive compensation from both the sales and mortgage components of the same transaction, subject only to the Commission's supervisory responsibility to "punish specific misconduct individually." . . . The Commission observed that N.J.S.A. 45:25–17(i) did not apply when the real estate broker originates the mortgage, since "he or she become a party, not a representative of a buyer." As to the real estate broker functioning for a fee as a mortgage broker or solicitor, the Commission noted:

> When a broker receives compensation for assisting in the placement of a mortgage, the compensation is paid by the mortgage originator, not the buyer. Thus, by receiving compensation for such services, the broker is not being paid for "representing" the buyer.

In reversing the Commission, the Appellate Division majority observed that whether the real estate broker was functioning as the mortgage issuer or the agent placing the mortgage loan, such functions were incompatible with the real estate broker's role as the seller's agent. . . .

Both the Commission's conclusion that a real estate broker placing a mortgage loan will be paid its fee by the lender, and the Appellate Division's conclusion that any such fee can be passed by the lender to the borrower, are sharply disputed by the Department of Banking. As intervenor before us, the Department asserts that is interpretation of

---

[2]The inquiry to the Commission was posited on the assumption that before the parties entered into the mortgage transaction, the real estate broker would fully disclose, to both buyer and seller, its dual role, its anticipated compensation, the nature and amount of all fees involved in the mortgage transaction, and the fact that the buyer is absolutely free to obtain mortgage financing from another source.

the Mortgage Bankers and Brokers Act prohibits the payment of fees by mortgage bankers to mortgage brokers for placing mortgages . . . . The department's position is that a mortgage broker may collect its fee from the borrower only in the form of application fees and discount points. . . .

In this connection there are related issues involving the propriety of payments by licensed mortgage bankers to real estate brokers not required to be licensed as mortgage brokers, and payments to sales personnel employed by such real estate brokers. . . .

For the reasons stated, the judgment of the Appellate Division is reversed and the matter is remanded to the Real Estate Commission and the Commissioner of Banking for hearings in accordance with this opinion. . . .

Case Reflections

1. Explain the "Shelternet" program formulated by First Boston.
2. The Mortgage Bankers Association of New Jersey claims that the "Shelternet" program is in violation of a New Jersey Statute. What does this statute prohibit?
3. How did the Supreme Court of New Jersey rule in this case?

SALISBURY V. CHAPMAN REALTY

465 N.E.2d 127 (Appellate Court of Illinois, Third District, 1984)

Liability exposure of franchisor

The plaintiffs appeal from the dismissal of their second amended complaint. In 1979 and 1980, the plaintiffs purchased real estate from Laurel Chapman, Jr., a partner of Chapman Realty and a licensed real estate broker. Laurel had originally purchased the property via four mortgage loans which were still outstanding at the time of the sales to the plaintiffs. The plaintiffs agreed to purchase the properties on installment contracts. Some of the plaintiffs were not told of the mortgages; others were not informed of the amount of the loans or the extent of Laurel's indebtedness. The plaintiffs made payments on the contracts, but Laurel failed to repay the mortgage loans. First Federal Savings and Loan Association of Ottawa foreclosed on the plaintiff's property. Laurel has absconded.

The plaintiffs filed a complaint naming Laurel's partners in Chapman Realty, and the franchisor, Realty World, as defendants. . . . The trial court granted the defendants' motion to dismiss holding that Realty World . . . could not be vicariously liable for Laurel's conduct because . . . Realty World was a franchisor and not a principal of Chapman Realty. . . .

Realty World and Chapman Realty are parties to a franchise agreement which specifically sets forth a relationship of franchisor/franchisee as opposed to principal/agent. In Slates v. International House of Pancakes Inc. (1980), . . . the court examined a franchise agreement with similar language and made the following observation:

> Where a sufficient degree of control and direction is manifested by the parent franchisor, an agency relationship may be created. Whether the relationship between a franchisor and a franchisee is that of principal and agent, at least insofar as the relationship affects a stranger to the franchise agreement, is dependent upon the intention of the parties as determined from the written agreement and the accompanying circumstances. The declaration of the parties in the agreement respecting the nature of the relationship created thereby are not controlling, however, and, as with contracts generally, the writings must be considered as a whole. . . .

[5] We find that Realty World did not exercise such complete control over Chapman Realty so as to negate the intent of the franchise agreement not to create a principal agent relationship. Realty World does not hire or fix the compensation of Chapman employees nor does it control the firm's day-to-day operation. In exchange for using Realty World's proprietary marks and goodwill, Chapman

agreed to conduct its business in accordance with Realty World's confidential operations manual. On a voluntary basis, Chapman could send its employees to training sessions conducted by Realty World. Chapman Realty agreed to maintain its office, furnishings and supplies according to standards set by Realty World. Finally, Realty World reserved the right to inspect Chapman's accounts at reasonable times. Realty World's control is considerable but not total. Chapman Realty maintains its individual identity and supervises its own operations subject to general standards set by Realty World. . . .

[6] [7] Apparent authority in an agent is such authority as the principal knowingly permits the agent to assume or which he holds his agent out as possessing. . . . There are no allegations in the plaintiffs' complaint which indicate that Realty World held Chapman Realty out as possessing the authority to act on Realty World's behalf as an agent. The complaint alleges only a franchisor/-franchisee relationship. In fact, the franchise agreement attached to the complaint as an exhibit, contains a clause which requires Chapman to prominently display a certificate in the office setting forth Chapman's status as an independent franchisee.

. . . The judgment of the circuit court of LaSalle County is affirmed insofar as it dismisses defendant Realty World.

Case Reflection

1. The issue in this case was whether or not Realty World could be held vicariously liable for the conduct of Chapman Realty. In what situation could Realty World be included as a defendant in this lawsuit? Why was Realty World dismissed as a defendant in this case?

CIAMPI V. RED CARPET CORPORATION OF AMERICA

213 Cal.Rptr. 388 (Court of Appeal, First District, Division 2, 1985)

Required initial disclosure by franchisor

After franchisor terminated franchisees for nonpayment of franchise and other fees, franchisees and their investment corporation brought action against franchisor, certain employees, and its president. Franchisor cross-complained. The Superior Court . . . found for franchisor. Franchisees appealed. The Court of Appeal . . . held that: (1) franchisor must be in compliance with provisions of section of Franchise Act which imposes liability for violation of other sections when it first contacts prospective franchisee about its franchises; (2) requisite disclosures should have been made at least 48 hours before franchisees paid consideration for franchises . . . ; (5) trial court committed reversible error by refusing to instruct jury on theory that franchisor was liable for misrepresentations of salesman; and (6) trial court should have given proposed instruction relating to section of Franchise Act which provides that any provision in contract for sale of franchise purporting to bind purchaser to waive compliance with Act is void.

Affirmed in part; and reversed in part.

I

. . .

Appellants sought relief for alleged violations of the Franchise Investment Law Act . . . hereinafter Franchise Act, . . .

[1] . . . Appellants testified that they signed the contracts to buy four franchises and paid consideration to Red Carpet on June 30, 1977. They claimed that as of that time they had not been told all the material facts which the Franchise Act requires the franchisor to disclose to a prospective franchisee. Appellants would not have agreed to buy the franchises had they been apprised of all the material facts, and they suffered damages as a result of their purchase.

A.

Appellants argued that respondents had a duty under the Franchise Act to disclose the following facts to them before June 30, 1977: (1) That sizeable deductions would be made from the portion of the service fee returned to the local councils to pay for the administrative expenses of the Red Carpet Council system. This deduction allegedly decreased significantly the amount of money available to the franchisee for advertising purposes; (2) that an assessment, which typically ranged between $300 and $1000 per month per franchise would be levied on appellants' franchises. This assessment in fact increased the cost of operating the Ciampi franchises by $1280 a month; (3) that if Red Carpet did not succeed in selling additional franchises in San Mateo appellants would not receive the main benefit of a Red Carpet franchise, to wit, the benefit of pooling their resources and business knowledge with other local brokers; (4) that Red Carpet would not finance the "big splash" promotion but instead would reimburse appellants for some of their expenses in arranging a "big splash"; (5) that this reimbursement would be made from the $1000 per franchise Red Carpet had obligated itself to deposit in the local council's reserve account when the franchises opened rather than in addition to this amount; (6) that Red Carpet would not advance funds for franchise office signs but instead would reimburse franchisees who purchased and installed acceptable signs at their offices; (7) that the video equipment and training tapes promised appellants would not be made available free of charge; (8) that unless Red Carpet succeeded in selling additional franchises in San Mateo, no training programs would be held in San Mateo but would instead be held at less convenient (from appellants' perspective) locations in the greater Bay Area; and (9) that Red Carpet had not contributed money to local councils in the past and had no intention of contributing such funds in the future.

Respondents introduced evidence that appellants had been apprised of most of these facts before the contracts were executed. They introduced evidence that appellants had read and initialed provisions in the contracts to the effect that the entire agreement of the parties was embodied in the contract and that no additional representations had been made by the franchisor's sales agents. They argued to the jury that they had satisfied their obligations under the Franchise Act by making the requisite disclosures to appellants before the contract became binding on July 29, 1977. . . .

The Franchise Act requires the franchisor to deliver a copy of the prospectus and franchise agreement at least 48 hours before the prospective franchisee manifests his intention to buy the franchise. . . . It provides that a civil action can be brought against any person "who offers or sells" a franchise without submitting a complete and accurate application to the Commissioner of Corporations. . . . "Offer" is defined as "includ[ing] every attempt to dispose of, or solicitation of an offer to buy, a franchise or interest in a franchise for value."

[2] . . . Respondents argue that . . . the franchisor . . . can comply with the section by delivering the requisite documents regardless of any inaccuracies contained therein. Under the interpretation of the Franchise Act suggested by respondents, the franchisor can comply . . . as long as the requisite disclosures are made to the prospective franchisee before the contract is formally executed. If respondents' position were adopted, a franchisor could submit a misleading prospectus to a prospective franchisee who in reliance thereon might make substantial expenditures to qualify as a franchisee (e.g., closing existing businesses, buying or leasing space for the franchise outlet, borrowing funds, etc.). The franchisor could put off disclosing the more unpleasant truths about the investment until the prospective franchisee had strong economic incentives not to withdraw from the contract. The franchisor would suffer no liability under the Franchise Act so long as the requisite disclosures were made before the contract was formally executed regardless of the amount of damage caused the prospective franchisee.

[3] [4] [5] . . . Logically, . . . the Franchise Act . . . must reasonably be understood to require that the franchisor be in compliance with the provisions of that section when it first contacts the prospective franchisee about its franchises. In this case, potential liability for violations . . . attached when respondents met with appellants . . . to discuss the sale of the Red Carpet franchises. . . . While subsequent disclosures might affect the amount of damages caused a prospective franchisee, such disclosures cannot be used to avoid liability . . .

B.

In their sixth cause of action appellants sought to recover for damages caused by alleged misrepresentations and omissions of material facts made by the franchise salesmen and found in the advertising materials they claimed they received . . .

[21] [22] The clear and stated purpose of the Franchise Act is to discourage franchisors and their agents from misrepresenting the nature of the franchise to prospective investors. This purpose would be ill served if the franchisor could avoid responsibility for misrepresentations by inserting a standard integration clause into a contract drafted by the franchisor. Contract law abounds with examples of individuals who have signed contracts containing such provisions not believing that the provisions would be enforced. The law is generally reluctant to permit them to deny the validity of those provisions at a later date. . . . The Legislature, however, intended to provide greater protection for prospective franchisees. . . . [The Act] must, therefore, be understood to void such provisions for purposes of determining liability under the Franchise Act. . . .

Case Reflections

1. What does the Franchise Act require? Why did Ciampi claim Red Carpet violated this Act?
2. Red Carpet claimed that it complied with the Franchise Act through the use of an "integra tion clause." What does this integration clause allow Red Carpet to do?
3. How did the Appellate Court rule in this case? What was the reasoning behind its decision?

PART

4

LEGAL ASPECTS OF REAL ESTATE DEVELOPMENT

CHAPTER 16

LAND USE REGULATION

LEARNING OBJECTIVES

After reading this chapter, you should be able to:

1. Understand the distinctions between private and public methods of land use control.
2. List and define each of the four major types of public land use controls.
3. Describe the effects of the Fifth Amendment and Fourteenth Amendment to the U.S. Constitution on the process of land use control.
4. List and define each of the basic elements of a zoning ordinance.
5. Understand the role that maps play in the implementation of land use plans and how zoning statutes and maps are "living" documents.
6. Distinguish between regulation of land use under the police powers of the states and taking private property for public benefit through the use of eminent domain.

KEY TERMS

Deed Restriction
Subdivision Covenant
Neighborhood Associations
Community Association
Police Power
Zoning Ordinance
Variance
Special Exceptions
Nonconforming Use
Rent Control
Eminent Domain
"Takings" Issue
Inverse Condemnation
Transfer Development Rights

Land use law in the U.S. is a complex web of rules and regulations, which are loosely strung between the pillars of constitutional law. The intricate structures of land use law were formed over centuries of strife and conflict. Property owners, who want complete freedom to use their land and buildings, represent one side of the conflict. A shifting constellation of interest groups formed at various times to represent particular public interests in the use of real property takes the opposing side of the struggle.

Land use restrictions generally fall into one of two broad groupings. Private land use control methods represent the earliest efforts to adjust the rights of individual landowners to the needs and desires of a community. Deed restrictions, subdivision covenants, and similar arrangements between individual landowners compose the first of these two groups. During the twentieth century, the rise of great cities has brought with it problems and difficulties that were not anticipated by the creators of private land use restrictions. These new challenges gave rise to a new group of public land use control techniques. The public land use control arsenal includes zoning ordinances, comprehensive master plans, development permits, and a host of other tools.

Finally, a third group of land use regulations is beginning to emerge from the public land use control group. This emerging category includes environmental and public safety regulations, historic preservation requirements, and similar measures.

In this chapter, we begin by looking at the historical development of land use regulation. We then examine the current state of the art. The chapter concludes with an analysis of some of the emerging trends in land use law.

PRIVATE LAND USE CONTROL METHODS

Most private restrictions on the use of property are created by placing the restrictions in a deed. For example, when a developer buys a forty-acre parcel of farm land and creates a housing subdivision on it, the deed to each lot might contain a standard set of covenants. By accepting the deed, the grantee will agree to use the property only for residential purposes, to permit only one structure to be built on the lot, and so forth. The purpose of the **deed restrictions** is to promote a harmonious, esthetically pleasing development, which will enhance the value of each of the lots in the development.

Deed Restrictions Provisions in individual deeds or for subdivisions which place restrictions on the use, development, and constuction of the premises.

The English courts were originally of two minds in interpreting deed convenants like the ones just described. If the court determined that the convenants were such that "touch and concern the land," then the covenants would be enforced as "covenants real." That is, the burden of the covenant, similar to the burden of an easement, would run with the land. The grantee whose deed contained the covenants and all subsequent grantees in the chain of title would be bound by the covenants in the original deed.

If the court determined that the restrictions were a matter of personal agreement between the grantor and grantee named in the deed, a different result was reached. Only those grantees who claimed title under a deed containing the covenants would be bound by them. When any grantee reconveyed the property to a subsequent owner, the convenants would lapse, unless they were included in the new deed. Whenever the covenants were left out of a deed (either intentionally or by mistake), the protective covenants became unenforceable.

In Chapter 13 we discussed the obligation of the seller, or the seller's agent, to disclose material facts concerning a property to potential buyers. Is the existence of restrictive covenants a material fact which must be disclosed? In *Large v. Cafferty Realty, Inc.* (851 P.2d 972, 1993) the court reversed a lower court ruling which had provided protection for the seller and his agent based on the concept of statutory constructive notice. This concept is based upon the notion that information about restrictive covenants, because they are a part of the public record, is equally available to buyers and sellers. The court held, however, that when the seller knows, or has reason to know, that the buyer does not know of the existence of covenants which make the property unsuitable for the buyer's purposes, then the seller or the seller's agent has an affirmative obligation to reveal this information.

SUBDIVISION REGULATIONS

The English courts had a disturbing tendency to view deed covenants as personal agreements between the grantor and grantee in the deed containing the covenants. In addition, American courts were often willing to follow these precedents. As a result, developers began to look for more reliable methods to maintain the esthetic qualities that enhance the value of their homes.

Subdivision covenants turned out to be an excellent vehicle for this purpose. Instead of placing the desired covenant restrictions in each deed, the developer can put them in the public record as part of the subdivision plat. Courts are generally more willing to accept subdivision covenants as "touching and concerning the land." As a result, subdivision covenants are a more dependable means of privately regulating the development of a new housing area, although as we see in the cases, even subdivision covenants are a less than perfect method for regulating development.

Subdivision Covenant Provisions for subdivisions which place restrictions on the use, development, and construction of premises within the subdivision.

COMMUNITY ASSOCIATIONS

A major drawback to subdivision covenants is the unwillingness of courts to enforce the covenants "in perpetuity." Many subdivision regulations have been declared void by the courts because by their terms they do not expire at some ascertainable time in the future. One method developers might use to avoid this outcome is to create, in the subdivision plat, a **neighborhood association.** When the neighborhood association, composed of all the property owners in the subdivision, has the authority to amend or revoke the subdivision covenants, the perpetuity problem is circumvented. Examples of use restrictions for a community association are included as Figure 16.1.

Neighborhood Association An association composed of all property owners in a neighborhood which has the authority to amend or revoke subdivision covenants.

COMMUNITY ASSOCIATION USE RESTRICTIONS

The Properties shall be used only for residential, recreational, and related purposes (which may include, without limitation, offices for any property manager retained by the Association or business offices for the Declarant, the Association or the Club) as may more particularly be set forth in this Declaration and amendments hereto. Any Supplemental Declaration or additional covenants imposed on the property within any neighborhood may impose stricter standards than those contained in this Article. The Association, acting through its Board of Directors, shall have standing and the power to enforce the standards contained in any declaration as if the provision were a guideline of the Association.

The Association, acting through its Board of Directors, shall have the authority to make and to enforce standards and restrictions governing the use of the Properties, in addition to those contained in these Use Restrictions, and to impose reasonable user fees for use of Common Area facilities. Those regulations and use restrictions shall be binding on all Owners and occupants until and unless overruled, canceled, or modified in a regular or special meeting of the Association by the vote of Voting Members representing a majority of the total votes in the Association and by the Class "B" Member, so long as that membership shall exist. Notwithstanding anything from application of the provisions of this Article so long as the Class "B" member owns any property described on Exhibits "__" or "__" primarily for development and/or resale, the Class "B" member shall have the right to disapprove any standards or restrictions governing the use of properties. Additional restrictions of a uniform and non-discriminating character may be approved by the Association for individual Neighborhoods to take into account special circumstances within those Neighborhoods.

Section 1. Signs No sign, billboard, or advertisement of any kind, including, without limitation, those of realtors, contractors, and subcontractors, shall be erected within the Properties without the written consent of the NCC, except as may be required by legal proceedings, and except signs, regardless of size, used by Declarant, it successors and assigns, and replacement of those signs (similar or otherwise). The NCC shall not grant permission to erect signs on any Unit after such Unit is improved and sold by the builder unless their erection is reasonably necessary to avert serious hardship to the Owner. If permission is granted to any Owner to erect a sign within the Properties, the NCC reserves the right to restrict the size, color, lettering, and location of such sign. Under no circumstances shall signs, flags, banners, or similar items advertising or providing directional information for activities being conducted outside the Properties be permitted within the Properties. No sign shall be nailed or otherwise attached to trees. No "open house" signs or signs of a similar import shall be permitted.

Section 2. Parking and Vehicular Restrictions Parking in the Properties shall be restricted to private automobiles and passenger vans, and only within the parking areas designed and/or designated for that purpose. No Owner shall conduct repairs (except in an emergency) or restorations of any motor vehicle, or other vehicle upon any portion of the Properties, except in an enclosed area with the doors to that area closed at all times.

No commercial vehicles, or campers, mobile homes, motorhomes, house trailers or trailers of any type, recreational vehicles, motorcycles, mopeds, boats, or vans, shall be permitted to be parked or to be stored at any place within the Properties, except in spaces for some or all of the above specifically designated by the Declarant. No Owner shall keep any vehicle on the Common Areas which is deemed a nuisance by the Board. For purposes of this Section, "commercial vehicles" shall mean those which are not designed and used for

FIGURE 16.1 COMMUNITY ASSOCIATION USE RESTRICTIONS

customary, personal/family purposes. The absence of commercial-type lettering or graphics on a vehicle shall not be dispositive of whether it is a commercial vehicle. The prohibitions on parking contained in this Section shall not apply to temporary parking of commercial vehicles such as for construction use or providing pick-up and delivery and other commercial services nor to any vehicles of the Declarant or the Club. No overnight on-street parking or parking on lawns shall be permitted.

Subject to applicable laws and ordinances, any vehicle parked in violation of these or other restrictions contained in these Use Restrictions or in the Rules and Regulations may be towed by the Association at the sole expense of the owner of the vehicle if the vehicle remains in violation for a period of 24 hours from the time a notice of violation is placed on the vehicle. The Association shall not be liable to the owner of that vehicle for trespass, conversion, or otherwise, nor guilty of any criminal act, by reason of the towing and once the notice is posted, neither its removal, nor failure of the owner to receive it for any other reason, shall be grounds for relief of any kind. For purposes of this paragraph, "vehicle" shall also mean campers, mobile homes, and trailers. An affidavit of the person posting the aforesaid notice stating that it was properly posted shall be conclusive evidence of proper posting.

Section 3. Occupants Bound All provisions of the Declaration, By-Laws, and of any Rules and Regulations or use restrictions promulgated pursuant thereto that govern the conduct of Owners and that provide for sanctions against Owners shall also apply to all occupants, guests, and invitees of any Unit. Every owner shall cause all occupants of the Owner's unit to comply with the Declaration, By-Laws, and the rules and regulations adopted pursuant thereto, and shall be responsible for all violations and losses to the Properties caused by those occupants, notwithstanding the fact that those occupants of a Unit are fully liable and may be sanctioned for any violation of the Declaration, By-Laws, and rules and regulations adopted pursuant thereto.

Section 4. Animals and Pets No animals, wildlife, livestock, reptiles, or poultry of any kind shall be raised, bred, or kept on any portion of the Properties, except that dogs, cats, or other usual and common adult household pets not to exceed a total of four (4) may be permitted in a Unit; however, limitations on pets may be more stringent within specific Neighborhoods. All pets shall be leashed when on the Common Area. Those pets which, in the sole discretion of the Association or any Neighborhood Association, endanger health, make objectionable noise, or constitute a nuisance or inconvenience to the Owners of other Units or the owner of any portion of the Properties shall be removed upon request of the Board. No pets shall be kept, bred, or maintained for any commercial purpose. Household pets shall at all times whenever they are outside a Unit be confined on a leash held by a responsible person. Pets shall only be permitted on the Common Areas if such portions thereof are so designated by the Association. All persons bringing a pet onto the Common Areas shall be responsible for immediately removing any solid waste of said pet.

Section 5. Nuisances No portion of the Properties shall be used, in whole or in part, for the storage of any property or thing that will cause it to appear to be in an unclean or untidy condition or that will be obnoxious to the eye; nor shall any substance, thing, or material be kept on any portion of the Properties that will emit foul or obnoxious odors or that will cause any noise or other condition that will or might disturb the peace, quiet, safety, comfort, or serenity of the occupants of surrounding property. No noxious, illegal or offensive activity shall be carried on upon any portion of the Properties, nor shall anything be done on the Properties tending to cause embarrassment, discomfort, annoyance, or nuisance to any person using any portion of the Properties. There shall not be maintained any plants or animals

FIGURE 16.1 COMMUNITY ASSOCIATION USE RESTRICTIONS *(continued)*

or device or thing of any sort whose activities or existence in any way is noxious, dangerous, unsightly, unpleasant, or of a nature that may diminish or destroy the enjoyment of the Properties. No outside burning of wood, leaves, trash, garbage, or household refuse shall be permitted within the Properties.

Section 6. Trash No rubbish, trash, garbage, or other waste material shall be kept or permitted on the Properties except in containers located in appropriate areas, if any, and no odor shall be permitted to arise from the containers so as to render the Properties or any portion thereof unsanitary, unsightly, offensive, or detrimental to any other property in the vicinity thereof or to its occupants. Appropriate flexibility shall be afforded food service operations, however. No clothing or household fabrics shall be hung, dried, or aired in a manner that is visible from any roadway, and no lumber, grass, shrub, or tree clippings, or trash shall be kept, stored, or allowed to accumulate on any portion of the Properties, except within an enclosed structure appropriately screened from view erected for that purpose, if any.

Section 7. Unsightly or Unkempt Conditions It shall be the responsibility of each Owner and the Club to prevent the development of any unclean, unhealthy, unsightly, or unkempt condition on his or her Unit, or the Club properties, respectively. The pursuit of hobbies or other activities, including specifically, without limiting the generality of the foregoing, the assembly and disassembly of mechanical devices, that might tend to cause disorderly, unsightly, or unkempt conditions, shall not be undertaken on any part of the Properties.

Section 8. Outside Installations No exterior antennas, aerials, satellite dishes, or other apparatus for the reception or transmission of television, radio, or other signals of any kind shall be placed, allowed, or maintained upon any portion of the Properties, including any Unit. The Declarant and/or the Association shall have the right, without obligation, to erect an aerial, satellite dish, or other apparatus for a master antenna or cable system for the benefit of all or a portion of the Properties, should master system or systems to be used by the Association require any such exterior apparatus. No radio transmissions of any kind shall be made from any building, Unit or Common Areas, except for communication equipment used by the Association and the Club.

Section 9. Subdivision of Unit and Time Sharing No Unit shall be subdivided or its boundary lines changed except with the prior written approval of the Board of Directors of the Association. The Board may permit a division in ownership of any Unit intended for a single family detached residence as shown on a Plat, but solely for the purpose of increasing the size of the Adjacent Units. In the event of a division in ownership of any Unit, the Owners among whom the ownership is divided shall be treated as co-owners of the divided Unit for purposes of voting and shall be jointly and severally liable for all assessments against the Unit hereunder. Declarant hereby expressly reserves the right to replat any Unit or Units owned by Declarant. Any such division, boundary line change, or replatting shall not be in violation of the applicable subdivision and zoning regulations.

No Unit shall be made subject to any type of time-share program, interval ownership, or similar program whereby the right to exclusive use of the Unit rotates among multiple owners or members of the program on a fixed or floating time schedule over a period of years.

Section 10. Driveways and Mailboxes All driveways and mailboxes shall be maintained in the style originally established or approved by Declarant. With respect to driveways, culverts installed therein shall be of a type and quality approved by Declarant and the grade of same shall be set by Declarant.

Section 11. Firearms The discharge of firearms within the Properties is prohibited except with the prior approval of the Board of Directors. The term "firearms" includes "B-B" guns,

FIGURE 16.1 COMMUNITY ASSOCIATION USE RESTRICTIONS (*continued*)

pellet guns, and other firearms of all types, regardless of size. Notwithstanding anything to the contrary contained herein or in the By-Laws, and Association shall not be obligated to take action to enforce this Section.

Section 12. Pools No above-ground pools shall be erected, constructed, or installed on any Unit except that above ground spas or jacuzzis may be permitted in designated Units with approval of the NCC or MC. Any in-ground pool to be constructed on any Unit shall be subject to the requirements of the MC, which include, but are not limited to the following: (a) Composition to be of material thoroughly tested and accepted by the industry for such construction; (b) Pool screening may not be visible from the street in front of the Unit; (c) All screening material shall be of a color in harmony with the exterior of the Unit. No raw aluminum color screen will be allowed.

Section 13. Irrigation No sprinkler or irrigation systems of any type that draw upon water from creeks, streams, rivers, lakes, ponds, wetlands, canals, or other ground or surface waters within the Properties shall be installed, constructed, or operated within the Properties by any Person, other than the Association and the Club, or to be utilized by any group of Units, unless prior written approval has been received from the NCC. All sprinkler and irrigation systems shall be subject to approval in accordance with Article__of this Declaration. This Section shall not apply to the Declarant, and it may not be amended without Declarant's written consent so long as Declarant has the right to add property in accordance with Article__, Section__. Declarant shall approve all irrigation systems for Neighborhoods, including one or more master irrigation wells.

Section 14. Tents, Trailers, and Temporary Structures Except as may be permitted by the NCC during initial construction within the Properties, no tent, utility shed, shack, trailer, outbuilding, basement, or other structure of a temporary nature shall be placed on any Unit.

Section 15. Wells and Drainage No private water system shall be constructed on any Unit except private irrigation wells for Single Family Units not to exceed three inches (3") in diameter approved by the NCC. Catch basins and drainage areas are for the purpose of natural flow of water only. No obstructions or debris shall be placed in these areas. No person other than Declarant or the Association may obstruct or channel the drainage flows after location and installation of drainage swales, storm sewers, or storm drains. Declarant hereby reserves for itself and the Association a perpetual easement across the Properties for the purpose of altering drainage and water flow and Declarant and the Association may require any Single Family Unit Owner or Neighborhood to treat any irrigation water which causes unsightly or unsanitary conditions.

Section 16. Tree Removal No trees shall be removed except for diseased or dead trees and trees needing to be removed to promote the growth of other trees or for safety reasons, unless approved in accordance with Article__of this Declaration. This Section shall not apply to the Club.

Section 17. Other Facilities Nothing shall be altered or constructed in or removed from the Properties, except upon the written consent of the MC.

Section 18. Insurance Rates Nothing shall be done or kept in the Common Area which will increase the rate of insurance on any property insured by the Association without the approval of the Board, nor shall anything be done or kept in any Unit which would result in the cancellation of insurance on any property insured by the Association or which would be in violation of any law.

Section 19. Sight Distance at Intersections All property located at street intersections shall be landscaped to permit safe sight across the street corners. No fence, wall, hedge,

FIGURE 16.1 COMMUNITY ASSOCIATION USE RESTRICTIONS (*continued*)

or shrub planting shall be placed or permitted to remain where it would create a traffic or sight problem.

Section 20. Utility Lines No overhead utility lines, including lines for cable television, shall be permitted within the Properties, except for temporary lines as required during construction and high voltage lines if required by law or for safety purposes.

Section 21. Air Conditioning Units Except as may be permitted by the Board or its designee, no window air conditioning units may be installed in a Unit.

Section 22. Lighting Except for seasonal decorative lights, which may be displayed between December 1 and January 10 only, all exterior lights must be approved in accordance with Article__of this Declaration.

Section 23. Artificial Vegetation, Exterior Sculpture, and Similar Items No artificial vegetation shall be permitted on the exterior of any portion of the Properties. Exterior sculpture, fountains, flags, and similar items must be approved in accordance with Article__of this Declaration; provided, however, that nothing herein shall prohibit the appropriate display of the American flag.

Section 24. Energy Conservation Equipment No solar energy collector panels or attendant hardware or other energy conservation equipment shall be constructed or installed on any Unit unless it is an integral and harmonious part of the architectural design of a structure, as determined in the sole discretion of the appropriate committee pursuant to Article___ hereof. Under no circumstances shall solar panels be installed that will be visible from any street in the Properties or from any portion of the Club properties.

Section 25. Preserves, Lakes, and Water Bodies All preserves within the Properties shall be left in their natural state and no alteration thereof or construction thereon shall be permitted. All lakes, ponds, and streams within the Properties, if any, shall be aesthetic amenities only, and no other use thereof, including, without limitation, swimming, boating, playing, or use of personal flotation devices, shall be permitted. Notwithstanding the above, the Board of Directors may permit on certain specified lakes, some boating with limitations to five (5) horsepower electric power engines and sail boats, and fishing by Owners, occupants of Units, and their accompanied guests subject to rules and regulations established by the Board. The Association shall not be responsible for any loss, damage, or injury to any person or property arising out of the authorized or unauthorized use of lakes, ponds, or streams within the Properties. This Section shall not restrict the right of the Club to permit other use of bodies of water within the Club property in connection with golf course play or other activities of the Club.

Section 26. Fences No dog runs, animal pens, or fences of any kind shall be permitted on any Unit except as approved in accordance with Article__of this Declaration.

Section 27. Business Use No trade or business may be conducted in or from any Unit, except that an Owner or occupant residing in a Unit may conduct business activities within the Unit so long as: (a) the existence or operation of the business activity is not apparent or detectable by sight, sound, or smell from outside the Unit; (b) the business activity conforms to all zoning requirements for the Properties; (c) the business activity does not involve persons coming onto the Properties who do not reside in the Properties or door-to-door solicitation of residents of the Properties; and (d) the business activity is consistent with the residential character of the Properties and does not constitute a nuisance, or a hazardous or offensive use, or threaten the security or safety of other residents of the Properties, as may be determined in the sole discretion of the Board. No garage sales shall be permitted.

FIGURE 16.1 COMMUNITY ASSOCIATION USE RESTRICTIONS (*continued*)

The terms "business" and "trade," as used in this provision, shall be construed to have their ordinary, generally accepted meanings, and shall include, without limitation, any occupation, work, or activity undertaken on an ongoing basis which involves the provision of goods or services to persons other than the provider's family and for which the provider receives a fee, compensation, or other form of consideration, regardless of whether: (i) such activity is engaged in full or part-time; (ii) such activity is intended to or does generate a profit; or (iii) a license is required therefor. Notwithstanding the above, the leasing of a Unit shall not be considered a trade or business within the meaning of this section. This section shall not apply to operation of the Club nor to any activity conducted by the Declarant with respect to its development and sale of the Properties or its use of any Units which it owns within the Properties nor to the property designated by the Declarant on any Plat as its sales office/model center location. As to this latter area, the Declarant or any purchaser of such property shall have the right, subject to applicable governmental ordinances, to utilize same for office/professional business uses.

Section 28. On-Site Fuel Storage On-site storage of gasoline or other fuels is prohibited on any part of the Properties, with the exception of up to five (5) gallons of fuel stored on each Unit for emergency purposes and operation of lawn mowers or similar tools or equipment; and the Association and the Club will be permitted to store fuel for operation of maintenance vehicles, generators, and similar equipment. Notwithstanding this provision, underground fuel tanks for storage of heating fuel for dwellings, pools, gas grills, and similar equipment may be permitted if approved in accordance with Article__.

Section 29. Golf Carts No gasoline-powered golf carts shall be operated within the Properties except as may be owned and operated by the Declarant, the Association, or the Club. All other golf carts shall be powered by electricity or by similar noncombustion means. Golf carts shall be stored only in garages serving the Owner's Unit or other areas specifically designed by the board as golf cart parking areas. No golf cart shall be placed, parked, or stored on the lawn of any Unit. No golf cart shall be operated on other than designated golf cart paths. All Owners shall register the golf carts with the Association (unless same have been leased from the Club) and shall keep same in good order and repair. No child under the age of sixteen (16) shall be permitted to operate a golf cart on the Properties.

Section 30. Leasing of Units (a) *Definition.* "Leasing," for purposes of this Declaration, is defined as regular, exclusive occupancy of a Unit by any person or persons other than the Owner for which the Owner receives any consideration or benefit, including, but not limited to a fee, service, gratuity, or emolument. (b) *Leasing Provisions.* (i) *General.* Units may be rented only in their entirety; no fraction or portion may be rented. There shall be no subleasing of Units or assignment of leases unless prior written approval is obtained from the Board of Directors. No transient tenants may be accommodated in a Unit. All leases shall be in writing except with the prior written consent of the Board of Directors. No Unit may be subject to more than one (1) lease in any twelve- (12-) month period, regardless of the lease term. The Owner must make available to the lessee copies of the Declaration, By-Laws, and the Rules and Regulations. (ii) *Compliance with Declaration, By-Laws, and Rules and Regulations.* Every Owner shall cause all occupants of his or her Unit to comply with the Declaration, By-Laws, and the Rules and Regulations adopted pursuant thereto, and shall be responsible for all violations and losses to the Common Areas caused by such occupants, notwithstanding the fact that such occupants of a Unit are fully liable and may be sanctioned for any violation of the Declaration, By-Laws, and Rules and Regulations adopted pursuant thereto. All leases of Units shall be automatically deemed to include a covenant on the part

FIGURE 16.1 COMMUNITY ASSOCIATION USE RESTRICTIONS (*continued*)

of the tenant to comply with, and be fully bound by, the provision of this Declaration and the Rules and Regulations of the Association. This Section shall also apply to Subleases of Units and assignments of leases.

Section 31. Storm Precautions No hurricane or storm shutters shall be permanently installed on any structure on a Unit unless first approved in accordance with Article__hereof. Hurricane or storm shutters may be installed temporarily, and other storm precautions may be taken to protect structures on a Unit, while the threat of a hurricane or similar storm is imminent; provided, all such shutters and other exterior alterations or additions made as a storm precaution shall be promptly removed once the storm or imminent threat of the storm has passed.

Section 32. Play Equipment, Strollers, Etc. All bicycles, tricycles, scooters, skateboards, and other play equipment, wading pools, baby strollers, and similar items shall be stored so as not to be visible from streets or property adjacent to the Unit. No such items shall be allowed to remain on the Common Area or on Units so as to be visible from adjacent property when not in use. Notwithstanding the above, the Board may, but shall not be obligated to, permit swing sets and similar permanent playground equipment to be erected on Units provided it is approved in accordance with Article__hereof.

Section 33. Basketball and Baseball Equipment No basketball hoops, backboards, or baseball cages shall be permitted.

Section 34. Window Coverings Reflective window coverings are prohibited. No awnings, canopies, or shutters shall be permanently installed on the exterior of any building unless first approved by the NCC or MC.

Section 35. Unit Maintenance Each Unit Owner undertakes or must designate a responsible firm or individual to undertake his general maintenance responsibilities, which responsibilities shall include, at a minimum, maintaining the exterior appearance of the Unit, safeguarding the Unit to prepare for hurricane or tropical storm watches and warnings by, among other things, removing any unfixed items on balconies and lanais, and repairing the Unit in the event of any damage therefrom. An Owner may designate a firm or individual to perform such functions for the Owner, but such designation shall not relieve the Owner of any responsibility hereunder. The name(s) and addresses of such firm or individual must be furnished to the Association. The designation of such firm or individual shall be subject to the approval of the Association.

Source: Judith H. Regan, "Sample Use Restrictions for a Community Association," The Practical Real Estate Lawyer, January 1993, pp. 83–93.

FIGURE 16.1 COMMUNITY ASSOCIATION USE RESTRICTIONS (*continued*)

Community Association An association composed of all property owners in a neighborhood, condominium or cooperative housing development which has the authority to amend or revoke covenants.

Community associations play an even stronger role in the management of condominium and cooperative housing developments. In these developments, the owners each have a fee simple absolute title to a defined air space unit within the development. In addition, the individual owners hold the common areas of the property (the roof, hallways, and grounds) as tenants in common. The common ownership of the real estate outside the individual air space units requires an active management structure.

Condominium associations, similar to cooperative housing corporations, draw their membership from the owners of the air space units. The associations are empowered to make decisions concerning assessments for maintenance and repairs in the common areas as well as to develop rules for the use of the common areas by owners and their guests. In addition, it is not uncommon for the bylaws of an owner's association to permit the adoption of rules concerning certain uses of the individual air space units.

It is not uncommon for subdivisions to have restrictive covenants relating to aesthetic considerations. Homeowner's associations, to enforce these restrictions, often employ an architectural review committee whose approval is needed prior to commencing construction on any home in the subdivision. Although the notion of architectural review is a generally accepted one, in *Point Farm Homeowner's Association, Inc. v. Evans* (1993 WL 257404 (Del. Ch.)) the court ruled in favor of a owner who began construction of a home without approval when the architectural review board objected to her use of vinyl siding. The court ruled that ". . . to the extent that architectural review is 'based on purely aesthetical considerations,' that review is considered arbitrary and capricious and therefore not reasonable." The court went on to add that "where the language used in the restrictive covenant empowering the committee is overly vague, imprecise, or so unclear as not to lend itself to even-handed application, then the grant of authority is normally not enforceable."

For example, many associations have attempted to prevent owners from owning pets or to exclude people below a certain age from occupancy in an air space unit. (The so-called adults-only developments.) Because the bylaws of community associations generally make the decision of a majority of owners binding upon all owners, prospective purchasers in these developments must study the association rules carefully.

At times, the decisions of community associations (or the requirements of subdivision covenants) may come into conflict with the U.S. Constitution or federal laws. For example, suppose that one of the covenants in a subdivision prohibits the sale of any lot to a black person. Under the Fourteenth Amendment, all Americans are entitled to the equal protection of the laws in any state. A number of cases have challenged subdivision covenants and association regulations that exclude members of a minority race from ownership.

The courts have been supportive of these challenges, although the private nature of the restrictions has caused judges some difficulty in dealing with the issue. The Constitution is generally construed as a document that limits the activity of government alone. Although states (and the federal government) are empowered by the U.S. Constitution to make laws that control the conduct of individuals, the Constitution itself is generally understood to apply only to the conduct of governmental bodies.

The earliest challenges to racial exclusivity were defended on exactly that basis. The proponents of racially exclusive subdivision covenants argued that the Constitution cannot prohibit individuals from deciding whom they choose to associate with, especially in the neighborhoods where the individuals doing the choosing reside. The Supreme Court met that argument with an elegant counterargument.

Shelley v. Kraemer

The Supreme Court agreed that racially exclusive private covenants were not violative of the equal protection clause of the Fourteenth Amendment. Enforcement of these covenants by a state or federal court, however, would violate the Constitution. The Supreme Court concluded that judicial enforcement of a racially exclusive covenant constitutes "state action," which violates the equal protection clause and is thus unconstitutional. In subsequent decisions, the Supreme Court has expanded this doctrine. Constitutional law now recognizes that the activities of private associations that have governmental approval or sanction can have a "chilling effect" on the exercise of the Constitutional rights of individuals. Because subdivisions and community associations are both recognized and sanctioned by local governments, any covenants that interfere with the rights of protected minorities are not only unenforceable, but also void under this interpretation of the Constitution.

PUBLIC LIMITATIONS ON LAND USE

We now turn our attention to the major issue in land use regulation, that of public control methods. As we have seen, even essentially private agreements may be subject to societal review by the court system. In the public arena, land use regulations are by definition the action of a governmental body. For that reason, these actions are the subject of more stringent constitutional review. Most issues in this area revolve around challenges based on either the Fourteenth Amendment, which guarantees due process of law, or the Fifth Amendment, which prohibits the government from "taking" private property for public use without just compensation. On occasion, however, issues of freedom of religion and free speech also become involved, especially when dealing with church property.

Public powers flow from one of four basic sources: (1) the police power to protect the public health, safety, and general welfare; (2) the power of eminent domain to take private property for public use with just compensation; (3) the power to tax; and (4) the power of the government, known as escheat, to claim property when an individual dies intestate (i.e., without a will) and no heirs can be located. Although the powers of taxation and escheat are important, the discussion in this chapter fo-

KEY POINTS

Restrictive covenants, like those discussed earlier in this chapter, are different and separate from zoning ordinances. When a private covenant is more restrictive than the zoning ordinance, the covenant will prevail. The zoning ordinance, however, remains enforceable, and the covenants do not change the requirements of a zoning ordinance. By the same token, activities permitted by covenants, but not allowed under current zoning laws, would not be permissible. In some instances, cities have tried to tie the two types of limitations together. This is sometimes done by making a zoning decision conditional on restrictions being placed in a deed or agreement. This practice falls into a category known as "contract" or "conditional" zoning, which, because such actions destroy the requirement for uniform treatment under the law since the restrictions would not apply to everyone in the zoning district, are prohibited.

cuses on eminent domain takings issues, police power regulatory issues, and the often gray area between them.

The most well-known application of **police power** in the land use regulation area is that of zoning. One central issue in zoning regulation is the applicability of language in the Fifth Amendment and Fourteenth Amendment of the Constitution. The Fourteenth Amendment states, in part, "[no person] shall be deprived of life, liberty or property without due process of law." The Fifth Amendment states, in part, "private property [shall not] be taken for public use without just compensation." The exact meaning of these words, when they are applied to zoning ordinances and other public land use regulations, has been extensively litigated.

Police Power The power of the government to protect the public health, safety, and general welfare.

During the 1920s, as **zoning ordinances** were first adopted by many cities, developers challenged the new ordinances on Fourteenth Amendment grounds. The argument was that zoning regulations that prohibit an owner from building an apartment house or factory on his or her property deprived the owner of a valuable property right without due process of law. The Supreme Court developed a two-prong test for dealing with this argument. To be valid, zoning ordinances must offer both substantive and procedural due process to the citizens of the community.

Zoning Ordinance Local ordinance which defines uses permitted in each zone, types of conditional uses, how zoning changes are to be made, and the appeals process which may be followed.

Substantive due process is usually measured using a "three-prong" test,[1] which requires that:

1. State regulations must advance the interests of the public generally, rather than those of a particular group or class.
2. The method used to accomplish the public purpose must be reasonably necessary.
3. The results must not be unduly burdensome on individuals.

Some have summarized this test as one in which the end must justify the means, and both the end and the means must be appropriate and proper.

The Supreme Court has no trouble agreeing that the public health, safety, and welfare are legitimate state interests and that cities can adopt regulations that advance these interests. Second, zoning regulations are required to be "reasonably necessary" for the maintenance of the legitimate state interests identified in the first part of the test. The Supreme Court generally permits state legislatures and city councils to decide what kinds of regulation are reasonably necessary for the promotion of legitimate state interests. Zoning regulations that pass muster on these two conditions will be deemed to provide substantive due process.

The second prong of the Supreme Court test is known as procedural due process. Procedural due process exists when two conditions are met. The first is that all property owners whose rights will be affected by a zoning ordinance must be informed of the proposed regulations before they take affect. In addition, property owners must be given the opportunity to appear before the decision-making body and state their case for or against the proposed regulations. The second requirement for procedural due process is an appeals procedure. A forum must be provided for property owners to appear and complain that a zoning regulation has been applied to them in an unreasonable or inappropriate manner.

[1]This test was developed in *Lawton v. Steele* [152 U.S. 133 (1894)] and is sometimes known simply as the Lawton test.

Zoning ordinances that afford both procedural and substantive due process to land owners will be deemed to be legitimate exercises of the "police power." Police power is the generic name for the right of states and cities to regulate the conduct of their citizens. Laws prohibiting murder, theft, and assault are all clear examples of the police power of the state. Zoning ordinances that provide both procedural and substantive due process will be placed in the same constitutional category as the criminal laws of the state or city.

A second attack against zoning regulations was made by referring to the Fifth Amendment, "private property [shall not] be taken for public use without just compensation." In the early years of zoning statutes, many developers claimed that the statutes resulted in a taking of their property by the state in order to promote the general welfare. These developers argued that because their property rights had been taken for a public use (general welfare), the city must pay just compensation, even if the zoning ordinance provides both substantive or procedural due process. This argument has proved to be a great deal more troublesome.

If a city condemns a forty-foot strip of land along the edge of a property owner's parcel and uses the land to build a public street, we should have no difficulty agreeing that the city must pay the owner for land it took. This is exactly the kind of taking of private property for public use of which the Fifth Amendment speaks. Suppose a developer comes to the city and asks to rezone a forty-acre parcel of farm land from agricultural zoning to residential zoning. Suppose further that the city agrees to rezone the land only if the developer will dedicate three forty-foot strips of land within the parcel for public streets. Is the city required to pay for the land dedicated by the developer for streets in the proposed subdivision? Surprisingly, the answer is no. Streets are a necessary part of the proposed subdivision development. Simply requiring the developer to include the streets in the planning and construction of the subdivision is an exercise of the city's police power.

From this example, we can see that the difference between the exercise of a city's police power (which does not require compensation to the property owner) and the taking of private property for public use (which does require compensation) is not easy to discover. Even when title to the property is transferred from a private owner to a public owner (as the streets in the subdivision will be), a taking has not necessarily occurred. In general, the Supreme Court has indicated that cities will be required to compensate landowners in only two situations:

1. The owner is deprived of any reasonable use of all (or substantially all) of the parcel.
2. The public use required of the property has no rational relationship to the legitimate state interests the city may advance under the use of its police power.

Virtually all land use regulations are based on the use of the police power of the state. This power enables the state, on behalf of its citizenry, to regulate the use of property when necessary to protect the health, safety, and general welfare of the public. In many instances, these regulations are clearly necessary and rarely challenged. The use of building codes and fire codes to ensure safe building methods, for example, is clearly necessary to protect the public. The concept of zoning, however, is often more controversial. By its very nature, the process of developing a master plan for a community and implementing it through zoning ordinances will create some "winners" and some "losers" among property owners. Although the community as a whole will benefit from such a process, some individuals will benefit far more than others. In the American scheme of things, this is simply a result of the "luck of the draw."

If a land use regulation system confers financial benefits on some owners and financial burdens on others, it seems logical that a means of transferring gains to those who suffer losses ought to be possible. This appealing concept is one with a fairly long, although unsuccessful, history.

"Worsenment" and "Betterment"

In the U.S., the primary controversies involving land use controls have generally been those surrounding proper definitions of due process and takings. We tend to think of an imaginary line that divides legitimate regulatory constraints under the police power of the state from restrictions that "go too far" and amount to a taking of the property being regulated. The majority of court decisions and the analytical efforts of researchers in the area have been attempts to define and redefine the position of this line.

The British approach to land use regulation involves a different concept. Because the British experiments occurred during roughly the same time as the American experience, they may provide some valuable insights. The British approach began with the passing of the Housing, Town Planning, Act of 1909. This act of Parliament combined city planning, zoning, and subdivision concepts into a single statute. The British were primarily concerned with devising a scheme that would not redistribute property wealth as a result of the planning process. Under the 1909 Act, local agencies were empowered to "recover from any person whose property is so increased in value one-half of the amount of that increase" caused by "the making of the town planning scheme."[2] The act balanced this by providing that any person "whose property is injuriously affected by the making of the town planning scheme shall . . . be entitled to obtain compensation."

Over the following sixty years, the act was refined and amended many times. Similar acts were also passed in several Canadian provinces, in several Australian states, and in New Zealand. None of them ever worked. This failure was caused by the simple fact that virtually no "betterment" gains were ever collected. Thus with no available funds, virtually no "worsenment" compensations were provided either. The failure, however, was not for want of effort. In typical British fashion, a commission was appointed to study the issue during 1941 and 1942 by the Churchill government. Meeting underground to avoid the Luftwaffe bombing raids, the Commission went on to make numerous revisions to the Act, which was amended and remained in place until the Thatcher administration. Even these efforts, however, failed to produce any significant results.

Although the British approach has a loyal following in the U.S., no similar legislation has ever been passed or even considered. As we shall see, however, some elements of the "betterment and worsenment" approach seem to have found their way into the American system of land use controls.

---

[2]See "Worsenment Mitigation and Betterment Recapture: The Issues in Historical Perspective" by Dean Misczynski, Chapter 1 in Joseph DiMento, ed., *Wipeouts and Their Mitigation.* Lincoln Institute of Land Policy, Cambridge, MA, 1990.

Zoning Basics

Until the late nineteenth century, virtually no formal land use controls existed in the U.S. The rapid expansion of urban areas after the Civil War increased the pressure to deal with mounting urban problems. Boston and Washington, D.C., along with several other cities, were the first to pass legislation regulating maximum tenement lot coverage and heights of buildings. In the early years of the twentieth century, a group known as the "Fifth Avenue Association" in New York City became concerned that the continued mixing of land uses threatened their retail business. This group of retailers pushed the nation's first comprehensive zoning ordinance through the New York City Council in 1916.

As zoning statutes spread across the U.S., a need for some type of uniformity developed. In response, the Department of Commerce drafted the *Standard State Zoning Enabling Act* in the 1920s, which has since been adopted, at least in part, by most states.

The basic purposes of zoning regulations are to avoid mixing "incompatible" uses; reduce crowding and building densities; and help promote the public health, safety, and general welfare. To accomplish this, most zoning ordinances cover at least the following subjects.

Permitted Uses

By dividing all potential land uses into categories, the most popular being dwellings, businesses, and industries (which are then generally divided into a series of subdivisions), uses that are thought to be incompatible are kept apart. For example, it seems reasonable to assume that mixing residential property with heavy industry in the same neighborhood would reduce the property values of both types, although for different reasons. Residential areas should be quiet and safe from hazards to residents. The presence of noisy trucks and equipment necessary for industrial operations would make an area less desirable for residential purposes. Industries operate best in areas where truck traffic and operating machines will be unlikely to injure children at play. In this instance, keeping these uses separate is in everyone's best interests.

Some zoning ordinances are cumulative, or "pyramidal," so that "higher" ranked uses are permitted in lower ranked areas. The usual rank order is residential (the highest rank), followed by commercial, and then industrial uses. The cumulative scheme is also applied within general categories. For example, single-family residential would be ranked higher than multi-family apartment houses. Thus a single-family residence, as the top-ranked use in the top-ranked category, could be located almost anywhere. To avoid the potential problems that can develop under such a system, many zoning ordinances are noncumulative, or exclusive, so only permitted uses are allowed in any zone.

Population Densities

Most ordinances limit population densities by establishing minimum lot sizes for dwellings. Larger cities have developed more elaborate regulations concerning multi-family developments.

Building Bulk

By requiring minimum yards along each lot boundary and by requiring structures to be set back a minimum distance from the lot line, the bulk of buildings is regulated. In commercial areas, the use of "floor-area" ratios and "usable open space" measures is common. Both are designed to allow the fairly dense development required in urban areas without overloading the traffic, water, and sewer systems. In highly developed areas, such as New York City, buildings must "step back" from the street as they go higher to allow sunlight to reach street level.

Offstreet Parking

Virtually all zoning ordinances require the provision of offstreet parking spaces in proportion to the type and density of use on a site. This avoids the additional public expense of providing wider streets and improves traffic flow. As with many aspects of zoning ordinances, public safety is a major issue with offstreet parking requirements. Highly congested streets are not only dangerous for pedestrians, but also they make it difficult for fire, ambulance, and police vehicles to get through.

Other Subjects

In addition to these basic elements, many zoning ordinances address such subjects as landscaping and other appearance items, sign placement and size, and even the preservation of scenic views and access to sunlight.

Zoning Maps

Maps are often used as a method to allow city planners and residents to visualize the relationship of various land uses. For most people, a visual depiction of spatial relationships provides a better understanding of the process used to create zoning districts. By the same token, zoning maps will also quickly highlight instances of poor planning, such as scattered, or fragmented, zones.

A zoning statute is the implementation phase of a general city planning process. For a zoning program to withstand challenges, it must be based on a rational, logical plan that was the result of a process that allowed adequate public input. A failure to address legitimate public needs or a failure to allow those needs to be articulated will often leave a plan and the zoning process that flows from it open to a "due process" challenge.

A zoning statute, like most laws, is a "living" document that requires continual interpretation and revision. The basics of zoning implementation are accomplished through a simple application of the statute by issuing, or refusing to issue, building permits. This system, however, is inadequate to address the challenges and disputes that frequently arise.

Appeals

In most states, each locality has a zoning board of appeals (sometimes called a board of adjustment) to hear appeals from zoning applicants. The appeal may result from a refusal to issue a building permit or from a refusal to authorize a different zoning for a particular parcel. The person requesting relief from a ruling may argue that the zoning administrator was mistaken or that the administrator has acted in an unreasonable, arbitrary, or capricious manner. As a general rule, all available "administrative remedies" must be exhausted before initiating a court suit. Remember, however, that zoning boards may only review and interpret the statutes as they currently exist. They are not empowered to alter the requirements or make exceptions except in certain situations.

Variances

Variance When a strict application of zoning requirements would create a hardship through no fault of the proprty owner, a variance may be granted with regard to specific zoning requirements.

Because zoning statutes are general procedures, they cannot anticipate every combination of circumstances that might arise. Land is infinitely varied in its terrain and features. Not all building sites, for example, allow for the exact placement of setbacks and side yards as specified by the statute. When a strict application of the zoning rules would result in an "unnecessary" or "undue" hardship owing to "unique circumstances," a **variance** may be requested. This variance power is generally administered by the same appeals board. Variances, however, should not be thought of as "exceptions" to the rules. A board may not, for example, allow an excluded use in a zone simply because it will be more profitable than the permitted use.

Special Exceptions

Special Exceptions An exception to normal zoning requirements, usually called "conditional uses", granted by a board of adjustment.

There are some instances, however, in which actual exceptions may be made. These exceptions, generally known as "conditional uses" or "special uses," follow a set of rules defined in the zoning statute. For example, churches or child care centers may be allowed in residential zones. The idea in using **special exceptions** is not to allow total freedom to the zoning board in determining what types or densities of uses should be allowed but rather to anticipate the need for a certain degree of flexibility in administering the statute.

Amendments

As cities grow and change, the original plan and zoning map may no longer be appropriate. Thus zoning statutes provide mechanisms to allow for continual reappraisal and, when necessary, changes. Similar to the process used to create the original zoning map, any "rezonings" must follow substantive procedures that allow for due process. This normally means notice to all potentially affected persons and public hearings.

Nonconforming Uses

Nonconforming Use A use that does not comply with the current zoning requirements but that existed prior to the time the zoning became effective.

As a general rule, legislation may not be retroactively enforced. Thus any uses in existence before the enactment of a zoning statute or a revision to the statute may continue to be used as **nonconforming uses.** Most statutes prohibit substantial expansion of such uses, do not allow nonconforming uses to be rebuilt if substantially destroyed, and may even require that they be "phased out" over some specified time period.

Zoning Applications

The general zoning approach has led to numerous applications and issues that constantly alter the framework of land use regulation. Some of the major issues that are a function of the zoning process are briefly described here.

Accessory Uses

The basic premise of zoning is that only certain uses are to be permitted in each zone. Modern business and technology, however, continually redefine the character of many uses, forcing zoning administrators to evaluate requests for what are called "accessory uses." For example, one case involved a dispute over the leasing of a 30,000-gallon liquid petroleum tank to a cooperative owned by local farmers in an area zoned for "general farming and accessory uses customarily incidental to general farming."[3]

Adult Uses

Two basic approaches have been used in this area. The first requires a concentration of adult establishments to create districts such as the infamous "combat zone" in Boston. The more popular approach, however, is to foster dispersal by requiring location in general commercial zones but not within a specified distance from a school, church, park, residential area, or other adult business.

Billboards and Signs

Most zoning ordinances have special provisions relating to the size and placement of signs for both on-premises and off-premises advertising. Overly restrictive ordinances, however, can be challenged on a takings claim.[4]

Dedications

One approach with growing popularity requires that developers, as a condition for obtaining approval for building permits, dedicate land for public uses, such as sidewalks, streets, and parks. Many dedication requirements provide that the improvements be put in place before dedication to the municipality. The use of dedications, however, has come under more scrutiny lately after the 1987 Nollan[5] case, in which the Supreme Court held that a public easement of passage on a beach could not be demanded as a condition for giving beachfront owners permission to enlarge their properties.

---

[3]*Farmington Township v. High Plains Cooperative* [460 N.W.2d 56 (Minn. App. 1990)].

[4]See *Georgia Outdoor Advertising, Inc. v. City of Waynesville* [900 F.2d 783 (4th Cir. 1990)], in which an ordinance that effectively prohibited all off-premises outdoor advertising signs in the city was held to be invalid.

[5]*Nollan v. California Costal Commission* [483 U.S. 825, 107 S.Ct. 3141].

Environmental Regulations

Local governments in locations that contain environmentally sensitive areas, such as beaches or wetlands, have enacted stringent regulations that must be adhered to by property owners. This is an area of growing controversy, especially in those cases in which "conservation" zones have been established that effectively prohibit any development. The Supreme Court heard a case involving conservation zoning during the 1992 term. In light of its recent rulings in similar cases, we expect the Supreme Court to find that a compensable taking has occurred.

Social Zoning

Village of Belle Terre v. Boraas

Regulations in this area cover a multitude of situations but generally relate to some notion of "family." Much attention in this area has been focused on the 1974 *Village of Belle Terre v. Boraas* [416 U.S. 1], in which a regulation that prohibited households consisting of more than two unrelated individuals was upheld by the Supreme Court. A related, and perhaps a more difficult, issue is that of group homes for the mentally retarded that seek to be located in single-family residential areas. Even more controversial are "prerelease" facilities for prison inmates.

Historic Preservation

Penn Central Tranportation Co. v. City of New York

The concept of historic preservation through land use regulation has been controversial since its inception. The general concept received a major boost when the Supreme Court, in *Penn Central Transportation Co. v. City of New York* [438 U.S. 104 (1978)], upheld the basic constitutionality of historic preservation land use regulations. This area, however, is highly complex because it involves not only exterior regulations, which prohibit demolishing or altering historic structures, but also, in a growing number of areas, interior regulations, which extend to the inside of structures.

In addition to the due process and takings issues, historic preservation regulations also bump into freedom of religion issues. Thus, on one basis or another, historic preservation regulations are almost constantly under assault. The future of the historic preservation movement, although well established, appears to be in some jeopardy based on some recent state rulings[6] and some analogies to the First English case, discussed later.

Special Districts

In an approach that combines some of the features of social zoning with historic preservation regulations, a few cities have begun to create "special districts" designed to protect neighborhoods threatened by change. New York City, for example, has 37 separate special districts, such as the Theater District, Fifth Avenue, Little Italy, and the Garment District.

---

[6]See United Artists Theater Circuit, Inc. v. City of Philadelphia, Philadelphia Historic Commission (595 A.2d C, 1991).

Vested Rights

At what point does a municipality lose its ability to enact changes in or enforce an existing land use regulation? Although the rules in this area are a bit complex, as a general rule, developments that have been started under an existing regulation cannot be halted by a change in the rules. In some situations, even an existing regulation may not be enforced if the municipality knew of a violation for a substantial period of time and failed to enforce its own regulations.

Moratoria

In some cases, municipalities, reacting to intense growth pressures, have instituted moratoria on new construction. Although this is a delicate area, owing to constitutional protections on our right to travel and thus live where we choose, if the municipality can show that the moratorium is "an integral part of the total zoning plan," temporary bans may be allowed.

Rent Control

Rent control regulations are possibly the most controversial of all police power regulations. In essence, the municipality must show that, if left alone, the market system would produce inequities for renters, so the city must intervene to protect the general welfare. Critics of this approach abound, as you might expect in a free market economic system. Advocates of the system, however, point to the many instances in which individuals, particularly retired persons on fixed incomes, have been able to stay in their residences only because of rent control.

Rent Control Ordinances which, under the police power, restrict the ability of property owners to increase rents.

EMINENT DOMAIN

As discussed earlier, the U.S. Constitution forbids the taking of private property by the government for public use without just compensation. It is common, however, for private property to be taken for public purposes, such as the building of roads, schools, and other public projects. So long as a "legitimate" public interest is advanced by the taking and just compensation is paid the former owner(s) of the property, the process is simply an exercise of the power of **eminent domain** through the process, or act, of condemnation.

Eminent Domain The right of governmental entities to take private property for public use or benefit.

When the government sets out to take private property, there are really only two basic issues that need to be addressed. First, does the intended use of the property advance a legitimate public interest. In most instances, this is self-evident, such as in the building of public schools, fire stations, and the like. In other instances, however, there may be some debate over the need to take private property.

The urban renewal programs in the U.S. were based on the need to assemble larger tracts of land in "slum" areas, which are often characterized by small lots owned by many individuals. Redevelopment of these areas, or "slum clearance" as it was more popularly referred to, was hindered by the practical difficulties of negotiating with many owners. Once word got out, of course, the remaining owners would hold out for higher prices. This, when combined with a generally inadequate public infrastructure, made redevelopment difficult if not impossible in many urban areas.

The solution to the problem was to use the public power of eminent domain to condemn the parcels. Once acquired, the government agency would assemble the many former lots into a few large lots and use them for either public purposes (many municipal sports stadiums were built in this fashion) or, in some cases, resell them to private developers.

KEY POINTS

Although the U.S. constitutional system in the area of eminent domain has served us well, the issue of "excess takings" can be cast in a different light. In Canada, for example, the rules are somewhat different. When Montreal decided to build a rapid transit system not only was the land necessary to build the tracks and stations taken, but also additional land around the station sites. Because the construction of the rapid transit system would greatly increase the value of land surrounding the station sites, this land was resold to developers at much higher prices. The revenue raised by these sales was used to fund much of the rapid transit system construction cost. In effect, the Canadian system allows a form of "betterment" recapture to fund the public works. In the U.S. system, only the land actually needed to construct the project may be taken. Anything beyond what is strictly necessary must remain with the original owner.

Critics of the program challenged it for failing to meet the public use mandate of eminent domain. The Supreme Court, in what is now regarded as a landmark ruling, held in *Berman v. Parker* [348 U.S. 26, 99 L.Ed. 27, 75 S.Ct. 98 (1954)] that:

> The concept of the public welfare is broad and inclusive. . . . The values it represents are spiritual as well as physical, aesthetic as well as monetary. It is within the power of the

KEY POINTS

When a rapid transit authority (RTA) was constructing a new subway line through a downtown area, they dug a tunnel for the subway rather than us the more disruptive "cut and cover" technique. As a result, the RTA needed only to acquire space at street level for an entrance to the new transit station. This was done by condemning a fairly narrow site. The owner of the site objected, stating that the RTA was making a claim to fee simple ownership when, by necessity, all that were needed was the surface and subsurface rights. What the owner wanted to retain was the air rights over the new station entrance, rights that were quite valuable in a densely developed urban area. After showing that the RTA's plans for the station entrance including footings large enough to hold a thirty-story building on top of the station entrance, the site owner's objection was upheld and the RTA was allowed only to take ownership up to thirty feet above street level.

> legislature to determine that the community should be beautiful as well as healthy, spacious as well as clean, well-balanced as well as carefully patrolled. . . . Once the object is within the authority of Congress, the right to realize it through the exercise of eminent domain is clear.

This ruling was widely interpreted as expanding the notion of "public use" to include that of "public benefit" and opened the door to more creative uses of eminent domain.

"Cloud of Condemnation" Issue

One somewhat minor, but still important, issue relating to eminent domain is that of properties that have been identified as the site of some future public project but that have not yet been taken. As a general rule, property is valued for just compensation purposes as of the date of the taking. What happens, however, if, because of the label as a "future site" of, say a landfill, the property declines in market value before the actual taking?

The historical solution was that property owners are not entitled to compensation for "incidental" damages, such as those caused by the planning process. More recent rulings, however, have tended to include compensation for changes in value as a result of the impending condemnation procedure. Keep in mind, however, that this sword cuts both ways. Increases in property value owing to announced public projects would be subject to the same type of analysis.

"Takings" Issue

Takings Issue Term applied to disputes regarding the point at which police power limitations become eminent domain takings and thus require just compensation.

However, in the **takings issue,** government officials still must choose between the two basic regulatory techniques—police power limitations (with no compensation) or eminent domain (with full compensation). Faced with this choice, the obvious reaction of most politicians is to attempt to stretch the limits of police power limitations as far as possible. Before the *Pennsylvania Coal Co. v. Mahon* [260 U.S. 393 (1922)] decision, the sole constitutional restriction on police power applications was the due process clause of the Fourteenth Amendment. In the *Penn Coal* case, Justice Holmes stated that "while property may be regulated to a certain extent, if regulation goes too far it will be recognized as a taking."

This notion of "going too far" revolutionized land use regulation in a legal sense. Ever since, the emphasis in the U.S. has been on trying to define the location of the line that represents the limit of police power regulation. Many commentators have noted, however, that the test for determining substantive due process and the many tests employed at various times to define a taking essentially boil down to the same thing. Although no clear "rule" exists for evaluating taking cases, a number of theories have been developed.[7] Perhaps the most popular of these theories is the *eco-*

---

[7] For an excellent review of these theories, see Susan E. Looper-Friedman, "Constitutional Rights as Property: The Supreme Court's Solution to the 'Takings Issue.'" *Columbia Journal of Environmental Law*, January 1990.

nomic loss theory, in which a taking can be found based on a "diminution in value." Although some courts have ruled that any diminution is sufficient, most rulings are based on a denial of any "reasonable" or "viable" use of property. Courts rarely use this theory, however, without first looking at the purpose of the regulation that caused the diminution.

Another theory is that of *enterprise-arbitration,* in which economic losses that result from government actions that benefit a government activity, such as severely restricting land uses near a municipal airport, would be compensable. Restrictions that result from government attempts to arbitrate disputes, such as prohibiting industrial uses in a residential area, would not be compensable. A more general version of this theory, called *harm-benefit theory,* has a much longer history and focuses on regulations designed to prevent harm to private owners, particularly those caused by "noxious uses." Under this theory, protective restrictions would be valid, but those that primarily confer a public benefit, such as historic preservation or open space zoning, would be found invalid. Many point to the language of the Penn Coal case, in which Holmes used the phrase "average reciprocity of advantage," in which a taking is held not to occur if the regulation confers an average reciprocity of advantage, such as that found by restricting uses of property that are public nuisances.

Finally, two fairly new theories have evolved based on recent supreme court rulings. The first of these, called *nexus theory,* holds that a taking may occur if the regulation, even though its purpose is proper, is not reasonably related to achieving that purpose. The last of the theories is called *balancing theory* and attempts to weigh the burdens imposed on individuals against the public purposes served by the regulation. The assumption appears to be that a system of regulations in which social gains outweigh private burdens must be inherently fair.

First English Evangelical Lutheran Church of Glendale v. County of Los Angeles

Regardless of the method used to find a taking, the use of takings analysis rather than substantive due process has one potential difference. A takings finding, because it would be found under the Fifth Amendment, requires just compensation be paid. Although this issue has been around for quite some time, most courts have avoided it by providing only the due process remedy of invalidating the regulation. In other words, if a taking was found to have occurred, the solution was to invalidate the zoning regulation and allow the desired use. During the 1987 term, however, the Supreme Court finally took up the issue of compensation with results that sent shock waves through many municipalities. In the now famous "First English" case, the court ruled that when a taking has occurred, even a temporary one, compensation must be paid because the Fifth Amendment is essentially "self-activating."

Inverse Condemnation Claims made to recover damages resulting from excessive regulation, nearby public uses, or damages remaining after an original eminent domain proceeding.

Inverse Condemnation

An area that is closely related to the general takings issue is that of ***inverse condemnation***. Traditionally inverse condemnation actions have been brought in two types of situations: first, when part of an owner's property has been taken and an action is brought to recover remaining damages, which may not have been covered in the original eminent domain proceeding; and second, claims may be made for damages when no property has been actually taken, but the owner claims damages owing to either excessive regulation or the effects of nearby public uses. For example, when aircraft fly overhead in an approach to a municipal airport, liability is usually established based on the notion that the continuing overflights amount to the taking of an easement. But what about the noise and pollution from a nearby highway? When no actual property has been taken, most courts have labeled the damages as "consequential" and thus not compensable.

Claims of inverse condemnation are usually based on the many state constitutions that provide for compensation for property that has been "taken or damaged" by public agencies. The addition of the "damaged" standard would seem to open the door for a wider interpretation, yet relatively few damage claims have been upheld. It remains to be seen whether or not the First English ruling will change the rules substantially in the takings area. Based on the state cases that have been heard since First English, however, it does not appear that courts are in a great rush to begin awarding compensation in takings cases.

When the actions of the government deprive a business of most of its customers, does this constitute an inverse condemnation of the property? In *Murphy v. City of Detroit* [1993 WL 288388 (Mich.App.)] the court held that although by condemning and tearing down 1,400 residences housing 17,000 people from the area surrounding a grocery store effectively eliminated most of the store's potential customers, their rights to possess their land and buildings were not taken, and thus there was no inverse condemnation. The store owners paid a premium for the location because of its proximity to a substantial base of customers. They assumed that their customer base would remain fairly constant and that the nearby land would continue to be used as it had in the past. Expectations, however, are not rights and the property owners have no control over how the owners of adjoining property choose to use their land.

TRANSFER DEVELOPMENT RIGHTS

One response to the "luck of the draw" nature of our system of land use controls is based on the notion that landownership is a bundle of rights that can be moved from one location to another. If land carries with it the inherent right to develop it or a privilege that government can convey to land, then the right (or privilege) has some value in and of itself. This notion is the basis for a system in which private landowners can buy or sell development rights in a market setting. Statutes to establish such a system are referred to as **transfer development rights** (TDR) ordinances.

Transfer Development Rights
A system in which all land carries with it inherent development rights which may be bought and/or sold by the land owner.

TDR systems are based on the notion of land having development rights. The closely related transfer development credits (TDC) approach is based on the notion of government-granted privileges. In practice, both types of systems function in much the same fashion. The major problem with land use regulation, as we have seen, is that of creating "winners" and "losers" as a result of the planning process. The use of a TDR/TDC system reduces the potentially harsh impact of zoning systems by defining certain "sending areas," in which rights may be sold, and "receiving areas," in which rights may be purchased. Thus owners of property in a sending area that is subject to restrictive use limitations may recover much, if not all, of their lost profits by selling the unused development rights to an owner in a receiving area.

The TDR system is fairly simple in concept, although fairly complex to administer. Owners of receiving sites have a specified base amount of permitted development and a specified amount of development that may be purchased in the form of TDRs.

The idea is simply to limit the total amount of development in an area without unduly penalizing any individual.

CONCLUSION

The history of land use regulation in the U.S. is, if nothing else, certainly controversial and confusing. The entire process can be thought of as a continuing battle between individual rights and public needs. As a result, permanent solutions are not likely to be found. As our notions of both individual freedoms and societal goals change over time, the legal system will adapt itself to the changing environment.

The British notion of "worsenment" and "betterment" is not really compatible with our constitutional system. Yet many elements of it have found their way into our system. For example, as of 1986, the use of fees and extractions charged to developers was expected to raise at least 25 percent of the cost of new schools. In California, the current five-year transportation plan calls for more than $700 million in privately funded projects. That number was zero only a few years ago.

Is the use of an increasing amount of private funding an example of creeping "betterment" thinking? After all, the basic notion in the British approach is to capture some of the gain in market value that results from government planning actions. It would appear that that is exactly what is happening. On the "worsenment" side of the ledger, does the recent First English ruling indicate that increased compensation is headed toward those who unduly suffer from harsh regulations? Perhaps so, but it is as yet too early to tell.

DISCUSSION QUESTIONS

1. Name the three groupings of land use restrictions and the types of regulations each includes.
2. How are private restrictions on the use of property created? How do subdivision covenants differ in this respect? What is the advantage of this method of recording land use restrictions?
3. What is a neighborhood association? What is the primary advantage of this type of control method?
4. If the U.S. Constitution itself applies only to the conduct of government bodies, how are racially exclusive private covenants in violation of the equal protection clause of the Fourteenth Amendment?
5. Describe the two-prong test developed by the Supreme Court to test the validity of zoning regulations said to be in violation of the due process clause of the Fourteenth Amendment.
6. In what two situations will the Supreme Court require a city to compensate a landowner for property restricted under police power actions?
7. What is the purpose of zoning regulations? Name and briefly discuss the subjects covered in most zoning ordinances.

8. Distinguish between a zoning *appeal* and a zoning *variance*. Between a *special exception* and a *nonconforming use*.
9. Discuss briefly each of the major issues addressed by the zoning process.
10. How did the Supreme Court ruling in *Berman v. Parker* affect the notion of "public use" as applied to eminent domain takings?
11. If a property's value is affected by eminent domain proceedings, will the amount of compensation granted to the landowner be reflective of the change in value?
12. Describe the various theories based on Supreme Court cases that are used to evaluate "taking" situations.
13. Explain the TDR/TDC system. What is the purpose of this system?

PENN CENTRAL TRANSPORTATION COMPANY V. CITY OF NEW YORK

438 U.S. 104, 98 S.Ct. 2646 (1978)

The "takings" issue as applied to historic preservation

Mr. Justice BRENNAN delivered the opinion of the Court.

The question presented is whether a city may, as part of a comprehensive program to preserve historic landmarks and historic districts, place restrictions on the development of individual historic landmarks—in addition to those imposed by applicable zoning ordinances—without effecting a "taking" requiring the payment of "just compensation." Specifically, we must decide whether the application of New York City's Landmarks Preservation Law to the parcel of land occupied by Grand Central Terminal has "taken" its owners' property in violation of the Fifth and Fourteenth Amendments.

I

A

Over the past 50 years, all 50 states and over 500 municipalities have enacted laws to encourage or require the preservation of buildings and areas with historic or aesthetic importance. These nationwide legislative efforts have been precipitated by two concerns. The first is recognition that, in recent years, large numbers of historic structures, landmarks, and areas have been destroyed without adequate consideration of either the values represented therein or the possibility of preserving the destroyed properties for use in economically productive ways. The second is a widely shared belief that structures with special historic, cultural, or architectural significance enhance the quality of life for all. Not only do these buildings and their workmanship represent the lessons of the past and embody precious features of our heritage, they serve as examples of quality for today. "[H]istoric conservation is but one aspect of the much larger problem, basically an environmental one, of enhancing—or perhaps developing for the first time—the quality of life for people."

New York City, responding to similar concerns and acting pursuant to a New York State enabling Act, adopted its Landmarks Preservation Law in 1965. *See* N.Y.C. Admin. Code, ch. 8-A, § 205-1.0 et seq. (1976). The city acted from the conviction that "the standing of [New York City] as a world-wide tourist center and world capital of business, culture and government" would be threatened if legislation were not enacted to protect historic landmarks and neighborhoods from precipitate decisions to destroy or fundamentally alter their character. § 205-1.0(a). The city believed that comprehensive measußres to safeguard desirable features of the existing urban fabric would benefit its citizens in a variety of ways: e.g., fostering "civic pride in the beauty and noble accomplishments of the past"; protecting and enhancing "the city's attractions to tourists and visitors"; "support-[ing] and stimul[ating] business and industry"; "strengthen[ing] the economy of the city"; and promoting "the use of historic districts, landmarks, interior landmarks and scenic landmarks for the education, pleasure and welfare of the people of the city." § 205-1.0(b).

The New York City law is typical of many urban landmark laws in that its primary method of achieving its goals is not by acquisitions of historic properties, but rather by involving public entities in land-use decisions affecting these properties and providing services, standards, controls, and incentives that will encourage preservation by private owners and users. While the law does place special restrictions on landmark properties as a necessary feature to the attainment of its larger objectives, the major theme of the law is to ensure the owners of any such properties both a "reasonable return" on their investments and maximum latitude to use their parcels for purposes not inconsistent with the preservation goals.

The operation of the law can be briefly summarized. The primary responsibility for administering the law is vested in the Landmarks Preservation Commission (Commission), a board based, 11-member agency assisted by a technical staff. The Commission first performs the function, critical to any landmark preservation effort, of identifying properties and areas that have "a special character or special historical or aesthetic interest or value as part of the development, heritage or cultural characteristics of the city, state or nation." § 207-1.0(n); see § 207-1.0(h). If the Commission determines, after giving all interested parties an opportunity to be heard, that a building or area satisfies the ordinance's criteria, it will designate a building to be a "landmark," situated on a particular "landmark site," or will designate an area to be a "historic district." After the Commission makes a designation, New York City's Board of Estimate, after considering the relationship of the designated property "to the master plan, the zoning resolution, projected public improvements and any plans for the renewal of the area involved," may modify or disapprove the designation, and the owner may seek judicial review of the final designation decision. Thus far, 31 historic districts and over 400 individual landmarks have been finally designated, and the process is a continuing one.

Final designation as a landmark results in restrictions upon the property owner's options concerning use of the landmark site. First, the law imposes a duty upon the owner to keep the exterior features of the building "in good repair" to assure that the law's objectives not be defeated by the landmark's falling into a state of irremediable disrepair. Second, the Commission must approve in advance any proposal to alter the exterior architectural features of the landmark or to construct any exterior improvement on the landmark site, thus ensuring that decisions concerning construction on the landmark site are made with due consideration of both the public interest in the maintenance of the structure and the landowner's interest in use of the property. In the event an owner wishes to alter a landmark site, three separate procedures are available through which administrative approval may be obtained. First, the owner may apply to the Commission for a "certificate of no effect on protected architectural features": that is, for an order approving the improvement or alteration on the ground that it will not change or affect any architectural feature of the landmark and will be in harmony therewith. Denial of the certificate is subject to judicial review.

Second, the owner may apply to the Commission for a certificate of "appropriateness." Such certificates will be granted if the Commission concludes—focusing upon aesthetic, historical, and architectural values—that the proposed construction on the landmark site would not unduly hinder the protection, enhancement, perpetuation, and use of the landmark. Again, denial of the certificate is subject to judicial review. Moreover, the owner who is denied either a certificate of no exterior effect or a certificate of appropriateness may submit an alternative or modified plan for approval. The final procedure—seeking a certificate of appropriateness on the ground of "insufficient return," provides special mechanisms, which vary depending on whether or not the landmark enjoys a tax exemption, to ensure that designation does not cause economic hardship.[1]

But this is not the only remedy available for owners of tax-exempt landmarks. As the case at bar illustrates, see infra, at 2658, if an owner files suit and establishes that he is incapable of earning a "reasonable return" on the site in its present state, he can be afforded judicial relief. Similarly, where a landmark owner who enjoys a tax exemption has demonstrated that the landmark structure, as restricted, is totally inadequate for the owner's "legitimate needs," the law has been held invalid as applied to that parcel. *See* Lutheran Church v. City of New York, 35 N.Y.2d 121, 359 N.Y.S.2d 7, 316 N.E.2d 305 (1974).

Although the designation of a landmark and landmark site restricts the owner's control over the parcel, designation also enhances the economic position of the landmark owner in one significant respect. Under New York City's zoning laws, owners of real property who have not developed their property to the full extent permitted by the applicable zoning laws are allowed to transfer development rights to contiguous parcels on the same city block. *See* New York City, Zoning Resolution Art. I, ch. 2, § 12-10 (1978) (definition of "zoning lot"). A 1968 ordinance gave the owners of landmark sites additional opportunities to transfer development rights to other parcels. Subject to a restriction that the floor area of the transferee lot may not be increased by more than 20% above its authorized level, the ordinance permitted transfers from a landmark parcel to property across the street or across a street intersection. In 1969, the law governing the conditions under which transfers from landmark parcels could occur was liberalized, apparently to ensure that the Landmark's Law would not unduly restrict the development options of the owners of Grand Central Terminal. . . .

[1]If the owner of a non–tax exempt parcel has been denied certificates of appropriateness for a proposed alteration and shows that he is not earning a reasonable return on the property in its present state, the Commission and other city agencies must assume the burden of developing a plan that will enable the landmark owner to earn a reasonable return on the landmark site. . . .

B

This case involves the application of New York City's Landmarks Preservation Law to Grand Central Terminal (Terminal). The Terminal, which is owned by the Penn Central Transportation Co. and its affiliates (Penn Central), is one of New York City's most famous buildings. Opened in 1913, it is regarded not only as providing an ingenious engineering solution to the problems presented by urban railroad stations, but also as a magnificent example of the French beaux-arts style.

The Terminal is located in midtown Manhattan. Its south facade faces 42d Street and that street's intersection with Park Avenue. At street level, the Terminal is bounded on the west by Vanderbilt Avenue, on the east by the Commodore Hotel, and on the north by the Pan-American Building. Although a 20-story office tower, to have been located above the Terminal, was part of the original design, the planned tower was never constructed. The Terminal itself is an eight-story structure which Penn Central uses as a railroad station and in which it rents space not needed for railroad purposes to a variety of commercial interests. The Terminal is one of a number of properties owned by appellant Penn Central in this area of midtown Manhattan. The others include the Barclay, Biltmore, Commodore, Roosevelt, and Waldorf-Astoria Hotels, the Pan-American Building and other office buildings along Park Avenue, and the Yale Club. At least eight of these are eligible to be recipients of development rights afforded the Terminal by virtue of landmark designation.

On August 2, 1967, following a public hearing, the Commission designated the Terminal a "landmark" and designated the "city tax block" it occupies a "landmark site." The Board of Estimate confirmed this action on September 21, 1967. Although appellant Penn Central had opposed the designation before the Commission, it did not seek judicial review of the final designation decision.

On January 22, 1968, appellant Penn Central, to increase its income, entered into a renewable 50-year lease and sublease agreement with appellant UGP Properties, Inc. (UGP), a wholly owned subsidiary of Union General Properties, Ltd., a United

Kingdom corporation. Under the terms of the agreement, UGP was to construct a multistory office building above the Terminal. UGP promised to pay Penn Central $1 million annually during construction and at least $3 million annually thereafter. The rentals would be offset in part by a loss of some $700,000 to $1 million in net rentals presently received from concessionaires displaced by the new building.

Appellants UGP and Penn Central then applied to the Commission for permission to construct an office building atop the Terminal. Two separate plans, both designed by architect Marcel Breuer and both apparently satisfying the terms of the applicable zoning ordinance, were submitted to the Commission for approval. The first, Breuer I, provided for the construction of a 55-story office building, to be cantilevered above the existing facade and to rest on the roof of the Terminal. The second, Breuer II Revised, called for tearing down a portion of the Terminal that included the 42d Street facade, stripping off some of the remaining features of the Terminal's facade, and constructing a 53-story office building. The Commission denied a certificate of no exterior effect on September 20, 1968. Appellants then applied for a certificate of "appropriateness" as to both proposals. After four days of hearings at which over 80 witnesses testified, the Commission denied this application as to both proposals.

The Commission's reasons for rejecting certificates respecting Breuer II Revised are summarized in the following statement: "To protect a Landmark, one does not tear it down. To perpetuate its architectural features, one does not strip them off." Record 2255. Breuer I, which would have preserved the existing vertical facades of the present structure, received more sympathetic consideration. The Commission first focused on the effect that the proposed tower would have on one desirable feature created by the present structure and its surroundings: the dramatic view of the Terminal from Park Avenue South. Although appellants had contended that the Pan-American Building had already destroyed the silhouette of the south facade and that one additional tower could do no further damage and might even provide a better background for the facade, the Commission disagreed, stating that it found the majestic approach from the south to be still unique in the city and that a 55-story tower atop the Terminal would be far more detrimental to its south facade than the Pan-American Building 375 feet away. Moreover, the Commission found that from closer vantage points the Pan Am Building and the other towers were largely cut off from view, which would not be the case of the mass on top of the Terminal planned under Breuer I. In conclusion, the Commission stated: "[We have] no fixed rule against making additions to designated buildings—it all depends on how they are done. . . . But to balance a 55-story office tower above a flamboyant Beaux-Arts facade seems nothing more than an aesthetic joke. Quite simply, the tower would overwhelm the Terminal by its sheer mass. The 'addition' would be four times as high as the existing structure and would reduce the Landmark itself to the status of a curiosity.

"Landmarks cannot be divorced from their settings—particularly when the setting is a dramatic and integral part of the original concept. The Terminal, in its setting, is a great example of urban design. Such examples are not so plentiful in New York City that we can afford to lose any of the few we have. And we must preserve them in a meaningful way—with alterations and additions of such character, scale, materials and mass as will protect, enhance and perpetuate the original design rather than overwhelm it."

Appellants did not seek judicial review of the denial of either certificate. Because the Terminal site enjoyed a tax exemption, remained suitable for its present and future uses, and was not the subject of a contract of sale, there were no further administrative remedies available to appellants as to the Breuer I and Breuer II Revised plans. *See* n. 13, *supra*. Further, appellants did not avail themselves of the opportunity to develop and submit other plans for the Commission's consideration and approval. Instead, appellants filed suit in New York Supreme Court, Trial Term, claiming, inter alia, that the application of the Landmarks Preservation Law had "taken" their property without just compensation in violation of the Fifth and Fourteenth Amendments and arbitrarily deprived them of their property without due process of law in violation of the Fourteenth Amendment. Appellants sought a declaratory judgment, injunctive relief barring the city from using the Landmarks Law to impede the construction of any structure that might otherwise lawfully be constructed on the Terminal site, and damages for the "temporary taking" that occurred between August 2, 1967, the designation date, and the date when the restrictions arising from the Landmarks Law would be lifted. The trial court granted the injunctive and declaratory relief, but severed the question of damages for a "temporary taking."

Appellees appealed, and the New York Supreme Court, Appellate Division, reversed. 50 A.D.2d 265, 377 N.Y.S.2d 20 (1975). The Appellate Division held that the restrictions on the development of the Terminal site were necessary to promote the legitimate public purpose of protecting landmarks and therefore that appellants could sustain their constitutional claims only by proof that the regulation deprived them of all reasonable beneficial use of the property. The Appellate Division held that the evidence appellants introduced at trial—"Statements of Revenues and Costs," purporting to show a net operating loss for the years 1969 and 1971, which were prepared for the instant litigation—had not satisfied their burden. . . .

The New York Court of Appeals affirmed. 42 N.Y.2d 324, 397 N.Y.S.2d 914, 366 N.E.2d 1271 (1977). That court summarily rejected any claim that the Landmarks Law had "taken" property without "just compensation," *id.*, at 329, 397 N.Y.S.2d, at 917, 366 N.E.2d, at 1274, indicating that there could be no "taking" since the law had not transferred control of the property to the city, but only restricted appellants' exploitation of it.

* * *

II

The issues presented by appellants are (1) whether the restrictions imposed by New York City's law upon appellants' exploitation of the Terminal site effect a "taking" of appellants' property for a public use within the meaning of the Fifth Amendment, which of course is made applicable to the States through the Fourteenth Amendment, *see* Chicago, B. & Q. R. Co. v. Chicago, 166 U.S. 226, 239, 17 S.Ct. 581, 585, 41 L.Ed. 979 (1897), and, (2), if so, whether the transferable development rights afforded appellants constitute "just compensation" within the meaning of the Fifth Amendment. We need only address the question whether a "taking" has occurred.

A

Before considering appellants' specific contentions, it will be useful to review the factors that have shaped the jurisprudence of the Fifth Amendment injunction "nor shall private property be taken for public use, without just compensation." The question of what constitutes a "taking" for purposes of the Fifth Amendment has proved to be a problem of considerable difficulty. While this Court has recognized that the "Fifth Amendment's guarantee . . . [is] designed to bar Government from forcing some people alone to bear public burdens which, in all fairness and justice should be borne by the public as a whole," Armstrong v. United States, 364 U.S. 40, 49, 80 S.Ct. 1563, 1569, 4 L.Ed.2d 1554 (1960), this Court, quite simply, has been unable to develop any "set formula" for determining when "justice and fairness" require that economic injuries caused by public action be compensated by the government, rather than remain disproportionately concentrated on a few persons. . . .

In engaging in these essentially ad hoc, factual inquiries, the Court's decisions have identified several factors that have particular significance. The economic impact of the regulation on the claimant and, particularly, the extent to which the regulation has interfered with distinct investment-backed expectations are, of course, relevant considerations. *See* Goldblatt v. Hempstead, *supra,* 369 U.S., at 594, 82 S.Ct., at 990. So, too, is the character of the governmental action. A "taking" may more readily be found when the interference with property can be characterized as a physical invasion by government, *see,* e.g., United States v. Causby, 328 U.S. 256, 66 S.Ct. 1062, 90 L.Ed. 1206 (1946), than when interference arises from some public program adjusting the benefits and burdens of economic life to promote the common good.

"Government hardly could go on if to some extent values incident to property could not be diminished without paying for every such change in the general law," Pennsylvania Coal Co. v. Mahon,

260 U.S. 393, 413, 43 S.Ct. 158, 159, 67 L.Ed. 322 (1922), and this Court has accordingly recognized, in a wide variety of contexts, that government may execute laws or programs that adversely affect recognized economic values. Exercises of the taxing power are one obvious example. A second are the decisions in which this Court has dismissed "taking" challenges on the ground that, while the challenged government action caused economic harm, it did not interfere with interests that were sufficiently bound up with the reasonable expectations of the claimant to constitute "property" for Fifth Amendment purposes. (Citations ommitted.)

* * *

Zoning laws generally do not affect existing uses of real property, but "taking" challenges have also been held to be without merit in a wide variety of situations when the challenged governmental actions prohibited a beneficial use to which individual parcels had previously been devoted and thus caused substantial individualized harm.

* * *

Finally, government actions that may be characterized as acquisitions of resources to permit or facilitate uniquely public functions have often been held to constitute "takings." United States v. Causby, 328 U.S. 256, 66 S.Ct. 1062, 90 L.Ed. 1206 (1946), is illustrative. In holding that direct overflights above the claimant's land, that destroyed the present use of the land as a chicken farm, constituted a "taking," Causby emphasized that Government had not "merely destroyed property [but was] using a part of it for the flight of its planes."

* * *

Appellants' final broad-based attack would have us treat the law as an instance, like that in United States v. Causby, in which government, acting in an enterprise capacity, has appropriated part of their property for some strictly governmental purpose. Apart from the fact that Causby was a case of invasion of airspace that destroyed the use of the farm beneath and this New York City law has in nowise impaired the present use of the Terminal, the Landmarks Law neither exploits appellants' parcel for city purposes nor facilitates nor arises from any entrepreneurial operations of the city. The situation is not remotely like that in Causby where the airspace above the property was in the flight pattern for military aircraft. The Landmarks Law's effect is simply to prohibit appellants or anyone else from occupying portions of the airspace above the Terminal, while permitting appellants to use the remainder of the parcel in a gainful fashion. This is no more an appropriation of property by government for its own uses than is a zoning law prohibiting, for "aesthetic" reasons, two or more adult theaters within a specified area, *see* Young v. American Mini Theatres, Inc., 427 U.S. 50, 96 S.Ct. 2440, 49 L.Ed.2d 310 (1976), or a safety regulation prohibiting excavations below a certain level.

* * *

Affirmed.

Case Reflections

1. On what grounds did plaintiff Penn Central sue the City of New York?
2. How did the alleged "Taking" occur? In other words, what act performed by the City of New York did Penn Central feel was in violation of the Constitution?
3. Did the Supreme Court of the United States agree or disagree with the position of Penn Central? What was the reasoning behind its decision?

VILLAGE OF BELLE TERRE
V.
BORAAS

416 U.S. 1, 94 S.Ct. 1536 (1974)

The Supreme Court allows a definition of "family" in a zoning ordinance

Mr. Justice DOUGLAS delivered the opinion of the Court.

Belle Terre is a village on Long Island's north shore of about 220 homes inhabited by 700 people. Its total land area is less than one square mile. It has restricted land use to one-family dwellings excluding lodging houses, boarding houses, fraternity houses, or multiple-dwelling houses. The word "family" as used in the ordinances means, "(o)ne or more persons related by blood, adoption, or marriage, living and cooking together as a single housekeeping unit, exclusive of household servants. A number of persons but not exceeding two (2) living and cooking together as a single housekeeping unit through not related by blood, adoption, or marriage shall be deemed to constitute a family."

Appellees, the Dickmans, are owners of a house in the village and leased it in December 1971 for a term of 18 months to Michael Truman. Later Bruce Boraas became a co-lessee. Then Anne Parish moved into the house along with three others. These six are students at nearby State University at Stony Brook and none is related to the other by blood, adoption, or marriage. When the village served the Dickmans with an "Order to Remedy Violations" of the ordinance, the owners plus three tenants thereupon brought this action under 42 U.S.C. § 1983 for an injunction and a judgment declaring the ordinance unconstitutional. The District Court held the ordinance constitutional, 367 F.Supp. 136, and the Court of Appeals reversed, one judge dissenting. 2 Cir., 476 F.2d 806. The case is here by appeal.

This case brings to this Court a different phase of local zoning regulations from those we have previously reviewed.

* * *

The present ordinance is challenged on several grounds: that it interferes with a person's right to travel; that it interferes with the right to migrate to and settle within a State; that it bars people who are uncongenial to the present residents; that it expresses the social preferences of the residents for groups that will be congenial to them; that social homogeneity is not a legitimate interest of government; that the restriction of those whom the neighbors do not like trenches on the newcomers' rights of privacy; that it is of no rightful concern to villagers whether the residents are married or unmarried; that the ordinance is antithetical to the Nation's experience, ideology, and self-perception as an open, egalitarian, and integrated society.

We find none of these reasons in the record before us.

* * *

It is said, however, that if two unmarried people can constitute a "family," there is no reason why three or four may not. But every line drawn by a legislature leaves some out that might well have been included.[5] That exercise of discretion, however, is a legislative, not a judicial, function.

* * *

The ordinance places no ban on other forms of association, for a "family" may, so far as the ordinance is concerned, entertain whomever it likes.

The regimes of boarding houses, fraternity houses, and the like present urban problems. More

[5]Mr. Justice Holmes made the point a half century ago. "When a legal distinction is determined, as no one doubts that it may be, between night and day, childhood and maturity, or any other extremes, a point has to be fixed or a line has to be drawn, or gradually picked out by successive decisions, to mark where the change takes place. Looked at by itself without regard to the necessity behind it the line or point seems arbitrary. It might as well or nearly as well be a little more to one side or the other. But when it is seen that a line or point there must be, and that there is no mathematical or logical way of fixing it precisely, the decision of the legislature must be accepted unless we can say that it is very wide of any reasonable mark." Louisville Gas & Electric Co. v. Coleman, 277 U.S. 32, 41, 48 S.Ct. 423, 426, 72 L.Ed. 770 (dissenting opinion).

people occupy a given space; more cars rather continuously pass by; more cars are parked; noise travels with crowds.

A quiet place where yards are wide, people few, and motor vehicles restricted are legitimate guidelines in a land-use project addressed to family needs. This goal is a permissible one within Berman v. Parker, supra. The police power is not confined to elimination of filth, stench, and unhealthy places. It is ample to lay out zones where family values, youth values, and the blessings of quiet seclusion and clean air make the area a sanctuary for people.

Reversed.

Case Reflections

1. What is the definition of "family" as put forth by the ordinance in question?
2. In your own words, state the issue to be decided by the Supreme Court in this case.
3. How did the Supreme Court rule in this case? How did the Court back up its decision?

FIRST ENGLISH EVANGELICAL LUTHERAN CHURCH OF GLENDALE V. COUNTY OF LOS ANGELES

482 U.S. 304, 107 S.Ct. 2378 (1987)

Is compensation due when there is a temporary "taking"?

In this case the California Court of Appeal held that a landowner who claims that his property has been "taken" by a land-use regulation may not recover damages for the time before it is finally determined that the regulation constitutes a "taking" of his property. We disagree, and conclude that in these circumstances the Fifth and Fourteenth Amendments to the United States Constitution would require compensation for that period. In 1957, appellant First English Evangelical Lutheran Church purchased a 21-acre parcel of land in a canyon along the banks of the Middle Fork of Mill Creek in the Angeles National Forest. The Middle Fork is the natural drainage channel for a watershed area owned by the National Forest Service. Twelve of the acres owned by the church are flat land, and contained a dining hall, two bunkhouses, a caretaker's lodge, an outdoor chapel, and a footbridge across the creek. The church operated on the site a campground, known as "Lutherglen," as a retreat center and a recreational area for handicapped children. In July 1977, a forest fire denuded the hills upstream from Lutherglen, destroying approximately 3860 acres of the watershed area and creating a serious flood hazard. Such flooding occurred on February 9 and 10, 1978, when a storm dropped 11 inches of rain in the watershed. The runoff from the storm overflowed the banks of the Mill Creek, flooding Lutherglen and destroying its buildings.

In response to the flooding of the canyon, appellee County of Los Angeles adopted Interim Ordinance No. 11,855 in January 1979. The ordinance provided that "[a] person shall not construct, reconstruct, place or enlarge any building or structure, any portion of which is, or will be, located within the outer boundary lines of the interim flood protection area located in Mill Creek Canyon. . . ." The ordinance was effective immediately because the county determined that it was "required for the immediate preservation of the public health and safety. . . ." The interim flood protection area described by the ordinance included the flat areas on either side of Mill Creek on which Lutherglen had stood. The church filed a complaint in the Superior Court of California a little more than a month after the ordinance was adopted. As subsequently amended, the complaint alleged two claims against the county and the Los Angeles County Flood Control District. The first alleged that the defendants were liable under Cal.Gov't Code Ann. § 835 (West 1980) for dangerous conditions on their upstream properties that contributed to the flooding of Lutherglen. As a part of this claim, appellant also alleged that "Ordinance No. 11,855 denies [appellant] all use of Lutherglen." App. 12, 49. The second claim sought to recover from the Flood District in inverse condemnation and in tort for engaging in cloud seed-ing during the storm that flooded Lutherglen. Appellant sought damages under each count for loss of use of Lutherglen. The defendants moved to strike the portions of the complaint alleging that the county's ordinance denied all use of Lutherglen, on the view that the California Supreme Court's decision in Agins v. Tiburon, 24 Cal.3d 266, 157 Cal.Rptr. 372, 598 P.2d 25 (1979), aff'd on other grounds, 447 U.S. 255, 100 S.Ct. 2138, 65 L.Ed.2d 106 (1980), rendered the allegation "entirely immaterial and irrelevant, [with] no bearing upon any conceivable cause of action herein."

In Agins v. Tiburon, *supra,* the Supreme Court of California decided that a landowner may not maintain an inverse condemnation suit in the courts of that State based upon a "regulatory" taking. In the court's view, maintenance of such a suit would allow a landowner to force the legislature to exercise its power of eminent domain. Under this decision, then, compensation is not required until the challenged regulation or ordinance has been held excessive in an action for declaratory relief or a writ of mandamus and the government has nevertheless decided to continue the regulation in effect. Based on this decision, the trial court in the present case granted the motion to strike the allegation that the church had been denied all use of Lutherglen. It explained that "a careful rereading of the Agins case persuades the Court that when an ordinance, even a nonzoning ordinance, deprives a person of the total use of his lands, his challenge to the ordinance is by way of declaratory relief or possibly mandamus." App. 26. Because the appellant alleged a regulatory taking and sought only damages, the allegation that the ordinance denied all use of Lutherglen was deemed irrelevant.

On appeal, the California Court of Appeal read the complaint as one seeking "damages for the uncompensated taking of all use of Lutherglen by County Ordinance No. 11,855. . . ." It too relied on the California Supreme Court's decision in Agins in rejecting the cause of action, declining appellant's invitation to reevaluate Agins in light of this Court's opinions in San Diego Gas & Electric Co. v. San Diego, 450 U.S. 621, 101 S.Ct. 1287, 67 L.Ed.2d 551 (1981) . . . It accordingly affirmed the trial court's decision to strike the allegations concerning appellee's ordinance. The Supreme Court of California denied review.

This appeal followed, and we noted probable jurisdiction. Appellant asks us to hold that the Supreme Court of California erred in Agins v. Tiburon in determining that the Fifth Amendment, as made applicable to the States through the Fourteenth Amendment, does not require compensation as a remedy for "temporary" regulatory takings—those regulatory takings which are ultimately invalidated by the courts. Four times this decade, we have considered similar claims and have found ourselves for one reason or another unable to consider the merits of the Agins rule. . . .

For the reasons explained below, however, we find the constitutional claim properly presented in this case, and hold that on these facts the California courts have decided the compensation question inconsistently with the requirements of the Fifth Amendment.

I

Concerns with finality left us unable to reach the remedial question in the earlier cases where we have been asked to consider the rule of Agins. In each of these cases, we concluded either that regulations considered to be in issue by the state court did not effect a taking, . . . or that the factual disputes yet to be resolved by state authorities might still lead to the conclusion that no taking had occurred. . . .Consideration of the remedial question in those circumstances, we concluded, would be premature.

The posture of the present case is quite different. Appellant's complaint alleged that "Ordinance No. 11,855 denies [it] all use of Lutherglen," and sought damages for this deprivation. In affirming the decision to strike this allegation, the Court of Appeal assumed that the complaint sought "damages for the uncompensated taking of all use of Lutherglen by County Ordinance No. 11,855." It relied on the California Supreme Court's Agins decision for the conclusion that "the remedy for a taking [is limited] to nonmonetary relief. . . ." The disposition of the case on these grounds isolates the remedial question for our consideration.

* * *

We reject appellee's suggestion that, regardless of the state court's treatment of the question, we must independently evaluate the adequacy of the complaint and resolve the takings claim on the merits before we can reach the remedial question. However "cryptic"—to use appellee's description—the allegations with respect to the taking were, the California courts deemed them sufficient to present the issue. We accordingly have no occasion to decide whether the ordinance at issue actually denied appellant all use of its property or whether the county might avoid the conclusion that a compensable taking had occurred by establishing that the denial of all use was insulated as a part of the State's authority to enact safety regulations. (Citations ommitted.) These questions, of course, remain open for decision on the remand we direct today. We now turn to the question of whether the Just Compensation Clause requires the government to pay for "temporary" regulatory takings.

II

Consideration of the compensation question must begin with direct reference to the language of the Fifth Amendment, which provides in relevant part that "private property [shall not] be taken for public use, without just compensation." As its language indicates, and as the Court has frequently noted, this provision does not prohibit the taking of private property, but instead places a condition on the exercise of that power. (Citations ommitted.) Thus, government action that works a taking of property rights necessarily implicates the "constitutional obligation to pay just compensation."

We have recognized that a landowner is entitled to bring an action in inverse condemnation as a result of "the self-executing character of the constitutional provision with respect to compensation. . . ." As noted in Justice BRENNAN's dissent in San Diego Gas & Electric Co., 450 U.S., at 654-655, 101 S.Ct., at 1305, it has been established at least since Jacobs v. United States, 290 U.S. 13, 54 S.Ct. 26, 78 L.Ed. 142 (1933), that claims for just compensation are grounded in the Constitution itself: "The suits were based on the right to recover just compensation for property taken by the United States for public use in the exercise of its power of eminent domain. That right was guaranteed by the Constitution. The fact that condemnation proceedings were not instituted and that the right was asserted in suits by the owners did not change the essential nature of the claim. The form of the remedy did not qualify the right. It rested upon the Fifth Amendment. Statutory recognition was not necessary. A promise to pay was not necessary. Such a promise was implied because of the duty imposed by the Amendment. The suits were thus founded upon the Constitution of the United States." *Id.*, at 16, 54 S.Ct., at 27.

* * *

[Prior] cases reflect the fact that "temporary" takings which, as here, deny a landowner all use of his property, are not different in kind from permanent takings, for which the Constitution clearly requires compensation.

* * *

Nothing we say today is intended to abrogate the principle that the decision to exercise the power of eminent domain is a legislative function, "for Congress and Congress alone to determine. . . ." Once a court determines that a taking has occurred, the government retains the whole range of options already available—amendment of the regulation, withdrawal of the invalidated regulation, or exercise of eminent domain. Thus we do not, as the Solicitor General suggests, "permit a court, at the behest of a private person, to require the . . . government to exercise the power of eminent domain. . . ." Brief for United States as Amicus Curiae 22. We merely hold that where the government's activities have already worked a taking of all use of property, no subsequent action by the government can relieve it of the duty to provide compensation for the period during which the taking was effective.

We also point out that the allegation of the complaint which we treat as true for purposes of our decision was that the ordinance in question denied appellant all use of its property. We limit our holding to the facts presented, and of course do not deal with the quite different questions that would arise in the case of normal delays in obtaining building permits, changes in zoning ordinances, variances, and the like which are not before us. We realize that even our present holding will undoubtedly lessen to some extent the freedom and flexibility of land-use planners and governing bodies of municipal corporations when enacting land-use regulations. But such consequences necessarily flow from any decision upholding a claim of constitutional right; many of the provisions of the Constitution are designed to limit the flexibility and freedom of governmental authorities and the Just Compensation Clause of the Fifth Amendment is one of them. As Justice Holmes aptly noted more than 50 years ago, "a strong public desire to improve the public condition is not enough to warrant achieving the desire by a shorter cut than the constitutional way of paying for the change." Pennsylvania Coal Co. v. Mahon, 260 U.S., at 416, 43 S.Ct., at 160.

Here we must assume that the Los Angeles County ordinances have denied appellant all use of its property for a considerable period of years, and we hold that invalidation of the ordinances without payment of fair value for the use of the property during this period of time would be a constitutionally insufficient remedy. The judgment of the California Court of Appeals is therefore reversed, and the case is remanded for further proceedings not inconsistent with this opinion.

It is so ordered.

Case Reflections

1. How did the County of Los Angeles supposedly "take" the property of the plaintiff?
2. State the issue before the Supreme Court in this case.
3. With which party did the Supreme Court side in this case? How did it justify its decision?

SHELLEY V. KRAEMER

334 U.S. 1, 68 S.Ct. 836 (1948)

Private agreements that violate the Constitution are unenforceable

Mr. Chief Justice VINSON delivered the opinion of the Court.

These cases present for our consideration questions relating to the validity of court enforcement of private agreements, generally described as restrictive covenants, which have as their purpose the exclusion of persons of designated race or color from the equal protection of the law. Basic constitutional issues of obvious importance have been raised.

The first of these cases comes to this Court on certiorari to the Supreme Court of Missouri. On February 16, 1911, thirty out of a total of thirty-nine owners of property fronting both sides of Labadie Avenue between Taylor Avenue and Cora Avenue in the city of St. Louis, signed an agreement, which was subsequently recorded, providing in part:

"***the said property is hereby restricted to the use and occupancy for the term of Fifty (50) years from this date, so that it shall be a condition all the time and whether recited and referred to as (sic) not in subsequent conveyances and shall attach to the land, as a condition precedent to the sale of the same, that hereafter no part of said property or any portion thereof shall be, for said term of Fifty-years, occupied by any person not of the Caucasian race, it being intended hereby to restrict the use of said property for said period of time against the occupancy as owners or tenants of any portion of said property for resident or other purpose by people of the Negro or Mongolian Race."

* * *

On August 11, 1945, pursuant to a contract of sale, petitioners Shelley, who are Negroes, for valuable consideration received from one Fitzgerald a warranty deed to the parcel in question. The trial court found that petitioners had no actual knowledge of the restrictive agreement at the time of the purchase.

On October 9, 1945, respondents, as owners of other property subject to the terms of the restrictive covenant, brought suit in Circuit Court of the city of St. Louis praying that petitioners Shelley be restrained from taking possession of the property and that judgment be entered divesting title out of petitioners Shelley and revesting title in the immediate grantor or in such other person as the court should direct. The trial court denied the requested relief on the ground that the restrictive agreement, upon which respondents based their action, had never become final and complete because it was the intention of the parties to that agreement that it was not to become effective until signed by all property owners in the district, and signatures of all the owners had never been obtained.

The Supreme Court of Missouri sitting en banc reversed and directed the trial court to grant the relief for which respondents had prayed. That court held the agreement effective and concluded that enforcement of its provisions violated no rights guaranteed to petitioners by the Federal Constitution. At the time the court rendered its decision, petitioners were occupying the property in question.

Petitioners have placed primary reliance on their contentions, first raised in the state courts, that judicial enforcement of the restrictive agreements in these cases has violated rights guaranteed to petitioners by the Fourteenth Amendment of the Federal Constitution and Acts of Congress passed pursuant to that Amendment. Specifically, petitioners urge that they have been denied the equal protection of the laws, deprived of property without due process of law, and have been denied privileges and immunities of citizens of the United States. We pass to a consideration of those issues.

I

Whether the equal protection clause of the Fourteenth Amendment inhibits judicial enforcement by state courts of restrictive covenants based on race or color is a question which this Court has not heretofore been called upon to consider. Only two cases have been decided by this Court which in any way have involved the enforcement of such agreements. The first of these was the case of Corrigan v. Buckley, 1926, 271 U.S. 323, 46 S.Ct. 521, 70 L.Ed. 969. There, suit was brought in the courts of the District of Columbia to enjoin a threatened violation of certain restrictive covenants relating to the lands situated in the city of Washington. Relief was granted, and the case was brought here on appeal. It is apparent that that case, which had originated in the federal courts and involved the enforcement of covenants on land located in the District of Columbia, could present no issues under the Fourteenth Amendment; for that Amendment by its terms applies only to the States. Nor was the question of the validity of court enforcement of the restrictive covenants under the Fifth Amendment properly before the Court, as the opinion of this Court specifically recognizes. The only constitutional issue which the appellants had raised in the lower courts, and hence the only constitutional issue before this Court on appeal, was the validity of the covenant agreements as such. This Court concluded that since the inhibitions of the constitutional provisions invoked, apply only to governmental action, as contrasted to action of private individuals, there was no showing that the covenants, which were simply agreements between private property owners, were invalid. Accordingly, the appeal was dismissed for want of a substantial question. Nothing in the opinion of this Court, therefore, may properly be regarded as an adjudication on the merits of the constitutional issues presented by these cases, which raise the question of the validity, not of the private agreements as such, but of the judicial enforcement of those agreements.

* * *

It cannot be doubted that among the civil rights intended to be protected from discriminatory state action by the Fourteenth Amendment are the rights to acquire, enjoy, own and dispose of property. Equality in the enjoyment of property rights was regarded by the framers of that Amendment as an essential pre-condition to the realization of other basic civil rights and liberties which the Amendment was intended to guarantee.

This Court has given specific recognition to the same principle.

It is likewise clear that restrictions on the right of occupancy of the sort sought to be created by the private agreements in these cases could not be squared with the requirements of the Fourteenth Amendment if imposed by state statute or local ordinance. We do not understand respondents to urge the contrary. (Citations ommitted.)

But the present cases, unlike those just discussed, do not involve action by state legislatures or city councils. Here the particular patterns of discrimination and the areas in which the restrictions are to operate, are determined, in the first instance, by the terms of agreements among private individuals. Participation of the State consists in the enforcement of the restrictions so defined. The crucial issue with which we are here confronted is whether this distinction removes these cases from the operation of the prohibitory provisions of the Fourteenth Amendment.

The short of the matter is that from the time of the adoption of the Fourteenth Amendment until the present, it has been the consistent ruling of this Court that the action of the States to which the Amendment has reference, includes action of state courts and state judicial officials. Although, in construing the terms of the Fourteenth Amendment, differences have from time to time been expressed as to whether particular types of state action may be said to offend the Amendment's prohibitory provisions, it has never been suggested that state court action is immunized from the operation of those provisions simply because the act is that of the judicial branch of the state government.

III

* * *

We have no doubt that there has been state action in these cases in the full and complete sense of the phrase. The undisputed facts disclose that petitioners were willing purchasers of properties upon which they desired to establish homes. The owners of the properties were willing sellers; and contracts of sale were accordingly consummated. It is clear that but for the active intervention of the state courts, supported by the full panoply of state power, petitioners would have been free to occupy the properties in question without restraint.

* * *

For the reasons stated, the judgment of the Supreme Court of Missouri and the judgment of the Supreme Court of Michigan must be reversed. Reversed.

Case Reflections

1. What is the issue to be decided by the Appellate Court in this case? Explain the significance of "state action" versus "private action."
2. How did the Supreme Court come to the conclusion that state action had occurred? What was its final ruling in this case?

CHAPTER 17

PRODUCT LIABILITY AND HOME OWNER'S WARRANTY

LEARNING OBJECTIVES

After reading this chapter, you should be able to:

1. Describe the nature of a claim in tort and list the three common forms these claims take.
2. Discuss the concept of privity as a defense to liability claims.
3. Understand the evolution of the strict products liability concept.
4. Understand how associations play a role in loss spreading and how home builders have used this approach.
5. Describe the nature of warranties, both implied and explicit, and the use of the merger doctrine as a defense to warranty claims.
6. Explain how Home Owner's Warranty (HOW) contracts mirror the doctrine of implied warranties.

KEY TERMS

Caveat Emptor

Stream of Commerce

Negligence

Strict Liability

Torts

Privity

Spreading the loss

Warranties

Uniform Commercial Code

Major Construction Defects

Services Exemption

> [T]hat by the Civil Law, every man is bound to warrant the thing that he selleth or conveyeth, albeit there be no expresse warranty, but the Common Law bindeth him not, unless there be a warranty either in Deed or in Law for *Caveat Emptor*
>
> *Coke on Littleton, 1633*

Caveat Emptor Literally, "Let the buyer beware." Often the standard of conduct in real property transactions.

Stream of Commerce Everyone who plays a role in producing a product and bringing it to the marketplace.

Thus it was that for nearly all of our history, English courts and courts of common-law jurisdictions in the U.S. have summed up the rights of a buyer in the purchase of a new or used home: ***caveat emptor.*** Earlier in this book, the issue of professional liability was examined in some detail.[1] To a large extent, the liability claims made against sellers, builders, or real estate professionals—most notably brokers—have been based on tort claims of negligence. In this chapter, we take a further look at tort theories and where they are leading us and introduce two new topics into this discussion. The first is that of strict liability, which has its most notable current applications in the field of products liability. Although strict liability concepts have mostly been confined to products placed into the **"stream of commerce"** by manufacturers, real estate has not completely escaped these notions. The second concept is that of warranties. Warranties generally flow from contracts, but this is not a hard and fast rule. As we see later, the areas of tort liability, including the concept of strict liability, and warranties appear to be making inroads into real property applications.

CLAIMS IN TORT

Historically tort actions have been based on personal injuries or injuries to property "other than itself." In other words, a situation must exist in which a personal injury has taken place or, by virtue of a product failure, some other property has been damaged or injured. To have a claim in tort, injury or additional damage had to be shown. Thus construction defects that posed no threat of injury or danger to other property could not be the basis of a tort claim.[2] Such claims have generally been called "disappointed commercial expectations" and have, for the main part, not been allowed to form the basis for claims in tort.

Liability claims that lie in tort have been based on some form of negligence (or fraud). Generally speaking, these claims take one of three forms:

> *Negligent misrepresentation.* When a property has been misrepresented in a material fashion such that the buyer suffers harm, a claim in tort may be available. To make such a claim, however, the injured party must show some fault with the actions, or in some cases the inactions, of the seller, builder, or broker.

---

[1] See Chapters 13 and 14.

[2] See, for example, *Redarowicz v. Ohlendorf* [92 Ill. 2d 171, 441 NE2d 324 (1982)], in which the Illinois Supreme Court held that a homeowner did not have a claim in tort against a builder whose improper construction caused the chimney and an adjoining brick wall to pull away from a structure.

Innocent misrepresentation. Some courts have extended the notion of misrepresentation to include those situations in which statements, even innocently made, may form the basis for a claim in tort. Under this standard, making a statement that later turns out to be false or misleading (assuming that the buyer is damaged by this statement) may lead to liability exposure.

Simple ***negligence.*** The newest standard to be placed in the sale of real property is that of the necessity to conduct a competent investigation of the property and disclose all material defects. In many ways, this standard is simply an affirmative extension of the misrepresentation forms. The difference is the active steps that must be taken by brokers to investigate and disclose.

Negligence The failure to do something which, under the circumstances, should have been done, or doing something which should not have been done, which causes injury to another.

Tort claims are subject to the statute of limitations. In housing, however, it is sometimes difficult to discover the existence of a latent defect until some event occurs that makes the existence of the defect obvious. In *Sewell v. Gregory* (371 S.E.2d 82, 1988) the court held that "the statute of limitation for a tort action arising from latent defects in the construction of a house begins to run when the injured parties knew, or by the exercise of reasonable diligence should have known, of the nature of their injury and its sources." This case involved a house that was constructed in 1975 and flooded in June, 1979 after heavy rains. After making various efforts to correct the flooding problem, the owners finally filed suit on December 21, 1983 claiming the builder to be strictly liable for selling a negligently designed and constructed house.

Many commentators in the field have pointed out that the innocent misrepresentation standard and the simple negligence standard, now seen in at least two states, amount to a form of strict liability. To press a claim of strict liability, no negligence or fault need be stated. The only necessary condition is that of injury or damage. Thus a strict liability claim may be made when an injury results from an action even though no fault is shown or claimed.

KEY POINTS

The general rule still followed in most states is that the seller, absent any attempt to conceal, must disclose only those facts that materially affect the value of a piece of property. The limitation to this rule, however, is that only those facts known to the seller and not discoverable by or accessible to a diligent buyer must be disclosed. This leads to many questions concerning the extent of the seller's knowledge. Some suggest that a limiting statement be placed in the sales agreement that, for example, "To the best (or actual) knowledge of the seller, without independent investigation, inquiry or review . . . " all material information has been disclosed.

STRICT PRODUCTS LIABILITY DOCTRINES

The notion that liability can accrue without fault is one that some claim actually predates the notion of negligence. In the eighteenth century, for example, all that was necessary to claim an action in trespass was proof of a direct physical invasion by the

Strict Liability Liability created based upon an injury to a party regardless of intent or fault. Negligence is not an element in determining strict liability.

defendant. Only in more recent years has the notion that fault must be shown become the prevailing theory in tort claims. Even then, however, many cases were based on the notion that there were exceptions to the negligence standard. At the turn of the century, courts began to look for ways to circumvent the requirement that negligence need be shown. One such device was that of *res ipsa loquitur,* in which the burden of proof shifts to the defendant once the plaintiff has shown that the accident that caused the injury is one that normally would not have occurred without negligence. Thus the plaintiff need only show an injury and the cause of that injury, and the defendant must then prove that he was *not* negligent. Such cases established the notion of a "presumption of negligence" and began the steady march toward **strict liability**.

Effects of "Privity"

Privity A direct contractual (or blood) relationship.

One of the major blockages to liability claims was the notion of privity between the injured party and the defendant. The **privity doctrine**, first established in 1842,[3] limits the class of people to whom a duty of care is owed to those with whom the manufacturer of a product is in contractual privity. Stated more simply, to press a claim against a manufacturer, the injured party must show the existence of a direct contractual relationship between himself and the manufacturer of the defective product. This notion gradually slid from view and was finally abolished as a defense with respect to manufacturers of personal property (or chattels) in 1916.[4] The privity defense, however, continued to appear in real property cases until 1956. In *Hanna v. Fletcher,*[5] the court rejected the notion that actions involving real property somehow differ from those involving personal property. Issues of liability, said the court, should be settled on the basis of facts and ". . . not by a legal fiction set up to bar a factual decision." As we see later, however, the issue of privity as a defense in real property cases has not completely gone away.

Strict Liability and the Construction Industry

The concept of strict liability, or products liability as it is often called, has perhaps its most likely real property area of application in the construction of new houses. Products liability doctrine was developed to protect consumers in what has become an "anonymous marketplace." How can one prove fault or negligence when a product is purchased from a retailer and manufactured in an industrial setting? Historic notions of privity and fault seem to have outlived their usefulness in such a setting. Thus the notion of finding fault was specifically eliminated in the famous case of *Greenman v. Yuba Power Products, Inc.,*[6] in which the user of a power tool was injured when

---

[3] *Winterbottom v. Wright* [10M. & W. 109, 152 Eng. Rep. 402 (1842)].

[4] In the landmark case of *McPherson v. Buick Motor Co.* [217 N.Y. 382, III N.E. 1050 (1916)], in which a defective wheel caused an accident, Buick Motor Co. claimed that the injured party lacked privity because the wheel was purchased from a wheel manufacturer, and Buick had merely installed it on the automobile.

[5] 231 F.2d 469 (D.C. Cir. 1956)

[6] 59 Cal. 2d 57, 377 P.2d 897 (1962)

KEY POINTS

Some commentators suggest the use of a survival and merger provision in the sales agreement to limit explicitly the representations that will survive closing. For example:

Only the warranties and representations and covenants contained in Section ____ shall survive the Closing, provided that any action based upon the failure of the representations or warranties set forth in Section ____ to be true must be commenced within six months after the date of the Closing. All other representations, warranties or covenants shall merge into and be superseded by the various documents executed and delivered at Closing and shall not survive the closing.

Northridge Company v. W.R. Grace and Company

a defective woodlathe malfunctioned and caused a piece of wood to fly out and strike Greenman in the head. Two new ideas, which have since been adopted by virtually every court in the U.S., were developed in *Greenman.* The first is the idea of a "stream of commerce," which includes everyone who played a role in producing the product. In an industrial society, products are often the result of a complex series of manufacturing processes. The final consumer should not have to determine which manufacturer actually caused the product to fail. Anyone in the stream thus becomes a possible target in a strict liability action.

Spreading the Loss Mass producers of products, as opposed to individual consumers, can afford to accept losses by spreading the loss among all consumers.

The second idea to surface was that of **spreading the loss**. Because consumers should have the right to rely on the quality of goods purchased in the marketplace, someone needs to insure their safety. Manufacturers, it is argued, can better afford to accept the burdens by spreading the loss among all consumers. Thus they can bear the losses far better than any individual consumer and should be placed in the position of doing so. This "loss spreading" doctrine at once provides the basis for shifting the liability burden from the consumer and creates an additional issue for courts to wrestle with. In addition to the issues relevant to the injury claim, courts must now take into consideration the ability of the manufacturer to spread the loss. This issue, although in many ways irrelevant to the specifies of the issue of liability, may turn out to be the single most distinguishing feature in real estate applications.

At the present time, there are two schools of thought with regard to strict liability claims involving real property. Until recently,[7] courts had hesitated to apply strict liability concepts to a real property setting. This reluctance was based on two issues.

1. Is an improvement on real property, a house, for example, a product in the normal sense of the term? This question calls for an examination of the history of construction methods, especially housing construction. As we have noted earlier, much of the impetus for strict products liability doctrines came from the Industrial Revolution, which introduced mass production techniques. The notion of *caveat emptor* was relaxed some time ago for consumer products. In part, this trend was based on the fact that consumers no longer had an opportunity to inspect products they were purchasing. In addition, buyers came more and more to rely on the skill, judgment, and knowledge of the seller when making purchases. Finally, the issue of

[7] Some commentators point to a 1965 case, *Shipper v. Levitt & Sons* [44 N.J. 70, 207 A.2d 314], as the first application of strict liability to defective improvements in real estate.

Berman v. Watergate West, Inc.

public safety prompted courts to adopt methods that would encourage producers to manufacture and sell only safe goods.

Some of these same forces have caused the lessening of strict applications of the *caveat emptor* standard in real estate. In the nineteenth century, builders were skilled artisans who worked closely with homeowners in constructing what was really a custom project. Homeowners not only monitored builders during every phase of the project, but also often demanded corrections or improvements before paying the builder. Under these circumstances, the notion of *caveat emptor* was appropriate. With the advent of mechanized equipment and modern construction techniques (which often include lower quality materials and questionable workmanship), home buyers gradually shifted to a position closer to that of a consumer. Gone was the one-on-one relationship between builder and owner, replaced by a relationship arguably little different from that between retailer and customer.

Although these arguments seem persuasive, the housing construction industry is characterized by diversity in methods, materials, and levels of sophistication. Some builders clearly fit the description of a manufacturer, or mass-producer, whereas others work in essentially the same manner as those of the nineteenth century. One distinction that may have some use is that between the custom builder and those who build on speculation. "Spec-built" housing comes much closer to a product in the traditional sense, whereas custom-built projects retain ties to nineteenth-century aspects of home building. The key is the degree of control exercised by the buyer. If the buyer is an active participant during the design and construction processes, it is harder to characterize her as a typical consumer.

2. Is the construction industry equipped to accept the loss-sharing aspect of strict products liability? This question is obviously closely related to the first but brings into perspective a different aspect of the housing construction industry. To the extent that the housing industry is characterized by small builders, and it is to a large degree, the notion of loss spreading has little merit. Over time, however, even a small builder can produce a significant number of houses. Is it fair that we exempt small builders from liability on the basis of size alone? If this doctrine were the dominant one, that is, if builders could avoid liability simply by remaining small, many would adopt strategies aimed at just such a result. The definitions in this area can be somewhat forced in nature. For example, one court found that a claim of strict liability was permissible against a builder even though he was not a "mass-producer" of homes.[8] In this instance, the builder had developed a tract of land with a dozen homes on it, which was, in the view of the court, enough evidence to indicate that he was a "professional builder."

The final issue in this discussion is that of "associations" of, in this case, home builders. If builders can join together in an association of some sort, does this not accomplish the loss-spreading ability needed to make strict liability concepts appropriate? Given that associations are possible,[9] it seems a wiser course for courts to assume that the industry will react to the demands placed on it by products liability.

---

[8] *Patitucci v. Drelich* [153 N.J. Super. 177, 379 A.2d 297 (1977)].

[9] To make risk spreading easier, Congress passed the Products Liability Risk Retention Act of 1980 [15 U.S.C. ss 3901–3904], which allows the formation of "risk retention groups," which may provide insurance on an interstate basis for organizations.

Although we will discuss the development of the role of associations in the context of homeowner warranties, this is exactly what has happened in the housing construction industry.

We began this discussion with a comment that the courts currently are holding to two sets of beliefs with regard to the appropriateness of applying strict products liability doctrines to housing. As you might suspect, one group of rulings continues to maintain that housing is not a product in the common sense of the word, and, when combined with the long-standing tradition of *caveat emptor*, strict product liability doctrines should not be applied. The other group of rulings has pushed housing further into the products liability camp. When faced with an obvious injury for which the recipient was not at fault, the courts tend to look for someone to provide restitution. As is the case with personal products, the issue of fault is not the dominant one. Rather it is the notion that an injury should not be borne by the consumer when the customer is clearly not at fault.

When a sixteen-month-old child was injured by scalding water caused by a builder's failure to install a hot water heater properly, the court quickly resorted to strict liability principles.[10] Lest anyone think that the doctrine would be applied only to instances of physical injuries, another court found a strict liability application involving a defective heating system installed in the home.[11] One interesting aspect of this case was that it involved a person who purchased the home from the original buyer six years after construction was completed. Instances like these will continue to appear. As in other applications of strict liability, courts must examine the facts and determine who should be held accountable for the situation. To expect that ancient doctrines such as *caveat emptor* and privity will offer any degree of insulation for the construction industry, especially in the area of housing, is to deny reality.

WARRANTY CONCEPTS IN REAL ESTATE

The developments in products liability to a large extent mirror those in **warranty** concepts. The doctrine of *caveat emptor* had effects in the application of warranties just as it did in negligence claims in tort. The basis for a distinction in warranty rights between real and personal property is the use of a deed. The home-buying process can be thought of as a two-step process of agreeing on a sales price through the use of a contract for sale and then transferring title by use of a deed. Historically the acceptance of a deed by the buyer ended the role of the seller. This process, often called the "merger" doctrine, assumes that all obligations the seller might have are merged into the deed.

Warranty A promise, covenant, or pledge made by a grantor to a grantee.

Claims of breach of implied warranties are often difficult to distinguish from tort claims. Earlier in this chapter the *Sewell v. Gregory* (371 S.E.2d 82) case, in which a tort claim was made against a builder several years after construction took place, was discussed. The home owners in that case also made claims of a breach of an implied warranty of habitability and fitness for use of the premises as a family home. The defendants used a lack of

[10] This was the basis for the *Schipper v. Levitt & Sons* case cited earlier.

[11] *Kriegler v. Eichler Homes, Inc.* [269 Cal. App. 2d 224, 74 Cal. Rept. 749 (1969)].

privity defense since the Sewells were the second owners of the house. The West Virginia court (quoting the Supreme Court of Wyoming) found that "[t]he purpose of a warranty is to protect innocent purchasers and hold builders accountable for their work. With that reasoning in mind, any reasoning which would arbitrarily interpose a first buyer as an obstruction to someone equally as deserving of recovery is incomprehensible . . . " Thus the builder was found to be potentially liable under both a tort claim **and** a breach of implied warranty claim.

In its strictest form, the merger doctrine denies recovery for breaches of warranties contained in the sales contract (except those that might have been also included in the deed). Thus express, or explicit, warranties the buyer might have included in the sales contract were lost after the closing. The *caveat emptor* standard also worked to deny any implied warranties. Housing consumers were clearly in an unacceptable situation, and courts began a slow process of relaxation of these twin doctrines.

"Collateral Promises" Exception

One of the ways that courts acted to relax the merger doctrine's undesirable effects was to broaden the notion of "unusual promises" made by builders that were deemed to be "collateral" to the deed. Although subject to case law interpretation, most courts now recognize any written warranties contained in the sales contract as collateral to the deed. The idea is that because warranties contained in the sales contract do not directly pertain to the transfer of title, they are necessarily collateral to the main purpose of the deed. This interpretation allows written warranties contained in the sales contract to survive the closing process. Without this exception, defects discovered after closing would not be subject to a claim against the builder, regardless of any promises made in the contract for sale.

Implied Warranties

Just as developments in consumer products caused shifts in the strict liability doctrine, the Industrial Revolution had a direct impact on warranty theories. One of the earliest findings of an implied warranty (as opposed to one expressly granted in a contract) was in a U.S. Supreme Court case in 1884.[12] When a buyer had no real opportunity to inspect a product before purchase, the courts began to impose what became known as the "implied warranty of merchantability" that a consumer could rely on. The **Uniform Commercial Code** (UCC), now adopted by all states except Louisiana, implies a warranty of merchantability in all transactions except real estate. The development of this doctrine was influenced by the notion of "reasonable expectations" that consumers have about the products they purchase but that are often not included in any written contract. The basic idea is that reasonable expectations about the quality and performance of a product can be assumed when operating in the marketplace. The promotion of public safety, especially in regard to food items, is also frequently stated as a reason for the implied warranty of merchantability.

Uniform Commercial Code Uniform statute adopted in most states which governs commercial transactions.

Although expressly excluded from the provisions of the UCC, real estate saw a similar development with regard to implied warranties between builder and buyer.

[12] *Kellog Bridge Co. v. Hamilton* [110 U.S. 108, 116 (1884)].

Similar to the consumer products area, real estate has seen implied warranties develop over time.

Warranty of Workmanlike Construction

As critics began to point out that consumers of a defective two-dollar fountain pen had more protection in the law than consumers of million-dollar houses, courts began to look for ways to back away from the strict *caveat emptor* standard. In what became known as the "implied warranty of workmanlike construction," courts began to impose a duty to comply with requirements that lenders mandated and regulations of municipalities to construct the house in a workmanlike manner. The application of these warranties, however, was severely limited because they were based on clauses actually contained in contracts. Eventually courts came to recognize an implied warranty, which encompassed the same requirements but based on principles seen in transactions of consumer goods rather than contract language.

Warranty of Habitability

Although the implied warranty of workmanlike construction (or skillful construction as it is sometimes called) is the equivalent of the implied warranty of merchantability found in consumer goods, another similar warranty was developed by some courts that is more uniquely suited to real estate. In addition to the notion of workmanlike construction, the notion developed that the structure should be "reasonably fit for occupancy as a place of abode." In some ways, this mimics the "implied fitness for use" warranty some courts have applied to consumer goods.

The concept embodied by these implied warranties is that a product should not only be free of defects (i.e., be constructed in a workmanlike fashion), but also should serve the purpose for which it was purchased. Thus a house must be safe and reasonably suitable for use as a dwelling.[13] The furnace, for example, must be capable of providing adequate heat in winter; in similar fashion, the house must be adequately insulated. In short, any feature that the court may deem to be necessary for use as a dwelling may be included in the notion of an implied warranty of habitability.

TORT AND WARRANTY LIABILITY CONCEPTS

In many ways, the development of strict products liability theories and implied warranties is intertwined. Some courts have held, for example, that implied warranties are really grounded in tort.[14] Although warranties have traditionally been subject to the privity requirements discussed earlier, many courts have not felt constrained by privity requirements. The lack of privity is still in use as a defense to implied war-

[13] Some courts use a stricter standard, which requires only that a dwelling be capable of use. In other words, the house has to be so damaged as to be unfit for habitation in order to press a claim. Other courts have adopted a compromise position based on the standard of a "substantial impairment."

[14] To confuse matters even more, these courts have gone on to impose the privity, notice, and waiver requirements of contracts.

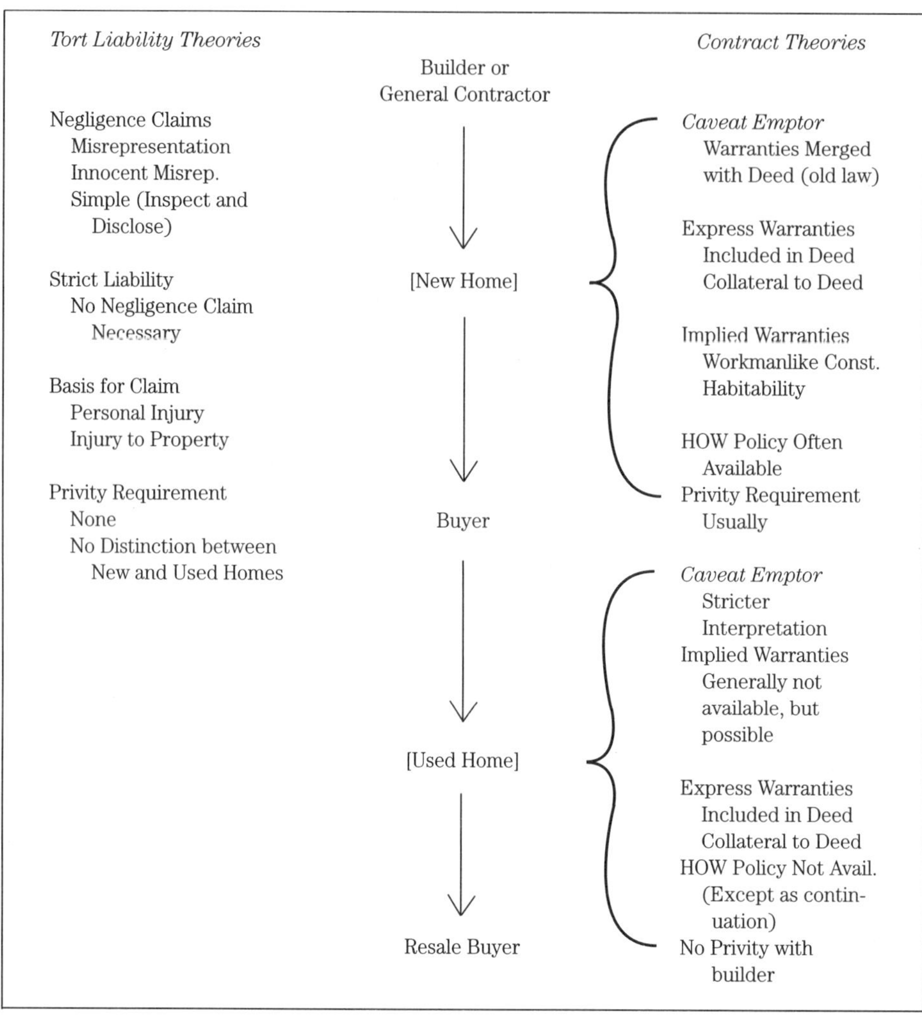

FIGURE 17.1 TORT AND CONTRACT LIABILITY CONCEPTS

ranty claims in some states. The future of this line of defense, however, seems to be in some doubt. Figure 17.1 provides a brief summary of the similarities and differences between warranty and tort claims of liability.

Notice and Waiver of Warranties

One feature found in warranty concepts is the ability to disclaim warranties, even implied warranties. Although disclaimers, because they are written by builders, must be interpreted in a fashion least favorable to their position, they are not considered inappropriate. The UCC requires that consumers be notified of any and all warranty disclaimers in a "clear and conspicuous" manner, and courts had tended to apply the same standards to builders.

The failure of a builder to disclaim warranties regarding specific features of a property can often prove to be costly. For example, a contractor was held strictly liable for a defective air conditioning unit installed in a poor location[15] even though this installation was caused by the owner's request for a modification late in the construction process. Had the builder disclaimed any warranties concerning the unit owing to its poor location and allowed the owner to accept or reject the decision, the strict liability claim may have been avoided. Remember, implied warranties are really just another form of strict liability in a different context. As we have seen, the rules in this entire area are ambiguous at best.

HOME OWNER'S WARRANTY CONTRACTS

In a development that many have characterized as an effort to restrict any common-law warranties that courts may decide to develop, the National Association of Home Builders (NAHB), whose members construct about one-half of all new housing in the U.S., established the Home Owner's Warranty (HOW) Program. If a builder wishes to participate in the HOW program, he must register with the HOW Corporation,[16] which administers the program. Participating builders agree to abide by HOW's construction and performance standards, which are developed and monitored by local warranty councils.

Rainwater v. National Home Insurance Company

For a one-time fee of $2 per $1000 of the closing price of the property, the builder warrants the workmanship and materials used for the first year of ownership. The program also covers plumbing, heating, electrical, and cooling systems during the first two years. Any major construction defects discovered during the first two years are also covered by the builder. During years three through ten of ownership, a private insurance contract is provided, which protects against major construction defects.[17]

The term **"major construction defects"** has been the source of many disputes by homeowners seeking coverage under the HOW program. A typical definition used would be:

Major Constuction Defects
Type of protection offered by HOW contracts which includes damages to major structural elements of a home.

> Actual damage to the load-bearing portions of the home (including damage due to Soil Movement [a specifically defined term in the contract]) that affects its load-bearing function and that vitally affects or is imminently likely to produce a vital effect on the use of the home for residential purposes.

If this language sounds familiar after reading the material on implied warranties, then you understand the purpose of HOW contracts. As we have seen, many courts have moved to provide home buyers with a set of implied warranties exactly like those expressly provided by HOW policies. Why then would a home buyer purchase such a contract? Two reasons come to mind:

1. The home buyer does not understand his rights under theories of implied warranties owed by builders.

---

[15] *Hamilton Fixture Company v. Anderson* [285 So. 2d 744 (Miss. Sup. Ct. 1973)].

[16] HOW was a fully owned subsidiary of NAHB until 1981, when ownership was transferred to participating builders on a mutual basis.

[17] Default by the builder on any obligation during the initial two-year period is also covered by this policy (although HOW may seek restitution from the builder for any costs incurred).

2. The home buyer wishes to have additional protection beyond that potentially available in a legal action.

Burley v. Homeowners Warranty Corporation

The first reason, although it may unfortunately be a common one, does little to justify the existence of the HOW program. The second reason, however, is more than adequate to justify the cost of obtaining a HOW policy when available. Two things can go wrong with an action to enforce a warranty, either express or implied. First, the jurisdiction may be one, and there are many, that still holds to fairly strict definitions of *caveat emptor* and merger theory or, possibly, allows privity as a defense.

Second, even if the homeowner is successful in pressing her claim, the builder may have inadequate resources to offer any real protection. Remember that many home builders are small businesses with little, if any, assets. For these reasons, the HOW program serves a valid purpose as an insurance policy for buyers of new homes.

Privity Revisited

Privity A direct contractual (or blood) relationship.

As you may recall from earlier in this chapter, the issue of contractual **privity** has at various times, and under various circumstances, presented a problem in pressing both tort and warranty (or contract) claims. As we have seen, privity as a defense died quite some time ago in the consumer products area. It still lingers on, however, in the real estate area.

McMillan v. Brune-Harpenau-Torbeck Builders, Inc.

This warranty discussion is predicated on the notion that the house purchased is of new construction. Thus privity usually exists between the builder (or general contractor) and buyer. The courts have generally been reluctant however, to extend implied warranties beyond the initial purchaser of homes. Thus a buyer of a "used" home, even one that is essentially new, may find herself without benefit of warranty protection.

There are two possible ways out of such a situation:

1. A court may hold (and some have) that privity is not strictly necessary to press a warranty claim.
2. A strict products liability approach, in which privity is not an issue, may be pursued.

KEY POINTS

One of the most troubling aspects of a strict application of the privity doctrine occurs when a "straw man" is used. Using a straw man involves having the original builder transfer title to an intermediary, a "sale" in name only. Thus the home buyer, even though he is the first "real" owner of the property, does not have privity with the builder. These schemes can become difficult to untangle when corporate subsidiaries are involved. For example, perhaps you bought a house from ABC Homes, which, because it had never been occupied, you assumed was a "new" home. Problems develop at a later date, and you try to press a claim against ABC Homes. Much to your dismay, you discover that ABC Homes "bought" the house from Acme Development using a short-term note that was paid off when you purchased the house; thus you lack privity with the true builder. Should the fact that ABC Homes and Acme Development, both corporations, share many common officers and members of their respective boards of directors make a difference?

The privity defense is still alive and quite well in a number of jurisdictions. In *Ellis v. Robert C. Morris, Inc.* (128 N.H. 358, 513 A.2d 951, 1986), for example, the court dismissed both a claim of breach of implied warranty of habitability and a claim in tort for negligence based on the absence of privity between a builder and subsequent owner. In this case, a home was first occupied in January, 1978 but sold by the end of the year to the original owner's employer. The employer in turn resold the house to Ellis in February 1979. In spite of the relatively short time frame, and the relationship between the parties, the New Hampshire court opted to " . . . depart from the traditional principles upon which contract and tort are predicated . . . " and took the position that " . . . allowing an action for breach of implied warranty in the absence of privity of contract [is] tantamount to imposing strict liability in tort. " Because lack of privity does not bar a negligence action, the court went on to find that builders have no tort duty to home buyers for economic loss—again reverting to an older position no longer held in the majority of states.

SERVICES EXEMPTION

Services Exemption The exemption from strict products liability doctrine for those who provide services as opposed to products.

One final topic should be included in our discussion, and that is the services/products distinction. As a general rule, those who provide services, as opposed to those who sell products, are exempt from strict products liability theories and implied warranty claims. At present, there is one major group in real estate that benefits from this exemption—architects. In a number of cases, architects have been held to be immune from strict liability[18] because they sell services rather than products. Thus a contractor may be held strictly liable for following an architect's defective plans, whereas the architect, absent a showing of negligence, would escape liability.

For most housing consumers, this exemption is not a matter of grave concern. Although builders may find little comfort in bearing the full responsibility while the person who in some cases may be the real culprit walks away, the housing consumer is still protected. The issue is raised here both as a point of information and to signal the emergence of what may be a new trend in the area.

CONCLUSIONS

Several commentators, searching for ways to shield builders and sellers from strict liability exposure, have begun to point to the role of real estate professionals, particularly real estate brokers and appraisers, as evidence that home buyers really do have access to adequate information concerning the property. The simple negligence standard described earlier in this chapter (and explained more fully in Chapter 12) would seem to add credence to this theory. After all, if real estate brokers are charged with an affirmative duty to inspect and disclose, does the seller still need to be saddled with strict liability exposure? At the very least, real estate brokers should share in the burden and, in fact, they are beginning to do just that. Although this development, similar to that concerning the services exemption for architects, should not

[18] See, for example, *K-Mart Corp. v. Midcon Realty Group of Conn., Ltd.* [489 F. Supp. 813 (D. Conn. 1980)].

overly concern housing consumers—it hardly matters who pays, as long as someone pays—the real estate brokers have much reason to be concerned.

If the attorneys for sellers or builders are successful in shifting some or even all of the responsibility to real estate professionals, the structure of the real estate brokerage industry will have to change. The most obvious way to change is to use an exemption already firmly established in the law—the services exemption. Real estate brokers can be characterized as sellers of a service at least as easily as architects who, after all, produce a physical set of plans.

Real estate brokers, in a very real sense, produce no product at all and should find refuge from strict liability, if not from negligence charges, by making the nature of their role more explicit. In other words, real estate brokers do not sell houses, they sell the service of finding buyers (or sellers) of houses and facilitating the transaction. Unfortunately, the continued use of agency relationships serves to confuse the issue.

DISCUSSION QUESTIONS

1. Historically what needed to exist before a tort claim could be filed? In what situation could a tort claim be used?
2. Claims on property in which liabilities lie in tort have historically been based on some form of negligence or fraud. Describe the three forms these claims tended to take.
3. At the turn of the century, courts began to use the notion of *res ipsa loquitor.* What was the purpose of this doctrine?
4. What is the privity doctrine?
5. In the famous case of *Greenman v. Yuba Power Products,* two new ideas surfaced: the "stream of commerce" and "spreading the loss" concepts. Discuss each of these ideas and the reasoning behind them.
6. Until recently courts have been hesitant to apply strict liability concepts to a real property setting. Why?
7. Historically the acceptance of a deed by the buyer ended the role of the seller. Explain this process, called the "merger doctrine."
8. As an attempt to relax the merger doctrine, the courts developed an interpretation known as the "collateral promises" exception. What is the idea behind this exception?
9. Similar to the consumer products area, real estate has developed implied warranties over time. Explain the "Warranty of Workmanlike Construction" and the "Warranty of Habitability."
10. Explain the Home Owner's Warranty (HOW) Program from the homeowner's perspective.
11. Aside from not understanding his rights under theories of implied warranties owed by builders, for what reason would a homeowner purchase a HOW policy?
12. Explain the service exemption as it applies to real estate. Who benefits most from this exemption?

NORTHRIDGE COMPANY V. W. R. GRACE AND COMPANY

471 N.W.2d 179 (1991)

Allows a claim in strict products liability to recover essentially economic losses involving asbestoes-containing product

The plaintiffs, Northridge Company and Southridge Company, filed a complaint against the defendant, W. R. Grace and Company, alleging breach of warranty and several tort claims based on the defendant's sale of Monokote, a fireproofing material, to the plaintiff's general contractor for use in the construction of the plaintiffs' shopping centers. The complaint alleges that the Monokote was in a defective condition and, because it contains asbestos, presented unreasonable danger to persons and property. The plaintiffs assert that the asbestos contaminated the building and they suffered damages by incurring expenses for inspection, testing and removal of Monokote and by a diminished value of the property.

The question we consider in this case is whether the plaintiffs' complaint states a tort claim for relief in strict products liability or negligence. The circuit court determined that the plaintiffs' claimed damages in this case did not result from " damage to other property" but instead were solely economic losses unrelated to any physical harm to property. . . . [T]he circuit court concluded that the "doctrine of economic loss" precludes the plaintiffs' tort claims of negligence and strict liability. According to the circuit court, "the doctrine of economic loss . . . provides that 'a commercial purchaser of a product cannot recover solely economic losses from the manufacturer under negligence or strict liability theories,' " . . . The circuit court thus denied recovery in tort when the only damage in this case was, in its view, to the product sold. The circuit court concluded that only a contract action for breach of warranty lies and that the statute of limitations barred the plaintiffs' warranty claim. The circuit court dismissed the plaintiffs' complaint, holding that it presented no claim upon which relief could be granted. . . .

[1] [2] [3] . . . The plaintiffs' shopping centers were built in 1970 and 1972 by a general contractor who is not a party to this action. The defendant sold Monokote to the general contractor, who applied it to the beams and columns of the buildings. Monokote contains asbestos. Because of an alleged health hazard created by the asbestos, the plaintiffs apparently initiated an asbestos abatement program in the shopping centers sometime in the mid-1980s. The plaintiffs subsequently sold the shopping centers in 1988. The plaintiffs allege that they expended funds in the asbestos abatement program, that the Monokote reduced the value of their property, and that they received a lower price on the sale of the shopping centers because the Monokote damaged the buildings.

[4] It is well-established law that under Wisconsin strict products liability law a plaintiff may recover for physical harm to property caused by a defect in the product that presents an unreasonable danger to persons or property. . . .

[5] Numerous cases support the rule that strict products liability law . . . and negligence law . . . apply to physical harm to property as well as to personal injury.

[6] The parties assume that Wisconsin has adopted some form of the "economic loss doctrine" which may preclude recovery in a negligence or strict products liability torts claim when the complainant's claim is characterized as solely economic loss. . . . "Economic loss" may be defined generally as "the diminution in the value of the product because it is inferior in quality and does not work for the general purposes for which it was manufactured and sold" . . . Economic loss has also been described in terms of direct economic loss and consequential economic loss.

. . . A complaint's remedy for economic loss alone, without a claim for personal injury or physical harm to property other than the defective product itself, generally lies in a breach of warranty claim, not in a claim in tort. . . .

[7] The plaintiffs assert that the Monokote caused asbestos contamination that has injured its other property. The plaintiffs argue that the contamination of the shopping centers with asbestos from the Monokote constitutes actual physical harm to their property. The plaintiffs urge that the

complaint is not that Monokote has broken down or failed to perform the functions for which it was purchased. The plaintiffs assert that the complaint focuses on what Monokote has done to the shopping centers: It has physically harmed the property causing an unreasonable risk to health and safety. The plaintiffs contend that these allegations of harm to property other than the Monokote itself are sufficient to defeat the motion to dismiss and to entitle the plaintiffs to an opportunity to prove their claims.

The defendant argues that the plaintiffs have not alleged any physical harm to either persons or property. The defendant argues that the plaintiffs' alleged losses are solely "economic," that is, that the product was allegedly of inferior quality. The defendants contend that the plaintiffs complain about damage to the product itself for which they are limited to contract remedies, not a tort remedy. According to the defendant, any losses suffered by the plaintiffs were incurred because the plaintiffs were dissatisfied with the product itself. Any expenses the plaintiffs incurred for asbestos abatement or any losses they incurred in the sale of the shopping centers were, according to the defendant, unrelated to "asbestos contamination" of the shopping centers and constitute solely economic losses which may not be recovered in strict products liability or negligence suits unless there is injury to person or property. The defendant emphasizes language in the plaintiffs' complaint referring to damage caused by the "mere presence" of the Monokote in the shopping centers. The defendant implies that any asbestos abatement programs the plaintiffs initiated were unnecessary and that the plaintiffs are using the asbestos as an excuse for disappointment in the sale price for their shopping centers. The defendant supports its argument with factual claims that the asbestos in Monokote poses no property or health risk and that the plaintiffs did not allege injury to any person by exposure to asbestos in the shopping malls.

We must assume, for the purposes of this review, that the plaintiffs' factual allegations and reasonable inferences drawn therefrom are true.[1] We must assume that the asbestos in Monokote creates a contaminant in the building that is a health hazard to the occupants of the building. . . .

The alleged damages in this case have characteristics associated with both economic loss and physical harm to property. The allegedly hazardous characteristic of the Monokote is its contamination of the buildings with asbestos. In this kind of case, no outwardly visible evidence of physical harm to the property exists. We infer from the complaint that the harm claimed is that the Monokote causes the air to contain particles of asbestos which are injurious to occupants of the buildings but invisible to the naked eye.

[8] In addition, the plaintiffs' claimed damages—expenses incurred to remove or replace the Monokote and the diminished value of their property due to the presence of the Monokote—appear to be the kind of damages typically associated with defects in the product itself and considered economic losses. The plaintiffs' strict products liability claim is not barred, however, simply because the plaintiffs seek damages for repair costs, replacement costs, decreased value, and lost profits in the sale of the centers. While economic loss is measured by repair costs, replacement costs, loss of profits, or diminution of value, the measure of damages does not determine whether the complaint is for physical harm or economic loss. . . . In other words, the fact that the measure of the plaintiffs' damages is economic does not transform the nature of its injury into a solely economic loss. . . . Physical harm to property may be measured by the cost of repairing the buildings to make them safe.

Commentators caution that distinguishing between economic loss and physical harm to property other than the product itself is often a difficult task, especially in cases involving substances

[1] The complaint claims damages to the property as follows: Plaintiffs have suffered harm including damage to and loss of use of their property, diminution of its value at resale, extensive costs for inspection, testing, repair, replacement and removal of asbestos and asbestos-containing products as well as for other measures necessary to abate the health hazard created by the presence of asbestos and asbestos-containing products in the Southridge and Northridge Premises. This harm has been caused solely by the presence of asbestos and asbestos-containing products in the Southridge Premises and Northridge Premises.

whose hazardous qualities are disputed.[2] Several courts have commented on the difficulty of trying to fit a claim for asbestos damage within the framework of physical harm or economic loss which has been established for more traditional tort and contract actions. . . . Nevertheless commentators and courts recognize the necessity of drawing a distinction between contract claims for economic loss and tort claims for physical harm to property. The parties' rights and defenses, such as notice, privity, and the statutes of limitations, may turn on whether the claim sounds in tort or contract.

The distinction between physical harm (tort actions) and economic loss (contract actions) is based on the traditional distinction between tort law and contract law. Tort law rests on obligations imposed by law; contract law rests on obligations imposed by bargain.

The gist of a strict products liability tort case is that the plaintiff has suffered personal injury or property damage caused by a defective product that posed an unreasonable risk of injury to person or property. Tort law is premised on safety. Public policy demands that the manufacturer and seller bear the responsibility for such injury to person or property.

[9] The principle of economic loss, on the other hand, is derived from the law of contract. Recovery for economic loss is intended to protect purchasers from losses suffered because a product failed in its intended use. Recovery for economic loss necessarily focuses on the bargain struck between the parties; warranty law is premised on protection of the bargain. Economic loss is defined, as we stated previously, as damages for inadequate value, because the product is inferior and does not work for the general purpose for which it was manufactured or sold. Liability for economic loss is based on express or implied representations manifesting the manufacturer's or seller's intent to guarantee the product. . . .

Thus defects of suitability and quality are redressed through contract actions and safety hazards through tort actions. . . .

Both parties cite decisions from other jurisdictions in which the courts struggled with characterizing the harm in cases alleging asbestos contamination of buildings. Many courts have upheld such complaints to be physical harm to property within strict products liability and negligence. . . . Other courts have concluded that where the complaining party has not really alleged contamination or physical harm to the building or where the risk of future injury from the product is remote and conjectural, the losses are economic losses, actionable in contract, not in negligence or strict products liability. . . .

With these principles in mind we examine the complaint in this case to determine whether the damages the plaintiffs allege are more akin to economic loss or physical harm to property.

The plaintiffs do not appear to assert in their tort counts in the complaint that the Monokote itself was inferior in quality or did not work for its intended purpose, the essence of a claim for economic loss. The plaintiffs are not dissatisfied with the quality of the Monokote as a fireproofing material. The plaintiffs' loss did not arise from deterioration or insufficient product value. The plaintiffs are not claiming damages because of injury to the product itself.

The essence of the plaintiffs' claim is that Monokote releases toxic substances in the environment thereby causing damage to the building and a health hazard to its occupants. The plaintiffs claim that their property has been physically altered by the defendant's product, whether or not such alteration is outwardly visible.

We conclude that the plaintiffs' allegation that the defendant's asbestos-containing product physically harmed the plaintiffs' building is the type of injury which is actionable under claims for relief in strict products liability and negligence. The principles and policies underlying strict products liability actions, namely, public safety and risk sharing, justify recognizing the tort claims.

[2] See, e.g., Comment, Asbestos in Schools and the Economic Loss Doctrine, 54 U.Chi.L.Rev. 277 (1987). That the distinction between strict products liability and warranty may be blurred may be explained by the fact that strict products liability in tort evolved from contract warranty theories; in many ways, strict products liability is a way of extending express or implied warranties to a remote purchaser.

For the reasons set forth, we reverse the order of the circuit court and remand the cause for further proceedings consistent with this opinion. The decision of the circuit court is reversed and the case remanded.

Case Reflections

1. What is W. R. Grace's relationship with the plaintiff Northridge Company? What specific damages are the plaintiffs suing for?
2. The defendants in this case claim that the plaintiffs' alleged losses are solely "economic." Explain the importance of this point.
3. How did the Supreme Court of Wisconsin rule in this case? What was the reasoning behind its decision?

BERMAN V. WATERGATE WEST, INC.

391 A.2d 1351 (1977–78)

Allows a strict products liability claim even though a breach of warranty claim was pressed. Note the dissenting opinion that this ruling opens real estate agents to strict liability

Appellant is a tenant-shareholder in the Watergate West housing cooperative. Appellees are Riverview Realty Corporation ("Riverview"), which is the company that marketed the cooperative apartments to the public, and Watergate West, Inc. ("Watergate West"), which is the cooperative itself. The suit was filed in 1971 for damages flowing from the breach of express and implied warranties. The complaint alleges that from the time appellant moved into the cooperative in 1969, her apartment was defective in many respects.

In 1976, a jury trial commenced. At the close of appellant's case, before either Watergate West or Riverview had presented their defenses, the trial court directed a verdict for both appellees, ruling that appellant had failed to show any contractual obligation on the part of Riverview, and had failed to prove damages. . . .

From one point of view this is a simple case. It involves a mass-produced product which allegedly reached the ultimate consumer in a defective state and caused property damage. In such circumstances, the law is clear that the consumer has a cause of action against all who participated in placing the product into the stream of commerce. The case, however, has not proved simple. Confusion arose partly because of the way in which the particular product was marketed (though a cooperative) and partly because of the use of one mischievously ambiguous word (warranty). In reversing, we do not pretend to deal with every issue which could be raised on the basis of the facts here. We wish only to clarify that the remedies of the injured consumer in such a situation do "not . . . depend upon the intricacies of the law of sales." Greenman v. Yuba Power Products, Inc. . . .

I. BACKGROUND

A developer of mass-produced housing has a number of choices as to how to market his completed product. One way in which that product can be marketed is as a cooperative. Where this is done, the developer does not sell the individual housing units directly to the ultimate consumer. Rather, the developer sells the whole building to a corporation (the " cooperative ") of which the ultimate consumer is a stockholder, and from which that consumer then rents an individual unit. The marketing of the Watergate West housing cooperative proceeded as follows.

In 1964, Watergate Improvements Associates ("WIA"), a limited partnership, was formed to sponsor a housing project. A subsidiary of WIA, Watergate Construction Corporation, was formed to build the cooperative. Another subsidiary of WIA, Riverview Realty Corporation, acted as sales agent. On August 24, 1967, before construction of the building began, Watergate West, the cooperative, was chartered. From that date until June 1969, when an independent board of directors was elected, WIA controlled Watergate West. On August 25, 1967, a prospectus was issued describing the project. . . .

Persons wishing to buy an interest in the planned cooperative signed the subscription and deposit agreement referred to in the prospectus. The agreement is, on its face, between the subscribing member and the cooperative, Watergate West. Appellant signed such an agreement on September 19, 1967. In 1969, after the cooperative was constructed, the subscribing members signed a Cooperative Apartment Proprietary Lease and Occupancy Agreement which gave them the right to occupy their apartments for 99 years in exchange for the payment of a monthly assessment. Like the stock subscription agreement, the lease is, on its face, between the subscribing member and the cooperative, Watergate West.

Appellant's lease agreement is dated January 14, 1969. On January 14, 1969, however, Watergate West did not own the building. As a result, appellant also signed a subsidiary agreement with Riverview whereby she agreed to remit monthly rent payments to Riverview if she should occupy her apartment before the cooperative acquired title to the building. Appellant moved into her apartment on January 28, 1969. The cooperative acquired title to the building on May 1, 1969.

II. THE PROCEEDINGS IN THE TRIAL COURT

As noted above, the complaint in this case alleges breach of express and implied warranties. More particularly, the complaint alleges that appellees breached these warranties by delivering to appellant an apartment containing numerous defective appliances; that these appliances included a defective air conditioning system; that this air conditioning system caused damage to the parquet floors, the wall, and the wool rug and pad in her bedroom; and "that said breaches of warranty have continued from the date of said agreement, January 14, 1969 to the present . . . (and) have rendered said apartment at least 50% Uninhabitable from January 1969 until the present."

Watergate West responded to this complaint as follows:

That on January 14, 1969, when the plaintiff first occupied her apartment . . . she occupied it as a tenant, and at that point all the defects alleged by her to exist, did exist. At that time she dealt exclusively with Riverview Realty Corporation, which was the agent for the promoters of the project. That Watergate West, Inc. did not become the owner of the building . . . until May 1, 1969, long after all of these defects had been noted and objected to.

Riverview answered the complaint by denying the existence of any express or implied warranties. In addition, Riverview filed a motion for summary judgment . . . alleging that Riverview could not be held liable on the contracts between appellant and Watergate West because "Riverview Realty Corporation acted as agent for Watergate West, Inc. in negotiating with the plaintiff and other purchasers of cooperative apartments in said building, and the fact of its agency and the identity of its principal were disclosed to the plaintiff."

. . . Watergate West contended that Riverview "(had not acted) as agents for Watergate West but (had acted) for themselves and the other promoters." Watergate West then went on to argue that appellant did have a valid cause of action against Riverview, because " at the time the building was conveyed (to Watergate West) it was defective in many respects, including the items alleged by the plaintiff herein."

Riverview's motion for summary judgment was denied and the case went to trial. At trial, appellant recounted the circumstances of her purchase of an interest in the cooperative. She then described the defects she found in the apartment when she moved in, the most serious of which was the malfunctioning of the air conditioning unit. According to appellant's testimony, the air conditioner created such serious humidity in her bedroom that she had to keep the door to that room closed and sleep in her living room for two years, until the unit was repaired. . . .

III. DISCUSSION

(A) The area of law which governs here is the law of products liability. That area of law has, in the past decade and a half, developed at a breathtaking pace. The field is succinctly described . . . in the following manner.

In general, products liability, in whatever form manifested, is viewed as an area of tort law, dealing with recourse for personal injury or property damage resulting from the use of a product, and in its broadest sense, it may cover actions for negligence, breach of warranty, or strict liability in tort. Over the years, numerous theories of recovery have evolved within the ambit of products liability, but these were refined and consolidated until the theory of strict liability evolved to complement the traditional warranty and negligence theories. Distinctions between the various doctrines of product liability as they presently exist frequently have more theoretical than practical significance . . .

The instant case is a suit for breach of express and implied warranty. Liability for breach of warranty "is a curious hybrid, born of the illicit intercourse of tort and contract. . . . " W. Prosser, Law of Torts s 95 at 634 (4th ed. 1971). Its evolution has been traced as follows.

Historically . . . an action for breach of warranty was essentially one in tort for deceit, differing, however, in that no knowledge on the part of the seller of the unfitness of the product had to be shown. Through changes in common-law pleading, an additional remedy for breach of warranty was found by the introduction of the method of declaring on warranty *Indebitatus assumpsit.* This action was predicated upon the contractual relation between the buyer and seller, and an implied promise of the seller to pay a fair amount for his failure to fulfill his implied promise or warranty. . . . However, by the adoption of *Assumpsit* as the almost exclusive remedy for breach of warranty, there was a transition of its status from tort to contract. . . .

As the excerpt makes clear, liability in warranty was gradually limited to cases involving contracts. This limitation undoubtedly served "to curtail the virtually limitless liabilities of the earlier law, perhaps, as some have suggested, to protect infant enterprises in the formative years of the industrial revolution." . . . As the infant enterprises of the early industrial revolution became the mass manufacturers of modern day society, however, the law of warranty began to shed its contractual trappings once more. Finally, in Greenman v. Yuba Power Products, Inc., . . . the California Supreme Court decided to discard the language of contract entirely. In that case, Chief Justice Traynor wrote:

Although . . . strict liability (for placing defective products into the stream of commerce) has usually been based on the theory of an express or implied warranty . . . the abandonment of the requirement of a contract . . . the recognition that the liability is not assumed by agreement but imposed by law . . . , and the refusal to permit (disclaimers) . . . make clear that the liability is not one governed by the law of contract warranties but by the law of strict liability in tort. . . .

Subsequent to the decision in Greenman v. Yuba Power Products, Inc. . . . the concept of strict liability in tort spread rapidly. . . .

It has been said that the current doctrines of implied warranty and strict liability in tort are but two labels for the same legal right and remedy, as the governing principles are identical. This to a large extent is true. The differences between strict liability in tort and implied warranty, if any, are conceptual. "Implied warranty recovery is based upon two factors: (a) The product or article in question has been transferred from the manufacturer's possession while in a 'defective' state * * * and (b) as a result of being 'defective,' the product causes personal injury or property damage." On the other hand, strict liability in tort is imposed on a manufacturer "when an article he places on the market * * * proves to have a defect that causes injury to a human being" or his property. Whether contract or tort, there is a liability imposed for injury caused by placing a defective product into the stream of commerce . . .

(B) The sale of an interest in a cooperative does not at first blush appear to fall within the purview of products liability law. Despite one court's characterization, the transaction does not strike one as a sale of "goods." . . . Yet even if we recognize to the sale of realty, the result is the same. For it is by now widely accepted that the law of products liability applies not only to the sale of goods, but also to the sale of newly constructed homes. Thus, in the leading case of Schipper v. Levitt & Sons, Inc., . . . , the Supreme Court of New Jersey wrote:

We consider that there are no meaningful distinctions between (the) mass production and sale of homes and the mass production and sale of automobiles and that the pertinent overriding policy considerations are the same. That being so, the warranty or strict liability principles . . . should be carried over into the realty field.

(C) . . . [I]f the sponsor of the Watergate project had been a single corporate entity, and the sponsor had built the complex itself and sold the individual units outright to the consumer, the sponsor would be liable under products liability theory to the extent the units proved defective.

The question before us today is where responsibility should be placed for damage caused by similar defects when the sponsor does not do business as a single corporation, but rather subdivides itself into a builder, an owner, and a vendor; and does not sell the units outright to the consumer, but rather transfers title to a cooperative and markets those units as proprietary leaseholds. The court below held that appellant had no cause of action against Riverview, as there was no contract between her and that corporation. There was also no contract between appellant and Watergate Improvement Associates. Nor was there any contract between appellant and Watergate Construction Corporation. Nevertheless, each one of those entities was an "integral part of the overall producing and marketing enterprise" that placed the defective product into the stream of commerce. . . . Accordingly, each one of them can be held accountable to the ultimate consumer for damage caused by the defective product.

(D) Whether the cooperative can or should also be held accountable is another question. In the present posture of this case, a decision regarding Watergate West's liability would be premature. Because of the arguments made on appeal, however, we think a few comments are warranted.

In many respects the cooperative is like any other landlord. . . . Admittedly, there are differences between Watergate West and other landlords. It does not appear, however, that these differences should have any significance in the present context.[1] Certainly, as regards the ability to redistribute or insure against loss caused by defective products, the cooperative is no differently situated than any other landlord. . . .

There is reason to believe that a landlord could be held strictly liable for damages caused to a tenant by defective equipment. . . . Moreover, in some circumstances this liability might attach even though the landlord acquired the building subsequent to installation of the equipment. . . .

On the other hand, where there appears to be nothing standing in the way of recovery from those who are primarily responsible for placing the defective products into the stream of commerce, some courts have declined to extend the law of products into the stream of commerce, some courts have declined to extend the law of products liability to its furthest reach. . . . Whether a similar result should obtain in the instant case, is a question which can be explored on remand.

Accordingly, the trial court's order is reversed and the case remanded for proceedings consistent with this opinion.

It is so order.

NEBEKER, Associate Judge, dissenting:

The thesis of the majority opinion is that one who is a part of the building and selling of homes, or, as the majority puts it, places them "into the stream of commerce," is liable for damage to the ultimate purchaser which results from defects in the property. Regardless of whether this is an accurate statement of the law in many jurisdictions, I submit that the proposition is wholly inapplicable to this case.

The record shows only that the appellee, Riverview Realty, was a real estate agent for the selling of the cooperative apartment for a company called Watergate Improvement Associates. The record does not show that Riverview was a builder, a seller or a manufacturer. There is absolutely no evidentiary support for the majority's assumption that Riverview was one and the same with the developers and builders of the project. Without evidence of such a connection, Riverview cannot be held liable for product defects on any theory. Not one of the many cases cited in the majority opinion holds that a real estate broker is liable to purchasers for damage resulting from defects in the

[1] Notably, the Javins court, which was among the first to extend products liability theory to the landlord-tenant field, made no distinction between cases involving cooperatives and conventional landlord-tenant cases, citing them indiscriminately alongside each other. . . .

real estate or the improvements, nor do I think the majority legitimately could intend to so hold. Nonetheless, given this record and the obvious effort to rule so broadly, that is precisely what the majority is holding. What the consequences of this holding will be on the present and projected efforts to provide housing in the National Capitol, I am not able to say. Surely this decision will come as a shock to those so engaged.

Accordingly, I must dissent.

Case Reflections

1. Why did plaintiff Berman bring suit against defendant Watergate West, Inc.? What type of claim was pressed by the plaintiff in the initial lawsuit?
2. What is the issue before the District of Columbia Court of Appeals?
3. Did the District of Columbia Court of Appeals allow the strict products liability claim to stand? Why or why not?

McMILLAN V. BRUNE-HARPENAU-TORBECK BUILDERS, INC.

455 N.E.2d 1276 (1983)

Holds that privity with builder is not necessary in a claim of negligence

SYLLABUS BY THE COURT

Privity of contract is not a necessary element of an action in negligence brought by a vendee of real property against the builder-vendor. (Insurance Co. v. Bonnie Built Homes . . . , to the extent inconsistent herewith, overruled.)

Plaintiffs-appellants, Allen and Rosemary McMillan and Lawrence and Cindy Raterman, own neighboring properties on Meigs Lane in Cincinnati, Ohio, having purchased their homes in late 1977 from the original purchasers. The real estate upon which the homes were constructed was developed by the Harper Realty Company which entered into a contractual relationship with defendant-appellee, the Harper Construction Company, in November 1971, wherein the latter was to serve as contractor for the real estate. Harper Realty Company sold the real estate to defendant-appellee Brune-Harpenau-Torbeck Builders, Inc., in January 1972, which constructed the homes and in turn sold them to the original purchasers sometime thereafter.

Landslide problems occurred on the properties subsequent to appellants' purchases, and appellants filed an action . . . in February 1981. The complaint alleged negligence in the placing, grading, and compacting of the fill material used to level the property, as well as concealment of the defect.

Appellees filed motions to dismiss the claims based on lack of privity, said motions being granted by the trial court in the form of summary judgment on October 23, 1981. . . . The court of appeals affirmed the trial court.

. . . [1] The issue presented in this case is whether privity of contract is a necessary element of an action in negligence brought by a vendee of real property against the builder-vendor. In overruling Insurance Co. v. Bonnie Built Homes (1980) . . . we hold today that privity of contract is not a necessary element of such an action. In Mitchem v. Johnson (1966) . . . this court stated in paragraph three of the syllabus:

> A duty is imposed by law upon a builder-vendor of a real property structure to construct the same in a workmanlike manner and to employ such care and skill in the choice of materials and work as will be commensurate with the gravity of the risk involved in protecting the structure against faults and hazards, including those inherent in its site. If the violation of that duty proximately causes a defect hidden from revelation by an inspection reasonably available to the vendee, the vendor is answerable to the vendee for the resulting damages.

In Mitchem, this duty ran only to the immediate vendee. No sound policy reasons exist to prevent the extension of this duty to all subsequent vendees as well.

Appellees urge us to reaffirm Bonnie Built Homes as being based on time-tested real property principals. Bonnie Built Homes was decided primarily on the rationale that an elimination of the privity element would render the vendor an insurer for all defects. It was felt that the vendor should not be held liable for all defects, because of "unforeseen ramifications."

Today's holding does not render the vendor an insurer for all defects, however remote. Nor are "unforeseen ramifications" an important consideration. Rather, vendors of real property will be held liable for damages proximately caused by their negligence in constructing, maintaining, or repairing the property sold. The duty spelled out in Mitchem runs now to all vendees, both original and subsequent.

[2] This standard of negligence will require vendees to prove the traditional negligence elements. The vendor is not to be held strictly liable for defects. Our holding establishes only the duty. Vendees still have the burden of proving the breach of that duty, proximate causation, and damages. As Justice William B. Brown pointed out in his dissenting opinion in Bonnie Built Homes: "Surely, to hold that a subsequent vendee * * * can bring an action in negligence against a builder-vendor is not equivalent to holding that such builder-vendor is an underwriter against economic loss not proximately caused by its negligence." . . .

[3] The extension of the duty of care in the real property context follows the trend of strong legal precedent in the area of products liability. . . . Notwithstanding claims to the contrary, privity of contract is no more valid a requirement in the context of real property than it is in the area of consumer products. Each may have defects undetectable even after reasonable investigation by the buyer. In either context, *caveat emptor* must give way to the negligence standard of liability.

Improved workmanship and accountability are promoted by an expansion of the scope of the duty as well. Were privity to be maintained as a necessary element for suits against vendors, it is conceivable that "strawman" vendees would be utilized by vendors to escape potential liability. The imposition of a negligence standard properly shifts the burden of loss to the negligent vendors. . . .

For the forgoing reasons, the judgment of the court of appeals is affirmed in part and reversed in part, and the cause is remanded to the trial court for a determination of the negligence claim.

Judgment accordingly. . . .

Case Reflections

1. For what reason did plaintiff McMillan sue defendant Brune-Harpenau-Torbeck Builders, Inc.?
2. The trial court in this case dismissed the plaintiff's claims based on lack of privity. What is the privity doctrine as applied to this case?
3. The issue to be decided in this case is whether or not privity is a necessary element of an action in negligence brought by a vendee of real property against a builder-vendor. How did the Supreme Court of Ohio rule on this issue?

RAINWATER
V.
NATIONAL HOME INSURANCE COMPANY

NATIONAL HOME INSURANCE COMPANY
V.
RAINWATER

1991 WL 169235 (4th Cir. [Va.]) (1991)

Is an arbitration award "final and binding" or only a prelude to litigation?

This appeal raises the question whether a home warranty contract provided for final and binding arbitration in disputes on coverage between a claimant and the underwriter, or whether the arbitration process was to be a mere interlude preceding litigation. The district court found the arbitration provision one for final and binding arbitration and in response to the claimant's petition for confirmation of the arbitration award, entered judgment for him based on his unchallenged cost of repairs. We affirm.

I

C. Phillip Rainwater purchased a house in McLean, Virginia, and as part of the purchase, obtained a Home Buyers Warranty Contract from Home Buyers Warranty ("HBW"), with defendant National Home Insurance Corp. ("NHIC") as the underwriter. The warranty covered certain defects in workmanship and materials, problems with electrical and plumbing systems, and certain qualified structural defects, all of which must first occur during the warranty period. The warranty also contained a section titled, "Section VII-Conciliation and Arbitration." This section provided that a homeowner in disagreement with a coverage decision by HBW or NHIC could "call for conciliation with [HBW] or an arbitration to be conducted by the American Arbitration Association (A.A.A.)," according to the rules of the AAA. This section further provided that "[t]he voluntary dispute settlement process provided herein shall be a condition precedent to the commencement of any litigation by any party to compel compliance with the warranty documents or to seek relief for any dispute arising out of this program."

Within a year of purchasing the house, Rainwater discovered a substantial crack in the foundation. He made a claim under the warranty, but NHIC denied the claim on the basis that the defect in the foundation did not first occur during the warranty period. In denying the claim, NHIC also informed Rainwater that he was required under the terms of the warranty to submit his claim to arbitration "prior to the commencement of litigation." Rainwater then requested arbitration, and sought to have the scope of the arbitration cover the issue of when the defect first occurred as well as whether the defect qualified as a "structural defect" under the warranty, and the reasonable cost of repair. . . . The arbitrator did not reach the reasonable cost question because he evidently believed that money damages could not be awarded as part of the arbitration.

After taking evidence the arbitrator issued an award finding that the defect first arose during the warranty period and that it was a qualified structural defect. NHIC appealed the award under AAA rules. In addition, Rainwater requested a modification of the award to provide for monetary damages of $206,500—the amount that Rainwater spent to have the defect repaired. The arbitrator modified the award by directing NHIC to complete the repairs within sixty days, but the request for specific damages was denied. The arbitrator's decision was upheld on appeal.

NHIC then filed this declaratory judgment action seeking a declaration that it was not liable under the warranty. Rainwater responded by filing a motion to dismiss and/or summary judgment and also filed a petition for confirmation of the arbitration award . . . NHIC answered the confirmation petition and moved to dismiss it. The district court consolidated the cases for oral argument and after a hearing granted both Rainwater's motion to dismiss NHIC's declaratory judgment action and his petition for confirmation. . . . This appeal by NHIC followed:

II

We begin by recognizing the "liberal federal policy favoring arbitration." . . . That policy holds that "any doubts concerning the scope of arbitrable issues should be resolved in favor of arbitration. . . ." . . . More important for our purposes, that policy also provides that once an arbitration award is made and the parties agree to entry of judgment then the award should be confirmed unless it was tainted by corruption, fraud, partiality, misconduct, or an arbitrator exceeded his authority. . . . And we note the presumption that one submits to arbitration, as opposed to mediation, precisely because of the binding quality of the process. . . . In sum, we approach the issues on appeal here guided by a congressional policy that favors and encourages arbitration precisely because it is thought to be a speedy, inexpensive and efficient way to resolve (as opposed to prolong) disputes without consuming court time.

A

The core question is whether the parties agreed to arbitration as a binding process, one that would bar litigation, or whether the agreement to arbitrate was simply a dispute settlement process that was a condition precedent to litigation. This determination is critical because the Federal Arbitration Act provides that " [i]f the parties in their agreement [to arbitrate] have agreed that a judgment of the court shall be entered upon the award made pursuant to the arbitration, . . . then at any time within one year . . . any party to the arbitration may apply to the court . . . for an order confirming the award, and thereupon the court must grant such an order [with exceptions not relevant here]." . . .

Thus, a court has jurisdiction to confirm an award only if the parties have agreed that the award is final. . . . The starting point of course is the agreement itself, since an agreement to arbitrate is a contract and must be interpreted like any other contract. . . . The warranty describes the following procedures to be followed in the event of a disagreement between a homeowner and underwriter on a claim:

Should the Builder or Homebuyer(s) disagree with the Insurer's decision to deny the claim . . . , the contesting party shall call for conciliation with [HBW] or an arbitration to be conducted by the American Arbitration Association (AAA),. . . . The conciliation and/or arbitration process will be conducted in accordance with the warranty conditions described herein and the rules and regulations of the AAA. . . . The voluntary dispute settlement process provided herein shall be a condition precedent to the commencement of any litigation by any party to compel compliance with the warrant documents or to seek relief for any dispute arising out of this program.

We note that this contract was drafted by NHIC and therefore should be construed against them when ambiguities are present. As support for his position, Rainwater points to the provision in the warranty that the "rules and regulations of the AAA" will apply. At the time of the arbitration, see AAA Rule 1 ("The parties shall be deemed to have agreed to these rules in the form in effect when the request for dispute settlement is received by the AAA."), Rule 26(c) of the AAA provided:

Unless the applicable law or the warranty program, the insurance policy, or another applicable document provides otherwise, the parties to these rules shall be deemed to have consented that judgment upon the arbitration award may be entered in any federal or state court having jurisdiction thereof.

Based on this rule, Rainwater argues that the arbitration award in his favor, issued pursuant to AAA rules, was intended to be final and consequently must be confirmed. The district court agreed, and so do we.

. . . [T]he test advanced by NHIC, that the parties must expressly agree that arbitration is "final" or "binding" before a court can look to the AAA rules, is one not supported by the cases. In fact, the decisions holding that reference to AAA rules as permitting entry of judgment are long standing. . . . Consequently, all parties are on notice, especially a sophisticated draftsman like NHIC, that resort to AAA arbitration will be deemed both binding and subject to entry of judgment unless the parties expressly stipulate to the contrary.

NHIC contends that the parties did expressly stipulate to the contrary. Citing the AAA rules that unless the warranty expresses "otherwise" consent to judgment will be presumed, NHIC points to a sentence which it contends shows "otherwise." That portion of the warranty states: "The voluntary dispute settlement process provided herein shall be a condition precedent to the commencement of any litigation by any party to compel compliance with the warrant documents or to seek relief for any dispute arising out of this program." The clause " shall be a condition precedent," NHIC maintains, is evidence that the parties contemplated future litigation and thus means that arbitration is not binding.

Though NHIC's claim has some surface appeal, we think that the "condition precedent" language cannot carry all the weight NHIC would ascribe to it. Traditionally, federal courts were hostile to arbitration clauses since it was thought they could be avoided at the whim of either party. . . . As a result, parties frequently included "condition precedent" language to make certain that the arbitration process ran its course before a federal court could entertain a suit. . . . Therefore, we read "condition precedent" to some extent as an artifact left over from the days of hostility toward arbitration. To the extent that the phrase has meaning, we find that it does not undermine the binding nature of arbitration, but instead applies to the confirmation process . . . or to other litigation in which the arbitration award would be final but just a sub-text in some larger litigation context. Accordingly, we affirm the district court's holding that the parties agreed that arbitration should be final and binding, and that as a result the arbitration award should be confirmed as made. . . .

Case Reflections

1. Discuss the facts leading up to the initial lawsuit filed by Rainwater in this case.
2. State the issue before the U.S. Court of Appeals in this case.
3. The Appellate Court agreed with Rainwater that the arbitration award was intended to be final and binding. How did it reach this decision?

BURLEY V. HOMEOWNERS WARRANTY CORPORATION

YEOMANS V. HOMEOWNERS WARRANTY CORPORATION

WATKINS V. HOMEOWNERS WARRANTY CORPORATION

1990 WL 304854 (S.D.Miss.) (1990)

A group of dissatisfied homeowners seek better coverage than the HOW program was designed to provide.

AMENDED MEMORANDUM OPINION AND ORDER

. . . Plaintiffs in these cases are homeowners who have brought suit against HOW and against CIGNA seeking to recover proceeds allegedly due under a major construction defect insurance policy issued pursuant to the Home Owner's Warranty program and insuring their respective residences. . . .

THE POLICY

The policy for each of the three homes is a single-premium, minimum premium insurance policy underwritten by CIGNA which provided coverage against major construction defects during years three through ten. Under the policy, "major construction defect" is defined as:

Actual damage to the load-bearing portions of the Home (including damage due to Soil Movement as defined below) which affects its load-bearing function and which vitally affects or is imminently likely to product a vital effect on the use of the Home for residential purposes.

Each of the present three lawsuits arises out of claims made during years three through ten of the

HOW warranty. The plaintiffs all allege entitlement to repair of their homes as a result of cracks, settlement and other defects which they claim amount to "major construction defects" under the policies at issue. In addition to their claims that defendants breached their policy obligations by their refusal to pay policy benefits, plaintiffs have asserted a variety of charges against defendants including breach of an implied covenant of good faith and fair dealing, breach of a fiduciary duty, fraud, intentional interference with protected property interests, unfair competition and deceptive trade practices, and bad faith denial of policy benefits. For defendants' alleged acts and omissions, plaintiffs seek to recover all premiums paid, all benefits provided by the policies, attorney's fees, prejudgment interest, and compensation for their embarrassment, humiliation and severe physical and emotional distress, as well as punitive damages.

THE HOW PROGRAM: ENROLLMENT AND COVERAGE

The HOW program . . . was created by the various builder members of the National Association of Home Builders, ostensibly to demonstrate their commitment to good workmanship and the construction of quality homes. HOW Corporation, one of the defendants in these cases, was formed to develop and administer the program. . . . HOW developed the plan for coverage, arranged for security to back the builder's warranty and arranged insurance coverage for the major construction defect coverage. That coverage was underwritten by CIGNA pursuant to an agreement between HOW and CIGNA. HOW was responsible to collect the premiums for the coverage and was to remit the appropriate premium to the insurer. In addition, HOW created and implemented Approved Standards for home construction to be followed by builders participating in the HOW program. HOW was also to recruit and register builders in the program and to screen those builders.

Under the Home Owner's Warranty Agreement itself, the builder is named as the warrantor under the warranty which is in effect for the first two years of the ten years of coverage. During that time, as set forth above, the builder warrants that the home will be free from defects under certain conditions. Thereafter, the major construction defect insurance policy becomes effective and remains in effect for years three through ten. Under that policy, the builder and HOW are listed as the insureds. Owners whose homes are enrolled in the HOW program, therefore, receive the benefit of the major construction defect coverage provided their builders.

Information regarding the HOW program and the coverage of the program is provided to registered builders by HOW who, in turn, provide prospective home buyers with the information they have acquired from HOW. HOW also conducts training seminars to educate builders concerning various facets of the program. Each builder is supplied with a complete supply of policy forms which prospective home buyers may review upon request. The builder is responsible for enrolling homes in the HOW program and causing the warranty and insurance coverage to be issued and is also responsible to pay the premium for the HOW warranty.

THE COVERAGE ISSUE

. . . "MAJOR CONSTRUCTION DEFECT"

Plaintiffs argue that because the definition of "major construction defect" in the policy does not include more than the load-bearing portion of the house, it is too restrictive. However, there is no theory of liability pursuant to which defendants can be held liable simply for providing coverage which is restrictive. In short, the coverage provided is the coverage that was contracted for.

Further, as to the definition of "major construction defect" in the policies under consideration, plaintiffs challenge the language as ambiguous. . . . Contrary to plaintiffs' assertion, while the policy does not cover every defect or purport to cover every defect, the provision is not meaningless. In fact, plaintiffs' retained experts have expressed their opinions that "major construction defects," as defined in the policy, exist in the residences of each of the plaintiffs.[1]

[1] The court notes plaintiffs' position that, consistent with the definition of "major structural defect" in the policy, the defects to their homes do "vitally affect the use of the home for residential purposes," since the damage has

HOW'S STATUS

HOW has moved for summary judgment contending that under the clear provisions of the home warranty documents, and in light of the strictly administrative functions it performs, it is not an insurer or warrantor under plaintiffs' policies and accordingly can have no liability to pay benefits or other damages based on a failure to pay policy benefits. Plaintiffs urge, though, that despite any statements to the contrary in HOW literature or the plaintiffs' policies, HOW held itself out to builders as an insurer under the program and should be treated as such for purposes of the plaintiffs' claims. . . . In support of this assertion, plaintiffs claim that HOW did much more than merely administer the HOW program. According to plaintiffs, HOW collected premiums from its builders and retained unto itself a portion of those premiums; HOW inspected homes in both the construction and claims phases of the program and further, reviewed claims and claims files. In addition, HOW participated in a conciliation procedure when disputes arose between homeowners and builders. Plaintiffs also deem it significant that HOW provided builders and homeowners with literature, brochures and pamphlets bearing the "HOW" logo and placed signs in front of enrolled homes advertising them as being covered by "HOW: Ten Years of Home Protection. " All of this conduct by HOW, plaintiffs aver, manifested to all reasonable observers of the program—including builders and the home buyers—that HOW itself was an insurer, when in actuality, unbeknownst to the builders and buyers, HOW had contracted with CIGNA for CIGNA to underwrite the HOW programs.

The court has reviewed the evidence pertaining to plaintiffs' claim that HOW is an insurer and concludes that neither the warranty/insurance documents, the HOW/CIGNA contract nor the conduct of HOW demonstrate that HOW is subject to the standards or duties of an insurer. . . . Additionally, the builder's limited warranty agreement issued to plaintiffs states that,

> [t]he National HOW Council and the Local HOW Council are not warrantors or insurers. Only the insurer named on page one is responsible for paying claims under the insurance coverage.

And, nowhere in the major construction defect policy is HOW listed as having any duties or responsibilities as an insurer; in fact, HOW is listed as an additional insured, along with the builder, under that coverage. . . .

In sum, therefore, HOW is not an insurer or warrantor with respect to the HOW program. Rather, it is the administrator of the program under which the builder issues a written warranty and CIGNA underwrites the major construction defect policies for years three through ten. It follows that while HOW can be subjected to liability for its activities relative to its administration of the program, it can have no liability to plaintiffs for their claims concerning the failure to pay policy benefits.

BAD FAITH DENIAL OF INSURANCE BENEFITS

Proof of a "bad faith" refusal to pay an insurance claim, so as to entitle the insureds to punitive damages, requires proof of both (1) the absence of a legitimate or arguable reason to deny the claim and (2) malicious conduct, gross negligence or reckless disregard of the rights of others, so as to constitute an independent tort. . . . In the case sub judice, plaintiffs claim to have proof to satisfy each of these elements. Yet, they contend that even if they are ultimately unable to prove lack of a legitimate or arguable reason for CIGNA's refusal to pay their claims, they may nevertheless establish their "bad faith" cause of action based on a course of conduct by the defendants toward plaintiffs and others.

Legitimate or Arguable Reason.

The court first notes plaintiffs' contention that defendants committed bad faith by refusing to give any reasonable interpretation to the policy definition of "major structural defect" so as to frustrate and bar plaintiffs' recovery of policy proceeds. The court has concluded . . . that plaintiffs' claims regarding policy interpretation are without merit. . . .

---

substantially affected and diminished the likelihood of attracting any potential purchasers. Yet, plaintiffs were advised in HOW literature provided to them prior to or at closing that " [e]vidence that damage has affected the value of the home does not necessarily demonstrate that the use of the home for residential purposes has been affected. "

HOW'S SCREENING OF BUILDERS

It is undisputed that one of HOW's administrative functions was the recruitment and screening of builders for enrollment in the HOW program. Plaintiffs purport to seek recovery based on an alleged failure by HOW to adequately screen the builders it enrolled in the program. According to plaintiffs, HOW conducted no inquiry into the qualifications of builders or of their knowledge of residence construction, but rather simply "loosely investigated" the builders' financial stability. Any failure by HOW in this regard cannot constitute a Cause of action for plaintiffs. An interesting analogy is provided by defendant HOW: such an assertion would be analogous to permitting an injured party to maintain a claim against a tortfeasor's automobile liability insurer for failure to screen more carefully the types of drivers insured. Such a cause of action is clearly not recognized by the courts of Mississippi.[2]

IMPLIED COVENANT OF GOOD FAITH AND FAIR DEALING

Plaintiffs' complaints charge that defendants breached an implied covenant of good faith and fair dealing by refusing to pay benefits due under the policies. As the court has concluded above, HOW, not being an insurer and not otherwise being in a contractual relation with the plaintiffs, can incur no liability under this theory advanced by plaintiffs and thus is entitled to summary judgment as to this claim. CIGNA is likewise entitled to judgment on this claim for the insurance contract at issue contain no implied covenant of good faith . . . CIGNA is therefore entitled to judgment on this claim.[3]

BREACH OF FIDUCIARY RELATIONSHIP

Plaintiffs allege in counts III and IV of their complaints respectively that CIGNA and HOW, by failing to ensure that plaintiffs received benefits under their policies' breached their fiduciary duties to plaintiffs. However, just as there is no implied covenant of good faith in a first-party insurance contract, there is no fiduciary relationship between an insurer and insured in a first-party contract. . . .

Plaintiffs next complain that the CIGNA brochure and HOW literature contained statements that misled plaintiffs concerning arbitration of claims submitted under the HOW program. Specifically, the Yeomans contend that they submitted to arbitration because they were misled by a representation in the brochure that if they elected to request arbitration, they " didn't have to accept the arbitrator's decision, but [the] builder [would be] obligated to comply with his ruling if [they did] accept it;" only after they had received two unfavorable arbitration decisions did they learn that under the HOW program, while arbitration is not binding on the homeowner for disputes arising during the first two years of the warranty, it is binding during years three through ten. Plaintiffs thus aver that they have suffered damage as a consequence of their reliance on the misrepresentation regarding arbitration. Apparently, defendants have not brought an action to confirm the arbitration award and plaintiffs, despite the fact of two unfavorable arbitration decisions, have filed this suit to recover benefits—the same benefits denied by the arbitrators; accordingly, the Yeomans cannot be said to have sustained any damage as a result of any representation regarding arbitration. It would therefore prove futile at this point to

[2] There is in the record, in any event, testimony of HOW representatives that HOW, on a random basis, examined and monitored prospective builders' construction practices to verify technical competence.

[3] Curiously, plaintiffs charge that under the HOW program, the builder is absolved from common law liability and statutory liability so that the existence of a HOW warranty operates to prevent them from asserting a claim directly against the builder. There is nothing whatsoever in the record to demonstrate that the HOW warranty is an exclusive remedy. In fact, the builders participating in the HOW program entered into an "Agreement of Builder and Local Warranty Council" which provides specifically that "Builder shall be responsible to defend against any claim or portion of a claim brought against Builder to recover on any basis other than that under the Certificate (or Insurance Coverage)." There thus appears to be nothing to preclude a homeowner's bringing a separate claim against a builder for construction defects to the extent permitted under Mississippi law.

permit the Yeomans to amend their complaint to allege a claim based on this alleged misrepresentation and as such, the amendment will not be granted.

Plaintiffs also request to be allowed to amend their complaint to assert a violation of . . . Mississippi's Consumer Protection Act. In particular, plaintiffs desire to allege a violation of section 75–24–5, which prohibits a provider of goods or services from representing that those goods or services have characteristics, benefits and uses that they do not have or representing that services are of a particular standard, quality or grade, if they are of another. The court concludes that the policy at issue in the case at bar is not a "good" or "service" and accordingly, the cited statute is inapplicable. In any event, a review of the literature of the defendants reveals that defendants made no representations which could subject them to liability under the statute even if it were applicable. . . .

CONCLUSION

It can be fairly said that plaintiffs brought their lawsuits attempting to base causes of action upon contentions that defendants drew a narrow definition of coverage and failed to underwrite the HOW program properly. With the sole exception of plaintiffs' claims for policy benefits, however, the causes of action alleged are either without basis in law or unsupported by the facts. Accordingly, it is ordered that HOW's motion for summary judgment is granted and CIGNA's motion for partial summary judgment and partial judgment on the pleadings is granted.

So ordered this the 9th day of February, 1990.

Case Reflections

1. Describe the policy purchased by the plaintiffs in this case. What is a "major construction defect" as defined under this policy?
2. On what grounds are the plaintiffs suing HOW Corporation and CIGNA Insurance Co.?
3. How did the District Court dismiss each of the above claims against the defendants?

CHAPTER 18

REAL ESTATE AS A SECURITY

LEARNING OBJECTIVES

After reading this chapter, you should be able to:

1. Describe the basic elements of a security as defined in the "Howey Test."
2. Define the role of the North American Securities Administrators Association (NASAA).
3. List the basic types of exemptions from state registration provisions.
4. List the basic types of exemptions from federal registration provisions.
5. Discuss the need for disclosure, the types of information that must be disclosed for real estate offerings, and who must comply.
6. List the basic types of investment opportunities available in real estate securities.

KEY TERMS

- Securitization
- Real Estate Investment Trust
- Investment Advisor
- Securities
- Howey Test
- NASAA
- Condominium Units
- Mortgage Backed Securities
- Time Shares
- Housing Cooperatives
- Partnerships

[J]ust as some things that look like real estate are securities, some things that look like securities are real estate.

L. Loss & J. Seligman, *Securities Regulation* 966

Securitization
Term which describes the process of converting an asset into a pool of securities which are then offered to investors.

Real Estate Investment Trust
Form of organization in which investors hold trust interest and enjoy profits based upon the trust's real estate related holdings.

Investment Advisor
A person "associated" with transactions involving securities as defined by the Investment Advisors Act of 1940.

Probably no other area in real estate has as much potential for changing our view of investing in real property as does that of **"securitization."** During the last decade, a virtual revolution has been taking place in the process of acquiring an interest in real estate for investment purposes. Traditionally we have thought of the process of investing in real estate as one involving the purchase of one or more properties through the use of equity (usually cash for a down payment) and debt. For the most part, investing in real estate was a game for those with fairly large amounts of cash (or other assets) available.

With the advent of **Real Estate Investment Trusts** (REITs), the ability to invest in commercial real estate became available to a much larger group of people. Unfortunately, many REITs suffered massive problems during the late 1970s and have not turned out to be the investment avenue they were designed to be. The concept of creating shares in pools of properties, however, has continued to gain popularity. As we see in this chapter, there are now many vehicles available for investing in real estate. Not only is it possible to become a partial "owner" of properties by pooling resources with others, the ability to participate in the issuing of debt has become widespread.

The dollar amounts involved in these investments are staggering and run into the billions of dollars. Obviously this aspect of real estate has become of major importance to even the most casual of investors—those maintaining individual retirement accounts (IRAs) to name but one example. The rules of this sort of investment game, however, are quite different from those of traditional investing. To purchase a rental property, still the most common real estate investment, is a fairly simple thing. No more complicated really than the purchase of a home. Taking this same property and creating securities based on its value, which are then offered for sale to others, is a much more complicated process.

The creation and offering for sale of securities is regulated at both the state and federal levels. The distinctions between securities brokers and real estate brokers that were discussed earlier in this book depend in large part on this regulatory environment. All aspects of the securities investment process are regulated in some fashion. Those offering the securities for sale, the broker-dealers and agents[1] helping with the market-making function, and the investors themselves are all under close scrutiny. In this chapter, we describe the registration issues, including disclosure requirements, and licensing requirements.

The registration and disclosure requirements are not without "teeth." Those failing to comply with the requirements face an array of civil and possible criminal penalties and liability exposure. The laws cover not only broker-dealers and agents, but also "associated persons" who may be used to make transactions in securities. Of particular importance to real estate professionals, who are often not licensed as securities brokers or dealers, is the coverage provided by the Investment Advisors Act of 1940, which provides a broad definition of **"investment advisors."** As the securiti-

[1]The terms "broker-dealer" and "agent" have fairly precise definitions in this context. See the material in Chapter 15 for more information.

zation of real estate continues to grow in importance, real estate agents will find themselves drawn ever closer to the role of an investment advisor. For those prepared for this change, this presents a great opportunity to expand the scope of traditional commercial real estate brokerage services. For those unprepared, this presents a great opportunity to suffer fairly severe penalties.

SECURITIES DEFINED

Reves v. Ernst & Young

One of the biggest problems with any investment, and this is particularly true in the real estate area, is deciding if the requirements for securities registration, disclosure, and licensing apply. The Securities Act of 1933, the main piece of federal legislation in this area, defines a **security** as "any interest or instrument commonly known as a 'security.'" This definition, like many contained in legislative acts, is not very helpful. The result has been a considerable body of judicial opinion attempting to define what is and is not a security.

Securities Investment contracts which meet the criteria for being considered a security.

The most well-known rule for defining a security is that found in *SEC v. W. J. Howey Co.* [328 U.S. 293 (1946)], a United States Supreme Court case, which established four elements that must be present for an investment contract to be considered a security:

1. Money must be invested.
2. The money must be invested in "a common enterprise."
3. There must be an expectation of profit.
4. The profit must result solely from the efforts of a third party.

Howey Test Four part test used by courts to decide when an investment contract is to be considered a security.

This test, called simply the **"Howey test,"** has been modified over the years.[2] Another test, commonly called the "risk capital test," is used by some state courts in which a security may exist even when the investor takes an active role in the enterprise (which would violate the fourth condition of the Howey test). Whichever test

KEY POINTS

The sale of unimproved land and residential lots has sometimes fallen within the securities framework. In several cases, courts have found that the prices paid for lots in housing projects were inflated as a result of claims made by the developer for future improvements to the entire development, for example, plans for parks, playgrounds, and pools. When deciding whether to apply federal securities laws in cases like this, courts rely primarily on any promises made, whether orally or in writing, by the developer. Thus the making of promises to make substantial improvements in the future, which might be an effective selling technique, may have severe ramifications should the unintended sale of an unregistered federal security, by an unlicensed individual, take place.

[2]The most recent modification was in *First Financial Federal Savings & Loan v. E. F. Hutton Mortgage Corporation* [834 F.2d 685, 689 (8th Cir. 1987)].

is applied in a particular case, there is no distinction made regarding applications to real estate investments. In other words, real estate is treated like any other investment in terms of defining potential applications of securities laws.

In what could be considered a classic land scheme, lots in Florida were sold to individuals, mostly residents of Puerto Rico. Even though some of the individuals selected their lots from a map which divided the development into "residential" and "commercial" sections, and the promoters emphasized the investment value of the land, the court refused to define the lot sales as the sale of a security. A simple sale of land, even for investment purposes, is not a security. The "strong and repeated suggestions" made by salespeople that the surrounding area would develop into a "thriving residential community," reasoned the court in *Rodriguez v. Banko Central Corporation* (990 F.2d 7, 1993), was not enough to conclude that the defendants were promising to construct a community. Such a promise, it should be noted, would be hard to believe since the development turned out to be located in a swamp unsuited for any type of development. Absent such a promise, the court could find no evidence of the type of "common enterprise" necessary under the *Howey* test.

REGISTRATION ISSUES

Securities laws require that all securities be either registered or exempt from registration requirements before being sold or offered for sale. Each state, and the federal government, has some form of registration provision. The most important feature of these registration requirements is the full **disclosure** of information regarding the nature and risks of the investment. These disclosure requirements are discussed in more detail in the next section. Here we take a closer look at both state and federal registration provisions.

Disclosure Requirements For securities, a complete disclosure of the nature and risks of the investment as well as information about the offeror.

State Registration Provisions

The registration of securities is covered in each state by provisions that vary somewhat in terms of their disclosure requirements and exemptions. Although the states vary in many specifics of securities laws, all are members of the North American Securities Administrators Association **(NASAA)**, which publishes guidelines for reviewing programs, including specific guidelines for real estate. The basic features of the NASAA real estate guidelines are summarized in Table 18.1. Some states have adopted these guidelines into formal regulations with statutory effect, whereas others follow them only informally. A few states, called "merit review" states, impose additional requirements beyond those of the NASAA guidelines on securities offered for sale.

NASAA The North American Securities Administrators Association which publishes guidelines for reviewing securities.

State Registration Exemptions

All securities laws provide for certain exemptions from coverage. Because the registration process can be expensive and time-consuming, being exempt from coverage can be quite important. Thus it becomes important to conform to the exemption requirements in effect at both the state and federal levels. These exemptions, it should

TABLE 18.1 NASAA GUIDELINES FOR REAL ESTATE SECURITIES

1. **Sponsor Qualifications**—minimum of two years real estate experience (four years if a service is offered). Appropriate financial strength (minimum net worth of $50,000 or 5% of all offerings sold up to a maximum of $1 million).
2. **Limits on Fees**—total fees ("front-end," operations and liquidation) must be reasonable.
3. **Conflicts of Interest**—the promoter (and affiliates) is restricted in offering services to the partnership. If allowed at all, services must be provided at equal or lower charges than available from nonaffiliates.
4. **Suitability Standards**—offerings are limited to sophisticated investors who understand the risks and will be able to benefit from the investment. Investors must have an annual salary of at least $30,000 and a net worth of at least $30,000 (not including home and automobiles) or $75,000 net worth (not including home or autos).
5. **Rights of Investors**—the investors must be given a set of rights (including voting, meeting, access to all records), and general partners may not be indemnified in such a way as to allow other than nonnegligent, good faith conduct.
6. **Disclosure and Marketing Requirements**—the literature, sales presentations, and advertising used to promote real estate securities is limited. The disclosure prospectus must conform to SEC requirements, which allow the use of forecast sonly under certain conditions and require that they be realistic and identify the assumptions used.
7. **Mortgage Pool Programs**—special provisions have been adopted (in 1983) relating to investment limitations and sponsor compensation for mortgage pool programs.
8. **Deferred Payments**—special provisions were also adopted to allow deferred, or installment, payments to investors under certain tightly regulated circumstances.
9. **REIT Guidelines**—special policy statements have also been adopted for real estate investment trusts, which are somewhat less comprehensive than the partnership guidelines.

be noted, cover only the registration requirements and do not exempt offerings from the disclosure provisions described later in this chapter.

There are generally three types of exemption offered by states:

1. *Limited Offering Exemption*. This exemption is based on the Uniform Securities Act, although it varies from state to state in its specifics. The requirements are meant to apply to situations in which small programs are offered for sale for a limited time. The definitions of "small" and "limited time," however, vary considerably. Generally the numbers of investors and sales, type of investment (limited partnerships are often not eligible), advertising (which is prohibited), and commissions paid are limited. The notion of "integration" becomes important in this context, but this concept is described in the federal exemptions section later.

   In 1980, the Small Business Investment Incentive Act was enacted, which called for the creation of uniform registration exemptions for use by small investors. Regulation D (discussed later) was developed by the SEC, and NASAA adopted a "Uniform Limited Offering Exemption" (ULOE) in 1983.

Although many states have adopted either a form of Regulation D or the ULOE, many have not or have made numerous modifications to these forms. Thus, at this point, no uniform exemption yet exists, although progress continues to be made.

2. *Offers to Existing Security Holders*. The Uniform Securities Act has a provision that allows offers to be made to existing holders of securities offered by the sponsor. Although this is usually used to make a "call" for additional funds, it can be used to offer a new or expanded security.
3. *Discretionary Exemptions*. Most states also offer a general exemption for those offerings for which registration is not necessary or appropriate for the protection of investors. These are generally handled on either a case-by-case basis or, in some instances, based on a set of rules issued by the state administrator. Often offers are allowed to wealthy, sophisticated investors or in cases in which numerical limits have been exceeded by only a small amount.

Federal Registration Provisions

In addition to the registration requirements of the states, the Securities Act of 1933 requires that all securities offered for sale must be registered or exempt from registration requirements. Although the state registration provisions can be time-consuming and expensive, adding federal registration requirements can make the offering of a security prohibitively expensive. Thus it becomes critically important to remain within the federal exemptions whenever possible.

Federal Registration Exemptions

There are only three basic types of exemptions from federal registration requirements. For simplicity, we discuss each of these in general terms. The specifics of federal registration and exemption provisions are well beyond the scope of this text. The intent here is to provide a general overview of the process.

Intrastate Exemption

The exemption that is most commonly relied on in the area of real estate securities is that available when both the issuer and the purchasers live or do business in the same state. To make it easier to determine if a particular offering will qualify for this "intrastate" exemption, the SEC has established a set of rules that, if adhered to, will provide the exemption.[3] There are four basic requirements for claiming an intrastate exemption:

1. All offers and sales for the security must take place in the same state where the issuer is incorporated or has its principal office.
2. To qualify as doing business in a state, the issuer must meet the three "80 percent" tests: At least 80 percent of gross revenues must come from the state, at least 80 percent of total assets must be located in the state; and at least 80 percent of the net proceeds of the offering must be used in the state.

[3]These provisions, called "safe-harbor" provisions, are contained in Rule 147.

3. No exempt securities may be resold to persons living outside the state for at least nine months after the last sale has been made.
4. The issuer must issue appropriate written instructions to purchasers and comply with other similar conditions.

KEY POINTS

When dealing with possible securities issues, it is important to keep in mind that there are really two issues involved. The first is the requirement that a seller of a security must be registered as a broker-dealer or be entitled to an exemption. The second is that the security itself must be registered or entitled to an exemption. Because the broker-dealer definition may include not only the seller, but also others who assist or participate in the sale, care must be taken. The potential liability for failure to register as a broker-dealer is severe when the sale of a security is involved. In addition to injunctions and criminal sanctions, suits for damages may be filed.

Private Placement Exemption

This exemption offers another commonly relied upon procedure for securities "not involving any public offering." As is the case with the intrastate exemption, the SEC has issued a set of conditions that, if met, will provide this exemption.[4] These rules limit the way in which securities may be offered for sale or resale and apply only to small issues, as described in the next section.

Small Issuer Exemption

The Securities Act of 1933 provided the SEC with broad powers to exempt offerings under $5 million from registration. This power has been defined in a series of rules (including those that apply to private placements). These rules, which specifically apply to real estate limited partnerships, place strict limits on the numbers and types of investors and the dollar amounts of securities offered during any twelve-month period. This issue limitation has led to the development of an additional set of rules to determine what constitutes a single issue of a security.

Integration of Offerings

The small issuer exemption is available only when offerings fall within the strict limits provided by the SEC. To avoid these limits, offerers may attempt to split projects into a series of smaller projects, each of which would qualify, rather than a single large project. To guard against this possibility, the SEC has developed the concept of "integration" to help define single offerings. Although the details of this concept are

---

[4] The original "safe-harbor" rule was Rule 146. In 1982, the SEC issued Regulation D, which replaced the existing rules in this area as well as the "small issuer" exemption.

beyond the scope of this coverage, the SEC views such things as the timing and proximity of real estate projects as well as borrowing by one project from another.[5]

Federal Registration Requirements

Should an offering of a security fail to qualify for one of the exemptions just listed, registration procedures for the type of program must be followed. These requirements are, as mentioned earlier, complex and time-consuming. Each type of registration has a set of information and a case law history pertaining to the registration process. In this section, we simply list and briefly describe the major types of registration forms and guides.

Real Estate Investment Trusts

REITs and other similar entities must register all securities using Form S-11. This requirement applies to all "issuers whose business is primarily that of acquiring and holding for investment real estate or interests in real estate . . . "

Real Estate Limited Partnerships

Goodman v. Epstein

Issues of securities that do not exceed an aggregate offering price of $7.5 million must register using Form S-18. This form is used by all issuers who meet the $7.5 million limit and was modified in 1982 to allow its use by real estate limited partnerships (RELPs) and other noncorporate issuers. RELPs must follow the SEC's "Guide 5" for registration requirements.

Condominium A form of multiple ownership in which each condominium owner receives a fee simple absolute estate in an individual air space unit (either a dwelling or an office space) and an undivided interest as tenant in common in the lands and structures which are within the boundaries of the condominium development and outside of the individual air space units.

Condominium Units

Certain **condominium units**, and other real estate developments may be subject to the registration provisions of the Securities Act of 1933. If so, any securities issued must be registered using information contained in Securities Act Release No. 5382.

DISCLOSURE REQUIREMENTS

Whenever securities are involved, the standards of conduct are stricter in terms of disclosure than those which apply to the sale of real estate. Any material misstatement or omission is unlawful under both federal and state securities laws. As was discussed in Chapter 15, the disclosure requirements, although severe, are generally accomplished through the use of materials prepared by third parties, usually accounting firms or attorneys. Thus for the broker or broker-dealer, the dis-

[5]Because these rules are so complex, the SEC offers a so-called "window" period starting six months before the first sale and ending six months after the last sale. If no other sales are made by the issuer during this period, offerings outside the window period will be ignored for integration purposes.

closure process may actually be less difficult and dangerous (in terms of potential liability exposure).

Brokers should be aware, however, of the need for disclosures of "material" information and what is generally deemed to be material. In the context of real estate offerings, the liability, rights, and liquidity positions of the general and limited partners; legislative environment (e.g., zoning, building codes, rent control); the experience and expertise of the developers, managers, or offerers; and the risks inherent in real estate must be disclosed. Many issuers use one of the many forms that have been developed in this area to provide this information to investors. Figure 18.1 is an example of a public limited partnership offering summary.

Woolridge Homes v. Bronze Tree, Inc.

When adequate disclosures are made by those offering securities, it is difficult for an investor to prevail in a claim of misrepresentation. In *Wentzka v. Gellman* (991 F.2d 423, 1993) an investor claimed misrepresentation when his investment in real estate limited partnerships went sour. The private placement memorandum specifically warned investors of the high degree of risk in such ventures, listing 11 factors to be considered. The investor made only a cursory reading of the memorandum due, he said, to its complexity and the assurances of his investment broker that such warnings were only "boilerplate." Even so, because the risks were disclosed to the investor, the misrepresentation claims were dismissed.

Even issues that are exempt from state or federal registration requirements must comply with the disclosure and antifraud provisions of securities laws. Failure to comply with these requirements may lead to civil or even criminal charges. Many attorneys now attempt to bring such charges under the state and federal Racketeer Influenced and Corrupt Organizations (RICO) Act of 1970,[6] which provides for treble

$6,916,800
44 Units of $157,200 Per Unit
One-Half and One-Quarter Units Available

Projected 2.7 to 1 Tax Write-Off in 1985
Projected Cumulative 1.5 to 1 Write-Off During Pay-in Period
Aggregate 2.1 to 1 Write-Off Through 1994 (Projected Date of Sale)

	One Unit		One-Half Unit		One-Quarter Unit	
Payment Date	Capital Contribution	Annual Projected Taxable Loss	Capital Contribution	Annual Projected Taxable Loss	Capital Contribution	Annual Projected Taxable Loss
Upon Subscription	$ 9,500	$ (25,538)	$ 4,750	$ (12,769)	$ 2,375	$ (6,385)
January 15, 1986	47,000	(70,687)	23,500	(35,343)	11,750	(17,671)
January 15, 1987	50,000	(68,633)	25,000	(34,317)	12,500	(17,159)
January 15, 1988	50,700	(63,083)	25,350	(31,541)	12,675	(15,770)
	$157,200	$(227,941)	$78,600	$(113,970)	$39,300	$(56,985)

FIGURE 18.1 EXAMPLE OF LIMITED PARTNERSHIP OFFERING (NAMES AND LOCATION DISGUISED)

[6]18 U.S.C. s 1961 *et. seq.*

a California Limited Partnership

August 28, 1985

General Partners:

1. The Partnership will acquire a seven year old shopping mall which contains 287,000 square feet of gross leasable area, situated on 32 acres of land, located on a major thoroughfare in , Florida. The anchor tenants include (91,000 square feet) and (30,000 square feet), on long term leases. The mall has over 70 tenants and parking for over 1,400 cars.

2. Approximately 70% of the gross leasable area is leased to major New York Stock Exchange or credit rated tenants. In addition to and tenants include (Premier Supermarket), Theaters, Shoes, and

3. 18 tenants paid percentage rents (additional rent based on store sales) aggregating over $100,000 in 1984.

4. The mall is located in Dade County, Florida, one of the fastest growing counties in the United States and home to approximately 100 *Fortune 500* companies.

5. The area is Dade County's fastest growing residential and commercial section.

6. Dade County shoppers rated the Number 1 general merchandise store and the Number 1 catalog showroom in the *Miami Herald* 1984 Shopper Survey.

7. The trade area in which the mall is located is a young, affluent one having an estimated average household income of $36,000, 27% higher than the national average.

8. Retail sales in Dade County grew between 1977 and 1984 at an annual compound rate of approximately 9.8%.

9. There is no mark-up by the Sponsor on the sale of the property to the Partnership.

10. Professional management of the center will be conducted by the number *seven* company in the United States in total shopping centers developed/acquired from 1982 through 1984, by gross leasable area, as reported in *National Mall Monitor.* Patrician manages over 60 shopping centers comprising 10,000,000 square feet of gross leasable area.

11. Projected 1.5 to 1 write-off during pay-in period aggregating a projected 2.1 to 1 write-off through December 31, 1994.

12. Limited Partners receive 99% of the operating profits, losses and cash flow. Upon sale of the property (or mortgage refinancing), Limited Partners receive 100% of the proceeds, up to an amount equal to their total investment ($157,200 per Unit) *plus* a preferred 12% cumulative cash on cash return on their investment (an additional $140,000 per Unit less prior distributions). Thereafter, Limited Partners receive 80% of the remaining proceeds and the General Partners receive 20% thereof.

13. The Partnership offers sheltered cash flow, significant capital appreciation potential and substantial tax benefits in the form of tax losses that can be used to offset taxable income from other sources.

This investment involves a high degree of risk. This material does not constitute an offer to sell nor is it a solicitation of an offer to buy any of the securities referred to. The securities may be offered and sold only through the use of an accurate, complete and current offering memorandum which contains information relevant to the risks and/or merits attendant to such an investment, which information is not contained in this document.

FIGURE 18.1 EXAMPLE OF LIMITED PARTNERSHIP OFFERING (NAMES AND LOCATION DISGUISED) *(continued)*

14. There are no tax preferences affecting alternative minimum tax or depreciation recapture upon sale of the property.

15. A "Big Eight" accounting firm reports on the accounting projections, prepares the Partnership tax returns and audits and renders an opinion on the Partnership's financial statements.

16. No interest is charged on the investor's promissory notes.

17. No letter of credit is required from investors.

18. No additional contributions are required from the investor for any purpose.

PRIOR SHOPPING CENTER ACQUISITIONS SPONSORED BY THE GENERAL PARTNERS

Location	Major Tenants	Gross Leasable Area	Purchase Price
		527,418 sq. ft.	$54,544,067
		565,600 sq. ft.	$45,000,000
		454,078 sq. ft.	$35,800,000
		497,380 sq. ft.	$35,000,000
		449,655 sq. ft.	$29,346,946
		304,000 sq. ft.	$27,763,000
		196,000 sq. ft.	$19,400,000
		287,000 sq. ft.	$19,489,750
		235,726 sq. ft.	$17,100,000
		219,949 sq. ft.	$17,100,000
		103,000 sq. ft.	$16,083,100
		296,550 sq. ft.	$15,800,000
		280,300 sq. ft.	$15,060,000
		224,868 sq. ft.	$15,000,000
		187,000 sq. ft.	$13,562,240
		228,520 sq. ft.	$13,000,000
		251,246 sq. ft.	$12,750,000
		205,000 sq. ft.	$12,000,000
		140,099 sq. ft.	$11,700,000
		258,364 sq. ft.	$11,625,000
		236,165 sq. ft.	$11,000,000
		213,553 sq. ft.	$10,835,000
		131,752 sq. ft.	$10,625,000
		133,480 sq. ft.	$10,100,000
		255,200 sq. ft.	$ 9,825,000
		202,000 sq. ft.	$ 8,975,000
		105,660 sq. ft.	$ 8,975,000
		229,984 sq. ft.	$ 8,500,000
		161,218 sq. ft.	$ 8,100,000
		134,000 sq. ft.	$ 7,800,000
		166,725 sq. ft.	$ 7,100,000
21 Additional Properties		2,455,023 sq. ft.	$94,780,000
		TOTAL—10,336,513 SQ. FT.	**$633,749,103**

FIGURE 18.1 EXAMPLE OF LIMITED PARTNERSHIP OFFERING (NAMES AND LOCATION DISGUISED) *(continued)*

SUMMARY OF THE OFFERING

This summary of certain provisions of the Private Placement Memorandum is intended only for quick reference and is not intended to be complete. The Private Placement Memorandum and accompanying Exhibits describe in detail numerous aspects of the transaction which are material to investors, and the following is, therefore, qualified in its entirety by reference to the full text of the Private Placement Memorandum.

GENERAL PARTNERS

are the sole general partners of the Partnership. Messrs. and have sponsored 45 other real estate partnerships which, in the aggregate, have acquired over 60 shopping centers, for approximately $600,000,000, comprising over 10,000,000 square feet of gross leasable area.

The , wholly owned by Messrs. , will manage the shopping center. Patrician ranks *seventh* in the United States in total shopping center gross leasable area developed or acquired for the period 1982 through 1984 as reported in the January 1985 issue of the *National Mall Monitor.*

PARTNERSHIP BUSINESS/THE PROPERTY

The Partnership has been formed to purchase, own and operate a shopping mall consisting of 287,000 square feet of gross leasable area, situated on 32 acres of land, located in , Dade County, Florida. The mall's anchor tenants include (91,000 square feet), (30,000 square feet), (28,000 square feet), and Theaters (22,300 square feet). Dade County is one of the fastest growing counties in the nation and the area population is expanding at the fastest rate within the county.

Florida is presently the eighth most populous state in the country. Over the ten year period ended 1980, the Florida population grew by 41% compared to the U.S. growth of 11.4%.

The property is located at the key intersection of Drive and Street in , approximately one mile west of an interchange of the Florida Turnpike. is situated five miles west of Coral Gables and Biscayne Bay. Drive is the major thoroughfare in the area and is developed with both commercial and multifamily developments. There is extensive residential and commercial development occuring and planned within the immediate area. Retail sales in Dade County grew 92% between 1977 and 1984.

, a New York Stock Exchange listed company, and its subsidiaries, are principally engaged in the sale of a wide range of general merchandise from a chain of discount stores throughout the world. As of January 26, 1985, operated over 2,500 stores. audited financial statements for the fiscal year ended January 26, 1985 reflect total assets of $9.3 billion, net worth of $3.1 billion, sales of $21.1 billion and net income of $499 million.

The initial term of the lease expires in 2002 and grants six five year renewal options. occupies approximately 91,000 square feet and is required to pay annual fixed rent of $295,300 plus percentage rent equal to 1% of annual sales at this location between $9,545,000 and $16,600,000 and 1/2 of 1% of sales in excess of $16,600,000. Sales at this location for the year ended November, 1984 were over $15,000,000.

, an American Stock Exchange listed company, is the largest catalog showroom operator in the State of Florida. In 1984 was voted the *Miami Herald's* Florida Company of the Year. is engaged in the operation of a chain of 35 catalog showrooms selling principally jewelry, watches, luggage and home electronics. The stores are located throughout the State of Florida. audited financial statement for the fiscal year ended June 30, 1984 reflect assets of $79.7 million, net worth of $46.7 million, sales of $145 million and net income of $6.8 million, an increase of approximately 17% and 23% over the prior year's sales and net income, respectively.

FIGURE 18.1 EXAMPLE OF LIMITED PARTNERSHIP OFFERING (NAMES AND LOCATION DISGUISED) *(continued)*

The initial term of the lease expires in 2003 and grants two 10 year renewal options. occupies 30,000 square feet of space and is required to pay annual fixed rent of $105,000 plus percentage rent equal to 1½% of annual sales at this location in excess of $7,000,000. Sales at this location for the year ended June, 1984 were $6,149,000.

was formerly a New York Stock Exchange listed company which went private in August, 1984. Its principal operations are in food distribution and speciality retailing. The company was the nation's third largest food wholesaler servicing 2,300 independent grocery customers, operating approximately 50 retail supermarkets and providing franchise services to over 900 Supermarkets. The latest audited financial statements dated June 25, 1983 reflect total assets of $468 million; net worth of $187 million; sales of $2.6 billion and net income of $34 million.

The initial term of the lease expires in 1998 and grants three options to extend the lease by an aggregate of 20 years. (doing business as a supermarket) occupies approximately 28,000 square feet, is currently in its first year of occupancy and is required to pay annual fixed rent of $109,200 plus percentage rent equal to 1½% of sales at this location in excess of $10,500,000.

ACQUISITION OF THE PROPERTY

will acquire the Property from the Sponsor for a purchase price of $19,489,750 (which is equivalent to the price paid by the Sponsor to the owner of the Property). The price is payable $3,189,750 in cash at closing and $16,300,000 by the Partnership executing and delivering at closing a nonrecourse purchase money wraparound note and mortgage, bearing a fixed interest rate of 16.75% per annum and maturing on December 31, 1988 with a refinancing option for a new loan which would mature on December 31, 1998 and bear annual interest at a rate which varies in accordance with changes in the six month U.S. Treasury Bill rate.

MANAGEMENT OF THE PROPERTY

Professional management of the Property will be conducted by which currently manages over 60 other shopping centers whose gross leasable area aggregates approximately 10,000,000 square feet.

TERMINATION OF THE OFFERING

The offering will terminate on or before September 30, 1985 (unless extended by the General Partners to October 31, 1985). Payments received from subscribers will be held in a segregated bank escrow account until the termination of the offering.

LIMITED PARTNERS' INTEREST

The Limited Partners will be investing an aggregate of $6,916,300 in the Partnership, which amount will be divided into 44 Units, and they will receive a 99% interest in operating profits, losses and cash flow. The General Partners will invest an aggregate of $69,866 in the Partnership for a 1% interest in operating profits, losses and cash flow. Upon sale of the property (or mortgage refinancing), the Limited Partners receive 100% of the proceeds up to an amount equal to their total investment plus a preferred 12% cumulative cash on cash return on their investment ($140,000 per Unit less prior distributions). Thereafter, Limited Partners receive 80% of the remaining proceeds and the General Partners receive 20% thereof.

No interest is charged on the Limited Partners' promissory notes, no letter of credit is required to secure the promissory note payments and the Limited Partners are not required to contribute any additional capital at any time beyond their capital contribution.

PROJECTED INVESTOR YIELDS

An investor's after tax Internal Rate of Return is projected to be approximately 29%, 33% and 37%, respectively, upon a projected sale of the Property on January 1, 1995, assuming annual property appreciation rates of 6%, 8% and 10%. (See page 7).

FIGURE 18.1 EXAMPLE OF LIMITED PARTNERSHIP OFFERING (NAMES AND LOCATION DISGUISED) *(continued)*

QUARTER UNIT

PROJECTED TAXABLE INCOME (LOSS) AND RELATED TAX EFFECT
SEPTEMBER 1985 TO DECEMBER 1994
FOR TAXPAYER AT 50% INCOME TAX BRACKET

FOR PURCHASE OF ¼ LIMITED PARTNERSHIP UNIT

Year	Capital Contribution	Cash Flow	Taxable Income (Loss)	After Tax Cash Generated By Loss	After Tax Cash Generated By Loss & Cash Flow	Cumulative After Tax Cash Generated	Cumulative Ratio Of Losses To Capital Contribution
1985	$ 2,375	$ 0	$ (6,385)	$ 3,193	$ 3,193	$ 3,193	2.7 :1
1986	11,750	0	(17,671)	8,835	8,835	12,028	1.7 :1
1987	12,500	0	(17,159)	8,580	8,580	20,608	1.5 :1
1988	12,675	0	(15,770)	7,885	7,885	28,493	1.5 :1
Subtotal 1985 to 1988	$39,300	$ 0	$(56,985)	$ 28,493	$ 28,493	$ 28,493	1.5 :1
1989	$ 0	$ 500	$ (6,729)	$ 3,365	$ 3,865	$ 32,358	1.6 :1
1990	0	875	(5,219)	2,609	3,484	35,842	1.8 :1
1991	0	1,250	(4,791)	2,396	3,646	39,488	1.9 :1
1992	0	1,875	(3,782)	1,891	3,766	43,254	2.0 :1
1993	0	2,375	(2,475)	1,238	3,613	46,867	2.0 :1
1994	0	2,990	(1,237)	618	3,608	50,475	2.1 :1
Total 1985 to 1994	$39,300	$ 9,865	$(81,218)	$ 40,610	$ 50,475	$ 50,475	

HALF UNIT

FOR PURCHASE OF ½ LIMITED PARTNERSHIP UNIT

Year	Capital Contribution	Cash Flow	Taxable Income (Loss)	After Tax Cash Generated By Loss	After Tax Cash Generated By Loss & Cash Flow	Cumulative After Tax Cash Generated	Cumulative Ratio Of Losses To Capital Contribution
1985	$ 4,750	$ 0	$ (12,769)	$ 6,385	$ 6,385	$ 6,385	2.7 :1
1986	23,500	0	(35,343)	17,671	17,671	24,056	1.7 :1
1987	25,000	0	(34,317)	17,159	17,159	41,215	1.5 :1
1988	25,350	0	(31,541)	15,770	15,770	56,985	1.5 :1
Subtotal 1985 to 1988	$78,600	$ 0	$(113,970)	$ 56,985	$ 56,985	$ 56,985	1.5 :1
1989	$ 0	$ 1,000	$ (13,458)	$ 6,729	$ 7,729	$ 64,714	1.6 :1
1990	0	1,750	(10,439)	5,219	6,969	71,683	1.8 :1
1991	0	2,500	(9,581)	4,791	7,291	78,974	1.9 :1
1992	0	3,750	(7,565)	3,782	7,532	86,506	2.0 :1
1993	0	4,750	(4,950)	2,475	7,225	93,731	2.0 :1
1994	0	5,981	(2,474)	1,237	7,218	100,949	2.1 :1
Total 1985 to 1994	$78,600	$19,731	$(162,437)	$ 81,218	$100,949	$100,949	

FIGURE 18.1 EXAMPLE OF LIMITED PARTNERSHIP OFFERING (NAMES AND LOCATION DISGUISED) *(continued)*

ONE UNIT

FOR PURCHASE OF ONE LIMITED PARTNERSHIP UNIT
PROJECTED TAXABLE INCOME (LOSS) AND RELATED TAX EFFECT
SEPTEMBER 1985 TO DECEMBER 1994

FOR TAXPAYER AT 50% INCOME TAX BRACKET

Year	Capital Contribution	Cash Flow	Taxable Income (Loss)	After Tax Cash Generated By Loss	After Tax Cash Generated By Loss & Cash Flow	Cumulative After Tax Cash Generated	Cumulative Ratio Of Losses To Capital Contribution
1985	$ 9,500	$ 0	$ (25,538)	$ 12,769	$ 12,769	$ 12,769	2.7 :1
1986	47,000	0	(70,687)	35,343	35,343	48,112	1.7 :1
1987	50,000	0	(68,633)	34,317	34,317	82,429	1.5 :1
1988	50,700	0	(63,083)	31,541	31,541	113,970	1.5 :1
Subtotal 1985 to 1988	$157,200	$ 0	$(227,941)	$113,970	$113,970	$113,970	1.5 :1
1989	$ 0	$ 2,000	$ (26,915)	$ 13,458	$ 15,458	$129,428	1.6 :1
1990	0	3,500	(20,879)	10,439	13,939	143,367	1.8 :1
1991	0	5,000	(19,161)	9,581	14,581	157,948	1.9 :1
1992	0	7,500	(15,130)	7,565	15,065	173,013	2.0 :1
1993	0	9,500	(9,899)	4,950	14,450	187,463	2.0 :1
1994	0	11,963	(4,949)	2,474	14,437	201,900	2.1 :1
Total 1985 to 1994	$157,200	$ 39,463	$(324,874)	$162,437	$201,900	$201,900	
		(B)		(A)			

PROJECTED RETURN TO A FULL UNIT PURCHASER AT 50% INCOME TAX BRACKET UPON A PROJECTED SALE AT JANUARY 1, 1995 ASSUMING VARIOUS RATES OF APPRECIATION PER YEAR

Assumed Appreciation Per Year	**6%**	**8%**	**10%**
Proceeds to Limited Partner	$324,429	$450,063	$596,771
Net Tax Due Upon Sale (at current capital gains rates)	106,313	131,440	160,782
Net Proceeds to Limited Partner Upon Sale	218,116	318,623	435,989
Plus: Tax Savings 1985-1994 [*See (A) above*]	162,437	162,437	162,437
Cash Flow 1985-1994 [*See (B) above*]	39,463	39,463	39,463
Total Benefits	420,016	520,523	637,889
Less: Capital Contribution	157,200	157,200	157,200
Net Benefits	**$262,816**	**$363,323**	**$480,689**
After Tax Internal Rate of Return	**29%**	**33%**	**37%**

FIGURE 18.1 EXAMPLE OF LIMITED PARTNERSHIP OFFERING (NAMES AND LOCATION DISGUISED) (*continued*)

damages. Even administrative sanctions by the SEC effectively end the ability of the issuer to operate in the securities area, either for a specific period or indefinitely.

KEY POINTS

The example limited partnership offering included in this chapter is an edited version (the names of the individuals and firms involved in this offering have been removed) of a summary that was mailed to potential investors. Although it is only a summary, notice the amount of information that has been disclosed about the property, the general partners, and the partnership agreement. Many "private" limited partnership offerings do not include either the amount of information or the level of detail seen in this offering. As an investor, you should always require the type of information seen in this offering summary *at a minimum.*

INVESTING IN REAL ESTATE SECURITIES

As we discussed at the beginning of this chapter, the process of investing in real estate is rapidly becoming "securitized." This process has already made some fundamental changes to the way we view real estate and promises to make even more dramatic changes, perhaps even affecting the real estate brokerage industry, in the near future. In the final sections of this chapter, we list and briefly describe each of the major investment areas in real estate that are potentially affected by securities laws. In some instances, the securitization process has been in place for many years. In others, the process is quite new or evolving rapidly.

Mortgages

The area of investing in mortgages involves numerous types and categories of in vestment instruments. One way of viewing these is to look at the basic form of the investment instruments available.

Single-Family Notes

Although most "notes" are considered to be securities by definition, mortgage notes held by single-family homeowners are generally an exception. Other forms of real estate transactions may, however, involve securities. This is especially true when multiple mortgage notes are grouped together into a pool, and participations in this pool are sold (see the following section).

Mortgage-Backed Securities A method for investors to participate in pools of mortgage instruments or notes issued by lenders.

Mortgage-Backed Securities

As discussed earlier, **mortgage-backed securities** are often created when groups of mortgage instruments or notes are pooled. These instruments, which have existed since at least the thirteenth century, have allowed the creation of a new market—commonly called a "secondary market"—in mortgages. In the U.S., loan originators in the 1920s began dealing with loan participations in which a part interest in the loan was sold by the mortgagee. The investors were paid when (and if) payments were made on the mortgages. Because such sales were considered to be a transfer of an equitable interest in the mortgage, investors sometimes found themselves embroiled in foreclosure actions in an attempt to recover their investment.

Today four basic types of securities are commonly created by the process of participating in mortgages and fall into two categories. Investors may acquire either debt or equity instruments.

> *Mortgage Backed Bonds (MBB).* These instruments are simply bonds, much like any corporate or government bond, issued based on the value of a pool of mortgages. Similar to any other bond, these instruments promise periodic payments at a stated interest rate and a repayment of the original bond amount upon maturity. Unfortunately, payment patterns such as this do not match up well with actual cash flows on the mortgages (i.e., the payments made to the mortgage issuers, which may include early repayment of loans) and, combined with some defaults in the pool, tend to make MBBs unpopular with issuers.

> *Mortgage Pay Through Bonds (MPTB).* These instruments represent a modification to the basic debt instrument a bond represents. Payments in a MPTB pass through to the investor and thus tend to vary a great deal over time as mortgages are paid off early. Remember that the average life of a mortgage is considerably shorter than its original term. One common figure used, although there are much better, more accurate methods to estimate early repayments, is approximately twelve years for an average life.

> *Mortgage Pass-Throughs (MPT).* These instruments are similar to the MPTBs described above but represent equity rather than debt. Although this distinction may appear to be minor, in fact it makes the issuance of securities much simpler and is thus a far more popular instrument than the MPTB. Although both MBBs and MPTBs are debt securities issued against an asset (i.e., the pool of mortgages), pass-throughs vest the investor with an ownership interest in the mortgage pool. Although some programs (called "straight" pass-throughs) exist in which the investor receives no guarantee of even a minimum payment, many pass-throughs carry some sort of protection.

> *Collateralized Mortgage Obligations (CMO).* The most recent form of mortgage-related security is the CMO. The CMO has all of the advantages of the pass-through form plus a form of "call protection." Call protection provides an assurance that the instrument will be repaid according to some predetermined schedule and will not be repaid (i.e., called) early. In essence, a CMO creates a series of securities of differing lengths based on the projected payment stream of the mortgage pool. This feature, plus the possibility of having the issuer realize a residual payment stream, which increases his return, has made CMOs popular. Although the mechanics of CMOs are fairly complex, most investors find the resulting products to be quite desirable.

The market for these securities now runs well into the billions of dollars, making them one of the largest types of real estate securities available. The popularity of these instruments has led to a continuing effort to develop new instruments (such as the CMO) and refine existing ones. Although MPTs and CMOs are "equity" investments, much effort is being expended in developing similar instruments based not on mortgage debt but on equity (or ownership) positions in pools of properties.

New Debt Instruments

In addition to the mortgage-based securities just described, several relatively new types of debt instruments (e.g., shared appreciation mortgages, shared equity mortgages, and percentage leases) may become the basis for securities. This area is evolving rapidly and, as one might expect, has led to a few contradictory court rulings.

Condominiums and Time Shares

Time Shares Real estate project, often taking a condominium form, in which investors purchase only a limited amount of time during which they may use the property each year.

Both condominiums and time share projects may be securities if profit rather than personal use is the primary objective of the purchase/investment. Before investing in a condominium or **time share** project or offering such a project for sale, an evaluation of the likelihood of security status should be conducted.

> The *Howey* test of a security described earlier in this Chapter includes a "common enterprise" requirement. The most common definition of common enterprise involves a "horizontal commonality" where all investors are pooled, giving up any claim to profits or losses from their particular investments in return for a pro rata share of the profits of the enterprise. In *Hocking v. Dubois* (885 F.2d 1449, 1989), this notion was applied to find that the purchase of a condominium unit in Hawaii where the purchaser participated in a rental pool would be considered to be a security transaction. In the *Hocking* case, the court stated that it would accept "either traditional horizontal commonality or, when no pooling among investors is present, a strict version of vertical commonality." Vertical commonality exists when "the profits and losses of the investor and investment promoter are interdependent." This definition, however, is not as popular with other courts and was specifically rejected in *Wals v. Fox Hill Development Corp* (1993 WL 303052 (E.D.Wis.)) in which an investment in a time-share estate was ruled to have failed the common enterprise prong of the *Howey* test and thus could not be considered a security.

Multiple Ownership Forms

There are many types of multiple ownership forms possible. Some of these, depending on the circumstances, may be treated as securities. Three of the most common types of multiple ownership are briefly examined here.

Primary Residences. When more than one person (other than a spouse) contributes to the purchase of a residence, a security could be created (see the "New Debt Instruments" discussion previously for similar information). The creation of a security is unlikely, however, because the profit motive is often missing, and no management efforts are provided by the additional investor.

Rental/Investment Properties. Because a profit motive is generally present in multiple ownership of rental and/or investment properties, the determination of security status often rests on the managerial efforts of the co-owners. If all share equally in the management efforts, or a third party is hired to manage the property, a security will generally not be created.

Housing Cooperatives. As in other multiple ownership situations, the determination of security status will rely on the factors discussed earlier. The most famous case in this area (*United Housing Foundation, Inc. v. Forman* [421 U.S. 837 (1975)]) was based on an application of the Howey test modified to include the concept of self-use or self-consumption. When the intent is to use or consume the property, the Court held that securities laws do not apply.[7]

United Housing Foundation, Inc. v. Forman

Housing Cooperative A form of multiunit housing in which a corporation owns the property and owners of shares in the corporation live in each of the units.

Partnerships

Perhaps the largest area of securities law applications to real estate is that of **partnerships**. The law in this area is often quite complex, and the intent here is only to summarize the basic rules that apply. In some instances, the applicability of securities laws is quite clear, whereas in others, there is a great deal of room for debate. As was discussed earlier, rulings in this area can make or break many projects, so it becomes quite important to follow the rules governing the creation of securities.

Partnership A legal relationship between two or more people which is formed for the purpose of owning real property or conducting a trade or business. Each of the partners is individually liable for payment of all of the partnership debts.

General Partnerships

Many times a general partnership (or joint venture) form is used primarily in hopes of avoiding securities laws. Although this approach may have some merit, the use of a general partnership form will not automatically avoid security status. The Courts have seemed to rely heavily on the management and control aspects of the partnership agreements in making this determination. Basically if an investor has little power, is inexperienced or unknowledgeable, or depends on the managerial ability of the promoter or manager to such an extent that he cannot be replaced, a security will be said to exist.[8]

Limited Partnerships

The rules discussed earlier in effect relate to a determination that a general partner is, in fact, a limited partner. Limited partnerships often involve security status because, by definition, the basic rules involving profit motive and managerial effort are met. The Revised Uniform Securities Act now includes limited partnership interests within the definition of a security. Just as the general partnership form does not automatically avoid security status, however, the limited partnership form does not automatically create a security. Three forms of partnerships are described here.

Stewart v. Germany

Private Partnerships. By definition, a private partnership is one which is not registered with the SEC. Registration requirements are described earlier in this chapter. Remember, however, that just because a partnership avoids the registration requirement does not mean it avoids the disclosure requirements.

---

[7]This finding was in spite of the fact that shares of stock had been issued that entitled the owners to purchase units in the housing project. The Court found, however, that a profit motive was not present either.

[8]See *Williamson v. Tucker* [645 F.2d 404 (5th Cir. 1981)].

Publicly Traded Partnership (PTPs). At one point in the mid-1980s, it appeared that PTPs would become a major investment vehicle. As PTPs failed to provide the expected returns and became increasingly difficult to trade, investors soon lost interest. These partnerships, which are registered with the SEC, are still active but have not been the market force that some predicted.

Master Limited Partnership (MLPs)

Large partnerships that are comprised of consolidated partnerships (or other assets), are publicly held, and are traded on an exchange or the over-the-counter (OTC) market are known as master limited partnerships. MLPs offer the benefits of other partnerships with added liquidity by being traded in open markets. There are numerous forms that MLPs can take (e.g., "roll-ups," "roll-outs," conversions, and initial offerings), but they are all clearly subject to securities laws. In many instances, the creation of a MLP is the result of tax avoidance strategies that are beyond the scope of this discussion.

Conventional Securities

There are numerous instances in which securities are created as a normal function of the investment process. Some of the more common forms are discussed briefly here:

Corporate Stock. Regular, or C, corporations may be used in many real estate applications. Changes in tax laws often alter the benefit-to-cost relationships for various investment ownership forms. Although the corporate form is generally avoided, there are instances in which its use is justified.

S Corporation Stock. An S corporation is basically a corporation taxed like a partnership (i.e., one that provides for a "flow through" of income directly to investors without taxation at the corporate level). Initially limits on passive income (such as rent) and the number of shareholders (maximum of fifteen) made its use for real estate nearly impossible. More recently, however, the passive income limitation was removed, and the number of shareholders was raised to thirty-five. These changes have made S corporations a much more attractive potential form for real estate investment.

Mutual Funds. Many types of investment companies are well suited to use as a form for real estate investment. Shares in various forms of mutual funds devoted entirely, or primarily, to real estate are commonly available.

Real Estate Investment Trusts (REITs). REITs are still the most common form of investment vehicle for real estate. REITs do not issue stock; rather they issue "Certificates of Beneficial Ownership," which, similar to shares of stock, are security instruments.

Exempt Holding Companies. The Tax Reform Act of 1986 created a category of companies[9] that can invest in leveraged real estate without being subject to the "unrelated business" tax, provided that they meet certain criteria. Such ex-

[9]Including public charities, private foundations, community chests, and certain foreign corporations.

empt holding companies can be organized by any organization, including ones that would not themselves qualify for the exemption. Thus a variety of such exempt holding companies can now be created.

Additional Security Forms

For the sake of making our discussion as complete as possible, a few additional forms that appear in security offerings for real estate investments should be mentioned. These are basically variations on forms already described but, because they carry specific labels, may cause confusion for investors. Thus each is briefly described here.

Split Benefit Syndications. The two primary sources of benefits for investors in real estate are periodic cash flows and appreciation. Some syndications have been created with two (or more) classes of investors who share in the cash flows, appreciation, or some combination of both. These syndications have been created to match the specific needs of groups of investors more closely.

Dequity Programs. Also called "hybrid programs," these programs attempt to combine the benefits of both equity investment and mortgage loan programs. These programs make mortgage loans on properties (or, in some instances, purchase loans from other lenders) and purchase other properties. Investors generally receive proceeds from both types of activities.

Specific Return Funds. Sponsors of some funds, in an effort to make the investment more appealing, have made promises of specific rates of return for investors. To do this, these funds often loan assets to other, usually affiliated, programs at specified interest rates. When the assets are sold, the sponsors have a stake in the proceeds. Because their investors have been guaranteed a specific return, however, there may be little if any profits left if the properties in the fund do not appreciate in value as projected.

Insured Partnerships. Similar to specific return funds, insured partnerships promise a specific rate of return to investors. The difference in these programs is that the insurance (or other guarantee) is provided by a third party, usually a financial institution. Although these partnerships are reasonably safe investments, the cost of the insurance tends to make the returns considerably lower than other partnerships.

One Hundred Percent Funds. This is really just another name for a "no-load" mutual fund in that the promise is that all funds will be invested. No fund is, of course, ever run without cost. Sponsors must earn a reasonable fee for creating and managing such funds. No-load funds often replace the initial, or front-end, fees with slightly higher management fees. In other instances, money may be borrowed from the sponsor to cover fees, and although the loan payments are usually subordinated to the return of investment, they will naturally reduce the return on investment.

Opportunity Funds. Often specific types of investments will become "bargains" as a result of economic or market conditions. For example, farm and ranch partnerships were formed a few years ago to take advantage of depressed prices in many parts of the U.S. Such funds are often referred to as "vulture funds."

Zero-Coupon Programs. In an effort to produce higher returns, some programs have used zero-coupon mortgages, which defer all payments until the loan matures. Using zero-coupon financing eliminates most of the benefits of property appreciation and replaces it with higher, but deferred, returns. Thus the net effect is negligible, and such programs have not done well in the market.

Repurchase Partnerships. One of the biggest problems with publicly traded partnerships has been a thin or nonexistent resale market. Once purchased, limited partnership interests generally cannot be resold without a substantial discount. To relieve this problem, some PTP sponsors have created programs that set aside a certain portion of cash flows for repurchase of partnership interests. Others have "redistribution" procedures, which allow some partners to receive additional interests from other partners in lieu of cash distributions. A few partnerships have even been created specifically to purchase partnership interests, presumably at a hefty discount, from other programs.

Foreign Programs. One of the inherent advantages of the entire "securitization" movement in real estate is that it opens the investment market to new categories of investors. Not the least of these are foreign investors who have drawn an increasing amount of attention. Many of the types of programs described here have increased their efforts to draw on foreign investors, and some have been created specifically with foreign investors in mind.

Other Investments

In addition to those already described, a few other potential investments that may take the form of securities need to be discussed. For the most part, these forms are not major players in the securities aspect of real estate investments, yet they cannot be ignored because they are present in the market.

Sale-Leasebacks. When a single investor buys and then leases back a property, a security is not involved. When there are multiple investors involved or when the lease payments are based on the revenues of the property (i.e., are some form of percentage payments), a security may have been created.

Franchises. Franchise agreements generally do not involve the creation of securities simply because the franchisee (or investor) provides the managerial efforts. When the franchisor provides most of the managerial efforts (or when a "pyramid" scheme is used[10]), a security may have been created.

Raw Land. Even though investing in raw land is often done with a profit motive, such investments generally do not involve securities. The promotional material

[10]See *SEC v. Glenn W. Turner Enterprises, Inc.* [348 F.Supp. 766 (D. Ore. 1972)] for an example of a pyramid franchise scheme.

used to attract investors, the representations made to investors, and the degree of control by investors are all factors that have led to rulings of security creation in some instances.

Campgrounds. Not-for-profit campground associations have become popular in some parts of the U.S. If the promoters expect to derive profit from the sale of the campgrounds to the associations (and also were the organizers of the associations and developers of the campgrounds), memberships in the associations have been ruled to be securities.

CONCLUSION

As you can tell from the length of this list, the potential effects of securities laws in the real estate area is immense. At this point, there appears to be little doubt that the forces that have pushed many aspects of real estate investing and lending toward securities markets and concepts will continue. The future of real estate will be closely intertwined with developments in the process of creating and marketing various forms of securities, including, no doubt, many that have not yet been conceived.

DISCUSSION QUESTIONS

1. Describe the basic elements of a security as defined in the "Howey Test."
2. Define the role of the North American Securities Administrators Association (NASAA).
3. List and describe the basic types of exemptions from state registration provisions.
4. List and briefly describe the basic types of exemptions from federal registration provisions.
5. Discuss the need for disclosure, the types of information that must be disclosed for real estate offerings, and who must comply.
6. Four basic types of securities are commonly created by the process of participating in mortgages. These four types fall into two categories: equity and debt. Briefly discuss each of the four types.
7. Possibly the largest area of securities law applications to real estate is that of partnerships. Distinguish between a general and a limited partnership. Additionally, discuss the three forms of partnerships described in the text.
8. Aside from those discussed in the chapter, generate a list of investment opportunities available in real estate securities.

REVES V. ERNST & YOUNG

110 S.Ct. 945 (1989–90)

Expands the definition of a "note" using the "family resemblance" test.

In order to raise money to support its general business operations, the Farmer's Cooperative of Arkansas and Oklahoma sold uncollateralized and uninsured promissory notes payable on demand by the holder. Offered to both Co-Op members and nonmembers and marketed as an "Investment Program," the notes paid a variable interest rate higher than that of local financial institutions. After the Co-Op filed for bankruptcy, petitioners, holders of the notes, filed suit in the District Court against the Co-Op's auditor, respondent's predecessor, alleging, inter alia, that it had violated the antifraud provisions of the Securities Exchange Act of 1934—which regulates certain specified instruments, including "any notes[s]"—and Arkansas' securities laws by intentionally failing to follow generally accepted accounting principles that would have made the Co-Op's insolvency apparent to potential note purchasers. Petitioners prevailed at trial, but the Court of Appeals reversed. Applying the test created in SEC v. W.J. Howey Co., . . . to determine whether an instrument is an "investment contract" to the determination whether the Co-Op's instruments were "notes," the court held that the notes were not securities under the 1934 Act or Arkansas law, and that the statutes' antifraud provisions therefore did not apply.

Held: The demand notes issued by the Co-Op fall under the "note" category of instruments that are "securities."

(a) Congress' purpose in enacting the securities laws was to regulate investments, in whatever form they are made and by whatever name they are called. However, notes are used in a variety of settings, not all of which involve investments. Thus, they are not securities per se, but must be defined using the "family resemblance" test. Under that test, a note is presumed to be a security unless it bears a strong resemblance, determined by examining four specified factors, to one of a judicially crafted list of categories of instrument that are not securities. If the instrument is not sufficiently similar to a listed item, a court must decide whether another category should be added by examining the same factors. The application of the Howey test to notes is rejected, since to hold that a "note" is not a "security" unless it meets a test designed for an entirely different variety of instrument would make the 1933 and 1934 Acts' enumeration of many types of instruments superfluous and would be inconsistent with Congress' intent in enacting the laws.

(b) Applying the family resemblance approach, the notes at issue are "securities." They do not resemble any of the enumerated categories of nonsecurities. Nor does an examination of the four relevant factors suggest that they should be treated as nonsecurities: (1) the Co-Op sold them to raise capital, and purchasers bought them to earn a profit in the form of interest, so that they are most naturally conceived as investments in a business enterprise; (2) there was "common trading" of the notes, which were offered and sold to a broad segment of the public; (3) the public reasonably perceived from advertisements for the notes that they were investments, and there were no countervailing factors that would have led a reasonable person to question this characterization; and (4) there was no risk-reducing factor that would make the application of the Securities Acts unnecessary, since the notes were uncollateralized and uninsured and would escape federal regulation entirely if the Acts were held not to apply. The lower court's argument that the demand nature of the notes is very uncharacteristic of a security is unpersuasive, since an instrument's liquidity does not eliminate the risk associated with securities.

(c) Respondent's contention that the notes fall within the statutory exception for "any note . . . which has a maturity at the time of issuance of not less than nine months" is rejected, since it rests entirely on the premise that Arkansas' statute of limitations for suits to collect demand notes—which are due immediately—is determinative of the notes' "maturity," as that term is used in the federal Securities Acts. The "maturity" of notes is a question of federal law, and Congress could not have intended that the Acts be applied differently to the same transactions depending on the accident of which State's law happens to applied.

(d) Since, as a matter of federal law, the words of the statutory exception are far from plain with regard to demand notes, the exclusion must be interpreted in accordance with the exception's purpose. Even assuming that Congress intended to create a bright-line rule exempting from coverage all notes of less than nine months' duration on the ground that short-term notes are sufficiently safe that the Securities Acts need not apply, that exemption would not cover the notes at issue here, which do not necessarily have short terms, since demand could just as easily be made years or decades into the future.

Reversed and remanded.

Case Reflections

1. Why is defendant Ernst & Young a party to this case?
2. Briefly describe the "family resemblance test " as outlined in the case.
3. Applying the family resemblance approach, do the demand notes issued by the Co-Op, in the eyes of the Supreme Court, fall within the "note" category of instruments that are securities? Explain.

WOOLDRIDGE HOMES, INC. V. BRONZE TREE, INC.

558 F.Supp. 1085 (1983)

The sale of a condominium unit as an "investment" meets the Howey test as a security.

Condominium purchaser brought action against vendor seeking rescission of purchase agreement and return of earnest money deposit plus accrued interest. On vendor's motion to dismiss, the District Court, Kane, J., held that: (1) the transaction was subject to federal securities laws, and (2) the complaint sufficiently stated a claim for breach of contract.
Motion denied.

MEMORANDUM OPINION AND ORDER

Plaintiff's . . . complaint alleges violations of federal and state securities laws . . . Defendant contends that the sale of the condominium unit which is the subject of this lawsuit is not a sale of a security or an investment contract and, therefore, the action cannot be one based on the securities laws. . . .

The complaint alleges that Robert E. Wooldridge received a solicitation letter . . . from Mountain Real Estate Association, Ltd., inviting offers in certain investment resort property located in Steamboat Village, Colorado. The condominium units to which the letter related were known as the Bronze Tree Condominiums. Wooldridge responded to the solicitation . . . and received a standard contract which he executed in the name of Wooldridge Homes . . . agreeing to make a $205,000 investment. Wooldridge tendered a $25,000 earnest money check which was deposited in an escrow account. A purchase agreement was entered "with the intent of making an investment in a growing resort community." Plaintiff maintains that it believed it was making a passive investment and anticipated little or no management of the unit would be required by it. . . . Sever, a principal of the sales agent, communicated by telephone and letter that plaintiff's investment was increasing in value. Plaintiff avers it expected to earn profits from the investment and relied on the efforts of defendant to do so. Plaintiff characterizes the investment as a common enterprise. By letter . . . defendant informed plaintiff that defendant was seeking construction financing and that financial institutions with whom defendant was dealing may contact plaintiff for financial information regarding plaintiff's credit worthiness. Plaintiff alleges that defendant was using plaintiff's contractual commitment under the purchase agreement, and other investors' contractual commitments under similar agreements, to obtain construction financing. Defendant was delayed in obtaining financing for a construction loan . . . and construction was unable to continue . . . Plaintiff claims that defendant represented through the sales agent that completion of the project was guaranteed . . . when in fact defendant contemplated or should have contemplated the delays in construction. Plaintiff seeks rescission of the purchase agreement and return of Wooldridge's earnest money deposit plus accrued interest.

[1] The parties agree that if this scheme can be characterized as a security or an investment contract, it must meet the three elements set forth in the paradigmatic case of Securities & Exchange Commission v. W. J. Howey Company . . .

INVESTMENT OF MONEY

Investment of money requires the investor to commit his assets to an enterprise or venture in such a manner as to subject himself to financial loss. . . . Neither side contends that there is any genuine dispute that this transaction qualifies as an investment of money.

COMMON ENTERPRISE

Defendant disputes that the common enterprise element is present in this action arguing that the fortunes of the condominium purchaser were not interwoven with and dependent upon the efforts and success of Bronze Tree, Inc. or any third party . . . Plaintiff contends that . . . the offer or sale coupled with an optional rental arrangement will constitute the offer of investment contracts.

. . . Defendant argues that the fortunes of the condominium purchaser are not interwoven with and dependent upon the efforts and success of Bronze Tree, Inc. or any third party. Specifically, defendant relies on the fact that its arrangement with Ski Country Enterprises, Inc. (a management company) to manage the common areas and to provide administrative and supervisory management for the complex was not to exceed two years, after which the owners of the individual condominium units were free to engage professional management as they desired. Further, defendant points out that after the initial two year contract, the rental of condominiums was strictly optional. In other words "[i]f an owner chooses to make their (sic) condominium available for rental purposes, they can enter into a Rental Agreement with Ski Country."

Here, defendant's activities come within . . . definitions of common enterprise. In attempting to obtain construction financing and by providing managerial services, however optional, the investors' profits are directly tied to the efforts of Bronze Tree, Inc. . . .

PROFITS SOLELY FROM THE EFFORTS OF OTHERS

Plaintiff maintains it had two independent bases for its expectations of profit in the condominium investment: capital appreciation, and rental income to be derived through the efforts of the defendant or third party. . . .

Although defendant concedes that plaintiff may have expected to receive some profit by virtue of the capital appreciation or rental income, defendant contends that this expectation was not derived solely from the effort of the promoter or a third party as is required under Howey. Defendant points to the fact that the increase in value of the condominium is inextricably tied to general economic factors, and that any representation made to plaintiff that the condominium would be a good "investment" is insufficient to establish the sale of a security. . . . In addition, defendant maintains that to the degree plaintiff expected profits from the efforts of Ski Country Enterprises, Inc., plaintiff would have to elect to use the services of Ski Country and would retain control over usage of the condominium by himself and his guests. Defendant concludes that this essential element of Howey is absent.

It is well settled that the term "solely" is not to be given a literal interpretation. . . . Therefore, reliance of investors on the promoter need not be total. . . . I hold that plaintiff has sufficiently met this third element of the Howey test and has plead the element of reliance sufficiently enough to withstand defendant's motion to dismiss.

[2] Having found that all three elements of the Howey test have been met, I find that this scheme falls within the definition of a security and is sub-

ject to the provisions of the acts. Defendant's motion to dismiss the securities claims is denied. . . .

Case Reflections

1. The defendant in this case may have chosen a rather "underhanded" method of obtaining financing for its project. Explain this method in your own words.
2. Can the project described in this case be characterized as a security or investment contract, thus making it subject to federal securities laws?

UNITED HOUSING FOUNDATION, INC. V. FORMAN

421 U.S. 837, 95 S.Ct. 2051 (1975)

Shares of "stock" that entitle the purchaser to lease an apartment are not securities.

Tenants of low income cooperative housing project brought suit and alleged violations of federal securities laws . . . The United States District Court . . . dismissed for lack of subject matter jurisdiction, and plaintiffs appealed. The Court of Appeals . . . reversed and remanded, and certiorari was granted. The Supreme Court, Mr. Justice Powell, held that shares of stock which entitled purchasers to lease an apartment in a state subsidized and supervised nonprofit housing cooperative were not "securities" within purview of Securities Act of 1933, and Securities Exchange Act of 1934; . . .

Respondents are 57 residents of Co-op City, a massive cooperative housing project in New York City, organized, financed, and constructed under the New York Private Housing Finance Law (Mitchell-Lama Act). They brought this action on behalf of all the apartment owners and derivatively on behalf of the housing corporation, alleging . . . violations of the antifraud provisions of the Securities Act of 1933 and of the Securities Exchange Act of 1934 (hereafter collectively Securities Acts), in connection with the sale to respondents of shares of the common stock of the cooperative housing corporation. Citing substantial increases in the tenants' monthly rental charges as a result of higher construction costs, respondents' claim centered on a Co-op City Information Bulletin issued in the project's initial stages, which allegedly misrepresented that the developers would absorb future cost increases due to such factors as inflation. Under the Mitchell-Lama Act, which was designed to encourage private developers to build low-cost cooperative housing, the State provides large, long-term low-interest mortgage loans and substantial tax exemptions, conditioned on step-by-step state supervision of the cooperative's development. Developers must agree to operate the facilities "on a nonprofit basis" and may lease apartments to only state-approved lessees whose incomes are below a certain level. The corporate petitioners in this case built, promoted, and presently control Co-op City: United Housing Foundation (UHF), a nonprofit membership corporation, initiated and sponsored the project; Riverbay, a nonprofit cooperative housing corporation, was organized by UHF to own and operate the land and buildings and issue the stock that is the subject of the instant action; and Community Securities, Inc. (CSI), UHF's wholly owned subsidiary, was the project's general contractor and sales agent. To acquire a Co-op City apartment a prospective purchaser must buy 18 shares of Riverbay stock for each room desired at $25 per share. The shares cannot be transferred to a nontenant, pledged, encumbered, or bequeathed (except to a surviving spouse), and do not convey voting rights based on the number owned (each apartment having one vote). On termination of occupancy a tenant must offer his stock to Riverbay at $25 per share, and in the unlikely event that Riverbay does not repurchase, the tenant cannot sell his shares for more than their original price, plus a fraction of the mortgage amortization that he has paid during his tenancy, and then only to a prospective tenant satisfying the statutory income eligibility requirements. Under the Co-op City lease arrangement the resident is committed to make monthly rental payments in accordance with the size, nature, and location of the apartment. The Securities Acts define a "security" as "any . . . stock, . . . investment contract, . . . or, in general, any interest or instrument commonly known as a security." Petitioners moved to dismiss the complaint for lack of federal jurisdiction, maintaining that the Riverbay stock did not constitute securities as thus defined. The District Court granted the motion to dismiss. The court of Appeals reversed, holding that (1) since the shares purchased were called "stock" the definitional sections of the Securities Acts were literally applicable and (2) the transaction was an investment contract under the Securities Acts, there being a profit expectation from rental reductions resulting from (i) the income produced by commercial facilities established for the use of Co-op City tenants; (ii) tax deductions for the portion of monthly rental charges allocable to interest payments on the mortgage; and (iii) savings based on the fact that Co-op City apartments cost substantially less than comparable nonsubsidized housing. Held: The shares of stock involved in this litigation do not constitute "securities" within the purview of the Securities Acts . . .

(a) When viewed as they must be in terms of their substance (the economic realities of the transaction) rather than their form, the instruments involved here were not shares of stock in the ordinary sense of conferring the right to receive "dividends contingent upon an apportionment of profits," . . . with the traditional characteristics of being negotiable, subject to pledge or hypothecation, conferring voting rights proportional to the number of shares owned, and possibility of appreciating in value. On the contrary, these instruments were purchased, not for making a profit, but for acquiring subsidized low-cost housing.

(b) A share in Riverbay does not constitute an "investment contract" as defined by the Securities Acts, a term which, like the term "any . . . instrument commonly known as a security," involves investment in a common venture premised on a reasonable expectation of profits to be derived from the entrepreneurial or managerial efforts of others. Here neither of the kinds of profits traditionally associated with securities were offered to respondents; instead, as indicated in the Information Bulletin, which stressed the "nonprofit" nature of the project, the focus was upon the acquisition of a place to live.

(c) Although deductible for tax purposes, the portion of rental charges applied to interest on the mortgage (benefits generally available to home mortgagors) does not constitute "profits," and, in any event, does not derive from the efforts of third parties.

(d) Low rent attributable to state financial subsidies no more embodies income or profit attributes than other types of government subsidies.

(e) Such income as might derive from Co-op City's leasing of commercial facilities within the housing project to be used to reduce tenant rentals (the prospect of which was never mentioned in the Information Bulletin) is too speculative and insubstantial to bring the entire transaction within the Securities Acts. These facilities were established, not for profit purposes, but to make essential services available to residents of the huge complex.

Case Reflections

1. Describe the terms and conditions of the "stock" issued by the Co-Op.
2. For what reason did the plaintiffs in this case file suit against United Housing Foundation? What is the issue before the Supreme Court in this case?
3. Were the shares of "stock" in question ruled by the Supreme Court to fall under the definition of a "security?" Why or why not?

STEWART V. GERMANY

631 F.Supp. 236 (1986)

Is a* general *partnership interest a security?

Buyer of general partnership interest brought action against other general partners and general partnership, alleging violations of federal and state securities law. Other general partners and partnership moved to dismiss suit . . . The District Court . . . held that: (1) genuine issues of fact precluded summary judgment as to whether general partnership interest was security; . . .

MEMORANDUM OPINION AND ORDER

The Court has before it the Motion of Defendants . . . (hereinafter sometimes referred to as "Managing General Partners") and the Natchez Hotel Company . . . , to Dismiss or for Judgment on the Pleadings. The issues raised by Defendants' Motion are whether Plaintiff's general partnership interest is a security, and, if so, whether the various statutes of limitation bar Plaintiff's federal and state securities claims against Defendants.

FACTS

This action arises out of the purchase by Plaintiff of a general partnership interest in the Natchez Hotel Company, a Mississippi general partnership ("the Partnership"), formed in September 1980 for the purpose of restoring, owning, developing and operating the Eola Hotel in Natchez, Mississippi. Defendants are, or have been, general partners of the partnership and the general partnership itself.

Plaintiff's First Amended Complaint . . . alleges violations of the Securities Act of 1933 . . . and Mississippi state securities laws. In essence, Plaintiff claims that her general partnership interest in the Natchez Hotel Company is a security and that Defendants, as managing general partners and controlling persons of the Natchez Hotel Company, violated federal and state securities laws by failing to register the offering of the alleged security; by\ failing to state material facts relating to the offering of the alleged security; by fraudulently misrepresenting or omitting material facts relating to the alleged security; and by breaching fiduciary duties owed by Defendants as managing general partners to Plaintiff. . . . As a result of Defendants' alleged securities violations, Plaintiff seeks rescission of her general partnership interest and return of all money paid for or on account of such securities, less any amounts received. Plaintiff also seeks dissolution of the Natchez Hotel Company, alleging that the partnership has operated at a loss since its inception as a result of mismanagement and that there is no substantial likelihood that it will ever operate profitably.

LAW

Is Plaintiff's general partnership interest a security?

[1] Defendants have moved to dismiss this suit . . . According to Defendants, Plaintiff did not purchase a security within the meaning of the Securities Act of 1933 or the Securities Exchange Act of 1934 . . . The Securities Act of 1933, 15 U.S.C. § 77b(1), defines "security" as: . . . any note, stock, treasury stock, bond, debenture, evidence of indebtedness, certificate of interest or participation in any profit-sharing agreement, collateral-trust certificate, preorganization certificate or subscription, transferable share, investment contract, voting-trust certificate, certificate of deposit for a security, fractional undivided interest in oil, gas or other mineral rights, or, in general, any interest or instrument commonly known as a "security" or any certificate of interest or participation in, temporary or interim certificate for, receipt for, guarantee of, or warrant or right to subscribe to or purchase, any of the foregoing.

To be a security, Plaintiff's general partnership interest must be an "investment contract."

According to the United States Supreme Court, an "investment contract" is a security if it is

> . . . a contract, transaction or scheme whereby a person invests his money in a common enter-

> prise and is led to expect profits solely from the efforts of a promoter or a third party.

The Fifth Circuit . . . elaborated on the Howey rule in the context of joint ventures and partnerships. According to Williamson, an interest in a joint venture or partnership may be a security if it involves: (1) an investment of money; (2) in a common enterprise; and (3) on an expectation of profits to be derived solely from the efforts of individuals other than the investor.

The Fifth Circuit also reiterated that the word "solely" . . . should not be read as a strict or literal limitation on the definition of an investment contract, but rather must be construed realistically so as to include within the definition those schemes which involve in substance, if not form, securities.

. . .

. . . The Fifth Circuit . . . reasoned that although "an investor who claims his general partnership interest is an investment contract has a difficult burden to overcome," a general partnership interest can be designated as a security if the investor can establish that:

(1) an agreement among the parties leaves so little power in the hands of the partner . . . that the arrangement in fact distributes power as would a limited partnership; or (2) the partner . . . is so inexperienced and unknowledgeable in business affairs that he is incapable of intelligently exercising his partnership . . . powers; or (3) the partner . . . is so dependent on some unique entrepreneurial or managerial ability of the promoter or manager that he cannot replace the manager or otherwise exercise meaningful partnership . . . powers.

. . . Defendants claim that the partnership agreement afforded each partner significant partnership powers and control; that Plaintiff warranted and represented to Defendants that she was experienced and knowledgeable in real estate investment and that she obtained qualified and experienced independent advice with respect to her investment (Art. III of the Partnership Agreement); and that neither Plaintiff nor the partnership depended upon the unique talents of any individual partner.

Plaintiff, on the other hand, claims that her general partnership interest is a security . . . because the real rights and powers of the general partners under the partnership agreement are severely restricted and because Plaintiff is an unsophisticated investor who relied upon the business acumen of the Defendants. In fact, Plaintiff claims that the only reason Defendants used the general partnership form was to achieve accelerated depreciation and maximum tax benefits and to satisfy the demands of financial institutions for total recourse debt and not to provide partners with managerial powers.

The Court is of the opinion that . . . there is a genuine issue of material fact concerning whether Plaintiff's general partnership interest is a security. Specifically, the Court finds that at least the following genuine issues of material fact preclude the entry of judgment on Defendants' claim that Plaintiff's general partnership interest is not a security: (1) whether the partnership agreement is structured such that the partners' powers are synonymous with those of a limited partner or; (2) whether the Plaintiff is so inexperienced or unknowledgeable in business affairs that she was incapable of intelligently exercising her partnership powers; or (3) whether the Plaintiff was so dependent on the unique entrepreneurial or managerial ability of the managing partners that she was unable to exercise meaningful partnership powers. . . .

Case Reflections

1. To be ruled a security, the plaintiff's general partnership interest must be an "investment contract." What is the definition of an "investment contract" according to the U.S. Supreme Court?
2. The Fifth Circuit Court also stated that a general partnership interest can be designated a security if the investor can establish one of three items. What are these items?

GOODMAN
V.
EPSTEIN

582 F.2d 388 (1971–78)

Is a* limited *partnership interest a security?

. . . Limited partners brought action against general partners seeking compensation for damages suffered as a result of failure of a limited partnership land development scheme alleging violations of the Securities Exchange Act, ... The United States District Court . . . entered judgment for general partners, and limited partners appealed. The Court of Appeals . . . held that: . . . (3) trial judge should have instructed jury that limited partners' interests in partnership constituted a "security,"

. . .

Affirmed in part; reversed in part and remanded.

. . .

HISTORY OF THE CASE

. . . When the suit finally was filed . . . plaintiffs sought total damages in the amount of $1,061,500, alleging that defendants had violated the federal securities laws (Count I) . . . A jury trial commenced . . . The trial lasted six full weeks and consumed some thirty trial days; the transcript of proceedings is more than 4000 pages in length, and there were in excess of 400 exhibits admitted into evidence. At the end of this considerable undertaking . . . the jury retired to deliberate in the late afternoon . . . About an hour later, the jury executed a sealed verdict which was unsealed and read in open court the next morning. The jury returned a general verdict in favor of each of the three defendants and against each of the four plaintiffs on each of the three Counts.

Plaintiffs now appeal from the judgment entered on this general verdict on grounds, not that the verdict was contrary to the substantial weight of the evidence, but that substantial mistakes of law and errors in the conduct of the trial on the part of the trial judge tipped the scales in favor of defendants in what was, otherwise, a close and complex case.

POSITIONS OF PARTIES ON APPEAL

Plaintiffs contend that the trial judge made substantial errors of law in each of four individual instructions which so prejudiced plaintiffs in regard to their Count I that a new trial on that Count should be mandated. . . .

(3) Whether a limited partnership interest constitutes security. . . .

Plaintiffs argue that a limited partnership interest is a security as a matter of law and that the trial judge's instructions improperly submitted to the jury the question of whether plaintiffs' interests constituted securities under the federal securities laws. Plaintiffs cite case law . . . holding that limited partnership interests constituted securities as a matter of law and then demonstrate that, under the Illinois law of limited partnership, the interests of the plaintiffs here met the test established by the Supreme Court for determining whether a financial interest is, in fact, a "security." Plaintiffs maintain that theirs was an "investment in a common venture premised on a reasonable expectation of profits to be derived from the entrepreneurial or managerial efforts of others."

Because . . . a limited partnership interest bears little resemblance to what lay jurors would consider a "security," plaintiffs contend that the submission of this issue to the jury, particularly in the face of the considerable weight of legal authorities to the contrary, was so prejudicial as to necessitate a new trial in that the jury's general verdict in favor of all defendants on Count I, the federal securities count, could easily have been premised on the conclusion that plaintiffs, as limited partners, did not hold "securities."

. . .

Defendants, of course, are not left speechless by these arguments by the plaintiffs. . . .

(3) Whether a limited partnership interest constitutes a security.

Defendants strenuously assert . . . no reversal is mandated because the trial judge was correct, in the circumstances of this case, in leaving to the jury the question whether a limited partnership interest constituted a security. They argue that there were factual disputes, eliciting conflicting evidence at trial, on at least two of the three factors to be considered in determining whether a financial interest is a security . . .

For the reasons stated below, we reverse the jury verdict entered in the District Court and remand for a new trial on Count I.

DISCUSSION

. . .

(3) Whether a limited partnership interest constitutes a security.

On the question of whether the trial judge incorrectly left for the jury the question of whether an interest in a limited partnership constituted a security, we agree with plaintiffs that the trial judge should have made that determination and directed the jury that the interest present in this case was, as a matter of law, a security.

The basic test which has been enunciated by the Supreme Court for determining the existence of a security involves three elements: (1) an investment in a common venture (2) premised on a reasonable expectation of profits (3) to be derived from the entrepreneurial or managerial efforts of others, United Housing Foundation, Inc. v. Forman . . . A limited partner's interest in a limited partnership established under Illinois law meets, on its face, all of these requirements. The actual D-E Westmont Limited Partnership Agreement (with its amendments) further confirms that the three requirements are met.

We recognize that, in evaluating a financial interest to determine whether an "investment contract," or security, exists, the substance of the transaction must be elevated over the form; that is, the existence or nonexistence of an "investment contract" must be determined from the actual facts and circumstances of the investment arrangement and not from the existence or nonexistence of a "stock certificate" alone. . . . It is this very consideration which has allowed numerous courts to determine that a limited partner's interest in a limited partnership is an "investment contract" or "security," even though it does not have the normal trappings of what a lay person may think of as a security. . . .

These courts recognized, as have the Securities and Exchange Commission[1] and several respected commentators,[2] that the very legal requirements for a limited partnership necessitate its including all of the attributes of a "security" in the interest bestowed upon one of limited partners.

We do not accept defendants' assertion that they raised sufficient factual questions to necessitate the trial judge's sending this issue to the jury. A summary perusal of the evidence adduced at trial reveals no debatable question of the plaintiffs' interests meeting all three of the Howey/Forman tests. . . .

Case Reflections

1. State the issues to be decided by the U.S. Court of Appeals in this case.
2. How did the U.S. Court of Appeals rule on each issue in this case?

---

[1]See S.E.C. Release No. 33-4877, August 8, 1967, which reads, in pertinent part:

Under the Federal Securities Laws, an offering of limited partnership interests and interests in joint or profit sharing real estate ventures generally constitutes an offering of a "profit sharing agreement" or an "investment contract" which is a "security" within the meaning of Section 2(1) of the Securities Act of 1933. . . .

. . . (I)f the promoters of a real estate syndication offer investors the opportunity to share in the profits of real estate syndications or similar ventures, particularly when there is no active participation in the management and operation of the scheme on the part of the investors, the promoters are, in effect, offering a "security." . . .

[2]Bromberg, for example, states:

Limited partners . . . are effectively precluded from participation in control by the threat of losing their limited liability. Perforce, they must rely on the investment efforts of general partners for profits. The investment contract concept is particularly applicable. (Citations omitted.) 1 Bromberg, Securities Law: Fraud, § 4.6(332), at 82.7 (1975)

Jennings and Marsh, in a particularly relevant section that interprets the effect of the Uniform Limited Partnership Act under which the D-E Westmont Limited Partnership was formed, state:

. . . (U)nder the Uniform Limited Partnership Act, a limited partner may not take part in the control of the business; he must remain a passive investor. Limited partnership interests thus fall squarely within the definition of a "security." . . . Jennings & Marsh, Securities Regulation 252 (1968).

CHAPTER 19

FUTURE TRENDS IN REAL ESTATE LAW

LEARNING OBJECTIVES

After reading this chapter, you should be able to:

1. List and describe the areas where change is already beginning to take place in real estate law.
2. Recognize the importance of disclosing all possible agency relationships to buyers and sellers and mandatory complete seller disclosure on potential agency liability exposure.
3. Understand the forces that may lead to more national real estate firms and the impact this will have on the real estate transaction process.
4. Describe the securitization process for real estate investments and its potential importance to small investors.
5. Recognize the potential conflict between efforts to defend individual liberties and the need to protect and preserve the environment.

KEY TERMS

Full Agency Disclosure

Seller Disclosure

Open MLS System

Hostile Takeover

Leveraged Buyout

Securitization

Systematic Risk

Unsystematic Risk

Portfolio Diversification

Takings Issue

Environmental Protection

Historic Preservation

The real estate industry is in the midst of what may prove to be a revolutionary restructuring. Many areas of the industry are now being pushed, often by legal challenges, to reexamine existing ways of conducting business. In this chapter, we try to look into the future a bit and predict where some of the most dramatic changes are likely to occur.

The areas where the process of change has already begun are agency and brokerage, professional liability, brokerage firm structure, land use controls, and securitization of real estate investments. Change will occur, of course, in many more areas than those discussed here. The aim of this discussion is simply to focus our attention on those areas that will potentially change the way the real estate industry docs business.

AGENCY AND BROKERAGE ISSUES

Perhaps no single area of the real estate industry is facing as much pressure as that of agency relationships. The single agency relationship, which has typified the brokerage industry, is rapidly giving way to a more comprehensive set of possible relationships between participants. As the number and complexity of these relationships expand, the need to inform the public becomes increasingly important. Thus we begin the discussion in this area with the issue of disclosure.

Agency Disclosure

Dismuke v. Edina Realty, Inc.

The question "who is my client?" is one that will simply not go away. In July, 1991, the National Association of Realtors (NAR) formed a task force to study the agency issue. Among its recommendations was to encourage, through legislation or regulation, increased written disclosure of agency relationships.[1] As we have seen earlier in this book, most states already require some form of written agency disclosure. The issue addressed by the task force recommendation is to expand the nature of the disclosure to include not only information about the agency relationship that is traditionally established, but also alternative relationships that could be established.

The single agency model, in which the seller is represented by all agents and subagents, currently dominates the industry, thus making it difficult for participants to be aware of the existence of alternatives. For example, buyer brokerage, although it is rapidly gaining popularity and recognition, is still a seldom used approach. A few areas in the U.S. have already begun to move toward **"full agency" disclosure** requirements. Figure 19.1 contains some examples of the disclosure forms used in these areas.

Full Agency Disclosure Disclosing not only the nature of the current agency relationship, but other possible agency relationships.

The movement toward full disclosure of alternative agency relationships is viewed by most industry participants as beneficial to the long-term growth and stability of the brokerage industry. Although there will be a period, not a lengthy one it is hoped, during which market participants will be confused about the changes taking place, in the long run the liability exposure of brokers and salespersons will be reduced by dealing with a more informed clientele.

[1]Portions of the *Report of the Presidential Advisory Group on Agency* are included as Appendix C.

NCR (No Carbon Required)

REAL ESTATE AGENCY DISCLOSURE

In a real estate transaction an agent generally represents either the Seller or the Buyer. When you enter into a discussion with a real estate agent, you need to understand the various relationships which can exist between you and the agent.

Listing agents represent the Seller. They are committed, contractually and by law, to act in the best interest of their principal, the Seller.

Since Seller and Buyer have adverse interests in a transaction, an agent cannot represent the interests of one party to the exclusion or detriment of the interests of the other party. Therefore - except in a Dual Agency situation with the express written consent of both parties - an agent representing the Seller cannot lawfully also represent the Buyer in the transaction.

If the Buyer wants the agent to act in his behalf, s/he can enter into an understanding with the agent whereby the agent agrees to represent the Buyer exclusively and not the Seller. The agent is referred to as a Buyer's Agent in such a transaction.

Under the law of agency, state laws, and the NATIONAL ASSOCIATION OF REALTORS® Code of Ethics, real estate agents have certain duties to their principals and other parties in a transaction, which are described below. These duties, however, do not relieve you from the responsibility to protect your own interests. Read carefully all agreements to ensure that they adequately express your understanding of the transaction. A real estate agent is qualified to advise on matters concerning real estate. If legal or tax advice is desired, consult a competent professional in that field.

SELLER'S AGENT'S DUTIES

A Seller's agent acts as the agent for the Seller only. Cooperating brokers and their salespersons can elect to be subagents of the Seller, usually through a multiple listing service. Seller's agents and subagents have certain obligations to the Seller, among which:

- A **fiduciary** duty of utmost care, integrity, honesty, confidentiality and loyalty in dealings with the Seller. The broker may never disclose confidential information, such as disclosing to a Buyer the price the Seller might accept.
- The duty to comply with the Seller's lawful instructions.
- A duty to account to the Seller for funds held for the benefit of the Seller.
- The duties discussed below under AGENT'S DUTIES TO ALL PARTIES
- A duty to comply with Fair Housing Laws.

BUYER'S AGENT'S DUTIES

A Buyer's agent acts as the agent for the Buyer only. An agent acting only for a Buyer, called Buyer's Agent or Buyer's Broker, has certain obligations to the Buyer, among which:

- A **fiduciary** duty of utmost care, integrity, honesty, confidentiality and loyalty in dealings with the Buyer. The broker may never disclose confidential information, such as disclosing to a Seller the price the Buyer might be willing to pay.
- The duty to comply with the Buyer's lawful instructions.
- The duty to account to the Buyer for funds held for the benefit of the Buyer.
- The duties discussed below under AGENT'S DUTIES TO ALL PARTIES.
- The duty to comply with Fair Housing Laws.

AGENT'S DUTIES IN A DUAL AGENCY RELATIONSHIP

A Dual Agency relationship can arise when a Buyer, represented by a Buyer's Agent, wishes to acquire a property listed by his/her agent. Since such Dual Agency creates conflicts of interest, the broker can only act as an intermediary between the parties. In a Dual Agency situation, the agent has the following obligations to both Seller and Buyer:

- A **fiduciary** duty of utmost care, integrity, honesty, confidentiality and loyalty in dealings with both Seller and Buyer. The broker may never disclose confidential information, such as disclosing to a Buyer the price the Seller might accept, or disclosing to a Seller the price the Buyer might be willing to pay.
- The duties discussed below under AGENT'S DUTIES TO ALL PARTIES.

AGENT'S DUTIES TO ALL PARTIES

In addition to the above described duties to their principals, agents have the following duties to all parties in a transaction, regardless of agency relationship:

- Diligent exercise of reasonable skill and care in performance of the agent's duties.
- A duty of "honest and fair dealing" and good faith.
- A duty to disclose all facts materially affecting the value or desirability of the property known to the agent.
- A duty to present all offers promptly.
- A duty to comply with Fair Housing Laws.

I/We acknowledge receipt of a copy of this disclosure.

Buyer / Seller ______________________ Date ______________

Buyer / Seller ______________________ Date ______________

Agent ______________________ By ______________________ Date ______________

CONFIRMATION OF AGENCY RELATIONSHIP

Property Address: ______________________________________

______________ is the AGENT of (check one below): (NAME OF LISTING AGENT)	______________ is the AGENT of (check one below): (NAME OF SELLING AGENT IF NOT THE SAME AS THE LISTING AGENT)
☐ THE SELLER EXCLUSIVELY; or ☐ BOTH THE BUYER AND THE SELLER	☐ THE BUYER EXCLUSIVELY; or ☐ THE SELLER EXCLUSIVELY; or ☐ BOTH THE BUYER AND THE SELLER

I/WE CONFIRM THE AGENCY AND ACKNOWLEDGE RECEIPT OF A COPY HEREOF.

Seller ______________ Date ________ Buyer ______________ Date ________

Seller ______________ Date ________ Buyer ______________ Date ________

Listing Agent ______________ By ______________ (Associate Licensee or Broker - Signature) Date ________

Selling Agent ______________ By ______________ (Associate Licensee or Broker - Signature) Date ________

FORM 110.51 (4-92) PROFESSIONAL PUBLISHING

FIGURE 19.1 EXAMPLES OF DISCLOSURE FORMS

DISCLOSURE REGARDING REAL ESTATE AGENCY RELATIONSHIPS

Before you enter into a discussion with a real estate agent regarding a real estate transaction, you should understand what type of agency relationship you wish to have with that agent.

New York State law requires real estate licensees who are acting as agents of buyers or sellers of property to advise the potential buyers or sellers with whom they work of the nature of their agency relationship and the rights and obligations it creates.

SELLER'S AGENT

If you are interested in selling real property, you can engage a real estate agent as a seller's agent. A seller's agent, including a listing agent under a listing agreement with the seller, acts solely on behalf of the seller. You can authorize a seller's agent to do other things including hire subagents, broker's agents or work with other agents, such as buyer's agents, on a cooperative basis. A subagent, or "cooperating agent," is one who has agreed to work with the seller's agent, often through a multiple listing service. A subagent may work in a different real estate office.

A seller's agent has, without limitation, the following fiduciary duties to the seller: reasonable care, undivided loyalty, confidentiality, full disclosure, obedience and a duty to account.

The obligations of an agent are also subject to any specific provisions set forth in an agreement between the agent and the seller.

In dealings with the buyer, a seller's agent should: (a) exercise reasonable skill and care in performance of the agent's duties: (b) deal honestly, fairly and in good faith; and (c) disclose all facts known to the agent materially affecting the value or desirability of the property, except as otherwise provided by law.

BUYER'S AGENT

If you are interested in buying real property, you can engage a real estate agent as a buyer's agent. A buyer's agent acts solely on behalf of the buyer. You can authorize a buyer's agent to do other things including hire subagents, broker's agents or work with other agents, such as seller's agents, on a cooperative basis.

A buyer's agent has, without limitation, the following fiduciary duties to the buyer: reasonable care, undivided loyalty, confidentiality, full disclosure, obedience and a duty to account.

The obligations of an agent are also subject to any specific provisions set forth in an agreement between the agent and the buyer.

In dealing with the seller, a buyer's agent should: (a) exercise reasonable skill and care in performance of the agent's duties: (b) deal honestly, fairly and in good faith; and (c) disclose all facts known to the agent materially affecting the value or desirability of the property, except as otherwise provided by law.

AGENT REPRESENTING BOTH SELLER AND BUYER

A real estate agent, acting directly or through an associated licensee, can be the agent of both the seller and the buyer in a transaction, but only with the knowledge and informed consent, in writing, of both the seller and the buyer.

In such a dual agency situation, the agent will not be able to provide the full range of fiduciary duties to the buyer and seller.

The obligations of an agent are also subject to any specific provisions set forth in an agreement between the agent and the buyer and seller.

An agent acting as a dual agent must explain carefully to both the buyer and seller that the agent is acting for the other party as well. The agent should also explain the possible effects of dual representation,

FIGURE 19.1 EXAMPLES OF DISCLOSURE FORMS *(continued)*

including that by consenting to the dual agency relationship the buyer and seller are giving up their rights to undivided loyalty.

A BUYER OR SELLER SHOULD CAREFULLY CONSIDER THE POSSIBLE CONSEQUENCES OF A DUAL AGENCY RELATIONSHIP BEFORE AGREEING TO SUCH REPRESENTATION.

GENERAL CONSIDERATIONS

You should carefully read all agreements to ensure that they adequately express your understanding of the transaction. A real estate agent is a person qualified to advise about real estate. If legal, tax or other advice is desired, consult a competent professional in that field.

Throughout the transaction you may receive more than one disclosure form. The law requires each agent assisting in the transaction to present you with this disclosure form. You should read its contents each time it is presented to you, considering the relationship between you and the real estate agent in your specific transaction.

ACKNOWLEDGMENT OF PROSPECTIVE BUYER

(1) I have received and read this disclosure notice.
(2) I understand that a seller's agent, including a listing agent, is the agent of the seller exclusively, unless the seller and buyer otherwise agree.
(3) I understand that subagents, including subagents participating in a multiple listing service, are agents of the seller exclusively.
(4) I understand that I may engage my own agent to be my buyer's agent.
(5) I understand that the agent presenting this form to me,

______________________________ of
(name of licensee)

______________________________ is
(name of firm)
(check applicable relationship)

______ an agent of the seller.

______ my agent as a buyer's agent.

Dated:__________________________

Buyer:__________________________

Dated:__________________________

Buyer:__________________________

ACKNOWLEDGMENT OF PROSPECTIVE SELLER

(1) I have received and read this disclosure notice.
(2) I understand that a seller's agent, including a listing agent, is the agent of the seller exclusively, unless the seller and buyer otherwise agree.
(3) I understand that subagents, including subagents participating in a multiple listing service, are agents of the seller exclusively.
(4) I understand that a buyer's agent is the agent of the buyer exclusively.
(5) I understand that the agent presenting this form to me.

______________________________ of
(name of licensee)

______________________________ is
(name of firm)
(check applicable relationship)

______ my agent as a seller's agent.

______ an agent of the buyer.

Dated:__________________________

Seller:__________________________

Dated:__________________________

Seller:__________________________

FIGURE 19.1 EXAMPLES OF DISCLOSURE FORMS *(continued)*

ACKNOWLEDGMENT OF PROSPECTIVE BUYER AND SELLER TO DUAL AGENCY

(1) I have received and read this disclosure notice.
(2) I understand that a dual agent will be working for both the seller and buyer.
(3) I understand that I may engage my own agent as a seller's agent or a buyer's agent.
(4) I understand that I am giving up my right to the agent's undivided loyalty.
(5) I have carefully considered the possible consequences of a dual agency relationship.
(6) I understand that the agent presenting this form to me,

____ of
(name of licensee)

____ is
(name of firm)

______a dual agent working for both the buyer and seller, acting as such with the consent of both the buyer and seller and following full disclosure to the buyer and seller.

Dated:_______________________________ Dated:_______________________________

Buyer:_______________________________ Seller:_______________________________

Dated:_______________________________ Dated:_______________________________

Buyer:_______________________________ Seller:_______________________________

ACKNOWLEDGMENT OF THE PARTIES TO THE CONTRACT

(1) I have received, read and understand this disclosure notice.

(2) I understand that ____ of
(name of licensee)

____ is
(name of firm)

(check applicable relationship)

_____an agent of the seller.

_____an agent of the buyer.

_____a dual agent working for both the buyer and seller, acting as such with the consent of both the buyer and seller and following full disclosure to the buyer and seller.

(3) I also understand that ____ of
(name of licensee)

____ is:
(name of firm)

(check applicable relationship)

_____an agent of the seller.

_____an agent of the buyer.

_____a dual agent working for both the buyer and seller, acting as such with the consent of both the buyer and seller and following full disclosure to the buyer and seller.

Dated:_______________________________ Dated:_______________________________

Buyer:_______________________________ Seller:_______________________________

Dated:_______________________________ Dated:_______________________________

Buyer:_______________________________ Seller:_______________________________

Use of the "Disclosure Regarding Real Estate Agency Relationships" is required by Section 443 of the Real Property Law of New York State.

FIGURE 19.1 EXAMPLES OF DISCLOSURE FORMS (*continued*)

DECLARATION PURSUANT TO SECTION 443 (3) (F) OF THE REAL PROPERTY LAW

STATE OF NEW YORK)
) ss. :
COUNTY OF)

________________________________(name), being duly sworn, deposes and says:

1. I am the principal broker/associate broker/licensed salesperson affiliated with ________________________________(name of agency).

2. I make this Affidavit in compliance with Section 443 (3) (F) of the New York State Real Property Law.

3. On the ______day of ________________, 199______ I presented to ____________________ (name of buyer or seller) the disclosure forms required pursuant to Section 443 of the Real Property Law. The form of the Disclosure Form as presented is attached to this statement.

4. The above named buyer/seller refused to execute an acknowledgement of the receipt of this disclosure form despite my request that it be executed.

5. A copy of this statement and additional copies of the Disclosure Form are being mailed to the person(s) named in paragraph 3, contemporaneously with the execution of this Affidavit.

____
(Name)

Sworn to before me this ________

day of ________________, 199 _____ .

____
Notary Public

IN-HOUSE TRANSACTION WAIVER FORM

"I/we hereby waive my/our right to fiduciary duties including, but not limited to undivided loyalty from any member of ________________________________ firm other than ____________________________ (sales associate) ________________________________ (name of supervising broker if agent is not a broker). I/we understand this waiver will in no way diminish the responsibility of the persons named above to act as my/our agent and provide me/us with fiduciary services including, but not limited to undivided loyalty. I further understand that this waiver allows other members of the __________________________ firm to act as agent for persons whose interest may be adverse to my/our interests and to provide them with the same fiduciary services"

FIGURE 19.1 EXAMPLES OF DISCLOSURE FORMS (*continued*)

EXCLUSIVE RIGHT TO REPRESENT BUYER AGREEMENT

This Agreement is made on ________________, 19_____ between ____

________________________________("Buyer") and ________________________________(firm name)________________("Agent").

In consideration of services and facilities, the Agent is hereby granted the right to represent the Buyer in the acquisition of real property. (As used in this Agreement, "acquistion of real property" shall include any purchase, option, exchange or lease of property or an agreement to do so.)

1. **TERM.** This Agreement commences when signed and, subject to Paragraph 6, terminates at _______ a.m./p.m. on ____________, 19___.

2. **RETAINER FEE.** The Agent, ________________________(firm name)________________________, acknowledges receipt of a retainer fee in the amount of ________________________________, which shall be subtracted from any compensation due the Agent under this Agreement. The retainer is non-refundable and is earned when paid.

3. **AGENT'S DUTIES.** (a)The Agent shall use professional real estate knowledge and skills to represent the Buyer in a diligent and effective manner and to locate property which is available for purchase and suitable to the Buyer; (b) if the Agent is not representing the seller, the Agent shall represent solely the interest of the Buyer in all negotiations and transactions regarding the acquisition of real property, and repudiate any agency or subagency relationship with the seller or the company representing the seller and shall not claim the subagency compensation offered to the selling broker in the Multiple Listing Service; (c) if the Agent represent the seller as well as the Buyer (i.e., disclosed dual agency), the Agent shall **not** disclose to the Buyer information obtained within the confidentiality and trust of the fiduciary relationship with the seller, nor disclose to the seller information similarly obtained from the Buyer, without the consent of the party adversely affected by the disclosure; (d) the Agent may represent other buyers who may be interested in the same property as the Buyer.

4. **BUYER'S DUTIES.** The Buyer shall: (a) work exclusively with the Agent during the term of this Agreement; (b) pay the Agent, directly or indirectly, the compensation set forth below; (c) comply with the reasonable requests of the Agent to supply any pertinent financial or personal data needed to fulfill the terms of this Agreement; (d) be available during Agent's regular working hours to view properties.

5. **PURPOSE.** The Buyer is retaining the Agent to acquire the following type of property: ________________________________

____

6. **COMPENSATION.** The Buyer shall pay the Agent (less the retainer fee) compensation of ________________________("Agent's Fee") in cash, if during the term of the Agreement, the Buyer enters into a contract to acquire any property, as described above, whether through the services of the Agent or otherwise. Any compensation paid to the Agent by the seller or a listing company shall be credited against the compensation due under this Agreement. This Agreement shall also apply to any property presented to the Buyer by the Agent during the term of the Agreement when a contract is entered into within ____ days after this Agreement expires unless the Purchaser enters into a subsequent "Exclusive Right to Represent Buyer Agreement" with another real estate broker, in which event no additional compensation shall be due under this Agreement. Any obligation to pay the Agent compensation incurred under this Agreement survives the termination of this Agreement.

7. **DISCLOSED DUAL AGENCY.** The Agent discloses that sellers may use the services of the Agent's sales associate(s) to represent them. When the Buyer and seller are each represented by the sales associate(s) of the Agent, this is called dual agency. Dual agency is permitted only when disclosed and with the knowledge and written consent of both parties. Disclosed dual agency limits the ability of the Agent and the sales associate(s) to represent either party fully and exclusively. For example, information obtained within the confidentiality and trust of the fiduciary relationship and shall not be disclosed without the prior written consent of the party adversely affected.
Check One: ☐ The Buyer consents to disclosed dual agency, **OR** ☐ the Buyer does not consent to disclosed dual agency, which means the Buyer chooses not to be shown and not to purchase any properties listed with the Agent.

8. **DISCLAIMER.** The Buyer acknowledges that the Agent is being retained solely as a real estate agent and is not an attorney, tax advisor, lender, appraiser, surveyor, structural engineer, home inspector or other professional service provider. The Buyer is advised to seek professional advice concerning the condition of the property or concerning legal and tax matters.

9. **EQUAL OPPORTUNITY.** Properties shall be shown and made available to the Buyer without regard to race, color, religion, sex, handicap, familial status or national origin as well as all classes protected by the laws of the United States, the Commonwealth of Virginia and applicable local jurisdictions.

10. **OTHER PROVISIONS.** ____

____.

11. **MISCELLANEOUS.** This Agreement, any exhibits and any addenda signed by the parties constitute the entire agreement between the parties and supersede any other written or oral agreements between the parties. This Agreement can only be modified in writing when signed by both parties. In any action or proceeding involving a dispute between the Buyer, the seller and/or the Agent, arising out of this Agreement, or to collect the Agent's Fee, the prevailing party shall be entitled to receive from the other party reasonable attorney's fees to be determined by the court or arbitrator(s).

(NOTE: The Buyer should consult with the sales associate of the Agent before visiting any resale or new homes or contacting any other REALTORS® representing sellers, to avoid the possibility of confusion over the agency relationship and misunderstandings about liability for compensation.)

	________________________________ Brokerage Firm(Agent)
________________________________(SEAL) Buyer's Signature	________________________________ Address
________________________________(SEAL) Buyer's Signature	________________________________ City, State, Zip Code
________________________________ Address	________________________________(SEAL) Broker/Sales Manager's Signature
________________________________ City, State, Zip Code	________________________________ Sale Associate's Printed name
Telephone: ____________ ____________ Work Home	Telephone: ____________ ____________ Work Home

REALTOR

NVAR -21-7/93

EQUAL HOUSING OPPORTUNITY

Prepared by the Northern Virginia Association of REALTORS Task Force, NVAR Standard Forms Committee and legal counsel.

FIGURE 19.1 EXAMPLES OF DISCLOSURE FORMS (*continued*)

BUYER AND SELLER AGENCY DISCLOSURE

When you enter into discussions with a real estate licensee member of the Northern Virginia Association of REALTORS®, Inc. ("REALTOR®") regarding a real estate transaction, from the outset you should understand what type of agency relationship or representation exists between you and the REALTOR®. All parties to a real estate transaction -- sellers, buyers, landlords, tenants, optionees, optionors--should understand the unique and valuable role of real estate licensees. This role has been defined over the years by both law and custom.

Virginia real estate licensees are required by the Real Estate Board (Regulation 6.3) to make prompt disclosure of their agency relationship to all actual and prospective parties to a transaction at the earliest practicable time. This disclosure must be in writing and must be acknowledged by the principals.

The REALTOR's® Duties

A REALTOR® and the REALTOR's® brokerage firm have a contractual agreement to act as the "agent" of the client, called the "principal." As an agent, a REALTOR® owes fiduciary duties of undivided loyalty, obedience, confidentiality, reasonable care, diligence, accounting and full disclosure to the principal. Nonetheless, even if a REALTOR® is contractually the agent of another party to a real estate transaction, the REALTOR® can still provide you with a variety of valuable information and assistance. For example, a REALTOR® can inform you about available properties and sources of financing, show you properties, assist you in submitting an offer and inform you about settlement procedures. But you should always keep in mind for whom the REALTOR® is acting as the agent in your transaction, and thus to whom that REALTOR® owes fiduciary duties.

Regardless of whose interests a REALTOR® represents, all REALTORS® are required by the REALTOR's® Code of Ethics to treat all parties fairly. Furthermore, REALTORS® are required by state law and regulation to present promptly all written offers and counteroffers, respond truthfully to questions concerning the property, disclose material facts known to them (unless obtained within their fiduciary relationship) and offer properties without discrimination.

Who Does the REALTOR® Represent?

In an individual real estate transaction, if the REALTOR® represents:

<u>The Seller</u> -- then a REALTOR® under a listing agreement with a seller acts as the agent for the seller. The listing company and all of its REALTORS®, and the selling company and all of its REALTORS® as subagents of the seller, would owe their fiduciary duties to the seller.

<u>The Buyer</u> -- then a REALTOR® under a contract with a buyer acts as the agent for that buyer only, as a "Buyer Broker/Agent," and the REALTOR® is <u>not</u> the seller's agent, even if the Sales Contract provides that the Seller or the Listing Company will pay the REALTOR® for services rendered to the buyer. A REALTOR® acting as the buyer's agent must disclaim the usual subagency offered by the listing agreement and must disclose the Buyer Broker/Agent relationship whenever dealing with the seller's REALTOR® or the seller.

<u>The Buyer AND the Seller</u> -- then a REALTOR®, either acting directly or through one or more of the brokerage firm's other REALTORS®, may be the agent of both the buyer and the seller, but <u>only</u> if the scope of the agency is limited by a written agreement and <u>only</u> with the express knowledge and written consent of both the buyer and the seller. A REALTOR® representing both the buyer and the seller <u>must disclose</u> all information regarding the agency relationship, including the limitation on the Agent's ability to represent either party fully and exclusively. For example, the REALTOR® <u>must not disclose</u> to either party, without the prior consent of the party adversely affected by the disclosure, any information obtained within the confidentiality and trust of the fiduciary relationship. More specifically, the REALTOR® must not tell the buyer that the seller will accept a price lower than the listing price, nor tell the seller that the buyer will pay a price higher than the price offered.

Principal's Responsibilities

The above duties of the REALTOR® in a real estate transaction do not relieve the buyers or the sellers from the responsibility to protect their own interests. You should carefully read all agreements to assure that they adequately express your understanding of the transaction. A REALTOR® is a person qualified to advise about real estate. If legal or tax advice is desired, consult a competent professional.

A principal should ensure that any existing agency relationship is disclosed to other principals and their agents. A buyer should also consult the buyer's REALTOR® before visiting any resale or new homes or contacting any other REALTORS® representing sellers, to avoid the possibility of confusion over the agency relationship.

You may receive more than one disclosure form, depending upon the number of REALTORS® assisting in the transaction. The law requires each agent with whom you have substantive discussions about specific property to present you with a written disclosure. You should read its contents each time it is presented to you, considering the relationship between you and the REALTOR® in your specific transaction.

WE ACKNOWLEDGE RECEIPT OF A COPY OF THIS DISCLOSURE AND THAT ____________________ (firm name)

AND ____________________ (Sales Associate) ARE WORKING AS: ☐ SELLER'S AGENT. ☐ BUYER'S AGENT.

______ / ____________________ Date / Buyer's or Seller's Signature ____________________ Brokerage Firm

______ / ____________________ Date / Buyer's or Seller's Signature ______ / By: ____________________ Date / Broker/Sales Manager

WE ACKNOWLEDGE THAT ____________________ (firm name) AND ____________________ (Sales Associate) ARE WORKING AS: ☐ SELLER'S AGENT. ☐ BUYER'S AGENT. ☐ AGENT REPRESENTING BOTH BUYER AND SELLER AND I/WE CONSENT TO SUCH AGENCY.

______ / ____________ Date / Buyer's Signature	______ / ____________ Date / Seller's Signature
______ / ____________ Date / Buyer's Signature	______ / ____________ Date / Seller's Signature
______ / ____________ Date / Buyer's Signature	______ / ____________ Date / Seller's Signature
______ / ____________ Date / Sales Associate	______ / ____________ Date / Sales Associate

REALTOR

EQUAL HOUSING OPPORTUNITY

NVAR - 22- 11/91

Prepared by the Northern Virginia Association of REALTORS Task Force, NVAR Standard Forms Committee and legal counsel.

FIGURE 19.1 EXAMPLES OF DISCLOSURE FORMS *(continued)*

EXHIBIT #4

BUYER BROKER/AGENT ADDENDUM TO SALES CONTRACT

This Addendum is made on ______________, 19___ to the Sales Contract dated ______________, 19___ between ____ ("Purchaser") and ____ ("Seller") for the purchase and sale of the Property located at ____.

[CHECK ONE BOX ONLY]

______________________ and ______________________
Sales Associate Selling Company
("Buyer Broker/Agent"):

☐ is the exclusive representative of the Purchaser and has no agency relationship, oral or written, expressed or implied, with the Seller and/or the Listing Company. By contract with the Purchaser, the Buyer Broker/Agent repudiates any agency or subagency relationship with the Seller or Listing Company.

☐ is associated with the Listing Company and, although acting on behalf of the Purchaser, has a fiduciary duty to the Seller as well and cannot fully and exclusively represent either party. To the extent that information is obtained by the Buyer Broker/Agent within the confidentiality and trust of the fiduciary relationship with one party, the Buyer Broker/Agent must not disclose such information to the other party without the prior consent of the party adversely affected by the disclosure. The parties hereby consent to the same agent representing both the Purchaser and the Seller.

WITNESS OUR SIGNATURES AND SEALS:

SELLER:		PURCHASER:	
____/____	____________ [SEAL]	____/____	____________ [SEAL]
Date	Signature	Date	Signature
____/____	____________ [SEAL]	____/____	____________ [SEAL]
Date	Signature	Date	Signature

To be used in with conjunction with NVAR Standard Forms: "Sales Contract" and "Exclusive Right to Represent Buyer Agreement."

NVAR - ___ -9/91

10

Prepared by the Northern Virginia Association of REALTORS Task Force, NVAR Standard Forms Committee and legal counsel.

FIGURE 19.1 EXAMPLES OF DISCLOSURE FORMS (*continued*)

Seller Disclosure

A similar, but distinctly different issue, **seller disclosure** concerns information about the property being offered for sale. Often the dissatisfaction that results in suits by purchasers against agents stems from problems, or unwanted surprises, regarding the features or condition of the property purchased. The agency disclosure issue discussed previously is usually a problem only if the purchaser is unhappy with her purchase and thinks that the agent(s) did not adequately protect her interests. To reduce the possibility of unwanted surprises for the purchaser, many people believe that a complete disclosure statement prepared by the seller should become a mandatory part of the sales process.

Seller Disclosure Information regarding the physical, and possibly locational, features of a property provided by the seller.

Seller disclosure forms are already in use in many areas of the U.S. The changes in this area are likely to take two forms. First, for the most part, seller disclosure forms are now voluntary. In some instances, individual firms or local Boards of Realtors may require their use. The trend in the future, and one advocated by NAR, will be to push for legislation mandating their use.

The second change involves the scope of the disclosure information. Most current forms concentrate on physical aspects of the property. Any known defects or problems must be disclosed to potential purchasers. In many instances, however, the real area of concern is not with the physical condition of the property but with such things as neighboring uses, environmental concerns, traffic noise and congestion, and other such potentially damaging locational aspects. For example, does a seller have the obligation to disclose, even though it could be discovered by the buyer, that from 7:15 until 8:30 every weekday morning there is a stream of rather fast-moving traffic on the otherwise quiet neighborhood street? Must the seller disclose that there is a race track a few blocks away that features loud stock car races every Friday night? How about the smell from a nearby factory that reaches noticeable proportions every summer? These and other similar questions may be quite important to a buyer, but how do you design a form that forces a seller to disclose such items?

Multiple Listing Services

Thompson v. Metropolitan Multi-List, Inc.

The same NAR task force discussed earlier in this chapter also made a series of recommendations concerning the operation of multiple listing services (MLS). The task force recommended that the mandatory subagency feature of current MLS agreements be dropped in favor of a "subagency optional" approach. In other words, rather than automatically making all agents using the MLS subagents of the seller, each agent or firm in the system may elect to represent the seller if they choose to. This change was recommended, and went into effect during 1992, primarily to allow for buyer brokerage operations.

In addition to this change, however, there is a likely change concerning access to MLS information. All MLS operations are "closed" systems, in that they are accessible only by members of the MLS. This, of course, is fair and equitable because members pay for the operation of the MLS. The issue now facing the industry, however, is that of allowing access to the system by outside persons or firms after payment of a fee. On the surface, this sounds like a minor issue. In fact, however, this approach could have major implications for those MLS operations now owned and operated by local Boards of Realtors. Because most MLS operations fall in this category, the real issue becomes whether or not it is permissible to "tie" membership in NAR to access to MLS.

As a result of the types of cases reported earlier in this book, in which mandatory NAR membership was held to be a restraint of trade issue when tied to MLS access, the issue of **"open" MLS** operations is likely to be a major one during the coming years. Realtors have often used access to the MLS as a marketing device for membership in NAR. This approach, however, seems to be in quite a bit of jeopardy. Thus it would appear that an open MLS approach will be seen more and more in the future.

Open MLS System
A multiple listing system which allows outside individuals, for a fee, to gain access to all information contained in the system.

Professional Liability

Quite a bit of space was devoted in this book to the issue of liability for real estate professionals. We do not repeat that discussion here. It is important, however, to gain a bit of perspective on this issue by "stepping back" from it to look for some general trends that might be developing.

After studying the areas of potential liability for real estate professionals, it would be easy to become discouraged about the prospect of working in the field. We believe, for example, that the trend is clearly toward an application of strict liability for real estate agents. There will be less and less need in the future to prove negligence by agents to win a claim. Merely demonstrating harm caused by the actions or inactions of an agent will be sufficient to prevail. This standard will be exacerbated by the almost daily increases in the areas included in the definition of consumer protection. In short, the rights of the consumer continue to expand, while the potential for liability exposure also increases.

If the industry fails to react to this changing legal environment, working in real estate may prove to be as difficult as medicine, with its high malpractice insurance premiums, but without the same level of compensation. Fortunately, however, the industry has begun to react to this threat. Changes in agency models and the adoption of agency disclosure requirements, mandatory seller disclosure, and arbitration agreements will all help to reduce the potential liability of real estate professionals. If these trends continue, the role of the real estate agent may begin to shift to one more like a securities broker in the U.S. or to resemble some of the roles seen in many foreign countries. In any case, the real estate agent as we have known him will not exist in the future. Rather a different role will evolve, a role that has not yet been clearly defined. The driving force behind this role change, however, without any doubt at all, is the changing legal environment.

KEY POINTS

A real estate transaction in the not too distant future may be quite different from one now. As a potential buyer, you will need to decide if you wish to have direct representation, and if so, what level of service you wish to pay for. Agents will be available to allow you to browse through listings (probably using computer-based information systems) and then inspect properties on your own. Or you can elect to have an agent personally take you around and provide additional information and help. Keep in mind that with an open MLS, optional subagency, and other changes, real estate agents may elect to offer only a subset of traditional services to customers at a presumably much lower cost.

REAL ESTATE FIRM STRUCTURE

Just as the role of the real estate agent will change during the coming decade, so too will the role of the real estate brokerage firm. As the role played by agents changes, there will be a considerable amount of pressure to change commission structures. Such things as "open" MLS systems, buyer brokerage, mandatory arbitration, and the like may cause consumers to reevaluate traditional payment amounts and methods. This in turn may lead to pressure on real estate firms to reposition themselves in the market or diversify to maintain or improve profit levels.

National Real Estate Firms

Currently in the U.S., most firms are either independently owned and operated or are part of some type of franchise operation. A few national real estate firms do exist, but the growth in this area has lagged far behind most predictions. Most areas of business in the U.S. have seen a great deal of merger activity. Almost daily we read of some sort of acquisition, **hostile** or friendly. Movies have been made about the process, and new terms like **"leveraged buyout"** have been added to our vocabulary. For the most part, however, real estate firms have escaped the attention of takeover artists. The questions we address here are: "Why have there been no major acquisitions of or by real estate firms?" and "Will this trend continue?"

The concept of a "takeover," as it is commonly used, refers only to publicly traded firms. Because few real estate firms and virtually no real estate brokerage firms are publicly traded, the notion of a takeover really does not apply. In addition, firms are usually taken over for one of two reasons: First, the firm has assets that are undervalued (i.e., the stock price of the firm does not reflect the true value of the firm), and if acquired, the assets could be sold off for a net gain over that paid to purchase the firm. This is highly unlikely to happen in real estate firms because most real estate firms, particularly brokerage firms, have few assets. The main assets of these firms are the people associated with the firm. Because these are often not even employees but rather independent contractors, there is little if any potential value in selling off the assets.

Hostile Takeover
A term which describes the process of acquiring a firm against the will of the current management by purchasing sufficient stock so as to have majority control.

Leveraged Buyout
The process of using the current assets of a takeover target as collateral for the debt used to acquire the firm.

The second reason for acquiring a firm is to broaden the scope of the parent firm. Often referred to as either vertical or horizontal integration, this concept allows a firm to diversify by adding compatible additional product lines or services (horizontal integration) or adding more components of the manufacturing process (vertical integration). The notion of diversification has long held some appeal for real estate firms. Real estate firms, especially in small markets, have often combined brokerage with appraisal, property management, and even insurance sales to broaden potential income sources and buffer the firm from market swings.

New Federal Trade Commission (FTC) rules would seem to open the door a bit for mergers in the mortgage banking area. Because, by definition, mortgages deal with real estate, the possibilities for mergers between mortgage banking (or mortgage brokerage) firms and real estate firms seem high. If this begins to happen, then the traditional independent firm structure in real estate brokerage (and appraisal, property management, and so forth) will begin to disappear because it is likely that mergers of this type would be successful only at the national, or perhaps regional, level.

In any case, increased diversification efforts are likely to occur in real estate firms. The types of seller disclosure statements described earlier, for example, may require the use of professionals to prepare them, much like the process of preparing an offering prospectus for a new stock or bond issuance or a partnership offering. Moving this task to a specialized group of individuals will offer another level of liability protection for agents and, perhaps more importantly, for sellers. Because it would also create a new field of business, somewhat of a cross between the role of the appraiser and the agent, with a little of the home inspection service as well, it may also change the shape of real estate firms in the future.

To summarize, we see the traditional real estate firm structure changing as the market demands higher levels of specialized services. Mergers or acquisitions by and of real estate firms is quite likely. These new firms will tend to be national, or at least regional, in scope and will probably become publicly traded. Franchises and referral networks, although they will continue to exist, will not play the expanded role many have predicted. That role will be played by a new breed of large national firms able to offer customers specialized services. The concept of "one stop shopping," in which the firm will offer all services needed to complete a transaction (brokerage, appraisal, mortgage lending, title insurance, and closing services) will come to real estate.

KEY POINTS

Just as consumers now have choices ranging from large discount stores to specialized boutiques when shopping for a pair of jeans, buyers or sellers of real estate may soon have a similar range of choices. Real estate firms will include very small operations offering personalized services and large firms offering help with all aspects of a transaction. To a small extent, this is already true. In the future, however, the large firms will grow into something like a "supermarket," whereas the small firms will continue to offer corner grocery store type services to a select clientele willing to pay a bit more for the higher level of personal attention.

SECURITIZATION OF REAL ESTATE INVESTMENTS

Securitization
Term which describes the process of converting an asset into a pool of securities which are then offered to investors.

The concept of **"securitization"** was discussed at some length in Chapter 18. The key to successful investment strategies for individuals and groups of individuals is diversification. Basic portfolio theory holds that there are two types of risk: *systematic* and unsystematic. **Systematic risk** is that risk inherent in the economic system as a whole. **Unsystematic,** or random, risk is caused by fluctuations in individual investments. For example, a particular firm may have a very good quarter or a very bad quarter and the stock price will vary accordingly. Fluctuations in interest rates will cause the value of debt instruments, like corporate bonds, to vary. By combining assets of different kinds, however, it is theoretically possible to avoid all unsystematic risk.

Historically real estate has played a minor role in **diversification strategies,** at least for individual investors. This is due to the simple fact that real estate is a relatively expensive asset to acquire and is also quite difficult to sell on short notice. Real estate investments take many forms—apartments, offices, retail stores, warehouses, and so forth. These properties may also be located in areas anywhere in the world. Treating real estate as a single category of investment is similar to treating stocks as a single category without regard to the type or location of the firm issuing the stock. Thus, unless the portfolio was large enough to include numerous properties, gaining diversification benefits from real estate has been difficult.

Systematic Risk Investment risk inherent in the economic system as a whole.

Unsystematic Risk The investment risk coused by flucuations of specific assets in a portfolio.

Portfolio Diversification The process of combining assets within a portfolio so as to reduce or eliminate unsystematic risk.

Because you can, as a general rule, buy as many shares of stock in a company as you wish, even relatively small investment portfolios can achieve at least modest diversification benefits by spreading investments out among numerous companies. There is ample evidence to indicate that real estate in general adds diversification benefits that cannot be obtained from any other source. Thus many people have looked for ways to include real estate in small portfolios. For the most part, small investors have chosen one of two routes to attain this goal: purchasing small properties or investing in real estate investment trusts (REITs). Small properties, even if you can afford several of them, present severe management difficulties and make it virtually impossible to obtain any geographic diversification benefits. Investing in REITs introduces another layer of management and leaves the investor using an investment in one portfolio (i.e., a REIT is essentially a portfolio of real estate investments) to provide diversification benefits in another. In short, the investor must not only analyze the strength of the properties owned by the REIT, but also the managerial skill of the REIT administrator. Publicly traded partnerships offer another investment avenue but one that also has many pitfalls at this time.

As the demand for investment opportunities in real estate continues to grow, more and more efforts to create securities based on the value of real estate assets will take place. The process of securitization of real estate will not only change the composition of many portfolios, but also it will change the nature of the real estate industry. It is quite possible that the traditional real estate brokerage function will be integrated into investment management firms or that specialized firms will be created that cater to security investors. Because real estate requires a high level of managerial expertise, these firms will resemble mortgage bankers in that they will acquire assets, securitize the assets and sell the securities, and retain the property (or asset) management function.

LAND USE CONTROLS

As discussed in Chapter 16, the issue of land use regulation in the U.S. has always been a contentious one. We see no changes in the types of debates that take place; in fact, we believe that the pace of change will increase a bit during the 1990s. The U.S. Supreme Court has shown a willingness to become involved in land use issues on a much larger scale than that seen previously. Trying to predict where the Supreme Court will go with its rulings is, of course, highly speculative at best. There are two issues, however, that will be in the forefront of these changes and will stir up quite a lot of controversy in the coming years: takings compensation and environmental and historic preservation.

Yee v. City of Escondido, California

Takings Issue Term applied to disputes regarding the point at which police power limitations become eminent domain takings and thus require just compensation.

Takings Compensation

The traditional remedy for a finding that a **"taking" of private property** has occurred, as discussed earlier in this book, has been simply to remove the offending land use limitation and allow the property owner the freedom to proceed with the desired activity. The trend now, however, appears to be headed toward a level of compensation for the time during which the taking occurred. In other words, if a taking (within the context of the Fifth Amendment to the U.S. Constitution) is found to have occurred, then the owner of the property must be compensated for the loss of use of his property during the time of the taking.

When carried to its logical, some would say illogical, conclusion, this would imply that cities and states must be careful in establishing regulations that limit property owner's rights. Zoning ordinances, for example, must be developed with care so as to avoid possible claims of uncompensated takings. Were this to occur on a large scale, government bodies would tend to err on the side of caution—knowing that an error could prove costly. This possibility, of course, alarms many groups involved with efforts to preserve and protect natural and historic sites.

Environmental and Historic Preservation

Lucas v. South Carolina Coastal Council

Environmental Protection Efforts by state and federal governments, primarily through statutes, to preserve and protect environmentally sensitive areas.

Historic Preservation A wide variety of programs and regulations designed to preserve and protect buildings and areas of particular historic significance.

It is highly ironic that the Court rulings in the takings area have tended to protect the rights of the individuals to the extent that, in effect, payments for errors must be made. Such a defense of individual liberties, however, may come into conflict with the desire to protect our sensitive **environmental** areas and **historic** properties from destruction. Thus, it is that a new set of battle lines have been drawn. On one side, we have the protectors of individual liberties against the power of the government, and on the other side are the defenders of the environment and history. What makes this battle so potentially fascinating is that, to a large extent, the individuals involved on both sides of this battle are the same people! In many instances, advocates for these positions have failed to notice the conflict between the positions and are, in effect, arguing with themselves.

CONCLUSION

The areas we have discussed in this chapter represent those for which signs of change are fairly evident. Certainly the possibility exists that significant change will take place in other areas as well. The real point of this discussion is to make clear the notion that real estate law, like our society as a whole, continues to evolve. Law is not static, and it certainly is not mundane. Real estate professionals will find themselves faced with an endless series of challenges, many of them resulting from changing interpretations of the law.

This book is designed to introduce students to the many ways in which our legal structure affects the real estate industry in its many facets. Careers in real estate offer a wide variety of interesting and challenging opportunities. The types of changes predicted here, or whatever changes end up taking place, will certainly have one predictable result for real estate professionals—the need to stay well informed about real estate law.

DISCUSSION QUESTIONS

1. Why is it so important to consumers that real estate agents disclose to them all possible legal relationships?
2. What effect would mandatory seller disclosure requirements potentially have on agent liability exposure?
3. What is an "open MLS," and why do you think NAR is so concerned about the possibility of dealing with them?
4. Why have real estate firms not been the target of takeover attempts?
5. What types of mergers or acquisitions are likely to occur for real estate brokerage firms? What impact would these have on the structure of the real estate brokerage industry?
6. Describe the portfolio diversification process. What role does the "securitization" of real properties play in this process?
7. Why do you think there is such a potential conflict between defenders of individual liberties and protectors of the environment in the field of land use controls?

THOMPSON
V.
METROPOLITAN MULTI-LIST, INC.

934 F.2d 1566 (1991)

The Court looks at the practice of "tying" NAR membership to MLS access

Real estate broker and brokers' association brought action against multilist real estate listing service and its owner to challenge requirement that broker be a member of real estate association branch in order to use multilist system. The United States District Court for the Northern District of Georgia, . . . entered summary judgment in favor of defendants. Broker and association appealed. The Court of Appeals, Johnson, Circuit Judge, held that: (1) association and broker had standing to litigate tying and group boycott claims, but only association had standing to litigate conspiracy to monopolize claim; (2) summary judgment was inappropriate with respect to tying and group boycott claims; and (3) listing service's membership requirements were illegal group boycott if service had sufficient market power.

Affirmed in part, reversed in part, and remanded.

This case arises on appeal following the district court's grant of summary judgment in favor of the defendants in this antitrust action.

I. STATEMENT OF THE CASE

A. Background Facts

Metropolitan Multi-List, Inc. ("Metro"), one of the defendants-appellees, is a wholly-owned subsidiary of the DeKalb Board of Realtors. Metro is a computerized multilist real estate listing system. . . . Brokers consider the use of a multilist system a necessity.

Metro provides the only multilist service which covers all of Atlanta. While First Multiple competes with Metro on the north side of Atlanta, there is little or no competition on the south side of Atlanta. On the south side of Atlanta, Metro carries the vast majority of listings and is utilized in most of the completed sales, measured both in dollar amounts and in raw numbers. Also, the vast majority of real estate brokers active in the area are members of Metro.

In order to use the Metro multilisting service a broker must become a Realtor. A Realtor is a broker (or a sales associate) who belongs to one of the local branches of the National Association of Realtors. Metro was an independent listing service until the DeKalb Board of Realtors acquired Metro and imposed the Realtor membership requirement upon those who would like to use the listing service.

There are four parties to this dispute. The two defendants are Metro and the DeKalb Board of Realtors; the two plaintiffs are Fletcher Thompson and the Empire Real Estate Board. Fletcher Thompson is a real estate broker who owns his own brokerage firm on the south side of Atlanta. He does not wish to join the Atlanta Board of Realtors.[1] He applied to use the Metro listing service but his application was denied solely because of his failure to join the Realtors. The defendants admit that when he joins the Realtors he will be allowed to use the listing service. The Empire Board was founded in 1939 as an African-American professional association because, at that time, the Realtors excluded African-Americans from membership. The Empire Board competes with the Board of Realtors and offers similar services, including a code of ethics and arbitration. The Empire Board is a predominantly African-American association which services a predominantly African-American clientele. Most of its members are located on the south side of Atlanta and most of its members traditionally represent buyers. The Empire Board alleges that, because of Metro's requirement that its members also belong to the Realtors, Empire is losing members. Some firms that otherwise would join the Empire Board cannot afford membership with both the Realtors and the Empire Board.

B. Procedural History

Plaintiffs filed their complaint on December 22, 1988, alleging antitrust and Fair Housing Act violations. Wendell White and others moved to intervene in this action, but the motion was denied. Following discovery, the parties filed cross motions for summary judgment. The district court granted defendants' summary judgment motion. The plaintiffs brought this timely appeal of the district court's dismissal of the antitrust claims.[2]

II. ANALYSIS

. . .

A. Standing

The question at the heart of standing analysis is whether the particular litigant before the court is entitled to have the court adjudicate the particular claim presented. . . . There are two plaintiffs to this action: Empire and Thompson; there are basically three different antitrust claims alleged: an illegal tying arrangement; a conspiracy to monopolize a market; and an illegal group boycott.

1. Empire's Standing to Litigate the Three Claims

[1] Empire is an unincorporated association. As such, it has standing to allege certain injuries suffered directly by the organization, . . . and standing to bring certain claims on behalf of its members.

Empire has standing to directly bring the tying claim. . . . Empire competes in the market for professional affiliation with the Realtors. Empire claims that it has lost members because the Realtors have entered an illegal tying arrangement with Metro which forces Empire members to drop their affiliation with Empire and join the Realtors. Assuming that Empire can prove these allegations, it has alleged a valid antitrust claim. See Section II C, *infra*. . . .

[2][3] Empire has standing to bring a suit on behalf of its members for the conspiracy to monopolize the multilist service market claim. . . . There is evidence in the record supporting Empire's assertion that nearly 40% of Empire's members also belong to the Realtors and use Metro. It is beyond dispute that, as consumers of the multilisting service, the Empire members may bring an action al-

---

[1]Although Metro is owned by the DeKalb Board of Realtors, Thompson and most of the members of the Empire Real Estate Board would be under the jurisdiction of the Atlanta Board of Realtors if they joined the Realtors.

[2]Because the plaintiffs have not specifically appealed the district court's disposition of the Fair Housing Act claims, the plaintiffs have waived any objection to summary judgment on this issue.

leging antitrust violations which force them to pay excessive fees. . . .

Empire also has standing to bring a suit on behalf of its members for the group boycott claim. Empire's members could bring a suit in their own right for the group boycott claim. There is evidence in the record that other members of Empire, including Thompson, would like to use Metro's multilist service but are ineligible because of the alleged group boycott. And Empire is asking for injunctive relief that is germane to the organization's purpose and could be brought by the association without the participation of the members.

2. Thompson's Standing to Litigate the Three Claims

[4][5] Thompson has standing to litigate the tying claim and the group boycott claim. Thompson applied to use Metro's multilist service but his application was denied because he refused to purchase the tied product, membership in the Realtors. Our circuit has recognized, in a related context, that an attempt to enter a market coupled with a showing of preparedness is sufficient to establish an injury in fact, which is one of the bases of standing. . . . Therefore, Thompson can litigate the validity of the entry barriers which prevented his use of the multilist service. These entry barriers constitute the bases of the tying claim and the group boycott claim. Moreover, the injuries which stem from Metro's ability to prevent Thompson from becoming a multilist service user are antitrust injuries and Thompson would be an efficient enforcer of the antitrust laws because the injuries are suffered directly.

[6] Thompson, however, lacks standing to litigate the conspiracy to monopolize claim. . . .

B. The Relevant Market

[7] On a very simplistic level, antitrust law is concerned with abuses of power by private actors in the marketplace. Therefore, before we can reach the larger question of whether Metro violated any of the antitrust laws, we must confront the threshold problem of defining the relevant market. Markets are defined in terms of two separate dimensions: products and geography. Once we have defined the relevant market, we can examine Metro's position within the market, determine Metro's "market power," and thereafter determine whether Metro had enough power within the marketplace to abuse its position.

It is undisputed that the relevant product market is the market for multilist services.[4] The parties, however, strongly dispute the geographic boundaries of that market. The plaintiffs argue that the relevant geographic market is the south side of Atlanta. The defendants argue that the relevant geographic market constitutes all of Atlanta. The district court ruled in favor of the defendants, stating that "[t]he relevant geographic market is not limited to the southside of Atlanta but encompasses the area of effective competition within which the defendants operate [which includes all of Atlanta.]"

[8][9] The Supreme Court in United States v. Philadelphia National Bank, 374 U.S. 321, 83 S.Ct. 1715, 10 L.Ed.2d 915 (1963), explained that the concept of a geographic market is essentially an economic concept in which the courts should examine "supplier-customer relations." . . . Courts, when they are defining the contours of a given market, should try to recall that the purpose of this task is to enable the courts to define market power. Thus we are required to exclude irrelevant information about purchasers and sellers who are not part of a market. By erroneously including potential sellers in a market when, in fact, those sellers are not members of that market, a court dilutes the defendant's role in the market and thereby risks erring in its ultimate determination of whether there has been an antitrust violation. . . . The process of defining a geographic market is more difficult when the courts are attempting to define a geographic market for something as intangible as information contained in data banks and conveyed via computers. While it is common to use the term "geographic market" in defining the parameters of a relevant market, it is misleading for courts to confine their analysis solely in geographic terms. . . . In the context of markets which deal in intangibles, the courts should examine transaction costs, transportation costs, and buyer preferences, as Philadelphia National Bank commanded, and

[4]As will be discussed subsequently, *see* section II C 1, *infra,* the parties do dispute whether there is a second product market, the market for professional affiliation.

thereby exclude all those potential sellers, regardless of where they are located, from the analysis of the market when buyers do not "practicably" turn to them for supplies. *Id.*

With this in mind, the district court erred in accepting Atlanta as the relevant geographic market. . . . On one hand, the defendant came forward with some evidence that Atlanta is a unitary market. But this was rebutted by the plaintiff who placed into the record considerable evidence suggesting that Atlanta is not a homogeneous real estate market and that real estate brokers specialize in different areas of the city. Moreover, the plaintiffs in this action, Empire and Thompson, specialize in real estate located on the south side of Atlanta. Therefore, the plaintiffs "can practicably turn for supplies" only to those multilist services which include south side listings. It is therefore inappropriate to resolve this dispute on a motion for summary judgment.

C. The Tying Claim

[10] The plaintiffs claim that Metro and the DeKalb Board of Realtors have been engaging in an unlawful tying arrangement. The plaintiffs allege that Metro's dominance in the market for multilist services allows it to force brokers into accepting the tied product, membership in the Realtors professional association in order to obtain the tying product, use of the multilist service.

Any alleged antitrust violation may be analyzed under either a per se rule or a rule of reason. This Court has held that unless the alleged anticompetitive behavior falls within a few narrow classes, the behavior should be analyzed under the rule of reason. See United States v. Realty Multi-List, Inc., 629 F.2d 1351 (5th Cir. 1980). . . . This Court has held that, unless the plaintiff is able to show all the elements of a per se tying claim, the claim must be analyzed under the rule of reason. *Id.* The four basic elements of a per se tying claim are: (1) that there are two separate products, a "tying" product and a "tied" product; (2) that those products are in fact "tied" together—that is, the buyer was forced to buy the tied product to get the tying product; (3) that the seller possesses sufficient economic power in the tying product market to coerce buyer acceptance of the tied product; and (4) involvement of a "not insubstantial" amount of interstate commerce in the market of the tied product. *Id.* at 1414. This Court in Keener v. Sizzler Family Steak Houses, 597 F.2d 453 (5th Cir. 1979), added a fifth requirement that the tying company have an economic interest in the tied product.

[11] Metro argued before the district court that summary judgment should be granted in its favor on all five elements of the tying claim. The district court granted summary judgment only on the coercion prong and the economic interest prong. Metro renews its argument for summary judgment on each of the elements of the claim in this Court. We therefore must analyze each element of the tying claim to determine if summary judgment was appropriate.

1. Two Separate Products or Services

Metro argues that there is only one relevant product, the market for multilist services, and that there are not two separate products. Metro concludes that if there are not two separate products there cannot be any illegal tie between them.

In determining whether there are two separate products, we are guided by Jefferson Parish Hospital District No. 2 v. Hyde, 466 U.S. 2, 104 S.Ct. 1551, 80 L.Ed.2d 2 (1984), which held that two products are separate for tying analysis when there are two separate markets for the product. . . . It is undisputed that multilist services constitute one product market. It is hotly disputed, however, whether there is a second, separate market for professional affiliation. . . .

[12] Metro's main argument is that multilist services are useless without the support services provided by the Realtors and that therefore the two services are actually one product. Metro argues that because brokers using a multilist service create various agency and a subagency arrangements, they would be hesitant to use these services if they had doubts about the ethics of the other brokers. Metro has placed considerable evidence in the record that the Realtors help reduce uncertainty and other transaction costs by providing a code of ethics and mandatory arbitration. Therefore, according to Metro, brokers utilizing the multilist service have less hesitancy because they know that should another broker use the multilist service unethically and "steal" a sale or a customer the Realtors will efficiently adjudicate the injured broker's complaint. Metro further states that it es-

sentially had a choice and could have structured its operations so that the code of ethics, arbitration, and other support services could have been either a direct part of the multilist service or an indirect part through the Realtors. Metro complains that it should not be penalized for structuring its business one way rather than another. However, both of Metro's arguments are irrelevant to the question of whether the market for professional affiliation is separate from the market for multilist services. Metro does not discuss billing practices, consumer preferences, consumer impressions, the cross-elasticity of the markets, or virtually anything relevant to the definition of whether there are separate markets.[6]

[13] Metro next argues that there is no market for professional affiliation because an individual who joins the Realtors gains nothing more than a status. Metro's argument can be interpreted in one of two ways. To the extent that Metro is claiming that services are somehow exempt from the antitrust laws, Metro's argument is meritless. . . . On the other hand, if Metro is claiming that the Realtors do not provide services and that by joining the Realtors one merely is gaining a "status," Metro is wrong to think that by calling a "service" a "status" one can actually alter legal relationships. Even if the Realtors offered no services[7] and a broker who joined the Realtors merely gained some added professional status, we would still need to answer the basic question of whether there is a market for this status. If there is not a market for this status, then it is not a separate product.

In the case at hand, all of the relevant evidence submitted on the question of whether there are two separate product markets indicates that the market for professional affiliation is separate from the market for multilist services. For example, there is evidence that the bill for joining the Realtors is separate from Metro's bill; that a broker can join the Realtors and choose not to use the multilist service; that, within Atlanta, there are at least two professional groups competing for members; that some local Realtor groups offer multilist services and some do not; that Metro was once an independent organization that was later purchased by the Realtors who imposed the Realtor membership requirement; and that in other markets, multilist services are independent of professional membership. *See* Federal Trade Commission Staff Report, The Residential Real Estate Brokerage Industry 116 (1983). (At the time of this report, there were at least 55 multilisting services operating in the United States that were independent of any local Realtor organization.) Based on these facts, we conclude that summary judgment in favor of the defendant on this element of the claim would be inappropriate.

2. Market Linkage

[14] The second step in the tying analysis is to determine if the two products are actually tied together. Tic-X-Press, 815 F.2d at 1415. The parties agree that a broker may not use Metro's multilisting service without joining the Realtors. Therefore, there is not any actual dispute over whether the markets are tied. . . .

3. Economic Coercion

[15] One of the bases of the district court's grant of summary judgment was its conclusion that the plaintiffs failed to produce sufficient evidence that Metro had enough economic power due to its multilist service to coerce brokers into joining the Realtors. . . .

The plaintiffs first must prove that Metro has sufficient market power within the relevant product market to coerce brokers into choosing the Realtors as their professional association if Metro so desires. We have already concluded that there is a material question of fact whether the tying market is that portion of multilisting services which contains listings on the south side of Atlanta or that portion of multilisting services which contains list-

[6]Metro raises a second argument, which is virtually indistinguishable from the first argument. Metro initially argues that a multilist service would be useless without the support services provided by the Realtors. Metro argues in the alternative that multilist services and the Realtors' other services are in fact one product because they function as one product. Such an argument, if it actually is distinct from the first argument, is nonetheless equally irrelevant to the question of whether the markets are in fact separate. . . .

[7]This assertion may come as a surprise to the members of the Realtors who pay several hundred dollars a year for membership and to the DeKalb Board of Realtors official, who, in an interrogatory, listed 27 services provided by the Realtors.

ings in Atlanta. Thus, this case needs to be remanded for this initial determination. On remand the district court should then use this definition of the relevant market to determine whether the plaintiffs have proven market power.

Metro argues that regardless of which set of boundaries defines the market, summary judgment is warranted because it lacks the requisite market power. . . .

The district court held that the plaintiffs have not demonstrated sufficient market power. There are two dimensions to its ruling. First, the district court held that there is no evidence in the record of the defendant's ability to force brokers to "alter their choice of professional associations." Second, the district court held that Metro has no "cost advantage . . . that cannot be duplicated." And, therefore, other groups could start a competing multilist system and challenge the defendant's market power.

Metro claims that it does not have any disproportionate market power because other multilist services compete with it and brokers can use alternatives to multilist systems. Metro claims that an individual who does not want to join the Realtors but nonetheless wants to use a multilist system could join First Multiple. And Metro claims that brokers could use other methods of determining what properties are for sale. . . .

In short, there is a material issue of fact as to whether the defendants have the necessary market power. There is evidence in the record suggesting that multilist systems are necessary, that there are few realistic substitutes, that there are entry barriers to the market, and that Metro may not have any competitors.

[16] To satisfy the coercion element of the claim, the plaintiffs need to show that Metro not only has this market power but also has wielded this market power to force brokers to alter their choice of professional associations. Metro denies wielding its market power and contends that there is no evidence in the record supporting this claim. However, it is undisputed that Metro requires brokers to join the Realtors. There also is evidence in the record stating that the expense of dual membership in trade groups can be prohibitive for some brokers, and that 400 of Empire's prospective and current members did not join Empire or quit Empire because of the prohibitive cost.[9] The record also contains the following affidavits: three affidavits stating that the individuals were members of the Realtors and of Empire and that they wanted to quit the Realtors but could not because Metro was too important to their business; three affidavits from Empire members stating that they would like to use Metro but they could not afford membership both in the Realtors and in Empire; seven affidavits from Realtor members who wanted to quit the Realtors and join Empire but could not afford either to lose their access to Metro or to pay a second set of dues for membership in a professional association; and one affidavit from an Empire member who would like to use Metro, evidently can afford membership in both the Realtors and Empire, but dislikes the Realtors because of their past history of discriminating against African-Americans. . . .

4. "Not Insubstantial" Effect on Interstate Commerce

[17] The plaintiffs also claim that they have demonstrated that the tie had more than an insubstantial effect on interstate commerce. . . . The plaintiffs claim there is sufficient evidence in the record to support this element of the claim. There is evidence that Empire has lost close to 400 members due to this allegedly illegal tying arrangement.[10] There is also evidence that Empire charges $75.00–175.00 in annual dues. The loss of just one year's dues from these members results in a loss of

[9]Metro dismisses Empire's affidavit about lost members as "conclusory, self-serving and factually unsupported." As for Metro's claim that the affidavit is self-serving, we would be surprised if any party ever submitted an affidavit that was not self-serving. . . . As for Metro's claim that the affidavit was factually unsupported, the affiant was an officer of Empire who spoke about her personal knowledge of the membership.

[10]The plaintiffs also claim that the dollar amounts are substantial because there is support in the record that Thompson and others have lost thousands of dollars in lost sales due to their lack of access to a multilisting service. This loss, however, is not a loss within the tied market because the tied market is the market for professional affiliation.

between $30,000.00–70,000.00 which is clearly substantial.[11]

5. The Economic Interest Question

The district court also granted summary judgment because the plaintiffs failed to show that Metro had an economic interest in the Atlanta Board of Realtors. The Realtors are structured like many organizations; all the local chapters of the Realtors belong to a state organization and each of the state organizations belongs to the national organization. Among the several local Realtor organizations in the greater Atlanta area are the Atlanta and DeKalb Board of Realtors. While Metro is wholly owned by the DeKalb Board of Realtors, Thompson and most, if not all, of Empire's members are within the jurisdiction of the Atlanta Board of Realtors and would have to join that Realtor association to use Metro.

. . . The plaintiffs imply that we should limit the economic interest prong to franchise cases. Although this standard has been applied only in franchise cases and the need for this rule appears to be best suited to such cases, we do not need to limit this economic interest prong to situations involving franchises,[12] because there is evidence in the record to support a finding that there was a sufficient economic interest.

We cannot say that Metro has "absolutely no interest" in the size of the Atlanta Board of Realtors. Because of the close nature of the relationships between all the Realtor organizations, Metro is benefited and therefore has an interest in having Thompson and the other Empire members join the Atlanta Board of Realtors. While Metro is owned by the DeKalb Board of Realtors, both the DeKalb and the Atlanta Boards belong to the Georgia and National Boards of Realtors. Moreover, a portion of every dollar paid to the local board is paid to the state and national boards. There is evidence in the record showing that the state and national boards then use the money to perform various services for the local boards. In an interrogatory, the DeKalb Board of Realtors listed nineteen benefits received from the Georgia Association of Realtors and seventeen benefits received from the National Association of Realtors. Moreover, the plaintiffs submitted an affidavit from an individual who attended a Georgia Association of Realtors meeting in which the group voted to send up to $15,000 to the DeKalb board to help in the defense of this action. Therefore, there is sufficient evidence in the record for us to conclude that Metro has something more than "absolutely no interest" in the size of the Atlanta Board of Realtors.

In conclusion, it appears that the plaintiffs have placed into the record sufficient evidence alleging the five prima facie elements of a per se tying violation.

D. The Group Boycott Claim

[18] The plaintiffs also complain about the restrictive membership policies adopted by Metro. The plaintiffs complain that Metro's requirement that its members belong to the Realtors violates the antitrust prohibition on group boycotts. Far from writing on a blank slate, we are faced with a considerable body of precedent explaining the group boycott effects of a Georgia-based multilist service's membership requirements. In the comprehensive opinion of United States v. Realty Multi-List, Inc., 629 F.2d 1351 (5th Cir. 1980), we noted that multilist services have many pro-competitive effects. Most importantly, multilist services help eliminate imperfections in the marketplace by increasing the availability of information. *Id.* at 1368. As a result of the pro-competitive effects inherent in multilist services, this Court recognized that it could not, as a matter of law, condemn the multilist service's membership criteria as a per se violation of the antitrust laws. *Id.* at 1369. The plaintiffs do not contest this application of Realty Multi-List to the case at hand. Following Realty Multi-List, we therefore hold that Metro's membership requirements are not per se antitrust violations.

[11]The plaintiffs could also prove a not insubstantial effect on the tying market by determining how much money the Realtors make from brokers who join the Realtors solely to use the multilist service.

[12]Arguably, though, the economic interest prong has already been implicitly limited to franchise cases because the economic interest prong has been ignored in non-franchise cases. . . .

The Realty Multi-List court, however, held that the membership requirements for a multilist organization can, under a rule of reason analysis, violate the antitrust laws. The Realty Multi-List court noted the significant economic harm that multilist services cause when they exclude brokers from their service. *Id.* at 1370–71. First, the excluded broker's listings will not be distributed as widely as possible, resulting in inefficient sales prices. Second, the exclusion reduces the competition among brokers and could result in less competition for brokerage fees. *Id.; see* also Federal Trade Commission Staff Report, The Residential Real Estate Brokerage Industry 151–55 (1983) (finding that discount brokers tend not to be members, for whatever reason, of multilisting services). "Thus, where a broker is excluded from a multiple listing service without an adequate justification in the competitive needs of the service, both the broker and the public are clearly harmed. [I]n these circumstances, the exclusion from the association will be found to violate Section 1 [of the Sherman Act]." Realty Multi-List, 629 F.2d at 1371 (emphasis added). Therefore, in order to determine whether summary judgment was warranted we must first determine whether Metro has the requisite market power, and second we must examine whether Metro has any justification in terms of fostering competitiveness for its entry requirements.

1. Market Power

[19] The district court granted summary judgment on the threshold question of market power. The district court noted that Realty Multi-List required an initial determination of whether the service has sufficient market power to justify this heightened scrutiny of its membership requirements. The rationale adopted by Realty Multi-List was that powerful market forces, essential to the economic survival of a competitor, must be open to all competitors. The question of market power is a factual one. *Id.* at 1373. In Realty Multi-List, we defined market power as a question of whether the multilist service has "sufficient economic importance that exclusion results in the denial of the opportunity to compete effectively on equal terms." *Id.* at 1373. Market power turns on the number of brokers who use the service, the total dollar amount of annual listings, and a comparison of the rate of sales using the multilisting service to the market as a whole. Realty Multi-List, 629 F.2d at 1373–74. It is important to note that the Court in Realty Multi-List assumed that testimony stating that the multilist system was used by the vast majority of brokers in the relevant geographic market and that it was very important to the economic survival of a brokerage was sufficient to constitute the requisite market power. *Id.* at 1374.

[20] In the case at bar, the district court erroneously granted summary judgment on the market power issue. . . . In short, there is sufficient contradictory evidence that summary judgment is inappropriate on this issue.

2. The Membership Requirements

[21] Metro argued to the district court, and renewed its argument in this Court, that it should be awarded summary judgment because even if it has sufficient market power its membership requirements are acceptable under Realty Multi-List. . . .

[22] The Realty Multi-List court held that, once the plaintiffs have shown the requisite market power, the multilist service must justify its restrictive membership requirements. The court noted that the restrictive membership requirements must be evaluated in light of an existing, extensive series of state laws and regulations. The court held that it is necessary to compare the proffered justification of the membership requirements to the state laws and if the multilist service's concern which motivated the restrictive membership requirements is already covered by state real estate brokerage law then the multilist service must "make a showing either that the legitimate needs of the service require protection in excess of that provided by the state or that the state does not adequately enforce its own regulations." *Id.* at 1380. The burden of proof is on the multilist service. *Id.* at 1380–81 n. 61. In the event that the concern underlying the membership requirements is a subject not covered by the regulations or the regulations are not enforced by the state, the court held that we must evaluate the suggested justification to see if it is "reasonably necessary to the accomplishment of the legitimate goals and narrowly tailored to that end." *Id.* at 1375.

Metro proffers two main justifications for requiring its users to join the Realtors. First, Metro

explains that Article 21 of the Realtor code of ethics imposes a "no soliciting" rule. Metro explains that few brokers would be willing to enter his or her client list into Metro's system without assurances that other brokers will not "steal" the list and solicit the clients directly. Metro explains that this justification is pro-competitive because the rule encourages more brokers to use the system and therefore increases the efficiencies of the market. Second, Metro explains that Article 14 of the Realtor code of ethics requires Realtors to arbitrate all disputes. Metro explains that this also encourages brokers to use the system because most disputes are over relatively small sums of money and traditional legal remedies are not cost effective for these disputes.

We therefore must examine the Realtor membership requirement in light of these two justifications and the Realty Multi-List standards. It is clear that Georgia state law does not impose any arbitration requirement in potential realtor disputes, . . . While the goal of inducing brokers to join the multilist system is a legitimate pro-competitive justification and the "no-solicitation" and arbitration rules are both reasonable and narrowly tailored to that end, this lawsuit is not questioning the validity of those two rules. The question before this Court is whether it is necessary to impose Realtor membership requirements in order to obtain the same ends. It is clear that the Realtor membership requirements are not narrowly tailored to the goal of inducing brokers to join the multilist system. Metro could easily impose its own "no solicitation" and arbitration rules on its members. Such rules would not constitute a group boycott and would achieve the same ends that Metro claims the Realtor membership requirements achieve.

Therefore, on remand, it is necessary to determine whether Metro has sufficient market power under Realty Multi-List. In the event that the district court finds that Metro has the market power, it must find that the Realtor membership requirements are an illegal group boycott.[13]

E. The Conspiracy to Monopolize Claim

[23] Finally, the plaintiffs bring a conspiracy claim under section 2 of the Sherman act. *See* 15 U.S.C.A. § 2 (1973).[14] There are three elements to a section 2 claim. The plaintiffs must prove: first, the existence of "concerted action by knowing participants," Key Enterprises of Delaware v. Venice Hospital, 919 F.2d 1550 (11th Cir.1990); second, a specific intent to monopolize, *id.;* and third, an overt act. *Id.*

[24] The plaintiffs argue that the record contains evidence of this conspiracy to monopolize. The plaintiffs allege that Metro was once an independent organization, that the owner of Metro met with important individuals in the National Association of Relators, that at this meeting the owner of Metro agreed to link with the DeKalb Relators because such a linkage would help in its competition against First Multiple. From this evidence, the plaintiffs argue that Metro intended to conspire to monopolize the multilisting market. With this monopoly as a base, the plaintiffs argue that Metro attempted to conspire to monopolize the market for professional associations. . . .

[25][26] Metro next argues that the district court correctly granted summary judgment on the intent to monopolize element of the claim. The record supports the defendants' assertion that the intent of the conspiracy was not anticompetitive because the purpose was to foster competition. Walter Scott, one of the early presidents of Metro, stated that he and the other members of the Metro board of directors decided to merge Metro into the DeKalb Realtors because the Metro board recognized the potential power of a multilist service within the real estate community and the Metro board was afraid that Metro would somehow be purchased by First Multiple. Scott claimed that the board was fearful because First Multiple, at that

[13]Of course, the Realtors are free on remand to raise other justifications for the realtor membership requirements.

[14]In their complaint, the plaintiffs also bring a conspiracy claim under section 1 of the Sherman Act. Despite the fact that section 1 claims are usually easier to prove, . . . the plaintiffs have abandoned their section 1 claims.

time, was an exclusive service[15] and the board feared the effect on the real estate community of an exclusive service's purchasing Metro and closing it to the vast majority of brokers. Thus, the Metro board merged itself with the Realtors in order to stay relatively open. The plaintiffs cannot point to anything in the record, nor could we find anything in the record, which suggests any other intent by those at the meeting, and the plaintiffs especially cannot find any anticompetitive intent by those at the meeting. Therefore, there is no material issue of fact appropriate for trial and we affirm the district court's grant of summary judgment to the defendants on this claim as a matter of law.[16]

[15]Following a Department of Justice lawsuit and a consent decree, First Multiple is now an open service.

[16]The district court, however, applied an erroneous summary judgment standard. . . .

III. CONCLUSION

We therefore affirm the district court on its grant of summary judgment in favor of the defendants on the conspiracy to monopolize claim. We reverse the district court on its grant of summary judgment in favor of the defendants on the tying claim and the group boycott claim. We remand this case to the district court for further proceedings not inconsistent with this option.

Case Reflections

1. One magazine article about this case suggested that, if similar cases across the country are lost by Realtor groups, the commission structure for residential brokerage could drop substantially. Why do you think the issues in this case could have such an impact?
2. What is "tying" in the context of providing services? What are the tests for finding that the services are tied together?
3. The court in this case placed an emphasis on the issue of "market power" with regard to the group boycott claim. What is market power in this context and why is it so critical?
4. Why have previous courts found that multi-list services are, in general, "pro-competitive?"

YEE
V.
CITY OF ESCONDIDO, CALIFORNIA

112 S.Ct. 1522 (1992)

A new look at rent control as an uncompensated "taking"

Mobile home park owners brought action and claimed that local rent control ordinance, when viewed against backdrop of California's Mobilehome Residency Law, amounted to physical occupation of their property entitling them to compensation under the takings clause. The Superior Court of San Diego County . . . sustained city's demurrer to complaint and dismissed the action. Mobile home park owners appealed. Eleven other cases were consolidated with the mobile home park owners' case. The Court of Appeal, 224 Cal.App.3d 1349, 274 Cal.Rptr. 551, affirmed. Petition for certiorari was filed in eight of the twelve cases. The Supreme Court, Justice O'Connor, held that: (1) the rent control ordinance did not amount to physical taking of park owners' property; (2) whether ordinance violated park owners' substantive due process rights was not properly before the Supreme Court; and (3) whether ordinance constituted regulatory taking was not properly before the Supreme Court.

Affirmed.

Justices Blackmun and Souter concurred in the judgment and filed opinions.

SYLLABUS

The Fifth Amendment's Takings Clause generally requires just compensation where the government authorizes a physical occupation of property. But where the Government merely regulates the property's use, compensation is required only if considerations such as the regulation's purpose or the extent to which it deprives the owner of the property's economic use suggests that the regulation has unfairly singled out the property owner to bear a burden that should be borne by the public as a whole. Petitioners, mobile home park owners in respondent Escondido, California, rent pads of land to mobile home owners. When the homes are sold, the new owners generally continue to rent the pads. Under the California Mobilehome Residency Law, the bases upon which a park owner may terminate a mobile home owner's tenancy are limited to, inter alia, nonpayment of rent and the park owner's desire to change the use of his land. The park owner may not require the removal of a mobile home when it is sold and may neither charge a transfer fee for the sale nor disapprove of a purchaser who is able to pay rent. The state law does not limit the rent the park owner may charge, but Escondido has a rent control ordinance setting mobile home rents back to their 1986 levels and prohibiting rent increases without the City Council's approval. The Superior Court dismissed lawsuits filed by petitioners and others challenging the ordinance, rejecting the argument that the ordinance effected a physical taking by depriving park owners of all use and occupancy of their property and granting to their tenants, and their tenants' successors, the right to physically permanently occupy and use the property. The Court of Appeal affirmed.

Held:

1. The rent control ordinance does not authorize an unwanted physical occupation of petitioners' property and thus does not amount to a per se taking. Petitioners' argument—that the rent control ordinance authorizes a physical taking because, coupled with the state law's restrictions, it increases a mobile home's value by giving the homeowner the right to occupy the pad indefinitely at a submarket rent—is unpersuasive. The government effects a physical taking only where it requires the landowner to submit to the physical occupation of his land. Here, petitioners have voluntarily rented their land to mobile home owners and are not required to continue to do so by either the City or the State. On their face, the laws at issue merely regulate petitioners' use of their land by regulating the relationship between landlord and tenant. Any transfer of wealth from park owners to incumbent mobile home owners in the form of submarket rent does not itself convert regulation into physical invasion. Additional contentions made by petitioners—that the ordinance benefits current mobile home owners but not future owners, who must purchase the homes at premiums resulting from the homes' increased value, and that the ordinance deprives petitioners of the ability to choose their incoming tenants—might have some bearing on whether the ordinance causes a regulatory taking, but have nothing to do with whether it causes a physical taking. Moreover, the finding in Loretto v. Teleprompter Manhattan CATV Corp., 458 U.S. 419, 439, n. 17, 102 S.Ct. 3164, 3178, n. 17, 73 L.Ed.2d 868—that a physical taking claim cannot be defeated by an argument that a landlord can avoid a statute's restrictions by ceasing to rent his property, because his ability to rent may not be conditioned on forfeiting the right to compensation for a physical occupation—has no relevance here, where there has been no physical taking. Since petitioners have made no attempt to change how their land is used, this case also presents no occasion to consider whether the statute, as applied, prevents them from making a change. Pp. 1528–1531.

2. Petitioners' claim that the ordinance constitutes a denial of substantive due process is not properly before this Court because it was not raised below or addressed by the state courts. The question whether this Court's customary refusal to consider claims not raised or addressed below is a jurisdictional or prudential rule need not be resolved here, because even if the rule were prudential, it would be adhered to in this case. Pp. 1531–1532.

3. Also improperly before this Court is petitioners' claim that the ordinance constitutes a regulatory taking. The regulatory taking claim is ripe for review; and the fact that it was not raised below does not mean that it could not be properly raised before this Court, since once petitioners properly raised a taking claim, they could have formulated, in this Court, any argument they liked in support

of that claim. Nonetheless, the claim will not be considered because, under this Court's Rule 14.1(a), only questions set forth, or fairly included, in the petition for certiorari are considered. Rule 14.1(a) is prudential, but is disregarded only where reasons of urgency or economy suggest the need to address the unpresented question in the case under consideration. The Rule provides the respondent with notice of the grounds on which certiorari is sought, thus relieving him of the expense of unnecessary litigation on the merits and the burden of opposing certiorari on unpresented questions. It also assists the Court in selecting the cases in which certiorari will be granted. By forcing the parties to focus on the questions the Court views as particularly important, the Rule enables the Court to use its resources efficiently. Petitioners' question presented was whether the lower court erred in finding no physical taking, and the regulatory taking claim is related to, but not fairly included in, that question. Thus, petitioners must overcome the very heavy presumption against consideration of the regulatory taking claim, which they have not done. While that claim is important, lower courts have not reached conflicting results on the claim as they have on the physical taking claim. Prudence also dictates awaiting a case in which the issue was fully litigated below, to have the benefit of developed arguments and lower court opinions squarely addressing the question. Thus, the regulatory taking issue should be left for the California courts to address in the first instance. Pp. 1531–1534. 224 Cal.App.3d 1349, 274 Cal.Rptr. 551 (1990), affirmed.

O'CONNOR, J., delivered the opinion of the Court, in which REHNQUIST, C. J., and WHITE, STEVENS, SCALIA, KENNEDY, and THOMAS, JJ., joined. BLACKMUN, J., and SOUTER, J., filed opinions concurring in the judgment.

Case Reflections

1. Why did the mobile home park owners characterize the rent control ordinance as a "physical taking" of their property in this case?
2. In Chapter 16 the issue of "substantive due process" was described. How might that claim apply in this case?
3. Although the Supreme Court refused to rule on the issue, it implied that a claim of a "regulatory taking" might be more appropriate in this case. What do you think might constitute a regulatory taking?

LUCAS V. SOUTH CAROLINA COASTAL COUNCIL

112 S.Ct. 2886 (1992)

One of the most controversial cases in recent years—environmental regulation as a "taking"

Owner of beachfront property brought action alleging that application of South Carolina Beachfront Management Act to his property constituted a taking without just compensation. The Common Pleas Court of Charleston County, Larry R. Patterson, Special Judge, awarded landowner damages and appeal was taken. The South Carolina Supreme Court, Toal, J., reversed, 304 S.C. 376, 404 S.E.2d 895. Certiorari was granted, 112 S.Ct. 436, and the Supreme Court, Justice Scalia held that: (1) property owner's claim was ripe for review, and (2) South Carolina Supreme Court erred in applying "harmful or noxious uses" principle to decide case.

Reversed and remanded.

Justice Kennedy, filed opinion concurring in the judgment. Justices Blackmun and Stevens filed separate dissenting opinions. Justice Souter filed separate statement.

Justice SCALIA delivered the opinion of the Court.

In 1986, petitioner David H. Lucas paid $975,000 for two residential lots on the Isle of Palms in Charleston County, South Carolina, on which he intended to build single-family homes. In 1988, however, the South Carolina Legislature enacted the Beachfront Management Act, S.C.Code §

48–39–250 et seq. (Supp.1990) (Act), which had the direct effect of barring petitioner from erecting any permanent habitable structures on his two parcels. See § 48–39–290(A). A state trial court found that this prohibition rendered Lucas's parcels "valueless." App. to Pet. for Cert. 37. This case requires us to decide whether the Act's dramatic effect on the economic value of Lucas's lots accomplished a taking of private property under the Fifth and Fourteenth Amendments requiring the payment of "just compensation." U.S. Const., Amdt. 5.

I.

A.

South Carolina's expressed interest in intensively managing development activities in the so-called "coastal zone" dates from 1977 when, in the aftermath of Congress's passage of the federal Coastal Zone Management Act of 1972 . . . , the legislature enacted a Coastal Zone Management Act of its own. . . . In its original form, the South Carolina Act required owners of coastal zone land that qualified as a "critical area" (defined in the legislation to include beaches and immediately adjacent sand dunes) to obtain a permit from the newly created South Carolina Coastal Council (respondent here) prior to committing the land to a "use other than the use the critical area was devoted to on [September 28, 1977]." . . . In the late 1970s, Lucas and others began extensive residential development of the Isle of Palms, a barrier island situated eastward of the City of Charleston. Toward the close of the development cycle for one residential subdivision known as "Beachwood East," Lucas in 1986 purchased the two lots at issue in this litigation for his own account. No portion of the lots, which were located approximately 300 feet from the beach, qualified as a "critical area" under the 1977 Act; accordingly, at the time Lucas acquired these parcels, he was not legally obliged to obtain a permit from the Council in advance of any development activity. His intention with respect to the lots was to do what the owners of the immediately adjacent parcels had already done: erect single-family residences. He commissioned architectural drawings for this purpose.

The Beachfront Management Act brought Lucas's plans to an abrupt end. Under that 1988 legislation, the Council was directed to establish a "baseline" connecting the landward-most "point[s] of erosion . . . during the past forty years" in the region of the Isle of Palms that includes Lucas's lots. . . . In action not challenged here, the Council fixed this baseline landward of Lucas's parcels. That was significant, for under the Act construction of occupiable improvements[2] was flatly prohibited seaward of a line drawn 20 feet landward of, and parallel to, the baseline, . . . The Act provided no exceptions.

B.

Lucas promptly filed suite in the South Carolina Court of Common Pleas, contending that the Beachfront Management Act's construction bar effected a taking of his property without just compensation. Lucas did not take issue with the validity of the Act as a lawful exercise of South Carolina's police power, but contended that the Act's complete extinguishment of his property's value entitled him to compensation regardless of whether the legislature had acted in furtherance of legitimate police power objectives. Following a bench trial, the court agreed. Among its factual determinations was the finding that "at the time Lucas purchased the two lots, both were zoned for single-family residential construction and . . . there were no restrictions imposed upon such use of the property by either the State of South Carolina, the County of Charleston, or the Town of the Isle of Palms." App. to Pet. for Cert. 36. The trial court further found that the Beachfront Management Act decreed a permanent ban on construction insofar as Lucas's lots were concerned, and that this prohibition "deprive[d] Lucas of any reasonable economic use of the lots, . . . eliminated the unrestricted right of use, and render[ed] them valueless." *Id.*, at 37. The court thus concluded that Lucas's properties had been "taken" by operation of the Act, and it ordered respondent to

[2]The Act did allow the construction of certain nonhabitable improvements, e.g., "wooden walkways no larger in width than six feet," and "small wooden decks no larger than 144 square feet." . . .

pay "just compensation" in the amount of $1,232,387.50. *Id.,* at 40. The Supreme Court of South Carolina reversed. It found dispositive what it described as Lucas's concession "that the Beachfront Management Act [was] properly and validly designed to preserve . . . South Carolina's beaches." 304 S.C. 376, 379, 404 S.E.2d 895, 896 (1991). Failing an attack on the validity of the statute as such, the court believed itself bound to accept the "uncontested . . . findings" of the South Carolina legislature that new construction in the coastal zone—such as petitioner intended—threatened this public resource. *Id.,* at 383, 404 S.E.2d, at 898. The Court ruled that when a regulation respecting the use of property is designed "to prevent serious public harm," . . . no compensation is owing under the Takings Clause regardless of the regulation's effect on the property's value. . . .

III.

A.

Prior to Justice Holmes' exposition in Pennsylvania Coal Co. v. Mahon, 260 U.S. 393, 43 S.Ct. 158, 67 L.Ed. 322 (1922), it was generally thought that the Takings Clause reached only a "direct appropriation" of property, Legal Tender Cases, 12 Wall. 457, 551, 20 L.Ed. 287 (1871), or the functional equivalent of a "practical ouster of [the owner's] possession." Transportation Co. v. Chicago, 99 U.S. 635, 642, 25 L.Ed. 336 (1879). *See also* Gibson v. United States, 166 U.S. 269, 275–276, 17 S.Ct. 578, 580, 41 L.Ed. 996 (1897). Justice Holmes recognized in Mahon, however, that if the protection against physical appropriations of private property was to be meaningfully enforced, the government's power to redefine the range of interests included in the ownership of property was necessarily constrained by constitutional limits. 260 U.S., at 414–415, 43 S.Ct., at 160. If, instead, the uses of private property were subject to unbridled, uncompensated qualification under the police power, "the natural tendency of human nature [would be] to extend the qualification more and more until at last private property disappear[ed]." *Id.,* at 415, 43 S.Ct., at 160. These considerations gave birth in that case to the oft-cited maxim that, "while property may be regulated to a certain extent, if regulation goes too far it will be recognized as a taking." *Ibid.*

[2] Nevertheless, our decision in Mahon offered little insight into when, and under what circumstances, a given regulation would be seen as going "too far" for purposes of the Fifth Amendment. In 70-odd years of succeeding "regulatory takings" jurisprudence, we have generally eschewed any " 'set formula' " for determining how far is too far, preferring to "engag[e] in . . . essentially ad hoc, factual inquiries." . . . We have, however, described at least two discrete categories of regulatory action as compensable without case-specific inquiry into the public interest advanced in support of the restraint. The first encompasses regulations that compel the property owner to suffer a physical "invasion" of his property. In general (at least with regard to permanent invasions), no matter how minute the intrusion, and no matter how weighty the public purpose behind it, we have required compensation. For example, in Loretto v. Teleprompter Manhattan CATV Corp., 458 U.S. 419, 102 S.Ct. 3164, 73 L.Ed.2d 868 (1982), we determined that New York's law requiring landlords to allow television cable companies to emplace cable facilities in their apartment buildings constituted a taking, *id.,* at 435–440, 102 S.Ct., at 3175–3178, even though the facilities occupied at most only 1 1/2 cubic feel of the landlords' property, *see id.,* at 438, n. 16, 102 S.Ct., at 3177. . . . The second situation in which we have found categorical treatment appropriate is where regulation denies all economically beneficial or productive use of land. *See* Agins, 447 U.S., at 260, 100 S.Ct., at 2141; *see also* Nollan v. California Coastal Comm'n, 483 U.S. 825, 834, 107 S.Ct. 3141, 3147, 97 L.Ed.2d 677 (1987); . . . As we have said on numerous occasions, the Fifth Amendment is violated when land-use regulation "does not substantially advance legitimate state interests or denies an owner economically viable use of his land." Agins, *supra,* 447 U.S., at 260, 100 S.Ct., at 2141 (citations omitted) (emphasis added). . . .

We have never set forth the justification for this rule. Perhaps it is simply, as Justice Brennan suggested, that total deprivation of beneficial use is, from the landowner's point of view, the equivalent of a physical appropriation. . . . Surely, at least, in the extraordinary circumstance when no productive or economically beneficial use of land is permitted, it is less realistic to indulge our usual assumption that the legislature is simply "adjusting the benefits and burdens of economic life," Penn Central Transportation Co., 438 U.S., at 124, 98 S.Ct., at 2659, in a manner that secures an "average reciprocity of advantage" to everyone concerned. Pennsylvania Coal Co. v. Mahon, 260 U.S., at 415, 43 S.Ct., at 160. And the functional basis for permitting the government, by regulation, to affect property values without compensation—that "Government hardly could go on if to some extent values incident to property could not be diminished without paying for every such change in the general law," *id.,* at 413, 43 S.Ct., at 159—does not apply to the relatively rare situations where the government has deprived a landowner of all economically beneficial uses.

On the other side of the balance, affirmatively supporting a compensation requirement, is the fact that regulations that leave the owner of land without economically beneficial or productive options for its use—typically, as here, by requiring land to be left substantially in its natural state—carry with them a heightened risk that private property is being pressed into some form of public service under the guise of mitigating serious public harm. *See,* e.g., Annicelli v. South Kingstown, 463 A.2d 133, 140–141 (R.I.1983) (prohibition on construction adjacent to beach justified on twin grounds of safety and "conservation of open space"); Morris County Land Improvement Co. v. Parisippany-Troy Hills Township, 40 N.J. 539, 552–553, 193 A.2d 232, 240 (1963) (prohibition on filling marshlands imposed in order to preserve region as water detention basin and create wildlife refuge). As Justice Brennan explained: "From the government's point of view, the benefits flowing to the public from preservation of open space through regulation may be equally great as from creating a wildlife refuge through formal condemnation or increasing electricity production through a dam project that floods private property." San Diego Gas & Elec. Co., *supra,* 450 U.S., at 652, 101 S.Ct., at 1304 (Brennan, J., dissenting). The many statutes on the books, both state and federal, that provide for the use of eminent domain to impose servitudes on private scenic lands preventing developmental uses, or to acquire such lands altogether, suggest the practical equivalence in this setting of negative regulation and appropriation. . . .

[3, 4] We think, in short, that there are good reasons for our frequently expressed belief that when the owner of real property has been called upon to sacrifice all economically beneficial uses in the name of the common good, that is, to leave his property economically idle, he has suffered a taking.[8]

---

[8]Justice STEVENS criticizes the "deprivation of all economically beneficial use" rule as "wholly arbitrary," in that "[the] landowner whose property is diminished in value 95 percent recovers nothing," while the landowner who suffers a complete elimination of value "recovers the land's full value." Post, at 2919. This analysis errs in its asumption that the landowner whose deprivation is one step short of complete is not entitiled to compensation. Such an owner might not be able to claim the benefit of our categorical formulation, but, as we have acknowledged time and again, "[t]he economic impact of the regulation on the claimant and . . . the extent to which the regulation has interfered with distinct investment-backed expectations" are keenly relevant to takings analysis generally. Penn Central Transportation Co. v. New York City, 438 U.S. 104,124,98 S. Ct. 2646, 2659, 57 L. Ed.2d 631 (1978). It is true that in at least some cases the landowner with 95 percent loss will get nothing, while the landowner with total loss will recover in full. But that occasional result is no more strange than the gross disparity between the landowner whose premises are taken for a highway (who recovers in full) and the landowner whose property is reduced to 5 percent of its former value by the highway (who recovers nothing).Takings law is full of these "all-or-nothing" situations. Justice STEVENS similarly misinterprets our focus on "developmental" uses of property (the uses proscribed by the Beachfront Management Act) as betraying an "assumption that the only uses of property cognizable under the Constitution are developmental uses." Post, at 2919,n.3. We make no such assumption. Though our prior takings cases evince an abiding concern for the productive use of, and economic investment in, land, there are plainly a number of noneconomic interests in land whose impairment will invite exceedingly close scrutiny under the Takings Clause. *See*, e.g., U.S. 419, 436, 102 S.Ct. 3164, 3176, 73 L.Ed.2d 868 (1982) (interest in excluding strangers from one's land.)

B.

[5, 6] The trial court found Lucas's two beachfront lots to have been rendered valueless by respondent's enforcement of the coastal-zone construction ban.[9] Under Lucas's theory of the case, which rested upon our "no economically viable use" statements, that finding entitled him to compensation. Lucas believed it unnecessary to take issue with either the purposes behind the Beachfront Management Act, or the means chosen by the South Carolina Legislature to effectuate those purposes. The South Carolina Supreme Court, however, thought otherwise. In its view, the Beachfront Management Act was no ordinary enactment, but involved an exercise of South Carolina's "police powers" to mitigate the harm to the public interest that petitioner's use of his land might occasion. 304 S.C., at 384, 404 S.E.2d, at 899. By neglecting to dispute the findings enumerated in the Act . . . or otherwise to challenge the legislature's purposes, petitioner "concede[d] that the beach/dune area of South Carolina's shores is an extremely valuable public resource; that the erection of new construction, inter alia, contributes to the erosion and destruction of this public resource; and that discouraging new construction in close proximity to the beach/dune area is necessary to prevent a great public harm." *Id.*, at 382–383, 404 S.E.2d, at 898. In the court's view, these concessions brought petitioner's challenge within a long line of this Court's cases sustaining against Due Process and Takings Clause challenges the State's use of its "police powers" to enjoin a property owner from activities akin to public nuisances. . . .

It is correct that many of our prior opinions have suggested that "harmful or noxious uses" of property may be proscribed by government regulation without the requirement of compensation. For a number of reasons, however, we think the South Carolina Supreme Court was too quick to conclude that that principle decides the present case. The "harmful or noxious uses" principle was the Court's early attempt to describe in theoretical terms why government may, consistent with the Takings Clause, affect property values by regulation without incurring an obligation to compensate—a reality we nowadays acknowledge explicitly with respect to the full scope of the State's police power. *See*, e.g., Penn Central Transportation Co., 438 U.S., at 125, 98 S.Ct., at 2659 (where State "reasonably conclude[s] that 'the health, safety, morals, or general welfare' would be promoted by prohibiting particular contemplated uses of land," compensation need not accompany prohibition); *see* also Nollan v. California Coastal Commission, 483 U.S., at 834–835, 107 S.Ct., . . .

The transition from early focus on control of "noxious" uses to our contemporary understanding of the broad realm within which government may regulate without compensation was an easy one, since the distinction between "harm-preventing" and "benefit-conferring" regulation is often in the eye of the beholder. It is quite possible, for example, to describe in either fashion the ecological, economic, and aesthetic concerns that inspired the South Carolina legislature in the present case. One could say that imposing a servitude on Lucas's land is necessary in order to prevent his use of it from "harming" South Carolina's ecological resources; or, instead, in order to achieve the "benefits" of an ecological preserve.[11] Compare, e.g., Claridge v. New Hampshire Wetlands Board, 125 N.H. 745, 752, 485 A.2d 287, 292 (1984) (owner may, without compensation, be barred from filling wetlands because landfilling would deprive adjacent coastal habitats and marine fisheries of ecological support), with e.g., Bartlett v. Zoning Comm'n of Old Lyme, 161 Conn. 24, 30, 282 A.2d 907, 910 (1971) (owner barred from filling tidal marshland must be compensated, despite municipality's "laudable" goal of "preserv[ing] marshlands from encroachment or destruction"). Whether one or the other of the competing characterizations will come to one's lips in a particular case depends primarily upon one's evaluation of the worth of competing uses of real estate. . . . Whether Lucas's construction of single-family residences on his

[9]This finding was the premise of the Petition for Certiorari, and since it was not challenged in the Brief in Opposition, we decline to entertain the argument in respondent's brief on the merits, see Brief for Respondent 45-50, that the finding was erroneous. Instead we decide the question presented under the same factual assumptions as did the Supreme Court of South Carolina. . . .

parcels should be described as bringing "harm" to South Carolina's adjacent ecological resources thus depends principally upon whether the describer believes that the State's use interest in nurturing those resources is so important that any competing adjacent use must yield.[12]

When it is understood that "prevention of harmful use" was merely our early formulation of the police power justification necessary to sustain (without compensation) any regulatory diminution in value; and that the distinction between regulation that "prevents harmful use" and that which "confers benefits" is difficult, if not impossible, to discern on an objective, value-free basis; it becomes self-evident that noxious-use logic cannot serve as a touchstone to distinguish regulatory "takings"—which require compensation—from regulatory deprivations that do not require compensation. A fortiori the legislature's recitation of a noxious-use justification cannot be the basis for departing from our categorical rule that total regulatory takings must be compensated. If it were, departure would virtually always be allowed. The South Carolina Supreme Court's approach would essentially nullify Mahon's affirmation of limits to the noncompensable exercise of the police power. Our cases provide no support for this: None of them that employed the logic of "harmful use" prevention to sustain a regulation involved an allegation that the regulation wholly eliminated the value of the claimant's land. . . .

[7] Where the State seeks to sustain regulation that deprives land of all economically beneficial use, we think it may resist compensation only if the logically antecedent inquiry into the nature of the owner's estate shows that the proscribed use interests were not part of his title to begin with.[14] This accords, we think, with our "takings" jurisprudence, which has traditionally been guided by the understandings of our citizens regarding the content of, and the State's power over, the "bundle of rights" that they acquire when they obtain title to property. It seems to us that the property owner necessarily expects the uses of his

[11]In the present case, in fact, some of the "[South Carolina] legislature's 'findings' " to which the South Carolina Supreme Court purported to defer in characterizing the purpose of the Act as "harm-preventing," 304 S.C. 376, 385, 404 S.E.2d 895, 900 (1991), seem to us phrased in "benefit-conferring" language instead. For example, they describe the importance of a construction ban in enhancing "South Carolina's annual tourism industry revenue," S.C. Code § 48–39–250(1)(b) (Supp.1991), in "provid[ing] habitat for numerous species of plants and animals, several of which are threatened or endangered," § 48–39–250(1)(c), and in "provid[ing] a natural healthy environment for the citizens of South Carolina to spend leisure time which serves their physical and mental well-being." § 48–39–250(1)(d). It would be pointless to make the outcome of this case hang upon this terminology, since the same interests could readily be described in "harm-preventing" fashion. Justice BLACKMUN, however, apparently insists that we must make the outcome hinge (exclusively) upon the South Carolina Legislature's other, "harm-preventing" characterizations, focusing on the declaration that "prohibitions on building in front of the setback line are necessary to protect people and property from storms, high tides, and beach erosion." Post, at 2906. He says "[n]othing in the record undermines [this] assessment," *ibid.*, apparently seeing no significance in the fact that the statute permits owners of existing structures to remain (and even to rebuild if their structures are not "destroyed beyond repair," S.C. Code Ann. § 48–39–290(B)), and in the fact that the 1990 amendment authorizes the Council to issue permits for new construction in violation of the uniform prohibition, *see* S.C. Code § 48–39–290(D)(1) (Supp. 1991).

[12]In Justice BLACKMUN's view, even with respect to regulations that deprive an owner of all developmental or economically beneficial land uses, the test for required compensation is whether the legislature has recited a harm-preventing justification for its action. *See* post, at 2906, 2910–2912. Since such a justification can be formulated in practically every case, this amounts to a test of whether the legislature has a stupid staff. We think the Takings Clause requires courts to do more than insist upon artful harm-preventing characterizations.

[14]Drawing on our First Amendment jurisprudence . . . Justice STEVENS would "loo[k] to the generality of a regulation of property" to determine whether compensation is owing. Post, at 2923. The Beachfront Management Act is general, in his view, because it "regulates the use of the coastline of the entire state." . . . Justice STEVENS' approach renders the Takings Clause little more than a particularized restatement of the Equal Protection Clause.

property to be restricted, from time to time, by various measures newly enacted by the State in legitimate exercise of its police powers; "[as] long recognized, some values are enjoyed under an implied limitation and must yield to the police power." Pennsylvania Coal Co. v. Mahon, 260 U.S., at 413, 43 S.Ct., at 159. And in the case of personal property, by reason of the State's traditionally high degree of control over commercial dealings, he ought to be aware of the possibility that new regulation might even render his property economically worthless (at least if the property's only economically productive use is sale or manufacture for sale), *see* Andrus v. Allard, 444 U.S. 51, 66–67, 100 S.Ct. 318, 327, 62 L.Ed.2d 210 (1979) (prohibition on sale of eagle feathers). In the case of land, however, we think the notion pressed by the Council that title is somehow held subject to the "implied limitation" that the State may subsequently eliminate all economically valuable use is inconsistent with the historical compact recorded in the Takings Clause that has become part of our constitutional culture.[15]

[8] Where "permanent physical occupation" of land is concerned, we have refused to allow the government to decree it anew (without compensation), no matter how weighty the asserted "public interests" involved, Loretto v. Teleprompter Manhattan CATV Corp., 458 U.S., at 426, 102 S.Ct., at 3171—though we assuredly would permit the government to assert a permanent easement that was a preexisting limitation upon the landowner's title. Compare Scranton v. Wheeler, 179 U.S. 141, 163, 21 S.Ct. 48, 57, 45 L.Ed. 126 (1900) (interests of "riparian owner in the submerged lands . . . bordering on a public navigable water" held subject to Government's navigational servitude), with Kaiser Aetna v. United States, 444 U.S., at 178–180, 100 S.Ct., at 392–393 (imposition of navigational servitude on marina created and rendered navigable at private expense held to constitute a taking). We believe similar treatment must be accorded confiscatory regulations, i.e., regulations that prohibit all economically beneficial use of land: Any limitation so severe cannot be newly legislated or decreed (without compensation), but must inhere in the title itself, in the restrictions that background principles of the State's law of property and nuisance already place upon land ownership. A law or decree with such an effect must, in other words, do no more than duplicate the result that could have been achieved in the courts—by adjacent landowners (or other uniquely affected persons) under the Sate's law of private nuisance, or by the State under its complementary power to abate nuisances that affect the public generally, or otherwise.[16]

[9] On this analysis, the owner of a lake bed, for example, would not be entitled to compensation when he is denied the requisite permit to engage in a landfilling operation that would have the effect of flooding others' land. Nor the corporate owner of a nuclear generating plant, when it is directed to remove all improvements from its land upon discovery that the plant sits astride an earthquake fault. Such regulatory action may well have the effect of eliminating the land's only economically productive use, but it does not proscribe a productive use that was previously permissible under relevant property and nuisance principles. The use of these properties for what are now expressly prohibited purposes was always unlawful, and (subject to other constitutional limitations) it was open to the State at any point to make the implication of those background principles of nuisance and property law explicit. . . . In light of our traditional resort to "existing rules or understandings that stem from an independent source such as state law" to define the range of interests that qualify for protection as "property" under the Fifth (and Fourteenth) Amendments, . . . this recognition that the Takings Clause does not require compensation

[15]After accusing us of "launch[ing] a missile to kill a mouse," post, at 2904, Justice BLACKMUN expends a good deal of throw-weight of his own on a noncombatant, arguing that our description of the "understanding" of land ownership that informs the Takings Clause is not supported by early American experience. That is largely true, but entirely irrelevant. . . .

[16]The principal "otherwise" that we have in mind is litigation absolving the State (or private parties) of liability for the destruction of "real and personal property, in cases of actual necessity, to prevent the spreading of a fire" or to forestall other grave threats to the lives and property of others. . . .

when an owner is barred from putting land to a use that is proscribed by those "existing rules or understandings" is surely unexceptional. When, however, a regulation that declares "off-limits" all economically productive or beneficial uses of land goes beyond what the relevant background principles would dictate, compensation must be paid to sustain it.[17]

The "total taking" inquiry we require today will ordinarily entail (as the application of state nuisance law ordinarily entails) analysis of, among other things, the degree of harm to public lands and resources, or adjacent private property, posed by the claimant's proposed activities, *see,* e.g., Restatement (Second) of Torts §§ 826, 827, the social value of the claimant's activities and their suitability to the locality in question, *see* e.g., *id.*, §§ 828(a) and (b), 831, and the relative ease with which the alleged harm can be avoided through measures taken by the claimant and the government (or adjacent private landowners) alike, *see* e.g., *i.d.,* §§ 827(e), 828(c), 830. The fact that a particular use has long been engaged in by similarly situated owners ordinarily imports a lack of any common-law prohibition (though changed circumstances or new knowledge may make what was previously permissible no longer so,) *see* Restatement (Second) of Torts, *supra,* § 827, comment g. So also does the fact that other landowners, similarly situated, are permitted to continue the use denied to the claimant.

It seems unlikely that common-law principles would have prevented the erection of any habitable or productive improvements on petitioner's land; they rarely support prohibition of the "essential use" of land, . . .

* * *

The judgment is reversed and the cause remanded for proceedings not inconsistent with this opinion.

So ordered.

[17]Of course, the State may elect to rescind its regulation and thereby avoid having to pay compensation for a permanent deprivation. *See* First English Evangelical Lutheran Church, 482 U.S., at 321, 107 S.Ct., at 2389. But "where the {regulation has} already worked a taking of all use of property, no subsequent action by the government can relieve it of the duty to provide compensation for the period during which the taking was effective." *Ibid.*

Case Reflections

1. The history of this case indicates that the trial court found that the plaintiff's property had been rendered "valueless" and thus a taking had occurred. The South Carolina Supreme Court ruled that, because Lucas did not contest the *purpose* of the ordinance, a taking could not have occurred. How did the U.S. Supreme Court resolve this conflict?
2. What remedies does the state have in settling this suit? How does the *First English* case (see Chapter 16) affect the outcome of this case?
3. The U.S. Supreme Court ties the "bundle of rights" concept to the takings issue to devise a new method of determining when a compensable taking has occurred. Explain this new method.

DISMUKE
V.
EDINA REALTY, INC.,

Failure to disclose agency status adequately certified as a class action

This action was commenced on May 5, 1992 by the named Plaintiffs on behalf of all others who sold property through Edina Realty, Inc. on or after May 1, 1986, in transactions in which Edina Realty acted as the agent for both the buyer and seller. Plaintiffs have alleged that Edina Realty failed to adequately disclose the existence, consequences and effect of this "dual agency."

Plaintiffs timely filed a motion for class certification, and on September 28, 1992, a certification hearing was conducted before the Honorable Gary Larson. . . .

Now, therefore, based upon all the files, records and proceedings herein, this Court, for purposes of the instant action, enters the following:

FINDINGS OF FACT

1. That Plaintiffs Phillip Dismuke, and Pamela and Joseph Gehlen, proposed class representatives (hereinafter "Sellers"), are individuals who entered into exclusive listing agreements with Defendant Edina Realty, Inc., in August 1989 and June 1991, respectively.
2. That Edina Realty is a Minnesota corporation, whose principal business is as a licensed real estate brokerage firm.
3. That pursuant to the terms of the exclusive listing agreements, Edina Realty agreed to act as Sellers' agent and fiduciary in connection with the sale of their respective homes.
4. That Sellers' respective properties were listed with Edina Realty sales associates ("listing agents").
5. That these properties were subsequently purchased by buyers who were also represented by Edina Realty sales associates ("selling agents").
6. That Edina Realty refers to the practice of representing both sellers and buyers as "in-house" transactions.
7. That Sellers allege that Edina Realty's practice of representing both buyers and sellers in the transfer of real property constitutes a "dual agency."
8. That Edina Realty associates disclose their representation on the purchase agreement by requiring both buyer and seller to initial the following:

   "Agency Disclosure:______________________________
   (selling agent)

   stipulates he or she is representing the ________ in this transaction. The listing agent or broker stipulates he or she is representing the seller in this transaction. Buyer and seller initial: Buyer(s) __________ Seller(s) ________"

9. That Edina Realty associates relied on this "Agency Disclosure" to disclose their representation of buyers and sellers.
10. That Sellers' admit that they initialed a form disclosure similar to the one reproduced above.
11. That Sellers allege that this written "Agency Disclosure" was inadequate, and failed to fully and adequately disclose the consequences and effect of Edina Realty's dual agency status.
12. That Sellers alleged that Edina Realty's standard and regular business practice was to rely solely on this "Agency Disclosure" to disclose the existence, consequences and effect of these "in-house" or "dual agency" transactions.
13. That Edina Realty received commissions in connection with these transactions and deducted the commissions from the sales proceeds otherwise paid to the Sellers.
14. That Sellers' evidential submissions establish that Edina Realty was involved in more than 4660 dual agency/in house transactions in the metropolitan area in 1990 alone.
15. That Sellers' counsel is well experienced in the area of complex litigation involving numerous claimants/parties, and that Edina Realty has not challenged the adequacy of Plaintiffs counsel.

CONCLUSIONS OF LAW

1. That the potential class, numbering more than 4500, is so numerous that joinder of all members is impracticable.
2. That there are questions of law common to the class, *e.g.,* whether Edina Realty's form disclosure constitutes an "affirmative written disclosure" as contemplated by Minn. Stat. Sec. 82.19, Subd. 5.
3. That the common questions of law to the class predominate over any question affecting only individual members.
4. That the claims of the representative parties are typical of the claims of the class.
5. That the representative parties will fairly and adequately assert and protect the interests of the class.

6. That the attorney for the representative parties will adequately represent the interests of the class.
7. That the representative parties do not have a conflict of interest in the maintenance of the class action.
8. That a class action will provide a fair and efficient method for adjudication of the controversy.
9. That the difficulties likely to be encountered in the management of the action as a class action are not so great as to preclude class action certification, as to certain specific issues presented in this litigation.
10. That the amount which may be recovered by individual class members is *not* so small in relation to the expense and effort of administering the action as to render a class action unjustifiable.
11. That the above-entitled action may be appropriately maintained as a class action under Minn.R.Civ.P. 23.02(c).

THE COURT HEREBY ORDERS:

1. That Plaintiffs' motion for conditional class Certification is GRANTED.
2. That the class is hereby conditionally certified pursuant to Minn.R.Civ.P. 23.02(c), thus permitting class members to "opt-out."
3. That the class shall be defined as those persons or entities that meet all of the following criteria:

   All persons or entities:
   A. Who listed real property for sale through Defendant Edina Realty, Inc. in transactions in which Defendant agreed to act as agent and fiduciary in connection with the sale of real property, *and*

   B. Who sold real property in a transaction on or after May 1, 1986 in which Defendant Edina Realty, Inc. acted as the agent and fiduciary for both the buyer and the seller to the transaction, *and*

   C. Who, as seller of real property, paid a commission to the Defendant Edina Realty, Inc. for services rendered in connection with the sale of real property.

4. That Plaintiffs Phillip Dismuke, Pamela Gehlen and Joseph Gehlen are certified as the representatives of the above-described class for purposes of maintaining this action.
5. That in making this Order, the Court retains all of its rights and authority to make other such orders affecting the class certification and procedural and managerial administration of this class action.
6. That Plaintiffs' and Defendant's counsel shall contact this Court within two weeks of the date of this Order to schedule a Status conference to discuss the procedural and managerial handling of this class action pursuant to Minn.R.Civ.P. 23.03 and Minn.R.Civ.P. 23.04.

Case Reflections

1. The material presented here is not really a "case" in the same sense as others that are included in this book. It is a preliminary finding that the action will be treated as a "class action" suit. Why is this determination potentially so important?
2. What is an "in-house" transaction as described in this document? What does the use of the term "in-house/dual agency" (see "Finding of Fact" 14) imply about the court's perception of this practice?
3. The agency disclosure statement used by the defendant is almost identical to the example statement included in Chapter 12. Why do you think the plaintiffs in this action find fault with this statement?

APPENDIX A

Sample Lease Clauses

§73.7 FURNISHED APARTMENT LEASE

This lease is made the _______ day of _______, 19 _____, by and between _______, herein called "Lessor," and _______, herein called "Lessee."

For and in consideration of the prompt payment of the rents by Lessee and the exact performance of the covenants hereinafter set forth by Lessee, Lessor does hereby lease to Lessee, and Lessee hereby hires from Lessor, that certain apartment No. _______, together with parking area No. _______, situated at _______, in the City of _____________, California, for the term of _______, commencing on the _______ day of _____________, 19 _____, and ending on the _____________ day of _____________, 19 _____, at the total rent of _____________ Dollars ($ _____________), payable at _____________, in installments of _____________ Dollars ($ _____________), each due and payable in advance on the _____________ day of each and every month during said term, which rent Lessee agrees to pay promptly in the manner set forth herein. Lessor hereby acknowledges receipt from Lessee of the sum of _____________ Dollars ($ _____________) in payment of the first installment of rent.

This lease is made by Lessor and is accepted by Lessee upon the following conditions, and it is agreed that each of the terms hereinafter specified shall be conditions as well as covenants. The breach, default, failure or violation of any one or more thereof shall, without limitation of his other rights, entitle Lessor to terminate this lease, re-enter and take over possession forthwith.

1. **Security Deposit.** As a further consideration for the execution of this lease by Lessor, and in addition to the rent agreed to be paid herein, Lessee agrees to pay Lessor the sum of $ _____________ as a partial security deposit upon the execution of this lease, the receipt of which is

hereby acknowledged. If Lessee shall promptly pay the rent as provided for herein, and if he shall comply with each and all of the terms and conditions of this written lease which are to be performed by Lessee during Lessee's entire tenancy, then in such event, upon the termination of this tenancy, and after the surrender of the possession of the leased premises according to the terms of this lease, in good and clean condition, reasonable wear and tear excepted, Lessor will refund to Lessee the said sum of $ ______________.

Security Deposit Not To Be Used as Last Month's Rent

2. **Utility Charges.** Lessee shall pay Lessor the rent hereinabove provided at any place specified by Lessor and, in addition thereto, shall pay when due all utility charges accruing or payable in connection with the use of said leased premises during said tenancy, except Lessor shall pay all charges for water.

3. **Use of Premises, Subletting, Surrender, Occupancy.** Lessee has examined and knows the condition of said premises, and has received the same in good order and repair, and hereby agrees: (a) to use said premises for living rooms and as a private residence only, (b) not to sell or assign this lease nor sublet said premises, or any part thereof without the written consent of Lessor first had and obtained, (c) to surrender possession of said premises at the expiration of this lease without further notice to quit, in as good condition as reasonable and careful use will permit, (d) that said premises will be occupied by no more than the following named adults ______________________________ and the following named children ______________________________ either as guest, lodger, roomer, boarder, licensee, or any other status, without, in each instance first obtaining the written consent of Lessor, and (e) to keep said premises in good condition and repair at his own expense.

4. **Lessee Waives Damages.** Lessee waives all rights under Section _______ of the _______ Code of the State of ______________, and agrees not to make any claim against Lessor and will hold Lessor harmless therefrom, for any loss or damage to any personal property belonging to Lessee or any of his guests or occupants, or for any injuries to Lessee or any of his guests or occupants.

5. **Termination on Default of Lessee.** Any failure on the part of Lessee to pay the rent, or any part thereof, or any failure on the part of Lessee to comply with any of the terms or conditions of this lease shall, at the election of Lessor, terminate this lease and all rights of Lessee hereunder.

6. **Right of Re-entry.** Upon termination of this lease in any manner, Lessor may re-enter the leased premises and remove any and all persons and property therefrom, and repossess and enjoy said premises again as of his first and former state. Lessee hereby waives all right to any notice from Lessor of his election to terminate this lease, or any demand for the payment of rent or for the possession of the leased premises. All remedies of Lessor under this lease are cumulative and are given without impairing any other rights or remedies of Lessor as provided by law.

7. **Reletting on Default of Lessee.** If Lessee shall be in default in the payment of the rent, or under any of the terms of this lease, or if Lessee shall vacate or abandon the premises or any part thereof (and absence of Lessee therefrom for a period of five days after such default shall be considered such an abandonment thereof), Lessor may, if he so elects, without terminating this lease re-enter said premises and remove all persons and property therefrom and take possession of said premises and

relet the same, or any part thereof, at such rental and upon such terms and conditions as he may deem proper, and apply the proceeds thereof, less the expenses, including the usual agent's commission, so incurred, upon the amount due from Lessee hereunder, and Lessee shall be liable for any deficiency. If Lessor shall take possession of the premises and relet the same, such reletting shall not operate as a termination of this lease unless Lessor so elects; nor shall such action by Lessor operate as a waiver of any other rights or remedies of Lessor.

8. **Liability of Lessee for Legal Responses.** If, upon failure of Lessee to pay the rent as aforesaid, or to comply with any of the other covenants, conditions, rules and regulations of this lease action should be brought or notice served on account thereof to enforce the payment of rent herein, or to recover possession of the premises, or to enforce any provision of this lease, or to obtain damages, Lessee agrees to pay Lessor reasonable costs and expenses in said action or for said notice, including attorneys fees, whether or not any such action proceeds to judgment.

9. **Right of Inspection.** Lessor shall have the right by himself or agent or with others, to enter the premises at reasonable hours to examine or exhibit the same, or to make such repairs and alterations as may be deemed necessary by Lessor for the safety and preservation of said building, and within the period of sixty days prior to the termination of this lease, to show the flat to prospective tenants.

10. **Liability of Lessee for Waste.** Lessee shall pay (a) for any expense, damage or repair occasioned by the stopping of waste pipes or overflow from bath tubs, closets, wash basins or sinks and (b) for damage to window panes, window shades, curtain rods, wall paper or any other damage to the interior of the leased premises and Lessee shall commit and suffer no waste to be committed therein and no change or alterations of the premises shall be made nor partitions erected nor walls papered without the consent in writing of the Lessor first had and obtained.

11. **Non-liability of Lessor.** Lessor shall not be liable for any damage occasioned by failure to keep the premises in repair, and shall not be liable for any damage done or occasioned by or from plumbing, gas, water, steam or other pipes or sewerage, or the bursting, leaking or running of any pipe, tank, wash stand, water closet or waste pipe, in, above, upon or about said building or premises, nor for damage occasioned by water, snow or ice being upon or coming through the roof, skylight, trap-door or otherwise, nor for any damage arising from the acts or neglects of co-tenants, or other occupants of the same building, or any owners or occupants of adjacent or contiguous property.

12. **Restrictions on Lessee's Activities.** Lessee agrees that said premises shall be used only for the purpose set forth above, and for no other purpose, and none of the rooms shall be offered for lease by placing notices on any door, window or wall of the building, not by advertising the same directly or indirectly in any newspaper, or otherwise, save and except with the written consent of the Lessor first had and obtained. There shall be no lounging, sitting upon, or unnecessary tarrying in or upon the front steps, the sidewalks, railings, stairways, halls, landings or other public places of the building by Lessee, members of his family, or other persons connected with the occupancy of the leased premises, and no provisions, milk, marketing, groceries or like merchandise shall be delivered into the premises through the front entrance of said building.

13. **Destruction of Premises.** If the premises shall be wrecked or destroyed by fire or by the elements or other causes so as to render them unfit for occupancy, or if the furnishings, if any, of Lessor be so damaged or destroyed as to be rendered un-

fit for use, this lease may thereupon be terminated, at the option of Lessor; but should the Lessor elect to repair or reconstruct said premises, and replace or repair said furnishings, he shall do so as speedily as possible, and should the damage be so extensive as to render the premises untenable, then the rent or a just and proportionate part thereof, according to the nature and extent of the damage, shall cease until the same shall be repaired by Lessor, but the Lessee shall in no case be entitled to compensation or damage on account of any annoyance or inconvenience in making said repairs, or on account of such destruction.

14. **Holdover Tenancy.** If Lessee shall holdover after the expiration of the term of this lease with the consent of Lessor, express or implied, such tenancy shall be from month to month only, and shall not be a renewal hereof, and Lessee agrees to pay rent and all other charges as hereinabove provided and also to comply with all the terms and convenants of this lease for the time Lessee holds over.

15. **Notices.** Lessor may serve any notice, required or desired to be given hereunder, on Lessee personally, or by sending the same through the United States mail, postage prepaid, to the address of Lessee specified herein.

16. **Entire Agreement.** The within lease constitutes the entire agreement between the parties and recites the entire consideration given and accepted by the parties, and no representations not expressed herein or endorsed hereon have been made by either party or their agents.

§85.5 ESCALATOR CLAUSE BASED ON VARIATION IN OPERATING COSTS AND TAXES*

(1) The tenant shall pay to the landlord for the demised premises during the term of this lease in lawful money of the United States the sum of Twelve Thousand Dollars ($12,000.00) for each lease year that this lease is in effect, as and for a minimum basic annual rental, which said sum shall be payable in equal monthly installments of One Thousand Dollars ($1,000.00) each, payable in advance and without notice commencing on January 1, 19 ____, being the first day of the first lease year of the term hereof.

(2) The minimum basic annual rental provided to be paid in paragraph (1) above is based upon a rate of $4.00 per square foot per annum occupied by the tenant under the terms of this lease, and it is expressly agreed by the parties hereto that the tenant will pay in addition to the said base rate an additional rental to cover the tenant's proportionate cost to the lessor during the preceding calendar year of all expenses paid and incurred for real estate and personal property taxes, heat, steam, fuel, labor, including all wages and salaries, social security taxes and other taxes which may be levied upon such wages and salaries, supplies, repairs, maintenance, painting, wall and window washing, laundry and towel service, tools and equipment (which are not required to be capitalized for federal income tax purposes), insurance, trash removal and all other items properly constituting direct operating costs according to standard accounting practices (hereinafter collectively referred to as the building operating costs) but not including depreciation of building or equipment, interest, income or excess profit taxes, cost of maintaining the landlord's corporate existence, franchise taxes, any expenditures required to be capitalized for federal income tax

purposes or office expenses, manager's fees or salaries of the landlord's executive officers or the cost of water used in operating air-conditioning equipment installed or which may be installed by the tenant or other tenants in the building.

It is further agreed by the parties hereto that the proportionate share of the building operating costs to be paid by the tenant shall be such portion of the total aggregate building operating costs to the landlord as the total usable space covered by this lease bears to the total usable space in the building, it being agreed that the usable space covered by this lease is _______ square feet and the total usable space in the building is _______ square feet.

(3) The landlord shall, as soon as conveniently possible after the effective date of this lease, and in any event not later than February 1, 19 _____, and thereafter at the expiration of each lease year during the term hereof or any extension thereof and not later than the first day of February of each such lease year, advise the tenant of the total building operating costs above referred to for the preceding calendar year, after which the tenant shall pay the additional rental indicated by these costs, which additional rental shall apply to the then current lease year, such new rates being applied to any months for which the rental shall then have been paid as well as the unexpired months of the current lease year, the adjustment for the then expired months to be made at the payment of the next succeeding monthly rental.

(4) For the protection of the tenant, the landlord shall maintain books of account which shall be open to the tenant at all reasonable times so that the tenant can determine that such costs have, in fact, been paid. Any disagreement with respect to any one or more of said charges if not satisfactorily settled between the landlord and the tenant shall be referred by either party to an independent certified public accountant to be mutually agreed upon and if such an accountant cannot be agreed upon, the American Arbitration Association may be asked by either party to select an arbitrator whose decision on the dispute will be final and binding upon both parties.

§ 80.4 PERCENTAGE STORE LEASE

Percentage Rental Provisions

(b-1) **Percentage Rental.** Lessee shall pay to Lessor sums of money equal to the following percentages of Gross Sales:

(b-2) **Gross Sales.** The term "Gross Sales" includes the total of all sales of merchandise, all charges for services for which charge is made, and all business transacted in, upon and from the premises during the term by Lessee and all others occupying the premises or any part thereof.

The term "Gross Sales" excludes bona fide refunds and credits for returns of merchandise, and the amounts turned over by Lessee to the State of Illinois on account of the "Retailers' Occupation Tax Act" of Illinois, approved June 28, 1933, and amendments thereto.

The Percentage Rental Provisions apply to all Gross Sales made for cash or upon credit, or partly for cash and partly upon credit, regardless of collections of charges for which credit is given, and to all sales, charges for services and business transacted for which orders are taken in or upon the premises during the term regardless of whether the merchandise is delivered, wholly or in part, and whether the services are rendered and the business is transacted in, from or upon the premises. Each sale, charge or business transaction upon installments, or a contract therefore, shall be treated as a gross sale for the full price or charge in the month during which such sale, charge or contract shall be made.

(b-3) **Records.** Lessee shall keep and preserve, during the term, full, complete and true records of all Gross Sales, in manner and form satisfactory to Lessor; shall permit Lessor or Lessor's representatives to examine or audit the records at any and all reasonable times, and shall, upon Lessor's request, explain the methods of keeping the records.

(b-4) **Monthly Statements.** On or before the tenth day of _______ 19____, and on or before the tenth day of each and every calendar month during the remainder of the term, and also on or before the tenth day of _______19____, Lessee shall prepare and deliver to Lessor at the place then fixed for the payment of Rent a sworn statement of Gross Sales during the preceding calendar month. With each such monthly Statement, Lessee shall pay to Lessor the Percentage Rental for the preceding month.

(b-5) **Annual Statements.** On or before the fifteenth day of _______, 19 ____, and on or before the same day of each _______ during the remainder of the term, and also on or before the same day of _______, 19 _____, Lessee shall deliver to Lessor at the place last fixed for the payment of Rent a statement, sworn to by Lessee or Lessee's authorized representative, showing Gross Sales during the year of the term ended on the last day of the last previous month. If Section (b-1) or any other provision of this lease, or the enforcement thereof by Lessor, requires accounting for Gross Sales and the payment of Percentage Rental for any period more than one month but less than twelve months, such shorter period shall be treated as one year for the purposes of an Annual Statement and the Statement shall be delivered to Lessor within fifteen days after termination of such shorter period. With each such Annual Statement or Statement for a shorter period, Lessee shall pay to Lessor any and all sums hereunder and then remaining unpaid for the entire period covered by such Statement.

(b-6) **Contesting Lessee's Statements.** If Lessor is not satisfied with any Monthly, Annual or other Statement, Lessor shall serve notice upon Lessee of Lessor's dissatisfaction within thirty days after Lessor's receipt of the Statement complained of, and it shall not be necessary for Lessor to specify therein the grounds for Lessor's dissatisfaction. Unless within ten days after service of Lessor's notice of dissatisfaction Lessee satisfies Lessor with respect to such statement, Lessor shall have the right to make an audit of all books and records of Lessee, including Lessee's bank accounts, which in any way pertain to or show Gross Sales. Such audit shall be made by a public accountant to be selected by Lessor, and all expenses of the audit shall be paid by Lessee if the report of the public accountant shows the statement complained of to have contained error prejudicial to Lessor's receipt of Rent in an amount equal to or greater than 1% of the amount of Rent reported by the Lessee's statement for the period of the audit; otherwise to be paid by Lessor. The final audit of the public accountant made pursuant to this Section (b-6) shall be conclusive upon the parties, and Lessee shall pay to Lessor within five days after a copy of the public accountant's final report has been delivered to Lessee the amount, if any, shown thereby to be due to Lessor. If Lessor makes any such audit, all Statements made by Lessee after the Statement complained of and until ten days after Lessor receives the final report of the public accountant shall be subject to Lessor's notice of dissatisfaction.

(b-7) **Failure to Deliver Statements.** If Lessee omits to prepare and deliver promptly any Monthly, Annual or other Statement required by the Percentage Rental Provisions, Lessor may elect to treat Lessee's omission as a substantive breach of this lease entitling Lessor to terminate this lease and Lessee's right to possession of the premises, or to make an audit of all books and records of Lessee, including Lessee's bank accounts, which in any way pertain to or show Gross Sales, and to prepare the statement or Statements which Lessee failed to prepare and deliver. Such audit shall be made and such Statement or Statements shall be prepared by a public accountant to be selected by Lessor. The Statement or Statements, so prepared, shall be conclusive on Lessee, and Lessee shall pay all expenses of the audit and other services.

(b-8) **Conduct of Business.** Lessee shall, during the entire term, continuously use the demised premises for the purpose stated in this lease, carrying on therein Lessee's business undertaking diligently, assiduously and energetically. Lessee shall maintain on the premises a substantial stock of goods, wares and merchandise and equipment, adequate to assure successful operation of Lessee's business, and shall employ clerks, salesmen and others sufficient for the service and convenience of customers. Lessee shall keep the premises open and available for business activity therein during all usual days and hours for such business in the vicinity except when prevented by strikes, fire, casualty or other causes beyond Lessee's reasonable control and except during reasonable periods for repairing, cleaning and decorating the premises. Lessee shall include the address and identity of its business activity in the demised premises in all advertisements made by Lessee in which the address and identity of any other local business activity of like character conducted by Lessee shall be mentioned, and shall not divert elsewhere any trade, commerce or business which ordinarily would be transacted by Lessee in or from the demised premises.

§88.13 LESSOR'S AND LESSEE'S OBLIGATIONS TO REPAIR—ANOTHER FORM

The Lessee shall at its own expense, throughout the term of this lease and so long as it shall remain in possession of the leased premises, keep and maintain in good repair all portions of the building or buildings located upon the leased premises, now or at any time hereafter during said term, including all fixtures and equipment, such as a sprinkler system, elevators and furnaces, and all other appurtenances, machinery and equipment therein which are wrought into and become part of the real estate, but not including articles of personal property which are capable of being removed without injury to the real estate, and shall also keep and maintain in good repair the sidewalk in front of the leased premises, whenever not so maintained by the City of _______________ or other public authority. It is understood that the preceding sentence does not require maintenance of said building or buildings and fixtures, equipment, appurtenances and machinery in perfect condition or a condition equal to new, but that the Lessee shall at all times keep and maintain the same in such condition as to minimize, so far as is practicable by usual care and repairs, the effects of use, decay, injury and destruction of said property, the lessors recognizing that certain depreciation by reason of increasing age and use is unavoidable. Such equipment as a sprinkler system of fire protection, elevators and all other appurtenances, machinery, equipment or fixtures in or about the leased premises shall be maintained and kept by the Lessee in such condition and repair as to meet the requirements of the Insurance Inspection Bureau, and the Lessee shall at its own expense rebuild or replace any of such appurtenances, machinery, equipment or fixtures (which are part of the real estate), which shall during the continuance of the term of his lease cease to be capable of safe use or operation and shall be incapable of repair or which shall be required or ordered to be rebuilt or replaced by any insurance or public authority. The Lessee shall also maintain throughout the time of its occupancy of the leased premises, all portions of said premises and of the machinery, equipment, fixtures and appurtenances therein, in a clean and sanitary condition. The Lessee shall be bound, so long as it shall remain in possession of the leased premises, to keep and maintain all portions of the premises, the improvements thereon and the appurtenances, machinery, equipment and fixtures therein in such condition as to prevent any loss, damage or injury to the persons, property, businesses, or occupations of any sublessees, persons permitted by the Lessee or its sublessees to be in or about the leased premises, owners, occupants and invitees of adjoining premises, and persons upon the adjacent portions of the street in front and the alley in rear of the leased premises as required by this sentence shall not constitute a breach of this lease.

Notwithstanding the other provisions hereof, the Lessee shall not be required to maintain the building now upon the leased premises, or any portion thereof which may be left after construction of a new building upon a part of the premises, in any better condition than at present until after ______________, 19_____.

§88.14 LESSOR'S AND LESSEE'S OBLIGATIONS TO REPAIR—LESSEE TO MAKE REPAIRS OF EVERY NATURE*

The Lessee shall, at his own expense, make all repairs and renewals necessary or advisable to keep said premises, both inside and outside, and all additions thereto, from deteriorating in value or condition, and the Lessor shall be absolutely exempt from making any repair or renewal or addition to said premises and their appurtenances during the term of this lease. The Lessee shall thoroughly paint all outside iron work about said premises at lease once in two years, it being intended that the purview of this clause shall extend to all repairs and renewals of whatsoever sort, which a judicious owner of said premises would make for the benefit of the same, including repainting, repairs of roof, sewerage, steam apparatus, elevators, gas fixtures, plumbing, and every other sort of repairs or renewals not herein specifically set down.

Source: Park, Leopold & Beyer, *West's Legal Forms,* Vol. 22 and Vol. 23. West Publishing Co., St. Paul, Minn. (1986)

APPENDIX B

Sample Mortgage Clauses

FUTURE ADVANCES CLAUSE

This mortgage contract provides for additional advances which may be made at the option of the Mortgagee and secured by the mortgage, and it is agreed that in the event of such advances the amount thereof may be added to the mortgage debt and shall increase the unpaid balance of the note hereby secured by the amount of such advance and shall be a part of said note indebtedness under all of the terms of said note and this contract as fully as if a new such note and contract were executed and delivered. An Additional Advance Agreement may be given and accepted for such advance and provision may be made for different monthly payments and a different interest rate and other express modifications of the contract, but in all other respects this contract shall remain in full force and effect as to said indebtedness, including all advances.
(West Legal Forms; vol. 22, sec. 63.26)

AFTER ACQUIRED PROPERTY CLAUSE

Together with all fixtures, chattels and articles of personal property now or hereafter attached to or used in connection with said premises, including but not limited to furnaces, boilers, oil burners, radiators and piping, plumbing and bathroom fixtures, refrigerators, air conditioning and sprinkling systems, sinks, stoves, ranges, awning, screens, gas and electric fixtures, kitchen cabinets, incinerators, plants and shrubs and all other equipment and machinery, appliances, fitting and fixtures of every kind in or used in the operation of the building(s) standing on said premises, together with any and all replacements thereof and additions thereto.
(West Legal Forms; vol. 22, sec. 63.14)

ACCELERATION CLAUSE

That the whole of said principal sum and interest shall become due at the option of the mortgagee; after default in the payment of any installment of principal or of interest for _______ days; or after default in the payment of any tax, water rate, sewer rent or assessment for _______ days after notice and demand; or after default after notice and demand either in assigning and delivering the policies insuring the buildings against loss by fire or in reimbursing and mortgagee for premiums paid on such insurance, as hereinbefore provided.
(West Legal Forms; vol. 22, sec. 63.6)

DUE ON TRANSFER CLAUSE

In the event that the mortgagors convey the title (legal, equitable or both) to all or any portion of said premises or in the event that such title becomes vested in a person other than the mortgagors in any manner whatsoever except under the power of eminent domain, that in any such case the entire unpaid principle of the note secured hereby with accrued interest thereon shall, at the option of the mortgagee at any time thereafter, become immediately due and payable without notice.
(West Legal Forms; vol. 22, sec. 63.69)

APPENDIX C

Report of the Presidential Advisory Group on Agency (Partial)

HISTORY/BACKGROUND

1985 Agency Task Force Report

In 1985, the President of the NATIONAL ASSOCIATION OF REALTORS®' appointed an Agency Task Force. This Task force was charged with studying the agency issue and formulating policy recommendations designed to reduce real estate brokers' potential liability for breaches of their agency obligations, and also to help dispel buyers' and sellers' confusion concerning the nature of a real estate broker's agency duties to his client.

From its research and deliberations, the Task Force made the following five factual conclusions:

1. There is an immediate and pressing need for clarification of the agency status of the real estate broker/salesperson vis-a-vis real estate seller and real estate buyer.
2. Identification of the agency status of the real estate broker/salesperson vis-a-vis the real estate seller and real estate buyer should occur at the first meeting between the broker/salesperson and the buyer concerning the buyer's specific real estate needs.
3. In those states where specific identification of the agency status of the real estate broker/salesperson vis-a-vis the real estate seller and real estate buyer is deemed desirable, identification should be mandated by law or regulation.
4. Disclosure of the agency status of the real estate broker/salesperson which is mandated should take the form of a standard Notice To Buyers.
5. The legislation and/or regulation mandating disclosure of the agency status of the broker/salesperson should also include incentives (a) to cause agency agreements between broker and

> buyer as well as broker and seller to be in writing and (b) to require the knowledge and consent of all parties when an agent of one party compensates the agent of the other party to a transaction.

Its ultimate recommendation was a disclosure program, to be developed and adopted on a state-by-state basis, that would require real estate brokers to disclose to prospective purchasers their agency status. To this end, the Task Force created suggested legislative and regulatory language to implement its conclusions.

Formation of Current Presidential Advisory Group on Agency

With the evolution of agency disclosure regulations and laws has come an increasing awareness among buyers and sellers of whom the real estate broker represents. The public and the real estate industry are becoming increasingly aware of alternative forms of agency relationships being practiced in the marketplace today. Concern has been expressed by NAR members regarding their ability to properly meet the developing desires of both buyers and sellers for representation in real estate transactions while working within the framework of traditional agency practice. Criticism has been directed at NAR's policies and procedures for not accommodating these alternative agency relationships.

On April 30, 1991, at NAR's Mid-Year Meeting, the Board of Directors approved a recommendation from the Professional Standards Committee that a Presidential Advisory Group on Agency be created to study various agency issues. In order to address these concerns of the NAR membership and to assess the challenges, problems and opportunities presented by the evolving agency issue, NAR's President appointed this Group. The Group was selected with the intent of bringing together members with a balanced perspective based on their background, types of brokerage experience and knowledge of varying agency practices that would help NAR further develop its policy on agency.

The twenty-two members of the Group represent a broad cross-section of the real estate industry. The Group is composed of commercial and industrial brokers, residential brokers, buyer's agents, real estate counselors, real estate educators, real estate regulators, property managers, appraisers, agency litigation consultants and expert witnesses, and executive officers and legal staff of state and local associations of REALTORS®. The members serve on many NAR Committees and are members of several affiliate organizations. They come from nineteen states representing all thirteen of the NAR regions and are active in market areas ranging from 60,000 to 2.5 million in population.

NAR's Group received staff support from the Legal Affairs Division, the State and Local Government Affairs Division and the Board Policy and Programs Division of the NATIONAL ASSOCIATION OF REALTORS®.

Presidential Advisory Group on Agency Charge

The charge of the Group was as follows:

> To determine alternative forms of agency relationships that are being or could be practiced in the real estate marketplace today.

- What are those alternatives?
- What are the benefits and weaknesses of each type?
- Are there impediments to those alternatives within our association or in the marketplace?

To recommend structural/policy changes needed to remove the impediments to alternative agency relationships where appropriate.

PROCESS

Methodology

At its first meeting in August, 1991, the Group decided that in order to fulfill its charge, the best method of information gathering would be to conduct a series of hearings. The Group felt that this format would be most appropriate for two reasons. First, it permitted the Group to undertake extensive information gathering to insure that all real estate industry interests and disciplines would have an opportunity for input. Second, as a result of this information collection process, the analysis of NAR's agency policies and the development of specific recommendations would be conducted with full understanding of the legal and ethical issues involved in agency relationships.

The hearings were held in 1991 and early 1992. The individuals and organizations invited to testify included buyer agency advocates, single agency advocates, state associations of REALTORS®, relocation companies, real estate attorneys, real estate educators, real estate regulators and a variety of real estate firms, including those offering exclusive buyer's agency, "traditional" agency operations, independents and franchises. The Group also reviewed a variety of individual states' agency legislation, industry publications, newspaper articles, real estate training manuals, surveys, reports and written testimony submitted by interested groups and individuals. After completing these hearings, the Group conducted their deliberations, analyzed the issues and drafted its final recommendations.

Types of Practice in the Marketplace Today

Currently the majority of real estate firms appear to be practicing one of the following types of agency relationships:

- Seller agency exclusively
- Buyer agency exclusively
- Seller agency and buyer agency, with disclosed dual agency for in-house sales
- Single agency

There are various advantages/disadvantages to each of these forms of agency relationships, some of which are highlighted below:

Seller Agency Exclusively

Advantages:

Traditional practice thus comfortable to most agents

Historical method of compensation in cooperating sales

Promoted through the MLS where a mandatory offer of subagency exists

Accommodates the sale of a company's own listings (in-house sale)

Disadvantages:

Increasing desire of consumers for buyer representation

Liability for the actions of the subagent flows to the Seller and Seller's agent

High potential for undisclosed dual agency

When a seller's subagent works with a buyer it results in an "unnatural" working relationship

Buyer Agency Exclusively

Advantages:

Eliminates the liability to the seller and listing agent for the actions of a sub-agent

Minimizes the possibility for a dual agency conflict

Promotes a more natural relationship for agents working with buyers

Agents know who they represent

Buyers have full representation

When broker's use exclusive buyer's contract, insures loyalty of the buyer

Disadvantages:

Focusing on one side of the transaction results in a limited client base

Resistance within the industry to new practices

Introduces compensation issues (1) as to whether seller or buyer pays buyer agent's fees and (2) whether listing agent will share his compensation

Lack of available training and education

Potential for new procuring cause issues

Potential conflict when two clients provide two offers on the same property at the same time

Broker has increased liability to buyer resulting from breach of fiduciary duties

If compensation is based on a percentage of the sales price, potential for a conflict of interest exists

Seller Agency and Buyer Agency with Disclosed Dual Agency for In-house Sales

Advantages:

Eliminates the possibility of undisclosed dual agency problems

More natural for agents and less disruptive to current practice

Reduces liability:

Seller and listing agent not liable for subagents

Buyer's agent not liable for acts of listing agent

Listing agent not liable for acts of buyer's agent

Disadvantages:

Under dual agency situations, neither buyer nor seller have full range of agency representation

Lack of available training and education

Disclosed dual agency is not well understood

Potential inability to sell in-house listing to a buyer who wants representation but refuses to allow dual agency

Single Agency, Whether Listing or Selling

Advantages:

Brokers can offer both seller and buyer agency

Allows full representation of client

Disadvantages:

Problems arise when buyer client wants to buy a company listing

Buyer cannot have agent representation if buying a company listing

Potential for undisclosed dual agency

Economic implications if company adopts policy not to show company listings to buyer clients

During its investigation into these various types of agency relationships, the Group identified the following impediments which exist within NAR and/or the real estate industry itself:

- Real estate practice is not always consistent with agency law
- NAR's MLS policy mandates an offer of subagency
- Lack of consumer and industry education and understanding of all alternative agency relationships

- Some specialty areas, such as property management, have differing needs with regards to agency representation
- Traditional method of compensation inhibits the use of various agency alternatives
- External factors such as appraisal and financial areas do not accommodate actual practices in the area of compensation
- Licensing structure allows for variations in state laws
- Liability issues vary with each agency alternative
- Professional standards problems in the following areas:

  Cooperation

  Procuring cause and

  Seller representation orientation of the Code of Ethics
- Resistance to change within the real estate industry

RECOMMENDATIONS

Findings of Fact

After careful review and analysis of the input received by the Group, it has reached the following findings of fact. These findings serve as a basis for the Group's recommendations.

- The day-to-day business practices of many real estate licensees do not conform to a strict interpretation of the law of agency. For example, many salespeople working as subagents for the seller develop de facto agency relationships with buyers.
- NAR's Code of Ethics is written with an emphasis towards seller agency.
- Buyer's agents have traditionally been more prevalent in firms that specialize in commercial, industrial, and farm and land brokerage.
- Consumers lack knowledge regarding the structure of the real estate industry and, in particular, agency relationships.
- The mandatory offer of subagency inhibits change from traditional agency practices.
- In many market areas, buyer agency relationships are not established in writing with exclusive buyer agency contracts.
- In some cases consumers do not understand the agency disclosures given to them.
- The creation of an agency relationship is practically unavoidable when the customer is a relative, close friend or business associate.

- Most real estate companies do not have a written, well defined company agency policy.
- There is much confusion/lack of understanding within NAR's membership regarding alternative agency relationships and how these practices might be incorporated into their offices.
- Unintended dual agency occurs in the marketplace with some frequency.
- Buyer's agency has not found acceptance in all market areas as demonstrated by a lack of cooperation especially in the area of compensation.
- State laws and licensing structures demand flexibility of NAR policies and practices to accommodate the state's varying needs.
- Agency disclosure is often limited to only that agency representation the broker is offering. Listing brokers rarely disclose to sellers: a) liability flowing from offers of subagency; b) the broker's office policy regarding cooperation with buyer's agent; c) compensation policies with cooperating brokers; and d) the full range of agency relationships available/legal within their state.
- Properly disclosed and consensual dual agency is prevalent in some markets and has not resulted in increased litigation or consumer complaints.
- NAR's guidelines for procuring cause disputes do not address buyer representation.

Framework for Solutions

The Group believed that any recommendations for change of industry practices or NAR policies must meet the following criteria in order for them to be meaningful and find acceptance:

- Protect freedom of choice of agency practices for REALTOR® members;
- Protect freedom of choice of agency relationships for buyers and sellers;
- Reflect the realities of today's marketplace;
- Preserve the ability for real estate companies to have in-house sales;
- Recognize the diversity and needs of the disciplines within NAR's membership;
- Establish a level playing field by eliminating barriers to competition for all forms of relationships;
- Maintain adequate accountability in brokerage practice to insure proper regulation of the industry and provide consumer protection; and
- Allow for future evolution of agency relationships.

Recommendations with Rationale

Recommendation #1

NAR's multiple listing policy shall be modified to delete the mandatory offer of subagency and make offers of subagency optional. Participants submitting listings to the MLS must, however, offer cooperation to other MLS participants in the form of subagency or cooperation with buyer agents or both. All offers of subagency or cooperation made through an MLS must include an offer of compensation.

Historically, NAR defined a multiple listing service (MLS) as a facility for the orderly correlation and dissemination of listing information among the participants so that they may better serve their clients and the public. That definition was later augmented to add that the MLS is a means by which one participant makes a blanket unilateral offer of subagency to other participants.

Defining an MLS exclusively in terms of the subagency relationships formed among the participants served the industry well for many years. That definition did not, however, take into account the role played by the buyer's agents. Although NAR's policy has always required that a buyer's agent be permitted to participate in a Board-owned MLS, the definition of an MLS has never accommodated a cooperative relationship between a listing broker and a buyer's agent. Rather, NAR's policy requires that a listing broker offer subagency as a condition of placing a listing in the MLS.

Some listing brokers may only wish to extend offers to buyer's agents to cooperate in the sale of a property. In order to accommodate this practice, the policy mandating an offer of subagency should be modified. MLS participants should be allowed to offer cooperation to other participants. Such cooperation could take the form of an offer of subagency or an offer of cooperation to buyer's agents or both.

Such a modification in policy was reviewed by NAR's counsel and was deemed to pose no significant risk to the ability to defend the requirement of membership as a condition of access to a Board's MLS.

Recommendation #2

NAR shall encourage State Associations to achieve through legislation or regulation state mandated agency disclosure which requires that all licensees provide timely, meaningful, written disclosure to consumers of all possible types of agency relationships (i.e., buyer agency, seller agency, disclosed dual agency, not types of listing agreements) available under state law and the most significant implications of choosing one type over another. This type of disclosure would permit consumers to make informed choices.

Timely: Disclosure to clients must take place prior to the time in which a listing agreement or contract is entered.

Disclosure to customers must take place prior to the time a licensee enters into substantive discussions with the customer regarding his real estate needs and his financial capabilities.

Meaningful: The disclosure must include all legal forms of agency relationships available under state law, even if the broker does not, as a matter of office policy, offer all of those agency relationships.

Typically the choices would be:

- representation of seller only;
- representation of buyer only; or
- representation of both buyer and seller as a disclosed dual agent for in-house transactions.

Sellers must be advised of the broker's office policies with respect to cooperation with other brokers if such policies could have more than an insubstantial impact on the marketing of the property or the principal's exposure to legal liability. For example, sellers should be informed whether the listing broker offers subagency to other brokers and about the legal liability that flows to the seller from subagency relationships; whether the listing broker cooperates with the buyer agents; or whether the listing broker may operate as a disclosed dual agent.

If a broker's policy permits it to function as a disclosed dual agent, he should so advise a seller at the time the listing is taken and obtain preliminary approval from the seller as to whether he would entertain a request from the agent to function as a dual agent. A broker should not, however, obtain blanket consent from the principal at that time to function as a dual agent. Informed consent to perform as a dual agent must be obtained from the principal only after the specific purchaser with whom the broker also seeks to establish an agency relationship has been identified. Unless otherwise provided by law[1], this would take place prior to the time the property is shown. If the consent from the seller is verbal, it should be confirmed in writing at the time the purchase offer is submitted.

The buyer's informed consent is also necessary in order to create a disclosed dual agency relationship. The buyer must understand and agree that his agent will also serve as the agent to the seller in the transaction. This understanding and agreement should be confirmed in writing by the buyer.

Disclosed dual agency is a viable agency alternative but only if full disclosure is made and all parties consent following such disclosure; similar to that as practiced in the legal profession.

Written: Each state should develop a standard disclosure form(s) that would be mandated for use by all licensees within the state. Disclosures should be mandatory in residential, commercial/industrial and property management/leasing transactions. The promulgation of a state form will provide licensees who use it with assurance that it is adequate, thereby insulating them from legal challenges over the sufficiency of the disclosure document.

NAR should amend Standards of Practice 21-13 and 21-14 to require that the disclosures be in writing.

Recommendation #3

NAR's policies shall be modified within one year to eliminate the emphasis on listing brokers and subagents and to remove any barriers to practice of alternative agency relationships.

The Code of Ethics and Multiple Listing Policy of NAR were developed at times in NAR's history before the spotlight was focused on agency relationships and before the increase in the practice of buyer agency. As a result, many of the policies reflect what could be perceived to be a bias toward the traditional agency relationship with brokers as agents of sellers utilizing subagents in cooperative transactions. Issues stemming from the practice of buyer agency are rarely addressed. This overall im-

[1]The California statute requires notice "as soon as practicable" and further requires confirmation of the dual agency relationship in the contract to purchase and sell or in a separate written document executed by the seller, buyer and the agent no later than the time the sales contract is signed by the buyer and seller, respectively.

balance needs to be corrected. Clear guidance is needed by all REALTOR® members regardless of the type of agency relationships they choose to practice. For example:

- Article 7

  Standards of Practice 7-1 and 7-2 should be expanded to address the presentation of counteroffers.

- Article 9

  Require disclosure by listing agents to clients of potential subagency liabilities.

  Standard of practice 9-5 should address compensation to any cooperating agent, whether subagent or buyer's agent.

- Article 11

  Develop a standard of practice defining "level of competent service" in light of the responsibilities of a buyer agent.

  Develop a Standard of Practice defining a field of competency for all disciplines such as buyer representation, tenant representation, appraisal, counseling or commercial brokerage.

- Article 19

  Determine whether Standard of Practice 19-1 applies only to a listing broker, and if yes, so state.

  Clarify Standard of Practice 19-5 to address whether words like "bought" fit the "true picture" test.

- Article 21

  Develop Standards of Practice similar to 21-3 and 21-8 to address solicitation of buyers who are subject to an exclusive representation agreement.

  Modify Standard of Practice 21-6 to speak in terms of clients and agents, not only property owners and their agents.

  Modify Standard of Practice 21-7 to reference "clients" rather than only sellers who are not subject to an exclusive agreement.

  Modify Standard of Practice 21-10 to address solicitation of "clients" in general or add language to address buyers and prospective buyers.

  Modify Standard of Practice 21-11 to include any buyer-client subject to an exclusive agreement.

  Determine whether Standard of Practice 21-15 is intended to include buyer agency as a "different type of service" and clarify accordingly.

- Article 22

  Clarify Article 22's obligations regarding negotiations with a buyer who is exclusively represented.

  Determine whether there are corresponding duties of buyer's agents under Standard of Practice 22-2 that apply when presenting counteroffers. Determine whether this Standard of Practice is appropriate when both parties are represented. Determine whether the Standard of Practice is appropriate in multiple offer situations.

Develop a Standard of Practice reinforcing Article 22's obligation to cooperation with buyer's agents and tenant's representatives.

- The procuring cause guidelines, "Arbitration Guidelines (Suggested Factors For Consideration by a Hearing Panel in Arbitration)", need to be augmented to address situations involving buyer's agents.

Recommendation #4

NAR shall encourage real estate firms to have a written company policy addressing agency relationships.

There is evidence that few real estate brokers have established a written office policy on agency. If they do exist, most office guidelines focus on the traditional listing/subagent relationship. Each brokerage firm should review all forms of agency relationships and make a conscious decision on which agency relationship best reflects the way it chooses to do business. Careful emphasis should be placed on the firm's decisions regarding in-house sales and sales/purchases from the personal account of the licensees, their friends or relatives. These areas pose the most conflicts within an office by encouraging undisclosed dual agency relationships. Undisclosed dual agency can result in suits for breach of fiduciary duties, rescission, damages, and regulatory discipline, including loss of license. An office policy should provide clear guidelines to broker and sales associates as to their duties and obligations in the selected agency structure.

It is critical that a clear understanding of agency relationships exist between the buyer and the agent working with the buyer. When a salesperson is working as a buyer's agent, it would be preferable for them to reduce to writing the terms of their relationship by, for example, use of an exclusive buyer agency agreement.

Recommendation #5

NAR shall emphasize the importance of education and training for all real estate licensees on the topic of agency and implement programs to accomplish this goal. State regulatory bodies that require prelicensing courses and core continuing education programs for licensees are encouraged to make agency programs part of the core requirement.

From the information gathered, it is clear that NAR's members and other licensees lack understanding regarding alternative agency relationships and are requesting education in this area. In order to achieve a full integration of agency practices in the marketplace, there must be full understanding of the issues by all real estate licensees. Education and training become the key to this evolution of agency relationships. Several ideas for educational activities include the following:

- That the NAR Legal Liability Series training program on agency, "Who's My Client," be updated to encompass education on the various agency relationships, including their duties and obligations, in existence in the marketplace today.

- That state/local associations be encouraged to utilize the NAR training program or to develop their own agency program for their members at the prelicensing, beginners and advanced levels of education.
- That the training program be promoted to the individual members through NAR, State and Local Associations.
- That the NAR training program be provided to professional liability insurance carriers in order to negotiate education premium credits.
- That the Graduate, REALTOR® Institute include, as one of its requirements, an element on agency.
- That education programs, including one on agency relationships, be incorporated into the menu of services provided through the new multi-board management program.
- That agency training be an educational program at all the NAR major meetings.
- That education on agency be encouraged through articles included in the NAR publications.
- That NAR encourage and assist the Institutes, Societies and Councils in providing agency education within their own structures.
- That training programs encourage, as a sound business practice, the sharing of compensation freely.

These educational endeavors should not be limited to only the real estate industry. Informed consent by definition requires that a consumer be knowledgeable about his choices of agency relationships. Educational products and programs for consumers also need to be developed and implemented. State and local associations may choose to develop consumer targeted brochures themselves or in conjunction with their state regulatory bodies.

Recommendation #6

NAR should use and encourage the use of the terms and definitions set forth in the Glossary uniformly throughout NAR's policies, programs and products.

It is clear that various terminology and definitions exist regarding agency relationships. This inconsistency in the language impedes education and knowledge. Therefore, NAR is encouraged to adopt those terms and definitions found in the Glossary and to use them in all NAR's publications, products and training programs. In addition, all the NAR policies should be reviewed and revised accordingly to comply with this terminology.

Future Developments

One of the goals of this report is to avoid establishing policies that would impede the development of new forms of representation. One example is the recent debate surrounding the "facilitator" concept which is currently being considered by some states.

By definition, facilitators would not establish an agency relationship with either the buyer or the seller. Instead, they would act as middlepersons owing no fiduciary obligation to either party. In this sense, they are true "brokers."

We believe that many of the implications of this concept and its future development remain unknown and require further study.

The Group conducted a preliminary examination of the "facilitator" relationship and made the following observations:

Advantages:

Reduces confusion as to who represents whom; there is no true "agent" relationship as defined in common law

May reduce liability by eliminating fiduciary duties

Disadvantages:

Buyers and sellers will not have their own representation

Problem with multiple purchase offers

Cannot switch from an agency relationship to a facilitator (e.g., originally employed as a listing agent with the corresponding fiduciary duties and when a buyer comes along, you cannot easily abandon this role to become a facilitator)

If compensation is based on a percentage of sale price, potential exists for conflict of interest

Liability: no case law established

Economic implications are unknown

Impediments:

Ability to obtain E&O Insurance

Requires many states to change license law and/or regulations

Difficulty integrating with existing agency relationships in the marketplace

Question regarding structuring of broker's compensation

Traditional MLS rules

Code of Ethics speaks in terms of agency relationships

Lack of knowledge, and resistance within the brokerage community, regulators, legislatures, the legal community and buyers/sellers.

We believe that NAR should work with interested groups and conduct a comprehensive study of the facilitator concept and provide information detailing its ramifications to State Associations for their consideration. Furthermore, NAR should offer assistance to State Associations who choose to explore the facilitator concept.

CONCLUSION

The recommendations in this report are founded on the principles of informed consent and freedom of choice. Buyers and sellers should be able to select from a range of options that relationship which best meets their needs. Likewise, real estate brokers should be able to choose which type of agency relationship(s) they wish to practice. This process of informed consent will also help to eliminate the hazards of undisclosed or accidental dual agency. These recommendations are designed to enhance the development of new relationships, not stifle their progress and will assist REALTORS® in responding to changes within the marketplace.

State laws, NAR policies and the mind-set of real estate licensees are often ill-prepared to deal with evolutions in the industry. When the 1986 Agency Task Force report was adopted by NAR, many felt that any type of agency disclosure was unnecessary and cumbersome. Today, some six years later, 44 states have mandatory agency disclosure and many states are now considering complete revisions of their state agency laws that would have been unimaginable just a few years ago. We believe this type of change is inevitable and desirable.

Although some of the recommendations are aimed at modifying NAR's policies and procedures to accommodate freedom of choice, the majority require action at the state and local level and by individual real estate offices. The NATIONAL ASSOCIATION OF REALTORS®, the Voice for Real Estate, should take a leading role in creating an environment that is responsive and adaptable to changes and growth in the industry. We believe the recommendations presented in this report support this concept.

APPENDIX D

Amendments to the Code of Ethics and Standards of Practice Effective January, 1993

National Association of REALTORS

NOTE TO READERS: This material is presented to illustrate the profound impact that changes in the legal environment are having on the methods of doing business in the real estate industry.

Where the word REALTORS® is used in this Code and Preamble, it shall be deemed to include REALTOR-ASSOCIATE®s.

While the Code of Ethics establishes obligations that may be higher than those mandated by law, in any instance where the Code of Ethics and the law conflict, the obligations of the law must take precedence.

PREAMBLE . . .

Under all is the land. Upon its wise utilization and widely allocated ownership depend the survival and growth of free institutions and of our civilization. REALTORS® should recognize that the interests of the nation and its citizens require the highest and best use of the land and the widest distribution of land ownership. They require the creation of adequate housing, the building of functioning cities, the development of productive industries and farms, and the preservation of a healthful environment.

Such interests impose obligations beyond those of ordinary commerce. They impose grave social responsibility and a patriotic duty to which REALTORS® should dedicate themselves, and for which they should be diligent in preparing themselves. REALTORS®, therefore, are zealous to maintain and improve the standards of their calling and share with their fellow REALTORS® a common responsibility for its integrity and honor. The term REALTOR® has come to connote competency, fairness, and high integrity resulting from adherence to a lofty ideal of moral conduct in business relations. No inducement of profit and no instruction from clients ever can justify departure from this ideal.

In the interpretation of this obligation, REALTORS® can take no safer guide than that which has been handed down through the centuries, embodied in the Golden Rule, "Whatsoever ye would that others should do to you, do ye even so to them."

Accepting this standard as their own, REALTORS® pledge to observe its spirit in all of their activities and to conduct their business in accordance with the tenets set forth below.

Articles 1 through 5 are aspirational and establish ideals REALTORS® should strive to attain.

ARTICLE 1

In justice to those who place their interests in a real estate professional's care, REALTORS® should endeavor to become and remain informed on matters affecting real estate in their community, the state, and nation ~~so that they may be able to contribute responsibly to public thinking on such matters.~~ (Amended 11/92)

ARTICLE 2

~~In justice to those who place their interests in a real estate professional's care, REALTORS® should endeavor always to be informed regarding laws, proposed legislation, governmental regulations, public policies, and current market conditions in order to be in a position to advise their clients properly.~~

In the interest of promoting cooperation and enhancing their professional image, REALTORS® are encouraged to refrain from unsolicited criticism of other real estate practitioners and, if an opinion is sought about another real estate practitioner, their business or their business practices, any opinion should be offered in an objective, professional manner. (Amended 11/92)

ARTICLE 3

REALTORS® should endeavor to eliminate in their communities any practices which could be damaging to the public or bring discredit to the real estate profession. REALTORS® should assist the governmental agency charged with regulating the practices of brokers and sales licensees in their states. (Amended 11/87)

ARTICLE 4

To prevent dissension and misunderstanding and to assure better service to the owner, REALTORS® should urge the exclusive listing of property unless contrary to the best interest of the owner. (Amended 11/87)

ARTICLE 5

In the best interests of society, of their associates, and their own businesses, REALTORS® should willingly share with other REALTORS® the lessons of their experience and study for the benefit of the public, and should be loyal to the Board of REALTORS® of their community and active in its work.

Articles 6 through 23 establish specific obligations. Failure to observe these requirements subject REALTORS® to disciplinary action.

ARTICLE 6

REALTORS® shall seek no unfair advantage over other REALTORS® and shall conduct their business so as to avoid controversies with other REALTORS®. (Amended 11/87)

• Standard of Practice 6-1

REALTORS® shall not misrepresent the availability of access to show or inspect a listed property. (Cross-reference Article 22.) (Amended 11/87)

~~• Standard of Practice 6-2~~

~~Article 6 is not intended to prohibit otherwise ethical, aggressive or innovative business practices. "Controversies", as used in Article 6, does not relate to disputes over commissions or divisions of commissions.~~ (Adopted 4/92)

ARTICLE 7

~~In accepting employment~~ When representing a buyer, seller, landlord, tenant, or other client as an agent, REALTORS® pledge themselves to protect and promote the interests of their client. This obligation of absolute fidelity to the client's interests is primary, but it does not relieve REALTORS® of their obligation to treat ~~fairly~~ all parties ~~to the transaction~~ honestly. When serving a buyer, seller, landlord, tenant or other party in a non-agency capacity, REALTORS® remain obligated to treat all parties honestly. (Amended 11/92)

• Standard of Practice 7-1(a)

REALTORS® shall submit offers and counter-offers as quickly as possible. (Adopted 11/92)

• Standard of Practice 7-1(b)

~~Unless agreed otherwise in writing,~~ When acting as listing brokers, REALTORS® shall continue to submit to the seller/landlord all offers and counter-offers until closing or execution of a lease unless the seller/landlord has waived this obligation in writing. ~~Unless the REALTOR® and the seller agree otherwise,~~ REALTORS® shall not be obligated to continue to market the property after an offer has been accepted by the seller/landlord. ~~Unless the subsequent offer is contingent upon the termination of an existing contract,~~ REALTORS® shall recommend that the sellers/landlords obtain the advice of legal counsel prior to acceptance of a subsequent offer except where the acceptance is contingent on the termination of the pre-existing purchase contract or lease. (Cross-reference Article 17.) (Amended 11/92)

• Standard of Practice 7-1(c)

REALTORS® acting as agents of buyers/tenants shall submit to buyers/tenants all offers and counter-offers until acceptance but have no obligation to continue to show properties to their clients after an offer has been accepted unless otherwise agreed in writing. REALTORS® acting as agents of buyers/tenants shall recommend that buyers/tenants obtain the advice of legal counsel if there is a question as to whether a pre-existing contract has been terminated. (Adopted 11/92)

• Standard of Practice 7-2

~~REALTORS®, acting as listing brokers, shall submit all offers to the seller as quickly as possible.~~
REALTORS®, when seeking to become a buyer/tenant representative, shall not mislead buyers or tenants as to savings or other benefits that might be realized through use of the REALTOR®'s services. (Amended 11/92)

• Standard of Practice 7-3

REALTORS®, in attempting to secure a listing, shall not deliberately mislead the owner as to market value.

• Standard of Practice 7-4

(Refer to Standard of Practice 22-1, which also relates to Article 7, Code of Ethics.)

• Standard of Practice 7-5

(Refer to Standard of Practice 22-2, which also relates to Article 7, Code of Ethics.)

• Standard of Practice 7-6

REALTORS®, when acting as principals in a real estate transaction, ~~cannot avoid their responsibilities under~~ remain obligated by the duties imposed by the Code of Ethics. (Amended 11/92)

• Standard of Practice 7-7

REALTORS® may represent the seller/landlord and buyer/tenant in the same transaction only after full disclosure to and with informed consent of both parties. (Cross-reference Article 9) (Adopted 11/92)

• Standard of Practice 7-8

The obligation of REALTORS® to preserve confidential information provided by their clients continues after the termination of the agency relationship. REALTORS® shall not knowingly, during or following the termination of a professional relationship with their client:

1. reveal confidential information of the client; or
2. use confidential information of the client to the disadvantage of the client; or
3. use confidential information of the client for the REALTORS®' advantage or the advantage of a third party unless the client consents after full disclosure unless:
   a. required by court order; or
   b. it is the intention of the client to commit a crime and the information is necessary to prevent the crime; or
   c. necessary to defend the REALTOR® or REALTOR®'s employees or associates against an accusation of wrongful conduct. (Cross-reference Article 9) (Adopted 11/92)

ARTICLE 8

In a transaction, REALTORS® shall not accept compensation from more than one party, even if permitted by law, without disclosure to all parties and the informed consent of the REALTOR®'s client or clients. ~~the full knowledge of all parties to the transaction.~~ (Amended 11/92)

ARTICLE 9

REALTORS® shall avoid exaggeration, misrepresentation, or concealment of pertinent facts relating to the property or the transaction. REALTORS® shall not, however, be obligated to discover latent defects in the property, or to advise on matters outside the scope of their real estate license, or to disclose facts which are confidential under the scope of agency duties owed to their clients. (Amended 11/92)

• Standard of Practice 9-1

REALTORS® shall not be parties to the naming of a false consideration in any document, unless it be the naming of an obviously nominal consideration.

• Standard of Practice 9-2

(Refer to Standard Practice 21-3, which also relates to Article 9, Code of Ethics.)

• Standard of Practice 9-3

(Refer to Standard of Practice 7-3, which also relates to Article 9, Code of Ethics.)

• Standard of Practice 9-4

REALTORS® shall not offer a service described as "free of charge" when the rendering of a service is contingent on the obtaining of a benefit such as a listing or commission.

• Standard of Practice 9-5

REALTORS® shall, with respect to the subagency of another REALTOR®, timely communicate any change of compensation for subagency services to the other REALTOR® prior to the time such REALTOR® produces a prospective buyer who has signed an offer to purchase the property for which the subagency has been offered through MLS or otherwise by the listing agency.

• Standard of Practice 9-6

REALTORS® shall disclose their REALTOR® status and contemplated personal interest, if any, when seeking information from another REALTOR® concerning real property. ~~for which the other REALTOR® is an agent or subagent~~ (Cross-reference to Article 12) (Amended 11/92)

• Standard of Practice 9-7

The offering of premiums, prizes, merchandise discounts or other inducements to list, ~~or~~ sell, purchase, or lease is not, in itself, unethical even if receipt of the benefit is contingent on listing, ~~or~~ purchasing, or leasing through the REALTOR® making the offer. However, REALTORS® must exercise care and candor in any such advertising or other public or private representations so that any party interested in receiving or otherwise benefiting from the REALTOR®'s offer will have clear, thorough, advance understanding of all the terms and conditions of the offer. The offering of any inducements to do business is subject to the limitations and restrictions of state law and the ethical obligations established by Article 9, as interpreted by any applicable Standard of Practice. (Amended 11/92)

• Standard of Practice 9-8

REALTORS® shall be obligated to discover and disclose adverse factors reasonably apparent to someone with expertise in only those areas required by their real estate licensing authority. Article 9 does not impose upon the REALTOR® the obligation of expertise in other professional or technical disciplines. (Cross-reference Article 11.) (Amended 11/86)

• Standard of Practice 9-9

REALTORS®, acting as listing brokers, have an affirmative obligation to disclose the existence of dual or variable rate commission arrangements (i.e., listings where one amount of commission is payable if the listing broker's firm is the procuring cause of sale and a different amount of commission is payable if the sale results through the efforts of the seller or a cooperating broker). The listing broker shall, as soon as practical, disclose the existence of such arrangements to potential cooperating brokers and shall, in response to inquiries from cooperating brokers, disclose the differential that would result in a cooperative transaction or in a sale that results through the efforts of the seller. (Amended 11/91)

• Standard of Practice 9-10(a)

When entering into listing contracts, REALTORS® must advise sellers/landlords of:

1. the REALTOR®'s general company policies regarding cooperation with subagents, buyer/tenant agents, or both;
2. the fact that buyer/tenant agents, even if compensated by the listing broker, or by the seller/landlord will represent the interests of buyers/tenants; and
3. any potential for the listing broker to act as a disclosed dual agent, e.g. buyer/tenant agent. (Adopted 11/92)

• Standard of Practice 9-10(b)

When entering into contracts to represent buyers/tenants, REALTORS® must advise potential clients of:

1. the REALTOR®'s general company policies regarding cooperation with other firms; and
2. any potential for the buyer/tenant representative to act as a disclosed dual agent, e.g. listing broker, subagent, landlord's agent, etc. (Adopted 11/92)

• Standard of Practice 9-11

Factors defined as "non-material" by law or regulation or which are expressly referenced in law or regulation as not being subject to disclosure are considered not "pertinent" for purposes of Article 9. (Adopted 11/92)

ARTICLE 10

REALTORS® shall not deny equal professional services to any person for reasons of race, color, religion, sex, handicap, familial status, or national origin. REALTORS® shall not be parties to any plan or agreement to discriminate against a person or persons on the basis of race, color, religion, sex, handicap, familial status, or national origin. (Amended 11/89)

ARTICLE 11

REALTORS® are expected to provide a level of competent service in keeping with the standards of practice in those fields in which the REALTOR® customarily engages.

REALTORS® shall not undertake to provide specialized professional services concerning a type of property or service that is outside their field of competence unless they engage the assistance of one who is competent on such types of property or service, or unless the facts are fully disclosed to the client. Any persons engaged to provide such assistance shall be so identified to the client and their contribution to the assignment should be set forth.

REALTORS® shall refer to the Standards of Practice of the National Association as to the degree of competence that a client has a right to expect the REALTOR® to possess, taking into consideration the complexity of the problem, the availability of expert assistance, and the opportunities for experience, available to the REALTOR®.

• Standard of Practice 11-1

Whenever REALTORS® submit an oral or written opinion of the value of real property for a fee, their opinion shall be supported by a memorandum in the file or an appraisal report, either of which shall include as a minimum the following:

1. Limiting conditions
2. Any existing or contemplated interest
3. Defined value
4. Date applicable
5. The estate appraised
6. A description of the property
7. The basis of the reasoning including applicable market data and/or capitalization computation

This report or memorandum shall be available to the Professional Standards Committee for a period of at least two years (beginning subsequent to final determination of the court if the appraisal is involved in litigation) to ensure compliance with Article 11 of the Code of Ethics of the NATIONAL ASSOCIATION OF REALTORS®.

• Standard of Practice 11-2

REALTORS® shall not undertake to make an appraisal when their employment or fee is contingent upon the amount of appraisal.

• Standard of Practice 11-3

REALTORS® engaged in real estate securities and syndications transactions are engaged in an activity subject to regulations beyond those governing real estate transactions generally, and therefore have the affirmative obligation to be informed of applicable federal and state laws, and rules and regulations regarding these types of transactions.

ARTICLE 12

REALTORS® shall not undertake to provide professional services concerning a property or its value where they have a present or contemplated interest unless such interest is specially disclosed to all affected parties.

• Standard of Practice 12-1

(Refer to Standards of Practice 9-4 and 16-1, which also relate to Article 12, Code of Ethics.) (Amended 5/84)

ARTICLE 13

REALTORS® shall not acquire an interest in or buy or present offers from themselves, any member of their immediate families, their firms or any member thereof, or any entities in which they have any ownership interest, any real property without making their true position known to the owner or the owner's agent. In selling property they own, or in which they have any interest, REALTORS® shall reveal their ownership or interest in writing to the purchaser or the purchaser's representative. (Amended 11/90)

• Standard of Practice 13-1

For the protection of all parties, the disclosures required by Article 13 shall be in writing and provided by REALTORS® prior to the signing of any contract. (Adopted 2/86)

ARTICLE 14

In the event of a controversy between REALTORS® associated with different firms, arising out of their relationship as REALTORS®, the REALTORS® shall submit the dispute to arbitration in accordance with the regulations of their Board or Boards rather than litigate the matter.

In the event clients of REALTORS® wish to arbitrate contractual disputes arising out of real estate transactions, REALTORS® shall arbitrate those disputes in accordance with the regulations of their Board, provided the clients agree to be bound by the decision.

(Amended 11/92)

• Standard of Practice 14-1

The filing of litigation and refusal to withdraw from it by REALTORS® in an arbitrable matter constitutes a refusal to arbitrate. (Adopted 2/86)

~~• Standard of Practice 14-2~~

~~The obligation to arbitrate mandated by Article 14 includes arbitration requests initiated by REALTORS®' clients. (Adopted 5/87)~~

• Standard of Practice ~~14-3~~ 14-2

Article 14 does not require REALTORS® to arbitrate in those circumstances when all parties to the dispute advise the Board in writing that they choose not to arbitrate before the Board. (Amended 11/92)

ARTICLE 15

If charged with unethical practice or asked to present evidence or to cooperate in any other way, in any disciplinary proceeding or investigation, REALTORS® shall place all pertinent facts before the proper tribunals of the Member Board or affiliated institute, society, or council in which membership is held and shall take no action to disrupt or obstruct such processes. (Amended 11/89)

• Standard of Practice 15-1

REALTORS® shall not be subject to disciplinary proceedings in more than one Board of REALTORS® with respect to alleged violations of the Code of Ethics relating to the same transaction.

• Standard of Practice 15-2

REALTORS® shall not make any unauthorized disclosure or dissemination of the allegations, findings, or decision developed in connection with an ethics hearing or appeal or in connection with an arbitration hearing or procedural review. (Amended 11/91)

• Standard of Practice 15-3

REALTORS® shall not obstruct the Board's investigative or disciplinary proceedings by instituting or threatening to institute actions for libel, slander or defamation against any party to a professional standards proceeding or their witnesses.
(Adopted 11/87)

• Standard of Practice 15-4

REALTORS® shall not intentionally impede the Board's investigative or disciplinary proceedings by filing multiple ethics complaints based on the same event or transaction. (Adopted 11/88)

ARTICLE 16

When acting as agents, REALTORS® shall not accept any commission, rebate, or profit on expenditures made for their principal, without the principal's knowledge and consent. (Amended 11/91)

• Standard of Practice 16-1

REALTORS® shall not recommend or suggest to a client or a customer the use of services of another organization or business entity in which they have a direct interest without disclosing such interest at the time of the recommendation or suggestion. (Amended 5/88)

• Standard of Practice 16-2

When acting as agents or subagents, REALTORS® shall disclose to a client or customer if there is any financial benefit or fee the REALTOR® or the REALTOR®'s firm may receive as a direct result of having recommended real estate products or services (e.g., homeowner's insurance, warranty programs, mortgage financing, title insurance, etc.) other than real estate referral fees. (Adopted 5/88)

ARTICLE 17

REALTORS® shall not engage in activities that constitute the unauthorized practice of law and shall recommend that legal counsel be obtained when the interest of any party to the transaction requires it.

ARTICLE 18

REALTORS® shall keep in a special account in an appropriate financial institution, separated from their own funds, monies coming into their possession in trust for other persons, such as escrows, trust funds, clients' monies, and other like items.

ARTICLE 19

REALTORS® shall be careful at all times to present a true picture in their advertising and representations to the public. REALTORS® shall also ensure that their professional status ~~as brokers~~ (e.g., broker, appraiser, property manager, etc.) or status as REALTORS® is clearly identifiable in any such advertising. (Amended 11/92)

• Standard of Practice 19-1

REALTORS® shall not ~~submit~~ offer for sale/lease or advertise property without authority., ~~and in any offering~~ When acting as listing brokers or as subagents, ~~the price quoted shall not be other than~~ REALTORS® shall not quote a price different from that agreed upon with the ~~owners~~ seller/landlord. (Amended 11/92)

• Standard of Practice 19-2

(Refer to Standard of Practice 9-4, which also relates to Article 19, Code of Ethics.)

• Standard of Practice 19-3

REALTORS®, when advertising unlisted real property for sale/lease in which they have an ownership interest, shall disclose their status as both owners/landlords and as REALTORS® or real estate licensees. (Amended 11/92)

• Standard of Practice 19-4

REALTORS® shall not advertise nor permit any person employed by or affiliated with them to advertise listed property without disclosing the name of the firm. (Adopted 11/86)

• Standard of Practice 19-5

Only REALTORS® as listing brokers, may claim to have "sold" the property, even when the sale resulted through the cooperative efforts of another broker. However, after transactions have closed, listing brokers may not prohibit successful cooperating brokers from advertising their "cooperation," "participation," or "assistance" in the transaction, or from making similar representations.

Only listing brokers are entitled to use the term "sold" on signs, in advertisements, and in other public representations. (Amended 11/89)

ARTICLE 20

REALTORS®, for the protection of all parties, shall see that financial obligations and commitments regarding real estate transactions are in writing, expressing the exact agreement of the parties. A copy of each agreement shall be furnished to each party upon their signing such agreement.

• Standard of Practice 20-1

At the time of signing or initialing, REALTORS® shall furnish to each party a copy of any document signed or initialed. (Adopted 5/86)

• Standard of Practice 20-2

For the protection of all parties, REALTORS® shall use reasonable care to ensure that documents pertaining to the purchase, ~~and~~ sale, or lease of real estate are kept current through the use of written extensions or amendments. (Amended 11/92)

ARTICLE 21

REALTORS® shall not engage in any practice or take any action inconsistent with the agency of other REALTORS®.

• Standard of Practice 21-1

Signs giving notice of property for sale, rent, lease, or exchange shall not be placed on property without ~~the~~ consent of the ~~owner~~ seller/landlord. (Amended 11/92)

• Standard of Practice 21-2

~~REALTORS® obtaining information from a listing broker about a specific property shall not convey this information to, nor invite the cooperation of a third party broker without the consent of the listing broker.~~ REALTORS® acting as subagents or as buyer/tenant agents, shall not attempt to extend a listing broker's offer of cooperation and/or compensation to other brokers without the consent of the listing broker. (Amended 11/92)

• Standard of Practice 21-3

REALTORS® shall not solicit a listing which is currently listed exclusively with another broker. However, if the listing broker, when asked by the REALTOR®, refuses to disclose the expiration date and nature of such listing; i.e., an exclusive right to sell, an exclusive agency, open listing, or other form of contractual agreement between the listing broker and the client, the REALTOR® may contact the owner to secure such information and may discuss the terms upon which the REALTOR® might take a future listing or, alternatively, may take a listing to become effective upon expiration of any existing exclusive listing. (Amended 11/86)

• Standard of Practice 21-4

REALTORS® shall not use information obtained by them from the listing broker, through offers to cooperate received through Multiple Listing Services or other sources authorized by the listing broker, for the purpose of creating a referral prospect to a third broker, or for creating a buyer/tenant prospect unless such use is authorized by the listing broker. (Amended 11/92)

• Standard of Practice 21-5

The fact that ~~a property~~ an agency agreement has been ~~listed exclusively~~ entered into with a REALTOR® shall not preclude or inhibit any other REALTOR® from ~~soliciting such listing~~ entering into a similar agreement after ~~its the~~ expiration of the prior agreement. (Amended 11/92)

• Standard of Practice 21-6

The fact that a ~~property owner~~ client has retained a REALTOR® as an ~~exclusive~~ agent in ~~respect of~~ one or more past transactions ~~creates no interest or agency which~~ does not precludes ~~or inhibits~~ other REALTORS® from seeking such ~~owner's~~ former client's future business. (Amended 11/92)

• Standard of Practice 21-7

REALTORS® shall be free to list property which is "open listed" at any time, but shall not knowingly obligate the seller to pay more than one commission except with the seller's knowledgeable consent. (Cross-reference Article 7.) (Amended 5/88)

• Standard of Practice 21-8

When REALTORS® are contacted by ~~owners~~ the client of another REALTOR® regarding the ~~sale of property that is exclusively listed with another broker~~, creation of an agency relationship to provide the same type of service, and REALTORS® have not directly or indirectly initiated ~~the~~ such discussions, ~~REALTORS®~~ they may discuss the terms upon which they might ~~take~~ enter into a future ~~listing~~ agency agreement or, alternatively, may ~~take a listing to~~ enter into an agency agreement which becomes effective upon expiration of any existing exclusive ~~listing~~ agreement. (Amended 11/92)

• Standard of Practice 21-9

In cooperative transactions REALTORS® shall compensate cooperating REALTORS® (principal brokers) and shall not compensate nor offer to compensate, directly or indirectly, any of the sales licensees employed by or affiliated with other REALTORS® without the prior express knowledge and consent of the cooperating broker.

• Standard of Practice 21-10

Article 21 does not preclude REALTORS® from making general announcements to ~~property owners~~ prospective clients describing their services and the terms of their availability even though some recipients may have ~~exclusively listed their property for sale or lease~~ entered into agency agreements with another REALTOR®. A general telephone canvas, general mailing or distribution addressed to all ~~property owners~~ prospective clients in a given geographical area or in a given profession, business, club, or organization, or other classification or group is deemed "general" for purposes of this standard.

Article 21 is intended to recognize as unethical two basic types of solicitations:

First, telephone or personal solicitations of property owners who have been identified by a real estate sign, multiple listing compilation, or other information service as having exclusively listed their property with another REALTOR®; and

Second, mail or other forms of written solicitations of ~~property owners~~ prospective clients whose properties are exclusively listed with another REALTOR® when such solicitations are not part of a general mailing but are directed specifically to property owners identified through compilations of current listings, "for sale" or "for rent" signs, or other sources of information required by Article 22 and Multiple Listing Service rules to be made available to other REALTORS® under offers of subagency or cooperation. (Amended 11/92)

• Standard of Practice 21-11

REALTORS®, prior to ~~accepting a listing~~, entering into an agency agreement, have an affirmative obligation to make reasonable efforts to determine whether the ~~property~~

client is subject to a current, valid exclusive ~~listing~~ agreement to provide the same type of real estate service. (Amended 11/92)

• Standard of Practice 21-12

REALTORS®, acting as agents of buyers or tenants, shall disclose that relationship to the seller/landlord's agent at first contact and shall provide written confirmation of that disclosure to the seller/landlord's agent not later than execution of a purchase agreement or lease. (Cross-reference Article 7.) (Amended 11/92)

• Standard of Practice 21-13

On unlisted property, REALTORS® acting as buyer/tenant agents ~~of buyers~~ shall disclose that relationship to the seller/landlord at first contact for that client and shall provide written confirmation of such disclosure to the seller/landlord not later than execution of any purchase or lease agreement.

REALTORS® shall make any request for anticipated compensation from the seller/landlord at first contact. (Cross-reference Article 7.) (Amended 11/92)

• Standard of Practice 21-14

REALTORS®, acting as agents of sellers/landlords or as subagents of ~~the~~ listing brokers, shall disclose that relationship to buyers/tenants as soon as practicable and shall provide written confirmation of such disclosure to buyers/tenants not later than execution of any purchase or lease agreement. (Amended 11/92)

• Standard of Practice 21-15

Article 21 does not preclude REALTORS® from contacting the client of another broker for the purpose of offering to provide, or entering into a contract to provide, a different type of real estate service unrelated to the type of service currently being provided (e.g., property management as opposed to brokerage). However, information received through a Multiple Listing Service or any other offer of cooperation may not be used to target ~~the property owners~~ clients of other REALTORS® to whom such offers to provide services ~~are~~ may be made. (Amended 11/92)

• Standard of Practice 21-16

REALTORS®, acting as subagents or buyer~~'s~~/tenant agents, shall not use the terms of an offer to purchase/lease to attempt to modify the listing broker's offer of compensation to subagents or buyer's agents nor make the submission of an executed offer to purchase/lease contingent on the listing broker's agreement to modify the offer of compensation. (Amended 11/92)

• Standard of Practice 21-17

Where property is listed on an open listing basis, REALTORS® acting as buyer/tenant agents may deal directly with the seller/landlord. (Adopted 11/92)

• Standard of Practice 21-18

All dealings concerning property exclusively listed, or with buyer/tenants who are exclusively represented shall be carried on with the client's agent, and not with the client, except with the consent of the client's agent. (Adopted 11/92)

ARTICLE 22

~~In the sale of property which is exclusively listed with a REALTOR®, REALTORS® shall utilize the services of other brokers upon mutually agreed upon terms when it is in the best interests of the client.~~

~~Negotiations concerning property which is listed exclusively shall be carried on with the listing broker, not with the owner, except with the consent of the listing broker.~~

REALTORS® shall cooperate with other brokers except when cooperation is not in the client's best interest. (Amended 11/92)

• Standard of Practice 22-1

It is the obligation of ~~the selling broker as~~ subagents ~~of the listing broker~~ to promptly disclose immediately all pertinent facts to ~~the listing broker~~ the principal's agent prior to as well as after ~~the contract~~ a purchase or lease agreement is executed. (Cross-reference to Article 9) (Adopted 11/92)

• Standard of Practice 22-2

REALTORS®~~, when~~ shall submit~~ting~~ offers ~~to the seller~~, and counter-offers, ~~shall present each~~ in an objective ~~and unbiased~~ manner. (Amended 11/92)

• Standard of Practice 22-3

REALTORS® shall disclose the existence of an accepted offer to any broker seeking cooperation. (Adopted 5/86)

• Standard of Practice 22-4

REALTORS®, acting as exclusive agents of sellers, establish the terms and conditions of offers to cooperate. Unless expressly indicated in offers to cooperate made through MLS or otherwise, a cooperating broker may not assume that the offer of cooperation includes an offer of compensation. Entitlement to compensation in a cooperative transaction must be agreed upon between a listing and cooperating broker prior to the time an offer to purchase the property is produced. (Adopted 11/88)

ARTICLE 23

REALTORS® shall not knowingly or recklessly make false or misleading statements about competitors, their businesses, or their business practices. (Amended 11/91)

The Code of Ethics was adopted in 1913. Amended at the Annual Convention in 1924, 1928, 1950, 1951, 1952, 1955, 1956, 1961, 1962, 1974, 1982, 1986, 1987, 1989, 1990, 1991, and 1992.

EXPLANATORY NOTES

(Amended 11/88)

The reader should be aware of the following policies which have been approved by the Board of Directors of the National Association:

In filing a charge of an alleged violation of the Code of Ethics by a REALTOR®, the charge shall read as an alleged violation of one or more Articles of the Code. A Standard of Practice may only be cited in support of the charge.

The Standards of Practice are not an integral part of the Code but rather serve to clarify the ethical obligations imposed by the various Articles. The Standards of Practice supplement, and do not substitute for, the Case Interpretations in *Interpretations of the Code of Ethics*.

Modifications to existing Standards of Practice and additional new Standards of Practice are approved from time to time. The reader is cautioned to ensure that the most recent publications are utilized.

Articles 1 through 5 are aspirational and establish ideals that a REALTOR® should strive to attain. Recognizing their subjective nature, these Articles shall not be used as the bases for charges of alleged unethical conduct or as the bases for disciplinary action.

TABLE OF CASES

End of chapter cases are in bold type. Cases included as case summaries are in italic type. Cases referenced in the text are in roman type. Page references are in roman type for all cases.

Pennsylvania Coal Co. v. Mahon, 260 U.S. 393 (Pa., 1922), 481, 482

Pilling v. Eastern and Pacific Enterprises Trust, 702 P.2d 1232 (Wash., 1985) 315, 394–350

Pinefda v. PMI Mortgage Insurance Co., 843 S.W.2d 660 (Tex., 1992), 256

Point Farm Homeowner's Association, Inc. v. Evans, 1993 WL 257404 (Del., 1993), 469

Prichard v. Reitz, 223 Cal.Rptr. 734 (Cal., 1986), 443

Property House, Inc. v. Kelley, 715 P.2d 805 (Haw., 1986), 359, 368–369

Queathem v. Quetham, 712 S.W.2d 703 (Mo., 1986), 207

Rainwater v. National Home Insurance Company, 1991 WL 169235 (Va., 1991), 509, 522–524

Redarowicz v. Ohlendorf, 441 N.E.2d 324 (Ill., 1982), 500

Reed v. King, 193 Cal.Rptr. 130 (Cal., 1983), 355, 365–366

Reves v. Ernst & Young, 110 S.Ct. 945 (Ark., 1990), 533, 554–555

Richardson v. Mustang Fuel Corp., 772 P.2d 1324 (Okla., 1989), 142

Rodriguez v. Banko Central Corporation, 990 F.2d 7 (P.R., 1993), 534

Rohauer v. Little, 736 P.2d 403 (Colo., 1987), 325, 350–351

Runyon v. Paley, 416 S.E. 2d 177 (N.C., 1992), 142, 160

Salisbury v. Chapman Realty, 465 N.E.2d 127 (Ill., 1984), 428, 452–453

San Francisco v. Grant Company, 227 Cal.Rptr. 154 (Cal., 1986), 131

Schackai v. Lagreco, 350 So.2d 1244 (La., 1977), 339, 347–348

Schaechter v. Regency Properties, Inc., 497 N.Y.S.2d 793 (N.Y., 1985), 423, 447

Schneider v. Schneider, 389 N.W.2d 835 (Wis., 1986), 105, 120

Schumacher v. Dept. of Professional Regulation, Div. of Real Estate, 611 So.2d 75 (Fla., 1992), 359

SEC v. W.J. Howey Co., 328 U.S. 293 (Fla., 1946), 533, 548, 549, 553

SEC v. Glenn W. Turner Enterprises, Inc., 348 F. Supp. 766 (Or., 1972), 552

Sedat, Inc. v. Fisher, 617 A.2d 1 (Pa., 1992), 31

Sewell v. Gregory, 371 S.E.2d 82 (W.Va., 1988), 501, 505

Shelley v. Kraemer, 68 S.Ct. 836 (Mo., 1948), 469, 495–497

Shellhammer and Shellhammer v. Lewallen and Lewallen, 770 F.2d 167 (Ohio, 1985), 382, 409–410

Shingleton v. N.C. Wildlife Resources Comm., 133 S.E. 2d 183 (N.C., 1963), 138, 145

Shipper v. Levitt & Sons, 207 A.2d 314 (N.J., 1965), 503, 505

Shockley v. Hoechst Celanese Corporation et. al., 1993 WL 241179 (S.C., 1993), 405

Smith v. Inman Realty Company, 846 S.W.2d 819 (Tenn., 1992), 357

South Burlington County NAACP v. Township of Mount Laural, 456 A.2d 390 (N.J., 1983), 383

South-Suburban Housing v. Greater South Suburban Board of Realtors, 935 F.2d 868 (Ill., 1991), 380

State Ex Rel. Fisher v. McNutt, 597 N.E.2d 539 (Ohio, 1992), 140, 152

State of Washington v. Black, 676 P.2d 963 (Wash., 1984), 361, 372–373

Stewart v. Germany, 631 F.Supp. 236 (Miss., 1986), 549, 559–560

Stoesser v. Shore Drive Partnership, 494 N.W.2d 204 (Wis., 1993), 33

Sutton v. Miller, 592 A.2d 83 (Pa., 1991), 185, 189

Swallows v. Laney, 691 P.2d 874 (N.M., 1984), 326, 346–347

Tanglewood East Homeowners v. Charles-Thomas, Inc., 849 F.2d 1568 (Tex., 1988), 404

Tennant v. Lawton, 615 P.2d 1305 (Wash., 1980), 443

Thompson v. Metropolitan Multi-List, Inc., 934 F.2d 1566 (Ga., 1991), 575, 581–590

Towne v. Porter Township Board, 460 N.W.2d 596 (Mich., 1990), 131, 155

United Artists Theater Circuit, Inc. v. City of Philadelphia, Philadelphia Historic Commission, 595 A.2d 6 (Pa., 1991), 478

GLOSSARY

Abatement A judicial act or order which is intended to terminate the activities of a land owner which have been declared to create a nuisance.

Acceptance Any act or communication which responds to the terms of an offer and creates a binding contract incorporating all of the material terms of the offer.

Adverse Possession A legal doctrine which permits a natural person to acquire title to real property by the continuous, open and hostile possession of the property.

Affirmative Defense A defense which must be raised by the defendant in a law suit in order to excuse the action complained of the plaintiff. The burden of proof in establishing an affirmative defense rests on the party who asserts it.

Agency The relationship between an agent and the party represented, or the principal.

Agency Disclosure A statement made to interested parties which indicates the existence of an agency relationship.

Agency Theory Concepts of fiduciary responsibility based upon agency law.

Agent A person who represents the interests of one person in dealings with others.

Air Rights The exclusive right to occupy, use and enjoy the air above a parcel of real property.

Allodial Ownership A set of absolute ownership rights in land which was created by the Roman Civil Code.

Annexation The legal principle which defines the mechanical processes required to convert an item of personal property into a fixture.

Anti-competitive Practices Actions by competitors whereby they agree to cooperate in the marketplace to form effective monopolies.

Arbitrator A neutral person whose function it is to hear the claims of parties and render a decision.

Assignment An agreement by which a lease tenant sells to another person the right of present possession enjoyed by the lease tenant, for the remaining period of the leasehold estate.

Assignment by Buyer Process of transferring contract rights to another person.

Associate Broker An individual who is licensed as a broker but who works under the guidance of a managing broker.

Attorney Opinions An opinion formed by reviewing the documents included in a title abstract of the property, and concluding that record title to the parcel belongs to the individual named in the opinion. The opinion will also mention any liens or encumbrances which may be asserted against the title of the record owner of the property.

Betterment The increase in property value which results from city planning activities.

Blockbusting The practice of enticing minorities to move into segregated neighborhoods in hopes of creating panic selling.

Boycotts An agreement not to use a firm's services. Permissable if done by customers, but generally illegal if done by competitors.

Breach of Contract The failure by one party to live up to the terms of a binding contract.

Broker In real estate, an agent licensed by the state to represent one party, usually the seller, in a transaction.

Building Bulk Concept used in some zoning ordinances to define the maximum total size of allowable structures.

Buyer Warranty Programs Various programs designed to provide some degree of protection for property purchasers.

Buyer Brokerage An agency relationship which is created between a potential property buyer and a broker.

Buyer Brokerage Fees Fees charged by buyer brokers based upon some combination of an hourly rate, a retainer, and/or a success fee.

Cashiers Check A check which is drawn by a depositary institution against funds held on deposit with the Federal Reserve or with another commercial bank.

Caveat Emptor Literally, "Let the buyer beware." Often the standard of conduct in real property transactions.

Caveat Vendor Literally, "Let the seller beware." May represent an emerging standard of conduct in real property transactions.

CERCLA Comprehensive Environmental Response, Compensation, and Liability Act (1980). Created the "superfund" to respond to releases of hazardous materials.

Certified Check A check which has been certified for payment by the bank the check is drawn on. The bank certifies the check by removing the funds needed for payment from the maker's account, and holding the funds in a separate account for payment to the person who presents the check.

Civil Code Legal Systems A type of legal system which relies mainly on laws drafted by national and regional legislatures to regulate the behavior of citizens.

Civil Law A philosphy of law which seeks to determine the ways things should be in order to construct a set of legal principles which results in a "just" society. In practice, Civil Law philosophies are most concerned with protecting the rights and privileges of citizens in a society.

Civil Rights Acts Series of laws passed by the U.S. Congress to prohibit discrimination based upon race, color, creed, religion, national origin, or other characteristics.

Closing Agent The person who collects, holds and disburses all the funds required for a real estate closing. The closing agent may also file all documents required to complete the transfer of record title which occurs at the closing.

Cloud of Condemnation The potential impact on market value that an announced plan to condem a property will have prior to the actual condemnation process.

Code of Ethics A statement of professional behavior to which all members of the National Association of REALTORS adhere.

Collateral Promises A concept in law which allows warranties made in the sales contract to survive the closing process and not be merged.

Collateralized Mortgage Obligations A mortgage-backed security with several securities of different lengths based upon the projected payment stream of the mortgage pool.

Commingling of Funds Allowing monies held by a broker as trustee to be mixed with other funds of the broker or firm.

Common Law Legal Systems A type of legal system which relies mainly on the legal opinions produced by judges to regulate the behavior of citizens.

Community Association An association composed of all property owners in a neighborhood, condominium or cooperative housing development which has the authority to amend or revoke covenants.

Complaint and Answer The major pleadings which describe the nature of the controversy between the parties to a law suit.

Condemnation The act of taking private property by the public under the power of eminent domain.

Condominium A form of multiple ownership in which each condominium owner receives a fee simple absolute estate in an individual air space unit (either a dwelling or commercial space) and an undivided interest as tenant in common in the lands and structures which are within the boundaries of the condominium development and outside of the individual air space units.

Consideration Any promise or performance which is made in exchange for a promise or performance by the another party to a contract.

Conspiracies A boycott against a firm by competing firms designed to force the firm to change its business practices or drive the firm out of the market.

Constitutions The basic document of government which describes the powers, procedures and limitations of governmental actions.

Contingency Clauses Statements inserted into a contract which allow one party to escape the terms of the contract upon certain conditions.

Contract A legally enforceable agreement between two or more persons.

Conversion Franchise An agreement by an existing business to become part of a franchise.

Cooperative A corporation which is formed for the purpose of owning and maintaining an aparment building. The shareholders of the corporation are limited to the occupants of the residential units in the development owned by the cooperative.

Corporate Stock Stock, either common or preferred, issued for sale by a regular (or "C") corporation.

Counteroffer Any communication, either written or oral, which responds to the terms of an offer by changing or amending one or more of the material terms of the offer. A counteroffer does not create a contract until it is accepted by the party receiving the counteroffer.

Covenant An agreement between two or more landowners which limits or restricts the ownership rights of the parties to the agreement.

Credit Discrimination The refusal to grant or extend credit based upon race, sex, religion, or other characteristics.

Cumulative Zoning Ordinance An ordinance in which permitted uses are ranked such that any "higher" use is permitted in all equal or "lower" ranked zones.

Dealers A securities dealer who, unlike a broker, is in the business of buying and selling for his own account.

Dedications Property and, in many cases, improvements deeded by developers to municipalities as a condition for obtaining building permits.

Deed of Trust A document conveying a power to sell real property to a public official (the Public Trustee) whenever the owner of the property fails or refuses to pay the sums due to a lender whose note is secured by the deed of trust.

Deed Restrictions Provisions in individual deeds or for subdivisions which place restrictions on the use, development, and construction of the premises.

Default The failure or refusal to comply with any material term or condition of a mortgage, or the promissory note which the mortgage secures.

Disclosure Requirements For securities, a complete disclosure of the nature and risks of the investment as well as information about the offeror.

Discount Brokerage Term applied to brokers who offer a limited set of services for a generally lower fee or commission.

Discretionary State Exemption General exemption from securities registration requirements offered by most states—usually handled on a case-by-case basis.

Diversity Jurisdiction The authority granted to Federal Courts by the U.S. Constitution to hear and resolve controversies between citizens of two or more different states.

Dominant Tenement The parcel of land which receives the benefit of an easement.

Dual Agency Created when an agent represents two parties who are in an adversarial relationship.

Due Diligence Reviews The environmental inspection of a property necessary to rely upon the "innocent landowner" defense against liability claims for hazardous materials found on a site.

Due Care Standard Standard of conduct which applies to the actions of an agent when dealing with his principal and the public.

Duress Operating under threat of harm, either physical or emotional.

Earnest Money Deposit A sum of money which accompanies an offer to purchase property as a sign of "good faith."

Easement A real property interest which gives the owner of the easement the right to subject the real property of another to a defined use or restriction on use.

Eminent Domain The right of governmental entities to take private property for public use or benefit.

Environmental Liability The liability of potentially responsible parties to pay all costs associated with the removal of hazardous materials.

Environmental Protection Efforts by state and federal governments, primarily through statutes, to preserve and protect environmentally sensitive areas.

Environmental Risk Management The process of conducting appropriate inspections and utilizing contractual provisions to provide protection against environmental liability.

Equitable Conversion Doctrine which holds that "what ought to be done is regarded as done" when a binding agreement is in place.

Equitable Remedies The right of a plaintiff in a law suit to obtain a judicial order requiring the defendant to perform, or refrain from performing, a specific act. Equitable remedies are only available to plaintiffs whose injury cannot be repaired by the payment of money damages.

Equity of Redemption In modern practice, this term refers to the difference between the fair market value of real property and the amounts currently due and owing to any mortgagees who have rights in the real property. At common law, the equity of redemption was the right of a borrower to redeem the property from the mortgagee after a foreclosure of the mortgage.

Escalator Clauses The provision of a commercial lease which permits increases in the rent paid by the tenant during the period of the lease.

Estoppel An equitable doctrine which requires a party to render a promised performance when another party has changed his or her position as a result of justifiable reliance upon the promise made by the party to whom the doctrine of estoppel is applied.

Exclusive Zoning Ordinance A zoning ordinance which only allows specific permitted uses within each zone.

Exclusive Agency Listing A listing agreement in which the seller reserves the right to sell the property without payment of a commission.

Exclusive Buyer Agency Contract Contract between a potential buyer and broker. Similar in concept to an exclusive agency listing contract between a seller and a broker.

Exclusive Right to Sell Listing A form of listing contract where the seller agrees to pay a commission to the broker in the event the property is sold regardless of who finds a buyer for the property.

Exempt Holding Company Companies which can invest in real estate without being subject to the unrelated business tax.

Fair Housing Acts The term applied to those sections of the Civil Rights Acts which specifically apply to housing issues.

Familial Status Provisions in the Fair Housing Amendments Act (1989) which prohibit discrimination against families and individuals with children in most housing situations.

Federal Registration Exemptions Three types of possible exemptions from securities registration requirements—Intrastate, Private Placement, and Small Issuer.

Fee Simple Estates The largest bundle of ownership rights available in the American law of real property.

Fee Tail Estates An archaic ownership estate which allows the owner to possess, use and enjoy land during his or her life; at the death of the fee tail tenant, the ownership estate automatically passes to the children of the decedent.

Feudal Tenure The right to possess and enjoy land which belongs to a military overlord. The feudal tenure was created in Europe after the collapse of the Roman Empire.

Fiduciary Obligations Obligations of accounting, confidentiality, diligence, disclosure, loyalty, obedience, and reasonable skill and care owed by an agent to a principal.

Fiduciary Relationship A relationship based upon trust and confidence between an agent and principal.

Fixtures Items which become real property through the process of attachment to land or buildings.

Flat Fee Brokerage A brokerage firm which charges, rather than a commission, a predetermined fee for services.

Foreclosure The process a lender must use to compel a borrower to sell real property and apply the proceeds of the sale towards the payments due to the lender.

Foreclosure by Public Sale The process by which the mortgagee in a lien theory jurisdiction is empowered to sell the real property encumbered by a mortgage, and apply the proceeds of the sale to the unpaid balance of the mortgage.

Franchise Agreements Contractual agreements between a franchisor and franchisee which spell out the rights and duties of each party.

Franchise Disclosure Statement A statement required by the FTC which discloses information about the franchisor, obligations the franchisee will incur, and important terms of the franchise agreement.

Fraud Deceitful practice with intent to deprive another of his right, or in some fashion do him injury.

Full Agency Disclosure Disclosing not only the nature of the current agency relationship, but other possible agency relationships.

Full Service Seller's Agent A broker who provides all normal services, as opposed to a discount or flat fee broker, to property sellers.

Future Interests An estate in land which conveys no ownership rights to the holder until an stated event in the future has occurred.

General Agency A relationship where the agent may act on behalf of the principal.

General Parnership A partnership arrangement in which there is only one type of partner and which does not offer liability protection.

Good Faith Purchaser for Value A person who gives money or some other thing of value in exchange for the conveyance of a real property interest, and has no notice or knowledge of any competing claims in the real property purchased.

Granting Clause The words in a deed which actually convey an ownership estate in real property from the grantor to the grantee of the deed.

Grantor/Grantee Index A record of deeds, mortgages and other documents affecting title to real property which records the documents alphabetically by the names of the parties to each document.

Habendum Clause The words in a deed which describe the nature of the ownership estate conveyed from the grantor to the grantee. Any limitations on the ownership estate should be included in the habendum clause.

Handicapped Access Rules Provisions in the Fair Housing Amendments which require all multifamily dwellings constructed after March 1991 to be accessible to handicapped persons.

Hazardous Substance Substances listed in 40 CFR Table 302.4 which can trigger CERCLA liability. There are currently well over 1,000 substances listed.

Historic Preservation A wide variety of programs and regulations designed to preserve and protect buildings and areas of particular historic significance.

Hold Over Tenancies The real property interest which is created when a lease tenant remains in possession of the premises after the expiration of the lease period.

Home Owner's Warranty Contract offered by some builders which warrants the workmanship, materials, and major construction elements for specified periods of time.

Horizontal Integration Acquiring additional product lines or services to diversify the operations of a firm.

Hostile Takeover A term which describes the process of acquiring a firm against the will of the current management by purchasing sufficient stock so as to have majority control.

Hourly Fee Fee sometimes charged by buyer brokers to insure at least some payment even when no property is purchased.

Housing Cooperative A form of multiunit housing in which a corporation owns the property and owners of shares in the corporation live in each of the units.

Howey Test Four part test used by courts to decide when an investment contract is to be considered a security.

Implied Warranty A warranty which may be granted to a consumer even though not expressly granted in a contract.

Implied Warranty of Habitability Warranty by a builder that a new home is free of major defects, or by a landlord in a residential lease that the premises are in good living condition.

Implied Warranty of Merchantability Based on the notion that a consumer has certain "reasonable expectations" about the quality and performance of a product.

Implied Warranty of Workmanlike Construction A warranty imposed upon builders that houses be constructed in "a workmanlike manner."

Indemnification Clause A contract provision designed to protect one party from potential liability for conditions not due to their actions.

Independent Contractor An individual working under the direction of another who exercises a limited degree of control.

Innocent Misrepresentation Actions or statements, even though innocently done, which may create a false impression in the mind of another concerning property.

Innocent Landowner Defense A current landowner may not be liable for clean-up costs due to hazardous materials if he can establish that he did not know, and had no reason to know, of the contamination.

Integration of Offerings Tests used to determine if a series of small securities offerings should be "integrated" and thus not eligible for the small issuer federal securities registration exemption.

***Inter Vivos* Gift** The transfer of property by a living donor who receives no compensation in exchange for making the transfer.

Intestate Succession The transfer of property to the heirs of a decedent who died without a valid will.

Intrastate Registration Exemption Exemption from federal securities registration available when both the issuer and purchasers live in the same state.

Inverse Condemnation Claims made to recover damages resulting from excessive regulation, nearby public uses, or damages remaining after an original eminent domain proceeding.

Investment Advisor A person "associated" with transactions involving securities as defined by the Investment Advisors Act of 1940.

Joint Tenancy A form of multiple ownership of real property in which each joint tenant owns an undivided interest in the property. At the death of any joint tenant, the undivided interest will pass to the surviving joint tenants.

Judgment An order issued by a trial judge providing a legal conclusion to the controversy which resulted in a law suit. The conclusion prescribed by the judgment is binding on all the parties to the law suit.

Judicial Opinion A legal document which explains how the law should be applied to the actions of the parties to a law suit, and describing the reasoning process employed by the judges who issued the opinion.

Junior Lien Holders Persons who hold liens in property which is encumbered by other liens which will be given priority in foreclosure or bankruptcy proceedings.

Lease Tenant The owner of a present possessory interest which ends at a definite date in the future.

Legal Injury Interference with the use of quiet enjoyment of another person's real property.

Legal Remedies The right of the plaintiff in a law suit to obtain an order requiring the defendant to pay a sum of money for damages when the defendant has committed a legal wrong against the plaintiff.

Legislative Enactments Laws established by Congress, or various state legislatures. Judges are required to interpret and apply the common law in the manner prescribed by legislative enactments.

Lender's Escrow Account Funds held by mortgage lenders which will be used to pay property tax bills and insurance premiums when those items become due in the future.

Leveraged Buyout The process of using the current assets of a takeover target as collateral for the debt used to acquire the firm.

License A personal property interest which permits the owner of the license to enter the land of another for a specific purpose.

Licensing Laws State Statutes which define the requirements for licensure, acceptable conduct of licensees, and establish a means of control.

Lien A contingent interest in real or personal property which secures the payment of a debt or obligation owed by the property owner to the lien holder.

Lien Theory Mortgage The rights and duties allocated by law to the parties to a mortgage, when the mortgage is considered to be a document which conveys no ownership rights in the property, but instead merely serves as security for the promise to repay a debt.

Life Tenant The owner of a present possessory interest in real property which continues until the death of the life tenant.

Life Estates A bundle of ownership rights which last only until the death of the owner.

Limited Liability The legal doctrine which holds that the liability of shareholders in a corporation, or limited partners in a limited partnership, is limited to the amount each shareholder or limited partner has invested in the entity.

Limited Offering Exemption A type of exemption from state securities registration requirements based upon the size of offerings and the amount of time they are available for sale.

Limited Partnership A partnership arrangement in which there are two types of partners—general and limited—which offers the limited partners liability protection.

Lis Pendens A notice filed for public record which informs the world that the owner of a described parcel of real property is the defendant in a law suit which may affect the title to the real property in the future.

Listing Agreement A contract between a seller and a broker which describes the terms and conditions under which the broker may collect a commission for his efforts.

Livery of Seisin The archaic ceremony used to transfer the right to occupy a parcel of land during the feudal period.

Local Franchise A term used to describe mergers and other cooperative agreements by small firms designed to provide franchise benefits at lower costs.

Major Construction Defects Type of protection offered by HOW contracts which includes damages to major structural elements of a home.

Mandatory Seller Disclosure A statement containing information about the physical condition of the property, environmental hazards, building and zoning code violations provided by the seller.

Marketable Title A title that is free from liens and encumbrances and which a reasonable purchaser, well informed as to the facts and their legal significance would, in the exercise ordinary prudence, be willing to accept and ought to accept.

Master Limited Partnership A form of publicly held and traded partnership which is generally made up of a group of limited partnerships.

Mergers A term used to describe mergers and other cooperative agreements by small firms designed to provide franchise benefits at lower costs.

Metes and Bounds A method of describing the physical boundaries of real property by starting at an identifiable location on the ground (The True Point of Beginning), and instructing the reader to travel a given distance in a prescribed direction.

Middleman An individual whose function it is to bring together a seller and a buyer but who does not enter into the negotiating process.

Mineral Rights The legal principles which define the ownership rights and duties of the person who removes (or will be permitted to remove) minerals beneath the surface of a parcel of real property.

Misrepresentation Statements or actions, whether intentional or not, which create a false impression in the mind of another and which may affect the purchase or sale decision.

Mortgage Backed Bonds Like a corporate bond, these instruments pay a stated interest rate and repay the original investment amount upon maturity.

Mortgage Backed Securities A method for investors to participate in pools of mortgage instruments or notes issued by lenders.

Mortgage Pass-Throughs The investor is vested with an ownership interest in the mortgage pool, thus the investment is considered an "equity" investment.

Mortgage Pay Through Bonds Payments into the mortgage pool, including principal repayments, pass through to the investors making these instruments have a much shorter average life.

Mortgagee A lender who receives a mortgage against real property to secure the future repayment of a debt to the lender contracted by the owner of the real property.

Mortgagor The owner of real property who gives a mortgage against the property in exchange for cash or something else of value.

Multiple Listing A cooperative agreement between brokers to share listings and split commissions.

Mutual Funds Funds in which multiple investors pool their funds for investment in a variety of opportunities, including real estate.

NAR The National Association of REALTORS, a voluntary trade organization of real estate brokers and salespersons.

NARELLO The National Association of Real Estate License Law Officials, made up of representatives of state real estate commissions.

NASSA The North American Securities Administrators Association which publishes guidelines for reviewing securities.

Natural Law A philosophy of law which seeks to examine the natural order of things and relationships in the world, in order to define the meaning of legal principles. In practice, Natural Law philosophies are most concerned with the duties and obligations of citizens in a society.

Negligence The failure to do something which, under the circumstances, should have been done, or doing something which should not have been done, which causes injury to another.

Negligent Misrepresentation Actions or statements caused by a failure to adhere to acceptable standards of conduct which create a false impression in the mind of another.

Negotiator One who represents another in deliberations, discussions or conferences upon the terms of a proposed agreement.

Neighborhood Associations An association composed of all property owners in a neighborhood which has the authority to amend or revoke subdivision covenants.

Net Leases Commercial leases in which the lease tenant is required to pay for some or all of the expenses of owning the property.

Nonconforming Use A use that does not comply with the current zoning requirements but that existed prior to the time the zoning became effective.

Notice and Waiver of Warranties The ability to disclaim warranties, even implied warranties, by placing a warranty waiver notice in a "clear and conspicuous" place.

Notice Statutes Recording statutes which award the record title in real property to the last good faith purchaser for value who records an instrument conveying the title.

Nuisance Activities of a landowner which interfere with the use or quiet enjoyment of neighboring parcels of real property.

Offer Any written or oral communication which is sufficiently definite in its terms as to indicate that the person making the offer intends to become bound by its terms.

Offer and Acceptance Initial communication by the offeror in contract formation process that, if accepted by the offeree, results in the creation of a binding contract.

Offers to Existing Security Holders A type of exemption from state securities registration requirements available when offers are restricted to only holders of existing securities issued by the sponsor.

Open Listing A unilateral contract where the seller agrees to pay a commission to any broker who sells the property.

Open MLS System A multiple listing system which allows outside individuals, for a fee, to gain access to all information contained in the system.

Ownership Rights The generic term applied to each of the individual rights included in the fee simple bundle of rights

Package Franchise A prepackaged business format including rules of operation and quality control standards.

Partition A legal proceeding which ends the common ownership of real property by dividing the real property into as many portions as there are undivided interests, and distributing the portions to each of the tenants in common or joint tenants. At the conclusion of a partition proceeding, each of the former joint or common tenants receives the sole ownership of property distributed through partition.

Partnership A legal relationship between two or more people which is formed for the purpose of owning real property or conducting a trade or business. Each of the partners is individually liable for payment of all of the partnership debts.

Patent A grant of fee simple absolute title in land which belongs to a sovereign nation at the time the patent is issued

Permitted Use A use which complys with the requirements of the area's zoning.

Personal Property The set of ownership rights and duties which are associated with everything which is not real property.

Physical Injury Injury to land or personal property of another person.

Police Power The power of the government to protect the public health, safety, and general welfare.

Portfolio Diversification The process of combining assets within a portfolio so as to reduce or eliminate unsystematic risk.

Possessory Rights The portion of the fee simple bundle of rights which allows the holder to possess, use and enjoy land in the present.

Potentially Responsible Party Individuals defined by CERCLA who may potentially be liable for all costs associated with the removal of hazardous materials from a site.

Price Fixing Actions by competing firms to mutually agree upon a fee or commission structure which will be charged by all firms in the market.

Private Placement Exemption Exemption from federal registration requirements for securities "not involving any public offering."

Private Limited Partnership A limited partnership which is not registered with the SEC.

Privity A direct contractual (or blood) relationship.

Procedural Due Process Constitutional requirement that processes which result in limiting property rights, or taking property, must follow procedures which safeguard the rights of all parties.

Procuring Cause The actions necessary to cause a transaction to take place.

Product Franchise An agreement which allows the franchisee to distribute a product manufactured under the control of the franchisor.

Promissory Estoppel An obligation which arises when a promise is made which the promisor should reasonably expect to induce action or forbearance of a definite and substantial character on the part of a promisee, and which does induce such action or forbearance. The obligation is binding if injustice can be avoided only by its enforcement.

Proration of Taxes The division of property tax payments between the buyer and seller of real property subject to the tax. The division is based on the number of days during the year that each party occupied the property.

Publicly Traded Partnerships Limited partnerships which have been registered with the SEC and can thus be traded on the open market.

Puffing Statements of opinion made by salespersons or brokers regarding features or characteristics of a property being offered for sale.

Purchase Contract A contract whereby a buyer obligates himself to purchase property under specified terms and conditions.

Quitclaim Deed A deed which releases any title to the real property described in the deed which the grantor may own. Quitclaim deeds are used primarily to correct defects in the record title to real property.

Race Statutes Recording statutes which award the record title in real property to the first person who records an instrument conveying the title.

Racial Steering The practice of showing certain properties for sale or rent to specific racial groups only.

Real Property The set of ownership rights and duties which are associated with land and buildings.

Real Estate Investment Trusts Form of organization in which investors hold trust interest and enjoy profits based on the trust's real estate related holdings.

Reciprocity Agreement Agreements between regulatory agencies of states to recognize the licenses issued by other states.

Record Title The ownership of real property which can be found by searching the public records of real property conveyances.

Redlining The practice of refusing to make loans in certain areas due to economic and/or racial composition. Often noted on maps by drawing a red line around the area.

Referral Networks A system which provides member brokers with referrals of sellers and/or buyers by brokers in other parts of the country.

Registration Exemptions Categories of securities which may be exempted from state and/or federal registration requirements.

Rehabilitation Act Act passed by Congress in 1973 designed to protect the handicapped.

Relocation Networks A system which provides member brokers with referrals of sellers and/or buyers by brokers in other parts of the country.

Reluctant Buyer Problem A buyer working with a buyer's broker who refuses to accept property located by the broker.

Rent Control Ordinances which, under the police power, restrict the ability of property owners to increase rents.

Rescission The legal doctrine which excuses both parties to a contract from performing the agreement, when the agreement was procured by fraud, or when both parties are mistaken as to the existence or lack of existence of a material fact.

Retainer Fee Fee sometimes charged by buyer brokers to insure at least some payment even when no property is purchased.

Revocation The withdrawal of an offer by the person making an offer. Revocation can occur at any time prior to the instant that the offer is accepted.

Right of Survivorship The rule of real property law which causes the ownership interest of a joint tenant to pass to surviving joint tenants at the death of any joint tenant

Risk Reduction A process of education, record keeping, and strict adherance to ethical standards of professional practice to reduce liability exposure.

S Corporation Stock Common stock issued by a corporation which meets the requirements so as to be taxed like a partnership.

Salesperson An indivdual licensed by the state to transact business under the supervision of a licensed broker.

SARA Superfund Amendments and Reauthorization Act (1986) which added the "innocent landowner" and "third party" defenses to CERCLA.

Securities Investment contracts which meet the criteria for being considered a security.

Securitization Term which describes the process of converting an asset into a pool of securities which are then offered to investors.

Security Interest The legally enforceable right to repossess and sell personal property which was previously purchased or financed in a transaction governed by the Uniform Commercial Code.

Seller Assurance Programs Programs adopted by some brokers to provide a guaranteed minimum purchase price if a buyer is not located within a specified time period.

Seller Disclosure Information regarding the physical, and possibly locational, features of a property provided by the seller.

Services Exemption The exemption from strict products liability doctrine for those who provide services as opposed to products.

Servient Tenement The parcel of land which is required to bear the burden of an easement.

Settlement Statement A statement of charges and payments made by the buyer and seller at a real estate closing

Severance The legal principle which defines the mechanical processes required to convert an item of real property into personal property.

Shingle Theory A standard of practice for securities dealors requiring that customers be treated with fairness.

Sign Ordinances City ordinances that prohibited the placement of "for sale" signs in the yards of houses in an attempt to limit racially motivated panic selling.

Small Issuer Exemption Exemption from federal securities registration for offers under $5 million which meet several tests including the integration of offerings requirements.

Special Agency A relatioship where the agent must operate within specific guidelines and may not obligate the principal.

Special Exceptions An exception to normal zoning requirements, usually called "conditional uses", granted by a board of adjustment.

Spreading the Loss Mass producers of products, as opposed to individual consumers, can afford to accept losses by spreading the loss among all consumers.

Standards of Practice Specific examples of acceptable conduct under the REALTOR's Code of Ethics.

Stare Decisis The legal principle which requires judges in each controversy to apply the law to the facts of the controversy in the same way the law was applied to similar facts in the past.

State Registration Exemptions Three general types of exemptions from state securities registration requirements—Limited Offering, Offers to Existing Holders, and Discretionary.

Statute of Frauds A statute adopted by the English Parliament which required that certain agreements must be in writing and signed by the party to be charged with performing the agreement. All

American states have adopted a version of the Statute of Frauds.

Stream of Commerce Everyone who plays a role in producing a product and bringing it to the marketplace.

Strict Liability Liability created based upon an injury to a party regardless of intent or fault. Negligence is not an element in determining strict liability.

Strict Foreclosure The process by which the mortgagee in a title theory jurisdiction acquires the fee simple title to the real property encumbered by a mortgage. After a strict foreclosure, the mortgagee acquires a title which is subject only to the mortgagor's right of redemption.

Subagency Optional An offer made by one broker to another to accept or reject a subagency relationship.

Subagent An agent who represents the interests of another agent.

Subdivision Covenant Provisions for subdivisions which place restrictions on the use, development, and construction of premises within the subdivision.

Subdivision Plat A document filed for record with an official of a local government unit which contains a map of all the building lots in the subdivision, and lists any restrictive covenants which apply to real property contained in the subdivision.

Sublease An agreement by which a lease tenant agrees to permit another person to use all or a portion of the right of present possession which belongs to the lease tenant.

Substantive Due Process Constitutional requirement that procedures which result in limiting or taking property rights provide adequate protection for the rights of all parties.

Success Fee Fee sometimes charged by buyer brokers based upon the location of a property acceptable to the buyer.

Summary Judgment An order of a trial judge which disposes of the controversy that resulted in a law suit prior to the trial of the law suit. A Summary Judgment can only be granted when the judge finds, as a matter of law, that there is no dispute about the facts of the controversy.

Supreme Law of the Land The legal doctrine established in the United States Constitution that the laws of the Federal Government take precedence over the laws of adopted by the government of any state.

Systematic Risk Investment risk inherent in the economic system as a whole.

Takings Issue Term applied to disputes regarding the point at which police power limitations become eminent domain takings and thus require just compensation.

Tax Proration The division of property taxes between the buyer and seller, based on the number of days during the year of closing each party occupied the property.

Tenancy in Common A form of multiple ownership of real property in which each tenant in common owns an undivided interest in the property. At the death of any tenant in common, the undivided interest will pass to the heirs of the deceased owner.

Testate Succession The transfer of property to the devisees and legatees of a decedent who died leaving a valid will.

Third Party Defense Defense added by SARA to CERCLA to help protect third party lenders from potential environmental liability.

Time is of the Essence A statement which describes the limited time during which an offer or contract will remain in effect.

Time Shares Real estate project, often taking a condominium form, in which investors purchase only a limited amount of time during which they may use the property each year.

Title Theory Mortgage The rights and duties allocated by law to the parties to a mortgage, when the mortgage is considered as a document which conveys ownership rights in the real property from the mortgagor to the mortgagee.

Title Abstract A written history of all documents filed for record which affect the ownership rights to a particular parcel of real property

Title Insurance An insurance policy which will pay the record owner of real property for any damage suffered as a result of liens or encumbrances of record against the property, unless the damage flows from a defect in record title which was excluded from the policy coverage.

Torts A legal wong committed upon a person or property independent of contract.

Trade Fixtures The legal doctrine applied to items of personal property installed in or upon real property which is leased for the purpose of conducting a trade or business. Items of personal property which meet the trade fixture definition retain their character as personalty, even though they are securely attached to a parcel of land or to a building.

Transfer Development Rights A system in which all land carries with it inherent development rights which may be bought and/or sold by the land owner.

Transfer Development Credits A system in which all land carries with it development priviledges granted by the government which may be bought and/or sold by the land owner.

Trust and Confidence Standard A fiduciary obligation by securities broker-dealers to disclose the cost to the dealer of securities offered for sale and the "best price" available.

Unbundled Services Brokerage A term applied to brokers who offer a "menu" of services which the client may select from.

Undue Influence Coercion by a dominant party in a relationship to gain benefits in a will or contract.

Uniform Vendor and Purchaser Risk Act State statute which places the risk of loss with the seller until title or possession has transferred to the buyer.

Uniform Commercial Code A model statute, now adopted by all states, which defines the rights and remedies of those engaged in the buying, selling and financing of goods.

Uniform Franchise Offering Circular An older format still used for providing the required disclosure of information by franchisors to potential franchisees.

Unilateral Contracts Legally enforceable agreements in which one party to the contract is not required to perform under the agreement until the other party has completed the performance required by the agreement.

Unsystematic Risk The investment risk caused by fluctuations of specific assets in a portfolio.

Variance When a strict application of zoning requirements would create a hardship through no fault of the property owner, a variance may be granted with regard to specific zoning requirements.

Verbal Contracts Created when a person's words or actions establish a contractual relationship between two parties.

Vertical Integration Adding other stages in the manufacturing process, or service provision process, so the firm becomes less dependent upon outside suppliers.

Void An agreement which is unenforceable against any party, because the agreement violates public policy.

Voidable An agreement which cannot be enforced against one of the parties, because that party lacked the capacity to make a valid contract, or because the agreement is so unreasonable that it shocks the conscience of the court where enforcement is sought.

Voluntary Transfers Transfers of property ownership rights which occur because the Grantor desires to transfer the ownership rights.

Warranty A promise, covenant, or pledge made by a grantor to a grantee.

Warranty Deed A deed conveying title to real property in which the grantor warrants the he or she actually possesses the title being conveyed. Warranty deeds are most commonly used to transfer title in exchange for payment of a purchase price.

Waste The legal doctrine which requires a life tenant to maintain the real property possessed by the life tenant in a state of good repair, for the benefit of holder of the remainder interest.

Worsenment The diminution of property value caused by city planning activities.

Zoning Ordinance Local ordinance which defines uses permitted in each zone, types of conditional uses, how zoning changes are to be made, and the appeals process which may be followed.

Zoning Board of Appeals Public board which hears appeals from individuals requesting relief from zoning or building code rulings.

Zoning Map Often an integral part of a zoning ordinance which describes and defines the boundaries of each zone.

INDEX